AF847550

Community Empowerment, Sustainable Cities, and Transformative Economies

Taha Chaiechi • Jacob Wood
Editors

Community Empowerment, Sustainable Cities, and Transformative Economies

Springer

Editors
Taha Chaiechi
College of Business, Law and Governance
James Cook University
Townsville, QLD, Australia

Jacob Wood
James Cook University
Singapore, Singapore

ISBN 978-981-16-5259-2 ISBN 978-981-16-5260-8 (eBook)
https://doi.org/10.1007/978-981-16-5260-8

© The Editor(s) (if applicable) and The Author(s), under exclusive license to Springer Nature Singapore Pte Ltd. 2022, corrected publication 2022
This work is subject to copyright. All rights are solely and exclusively licensed by the Publisher, whether the whole or part of the material is concerned, specifically the rights of translation, reprinting, reuse of illustrations, recitation, broadcasting, reproduction on microfilms or in any other physical way, and transmission or information storage and retrieval, electronic adaptation, computer software, or by similar or dissimilar methodology now known or hereafter developed.
The use of general descriptive names, registered names, trademarks, service marks, etc. in this publication does not imply, even in the absence of a specific statement, that such names are exempt from the relevant protective laws and regulations and therefore free for general use.
The publisher, the authors and the editors are safe to assume that the advice and information in this book are believed to be true and accurate at the date of publication. Neither the publisher nor the authors or the editors give a warranty, expressed or implied, with respect to the material contained herein or for any errors or omissions that may have been made. The publisher remains neutral with regard to jurisdictional claims in published maps and institutional affiliations.

This Springer imprint is published by the registered company Springer Nature Singapore Pte Ltd.
The registered company address is: 152 Beach Road, #21-01/04 Gateway East, Singapore 189721, Singapore

International Conference on Business, Economics, Management, and Sustainability (BEMAS) 2–3 July 2021

Organised by the Centre for International Trade and Business in Asia (CITBA) at James Cook University, Australia

Organisation

General Chair

Taha Chaiechi, James Cook University, Australia

The Scientific Committee

Jacob Wood	Josephine Pryce	Riccardo Welters
Emiel Eijdenberg	Thirumaran K	Breda McCarthy
Rachel Hay	Caroline Wong	Simona Azzali
Diane Jarvis	Tracey Mahony	Daniel Grainger

Registration and Finance Chair	Diana Castorina
Conference Coordinator	Dwi Sugiharti
Internal Consultant	Fiona Whittenbury
Videoconference & Audiovisual Specialist	Anders Thornblad
Senior Media Liaison Officer	Linden Woodward
CBLG Research[a]	Belinda Wilson
JCU Advancement Services[a]	Viv Sonntag

[a]*CBLG* College of Business,Law, and Governance, *JCU* James Cook University,Australia

Session Chairs

Diana Castorina	Breda McCarthy	Emiel Eijdenberg
Riccardo Welters	Dwi Sugiharti	Graeme Cotter
Josephine Pryce	Thirumaran K	Denis Tolkach
Diane Jarvis	Simona Azzali	James Juniper

The Panel of Keynote Speakers:

Cr Bob Manning OAM	Mayor of Cairns, Cairns Regional Council
Professor Stephen Boyle	Dean, College of Business, Law, and Governance, JCU
Professor Peter Case	Professor of Management, JCU and Bristol Business School
Ms Kasy Chambers	Executive Director, Anglicare Australia
Professor Hurriyet Babacan	Research Director, The Rural Economies Centre of Excellence, The Cairns Institute, JCU
Mr Michael Levie	Hotelier and Co-Founder of citizenM hotels
Adj. Professor Warwick Powel	Chairman of Smart Trade Networks and Queensland University of Technology

Preface

Following the successful international Urban Thinkers Campus (UTC) event in 2019 organised by the Centre for International Trade and Business in Asia (CITBA), College of Business, Law, and Governance (CBLG), James Cook University, Australia, the Centre is pleased to announce the International Conference on Business, Economics, Management, and Sustainability (BEMAS) on 02–03 July 2021 in Cairns, Australia. This year's conference is organised to be held in a hybrid format. All sessions are set up to be held on campus and online, allowing international participation.

The International Conference on Business, Economics, Management, and Sustainability (BEMAS) aims to bring together multidisciplinary scholars from around the globe to share methods and ideas for building a transformative economy and develop a comprehensive metric and measurable definitions of a resilient economy. The theme of the conference is: Community Empowerment, Sustainable Cities, and Transformative Economies. The conference also includes five tracks:

- Urban Planning, Public Spaces and Sustainable Economic Growth
- Understanding the Principles of Resilient Economies
- Society and Community-Based Initiatives in the Time of Crisis
- Business, Management and Sustainable Path to 2030 Agenda
- Sustainable Marketing, Community, and the Planet

The conference attracted full research papers, practitioner papers, research notes, scoping review papers, and case studies. The conference organiser, CITBA, requires that all submitted conference papers go through a blind peer-review process and evaluation based on originality, research depth and quality, and relevance to the theme of the conference and/or the conference tracks listed above. Accepted papers that have successfully completed the peer-review process are presented at the conference, and a selected number of those papers are published in this conference proceeding. The organisers of BEMAS would like to thank:

- The scientific committee of the conference for their help and their important contribution to the double-blind peer-review process

- The Organising Committee (full names listed on the previous page), including the Scientific Committee, Conference Coordinator, the Internal Consultant, Session Chairs, Registration and Finance Chair, and Videoconference & Audio Specialist for carrying out the tremendous workload in organising and synchronising different activities and processes
- The College of Business, Law, and Governance (CBLG) Professional team, CBLG Research, CBLG and JCU central Marketing teams, and JCU Media Liaison team for their ongoing support of the conference
- The local businesses and professionals for their contributions and presentations
- The outstanding keynote speakers for sharing their wisdom and inspiring ideas

Townsville, Australia
July 2021

Taha Chaiechi

Contents

Foreword- Sustainable and Resilient Economies, Theoretical Considerations

Taha Chaiechi

The orthodox methods of addressing external risks, such as climate change, public health emergencies and unsustainable growth, are no longer adequate. In the new millennium, these frequent external shocks have resulted in substantial economic losses, recessions, and loss of well-being and even lives. Methods that have been used in addressing these issues in the forms of climate adaptation plans, national strategies, public health emergency contingency planning, and sustainable development plans and strategies have one thing in common; they largely ignore the ongoing structural changes associated with economic development. Furthermore, these methods have also failed to account for evolving industries' composition and new comparative advantages and skills.

Moreover, vulnerable communities that tend to experience higher susceptibility to external risks have been largely ignored in incremental adaptation plans. Vulnerable communities and areas require different adaptive responses to climate risk and possess the unlocked adaptive capacity that can motivate different patterns of sustainable development to achieve the goals of the 2030 Agenda. Therefore, it is essential to view transformative growth and fundamental reorientation of economic resources as integral parts of the solution. Social disorganisation and vulnerability are other undesired outcomes of the unpredictable and widespread external economic shocks. This is due to a sudden and tough competition between members of society to acquire precious resources, most of which may be depleted during unprecedented events such as natural disasters or pandemics, resulting in an even more chaotic and disorganised condition.

Joseph Schumpeter (1942, 1961) emphasised that economic success is an evolving process and change-oriented. In particular, Schumpeter's perennial 'gale of "creative destruction" could not be more relevant today. As the global economy is

T. Chaiechi (✉)
College of Business, Law and Governance, James Cook University, Townsville, QLD, Australia
e-mail: Taha.chaiechi@jcu.edu.au

© The Author(s), under exclusive license to Springer Nature Singapore Pte Ltd. 2022
T. Chaiechi, J. Wood (eds.), *Community Empowerment, Sustainable Cities, and Transformative Economies*, https://doi.org/10.1007/978-981-16-5260-8_1

undergoing a fundamental transformation due to the COVID pandemic, not only are economic growth dynamics changing, but even the geography of economic activities is shifting. The disruption (or the destruction) caused by the pandemic are creating transformative challenges and opportunities for communities, economies, and regions, adding new layers of complexities to the concept of sustainability. So the question is: does achieving sustainable development make for apt designation as a wicked problem? A wicked problem is referred to as a problem that is difficult or impossible to solve due to competing, conflicting, and changing priorities that are often difficult to recognise. Probably the "impossible to solve" component is rather an overstatement; nevertheless, this notion seems to be applicable when dealing with the concept of sustainable development, where there is an apparent tension between the goals and priorities that tie back into the three pillars of sustainability (aka People, Planet, Profit) as shown in Fig. 1.

Each of these pillars has its own set of priorities and objectives that are not only reasonable and often necessary, some of which may be competing at best or contradictory at worst.

But what about the concept of resilience? Economic resilience can be either inherent or adaptive. Inherent resilience is routinely provided through resource allocation, and adaptive resilience is generally the system's ability to maintain functionality after being shocked. Economic resilience is operative in three levels: micro-, meso-, and macro-level (Fig. 2).

While the concept of sustainability has become well established in scholarly works in the past several years, economic resilience is poorly understood, and the concept is under-researched. One reason for this may be due to the fact that most classical economic models focus on equilibrium condition, whereas economic

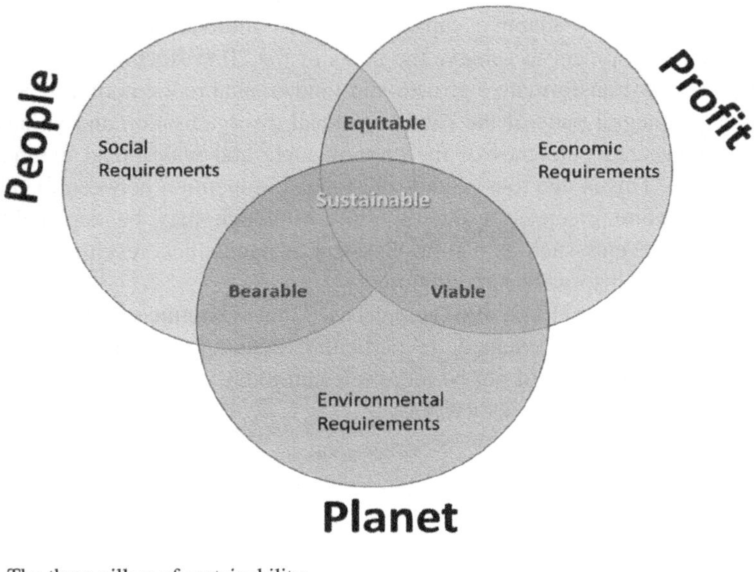

Fig. 1 The three pillars of sustainability

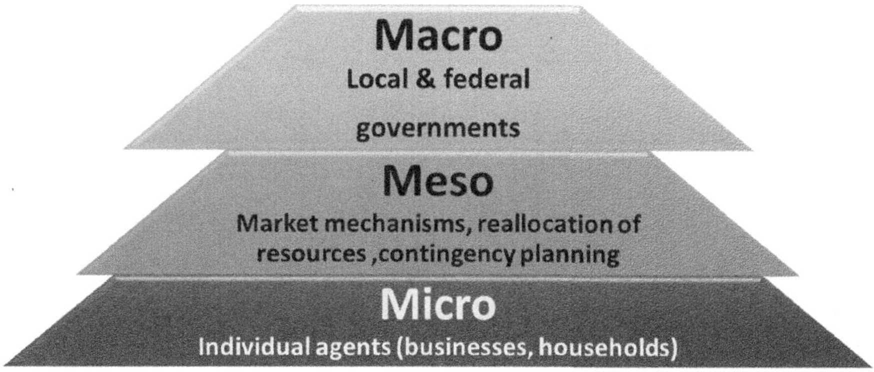

Fig. 2 Resilience from systems' perspective, source: author's generated

resilience refers to the capacity to adapt to new conditions, and as such, it would be challenging to integrate the concept of resilience into the classical theories (Chaiechi & Nguyen, 2021). Nonetheless, contemporary economic schools of thoughts, such as post-Keynesians (PK) have repeatedly focused on out-of-equilibrium phenomena where change is a given part of the economic processes. Accordingly, the PK methodologies are perceived to be especially suitable for sustainability studies.

Furthermore, achieving more moderate business cycle fluctuations is often quoted as a macroeconomic goal. A large body of literature frequently cited better macroeconomic policies and more reliable financial market instruments to help rid of severe fluctuations in economic activities (business cycles). And while more advanced economies have shown a seeming ability to recover from external shocks in the past relatively quickly, the severe COVID-19 recessionary pressure has exposed superficial evidence of resilience within economic systems (Chaiechi & Nguyen, 2021). As demonstrated in Fig. 3, higher levels of resilience will lower the magnitude and size of exogenous shocks preventing full swing economic losses.

But are sustainability and resilience the two sides of the same coin? There are indeed certain similarities between the two concepts. Both concepts are used to describe a system ranging from the global economy to individual decision-maker units. Furthermore, both concepts focus on systems' survivability under normal conditions or in response to disturbances (external shocks). Despite the similarities, there are distinct differences between the two concepts. For example, sustainability initiatives tend to focus on preserving traditional methods and practices of utilising limited resources. In contrast, resilience initiatives tend to focus on adapting to new conditions.

Further, resilience tends to prioritise processes of systems or features, whereas sustainability prioritises outcomes of those system's (Park et al., 2013). While it is true that neglecting similarities and differences between the two doctrines may blindside policymakers and prevent them from recognising the importance of capitalising on synergies, there seems to be a need to put aside this discourse of similarity and differences and start to think about these two concepts as intertwined

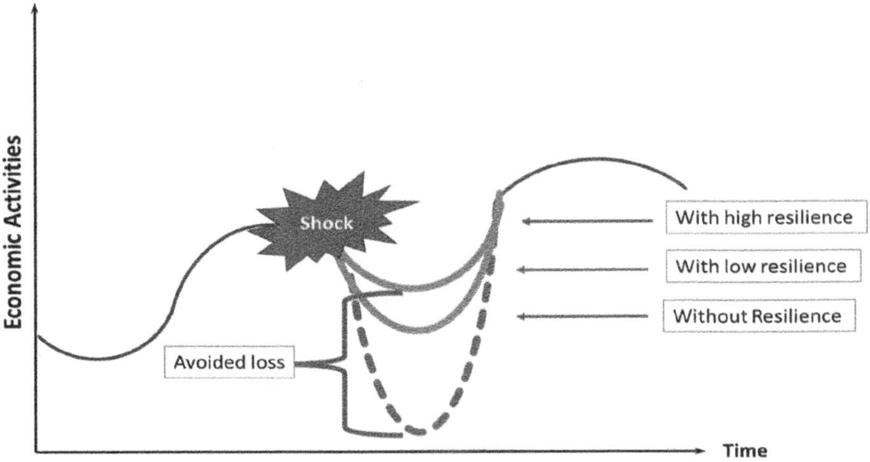

Fig. 3 Business cycle, resilience and the avoided economic losses, source: author

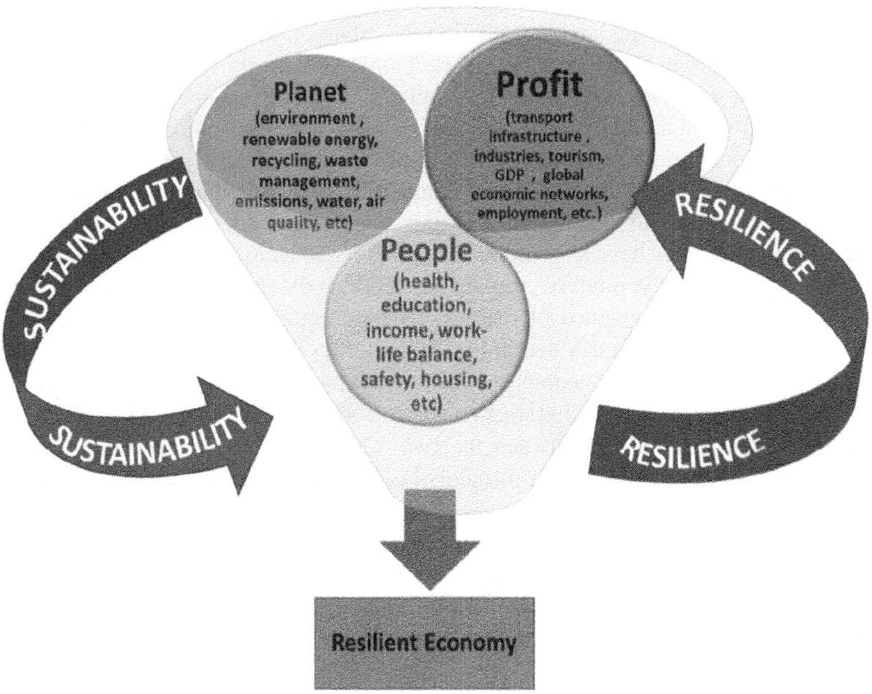

Fig. 4 proposed DNA structure for a resilient economy, source: author

(Fig. 4). Accordingly, I argue that a further entwining of economic resilience and sustainable development could produce a shared epistemology applicable across multiple academic disicplinaes and capable of unlocking hidden capacities that have been overlooked otherwise. There is a need to develop more progressive sounding themes through the recalibration of our deepest held economic assumptions to provoke a paradigmatic change in how we formulate driving factors of economic growth. New methods should place a premium on empowering communities and building resilient economies; for businesses, increased efficiency should no longer be the primary goal. They need to plan and design for resilience.

Accordingly, *Community Empowerment, Sustainable Cities, and Transformative Economies* take a multi-disciplinary approach to look at changing economies, challenges, and opportunities, focusing on community-driven development, unlocking the adaptive capacity of vulnerable communities, sustainable cities, regional competitiveness, and emerging practices for inclusive, transformative and resilient growth. No other book presents such a prolific collection of theoretical and empirical frameworks to evaluate the quality of sustainability and resilience research in theory and practice, with a special focus on external and emerging sources of risks (such as climate change and pandemics).

Each chapter is written by leading experts in the field or by doctoral research candidates and is intended to stand independently. Furthermore, the chapters provide an aspiring contribution to the complicated yet critical debates of our time. Despite the topic diversity of the chapters in this collection, one common denominator appears to be the focus on expansive resilience and sustainability discourses and the importance of the mobilisation of resilience knowledge.

References

Chaiechi, T., & Nguyen, T. (2021). Measuring urban economic resilience of two tropical cities, using impulse response analysis. *Bulletin of Applied Economics, 8*(1), 59–79. https://doi.org/10.47260/bae/814

Park, J., Seager, T. P., Rao, P. S. C., Convertino, M., & Linkov, I. (2013). Integrating risk and resilience approaches to catastrophe management in engineering systems. *Risk Analysis, 33*, 356–367. https://doi.org/10.1111/j.1539-6924.2012.01885.x

Schumpeter, J. A., (1942). *Capitalism, socialism, and democracy*. University of Illinois at Urbana-Champaign's Academy for Entrepreneurial Leadership Historical Research Reference in Entrepreneurship, Available at SSRN: https://ssrn.com/abstract=1496200

Schumpeter, J. A. (1961). *The theory of economic development* (3rd ed.). Oxford University Press.

Conference Keynote- After COVID-19: Building Inclusive and Sustainable Economies for Resilience

Hurriyet Babacan

Abstract COVID-19 has exposed the vulnerabilities and structural weaknesses of economic and social systems. The two major challenges of our economic systems are ecological degradation and limits the to the capacity of Earth and the immense social disparities and inequalities. It is now time to re-think and imagine our economic and social systems for a better world. In order for progress to occur we need to critique our existing economic approaches based on growth and unsustained consumption and production models. This article provides an outline of the dominant growth paradigm and outlines the key critiques of these approaches. Alternative ways to think about inclusive and ecologically sustainable economic development are considered, particularly focusing on inclusive economies and ecological economies. COVID-19 efforts are linked with resilience and adaptation. This article argues that it is critical that we go beyond the absorption of shock approaches to transformative economic development and major reforms to our economic and political systems.

Keywords Inclusive economic development · Resilience · Ecological sustainability · COVID-19

1 Introduction

The global pandemic of the coronavirus disease 2019 (COVID-19) has exposed the vulnerabilities of individuals, societies and economies and has amplified existing inequalities (Babacan et al., 2020; Babacan & Lewis, 2019). The pandemic has exposed the structural weaknesses of economic and social systems, "revealing numerous problems including unstable supply chains, unjust social provisioning of essentials, profiteering, precarious employment, inequities and pollution" (Spash, 2020:1). The Sustainable Development Goals is an urgent call for action for the

H. Babacan (✉)
Rural Economies Centre of Excellence, The Cairns Institute, James Cook University, Townsville, Australia
e-mail: hurriyet.babacan@jcu.edu.au

© The Author(s), under exclusive license to Springer Nature Singapore Pte Ltd. 2022
T. Chaiechi, J. Wood (eds.), *Community Empowerment, Sustainable Cities, and Transformative Economies*, https://doi.org/10.1007/978-981-16-5260-8_2

international community with 17 goals as focus areas facing the planet and societies (UN, 2015). The pandemic has exacerbated the global challenges. Humanity now faces a 'triple conjuncture' of global crises: climate change and ecological breakdown; a systemic crisis of global capitalism; and the current global Coronavirus pandemic (Gills, 2020). The implications of COVID-19 in going forward are vast and there are calls, from different sectors, for a rethink of how economic and social activities are organized (OECD, 2020; Spash, 2020).

Major questions arise about what shape does recovery, adaptation and resilience should take. The impact of the pandemic has reinforced existing inequalities within and between countries and is giving rise to asymmetric recovery. Technological change has accelerated through the crisis and is giving rise to societal polarization. Significant doubts have been raised about building on a flawed and structurally weakened economic systems (Gills, 2020; Helm, 2020). Rather than simply revert to 'business as usual', the desire for change, to be resilient has been termed *'build back better' and 'build broader'* (WRI, 2020; OECD, 2020). The questions arise of 'build better for whom' and how do we progress to systems that are inclusive and ecologically sustainable (Chmutina & Cheek, 2021).

This chapter addresses explores the key challenges for developing transformative economic resilience in the post-COVID-era. It critiques the existing economic ideas and argues that current structures have resulted in pursuing growth at all costs, with significant environmental damage and immense social inequalities. The chapter explores the emerging ideas of inclusive and ecological economies as useful pathways to developing resilient economies for the future. Utilising research conducted by the author, key learnings about resilience is outlined. The chapter concludes with what can be undertaken for transformative change.

2 The Growth Paradigm

Economic growth has been the primary goal of economic policy for over that last seven decades where measure of economic success has been sought in rising national income and gross domestic product (GDP) raising standard of living, increasing profits, improving employment and household incomes (Ramos & Hynes, 2019). Described as the "ideology of post-war capitalism", neo-classical economics assumes that is possible to have unlimited growth as a way to prosperity (Ikerd, 2014). Referred to as the 'cult of growth' (Pilling, 2018), the growth paradigm produced a powerful and widely shared notion that growth was desirable and limitless (Macekura, 2020). Statistical arguments advance ideological positions (Macekura, 2020). For this reason, progress was measured by the growth of the economy, using GDP as a measure of wealth of a society (Rogge & Van Nijverseel, 2018). Certain statistics measuring growth were given primacy in political and public life but they do tell us about the quality of life and what people value (Pilling, 2018). Measures such as GDP are increasingly being criticized as a measure of progress and is not correlating to wellbeing (Macekura, 2020; OECD, 2019). What is collected and measured in relation to economic growth is deliberate and the way value was assigned made key assumptions. For example, negative expenditures (e.g. armament, defence) grew GPD while the costs to the environment, women's unpaid labour were not included while unproductive financial services were (Shaik & Tomak, 1994; Waring, 1999).

Increasingly coming under pressure, the global pursuit of economic growth has been criticized as it has deepened wealth and social disparities and threatens the ecological basis for human civilization. The critiques of growth were twofold: ecological critiques and development critiques focusing on costs to human wellbeing and deepening inequalities. Ecological arguments focused on the costs of growth and production such as air and water pollution, erosion, industrial waste, deforestation, and climate change.

The pursuit of growth, it was argued, reduced rather than increase welfare as early as the 1960s (Mishan, 1967, 1977). While growth produced material abundance its distribution was problematic, creating wealth disparities, poverty and unemployment. It was also noted the consumption of material goods did not, in themselves, bring individual fulfillment and its pursuit has created undesirable social impacts. Gender focused critiques argued the invisibility of women's contribution to society, particularly in the form of unpaid labour. The key discontents of growth focused economic development are:

- Weak systems for growth and unstable systems e.g. financial crash of 2008, periods of contraction and expansion;
- False view that there is a trade-off between growth, efficiency and productivity with human and social development;
- Growth not equating to sustainable expansion of productive capacity, wealth or income;
- Stagnant private sector investment in many areas with public sector substitution;
- Public sector bearing risk in public-private partnerships;
- Stagnating living standards and rising inequality (poverty, income and wealth disparities; access to education, increase in household debt, trend towards declining wages);
- Labour market insecurity and precarious nature of work and declining wages in many countries;
- Environmental and planetary critical limits (waste, climate change, pollution, emissions, bio-diversity loss);
- The 'trickle down economics' has not worked.' This is based on the assumption that if the economy grows that everyone will benefit. The wealth and resources of growth has not 'tricked down' and economic systems are fundamentally unfair;
- Competitive forms of economy are better than collaborative ones;
- Unsustainable consumption and values of greed and instant gratification undermine social cohesion and trust;
- Political systems fail to correct market failures and imperfections;
- Confusion of the wealth of a nation with those of individuals who are rent seeking rather than wealth creation;

- Masks exploitation in the creation of wealth;
- Neo-liberal processes and governmentalities that have entrenched market ethic and contractual relations as the most efficient means to organize society (Babacan, 2021; Birch & Siemiatycki, 2016; Jacobs & Mazzucato, 2016; Kar et al., 2013; Spash, 2020; Stiglitz, 2012)

These critiques have led to focusing on the links between rising inequality, unsustainable natural resource use and the fragility of growth. Pilling argues that the steadfast loyalty to growth is informing misguided policies – and contributing to a rising mistrust of experts that is shaking the very foundations of our democracy (Pilling, 2018). The 'grow first and clean later; grow first and distribute later' approach to the economy is no longer sustainable (OECD, 2020). Achieving sustainable economic development has been hampered by current growth focused economic approaches and the trade-offs in favour of economic growth over social well-being and ecological viability (Gupta & Vegelin, 2016; Spash, 2020). COVID-19 has exposed the structural flaws of economic systems and a growing recognition to do things differently. The sentiment expressed by George Soros (2015), "economic theory needs to be rethought from the ground-up" is relevant here.

3 Economic and Social Impacts of COVID-19

While there are signs of global recovery, the pandemic will continue to have impacts, affecting the most vulnerable. Key areas of these impacts include:

Labour market scarring. The ILO estimates 8% of global working hours were lost in 2020 equivalent to 255 million full-time jobs with continued losses into 2021 (ILO, 2021:1). These have been across different sectors. For example, in Australia job losses were – 15.3% in higher education, –5.1% in tourism, –6.1% in retail, 23.9% in air, water and road transport and 15.2% in accommodation (ABS, 2021).

Finances and poverty: 120 million have been pushed into extreme poverty (IMF, 2020). Even significant segments of populations in developed nations experienced hardship. 12% identified that their household finances had worsened since 2020, 20% took actions to support basic living expenses and 13% were unable to pay at least one bill in the last 3 months (to Mach 2021) (ABS, 2021a).

Social determinant of health impacts: the pandemic has challenged the stretched health systems and widened global inequities in health. Access to medical health, vaccines and hospital care, social protections, exposure and transmission risks, death rates have been uneven across the global North and South and also within countries, based on severe global health inequalities (Babacan, 2021; Jensen et al., 2021). The physical and mental health stresses of the pandemic will have long term and continuing consequences. For example, one year since the pandemic, in a national survey in Australia, participants identified worsening health outcomes (18% worse physical health and 20% with worse mental health) (ABS, 2021).

Digital divide: at a time when COVID-19 accelerated the use of digital technologies, access to internet, digital devices and digital skills impacted on those who were the most vulnerable (Babacan et al., 2020). Based on economic vulnerability, Roese (2021) estimates that 74% of people with low vulnerability had access to the internet globally, while only 24% of those who were highly vulnerable had internet access, assessing that the challenges of digital exclusion will be significant for economic and social progress. The Australian Digital Inclusion Index (ADII) sees inclusion as relating to access, affordability and ability. They conclude "The benefits of the digital economy cannot be shared when some members of the community are still facing real barriers to online participation" (ADII, 2019:5).

The Word Bank (2020) indicates that many of the people and places considered 'disadvantage before COVID-19, have been hardest hit by consequences of the pandemic. UNDP identifies the potential for deepening inequality. "Part of the reason climate change and disasters are disequalizing is that inequality exists in the first place; they run along, exploit and deepen existing social and economic fault lines" (UNDP, 2019:179). These impacts raise complex questions about pathways to social and economic recovery and resilience. Unless appropriate systems and policies that promote fair distribution of resources and overcome social and economic exclusion are in place, the result will be unequal patterns of recovery, posing significant social and economic risks.

4 Transformative Resilience

The COVID-19 pandemic has created a deep and lasting damage to the social and economic fabric of our societies. Developing an effective framework to address COVID-19 is complex and will involve making choices about resources and actions for the short and long term (Babacan et al., 2020). Much effort has gone into recovery and adaptation. Some fundamental principles need to be used to guide response and recovery efforts. As noted by Hogan & Drew (2020:3) "recovery must be about doing high impact interventions and high return investments, as well addressing inequalities and weaknesses in capacities and capabilities that will constrain recovery. It must be about investing in 'people and places', and making the most our social, cultural and regional diversity.

Resilience is defined in many ways. It refers to "the capacity of given places to resist shocks, recover from unexpected events and sustain a long-term developmental growth path" (Di Caro, 2017: 94). Resilience is often linked with vulnerability, absorption of shock and thriving under uncertainty. Resilience is not only about coping with adversity but to be able to thrive and maximise the full potential of communities and individuals. Social capital, social cohesion, sense of belonging and community spirit, trusted sources of information, ability to collaborate, diversity of economic and other resources available to the community, governance and institutions are key factors in resilience (Dale et al., 2014; Kulig et al., 2013). At the individual level it is about being adaptive, having hope, capability to imagine and innovate and the capacity to respond to opportunity (Nemeth & Olivier, 2017). Adaptive capacity is distributed across systems, relationships and organisations (Babacan et al., 2020). In that sense resilience, adaptive capacity and innovation "should not be viewed as a singular, isolated trait of a person, family, or community, but rather as a broader and multifaceted capacity" (Masten & Motti-Stefanidi, 2020:5).

Resilience can perpatuate existing inequalities (Babacan et al., 2020). OECD (2014:6-7) identifies a useful framework for strengthening different types of capacities:

- *Absorptive capacity*: The ability of a system to prepare for, mitigate or prevent negativeimpacts,using predetermined coping responses in order to preserve and restore essential basic structures and functions.This includes coping mechanisms used during periods of shock.
- *Adaptive capacity*: The ability of a system to adjust, modify or change its characteristics and actions to moderate potential future damage and to take advantage of opportunities, so that it cancontinue to functionwithout major qualitative changes in function or structural identity.
- *Transformative capacity*: The ability to create a fundamentally new system so that the shock will no longer have any impact. This can be necessary when ecological, economic or social structures make the existing system untenable.

It is this transformative capacity that is critical for addressing ecological and inclusive economic resilience. If there is to be a better build, then the focus of effort for resilience needs to be transformative approaches, of systems, processes and capacities.

COVID-19 has seen the acceleration of industry 4.0, fourth industrial revolution (Dollar, 2020). This is based on digital ecoomy, platmofrm economy of many broker firms and changes to the nature of jobs. "what's going on is that work is being disconnected from jobs, and jobs and work are being disconnected from companies, which are increasingly becoming platforms" (Friedman cited in Schwartz et al., 2019:3). COVID-19 has hastened the use of technologies due to shifting to online services (e.g. health, education, shopping, entertainment), automation uptake due to labour supply contraints (costs, lock down, mobility, skills); employers seeing different work options and business models of employment and the need to be agile. These pose major challenges for economic development pathways and further polarisation.

Key considerations in the looking at resilience is how the trade off between long and term outcomes, and how much weight is given to addressing the immediate and the longer term with inter-generational implications. Another key issue is the performance versus structural elements of resilience. Often, measures such as GDP are used (stemming from the growth paradigm outlined above), which says says little about the structures that underlie the system (Regibeau & Rockett, 2013). Additionally, there are considerations about the speed of recovery versus sustainability. There may be emphasis on growth rather than creation of systems that are better able to withstand economic disruption and produce equitable and sustainable outcomes (Brown & Greenbaum, 2016).

5 Alternatives for Transformative Resilience

'The economy is not real. It is merely one way of imagining our world.' (Pilling, 2018)

It is well known that the COVID-19 pandemic is having important distributional and generational effects that amplify pre-existing social inequalities (Bonaccorsi et al., 2020). Shocks and disruptions have disproportionate impacts on population with intersecting factors impacting on resilience (OECD, 2020). The idea of 'building better' post COVID-19 is a chance to inclusive and sustainable economic systems which will be more resilient in the long term. There are diverse ideas of transformative change. The key challenges that face society is ecological sustainability and social inequality. A new way to imagine our world and the opportunity to have new forms of economy has arisen.

Two broad theories are emerging as possible ways for transformative resilience. These are inclusive economies and ecological (green) economies.

Inclusive economies: The growth paradigm presents economy as a tension between inclusion/equity and efficiency and growth. It was assumed that economic growth is hindered by considerations equality and disadvantage. The conventional thinking of the 'trickle down,' where the natural cycle of wealth accumulation at the top will eventually filter down to lift up the poor, is increasingly discounted (Piketty, 2014). There is evidence to show the inequality hinders economic growth through a range of demand and supply side factors (Berg & Ostry, 2011; Stiglitz, 2012). As Dua et al. (2021:10) posits "the perceived tension between inclusion and growth—and the false belief that they should be addressed separately—has hampered efforts to pursue and achieve inclusive growth". Inequality also hinders economic development as it erodes social cohesion and lack of collaboration to protect common resources (Cushing et al., 2015). These critiques saw the development of concepts such as pro-poor growth and inclusive economic growth, which espoused the idea of poverty reduction and for members of society to contribute and benefit from economic growth (Aoyagi & Ganelli, 2015; Benner & Pastor, 2016; Ramos & Hynes, 2019).

In the post COVID-19 era, there are calls for a re-balancing of efficiency, inclusion and resilience argument throughout the economy (Spash, 2020). Traditionally, the purpose of the social economy has been seen to "repair" social problems and forms of social exclusion experienced by vulnerable groups. OECD argues that the social economy can develop a much larger role in the post-COVID phase to inspire transformation to a more inclusive and sustainable economy and society. (OECD, 2020). There are suggestions that inclusive economic development should start from the most 'disadvantage out' (Yunus Centre, 2020:19). These ideas of economic development from bottom up is echoed elsewhere. For example, the

Rockefeller Foundation inclusive economies framework posit that "When we invest in making economies more equitable from the bottom up, or the middle class out, economic growth is likely to be better for everyone's pocketbooks, for longer periods" (Pacetti, 2016).

Inclusive economies work can be considered as in its infancy. Some of the emerging work is still shackled by the growth paradigms. The inclusive growth accepts the market liberal framing and is not progressive to address inclusion challenges. Moreover, it does not enable options for where there is no or negative growth and does not sufficiently address environmental degradation (Burch & McInroy, 2018). The Rockefeller Foundation posits that there is a need to go beyond the equity-growth dichotomy and consider a framework for inclusive economies, defined as those that "expand opportunities for more broadly shared prosperity, especially for those facing the greatest barriers to advancing their well-being" (Benner & Pastor, 2016:6). The authors outline five characteristics of an inclusive economy: equitable, participatory, growing, sustainable and stable (Benner & Pastor, 2016). The Centre for Local Economic Strategies (CLES, 2020) advocates a community wealth building strategy to address inequality and identifies pillars for transformed economic systems recovery and resilience. These are include fair employment and just labour markets, progressive procurement of goods and services, plural ownership of the economy, socially just use of land and property and making financial power work for local places.

Adopting an inclusive economies approach, as contrasted to the inclusive growth, fundamentally urges a global and country system scale transformation and enables consideration of a range of ideas about imagining the economy through considerations of inclusion, gender, ecology, new local economies, participation and development which contribute to inclusion and sustainability. The imperative to move to inclusive economies is that a a less divided society, an economy with more equality, performs better on a wider range of indicators of quality of life (Stiglitz, 2012).

Green economies: Decades of scientific scholarship indicates that the current rates of growth are not sustainable and that we have reached the limits of our planet with bio-diversity loss, global warming and carbon emissions, water and air pollution, deforestation, erosion and waste (Helm, 2020; Kallis et al., 2013). Despite global summits, and agreements, it is clear that sustainability targets will not be met (Helm, 2020). There is increasing recognition that we need to reorient the post-coronavirus economy for ecological sustainability. The costs of natural resource depletion and damage to the environment as been treated as an externality in the economic systems and not priced into economic activity. The recent ideas of green growth is gaining traction which has the central tenet that "by full-pricing resource overexploitation, greenhouse gas emissions and pollution in markets' economic progress and environmental protection can be achieved in tandem" (Taherzadeh, 2021:1). This policy response to climate change and environmental challenges ignores the concept that growth is bounded by resource scarcity and the biophysical limits of the planet (Meckling & Allan, 2020).

Ecological economics questions unlimited growth with global finite resources (Spash, 2020; Washington & Maloney, 2020) and identifies a range of challenges:

- Continued subsidy and industry supports for fossil fuels and polluting industries;
- Polluters are not paying;
- Lack of capital investment in green economy options (research, infrastructure, economic development initiatives;
- Decoupling of growth, GDP and unsustainable consumption from environmental concerns;
- Unsustainable patterns of agricultural and industrial production contributing to increased emissions;
- Intergenerational impacts of environmental damage;
- Impacts of global population growth on natural resources;
- Commodification of nature and non-recognition of non-market values attributed to natural assets;
- Reducing waste and recycling;
- How to move to a sustainable consumption;
- Critiques that technological progress will mitigate environmental degradation or can innovate quick enough to address the massive environmental challenges; (Bennett, 2020; Best et al., 2020; Coady et al., 2017; Helm, 2020; Spash, 2020; Taherzadeh, 2021; Washington & Maloney, 2020).

A number of models emerge in ecological economics as a way forward including steady growth economy, de-growth, circular economy, sharing economy and the doughnut economy (Washington & Maloney, 2020). These alternative ecological models challenge the economic growth model and encourage sustainable resource use, reduce waste, reuse and recycle, and nudge sustainable consumption models.

The environmental impacts of COVID-19 have been variable. The slowing of the economy, the lockdown, reduced travel and transport witnessed a decline in emissions, air pollution, energy use, improved water quality during COVID-19 (Helm, 2020; Lenzen et al., 2020). Although temporary, it is estimated that the level of daily global CO2 emissions fell by approximately 4–7% (Le Qúefe et al., 2020). The period also confirmed the correlation between consumption, GPD and the environment (Helm, 2020). The monetary easing, as governments reduced interest rates, saw impacts on housing and land, with higher prices for property and land. This led to an increased use of marginal lands for agriculture rather than leaving in natural state (Helm, 2020).

The major contribution of ecological economics in the post COVID -19 is the recognition that the impacts of economic expansion on the environment cannot be alleviated by market forces or technological progress alone (Bennett, 2020; Spash, 2020). The current ecological crisis invites an examination of capitalism as the root cause of unsustainable consumption patterns and production practices (Weidmann et al., 2020). This will require a break-free from anthropocentrism toward ecocentrism and develop ecological economic ethics with principles such as de-commodifying nature, Earth jurisprudence, commitments to non-human aspects of the planet, limits to growth, and equity and social justice (Washington & Maloney, 2020).

6 Conclusion

COVID-19 crisis has provided a shake up to the world. We have the opportunity to build better and broader. The challenge will be not reverting back to the usual, pushback from vested interests who benefit from existing systems, working out global and national goals and power conflicts, developing strong governance and effective institutions for change and reactive mindsets (Jerneck & Olsson, 2008; Sjostedt, 2015).

There is urgency for a re-think and action as the world deliberates with recovery efforts. This is now a time to re-examine what system – scale reforms are needed in economic systems with a view to inclusive and sustainable economies. Areas of focus include labour market and wage structures, production systems, monetary and tax systems and discourses we have about the economy. As noted by Stiglitz (2012), incrementalism and minor tweaks to our economic and political systems will be inadequate to bring about the needed change and a fundamental shift in approach is needed.

There is a significant body of literature on resilience practice and place-based economic transformation initiatives. They go the core of interlinking economic, social and environmental factors and undertaking a holistic systems and vulnerability analysis; developing capacity and capabiilites; working at different scales from the individual, household, to regional, national and international; increasing social capital; supporting non-traditional leadership; particpatory processes in key decision making structures; nudging policy making in the right direction; ensuring resilience efforts go into different systems in an integrated manner; developing a dynamic public sector; social protections and safety nets; green stimulus investments, building local vision and consensus (Babacan et al., 2020; Gupta et al., 2021; OECD, 2020; Yunus Centre, 2020).

There is a lot at stake. A return to business as usual is not acceptable as it lead to a vicious cycle of ecological degradation, wider scale inequality and further vulnerability of populations and nature. The COVID-19 recovery approaches of absorption of shock will only retain the status quo. Building better has to be about the interests of the planet and those who are vulnerable and marginalised. Transformative resilience has to be at the heart of our efforts for a better world during and after COVID-19.

References

ABS. (2021). *Tourism satellite accounts*, Australian Bureau of Statistics., https://www.abs.gov.au/statistics/economy/national-accounts/tourism-satellite-accounts-quarterly-tourism-labour-statistics-australia-experimental-estimates/latest-release Accessed 1 July 2021.

ABS. (2021a). *Household impacts of COVID-19 survey*, Australian Bureau of Statistics, . https://www.abs.gov.au/statistics/people/people-and-communities/household-impacts-covid-19-survey/latest-release Accessed 1 July 2021.

ADII. (2019). *Measuring Australia's digital divide,* The Australian Digital Inclusion Index, , https://apo.org.au/node/255341 Accessed 1 July 2021.
Aoyagi, C., & Ganelli, G. (2015). *Asia's quest for inclusive growth revisited* (Working Paper No. 15). International Monetary Fund, Asia and Pacific Department, Washington D.C.
Babacan, H. (2021). Public-private partnerships for global health. In R. Haring, I. Kickbusch, D. Ganten, & M. Moeti (Eds.), *Handbook of Global Health* (pp. 1–34). Springer Publishers.
Babacan, H., & Lewis, E. (2019). *Gender responsive alternatives to climate change, global report.* Ethos of Engagement and Action Aid.
Babacan, H., McHugh, J., & Dale, A. (2020). *Cairns local rapid needs assessment: Social impacts of COVID-19.* Cairns Regional Council and James Cook University.
Benner, C. & Pastor, M. (2016). *Inclusive Economy Indicators*, Rockefeller Foundation., https://www.rockefellerfoundation.org/report/inclusive-economies-indicators-full-report/ Accessed 3 July 2021.
Bennett, J. (2020). Reorienting the post-coronavirus economy for ecological sustainability. *Journal of Australian Political Economy, 85*, 212–218.
Berg, A. G., & Ostry, J. D. (2011). *Inequality and unsustainable growth: Two sides of the same coin?* International Monetary Fund.
Best, R., Burke, P. J., & Jotzo, F. (2020). Carbon pricing efficacy: Cross-country evidence. *Environmental and Resource Economics, 77*, 69–94.
Birch, K., & Siemiatycki, M. (2016). Neoliberalism and the geographies of marketization: The entangling of state and markets. *Progress in Human Geography, 40*(2), 177–198.
Bonaccorsi, G., Pierri, F., Cinelli, M., Flori, A., Galeazzi, A., Porcelli, F., Schmidt, A. L., Valensise, C. M., Scala, A., Quattrociocchi, W., & Pammolli, F. (2020). Economic and social consequences of human mobility restrictions under COVID-19. *Proceedings of the National Academy of Sciences, 117*(27), 15530–15535.
Brown, L., & Greenbaum, R. T. (2016). The role of industrial diversity in economic resilience: An empirical examination across 35 years. *Journal of Urban Studies, 54*(6), 1347–1366.
Burch, D., & McInroy, N. (2018). *We need an inclusive economy not inclusive growth*, Centre for Local Economic Strategies, . https://cles.org.uk/wp-content/uploads/2020/04/Rescue-recover-reform-FINAL.pdf Accessed 3 July 2021.
Chmutina, K., & Cheek, W. (2021). *Build back better for whom? How neoliberalism (re) creates disaster risks*, I. https://www.currentaffairs.org/2021/01/build-back-better-for-whom-how-neo liberalism-recreates-disaster-risks Accessed 1 July 2021.
CLES. (2020). *Rescue, recover and reform. A framework for new local economic practice in the era of COVID-19.* Centre for Local Economic Strategies.
Coady, D., Parry, I., Sears, L., & Shang, B. (2017). How large are global fossil fuel subsidies? *World Development, 91*, 11–27.
Cushing, L., Morello-Frosch, R., Wander, M., & Pastor, M. (2015). The haves, the have-nots, and the health of everyone: The relationship between social inequality and environmental quality. *Annual Review of Public Health, 36*, 193–209.
Dale, A., Vella, K., Potts, R., Voyce, B., Stevenson, B., Cottrel, A., King, D., Babacan, H., Boon, H., Gooch, M., & Pert, P. (2014). *Applying social resilience concepts and indicators to support climate adaptation in tropical North Queensland, Australia: Benchmark evidence base.* James Cook University.
Di Caro, P. (2017). Testing and explaining economic resilience with an application to Italian regions. *Papers in Regional Science, 96*(1), 93–113.
Dollar, D. (2020). The future of global supply chains: What are the implications for international trade? In B. Coulbally, K. Dervis, H. Kharas, & Z. Qureshi (Eds.), *Reimagining the global economy*. Brookings Institute.
Dua, A., Mike-Kerlin, J., Law, J., McKinney, B., Noel, N., & Stewart, S. (2021). *The case for inclusive growth.* McKinsey and Company.
Gills, B. (2020). Deep restoration: From the great implosion to the great awakening. *Globalizations, 17*(4), 577–579.

Gupta, J., Bavinck, M., Ros-Tonen, M., Asubonteng, K., Bosch, H., van Ewijk, E., Hordijk, M., van Leynseele, Y., Cordozo, M. L., Miedema, E., Pouw, N., Rammelt, C., Scholtens, J., Vegelin, C., & Verrest, H. (2021). COVID-19, poverty and inclusive development. *World Development, 145*, 105527.

Gupta, J., & Vegelin, C. (2016). Sustainable development goals and inclusive development. *International Environmental Agreements: Politics, Law and Economics, 16*, 433–448.

Helm, D. (2020). The environmental impacts of the coronavirus. *Environmental and Resource Economics, 76*, 21–38.

Hogan, M., & Drew, C. (2020) *Recovering from Covid-19 by investing in people and places,* Australia Together, . https://static1.squarespace.com/static/5eccbe4ec6fa01358cfceb8b/t/5ee1a0575a315a4e35ea5d9f/1591844957587/AustraliaTogether+1-6-20+v.0.1.pdf Accessed 1 July 2021.

Ikerd, J. (2014). Limits to economic growth. *Journal of Agriculture, Food Systems, and Community Development, 4*(3), 15–18.

ILO. (2021). ILO monitor: COVID-19 and the world of work, International Labour Organisation., https://www.ilo.org/wcmsp5/groups/public/%2D%2D-dgreports/%2D%2D-dcomm/ documents/ briefingnote/ wcms_767028.pdf Accessed 30 June 2021.

IMF. (2020). *Inequality in the time of COVID-19*. International Monetary Fund, Washington DC.

Jacobs, M., & Mazzucato, M. (2016). *Rethinking capitalism: Economics and policy for sustainable and inclusive growth*. Wiley.

Jensen, N., Kelly, A. H., & Avendano, M. (2021). The COVID-19 pandemic underscores the need for an equity-focused global health agenda. *Humanities and Social Science Communications, 8*, 15.

Jerneck, A., & Olsson, L. (2008). Adaptation and the poor: Development, resilience and transition. *Climate Policy, 8*, 170–182.

Kallis, G., Gomez-Baggethun, E., & Zografos, C. (2013). To value or not to value? That is not the question. *Ecological Economics, 94*, 97–105.

Kar, S., Pritchett, L., Raihan, S., & Sen, K. (2013). Looking for a break: Identifying transitions in growth regimes. *Journal of Macroeconomics, 38*(Part B), 151–166.

Kulig, J. C., Edge, D. S., Townshend, I., Lightfoot, N., & Reimer, W. (2013). Community resiliency: Emerging theoretical insights. *Journal of Community Psychology, 41*(6), 758–775.

Le Qúeŕe, C., Jackson, R. B., Jones, M. W., Smith, A. J. P., Abernethy, S., Andrew, R. M., De-Gol, A. J., Willis, D. R., Shan, Y., Canadell, J. G., Friedlingstein, P., Creutzig, F., & Peters, G. P. (2020). Temporary reduction in daily global CO2 emissions during the COVID-19 forced confinement. *Nature Climate Change, 10*, 47–653.

Lenzen, M., Li, M., Malik, A., Pomponi, F., Sun, Y.-Y., Wiedmann, T., Faturay, F., Fry, J., Gallego, B., Geschke, A., Gómez-Paredes, J., Kanemoto, K., Kenway, S., Nansai, K., Prokopenko, M., Wakiyama, T., Wang, Y., & Yousefzadeh, M. (2020). Global socio-economic losses and environmental gains from the coronavirus pandemic. *PLoS One, 15*(7), e0235654.

Macekura, S. J. (2020). *The mismeasure of progress: Economic growth and its critics*. University of Chicago Press.

Masten, A. S., & Motti-Stefanidi, F. (2020). Multisystem resilience for children and youth in disaster: Reflections in the context of COVID-19. *Adversity and Resilience Science*, 1–12.

Meckling, J., & Allan, B. B. (2020). The evolution of ideas in global climate policy. *Nature Climate Change, 10*, 434–438.

Mishan, E. J. (1967). *The costs of economic growth*. Staples.

Mishan, E. J. (1977). *The economic growth debate: An assessment*. Allen and Unwin.

Nemeth, D. G., & Olivier, T. W. (2017). *Innovative approaches to individual and community resilience: From theory to practice*. Elsevier Academic Press.

OECD. (2014). Guidelines for resilience systems analysis, Organisation for Economic Co-operation and Development Publishing, . https://www.oecd.org/dac/Resilience%20Systems%20Analysis%20FINAL.pdf Accessed 29 June 2021.

OECD. (2019). Beyond growth: Towards a new economic approach, new approaches to economic challenges, OECD Publishing, , https://doi.org/10.1787/33a25ba3-en. Accessed 28 June 2021.
OECD. (2020). *Social economy and the COVID-19 crisis: current and future roles, Organisation for Economic Development and Co-operation*, Paris. https://www.oecd.org/coronavirus/policy-responses/social-economy-and-the-covid-19-crisis-current-and-future-roles-f904b89f/ Accessed 28 June 2021.
Pacetti, E.G. (2016). *The five characteristics of an inclusive economy: Getting beyond the equity-growth dichotomy,* Rockefeller Foundation., https://www.rockefellerfoundation.org/blog/five-characteristics-inclusive-economy-getting-beyond-equity-growth-dichotomy/ Accessed 29 June 2021.
Piketty, T. (2014). *Capital in the twenty-first century*. Belknap Press.
Pilling, D. (2018). *The growth delusion: The wealth and Well-being of nations*. Bloomsbury Publishing.
Ramos, G., & Hynes, W. (2019). *Beyond growth: Towards a new economic approach*, OECD Publishing. https://www.oecd.org/naec/averting-systemic-collapse/SG-NAEC(2019)3_Beyond%20Growth.pdf Accessed 28 June 2021.
Regibeau, P., & Rockett, K. (2013). Economic analysis of resilience: A framework for local policy response based on new case studies, Journal of Innovation Economics, vol. 0(1), 107–147.
Roese, J. (2021). *COVID-19 exposed the digital divide. Here's how we can close it,* World Economic Forum. https://www.weforum.org/agenda/2021/01/covid-digital-divide-learning-education/ Accessed 30 June 2021.
Rogge, N., & Van Nijverseel, I. (2018). Quality of life in the European Union: A multidimensional analysis. *Social Indicators Research, 141*(2), 765–789.
Schwartz, J., Hatfield, S., Jones, R., & Anderson, S. (2019). *What is the future of work? Redefining work, workforces and workplaces*. Deloitte Insights.
Shaik, A., & Tomak, A. (1994). *Measuring the wealth of nations: The political economy of national accounting*. Cambridge University Press.
Sjostedt, M. (2015). Resilience revisited: Taking institutional theory seriously. *Ecology and Society, 20*, 23.
Soros, G. (2015). *Why we need to rethink economics*, interview, Institute for New Economic Thinking, New York. https://www.ineteconomics.org/perspectives/videos/why-we-need-to-rethink-economics Accessed 29 June 2021.
Spash, C. L. (2020). 'The economy' as if people mattered: Revisiting critiques of economic growth in a time. *Globalizations*. https://doi.org/10.1080/14747731.2020.1761612
Stiglitz, J. (2012). *The price of inequality*. Penguin Books.
Taherzadeh, O. (2021). Promise of a green economic recovery post-Covid: Trojan horse or turning point? *Global Sustainability, 4*(e2), 1–6.
UN. (2015). *Sustainable development goals*. Department of Economic and Social Affairs, United Nations. https://sdgs.un.org/goals Accessed 29 June 2021
UNDP. (2019). *Human development report 2019: Beyond income, beyond averages, beyond today*. United Nations Development Programme.
Waring, M. (1999). *Counting for nothing: What men value and what women are worth*. University of Toronto Press.
Washington, H., & Maloney, M. (2020). The need for ecological ethics in a new ecological economics. *Ecological Economics, 169*.
Weidmann, T., Lenzen M., KeyBer L. T., & Steinberger J. K. (2020). Scientists' warning on affluence. *Nature Communications, 11*, 3107. https://doi.org/10.1038/s41467-020-16941-y.
World Bank. (2020). *Poverty and distributional impacts of COVID-19: Potential channels of impact and mitigating Policies*, World Bank, . https://www.worldbank.org/en/topic/poverty/brief/poverty-and-distributional-impacts-of-covid-19-potential-channels-of-impact-and-mitigating-policies Accessed 2 July 2020.
WRI. (2020). *Build back better: Perspectives on COVID-19 response and recovery*, World Resources Institute. https://www.wri.org/events/2020/04/build-back-better-perspectives-covid-19-response-recovery Accessed 1 July 2020.
Yunus Centre. (2020). *Roadmap to recovery and regeneration*. Griffith University.

An MMT Perspective on How Agenda 30 Could Be Implemented in Australia

James Juniper

Abstract Covid-19 has shown that governments with monetary sovereignty can turn the tap off quickly, if they must, and just as easily turn the tap back on. This has been coupled with a new appreciation for the ability of a sovereign economy to operate effectively despite large levels of net government (and net foreign) debt as a proportion of GDP, reconfirming the experience of those governments during WWII, when debt was used as an instrument to curb consumption and to redirect productive resources and research activity into investment in new capacity and new technology to support the war effort (viz the Agenda 30 strategic policy goals).

A similar imperative now confronts nations as they direct resources into a sustainable transformation of the economy. This paper will contribute to these policy objectives by examining the respective economic roles to be played in this transformation by the Job Guarantee, the Green New Deal, and what Mazzucato chooses to call "mission-oriented finance"! In this context, a range of metrics for guiding policy is also evaluated.

Keywords Modern monetary theory · Agenda 30 · Green new Deal · Job guarantee · Mission-oriented finance · Short-changing nature

1 Introduction

The main purpose of this paper is to clarify both the rationale for, and policy objectives underpinning, a range of interventions recently advocated by Modern Monetary Theorists (MMTs), within the context of the UN's Agenda 30 strategic policy goals. Specifically, it will address the Job Guarantee (JG) as an anti-inflationary instrument and the Green New Deal (GND) as a means for redirection of resources and capital investment.

J. Juniper (✉)
Newcastle Business School, College of Human and Social Futures, The University of Newcastle, Callaghan, NSW, Australia
e-mail: James.juniper@newcastle.edu.au

© The Author(s), under exclusive license to Springer Nature Singapore Pte Ltd. 2022

T. Chaiechi, J. Wood (eds.), *Community Empowerment, Sustainable Cities, and Transformative Economies*, https://doi.org/10.1007/978-981-16-5260-8_3

However, I intend to achieve this clarification within an academic context where it has become fashionable to question MMT for its on-going adherence to supposedly inadequate or erroneous theoretical principles. Much like much like Marc Antony in Shakespeare's Julius Caesar, who guilefully claimed that he came "to bury Ceasar not to praise him", for although Brutus (along with Georg Friedrich Knapp and Abba Lerner) was purportedly an honourable man, MMT is faulted on a fundamental level for its less than honourable fidelity to the principles of (i) neo-Chartalism; and, (ii) Functional Finance.

The first theoretical allegiance is criticised on the basis of a broader Post Keynesian or Marxist interpretation of "money with no intrinsic value", which questions the notion that stability in the value of money, when it functions as both a unit of account and a store of value, can be guaranteed solely by the legislated requirement that it be used for the payment of outstanding tax obligations (Lapavitsas & Aguila, 2020, is representative on this strand of critique). The second allegiance is questioned by so-called Structuralists, on the basis that current account deficits and cumulative net foreign indebtedness *do matter*, especially for emerging economies, which suffer from being situated low in the global currency hierarchy, plagued by a narrow, commodity-based admixture of exports, while subject to a rapidly destabilising pass-through of exchange rate fluctuations onto tradeable goods prices (for examples of this Structuralist critique, see Prates, 2020; Vernengo & Caldentey, 2019, for critiques, and Carnevali et al., 2020 for a discussion of strategic pass-through as a generalisation of the Marshall-Lerner conditions).

With the intention of clearing the way for a more focused discussion of macroeconomic policy options, I wanted to briefly respond to the above-mentioned criticism of MMT's theoretical foundations. To begin with, I wanted to highlight the fact that, in the 1980s, the Australian tradition of MMT developed within an environment where many mainstream and more left-wing economists adopted what were effectively *Structuralist* arguments to argue that a return to policies of full employment that were temporarily abandoned in the last year of the Whitlam Labour Government, was prevented by a "Balance-of-Payments Constraint". When Hawke-Keating Labor Government was returned to power in the early 80s, Treasurer Paul Keating, largely mirrored then ex-Prime-Minister John Howard's obsession with the rising level of foreign debt.

In Australia, back in the 80s, a series of inter-linked Structuralist arguments that legitimised a sustained assault on the wages and conditions of Australian workers, and ultimately, the level of trade union influence. However, the biggest impact on the industrial working class could be sheeted home to rising labour underutilisation (a combination of rising unemployment and 'precariousness'). With the clear intention of reducing the "real wage overhang," workers were encouraged to trade-off increases in the 'social wage' for cuts to real wages as a means of restoring the international competitiveness of Australian goods and services.

In grappling with these problems, progressive economists often (incorrectly) applied Kaldor-Thirlwall multiplier models of trade to the case of *floating* rather than *fixed* exchange rates (McCombie & Thirlwall, 1994). On this view, income elasticities of demand dominate in their effects over exchange-rate related price-elasticities. A country like Australia is seen to have a high income-elasticity of demand for imports whereas the rest of the world has relatively low income-elasticities of demand for Australian exports. Accordingly, if Australia were to grow too rapidly compared with rates of growth exhibited by our major trading partners, the current account deficit would widen dramatically. "Stop-Go" policies would be the inevitable result.

Within the Commonwealth Government bureaucracy, it was commonplace for economists to refer to the "twin deficits" hypothesis, which viewed total public sector debt as the main driver of deficits on the current account. Similar views were actively promoted by supposedly 'left wing' economists in the National Institute of Economic and Industry Research, officials at the OECD, and members of Secretariat of the tripartite Australian Economic Planning and Advisory Commission. At around the same time, there was much-heated debate about "Dutch Disease" (i.e., the "crowding out" of other industries when the resource-sector expanded) and the "J-curve" effect in Australia (which arises when an exchange-rate depreciation initially worsens the trade deficit before contributing to a gradual increase in net exports).

Both Marxist and Post Keynesian critics of MMT have emphasised the importance of the global currency hierarchy, the determinants of *effective* sovereignty, and the influence of conventions and confidence in the whole monetary system as having some bearing on the value of money. And Chartalist views have been questioned on the dubious basis that spot/forward contracts were developed before effective principles of taxation were formalised. It has been claimed that many developing economies simply "will not find foreign demand for their currencies".

Kaltenbrunner (2019) has attempted to achieve an integration of what she calls the 'horizontalist' or structuralist position and 'verticalist' interpretations of monetary policy in open economies (the work of Lavoie, 2000, 2002–03 can be seen as illustrative of the 'verticalist' position, especially in his interpretation of the covered interest parity condition). To this end, she has identified three structural factors that determine the ability of a country to meet outstanding external obligations (and thus, the liquidity premium on its currency); namely: (i) a country's total stock of net (short-term) external obligations (expressed as a proportion of GDP); (ii) the proportion of its liabilities denominated in foreign currency and the possible existence of other liabilities to foreign investors; (iii) a country's ability to meet its outstanding liabilities through "forcing a cash flow in its favour" either through the income generation process (including income from previous rounds of lending) and/or dealing and trading in capital assets and financial instruments; and finally, if current cash flows are insufficient to meet outstanding obligations, (iv) the ability to "make positions" (i.e. to refinance existing debt and/or to liquidate assets).

The question for policy makers is whether a country exposed to external pressures in each of these three ways, can put together a cluster of policy interventions, including capital controls, to counter any likely shocks (while recognzing the fact that floating exchange rates ensure greater levels of autonomy in the pursuit of effective fiscal policy). This is where consideration must be given to a range of policy instruments that help to develop and diversify the economic and trading base.

Personally, I see a *strong resonance* between Marxist views on the credit system, when it fails to work as a means of payment, and Minsky's notions of financial instability, which have long been accepted by MMT advocates. By the same token, I see little difference between Marx's conception of money with no intrinsic value and Chartalist efforts to explain how a stable value for the national currency can be established (see Campbell, 2017, for a comprehernsive discussion of Marx's views on money with no intrnsic value).

In the next section of the paper, I will examine the Job Guarantee (JG). This will be followed by an interpretation of the Green New Deal (GND) as a policy for controlling inflationary pressures in the long run while achieving dramatic changes in the resource base. Australian MMT researchers would insist that a raft of supplementary policies (apart from but including capital controls) can also be adopted as supplements in the pursuit of full employment, including tax policy, industry policy and a strategic commitment to industrial development on the basis of competencies.

2 The Job Guarantee in a "Nutshell"

The JG is premised on the fact that only the national government (as the issuer of fiat currency) can create *Net Financial Assets* (NFA) through deficit spending. To avoid any under-employment of labour and productive capacity, the flow of NFA must match non-Government sector's desire to net save. Otherwise, there would be a shortfall in effective demand. Jobs created through the issue of NFA would be paid at minimum wage and designed so that they do not directly compete with those to be subsequently created within the domestic private sector via the multiplier.

The JG labour-force thus functions as a "buffer stock" whose primary role is that of an anti-inflationary instrument. This is because the uneven distribution and persistence of underemployment mean that traditional policies of public investment would otherwise meet inflationary bottlenecks well before full employment is reached (Mitchell & Juniper, 2007).

Mitchell (2020) explains how a JG operates as a superior means for the control of inflation when compared to the mainstream pursuit of a non-accelerating inflation rate of unemployment (NAIRU). The effectiveness of inflation policies based on NAIRU can and has been undermined by: (i) the continual movement of workers out of short term into long-term unemployment; and, (ii) the dramatic rise in the proportion of those in precarious employment. In the more technical literature on inflation, these combined effects are said to have contributed to the development of a "horizontal" Phillips Curve.

Figure 1., below, suggests how the JG could operate by comparing three positions on the traditional Phillips Curve, which depicts trade-offs between realised inflation and unemployment. Governments increase effective demand in response to high unemployment in position *A*, moving to position *B*, at the cost of a rise in inflation

Fig. 1 The job guarantee and the Phillips curve
Source: Mitchell, Wray, Watts (2019). Fig. 19.3: 309

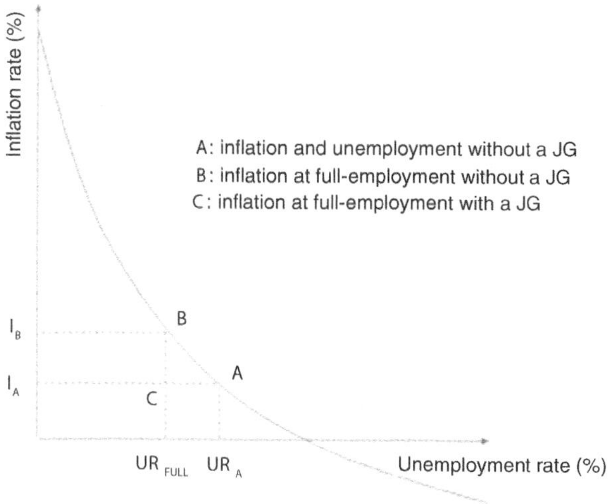

from I_A to I_B. If a JG were put into place, the economy could instead move to position *C*, achieving full employment at the original rate of inflation.

3 The Green New Deal in a "Nutshell"

Where the JG is a short-run anti-inflationary mechanism, the Green New Deal (GND) is a log-run anti-inflationary mechanism for achieving a dramatic transformation in the economy through intervention in the process of capital accumulation. The GND adopts the methodology originally proposed by J. M. Keynes in his pamphlet on *How to Pay for the War* in the context of responding on a massive scale to environmental problems such as climate change (Nersisyan & Wray, 2019).

Under this modern version of the scheme, the stages to be followed are first to estimate the "costs" of the GND in terms of resource requirements; second, to assesses resource availability that can be devoted to implementing GND projects. This includes mobilisation of unutilised and underutilised resources, plus shifting of resources away from current destructive and inefficient uses into GND projects. Here, the main problem that could arise is that of inflation if sufficient resources cannot be diverted to the GND. Accordingly, the scheme also proposes a series of anti-inflationary measures, which could include well-targeted taxes, wage and price controls, rationing, and voluntary saving. During WWII, voluntary saving was accomplished, both Great Britain and the US, through the issuance of war bonds to *all* classes in society. This combination of policy interventions is summarised in Fig. 2., below.

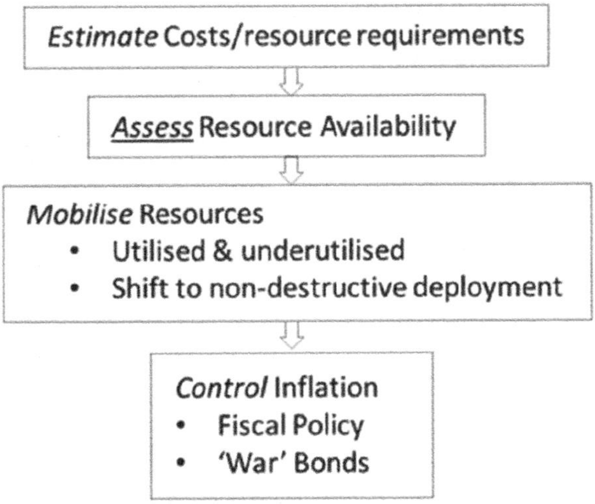

Fig. 2 The green new deal in a Nutshell

4 Industry-Policies and Economic Development

Through a historical and political analysis of the East Asian development model, Amsden and Wade have highlighted the difficulties faced by developing economies located at some distance from the frontier of best practice yet still want to tilt the "playing field" away from existing configurations of comparative advantage. Amsden (1989) emphasises the need for a strong state to impose a binding condition of reciprocity on corporations and sectors that benefit from a variety of subsidies designed to influence the path of capital accumulation. Wade (1990) attends to the complexity of "governed market" interventions that might appear to be even-handed in regard to trade versus non-traded, or import-substituting rather than export-oriented industries (conditions which he describes as those of a "simulated free-market"), yet nevertheless still provide incentives for advancement.

The work of Felipe et al., (2012) builds on the competency-based economic analysis of strategic development. This research updates work originally conducted by Hidalgo & Hausman (2009) using another set of data encompassing 5107 products and 124 countries. A minimal spanning tree is constructed for global trade based on proximity links between different products. Production of traded goods located at the centre of the network is seen to require a more diverse and non-ubiquitous but unobservable set of competencies. In countries such as India and China, policymakers seem to have been able to exploit available proximity links in their efforts to expand both the scale and scope of what is being produced and traded.

More recently, Barry Naughten (2021) has identified a shift in Chinese industry policy away from sectoral policies for strategic emerging industries towards policies that promote core digital technologies that, if successful, would enable China to leap-frog ahead of EU and US industries in a selected range of key domains (including digital fabrication and production, quantum computation, AI, and machine-learning, big data and the internet-of-things). Understandably, Naughten is reluctant to evaluate the success or failure of these initiatives, remarking that insufficient evidence has yet been amassed to make such judgements. He describes at some length the Industry Guidance Funds (IGF) that China deploys to coordinate different forms of investment at all levels of government—national, provincial, and local—in innovation, infrastructure, and commercialisation of these technologies—while identifying potential sites of failure and emerging risk.

Along similar lines, Mazzucato and Wray (2015) have emphasised the important policy role of State Investment Banks for "entrepreneurial states" wishing to engage in counter-cyclical expenditure, capital development, and new venture support. In particular, they describe an over-arching process of "mission-oriented" finance instantiated by Eisenhower's efforts to "land a man on the moon" before the Soviet Union. The interventions of a variety of agencies—both public and private, including the newly formed NASA and DARPA—were orchestrated to achieve this set of aims, through the injection of finance at each stage in the innovation chain (i.e., from research, through concept invention, early-stage technology development, and product development, into final production and marketing). If successful, China's IGFs would fulfil all of these requirements. This same kind of coordinated approach could readily be harnessed to achieve ecological rather than military and geo-political goals.

5 Metrics for Short-Changing Nature

In a talk I recently gave to members of MMT-Australia I focused on the limitations of mainstream approaches to Ecological Economics, focusing on the modified neoclassical framework of Pearce and Turner (1990). My major concern was to question those who saw policies for full-employment as being in contradiction with interventions designed to achieve ecological sustainability. However, I also questioned the notion of environmental capital, which featured in Pearce and Turner's '4 Capitals' model of sustainability. Accordingly, I turned to Marx's concept of 'fictitious capital', which he applied both to human capital (with labour services being capitalised into a 'stock' using a discount rate that simply reflected the rate of exploitation) and to the capitalisation of fictitious structures of money taking the form of credit as a means of payment, that were increasingly divorced from real processes of capital accumulation. I suggested that environmental capital could be viewed as an equally fictitious concept, insofar as it attempted to 'capitalise' ill-defined flows of 'environmental services.

I moved on to the need to build more rigorous bridges between Value Theory (understood in terms of Classical rather than Neoclassical Political Economy) and sustainability metrics (which adequately accounted for the 'short-changing' of nature). In the Classical system, prices are determined by socially necessary labour time, including the application of the labour embodied in productive capital. However, from a sustainability perspective, this should include the labour time required to recycle renewable resources, reduce other forms of waste, mitigate the impact of

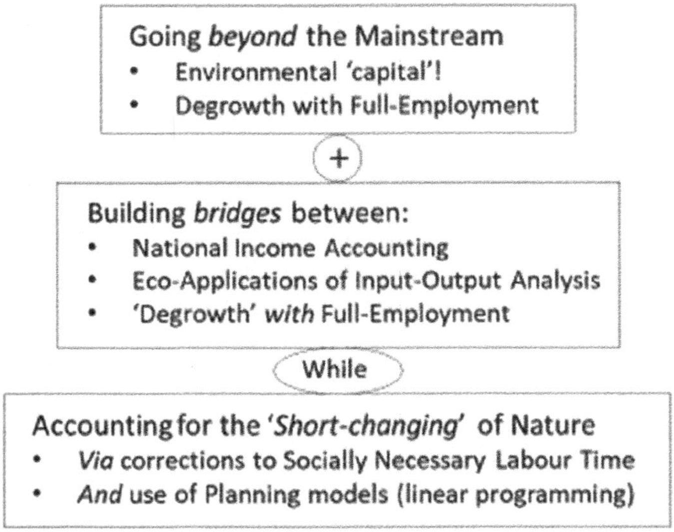

Fig. 3 Metrics for eclogical sustainability
Source: Author's Zoom presentation to MMT-Australia, 20 May, 2020

pollution, and discover substitutes for non-renewable resources whose stocks were being depleted (as argued by Moore, 2017).

To this end, I emphasised the proximity between this Classical theory of reproduction pricing, Leontief's Input-Output Analysis (which has been taken up by a whole generation of Industrial Ecologists), and national accounting conventions for the measurement of GDP (on the former see Schmelev, 2012, along with Suh and Kagawa, 2005; on the latter see UN Statistics Division, 2020; Flaschel, 2010). I then suggested that metrics for sustainability could be constructed by adopting techniques of linear programming that had been developed by mathematical economists and planners in the former Soviet Union, because these techniques were also grounded in the labour theory of value. At the time I was unaware that Paul Cockshott (2010) and his PhD student, Jan Dapprich (2020), had already pursued this approach to sustainability modelling, using modern software, while building on the research of Kantorovich (1939, 1965) and Novozhilov (1970) (also see Ellman, 1968 and Holubnychy, 1982).

For convenience, the various elements of what has been proposed above, are brought together in the Fig. 3., above.

6 Conclusion

By way of a recapitulation, let me suggest that policies such as the JG and the GND complement one another and, in combination, demonstrate ways that Agenda 30 *can be* successfully implemented both in Australia and elsewhere. I went on to argue that the Job Guarantee could serve as a short-run inflation control mechanism while promoting full-allocation and processes of capital accumulation, to achieve sustainability objectives while avoiding inflationary pressures over the long-run.

In arguing for this position, I also wanted to highlight the fact that MMT is and has always been cognisant of difficulties faced by 'emerging economies. For this reason, I also considered a raft of industry policies that could assist developing nations in their efforts to progress up the technology and productivity ladder (even leaving the existing technology frontier behind them in their wake), while diversifying their trade activity. Industry policy can take a long time to come to fruition and some merging economies may be exposed to difficulty when servicing ballooning foreign debt. Under these circumstances capital controls may also fail to stem the tide of increasing financial obligation. However, as Kaltenbrunner (2019), explains, only a certain number of emerging economies would fall into this category. MMT advocates maintain that the loss of fiscal autonomy that would result from any move towards a fixed or 'dollarised' exchange-rate, would unfortunately be a heavy price to pay for the achievement of currency stability, even in the short-run.

Finally, I touched on ways that sustainability metrics could be developed using techniques of linear programming that deployed a modified labour theory of value approach to account for various ways in which nature was being 'short-changed'. In this way, programmes to achieve full-employment could be designed to complement efforts to transform productive activity in ways that met ecological sustainability objectives.

References

Amsden, Alice H. (1989). Asia's next giant: South Korea and late industrialisation. : Oxford University Press.

Campbell, M. (2017). Marx's transition to money with no intrinsic value in capital, chapter 3. *Continental Thought and Freedom: 150 years of Capital, 1*(4), 207–230.

Carnevali, E., Fontana, G., & Passarella, M. V. (2020). Assessing the Marshall–Lerner condition within a stock-flow consistent model. *Cambridge Journal of Economics, 44*, 891–918.

Cockshott, P. (2010, January). Von Mises, Kantorovich and in-natura calculation. *European Journal of Economics and Economic Policies, INTERVENTION, 7*(1), 167–199.

Dapprich, J. P. (2020). *Rationality and distribution in the socialist economy*. PhD thesis. http://theses.gla.ac.uk/81793/.

Ellman. (1968). Novozhilov's book: A note. *Soviet Studies, 20*(1), 152–154.

Felipe, J., Kumar, U., Abdon, A., & Bacate, M. (2012). Product complexity and economic development. *Structural Change and Economic Dynamics, 23*(1), 36–68. Available from Journals - Jesus Felipe.

Flaschel, P. (2010). *Topics in classical Micro- and macroeconomics elements of a critique of Neoricardian theory*. Springer.

Hidalgo, C., & Hausmann, R. (2009). The building blocks of economic complexity. *Proceedings of the National Academy of Sciences of the United States of America, 106*(26), 10570–10575.

Holubnychy, V. (1982). Novozhilov's theory of value. In I. Koropckyj (Ed.), *Soviet regional economics: Selected works of Vsevolod Holubnychy* (pp. 381–484). Canadian Institute of

Ukranian Studies/Hignell Printing. Available at https://diasporiana.org.ua/wp-content/uploads/books/20677/file.pdf
Kaltenbrunner, A. (2019, November – April). How to interpret the forward rate in the foreign exchange market? Horizontalists vs. Structuralists in the open economy. *Revista de Economí Política y Desarrollo, 1*(2), 7–23.
Kantorovich, L. V. (1939 [1960]). Mathematicheskie Metody Organizatsii i Planirovania Proizvodstva, Leningrad: Leningrad state university publishers. (Trans.) mathematical methods in the organisation and planning of production. *Management Science, 6*(4), 366–422.
Kantorovich, L. V. (1965). (trans. P.F. Knightsfield), *The best use of economic resources*. Oxford: Pergamon Press.
Lapavitsas, C., & Aguila, N. (2020). Modern monetary theory on money, sovereignty, and policy: A marxist critique with reference to the Eurozone and Greece. *The Japanese Political Economy, 46*(4), 300–326.
Lavoie, M. (2000). A post Keynesian view of interest parity theorems. *Journal of Post Keynesian Economics, 23*(1), 163–179.
Lavoie, M. (2002). Interest parity, risk Premia, and post Keynesian analysis. *Journal of Post Keynesian Economics, 25*(2), 237–249.
Mazzucato, M., & Wray, L. R. (2015). *Financing the capital development of the economy: a Keynes-Schumpeter-Minsky synthesis*, Levy Economics Institute, Working Paper No. 837.
McCombie, J. S. L., & Thirlwall, A. P. (1994). *Economic growth and the balance of payments constraint*. Macmillan.
Mitchell, W. (2020). The job guarantee and the Phillips curve. *The Japanese Political Economy, 46*(4), 240–260.
Mitchell, W., & Juniper, J. (2007). Towards a spatial Keynesian macroeconomics, chapter 10. In P. Arestis & G. Zezza (Eds.), *Advances in monetary policy and macroeconomics*. Palgrave/Macmillan.
Mitchell, W., Randall Wray, L., & Watts, M. (2019). *Macroeconomics*. Macmillan-Red Globe Press.
Moore, J. W. (2017). Metabolic rift or metabolic shift? *Theory & society, 46*, 285–318.
Naughten, B. (2021). *The rise of China's industrial policy 1978 to 2020*. D.R. Universidad Nacional Autónoma de México.
Nersisyan, Y. & L. R. Wray (2019, May). *How to pay for the green new deal*. Levy Economics Institute Working Paper No. 931.
Novozhilov, V. V. (1970). *Problems of cost-benefit analysis in optimal planning* (Trans. H. McQuiston), White Plains, N.Y.: International Arts and Sciences Press.
Pearce, D. W., & Turner, R. K. (1990). *Economics of natural resources and the environment*. Johns Hopkins University Press.
Prates, D. (2020). Beyond modern money theory: A post-Keynesian approach to the currency hierarchy, monetary sovereignty, and policy space. *Review of Keynesian Economics, 8*(4), 494–511.
Shmelev, S. E. (2012). Industrial economics, chapter 2. In *Ecological economics: Sustainability in practice* (pp. 19–34). Springer Publishers.
Suh, S., & Kagawa, S. (2005). Industrial ecology and input-output economics: An introduction. *Economic Systems Research, December, 17*(4), 349–364.
United Nations Statistics Division (UNSD). (2020). *SDG indicators – global indicator framework for the sustainable development goals and targets of the 2030 agenda for sustainable development*. https://unstats.un.org/sdgs/indicators/indicators-list/
Vernengo, M., &Caldentey, E. P. (2019). *Modern Money Theory (MMT) in the tropics: Functional finance in developing countries*. Political Economy Research Institute. University of Massachusetts, Amhearst, Working Paper No. 495.
Wade, R. (1990). *Governing the market: Economic theory and the role of government in east Asian industrialization*. Princeton University Press.

How Resilient Is the Investment Climate in Australia? Unpacking the Driving Factors

Michael Koczyrkewycz, Taha Chaiechi, and Rabiul Beg

Abstract A resilient economy is the ultimate aspiration of Government authorities and legislators. Economic recovery, one of the cornerstones of economic resilience, measures the speed at which a system recovers from an exogenous and adverse shock. This paper focuses on the resilience of private sector investment within Australia to test its adaptability and absorbability against external shocks. This paper utilises a Kaleckian-Post Keynesian approach to investment, whereby capacity utilisation, profit share, interest rates, and productivity growth are contributing factors. Research, however, has provided evidence that the incorporation of financial development and fiscal policy within the investment model has been largely ignored within the literature. Accordingly, this paper incorporates such indicators to capture their role in modelling approaches. Using annual historical data from 1980 to 2015, this paper adopts a Vector Error Correction Model (VECM), Impulse Response Functions (IRF) and Variance Decompositions (VD) to examine investment's resilience against external disturbances. Results show that both long and short-run unidirectional causality between investment and the explanatory variables was evident, by identifying cointegrating vectors. The results confirm that government expenditure is the more powerful mechanism of the two, suggesting that a permanent incorporation into the model should be taken seriously. A simulated onetime shock upon the explanatory variables towards investment shows volatile and positive long-lasting reactions, with no sign of returning to pre-shock levels in the long-run. The results showed the changes in profit and the private sector's productive capacity are

M. Koczyrkewycz (✉)
College of Business, Law and Governance, James Cook University, Cairns, QLD, Australia
e-mail: michael.koczyrkewycz@my.jcu.edu.au

T. Chaiechi
College of Business, Law and Governance, James Cook University, Townsville, QLD, Australia
e-mail: taha.chaiechi@jcu.edu.au

R. Beg
College of Business, Law and Governance, Bebegu Yumba Campus, James Cook University, Townsville, QLD, Australia
e-mail: rabiul.beg@jcu.edu.au

© The Author(s), under exclusive license to Springer Nature Singapore Pte Ltd. 2022

T. Chaiechi, J. Wood (eds.), *Community Empowerment, Sustainable Cities, and Transformative Economies*, https://doi.org/10.1007/978-981-16-5260-8_4

the most important indicators capable of explaining variations in private sector investment decisions in Australia.

Keywords Economic resilience · Adaptability · Speed of recovery · Investment · Kaleckian-Post Keynesian

1 Introduction

While the concept of externalities (i.e., outcomes of market failure) goes back to the early twentieth century, discussions around externalities of climate change (e.g., environmental degradation, air and water pollution etc.) or externalities of highly infectious transmitted diseases (such as the COVID-19 pandemic) has emerged in the environmental and health economics literature in the recent decades. Negative externalities emanating from natural disasters, financial shocks, and public health emergencies have shifted how the private sector makes decisions about investing (Chaiechi & Nguyen, 2021). Understanding this shift is essential because, unlike classical economics, Keynesian and Post-Keynesian frameworks perceive investment as the main engine of economic growth and full employment. Indeed, Michal Kalecki and John Maynard Keynes were the first to emphasise the importance of investment, within theoretical frameworks, in determining aggregate demand and output. Accordingly, a country's ability to achieve economic development depends upon its private sector capability and willingness to invest. Therefore, investment is placed at the centre stage to stimulate aggregate demand (see Keynes, 1936 as the pioneering work). A decline in investment levels would lower aggregate demand, adversely affecting employment levels and business continuity, and therefore, investment remains the crucial factor in building and growing a strong economy. One of the factors influencing investment levels is the investors' confidence or willingness to engage in investment opportunities based on their perception of risk and return.

As of 2016, Australia enjoyed 25 years of continuous positive economic growth, the only developed nation to do so (Australian Government, 2016). As seen in Fig. 1, the annualised percentage growth of GDP shows that some behaviours align with investment annualised growth, with noticeable joint dips in 1983, 1987 (the commodity crisis), 1991/1992, 2001 and 2009 (GFC). Furthermore, Australia's investment has faced cyclical backlashes from exogenous shocks more recently, such as adverse impacts from climate change (floods in 2019 and bushfires in 2019–2020) and the COVID-19 pandemic in 2020, to name a few. In line with such impacts, investment declined −5.9% in June 2020, rebounding to 3.9% in December 2020, the strongest rise since September 2017 (ABS, 2020).

Evidence shows investor confidence is adversely reactional to uncertainty (Krugman, 1988; Mian & Sufi, 2014) and unexpected turns of events (Angeletos & Lian, 2020) such as natural/financial disasters and public health emergencies. As such, this paper posits that investor confidence starts with resilience, as seen via the

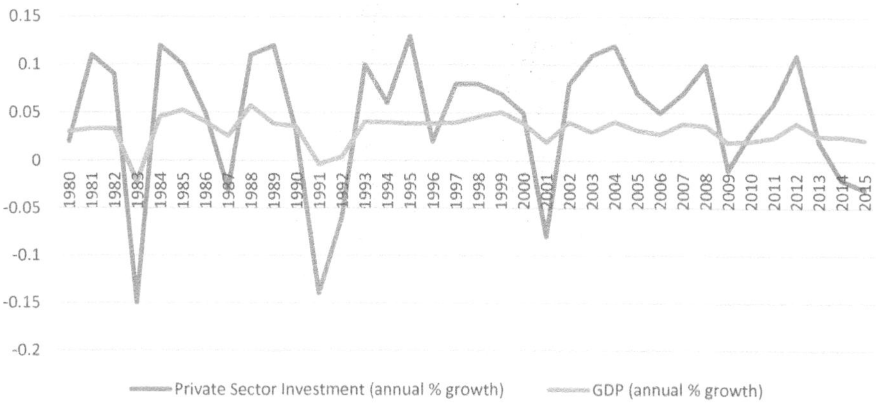

Fig. 1 Private sector investment (% GDP and annual growth) and GDP (annual % growth) Australia: 1980–2015
Source: International Monetary Fund: Fiscal Affairs, OECD and World Bank

Global Commission on Adaptation, estimating high investment return rates in areas with high resilience (Larsfalten, 2020). While literature around economic resilience is limited, such a mechanism is referred to as the inherent or adaptive ability to absorb, adapt and recover from external shocks (Holling, 1973; Rose, 2004; Milenti, 1999, P1). Therefore, this paper aims to investigate the resilience of investment in Australia after an exogenous shock.

In redefining Kalecki's investment model, this paper will build upon the works of Bhaduri and Marglin (1990), Stockhammer and Onaran (2004) and Chaiechi (2012), whereby capacity utilisation, profit share, interest rates, and productivity growth are driving factors. Chaiechi (2012) has provided evidence that the incorporation of financial development and fiscal policy within the investment model has been largely ignored within the literature. As such, there is scope to incorporate a more intuitive measure of capturing financial market developments into the model, alongside a more traditional fiscal policy measure. Financial market developments, and its role in promoting growth, is defined by market costs and imperfections (Cihak et al., 2012). Markets infer costs by obtaining and processing investment information in the form of transacting goods and services with the use of financial instruments, while market imperfections negatively influence society's savings ability to those with best projects and ideas, curtailing rotational economic development and constraining living standard improvements. Investment growth leads to the creation of financial contracts, intermediaries and markets, leading to positive impacts on economic growth through reduced costings (Cihak et al., 2012). Financial development occurs when intermediaries and markets mitigate the effects of limited enforcement, transition costs and imperfect information (Cihak et al., 2012). Although Keynesian and Post-Keynesian schools view the promotion of investment as key in driving economic growth, the transmission mechanisms between finance and investment have been mostly overlooked (Nazlioglu et al., 2009).

When compared to monetary policy, fiscal policy has received less attention as to its effects upon economic growth (Afonso & Sousa, 2012). Expanding fiscal policy can positively influence investment, also known as crowding in, leading to growth in real GDP. However, the reverse may hold true, whereby a crowding-out effect may negatively impact growth (Akinlo & Oyeleke, 2018). These findings can be mixed, whereby Laopodis (2001) finds evidence of a crowding-in effect within some economies and a crowding-out effect within others. Literature tends to focus on the effects of government spending on either private or public investment, including introducing categories of government expenditures, with each presenting conflicting results. After careful review of the literature, the incorporation of both indicators within such an investment model, more so to test adaptability and absorbability against external shocks, will be a first.

2 Literature Review

Negative externalities such as climate change and public health emergencies would impact every business and investor globally, forcing them to recalibrate their investment decisions by continuously incorporating new realities into their business modelling. While there is abundant literature around the private sector's role in creating jobs, making investment decisions, and inducing economic growth, studies focusing on the strength and adaptability of private sector investment decisions are rather limited. Chaiechi and Nguyen (2021) argue that since classical economics is primarily concerned with equilibrium conditions, it cannot provide suitable frameworks to explore the concept of resilience. The authors argue that Post-Keynesian economics provides the most appropriate framework for analysing economic resilience. Their established frameworks and methods for out-of-equilibrium phenomena in contemporary economic theories are commonly utilised. Using policy and climate scenario analysis, Emodi et al. (2018, 2019) focused on Australia's Energy Industry. They explored investment capacity expansion under different scenarios, especially when the system is faced with increased demand. They found if the private sector switches to better energy efficiency measures, the high cost of investment in the short-run would be largely offset by cost savings in the long-run.

Briguglio et al. (2005) show three definition senses are incorporated within the literature: the ability to recover quickly after a shock, withstanding the shock and shock avoidance effect. The authors establish a resilience index, relating shock-absorbing and shock-counteracting functions through social development, good governance, microeconomic market stability and macroeconomic stability. Of the 102 countries under analysis via the resilience index, Briguglio et al. show that Australia is ranked the sixth most resilient economy in periods 2001–2003. The top 5 most resilient countries were Iceland, New Zealand, Singapore, United States, and Denmark.

In analysing the mechanisms behind strengthening economic resilience, Caldera-Sánchez et al. (2016) gain insights from post-1970 records of severe recessions and financial crises. The study summarises a large sample of OECD and non-OECD economies during 1970–2014, investigating growth-related financial fragility. The authors found that more effective Governments benefit from fewer severe recessions and higher economic growth. Also, economic resilience can be strengthened by exploring the role of policies within an economy that can mitigate the consequences and risks of severe crises. Concerning exogenous shocks, only a limited number of studies have examined investment sensitivity (Chaiechi et al., 2006; Go, 1994; Greenwood et al., 1988). Such literature shows a significant vulnerability to unexpected events. A more recent study from Hassan and Othman (2015) investigates the resilience of private sector investment within selected Malaysian economic sectors from 1995–2012. The study finds Malaysia's economic resilience required strengthening post-2012 to avoid economic vulnerability and encourage investment. The authors conclude that market efficiency and macroeconomic stability were considered the two main strategies for establishing a resilient economy that encourages investment.

Impacts of variations in financial markets and government policies such as fiscal policy upon investment is also important. Financial market developments impact private sector investment. It can be used as a marker to define improvements in the quality, quantity, and efficiency of intermediary services, leading to higher investment levels (Chaiechi, 2012). King and Levine (1993a, 1993b) found that high levels of financial development correlate with efficiency improvements, physical capital accumulation, investment and economic growth, using cross-country regression methods. Bloch and Tang (2003) showed mixed results with the analysis of 75 countries during 1960–1990, whereby 26 economies showed a positive correlation between financial development and investment. Only one economy showed statistical significance, while 49 economies showed a negative relationship, with 21 showing statistical significance.

In analysing the influence of fiscal policy upon private sector investment, Alesina et al. (2002) find a sizeable crowding-out effect, using a panel of OECD countries, showing a link between fiscal policy to profits and wages. The study also concluded that Government employment places wage pressures for private industry and various taxes, creating a crowding-out effect upon profits. Overall, however, the study finds that government expenditure's effects overshadow the effects of taxes upon investment. Counter to these findings, Marattin and Salotti (2011) found that Government expenditure shocks positively affected private sector investment within 14 EU countries, whereby a crowding-in effect was identified. In comparing expenditure and taxation, Arin (2004) shows that changes in expenditure have a greater impact on private sector investment than changes in taxation, using a panel data set of G-7 countries. Arin shows that taxes on household income interfere with individuals' leisure and labour choices, creating distortions on output.

3 The Empirical Model

Kalecki provided three evolutions in investment theory, he: (1) placed aggregate investment as a function of gross profitability and interest rates (Kalecki, 1933); (2) defined investment as a function of profit gaps, capital stock gaps and cash flow (Kalecki, 1943); and (3) assumed investment depends on marginal profitability (Kalecki, 1968). In redefining Kalecki's approach to investment, this paper builds upon the works of Bhaduri and Marglin (1990), Stockhammer and Onaran (Stockhammer & Onaran, 2004) and Chaiechi (2012), whereby capacity utilisation, profit share, interest rates, and productivity growth are driving factors. Additionally, Chaiechi provided evidence that the incorporation of financial development and the role of government policy within the selected investment model has been largely ignored within the literature. As such, the investment function within this paper will be augmented with the incorporation of financial development (*fd*) and fiscal policy (*fp*) term. Accordingly, our empirical investment model is presented as follows:

$$\text{Investment}: I_t = a_0 + a_1 ut_{t-1} + a_2 p_{t-1} + a_3 ir_t + a_4 pg_{t-1} + a_5 fd_t + a_6 fp_t + \varepsilon_t \quad (1)$$

I_t: Investment (i)
ut_t: Capacity utilisation (ii)
p_t: Profit share (iii)
ir_t: Interest rate (iv)
pg_t: Productivity growth (v)
fd_t: Financial development indicator (vi)
fp_t: Fiscal policy indicator (vii)
ε_t: Random disturbance term with certain properties
a_i: $i = 0, 1, 2, 3, 4, 5$ and 6 are unknown parameters to be estimated.
t: Time index

The dependent variable investment is calculated as a ratio of *I/Y*, whereby *Y* is nominal gross domestic product (NGDP). Following Dutt (1992), capacity utilisation is calculated as the ratio of *Y/K* whereby *K* is stock of capital. Profit share is calculated as the rate of profit (p_t) as $pr = (1\text{-}Wb)u$, where *W* is the real wage rate, *b* is the full ratio of labour to NGDP, and *u* is the rate of profit. Interest rate is directly determined by commercial and central bank liquidity holdings, wealth organisations and other holders. Interest rates will be defined as real interest rates, captured as the lending interest rate adjusted by the GDP deflator. Productivity growth is defined as the change through the *K/L* ratio, whereby *L* is defined as labour, holding a positive function towards investment and capacity utilisation. Financial development is defined as the stock market turnover ratio (SMTR), calculated as the total value of shares traded during the period divided by average market capitalisation. Defined as an efficiency indicator within financial markets, this ratio is often met with a higher turnover ratio due to higher liquidity (Svirydzenda, 2016). Fiscal policy is defined as changes in government expenditure, expressed as *GE/Y*.

4 Data Sources

Relevant Australian data sets were obtained from the following trusted sources as per described in Table 1. The data is collected annually for periods 1980–2015.

5 Estimation Techniques and Results

Using EViews 10 software, this paper adopts time series analysis techniques and processes, including preliminary tests for stationarity, lag selection, cointegration, Vector Error Correction Models (VECM), and post estimation tests Granger causality/block exogeneity. Furthermore, to capture investment's resilience against external shocks, Impulse Response Functions (IRF) and Variance Decomposition (VD) are adopted.

5.1 *Testing for Stationarity*

In analysing whether the series is stationary, the Augmented Dickey-Fuller (ADF) and Phillips-Perron (PP) testing methods are used. Both tests differ mainly in how they handle serial correlation in the test regressions, while PP uses non-parametric corrections (Dickey & Fuller, 1979 Dickey & Fuller, 1981 Phillips & Perron, 1988).

Table 1 Data sources. 1980–2015

Variables	Calculation	Data sources
Investment	Investment/Nominal GDP Ratio	World Development Indicators – World Bank
Capacity Utilisation	Nominal GDP/Stock of Capital Ratio	World Development Indicators – World Bank, IMF Fiscal Affairs Department
Profit Share	(1-Wb)u	Australian Bureau of Statistics, Australian Tax Office, Penn World Table
Interest Rate	Lending Interest Rate, GDP Deflator Adjusted	World Development Indicators – World Bank
Productivity Growth	Stock of Capital/Labour Ratio	IMF Fiscal Affairs Department, Australian Bureau of Statistics
Financial Development Indicator	Total Value of Shares Traded/ Average Market Capitalisation Ratio	Global Financial Development Database – World Bank
Fiscal Policy Indicator	Government Expenditure/Nominal GDP Ratio	World Development Indicators – World Bank
Nominal GDP	Nominal Gross Domestic Product	World Development Indicators – World Bank

Descriptive statistics are presented in Appendix 1, while Table 2 shows the stationary test results. The ADF and PP produce similar results, whereby all level series show a unit root at the 1% significance level.

5.2 Johansen Cointegration Tests

Engle and Granger (1987) argued that two or more time-series I(1) variables could be cointegrated if it can be proved that there is a relationship between the variables. Accordingly, this paper tested for the evidence of cointegration using Johansen's (1995) method with summary results presented in Table 3.

While both Trace statistics and Max Eigenvalues are important components of Johansen's test, Lütkepohl et al. (2001) argue that the trace test suffers from size distortion issues when applied to smaller series. As such, the Max Eigenvalues statistic is a more accurate representation. As seen in Table 2, the minimum cointegrating vectors are reported as two.

5.3 Vector Error Correction Model

Since our series are cointegrated, this paper adopts the Vector Error Correction Model (VECM) with cointegration relations embedded into its specification. Accordingly, the VECM restricts the long-run behaviour between variables by converging to their cointegrated relationship. The cointegration term is also known as the error correction term or ECT. Since there are at least two cointegrating vectors in the series, at least two ECT terms exist in the VECM. However, as this paper is interested in the investment model, the following will focus on the ECT contained within Eq. (2). Optimum lag length selection criteria were tested, and lag 3 was found to be the appropriate lag based on the AIC and HQ criteria. The VECM uses Least Squares (Gauss-Newton/Marquardt steps). The analysis of Eq. (2) required the following foresight: capacity utilisation is not incorporated within the ECT and the signs of the coefficients are reversed in the long-run as $ECT = 0$.

$$ECT1_{t-1} = -\left(\begin{array}{cccccc} & +1.77IR_{t-1} & +0.5PG_{t-1} & +0.02SMTR_{t-1} & +6.90GE_{t-1} & +0.84) \\ 1.00INV_{t-1}+0.95P_{t-1}(0.42)[2.26] & (0.40) & (0.39) & (0.05) & (0.37) & \\ & [4.34] & [1.31] & [0.38] & [-18.58] & \end{array} \right. \quad (2)$$

The coefficients of profit share, interest rates, productivity growth, and stock market turnover are all negative in sign. Only profit share and interest rates are statistically significant at the 5% level. As such, a 1% increase in profit share will

Table 2 Stationarity results. 1980–2015

	ADF				PP			
	Level		First difference		Level		First difference	
Variable	Intercept	Trend	Intercept	Trend	Intercept	Trend	Intercept	Trend
INV		−3.21(0.10)		−5.77***(0.02)		−3.21(0.10)		−5.78***(0.00)
UT		−0.47(0.98)		−4.45***(0.02)		−0.81(0.95)		−4.47***(0.00)
P		−2.30(0.42)		−6.46***(0.00)		−2.35(0.39)		−6.70***(0.02)
IR	−1.94(0.31)		−4.79***(0.00)		−2.39(0.10)		−8.09***(0.00)	
PG		−2.63(0.26)		−7.19***(0.00)		−2.41(0.36)		−8.28***(0.00)
SMTR		−2.28(0.43)		−8.94***(0.02)		−2.03(0.56)		−9.19***(0.00)
GE		−2.76(0.22)		−3.82***(0.00)		−2.76(0.22)		−3.82***(0.00)

*** Significant at 1%, ** Significant at 5%, * Significant at 10%, MacKinnon (1996) one-sided p-values. *INV* Investment, *UT* Capacity Utilisation, *P* Profit Share, *IR* Interest Rate, *PG* Productivity Growth, *SMTR* Stock Market Turnover Ratio, *GE* Government Expenditure

Table 3 Johansen testing investment equation: 1980–2015

INV = f(UT, P, IR, PG, SMTR, GE)					
Data Trend	None	None	Linear	Linear	Quadratic
Test type	No intercept	Intercept	Intercept	Intercept	Intercept
MHM:0.01	No trend	No trend	No trend	Trend	Trend
Trace	4	4	5	5	4
Max	2	3	2	3	3

INV Investment, *UT* Capacity Utilisation, *P* Profit Share, *IR* Interest Rate, *PG* Productivity Growth, *SMTR* Stock Market Turnover Ratio, *GE* Government Expenditure

decrease investment by 0.95% in the long-run in simple interpretation. In line with economic theory, interest rates hold a negative and significant unidirectional causal relationship with investment in the long-run. Government expenditure holds a strong positive causal relationship, exhibiting a crowding-in effect upon investment in the long-run. Short-run dynamics are captured through individual coefficients of the differentiated terms in the VECM model. Due to space restriction, short-run individual lagged coefficients and their statistical significance are not supplied in this paper; however, can be provided upon request. In analysing the short-run dynamics and their sign, derived from the long-run model, the VECM can be written as Eq. (3):

$$\begin{aligned} \Delta INV_t = & -0.68ECT1_{t-1} + 0.28ECT2_{t-1} - 0.06\Delta INV_{t-1} - 0.44\Delta INV_{t-2} \\ & + 0.09\Delta UT_{t-1} + 0.06\,\Delta UT_{t-2} + 0.42\Delta P_{t-1} + 0.38\Delta P_{t-2} \\ & + 0.11\Delta IR_{t-1} + 0.07\Delta IR_{t-2} - 0.21\Delta PG_{t-1} + 0.08\Delta PG_{t-2} \\ & - 0.03\Delta SMTR_{t-1} - 0.02\Delta SMTR_{t-2} - 0.35\Delta GE_{t-1} - 0.51\Delta GE_{t-2} \\ & - 0.002 \end{aligned} \tag{3}$$

The $ECT1_{t\,-\,1}$ shows the speed to which the model returns to equilibrium following an exogenous shock, whereby 68% of departures from long-run equilibrium is corrected in each period at the 1% significance level, being annual. Table 4 shows the joint significance of the explanatory variables in Eq. (3) in the short-run. Residual testing shows the VECM is correctly specified in the sense that there is no serial correlation, no heteroskedasticity and the variables are normally distributed.

5.4 *Impulse Response Analysis*

Impulse response analysis is a great way to examine the reaction of the model variables to exogenous shocks and disturbances. As such, this section investigates the resilience of investment by measuring the impulse responses towards a simulated Cholesky one standard deviation (S.D.) shock upon the explanatory variables over a 20-year period. While shocks will be permanent due to the nonstationary series, the IRFs will still provide insights into the absorbability and recoverability of investment towards such simulated shocks.

Table 4 VECM Granger Causality/Block Exogeneity Wald Test: 1980 – 2015

Dependent Variable: D(INV)			
Excluded	Chi-sq	df	Prob.
D(UT)	0.55	2	0.76
D(P)	25.71	2	0.00
D(IR)	3.49	2	0.17
D(PG)	12.47	2	0.00
D(SMTR)	7.78	2	0.02
D(GE)	25.01	2	0.00
All	124.76	12	0.00

D(INV) (Differenced) Investment, *D(UT)* (Differenced) Capacity Utilisation, *D(P)* (Differenced) Profit Share, *D(IR)* (Differenced) Interest Rate, *D(PG)* (Differenced) Productivity Growth, *D(SMTR)* (Differenced) Stock Market Turnover Ratio, *D(GE)* (Differenced) Government Expenditure. All = joint Wald Test

Figure 2 and Appendix 2 show the results of the IRF analysis. The results show shocks contemporaneously influence investment to any one variable in the model. The response of investment to a one standard deviation shock in profit share (P) and productivity growth (PG) is immediate and positive, lasting about 3–4 years and then fluctuating until it becomes steady after almost 10–12 years. In the case of shocks in the financial market indicator (SMTR) and the government expenditure (GE), investment delays in reacting to shocks for about 2–3 years. The investment then reacts positively in a cyclical manner before it becomes somewhat steady after 14–16 years. Another interesting reading from the results is investment response to a one standard deviation shock to interest rates (IR) and capacity utilisation (UT). The investment shows an erratic reaction to both shocks for about 6 years before becoming stable. The investment reaction to the shock in interest rate is not typical for the post-shock years 3–6. This inconsistency may be due to Australian businesses' investment decisions not being affected by changes to the cost of borrowings (Lane & Rosewell, 2015; Sharpe & Suarez, 2014), as the investment itself is a heterogeneous activity. Also, the spread of interest rates paid by companies, since the GFC, at the top and bottom of the distribution spreads has widened, causing a significant inverse relationship between the cost of debt and corporate investment, which is not captured in this study (Hambur & Cava, 2018). Arguably, Fig. 2 displays simple line estimates, whereby the statistical significance of Eq. 2 governs the range of the IRFs.

5.5 *Variance Decomposition*

As per Sims (1980), variance decomposition indicates the magnitude of the predicted error variance for the series, accounted for by innovations from each independent variable over different time-periods (Shahbaz, 2012). Pesaran and Shin (1998) show that this method shows proportional contribution in one variable

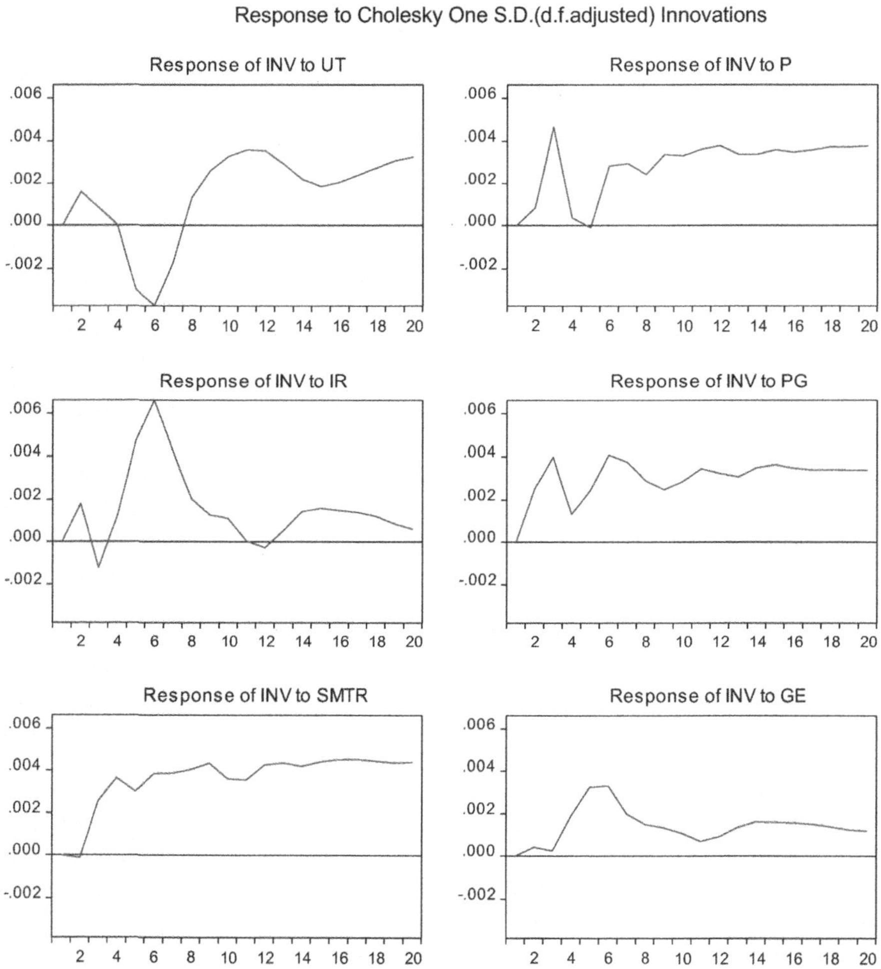

Fig. 2 Impulse Responses on a shock to the explanatory variables towards Investment: Australia: 1980–2015 Cholesky Ordering: INV Z P IR GX SMTR GE. *INV* Investment, *Z* Capacity Utilisation, *P* Profit Share, *IR* Interest Rate, *GX* Productivity Growth, *SMTR* Stock Market Turnover Ratio, *GE* Government Expenditure

due to innovative stemming in other variables. Such impulses can measure the recovery or adjustment speed (an important aspect of resilience) after orthogonal uncorrelated shocks (Chaiechi & Nguyen, 2021). Drawing on our time series data, Sim's Cholesky decomposition techniques were incorporated to measure the variables' compositional speed adjustments in response to simulated shocks. In analysing the results in Table 5, the columns show orthogonal shocks as a percentage of the forecast variance, decomposing total variances into percentages attributable to each shock to the sum of 100%. The share of the forecast-error variance attributable to investment varies between 3%–31.37%.

Table 5 Variance decomposition investment equation: 1980–2015

Variance Decomposition of UT:									Variance Decomposition of P:								
Period	S.E.	INV	UT	P	IR	PG	SMTR	GE	Period	S.E.	INV	UT	P	IR	PG	SMTR	GE
1	0.01	6.6	93.4	0	0	0	0	0	1	0.01	28.57	32.09	39.33	0	0	0	0
2	0.01	10.67	80.75	0.46	3.12	1.88	3.03	0.09	2	0.01	31.37	27.93	28.86	6.15	1.31	2.66	1.73
3	0.01	10.33	70.51	0.67	9.99	2.32	6.05	0.13	3	0.02	21.22	19.85	26.34	17.94	0.98	12.49	1.18
4	0.02	9.2	49.94	8.55	7.76	2.53	21.25	0.77	4	0.02	14.45	13.91	27.9	12.24	0.69	29.2	1.62
5	0.02	10.92	29.45	20.97	6.72	1.53	29.97	0.44	5	0.02	13.84	11.68	30.72	10.45	0.68	31.27	1.36
20	0.04	15.4	13.34	28.08	11.96	1.99	28.33	0.89	20	0.03	16.61	10.31	29.46	11.59	1.59	29.01	1.43

Variance Decomposition of IR:									Variance Decomposition of PG:								
Period	S.E.	INV	UT	P	IR	PG	SMTR	GE	Period	S.E.	INV	UT	P	IR	PG	SMTR	GE
1	0.01	10.41	3.74	4.73	81.12	0	0	0	1	0.02	4.04	15.55	21.97	3.1	55.35	0	0
2	0.01	5.4	4.95	2.74	45.2	34.67	7.04	0	2	0.02	3.57	14.15	27.91	3.52	49.12	1.57	0.16
3	0.02	4.39	3.2	13.23	28.42	18.71	29.85	2.19	3	0.02	4.03	15.26	26.34	3.32	48.82	2	0.23
4	0.02	3.9	2.83	12.89	28.57	22.07	27.4	2.33	4	0.02	7.31	13.62	26.98	6.51	42.46	2.88	0.24
5	0.02	6.46	4.4	14.16	29.47	17.53	26.15	1.83	5	0.02	11.3	12.29	26.92	6.83	38.06	2.63	1.97
20	0.03	10.6	8.26	16	29.71	11.04	22.44	1.96	20	0.03	10.91	12.25	23.51	16.46	26.31	8.46	2.1

Variance Decomposition of SMTR:									Variance Decomposition of GE:								
Period	S.E.	INV	UT	P	IR	PG	SMTR	GE	Period	S.E.	INV	UT	P	IR	PG	SMTR	GE
1	0.14	3.02	1	19.68	11.03	5.23	60.04	0	1	0.01	12.65	12.35	8.95	41.26	3.34	1.18	20.28
2	0.16	2.55	0.79	23.91	14.09	4.73	53.89	0.03	2	0.01	10.44	33.75	6.97	30.89	5.2	1.75	11
3	0.18	3.77	0.66	25.88	12.14	4.17	53.07	0.3	3	0.01	11.93	29.97	6.9	34.27	4.2	1.63	11.1
4	0.19	3.99	0.58	29.52	11.15	4.05	50.44	0.26	4	0.01	13.43	29.07	7.71	31.66	5.44	1.94	10.74
5	0.2	4.38	0.79	29.6	11.42	3.75	49.8	0.26	5	0.02	11.91	30.11	7.04	29.09	5.25	7.25	9.36
20	0.24	7.8	4.02	30.16	12.34	3.53	41.58	0.58	20	0.02	10.9	28.08	8.25	27.64	4.69	13.55	6.89

Cholesky Ordering: INV, UT, P, IR, PG, SMTR, GE. Where *INV* Investment, *UT* Capacity Utilisation, *P* Profit Share, *IR* Interest Rate, *PG* Productivity Growth, *SMTR* Stock Market Turnover Ratio, *GE* Government Expenditure

In analysing capacity utilisation at year 5, the fluctuation in capacity utilisation itself explained 29.45% of its total variance, whereas investment accounted for 10.92%. In analysing year 20, the fluctuation in capacity utilisation itself explained 13.34% of its total variance, whereas investment accounted for 15.40%. As such, the results suggest the investment is highly sensitive to changes in capacity utilisation, whereby external shocks in production efficiency will influence the stability of investment into year 20 and increase over time. Similar to the results of capacity utilisation, investment reacts strongly to changes in profit share. In particular, the results reveal that the fluctuation in profit share itself explained 39.33% and 28.86% of its total variance in year 1 and 2, whereas investment accounted for 25.57% and 31.37%, respectively.

5.6 Conclusions

This paper aimed to investigate the resilience of investment in Australia in the presence of exogenous shocks, utilising a Kaleckian Post-Keynesian approach. A more intuitive measure of financial development was incorporated in the model to better capture government and financial markets' roles in influencing investment decisions, alongside a more traditional fiscal policy measure. Primarily, by using time series annual data (1980–2015), this paper utilised the VECM estimation technique to test for dynamic interactions between the incorporated investment model variables, with the more notable results showing a significant ECT and joint short-run Granger causality results.

The incorporated financial development and fiscal policy indicators produced differing results, with stock market turnover holding a negative and insignificant long-run relationship towards investment, while showing a weak, negative and significant causal relationship towards investment in the short-run. On the other hand, government expenditure held a strong crowding-in effect in the long-run and a moderate crowding-out effect in the short-run. This is an important result for decision makers, as governmental spending through targeted policies is said to have strong and differing implications in both periods. Overall, the results show that the incorporation of both indicators into such a targeted investment model is warranted. Government expenditure was found to be the more powerful mechanism of the two, suggesting that such permanent incorporation into the model should be taken seriously.

After preliminary analysis and performing appropriate diagnostic tests, the paper analysed the resilience of investment using impulse response analysis and variance decomposition to test adaptability, absorbability, and recoverability from shocks. Impulse response analysis was adopted to test for the absorbability and recoverability of investment in the face of external shocks. We found evidence that investors react positively and cyclically to changes in profit, productivity, and financial markets via impulse response analysis. The investment appears to benefit from improvements in these variables, absorbing the shocks and obtaining stability in the short-run (5–6 years). Furthermore, the variance decomposition technique was used to determine the influence of model variables on investment and their ability in explaining the variability in the investment level over time. The results showed that the changes in profitability and the private sector's productive capacity can explain investment level variations in Australia.

The impulse response analysis and variance decomposition results hold significance, as the ECT shows a strong long-run relationship between investment and the explanatory variables. With this in hand, the evidence-based information provides investors better information to make informed decisions in both the short and long-run. After careful review of the literature, incorporating both indicators within such an investment model, more so to test adaptability and absorbability against external shocks, was a first. Put simply, this paper estimated the resilience of the private sector with the Australian economy. It incorporated the role of financial development and fiscal policy upon an augmented Kaleckian-Post Keynesian investment model. As such, the evidence-based information provided in this paper provides policymakers with an understanding of the channels through which the private sector's investment decisions could be affected, providing an opportunity to incorporate resilience thinking into policymaking.

Appendix 1 *Descriptive Statistics. Australia: 1980–2015*

Statistics	INV	UT	P	IR	PG	SMTR	GE
Mean	0.25	0.42	0.52	0.05	0.04	0.52	0.25
Median	0.26	0.43	0.53	0.05	0.04	0.52	0.25
Maximum	0.28	0.51	0.58	0.10	0.14	1.12	0.27
Minimum	0.22	0.32	0.43	0.00	−0.01	0.10	0.21
Std. dev.	0.02	0.06	0.04	0.03	0.03	0.26	0.01
Skewness	−0.39	−0.11	−0.26	0.00	0.92	0.22	−0.77
Kurtosis	2.17	1.46	1.79	2.04	3.91	2.30	2.87
J-B.	1.92	3.62	2.60	1.39	6.34	1.02	3.56
Prob.	0.38	0.16	0.27	0.50	0.04	0.60	0.17
Ob.	36	36	36	36	36	36	36

INV Investment, *UT* Capacity Utilisation, *P* Profit Share, *IR* Interest Rate, *PG* Productivity Growth, *SMTR* Stock Market Turnover Ratio, *GE* Government Expenditure

Appendix 2 *Responses of INV to Cholesky One S.D. (d.f. Adjusted) Innovations, Australia: 1980–2015*

Period	UT	P	IR	PG	SMTR	GE
1	0.0000	0.0000	0.0000	0.0000	0.0000	0.0000
2	0.0016	0.0008	0.0018	0.0026	−0.0001	0.0004
3	0.0008	0.0047	−0.0012	0.0040	0.0025	0.0002
4	0.0000	0.0004	0.0012	0.0013	0.0037	0.0019
5	−0.0030	−0.0001	0.0047	0.0025	0.0030	0.0033
6	−0.0038	0.0028	0.0066	0.0041	0.0039	0.0033
7	−0.0017	0.0030	0.0043	0.0038	0.0039	0.0020
8	0.0013	0.0024	0.0021	0.0029	0.0040	0.0015
9	0.0026	0.0034	0.0013	0.0025	0.0043	0.0013
10	0.0033	0.0033	0.0011	0.0029	0.0036	0.0011
11	0.0036	0.0036	0.0000	0.0035	0.0036	0.0007
12	0.0036	0.0038	−0.0003	0.0033	0.0043	0.0009
13	0.0029	0.0034	0.0005	0.0031	0.0044	0.0013
14	0.0022	0.0034	0.0014	0.0035	0.0042	0.0016

(continued)

Period	UT	P	IR	PG	SMTR	GE
15	0.0019	0.0036	0.0016	0.0037	0.0044	0.0016
16	0.0021	0.0035	0.0015	0.0035	0.0045	0.0016
17	0.0024	0.0036	0.0014	0.0034	0.0045	0.0015
18	0.0028	0.0037	0.0012	0.0034	0.0044	0.0014
19	0.0031	0.0037	0.0009	0.0034	0.0044	0.0012
20	0.0033	0.0038	0.0006	0.0034	0.0044	0.0012

Cholesky Ordering: INV, UT, P, IR, PG, SMTR, GE. *INV* Investment, *UT* Capacity Utilisation, *P* Profit Share, *IR* Interest Rate, *PG* Productivity Growth, *SMTR* Stock Market Turnover Ratio, *GE* Government Expenditure

References

ABS. (2020). *Australian National Accounts: National Income, Expenditure and Product: Quarterly estimates of key economic flows in Australia, including gross domestic product (GDP), consumption, investment, income and saving.* Retrieved from https://www.abs.gov.au/statistics/economy/national-accounts/australian-national-accounts-national-income-expenditure-and-product/latest-release

Afonso, A., & Sousa, R. (2012). The macroeconomic effects of fiscal policy. *Applied Economics, 44*(34), 4439–4454.

Akinlo, T., & Oyeleke, O. J. (2018). Effects of government expenditure on private investment in Nigerian Economy (1980–2016). *Emerging Economy Studies, 4*(2), 147–156.

Alesina, A., Ardagna, R., Perotti, R., & Schiantarelli, F. (2002). Fiscal policy, profits, and investment. *The American Economic Review, 92*, 571–589.

Angeletos, G., & Lian, C. (2020). *Confidence and the propagation of demand shocks.* Retrieved from https://economics.mit.edu/files/16734

Arin, K. (2004). Fiscal policy, private investment and economic growth: Evidence from G-7 countries. *SSRN Electronic Journal.* https://doi.org/10.2139/ssrn.438785

Australian Government. (2016). *Budget 2016–2017.* Retrieved from http://www.budget.gov.au/2016-17/content/bp1/html/bp1_bs3-01.htm

Bhaduri, A., & Marglin, S. (1990). Unemployment and the real wage: The economic basis for contesting political ideologies. *Cambridge Journal of Economics, 14*(4), 375–393.

Bloch, H., & Tang, S. (2003). The role of financial development in economic growth. *Progress in Development Studies, 3*(3), 243–251.

Briguglio, L., Cordina, G., Garrugia, N., & Vella, S. (2005). *Conceptualising and measuring economic resilience: Pacific islands regional integration and governance.* ANU Press.

Caldera-Sánchez, A., Serres, A., Gori, F., Hermansen, M., & Röhn, O. (2016). Strengthening economic resilience: Insights from the post-1970 record of severe recessions and financial crises. *OECD economic policy paper*, 20.

Chaiechi, T. (2012). Financial development shocks and contemporaneous feedback effect on key macroeconomic indications: A post Keynesian time series analysis. *Economic Modelling, 29*, 487–501.

Chaiechi, T., Juniper, J., & Mitchell, B. (2006). *Dynamic investment and financial development, application of Kaleckian, Post-Keynesian model.* Paper presented at the Centre of Full Employment and Equity Conference Newcastle, NSW.

Chaiechi, T., & Nguyen, N. (2021). Measuring urban economic resilience of two tropical cities, using impulse response analysis. *Bulletin of Applied Economics, 8*(1), 59–79.

Cihak, M., Demirgüç-Kunt, A.D., Feyen, E., & Levine, R. (2012). *Bench marketing Financial Systems around the World.* Policy Research working paper (No. WPS 6175). Washington, D.C.: World Bank.

Dickey, D., & Fuller, W. (1979). Distribution of the estimators for autoregressive time series with a unit root. *Journal of the American Statistical Association, 74*(366), 427–431.

Dickey, D. A., & Fuller, W. A. (1981). Likelihood ratio statistics for autoregressive time series with a unit root. *Econometrica, 49*, 1057–1072.

Dutt, A. (1992). *Rentiers in post-Keynesian models. In recent developments in post-Keynesian economics*. Edward Elgar.

Emodi, N., Chaiechi, T., & Beg, A. B. M. (2018). The impact of climate change on electricity demand in Australia. *Energy & Environment, 29*(7), 1263–1297.

Emodi, N., Chaiechi, T., & Beg, A. B. M. (2019). A techno-economic and environmental assessment of long-term energy policies and climate variability impact on the energy system. *Energy Policy, 128*(May 2019), 329–346.

Engle, R., & Granger, C. W. J. (1987). Co-integration and error correction: Representation, estimation, and testing. *Econometrica, 55*(2), 251–276.

Go, D. (1994). External shocks, adjustment policies and investment in a developing economy: Illustrations from a forward-looking CGE model of the Philippines. *Journal of Development Economics, 44*(2), 229–261.

Greenwood, J., Hercowitz, Z., & Huffman, G. (1988). Investment, capacity utilisation, and the real business cycle, american economic review. *American Economic Review, 78*(3), 402–417.

Hambur, J., & Cava, G. (2018). *Do interest rates affect business investment? Evidence from Australian company-level data*. Reserve Bank of Australia.

Hassan, S., & Othman, Z. (2015). The effect of economic resilience on private investment in selected malaysian economic sectors. *Mediterranean Journal of Social Sciences, 6*(6), 374–380.

Holling, C. (1973). Resilience and stability of ecological systems. *Annual Review of Ecology and Systematics, 4*, 1–23.

Johansen, S. (1995). *Likelihood-based inference in cointegrated vector autoregressive models.* Oxford University Press.

Kalecki, M. (1933). *Proba Teorii Koniunktury.* Institute for the Study of Business Cycles and Prices.

Kalecki, M. (1943). *Studies in economic dynamics*. George Allen & Unwin.

Kalecki, M. (1968). Business cycle reconsidered. *Economic Journal, 78*(2), 263–276.

Keynes, J. (1936). *The general theory of employment, interest and money*. MacMillian.

King, R., & Levine, R. (1993a). Finance and growth: Schumpeter might be right. *The Quarterly Journal of Economics, 108*, 717–737.

King, R., & Levine, R. (1993b). Finance, entrepreneurship and growth theory and evidence. *Journal of Monetary Economics, 32*(3), 513–542.

Krugman, P. (1988). *Deindustrialisation, reindustrialisation, and the real exchange rate*. Working Paper 2586.

Lane, K., & Rosewell, T. (2015). *Firms' investment decisions and interest rates*. RBA Bulletin, June, pp 1–7.

Laopodis, N. T. (2001). Effects of government spending on private investment. *Applied Economics, 33*, 1563–1577.

Larsfalten, C. (2020). *Why investment in resilience is good for business*. Received from https://gca.org/why-investing-in-resilience-is-good-for-business/

Lütkepohl, P., Hubrich, K., & Saikkonen, P. (2001). A review of systems cointegration tests. *Econometric Reviews, 20*, 247–318.

MacKinnon, J. (1996). Numerical distribution functions for unit root and cointegration tests. *Journal of Applied Econometrics, 11*(6), 601–618.

Marattin, L., & Salotti, S. (2011). *On the usefulness of government spending in the EU area*. MPRA Paper No. 24906.

Mian, A., & Sufi, A. (2014). What explains the 2007–2009 drop in employment? *Econometrica, 82* (6), 2197–2223.

Milenti, D. (1999). *Disasters by design: A reassessment of natural hazards in the United States*. Joseph Henry Press.

Nazlioglu, S., Yalama, A., & Aslan, M. (2009). Financial development and investment: Cointegration and causality analysis for the case of Turkey. *International Journal of Economic Perspectives, 3*(2), 107–119.

Pesaran, M., & Shin, P. (1998). Generalised impulse response analysis in leaner multivariate models. *Economic Letters, 58*, 17–29.

Phillips, P., & Perron, P. (1988). Testing for a unit root in time series regression. *Biometrika, 75*(2), 335–346.

Rose, A. (2004). Defining and measuring economic resilience to disasters. *Disaster Prevention and Management, 13*(4), 307–314.

Shahbaz, M. (2012). Does trade openness affect long run growth? Cointegration, causality and forecast error variance decomposition tests for Pakistan. *Economic Modelling, 29*, 2325–2339.

Sharpe, S.A., & Suarez, G.A. (2014). *Why isn't investment more sensitive to interest rates: Evidence from surveys*. Board of Governors of the Federal Reserve System Finance and Economics Discussion, Series No 2014–002.

Sims, C. (1980). Macroeconomics and reality. *Econometrica, 48*(1), 1–48.

Stockhammer, E., & Onaran, O. (2004). Accumulation, distribution and employment: A structural VAR approach to a Kaleckian macro-model. *Structural Change and Economic Dynamics, 15* (4), 421–247.

Svirydzenda, K. (2016). *Introducing a New Broad-Based Index of Financial Development*. IMF Working Paper, Strategy, Policy, and Review Department. WP16/15.

Economic Resilience During COVID-19's First Year: Case Studies of Costa Rica, Dominican Republic and Panama

Adriana Chacón and Sandro Zolezzi

Abstract During the last two decades, the services sector has become increasingly important for the world's economy. Technological advances have played a key role in lowering communication costs and have also enabled the development of new ways to deliver services. Some countries have been able to take advantage of this new wave, transforming their economies and becoming more resilient towards external shocks. For example, instead of depending mainly on tourism, some countries have diversified their services exports, offering services with greater added value, knowledge-intensive and focused more on information and communications technologies (ICT). These changes have also provided more opportunities for higher income, productivity, employment, investment, and trade. Services are also crucial for achieving the 2030 Sustainable Development Goals. But last year, the world economy probably shrank by 4.3 percent, a setback matched only by the Depression and the two world wars, according to the World Bank. For most countries, the COVID-19 pandemic is one of their biggest challenges. However, some services exports have continued and, in some cases, grew compared to 2019. Preliminary results regarding foreign trade have shown that the services sector has responded effectively to the COVID-19 pandemic. The paper focuses on three countries: Costa Rica, the Dominican Republic, and Panama, which are close competitors and heavily rely on their tourism sector. In the first three quarters of 2020: Costa Rica increased its' exports of knowledge-intensive services, while Panama increased its' exports of transport services and the Dominican Republic, on the other hand, according to preliminary data, is still heavily relying on exports of travel services.

Keywords Economic resilience · Service sector · Pandemic · Knowledge-intensive · Added value

---

A. Chacón (✉) · S. Zolezzi
CINDE, Torre Universal, San José, Costa Rica
e-mail: achacon@cinde.org; szolezzi@cinde.org

© The Author(s), under exclusive license to Springer Nature Singapore Pte Ltd. 2022
T. Chaiechi, J. Wood (eds.), *Community Empowerment, Sustainable Cities, and Transformative Economies*, https://doi.org/10.1007/978-981-16-5260-8_5

1 Introduction

Globally, trade in services reached $5.8 trillion in 2018. This was an all-time high, confirming the dynamism of services exports, higher than for goods. In developing economies, services' exports grew 7.6 per cent annually between 2005 and 2018, increasing services' direct contribution to total exports from 14 to 17 per cent (UNCTAD, 2020). These trends come short of reflecting the full importance of trade in services. There is substantial value-added of services, which is not captured in these data, incorporated in goods exports, from services intermediate inputs and from services bundled with goods.

Direct exports from services accounted for 14 per cent of total exports in developing economies in 2011; services represented a much higher share of the value-added in total exports: 32 per cent (Antunes, 2020a). Close to two-thirds of the growth of services value-added in exports is due to an increase in services embodied in exports of all sectors, according to Antunes (2020a). Also, for a set of selected economies, when considering services activities within manufacturing firms, services to overall exports were close to two-thirds. This places trade in services at the same level as services output, jobs, and investment (Antunes, 2020a). In 2017, services globally achieved 68 per cent of output, 51 per cent of jobs and 50 per cent of foreign direct investment. This prevalence also occurs in developing economies where services were responsible for 56 per cent of output and 46 per cent of jobs (Antunes, 2020a).

Through these indirect roles, services can induce efficiency and effectiveness, reduction of productive and trade barriers, and contribute to more productivity, increased production and export capacity and higher participation in global value chains (Antunes, 2020a). This highlights that the services sector is not an alternative to agriculture or industrial development but rather provides key means to complement and strengthen agriculture and industrialisation strategies. This can also induce a structural transformation that may favour sectors that tend to have higher productivity and thereby enhance the above-mentioned effects. A stronger services sector, namely through increased value-added services in all economic sectors, can be particularly relevant for a more resilient economy (Antunes, 2020b).

Trade-in services are more resilient than the trade in goods to foreign income shocks. For instance, according to Ariu, 2016 during the 2008–2009 crisis, trade in goods fell by 30 per cent, and in contrast, trade in business, telecommunication and financial services continued growing at their pre-crisis rates and only services related to transport declined. Additionally, transport services dropped similarly to trade in goods, while professional, financial, and telecommunication services continued to grow rapidly. Ariu (2016) explains that services represent essential inputs for the production process, that their flow must be continuous, and that they cannot be stored, nor can they be easily modified in reaction to fluctuations in output. Therefore, even during the crisis, firms continued importing services that provided fundamental production inputs. The decrease was mostly due to a reduction in durable and capital goods for trade in goods, while consumable goods declined more smoothly. During this pandemic, the opposite has happened!

The services sector is more likely to be marked by market failures, and therefore to be subject to government regulation. Francois and Hoekman (2010) found some examples of market failures in the services sector, such as natural monopolies (rail transport, electricity distribution), network externalities (telecommunications) and asymmetric information (healthcare, finance). They stated that government intervention in the services sectors where market failures exist can improve economic efficiency. This intervention typically takes the form of regulations that affect, among other economic outcomes, competition, and market entry. This is not to argue that there are no domestic regulations on goods, but that they seem to be far more visible in the services sectors.

These regulations differ widely among different economies and affect the ease of trading the regulated services. While regulatory authorities may have no desire to restrict trade, differences in regulations can create conditions that impede more trade than desirable (Sykes, 1999). This may be another reason for the low share of cross border services trade in the world, and for the need to turn to other ways of supplying foreign markets, notably through the commercial presence of foreign suppliers (mode 3 of the General Agreement on Trade in Services – GATS).

An important characteristic differentiating trade in services from trade in goods is the "proximity burden" (Francois & Hoekman, 2010). Unlike a trade in goods, many services require that supplier and consumer be within close proximity. This means that proximity has a disproportionately larger adverse effect on trade in services than trade in goods (Anderson et al., 2014). The proximity burden may also require more bundling of local presence with cross-border provision of services than is the case with goods. For example, even if the service may be amenable to cross-border supply, the potential exporter of services may still need to establish a commercial presence in the destination market to be able to attract interest from potential purchasers. However, it should be noted that digitalisation is likely to decrease this burden, as technological changes make more and more services deliverable electronically.

The rapid acceleration of digital transformation has had profound implications for services trade but the benefits of digitalisation risk being derailed by existing and emerging trade barriers. The OECD Digital Services Trade Restrictiveness Index (Digital STRI) is a new tool that identifies, catalogues, and quantifies cross-cutting barriers that affect services traded digitally. It consists of two components, the regulatory database and indices, which bring together comparable information from 44 countries. The Digital STRI shows a diverse and complex global regulatory environment affecting trade in digitally enabled services. Over the past years, the index shows an increasingly regulated environment, highlighting that further international cooperation and dialogue are needed to maximise digitalisation benefits. In the 2020 report, Costa Rica showed the lowest STRI index (Panama and the Dominican Republic are not included), which implies fewer restrictions to export digital services (Ferencz & OECD, 2019).

In 2019, the value of world merchandise trade declined by 2.8 per cent, after two consecutive years of increase. Global exports amounted to $18.9 trillion. Considering COVID-19, quarter two of 2020 saw a precipitous decline before being nowcast to rebound somewhat in quarter three. Despite this recovery, a year-on-year decrease of 11.9 per cent is nowcast for the third quarter of 2020 (UNCTAD, 2020).

After a modest rise of 1.9 per cent in 2019, world services exports dropped sharply in the first two quarters of 2020 when the COVID-19 pandemic hit. They showed signs of a recovery in the third quarter. However, a decline of 19.9 per cent year-on-year is still nowcast for the third quarter of 2020. In 2019, global services exports were valued at $6.1 trillion, representing one-quarter of the value of total exports, including goods, and 7 per cent of world GDP. In more than half of the world economies, their share in Gross Domestic Product (GDP) was larger than 10 per cent. With $876 billion worth of services sold internationally, the United States of America remained the world's leading exporter, accounting for 14 per cent of global services exports. China, the leading exporter among developing economies, ranked fifth overall, with $283 billion of services sold. All top five services exporters from the developing world were Asian. In 2019, they held a world market share of almost 15 per cent, the same as all other developing economies combined (UNCTAD, 2020). According to the World Development Indicators database, in 2018 and compared to 1997, Costa Rica increased from 52 per cent to 69 per cent of value-added services as a percentage of its' GDP, Panama decreased from 69 per cent to 65 per cent, and the Dominican Republic also increased from 51 per cent to 59 per cent (shown on Fig. 1).

Before COVID-19, travel and tourism had become one of the most important sectors in the world economy, accounting for 10 per cent of global GDP and more than 320 million jobs worldwide. In 1950, at the dawn of the jet age, just 25 million people took foreign trips. By 2019, that number had reached 1.5 billion, and the travel and tourism sector had grown to almost too big-to-fail proportions for many economies (Behsudi, 2020). The global pandemic, the first of its scale in a new era of interconnectedness, has put 100 million jobs at risk, many in micro, small, and medium-sized enterprises that employ a high share of women, who represent 54 per cent of the tourism workforce, according to the United Nations World Tourism

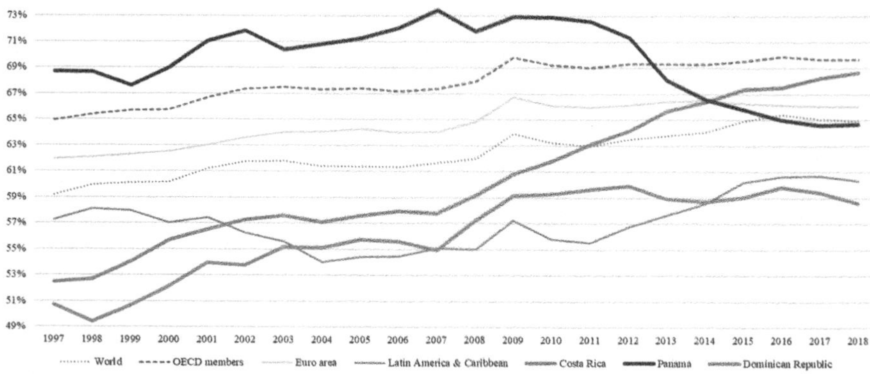

Fig. 1 Services, value-added (per cent of GDP), 1997–2018
Source: World Development Indicators, March 2021

Organization (Behsudi, 2020). Tourism-dependent countries will likely feel the negative impacts of the crisis for much longer than other economies. Contact-intensive services key to the tourism and travel sectors are disproportionately affected by the pandemic and will continue to struggle until people feel safe to travel massively again (Behsudi, 2020). Tourism receipts worldwide are not expected to recover to 2019 levels until 2023. In the first half of 2020, tourist arrivals fell globally by more than 65 per cent, with a near halt since April–compared with 8 per cent during the global financial crisis and 17 per cent amid the SARS epidemic of 2003, according to ongoing research on tourism in a post-pandemic world (Behsudi, 2020).

At the same time, information and communications technologies (ICTs) are one of the main drivers of global economic growth (Aboal & Tacsir, 2018). Technological innovations, coupled with new business models, have changed the nature and structure of services. ICT development means that economies of scale have become important in ICT-enabled services sectors, as the marginal cost of providing an additional unit approaches zero (Fontagné et al., 2015). The input of professional scientific and technical services into agriculture, mining, utilities, and construction are making sizeable contributions to the growth of those sectors (Hallward-Driemeier & Nayyar, 2018). One outcome of this has been increased interest in identifying services sectors that are "potentially ICT-enabled" (Borga & Howell, 2014). These sectors include: financial and insurance services, charges for the use of intellectual property, audiovisual and related products, telecommunications, computer and information services, research and development (R&D) services, professional and management consulting services, and architectural and engineering services.

According to the World Trade Organization (2019), the information and telecommunications sector has seen a growth in productivity that is faster than that in manufacturing in many economies, and the same pattern of higher growth than in manufacturing is observed in professional service activities. Productivity in financial and insurance activities has also grown faster than in manufacturing. This pattern appears consistent with what has been argued by Aboal and Tacsir (2018) to be the larger role played by rapid advancements in ICT in services than in manufacturing. This higher productivity growth in services enabled by the ICT sector could allay fears that secular or long-term growth of the services sector in many economies will come at the expense of slowing overall growth.

In the context of the COVID-19 pandemic, in the face of disruption of global value chains and the sharp contraction of the demand, world trade in goods and services experienced a sharp drop in the first half of 2020 and incipient recovery in the second semester. The volume of the world trade in goods would fall around 9 per cent in 2020, less than the collapse registered in 2009 during the world financial crisis (−13 per cent) (CEPAL, 2021).

Central America is the most commercially integrated subregion of Latin America and the Caribbean: intraregional exports represent approximately 30 per cent of its total exports, and the subregion constitutes its main export destination after the United States. Despite this high level of integration in gross exports, the subregional input-output matrix shows that trade in goods and services is less in terms of added value. Likewise, patterns of differentiated commercial insertion vary between countries (CEPAL, 2020).

The levels of intraregional added value incorporated in exports to intraregional markets are generally low. Secondly, there are different profiles of commercial participation and generation of value through exports and imports. For example, Mexico is a net supplier of primary and secondary goods but demands services; Costa Rica is a net supplier of secondary goods and services and demands primary goods; Guatemala and Nicaragua supply primary goods and demand secondary goods and tertiary; Panama is a net service provider but demands mainly primary and secondary goods, and El Salvador, Honduras and the Dominican Republic are net demanders of both services and primary and secondary goods (CEPAL, 2020).

In 2020 the economies of Central America and the Dominican Republic suffered a deep and generalised contraction, which in most cases were the most severe observed in several decades. CEPAL estimates that the average GDP contracted 6.1 per cent, after 10 years of uninterrupted expansion. The fall is mainly explained by the measures of restriction of mobility and closure of activities, which were implemented in greater or lesser extent in each country of the subregion to contain the spread of COVID-19 disease, as well as a notable contraction in external demand (CEPAL, 2021).

Exports of services recorded an average year-on-year reduction of 37.6 per cent as of the third quarter of 2020, mainly due to the strong collapse of the tourism sector in the context of the pandemic. The Dominican Republic reported the deepest drop (56.2 per cent year-on-year). Tourism has an important weight in Costa Rica and Panama's GDP (12 per cent and 13.6 per cent respectively) (WTTC, 2019). Income from travel in the subregion contracted by 64.2 per cent in the third quarter. In contrast, the flows of remittances to Central America and the Dominican Republic countries would report growth of 10 per cent year-on-year in the first 9 months of 2020 (CEPAL, 2021).

2 Case Studies

2.1 Costa Rica

Costa Rica is a small economy located in Central America that initially specialised in exporting a few primary products (e.g., coffee, bananas, sugar, and beef) to its neighbours. Costa Rica has experienced consistent growth and diversification in its exports of goods. Costa Rica exported 1.859 different products to 151 destination countries in 2020, from 4 products destined only to the Central America region in the 1980s. The relative share of exports of traditional goods (include coffee, banana, meat, and sugar) has fallen significantly, representing 67 per cent in 1986 to 14 per cent in 2020. Non-tourism services exports have grown 20-fold since 1995: from $165 million to $5.5 billion in 2019. Exports of goods and services have grown at an average annual rate of 5.7 per cent from 2009 to 2019: exports of goods 4.7 per cent and exports of services: 7.2 per cent. In 2019, services exports represented 45 per cent of total exports from Costa Rica (Banco Central de Costa Rica, 2020).

The arrival of major Information Technology company Intel, in the late 1990s, helped the country forge a worldwide reputation as a place for investment. The demonstration effect has worked. Foreign firms face greater uncertainties than domestic firms in the host country; they may have strong incentives to follow previous investors because of the signal they send to the host country's reliability (Krugman, 1997). Since then, much has happened, and Costa Rica has developed a strong track record of foreign direct investment companies in medical devices manufacturing, BP, and IT services sectors (knowledge and technology-intensive products and services).

Foreign direct investment has driven a demand for improved education and training standards, fostering learning among workers, management, and production, therefore improving the business environment in Costa Rica (OECD, 2013). The increasing dynamism in the arrival of Information technology-enabled multinational companies began in 2004, when Procter & Gamble transformed its operations in Costa Rica into one of its three business hubs. At the same time, it decided to globally outsource inside Information technology activities to Hewlett-Packard and inside human resources activities to IBM. With this signal, three flagship companies started operations in the country that same year based on the strategic decision of only one of them.

The increase in foreign direct investment inflows to the business services industry, including the information technology-enabled sector, after 2009 can partly be explained by the liberalisation of the telecommunication sector due to Dominican Republic-Central America Free Trade Agreement (CAFTA-DR). Since then, Costa Rica has progressively opened the telecommunication sector, including private network services, internet services, and mobile wireless services, which are now open to competition. Most of the foreign investment and reinvestment in the business services sector after 2009 was made by companies from the USA in shared services, including Procter & Gamble, Hewlett-Packard, IBM, National Instruments, Thomson Reuters, and Wal-Mart (World Bank, 2014). Exports of knowledge-intensive services have represented around 50 per cent of total services exports from 2015–2019, while travel represented around 40 per cent in the same period (shown in Fig. 2). In 2020, in the first three quarters, exports of services were affected by the COVID-19 pandemic, and travel decreased to 23 per cent while knowledge-intensive increased to 70 per cent (see Fig. 2). Knowledge-intensive services exports include: insurance and pensions; financial charges for use of intellectual property; telecommunications, computing and information; and other business.

2.2 *Dominican Republic*

In the past 25 years, the Dominican Republic has experienced a period of strong economic growth. The economy maintained its rapid expansion in the years leading

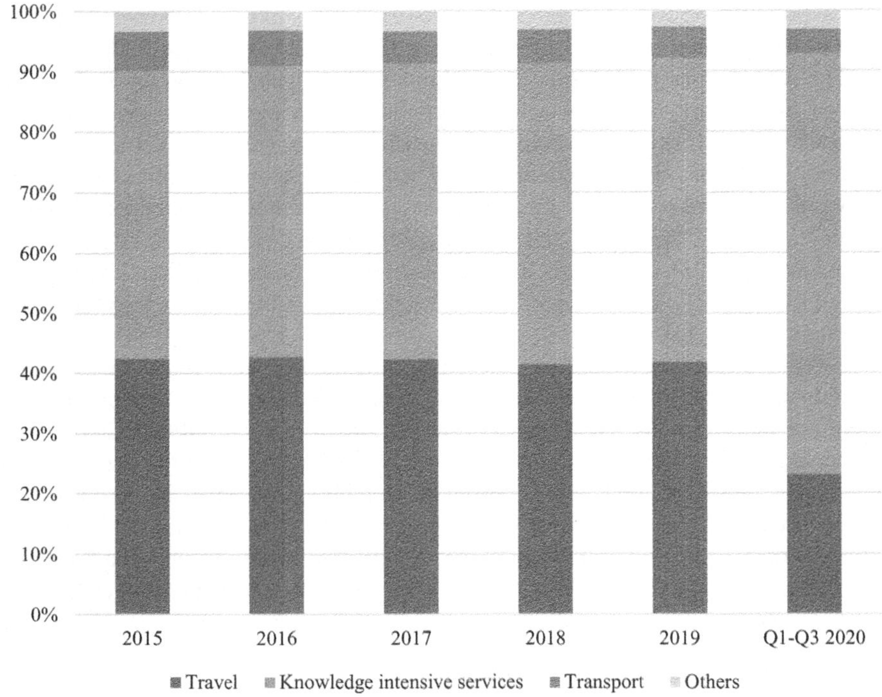

Fig. 2 Costa Rica: Exports of services (per cent of all services exports), 2015- Q1-Q3 2020
Sources: ITC, UNCTAD, WTO trade in services database based on International Monetary Fund statistics

up to the COVID-19 pandemic; between 2015 and 2019, the annual growth rate of the Dominican GDP averaged 6.1 per cent. Tourism, remittances, foreign direct investment, mining revenues, free zones, and telecommunications helped make the Dominican Republic one of the fastest expanding economies in the Latin America and Caribbean region (World Bank, 2020).

The Dominican Republic is an attractive tourist destination in the Caribbean, characterised by its white-sand beaches, clear waters, recreational opportunities, and vast cultural wealth. For decades, the country has made efforts to efficiently take advantage of its comparative advantages and improve the competitiveness of the sector, but it was not until the 1990s, specifically, from the year 1995 with the entry into force of Law No. 16-95 on Foreign Investment, when the tourist industry was consolidated as a core activity within the Dominican economy (Banco Central de la República Dominicana, 2021). The travel sector has represented around 80 per cent of total exports of services in the year 2015–2019 (Fig. 3), but in the first three quarters of 2020 this percentage dropped to 64 per cent as the continued absence of business travel and surge in COVID-19 cases has directly impacted the travel industry.

The evolution of the hotel, bar and restaurant industry has played an important role in the transformation of the national productive apparatus, with an average growth of the real added value of this activity of 5.9 per cent in the last three decades, especially

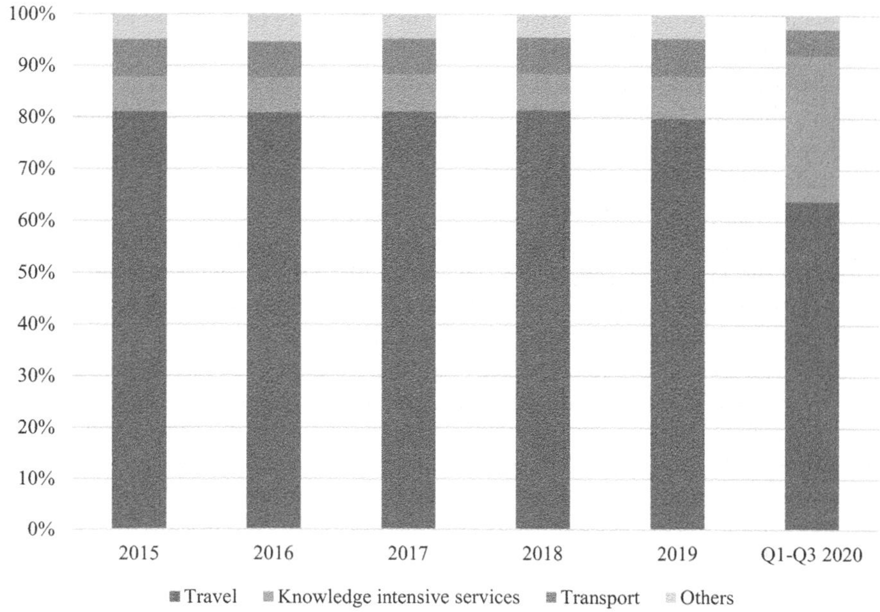

Fig. 3 Dominican Republic: Exports of services (per cent of all services exports), 2015- Q1-Q3 2020
Sources: ITC, UNCTAD, WTO trade in services database based on International Monetary Fund statistics

because of a multiplier effect on the demand for local goods and services and on the generation of jobs, as well as its high incidence in the country's total exports. In this sense, it is relevant to evaluate the performance of this activity in the Dominican Republic in recent years and especially, in the face of an adverse international context impacted by the COVID-19 pandemic, as well as the recovery expectations of the neuralgic industry for the country (Banco Central de la República Dominicana, 2021).

Additionally, the referred sector contributes to the flow of foreign exchange and the balance of payments balance by attracting foreign direct investment. During the 2010–2019 period, foreign direct investment destined for tourism reached the amount of US $ 4911.2 million, equivalent to 19.4 per cent of the total received in these years. Specifically, it is relevant to note the notable increase in the contribution of this component compared to the total during the last decade, going from a weighting of 8.9 per cent in 2010 to 29.3 per cent in 2019 (Banco Central de la República Dominicana, 2021).

2.3 *Panama*

Since 1990 Panama has led the region in economic growth rate, 5.9 per cent on average per year in the period 1990-2011. At the same time, Panama has undergone a structural transformation of its economy, in which the construction, financial and logistics services, as well as retail and wholesaling sectors have made the greatest contribution to growth (Beteta & Moreno Brid, 2014).

According to Hausmann et al. (2016), 57 per cent of the entire contribution to economic growth of Panama in the period 2010–2015 occurred in three sectors: transportation, construction and retail and wholesale trade.

According to the Contraloría General de la República de Panamá (2021) during 2020, the total production of goods and services in the Panamanian economy, measured through GDP, reflected a contraction of 17.9 per cent compared to 2019 when the GDP was in the order of 43,032.8 million balboas (which is pegged to and fully convertible to the US dollar, i.e., the exchange rate is 1:1).

However, among the relevant activities that sustained the performance of the national economy and marked a positive dynamic from January to December 2020, were the government services with 9.9 per cent accumulated growth due to the hiring of collaborators in the health, education and public security sectors, necessary to attend the health crisis; private health services with a growth of 4.7 per cent, while the agricultural activity showed an increase of 3 per cent, fishing grew 12.2 per cent and exploitation from mines and quarries 34.1 per cent (Contraloría General de la República de Panamá, 2021). Other specific activities which during the same period presented a favorable performance: in the transportation sector, positive rates were recorded in revenues of the Canal by toll in 1.7 per cent; movement of TEU containers in 5.3 per cent; while the agricultural production showed an increase in FOB banana exports by 10 per cent; fish and fish fillets at 23 per cent; in mines and quarry, a growth was reflected in the export of copper minerals and their concentrates in 34.4 per cent (Contraloría General de la República de Panamá, 2021). In domestic trade, the sale of marine fuel in ports of 3.6 per cent (Contraloría General de la República de Panamá, 2021). As shown on Fig. 4, transport has one of the highest percentages of participation in the exports of services, from 2015 to 2019 it reached around 50 per cent. During the first two quarters of 2020, the services exports of transport reached 60 per cent (Fig. 4).

The negative impact was reflected in the substantial decrease in activities of the manufacturing industries (−22.2 per cent), construction (−51.9 per cent), wholesale and retail trade (−19.4 per cent); hotels and restaurants (−55.8 per cent); transportation, storage, and communications (−6.2 per cent) and real estate, business, and rental activities (−30.8 per cent) (Contraloría General de la República de Panamá, 2021).

3 Performance during the 2020 Pandemic

March 2021 marked 1 year since the COVID-19 pandemic reached the Central American region: March first in Dominican Republic, March sixth in Costa Rica and March ninth in Panama. Although the threats are the same, the national contexts matter a lot in the results, the virus is the same, but the countries are not. In Latin

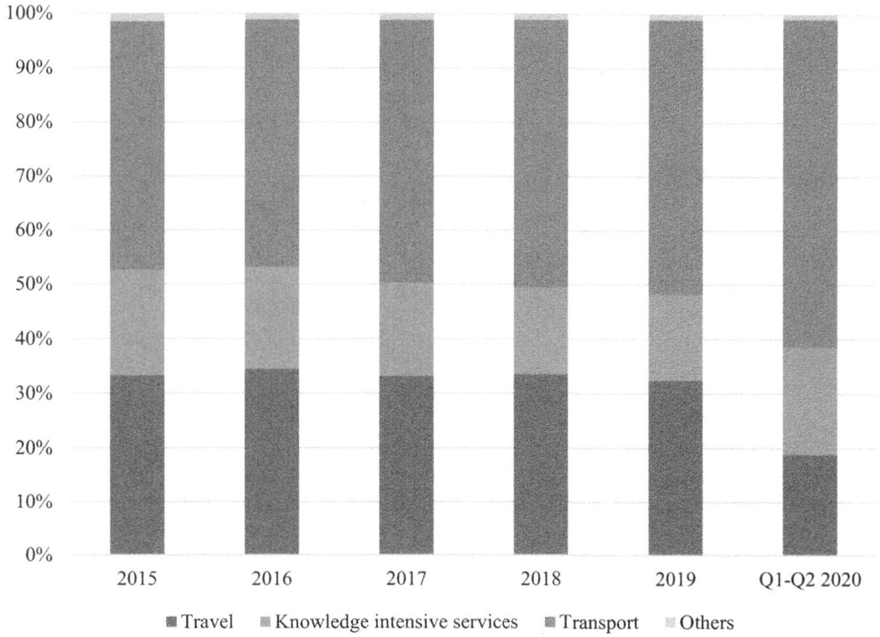

Fig. 4 Panama: Exports of services (per cent of all services exports), 2015- Q1-Q2 2020
Sources: ITC, UNCTAD, WTO trade in services database based on International Monetary Fund statistics

America, although there is only 8 per cent of the world's population, 26.54 per cent of deaths from COVID-19 have been accounted for to date (March, 2021). And economically, the region had a drop of −7.4 per cent in Gross Domestic Product, while the United States registered a drop of −3.4 per cent, Canada −5.5 per cent or the Euro region −7.2 per cent, according to the data from the International Monetary Fund for 2020.

The pandemic has cost lives and has also had a socially and economically negative impact. Although there are differences between countries, evaluating this first pandemic year, differentiating performances in the region, according to minimising the cost in lives and the economic costs and divided in 4 categories; according to INCAE, and García (2021) (see Fig. 5):

1. Countries with a good performance during the crisis, since they managed to minimise the cost in lives with a lethality lower than 2.21 per cent, and they also minimised the economic cost such as Uruguay, **Costa Rica**, Paraguay, and the **Dominican Republic**.
2. Countries with a high economic cost, higher than that of the region, maintained a fatality rate lower than the average fatality associated with the disease (2.21 per cent), such as **Panama**.

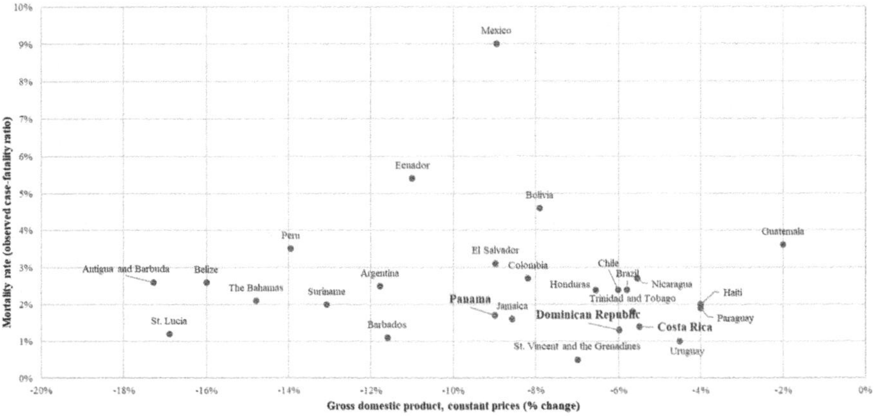

Fig. 5 GDP (constant prices, per cent change) versus mortality rate
Source: International Monetary Fund, World Economic Outlook Database, October 2020 & Coronavirus Resource Center, Johns Hopkins University & Medicine, March 2021

3. Countries that minimised the economic cost such as Guatemala, Nicaragua, Brazil, Chile, and Honduras; but that its fatality rate was higher than that observed in the world.
4. And finally, countries that had high levels of fatality and high levels of economic losses such as Colombia, El Salvador, Bolivia, Argentina, Peru, Ecuador, and Mexico. In this group is the country with the greatest drop in its GDP, with −13.94 per cent which is Peru; and the country with the highest fatality reported with 8.83 per cent which is Mexico.

The three case study countries: Costa Rica, Dominican Republic and Panama have been hard-hit by the pandemic, but their economic resilience has been very different. As mentioned before tourism has an important weight in their GDP, and in the share of their services exports. The travel industry on year 2019 represented almost 80 per cent of the services exports of Dominican Republic, 42 per cent of Costa Rica and 32 per cent of Panama (as shown on Table 1).

Due to the global expansion of the COVID-19 pandemic, from January to October 2020, international tourist arrivals worldwide fell by 72 per cent compared to the same period in 2019. The COVID-19 pandemic, disease caused by this virus was the main cause of year-on-year decreases that reached 82 per cent in the Asia-Pacific region and 68 per cent in America and Europe (UNWTO, 2020). The travel industry has been hit hard by the pandemic, countries shutting down their boarders and setting up traveling restrictions, and because of its' nature is one of the activities that cannot be done remotely. In 2019, the Dominican Republic was the fifth country in Latin America and the Caribbean with the highest receipts of international tourism, as a percentage of total exports (Fig. 6). The Dominican Republic accounted for 37 per cent of international tourism receipts of its total exports in 2019, while Panama was 25 per cent and Costa Rica 19 per cent (Fig. 6).

Table 1 Analysis of services exports of Costa Rica, Panama, and Dominican Republic, year 2019 and Q1-Q3 of year 2020

Indicators (% of all service exports)	Costa Rica		Panama		Dominican Republic	
	2019	Q1-Q3 2020	2019	Q1-Q2 2020	2019	Q1-Q3 2020
Knowledge-intensive Services	50.3%	69.9%	15.9%	19.7%	8.3%	28.3%
Travel	41.8%	23.1%	32.4%	18.9%	79.9%	64.0%
Transport	5.2%	4.0%	50.6%	60.4%	7.2%	5.1%
Manufacturing Services on physical inputs owned by others	1.3%	1.5%	0.0%	0.0%	0.6%	0.7%
Maintenance and repair services	1.1%	1.2%	0.1%	0.1%	0.0%	0.0%
Other services	0.3%	0.3%	0.9%	0.8%	4.0%	1.9%
Total service exports	100.0%	100.0%	100.0%	100.0%	100.0%	100.0%
Total service exports YOY growth rate	4.5%	−24.4%	1.1%	−34.5%	0.7%	−56.2%
Knowledge intensive services YOY growth rate	5.3%	5.8%	0.2%	−14.6%	16.1%	14.7%
Travel YOY growth rate	5.4%	−58.3%	−2.1%	−71.8%	−1.2%	−65.2%

Sources: ITC, UNCTAD, WTO trade in services database based on International Monetary Fund statistics. Detailed information included in the Annexes section

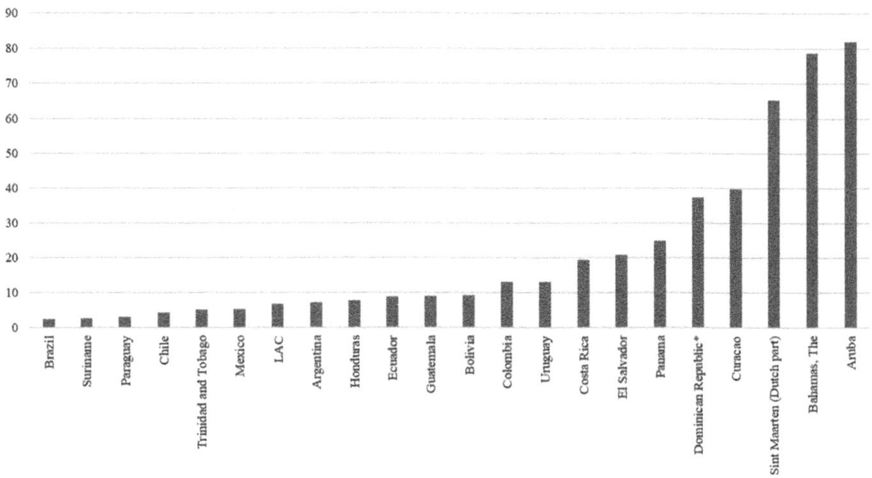

Fig. 6 International tourism, receipts (per cent of total exports), 2019
Source: World Tourism Organization, Yearbook of Tourism Statistics, Compendium of Tourism Statistics and data files, and IMF and World Bank exports estimates, 2019 (*Dominican Republic data of 2018)

The transportation and logistics industries were also affected by boarder closures and restrictions on travel and transport to contain the virus, important supply chains in the logistic and transportation industry were hampered, though differently across air, freight, and sea sectors. The negative impact on the liner shipping connectivity levels of Latin America and the Caribbean seemed less severe in the first and second quarter of 2020 (UNCTAD, 2020). The port of Colon in Panama experienced a considerable increase in the values of all the components used to measure its liner shipping connectivity, except for the maximum capacity of container ships calling at the port during both first and second quarter of 2020. Liner shipping connectivity levels improved with the number of liner shipping operators increasing from 6 in Q1 of 2019 to 12 in Q2 of 2020. It was achieved during the pandemic and even though the port experienced a 4.2 per cent drop in container traffic between January and May 2020. Panama's services exports on transports on 2019 represented 50 per cent of its' total services exports and in Q1-Q2 60 per cent (see Table 1).

Panama has a long-term vision whose objective is to become the main logistics service centre; it increased labour productivity compared to that of the United States, going from 30 per cent in 1970 to 40 per cent in 2017, thanks to the institutional framework created after the delivery of the canal in 1999. This vision has guided its public policies. The Dominican Republic, as mentioned before, tourism has come to play a vital role in the economy. Meanwhile, Costa Rica has embarked on a process of transformation of its productive structure, betting on exports of goods and services with high added value and achieving, together with Mexico, becoming an economy where two thirds of its exports are manufactures (Carranza et al., 2020).

Two notable facts, before the pandemic, are related to value-added services exports of Costa Rica. First, knowledge-intensive services exports have grown more than six-fold since 2000. Costa Rican IT and IT-enabled services exports reached more than $4.8 billions in 2019 (+5.3 growth) and the USA market accounted for 65 per cent of total Costa Rican knowledge-intensive services exports. Costa Rica leads this kind of export of services in Latin America as a percentage of GDP (7 per cent). Second, Costa Rica is a net exporter of services. Its trade balance surplus reached nearly 10 per cent of GDP in 2019, and for the rest of Latin America it resulted in an average deficit of 1 per cent of GDP (TradeMap, 2020). As shown on Table 1, Costa Rica's exports of knowledge-intensive services accounted for 50 per cent of total services export in 2019, and for Q1-Q3 of 2020 almost 70 per cent. Costa Rica's long-term investment in human capital and technology has provided more opportunities for greater income, productivity, employment, investment, and trade (OECD, 2012).

4 Discussion and Conclusion

As countries reel under the pandemic's economic impact, the services sector can help turn the tide by creating opportunities for greater income, food security, productivity, employment, investment, and trade. *Servicification*—putting a premium on the role of trade in services to power national economies—needs to be a key element of countries' strategies for recovery from COVID-19. But for services to serve societies and economies, countries need inclusive, coherent, and fitting policies. Particularly developing countries and least developed countries need support to strengthen and upgrade their services. With developing countries relying more on traditional services and developed countries depending on knowledge-intensive ones, the landscape is not even. Dealing with the pandemic has underscored the need to mind the structural gap between developed and developing countries. It is critical to promote key services inputs that transform the economy and trade in developing countries (UNCTAD, 2020).

From the three case studies of Costa Rica, Panama, and the Dominican Republic, which have heavily relied on their tourism sector in the past and although the results are preliminary, in the first three quarters of 2020 the travel service exports were affected the most (compared to other services exports). The difference between the three countries, regarding service exports, varied: Costa Rica increased its' exports of knowledge-intensive services from 50 per cent in 2019 to 70 percent in the first three quarters of 2020 (as a percentage of the total service exports), while Panama increased its' service exports in transport from 51 per cent to 60 per cent in the first two quarters of 2020. The Dominican Republic, on the other hand, according to preliminary data is still heavily relying on travel export services, but it decreased from 80 per cent in 2019 to 64% in the first three quarters of 2020 (as shown in Table 1).

In 2021, the availability of vaccines against COVID-19 would facilitate the recovery of foreign trade in the world and the Central American and the Dominican Republic region. Even with the introduction of the vaccine globally, it is likely that the effective access to it is slower and with limited coverage in the Central American and the Dominican Republic economies, which would result in the persistence of a certain reluctance to travel, with a negative impact on the tourism sector and, therefore, in the export of services during most of the year. After the favourable rise for the region in 2020, the terms of trade would remain relatively stable in 2021 (CEPAL, 2021).

For the next few years, the services sector will continue as a significant player on the world economic stage. Under this premise, Latin America and the Caribbean countries have the traces to be relevant players and understand that within the framework of a sector that must have high productivity, added value, innovation, and a total use of new technologies. All of this will lead, as is to be expected, in higher productivity rates, greater international trade flows, foreign capital inflows and increased employment.

For Costa Rica, Panama and the Dominican Republic investment incentives not only have helped attracting new projects, but also to retain them for many years, creating more and better jobs. The fourth industrial revolution is transforming the skills that the global human capital requires, which has caused job destruction, creation of new ones, and transformation of others. New technologies such as smart and autonomous systems, and automation fueled by big data and machine learning have emerged. The COVID-19 pandemic has fast-tracked the transformative power of those digital technologies. Governments must be prepared to offer innovative incentives that allow companies to evolve towards the knowledge economy.

Annexes

List of services exported by Costa Rica (US$000's)

Code	Service label	2015	2016	2017	2018	2019	CAGR	Share 2019	Q1-Q3 2020	Share 2020
S	**All services**	**7,693,597**	**8,537,127**	**8,631,700**	**9,090,500**	**9,503,094**	**5.4%**	**100%**	**5,366,964**	**100%**
4	Travel	3,266,478	3,648,357	3,656,034	3,772,508	3,976,691	5.0%	42%	1,239,855	23%
4.1	Travel, Business	541,725	492,093	327,195	340,667	350,722	−10.3%	9%		
4.2	Travel, Personal	2,724,753	3,156,264	3,328,839	3,431,841	3,625,969	7.4%	91%		
10	Other business services	2,606,835	2,924,993	2,968,856	3,194,702	3,346,510	6.4%	35%	2,654,140	49%
10.1	Research and development (R&D)	155,028	169,195	152,275	168,000	172,000	2.6%	5%		
10.2	Professional and management consulting services	2,187,793	2,538,755	2,654,655	2,845,490	2,987,503	8.1%	89%		
10.3	Technical, trade-related, and other business services	264,015	217,043	161,926	181,212	187,007	−8.3%	6%		
9	Telecommunications, computer, and information services	1,001,667	1,094,730	1,163,436	1,246,430	1,334,181	7.4%	14%	1,030,588	19%
9.1	Telecommunications services	12,843	11,546	13,132	12,411	12,011	−1.7%	1%		
9.2	Computer services	928,075	993,953	1,076,400	1,154,937	1,237,064	7.4%	93%		
9.3	Information services	60,750	89,230	73,904	79,082	85,106	8.8%	6%		
3	Transport	496,066	503,337	454,739	501,960	495,929	0.0%	5%	212,391	4%
3.1	Sea transport	172,439	190,976	170,431	170,913	170,314	−0.3%	34%		
3.2	Air transport	280,579	266,239	243,016	294,377	280,166	0.0%	56%		
3.3	Other modes of transport (other than sea and air)	39,232	38,841	26,985	27,967	28,471	−7.7%	6%		
3.4	Postal and courier services	3,815	7,282	14,307	8,703	16,978	45.2%	3%		

1	Manufacturing services on physical inputs owned by others	149,092	136,873	151,427	139,475	121,279	−5.0%	1%	82,953	2%
2	Maintenance and repair services n.i.e.	81,125	103,220	107,819	117,683	101,436	5.7%	1%	64,407	1%
7	Financial services	65,306	89,553	90,032	85,439	87,388	7.6%	1%	57,582	1%
7.1	Explicitly charged and other financial services	57,980	81,448	80,093	75,430	70,259	4.9%	80%		
7.2	Financial intermediation services indirectly measured (FISIM)	7,326	8,105	9,939	10,009	17,129	23.7%	20%		
12	Government goods and services n.i.e.	24,606	29,025	31,831	23,969	31,049	6.0%	0%	18,436	0%
8	Charges for the use of intellectual property n.i.e.	436	5,371	5,639	5,921	6,218	94.3%	0%	4,696	0%
6	Insurance and pension services	1,986	1,668	1,886	2,413	2,413	5.0%	0%	1,916	0%
6.1	Direct insurance	0	0	0	0	0		0%		
6.2	Reinsurance	1,986	1,668	1,886	2,413	2,413	5.0%	100%		
11	Personal, cultural, and recreational services	0	0	0	0	0		0%	0	0%
Knowledge intensive services (% of all service exports)		47.8%	48.2%	49.0%	49.9%	50.3%			69.9%	
Knowledge intensive services YOY Growth			12.0%	2.8%	7.2%	5.3%			5.8%	

Sources: ITC, UNCTAD, WTO trade in services database based on International Monetary Fund statistics. 2020 data based on BCCR

List of services exported by Panama (US$000's)

Code	Service label	2015	2016	2017	2018	2019	CAGR	Share 2019	Q1-Q2 2020	Share 2020
S	**All services**	**11,865,500**	**12,276,826**	**13,325,965**	**13,782,251**	**13,932,594**	**4.1%**	**100%**	**4,706,829**	**100%**
4	Travel	3,948,200	4,234,315	4,422,040	4,616,857	4,521,107	3.4%	32%	890,737	19%
4.1	Travel, Business	107,600	110,777	151,936	163,433	182,136	14.1%	4%	28,942	3%
4.2	Travel, Personal	3,840,600	4,123,538	4,270,104	4,453,424	4,338,970	3.1%	96%	861,795	97%
1	Manufacturing services on physical inputs owned by others	0	0	0	0	0	0.0%	0%	0	0%
3	Transport	5,440,300	5,604,252	6,459,000	6,814,500	7,056,741	6.7%	51%	2,844,241	60%
3.1	Sea transport	3,417,200	3,351,960	3,856,064	4,071,145	4,292,451	5.9%	61%	2,202,811	77%
3.2	Air transport	1,946,500	2,173,165	2,523,815	2,664,070	2,684,991	8.4%	38%	610,629	21%
3.3	Other modes of transport (other than sea and air)	0	0	0	0	0	0.0%	0%	0	0%
3.4	Postal and courier services	76,600	79,127	79,125	79,338	79,298	0.9%	1%	30,802	1%
2	Maintenance and repair services n.i.e.	16,700	15,023	16,124	16,425	16,400	-0.5%	0%	7,000	0%
9	Telecommunications, computer, and information services	285,500	300,959	294,081	298,605	303,204	1.5%	2%	153,150	3%
9.1	Telecommunications services	253,300	270,107	257,874	264,027	268,950	1.5%	89%	135,900	89%
9.2	Computer services	24,400	22,900	28,302	26,650	26,356	1.9%	9%	13,411	9%
9.3	Information services	7,800	7,952	7,905	7,929	7,899	0.3%	3%	3,839	3%
10	Other business services	546,700	504,445	514,648	530,740	551,580	0.2%	4%	129,246	3%
10.1	Research and development (R&D)	15,600	16,602	16,396	16,146	16,480	1.4%	3%	7,090	5%
10.2	Professional and management consulting services	324,600	325,807	334,175	335,734	342,410	1.3%	62%	85,176	66%

10.3	Technical, trade-related, and other business services	206,500	162,036	164,077	178,860	192,690	−1.7%	35%	36,980	29%
12	Government goods and services n. i.e.	107,500	112,947	123,828	117,901	116,084	1.9%	1%	33,895	1%
7	Financial services	1,244,400	1,269,381	1,222,577	1,128,943	1,082,422	−3.4%	8%	545,315	12%
7.1	Explicitly charged and other financial services	549,300	520,272	449,146	391,985	380,239	−8.8%	35%	235,261	43%
7.2	Financial intermediation services indirectly measured (FISIM)	695,100	749,109	773,431	736,958	702,183	0.3%	65%	310,054	57%
6	Insurance and pension services	225,700	226,727	262,771	230,397	264,946	4.1%	2%	99,380	2%
6.1	Direct insurance	84,800	73,774	81,770	75,667	75,222	−3.0%	28%	43,994	44%
6.2	Reinsurance	97,400	94,294	121,967	106,070	132,546	8.0%	50%	45,445	46%
6.3	Auxiliary insurance services	43,500	58,659	59,033	48,659	57,177	7.1%	22%	9,942	10%
8	Charges for the use of intellectual property n.i.e.	5,900	3,700	3,800	21,700	12,722	21.2%	0%	1,967	0%
11	Personal, cultural, and recreational services	44,600	5,080	7,092	6,132	7,390	−36.2%	0%	1,898	0%
Knowledge intensive services (% of all service exports)		19.5%	18.8%	17.2%	16.0%	15.9%			19.7%	
Knowledge intensive services YOY Growth			−0.1%	−0.3%	−3.8%	0.2%			−14.6%	

Sources: ITC, UNCTAD, WTO trade in Services database based on International Monetary Fund statistics. 2020 data based on CGR of Panama

List of services exported by Dominican Republic (US$000's)

Code	Service label	2015	2016	2017	2018	2019	CAGR	Share 2019	Q1-Q3 2020	Share 2020
S	**All services**	**7,541,800**	**8,309,200**	**8,856,800**	**9,284,100**	**9,345,600**	**5.5%**	**100%**	**3,136,400**	**100%**
4	Travel	6,115,900	6,719,600	7,184,100	7,560,700	7,468,100	5.1%	80%	2,005,800	64%
4.1	Travel, Business	55,800	58,400	66,200	72,000	72,800	6.9%	1%		
4.2	Travel, Personal	6,060,100	6,661,200	7,117,900	7,488,700	7,395,300	5.1%	99%		
10	Other business services	273,000	336,100	404,300	432,000	558,100	19.6%	6%	667,343	21%
10.1	Research and development (R&D)	6,900	8,000	7,600	7,900	7,800	3.1%	1%		
10.2	Professional and management consulting services	23,100	28,200	27,100	26,200	24,400	1.4%	4%		
10.3	Technical, trade-related, and other business services	243,000	299,900	369,600	397,900	525,900	21.3%	94%		
9	Telecommunications, computer, and information services	168,300	147,200	130,100	116,200	91,000	−14.2%	1%	78,033	2%
9.1	Telecommunications services	114,500	99,900	95,300	81,200	67,500	−12.4%	74%		
9.2	Computer services	53,800	47,300	34,800	35,000	23,500	−18.7%	26%		
9.3	Information services	0	0	0	0	0	0.0%	0%		
3	Transport	547,700	581,000	609,600	649,100	674,700	5.4%	7%	159,000	5%
3.1	Sea transport	103,300	108,600	117,300	143,100	159,000	11.4%	24%		
3.2	Air transport	441,800	472,400	492,300	506,000	515,700	3.9%	76%		
3.3	Other modes of transport (other than sea and air)	0	0	0	0	0	0.0%	0%		
3.4	Postal and courier services	2,600	0	0	0	0	0.0%	0%		
1	Manufacturing services on physical inputs owned by others	79,000	74,700	58,000	54,500	55,400	−8.5%	1%	22,800	1%
2	Maintenance and repair services n.i.e.	0	0	0	0	0	0.0%	0%	0	0%
7	Financial services	29,600	39,000	46,100	41,100	45,700	11.5%	0%	50,942	2%

7.1	Explicitly charged and other financial services	22,600	31,900	40,900	36,500	36,500	12.7%	80%		
7.2	Financial intermediation services indirectly measured (FISIM)	7,000	7,100	5,200	4,600	9,200	7.1%	20%		
12	Government goods and services n.i.e.	274,400	320,700	315,100	317,400	314,300	3.5%	3%		0%
8	Charges for the use of intellectual property n.i.e.	0	0	0	0	0	0.0%	0%	0	0%
6	Insurance and pension services	45,300	47,700	68,600	78,100	80,200	15.4%	0%	92,511	3%
6.1	Direct insurance	45,300	47,700	68,600	78,100	80,200	100.0%	0%		
6.2	Reinsurance	0	0	0	0	0	0.0%	0%		
11	Personal, cultural, and recreational services	8,600	43,200	40,900	35,000	58,100	61.2%	1%	59,971	2%
Knowledge intensive services (% of all service exports)		6.8%	6.9%	7.3%	7.2%	8.3%			28.3%	
Knowledge intensive services YOY Growth			10.4%	13.9%	2.8%	16.1%			14.7%	

Sources: ITC, UNCTAD, WTO trade in Services database based on International Monetary Fund statistics. 2020 data based on BCRD

References

Aboal, D., & Tacsir, E. (2018). Innovation and productivity in services and manufacturing: The role of ICT. *Industrial and Corporate Change, 27*(2), 221–241. https://doi.org/10.1093/icc/dtx030

Anderson, J., Milot, C., & Yotov, Y. (2014). How much does geography deflect services trade? Canadian answers. *International Economic Review, w 55*(3), 791–818. https://doi.org/10.1111/iere.12071

Antunes, B. (Ed.). (2020a, August 19a). *Measurement of services value-added in exports and analysis of related services and trade policies*. Retrieved May 10, 2021, from https://unctad.org/project/measurement-services-value-added-exports-and-analysis-related-services-and-trade-policies

Antunes, B. (2020b, November 6b). *Services sector vital to COVID-19 economic recovery | UNCTAD*. UNCTAD. https://unctad.org/news/services-sector-vital-covid-19-economic-recovery

Ariu, A. (2016). Crisis-proof services: Why trade in services did not suffer during the 2008–2009 collapse. *Journal of International Economics, 98*, 138–149. https://doi.org/10.1016/j.jinteco.2015.09.002

Banco Central de Costa Rica. (2020). Retrieved May 10, 2021, from https://www.bccr.fi.cr/SitePages/Inicio.aspx

Banco Central de la República Dominicana. (2021, January 7). *Importancia del turismo en República Dominicana*. https://www.bancentral.gov.do/a/d/5003-importancia-del-turismo-en-republica-dominicana

Behsudi, A. (2020, December). *Impact of the pandemic on tourism – IMF F&D*. International Monetary Fund. https://www.imf.org/external/pubs/ft/fandd/2020/12/impact-of-the-pandemic-on-tourism-behsudi.htm#: per cent7E:text=The per cent20global per cent20pandemic per cent2C per cent20the per cent20first, world per cent20Tourism per cent20Organization per cent20 (UNWTO).

Beteta, H. E., & Moreno Brid, J. C. (2014). *Cambio estructural y crecimiento en Centroamérica y la República Dominicana: Un balance de dos décadas, 1990–2011*. CEPAL.

Borga, M., & Howell, K. (2014). The comprehensive restructuring of the international economic accounts: Changes in definitions, classifications, and presentations. *Survey of Current Business, 94*(March), 1–19. Available at http://bea.gov/scb/pdf/2014/03percent20March/0314_restructuring_the_international_economic_accounts.pdf

Carranza, L., de la Torre, A., Ize, A., Alfaro, L., Kanczuk, F., Perry, G., Guzmán, C., Benavides, J., Meller, P., Engel, E., Lustig, N., Olarreaga, M., & Levy Yeyati, E. (2020, November 12). *El desafío del desarrollo en América Latina. Políticas para una región más productiva, integrada e inclusiva*. CAF. Retrieved from http://scioteca.caf.com/handle/123456789/1659

Comisión Económica para América Latina y el Caribe (CEPAL). (2020, October). *Estudio Económico de América Latina y el Caribe* (No. 9789211220506). CEPAL. https://www.cepal.org/es/publicaciones/46070-estudio-economico-america-latina-caribe-2020-principales-condicionantes

Comisión Económica para América Latina y el Caribe (CEPAL), Orozco, R. C., & Torres González, L. D. (2021, January). *Redes intersectoriales de comercio entre Centroamérica, México y la República Dominicana: un análisis desde la perspectiva de la teoría de redes sociales* (Documentos de Proyectos). CEPAL. https://repositorio.cepal.org/handle/11362/46617

Contraloría General de la República de Panamá. (2021, March). *Cifras Estimadas Del Producto Interno Bruto De La República, A Precios Corrientes Y En Medidas De Volumen Encadenadas Con Año De Referencia 2007, ANUAL Y TRIMESTRAL: AÑO 2020*. Instituto Nacional de Estadística y Censo. https://www.inec.gob.pa/archivos/P0705547520210301110152COMENTARIO.pdf

Ferencz, J., & OECD. (2019). The OECD digital services trade restrictiveness index. *OECD Trade Policy Papers, 221*, 1–21. https://doi.org/10.1787/16ed2d78-en

Fontagné, L., Orefice, G., Piermartini, R., & Rocha, N. (2015). Product standards and margins of trade: Firmlevel evidence. *Journal of International Economics, 97*(1), 29–44.
Francois, J., & Hoekman, B. (2010). Services trade and policy. *Journal of Economic Literature, 48* (3), 642–692. https://doi.org/10.1257/jel.48.3.642
Hallward-Driemeier, M., & Nayyar, G. (2018). *Trouble in the making?: The future of manufacturing-led development.* World Bank.
Hausmann, R., Espinoza, L. & Santos, M.A., (2016). Shifting gears: A growth diagnostic of Panama. Copy at http://www.tinyurl.com/kwucd7t
INCAE, & García, J. (2021, March 1). *Un año de pandemia.* INCAE. https://www.incae.edu/es/blog/2021/03/01/un-ano-de-pandemia.html?seccion=clacds
Krugman, P. R. (1997). Good news from Ireland: A geographical perspective. *International Perspective on the Irish Economy*, 38–53.
OECD. (2012). *Attracting knowledge-intensive FDI to Costa Rica: Challenges and policy options.* Organisation for Economic Co-operation and Development. http://www.oecd.org/countries/costarica/E-book%20FDI%20to%20Costa%20Rica.pdf
OECD. (2013). *Investment policy reviews: Costa Rica 2013.* OECD Publishing.
Sykes, A. (1999). Regulatory protectionism and the law of international trade. *The University of Chicago Law Review, 66*(1), 1–46. https://doi.org/10.2307/1600385
TradeMap. (2020). *Trade statistics for international business development from International Trade Center.* https://www.trademap.org/
UNCTAD. (2020, December 7). Total merchandise trade. UNCTAD E-Handbook of Statistics 2020. https://stats.unctad.org/handbook/MerchandiseTrade/Total.html
World Bank. (2014, June 13). Costa Rica Five years after CAFTA-DR assessing early results for the Costa Rican economy. Costa Rica and Panama country management unit, poverty reduction and economic management, Latin America and the Caribbean Region.
World Bank. (2020, October 29). *Overview.* https://www.worldbank.org/en/country/dominicanrepublic/overview
World Tourism Organization (UNWTO). (2020, December). *UNWTO World Tourism Barometer* (No. 1728–9246). UNWTO. https://doi.org/10.18111/wtobarometereng
World Trade Organization. (2019, November). *World Trade Report 2019: The future of services trade.* https://www.wto.org/english/res_e/booksp_e/00_wtr19_e.pdf
World Travel & Tourism Council (WTTC). (2019). *Travel & Tourism Economic Impact. World Travel & Tourism Council (WTTC). WTTC Data Gateway.* https://wttc.org/Research/Economic-Impact/Data-Gateway

Entrepreneurship, Knowledge-Economy and Economic Success of Cities: A Scoping Review and Thematic Analysis

Taha Chaiechi and Emiel L. Eijdenberg

Abstract The existing literature on the interplay between entrepreneurship, knowledge-based economy and urban economic prosperity has often portrayed a predictable relationship between entrepreneurship and economic growth, yet the arguments are mainly broad-brush. It appears that most studies fail to pay adequate attention to the dynamic forces of positive externalities and mechanisms through which they affect the sources of economic growth in cities. This paper adopts a scoping review approach to determine the scope, coverage, knowledge gap and context of the existing literature on the topic. The paper further uses thematic analysis to identify, analyse and report the patterns in the reviewed literature. The paper finds that the literature relating to the entrepreneurship–growth nexus determinants is sporadic and less structured. The paper concludes that the multidimensionality of this complicated relationship requires a more systematic understanding of the dynamic interaction between factors such as innovation, urbanisation and technology. Additionally, this scoping review finds that while migration and industry clusters are growing phenomena in both developed and developing countries, their effects on entrepreneurial activities and growth have yet to receive sufficient attention. Finally, the paper finds a paucity of comparative studies on the multi-level interactions of entrepreneurial activities at the industry–city–country level.

Keywords Entrepreneurship · Knowledge-economy · City prosperity · Urban economic growth · Scoping review · Thematic analysis

---

T. Chaiechi (✉)
College of Business, Law and Governance, James Cook University, Townsville, QLD, Australia
e-mail: taha.chaiechi@jcu.edu.au

E. L. Eijdenberg
JCU Singapore Business School, James Cook University, Singapore, Singapore
e-mail: emiel.eijdenberg@jcu.edu.au

© The Author(s), under exclusive license to Springer Nature Singapore Pte Ltd. 2022
T. Chaiechi, J. Wood (eds.), *Community Empowerment, Sustainable Cities, and Transformative Economies*, https://doi.org/10.1007/978-981-16-5260-8_6

1 Introduction

Despite the commonly held view that entrepreneurship fosters job creation and economic growth (Acs & Szerb, 2007; Baptista et al., 2008; Malchow-Møller et al., 2011), little is known about how and if entrepreneurship improves economic resilience or urban prosperity, particularly from an urban economics perspective. At the macro and meso levels, the literature has often portrayed an entirely predictable relationship between entrepreneurship and economic growth (Acs & Szerb, 2007; Baumol et al., 2007; Wennekers & Thurik, 1999). At the micro-level, the literature has more often than not focused on *why* entrepreneurs choose to locate in urban areas or on what aspects of urban areas attract entrepreneurs to relocate (cf. Choongo et al., 2020; Rooks et al., 2016). These arguments are either broad-brush or fail to pay adequate attention to the dynamic forces of externalities, such as innovation and knowledge spillovers. For example, the knowledge spillover theory of entrepreneurship explains how disseminating non-rival knowledge amongst firms leads to improvements in endogenous growth foundations. However, apart from some recent notable studies (e.g. Cohen & Muñoz, 2015; Rodrigues & Franco, 2018), entrepreneurial actions and mechanisms affecting the sources of economic growth in cities and urban areas are not fully discussed in the literature.

Entrepreneurship was not considered essential in classical and neoclassical theories. Neoclassical growth theory, for example, failed to consider or design a mechanism to explain either technological advancements or entrepreneurship effects as potential sources of economic growth (see Solow, 1956). Classical models primarily relied on capital investment in the large manufacturing sector rather than new and small businesses. Upon the emergence of the endogenous growth theory in the 1980s (see Romer, 1986, 1990), many economists' attention shifted towards human capital, innovation and knowledge as essential drivers of economic growth. These economists held the view that the domestic economy grows endogenously, a belief that also gave birth to the concept of (positive) externalities and spillover effects of knowledge and innovation in inducing economic development. As economists began to focus on knowledge and innovation spillovers, Lucas (1988) demonstrated how city economies benefit from local spillovers. Lucas viewed cities as a collection of production factors (capital, labour and land) clustered in one location where the production is concentrated and facilitated.

Two other important works that placed innovation and entrepreneurship at the centre of evolutionary economics are Joseph Schumpeter's *Capitalism, Socialism and Democracy* (1942) and the *Theory of Economic Development* (1961). Schumpeter believed that economic success is an evolving process that is change-oriented and innovation-based. In the Schumpeterian view, this evolving process based on entrepreneurship and the emergence of new businesses is the key to the survival of capitalism. This belief is rooted in Schumpeter (1942)'s perennial 'gale of creative destruction':

> . . . The opening up of new markets, foreign or domestic, and the organisational development from the craft shop and factory to such concerns as U.S. Steel illustrate the process of

> industrial mutation that incessantly revolutionises the economic structure from within, incessantly destroying the old one, incessantly creating a new one. This process of Creative Destruction is an essential fact about capitalism. It is what capitalism consists in and what every capitalist concern has got to live in. (p. 83)

Profit-driven entrepreneurs introduce new products, services or technologies and compete with other firms in the marketplace, an interaction that will usually result in lower prices, higher quality, better features and greater customer satisfaction.

> The fundamental impulse that sets and keeps the capitalist engine in motion comes from the new 'consumers' goods, the new methods of production or transportation, the new markets, the new forms of industrial organisation that capitalist enterprise creates. (p. 83)

It did not take long before entrepreneurship activities were hailed not only by academics (Baumol, 1968; Shane & Venkataraman, 2000; Wiklund & Davidsson, 2011) but were also highly praised by politicians and governments worldwide. Governments began to view entrepreneurship as an essential catalyst in creating more jobs within the economy (Michael & Pearce II, 2009; Ribeiro-Soriano & Galindo-Martín, 2012). Hence, they continue their support for innovative start-ups and help them grow through different means, including attractive financial resources, favourable policies and training programs (Buffart et al., 2020; Rasmussen & Gulbrandsen, 2012; Stephan et al., 2015). Nonetheless, 41% of start-ups seem to be in a 'red zone', where they are only a few months away from running out of cash completely.[1]

Following the emergence of conflicting evidence, some authors began to dive deeper into investigating entrepreneurship's economic impacts. The seminal works of Birch (1979) and Davidsson et al. (1998) offered empirical evidence to show that small businesses make uneven contributions to net job creation within the economy. These findings were later corroborated in the works of Audretsch and Fritsch (2002) and van Stel and Storey (2004), who discussed how the relationship between start-ups and employment varied across different regions. More recent studies have found that it is mainly new firms rather than small ones that increase employment levels within economies (Haltiwanger et al., 2013), and while entrepreneurial firms do not seem to change the average wage levels (Malchow-Møller et al., 2009), wages paid by newly-established firms have been found to be up to 8% lower than those paid by older firms of similar size (Brixy et al., 2007). It has also been argued that these new jobs are sometimes poor quality (Coad et al., 2014). These observations leverage the potential of a paradox between the macroeconomic goal of 'job creation' and the quality of jobs. However, further investigation and timely insights into an array of potential economic outcomes are necessary.

Apart from job creation as a significant factor for economic growth in cities (i.e. urban prosperity and 'city economy'), cities can grow in many different ways. Understanding the interplay between urban economy, economic prosperity, knowledge-based economy and entrepreneurship (as portrayed in Fig. 1) is essential

---

[1] https://www.weforum.org/agenda/2020/06/4-ways-governments-can-support-start-ups-and-save-their-economies/

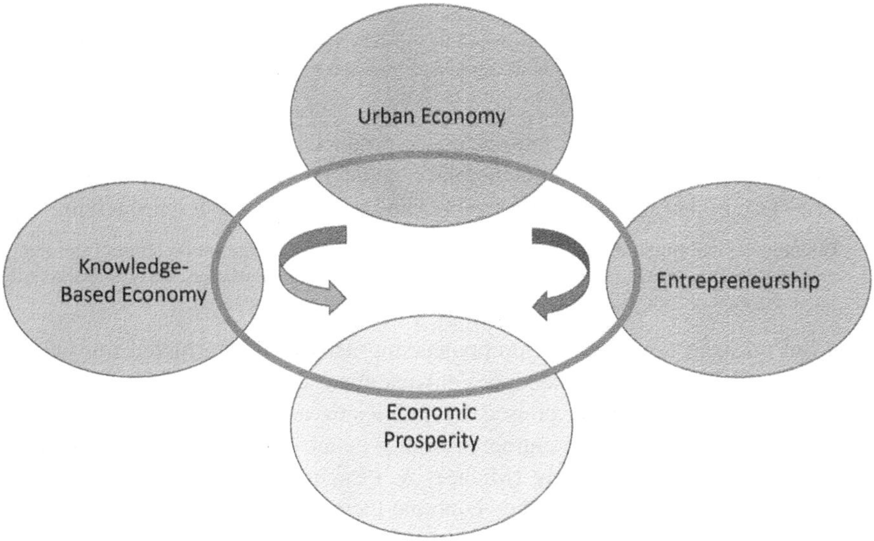

Fig. 1 The assumed interplay between city economy and urban prosperity through entrepreneurship and knowledge-based development

to comprehend the channels through which urban economic growth and prosperity can be achieved.

Accordingly, this paper adopts a scoping review approach to determine the scope, coverage and knowledge gaps in the existing literature on the interplay between entrepreneurship, knowledge-based development (KBD) and urban economic growth and prosperity. Because our topic involves an array of disciplines and sub-disciplines, this scoping review allows the authors to examine emerging evidence that could address and inform practice and research. Therefore, this paper does not attempt to synthesise findings or assess the quality of the literature included in the review.

2 Methods

To investigate the extent and variety of existing approaches to explore the relationship between entrepreneurship, knowledge and urban economics, this paper follows Arksey and O'Malley's (2005) method of conducting a scoping review. It begins by establishing a broad guiding question to shape the search strategy. To generate a literature profile on our topic and identify gaps, we follow five scoping steps – setting up an *a priori* protocol, searching, screening, data charting and data analysis.

To establish review strategies, an *a priori* protocol was developed. The protocol included constructing a guiding (research) question, identifying qualifying criteria, searching strategies and reporting and presentation techniques.

Table 1 Inclusion and exclusion criteria

Criterion	Inclusion	Exclusion
Year of publications	1990–2020	Studies outside this period
Search language	English	Non-English literature
Type of literature	Peer-reviewed original research, conference proceedings, working papers, and governmental reports	Editorials, opinion articles, action research articles, books and non-scholarly sources
Concept	All relevant studies that discuss any or the combination of factors pertinent to entrepreneurship, knowledge economy, city prosperity and economic growth and provide practical and transparent evaluation frameworks	Studies without practical focus
Coverage	Allowed great coverage of academic disciplines	Nil
Relevance	Title and abstract relevant to the guiding question	Irrelevant titles and abstracts

A well-constructed guiding question was important to our search and review processes. Accordingly, our question's elements were defined, and the question was tested and refined as necessary. Ultimately, our guiding question was 'What is the relationship between entrepreneurship, knowledge economy, city prosperity and economic growth?' The search strategy involved utilising search engines such as Google Scholar and the James Cook University library database. Specific qualifying criteria were developed (listed in Table 1), primarily based on the relevance of titles and abstracts to the guiding question. An initial time span of 1990–2020 was deemed appropriate, as entrepreneurship gained impetus in the literature after the emergence of the endogenous growth theory in 1986.

The principal investigator performed the search for titles and abstracts. Following Chaiechi (2020), the primary search was conducted manually, and after going through over 600 search results, 108 studies were selected. A staged approach was taken in evaluating and analysing the studies (see Fig. 2). Following the second round of screening and checking for duplicates and full-text availability, 106 articles met the eligibility criteria based on relevance, coverage and concept.

2.1 *Research Profiling*

A thorough and methodical review is an essential part of generating new knowledge, and a key aspect of a comprehensive scoping review is literature profiling. Profiling provides a valid basis for analysing the theme-based attributes of the selected studies (Mustafee et al., 2010; Gaffar et al., 2015; Coursaris & Bontis, 2012). The next step was to scan the collected articles and group them based on (1) discipline specifics

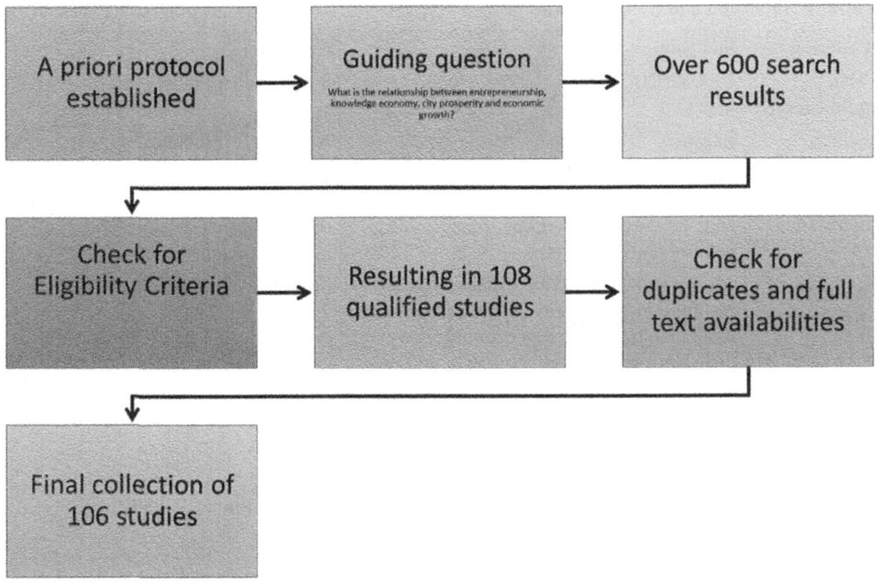

Fig. 2 The flowchart incorporating an *a priori* protocol for the scoping review

(subject areas), (2) dissemination specifics, and (3) research methods specifics. Together, these classifications uncovered topical relationships, the parallel existence of discrete knowledge sources and complementary capabilities academic fields have contributed to the research domain.

By determining the subject areas of the selected articles, we better identified the diversity of research disciplines in our sample. The subject areas were initially determined with a script based on the authors' discipline identifier or departmental information, which resulted in over 20 categories. They were then regrouped into macro-categories to better represent the academic fields. These macro-categories and the percentage of publications falling into each discipline are presented in Fig. 2.

Figure 3 shows the three major contributing disciplines focusing on the relationship between the key concepts of entrepreneurship, knowledge, city prosperity and economic growth. These are:

1. Economics (including urban economics), accounting for 27% of the collected articles
2. Planning, accounting for 21% of the collected articles
3. Entrepreneurship, accounting for 14% of the collected articles

While there are different modalities in which these three disciplines perform, their collective attention to the relationship between our key topic areas indicates the growing importance of a multidisciplinary approach to entrepreneurship, knowledge, urban prosperity and economic growth. Other identified disciplines include Technology and Innovation (accounting for 11% of the collected articles), Regional

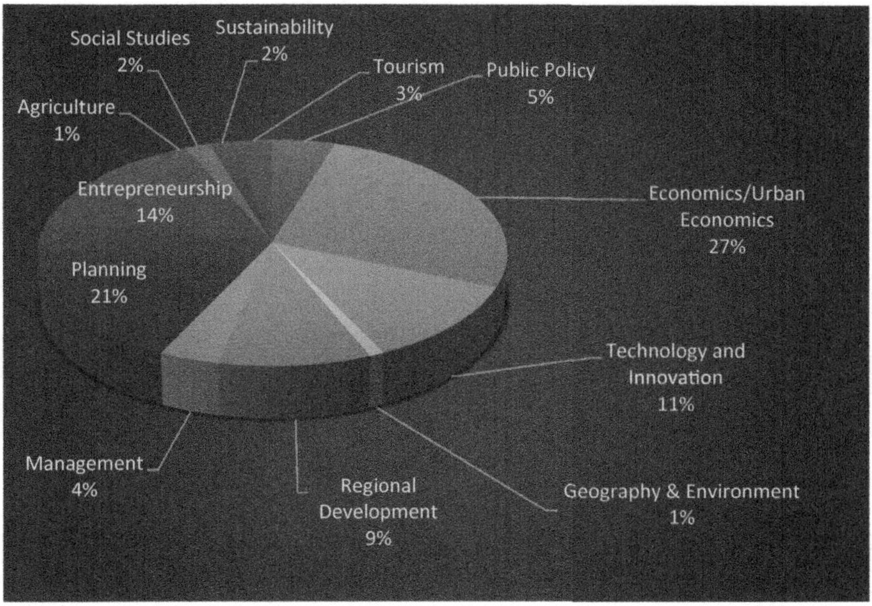

Fig. 3 The diversity of research disciplines appearing in the selected sample ($n = 106$)

Development (accounting for 9% of the collected articles) and Public Policy (accounting for 5% of the collected articles).

The next category to explore was the dissemination specifics of the collected articles. As presented in Fig. 3, this paper looked at the year of publication and the frequency of publication, highlighting the popularity and the impetus the topic area has been gaining during the selected timeframe.

Figure 4 shows the topic area was little discussed in the early 2000s, with only occasional publications focusing on the complex relationship between our concepts of interest. The research in the topic area seems to greatly increase around 2014, after which a steady upward trend occurred. The earliest work in our collected sample was published in 2001, and the second earliest was published in 2002, with no publications found in 2003–2005.

The final step in the research profiling of the collected articles was identifying research design formats, methods, data analysis and application domains over the years to specify concepts and uncover research paradigms. In light of the above inquiry, we found a balanced distribution between qualitative and quantitative approaches within the sample. The distribution of applied methods is presented in Fig. 5.

We further discovered methodological pluralism in the sample. Figure 5 shows that some articles employed various quantitative and qualitative methods. Deductive reasoning and regression analysis were the first and second most predominant approaches in the sample collected, found in 45% and 23% of the articles, respectively. Various regression models were applied, including ordinary least squares

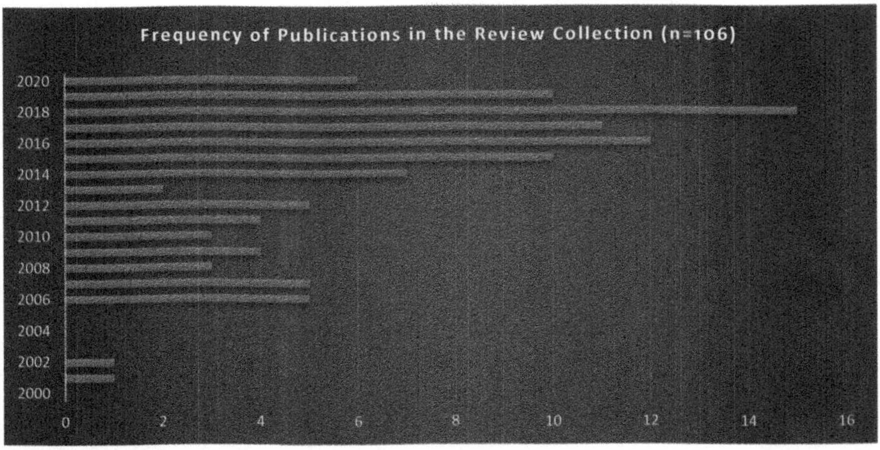

Fig. 4 Publication years and the frequency of publications

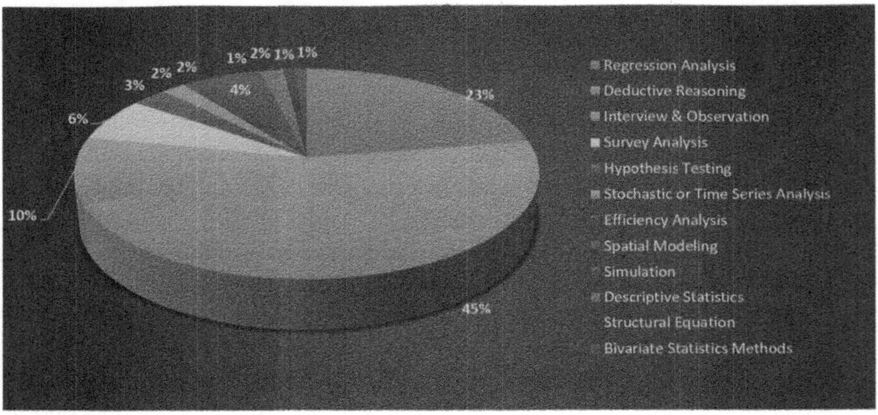

Fig. 5 The percentage and the diversity of methods and data analysis used in the collected sample ($n = 106$)

(OLS) regression, spatial regression, panel regression and logit and probit regression. Interviews combined with observation and survey analysis were other significantly used methods, each comprising 10% and 6% of articles, correspondingly. The evolution of urban entrepreneurship studies focusing on economic growth and knowledge economy is shown in Fig. 6. The figure shows that the increase in the application of various contemporary methods started in 2007. The summary of methods reveals that deductive reasoning and regression analysis were the most frequently used approaches and appear to gain popularity over time.

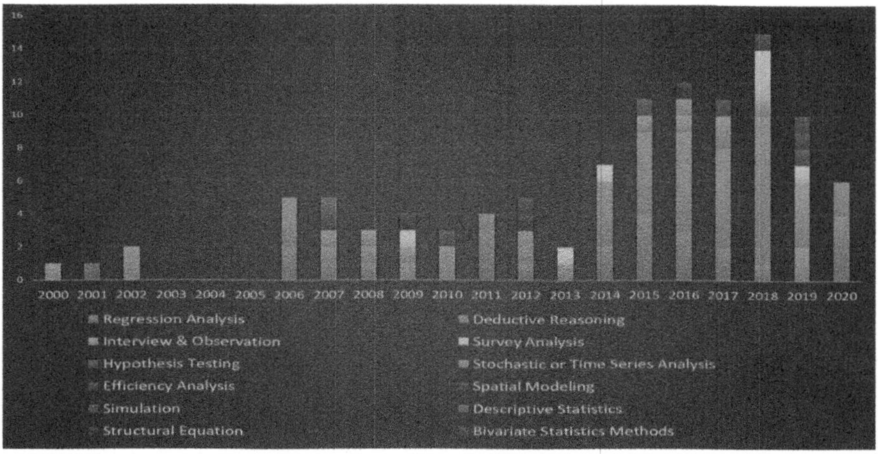

Fig. 6 Application of various contemporary methods in the sample over the search period

2.2 *Themes Identification*

Upon completing literature profiling, this paper followed Braun and Clarke (2006) to explore the sample further and identify emerging themes. This step required an initial coding process to fragment the data to identify themes and relationships. The coding of the articles is important, as it leads to data-driven interpretations. For accuracy, the process was accomplished using NVivo 12 Plus, qualitative data analysis software that accommodates a wide range of qualitative research methods, such as scoping reviews.

After importing all 106 articles into NVivo 12 Plus, the researchers conducted an initial auto-coding or machine-classified coding, a feature based on machine pattern recognition and emulation. This stage was fully automated and unsupervised. The auto-coding results gave an initial impression of the review articles. In this stage, the authors immersed themselves in the data (following Braun & Clarke, 2006) and improved their understanding of the content. Following this step, the researchers conducted open coding (following Strauss & Corbin, 1990). This step involved vetting coding results by un-coding what may have been inappropriately and inadequately coded and then creating codes based on the qualitative data itself.

The TreeMap in Fig. 7 shows the open coding hierarchy results based on how they relate to one another. In this chart, the size of the rectangles represents the amount of coding references in the data; thus, larger rectangles represent parent themes (main topics), and nested rectangles represent child themes (sub-themes) and their association with parent themes. In our dataset, the parent themes include innovation, knowledge, social, urban, entrepreneurship, resources, policy, community, sustainability, regionality and resilience. The main sub-themes include human capital, KBD, spillover, values, public, business and economy. Because effective

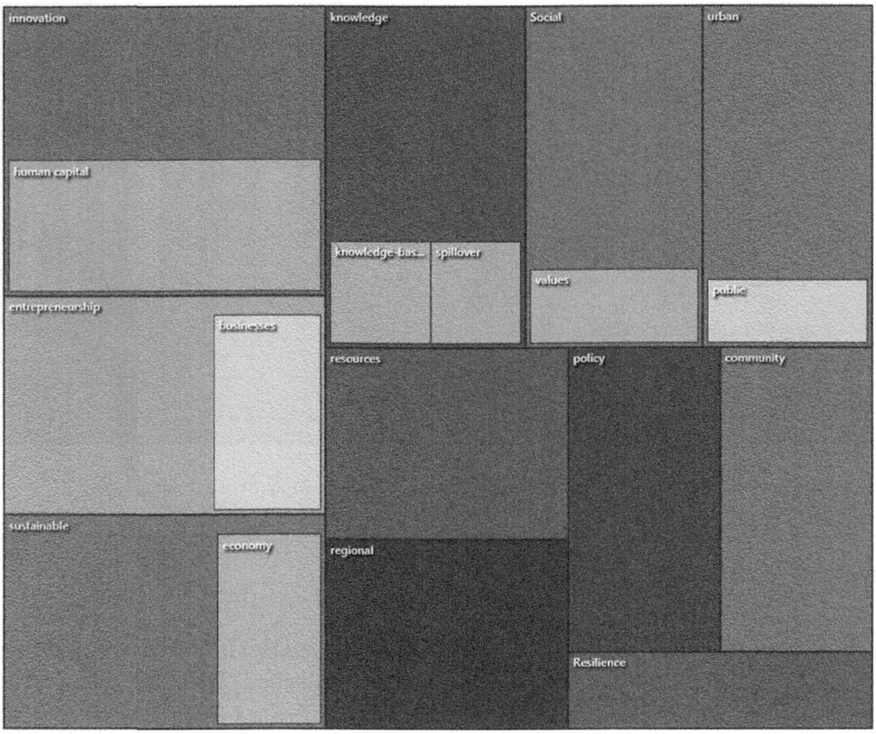

Fig. 7 TreeMap, open thematic coding

labelling becomes difficult as the rectangles get smaller, only the most prominent values (parent and main sub-parent categories) are labelled in Fig. 7.

2.3 Social Capital

Since the emergence of the notion of social capital in the literature in the 1980s, the concept has gained a great deal of currency as a key determinant of economic development. The inclusion of social capital in conceptual, theoretical and empirical literature has been a welcome addition to a rather limited perspective on economic growth and prosperity drivers. Various types of capital, including social and human capital, have been identified as drivers of economic growth and entrepreneurship in several selected studies, such as Audretsch and Keilbach (2007), Glaeser and Redlick (2009), Storper and Scott (2009), Doh and McNeely (2012), Kebede and Bokelmann (2017), Roos (2017), and Sorenson (2018).

Doh and McNeely (2012) provide supportive evidence for the importance of associating social capital with economic development, emphasising the significant indirect effect of entrepreneurship on generating economic development.

Fig. 8 Word cloud generated in NVivo 12 Plus using the selected articles with a focus on the social capital theme

Surprisingly, however, the study finds a negative interaction between social capital and entrepreneurship, calling for subsequent studies to examine the relationship more explicitly. Some studies have linked entrepreneurship to new employment opportunities that would alleviate urban poverty and inequality. For example, Kebede and Bokelmann (2017) applies a network approach to social capital in Addis Ababa to investigate this relationship. The study found that while street vendors were mostly homogenous in terms of cultural values and religion, entrepreneurs exhibited heterophilous tendencies towards education, occupation, income and age.

In order to better understand how social capital was presented in the selected articles, we generated a word frequency cloud using NVivo 12 Plus. Figure 8 is a graphical representation of word frequency in the articles connected to the theme of social capital. The word cloud displays the 100 most frequently used words in the selected articles, and the size of each word indicates its greater dominance.[2] Fig. 8 shows that most of these articles have also paid great attention to the concepts of

[2]https://help-nv.qsrinternational.com/12/win/v12.1.99-d3ea61/Content/queries/word-frequency-query.htm

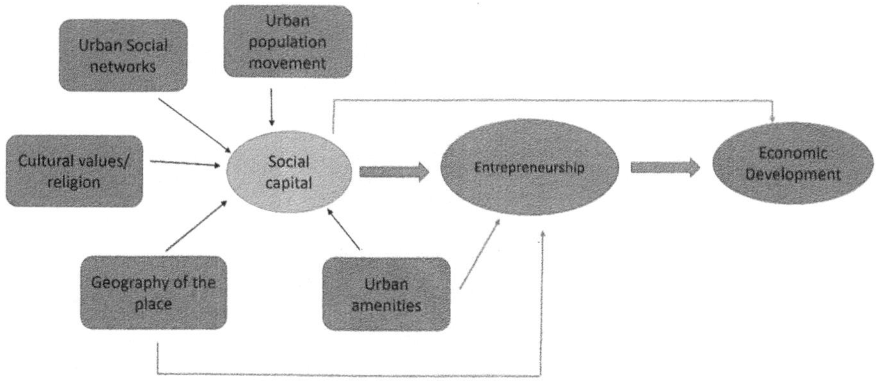

Fig. 9 The conceptual mechanism through which social capital impacts economic development. (Source: Developed by the authors based on the literature in the sample)

urban, economic growth, intellectuality and knowledge. While word clouds do not form the central part of the thematic analysis, it is important to note that they certainly supplement the insight gained from a close reading of the literature, as noted below.

Apart from cultural values that may result in social ties, the concept of social capital has also been identified as place-specific, where migrating out of and into a region impacts the construct of social ties (Glaeser & Redlick, 2009; Sorenson, 2018). If people expect to leave a neighbourhood or a place, they will have less of a tendency to form social ties. This phenomenon is economically important, as it may result in the decline of neighbourhoods due to a lack of investment in social capital. This may eventually result in the loss of government subsidies for those neighbourhoods, thus affecting the residents' social welfare. Glaeser and Redlick (2009) test this hypothesis and find little evidence to support a connection between social capital investment and out-migration across metropolitan areas. However, the study finds substantial evidence showing that growing urban areas attract greater human capital. Another study that ties the power of social capital to place is that of Sorenson (2018). Sorenson investigates the geography of social networks and their impact on entrepreneurs and argues that social ties tend to exist in physical and social spaces. The study also highlights the importance of social capital in supporting entrepreneurs by providing them with information about acquiring resources, career paths and amenities relevant to entrepreneurs.

Amenities are also discussed in Storper and Scott (2009) and are assumed to have a potent effect on urban population movements and the nature of jobs. The authors argue that urban prosperity must be directly linked to the economic geography of production and firms' agglomeration. The paper strongly suggests that most of the literature relating to urban policy agendas and advocacy groups ignores urban economic and social inequality. The following conceptual framework (Fig. 9) provides an overall summary of the demonstrated mechanisms, distinctions and ideas in the articles connected to the theme of social capital.

2.4 *Knowledge-Economy and Human Capital*

Since the emergence of endogenous growth theory in the 1980s and as an alternative response to classical and exogenous growth theory, the role of knowledge and its inter-temporal spillover effects in inducing economic growth has been hypothesised and tested in a plethora of publications. While much remains to be discovered, the positive spillover effect of knowledge is undisputed in the literature. The studies that focused on the role of knowledge and human capital in our sample include Lambooy and Boschma (2001), Audretsch and Keilbach (2007), Audretsch and Keilbach (2008), Yigitcanlar et al. (2008), Yigitcanlar (2010), Hendarmana and Tjakraatmadjab (2012), Moreno and Miguelez (2012), Sarimin (2014), Benneworth and Ratinho (2014), Yigitcanlar and Sarimin (2011), Attar (2015), Russ et al. (2017), Braunerhjelm et al. (2016), Kolehmainen et al. (2015), Yigitcanlar and Bulu (2016), Roos (2017), Yigitcanlar, Laasonen and Kolehmainen (2017), Faggian et al. (2017), Chang et al. (2018), Batabyal et al. (2018), Pyka et al. (2019), Lindemann (2019), and Williams (2019).

Similar to the approach taken for social capital, a word frequency cloud was generated for the articles connected to the theme of a knowledge-based economy and human capital; see Fig. 10 for the graphical representation. Many of the high-frequency words in this figure do not come as a surprise, such as knowledge, innovation, cities, regions and economics.

The role of knowledge and workers' skills in supporting production and firms' activities is rooted in the works of Lucas (1988) and Schumpeter (1942, 1961); this was later referred to as human capital in the literature. This term lends itself to creating one of the most widespread labels of modern economics, 'knowledge economy', where knowledge is paramount. Faggian et al. (2017) state that while the importance of knowledge is undisputed in modern society, what is unclear is whether all knowledge is significant in inducing economic growth and contributing to economic development in the same way. They find that while human capital is conducive to employment growth, creativity and innovation levels do not appear to contribute as much.

van Winden et al. (2007) argue that while the evidence supports the positive role knowledge plays in European cities' success, not all cities benefit from knowledge proportionately. They state that the extent of prosperity depends on several factors, such as industrial structure, urban amenities, social constructs, diversity and the ability to develop human capital. Some other studies in the collected sample envisage KBD as not only a central source of structuring development strategies (Yigitcanlar, 2010; Yigitcanlar et al., 2017) but also as a guiding framework to build sustainable and smart cities of the future (Chang et al., 2018) and multimedia super-corridors (Yigitcanlar & Sarimin, 2011). Braunerhjelm et al. (2016) assume

Fig. 10 Word cloud generated in Nvivo 12 Plus using the selected articles with a focus on knowledge economy and human capital

knowledge flows are entrenched in labour mobility, resulting in new knowledge creation. They find a robust and positive relationship between labour mobility and entrepreneurship. A few studies in the sample focused on knowledge adoption in rural and urban agriculture settings by focusing on the agricultural technology–knowledge ratio (Batabyal et al., 2018), the role of knowledge in industrial revolutions (Attar, 2015) and the role of community knowledge in urban agriculture (Lindemann, 2019) and rural development (Kolehmainen et al., 2015). Like the previous theme, the following conceptual framework (Fig. 11) was developed to provide an overall summary of the demonstrated mechanisms, distinctions and ideas in the articles connected to the theme of knowledge and human capital.

2.5 Resilience as a New Paradigm

Following Jackson and Mazzei (2013), St. Pierre (2000) and St. Pierre and Jackson (2014), in the final stage of the analysis we adopted the 'thinking with theory' approach, a philosophical approach in qualitative research that is contrary to the

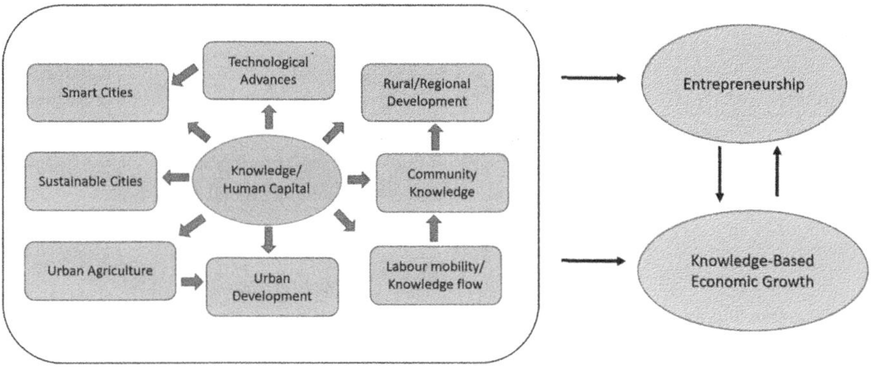

Fig. 11 The conceptual mechanism through which knowledge and human capital impacts economic growth. (Source: Developed by the authors based on the literature in the sample)

positivist approach and interpretive imperatives. Employing the theory approach allowed the authors to view the data across multiple perspectives, just as Jackson and Mazzei (2013) challenged simplistic treatments of qualitative data and argued that uncovering complex relationships requires taking steps beyond mechanistic coding and writing up transparent narratives. Accordingly, we took a step away from conventional analysis by analysing the collected literature again through the lens of the emerging and important theme of resilience. The term 'resilience' was not included in the search strategy or the guiding question. Still, during the stages of theme identification, the authors actively looked for 'resilience' as a recurring concept. Although it was not expected to appear in the search results, the concept of resilience is one of the most relevant and essential emerging themes in the research domain. In particular, resilience is considered a necessary trait for entrepreneurs (Korber & McNaughton, 2018). It helps businesses reimagine the way they see setbacks and devise mechanisms to pull through crises. We were interested in seeing if any of the collected articles tried to connect resilience and entrepreneurship.

Using NVivo, we analysed the sample to search for resilience in the articles. Of 106 articles, only 34 referred to the concept of resilience, and only nine used the word 'resilience' three or more times (see Table 2).

Figure 12 is a sunburst chart that shows the most prominent contributing themes from the selected articles in a hierarchy of multiple levels, focusing on resilience. The prominent themes (parent codes) in these articles include (but are not limited to) sustainability, entrepreneurship, knowledge, innovation and communities. The lengths of the slices in the chart reflect the portion of the contribution of the whole. The main ring is sliced up and divided into angular sweeps representing nested hierarchy levels (child codes). Child codes in the hierarchy include (but are not limited to) resilient community food systems, sustainable development goals, social wealth, social obligations, wealth and global competitiveness. Colour saturation delineates themes that are distinctly different.

Table 2 The only studies in the sample of 106 articles mention or investigate the concept of resilience

Main title	Top keywords	References to resilience
Challenges of transformation innovation re-bundling and traditional manufacturing in Canada's technology triangle	Technology triangle	9
	Manufacturing sector	
	Global financial crisis	
	Re-bundling	
	Innovation practices and strategies	
Entrepreneurship as resourcing	Resilience	43
	Entrepreneurship	
	Economic crisis	
	Discovery view	
	Environmental crisis	
Gardens and green spaces placemaking and black entrepreneurialism in Ohio	Community development	9
	Urban food production	
	Creative placemaking	
	Urban agriculture	
	Urban planning	
Global reversal, regional revival	Regional development	3
	Entrepreneurship	
	Innovation	
	Global networks	
	Mobility	
Impact assessment of entrepreneurial zones on local economic outcomes	Entrepreneurial zones	5
	Entrepreneurship	
	Local development	
	Local government units	
Knowledge-based, smart and sustainable cities: A provocation for a conceptual framework	Sustainable cities	7
	Smart cities	
	Sustainability assessment	
	Knowledge-based development urban living labs	
Slums and prosperity: A complex, dynamic pathway of intervention	Resilience	5
	Intervention	
	Informal	
	Slums	
Tourism diversification and its implications for smart specialisation	Tourism diversification	9
	Smart specialisation	
	Tourism innovation	

(continued)

Table 2 (continued)

Main title	Top keywords	References to resilience
	Related variety	
Urban virtues and the innovative city: An experiment in placing innovation in Edmonton, Canada	Community engagement	3
	Innovation	
	Negative place narratives	
	Urban touring	

Source: Generated by the authors using NVivo 12 Plus word analysis

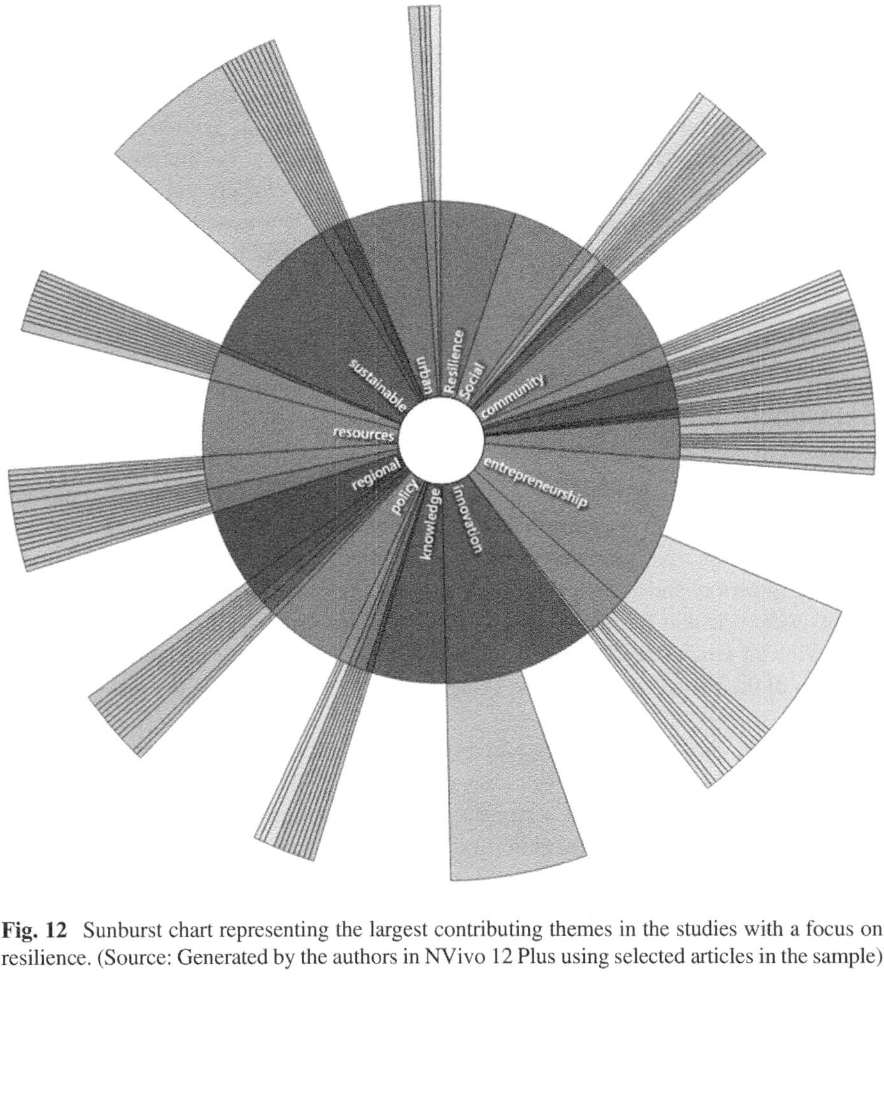

Fig. 12 Sunburst chart representing the largest contributing themes in the studies with a focus on resilience. (Source: Generated by the authors in NVivo 12 Plus using selected articles in the sample)

2.6 *Identified Research Gaps*

Entrepreneurship largely exists in urban and metropolitan areas due to agglomeration economies, access to resources and social networks (Freire-Gibb & Nielsen, 2014; Glaeser et al., 2010; Glaeser et al., 2015). The choice of location is an important firm decision and is part of spatial strategies. The principles of urban economics and Alfred Weber's theory of location of industries (Weber, 1909) confirm why firms compete for a location or pay for location-based intelligence. Nevertheless, there seems to be a lack of attention to the relationship between urban locations of firms and the success of entrepreneurs resulting in urban prosperity and economic growth.

While a limited number of studies in our sample indicated that the growth impacts of entrepreneurial activities are intensified in cities and urban areas, the determinants of an entrepreneurship–growth nexus, particularly in urban and metro areas, have been examined sporadically. This review finds a need for systematic scholarship around multi-level interactions between locational decisions, knowledge-based initiatives, human capital and urban and economic prosperity. Furthermore, there is a lack of evidence to support the impact of industry clusters on entrepreneurial activities and growth. Finally, this review finds there is a paucity of studies investigating the resilience of entrepreneurs and business continuity to better develop urban economies.

3 Conclusion

This paper adopted a scoping review approach to determine the scope, coverage and knowledge gaps in the existing literature on the interplay between urban economy, economic prosperity, knowledge-based economy and entrepreneurship. Using a guiding question and an a priori protocol, 106 relevant articles from 600 search results were selected for the review. Without attempting to synthesise the findings of the reviewed articles or assess the quality of the literature, we conducted a thematic analysis of the collected documents using NVivo 12 Plus software to assess appraisal themes.

This paper is among the first to bridge the scholarly disconnection between entrepreneurship and urban economics as a research field. Due to pressing global issues, such as migration and urbanisation due to changing socio-economic conditions such as lack of employment in rural areas versus the availability of employment in urban areas and ecologic conditions such as deforestation, drought and the effects of climate change (United Nations, 2020), the role of entrepreneurs is becoming more important. Seen as important economic actors and job creators (Acs & Szerb, 2007; Baptista et al., 2008; Malchow-Møller et al., 2011), entrepreneurs and their locational decisions, their use and development of innovation, their human capital and their urban prosperity are key factors found in this study that pave the way for future researchers to perform more thorough studies. Taking these key factors as points of departure in entrepreneurship research, more thorough analyses at the micro (i.e. individual entrepreneurs) and meso (i.e. entrepreneurs' firms) levels would lead to fruitful insights about, for example, what entrepreneurs consider when deciding on an urban location; what kind of innovations entrepreneurs use (e.g. artificial intelligence, fintech, frugal innovations) to grow their firms in different types of (urban) areas; and how entrepreneurs source skilled employees to work in their firms.

Acknowledgments This manuscript is supported by the JCUS–JCUA cross-collaboration grant IRG 20200008.

References

Acs, Z. J., & Szerb, L. (2007). Entrepreneurship, economic growth and public policy. *Small Business Economics, 28*(2), 109–122.

Arksey, H., & O'Malley, L. (2005). Scoping studies: Towards a methodological framework. *International Journal of Social Research Methodology, 8*(1), 19–32. https://doi.org/10.1080/1364557032000119616

Attar, M. A. (2015). Entrepreneurship, knowledge, and the industrial revolution. *Economics, 9*(1), 20150003. https://doi.org/10.5018/economics-ejournal.ja.2015-3

Audretsch, D. B., & Fritsch, M. (2002). *Growth Regimes Over Time and Space Regional Studies, 36*, 113–124.

Audretsch, D., & Keilbach, M. (2007). The localisation of entrepreneurship capital: Evidence from Germany. *Papers in Regional Science, 86*(3), 351–365.

Audretsch, D., & Keilbach, M. (2008). Resolving the knowledge paradox: Knowledge-spillover entrepreneurship and economic growth. *Research Policy, 37*(10), 1697–1705.

Baptista, R., Escária, V., & Madruga, P. (2008). Entrepreneurship, regional development and job creation: The case of Portugal. *Small Business Economics, 30*(1), 49–58.

Batabyal, K., Banerjee, A., Pal, S., Dey, S., Joardar, S. N., Samanta, I., Isore, D. P., & Singh, A. D. (2018). Detection, characterization, and antibiogram of extended-spectrum betalactamase Escherichia coli isolated from bovine milk samples in West Bengal. *India Vet World, 11*, 1423–1427.

Baumol, W. J. (1968). Entrepreneurship in economic theory. *The American Economic Review, 58* (2), 64–71.

Baumol, W. J., Litan, R., & Schramm, C. (2007). *Good capitalism, bad capitalism, and the economics of growth and prosperity*. Yale University Press.

Benneworth, P., & Ratinho, T. (2014). Regional innovation culture in the social knowledge economy. In R. Rutten, P. Benneworth, D. Irawati, & F. Boekema (Eds.), *The social dynamics of innovation networks* (pp. 239–256). Routledge.

Braun, V., & Clarke, V. (2006). Using thematic analysis in psychology. *Qualitative Research in Psychology, 3*, 77–101. https://doi.org/10.1191/1478088706qp063oa

Braunerhjelm, P., Ding, D., & Thulin, P. (2016). Labour as a knowledge carrier: How increased mobility influences entrepreneurship. *The Journal of Technology Transfer, 41*(6), 1308–1326.

Brixy, U., Kohaut, S., & Schnabel, C. (2007). Do newly founded firms pay lower wages? First evidence from Germany. *Small Business Economics, 29*, 161–171.

Buffart, M., Croidieu, G., Kim, P. H., & Bowman, R. (2020). Even winners need to learn: How government entrepreneurship programs can support innovative ventures. *Research Policy, 49*(10), 104052.

Chaiechi, T. (2020). Sustainable tropical cities: A scoping review of multidisciplinary methods for urban planning. *ETropic: Electronic Journal of Studies in the Tropics, 19*(2), 25–51.
Chang, A. J., Kim, N. S., Hireed, H., et al. (2018). Chang et al. reply. *Nature, 561*(E41). https://doi.org/10.1038/s41586-018-0547-7
Choongo, P., Eijdenberg, E. L., Chabala, M., Lungu, J., & Taylor, T. K. (2020). The evolution of urban entrepreneurship in Zambia. In M. Iftikhar, J. Justice, & D. Audretsch (Eds.), *The urban book series. Urban studies and entrepreneurship* (pp. 249–269). Springer.
Coad, A., Daunfeldt, S. O., Hölzl, W., Johansson, D., & Nightingale, P. (2014). High-growth firms: Introduction to the special section. *Industrial and Corporate Change, 23*(1), 91–112. https://doi.org/10.1093/icc/dtt052
Cohen, B., & Muñoz, P. (2015). Toward a theory of purpose-driven urban entrepreneurship. *Organization & Environment, 28*(3), 264–285.
Coursaris, C. K., & Bontis, N. (2012). A meta review of HCI literature: Citation impact and research productivity rankings. In *SIGHCI 2012 proceedings* (Paper 9).
Davidsson, P., Lindmark, L., & Olofsson, C. (1998). The extent of overestimation of small firm job creation: An empirical examination of the 'regression bias'. *Small Business Economics, 10*, 87–100.
Doh, S., & McNeely, C. (2012). A multi-dimensional perspective on social capital and economic development: An exploratory analysis. *The Annals of Regional Science, 49*(3), 821–843.
Faggian, A., Partridge, M., & Malecki, E. (2017). Creating an environment for economic growth: Creativity, entrepreneurship or human capital? *International Journal of Urban and Regional Research, 41*(6), 997–1009.
Freire-Gibb, L. C., & Nielsen, K. (2014). Entrepreneurship within urban and rural areas: Creative people and social networks. *Regional Studies, 48*(1), 139–153.
Gaffar, A., Deshpande, A., Bandara, W., & Mathiesen, P. (2015). Importance of literature profiling: An archival analysis with illustrative examples for IS researchers. In *PACIS 2015 proceedings* (Paper 103).
Glaeser, E., & Redlick, C. (2009). Social capital and urban growth. National Bureau of economic research. *International Regional Science Review, 32*(3), 264–299. https://doi.org/10.1177/0160017609336079
Glaeser, E. L., Kerr, S. P., & Kerr, W. R. (2015). Entrepreneurship and urban growth: An empirical assessment with historical mines. *Review of Economics and Statistics, 97*(2), 498–520.
Glaeser, E. L., Rosenthal, S. S., & Strange, W. C. (2010). Urban economics and entrepreneurship. *Journal of Urban Economics, 67*(1), 1–14.
Haltiwanger, J., Jarmin, R. S., & Miranda, J. (2013). Who creates jobs? Small versus large versus young. *The Review of Economics and Statistics, 95*(2), 347–361. https://doi.org/10.1162/REST_a_00288
Hendarmana, A. F., & Tjakraatmadjab, J. H. (2012). Relationship among soft skills, hard skills, and innovativeness of knowledge Workers in the Knowledge Economy era. *Procedia - Social and Behavioral Sciences, 52*(2012), 35–44.
Jackson, A. Y., & Mazzei, L. A. (2013). Plugging one text into another: Thinking with theory in qualitative research. *Qualitative Inquiry, 19*(4), 261–271.
Kebede, S. W., & Bokelmann, W. (2017). African indigenous vegetables and their production practices: Evidence from the HORTINLEA survey in Kenya. *Agrotechnology, 6*, 170. https://doi.org/10.4172/2168-9881.1000170
Kolehmainen, N., Ramsay, C., McKee, L., Missiuna, C., Owen, C., & Francis, J. (2015). Participation in physical play and leisure in children with motor impairments: Mixed-methods study to generate evidence for developing an intervention. *Physical Therapy, 95*(10), 1374–1386. https://doi.org/10.2522/ptj.20140404
Korber, S., & McNaughton, R. B. (2018). Resilience and entrepreneurship: A systematic literature review. *International Journal of Entrepreneurial Behavior & Research, 24*(7), 1129–1154.

Laasonen, V., & Kolehmainen, J. (2017). Capabilities in knowledge-based regional development – Towards a dynamic framework. *European Planning Studies, 25*(10), 1673–1692. https://doi.org/10.1080/09654313.2017.1337727

Lambooy, J., & Boschma, R. (2001). Evolutionary economics and regional policy. *The Annals of Regional Science, 35*, 113–131. https://doi.org/10.1007/s001680000033

Lindemann, J. (2019). Gardens and green spaces: Placemaking and black entrepreneurialism in Cleveland. *Ohio Agric Hum Values, 36*, 867–878. https://doi.org/10.1007/s10460-019-09947-w

Lucas, R. E., Jr. (1988). On the mechanisms of economic development. *Journal of Monetary Economics, 22*, 3–42.

Malchow-Møller, N., Munch, J., Schroll, S., & Skaksen, J. (2009). Explaining cross-country differences in attitudes towards immigration in the EU-15. *Social Indicators Research, 91*(3), 371–390.

Malchow-Møller, N., Schjerning, B., & Sørensen, A. (2011). Entrepreneurship, job creation and wage growth. *Small Business Economics, 36*(1), 15–32.

Michael, S. C., & Pearce, J. A. (2009). The need for innovation as a rationale for government involvement in entrepreneurship. *Entrepreneurship and Regional Development, 21*(3), 285–302.

Moreno, R., & Miguélez, E. (2012). A relational approach to the geography of innovation: A typology of regions. *Journal of Economic Surveys, 26*(3), 492–516.

Mustafee, N., Katsaliaki, K., & Taylor, S. J. E. (2010). Profiling literature in healthcare simulation. *Simulation, 86*(8–9), 543–558. https://doi.org/10.1177/0037549709359090

Pyka, A., Kudic, M., & Müller, M. (2019). Systemic interventions in regional innovation systems: Entrepreneurship, knowledge accumulation and regional innovation. *Regional Studies, 53*(9), 1321–1332.

Rasmussen, E., & Gulbrandsen, M. (2012). Government support programmes to promote academic entrepreneurship: A principal–agent perspective. *European Planning Studies, 20*(4), 527–546.

Ribeiro-Soriano, D., & Galindo-Martín, M. Á. (2012). Government policies to support entrepreneurship. *Entrepreneurship & Regional Development, 24*(9–10), 861–864.

Rodrigues, M., & Franco, M. (2018). Importance of living labs in urban entrepreneurship: A Portuguese case study. *Journal of Cleaner Production, 180*, 780–789.

Romer, P. (1986). Increasing returns and long run growth. *Journal of Political Economy, 94*, 1002–1037.

Romer, P. (1990). Endogenous technological change. *Journal of Political Economy, 98*, S71–S102.

Rooks, G., Klyver, K., & Sserwanga, A. (2016). The context of social capital: A comparison of rural and urban entrepreneurs in Uganda. *Entrepreneurship Theory and Practice, 40*(1), 111–130.

Roos, G. (2017). Knowledge management, intellectual capital, structural holes, economic complexity and national prosperity. *Journal of Intellectual Capital, 18*(4), 745–770.

Russ, M., Bansal, G., & Parrillo, A. (2017). The "knowledge city" and the "experience city": The main, mediating, and moderating effects of education on income and economic inequality. *Journal of the Knowledge Economy, 8*(3), 804–829.

Schumpeter, J. A. (1942). *Capitalism, socialism, and democracy*. University of Illinois at Urbana-Champaign's Academy for Entrepreneurial Leadership Historical Research Reference in Entrepreneurship. Available at SSRN: https://ssrn.com/abstract=1496200

Schumpeter, J. A. (1961). *The theory of economic development* (3rd ed.). Oxford University Press.

Shane, S., & Venkataraman, S. (2000). The promise of entrepreneurship as a field of research. *Academy of Management Review, 25*(1), 217–226.

Solow, R. M. (1956). A contribution to the theory of economic growth. *Quarterly Journal of Economics, 70*(1), 65–94.

Sorenson, O. (2018). Social networks and the geography of entrepreneurship. *Small Business Economics, 51*, 527–537. https://doi.org/10.1007/s11187-018-0076-7

St. Pierre, E. A. (2000). Poststructural feminism in education: An overview. *Qualitative Studies in Education, 13*(5), 477–515.

St. Pierre, E. A., & Jackson, A. Y. (2014). Qualitative data analysis after coding. *Qualitative Inquiry, 20*(6), 715–719.

Stel, A. V., & Storey, D. (2004). The link between firm births and job creation: Is there a Upas tree effect? *Regional Studies, 38*(8), 893–909. https://doi.org/10.1080/0034340042000280929

Stephan, U., Uhlaner, L. M., & Stride, C. (2015). Institutions and social entrepreneurship: The role of institutional voids, institutional support, and institutional configurations. *Journal of International Business Studies, 46*(3), 308–331.

Storper, M., & Scott, A. J. (2009). Rethinking human capital, creativity and urban growth. *Journal of Economic Geography, 9*(2), 147–167. https://doi.org/10.1093/jeg/lbn052

Strauss, A., & Corbin, J. M. (1990). *Basics of qualitative research: Grounded theory procedures and techniques*. Sage.

United Nations. (2020). *Sustainable development topics.* https://sdgs.un.org/topics

Weber, A. (1909). *Theory of the location of industries* (C. J. Friedrich, Trans.). University of Chicago Press.

Wennekers, S., & Thurik, R. (1999). Linking entrepreneurship and economic growth. *Small Business Economics, 13*(1), 27–56.

van Winden, W., van den Berg, L., & Pol, P. (2007). European cities in the knowledge economy: Towards a typology. *Urban Studies, 44*(3), 525–549. https://doi.org/10.1080/00420980601131886

Wiklund, J., Davidsson, P., Audretsch, D. B., & Karlsson, C. (2011). The future of entrepreneurship research. *Entrepreneurship Theory and Practice, 35*(1), 1–9. https://doi.org/10.1111/j.1540-6520.2010.00420.x

Williams, R. C. (2019). European conference on innovation and entrepreneurship. *Reading*. https://doi.org/10.34190/ECIE.19.123

Yigitcanlar, T. (2010). Making space and place for the knowledge economy. *European Planning Studies, 18*(11), 1769–1786.

Yigitcanlar, T., Baum, S., & Horton, S. (2007). Attracting and retaining knowledge workers in knowledge cities. *Journal of Knowledge Management, 11*(5), 6–17.

Yigitcanlar, T., & Bulu, M. (2016). Urban knowledge and innovation spaces. *Journal of Urban Technology, 23*(1), 1–9. https://doi.org/10.1080/10630732.2016.1164443

Yigitcanlar, T., Edvardsson, I. R., Johannesson, H., Kamruzzaman, M., Ioppolo, G., & Pancholi, S. (2017). Knowledge-based development dynamics in less favoured regions: Insights from Australian and Icelandic university towns. *European Planning Studies, 25*(12), 2272–2292. https://doi.org/10.1080/09654313.2017.1358699

Yigitcanlar, T., & Sarimin, M. (2011). The role of universities in building prosperous knowledge cities. *Built Environment, 37*(3), 260–280.

Yigitcanlar, T., Velibeyoglu, K., & Martinez-Fernandez, C. (2008). Rising knowledge cities: The role of urban knowledge precincts. *Journal of Knowledge Management, 12*(5), 8–20. https://doi.org/10.1108/13673270810902902

Urbanisation and Sustainable Development: Econometric Evidence from Australia

Janet Dzator, Alex O. Acheampong, and Michael Dzator

Abstract This study examines the effect of urbanisation on economic growth and carbon emissions in Australia for the period 1960–2019 using Cobb-Douglas production function with a Fully Modified Ordinary Least Squares and Dynamic Ordinary Least Squares estimators. The findings indicate that while urbanisation has a significant negative effect on economic growth, it has a significant positive effect on Australia's carbon emissions. Other factors such as physical capital and labour were found to have a significant positive impact on economic growth, while trade openness has a significant negative effect on economic growth. Our findings suggest that energy consumption and foreign direct investment do not affect Australia's economic growth. Further, our results validate the Environmental Kuznets Curve in Australia, while other factors such as energy consumption and population growths were found to worsen carbon emissions. It was also revealed that trade openness and foreign direct investment (FDI) are not insignificant contributors to carbon emissions in Australia. The policy implications are discussed.

J. Dzator (✉)
Newcastle Business School, University of Newcastle, Callaghan, NSW, Australia

Centre for African Research, Engagement and Partnerships (CARE-P), University of Newcastle, Callaghan, NSW, Australia

Australia Africa Universities Network (AAUN) Partner, University of Wollongong, Wollongong, Australia
e-mail: Janet.Dzator@newcastle.edu.au

A. O. Acheampong
Newcastle Business School, University of Newcastle, Callaghan, NSW, Australia

Centre for African Research, Engagement and Partnerships (CARE-P), University of Newcastle, Callaghan, NSW, Australia

M. Dzator
Centre for African Research, Engagement and Partnerships (CARE-P), University of Newcastle, Callaghan, NSW, Australia

SAE, Central Queensland University, Mackay, QLD, Australia

Australia Africa Universities Network (AAUN) Partner, University of Wollongong, Wollongong, Australia

© The Author(s), under exclusive license to Springer Nature Singapore Pte Ltd. 2022
T. Chaiechi, J. Wood (eds.), *Community Empowerment, Sustainable Cities, and Transformative Economies*, https://doi.org/10.1007/978-981-16-5260-8_7

Keywords Australia · Urbanisation · Carbon emissions · Economic growth · Sustainable development

1 Introduction

This paper examines the effect of urbanisation on economic growth and carbon emissions in Australia. Urbanisation is an economic and social modernisation phenomenon (Poumanyvong & Kaneko, 2010). This definition suggests that urbanisation is associated with the movement of people from rural areas to urban areas and a process of structural transformation of rural areas into urban areas (Poumanyvong & Kaneko, 2010). Globally, more people live in urban areas compared to rural areas. For instance, the United Nation (2018) report indicate that 55% the world's population reside in urban areas in 2018; however, 30% of the world's population was urban in 1950. The United Nation (2018) projected that 68% of the world's population would live in urban areas by 2050. The global increase in the number of people in urban areas is not different from Australia's case. Australia remains one of the most urbanised countries in the world. According to United Nations data, in 2015, the percentage of the Australian population living in urban areas was 89.4%; by 90.1% in 2020 and by 2025 is expected to reach 90.6%.

Rapid urbanisation in Australia and across the globe is associated with more resource use and additional pressure on the already fragile ecosystem due to the development of additional urban infrastructure to support the urban areas' unprecedented growth (Poumanyvong & Kaneko, 2010). Thus, changes that occur in urbanisation can affect economic growth and carbon emissions (Sadorsky, 2014). For instance, some scholars argue that urbanisation influence economic growth; however, the argument remains conflicting (Nguyen, 2018). One school of thought argue that urbanisation serves as an engine of economic growth. For instance, Bertinelli and Black (2004) argue that urbanisation generates economic growth. It structures the economy and society by providing opportunities for people to access educational services, employment, and health. Urbanisation also promotes economic growth as it allows countries to have advantages in transaction costs, economies of scale, and internal specialisation (Nguyen, 2018). Furthermore, urbanisation generates positive externalities such as increasing remittance, transfer of technology, skills, which can improve areas where migrant have left (Calì, 2008; Nguyen, 2018; Sasin & McKenzie, 2007). The second strand of the literature argues that urbanisation may have a U-shaped relationship with economic growth (Henderson, 2003; Nguyen, 2018). Thus, at the initial stage of economic development, urbanisation retards economic growth, while at the advanced stage of economic development, urbanisation improves economic growth. It is also argued that urbanisation can impede economic growth if urbanisation stresses the existing infrastructure (Alam et al., 2007). Lastly, some studies have indicated that urbanisation has no effect on economic growth. For instance, Bloom et al. (2008) suggested that urbanisation do not influence economic growth, especially in developing countries.

Besides, urbanisation is argued to influence the environment; however, its impact on carbon emissions is not known in advance. For instance, the Ecological Modernization Theory (EMT) stipulates an inverted U-shaped relationship between urbanisation and carbon emissions. Thus, the EMT argues that environmental problems such as carbon emissions increase as society becomes modernised and seek to address such environmental problems at the later stage of economic development (Poumanyvong & Kaneko, 2010; Sadorsky, 2014). The implication is that at the advanced stage of economic development with efficient technology, urban agglomeration and knowledge spillover effect, societies seek to minimise environmental problems such as mitigating carbon emissions compared to the lower stage of economic development (Gouldson & Murphy, 1997; Mol & Spaargaren, 2000; Poumanyvong & Kaneko, 2010). Like the EMT, the Urban Environmental Transition Theory (UETT) suggests that environmental problems differ across different economic development stages at the city level (McGranahan, 2010). Thus, as cities become prosperous by increasing production, environmental problems also increase; however, as cities become wealthier or at the advanced stage of development, environmental problems reduce as results of improvement in environmental regulation, technological progress, and structural change in the economy (Poumanyvong & Kaneko, 2010; Sadorsky, 2014). Both the EMT and UETT argue that urbanisation can negatively affect the environment, and hence the net impact of urbanisation on carbon emissions is indeterminate (Sadorsky, 2014). The findings of existing empirical studies remains conflicting. For instance, some studies revealed that urbanisation increases carbon emissions (Liu & Bae, 2018; Poumanyvong & Kaneko, 2010; Wang et al., 2016; Zhang & Lin, 2012). Another strand of the literature indicated that urbanisation reduces carbon emissions (Acheampong, 2019; Adams et al., 2020; Poumanyvong & Kaneko, 2010; Sadorsky, 2014), while the last strand indicated that an inverted U-shaped relationship exists between urbanisation and carbon emissions (Bekhet & Othman, 2017).

This study's motivation is rooted in the inconsistency in the empirical findings coupled with limited empirical studies that simultaneously examine the effect of urbanisation on economic growth and carbon emissions in Australia. This study, therefore, examines the impact of urbanisation on economic growth and carbon emissions in Australia for the period 1960–2019 using Fully Modified Ordinary Least Squares (FMOLS) and Dynamic Ordinary Least Squares (DOLS) models. Some scholars (Poumanyvong & Kaneko, 2010; Sadorsky, 2014) suggest that investigating the role of urbanisation on economic growth and carbon emissions is critical because if urbanisation is found to increase carbon emissions, this can affect forecasting models and climate change policy in Australia. Thus, earlier forecasting models of Australia's carbon emissions that failed to consider the impact of urbanisation on carbon emissions may generate unreliable information if urbanisation does actually affect carbon dioxide emissions. Policies based on models that omit urbanisation may also be inefficient. Contrarily, if urbanisation is found to mitigate carbon emissions, then modelling the economic and environmental effect of Australia's urbanisation would improve urban planners understanding of the contributing role of urbanisation to sustainable development and help implement sustainable urban policies in the short and long run.

The rest of the paper is outlined as follows: Section 2 presents the methodology and data, while Sect. 3 presents the empirical results. Section 4 presents the conclusions and policy implications.

2 Methodology and Data

2.1 Empirical Model for Economic Growth

This study uses Cobb-Douglas production function framework to examine the effect of urbanisation on Australia's economic growth. Following existing studies such as Omri and Kahouli (2014) and Shahbaz et al. (2013), economic growth is specified in Eq. (1) as a function of capital (K), labour (LAB), energy consumption, (ENER) urbanisation (URBP), trade openness (TRAD) and foreign direct investment (FDI). The subscript t refers to time.

$$GDPC_t = f(K_t, LAB_t, ENER_t, URBP_t, TRAD_t, FDI_t) \tag{1}$$

For empirical estimation, the reduced-form of the log-linear empirical model for the estimation is given as:

$$\begin{aligned} lnGDPC_t = {} & \theta_0 + \theta_1 lnK_t + \theta_2 lnLAB_t + \theta_3 lnENER_t + \theta_4 lnURBP_t \\ & + \theta_5 lnTRAD_t + \theta_6 lnFDI_t + \mu_t \end{aligned} \tag{2}$$

From Eq. (2), $lnGDPC_t$ denotes the log of economic growth. lnK_t indicates the log of physical capital, $lnLAB_t$ represents the log of labour, $lnENER_t$ represents the log of energy consumption, $lnURBP_t$ denotes urbanisation, $lnTRAD_t$ represents the log of trade openness and $lnFDI_t$ denotes the log of foreign direct investment. The term μ_t is the error term, which is assumed to be normally distributed, and the subscript t refers to time. In this study, we expect physical capital and labour to have a positive effect on economic growth and hence $\theta_1 > 0$ *and* $\theta_2 > 0$ (Omri, 2013; Solow, 1956). Also, we expect the relationship between energy consumption and economic growth to be positive and hence $\theta_3 > 0$ (Nasreen & Anwar, 2014; Omri, 2013, 2014). We hypotheses that urbanisation has a positive effect on economic growth and hence $\theta_4 > 0$ (Henderson, 2003; Nguyen, 2018). We also expect trade openness and foreign direct investment to increase economic growth and hence $\theta_5 > 0$ *and* $\theta_6 > 0$ (Brueckner & Lederman, 2015; Pandya & Sisombat, 2017; Sakyi et al., 2017).

2.2 Empirical Model for Carbon Emissions

Following Shahbaz et al. (2017), we state that carbon emission is a function of economic growth, population, urbanisation, trade openness and foreign direct investment. Therefore, the carbon emissions function is as indicated in Eq. (3):

$$CO2kt_t = f(GDPC_t, POPG_t, ENER_t, URBP_t, TRAD_t, FDI_t) \tag{3}$$

Where GDPC represents economic growth, POPG represents population growth and other variables remained as defined above. For empirical estimation, the log-linear form of the empirical equation is specified in Eq. (3). Following the argument on the Environmental Kuznets curve (EKC) hypothesis (Acheampong, 2019; Stern, 2004; Stern & Common, 2001), we also augment Eq. (1) with the squared of economic growth. The EKC hypothesis suggests that there an inverted U-shaped relationship between economic growth and environment. Thus, at the initial stage of economic development, environmental degradation and pollution increase but after a certain threshold of economic development, environmental quality improves (Grossman & Krueger, 1995). Analysing the impact of urbanisation on carbon emissions within the framework of the EKC is important since at the advanced stage of countries' economic development, urbanisation could spur technological development, which is critical for addressing carbon emissions (Poumanyvong & Kaneko, 2010).

$$\begin{aligned} lnCO2kt_t = {} & \alpha_1 + \beta_1 lnGDPC_t + \beta_2 \ln GDPC^2{}_t + \beta_3 lnPOPG_t + \beta_4 lnENER_t \\ & + \beta_5 lnURBP_t + \beta_6 lnTRAD_t + \beta_7 lnFDI_t + \varepsilon_t \end{aligned} \tag{4}$$

In Eq. (4), $lnCO2kt_t$ indicates the log of carbon emissions. $lnGDPC_t$ and $lnGDPC^2{}_t$ denote the log of the main term and squared term of economic growth, respectively. $POPG_t$ indicates population growth, $lnENER_t$ represents the log of energy consumption, $lnURBP_t$ denotes urbanisation, $lnTRAD_t$ represents the log of trade openness and $lnFDI_t$ denotes the log of foreign direct investment. The term ε_t is the error term, which is assumed to be normally distributed. If the EKC is valid, then $\beta_1 < 0$ and $\beta_2 > 0$, otherwise $\beta_1 > 0$ and $\beta_2 < 0$ (Acheampong, 2019; Acheampong et al., 2020; Shahbaz et al., 2018). We also expect the population to increase carbon emissions and hence $\beta_3 > 0$. Energy consumption is expected to increase carbon emissions and hence $\beta_4 > 0$ (Sadorsky, 2014). We hypothesis that urbanisation mitigates carbon emissions and hence $\beta_5 < 0$ (Poumanyvong & Kaneko, 2010). We also expect that trade openness and foreign direct investment reduce carbon emissions and hence $\beta_6 <0$ and $\beta_1 < 0$ (Antweiler et al., 2001; Doytch & Uctum, 2016).

2.3 Estimation Strategies

Given that this study examines the long-run effect of urbanisation on economic growth and urbanisation, we follow Mahjabeen et al. (2020) and Sarkodie and Strezov (2018) to estimate the above equations using the Pedroni (2001a, 2001b) Fully Modified Ordinary Least Squares (FMOLS) and Dynamic Ordinary Least Squares (DOLS). Unlike the conventional econometric technique such Ordinary Least Squares, applying FMOLS in this study is essential since it addresses econometrics issues such as serial correlation and endogeneity among the regressors (Bhattacharya et al., 2017). Pedroni (2001a) also argued that the FMOLS provides consistent estimates of the cointegrating vector's sample mean in the presence of heterogeneity in the cointegration relationship. Like the FMOLS, the Pedroni (2001b) DOLS controls for endogeneity, serial correlation and generates unbiased estimates. Both FMOLS and DOLS are employed to estimate the long-run output and carbon emissions elasticities.

2.4 Data

This study uses a annual time series dataset for the period 1960–2019. The data on economic growth is measured using GDP per capita (constant 2010 US$), carbon emissions measured CO2 emissions (kt), energy consumption measured in kg of oil equivalent per capita, urbanisation measured in urban population as % of the total population, physical capital measured in gross fixed capital formation (constant 2010 US$), labour measured in the total labour force, population growth measured in annual percentage of population growth, trade openness measured trade as a percentage of GDP and foreign direct investment measured FDI Net Inflows (% of GDP). These variables were obtained from the World Development Indicators (WDI) database. The variables were transformed into their natural logarithm, except population growth.

Table 1 presents the descriptive statistics for the variables. From the descriptive statistics, carbon emissions have a negative mean of 12.354%. Economic growth and population growth have a mean of 10.467% and 1.531%, respectively. Energy consumption has a mean of 8.455%, and urbanisation has a mean of 4.439%. Physical capital and labour have a mean of 25.507% and 16.170%, respectively. Trade openness and foreign direct investment have a mean of 3.518% and 0.698%, respectively. The Jarque-Bera statistics indicate that foreign direct investment, trade openness, energy consumption, urbanisation and population growth are not normally distributed, while physical capital, labour economic growth are normally distributed.

Table 1 Descriptive statistics for the variables used in the model

	lnco2kt	lngdpc	lngdpc2	popg	lnfdi	lntrad	lnurbp	lnener	lngfc	lnlab
Mean	12.354	10.467	109.671	1.531	0.698	3.518	4.439	8.455	25.507	16.170
Median	12.473	10.466	109.543	1.480	0.939	3.485	4.442	8.475	25.460	16.157
Maximum	12.886	10.954	119.992	3.380	1.947	3.824	4.456	8.694	26.635	16.418
Minimum	11.387	9.865	97.319	0.625	−1.552	3.211	4.401	8.027	24.204	15.955
Std. dev.	0.436	0.329	6.875	0.454	0.752	0.192	0.012	0.184	0.736	0.148
Skewness	−0.664	−0.129	−0.089	1.363	−1.115	−0.005	−1.267	−0.796	0.040	0.099
Kurtosis	2.349	1.882	1.855	6.317	4.281	1.530	4.229	2.653	1.837	1.657
Jarque-Bera	5.201	3.293	3.359	45.327	13.498	5.400	19.830	6.190	3.395	2.303
Probability	0.074	0.193	0.186	0.000	0.001	0.067	0.000	0.045	0.183	0.316

where lnco2kt represents carbon emissions, lngdpc represents economic growth, lngdpc2 represents economic growth squared, popg represent population, lnfdi represents foreign direct investment, lntrade represents trade openness. Lnurbp represents urbanisation, lnener represents energy consumption; lngfc represents physical capital and lnlab represents labour

3 Empirical Results

3.1 Unit Root Test

Table 2 displays the results of the unit root test. We check the stationarity properties of the variables using the Augmented Dickey-Fuller (ADF) (Dickey & Fuller, 1979) and Philips-Perron (PP) (Phillips & Perron, 1988) tests before estimating the empirical models. The results from the ADF and PP indicate that economic growth, economic growth squared, physical capital, labour, trade openness, population growth and urbanisation are non-stationary at levels. At the same time, carbon emissions, energy consumption and foreign direct investment are stationary at levels. At first difference, ADF and PP suggest that all the variables are stationary.

3.2 Long-Run Estimates for Economic Growth

Table 3 presents the FMOLS and DOLS results for the economic growth. The results from both FMOLS and DOLS estimators suggest that urbanisation has a significant negative effect (−6.0546 (FMOLS) and − 5.519 (DOLS)) on economic growth. This result implies that urbanisation is detrimental to Australia's economic growth. This result can be explained using Lipton (1977) urban bias theory. The urban bias theory argues that over-concentration of scarce resources in the urban sector at the expense of rural areas keeps urban areas that already have a larger share of the national income better off, with rural areas descending into an increasing worsening

Table 2 Stationarity tests of the variables used in estimation

	Levels		1st difference	
Variables	ADF	PP	ADF	PP
Lnco2kt	-4.074^{***}	-6.044^{***}	-6.451^{***}	-6.541^{***}
Lnener	-3.114^{**}	-3.449^{**}	-7.760^{***}	-7.798^{***}
Lnfdi	-4.246^{***}	-4.461^{***}	-11.832^{***}	-16.499^{***}
Lngdpc	−1.667	−1.599	-6.338^{***}	-6.330^{***}
lngdpc2	−1.434	−1.375	-6.385^{***}	-6.360^{***}
Lngfc	−1.273	−1.247	-6.203^{***}	-6.115^{***}
Lnlab	1.724	1.524	-3.993^{***}	-3.941^{***}
Lntrad	−0.622	−0.245	-8.387^{***}	-8.973^{***}
Popg	−2.438	-4.882^{***}	-9.914^{***}	-13.379^{***}
Lnurbp	−1.152	-3.267^{**}	-2.787^{*}	-2.783^{*}

$p < 0.10$, $^{**}p < 0.05$, $^{***}p < 0.01$; where lnco2kt represents carbon emissions, lngdpc represents economic growth, lngdpc2 represents economic growth squared, popg represent population, lnfdi represents foreign direct investment, lntrade represents trade openness. Lnurbp represents urbanisation, lnener represents energy consumption; lngfc represents physical capital and lnlab represents labour

Table 3 FMOLS and DOLS results for Economic Growth

Variable	Coefficient	Std. Error	t-Statistic	P-value	Coefficient	Std. Error	t-Statistic	P-value
	FMOLS				**DOLS**			
Lngfc	0.202***	0.043	4.660	0.000	0.191***	0.047	4.057	0.001
Lnlab	0.664***	0.144	4.615	0.000	0.676***	0.152	4.436	0.000
Lntrad	−0.088*	0.048	−1.849	0.083	−0.079	0.059	−1.356	0.192
Lnfdi	0.000	0.004	0.044	0.966	0.001	0.005	0.183	0.857
Lnener	−0.008	0.079	−0.097	0.924	0.026	0.096	0.271	0.789
Lnurbp	−6.046***	0.694	−8.708	0.000	−5.519***	0.792	−6.966	0.000
Constant	21.990	2.870	7.663	0.000	19.412	3.462	5.607	0.000
R^2	0.997				0.998			
Adj R^2	0.996				0.997			

$p < 0.10$, ** $p < 0.05$, *** $p < 0.01$. where lngfc represents physical capital, lnlab represents labour, lntrade represents trade openness, lnfdi represents foreign direct investment, lnener represents energy consumption and lnurbp represents urbanisation income inequality (Lipton, 1977). The inequality between the urban and rural areas hampers economic growth. Similarly, Weede (1987) argues that countries with large income inequality between urban and rural areas suffer from urban bias and found that urban bias retards economic growth.

This result contradicts the findings of (Bertinelli & Black, 2004; Henderson, 2003; Nguyen, 2018), which revealed that urbanisation promotes economic growth. The results further indicate that physical capital and labour have a significant positive impact on economic growth, whiles trade openness has a significant negative impact on economic growth. It is observed that energy consumption and foreign direct investment have no statistically significant impact on economic growth.

3.3 Long-Run Estimates for Carbon Emissions

Table 4 displays the FMOLS and DOLS estimates for carbon emissions. The results from both FMOLS and DOLS estimators suggest that urbanisation has a significant positive effect on carbon emissions. This result indicates that urbanisation is an important contributor to carbon emissions. Urbanisation in generating carbon emissions in Australia implies that urbanisation results in traffic congestions and overcrowding, consequently increasing energy consumption and carbon emissions (Breheny, 2001; Poumanyvong & Kaneko, 2010; Rudlin & Falk, 1999). This finding is consistent with the results of Wang et al. (2016), Zhang and Lin (2012) and Wu et al. (2016), which revealed that urbanisation contributes to higher carbon emissions. The results also indicate that the main term of economic growth and its squared term has a significant positive and negative effect on carbon emissions. This validates the environmental Kuznets curve in Australia, and hence economic growth will improve carbon emissions in the long term. This result is consistent with the findings (see Ahmad et al., 2017; Apergis & Ozturk, 2015; Apergis & Payne, 2009, 2010; Ben Jebli et al., 2016).

Other factors such as energy consumption and population growths have a significant positive effect on carbon emissions. A unit increase in energy consumption will result in about 75 to 81 units of increase carbon dioxide (based on the DOLS and FMOLS estimates, respectively). Thus, a consistent increase in population and excessive use of energy would increase Australia's carbon emissions. Our results are in line with the results of Dzator and Acheampong (2020) and Shahbaz et al. (2017), which indicated that population and energy consumption are major contributors to carbon emissions. The results suggest that trade openness and FDI have insignificant effects on carbon emissions. Still, this finding contradicts Shahbaz et al. (2017) findings which argue that globalisation plays a significant role in mitigating carbon emissions in Australia.

Table 4 FMOLS and DOLS results for Carbon Emissions

Variable	Coefficient	Std. Error	t-Statistic	P-value	Coefficient	Std. Error	t-Statistic	P-value
	FMOLS				**DOLS**			
Lngdpc	19.705***	2.835	6.950	0.000	19.830***	3.531	5.616	0.000
lngdpc2	−0.899***	0.132	−6.824	0.000	−0.903***	0.164	−5.503	0.000
Lnener	0.808***	0.156	5.192	0.000	0.735***	0.195	3.766	0.001
Popg	0.031**	0.011	2.698	0.011	0.025*	0.014	1.738	0.091
Lnfdi	−0.007	0.007	−0.952	0.348	−0.007	0.009	−0.805	0.426
Lntrad	0.119	0.095	1.249	0.220	0.091	0.120	0.763	0.450
lnurbp	5.261***	0.710	7.405	0.000	5.372***	0.856	6.277	0.000
Constant	−125.957	14.643	−8.602	0.000	−126.648	17.874	−7.086	0.000
R^2	0.992				0.993			
Adj R^2	0.990				0.992			

$p < 0.10$, ** $p < 0.05$, *** $p < 0.01$. where lngdpc represents economic growth, lngdpc2 represents economic growth squared, lnener represents energy consumption, popg represent population, lnfdi represents foreign direct investment, lntrade represents trade openness and lnurbp represents urbanisation

4 Conclusion and Policy Implications

This study examines the effect of urbanisation on economic growth and carbon emissions in Australia for the period 1960–2019 using FMOLS and DOLS. The findings indicate that while urbanisation has a significant negative effect on economic growth, it has a significant positive effect on Australia's carbon emissions. Other factors such as physical capital and labour were found to have a significant positive impact on economic growth, while trade openness has a significant negative effect on economic growth. Our findings suggest that energy consumption and foreign direct investment do not affect Australia's economic growth. Further, our results validate the environmental Kuznets curve in Australia. Thus, at the initial stage of economic development, environmental degradation and pollution increase but after a certain threshold of economic development, environmental quality improves (Grossman & Krueger, 1995). Therefore, given the advanced stage of Australia's economic development, its economic growth contributes to carbon emissions mitigation. Our findings suggest that other factors such as energy consumption and population growths worsen carbon emissions. It was also revealed that trade openness and FDI are not insignificant contributors to carbon emissions in Australia.

These results have important policy implications for decarbonising Australia's economy while achieving robust economic growth. Our results show that urbanisation reduces economic growth while increasing carbon emissions and suggest that Australia's urbanisation is unsustainable. This indicates that Australia's rapid urbanisation will be associated with excess use of resources such as energy due to the expansion of urban infrastructure facilities. Therefore, to decarbonise the economy, urban planners must develop energy-efficient and sustainable urban infrastructure systems to improve their efficient use of energy. Another implication of the study is that drastic policies must be implemented to reduce the ever-increasing population in urban areas across the countries. Our findings indicate that economic growth would contribute to carbon emissions mitigating policies. This requires improving energy efficiency, transitioning towards renewable energy, and implementing policies to maintain population growth in Australia.

References

Acheampong, A. O. (2019). Modelling for insight: Does financial development improve environmental quality? *Energy Economics, 83*, 156–179. https://doi.org/10.1016/j.eneco.2019.06.025

Acheampong, A. O., Amponsah, M., & Boateng, E. (2020). Does financial development mitigate carbon emissions? Evidence from heterogeneous financial economies. *Energy Economics, 88*, 104768. https://doi.org/10.1016/j.eneco.2020.104768

Adams, S., Boateng, E., & Acheampong, A. O. (2020). Transport energy consumption and environmental quality: Does urbanisation matter? *Science of the Total Environment, 744*, 140617. https://doi.org/10.1016/j.scitotenv.2020.140617

Ahmad, N., Du, L., Lu, J., Wang, J., Li, H.-Z., & Hashmi, M. Z. (2017). Modelling the CO2 emissions and economic growth in Croatia: Is there any environmental Kuznets curve? *Energy, 123*, 164–172. https://doi.org/10.1016/j.energy.2016.12.106

Alam, S., Fatima, A., & Butt, M. S. (2007). Sustainable development in Pakistan in the context of energy consumption demand and environmental degradation. *Journal of Asian Economics, 18* (5), 825–837.

Antweiler, W., Copeland, B. R., & Taylor, M. S. (2001). Is free trade good for the environment? *The American Economic Review, 91*(4), 877–908. Retrieved from http://www.jstor.org/stable/2677817

Apergis, N., & Ozturk, I. (2015). Testing environmental Kuznets curve hypothesis in Asian countries. *Ecological Indicators, 52*(Supplement C), 16–22. https://doi.org/10.1016/j.ecolind.2014.11.026

Apergis, N., & Payne, J. E. (2009). CO2 emissions, energy usage, and output in Central America. *Energy Policy, 37*(8), 3282–3286. https://doi.org/10.1016/j.enpol.2009.03.048

Apergis, N., & Payne, J. E. (2010). The emissions, energy consumption, and growth nexus: Evidence from the commonwealth of independent states. *Energy Policy, 38*(1), 650–655. https://doi.org/10.1016/j.enpol.2009.08.029

Bekhet, H. A., & Othman, N. S. (2017). Impact of urbanisation growth on Malaysia CO2 emissions: Evidence from the dynamic relationship. *Journal of Cleaner Production, 154*, 374–388. https://doi.org/10.1016/j.jclepro.2017.03.174

Ben Jebli, M., Ben Youssef, S., & Ozturk, I. (2016). Testing environmental Kuznets curve hypothesis: The role of renewable and non-renewable energy consumption and trade in OECD countries. *Ecological Indicators, 60*, 824–831. https://doi.org/10.1016/j.ecolind.2015.08.031

Bertinelli, L., & Black, D. (2004). Urbanisation and growth. *Journal of Urban Economics, 56*(1), 80–96.

Bhattacharya, M., Awaworyi Churchill, S., & Paramati, S. R. (2017). The dynamic impact of renewable energy and institutions on economic output and CO2 emissions across regions. *Renewable Energy, 111*, 157–167. https://doi.org/10.1016/j.renene.2017.03.102

Bloom, D. E., Canning, D., & Fink, G. (2008). Urbanisation and the wealth of nations. *Science, 319* (5864), 772–775.

Breheny, M. (2001). *Densities and sustainable cities: The UK experience*. Cities for the new millennium, 39–51.

Brueckner, M., & Lederman, D. (2015). Trade openness and economic growth: Panel data evidence from sub-Saharan Africa. *Economica, 82*, 1302–1323.

Calì, M. (2008). *Urbanisation, inequality and economic growth: Evidence from Indian states and towns. Background note for the World Development Report*. Overseas Development Institute.

Dickey, D. A., & Fuller, W. A. (1979). Distribution of the estimators for autoregressive time series with a unit root. *Journal of the American Statistical Association, 74*(366), 427–431. https://doi.org/10.2307/2286348

Doytch, N., & Uctum, M. (2016). Globalisation and the environmental impact of sectoral FDI. *Economic Systems, 40*(4), 582–594. https://doi.org/10.1016/j.ecosys.2016.02.005

Dzator, J., & Acheampong, A. O. (2020). The impact of energy innovation on carbon emission mitigation: An empirical evidence from OECD countries. In C. M. Hussain (Ed.), *Handbook of environmental materials management* (pp. 1–19). Springer International Publishing.

Gouldson, A., & Murphy, J. (1997). Ecological modernisation: Economic restructuring and the environment. *The Political Quarterly, 68*(5), 74–86.

Grossman, G. M., & Krueger, A. B. (1995). Economic growth and the environment. *The Quarterly Journal of Economics, 110*(2), 353–377. https://doi.org/10.2307/2118443

Henderson, V. (2003). The urbanisation process and economic growth: The so-what question. *Journal of Economic Growth, 8*(1), 47–71.

Lipton, M. (1977). In T. Smith (Ed.), *Why poor people stay poor: A study of urban bias in world development*. Australian National University Press.

Liu, X., & Bae, J. (2018). Urbanisation and industrialisation impact of CO2 emissions in China. *Journal of Cleaner Production, 172*, 178–186. https://doi.org/10.1016/j.jclepro.2017.10.156

Mahjabeen, Shah, S. Z. A., Chughtai, S., & Simonetti, B. (2020). Renewable energy, institutional stability, environment and economic growth nexus of D-8 countries. *Energy Strategy Reviews, 29*, 100484. https://doi.org/10.1016/j.esr.2020.100484

McGranahan, G. (2010). *The citizens at risk: From urban sanitation to sustainable cities.* Earthscan.

Mol, A. P. J., & Spaargaren, G. (2000). Ecological modernisation theory in debate: A review. *Environmental Politics, 9*(1), 17–49. https://doi.org/10.1080/09644010008414511

Nasreen, S., & Anwar, S. (2014). Causal relationship between trade openness, economic growth and energy consumption: A panel data analysis of Asian countries. *Energy Policy, 69*, 82–91. https://doi.org/10.1016/j.enpol.2014.02.009

Nguyen, H. M. (2018). The relationship between urbanisation and economic growth: An empirical study on ASEAN countries. *International Journal of Social Economics.*

Omri, A. (2013). CO2 emissions, energy consumption and economic growth nexus in MENA countries: Evidence from simultaneous equations models. *Energy Economics, 40*, 657–664. https://doi.org/10.1016/j.eneco.2013.09.003

Omri, A. (2014). An international literature survey on energy-economic growth nexus: Evidence from country-specific studies. *Renewable and Sustainable Energy Reviews, 38*(Supplement C), 951–959. https://doi.org/10.1016/j.rser.2014.07.084

Omri, A., & Kahouli, B. (2014). Causal relationships between energy consumption, foreign direct investment and economic growth: Fresh evidence from dynamic simultaneous-equations models. *Energy Policy, 67*, 913–922. https://doi.org/10.1016/j.enpol.2013.11.067

Pandya, V., & Sisombat, S. (2017). Impacts of foreign direct investment on economic growth: Empirical evidence from Australian economy. *International Journal of Economics and Finance, 9*(5), 121–131.

Pedroni, P. (2001a). Fully modified OLS for heterogeneous cointegrated panels. In *Non-stationary panels, panel cointegration, and dynamic panels*. Emerald Group Publishing Limited.

Pedroni, P. (2001b). Purchasing power parity tests in cointegrated panels. *Review of Economics and Statistics, 83*(4), 727–731.

Phillips, P. C., & Perron, P. (1988). Testing for a unit root in time series regression. *Biometrika, 75* (2), 335–346.

Poumanyvong, P., & Kaneko, S. (2010). Does urbanisation lead to less energy use and lower CO2 emissions? A cross-country analysis. *Ecological Economics, 70*(2), 434–444. https://doi.org/10.1016/j.ecolecon.2010.09.029

Rudlin, D., & Falk, N. (1999). *Building the 21st century home: The sustainable urban neighbourhood.* Butterworth-Heinemann.

Sadorsky, P. (2014). The effect of urbanisation on CO2 emissions in emerging economies. *Energy Economics, 41*, 147–153. https://doi.org/10.1016/j.eneco.2013.11.007

Sakyi, D., Villaverde, J., Maza, A., & Bonuedi, I. (2017). The effects of trade and trade facilitation on economic growth in Africa. *African Development Review, 29*(2), 350–361.

Sarkodie, S. A., & Strezov, V. (2018). Assessment of contribution of Australia's energy production to CO2 emissions and environmental degradation using statistical dynamic approach. *Science of the Total Environment, 639*, 888–899. https://doi.org/10.1016/j.scitotenv.2018.05.204

Sasin, M. J., & McKenzie, D. (2007). *Migration, remittances, poverty, and human capital: conceptual and empirical challenges.*

Shahbaz, M., Bhattacharya, M., & Ahmed, K. (2017). CO2 emissions in Australia: Economic and non-economic drivers in the long-run. *Applied Economics, 49*(13), 1273–1286.

Shahbaz, M., Khan, S., & Tahir, M. I. (2013). The dynamic links between energy consumption, economic growth, financial development and trade in China: Fresh evidence from multivariate framework analysis. *Energy Economics, 40*, 8–21. https://doi.org/10.1016/j.eneco.2013.06.006

Shahbaz, M., Nasir, M. A., & Roubaud, D. (2018). Environmental degradation in France: The effects of FDI, financial development, and energy innovations. *Energy Economics, 74*, 843–857. https://doi.org/10.1016/j.eneco.2018.07.020

Solow, R. M. (1956). A contribution to the theory of economic growth. *The Quarterly Journal of Economics, 70*(1), 65–94.

Stern, D. I. (2004). The rise and fall of the environmental Kuznets curve. *World Development, 32* (8), 1419–1439. https://doi.org/10.1016/j.worlddev.2004.03.004

Stern, D. I., & Common, M. S. (2001). Is there an environmental Kuznets curve for sulfur? *Journal of Environmental Economics and Management, 41*(2), 162–178. https://doi.org/10.1006/jeem.2000.1132

Wang, Q., Wu, S.-D., Zeng, Y.-E., & Wu, B.-W. (2016). Exploring the relationship between urbanisation, energy consumption, and CO2 emissions in different provinces of China. *Renewable and Sustainable Energy Reviews, 54*, 1563–1579. https://doi.org/10.1016/j.rser.2015.10.090

Weede, E. (1987). Urban Bias and economic growth in cross-National Perspective. *International Journal of Comparative Sociology, 28*(1–2), 30–42.

Wu, Y., Shen, J., Zhang, X., Skitmore, M., & Lu, W. (2016). The impact of urbanisation on carbon emissions in developing countries: A Chinese study based on the U-Kaya method. *Journal of Cleaner Production, 135*, 589–603. https://doi.org/10.1016/j.jclepro.2016.06.121

Zhang, C., & Lin, Y. (2012). Panel estimation for urbanisation, energy consumption and CO2 emissions: A regional analysis in China. *Energy Policy, 49*, 488–498. https://doi.org/10.1016/j.enpol.2012.06.048

Application of Data Analysis and Big Data in Auditing

Vahid Biglari and Zahra Pourabedin

Abstract The rapid advancement in technology and increase in business information has challenged traditional auditing methods. This paper aims to review big data analysis and its integration in the audit process. The research uses secondary research to systematically review the literature on big data analysis in the accounting profession.

The findings show that auditors rely on big data analysis tools to increase the depth and quality of their assurance services. Hence using big data analysis helps to promote legitimacy and social trust to auditing firms. Despite the relative growth of technology in the auditing profession and extensive research in the big data analysis field, there are not enough academic studies on big data analysis. This research is among the first to examine and clarify big data analysis in auditing and the challenges and opportunities that arise from it.

Keywords Audit · Big data · Big data analysis · New technologies · Social legitimacy

1 Introduction

In today's world, data is generated from a variety of sources, and the rapid growth of technology has led to increased production rates and created large volumes of data. Such a large volume of data has enabled evolutionary advances in various scientific and industrial fields. Big data is frequently claimed to have a transformative effect on businesses and economies (Einav & Levin, 2014).

V. Biglari (✉)
University of Newcastle Singapore, Suntec City, Singapore
e-mail: vahid.biglari@newcastle.edu.au

Z. Pourabedin
James Cook University, Singapore, Singapore
e-mail: zahra.pourabedin@jcu.edu.au

© The Author(s), under exclusive license to Springer Nature Singapore Pte Ltd. 2022

T. Chaiechi, J. Wood (eds.), *Community Empowerment, Sustainable Cities, and Transformative Economies*, https://doi.org/10.1007/978-981-16-5260-8_8

Since auditing is essentially an information-based industry, big data analytics developments can potentially change the audit environment (Appelbaum et al., 2017). Nevertheless, unlike other disciplines, such techniques have not been commonly used in the audit field. Although some leading companies are implementing big data analysis techniques, the lack of progress in this area is surprising. This is because, in the auditing profession, there are unique challenges in data processing and analysis. Due to the increasing information growth, auditors' use of new techniques and technologies is inevitable (Alles, 2015). Currently, big data, and data analysis applications are growing in audit services. Large investment companies pay special attention to use data analysis, which is a great promise for effective implementation of audit projects. On the other hand, financial crises and scandals have raised criticisms against audit firms questioning the social legitimacy of the profession. This has shattered the trust between the community and auditors. Thus, the role of new audit technologies is not only to restore trust through method change, but it also presents a picture of the audit as a reviewed and desirable service compared to the previous incomplete service.

Although data analysis is widely used in many industries, the auditing profession lags other businesses in applying it. Data analysis is expanding in the auditing profession and related technologies. Regarding the application of data analysis in auditing, it is necessary to explain two basic points. First, why is data analysis used in financial statements audit and how it can save audit time and improve audit quality. Second, the problems and challenges of data analysis technology in auditing and conclude with some suggested remedies. This paper will discuss the above points to draw a concept map to promote big data application in auditing.

This paper emphasises that applying big data analytics can add value to the auditing profession, especially when rigorous analytical methods are combined with auditing techniques and expert judgment (Gepp et al., 2018). By using advanced technologies, auditors can audit complex high-end business environments. Technologies help auditors to make professional judgments (Power, 1995). Because the audit profession is based on the concept of adequate and appropriate audit evidence, by obtaining and handling more audit evidence, auditors can achieve more accurate audit opinion. The use of such big data technologies would help maintain the auditing profession's social legitimacy (Robson et al., 2007).

Researchers argue that a paradigm shift is needed to understand the quantification and measure the economic and social impact of big data analytics in the audit environment (Vasarhelyi et al., 2015). Therefore, big data analytics as an area of Innovation in auditing has become important, and recently the audit profession has become interested in using big data tools to audit financial statements (Salijeni, 2019). Undoubtedly, the use of information technology affects the audit quality and cost. If new technologies are not used, it will not be long before the audit profession faces serious threats and the efficiency and effectiveness that stakeholders expect from the audit will not be provided.

There are not many studies in the field of big data analysis in auditing (Gepp et al., 2018). Studies that focus on the application of big data in financial accounting are unlikely to provide benefits and challenges of using big data in auditing. Also, other available work usually focuses on financial distress modelling (Kim & Upneja, 2014), financial fraud modelling (West & Bhattacharya, 2016), and stock market prediction (Nardo et al., 2016) and quantitative modelling (Xiao et al., 2015), which do not offer implications for using big data in auditing. This study aims to clarify the issue of big data analysis in auditing and the challenges and opportunities that arise from it.

The next section describes the research method and examines the concept of big data analytics in auditing. After that, the theoretical foundations of the research background is discussed. Next, solutions for implementing big data analysis, unique features of big data analysis, and obstacles and challenges of using big data analysis in auditing are reviewed. Finally, a general conclusion is presented, and brief analysis of auditing technology's unsettled conditions is presented.

2 Method

According to Littell et al. (2008), a systematic review "aims to comprehensively locate and synthesize research that bears on a particular question, using organized, transparent, and replicable procedures at each step in the process" to identify, in our case, the contributions in the field of big data in auditing. Thus, our review provides an interdisciplinary and international overview of the current understanding of using big data in an audit. Fink (2019) proposes four steps for a systematic review, which we used as a foundation and which we enriched by using the structure proposed by Tranfield et al. (2003). In the first step, research questions, the bibliographic article databases and websites, as well as the appropriate search terms were selected. Then, practical review criteria were used to include or exclude relevant literature. Next, methodological review criteria were developed and applied. Finally, the findings were synthesized.

The search within the databases (not including Google Scholar) yields 88 hits. By using the inclusion and exclusion criteria, we limit the sources to 53 results, including 8 double publications, which are excluded. The search in Google Scholar yields 45 hits; 18 of these are relevant. Of these relevant studies, 15 are also found within the other databases. In total, 48 publications are included in the analysis. The oldest source analyzed is published in 1982; the most recent one is from 2020. The majority of the publications are published after 2012. Thus, it appears that the topic is becoming more important and increasing interest within the research community.

3 Big Data

In general, big data goes back to large and complex datasets that are difficult to process using database systems or traditional data processing software (Cockcroft & Russell, 2018). Big data is usually defined by five words beginning with "V". They are Volume, Variety, Velocity, Veracity, and Value (Cappa et al., 2021). Volume refers to a very large set of data that traditional tools are not able to analyse. Variety refers to structured, unstructured, and semi-structured data types such as half text data, video images and other forms of data. Velocity, which is increasingly growing, refers to the frequency at which new information becomes available. The quality and accessibility, and relevance of data can change dramatically over time, referred to as Veracity. Finally, the value refers to the usefulness of analysing this data. (Shukla & Mattar, 2019).

4 Big Data Analysis in Auditing

In recent years, four major auditing firms and many of the world's top audit firms have invested in big data analysis tools. Among the advanced tools of big data analysis used by auditing companies are Society Consulting and Bluestone. In addition, Hallo is an internal analysis tool, and application software uses algorithms to make big data analysis possible. Smaller auditing firms use other big data analytics software such as Lavastorm, Spotlight and Alteryx (ICAEW, 2016). While auditing companies are actively developing and testing big data analysis tools, professional organizations, standard setters, and legislators are pursuing initiatives to use big data analysis and discuss its impact on auditing standards (FRC, 2017).

Studies show that audit firms incentives to develop new technologies is influenced by two factors. First, audit firms are willing to comply with legal requirements and are concerned about understanding and using different technologies to better perform their role. Second, audit firms seek to maximize their business profits and use new auditing technologies to enhance assurance services, thereby increasing their profits and revenue (Robson et al., 2007).

Auditors generally think that advances in audit technology include evolvements in audit techniques, resulting in higher audit quality. Following such advances, the audit process requires formalisation, "continuous objectification and simplification" (Newton & Ashton, 1989). Given the risks that threaten audit firms, it is important to use more structured methods to increase productivity and cost savings and manage the time performing audits, leading to providing audit services with a high degree of individual judgment. The formalization of the audit process means the use of tools such as electronic worksheets and computer-assisted auditing techniques to assist auditors in making professional and specialized decisions (Power, 2003). Regarding objectivity, it can be said that expertise and professional judgments are facilitated by coding in technology, and auditors can achieve similar auditing judgments. In addition, technological changes seek to codify and simplify auditor judgments (Newton & Ashton, 1989).

Big data analysis in auditing is the science and art of detecting and analysing patterns, identifying anomalies, and extracting other useful information from the underlying or relevant data through analysis, modelling, and visualization to enhance audit performance (FRC, 2017).

While the use of big data analysis in auditing is just the beginning, audit analysis is not new(Salijeni, 2019). Audit firms have used computer-based and non-computer-based analytics tools since the 1960s. Some companies have developed analytical review techniques and computer-aided auditing techniques. In the 1990s, information systems such as the SAP were developed to store larger data warehouses for data storage and management and provide information flow between different organisation units. Such systems were classified as enterprise resource planning (ERP) systems. Using available information, such advances in technology can pave the way for real-time auditing, which is referred to as continuous audit.

With the development of ERP and the increase in data storage capacity, customers' accumulated data increased both in volume and variety. It included structured and unstructured information. At this stage, the focus of the audit methodology is to understand the customer business to evaluate Potential Audit Risks became known as Business Risk Audit (BRA). BRA Includes the pervasive use of technology in the audit process. Therefore, the development of technological tools that can record data faced the business environment with a digital phenomenon called big data (Salijeni, 2019).

5 Theoretical Foundations and Research Background

The social relevance of auditing depends on building trust among key stakeholders (Carter et al., 2015). In times of crisis and when trust in auditing is shattered, auditors are lost in negotiating and rebuilding trust. The use of big data analysis in the Auditing field can be used as a tool through which the auditing profession maintains its social connections and legitimacy (Power, 2003). Based on modern institutional theory, legitimacy is related to how organizations interact with beliefs, norms, communicate the rules and standards of a particular environment. In auditing, legitimacy can mean that many stakeholders' methods or techniques are overlooked because they are desirable and appropriate. Therefore, legitimacy is appropriate as a concept to explain organizational behaviour and change (Suchman, 1995).

Suchman (1995) considers legitimacy to have three distinct but related dimensions. These three dimensions are practical legitimacy, moral legitimacy, and cognitive legitimacy. Practical legitimacy is achieved when the stakeholders of the organization believe that the activities and programs of the organization are designed in a way that best serves their interests. Positive and constructive evaluation of the organization and its activities generates moral legitimacy. This means that external groups evaluate the organisation's activities, not in terms of whether it brings them special benefits but in terms of whether "the right thing is done" according to social norms and values. For example, the organization's actions to protect the environment are the goal of social legitimacy. According to Suchman (1995), cognitive legitimacy is the ultimate and most difficult form of achieving legitimacy. In this type of legitimacy, the organization and its activities are accepted as necessary and inevitable. This type of legitimacy is based on gaining a relatively accurate knowledge of the organization and its operations (Suchman, 1995). Because big data analysis is in its infancy. The focus is on gaining practical and moral legitimacy. Rhetorical strategies can be useful in gaining this kind of legitimacy (FRC, 2017).

In the following, we describe three distinct theoretical structures related to the discussion. These theoretical structures are rhetorical strategies, identity regulation and environmental affordance that are used to understand the use and analysis of big data in auditing. The first two theoretical structures, namely rhetorical strategy and identity regulation, have been extracted from the new institutional theory. Because these Structures show two distinct theoretical perspectives, they are used to provide a richer understanding of phenomena by considering the role of material objects such as technology (Salijeni, 2019).

The survival of audit firms depends on their social legitimacy. Therefore, companies actively take actions that are socially acceptable and desirable. Advances such as big data analysis is part of the 'companies' efforts to meet expectations. However, the introduction of big data analysis into the field of auditing is not an easy way to conduct audits, and auditing firms need to convince their respective auditors that big data analysis is socially desirable and appropriate and thus increases their legitimacy.

In addition, from the point of view of modern institutional theory, the methods used by auditors during the audit have a great impact on how they judge professionally. Auditing firms seek to gain legitimacy by changing audit practices. Such a strategic move Affect the role of auditors and audit procedures. Therefore, based on the new institutional theory, understanding how the advanced auditing methods change auditors' identity can explain how big data analysis is used in the audit process (Robson et al., 2007). In addition, auditors use audit tools when conducting audits. Technologies are among the tools that can affect audit procedures.

Therefore, the theoretical structure of environmental capabilities can be considered to overcome the limitations of the new institutional theory that ignores the role of material objects and their effect on the reconfiguration of social practices and spaces. These three theoretical structures complement each other for a deeper understanding of the emergence of big data analysis in the field of auditing (Salijeni, 2019).

6 Rhetorical Strategies Help to Gain Legitimacy

Rhetoric is a tool that uses language to persuade others (Suddaby & Greenwood, 2005). Auditors state their goals of using technology and clarify the benefits of technology to stakeholders to gain legitimacy. In many cases, the rhetoric is designed in such a way that the auditors use technology to express the problems they intend to solve (Power, 1996).

In times of crisis, sometimes auditors use blame game as a rhetorical method of defending the profession. In fact, by showing and blaming the weakness of regulatory guidelines and auditing standards and the weakness of customer management structures, the auditors tried to turn the blame from themselves. Blame games can serve as a strategy for maintaining moral legitimacy (Whittle et al., 2016). There is a limited understanding of the rhetoric used to legitimize the use of audit technologies. To promote big data analysis, audit firms need to identify organizational terms that can demonstrate inconsistencies or shortcomings in the underlying audit profession. These terms can include lack of audit quality or the need for added value for clients (Khalifa et al., 2007). Suddaby and Greenwood (2005) argues that identifying such organizational vocabularies are not enough to persuade stakeholders to make technological improvements. Given the major concerns of uncertainty in the use of new technologies, auditors should also use rhetoric tools to reduce concerns about the uncertainty of new technologies.

7 Identification

Applying big data analysis in the audit process leads to changes in auditing practices. This requires auditors to reconsider their role in light of new methodologies and technologies (Robson et al., 2007). Applying big data analysis brings new credibility and identity to auditors. Through this technology, auditors can provide more reliable opinion.

Auditing companies can go beyond mere auditing and provide unique services concerning clients as business consultants. Although this may not be pleasant for supervisors because of the potential for impairment of the auditor's independence, since this technology improves objectivity and reliability in methods and opinions, the audit profession can develop other measures to face concerns about declining independence. However, the use of big data analytics is a tool through which auditors are encouraged to recover their identities. Rhetorical methods can also be used to create identity changes.

Auditors can use rhetorical tools to communicate their developed capabilities to the community, thereby gaining and increasing legitimacy and achieving profitability (Salijeni, 2019).

8 Environmental Capability Theory

From a sociological point of view, it is emphasized that social and socially inseparable material objects believe that organizational methods emerge from the fusion of human communities and material objects. Humans communicate directly with the environment through objects and tools, shaping the environment in a way that suits them. In addition, the capabilities of the environment are considered as opportunities for activity (Orlikowski, 2007). This sociological perspective has been considered in IT studies and organizational studies but has not been developed in audit research

(Jones, 2014). Separation of society from material objects is common in audit research. However, some researchers have examined audit technology as a social structure that is a product of interactions between different groups of people. Considering the human community around audit firms helps to understand better how to select specific audit methods such as audit tests and analytical methods (Robson et al., 2007). Technology in auditing can enable the auditor to perform tasks and implement specific methods, thus giving better professional judgment. Managers of audit firms should ensure that technologies are designed to assist auditors to effectively achieve audit objectives. Power (2003) states that material objects (audit technologies) in auditing have both a symbolic and a technical role in gaining social legitimacy. These technologies can be developed by auditors' competence and expertise to create social and economic capital. Such development changes the identity of auditors.

Since 2012, North American researchers and lawmakers have made suggestions to use big data in auditing. In 2013, IASB emphasised the importance of technologies and the potential impact of big data on financial statements auditing. In the same year, AICPA published an article titled "Audit Evolution: From a Traditional Approach to Future Auditing" that questioned the current state of auditing and prioritized the data-based audit approach. UK professional organizations have demonstrated in their discussions how the widespread use of big data can potentially change the audit environment (Salijeni, 2019). Researchers have also conducted studies in this area. Studies that focus on big data, on the one hand, refer to the opportunity to use it as audit evidence. On the other hand, it has raised other concerns about the integrity of such information. These studies explained the potential benefits of big data analysis in the audit process and the implications of big data analysis on the nature of audit evidence, including its impact on auditors' judgment (Alles & Gray, 2016).

Shukla and Mattar (2019) examined Barriers to Applying Big Data Analysis in Sustained Auditing and found that a lack of auditors understanding of the value of investing in big data is among barriers to using big data analysis in audit companies.

Salijeni (2019) argued that audit firms use big data analytics to gain social legitimacy. Receiving big data analysis leads to increased audit quality and improved auditor services. Alles and Gray (2016) showed that big data includes financial and non-financial data, structured and unstructured, Intra-organizational and extra-organizational and different data types in very high volume beyond the audits' current technical capabilities. They explained that big data in auditing can be conceptualized in two ways (access to big data and big data analysis techniques).

Alles and Gray (2016) stated that audit companies have been operating for a long time in section A of the figure above. Auditors use traditional tools such as Excel, ACL and IDEA to analyse financial and accounting data. However, recent advances in the use of non-financial data, and have been included in Part C in Fig. 1. Data analysis techniques have also advanced, as shown in the figure. The auditors have also entered section B of the table. However, Alles and Gray (2016) believe that big data analysis in auditing should go as far as Part D of the table above. The analysis of this data should be done using advanced analysis tools such as machine learning for

		Big Data Analysis Techniques	
		Traditional (Excel, IDEA, ACL)	Developed (visualization, Predictive Analysis)
Data Sources	Traditional (accounting and finance)	A → (to B); ↓ (to C)	B
	Developed (non-financial, Big data)	C	D

Fig. 1 Conceptualizing the progress of big data analysis in auditing (Alles & Gray, 2016)

visualization and predictive analysis. To gain more insight from the clients, the clients' current situation can be evaluated and predict their future condition. In fact, the optimal audit process includes all four parts A, B, C and D (in Fig. 1).

Vasarhelyi et al. (2015) argued that changes in technology and the use of ERPs such as Oracle and SAP make big data available, and this is an opportunity to change the paradigm in terms of how transactions are measured and recorded. Yoon et al. (2015) argued that big data evidence is complementary to audit purposes and requires careful consideration to match it with what constitutes audit evidence. They argued that because big data provides a large amount of diverse real-time data, it helps to provide sufficient evidence. On the other hand, noise in big data reduces the reliability of this evidence. Accordingly, to achieve value, big data must be used in conjunction with other traditional audit evidence. Examining the reliability and relevance of big data is a challenge since identifying the data source is often difficult.

Brown-Liburd et al. (2015) showed that big data analysis potentially deals with some aspects of audit performance, such as risk assessment. They related analytical methods and tests. Cao et al. (2015) argued that big data analysis create patterns and trends to provide auditors with faster access to messy data. They argued that data exchanged on social media, videos, text images and text messages could be useful as audit evidence to confirm the existence of events. In addition, Griffin and Wright (2015) suggest that big data should be included in the audit process as soon as possible because of the possibility of not entering the field in a timely manner creates a serious risk for the audit profession. Alles (2015) believes that auditors need to adapt to their clients' day-to-day techniques to maintain their credibility.

Krahel and Titera (2015) argue that accounting and auditing standards have not evolved with technological changes, and they continue to emphasize traditional methods of manual collection and statistical sampling. However, big data analysis tools enable auditors to test all transactions, thereby increasing the auditing and accounting value. Chang et al. (2014) argue that social media, political debate blogs, company announcements, digital journalism, mobile phones, home entertainment, online games, online financial services, online shopping, social advertising, and social commerce are just some of the new areas that can be explored in audit research.

Although big data analysis provides many opportunities for auditors to better understand the audited entity, some issues such as information ambiguity, excessive information and inability to separate information and not identifying information patterns can undermine the benefits of using big data analytics concerning auditing-related economics (Salijeni, 2019). Note that big data analysis as a paradigm shift can be difficult to apply in the audit process. In this regard, it has been suggested to Integrate big data analytics with formal auditing standards to eliminate uncertainty in some areas of judgment and reduce problems. However, existing audit standards do not appear to restrict auditors from using big data (Brown-Liburd et al., 2015).

9 Perform Big Data Analysis Through the Process of Extraction, Conversion, and Execution

Big data analysis is a set of tools that provide various analytical capabilities. Big data analytics enables auditors to collect and process large amounts of data that can be used as audit evidence. Using the big data analytics tools, auditors collect data from various customer ERPs sources and analyse all transactions in a single population. In fact, big data analysis allows auditors to consider a wider range of data collection and analysis. This increases the auditor's confidence in the audit evidence's adequacy and appropriateness, which affects the auditor's comments.

In some cases, auditors do not collect and process all customer transactions. They are available according to the constraints of benefit, cost, and time. They gather as much evidence as possible to confirm or disprove the financial statements claims, which is a major challenge for auditors, especially when the quality of auditing by other institutions and stakeholders is benchmarked (Leonardi, 2013). Gathering audit evidence is especially important in relation to fraud risk factors and evaluating internal controls. Big data analysis is an opportunity to address the challenges posed by poor audit evidence in these areas (fraud risk and internal controls).

According to Salijeni (2019), before auditors access the analyzed data, there should be a special process called ETL. This process has three steps, Extraction, Transformation and Load. In the first step, the data is extracted from the customer database. In the next step, the obtained data is transformed into a common data model. This data is then loaded into a data analysis tool. This analysis tool is used to capture some of the flows identified by the audit team. The output of this tool is the analysed data received by the audit team. The ETL process demonstrates how macro data analysis facilitates data collection and processing in the audit process. In addition, it shows what role data analysts play and how they relate to auditors in the audit process (Fig. 2).

The first step in the ETL process involves extracting data from the 'client's ERP system. Data can be found in Exclusive customer or third-party storages. In this regard, cloud computing capabilities can be used. Based on audit objectives, the nature of the data and the nature of the customer auditor seeks to obtain information that can be used as audit evidence to support the financial statements. Auditors

Restructuring	Environment capability
Step 1: Script extraction and data analysis	Extent of operations with 100% processing of transactions
Step 2: Convert scripts and analyse data	Depth of operation with automatic audit method
Step 3: Implementation (visualization tools and auditors)	Professional judgement with visualization

Fig. 2 ETL Process includes extraction. Conversion and implementation in the audit process

decide what audit procedures should be used to judge these statements. The role of analysts in data collection and processing is clear.

The purpose of the audit evidence is to provide a basis for the auditor's comments. Usually, audit analysts want to complete a standard questionnaire. In this questionnaire, auditors specify the required data and the audit methods and tests that should be performed. Analysts use scripts to extract data needed by auditors. At this stage, data are collected in various forms.

The second step is conversion. Information collected from different sources and databases is converted into a single format or similar formats. In fact, the data becomes a shared data model. This is done to link the data. Analysts typically use scripts to convert data into audit file formats, leading to specific audit procedures.

The third step is to execute the converted data with the audit firm's proprietary big data analysis tools (in which the audit procedures are performed automatically). At this stage, visualization tools are used to help analyse large volumes of processed data (Salijeni, 2019). Some visualization tools used by audit firms include Spotfire and Lavastorm, Qlik, Powerview (ICAEW, 2016). In the next section, we discuss the unique features of big data analysis and how big data analysis helps auditors collect and process data.

- The extent of operations with 100% processing of transactions

The use of Structured Query Language (SQL) and scripts provide a place to collect large amounts of data in the audit process. In fact, one of the advantages of big data analytics is that it provides auditors with a wider range of information collected through different resources and wider coverage, which is one of the salient features of big data analytics. Big data analysis helps auditors evaluate highly subjective areas cost-effectively by collecting real-time data and providing quality information, leading to more professional judgment. It should be noted that the collection of big data is not considered as audit evidence until the tests are performed on the transactions. The validity of the analysis is established since, in the statistical sampling, a part of the transactions is examined; auditors are always concerned that the sample selected is not a good fit for the entire population. Big data analysis addresses this concern and affects the position of auditors in the company. In addition, if the customer databases have different formats, the challenge is how to convert it and make that data in a format that is compatible with the auditing firm's ERPs so that transactions can be processed for auditing purpose. Thus, big data analysis has unique features that break the limitations of statistical consolidation and increase audit quality (Salijeni, 2019).

- Depth of operation

Another challenge that auditors face is how to deal with appropriate audit evidence (Power, 2003). This goes back to the depth of the evidence. Big data analytics changes the way audit evidence is processed and analysed and enhances auditors' processing power. Scripts are an important feature in big data analysis that leads to the automation of audit procedures and sometimes blurs the line between control tests and substantive tests.

Scripts are commands written in a computer coding language that can be used to collect and analyze data. These scripts are written based on auditor needs. For example, SQL is a form of script that is used to extract information from databases or data warehouses. Usually, customers who have ERP systems use databases to store large amounts of data related to their business operations. SQL can extract meaningful data through scripts that examine databases. Scripts are also used to perform some audit procedures (Salijeni, 2019). However, since auditors have limited skills in script programming, a specialized team of data analysts and IT auditors is usually required to design and use high-level programming languages such as Python and R to design scripts that perform the audit tests (ICAEW, 2016). Thus, auditors can collect, process, and analyze big data to perform audit procedures to meet specific audit objectives. In addition, since all trades are analysed, the level of confidence in statistical sampling is increased. Macro data analysis with the help of scripts allows you to perform both substantive and control tests together. Such a combination increases productivity. Some argue that big data analysis is more of a method for substantive tests than for control tests because 100% of trades can be analysed and Completed without control tests (Salijeni, 2019).

- Visualization tools

Another feature of big data analysis that is important in improving the audit process is the use of visualization tools. These tools summarize information in displayable graphical forms. Auditors should consider data from areas that are relevant to the audit process, such as high-risk areas. Excel can also be considered as a low-level visualization tool when it presents pivot tables. Since working with Excel is simple, auditors can use it without assistance. However, there are sophisticated visualization tools used in big data analysis. Because real-time data analytics is available, any updates to the customer's database relating to financial statements can be quickly viewed and tracked with the help of visualization tools.

The visual forms provided can be a basis for discussion with customers. Visual outputs come in a variety of shapes, such as graphs and basic charts, and colour. Colours can draw attention to areas of concern so auditors and clients can act where needed. Visualization helps auditors to look at potential evidence from different angles. This could potentially alter the auditor's professional judgment, reflecting the psychoanalytic impact of the big data analysis (Salijeni, 2019). The ability to visualize puts big data analysis above statistical sampling. In interacting with clients, auditors can demonstrate their expertise in a variety of matters. In addition, visualization by visually displaying red flags and strengths and weaknesses allows auditors to focus professionally on key data in the audit process to make professional judgments, thus increasing audit quality. With this tool's help, all customer transactions can be examined immediately, and what is unusual can be identified quickly (Burri, 2008). Visualisation as a source of knowledge creates additional insight to the auditor, generating added value for customers (IAASB, 2016). This insight provides an opportunity for auditors to reap the economic benefits associated with auditing and consulting. Visualization tools help auditors confidently discuss risk areas related to client operations (Salijeni, 2019).

10 Challenges and Barriers in Applying Big Data Analysis

Although big data analysis is theoretically possible, it is very difficult to implement; this section explains the most important obstacles and challenges of using big data analysis systems. In the following, we will consider the obstacles posed by them.

1. *Lack of understanding the value of using big data analysis:* Lack of audit firms understanding of the value of investing in technologies such as big data analysis is a major obstacle of using this technology (Shukla & Mattar, 2019). Using a big data analysis system initially face many costs and challenges. Its benefits are not apparent in the short term. For this reason, it is challenging to convince audit companies to invest in such technologies (Lee, 2017).
2. *Financial constraints:* financing the operating costs of Big data analysis systems is a problem. The researchers found that the lack of funding for information technology in companies' supply chain is the main obstacle to adopting information technology.

   Because big data analysis requires advanced expertise and facilities to retrieve, store and analyse large volumes of data, initially it requires significant costs, including costs such as staff training, changes in the organisation's structure, upgrading of IT equipment and infrastructure, as well as running costs related to storing and analysing large volumes of data (Shukla & Mattar, 2019).
3. *Lack of top management commitment:* Zhang et al. (2017) showed that one of the major obstacles is that the use of big data analytics for top management is not a high priority. Managers often prioritize other competitive initiatives. Immature technology and lack of skilled labour can justify management's lack of commitment. The lack of top management commitment in adopting the big data analysis system affects the budget allocated to technology and the lack of necessary infrastructure.

4. *Organizational resistance to change:* The use of big data analysis system also requires a fundamentally different organizational trend. Individuals and organizations resist change. They are satisfied with their work's current process and are not willing to try new ways of doing things. They lack a general understanding of how big data analytics can improve business performance figures. Microdata analysis requires extensive changes in perspective, organizational strategy, and culture.
5. *Current systems in auditing:* Applying big data analysis requires changing existing systems, and this change does not happen overnight. Existing systems in subcontracting companies can slow down the process of deploying big data analytics. Therefore, they are considered as an obstacle (Zhang et al., 2017).
6. *complexities of data management:* The complexity of big data makes it very difficult to manage due to the rapid growth of data, the variety of data sources and forms, and the structural nature of the data. Running the storage process, achieving valuable and valid data identifying relevant information and deleting irrelevant information, and integrating the quality and relevance of existing data and data analysis is very complex. Therefore, companies are reluctant to adopt big data analysis.
7. *Low data quality:* Because big data contains a huge amount of structured and unstructured data from various sources, probably part of it does not meet the quality required for audit evidence. In addition, data quality might be impaired through challenges faced in. data recording, analysis, and visualisation process. Poor quality data is not valuable and may even lead to incorrect decisions. This leads to the reluctance of audit firms to adopt big data analysis.
8. *Concerns about data security:* Concerns about information confidentiality and security against cyber-attacks are among the most important obstacles to adopting a macro data analysis system. Unauthorized access to data may call into question the credibility and legitimacy of the audit firm. Therefore, data security is very important and worrying about maintaining this security is an obstacle to accepting the big data analysis system (Shukla & Mattar, 2019).
9. *Legal and ethical challenges:* Unauthorized collection and use of personal data has legal and ethical consequences. Getting as much relevant data as possible can be very lucrative, but it raises red flags in terms of privacy (Brohi et al., 2016).
10. *Lack of knowledge sharing:* Companies may be afraid to share their information due to security and privacy concerns. The unwillingness to share knowledge is a barrier to accepting big data analysis. Audit firms need the information to get the most out of big data analysis. Data suppliers, analysts, and auditors' ability to work together is a key condition for overcoming fragmentation and creating a big data analysis system (Shukla & Mattar, 2019).
11. *Lack of necessary infrastructure:* Poor IT infrastructure is a major barrier to accepting big data analysis. The current technologies used in most audit firms are not designed to meet the growing need for big data analytics (Zhang et al., 2017). There are challenges such as increasing data security and data management with the right infrastructure.

12. *Lack of Experts:* Numerous studies have highlighted the need for top professionals and data management experts to apply big data analysis. Because big data analysis is still in its infancy stage. Many auditors and staff do not have the technological and analytical skills necessary to accept big data analytics (Lee, 2017).
13. *Immature technology:* Macro data analysis technology is relatively new and needs further development. Faster and more efficient analyses are needed to properly perform big data analysis. Organizations are likely to be more willing to accept big data analytics as they further develop the technology and reduce the risks associated with it.
14. *Challenges of Continuous Information Growth:* The need for more powerful computers and methods for analyzing and filtering meaningful information from the big data set is a serious obstacle. Few organizations have access to powerful computers to analyse such datasets (Brohi et al., 2016). This has been an important challenge that many data mining software has not been able to solve, how to extract knowledge from big data and put it in the hands of managers to make better and more informed decisions. The continuous growth of data and the need to analyse and provide timely and accurate information to -makers are major challenges in big data analysis (Shukla & Mattar, 2019).

11 Discussion and Conclusion

Advances in technology caused the business world to face ever-increasing data and information. The complex data can provide a valuable opportunity to grow and gain a competitive advantage in multiple markets. There is no doubt that access to the big data set, which is constantly updated and includes non-traditional information, will greatly value audit performance. Because big data has a huge volume and is growing and changing rapidly, it is not appropriate to use traditional tools to analyse it. However, the auditing profession has not made the necessary investment in big data analysis tools and techniques. The issue of lack of audit quality after the financial crisis has been an important issue among regulators and standardisers. The use of new technologies can reduce professional scepticism, increasing the quality of auditing and restore the lost legitimacy and trust in the profession.

This article examined the application of big data analysis and its technical and symbolic consequences. The use of big data analysis tools leads to an increase in the audit process's breadth and depth, which improves the audit quality and creates added value for the audit clients, followed by increasing social legitimacy and relative trust in auditing. Such technological developments require auditors to reconstruct their professional identities. It should be noted that the audit environment is complex and political, and the legitimacy of big data analysis in auditing can be achieved when these technologies are linked to cultural values in the audit field. To do this, the auditing profession must, through rhetorical strategies, create the necessary legitimacy and place big data analysis at the heart of the audit process by trying to reform standards and regulations.

Despite the relative growth of technology in the auditing profession at the international level and conducting a lot of research in the field of big data analysis, there are not enough academic studies on big data analysis in auditing. This research is the first step in examining and clarifying the issue of big data analysis in auditing and the challenges and opportunities arising from it. Although the value of big data analysis in auditing has been proven, insufficient investment has been made to use such technologies in the auditing profession. The use of such technologies by auditing firms requires high costs of building the necessary infrastructure and scrapping old systems. Due to the high costs associated with using big data technologies, audit firms may not be willing to accept such costs, especially since these technologies are still immature and auditing companies do not have the necessary understanding of the value of investing in such technologies. Another reason for the backwardness of the auditing profession's technologies is that not many auditors are skilled in the field of information technology and its advanced techniques. This is due to the lack of technology education for accounting students in universities. It is necessary to make investments and arrangements to promote information technology education in universities.

The findings implies that in auditing, big data helps the auditor to substantiate management claims by providing extensive information and improving audit commentary and reporting, thus transforming the legitimacy and efficiency of the auditing profession. In addition to opportunities, big data also presents a number of challenges for accountants and auditors. Changing the traditional pattern of the auditor in handling financial statements, performing complex and excessive calculations, as well as the confidentiality of big data, are examples of the challenges mentioned. On the other hand, big data creates gaps between traditional data analysis in current continuous auditing and the analysis required for continuous big data auditing, creating problems for continuous auditors such as collecting and handling large, heterogeneous and erratic data. The insights gained from this study can be used by academics and the auditing profession to better understand big data analytics tools, the social benefits of using it, and the challenges associated with it so that these groups can overcome barriers to using big data analytics in the audit profession.

References

Alles, M., & Gray, G. L. (2016). Incorporating big data in audits: Identifying inhibitors and a research agenda to address those inhibitors. *International Journal of Accounting Information Systems, 22*, 44–59.

Alles, M. G. (2015). Drivers of the use and facilitators and obstacles of the evolution of big data by the audit profession. *Accounting Horizons, 29*(2), 439–449.

Appelbaum, D., et al. (2017). Big data and analytics in the modern audit engagement: Research needs. *Auditing: A Journal of Practice & Theory, 36*(4), 1–27.

Brohi, S. N., et al. (2016). Identifying and analyzing the transient and permanent barriers for big data. *Journal of Engineering Science and Technology, 11*(12), 1793–1807.
Brown-Liburd, H., et al. (2015). Behavioral implications of big Data's impact on audit judgment and decision making and future research directions. *Accounting Horizons, 29*(2), 451–468.
Burri, R. V. (2008). Doing distinctions: Boundary work and symbolic capital in radiology. *Social Studies of Science, 38*(1), 35–62.
Cao, M., Chychyla, R., & Stewart, T. (2015). Big data analytics in financial statement audits. *Accounting Horizons, 29*(2), 423–429.
Cappa, F., et al. (2021). Big data for creating and capturing value in the digitalized environment: Unpacking the effects of volume, variety, and veracity on firm performance. *Journal of Product Innovation Management, 38*(1), 49–67.
Carter, C., et al. (2015). Annexing new audit spaces: Challenges and adaptations. *Accounting, Auditing & Accountability Journal.*
Chang, R. M., et al. (2014). Understanding the paradigm shift to computational social science in the presence of big data. *Decision Support Systems, 63*, 67–80.
Cockcroft, S., & Russell, M. (2018). Big data opportunities for accounting and finance practice and research. *Australian Accounting Review, 28*(3), 323–333.
Einav, L., & Levin, J. (2014). Economics in the age of big data. *Science, 346*(6210).
Fink, A. (2019). *Conducting research literature reviews: From the internet to paper.* Sage publications.
FRC. (2017). *Audit quality thematic review: The use of data analytics in the audit of financial statements.* Financial Reporting Council Limited.
Gepp, A., et al. (2018). Big data techniques in auditing research and practice: Current trends and future opportunities. *Journal of Accounting Literature, 40*, 102–115.
Griffin, P. A., & Wright, A. M. (2015). Commentaries on big Data's importance for accounting and auditing. *Accounting Horizons, 29*(2), 377–379.
IAASB. (2016). *Exploring the growing use of Technology in the Audit, with a focus on data analytics.* IFAC.
ICAEW. (2016). *Data analytics for external auditors.* Institute of Chartered Accountants England and Wales.
Jones, M. (2014). A matter of life and death. *MIS Quarterly, 38*(3), 895–A896.
Khalifa, R., et al. (2007). Discourse and audit change: Transformations in methodology in the professional audit field. *Accounting, Auditing & Accountability Journal.*
Kim, S. Y., & Upneja, A. (2014). Predicting restaurant financial distress using decision tree and AdaBoosted decision tree models. *Economic Modelling, 36*, 354–362.
Krahel, J. P., & Titera, W. R. (2015). Consequences of big data and formalization on accounting and auditing standards. *Accounting Horizons, 29*(2), 409–422.
Lee, I. (2017). Big data: Dimensions, evolution, impacts, and challenges. *Business Horizons, 60*(3), 293–303.
Leonardi, P. M. (2013). Theoretical foundations for the study of sociomateriality. *Information and Organization, 23*(2), 59–76.
Littell, J. H., Corcoran, J., & Pillai, V. (2008). *Systematic reviews and meta-analysis.* Oxford University Press.
Nardo, M., et al. (2016). Walking down wall street with a tablet: A survey of stock market predictions using the web. *Journal of Economic Surveys, 30*(2), 356–369.
Newton, J. D., & Ashton, R. H. (1989). The association between audit technology and audit delay. *Auditing-a Journal of Practice & Theory, 8*, 22–37.
Orlikowski, W. J. (2007). Sociomaterial practices: Exploring technology at work. *Organization Studies, 28*(9), 1435–1448.
Power, M. (1995). Auditing, expertise and the sociology of technique. *Critical Perspectives on Accounting, 6*(4), 317–339.
Power, M. (1996). Making things auditable. *Accounting, Organizations and Society, 21*(2–3), 289–315.

Power, M. K. (2003). Auditing and the production of legitimacy. *Accounting, Organizations and Society, 28*(4), 379–394.

Robson, K., et al. (2007). Transforming audit technologies: Business risk audit methodologies and the audit field. *Accounting, Organizations and Society, 32*(4–5), 409–438.

Salijeni, G. (2019). *Big Data Analytics and the Social Relevance of Auditing: An Exploratory Study*. The University of Manchester.

Shukla, M., & Mattar, L. (2019). Next generation smart sustainable auditing systems using big data analytics: Understanding the interaction of critical barriers. *Computers & Industrial Engineering, 128*, 1015–1026.

Suchman, M. C. (1995). Managing legitimacy: Strategic and institutional approaches. *Academy of Management Review, 20*(3), 571–610.

Suddaby, R., & Greenwood, R. (2005). Rhetorical strategies of legitimacy. *Administrative Science Quarterly, 50*(1), 35–67.

Tranfield, D., et al. (2003). Towards a methodology for developing evidence-informed management knowledge by means of systematic review. *British Journal of Management, 14*(3), 207–222.

Vasarhelyi, M. A., et al. (2015). Big data in accounting: An overview. *Accounting Horizons, 29*(2), 381–396.

West, J., & Bhattacharya, M. (2016). Intelligent financial fraud detection: a comprehensive review. *Computers & Security, 57*, 47–66.

Whittle, A., et al. (2016). The 'Big Four'in the spotlight: Accountability and professional legitimacy in the UK audit market. *Journal of Professions and Organization, 3*(2), 119–141.

Xiao, S., et al. (2015). European option pricing with a fast fourier transform algorithm for big data analysis. *IEEE Transactions on Industrial Informatics, 12*(3), 1219–1231.

Yoon, K., et al. (2015). Big data as complementary audit evidence. *Accounting Horizons, 29*(2), 431–438.

Zhang, Y., et al. (2017). A big data analytics architecture for cleaner manufacturing and maintenance processes of complex products. *Journal of Cleaner Production, 142*, 626–641.

Urbanisation and Well-Being of Ageing Population in the Twenty-first Century: A Scoping Review of Available Assessment Tools

Simona Azzali, André Siew Yeong Yew, Taha Chaiechi, and Caroline Wong

Abstract Ageing population and urbanisation are two global trends that together comprise major forces shaping the twenty-first Century. Cities are growing, and so are their share of ageing population. In 2019, the world's population aged 60 years or over numbered 703 million and is projected to double to 1.5 billion by 2050 (UN, 2019). By then, 1 in 6 people will be over 65 years of age (UN, 2019).

Urban areas have already started experiencing the challenges of providing services and infrastructure to support ageing residents' well-being and necessities. In practical terms, an age-friendly city adapts its structures and services to be accessible to and inclusive of senior citizens with varying needs and capacities. However, the global ageing population is a major concern for economists and policymakers since it has numerous economic and financial implications affecting economic growth, public healthcare, and social support systems.

After an initial search that included 466 items from a variety of sources of available evidence, this research adopted a scoping review following the work of (Arskey, O'Malley Int J Social Res Methodol 8:19–32, 2005) in order to map the key concepts underpinning population ageing, well-being, and urbanisation. In particular, the review seeks to examine various ageing well-being assessment tools (qualitative and quantitative) so as to define the recurrent indicators, criteria, areas covered and what is missing. This review was complemented by a summary of the research findings and research gaps in existing literature pertaining to the well-being of the ageing population. The review has highlighted four critical characteristics of a pragmatic well-being assessment model for the ageing population, including the need for individualisation to a specific context, the subjective and objective relevance, flexibility in choosing the appropriate frameworks, and the importance to narrate the progressive status in the

S. Azzali (✉) · A. S. Y. Yew · C. Wong
James Cook University Singapore, Sims Drive, Singapore
e-mail: simona.azzali@jcu.edu.au; caroline.wong@jcu.edu.au

T. Chaiechi
College of Business, Law and Governance, James Cook University, Townsville, QLD, Australia
e-mail: taha.chaiechi@jcu.edu.au

© The Author(s), under exclusive license to Springer Nature Singapore Pte Ltd. 2022
T. Chaiechi, J. Wood (eds.), *Community Empowerment, Sustainable Cities, and Transformative Economies*, https://doi.org/10.1007/978-981-16-5260-8_9

well-being of an individual over time. In a fast ageing world, this review helps in capacity-building and design thinking by bridging academic knowledge and real-world planning and design endeavours.

Keywords Urbanisation · Age-friendly · Well-being assessment tools · Scoping review · Healthy cities

1 Introduction

In Singapore, one in four Singapore residents (UOB Global Economics & Markets Research, 2018) and about 40% of the workforce would be 65 and-over (Prime Minister's Office Strategy Group National Population and Talent Division, 2018) by 2030. The rapid ageing population has prompted the government to come out with an action plan for successful ageing in 2016 that charts the way forward for Singaporeans to age more confidently and gracefully (Singapore Ministry of Health, 2016). Singapore has continually made efforts to provide for a quality healthy ageing environment through investment in elderly health and social care, assistive housing and age-friendly urbanisation (National Population & Talent Division, 2013). However, the context in which the ageing population live is also changing with evolving needs among different ageing sub-populations (Singapore Ministry of Health, 2016).

While the government attempts to adapt its age-friendly infrastructure and services to be accessible and inclusive of senior citizens with varying needs, the urbanisation strategies remain a concern for various stakeholders as the city-state's urban planning leans towards a 'help--them--now' strategy (Yew, 2020) often perceived as didactic, standard-upgrade and choice-expansion in public housing and social environment (Harrison, 1997). This might not be sufficient to address the evolving needs of the ageing population in Singapore. The nature of the Singaporean environment for living, working, and playing has evolved beyond global benchmarks set by the United Nations and World Health Organization (WHO)'s Age-Friendly Environment comprehensive guidelines (Yew, 2020).

In its constitution, the World Health Organisation (WHO) defines health as "a state of complete physical, mental and social wellbeing and not merely the absence of disease or infirmity" (WHO, 1948). This is consistent with the biopsychosocial model of health, which considers physiological, psychological and social factors in health and illness, and interactions between these factors. It differs from the traditional medical model, which defines health as the absence of illness or disease and emphasises the role of clinical diagnosis and intervention. The WHO definition links health explicitly with wellbeing, and conceptualises health as a human right requiring physical and social resources to achieve and maintain. It is therefore pertinent for Singapore to monitor its strategies towards enhancing the well-being of its ageing population to ensure sustainable results and returns, and confidence in the stakeholders. Having an assessment tool for the well-being of ageing population could provide insights to the developmental status thereby making forecasting beneficial for aged care planning and governance.

Therefore, in this literature review, we seek to identify the availability of well-being assessment tools for the ageing population (qualitative and quantitative). We also seek to examine the concepts, processes, structures, indicators and criteria covered in well-being appraisal. The identification of successful tools can help policymakers examine and improve existing urban planning strategies in ageing population. Any inadequacy in certain aspects of a tool would provide opportunities for improvement or adaptation of existing tool to suit Singapore.

Accordingly, this paper is organised as follows. Firstly, we focus on the methodology by searching and filtering literature on assessment of well-being in ageing population. Secondly, we text screen the preliminary search results to ascertain relevant assessment tools. The ascertained literature is then reviewed in detail to identify each of their concepts, assessment processes, areas of interest, structure and indicators of measures. These findings form the basis for understanding the nature of well-being assessment and the measurement approaches. In addition, we aim to identify any strengths or pitfalls among these tools based on the findings. Finally, we seek to gain insights on the nature of an optimum well-being assessment, one that could provide monitoring and forecasting capacities, and that has the potential to help Singapore in developing sustainable urbanisation strategies towards enhancement of well-being in its ageing population.

2 Methodology

Chaiechi (2020) adopts Arksey & O'Malley (2005) scoping approach (see Table 1) in the investigation for a multidisciplinary influence approach in scoping review for sustainable urbanism, and develops a methodology framework to map existing literature across a wide range of studies in urban development. In this review, while we base our investigation on Chaiechi's framework to provide an overview of existing research evidence and methods used in measuring or assessing the well-being of the ageing population, we also seek to identify the strengths and limitations of those methods. Our goal is to determine the most practical methods of well-being assessment for the ageing population.

Chaiechi's scoping review framework is selected because of its inherent emphasis on multi-dimensional integration of socio-cultural, economic and environmental factors in developing sustainable urban models and planning policies. Our goal is to be inclusive of assessments that encompass all these factors for the well-being of ageing population in establishing sustainable urban policies.

2.1 A Priori

Following Chaiechi's (2020) *a priori* protocol for study selection in Fig. 1, we developed a similar process. The point of departure in this study is that the exclusion

Table 1 Scoping review by Arksey & O'Malley (2005)

Step 1: Identification of the guiding question	Guiding questions are to be broad in nature as they seek to provide breadth of coverage. Identifying the guiding question provides the roadmap for subsequent stages.
Step 2: Identification of relevant sources	Steps 2 consists in identifying the relevant literature and developing a decision plan for where to search, which terms to use, which sources are to be searched, time span, and language. Comprehensiveness and breadth is important in the search.
Step 3: Selection of the sources	Literature selection involves identification of inclusion and exclusion criteria. These criteria are based on the specifics of the guiding question.
Step 4: Charting the data	A data-charting form is developed and used to extract data from each item. A narrative review is used to extract contextual information from each item.
Step 5: Collating, summarizing, and reporting results	An analytic framework is used to provide an overview of the breadth of the literature. An analysis of the extent and nature of studies is outline using tables and diagrams. A thematic analysis is then presented.
Step 6: Consultation (optional and not included in this study)	Provides opportunities for stakeholder involvement to provide insights beyond those in the literature.

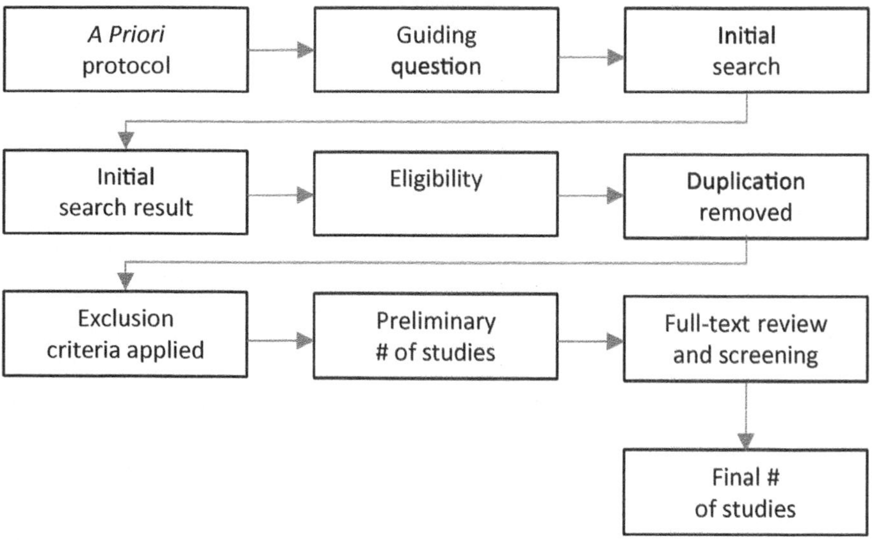

Fig. 1 A priori protocol and selection process. (Chaiechi, 2020)

criteria are applied simultaneously during our initial search utilising JCU Library's upgraded search filters.

The modified process is illustrated in Fig. 2.

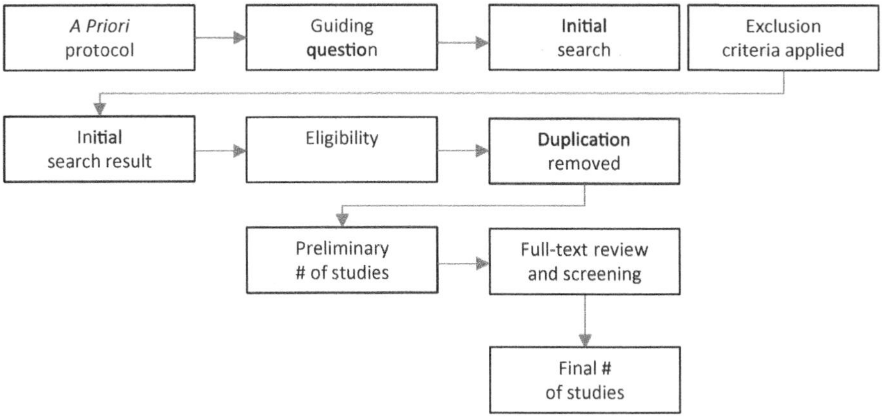

Fig. 2 Modified a priori protocol and selection process

2.2 *The Guiding Question*

To initiate the search, we needed a query framework as our basis to search for assessment tools that are available and usable, or been tested. This query framework must encompass the three parameters of "ageing population", "well-being", and "assessment". The guiding question formulated for our scoping review is, "What are the most practical methods of well-being assessment for the ageing population?"

2.3 *Eligibility Criteria*

The purpose of this review is to identify practical methods in the measurement or assessment of well-being for ageing population. We formulated specific fundamental inclusion criteria listed in Table 2. In the selection of the time-span, we pivoted our search to the initiation of the *World Health Organization Active Ageing* policy framework in 2002 (WHO, 2002). This framework was later replaced by *Healthy Ageing* in 2015 (WHO, 2015) and subsequently by Health General Assembly endorsement of the *Global Strategy and Action Plan on Ageing & Health* (WHO, 2016). In 2017, an addendum to the action plan with 10 *Priorities Towards a Decade of Healthy Ageing* (WHO Department of Ageing and Life Course, 2017) was published. The year 2002 is determined as a significant time marker as this was the year when WHO's terminology, definitions and initiatives on ageing are benchmarked.

We further applied a filter by keywords with *Title* and *Abstract* based on the three parameters in the guiding question. Common variations in spelling, synonym and terminology of the parameters were permitted, as shown in the *Keywords* column of Table 3.

Table 2 Eligibility criteria

Criterion	Inclusion	Remarks
Publication year	Since 2002	WHO Active Ageing initiation year
Language	English	
Type of literature	Scholarly materials, Peer-reviewed: Books/ eBooks Book Chapters Conference Proceedings Journals/ eJournals Journal Articles	Excluded: Newspaper articles Book reviews Dissertations/ Theses
Concept	Studies that discuss well-being assessment of ageing population	
Coverage (Disciplines)	All	
Relevance	Titles and Abstracts	

Table 3 Search by parameter keywords

	Relevance	Keywords	Contains	Search 1	Search 2	Search 3
	Title	well-being, wellbeing	any of these words	☒	☒	☒
AND	*Title*	measure, assess	any of these words	☒	☒	☒
AND	*Title*	older, elderly, ageing, aging	any of these words	☒	☐	☐
AND	*Abstract*	well-being	–	☒	☒	☒
OR	*Abstract*	wellbeing	–	☒	☒	☒
AND	*Abstract*	measure	–	☒	☒	☒
OR	*Abstract*	assess	–	☒	☒	☒
AND	*Abstract*	older	–	☒	☐	☒
OR	*Abstract*	elderly	–	☒	☐	☒
OR	*Abstract*	ageing	–	☒	☐	☒
OR	*Abstract*	aging	–	☒	☐	☒
Initial search results				12	466	33
Duplications (removed)				–	–	4
Screening based on relevance to guiding question (removed)				–	–	18
Preliminary number of studies for full-text review & screening				–	–	11

2.4 Search Objectives

As shown in Table 3, our Search 1 was based completely on our guiding question. This search was parameters-specific within the *Title* and *Abstract*. In Search 2, we investigated the impact of excluding the age parameter from the search, with an inquiry on the extent of contemporary studies on well-being assessments for the general population.

In Search 3, we considered the possibility of a non-descriptive *Title* or one with alternate terminology for the ageing population. For example, in his paper to illustrate Singapore's ageing population that is living longer with unique criteria in living, Yew (2020) distinguishes this population as the Singapore Extended Lifespan Population (SELP) in its *Title*. Furthermore, he refers to this group as the 65 and-over population. Hence, in Search 3, ensuring we capture publications with nomenclature variations, we omitted "ageing" in the search relevance for *Title*. This also allows us to capture literature on the well-being of adults transitioning to next phase of life in longitudinal studies within the general population, but their *Title* may not include "ageing". We further evaluated the relevance of these studies in the final round of full-text review and screening.

2.5 Search Results

By comparing the initial search results of Search 1 (12 items) and Search 2 (466 items), it is apparent that there were significantly more research done for the general population well-being and potentially more assessment methodologies developed too. Through a broad overview of the titles in Search 2, the topics were diverse and encompassed assessments varying from clinical well-being in adolescents to subjective perception of financial well-being in retiring adults. The gap in the results is evident as there is a lack of research on the assessments of well-being in the ageing population.

In Search 3, omitting the 'age' parameter in *Title* has favoured our special consideration for the absence of or alternate age terminologies. The thirty-three results in Search 3 encompass all those from Search 1. Therefore, we concluded that the preliminary results from Search 3 were adequate to proceed with the first round of eligibility screening. This step is conducted through a manual inspection of each paper's title and abstract, and selected based on the relevance to our guiding question. Eighteen papers are disqualified for the reasons listed below (Table 4).

The remaining eleven papers include nine research papers from various disciplines (Fig. 3), of which two are in tandem feasibility investigation (Reijula, et al., 2009) and follow-up report (Reijula, et al., 2010) of one study. Among these, one search result is a supplemental introduction to well-being indexes by Goodwin & Krause (2017) in preparation for their discussion on challenges and opporunities linked with summary measures of well-being in later life at the 2017 IAGG World Congress symposium.[1] The last paper omitted is a result brief by Daaleman et al.

[1]Goodwin & Krause (2017) provided an advance briefing on EU/UNECE Active Ageing Index (AAI), the HelpAge Global AgeWatch Index, and the AARP's Livability Index. Also in the brief, United Kingdom's Well-being in Later Life (WILL) Index and WHO's indicaors of age-friendly cities were mentioned by name as measure summary with potentials in serving the public good.

Table 4 Disqualified researches

General population comparative study in well-being and measures (4 disqualifications): (i) Mental well-being based on self-reported health (SRH) cross-sectional survey of general population in Coventry, UK, Putz et al. (2019). (ii) Comparison methods of measure in subjective well-being, evaluative and experienced based, in a sample of the US general population, Dolan (2017). (iii) Co-relationship between measures of perceived control and subjective well-beings in adults age 18–88 in 256 participants in south-eastern part of US, Owusu-Ansah (2008). (iv) Measurment and comparison of risk-taking tendency in relationship to age in a self-report rating study across age groups, Rolison & Pachur (2016).
Measurement of a specific factor in relation to elderly well-being (2): These studies focused on the comparison of psychometric measurement reliability: (i) Comparison of two psychometric measures approaches (well- and ill-defined) in the measurement of everyday cognition of older adults in reasonsing, basic knowledge and memory, Allaire & Marsiske (2002). (ii) Comparison of two psychometric measures of wisdom to determine their reliability in prediciting forgiveness and psychological well-being in older adults, Taylor et al. (2011).
Retirement transition influenced well-being (3) Dulin et al. (2011), Richardson et al. (2019) and Wells et al. (2010).
Clinical or long-term care well-being (2) Edvardsson, et al. (2019) and Nieboer & Cramm (2020)
Medicine related well-being (4): (i) Vaginal ageing in post-menopausal women, Huang et al., (2015). (ii) Arterary stiffness in relation to cardiovascular mortality in ageing patients, Nilsson et al. (2017). (iii) Co-relation in switching hand preference side with well-being in older adults, Porac & Searleman (2002). (iv) Effect of museum-based social prescribed intervention on the well-being in older adults, Thomson et al. (2018).
Well-being in older children or adolescents (2) Chan D. et al. (2019) and Smees et al. (2020)
Well-being in elderly robotic users (1) Kortner, et al. (2012)

(2002) on the Spirituality Index of Well-Being (SIWB) they had developed and tested in a Kansas elderly patient community population, but provided no discussions on their research. Our final search result is left with eight research studies in the assessment of well-beings of older adults.

3 Findings

While the main findings are summarised in Table 7, what follows is a detailed and comprehensive review of the contribution of each of the selected research works.

Burton et al. (2011) in the United Kingdom developed a Neighbourhood Design Characteristics Checklist (NeDeCC) to examine the links and relationship between

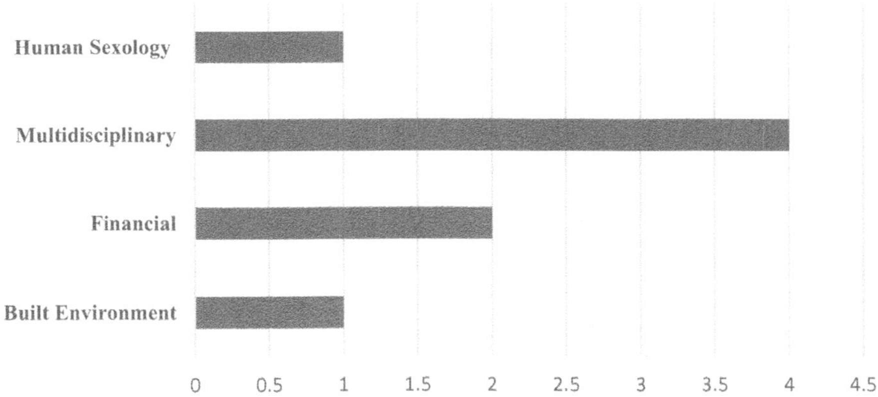

Fig. 3 Nature of well-being studies

Table 5 Burton et al. (2011) NeDeCC summary

Location relative to residence	Individual's residence	Adjacent Street	Wider Neighbourhood
No. of urban design characteristics examined	4	9	12
Source for urban designcharacteristics	urban design guidance texts & standards		
Well-being constructs measured in ea. location	14 (6 functional, 4 social & 4 emotional)		
Source for well-being constructs	literature reviews & focus group discussions with senior citizens		
Construct measurement	Self-reported and perception		

25 urban residential design characteristics and 14 place-related well-being constructs in older residents (Table 5). An overview of the NeDeCC design characteristics and well-being constructs is summarised in Table 4. Results show wide range of links and relationships and no conclusions can be drawn properly. However, Burton et al. (2011) suggest the potential of non-linear relationships, and the importance of meaningful calibration of measures where urban design characteristics are measured using correlated well-being outcomes. The authors indicated that NeDeCC is reflective on the nature of the built environment, but it is not as successful in detecting relationships with well-being dimensions.

To enhance the economic evaluation for fair allocations of health and social care services in the Netherlands, Hackert et al. (2020) developed the Well-being of Older People (WOOP) measure as a comprehensive well-being measure with attention for domains relevant to the senior citizens. Hackert et al. argue existing measures may either lack suitability in economic evaluations, or relevance to senior citizens. This review reports the validity and reliability of WOOP, which consists of nine domains (physical health, mental health, social contact, receive support, acceptance and resilience, feeling useful, independence, making ends meet, and living situation) based on a prior Q-methodology (subjectivity) study on senior citizens' five views on well-being (Hackert et al., 2019). Respondents self-report on their functioning for each item on a scale of 1-poor to 5-excellent through online surveys.

Based on literature reviews and evaluations of existing measures, Hackert et al. (2019) test the health component of WOOP against EuroQoL Five Dimensionality Questionnaire (EQ-5D), EuroQoL Visual Analogue Scale (EQ-VAS), Barthel Index, and the Physical health and Mental health Component Score (SF-12PCS and SF-12PCS MCS). The well-being component is tested against ICEpop CAPability measure for seniors (ICECAP-O), the Satisfaction with Life Scale (SWLS), and Cantril's Ladder. Based on their first validity and reliability tests, the authors find and conclude that WOOP seems to capture aspects relevant to the well-being of senior citizens adequately but, requires further studies for use in economic evaluations in care services.

Mitra et al. (2020) develop a measure of well-being at older ages that is multi-dimensional and disability inclusive. After reviewing data from two national U.-S. surveys, the researchers identified five dimensions of well-being: material wellbeing, health status, personal activities, social connections/relationships, and economic security. Mitra et al. (2020)'s data review and well-being dimensions are summarised in Table 6.

As Mitra et al.'s study is based on human development of disability, health and well-being; a capability approach where well-being is comprised of capabilities and functionings, the threshold was set for 13 individual indicators. An individual was considered to experience well-being when an individual has met or exceeded a set of thresholds. Their major findings are, 1.) Persons with disabilities are significantly less likely to experience well-being at older ages, and 2.) Well-being for older persons varies by disability status across the dimensions, among others that highlight the need for inclusion persons with disability.

Table 6 Mitra et al. (2020) data source & review summary

Source for data reviewed	U.S. national surveys
Data 1	Panel Study on Income Dynamics (PSID)
content extracted	social, economic and health factors
Data 2	Disability and Use of Time (DUST)
content extracted	disability and well-being of older couples
Identifications made:	
well-being dimensions	5
well-being indicators	13

[a]DUST (McGonagle, Schoeni, Sastry, & Freedman, 2012) is a supplemental survey report to PSID with disability inclusiveness

In Finland, upon completion with positive outcome of a 2 weeks Con-Dis[2] device feasibility study (Reijula, et al., 2009), Reijula et al. proceeded in measuring the well-being in 10 Finnish elderly patients in the morning and evening with Con-Dis (Reijula, et al., 2010) over a 4 weeks period. A pedometer was used in conjunction to monitor individual's activities outdoor. Individual's general health was also monitored twice daily with measurement of blood pressure and heart rate. Their findings indicate the potential applicability of Con-Dis device and show correlations of the perceived level of well-being in mood and quality of life to outdoor activities.

Sexton et al. (2016) compared and determined the validity of two old adult population survey studies (with and without intellectual disability) in Ireland, using measures based on two dimensions in emotional well-being and self-determination, considered as the holistic approach to quality of life (QOL), of Schalock's Quality of Life Framework. Emotional well-being comprises contentment (moods, satisfaction), self-concept, lack of stress, and self-determination, which comprises autonomy/personal control, goals and personal values, and choice. The data of the two population are from face-to-face computer-assisted personal interview and self-completion questionnaire survey. Through content analysis, they compared 15 QOL measures (nine emotional well-being and six self-determination) and determined that the QOL measures are different between the two groups. The researchers conclude the QOL measures of general old adult population is non-inclusive of those with intellectual disability and they recommend research to address inclusive measurement of QOL and as they recognise it as a key challenge regardless of the population of interest, especially for ageing population with diminishing cognitive ability.

Besides general well-being, specific aspects in life are taken as contributors to life satisfaction, such as financial, sexual and spiritual well-beings. While taking other personal factors (life transitions, health, employment and socio-demography) as covariates, Chan et al. (2002) investigate the changes in the subjective and objective economic well-being of older adults in a longitudinal study in Singapore (1995–1999) and Taiwan (1989–1993). Using population surveys from Singapore (1995) and Taiwan (1989) with income information as to their baseline for economic status, Chan et al. re-interviewed samples of the surveyed elderlies to establish the changes of their subjective and objective well-beings after 4 years, by comparing their before-and-after perceived financial adequacy and actual income levels. The researchers found fluctuations of subjective and objective well-beings over the period, with fluctuations being dependent on some of the covariates included in the study. As the subjective well-being is captured by respondents' evaluations of their financial adequacy based on their household total income, Chan et al. highlight the need for measuring multiple economic dimensions in determining the economic

[2] An electronic self-reporting device carried by subjects with three input buttons of happy, neutral and unhappy, that records evaluations on perceived levels of well-being in mood, pain, and quality of life.

well-beings as the sources of income of the respondents varies (welfare, continuing employment, children's support, pension, et cetera).

Using similar financial framework, Tenney and Kalenkoski (2019) investigated the relationship between subjective and objective measures of financial well-being among senior Americans in a cross-sectional analysis. Instead of using income changes as objective measure, the authors use three financial ratios in liquidity, investment and debt-to-asset. These ratios are typically utilised by financial planners to evaluate the financial health of a client. Relying on a 2014 human and retirement study survey in conjunction with a single-question satisfaction questionnaire, Tenney and Kalenkoski find that investment ratio is positively associated with the subjective financial well-being. Other covariates (age, marital status, retirment status, et cetera) play a role in the perceived satisfaction, at various degrees of influence, of respondents' financial conditions. Authors highlight other objective measure of financial ratios are available and financial planners should not rely on them to tell the full story of financial well-being.

In this final article of our search result, Stulhofer et al. (2019) set out to develop a multi-dimensional measure and validate it in population samples across Norway, Denmark, Belgium and Portugal. Authors recognise the lack of research and validated measures on sexual well-being in older adults. Through literature review, they conceptualise sexual well-being measure to include five dimensions in emotional intimacy, sexual intimacy, perceived sexual compatibility, absence of sexual distress and sexual satisfaction, and presented them in a questionnaire of self-report on frequency and subjective evaluations of individual's sexual activities. The data results were evaluated using several other constructs that have been proven to be related to sexual satisfaction. Stulhofer's sexual well-being measure is found to be invariant across the four cultures, which Stulhofer highlights as a limitation in comprehensive applicability of the measure, and corroborated the findings from earlier sexual well-being studies, based traditionally on sexual problematic behaviour and dysfunction models, in general.

4 Discussion

Based on our review, we made the following observations on the structure of the research processes, identifications of certain commonalities, and derivations.

4.1 Multi-dimensionality of well-being

There is consensus that well-being has multiple aspects and the majority calls these aspects dimensions, whereas Burton et al. (2011) refers to them as constructs and Hackert et al. (2019) domains. For ease of discussion, we will continue to refer to these aspects as dimensions. Hence, well-being is multi-dimensional.

4.2 Establishing the Well-being Framework

Except in Reijula et al. (2009, 2010) Con-Dis device applicability studies, well-being measurement papers begin with identifying an established well-being concept framework, either one or multiple from where their dimensions are derived, evaluated and selected. Selection methods include literature review, content analysis, and further supplementing their process with separate focus group studies and statistical relevance tests. Based on the origin of the framework, dimensions may or may not be categorised under broader domains. One or more measurable indicators are then identified for each dimensions in all studies. For example, indicator- activities for enjoyment, is one of several indicators for the dimension- personal activities in Mitra et al. (2020).

4.3 Dichotomy in Measurement of Well-being: Data Source and Its Influence in Dimensions Selection

There is a source for data in each research, which is either field-collected through interviews and surveys, or acquired from records of a population survey, or in combination. There is evidence that data influence dimension selections. In Mitra et al. (2020), through content analysis of the survey data, only five of the eight dimensions from the Report by the Commission on Measurement of Economic Performance and Social Progress Stiglitz et al.(2009) were selected as relevant for study. On the other hand, Hackert et al. (2019) Q-methodology subjective survey on older people's view on well-being is a precursor to the 2020 well-being data collection and measurement of subjective well-being. The framework/dimensions shaped the data collection in this case.

There is a dichotomy in the approach towards the measurement of well-being. In their investigations, Mitra et al. (2020) and Reijula et al. (2009) measured the functionings and capabilities, or achievements, based on human development model to determine the well-being of individuals, whereas Burton et al. (2011) and Hackert et al. (2019) assessed subjective perceived well-being. Sexton et al. (2016)'s data and content allowed the investigation to proceed with both approaches. Hence, it is evident that the nature of the data influences dimensions selection process and the choice of measurement approach. The observations on well-being frameworks, dimensions and selection methods, data, locations and measurement approach in each well-being measurement research are summarised in Table 5.

Based on the above observations, it is common practice to determine the (1.) Well-being framework/s, (2.) Data and its nature, (3.) Dimensions, and (4.) Measurement approach, but not necessarily in that order. There is indication of a potential tripartitie influence among dimensions, data and measurement approach in the engineering of the well-being measurement method. Data and its nature determined the dimensions and measurement approach in Mitra et al. (2020) and Sexton et al. (2016). In the absence of data (Burton et al., 2011; Hackert et al.,

(2020), the framework/dimensions determined the measurement approach and the nature of data to be collected.

4.4 Socio-demographic Covariates & Relevance

Socio-demographics are taken as covariates in the studies, especially in financial well-being (Chan A. et al., 2002; Tenney & Kalenkoski, 2019). There is consensus across the studies that socio-demographic covariates influence but varies in their impact on the type of well-being in discussion, particularly in subjective or perceived well-being (Chan A. et al., 2002). For example, education level demonstrated impact on perceived financial well-being in older adults (Tenney & Kalenkoski, 2019), but reported no correlation with sexual well-being (Stulhofer et al., 2019). From the longitudinal study on financial well-being in older adults, Chan et al. (2002) suggest observable changes in the priority or importance of each dimension as a person age. Culminated with socio-demographic covariates' varying influence discussed before, it seems the method of selecting the dimensions of well-being needs to accommodate the socio-demography of the specific ageing population and shall be re-evaluated for its applicability to the same group after a certain period, which suggests that well-being assessments are periodic with continuity to ascertain relevance with the population in discussion.

The selected literature in the review also suggests well-being in the ageing population is a topic prevalent in developed countries (Fig. 4). This, however, could be a result of the deducible dimensions available within urban frameworks and urban lifestyles. The dimensions and indicators selected in a study need to be relevant to the population in question. This echoes our observation that well-being assessments are socio-demography specific.

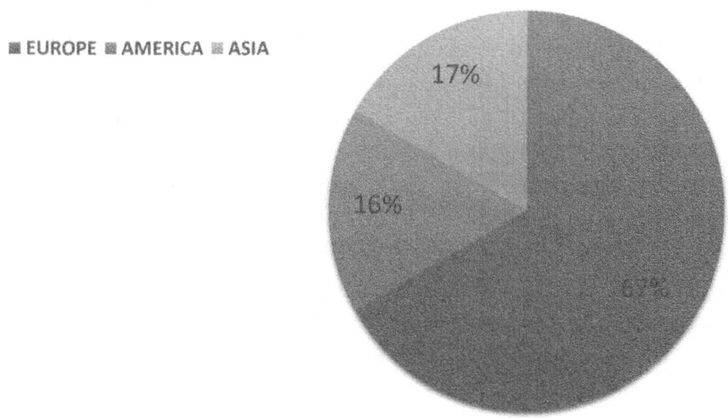

Fig. 4 Geographical scope of the selected studies

4.5 Assessment Model and Future Work

Based on our findings and observations, we can infer that a pragmatic well-being assessment model for the ageing population should possess four critical characteristics. With these characteristics identified, a possible next task would be to develop an assessment model followed by (1.) A feasibility test with a focus group and, upon positive result, (2.) A validity study of the findings using the model against established well-being indices or scales in a population sample. The latter study can potentially incorporate a comparative well-being evaluation of residents at selected estates and neighbourhoods. The four identified characteristics are as follow:

1. *Individualisation*

Regardless of the type of well-beings discussed, socio-demographic covariates influence both subjective and objective well-beings, each at various degrees under different circumstances and locations. Chan et al. (2002) show perception of financial adequacy differs in Singapore and Taiwan older populations. The perception also varies across gender, ethnicity and education levels. The individualisation of the well-being assessment is apparent and indisputable. Especially with Burton et al. (2011)'s suggestion of a non-linear relationship between dimensions and the environment, individualised assessment is not subjugated to pre-dominant social behaviors. By individualisation of the assessment, unintentional exclusions such as that of persons with disability (Mitra et al., 2020; Sexton et al., 2016) are unlikely to become potential problem.

2. *Temporal continuity and life-event influence reflective*

Chan et al. (2002)'s study indicates that financial well-being dimensions of priority and importance change over time in the only longitudinal study in this search and review. This study also finds life transition in retirement influencing the perceived well-being in the Singapore population sample, but not in Taiwan. It also finds that perceived financial hardship is associated with widowhood in women in Singapore and Taiwan, more so than men. Hence, it is important for an informative well-being assessment to narrate the progressive status in the well-being of an individual over time. This is especially crucial for caregivers to gain insights how to enhance the well-beings of an individual under their continuous care.

3. *Subjective and objective relevance*

The dichotomy of subjective and objective perceptions of well-being is prevalent in the literature as identified in the measurement approach of Table 7. Some emphasise either subjective importance or objective achievement, while some take combination approach. Burton et al. (2011) and Hackert et al. (2020) also ensure the validity of the perceived importance or relevance in the selected dimensions. Therefore, an encompassing assessment must incorporate the subjectivity and objectivity in the relevance and measurement of the dimensions.

4. *Framework independent and multi-dimensions adaptive*

Multiple frameworks have been explored in the research being reviewed, each latent in field/s of interest ranging from comprehensive to personal sexual well-beings. It is only logical for the assessment to investigate the relevant audiences both to subjective and objective. Burton et al. (2011) identify the values and shortcomings of various frameworks in the beginning of their article before filtering to fourteen dimensions. Mitra et al. (2020) select five of eight dimensions from Stiglitz, Sen and Fitoussi's social progress report (2009). Both selection processes are based on relevance of frameworks and dimensions to the target population. A pragmatic assessment would have the flexibility in choosing the appropriate frameworks relevant to the individual in question, and provide the capacity in expansion, or contraction, on the selection or deselection process of dimensions.

5 Conclusions

In order to find the most practical methods in measuring and assessing the well-being of the ageing-population since to the initiation of Acitve Ageing, we applied a scoping review based on *a priori* protocol and search process for multidisciplinary scoping review for sustainable urbanism- a methodology framework to map existing literature across a wide range of studies in urban development. The process has proven its applicability in our preliminary literature scoping but with limits. The search and review of the results yielded various and potentially an array of well-being frameworks, by which a well-being assessment discourse could be based on. Our observations indicate that further refinement in search keywords to include domain or category, and dimensions will not be productive as they are well-being framework dependent; different frameworks identify and name the domains and dimensions differently, and particularly so for the latter.

It is also evident from the results that more attention is required to examine the well-being of the ageing population. There is a big gap in the literature between the well-being of the general population and ageing population. In addition, the lack in the inclusiveness of studies for the disabled, which includes ageing population with developing physical and mental disabilities, is highlighted in some of the studies.

The scoping review further reveals indication of a tripatite influencing relationship among the framework, data and measurment approach in the engineering of an well-being assessment method. The authors conclude that the practicality of an assessment method is dependent on the co-relationship of the well-being framework and the nature of the data, and more research with disability inclusiveness is required to fill the void of the well-being of ageing population.

Based on the results of our review, there is no conclusive evidence of established practical methods in measuring the well-being of ageing population. These measuring methods are still in their infancy stages of development. The reference well-being frameworks and their respective dimensions are still being tested for relevance

Table 7 Well-being frameworks, dimensions & selection methods, data, locations and measurement approach observed in review

				No. of *dimensions*					
Study	Authors	Well-being framework/s referenced	Nature of well-being in study	in framework	selected	Selection methods	*Data*	Geographic location	*Measurement approach*
1	Burton et al. (2011)	Multiple	Built environment	14	14	literature review content analysis focus group studies	Survey	United Kingdom	Subjective
2	Chan A. et al. (2002)	Subjective: MultipleObjective: Multiple	Financial	1	1	literature review data content analysis	Records & re-interview	Singapore Taiwan	Combination
3	Hackert et al. (2020)	Hackert et al. (2019)	Comprehensive	9	9	Q-methodology survey	Survey	The Netherlands	Subjective
4	Mitra et al. (2020)	Stiglitz et al. (2009)	Comprehensive	8	5	data content analysis	Records	United States	Achievement
5 a/b	Reijula et al. (2009, 2010)	n.a.	Comprehensive	1	1	n.a.	Con-dis	Finland	Achievement
6	Sexton et al. (2016)		Comprehensive	15	15	content analysis acceptability & relevance test	Records	Ireland	Combination
7	Stuholfer et al. (2019)	Multiple	Sexual	5	5	literature review	Survey	Norway Denmark Belgium Portugal	Combination
8	Tenney and Kalenkoski (2019)	Subjective: n.a. Objective: Multiple	Financial	multiple	3	literature review data content analysis	Records & 1-question	United States	Combination

Note: Goodwin & Krause (2017) is omitted from this list as it is a pre-symposium briefing. No research, methodology or findings are presented to the ageing population. The availability of different frameworks, domains and multi-dimensionality of well-being also complicate our scoping exercise. It is apparent that all the researches demonstrate distinguish effort in co-relating their well-being frameworks and dimensions with their data and its content, or vice versa. Despite not identifying practical methods in this scoping exercise, we identified that a practical well-being assessment method must have a well-being framework with dimensions correlating to the data and its inherent nature.

With the newly identified characteristics for well-being assessment of ageing population, our goal is to develop an assessment tool that could overcome the framework and dimension relevance, and other issues mentioned, in our next phase of work and test its feasibility in the field. We aim to develop a tool that is inclusive and meaningful to individuals as well as caregivers; one that is adaptive to socio-demography, geography, environment, and other external factors. This tool is also one that provides continuity to aid in sustainable planning and development especially in the governance of friendly ageing urbanism (Table 7).

References

Allaire, J. C., & Marsiske, M. (2002). Well- and Ill-defined measures of everyday cognition relationship to older adults' initellectual ability and functional status. *Psychology and Aging, 17*(1), 101–115. https://doi.org/10.1037/0882-7974.17.1.101

Arksey, H., & O'Malley, L. (2005). Scoping studies: towards a methodological framework. *International Journal of Social Research Methodology, 8*(1), 19–32. https://doi.org/10.1080/1364557032000119616

Burton, E. J., Mitchell, L., & Stride, C. B. (2011). Good places for ageing in place: Development of objective built environment measures for investigating links with older people's wellbeing. *BMC Public Health, 11*(1), 839. https://doi.org/10.1186/1471-2458-11-839

Chaiechi, T. (2020). Sustainable tropical cities: A scoping review of multidisciplinary mehtods for urban planning. *eTropic: Electronic Journal of Studies In The Tropics, 19*(2). https://doi.org/10.25120/etropic.19.2.2020.3743

Chan, A., Ofstedal, M. B., & Hermalin, A. I. (2002). Changes in subjective and objective measures of economic well-being and their interrelationship among the elderly in Singapore and Taiwan. *Social Inidcators Research, 57*(3), 263–300. Retrieved from http://www.jstor.org/stable/27526994

Chan, D. W., Chan, L.-K., & Sun, X. (2019). Developing a brief version of Ryff's scale to assess the psychological well-being of adolescents in Hong Kong. *European Journal of Psychological Assessment, 35*(3), 414–422. https://doi.org/10.1027/1015-5759/a000403

Daaleman, T. P., Frey, B. B., & Studenski, S. A. (2002). Spirituality index of well-being scale: development and testing of a new measure. *The Journal of Family Practice, 51*(11), 952.

Dolan, P., Kudrna, L., & Stone, A. (2017). The measure matters: An investigation of evaluative and experience-based measure of wellbeing in time use data. *Social Indicators Research, 134*(1), 57–73. https://doi.org/10.1007/s11205-016-1429-8

Dulin, P. L., Stephens, C., Alpass, F., Hill, R. D., & Stevenson, B. (2011). The impact of socio-contextual, physical and lifestyle variables on measures of physical and psychological wellbeing among Māori and non-Māori: The New Zealand Health, Work and Retirement Study. *Ageing & Society, 31*(8), 1406–1424. https://doi.org/10.1017/S0144686X10001479

Edvardsson, D., Baxter, R., Corneliusson, L., Anderson, R. A., Beeber, A., Boas, P. V., . . . Zuniga, F. (2019). Advancing long-term care science through using common data elements: Candidate measures for care outcomes of personhood, well-being, and quality of life. *Gerontology and Geriatric Medicine*. https://doi.org/10.1177/2333721419842672

Goodwin, J., & Krause, B. (2017). Challenges and Opportunities Linked with Summary Measures of Well-being in Later Life. *Innovation in Aging, 1*(suppl_1), 959. https://doi.org/10.1093/geroni/igx004.3453

Hackert, M. Q., Brouwer, W. B., Hoefman, R. J., & van Exel, J. (2019). Views of older people in the Netherlands on wellbeing: A Q-methodology. *Social Science and Medicine, 240*, 112535. https://doi.org/10.1016/j.socscimed.2019.112535

Hackert, M. Q., van Excel, J., & Brouwer, W. B. (2020). Well-being of Older People (WOOP): Quantitative validation of a new outcome measure for use in economic evaluations. *Social Science & Medicine, 259*, 113109. https://doi.org/10.1016/j.socscimed.2020.113109

Harrison, J. D. (1997). Housing for the ageing population of Singapore. *Ageing International, 23*(3), 32–48. https://doi.org/10.1007/s12126-997-1003-4

Huang, A. J., Gregorich, S. E., Kuppermann, M., Nakagawa, S., Van den Eeden, S. K., Brown, J. S., ... Steward, A. L. (2015). Day-to-Day impact of vaginal aging questionnaire: A multidimensional measure of the impact of vaginal symptoms on functioning and well-being in postmenopausal women. *Menopause- The Journal of the North American Menopause Society, 22*(2), 144–154. https://doi.org/10.1097/gme.0000000000000281

Kortner, T., Schmid, A., Batko-Klein, D., Gisinger, C., Huber, A., Lammer, L., & Markus, V. (2012). How social robots make older users really feel well – a method to assess users' concepts of a social robotic assistant. In S. Ge, O. Khatib, J.-J. Cabibihan, R. Simmons, & M.-A. Williams (Eds.), *Social robotics, ICSR 2012. 7621* (pp. 138–147). Springer. https://doi.org/10.1007/978-3-642-34103-8_14

McGonagle, K. A., Schoeni, R. F., Sastry, N., & Freedman, V. A. (2012). The panel study of income dynamics: Overview, recent innovations, and potential for life course research. *Longitudinal and Life Course Studies 2012, 3*(2), 268–284. Retrieved from https://psidonline.isr.umich.edu/

Mitra, S., Brucker, D. L., & Jajtner, K. M. (2020). Wellbeing at older ages: Towards an inclusive and multidimensional measure. *Disability and Health Journal, 13*(4), 100926. https://doi.org/10.1016/j.dhjo.2020.100926

National Population & Talent Division. (2013). *A sustainable population for a dynamic Singapore*. Strategy Group in The Prime Minsiter's Office.

Nieboer, A. P., & Cramm, J. M. (2020). Validation of the SPF-Q, an instrument to assess the quality of production functions to achieve well-being, among multimorbid patients. *Health and Quality of Life Outcomes, 18*, 1–10. https://doi.org/10.1186/s12955-020-01573-z

Nilsson, P., Gottsater, M., & Fatehali, A.-H. (2017). P23 prediction of total and causes-specific mortality incidence as well as cardiovascular morbidity by use of non-invasive measurement of carotid-femoral pulse wave velocity as a measure of arterial stiffness. *Artery Research, 20*(C). https://doi.org/10.1016/j.artres.2017.10.164

Owusu-Ansah, F. E. (2008). Control perceptions and control appraisal: Relation to measures of subjective well-being. *Ghana Medical Journal, 42*(2), 61–67. https://doi.org/10.4314/gmj.v42i2.43597

Porac, C., & Searleman, A. (2002). The effects of hand preference side and hand preference switch history on measures of psychological and physical well-being and cognitive performance in a sample of older adult right-and left-handers. *Neuropsychologia, 40*(12), 2074–2083. https://doi.org/10.1016/S0028-3932(02)00058-1

Prime Minister's Office Strategy Group National Population and Talent Division. (2018). *Population in brief 2018*. NPTD.

Putz, R., Clarke, A., Hamborg, T., & Franco, O. (2019). What factors are associated with a validated measure of mental wellbeing in the general population in Coventry? A stratified random cross sectional suvey. *Journal of Epidemoilogy & Community Health, 65*(Suppl 2). https://doi.org/10.1136/jech.2011.143586.31

Reijula, J., Rosendahl, T., Reijula, K., Roilas, P., Roilas, H., & Sepponen, R. (2009). A new method to assess perceived well-being among elderly people- a feasibility study. *BMC Geriatrics, 9*(1), 55. https://doi.org/10.1186/1471-2318-9-55

Reijula, J., Rosendahl, T., Reijula, K., Roilas, P., Roilas, H., & Sepponen, R. (2010). A new method to assess perceived well-being among elderly people- a follow-up study. *International Journal On Smart Sensing and Intelligent Systems, 3*(2), 130–145. https://doi.org/10.21307/ijssis-2017-385

Richardson, S., Carr, E., Netuveli, G., & Sacker, A. (2019). Country-level welfare-state measures and change in wellbeing following work exit in early old age: evidence from 16 European countries. *International Journal of Epidemiology, 48*(2), 389–401. https://doi.org/10.1093/ije/dyy205

Rolison, J. J., & Pachur, T. (2016). How well do we know our inner daredevil? Probing the relationship between self-report and behavioral measures of risk taking. *Journal of Behavioral Decision Making, 30*(2), 647–657. https://doi.org/10.1002/bdm.1979

Sexton, E., O'Donovan, M.-A., Mulryan, N., McCallion, P., & McCarron, M. (2016). Whose quality of life? A comparison of measures of self-determination and emotional wellbeing in research with older adults with and without intellectual disability. *Journal of Intellectual & Development Disability, 41*(4), 324–337. https://doi.org/10.3109/13668250.2016.1213377

Singapore Ministry of Health. (2016). *What the action plan is all about?* Retrieved 28 Mar, 2021, from https://www.moh.gov.sg/ifeelyoungsg/about/what-is-the-action-plan-about

Smees, R., Rinaldi, L. J., & Simner, J. (2020). Well-being measures for younger children. *Psychological Assessment, 32*(2), 154–169. https://doi.org/10.1037/pas0000768

Stiglitz, J. E., Sen, A., & Fitoussi, J.-P. (2009). Report by the commission on the measurement of economic performance and social progress. : Commission on the Measurement of Economic Performance and Social Progress. Retrieved 04 Mar, 2021, from https://www.researchgate.net/publication/258260767_Report_of_the_Commission_on_the_Measurement_of_Economic_Performance_and_Social_Progress_CMEPSP

Stulhofer, A., Jurin, T., Graham, C., Enzlin, P., & Traeen, B. (2019). Sexual well-being in older men and women: Construction and validation of a multi-dimensional measure in four european countries. *Journal of Happiness Studies, 20*(7), 2329–2350. https://doi.org/10.1007/s10902-018-0049-1

Taylor, M., Bates, G., & Webster, J. D. (2011). Comparing the psychometric propoerties of two measures of wisdom: Predicting forgiveness and psychological well-being with the Self-Assessed Wisdom Scale (SAWS) and the Three Dimensional Wisdom Scale (3D-WS). *Experimental Aging Research, 37*(2), 129–141. https://doi.org/10.1080/0361073X.2011.554508

Tenney, J. A., & Kalenkoski, C. M. (2019). Financial ratios and financial satisfaction: Exploring associations between objective and sub jective measures of financial well-being among older Americans. *Journal of Financial Counseling and Planning, 30*(2), 231–243. https://doi.org/10.1891/1052-3073.30.2.231

Thomson, L. J., Lockyer, B., Carmic, P. M., & Chatterjee, H. J. (2018). Effects of a museum-based social prescription intervention on quantitative measures of psychological wellbeing in older adults. *Perspectives in Public Health, 138*(1). https://doi.org/10.1177/1757913917737563

UOB Global Economics & Markets Research. (2018). *Singapore focus: Reaching a demographic crossroad in 2018*. United Overseas Bank.

Wells, Y., De Vaus, D., Kendig, H., & Quine, S. (2010, January 06). Health and wellbeing through work and retirement transitions in mature age: Understanding pre—post and retrospective measures of change. *The International Jounral of Aging and Human Development, 69*(4), 287–310. https://doi.org/10.2190/AG.69.4.c

WHO. (1948). *Constitution*. Retrieved from https://www.who.int/about/who-we-are/constitution

WHO. (2002). *Active ageing: A policy framerwork*. World Health Organization. Retrieved from https://apps.who.int/iris/bitstream/handle/10665/67215/WHO_NMH_NPH_02.8.pdf;jsessionid=3B6BF11FC359A5D9A37AB0AEF7F2202F?sequence=1

WHO. (2015). *WHO Measuring the age-friendliness of cities: A guide to using core indicators.* Retrieved from World Health Organization: https://www.who.int/ageing/publications/measuring-cities-age-friendliness/en/

WHO. (2016). *Global strategy and action plan on ageing & health.* World Health Organization. Retrieved from https://www.who.int/ageing/WHO-GSAP-2017.pdf?ua=1

WHO Department of Ageing and Life Course. (2017). *10 Priorities towards a decade of healthy ageing.* World Health Organization. Retrieved from https://www.who.int/ageing/WHO-ALC-10-priorities.pdf?ua=1

Yew, A. S. (2020). Re-thinking urban planning for Singapore's extended lifespan population of 2050- A league of its own. *eTropic: Electronic Journal of Studies In The Tropics, 19*(2), 249–273. https://doi.org/10.25120/etropic.19.2.2020.3744

Finding a Balance Between Quiet Work and Being Social: Exploring Coworking Space Needs of Digital Nomads in Terms of Amenities and Community

Bianca de Loryn

Abstract Portable computers and wireless internet have transformed white-collar work and made the digital nomad lifestyle possible, which is to work online from almost anywhere on the planet. This research examines the requirements nomadic online freelancers and location-independent small business owners (digital nomads) have in terms of amenities and community in a coworking space, but also how they are willing to pay for these services. Coworking spaces (shared offices) provide a workspace outside the home as well as networking opportunities with other digital nomads. This study builds on Lucia Parrino's (2015) study on proximity and collaboration in coworking spaces in Milan. The case study is based on interviews with 19 digital nomads and three coworking space employees who lived and worked in Chiang Mai, Thailand, in 2019. The focus lies on the digital nomad experience; the coworking space employees were interviewed to gain an additional perspective on the digital nomad lifestyle. The results demonstrate that there are three distinct groups of digital nomads in terms of workspace usage who nevertheless share a number of expectations as to must-have features of a coworking space. These include ergonomic furniture and a quiet atmosphere, community and networking activities, and the desire for a balance between work and play. Participants also discussed the need to constantly seek out new workspaces as well as alternative payment options in terms of workspace usage, for example via food purchases or room rates. While the fieldwork was conducted before the COVID-19 pandemic, the findings are also relevant for the post-COVID-19 era that has drawn many remote workers out of the capital cities and into regional towns. As such, this research could help businesses attract a wider range of clients to their coworking spaces.

Keywords Coworking space · Digital nomads · Remote work · Online worker · Online freelancer · Community

B. de Loryn (✉)
JCU Cairns, Nguma-bada Campus, Smithfield, QLD, Australia
e-mail: bianca.deloryn@my.jcu.edu.au

© The Author(s), under exclusive license to Springer Nature Singapore Pte Ltd. 2022

T. Chaiechi, J. Wood (eds.), *Community Empowerment, Sustainable Cities, and Transformative Economies*, https://doi.org/10.1007/978-981-16-5260-8_10

1 Introduction

Remote workers have several options when it comes to choosing a workspace, such as one's home or accommodation, coworking spaces, cafes, libraries and other public spaces. The most cost-effective solution is to work from home (or one's accommodation), as there is no extra cost to commute to the workplace and the rent (or room rate) is already paid. However, using one's home or accommodation as office space can result in loneliness and isolation (King, 2017; Moriset, 2013; Orel, 2019; Orel & Dvouletý, 2020; Thompson, 2019a, b). Working from home can also create a vicious cycle in which there is only work and little time for other experiences (Spinuzzi, 2012). This paper focuses on what matters to nomadic online freelancers and location-independent small business owners – or 'digital nomads' – in regard to workspaces away from the home, with a focus on coworking spaces. The aim is to help businesses that are interested in offering coworking services make better informed decisions when it comes to creating a more attractive coworking experience. This research builds on Lucia Parrino's (2015) study on proximity and collaboration in coworking spaces in Milan, Italy, and on Merkel's (2015) paper about the importance of coworking hosts. Some of the coworking spaces in Parrino's study offered not much more than a desk and a chair for their clients. In consequence, coworkers were in geographic proximity to people from a similar background, but they still remained isolated. Other coworking spaces in the same study offered not only spatial but also social proximity, as coworking hosts encouraged their clients to engage in networking activities (Parrino, 2015). Parrino's conclusion – that people who work next to each other need a mediator to develop social ties – points to the importance of active community-building for the success of a coworking space.

This case study explores the coworking space needs of nomadic online freelancers and small business owners in terms of amenities and community. It is based on semi-structured qualitative interviews with 19 digital nomads and three coworking hosts who were living and working in Chiang Mai, Thailand, for at least 3 weeks in 2019. The location independent remote workers mostly had a European, American or Australian background and were freelancers or small business owners. Interviewees were asked how they structured their workday, how important coworking spaces were for them and to name the most important features in a coworking space. For the analysis, an open coding process based on Corbin and Strauss (1990, 2015) was used. Interviewee replies were categorised in regard to how frequently coworking spaces were used by the participants, and later "broken down into specific properties and their dimensions" (Corbin & Strauss, 1990, p. 12). This was complemented by separately coding statements in regard to features and usage of coworking spaces, cafes and working from home and sorting them by frequency in separate tables ("Interviewees by Coworking Space Usage" and "Coworking Spaces, Cafes and Working from Home"). In terms of frequency, the most discussed issue was the need for ergonomic furniture which was mentioned by seven out of 19 digital nomads. This was followed by "a quiet environment" and "community" (in the sense of sharing a space with like-minded people), which was important to six out of 19 interviewees. The research participants also elaborated on payment for workspaces by means of membership fees or indirect payment, for example via their food bill.

In terms of actual coworking space usage, only two participants confirmed they were committed members and would go at least three times per week. For the purposes of this research, these people will be called "all-inclusive nomads" from now on, because they were looking for the full range of coworking services, which included the actual workspace as well as social activities. A larger group of (seven) "independent nomads" preferred to avoid coworking spaces altogether and instead opted to work in cafés, libraries or their accommodation. Ten research participants can be classified as "flexible nomads", as they make use of coworking spaces as well as other workspaces.

I will now proceed to define the term "digital nomads" in the context of this research and explain why Chiang Mai, Thailand, is an important digital nomad hotspot. I will then give an overview over current literature in regard to coworking spaces and the role of community in a coworking context. This is followed by an overview over the methods used for this study and the discussion of the most frequently named issues in regard to coworking space usage, the coworking community and payment for coworking services. This article closes with conclusions, recommendations and suggestions for further research.

2 Defining Digital Nomads, the City of Chiang Mai and Coworking Spaces

The technological advances of the early twenty-first century have helped to transform how people in many white-collar professions live and work. Portable computers, internet-enabled mobile phones, wireless internet and online job opportunities such as teaching English online, online marketing or software programming have given the well-educated middle class of (mostly) Western nations (Haking, 2017, p. 27; Mouratidis, 2018, p. 22; Reichenberger, 2018, p. 369; Thompson, 2018, p. 14) visa-free access to many countries of the world (Henley & Partners, 2021). This allows them to work anywhere and anytime by choice, and not because they are required to do so (Mouratidis, 2018, p. 7). These people go by a number of names, such as "location independent freelancers" (Müller, 2016), "wanderlusting internet entrepreneurs" (Sutherland & Jarrahi, 2017) or simply "digital nomads" (Haking, 2017; Müller, 2016; Reichenberger, 2018). The context behind digital nomadism is that performing the role of an employee in a well-paid nine-to-five job in a centrally located open plan office, while paying off one's home loan (Green, 2020), is not as rewarding as a "a location-independent and self-determined life" (Müller, 2016, p. 344). For digital nomads, other aspects are more important than the maximisation of their income, such as the "quest for holistic freedom in work and leisure" (Reichenberger, 2018). This case study is based Reichenberger's definition, "[d]igital nomads are individuals who achieve location independence by conducting their work in an online environment, transferring this independence to mobility by not consistently working in one designated personal office space but using the possibility to simultaneously work and travel." (Reichenberger, 2018, p. 371). For a digital nomad, "Internet availability, Climate and Natural surroundings, Cost of living, Community, Culture and Language, Accessibility, Timezone, and Safety" (Lee et al., 2019, p. 142: 148) all have a part to play, as this lifestyle is equally defined by work and leisure. Since the beginning of the COVID-19 pandemic, international travel has become more complicated due to travel restrictions and local lockdowns, even for those considered "privileged" due to their "strong" (Mancinelli, 2020, p. 425) or "powerful" (Thompson, 2018, p. 14), mostly Western passports. Some researchers, however, argue that the pandemic could provide an opportunity for independent professionals and for remote employees to try out the digital nomad lifestyle (de Almeida et al., 2021).

Bali in Indonesia (Haking, 2017; Richards, 2015) and Chiang Mai in Thailand (Green, 2020; Sutherland & Jarrahi, 2017; Thompson, 2019a) have become popular digital nomad destinations over the years. Thailand in general is a popular tourist destination in its own right, with 39 million international visitors in 2019. In the same year, 11 million visitors arrived from China, 6.5 million from Europe, 1.4 million from North America and almost 900,000 from Australia and New Zealand (Ministry of Tourism and Sports, 2019). This is important in the context that digital nomads generally travel on tourist visas. In 2019, citizens from 56 countries, including the United States and Australia, were permitted to visit Thailand for 30 days without a visa and for 90 days on a tourist visa (Royal Thai Embassy London, 2019). In terms of Chiang Mai as a digital nomad destination, Thompson argues that the city is "the most popular location with digital nomad communities" (2018, p. 17) as it "responds to the infrastructural needs of mobile subjects and tourism mobilities" (Green, 2020, p. 435), such as affordable accommodation, coworking spaces, restaurants and laptop-friendly cafes.

Traveling is certainly an important aspect of the digital nomad lifestyle, but so is doing digital work. The easiest and most economical solution would be to work from home, as this mode of working does not incur any additional costs. However, outside of pandemic restrictions, especially cafes and coworking spaces are popular with digital nomads as they do not only offer a workspace away from the home, but also, for some, an escape from loneliness and isolation (King, 2017; Moriset, 2013; Orel, 2019; Orel & Dvouletý, 2020; Thompson, 2019a, b).

Coworking is "the practice of working individually in a shared environment" (Gandini, 2015, p. 195). It is "the practice of working alongside one another in flexible, shared work settings" (Merkel, 2015, pp. 122) or "working on different projects in the same shared space" (Spinuzzi, 2012, p. 417). Coworking as a business is a relatively new development which began in the early 2000s in the bohemian environment of the San Francisco arts scene (Gandini, 2015).[1] The first two coworking spaces, *Spiral Muse* and *Hat Factory*, were opened in 2005 and 2006, respectively (Neuberg, 2021). The Coworking Wiki (2008) "a free, community-owned and operated resource for everyone involved or interested in the world of coworking" explains that *Hat Factory* was a "venue (with good coffee and wifi!) for independent consultants, workers, students, social geeks, vloggers and cultured folks to come work, relax, collaborate". These coworking pioneers have triggered an avalanche of similar workspaces around the world, with *Fishburners* opening in Brisbane in 2011 (Fishburners.org) and *Punspace*, the first coworking space in Chiang Mai, Thailand, launching in 2013 (Punspace, 2021). To give an example for pricing and services, coworking spaces in Chiang Mai in late 2019 offered memberships which included access to workspaces and social activities ranging from day passes for 189–289 Thai Baht (AUD $8.13–$12.43) to 24/7 monthly memberships for 3299–3899 Thai Baht (AUD $142–168). Included in the membership was a shared desk ("hot desk") and access to a shared kitchen with a fridge, free coffee and biscuits. There were quiet workspaces as well as "social" spaces, such as a garden or kitchen. In addition, at least one restaurant or café was located directly outside the building or within walking distance. Some coworking spaces offer rooms for rent nearby or on the same premises, which transforms the business into a "coworking and coliving space" or a 'co-living space' (Bouncken et al., 2016; von Zumbusch & Lalicic, 2020, p. 446).

There are two aspects that make coworking stand out from regular office work: Firstly, coworking space users do not necessarily work for the same company. Many coworkers are freelancers, micro-business owners or self-employed, though not necessarily digital nomads (Parrino, 2015). Instead, in these spaces, coworkers "operate as 'complementary' figures rather than potential competitors," writes Gandini (2015, p. 198). The other key difference between a coworking space and a "regular" office is the coworking host. According to Merkel (2015), coworking hosts may be the owners or operators of the business; sometimes there are also "professional community managers" (p. 122). A coworking host is the crucial link that turns people working alongside each other into a community of like-minded spirits, that is willing to share and collaborate (Merkel, 2015). Coworking hosts are curators of a community that needs "to be pro-actively developed" as this is "unlikely to happen by chance" (Brown, 2017, p. 121), and they need to encourage people to create "collaborative relationships" (Parrino, 2015, p. 269). In this research, community is defined in two ways: (1) working together in a place that offers social spaces such as a kitchen, a courtyard or a garden where informal networking is encouraged (Spinuzzi, 2012), but also (2) social events curated by the coworking hosts, such as networking lunches or evening activities (see Table 4 for more examples).

To sum up this literature review, the digital nomad lifestyle is defined by a holistic outlook on work and travel, with Chiang Mai serving as an important, though

[1] In contrast, "virtual coworking" is working together on a project in a team whose members are located around the world (Tucker et al., 2005).

temporary, base for location independent remote workers. Coworking spaces have a role to play in the digital nomad experience, especially when it comes to networking with other location independent free lancers and small business owners. In the following section I will describe the methods used in this research before I discuss the research outcomes in detail.

3 Methods

My social constructivist worldview is based on the observation that "[m]embers of a society together invent the properties of the world" (Kim, 2001, p. 3). Meaning is "co-created between the researcher and the participant" with the interview creating a "fusion of ideas" between the interviewer and interviewees (Vandermause & Fleming, 2011, pp. 369–370). A semi-structured qualitative approach was chosen in order to "offer a balance between flexibility and control while giving reassurance that the aims of the study could be achieved" (Walker, 2011, p. 20). The study is based on 22 interviews with 19 digital nomads and three coworking hosts. All participants lived in Chiang Mai for at least 3 weeks in 2019. The interviews were audio recorded in November and December 2019 in membership-based coworking spaces, coworking cafes that did not charge membership fees, and in "regular" cafes and restaurants in Chiang Mai, Thailand. Seven interviews were conducted via video conferencing, as the researcher and some of the participants had already left Chiang Mai at the time of the interview. The interviewees were from the Americas, Europe and Australia; one digital nomad was from the Philippines and one coworking host was from Thailand (see Table 1 for an overview over the research participants). The age range among the digital nomads was 25 to 49 years, with a median age of 32 years. The coworking hosts were aged in their 30s. The group consisted of 12 women and 10 men. There were no remote employees among the digital nomads; all were either freelancers or small business owners. The professions were gendered in the sense that only the women were involved in teaching, accounting, psychology, writing services and graphic design. Three of the men were freelance computer programmers. Both women and men offered event planning, web design and photography services or sold goods online. The interviews were explorative in nature and discussed a number of topics in regard to how location independent remote workers live and work. This included questions about daily routines and the importance of coworking spaces, such as, "How important are coworking spaces for you? If so, how often do you use them?" and, "What is the most important thing about a coworking space for you?". The names have been replaced by pseudonyms in order to protect the confidentiality of the research participants. The professions and nationalities have not been changed.

For this paper, I used open coding as developed by Corbin and Strauss (Corbin & Strauss, 1990, p. 12; 2015, p. 220). I started the analysis by categorising interviewee replies based on usage of coworking spaces (see Table 2). In a second step I coded the interviews based on statements made in regard to (1) membership-based

Table 1 Research participants

#	Pseudonym	Gender	Age	Nationality	Employment status	Current profession
1	Cara	F	25	Australia (has UK work permit)	Freelancer	Photographer
2	Sophie	F	26	United States	Freelancer/ small business owner	1. Branding and web design, 2. online retailer
3	Katherine	F	27	Australia	Freelancer	Journalist/writer
4	Emily	F	30	United Kingdom	Small business owner	Online retailer
5	Yasmin	F	31	Germany	Small business owner	1. Online retailer, 2. co-owner of a tax accountancy
6	Lorain	F	31	United States	Freelancer	1. Event planner, 2. online English teacher
7	Lola	F	32	Brazil	Freelancer	Online psychologist
8	Amanda	F	34	Finland	Freelancer	Graphic designer
9	Marcelina	F	39	Germany, Poland	Small business owner	Co-owner of a media company
10	Sarah	F	39	Philippines	Freelancer	Journalist/writer
11	Jessica	F	42	United States (ethnic Chinese-American)	Freelancer	Online English teacher
12	Fabiano	M	25	Italy	Freelancer	Computer programmer
13	Sven	M	26	Italy	Freelancer	Computer programmer
14	Andreas	M	28	Germany	Small business owner	Online retailer
15	Brad	M	33	Canada (ethnic Chinese-Canadian)	Small business owner	1. Online retailer, 2. ecommerce coach
16	Daniel	M	37	Australia	Freelancer	Computer programmer
17	Markus	M	38	Germany	Freelancer/ small business owner	1. Photographer, 2. online courses for photographers
18	Thomas	M	39	Germany	Freelancer/ small business owner	1. Podcast creator, 2. event planner, 3. architect
19	Yoshi	M	49	United States, Japan	Freelancer	Web designer
20	Lamai	M	30s	Thailand	Full-time employee	Coworking host
21	Jack	M	30s	Ireland	Remote employee	Coworking host
22	Karsten	M	30s	Germany	Co-owner	Coworking host

Table 2 Interviewees by coworking space usage

User status (Number of participants)	Workspace usage	Number of participants
All-inclusive nomads - committed coworking space users **(2)**	Regular users, going at least three times per week	**(2)**
Flexible nomads - *sometimes use coworking spaces (10)*	Depending on the location[a]	**(7)**
	Uses coworking spaces for other reasons (e.g. variety)	**(3)**
Independent nomads - *do not use coworking spaces (7)*	Working in different locations, such as accommodation, cafes, (free) coworking cafes	**(4)**
	Work from their accommodation only	**(2)**
	Former coworking space user, now working in cafes only (= more variety)	**(1)**
Total: (19)		**Total: (19)**

[a]Some places might have affordable coworking spaces, while others might have laptop-friendly cafes

Table 3 Coworking spaces, cafes and working from home – frequently mentioned topics sorted by frequency

Working in (Membership-based) coworking spaces	Working in cafes or (free) coworking cafes	Working from home
Ergonomic furniture (e.g., chairs, standing desks) (7)	Prefer to pay for food or coffee instead of membership (4)	Goes to networking activities that are published on Facebook (1)
Quiet environment (6)		Quiet environment (1)
Participating in the community, "the social atmosphere," social/networking activities (6)	More variety (4)	No need to commute (1)
Goes to coworking spaces for meetups/networking activities (5)	Do not mind paying a little more for food in a coworking café or for a special coworking event (3)	Working at home is free (1)
A balance between quiet time or quiet places for work and social activities is important (4)	Doesn't feel like an office, "casual feeling" (2)	
Too much socialising can detract from work, don't feel very productive there (3)		
Meeting other people from the same industry (3)		
Should have good (wireless) internet (3)	Should have good (wireless) internet (1)	

coworking spaces, (2) cafes and free coworking cafes and (3) working from home. The responses where then sorted by frequency. Table 3 shows the most popular issues raised, whereas Table 5 describes other topics that were mentioned by one or two interviewees only. Issues mentioned by coworking hosts have been coded separately as they provide a perspective that was different from the digital nomad worldview. In the following section, I will discuss the most frequently named aspects and features that digital nomads have mentioned in terms of coworking space usage.

4 Discussion

When it comes to their preferred workplace, all but two digital nomads in this case study do not permanently work from their accommodation, even though working from home is "free". Out of 19 digital nomad interviewees, ten flexible nomads stated that they would use a range of different workspaces, which included cafes, libraries and coworking spaces. In addition, I interviewed two all-inclusive nomads who stated that they were committed coworking space members (at least three times per week). The remaining seven independent nomads generally avoided coworking spaces, with only two of them stating that they exclusively worked from home. In terms of coworking space usage by gender, the three coworking hosts reported that the majority of their clients were male (host #1) and that the male-to-female ratio was even (hosts #2 and #3). Host #3 added that other coworking spaces in Chiang Mai seemed to be more male-dominated than the business he was working at. This points to Chiang Mai coworking spaces being somewhat more inviting to male users, who, after all, have found their niche in professions that do not need a lot of verbal communication (unlike the female English teachers, for example). The topics that were mentioned most frequently in regard to features and amenities were the need for ergonomic furniture (such as comfortable chairs and tables) and a quiet environment, participating in the community and social activities, and the importance of finding a balance between work and social activities (see Table 3). Finally, a number of other factors were mentioned, such as the "nomadic urge", local factors such as laptop-friendliness of a place and alternatives to charging "direct" membership fees.

4.1 Ergonomic Furniture and a Quiet Environment

The most discussed topic in terms of coworking spaces was ergonomic furniture (see Table 3). It should seem obvious that coworking spaces should have comfortable chairs and tables. However, according to the research participant with the pseudonym 'Lola', a psychologist from Brazil, only a few of the coworking spaces she has seen have ergonomic chairs. This is also confirmed by online-shop owner 'Emily' from the United Kingdom. Emily could be considered a flexible nomad who chooses her workspaces based on local considerations. During her stay in Bali earlier in 2019, Emily signed up for a coworking space which left a lot to be desired. According to Emily, "to work there, which we did a few of times, was awful. The chairs were awful, Wi-Fi was awful, so loud." Other ergonomic must-haves are "good tables" (Sven) and standing desks (Markus). Three participants mentioned they needed good internet. Aside from ergonomics, the second-most named issue is a quiet work environment. Katherine, a travel writer from Australia and an "all-inclusive nomad", said she needs

> a very quiet space where I can be productive. Like having a productive space is the most important thing for me because I find it really difficult to get into that focus zone. Once I find my space it's like, heaven.

This is also supported by Markus ("I like it to have it a bit quieter and rather talk to people on the meetups") and coworking host #3, who declared that a "quiet [space] and good seating and, not too cold a/c" were essential for his business. Sometimes, however, people need a quiet space just for themselves. "Like, if you have meetings, which require a silent environment. Sometimes the home is the only place where you actually can really do it," said Sven from Italy, a computer programmer. This is also supported by the Lola (a psychologist) and Lorain and Jennifer (English teachers) who at times also need a quiet, private space in order to talk to their customers, and this quiet space is currently their apartment.

4.2 Community and Social Activities

As mentioned in the literature review, digital nomads are only short term visitors in Chiang Mai, Thailand. According to Fabiano, a computer programmer from Italy, who generally travels alone, becoming a member of a coworking space can alleviate loneliness. Fabiano, who could be classified as a flexible nomad, said that trying to work from his apartment was not for him:

> I initially thought, okay, working from home, perfectly fine. Doesn't cost anything. I have anything I need at home [. . .] and after work I see my friends, and everything [is] fine. And then at some point I figured out, wow, that really sucks.

Sven, another computer programmer from Italy, is also looking for company when he arrives at a new place. Sven adds that coworking spaces are a good place to go even for those who find it hard to connect with others. "It doesn't matter how introvert you are, you will automatically meet new people there. Because it is just part of that community," he said. Joining a coworking space offers instant access to a community of people who engage in online work. Community "refers to the possible relational implications of the co-location of workers within the same space [. . .] in which relationships and interpersonal interaction can develop, not necessarily with effects in terms of professional relations and exchange of knowledge" (Parrino, 2015). This means that coworking space users may have a financial benefit by becoming a part of the community, but this is not the primary reason why they look for company. Yasmin, an accountant and online retailer from Germany, is one of only two all-inclusive nomads in this research. She confirmed that she and her partner generally used coworking spaces about five times a week, and "[w]e use the

Table 4 Community activities in Chiang Mai coworking spaces in 2019

Weekly	Bi-weekly or monthly	One-time only events
Networking lunches with preordered (and prepaid) food	One-hour introductory Thai lesson	Presentations/workshops by coworking space users
Meetups for people with online shops on Amazon.com	After-work drinks (soft-drinks and alcohol paid for via an honesty system)	
Evening networking function in collaboration with a Facebook group[a]	Movie nights	

[a]Free event at a (free) coworking café, drinks were sold at the licensed bar

coworking spaces for the community. Community plays a major role for us." Emily from the United Kingdom added that the informal networking in social spaces matters to her as well, such as

> just talking to someone while you get a cup of coffee. Or, I don't know, me and my husband having a conversation about something and there is someone joining in. That, to me, is why I go. I don't go there to be in a silent bubble, where I just, I probably, if I did that, I'd be at home to do that.

In total, six out of 19 digital nomads explicitly stated that the community aspects of a coworking space were important for them. Markus (a photographer) and Thomas (a podcaster and event planner), both from Germany, said they enjoyed sharing a workspace with people from a similar line of work. This is also confirmed by Brad, an online retailer from Canada, who said that "coworking spaces, also, the environment, everyone is working. And it really pushes you to, you know, get, first of all, get ideas, but also execute those ideas." More than that, some coworking spaces see social events such as regular "power lunches" or after-work drinks as a part of their core activities. Five female digital nomads stated they would only use coworking spaces for social events, and sometimes they would only go if friends were going as well. These female nomads have no interest in using the coworking spaces for work. Instead, they go there to meet people. Emily from the United Kingdom explained that "[w]e went to a few [coworking spaces] in Canggu and Bali, which we had really good experiences with. We actually selected one because of its events, and not because of the work." In order to do their daily work, though, they realised that "the cafes in Canggu were so good that we just worked in a café and then went to the events [in the coworking spaces]." Emily added that this particular coworking space offered a "social membership [...] so you could just go to the events. Very clever." In Chiang Mai, Emily did not sign up for a coworking space because she found social events via other sources, such as local Facebook groups.

4.3 Coworking Spaces – The Importance of Finding a Balance

Several interviewees lamented that coworking spaces did not always succeed in providing a balance between creating a quiet workplace as well as a sense of community. Coworking host #2 mentioned that not all coworking spaces encouraged community building, as "[s]ome places I have been to, they don't offer community, they don't try to promote it. And people sometimes arrive, and they just don't meet people, and they kind of, they miss out." Parrino (2015) observed similar challenges in coworking spaces in Milan. Even though people were working next to each other, they did not try get to know their fellow workers or organise community activities themselves without the intervention of a coworking host. This was only different in places where social activities were already being offered. Too much community, on the other hand, may also have its downsides. Sven from Italy mentioned that some coworking spaces were going a bit too far in this respect. He reflected that, "I mean at some point [. . .] I was really thinking 'wow, I am only coming to the coworking space to meet my friends, and then I need to go home later to do work'". This was echoed by Lola from Brazil, an independent nomad who generally did not use coworking spaces. Lola also did not think that she was productive at coworking spaces and preferred to work in cafes instead. Reminiscing on her experience in a coworking space in Ko Lanta, Thailand, all-inclusive nomad Yasmin from Germany stated that "they have events almost every night. In a way you almost fear that if you don't participate, you are somehow excluded [from the community]. But I liked it." These comments demonstrate that it can be difficult to find a balance between quiet work and community aspects. In the end, it is up to the coworking host to encourage an environment that creates the kind of community they envision for their business.

4.4 The Nomadic Urge, Local Factors and Membership Fees

According to Brad from Canada, an important part of his nomadic life is to "keep it all fresh". Loyalty to a certain workspace or business for him is replaced by a spirit of exploration. Six of the digital nomads in this study have subscribed to a similar outlook on their work week: Cara, a photographer from Australia, generally starts her day by working at her hostel, followed by lunch at a café, then back to her hostel in the afternoon. Lorain from the United States said she works in three different places per week, whereas Sven from Italy declared that it "gets repetitive being in the same place all over again." However, he added that "I would just consider going for a few days or a week or so, to a coworking space, if I like it." There is a solution to this matter that has already been tried and proven in Chiang Mai and that seems to work at least for Sophie from the United States. Sophie, who sells meditation products online, explicitly commended one coworking business in Chiang Mai because it had several branches, among them one "social" coworking space with a garden, and another, "quieter" branch also within walking distance. Even one of the all-inclusive nomads uses coworking spaces "only" three times per week, which means that a committed coworking space user like her works elsewhere on a regular basis. Apart from avoiding repetitiveness in one's work week, there are also local factors that come into play. Fabiano from Italy, for example, uses a coworking space in Sofia, Bulgaria, but not in Chiang Mai. Fabiano said that

> [in Sofia, Bulgaria] they don't have so many cafés that are laptop friendly and have, you know, power outlets, internet, everything you need. In Chiang Mai it is definitely the opposite. It's full of cafes where you can work from. It is a beautiful place for nomads to do work. And a lot of café are just like coworking spaces. That's why I basically don't need a coworking space right now. So, I rather just save the money and, also, I like it more to work in cafes because it doesn't feel as [like an] office.

Saving money was also an issue for Amanda from Finland, who used a coworking-coliving space during her 2019 stay in Chiang Mai. She said she did not generally go to a coworking space when in Canada, for example, because she found the membership fees in Canada too expensive. In line with Amanda's statement, the majority of the group (six interviewees) preferred to pay for their workspace not via membership fees but rather by other means, such as via their food and drinks bill. Some of them were also willing to pay a little more than in a "regular" café. I met Fabiano and Sven in a coworking café that served upmarket food and drinks, and Cara visited an upmarket café in Chiang Mai because a local expat had organised a "coworking day" at this location via Facebook earlier. Another business offered combined coliving and coworking. By paying the room rate, both Amanda from Finland and Andreas from Germany received access to the in-house coworking space. This shows that financing a coworking space via a membership model might not be the most attractive option for all potential coworking customers. Table 5 sums up a number of issues that only one or two participants have addressed in regard to working in cafes, coworking spaces and at home. Overall, though, many of the research participants shared a similar outlook on key points such as ergonomic furniture, a quiet environment and the importance of finding a middle ground between quiet work and community activities.

5 Conclusions and Recommendations

Finding a comfortable workspace outside their home (or their temporary accommodation) is an important issue for nomadic online freelancers and small business owners, who also go by the name of "digital nomads". This article has discussed coworking space needs of digital nomads in terms of amenities and community and the way they are willing to pay for these services. Twenty-two research participants who originated mostly from North America, Europe and Australia were interviewed in a qualitative, semi-structured approach. After using open coding based on Corbin and Strauss (1990, 2015) digital nomads were categorized in three different groups: (1) independent nomads, who generally do not use coworking spaces, (2) flexible

Table 5 Coworking spaces, cafes and working from home – other issues, sorted by frequency

Working in (membership-based) coworking spaces	Working in cafes or (free) coworking cafes
Don't mind that membership fees are charged (2)	You can have your food on the table while your work (1)
Variety: Some coworking spaces have several branches or can be used as alternative to working in cafes (2)	Quiet environment (1)
Nice to have: 'Skype rooms'/enclosed spaces for calls to clients or for teaching (2)	Some cafes are just like coworking spaces (1)
Aircon (2)	Good food (1)
Nice to have rooms for audio or video editing (1)	Ergonomic furniture is important (1)
Not sure where to store belongings when going out for a meal (1)	Ergonomic furniture is not important (1)
One should be able to hire external monitors (1)	Escape loneliness (1)
If they don't serve food, restaurants or cafes should be nearby (1)	
Some coworking spaces do not even have free coffee (1)	
Should not be too crowded (1)	
Going to a coworking spaces helps create a routine (1)	
Coworking spaces are an alternative if there is an internet outage in their accommodation (1)	
Escape loneliness, good for introverts (1)	

nomads, who see a coworking space as one of several options, and (3) all-inclusive nomads, who are willing to pay for the full range of services that a membership-based coworking space provides.

This research focused on (in-person) coworking spaces as an example for workspaces outside the home. Coworking spaces offer a desk to work from as well as access to networking opportunities with other remote workers. When it comes to desired coworking space features, ergonomic furniture was an important aspect for some, but not all of the research participants. Of similar importance was the desire to find a balance between the social aspects of the coworking space experience, such as community and networking activities (networking lunches, after-work drinks etc.), but also the need to work in a quiet environment. Some participants stressed that for some tasks, such as meetings with clients, working from one's accommodation is the best solution, as it provides the quiet surroundings and the privacy needed for some tasks. In terms of payment for workspaces, the research participants generally preferred to pay indirectly for their workspaces, for example via their food bill or other services such as the room rate in a coliving-coworking space. Finally, the "nomadic urge" of the digital nomads should not be overlooked as it resulted in less customer loyalty in terms of workspaces in general.

In terms of recommendations for current or future coworking businesses, coworking hosts might want to discuss ergonomics as well as the desired balance between community building and a quiet environment with their clients. This could help to identify the needs of the local coworking community. It might also be beneficial to find out which community activities the majority of current coworking customers are interested in, also in view of attracting the larger group of prospective clients that are mainly interested in community activities. Coworking spaces might want to offer different membership levels such as social memberships for the larger group of flexible nomads who are primarily looking for networking activities and who do not need access to the workspaces on a daily basis. Finally, in terms of the "nomadic urge", it might be beneficial for businesses in a similar space to collaborate in order to make it easier for prospective clients to use different workspaces.

In regard to opportunities for further research it would be interesting to investigate how much digital nomads are willing to pay for full-time and social membership fees and, in regard to the gendered nature of some professions, if and how coworking spaces could be made more attractive to female users.

Funding This research was funded by a Postgraduate Research Scholarship from James Cook University, Cairns.

References

Bouncken, R. B., Clauss, T., & Reuschl, A. J. (2016). *Coworking-spaces in Asia: A business model design perspective*. SMS.

Brown, J. (2017). Curating the "third place"? Coworking and the mediation of creativity. *Geoforum, 82*, 112–126. https://doi.org/10.1016/j.geoforum.2017.04.006

Corbin, J. M., & Strauss, A. (1990). Grounded theory research: Procedures, canons, and evaluative criteria. *Qualitative Sociology*, 3–21.

Corbin, J. M., & Strauss, A. L. (2015). *Basics of qualitative research: Techniques and procedures for developing grounded theory* (4th ed.). Sage.

Coworking Wiki. (2008). Retrieved from https://wiki.coworking.org/w/page/16583854/HatFactory

de Almeida, M. A., Correia, A., Schneider, D., & de Souza, J. M. (2021). *COVID-19 as opportunity to test digital nomad lifestyle*. Paper presented at the proceedings of the 2021 IEEE 24th international conference on computer supported cooperative work in design.

Fishburners.org. *Fishburners – Where startups grow: From UQ to Silicon Valley and Back again*. Retrieved from https://web.library.uq.edu.au/files/50802/Copy%20of%20Marc%20-%20Fishburners%20Pitch%20Deck%20%281%29.pdf

Gandini, A. (2015). The rise of coworking spaces: A literature review. *Ephemera: Theory & Politics in Organization, 15*(1), 193–205.

Green, P. (2020). Disruptions of self, place and mobility: Digital nomads in Chiang Mai, Thailand. *Mobilities, 15*(3), 431–445. https://doi.org/10.1080/17450101.2020.1723253

Haking, J. (2017). *Digital nomad lifestyle: A field study in Bali.* Master of Science, KTH Royal Institute of Technology, Stockholm.

Henley & Partners. (2021). *Henley & Partners passport index.* Retrieved from https://www.henleypassportindex.com/passport

Kim, B. (2001). Social constructivism. *Emerging Perspectives on Learning, Teaching, and Technology, 1*(1), 16.

King, S. (2017). Co-working is not about workspace – It's about feeling less lonely. *Harvard Business Review, 16*(1), 2–6.

Lee, A., Toombs, A. L., Erickson, I., Nemer, D., Ho, Y.-A., Jo, E., & Guo, Z. (2019). The social infrastructure of co-spaces: Home, work, and sociable places for digital nomads. *Proceedings of the ACM on Human-Computer Interaction, 3*(CSCW), 1–23.

Mancinelli, F. (2020). Digital nomads: Freedom, responsibility and the neoliberal order. *Information Technology & Tourism*, 1–21. https://doi.org/10.1007/s40558-020-00174-2
Merkel, J. (2015). Coworking in the city. *Ephemera, 15*(1), 121–139.
Ministry of Tourism and Sports. (2019). *Tourism receipts from international tourist arrivals*, January–December 2019. Retrieved from https://www.mots.go.th/more_news_new.php?cid=615
Moriset, B. (2013). *Building new places of the creative economy. The rise of coworking spaces.*
Mouratidis, G. (2018). *Digital nomads: Travel, remote work and alternative lifestyles.* Master of Applied Cultural Analysis, Lund University, Lund.
Müller, A. (2016). The digital nomad: Buzzword or research category? *Transnational Social Review*, 344–348. https://doi.org/10.1080/21931674.2016.1229930
Neuberg, B. (2021). *The start of coworking* (From the guy that started it). Retrieved from http://codinginparadise.org/ebooks/html/blog/start_of_coworking.html
Orel, M. (2019). Coworking environments and digital nomadism: Balancing work and leisure whilst on the move. *World Leisure Journal, 61*(3), 215–227. https://doi.org/10.1080/16078055.2019.1639275
Orel, M., & Dvouletý, O. (2020). Transformative changes and developments of the coworking model: A narrative review. *Technological Progress, Inequality and Entrepreneurship*, 9–27. https://doi.org/10.1007/978-3-030-26245-7_2
Parrino, L. (2015). Coworking: Assessing the role of proximity in knowledge exchange. *Knowledge Management Research & Practice, 13*(3), 261–271. https://doi.org/10.1057/kmrp.2013.47
Punspace. (2021). *First coworking space in Chiang Mai since 2013.* Retrieved from https://www.instagram.com/punspace/?hl=en
Reichenberger, I. (2018). Digital nomads – A quest for holistic freedom in work and leisure. *Annals of Leisure Research*, 364–380. https://doi.org/10.1080/11745398.2017.1358098
Richards, G. (2015). The new global nomads: Youth travel in a globalizing world. *Tourism Recreation Research, 40*(3), 340–352.
Royal Thai Embassy London. (2019). *Tourist Visa*. Retrieved from https://london.thaiembassy.org/en/publicservice/84451-tourist-visa
Spinuzzi, C. (2012). Working alone together: Coworking as emergent collaborative activity. *Journal of Business and Technical Communication, 26*(4), 399–441. https://doi.org/10.1177%2F1050651912444070
Sutherland, W., & Jarrahi, M. H. (2017). The gig economy and information infrastructure: The case of the digital nomad community. *Proceedings of the ACM on Human-Computer Interaction, 97.* https://doi.org/10.1145/3134732
Thompson, B. Y. (2018). Digital nomads: Employment in the online gig economy. *Glocalism: Journal of Culture, Politics and Innovation*, 1. https://doi.org/10.12893/gjcpi.2018.1.11
Thompson, B. Y. (2019a). The digital nomad lifestyle: (Remote) work/leisure balance, privilege, and constructed community. *International Journal of the Sociology of Leisure*, 1–16. https://doi.org/10.1007/s41978-018-00030-y
Thompson, B. Y. (2019b). 'I get my lovin' on the run': Digital nomads, constant travel, and nurturing romantic relationships. In A. Gorman-Murray & C. J. Nash (Eds.), *The geographies of digital sexualities*. https://doi.org/10.1007/978-981-13-6876-9_5
Tucker, E., Kao, T., & Verma, N. (2005). Next-generation talent management. *Business Credit, 107*, 20–27.
Vandermause, R. K., & Fleming, S. E. (2011). Philosophical hermeneutic interviewing. *International Journal of Qualitative Methods, 10*(4), 367–377.
von Zumbusch, J. S. H., & Lalicic, L. (2020). The role of co-living spaces in digital nomads' well-being. *Information Technology & Tourism, 22*(3), 439–453. https://doi.org/10.1007/s40558-020-00182-2
Walker, W. (2011). Hermeneutic inquiry: Insights into the process of interviewing. *Nurse Researcher, 18*(2).

Growing Strangler Figs in Coconuts. Ideation of Carbon-Negative, Living Infrastructure

Damian Settle and Lucas Cernusak

Abstract Carbon-negative, Living Infrastructure has the potential to generate revenue, draw down atmospheric carbon and benefit both human health and biodiversity whilst cooling cities and strengthening urban climate resilience. Living Root Bridges (LRBs) are the most well-known examples of living infrastructure. LRBs are functional pedestrian bridges formed from the living aerial roots of Strangler fig trees (*Ficus* subgen. *Urostigma*). Unfortunately, the 50–100 year gestation period required to 'grow' a LRB installation renders their integration into urban spaces untenable. However, it may be possible to significantly reduce LRB construction times if conditions favourable to inter-specific anastomosis are provided. A significant challenge is to first identify a growth media capable of providing moisture and nutrients whilst Strangler figs are suspended supra-situ.

Whole coconuts are readily available across the tropics. Coir fibres extracted from the mesocarp of coconut husks have proven to be a suitable growth media for containerised plant production. However, no previous studies have investigated the potential of using whole, unhusked coconuts as plant growth containers.

This study investigates the potential for whole coconuts to be used as growth containment units for a common Strangler fig, *Ficus benjamina*. Strangler fig cuttings were grown in five whole-coconut treatments; high-quality potting mix, coarse sand, retted coconuts, perforated and unperforated coconuts. No significant between-treatment difference was observed in the three parameters studied, diametric growth, leaf count and mass accumulation. Whole, untreated coconuts are a suitable medium for the production of Strangler figs. The widespread availability of whole coconuts makes them an ideal growth containment option for accelerated construction of ultra-low-cost, carbon-negative, living infrastructure.

The integration of carbon-negative, self-repairing Living Infrastructure into urban spaces represents a low-cost opportunity to provide climate-resilient infrastructure whilst simultaneously cooling cities and enabling greater access to green spaces.

D. Settle (✉) · L. Cernusak
College of Science and Engineering, James Cook University, Cairns, QLD, Australia
e-mail: damian.settle@my.jcu.edu.au; lucas.cernusak@jcu.edu.au

© The Author(s), under exclusive license to Springer Nature Singapore Pte Ltd. 2022
T. Chaiechi, J. Wood (eds.), *Community Empowerment, Sustainable Cities, and Transformative Economies*, https://doi.org/10.1007/978-981-16-5260-8_11

Living Infrastructure instillations in tropical urban spaces such as Cairns or Singapore may also have the potential to become popular tourism attractions.

Keywords Living Root Bridge · Strangler fig · *Urostigma* · Coconut · Living infrastructure

1 Introduction

Cities are the primary drivers of anthropogenic climate change, generating around 75% of all global climate emissions. Cities are simultaneously also disproportionately at risk from the effects of anthropogenic climate change (World Bank, 2010; Seto et al., 2014; UN-HABITAT, 2016; Reckien et al., 2017; Pervin et al., 2020). Accelerated rise in sea levels and increases in ocean surface temperatures will lead to intensification in the frequency and severity of tropical and extratropical cyclones, larger extreme waves and storm surges, altered precipitation and ocean acidification (Nicholls, 1995; Hunt & Watkiss, 2011; Un-Habitat, 2021). Urban heating due to anthropogenic climate change already claims over 150,000 lives annually (Patz et al., 2005), with this number expected to increase 12 ~ 15 times by the 2050s (Varquez et al., 2020).

By 2050 some 68% of the world's population will live in urban areas (United Nations, 2018). Some 2 Billion of these will suffer chronic disadvantage and be forced into informal settlements across the most fragile urban spaces, such as mountainsides or floodplains (United Nations, 2018, 2019; Satterthwaite et al., 2020). These disadvantaged urban communities will bear the brunt of climate change in the form of floods, landslides, and extreme heat (Nicholls, 1995; McGranahan et al., 2012; United Nations, 2019). Disadvantaged urban communities are also disproportionately impacted by urban heating (urban heat island effect) due to limited access to urban green spaces; with which daily contact is recognised as vital for human health and economic growth (Bowler et al., 2010a, b; Gill et al., 2018; Włodarczyk-Marciniak et al., 2020). Infrastructure assets to the value of US$35 trillion will be exposed to flooding annually (World Bank, 2010; Un-Habitat, 2021). Concurrently, spending on infrastructure must increase from around $3 trillion a year to over $8 trillion by 2030 if we are to achieve the Paris Agreement's <2 °C climate change goal.

Developing and financing climate-resilient infrastructure is critical to maintaining communities and economies' integrity (Harding et al., 2017; Ambrosio et al., 2020; Satterthwaite et al., 2020). However, increases in temperature, precipitation, relative humidity, and atmospheric carbon concentrations will accelerate infrastructure deterioration. Even concrete carbonation-induced corrosion risk, is expected to rise by 400% (Wang et al., 2012; Nasr et al., 2020). As such, all new urban infrastructure projects will be increasingly required to consider climate resilience capacity and human health effect considerations in their tender, greatly inflating project delivery and ongoing maintenance costs (Bivens, 2014; Nasr et al., 2020). It is highly unlikely that even moderately disadvantaged communities will benefit from future investment in increasingly expensive, climate-resilient municipal infrastructure.

Thus, there is a critical need for radical innovation in tropical municipal infrastructure to provide low-cost, climate-resilient options to those who need it most, whilst simultaneously identifying innovative methods to cool cities and provide greater access to green spaces.

Carbon-negative, Living Infrastructure is a low-cost and inherently sustainable technology with the potential to simultaneously address many of these problems. The establishment of Living Infrastructure instalments, such as LRB in urban areas, can draw down and fix significant amounts of atmospheric carbon in unused, empty void spaces (e.g., above streets, carparks, buildings) that are entirely overlooked as suitable for tree growth. Payments from carbon sequestration and tourism combined with savings achieved from ecosystem services and other flow-on benefits, may provide transformative economic opportunities for tropical communities.

Unfortunately, the multi-decade construction times required to construct LRBs, renders any potential investment untenable. If construction, times can be reduced to a reasonable time frame; however, the benefits listed above could be realised and transformational change to urban spaces made possible.

This study aims to use an ideation process to explore the opportunity to accelerate the construction of low-cost, carbon-negative, Living Infrastructure by using whole coconuts as plant-growth containment units. Accordingly, the paper is structured as follows. Section 1.1 provides an overview of Living Root Bridges, Sect. 1.2 introduces Strangler figs, Sect. 1.3 highlights the abundance of Strangler figs in tropical urban spaces, Sect. 1.4 discusses anastomosis in Strangler figs. Section 1.5 discusses the attributes that highlight whole coconuts' potential for use as low-cost growth containment units for Strangler figs, from which carbon-negative infrastructure is formed.

1.1 Living Root Bridges – Background Information

As found in India (Fig. 1a, b) and Indonesia (Fig. 1c), LRBs are the most well-known examples of living infrastructure. LRBs are functional suspension bridges constructed entirely from intertwined, fused, living aerial roots of Strangler figs (*Ficus* subgenus *Urostigma* (*Moreaceae*)). LRBs are both a man-made technology and a specialised form of horticulture. In both countries, LRBs are typically located above remote, seasonally flooded rivers or fast-flowing water. LRBs can span over 50 m and support the weight of more than 100 people (Shankar, 2015; Chaudhuri et al., 2016; Ludwig et al., 2019; Middleton et al., 2020).

Constructed without modern engineering skills or equipment over a period of 50–100 years, LRBs survive for centuries (Yule, 1844; Chaudhuri et al., 2016; Ludwig et al., 2019). Not only are LRBs demonstrably longer-lasting than contemporary construction materials, they are carbon negative, that is, they absorb CO_2. Rather than generating CO_2 emissions like steel and concrete, LRB reduces CO_2.

Fig. 1 (**a**) a Double Decker LRB in Nongriat village and (**b**) Mawlynnong village in East Khasi Hills district, Mehalaya, India; (**c**) a LRB with younger aerial roots in the foreground, Bayang Utara District, Pesisir Selatan Regency, West Sumatra, Indonesia. Photos by (**a**) and (**b**) P. Jeganathan, distributed under a CC-BY 2.0 license, (**c**) sumbarprov.go.id, distributed under a CC BY-SA 4.0 license

Table 1 CO_2 emissions per cubic meter of material

Material	CO_2 kg m^3	
Steel (low carbon)	25,000	Li et al. (2018)
Concrete	650	Li et al. (2018)
LRB (*Ficus benjamina*)	**−325**	Zanne et al. (2009)

For every one cubic meter of LRB, approximately 325 kg of atmospheric carbon is sequestered (Table 1).

The primary inputs for LRB construction, germplasm, atmospheric carbon and sunlight, are all available for (effectively) free. LRBs are effectively constructed without cost. The only significant cost is time. Before LRBs or Living Infrastructure can be considered viable options for tropical cities, methods must be identified to significantly reduce construction times, from 50–100 years to time frames more amenable to modern societal needs.

1.2 Living Root Bridges and Tourism

LRBs were first brought to the attention of the west by Yule (1844) and have since enjoyed extensive media presence, ranging from books, blogs, TV documentaries and social media. The 'Double-Decker' LRB connecting Nongriat and Umshiang villages in Meghalaya, India is particularly popular among tourists and is the subject of hundreds of YouTube videos and documentaries. LRBs are regularly described in terms such as "*one of the finest human creations*" (Yule, 1844), "*...as if I had stepped into Tolkien's Middle Earth.*", "*...a shapeshifting fantasy world*" (Galbraith, 2013), "*simply awesome and mesmerising.*" (Prajwal, 2016), "*...Will Blow Your Mind!*", "*...nothing short of breathtaking*" (Binayak, 2017), "*organic gnarliness*" (Marks, 2019). The popularity of LRBs as tourism experiences, has stimulated significant economic growth for the villages is these regions (Nayak & Mishra, 2013; Ismul, 2017; Candra et al., 2019; Shillong, 2019; Middleton et al., 2020). Integrating LRBs or other Living Infrastructure into accessible cities such as Cairns or Singapore could become a major tourist attraction.

1.3 Strangler Figs

Ficus subgenus *Urostigma* trees from which all LRBs are constructed are commonly known as Banyans or Strangler figs. Found naturally throughout Australia Asia, Africa and South America, these trees are facultative hemiepiphytes generally begin life as a tiny seed deposited by a bird in the canopy of a host tree. Soon after germination, a small epiphytic fig emerges and produces a single aerial root (Fig. 2a). This first aerial roots grow slowly down the side of the host tree until reaching the substrate. The epiphytic fig, now able to access moisture and nutrition,

Fig. 2 Strangler figs begin as (**a**) an epiphyte on a host tree; (**b**) having reached the substrate the now hemiepiphyte begins to constrict it's host; (**c**) the Strangler eventually kills it's host; (**d**) the free-standing the Strangler fig transitions into a Banyan by growing a broad canopy, producing numerous aerial roots which form secondary trunks. Photos by (**a**) John Robert McPherson, distributed under a CC BY-SA 4.0 license (**b**) Woodard 1998, public domain (**c**) Gzzz, distributed under a CC BY-SA 4.0 license (**d**) Delonix, distributed under a CC BY-SA 3.0 license

grows rapidly and produces abundant secondary aerial roots, which grow (lengthen) up to 3 m per year (Moles et al., 2019) (Fig. 2b). These aerial roots wrap around the host tree, fuse into each other and thicken to form a lattice-like scaffold, enmeshing the host tree. Ultimately, being deprived of water and nutrient transportability, the host tree will usually perish (Fig. 2c). The free-standing Strangler fig tree continues to grow, forming a vast canopy, from which it produces further aerial roots. These roots may form multiple secondary trunks transforming the fig into a broad free-standing Banyan. Alternatively the roots may strangle multiple adjacent host trees (Fig. 2d). It is these interlocking aerial roots that are used to form LRBs.

1.4 Strangler Figs in Cities

Strangler fig trees readily exploit extreme niches and will freely colonise urban and built environments (Fig. 4) (Zimmermann et al., 1968; Putz & Holbrook, 1986, 1989; Harrison & Shanahan, 2005; Jim & Chen, 2011; Jim, 2014, 2018; Okamoto, 2015).

Cairns City occupies a place traditionally known as '*Gimuy*' by the Gimuy-walubarra yidi traditional owners, which translates to '*place of the Strangler fig tree*' and is also the name for the strangler fig species *Ficus albipila* (Exley et al., 2018; Cairns Regional Council, 2020; Bresson, 2021). Since the late 1800s, representations of the Cairns hinterland region have been dominated by the ~50 m tall, 500-year-old, giant Curtain Fig Tree (Fig. 3c, e) (Thorp, 2005, 2007). Often described as evoking *"a sense of awe, wonder, amazement and curiosity"* (Queensland Government, 2016; National Trust, 2019), commercial tours to this tree have been operating since the 1920s. Around 180,000 tourists visited this tree prior to the pandemic each year (Thorp, 2005; Queensland Government, 2016).

Today Cairns city is punctuated by innumerable Strangler fig-trees, ranging from <1 cm to true giants (*Personal Observations*). Many have been incorporated into the avenues, parks and esplanades, several have even been integrated into children's playgrounds. Similarly, Central Hong Kong, is home to thousands of Strangler figs. In one of the most densely populated urban spaces on the planet, Strangler figs are found growing directly on vertical concrete walls or along historic stone walls (Corlett, 2006; Jim, 2010; Jim & Chen, 2011).

Hougang New Town is Singapore's largest public housing estate. At any one time, around 25% of buildings in this district are colonised by Strangler fig trees (Wee, 1990; Lok et al., 2013).

Thus, the Strangler figs from which LRBs are constructed are very well adapted to tropical city environments.

1.5 Anastomosis of Strangler Figs

Due to competition for limited resources (light, water, nutrients, pollinators, seed dispersers, etc.), the growth of trees growing too close to one another will be impeded (Tilman et al., 1982; Weiner & Thomas, 1986). In contrast, Strangler figs have the capacity to bypass competition through a form of cooperation. When two Strangler figs grow close together and the branches or aerial roots touch, those organs often fuse and the trees become extensions of the same organism (Fig. 4). Multiple Strangler figs trees can fuse together to form (what appears as) one single tree

Fig. 3 (**a** and **b**) fused aerial roots of a Strangler fig; (**c**) the 50 m tall Curtain Fig Tree, protruding above the rainforest canopy; (**d**) Strangler fig forming a living tunnel in Bali Indonesia; (**e**) the base of the Curtain Fig Tree. Photos by (**a** and **b**) Source: authors; (**c**) Martin Gloss, distributed under a CC BY-SA 3.0 license, (**d**) Chrissy. H., distributed under a CC BY-NC-SA 2.0 license, (**e**) Dagmar Hollmann, distributed under a CC-BY-SA-4.0 license

Fig. 4 An example of anastomosis. Two large Strangler fig trees (*Ficus benjamina*), growing on opposite ends of a brick structure, in suburban Cairns. The strangling aerial roots have anastomosed and the two trees now function as one living organism. (Source: authors)

(Rao, 1966; Zimmermann et al., 1968). The process that allows Strangler figs to naturally fuse together and exchange resources are known as 'anastomosis'. It is by harnessing and augmenting anastomosis, the incredible adaptive capacity of Strangler figs to fuse/merge, that accelerated construction of Living Infrastructure could be readily achieved.

Suspending multiple Strangler fig seedlings across an impending geographic feature (street, river, housing, etc.) would facilitate anastomosis between the individual trees in a series and at regular spacings. Anastomosed trees would form one long, linear tree that doubles as a bridge (Fig. 1a–c), or a tunnel (Fig. 3c) or even housing. This trait, combined with Strangler fig's highly plastic growth habit, a predilection for exploiting tropical cities, strong spiritual significance, and demonstrated capacity to form functional, Living Infrastructure, highlights Strangler figs' suitability to be utilised in Living Infrastructure projects integrated into tropical urban spaces.

A fundamental first step in the ideation of accelerated Living Infrastructure construction is to identify a growth containment media suitable for Strangler fig trees. The ideal growing medium for suspended Strangler figs would need to retain adequate moisture for tree survival while simultaneously providing basic nutritional requirements until such point as anastomosis occurs and water and nutrients can be transferred between individuals. Using a design thinking approach to empathise with end-users, it is imperative to identify an ultra-low-cost growing media readily available to even disadvantaged urban communities.

1.6 Whole Coconuts

Whole coconuts (*Cocos nucifera L.* [Arecaceae]) may be an ideal growing media for Strangler figs. The inner fibres of coconut husks have been increasingly adopted for use in horticulture. Coconut husks are shredded, and the inner fibres are extracted to produce coir. Coir fibres are used as a low-cost growth media for food crops, floriculture, and forestry (Offord et al., 1998; Rose & Haase, 2000; Vavrina et al., 2002; Meerow, 2007). Coir is recognised as a low-cost soil alternative for containerised plant production. It is rich in micronutrients, potassium, iron, zinc, copper, manganese and available boron (Abad et al., 2002; Vavrina et al., 2002; Meerow, 2007).

Coir is produced in over 90 countries, with the Philippines, Indonesia and India being the world's largest producers (Alonge & Adetunji, 2011; Pham, 2016). Despite the abundance of coconut trees in Australia, there is little commercial demand for coconut fruit (Wilson, 2017).

Whole, intact coconuts, not shredded into coir fibres, may be ideal growth containment units for Strangler figs. Not only do the inner coir layers contain nutrients and absorb moisture, the outer skin (exocarp) (Fig. 5a) of the coconut is relatively impervious to desiccation (Konduru et al., 1999; Fowler & Marsden, 2013), suggesting that whole coconut would be able to absorb and retain moisture. Furthermore, the endosperm (meat) (Fig. 6a) is high in fat, sucrose and glucose (Yong et al., 2009; Yalegama et al., 2013), which may further benefit Strangler fig growth.

This study investigates the suitability of whole coconuts for use as ultra-low-cost, biodegradable growth containers for living-infrastructure-building Strangler figs.

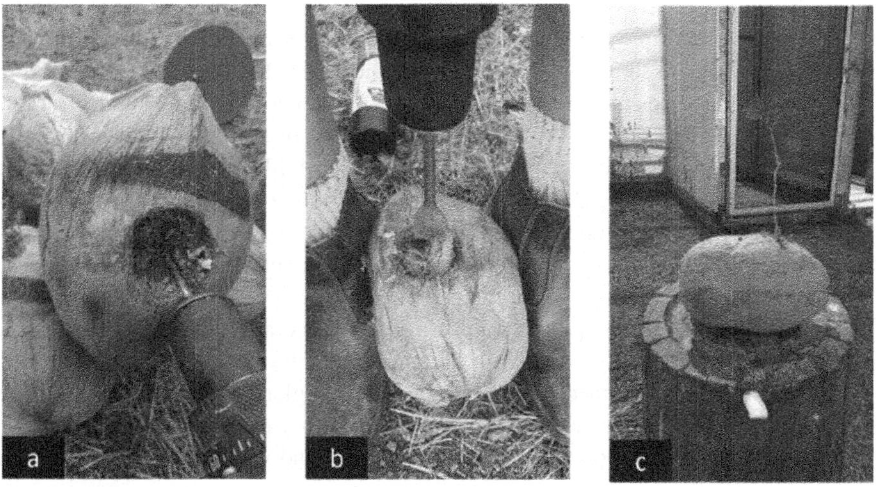

Fig. 5 Coconut treatments used in this experiment; (**a**) a cylindrical plug was removed from each coconut (**b**) the endocarp (shell) was punctured in the three internal treatments (Good_Soil, Poor_Soil and No_Soil) (**c**) *F. benjamina* cuttings were planted directly into the coconuts. (Source: authors)

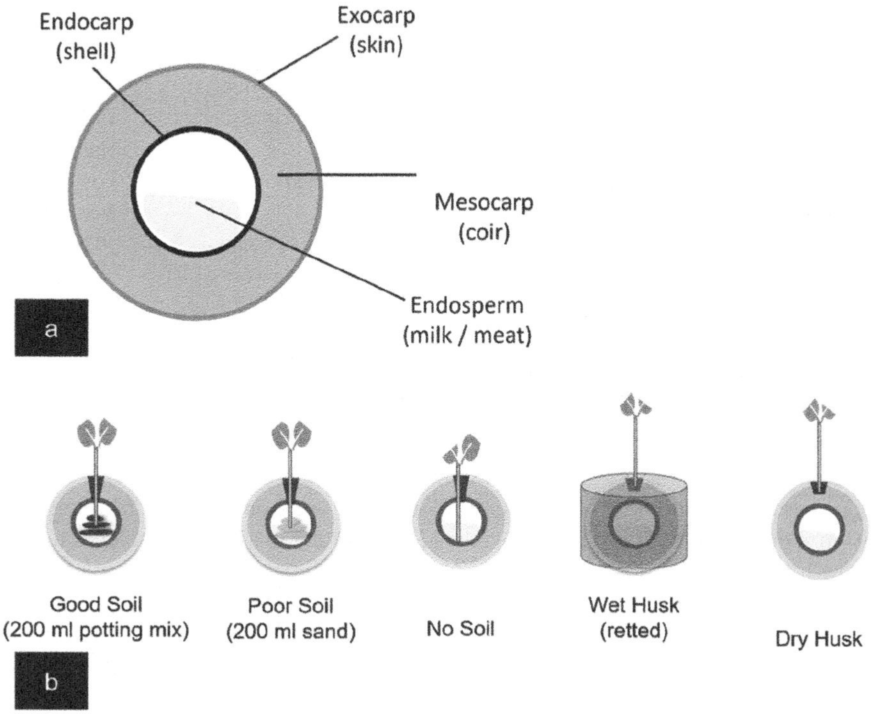

Fig. 6 Schematic of (**a**) transverse section of a whole coconut and (**b**) the five treatments used in this experiment

2 Methods

Ficus benjamina L., (Weeping fig) was selected as a representative species of *Ficus* subgen. *Urostigma*, due to its presence in most tropical cites (Mc Pherson, 1999; Guevara-Escobar et al., 2007; Jim, 2010; Lok et al., 2013). The study was conducted at the Environmental Research Centre of James Cook University, Cairns Australia, 16°48′57.01″S 145°41′2.40″E.

2.1 Experimental Design and Sampling Procedure

Ficus benjamina propagation material was selected from a mature (~20 years) *F. benjamina* located on James Cook University's Nguma-bada campus, Smithfield, Cairns. Cuttings were ~ 30 cm in length and removed from the terminal end of branchlets. Cuttings were transported in semi-transparent polythene bags to prevent desiccation. No rooting hormone was used in this experiment (Table 2).

Table 2 Five coconut-substrate treatments and their relative cost utilised in this study

	Treatment	Condition	Relative cost
Internal	Good_Soil	200 ml potting mix (AUD$70 m^3)	Very high
	Poor_Soil	200 ml sand (AUD$60 m^3)	High
	No_Soil	No substrate	High
External	Wet_Husk	Only mesocarp (saturated)	Low
	Dry_Husk	Only mesocarp	Very low

The endocarp of Internal treatments Good_Soil, Poor_Soil and No_Soil was punctured. External treatments Wet_Husk and Dry_Husk did not have the endocarp punctured

2.2 Coconut Treatments

Fallen, mature coconuts were collected from a seed-grown orchard in Palm Cove, Queensland, 16°45′2.92″S, 145°39′48.48″E. The plantation is not irrigated and lies approximately 1 km west of the ocean. Trees had an approximate mean height of 30 m. For this study, individual coconut (fruit) volume was not considered to be a growth affecting factor.

All coconuts were prepared by removing a single, cylindrical 'plug' from the external husk (exocarp and mesocarp) using a 54 * 25.2 mm (W * L) hole saw (Fig. 6a–c). The plug was removed from the centre of the tallest lobe (*whole coconuts have three lobes; generally one is somewhat larger* (Nijaguna, 1988; Alonge & Adetunji, 2011). Coconuts were subsequently treated in five different methods for the experiments, each with 15 replicates. Three treatments were prepared by puncturing the internal coconut shell (the endocarp), directly below the plug-hole, using a 32 mm spade drill-bit. This process exposed the internal cavity and the white coconut meat (the endosperm). Two external treatments did not have the endocarp punctured (Fig. 6).

The internal cavity space of treatment Good_Soil was partially filled with 200 ml of high-quality potting mix. Poor_Soil treatment had 200 ml of coarse river sand added to the cavity space. No media was added to the No_Soil treatment (Fig. 6b). Retting of coconuts (submergence in water) is a common practice in the preparation of coir (Konduru et al., 1999; Fowler & Marsden, 2013). Coconuts of Wet_Husk treatment were retted for seven days immediately prior to the beginning of the experiment. No additional modification was made to Dry_Husk treatment coconuts (Fig. 6b). For treatments Good_Soil and Poor_Soil, cuttings were inserted into to a depth where the cutting base aligned approximately with the centre of the internal cavity space. The bases of No_Soil treatment cuttings abutted the coconut endosperm. For the two external treatments (Wet_Husk and Dry_Husk), cuttings were inserted to the bottom of the plug-hole only (~25 mm). The bases of the cuttings were in contact with the mesocarp. All cuttings were kept upright by loosely packing the plug space with sugarcane mulch.

2.3 Relative Cost

Costs of each treatment type were ranked from very high to very low. Three factors affect the relative cost estimation for each treatment, namely the technical skill and physical effort required, the time it takes to prepare the treatment, and soil media's added cost. Puncturing the endocarp of the three internal treatments requires greater technical skill, additional tools and extra work effort. High quality and low-quality media were added into the cavities of treatments Good_Soil and Poor_Soil, respectively. Therefore, these treatments are considered higher in cost than No_Soil, to which soil was not added. Retting coconuts required additional time and labour and therefore is higher in cost than Dry_Husk, which required almost no skill or preparation inputs and is therefore considered the lowest cost (Fig. 6b).

2.4 Experimental Design and Statistical Analysis

Fifteen replicates were made for each of the five coconut treatments (n = 75). All replicates were housed in the same greenhouse. Coconuts were arranged in rows of five, with each row containing one replicate of each of the treatments (total of 15 rows). The position of each treatment within row, was progressively stepped across one position between rows (Fig. 7a). Each treatment location was repeated three times to ensure light, moisture and temperature were equal across all treatments.

Three parameters were studied, diametric growth (increase in stem width) and leaf count (number of new leaves) and mass (change in mass of cutting-coconut units). Basal diameters of cuttings were measured using DIGIMATIC series 500 digital callipers. All diameter measurements were taken level with external coconut husk surface, east-to-west. Coconuts mass was measured to 0.01 kg using OHAUS Defender 3000 digital scales (Fig. 7b).

Leaf number was counted manually, with only fully formed leaves included. Increases in basal diameter (width), leaf growth and mass accumulation were determined by subtracting the original mass values from the final mass values. In this experiment, biomass accumulation of cuttings was not examined due to the difficulty in separating roots from mesocarp. Statistical analysis was conducted in R (R Core Team, 2011) and figures were produced using the package ggplot2 (Wickham, 2009).

3 Results

For the 3 months preceding the experiment, March to May 2020, the meteorological conditions were characterised by lower rainfall and higher temperatures than the average climate factors for tropical North-eastern Australia's early dry season. Total

Fig. 7 (**a**) Whole coconut treatment were arranged in rows of five and stepped one space each row (e.g. Pink stripe). (**b**) Basal diameters of cuttings were measured using digital callipers, level with external coconut husk surface. Coconuts mass was measured using digital scales

Table 3 Climate averages for the 3 months preceding the experiment compared to long term climate averages for those months

Month	t (min)	t (Max)	Mean T	Long-term monthly means (°C)	ΔMean T	Rainfall (mm)	Rainfall month means (mm)	Δ Rainfall difference (mm)
March	28	34.2	31.3	30.6	0.7	134.4	416.3	−281.9
April	28.4	31.9	30.7	29.3	1.4	53.8	191.7	−137.9
May	20.3	31.3	27.5	27.7	−0.2	151.4	91.5	59.9

Temperatures were hotter and rainfall lower than averages recorded from closest publicly available weather station on the same altitude, Cairns Airport Climate data was obtained from the Australian Bureau of Meteorology (http://www.bom.gov.au/)

rainfall for the period preceding the project was 49% below average (339.6 mm c.f. 699.5 mm). With the exception of May, monthly mean-maximum temperatures were higher than long-term monthly means (Table 3).

F. benjamina cuttings were grown in whole coconuts for a 16-week period. Total diametric growth was highest in Wet_Husk and lowest in No_Soil (Table 4). Wet_Husk also exhibited the highest total leaf count. Total mass gains were highest in No_Soil treatment and lowest in Wet_Husk (Table 4).

Table 4 The overall, total leaf count, total diametric growth and total of *Ficus benjamina* grown in five coconut-substrate treatments, potting mix, (Good_Soil), sand, (Poor_Soil), punctured internal void space (No_Soil), retted coconut (Wet_Husk) and coconut with no treatment other than planting hole (Dry_Husk)

Treatment	Leaf count	Total diametric growth (mm)	Total mass accumulation (kg)
Good_Soil	97	16.66	14.88
Poor_Soil	71	17.84	16.01
No_Soil	60	15.28	25.33
Wet_Husk	103	28.72	10.71
Dry_Husk	80	22.38	13.91
Total	411	100.88	80.84

Table 5 The mean diametric growth of *Ficus Benjamina* cuttings grown inside five coconut-substrate treatments

Treatment	Mean diametric growth ± σ (mm)
Good_Soil	2.0 ± 1.2
Poor_Soil	1.4 ± 1
No_Soil	1.6 ± 1.4
Wet_Husk	2.3 ± 1
Dry_Husk	1.8 ± 1.1

3.1 Diametric Growth

Mean diametric growth was highest in Wet_Husk and lowest in Poor_Soil (Table 5). Basal Diameter was not normally distributed. A Kruskal-Wallis test by rank was utilised as a non-parametric test to determine no significant differences between the Diametric Growth means of the five treatments (Kruskal-Wallis chi-squared (*4*) 1.0693, $p = 0.899$).

3.2 Leaf Count

Mean leaf production was highest in Wet_Husk followed by Good_Soil, Dry_Husk, Poor_Soil and No_Soil. A total of 353 individual leaves were produced across the trial, a mean of 5.9 leaves per cutting (Table 6). Leaf Count data was not normally distributed. A Kruskal-Wallis test by rank was utilised as a non-parametric alternative to one-way ANOVA. No significant differences (Chi square = (4) 4.7375, $p = 0.3153$) were found between the mean number of leaves in the five treatments (Fig. 8).

Table 6 Leaf count of *F. benjamina* cuttings grown inside five coconut-substrate treatments

Treatment	Mean number of leaves ± σ (mm)	Total
Good_Soil	5.6 ± 4.5	97
Bad_Soil	4.3 ± 4.3	71
No_Soil	2.7 ± 2.8	60
Wet husk	6.9 ± 4.1	103
Dry husk	4.0 ± 4.7	80

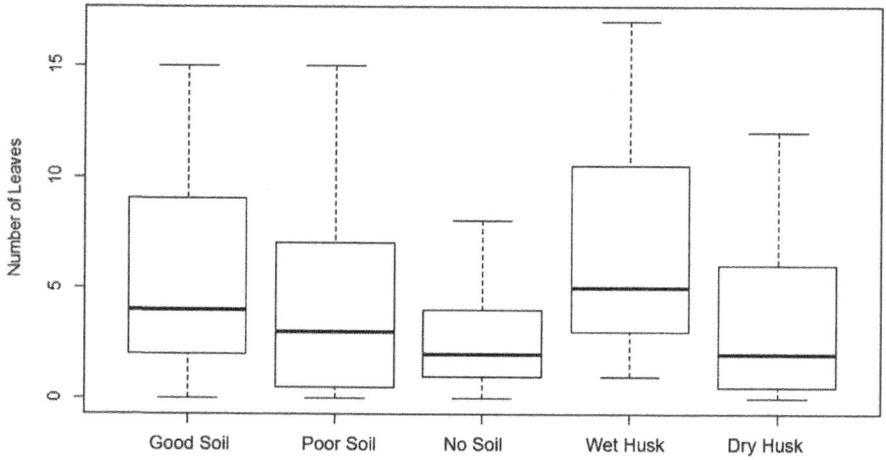

Fig. 8 Boxplot shows no significant difference in mean number of leaves between five coconut-media treatments of *Ficus benjamina*. Horizontal bars are treatment medians. Boxes show first and third quartiles. Error bars are standard error of means

3.3 Mass Accumulation

Mean mass accumulation of coconuts plus cuttings, in proportion to the initial weight of coconut-cutting treatments, was highest in No_Soil (1.72 kg), followed by Poor_Soil, (1.67 kg) Good_Soil (1.35 kg) and Dry_Husk (1.44 kg). Wet_Husk exhibited the lowest mean accumulation of mass in proportion to its initial weight (1.18 kg) (Fig. 9). A one-way ANOVA determined no significant difference between the mean mass of the five treatments ($F(4)$ 0.588, $p = 0.673$).

4 Discussion

F. benjamina cuttings were successfully propagated directly in whole coconuts. This analysis supports the theory that whole coconuts are suitable for the propagation of *Ficus* subgen. *Urostigma spp.* Strangler fig cuttings grown directly in and on whole

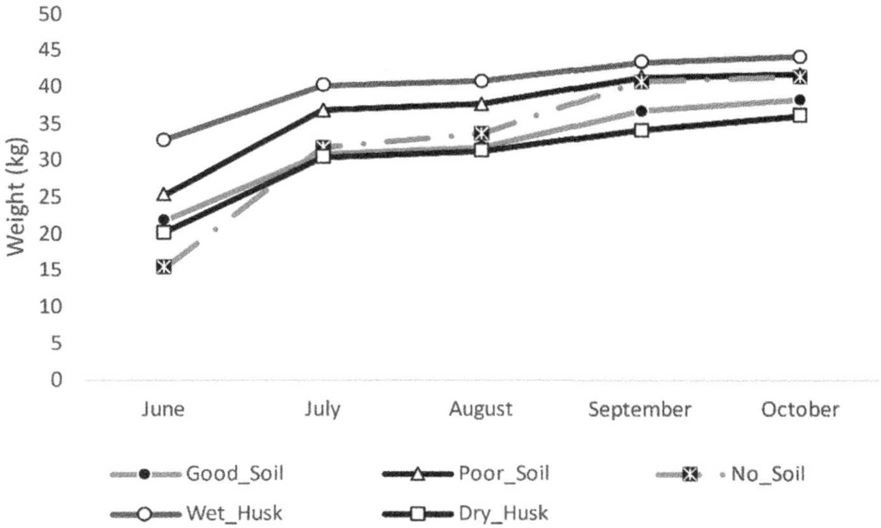

Fig. 9 Lineplot demonstrating the accumulation of mass (kg) in five coconut-*F. benjamina* treatments over a 4-month period. Mass is primary due to water absorption and not cutting growth

coconut mesocarp were equally productive as treatments containing the addition of media, both high and low quality. The spongy mesocarp layer (coir) of coconuts is sufficient for the growth of *F. benjamina.*

The results of this experiment support previous studies showing that vegetative propagation of *Ficus* subgen. *Urostigma spp.*, is possible in a wide range of media, including coarse and non-sterile sand (Danthu et al., 2002; Kshatri et al., 2005; Calin & Băla, 2013; Topacoglu et al., 2016) and high-quality potting mix (Trillas et al., 1981). However, the results of this experiment also indicate that whole, unhusked coconuts are equally beneficial as specific media mixes for the production of Strangler figs.

Although differences between the means of the three treatment parameters were not significant, there were common patterns. Wet_Husk exhibited the highest mean leaf productivity and the greatest diametric growth and the lowest absorption of water. Prior to experiment commencement, Wet_Husk coconuts were retted for 1 week. Retting of coconut husk is common practice in coir production as the mesocarp fibres are more-readily separated (Konduru et al., 1999; Fowler & Marsden, 2013). The pre-moistened fibres of Wet_Husk treatment may provide a boost to Strangler fig cuttings and promote growth by providing additional moisture and nutrition.

This project was constrained by both time and budget. Therefore, it should only be considered an exploratory investigation of the potential for whole coconuts to act as a suitable growth media for Strangler figs. In this experiment, a uniform size plug, 54 * 25.2 mm (W * L) was removed from each coconut to allow water to penetrate the mesocarp layer, resulting in mean water absorption of around one litre per coconut. Although this diameter opening appeared to be satisfactory for water penetration, further research is required to determine if this size is optimal for supporting Strangler fig growth over a longer-term. Simply scoring the exocarp and inserting germplasm directly into the husk without removing a plug, may be equally effective in allowing moisture penetration. Such a design may allow multiple plants to be produced per coconut, further accelerating LRB construction times.

Based on the results from this study, whole coconuts with little to no treatment appear to be a very effective growth medium for the propagation of *Ficus* subgnen. *Urostigma spp.* Growing Strangler figs in whole coconuts is likely to dramatically reduce the construction time of LRBs. Suspending multiple individual Strangler fig cuttings, growing in whole coconuts, above an impending geographic feature (street, river, housing etc.), and arranging the coconuts in close, uniform spacings (e.g., 2 m), would allow for rapid inter-tree anastomosis. Individual Strangler figs would readily merge, anastomose and form one long, living linear structure (e.g. bridge, tunnel, boardwalk, etc.). Such a design would likely produce a LRB in just several years, providing rapid integration into modern urban spaces.

When viewed through a Design Thinking lens, to empathise with end users; *simply awesome and mesmerising* Living Infrastructure formed of *organic gnarliness* that *Will Blow Your Mind* represents a unique solution for promoting economic growth, social inclusion, empowering communities and building resilience in communities. Cities such as Cairns and Singapore are uniquely positioned to benefit from this technology, particular as we return to the new normal and seek innovative strategies to rebuild hard-hit tourism industries.

5 Limitations of the Study

The methodological choices used in this project were constrained by lack of any previous research into using whole coconuts as a plant growth medium. Repeating the project over a longer duration, with multiple Strangler fig species and increased replication, may provide identifiable differences in productivity gains of the parameter means. Retting coconuts may represent a superior treatment for the production of Strangler figs. Future research with larger sample sizes and longer treatment times may be sensitive enough to detect differences.

The next phase in the design thinking process is building functional, accessible prototypes to gather and incorporate user feedback and data (Buchenau & Suri, 2000; Buxton, 2007; Brown, 2017). Future research into Living Infrastructure construction methodologies is needed to identify the most suitable Stranger figs species, along with optimal spacings for coconut containment units. Construction times, costs and structural engineering requirements will need quantification. In order to determine carbon market potential, accurate estimates of carbon sequestration rates will also be required. As wood is 50% carbon by weight (Lamlom & Savidge, 2003; Settle et al., 2012), it is likely that LRBs carbon storage potential is equal to the largest trees on earth (Keith et al., 2009; Jones & O'hara, 2011).

6 Conclusion

This study was conducted as a pilot project to partially satisfy the requirements of a Master of Science. The paper demonstrates that whole coconuts are suitable for the propagation of a pan-tropical distributed *Ficus subgen. Urostigma species.* The addition of any media into the internal void spaces of coconut does not increase growth of *F. benjamina* cuttings. Gains in productivity can be equally achieved with cuttings growing directly in the spongy mesocarp fibres of coconuts. Whole, unhusked coconuts are inexpensive, readily obtainable and environmentally friendly. When considering availability, cost and environmental impact, and productivity, the authors' opinion that the whole coconut represents a superior growth medium than other substrate and pot choices. Further research into the number of individual Strangler figs that can be grown simultaneously in whole coconuts is required. Living Infrastructure construction prototypes are also required.

This study posits a fundamental first step in the ideation of accelerated construction of Living Infrastructure and identifies a suitable growth containment media for Strangler fig trees.

It is beyond the scope of this study to make broad generalisations regarding the suitability of whole coconuts for genus and species outside of *Ficus* subgen. *Urostigma.* However, considering coir has been demonstrated as suitable for a range of species and cultivars, it is not unreasonable to expect that whole coconut would have potential as a low cost, environmentally friendly growth medium for a wide range of plant species.

References

Abad, M., Noguera, P., Puchades, R., Maquieira, A., & Noguera, V. (2002). Physico-chemical and chemical properties of some coconut coir dusts for use as a peat substitute for containerised ornamental plants. *Bioresource Technology, 82*, 241–245.

Alonge, A. F., & Adetunji, W. B. (2011). Properties of coconut (Cocos nucifera L.) relevant to its dehusking. *Journal of Agricultural Science and Technology A, 1*, 1089–1094.

Ambrosio, N., Kim, Y. H., Swann, S., & Wang, Z. (2020). *Addressing climate risk in financial decision making* (Colker RBT-OCI, Ed., pp. 123–142). Butterworth-Heinemann.

Binayak, P. (2017). India's amazing living root bridges will blow your mind. *Culture trip.*

Bivens, J. (2014). *The short- and long-term impact of infrastructure investments on employment and economic activity in the U.S. economy*. Washington, DC, 20433, USA.

Bowler, D. E., Buyung-Ali, L., Knight, T. M., & Pullin, A. S. (2010a). Urban greening to cool towns and cities: A systematic review of the empirical evidence. *Landscape and Urban Planning, 97*, 147–155.

Bowler, D. E., Buyung-Ali, L. M., Knight, T. M., & Pullin, A. S. (2010b). A systematic review of evidence for the added benefits to health of exposure to natural environments. *BMC Public Health, 10*, 456.

Bresson, M. (2021). Tjapukai cultural renewal in the Kuranda Region of Queensland. *The Oral History Association of Australia Journal.*

Brown, T. (2017). *Design thinking – IDEO U.*

Buchenau, M., & Suri, J. F. (2000). Experience prototyping. In *Proceedings of the conference on designing interactive systems: Processes, practices, methods, and techniques, DIS*: 424–433.
Buxton, B. (2007). *Sketching user experiences: Getting the design right and the right design*. Elsevier.
Cairns Regional Council. (2020). *Indigenous culture and history. Indigenous culture and history*.
Calin, A. C., & Băla, M. (2013). Effects of different rooting substrates and rooting growth enhancers on the rooting of Ficus benjamina cuttings. *Review on Agriculture and Rural Development, 2*, 109–113.
Candra, Y., Mayora, E., Okta, H., & Putra, A. (2019). *Analisis Faktor Revisit Intention Wisnus Di Kawasan Jembatan Akar Kabupaten Pesisir Selatan, 10*, 9.
Chaudhuri, P., Bhattacharyya, S., & Samal, A. C. (2016). Living Root Bridge: A potential no cost eco-technology for mitigating rural communication problems. *International Journal of Experimental Research and Review, 5*, 33–35.
Corlett, R. T. (2006). Figs (Ficus, Moraceae) in urban Hong Kong, South China. *Biotropica, 38*, 116–121.
Danthu, P., Soloviev, P., Gaye, A., Sarr, A., Seck, M., & Thomas, I. (2002). Vegetative propagation of some West African Ficus species by cuttings. *Agroforestry Systems, 55*, 57–63.
Delonix. (2013). *Banyan tree at the valley school, Bangalore*. Wikimedia Commons.
Exley, B., Whatman, S., & Singh, P. (2018). Postcolonial, decolonial research dilemmas: Fieldwork in Australian indigenous contexts. *Qualitative Research, 18*, 526–537.
Fowler, G. J., & Marsden, F. (2013). The retting of coconut husk for the production of coir. *Journal of the Indian Institute of Science, 7*, 39.
Galbraith, E. (2013). Living beauty in the Indian jungle. *EthnoTraveler Magazine*.
Gill, S. E., Handley, J. F., Ennos, A. R., & Pauleit, S. (2018). Adapting cities for climate change: The role of the green infrastructure. In *Planning for climate change: A reader in green infrastructure and sustainable design for resilient cities* (pp. 195–205). Alexandrine Press.
Guevara-Escobar, A., González-Sosa, E., Véliz-Chávez, C., Ventura-Ramos, E., & Ramos-Salinas, M. (2007). Rainfall interception and distribution patterns of gross precipitation around an isolated Ficus benjamina tree in an urban area. *Journal of Hydrology, 333*, 532–541.
Harding, S., Trewin, D., Penny, A., Ziembicki, M., Dale, A., Ustan, T. S., Tan, D., Waltham, N., Laurance, W. F., & Ceclia, R. (2017). *State of the tropics 2017 report: Sustainable infrastructure in the tropics*. James Cook University.
Harrison, R. D., & Shanahan, M. (2005). Seventy-seven ways to be a fig: Overview of a diverse plant assemblage. In *Pollination ecology and the rain forest* (pp. 111–127). Springer.
Hunt, A., & Watkiss, P. (2011). Climate change impacts and adaptation in cities: A review of the literature. *Climatic Change, 104*, 13–49.
Ismul, A. (2017). POTRET PENGELOLAAN PARIWISATA DI OBYEK WISATA JEMBATAN AKAR (Studi Terhadap: Pelaku Obyek Wisata Jembatan Akar Kenagarian Puluik-Puluik Kecamatan IV Nagari Bayang Utara Kabupaten Pesisir Selatan).
Jim, C. Y. (2010). Old masonry walls as ruderal habitats for biodiversity conservation and enhancement in urban Hong Kong. In *Urban biodiversity and design*.
Jim, C. Y. (2014). Ecology and conservation of strangler figs in urban wall habitats. *Urban Ecosystem, 17*, 405–426.
Jim, C. Y. (2018). Epiphytic strangler trees colonising extreme habitats of building envelopes in Hong Kong. *Landscape and Urban Planning, 178*, 281–291.
Jim, C. Y., & Chen, W. Y. (2011). Bioreceptivity of buildings for spontaneous arboreal flora in compact city environment. *Urban Forestry and Urban Greening, 10*, 19–28.
Jones, D. A., & O'hara, K. L. (2011). Carbon density in managed coast redwood stands: Implications for forest carbon estimation. *Forestry, 85*, 99–110.
Keith, H., Mackey, B. G., & Lindenmayer, D. B. (2009). Re-evaluation of forest biomass carbon stocks and lessons from the world's most carbon-dense forests. *Proceedings of the National Academy of Sciences of the United States of America, 106*, 11635–11640.

Konduru, S., Evans, M. R., & Stamps, R. H. (1999). Coconut husk and processing effects on chemical and physical properties of coconut coir dust. *HortScience, 34*, 88–90.

Kshatri, B. B., Kemp, P. D., & Devkota, J. H. N. R. (2005). Vegetative propagation of Ficus benjamina using non-sterile sand and hardwood cuttings. *Agronomy NZ, 35*, 19–22.

Lamlom, S. H., & Savidge, R. A. (2003). A reassessment of carbon content in wood: Variation within and between 41 North American species. *Biomass and Bioenergy, 25*, 381–388.

Li, M., Zhong, R., Zhu, S., Ramsay, L. C., Li, F., & Coyte, P. C. (2018). Access to community living infrastructure and its impact on the establishment of community-based day care centres for seniors in rural China. *International Journal of Environmental Research and Public Health, 15*, 1184.

Lok, A., Ang, W. F., Ng, B. Y. Q., Leong, T. M., Yeo, C. K., & Tan, H. T. W. (2013). *Native fig species as a keystone resource for the Singapore urban environment*. Raffles Museum of Biodiversity Research, National University of Singapore.

Ludwig, F., Middleton, W., Gallenmüller, F., Rogers, P., & Speck, T. (2019). Living bridges using aerial roots of ficus elastica – An interdisciplinary perspective. *Scientific Reports, 9*.

Marks, A. (2019). Living root bridges. *Tribes*.

McGranahan, G., Balk, D. & Anderson, B. (2012). The rising tide: Assessing the risks of climate change and human settlements in low elevation coastal zones. In J. Bicknell, D. Dodman, & D. Satterthwaite (Eds.), *Adapting cities to climate change: Understanding and addressing the development challenges* (pp. 1–397). London: Routledge. https://doi.org/10.4324/9781849770361.

Mc Pherson, J. R. (1999). Studies in urban ecology: Strangler figs in the urban parklands of Brisbane, Queensland, Australia. *Australian Geographical Studies, 37*, 214–229.

Meerow, A. W. (2007). Coir dust, a viable alternative to peat moss performance of coir dust as a plant growth medium. *Greenhouse Product News, 1*, 2–7.

Middleton, W., Habibi, A., Shankar, S., & Ludwig, F. (2020). Characterising regenerative aspects of living root bridges. *Sustainability (Switzerland), 12*.

Moles, A. T., Jagdish, A., Wu, Y., Gooley, S., Dalrymple, R. L., Feng, P., Auld, J., Badgery, G., Balding, M., & Bell, A. (2019). From dangerous branches to urban banyan: Facilitating aerial root growth of Ficus rubiginosa. *PLoS One, 14*, e0226845.

Nasr, A., Kjellström, E., Björnsson, I., Honfi, D., Ivanov, O. L., & Johansson, J. (2020). Bridges in a changing climate: A study of the potential impacts of climate change on bridges and their possible adaptations. *Structure and Infrastructure Engineering, 16*, 738–749.

National Trust. (2019). *National trust – white fig (Ficus virens)*. Canberra, Australia.

Nayak, P., & Mishra, S. K. (2013). Problems and prospects of promoting tourism in Meghalaya. In *Promotion of international tourism circuits in North East India: Prospects, priorities and strategic options* (pp. 1–13).

Nicholls, R. J. (1995). Coastal megacities and climate change. *GeoJournal, 37*, 369–379.

Nijaguna, B. T. (1988). Coconut dehusker. *Journal of Food Engineering, 8*, 287–301.

Offord, C. A., Muir, S., & Tyler, J. L. (1998). Growth of selected Australian plants in soilless media using coir as a substitute for peat. *Australian Journal of Experimental Agriculture, 38*, 879–887.

Okamoto, K. W. (2015). The dynamics of strangling among forest trees. *Journal of Theoretical Biology, 384*, 95–104.

Patz, J. A., Campbell-Lendrum, D., Holloway, T., & Foley, J. A. (2005). Impact of regional climate change on human health. *Nature, 438*, 310–317.

Pervin, I. A., Rahman, S. M. M., Nepal, M., Haque, A. K. E., Karim, H., & Dhakal, G. (2020). Adapting to urban flooding: A case of two cities in South Asia. *Water Policy, 22*, 162–188.

Pham, L. J. (2016). Chapter 9: Coconut (Cocos nucifera). In T. A. McKeon, D. G. Hayes, D. F. Hildebrand, & R. J. Weselake (Eds.), *Industrial oil crops* (pp. 231–242). AOCS Press.

Prajwal, N. (2016). The mesmerising double decker living root bridge! *Instagram*.

Putz, F. E., & Holbrook, N. M. (1986). Notes on the natural history of hemiepiphytes. *Selbyana, 9*, 61–69.

Putz, F. E., & Holbrook, N. M. (1989). Strangler fig rooting habits and nutrient relations in the Llanos of Venezuela. *American Journal of Botany, 76*, 781–788.

Queensland Government. (2016). *The curtain fig tree*. Brisbane.

R Core Team. (2011). *R: A language and environment for statistical computing*.

Rao, A. N. (1966). Developmental anatomy of natural root grafts in Ficus globosa. *Australian Journal of Botany, 14*, 269–276.

Reckien, D., Creutzig, F., Fernandez, B., Lwasa, S., Tovar-Restrepo, M., Mcevoy, D., & Satterthwaite, D. (2017). Climate change, equity and the sustainable development goals: An urban perspective. *Environment and Urbanisation, 29*, 159–182.

Rose, R., & Haase, D. L. (2000). The use of coir as a containerised growing medium for Douglas-fir seedlings. *Native Plants Journal, 1*, 107–111.

Satterthwaite, D., Archer, D., Colenbrander, S., Dodman, D., Hardoy, J., Mitlin, D., & Patel, S. (2020). Building resilience to climate change in informal settlements. *One Earth, 2*, 143–156.

Seto, K. C., Dhakal, S., Bigio, A., Blanco, H., Delgado, G. C., Dewar, D., Huang, L., Inaba, A., Kansal, A., & Lwasa, S. (2014). *Human settlements, infrastructure and spatial planning*.

Settle, D. J., Page, T., Bush, D., Doran, J., Sethy, M., & Viji, I. (2012). Basic density, diameter and radial variation of Vanuatu Whitewood (Endospermum medullosum). Potential for breeding in a low density, tropical hardwood. *International Forestry Review, 14*, 463–473.

Shankar, S. (2015). Living root bridges: State of knowledge, fundamental research and future application. In *IABSE conference, Geneva 2015: Structural engineering: Providing solutions to global challenges – Report* (pp. 1974–1981).

Shillong. (2019). Tourists flock to Meghalaya, Scotland of the East – Telegraph India. *The Telegraph Online*.

Thorp, J. (2007). Tourism in Cairns: Image and product. *Journal of Australian studies, 31*, 107–113.

Thorp, J. M. (2005). *The development of the tourism cultural landscape of the Cairns Region, 1890–1970*.

Tilman, D., Kilham, S. S., & Kilham, P. (1982). Phytoplankton community ecology: The role of limiting nutrients. *Annual Review of Ecology and Systematics, 13*, 349–372.

Topacoglu, O., Sevik, H., Guney, K., Unal, C., Akkuzu, E., & Sivacioglu, A. (2016). Effect of rooting hormones on the rooting capability of Ficus benjamina L. cuttings. *Šumarski list, 140*, 39–44.

Trillas, M. I., Lorenzo, P., Sant, M. D., & Aguilà, J. F. (1981). Influence of the substrate on Ficus benjamina growth. *Symposium on Substrates in Horticulture other than Soils In Situ, 126*, 303–310.

UN-HABITAT. (2016). *World cities report 2016*. United Nations Publications.

UN-HABITAT. (2021). *The impacts of climate change upon urban areas* (pp. 82–107). Cities and Climate Change.

United Nations. (2018). *The world's cities in 2018* (pp. 1–34). Department of Economic and Social Affairs, Population Division, World Urbanization Prospects.

United Nations. (2019). *UN News – Cities: A "cause of and solution to" climate change*.

Varquez, A. C. G., Darmanto, N. S., Honda, Y., Ihara, T., & Kanda, M. (2020). Future increase in elderly heat-related mortality of a rapidly growing Asian megacity. *Scientific Reports, 10*, 9304.

Vavrina, C. S., Arenas, M., Cornell, J. A., Hanlon, E. A., & Hochmuth, G. J. (2002). Coir as an alternative to peat in media for tomato transplant production. *HortScience, 37*, 309–312.

Wang, X., Stewart, M. G., & Nguyen, M. (2012). Impact of climate change on corrosion and damage to concrete infrastructure in Australia. *Climatic Change, 110*, 941–957.

Wee, Y. C. (1990). *Country report: Singapore. Ficus spp. on highrise buildings in Singapore*: 37–39.

Weiner, J., & Thomas, S. C. (1986). Size variability and competition in plant monocultures. *Oikos*, 211–222.

Wickham, H. (2009). *Elegant graphics for data analysis*.

Wilson, C. (2017). Australia has a lot of coconut palms – So why don't we have a coconut industry? *ABC News*.

Włodarczyk-Marciniak, R., Sikorska, D., & Krauze, K. (2020). Residents' awareness of the role of informal green spaces in a post-industrial city, with a focus on regulating services and urban adaptation potential. *Sustainable Cities and Society, 59*, 102236.

Woodard, P. (1998). Native Elm & Strangler – Richmond River. *Wikimedia Commons*.

World Bank. (2010). *Climate risks and adaptation in Asian coastal megacities: A synthesis report*: 1–120.

Yalegama, L. L. W. C., Nedra Karunaratne, D., Sivakanesan, R., & Jayasekara, C. (2013). Chemical and functional properties of fibre concentrates obtained from by-products of coconut kernel. *Food Chemistry, 141*, 124–130.

Yong, J. W., Ge, L., Ng, Y. F., & Tan, S. N. (2009). The chemical composition and biological properties of coconut (Cocos nucifera L.) water. *Molecules, 14*, 5144–5164.

Yule, H. (1844). The journal of the Asiatic Society of Bengal. *XIII*, 1832–1936.

Zanne, A. E., Lopez-Gonzalez, G., Coomes, D. A., Ilic, J., Jansen, S., Lewis, S. L., Miller, R. B., Swenson, N. G., Wiemann, M. C., & Chave, J. (2009). Global wood density database. In *Data from: Towards a worldwide wood economics spectrum*. Dryad Digital Repository.

Zimmermann, M. H., Wardrop, A. B., & Tomlinson, P. B. (1968). Tension wood in aerial roots of Ficus benjamina L. *Wood Science and Technology, 2*, 95–104.

Is a Low and Fixed Price for Mitigation Credits Effective in Reducing Deforestation Emissions?

Fiona Ryan

Abstract *Reducing emissions from deforestation and forest degradation* (REDD+) involves payments for emissions reduction in terms of tonnes of Carbon known as Results-Based Payments (RBP). RBPs were envisaged as covering the opportunity and transaction/implementation costs of not converting the forest to other land uses such as oil palm or beef production by providing alternative development pathways. Most REDD+ funding has come from official development assistance (ODA) where funders have benchmarked payments for results at US$ 5/tCO2-e or sometimes US$ 10/tCO2-e. These prices are far below most estimates of the net costs of ending deforestation. Despite REDD+ being designed to fit into an international emissions trading context, the international environment makes it uncertain that international emissions trading under Article 6 of the Paris Agreement will generate a price for REDD+ RBPs necessary to meet the costs of reducing emissions in developing countries. The study examines the peer-reviewed literature and materials produced by various stakeholders on low and fixed benchmark prices for REDD+ RBPs and will conduct a Strengths, Weaknesses, Opportunities, Threats (SWOT) analysis to determine likely outcomes. It concludes that low prices for REDD+ RBPs will substantially continue deforestation because of loss of country ownership, loss of stakeholder support for an alternative development pathway, and shifting of the burden of emissions reduction to developing countries. Low fixed prices result in serious equity and justice concerns for people in tropical forest countries. In the absence of a viable compliance market for REDD+, greater expenditure on REDD+ RBPs is justified, in particular, because it enables a higher price for RBPs.

Keywords REDD+ · Climate change · Results-based-payments · Carbon pricing · Deforestation · Development assistance

F. Ryan (✉)
Independent Scholar, Edge Hill, QLD, Australia

© The Author(s), under exclusive license to Springer Nature Singapore Pte Ltd. 2022

T. Chaiechi, J. Wood (eds.), *Community Empowerment, Sustainable Cities, and Transformative Economies*, https://doi.org/10.1007/978-981-16-5260-8_12

1 Introduction

Deforestation in the tropics generates about 11% of global greenhouse gas emissions, See Fig. 2 (Smith et al., 2014). Consequently, there has been an increasing focus on reducing emissions from tropical deforestation. This was reflected in the establishment of international arrangements to reduce deforestation to mitigate climate change. The most prominent of these was the UN reducing emissions from deforestation, forest degradation, conservation, sustainable management of forests, and enhancement of forest carbon stocks, also known as UN- REDD+ established in 2008 after a submission from Costa Rica and Papua New Guinea (2005) to the United Nations Framework Convention for Climate Change (UNFCCC). They proposed drastically cutting their emissions from deforestation if wealthy countries provided sufficient funds to enable them to implement these reductions (Fig. 1).

To ensure REDD+ did not produce negative ecological or social outcomes, the Cancun Safeguards were adopted by the UNFCCC in 2010, and this was formalised in the Warsaw Framework for REDD+ in 2013 subsequent UNFCCC decisions (Martius et al., 2018, p. 24). The original hopes for a quick end to emissions from deforestation have not been achieved despite initial high expectations. There has been patchy achievement of many of REDD+ objectives (Sills et al., 2014) (Fig. 2).

It was envisaged that RBPs would be funded through international emissions trading for compliance by developed countries with national emissions targets. However, REDD+ RBPs were not included in national emissions trading

Fig. 1 Image of deforestation in Indonesia. (Note: Rainforest Action Network (2018) CC BY-NC 2.0)

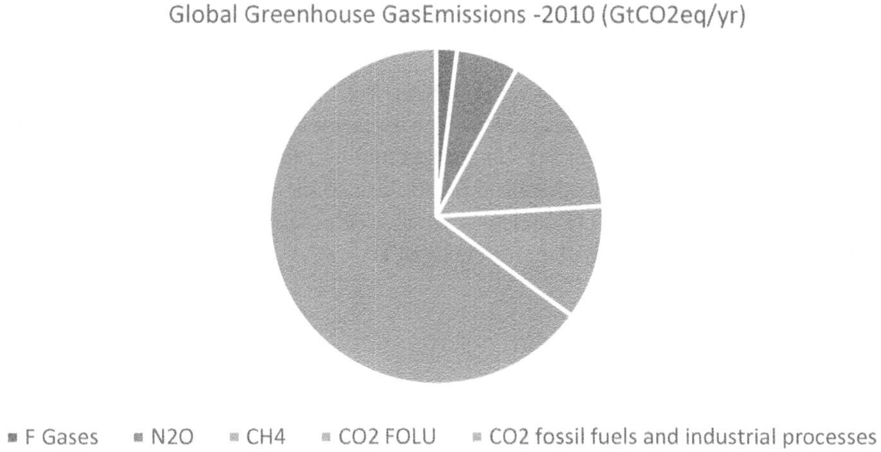

Fig. 2 Global anthropogenic greenhouse gas emissions major sectors and gases 2010. (Source: authors generated from data from Smith et al., 2014)

compliance markets under the Kyoto Protocol, which expired in 2020. It is uncertain that REDD+ will be included in international emissions trading for compliance in the rules for the 2015 Paris Agreement due to be finalised in 2021. The expected demand for REDD+ credits is reduced by the lack of effort required to meet weak Paris commitments and by the exclusion of international offsets from the EU emissions trading scheme. Also, the future US policy on offsets and public funding for REDD+ is uncertain. It is possible that low prices may continue in compliance markets if demand remains low. The current low price for RBPs, financed from ODA (Ryan, 2019) and sourced from funding institutions such as the Green Climate Fund may prefigure the future of compliance REDD+ due to low demand for international offsets.

This study examines reducing emissions from deforestation rather than the other components of REDD+ such as forest degradation or conservation, sustainable management of forests, and enhancement of forest carbon stocks. However, REDD+ is not being implemented as envisaged in previous studies with regards to RBP pricing. This study looks at the current situation and endeavours to fill that gap. The OECD definition of ODA requires it contribute to the economic development and welfare of developing countries (Ryan, 2019). Almost all climate finance from development finance institutions is counted as ODA (Ryan, 2019), therefore those institutions that are undertaking REDD+ RBP programs are also evaluated on their contribution to the economic development and welfare of developing countries in addition to reducing emissions from deforestation. A SWOT (strengths, weaknesses, opportunities, threats) method of analysis is adopted.

1.1 Layout of the Article

The key aims of this study are shown in Sect. 1.2, followed by Sect. 1.3, outlining the scope of this study. Section 2 contains an assessment of the literature divided into the major concepts and issues relevant to meeting the studies aims. Section 3 covers the methodology and the justification for the use of the SWOT analysis. Section 4 gives the results of the SWOT analysis, which is summarised in Table 1. Section 5 is the conclusion, followed by the references in Sect. 6.

1.2 The Key Aims

The aim of this study is to determine the likely relative effectiveness of a fixed and low price of the Carbon price for REDD+ RBPs compared to other flexible pricing options based on marginal abatement costs. The evaluation focuses on the effectiveness of the achievement of two key sub-aims;

1. emissions reductions from deforestation, and
2. the economic development and welfare of developing countries.

1.3 Scope of This Study

This paper looks at REDD+ from how it was originally envisaged as an incentive payment for environmental services to stakeholder in tropical forest countries. It also looks at whether REDD+ RBP prices are sufficient to provide the necessary incentives to meet aspirations to reduce emissions from deforestation. The focus is on REDD+ activities that make payments for emissions reductions at national and jurisdictional scales and are financed from public sources such as bilateral official development assistance or multilateral financial institutions such as the World Bank or the Green Climate Fund. Currently, REDD+ RBPs have not been made for any UNFCCC compliance market (Lujan & Silva-Chavez, 2018). The International Civil Aviation Organisation (ICAO) carbon offsets system is likely to generate a market

Table 1 Economic incentives rationale underlying REDD+ theories of change (Angelsen et al., 2018)

Rationale	Description	Main policy	Underlying ideology	Key proponents
Economic incentives	Excessive emissions are a market failure, to be corrected through payment for environmental services (PES)	Payments for environmental services (PES/market approach)	Neoclassical environmental economics (rational choice); 'bioenvironmentalists' (Hiraldo & Tanner, 2012)	Key donors, World Bank, UN-REDD, Green Climate Fund (GCF), many NGOs

for REDD+ credits post 2020 (Lujan & Silva-Chavez, 2018), but little is known of its likely effects. Projects that are local in scale and financed by the private sector through the voluntary carbon market are not examined in this paper.

REDD+ phases 1-Readiness and 2-Implementation activities such as institutional strengthening and the implementation of monitoring, reporting, and verification regimes are rarely conditional; that is, they are not paid on results. These and other non-conditional REDD+ activities are outside the scope of this paper. Phase 3, Results-based finance, is the focus here. ODA financed REDD+ RBPs are seen as pilots for international compliance markets that may ultimately be established.

2 Assessment of the Literature

There has been some reduction in emissions from deforestation from an average of 4.3 Gt CO2 year^{-1} during 1991–2000, to an average of 2.9 Gt CO2 year^{-1} during the period 2016–2020 (Tubiello et al., 2020). FAO (2020) predicts that on current trends, it will take another 25 years to reach the United Nations 2030 Agenda, SDG 15 goal (United Nations General Assembly, 2015) of ending deforestation, the original target year is 2020.

Many different REDD+ approaches have been tried. However, the essential feature of the REDD+ theory of change is conditionality or payment for results. This has rarely been applied in practice (Martius et al., 2018). Conditional payments are often known as results-based payments (RBPs) where the funds are paid to achieve emissions reductions measured against a baseline.

REDD+ RBPs are meant to incentivise developing countries to significantly reduce deforestation (Martius et al., 2018). Payments set by the main public funding institutions are set at US$5/t CO2-e, with Norway paying US$ 10/tCO2-e in recent agreements (Lujan & Silva-Chavez, 2018; Clouse, 2020). By contrast, Rakatma et al. (2017) found that average total REDD costs to recipient countries of US$24.87/tCO2-e. Significantly, no studies have been published that examine the outcomes of publicly financed REDD+ RBP activities financed at the current benchmark prices.

Busch and Engelmann (2015), using revealed preference analysis, projected that tropical deforestation will release 169 GtCO2 to the atmosphere from 2016–2050, one-sixth of the global carbon budget to keep global warming under 2 °C. They estimated that a global carbon price of $20/tCO2 from 2016–2050 would reduce emissions from tropical deforestation by 41 GtCO2 while a carbon price of $50/tCO2 would avoid 77 GtCO2.

Many studies have calculated the marginal abatement costs of avoided deforestation (Seymour, 2016). Benchmarked payments for results prices of US$ 5/tCO2-e or sometimes US$ 10/tCO2-e are far below most estimates of the opportunity cost and other net costs that would result from substantially reducing deforestation.

However, there has been little discussion of publicly financed REDD+ activities when prices are fixed below net abatement costs and funded from limited public sources. Kohl et al. (2020) concluded that current prices for REDD+ were insufficient to cover measurement, reporting and verification (MRV) costs and recommended reducing MRV requirements. However, Kohl et al. (2020) did not focus on opportunity cost, which is a major theoretical concern of this paper. The low and fixed RBP prices do not conform to the incentive rationale for the theory of change for REDD+ described in Table 1. Much of the literature looks at the vision for REDD+ as it was conceived with a market-based system with flexible prices meeting a substantial global demand for emissions reduction. Most studies concerning REDD+ were produced before 2014 before the current REDD+ system was formalised in the Warsaw Framework for REDD+ and subsequent UNFCCC decisions. This study examines the implications for the current situation where REDD+ RBPs are set at a low inflexible price. This crucial deviation from the REDD+ theory of change is poorly covered in the literature.

2.1 Theoretical Issues Identified in the Literature

The literature review uncovered issues and assumptions relevant to the likely outcomes and impacts of low and fixed prices REDD+ RBPs.

2.1.1 Rationale for REDD+

The are many ideological rationales for the REDD+ RBPs Theory of Change. The core rationale or theory of change is the economic incentives rationale found in Table 1. from Angelsen et al. (2018). Other concepts within which REDD+ RBP prices are discussed, include; global- public- goods- theory, the concepts of mutual-benefit and country ownership.

2.1.2 The Economic Incentives Rationale for REDD+

The key rationale used here to evaluate the low fixed price for RBPs is the economic incentives rationale under which excessive emissions are seen as a market failure. The policy solution is payment for environmental services (PES) through a market approach (RBPs in this context). The underlying ideology is neoclassical environmental economics based on concepts such as rational choice, "bioenvironmentalists" (Hiraldo & Tanner, 2012). Conditionality is the key component of PES or RBPs. Payments are only made if ex-post monitoring shows a reduction in deforestation below a certain baseline (Seymour, 2016).

2.1.3 Global Public Goods

The theoretical justification for REDD+ as well as other emissions trading offsets or climate finance arises from the theory of public goods. Climate mitigation meets the Samuelson (1954) criteria for a public good of being: (1) Non-rival in that everyone benefits and (2) non-excludable in that enjoying the benefit of a stable climate does not lessen the benefit to other individuals and that it is impossible to prevent someone from enjoying these benefits. It is also global, so that REDD+ results, as with other climate change mitigation, has benefits around the globe.

2.1.4 Mutual Benefit

Kaul et al. (1999) claim that to achieve durable and significant international cooperation outcomes on global public goods, all parties must be better off. Compensatory payments are crucial to any strategy on public goods where the priorities of the stakeholders diverge.

For REDD+ to meet this criterion, the payment for results should also compensate the full cost to the host country, that is, the opportunity cost plus the transaction and implementation cost less co-benefits. Developing and developed countries have different priorities; therefore, compensation for the net cost to the developing country is necessary for durable emissions reductions. The official REDD+ provisions (see below) were much more reserved about the point of full compensation of opportunity costs (only citing 'positive incentives', see UNFCCC 2011, Add.1; App. 1:26) It also was not clear about Carbon offsets in particular (Angelsen, 2017) Juan Chang a Deputy Director of the Green Climate Fund (GCF), the financial mechanism for the UNFCCC is quoted as saying:

> "For some people, REDD+ is a compensation mechanism that pays for not cutting down forests," he said. "To me that's the wrong definition. It makes the system fragile and subject to so many changes that it becomes unsustainable. However, if we look at REDD+ as a transition in which you're providing sustainable livelihoods as opposed to unsustainable activities, then there is a point where you do not depend on the payments that REDD+ provides to sustain your livelihoods and keep the forest" (Clouse, 2020)

This opens the question of what is an adequate, sustainable livelihood and what happens if the stakeholder chooses the deforestation route to development rather than a less prosperous but sustainable livelihood offered through REDD+.

2.1.5 Country Ownership

Country ownership is an increasingly discussed concept in ODA in which developing countries set their own agenda for the implementation of ODA. It is related to the idea of country ownership facilitated by mutual benefit which facilitates the maintenance of support for the activity within the host country. It is a concept established by international agreements such as the Paris Declaration on Aid Effectiveness and the Accra Agenda for Action (OECD, 2021a). A decline in-country ownership can negate the gains made in REDD+ projects. If countries receive inadequate compensation, then the prospect of deforestation and agricultural expansion becomes a more attractive alternative.

3 Methodology

This study begins with a literature search using various JCU databases and google scholar. Many of the references are from the grey literature because it discusses institutional arrangements surrounding the United Nations Framework Convention on Climate Change (UNFCCC). Some were sourced from the stakeholder organisations themselves and others were news items that had informative quotes from people who work in the field.

As indicated in the introduction, the SWOT (strengths, weaknesses, opportunities, threats) framework has been utilised in this study as the principal analytical tool to analyse the complexities of a fixed but low price for REDD+ RBPs from public sources. SWOT analysis is a very widely used strategic decision-making tool applied to many entities ranging from commercial firms to countries and its use and prominent place in the strategic literature substantiated by Helm and Nixon (2010). Although they did point out that there are issues with SWOT not ranking factors and that further research and theory building was warranted. Sub-aim 2 of this study involves numerous stakeholders that are likely to be affected in many ways. Fertel et al. (2013) stated that the SWOT framework is particularly suitable for aiding in strategic decisions concerning climate change which involve maximising several different objectives. Much of the evaluation of low and fixed RBP prices uses the key theoretical concepts and theories identified in the literature search listed in Sect. 2.

Apart from abatement costs and RBP prices, most of the data is qualitative. SWOT is useful for dealing with qualitative data from a number of sources (Gurel & Tat, 2017).

The organisations that set the pricing for the REDD+ RBP and provide most of the funding are public finance institutions such as Green Climate Fund; Forest Investment Program administered through the World Bank and bilateral institutions such as Norway's International Climate and Forest Initiative (NICFI). The internal and external factors are identified. The main internal factor is the decision as to whether these organisations should stay with low fixed prices for RBPs or whether they should opt for a more flexible price structure. Factors external to these organisations include prices in commodity markets and the existence of viable market for compliance carbon offsets that include REDD+ activities, or removal of commodities associated with deforestation from global supply chains. As almost all climate finance from these institutions is counted as ODA by the OECD (Ryan, 2019), these organisations are also evaluated on their contributions to developing countries' economic development and welfare as required by the OECD for ODA. Evaluating the efficacy of REDD+ in reducing emissions, deforestation and forest degradation is the other main aim of the SWOT analysis.

4 Results

A Strengths, Weaknesses, Opportunities and Threats (SWOT) analysis was conducted with an emphasis on how low and fixed RBPs can be analysed using the theoretical frameworks and concepts outlined above. The SWOT analysis is summarised in Table 2. Many of the strengths, weaknesses, opportunities and threats share common causal factors. As an example, indigenous-peoples-and-local-communities concerns are a subset of the many country ownership issues. Nevertheless, they were sufficiently distinct issues to warrant separate designation.

4.1 Strengths

4.1.1 Lower Investment Is Required for a Given Amount of Emissions Reductions from Deforestation. This Leaves More Funds Available for Other ODA and Climate Sectors Because of the Likely Restricted Future Volume of ODA

Less funds diverted from other ODA sectors to finance global public goods. The Paris Agreement has a goal of $100 billion per year by 2020 until 2025 to support developing countries climate change efforts. This consists of public finance and private finance directly mobilised by governments. Public finance has overwhelmingly been sourced from ODA. The comprehensive ODA figures compiled by the OECD (2021b) show net ODA was $152 billion in 2019. Private finance directly mobilised has been minor for REDD+ (Lujan & Silva-Chavez, 2018). Half of the $100 billion goals was specified to fund adaptation. Therefore, support for mitigation in all sectors under this provision would be limited to $50 billion per year. If we limit the amount of REDD+ funding to around 30% of total support in line with its potential contribution to global mitigation, which Angelsen et al. (2018) consider fair, that puts a limit of $15 billion per year that could be diverted from other ODA categories into finance for REDD+ RBPs.

A theoretical justification for REDD+ and other international mitigation activities arises from the theory of public goods. Climate mitigation meets the Samuelson (1954) criteria for a public good of being both non-rival and non-excludable. REDD + results, as with other climate change mitigation measures, have benefits worldwide. However, when developing countries suffer net costs for climate mitigation, this has significant equity and durability implications (Ryngaert, 2016; Kaul et al., 1999). The low price facilitates limiting the diversion of aid from other sectors. This

Table 2 Summary of SWOT analysis of low fixed RBP prices

Strengths	**Opportunities**
Lower investment is required for a given amount of emissions reductions from deforestation. This leaves more funds available for other ODA and climate sectors. Less burden on developing countries to provide global public goods.	If the compliance market for REDD+ RBPs become widespread, compliance RBPs may replace low priced payments from ODA, leaving more funds available for other ODA sectors.
Raising the price does not result in greater payments in total because the total volume of REDD+ payments is capped by a budget from DFIs.	
Weaknesses	**Threats**
Does not align with the concept of country ownership.	If returns to agriculture, including wood pellets and bioenergy, increase it may require greater payment to maintain country ownership, but a fixed price means the donor cannot respond with a higher price to cover increasing stakeholder opportunity costs.
A low price for RBPs results in a lower return from forest conservation compared with other land uses to relevant stakeholders.	The ineffectiveness of REDD+ based on low fixed prices may lead to greater efforts to remove deforestation related products from global supply chains. Thus, shifting the burden of mitigation on to developing countries.
Fewer funds available to deal with equity issues such as support for local communities and indigenous peoples.	
A low price means that forest conservation is restricted to areas that have low opportunity cost, which is often indigenous land, this has serious equity implications.	
Developing countries burdened with financing a global common good.	
Widening the gap in Carbon prices leads to a lessening of the efficiency to the transition to a low Carbon economy.	
Current pilot programs are not representative of likely future compliance markets.	

strength is relevant to the economic development and welfare of developing countries.

4.1.2 Raising the Price Does Not Mean Greater Payments Overall Because the Total Volume of Payments Is Capped by a Budget

The rule is the higher the price, the smaller the proportion of emissions reductions achieved that are funded. With a lower price, a greater volume of emissions reductions can be funded. A higher price could lead to a smaller number of countries receiving RBPs as a result of fewer hectares being preserved. This could create resentment in the countries that do not receive RBPs. The sharing of funds between countries has been an issue with the Kyoto Protocol's Clean Development Mechanism (Agbonifo, 2017). Similarly, a variable price is likely to result in resentment with host countries receiving different prices. These resentments are unlikely to facilitate emissions reductions.

4.2 Weaknesses

4.2.1 Does Not Align with the Concept of Country Ownership

The lack of compensation for lost economic gain and transaction costs from deforestation can create resentment among stakeholders and endanger forest protection's long-term viability. Expectations of significant REDD+ funding drove many countries participation (Brockhaus et al., 2017). Country ownership is an increasingly important concept in which developing countries set their own agenda for ODA in general. If countries receive inadequate compensation, then the prospect of deforestation and agricultural expansion becomes a more attractive option. A decline in-country ownership is a major threat to REDD+ goals. A cogent current example is that the Brazilian Government has recently cut back on environmental regulation and enforcement to prevent deforestation. The current low RBPs paid to Brazil have proved not to be sufficient incentive. At the same time, Brazil has requested $10 billion per year to reduce deforestation (GOB, 2020). As the expectations of the level of developed country support decline, support for policies and measures that reduce deforestation may be declining in Indonesia. Jong (2020) reported that Indonesia has degazetted 26 million ha of protected forest over the last 20 years. REDD+ set up expectations of compensation and alternative development pathways within forested countries (NORAD, 2011). When REDD+ does not live up to these expectations, support within those countries for reducing emissions from deforestation will likely fall relative to the desire for agricultural development and other extractive activities. Thus, there is currently a "narrative of disappointment" from leaders of host countries (Seymour, 2016).

Country ownership sometimes includes participation by stakeholders (Smithers, 2011), including subnational governments, agricultural commodity producers, local communities and indigenous peoples. Brimont et al. (2017) found that for a REDD+ activity in Madagascar, the compensation given to local people was one-seventh what their economic losses from not deforesting were. Such outcomes associated with inadequate funding are likely to create resentment in the local population against REDD+ activities, endangering their long-term viability. This weakness applies to the aim of long-term emissions reductions and economic development and welfare in developing countries.

4.2.2 A Fixed and Lower Price for RBPs Results in a High Probability of a Lower Return from Forest Conservation Compared with Other Land Uses for Relevant Stakeholders

There are fewer incentives to protect forest than if the price was flexible and responsive to markets (High-level commission, 2014). In the incentive rationale framework, this is ascribed to externalities not being fully internalised. This weakness applies to emissions reductions.

4.2.3 Fewer Funds Are Available to Deal with Equity Issues Such as the Compensation of Local Communities and Indigenous Peoples

Less funding for community-based activities such as forest planning or land tenure initiatives violates the "empower local people, women and marginalised groups" rationale (Angelsen, 2017).

Donor funding is insufficient and is vulnerable to political fluctuations (Angelsen et al., 2018). Global estimates of finance pledged or committed to support REDD+ efforts are US$ 1.1–2.7 billion per year (Norman & Nakhooda, 2014; Olesen et al., 2018) – the broad range is primarily due to different REDD+ definitions. By some estimates, the world needs at least US$ 15 billion per year, compared to the US$ 1–2 billion currently available (Norman & Nakhooda, 2014). By these measures, funding is an order of magnitude too low. This considers estimates by the Eliasch Review (Eliasch, 2008) that by 2030, the cost to halve emissions from the forest sector could be around US$ 17–33 billion per year, including global carbon trading. Morris and Stevenson estimated that by 2020 the cost to halve deforestation is between US$ 15 and US$ 60 billion. Increased funding from ODA has been justified using the argument that only 3% of climate funding goes to such land-oriented climate solutions, less than a tenth of what could be considered a fair share (Global Environment Facility, 2018). If implemented, this would go a long way to narrowing the funding gap between what is needed and what is currently available.

The 2020 Green Climate Fund (GCF) RBP payment to Indonesia included US$ 93.4 million for decentralised sustainable forest governance (GCF, 2020). There are 9.2 million households in forest areas, and that amounts to less than US$ 10 per household. Optimal ecological and social outcomes routinely require intensive community consultation processes. It is difficult to see how this level of funding can deliver the equitable forest governance required for the Forest Management Unit program, which gives rights to forest-dependent peoples. This weakness applies to developing countries' economic development and welfare, which may reduce emissions reductions in the longer term.

4.2.4 A Low Price Means That Forest Conservation Is Restricted to Areas That Have Low Opportunity Costs which Is Often Indigenous Land

This has serious equity considerations (Sloan et al., 2018). It also has implications for the "empowering local people" rationale described by Angelsen (2017). As such, it inhibits the economic development and welfare of the host country.

4.2.5 Developing Countries Finance a Global Common Good at a Net Cost to Themselves

This violates the principle of Common-but- differential- responsibilities- and-respective-capabilities (CBDR-RC) as developing countries bear the cost (UNFCCC, 1992).

4.2.6 Widening the Gap in Carbon Prices Leads to a Lessening of the Efficiency to the Transition to a Low Carbon Economy

RBPs were envisaged as covering the net cost of not converting the forest to other land uses such as oil palm or beef production. However, major public funders of REDD+ have benchmarked payments for results at US$ 5/t CO2-e (note: Norway pays US$ 10/tCO2-e in some cases). RBP payments at these prices are far below most estimates of the opportunity costs plus the transaction/management costs less net co-benefits which in the examples above of Rakatma et al. (2017) and Busch and Engelmann (2015) above, generally vary between US$ 20/tCO2-e and 50/tCO2-e of reducing deforestation.

Narrowing the range of carbon prices leads to greater efficiency under certain simple conditions because it ensures firms equalise marginal abatement costs across emissions sectors, a necessary condition for an efficient transition (Nordhaus, 1991, cited in High-Level Commission on Carbon Prices, 2017).

Globally carbon prices still vary widely from US$1/tCO2-e to $119/tCO2-e with the average of carbon prices being above US $10/tCO2-e. However, the High-Level Commission on Carbon Prices (2017) has estimated that if the world is to stay below the Paris Agreement temperature goal then a Carbon price is needed of US$40 to US $80/tCO2-e by 2020 and US$50 to US$100/tCO2-e by 2030. The International Energy Agency recommends a Carbon price of US$75 to US$100/tCO2-e (World Bank, 2020).

The 5 US$/tCO2 price from the GCF and the FCPF REDD+ RBPs is at the low end of the range of Carbon prices that are increasingly being introduced. Development finance institutions also use shadow prices with which to evaluate projects. The IDA uses a shadow price of US$40/tCO2-e and US$80/tCO2-e to do evaluations of projects (World Bank, 2017). The World Bank (2017) maintains that this shadow price was designed to match the High Level Commission on Carbon Prices (2017) recommendation. This shows a large difference between its shadow price for Carbon and the usual REDD+ RBPs price of US$5/tCO2 and it contradicts the High Level Commissions (2017) observation that equalising the marginal abatement cost across the sources and sectors will ease the transition to a low carbon economy.

I have not been able to find a stated explanation for the use of the US$5/tCO2 benchmark price set by the FCPF of the World Bank or any other donor. FCPF ignored The Forest Carbon Partnership Facility (2012) working group, which had recommended a negotiated price based on willingness to pay and consisting of a combination of fixed and floating proportions where feasible. This lack of transparency on how the $5/tCO2 fixed price was introduced contradicts the High-Level Commissions (2017) recommendation that policy should be transparent and "predictably flexible":

Frances Seymour, the distinguished senior fellow at the World Resources Institute (WRI), was quoted in Clouse (2020) as saying the price-setting was based on unbalanced negotiations between development finance institutions (DFI) and host countries. This weakness is particularly relevant to emissions reductions as its economic effects apply to both developed and developing economies.

4.3 Opportunities

4.3.1 If Compliance Markets for REDD+ RBPs Become Widespread, Compliance RBPs May Replace Low Priced Payments from ODA, Leaving More Available for Other ODA Sectors

The GCF does not pay REDD+ RBPs if RPBs have been paid from other sources for the same emissions reductions (Green Climate Fund, 2017). If mitigation funding comes from sources other than ODA, that contributes to developing countries' economic development.

4.4 Threats

4.4.1 If Returns to Agriculture Increase It May Require Greater Payment to Maintain Country Ownership But a Fixed Price Means the Donor Cannot Pay a Higher Price to Cover Net Costs

Under the economic incentives rationale of REDD+ this puts at risk the continued implementation of the policy and measures required to prevent deforestation. Through changes such as increasing commodity prices, the balance of incentive can shift from REDD+ RBP forest preservation to deforestation for agriculture which threatens increased emissions.

4.4.2 The Ineffectiveness of REDD+ Based on Low Fixed Prices May Lead to Greater Efforts to Remove Deforestation Related Products from Global Supply Chains, Shifting the Burden of Mitigation to Developing Countries

This will shift the burden of emissions reductions from developed to developing countries with even less effort to compensate developing countries to provide a global public good which violates the UNFCCC principle of Common but Differentiated Responsibilities and Respective Capabilities (CBDR RC) raising many equity issues (Ryngaert, 2016) and is therefore detrimental to the economic development and welfare of developing countries.

4.4.3 Current Pilot Programs Are Not Representative of Future Compliance Markets

The RBP price for these pilot programs may be grossly unrepresentative of the prices available in any future compliance market once it is established. Particular issues would be, insufficient resources and lack of experience for stakeholders negotiating prices for RBPs. This threatens the development and welfare of developing countries.

5 Conclusion

REDD+ RPBs were envisaged as a market mechanism for reducing emissions from forest destruction. In the absence of a UNFCCC compliance carbon market, public institutions have financed pilot projects funded from donor ODA budgets. This has resulted in a limited budget for REDD+ RBPs, with prices paid being low and inflexible. The SWOT analysis carried out in this study identified a number of implications of the current situation for future emissions reductions and the development and welfare of developing countries. The development finance institutions have never explained the choice of a low and fixed price. The SWOT analysis highlighted a possible explanation that a minimal Carbon price enabled the DFIs to attribute their REDD+ RBPs to a greater volume of emissions reductions. It also facilitates the funding of a greater number of countries at a single price, thus reducing the likelihood of resentful stakeholders.

Conversely, the funding per country is small. The abandonment of the principle of REDD+ fully covering opportunity and transaction/implementation cost, less the co-benefits of ending deforestation, has reduced pressure to divert ODA to REDD+. Notwithstanding, the issue of aid diversion applies to all climate finance and not just REDD+.

The introduction of REDD+, created expectations that have not been met due largely to a lack of funding. Subsequent disillusionment of REDD+ stakeholders may seriously impede it meeting its goal in the coming years. The lack of funds will disadvantage vulnerable groups such as indigenous people and local communities because there are less funds to provide forest and land use planning and alternative livelihoods to deforestation or other benefits such as land tenure clarification. Developing countries are being asked to provide a global public good, climate mitigation, which is in contravention to established climate justice principles such as CBDR RC. This study concludes that a low fixed price is not efficient, equitable or durable especially as developing country expectations that were raised of fair prices for REDD+ RBPs diminish. In the absence of an effective compliance market for REDD+, it is recommended that flexible prices sufficient to cover costs be established in combination with a greatly expanded REDD+ RBP budget from public sources, which do not divert funds from other ODA sectors. The literature to date has proceeded on the assumption that REDD+ RBPs cover or exceed the full marginal abatement costs, up to a carbon price set by markets. The economic incentives rationale would predict failure if host country costs are not covered. New research should investigate the likely results of REDD+ RBPs if prices are inflexible and do not reflect marginal abatement costs. Work should be carried out on the extent to which claimed emissions reductions are not additional, that is they occurred at zero cost to the stakeholders. However, other factors not related directly to RBP pricing may be at play and so expertise from other fields may contribute to the analysis, including but not limited to; international relations, political economy analysis, strategic decision making, theorists in government and administration, and development economics.

References

Agbonifo, P. (2017). The pursuit of climate protection and the uneven global distribution of clean development mechanism (CDM) projects: Lesson from least developed countries (LDCS). *European Journal of Sustainable Development, 6*(1), 139. https://doi.org/10.14207/ejsd.2017.v6n1p139

Angelsen, A. (2017). REDD+ as results-based aid: General lessons and bilateral agreements of Norway. *Review of Development Economics, 21*(2), 237–264. https://doi.org/10.1111/rode.12271

Angelsen, A., Martius, C., De Sy, V., Duchelle, A. E., Larson, A. M., & Pham, T. T. (Eds.). (2018). *Transforming REDD+: Lessons and new directions*. CIFOR.

Brimont, L., Ezzina de Blas, D., & Kasenty, A. (2017). The cost of making compensation payments to local forest populations in a REDD+ pilot project in Madagascar. *Madagascar Conservation and Development, 12*(1), 161045.

Brockhaus, M., Korhonen-Kurki, K., Sehring, J., Di Gregorio, M., Assembe-Mvondo, S., Babon, A., Bekele, M., Gebara, M. F., Khatri, D. B., Kambire, H., Kengoum, F., Kweka, D., Menton, M., Moeliono, M., Paudel, N. S., Pham, T. T., Resosudarmo, I. A. P., Sitoe, A., Wunder, S., & Zida, N. (2017). REDD+, transformational change and the promise of performance-based payments: A qualitative comparative analysis. *Climate Policy, 17*(6), 708–730. https://doi.org/10.1080/14693062.2016.1169392

Busch, J., & Engelmann, J. (2015). The future of forests: Emissions from tropical deforestation with and without a carbon rice, 2016–2050. In *CGD Climate and Forest Paper Series #22* (Working Paper 411). CGD.

Clouse, C. (2020, July 15). In the battle to save forests, a make-or-break moment for REDD+. *Mongabay*. Series–Global Forests. https://news.mongabay.com/2020/07/in-the-battle-to-save-forests-a-make-or-break-moment-for-redd/

Costa Rica and Papua New Guinea. (2005). *Reducing emissions from deforestation in developing countries: Approaches to stimulate action, submissions from parties*. Conference of the parties eleventh session Montreal. 28 November to 9 December. https://unfccc.int/resource/docs/2005/cop11/eng/misc01.pdf

Eliasch, J. (2008). *The eliasch review, climate change: Financing global forests*. Earthscan/James & James. https://assets.publishing.service.gov.uk/government/uploads/system/uploads/attachment_data/file/228833/9780108507632.pdf

FAO (UN Food and Agriculture Organisation). (2020). *Global forest resources assessment 2020: Main report*. Rome. https://doi.org/10.4060/ca9825en

Fertel, C., Bahn, O., Vaillancourt, K., & Waaub, J. (2013). Canadian energy and climate policies: A SWOT analysis in search of federal/provincial coherence. *Energy Policy, 63*. https://doi.org/10.1016/j.enpol.2013.09.057

Forest Carbon Partnership Facility. (2012). *5a. Recommendations of the Working Group on Methodological and Pricing Approach, Fourth Meeting of the Carbon Fund (CF4)*, Santa Marta, Colombia, June 24–25, 2012.

Global Environment Facility. (2018, September 13). *News*, Retrieved May 8, 2021, https://www.thegef.org/news/global-business-government-and-agricultural-leaders-announce-land-focused-commitments-mitigate

Government of Brazil (GOB). (2020). *Brazil's nationally determined contribution (NDC)*. Paris Agreement. UNFCCC. https://www4.unfccc.int/sites/ndcstaging/PublishedDocuments/Brazil%20First/Brazil%20First%20NDC%20(Updated%20submission).pdf

Green Climate Fund (GCF). (2017, June 26). *Pilot Programme for REDD+ results based payments*. GCF/B.17/13. https://www.greenclimate.fund/sites/default/files/gcf-b17-13.pdf. Green Climate Fund.

Green Climate Fund (GCF). (2020, August 21). *FP130: Indonesia REDD-plus RBP for results period 2014–2016*. Decision B.26/02.

Gurel, E., & Tat, M. (2017). SWOT analysis: A theoretical review. *The Journal of International Social Research, 10*(51). https://doi.org/10.17719/jisr.2017.1832

Helm, M., & Nixon, J. (2010). Exploring SWOT analysis – Where are we now? – A review of academic research from the last decade. *Journal of Strategy and Management, 3*(3), 215.

High-Level Commission on Carbon Prices. (2017). *Report of the high-level commission on carbon prices*. World Bank.

Hiraldo, R., & Tanner, T. M. (2012). The role of ideologies in framing the REDD+agenda. In A. Angelsen, M. Brockhaus, W. D. Sunderlin, & L. V. Verchot (Eds.), *Analysing REDD+: Challenges and choices* (pp. 37–38). Center for International Forestry Research (CIFOR).

Jong, H., (2020, April 22). Obstacles abound in bid to protect forests and cut emissions. *Mongabay*. https://news.mongabay.com/2020/04/obstacles-abound-in-bid-to-protect-indonesias-forests-and-cut-emissions/

Kaul, I., Grunberg, I., & Stern, M. A. (1999). Defining global public goods. In *Global public goods: International cooperation in the 21st century*. ISBN:0-19-513051-0 (cloth); ISBN:0-19-513052-9 (paper).

Köhl, M., Neupane, P., & Mundhenk, P. (2020). REDD+ measurement, reporting and verification – A cost trap? Implications for financing REDD+MRV costs by result-based payments. *Ecological Economics, 168*, 2020. https://doi.org/10.1016/j.ecolecon.2019.106513

Lujan, B., & Silva-Chávez, G. (2018). *Mapping forest finance: A landscape of available sources of finance for REDD+ and climate action in forests*. Environmental Defence Fund.

Martius, C., Angelsen, A., Larson, A. M., Pham, T. T., Sonwa, D. J., & Belcher, B. (2018). Pathway to impact. Is REDD+ a viable theory change? In A. Angelsen, C. Martius, V. De Sy, A. E. Duchelle, A. M. Larson, & T. T. Pham (Eds.), *Transforming REDD+: Lessons and new directions*. CIFOR.

NORAD. (2011). *Real-time evaluation of Norway's international climate and forest initiative contributions to national REDD+ processes 2007–2010 country report: Brazil.*

Norman, M., & Nakhooda, S. (2014). *The state of REDD+ finance*. Center for Global Development.

Organisation for Economic Co-operation and Development (OECD). (2021a, March 15). *Paris Declaration and Accra Agenda for Action*. OECD. http://www.oecd.org/dac/effectiveness/parisdeclarationandaccraagendaforaction.htm#:~:text=The%20Paris%20Declaration%20outlines%20the%20following%20five%20fundamental,align%20behind%20these%20objectives%20and%20use%20local%20systems. 15 Mar 2021.

Organisation for Economic Co-operation and Development (OECD). (2021b, May 14). *Official development assistance (ODA)*. OECD. https://www.oecd.org/dac/financing-sustainable-development/development-finance-standards/official-development-assistance.htm

Olesen, A,. Böttcher, H,. Siemons, A,. Herrmann, L,. Martius, C,. Roman-Cuesta, R, M,. Atmadja, S,. Hansen, D, S,. Andersen, S, P,. Georgiev, I,. Bager, S, L,. Schwöppe, C,. & Wunder, S. (2018). *Study on EU financing of REDD+ related activities, and results-based payments pre and post 2020: Sources, cost-effectiveness and fair allocation of incentives*. Luxembourg: European Commission, DG Environment/Climate Action.

Rainforest Action Network. (2018). *Cargill's problems with palm oil.* CC BY-NC 2.0. https://www.ran.org/wp-content/uploads/2018/06/cargills_problems_with_palm_oil_low.pdf

Rakatama, A., Pandit, R., Ma, C., & Iftekhar, S. (2017). *The costs and benefits of REDD+: A review of the literature* (Forest Policy and Economics 75) (pp. 103–111). Elsevier.

Ryan, F. (2019, April 24). *Separating climate finance and ODA, DEVPOLICYBLOG*. Crawford School of Public Policy, Australian National University. https://devpolicy.org/separating-climate-finance-and-oda-20190424/

Ryngaert, C. (2016). Climate change mitigation techniques and international law: Assessing the externalities of reforestation and geo-engineering. *Ratio Juris, 30*(3), 273–289. https://doi.org/10.1111/raju.12154

Samuelson, P. A. (1954). The pure theory of public expenditure. *Review of Economics and Statistics, 36*(4), 387–89. https://doi.org/10.2307/1925895. JSTOR 1925895. S2CID 153571905.

Seymour, F. (2016). *Why forests? Why now? The science, economics, and politics of tropical forests and climate change*. Seymour, F., Busch, J. P., Includes bibliographic references. ISBN: 978-1-933286-85-3987654321.

Sills, E. O., Atmadja, S. S., de Sassi, C., Duchelle, A. E., Kweka, D. L., Resosudarmo, I. A. P., & Sunderlin, W. D. (Eds.). (2014). *REDD+ on the ground: A case book of subnational initiatives across the globe*. CIFOR.

Sloan, S., Pereira, J. C., Labbate, G., Asner, G., & Imbach, P. (2018). The cost and distribution of forest conservation for national emissions reductions. *Global Environmental Change, 53*, 39–51.

Smith, P. M., Bustamante, H., Ahammad, H., Clark, H., Dong, E. A., Elsiddig, H., Haberl, R., Harper, J., House, M., Jafari, O., Masera, C., Mbow, N. H., Ravindranath, C. W., Rice, C., Abad, A., Romanovskaya, F., Sperling, & Tubiello, F. (2014). Agriculture, forestry and other land use (AFOLU). In Contribution of Working Group III to the Fifth Assessment Report of the Intergovernmental Panel on Climate Change, O. R. Edenhofer, Y. Pichs-Madruga, E. Sokona, S. Farahani, K. Kadner, A. Seyboth, I. Adler, S. Baum, P. Brunner, B. Eickemeier, J. Kriemann, S. Savolainen, C. Schlömer, T. von Stechow, T. Zwickel, & J. C. Minx (Eds.), *Climate change 2014: Mitigation of climate change*. Cambridge University Press.

Smithers, N. (2011). *The importance of stakeholder ownership for capacity development results*. World Bank Institute.

Tubiello, F. N., Pekkarinen, A., Marklund, L., Wanner, N., Conchedda, G., Federici, S., Rossi, S., & Grassi, G. (2020). Carbon emissions and removals by forests: New estimates 1990–2020. *Earth System Science Data Discussion*. https://doi.org/10.5194/essd-2020-203

United Nations Framework Convention on Climate Change (UNFCCC). (1992). https://unfccc.int/files/essential_background/background_publications_htmlpdf/application/pdf/conveng.pdf

United Nations General Assembly. (2015, September 25). *Transforming our world: The 2030 agenda for sustainable development*. Resolution adopted by the General Assembly. https://sustainabledevelopment.un.org/content/documents/21252030%20Agenda%20for%20Sustainable%20Development%20web.pdf

World Bank. (2017, November 12). *Guidance note on shadow price of Carbon in economic analysis*. https://pubdocs.worldbank.org/en/911381516303509498/2017-Shadow-Price-of-Carbon-Guidance-Note-FINAL-CLEARED.pdf

World Bank. (2020, May). *State and trends of carbon pricing 2020*. World Bank. https://doi.org/10.1596/978-1-4648-1586-7. License: Creative Commons Attribution CC BY 3.0 IGO.

Vietnam and Motorcycles: Dialectics and Commensurate Adaptations

Quang Chinh Nguyen, Sanjay Mishra, Dyen Thanh My Nguyen, and Duyen Hong Thuc Nguyen

Abstract Due to rapid urbanisation, mixed traffic in Vietnam's megacities is getting worse. Dialectics remain unsolved as communities persist with their two-wheel figurehead while the government frames taxonomy and substitution. Driven by the need for reconciliations, the proposed empirical research aims to fill the knowledge gap and to contribute to the Sustainable Path to 2030 Agenda.

The study explored values and threats in relation to motorcycle, proposed solutions to the dialectic, probed for community readiness, and weighted predictors against adaptation. Sequential Exploratory Mixed Methodology was followed to develop a new theory. System data input was collected from three sources: documentary review, qualitative expert interviews, and quantitative survey using questionnaires of 100 variables. More than 700 responses from Hanoi and Ho Chi Minh City facilitated the analytics threading four techniques of: Ordinal Logistic Regression with Factors Input, Generalised Linear Models with Ordinal Logistic Response, Spearman's correlations, and Exploratory Factor Analysis.

Benchmarking between four analytical methods resulted in more than 80 coinciding associations between community acceptance and its determinants that enable a

The original version of this chapter was revised: This chapter was inadvertently published with incorrect author's name "Tasya Aspiranti" instead of "Dyen Thanh My Nguyen" which has been corrected now. The correction to this chapter is available at https://doi.org/10.1007/978-981-16-5260-8_39

Q. C. Nguyen (✉)
Midwest University, Wentzville, MO, USA
e-mail: quangscd@gmail.com

S. Mishra
School of Business, University of Kansas, Lawrence, KS, USA

D. T. M. Nguyen
FPT University, Ho Chi Minh City, Vietnam

D. H. T. Nguyen
Industrial University of Ho Chi Minh City, Ho Chi Minh City, Vietnam

© The Author(s), under exclusive license to Springer Nature Singapore Pte Ltd. 2022, corrected publication 2022

T. Chaiechi, J. Wood (eds.), *Community Empowerment, Sustainable Cities, and Transformative Economies*, https://doi.org/10.1007/978-981-16-5260-8_13

better understanding of the issues related to motorcycles. Emerging determinants include propaganda/education, public bus operation, infrastructure/travel patterns, and regulations change.

Keywords Bus · Community empowerment · Motorcycle · Sustainable city · Vietnam traffic

1 Introduction

1.1 Background

Motorcycle ownership in Vietnam has been increasing for the last two decades and globally is second to Taiwan (Boltze & Vu, 2016, pp. 205–206). In Ho Chi Minh City (HCMC), the *Houtrans* survey in 2002 showed that more than 90% of households owned motorcycles and 53% owned two or more motorcycles. A study in Hanoi showed that private vehicle users tend to continue using their vehicles despite the public transport being developed in the city (Nguyen et al., 2018, p. 118). Nguyen & Yoshitaka (2018, pp. 1, 6) reported the difficulty in introducing BRT to Hanoi as it was not attractive to working and school-age populations. Fujii and Van Hong (2009, p. 98) highlighted that only 5% of trips in HCMC occur by bus, whereas almost all the rest are by motorcycle. Dapice et al. (2010, pp. 3–8) reported that HCMC residents rely heavily on the motorcycle and little on public buses. More recently, Chu and Thi (2017, p. 26) found that public transport in Hanoi and Ho Chi Minh City only meets 7–10% and 9.8% of demand, respectively. Thus this is forcing more than 90% to travel by motorcycles and other personal transportation means.

Motorcycle holds an important role in rural areas or areas lacking public transport services (Hoang & Okamura, 2018, p. 164), with its advantages of lower costs and less space needed for driving and parking compared to other vehicles (Tien-Pen et al., 2003, p. 50). However, megacities over the developing world have been facing increased traffic problems, which strongly call for sustainable traffic management (Boltze & Vu, 2016, p. 205; Bakker et al., 2017, p. 1). In Vietnam, the strong process of urbanisation, the non-synchronous infrastructure system and urban planning, and poor awareness of traffic participants make the traffic in Ho Chi Minh City and Hanoi worse (Chu & Thi, 2017, p. 26). Currently, in Hanoi, there are extreme opinions that "motorcycles are the enemies of urban traffic''[and] "adverse effects have led to Hanoi's decision to stop using motorbikes and suspect the rationality of motorcycles in the (inner) city" (Tran, 2019, pp. 89, 90, 93).

The debate persists for years in Vietnam: sustainable cities foster public transport; in contrast, the community prefers private motorcycle. Discussing this division in views, Fujii and Van Hong (2009, p. 98) evaluated the bus service in HCMC as neutral in all three aspects of symbolic, instrumental, and social orderliness. They suggested a combination of "hard" measures such as improving the quality of the bus service and "soft" measures like mobility management. However, mobility management has not received much attention in research. There is a serious shortage of research that conveys the definition and the impact of these "hard" and "soft" measures.

1.2 Research Objectives

This proposed study has three major goals:

- First, because public transport and private motorcycle continue to polarise the unsolved dilemma, this research aims to fill the research gap and give solutions to the dialectic.
- Second, the paper builds on the United Nations (UN) 2030 Agenda term of community empowerment: the experiment galvanises the inclusion of low-class communities to sustainable city transport information, gives motorcyclists fair access to the survey, and shapes their voluntariness for metropolitan public transport. The study also reflects the UN Goal 11.2: "to provide access to safe, affordable, accessible and sustainable transport systems for all, improving road safety, notably by expanding public transport, with special attention to the needs of those in vulnerable situations."
- Third, the study builds on prior research by using contemporary quantitative input to test previous notions on the perceived values of motorcyclists.

The research context embroiders the two largest megacities in Vietnam: Hanoi and HCMC. Both deductive and inductive approaches are adopted.

2 Materials and Methods

This paper uses Sequential exploratory mixed methodology to achieve the research objectives. The methodology involves more than one phase of data collection and analysis. Herewith, the empirical problem-solving research "threads" through the sequence of "Qualitative First, Quantitative Later." This methodology was also posited by Tracy (2013, pp. 5, 25) and Jonker and Pennink (2010, p. 90).

Qualitatively first, this study convened three sources of input to increase the content validity: (a) documentary review with selected secondary data; (b) qualitative expert interviews; and (c) authors-generating potential factors that may influence the motorcyclists' mobility behaviour. In Sects. 2.1 and 2.2, qualitative insights from documentary review and expert interviews were added to variable groups for subsequent quantitative analyses. The authors also contributed input variables into the experiment based on their own experiences. A comprehensive list of key variables formulated from three sources of input is summarised in Table 1 of Sect. 2.3.

Quantitatively, data collection followed its preceding qualitative latent variables to compute correlations, factoring, and confirmatory regression on synchronising motorcyclists' behaviour with sustainable city network. Quantitative discussion is presented in Sect. 2.5.

Saunders et al. (2016, pp. 164, 178) classified several research strategies into their onion layers, from which experiment – studying the probability of a change in an

Table 1 List of key predictors and latent variables with coding[a]

A1	PERCEIVED USEFULNESS											
	PU1	PU2	PU3	PU4	PU5							
	CULTURE-BOUND COMFORT											
	CBC1	CBC2	CBC3	CBC4	CBC5							
	PERCEIVED EASE OF USE											
	PEU1	PEU2	PEU3	PEU4								
	REASONS AGAINST SUBSTITUTION											
	RAS1	RAS2	RAS3	RAS4	RAS5							
A2	CONGESTION											
	CG1	CG2	CG3	CG4	CG5	CG6	CG7	CG8	CG9	CG10	CG11	
	ENVIRONMENTAL POLLUTION											
	EP1	EP2	EP3	EP4								
	ACCIDENT AND SAFETY											
	AS1	AS2	AS3	AS4	AS5	AS6						
	OTHER TRANSPORT MODE											
	OTM1	OTM2	OTM3									
	POLICIES											
	PO1	PO2	PO3	PO4								
A3	PUBLIC BUS OPERATION IMPROVEMENT											
	PBO1	PBO2	PBO3	PBO4	PBO5	PBO6	…………………………			PBO11	PBO12	PBO13
	INFRASTRUCTURE / TRAVEL PATTERNS IMPROVEMENT											
	ITP1	ITP2	ITP3	ITP4	ITP5	ITP6						
	REGULATION CHANGES											
	RGL1	RGL2	RGL3	RGL4	RGL5	RGL6	………....		RGL10	RGL11		
	PROPAGANDA/EDUCATION IMPLEMENTATION											
	PEI1	PEI2	PEI3	PEI4	PEI5	PEI6	PEI7					

A4	RECONCILED/PERCEIVED EASE OF USE											
	RPEU1	RPEU2	RPEU3	RPEU4	RPEU5							
	RECONCILED/PERCEIVED USEFULNESS											
	RPU1	RPU2	RPU3	RPU4								
	COMMUNITY ACTUAL USAGE											
	CAU1	CAU2	CAU3	CAU4	CAU5	CAU6	CAU7					

A1 Community psychology and culture, A2 Government/institutional concern, A3 Tentative solutions
A4 Community adapted behavior
[a]This is a self-generated product by the study authors. For full explanation of variables, refer to the Appendix C

independent variable causing a change in a dependent variable – was applied as the backbone of this paper. Moreover, the study adopted three other research strategies: first, the research uses archival and documentary research strategy through a literature review of secondary data such as media sources and online articles. In addition, as Saunders, et al. (2016, p. 184) recommended documentary strategy to be combined with another – for example, alongside a grounded theory strategy based on qualitative interviews – expert interview therefore becomes the second strategy of this research. Survey using questionnaires is the third strategy of this research, allowing quantitative data to suggest possible reasons for particular relationships between variables and to produce models of these relationships (Saunders et al., 2016, p. 182).

2.1 Documentary Review and Input Materials

In Vietnam, according to the National Traffic Safety Committee, traffic congestion annually causes a loss of 1.34 billion USD (Nguyen et al., 2019, p. 112). Professor Nguyen Minh Hoa highlighted this at HCMC University of Social Sciences and Humanities (reproduced by Boltze & Vu, 2016, p. 206) – Congestion is added to variable groups A2. From 2008 to 2017, nationwide, 1379 traffic jams were lasting over 1 h, of which 336 occurred in Hanoi, accounting for 24.4% and 227 in Ho Chi Minh City, accounting for 16.5% (Chu & Thi, 2017, p. 26). The traffic fatality rate in Vietnam is extremely high; about 13.4 deaths per 100,000 population and motorcycles are involved in 75% of the total accidents (Tuan, V.A., Motorcycle Accidents in Vietnam, United Nations Roundtable on Safety Issues of Two-wheeled Vehicles, Geneva, 2015 – reproduced by Boltze & Vu, 2016, p. 206) – Accident is added to variable group A2. Traffic mixed with the motorcycle will become more hazardous under interruption caused by motorcycle [and] therefore requiring more effort to enhance safety (Tien-Pen et al., 2003, pp. 01, 50) – Safety is added to variable group A2 as AS1-5 series. Automobile-related social cost factors also include traffic air pollution (Shibata, 2007, p. 87). Vietnam is also one of the developing countries in Asia that suffers excessive noise emission from road traffic. To date, there has not been any proper measure to cope with the situation, and Vietnam does not have a national noise policy (Phan et al., 2008) – Noise pollution is added to variable group A2 as EP2; legal framework against noise pollution is added to variable group A2 as EP3.

According to Tran (2019), the factors influencing motorcycle use in Vietnam may be classified into the following categories: (1) Socio-demographic; (2) Travel pattern; (3) Contextual; and (4) Psychological (Hoang & Okamura, 2018, p. 163). Finally, not only for economic reasons but also because of the cultural conception in Vietnam, the ownership of a private transport vehicle is considered a symbol of the social status of the inhabitants only less than their homeownership (Tran, 2019, p. 89) – Culture-bound comfort is added to variable group A1 as CBC4, CBC5.

Shibata (2007) prioritised public buses as an immediate solution to traffic congestion in developing metropolises, rather than rapid mass transit (MRT) – MRT network is added to variable group A3 as RGL9. Professor Nguyen Minh Hoa – head of the Urban Studies Faculty of the HCMC University of Social Sciences and Humanities – highlighted that only 1.7–2% of the total area of urban land is used for traffic in Ho Chi Minh City (cited/reproduced by Boltze & Vu, 2016, p. 206) – Surface area for traffic is added to variable group A3 as ITP1. Chu and Thi (2017, p. 30) reported additional figures that road density reaches only 3.89 km/km^2 in Hanoi, and 3.88 km/km^2 in HCMC. Boltze and Vu (2016, pp. 208–212) added transit-oriented development as one of the most effective and long-term strategies, along with land use planning – Transit-oriented development is added to variable group A3 as RGL9. Similarly, Ho and Yamamoto (2011, p. 01) agreed with all ideas that bus coverage, bus operators' attitudes, and land use issues are important factors to vehicle ownership behaviour – Bus coverage is added to variable group A3 as PBO1, PBO2; bus operators' attitude is added as variables PBO7, PBO11, PBO12, PEI7; land use is added as ITP1. Boltze and Vu (2016, pp. 208–212) added that, recently, Hanoi had applied flextime to avoid congestion at peak hours – Flexible work hour is added to variable group A3 as RGL10. They also supported the concept of intermodal travel through the provision of Park-and-Ride, Bike-and-Ride, dynamically and situation-responsive infrastructure, intelligent transport systems in urban public transport such as pre-trip and in-trip information services, electronic displays, electronic tickets, security cameras – Intermodal travel patterns, park-and-ride, bike-and-ride are added to variable group A3 as ITP5; dynamic and situation-responsive infrastructure is added as variables ITP2, ITP3, ITP6; intelligent transport system is added as variable PBO5, PBO6.

An analysis of peer-reviewed literature on transport policy found that fewer than 10% of papers engaged in debates about policy aims and two-thirds of papers did not engage with real-world policies examples (Bakker et al., 2017, p. 2 – citing: Marsden, G.; Reardon, L. Questions of Governance: Rethinking the Study of Transportation Policy). Tough policies may sound excellent on paper, but it would probably take a long time to put these into practice (Shibata, 2007, p. 86). Considering the same discipline, 1300 motorcycles a working day were registered and added in HCMC (Dapice et al., 2010, p. 3) – policy and registration are added to variable group A3 as RGL1, RGL2, RGL5, and RGL6.

2.2 *Expert Interviews and Input Materials*

In addition to the input from the documentary review presented in Sect. 2.1, expert interviews were also conducted by the author in the first quarter of 2021 to collect additional contemporary input. Data currency and consistency are the essences at this stage. The saturation method was applied to the interviews to the point at which the data became repetitive, and no major new insights were gained. Interviews were post-coded.

Three representatives were selected as face-to-face interviewees: (1) a professor at University in Hanoi with a transport engineering background; (2) a high-rank project officer at HCMC Metro Line project under construction and commissioning; and (3) a high-rank Government official at HCMC Construction Department. Results of three interviews were imported to the list of variables whenever those opinion leaders agreed on the ideas or with the documentary review. Emerging families of results from the interviews included the unavoidable necessity for motorcycles, inevitable public networking and soft combination between transport modes rather than substitution. Specific results of the interviews involved the following variables: PU1, CBC4, PEU4, RAS2, CG2, CG3, CG5, CG6, CG7, CG9, EP1, EP2, EP3, EP4, AS1, AS2, AS3, AS4, AS5, OTM2, PO2, PO3, PBO1, PBO2, PBO7, PBO9, PBO11, PBO12, PBO13, ITP1, ITP2, ITP4, RGL4, RGL9, RGL11, PEI1, PEI7, RPEU1, RPEU2, RPU3, CAU4, CAU5, and CAU7. For a general understanding of each variable, please see Table 1 in Sect. 2.3; for a full description of all 100 variables, refer to Appendix C.

2.3 The Hypothetical Model

The proposed predictive model incorporates all variables imported from the three sources – documentary review, qualitative expert interviews, and authors-generating potential factors. There are 100 ordinal variables clustered into four groups: group A1 explores the perceived values of motorcycle in the mind of low-class communities; group A2 + A3 proposes "hard and soft" commensurate accommodations for resilient transport modes; and group A4 probes adaptation behaviour from vulnerable communities of motorcyclists.

Table 1 presents all candidate predictor variables and outcome variables under the form of codes. Adjacency between four groups is depicted; however, associations between component variables are not assumed at this stage by not duplicating the model under space constraint. At the end of the paper and subsequent to statistical inferences, re-modelling and specificity will shape the conclusions.

2.4 Quantitative Data Survey

Key variables of this study follow the 5-level Likert-style ordinal scale, translated into 100 bilingual rating questions. The self-completed questionnaire was designed to collect quantitative data. We pilot tested the draft of the questionnaire by sharing it with a dozen experts and informants who are similar to the responsive target for comments on the representativeness and suitability of the questions (Saunders et al., 2016). Based on comments from the pilot test, the questionnaire was refined before delivering to mass media.

Calculation of the sample size n follows the formula by Hair et al. (2017, p. 149):

$$n = \left(Z_{B,\mathrm{CL}}^2\right) \cdot \left(\frac{\sigma^2}{e^2}\right) \tag{1}$$

where

$Z_{B,CL}$ = The standardised z-value associated with the level of confidence
σ_μ = Estimate of the population standard deviation based on some type of prior information
e = Acceptable tolerance level of error (stated in percentage points)

Based on our previous experience: with an estimated value of $\sigma = 1.05$ (at 5-level Likert scale); $e = 0.1$; $z = 1.96$ (95% confidence); a round figure of n would be 450, which is smaller than the actual number of 700 records received.

Hanoi and HCMC are the two geographic zones in context. Invitations to surveys were sent to snowball facilitators and seven panels of students and blue-collar employees – the two most crowded panels of motorcyclists in Vietnam. Google Forms, Facebook combined with Emails were used as the medium for survey matching the culture of target respondents. Three links of Google Forms were created to monitor different zones, as indicated in the footnotes.[1] Out of the more than 700 responses received, 609 entries were usable after screening and cleaning. This is higher than the required sample size.

2.5 *Analytical Methods*

The paper combines four techniques before drawing conclusions on the correlations between predictors and latent responses to adaptations. To solve the dialectic rather than plunge into theoretical statistics, each of these four methods is briefly summarised hereinafter;

First Route: Ordinal Logistic Regression with Factors Input
For ordinal categories, there are several different commonly used models. The paper uses Ordinal Logistic Regression (OLR) as the first route to determine the associations between variables. The log odds (or logit) of the outcome is modelled as linear in the regression parameters. The proportional odds model is the usual (or default) form of ordinal logistic regression provided by statistical software. Dobson & Barnett (2018, p. 190) stated: The proportional odds model is based on the assumption that the effects of the covariates $x_1,\ldots,x_{p-1}$ are the same for all categories on the logarithmic scale, presented as:

[1] Three links to Google Forms with questionnaire were:
Link 1: https://forms.gle/yQPq3SkqXfDy9YNq5
Link 2: https://forms.gle/H2guGikfhxL3sj4t6
Link 3: https://forms.gle/TgDDNdfZDQFgZVaM8

$$\log \frac{\pi_1 + \ldots + \pi_j}{\pi_{j+1} + \ldots + \pi_J} = \beta_{0j} + \beta_1 x_1 + \ldots + \beta_{p-1} x_{p-1} \tag{2}$$

On the log-odds scale, the probabilities for categories are represented by parallel lines. The odds ratio associated with one unit increase in an explanatory variable x_k is $\exp(\beta_k)$, where $k = 1,\ldots, p - 1$. The coefficients for predictors in logistic regression analysis are presented in two forms in most software and in publication: (a) B_1 coefficient indicates the linear increment in the logit for a one-unit increment in the predictor; and (b) the coefficients for the predictors presented as odds ratios. The odds ratio would tell by what amount the odds of being in the case group are multiplied when the predictor is incremented by a value of one unit (Cohen et al., 2003, p. 492).

This paper applied Ordinal Logistic Regression with Factors Input, using SPSS software, iteratively between different pairs of groups: A1-A4, A1-A3, A2-A3, A2-A4, and A3-A4. Model Fitting, Goodness of Fit, Test of Parallel Lines, Parameter Estimates and other constraints are repeatedly considered. Benchmarking of selected results between four methods is presented in Sect. 3.

Second Route: Generalised Linear Models with Ordinal Logistic Response and Covariates

Generalised Linear Models (GLM) are a natural generalisation of the classical linear model, using maximum likelihood methods to estimate model parameters (Kleinbaum & Klein, 2002, p. 341) and allowing to work with data for which the mean of the dependent variable is a nonlinear function of the regression parameters, and the response variable is not normally distributed (Dunteman & Ho, 2006, p. 18). Given the mean response E(Y) and $g(\mu)$ as a function of the mean response, GLM with p independent variables can be expressed as $g(\mu)$ equals β_0 plus the summation of the p independent variables times their beta coefficients (Kleinbaum & Klein, 2002, p. 342):

$$g(\mu) = \beta_0 + \sum_{h=1}^{p} \beta_h X_h \tag{3}$$

Third Route: Spearman's Correlations

The Spearman's rho (r) correlation is used frequently with ordinal data, correlating ranks between two ordered variables and based on the concept of concordant and discordant pairs. It does not require the assumption of a bivariate normal distribution, yet by incorporating order, most producing a range from −1.0 (a perfect negative relationship) to +1.0 (a perfect positive one). As a special form of Pearson's product-moment Correlation, rho's strengths outweigh its weaknesses (Cooper & Schindler, 2014, p. 497). For this study, Spearman's correlations between 100 ordinal variables were calculated. Benchmarking of selected results among four routes is presented in Sect. 3.

Fourth Route: Exploratory Factor Analysis (EFA)
This analytical method is associated with theory development and exploratory nature, examining correlations among variables. Components or factors are simply aggregates of correlated variables which are simply empirically associated. There are two general classes of rotation: orthogonal and oblique. This paper uses orthogonal rotation where all the factors are uncorrelated with each other, and a loading matrix between observed variables and factors is produced (Tabachnick & Fidell, 2013, p. 614) as long as EFA is used descriptively to summarise the relationships in a large set of observed variables, assumptions regarding the distributions of variables are not in force. This study uses Principal Component Analysis, where multicollinearity is not a problem because there is no need to invert a matrix (Tabachnick & Fidell, 2013, pp. 618, 619).

EFA was combined with other methods of Ordinal Logistic Regression with Factors Input, Generalised Linear Models with Ordinal Logistic Response, and Spearman's Correlations. EFA contributes to the remodelling and shapes the conclusions. The final model (re-modelling from Table 1) of associations is presented in Sect. 3.

3 Results

3.1 Ordinal Logistic Vs. Spearman Vs. Generalised Linear Models

As mentioned in Sect. 2.5, this study uses four statistical techniques to identify the relations between predictors and latent responses to adaptations. Spearman's Correlation was the first gate filter. A total number of 3312 Spearman's correlation tests were calculated. These include 448 tests among group A1 and A2; 576 tests among A1 and A3; 256 tests among A1 and A4; 1008 tests among A2 and A3; 448 tests among A2 and A4; and 576 tests among A3 and A4. Satisfactory output from the first gate filter was then moved to the second skimmer using OLR and GLM techniques. To conclude correlations, pairs of variables must additionally: (a) satisfy at least the key criteria of one of these two techniques; and (b) not rejecting any key parameters of the threefold OLR–Spearman–GLM. A total number of 303 triple tests were done at the second skimmer. Due to space constraint, this paper cannot show all processes and results. Only one example is presented hereinafter: Table 2 illustrates the variable RPU4 computed against selected variables of group A3.

Table 2 Triple tests between OLR–Spearman–GLM[a]: an example of RPU4 versus group A3

RPU4 vs. A3													
Ordinal Logistic Regression with Factors Input							Spearman's Correlation Result		Generalised Linear Model with Covariates Input				
Parameter Estimates (All IVs)			Sig. (MFI) <0.05	Sig. (GoF) >0.05	Pseudo R-Square (N)	Sig. (ToPL) (>0.05)			Test of Model Effects	Parameter Estimates (All IVs)		Max in PE	Exp(B)
Factor	Estimate	Sig (<0.05)					Factor	Corr.	Sig (<0.05)	Sig (<0.05)	B		
[PBO1=2]	-2.25	0.00	0.00	0.06	0.15	0.23	PBO1	0.36	0.00	0.00	0.44	PBO1	1.56
[PBO2=1]	-1.71	0.04	0.00	0.08	0.11	0.08	PBO2	0.31	0.18	0.18	0.14		
[PBO3=1]	-100.08	0.00	0.00	0.00	0.07	0.00	PBO3	0.23	0.66	0.66	-0.06		
[PBO8=2]	-3.86	0.00	0.00	0.27	0.13	0.17	PBO8	0.32	0.02	0.02	0.36	PBO8	1.43
[PEI2=1]	-4.35	0.03	0.00	0.04	0.12	0.01	PEI2	0.33	0.01	0.01	0.44	PEI2	1.55
[RGL11=1]	-2.49	0.00	0.00	0.00	0.09	0.00	RGL11	0.25	0.01	0.01	0.22		
[RGL3=2]	-2.26	0.00	0.00	0.00	0.14	0.03	RGL3	0.24	0.02	0.02	0.24	RGL3	1.27
[RGL6=3]	-1.02	0.02	0.00	0.05	0.08	0.89	RGL6	0.15	0.04	0.04	0.19	RGL6	1.21
[RGL8=2]	0.97	0.08	0.00	0.00	0.04	0.00	RGL8	0.12	0.21	0.21	-0.09		
[RGL9=1]	-3.22	0.01	0.00	0.00	0.08	0.00	RGL9	0.25	0.84	0.84	0.02		
[ITP5=1]	-3.22	0.08	0.00	0.00	0.14	0.00	ITP5	0.35	0.04	0.04	0.27	ITP5	1.31
[PEI4=1]	21.93	0.99	0.00	0.00	0.08	0.00	PEI4	0.26	0.03	0.03	-0.39	PEI4	0.67
[PEI6=2]	-1.02	0.07	0.00	0.00	0.09	0.04	PEI6	0.29	0.02	0.02	0.23	PEI6	1.25
[PEI7=1]	-6.45	0.16	0.00	0.02	0.11	0.00	PEI7	0.30	0.03	0.03	0.34	PEI7	1.41
[RGL11=1]	-2.49	0.00	0.00	0.00	0.09	0.00	RGL11	0.25	0.01	0.01	0.22	RGL11	1.25

Note: Green color means "satisfying the requirements." Red color means "rejected"
[a]This is a self-generated product by the authors. For general standing of each factor, see Table 1 in Sect. 2.3; for full details of all 100 variables, please refer to the Appendix C
MFI Model Fitting Information _ constraint Sig < 0.05, ToPL Test of Parallel Line _ expect Sig > 0.05
Pseudo R-Square (Nagelkerke) _ expect high, Corr. Spearman's Correlation _ constraint >0.3
GoF Goodness of Fit _ expect Sig (Pearson) > 0.05, Exp(B) Exponential value _ expect >1
Parameter Estimates (All Independent Variables) _ constraint Sig < 0.05
Max in PE Max in Parameter Estimates _ benchmark between OLR marginal and GLM

3.2 *Exploratory Factor Analyses*

Reliability test and Exploratory factor analysis is the fourth method that portrays the conclusion of this paper. The study involves 100 variables, divided into four groups and 16 sub-groups. As for the reliability test, Cronbach's Alpha repeated 16 times to measure the internal consistency of all sub-groups. For each sub-group, the process involved two rounds. The first round eliminated inappropriate variables if any; the second round transferred eligible variables to EFA. Through 16 processes, four variables were eliminated: PU5, CBC1, CBC5, and RGL4. All other variables and sub-groups met the requirements of inter-correlations within groups.

Exploratory factor analyses continued checking dimensionality, formulated components and shaped the correlation structure. Four comprehensive EFAs were computed to four groups. Due to space constraint, this paper cannot show all processes and results. One example is presented hereinafter: Table 3 presents

Table 3 Cronbach's Alpha and EFA: combined figures within-group A4

Sub-groups and Variables[a]	1st round Cronbach's Alpha	Corrected item – total correlation	Cronbach's Alpha if item deleted	Deleted items after first round	2nd round Cronbach's Alpha	EFA test – rotated component matrix[b]			
						KMO and Bartlett's test of sphericity (Sig.)		Component	Coefficients
RPEU	0.84				0.84	KMO (group A4) 0.93	Bartlett's test of Sphericity (sig.) 0.00		
RPEU1		0.65	0.81	–				2	0.71
RPEU2		0.70	0.79	–				2	0.76
RPEU3		0.64	0.81	–				2	0.74
RPEU4		0.61	0.82	–				2	0.66
RPEU5		0.64	0.81	–				2	0.62
RPU	0.79				0.79				
RPU1		0.52	0.80	–				1	0.76
RPU2		0.60	0.74	–				1	0.66
RPU3		0.64	0.73	–				1	0.59
RPU4		0.69	0.70	–				1	0.63
CAU	0.87				0.87				
CAU1		0.64	0.86	–				1	0.71
CAU2		0.68	0.86	–				1	0.67
CAU3		0.56	0.87	–				1	0.64
CAU4		0.70	0.85	–				3	0.71
CAU5		0.68	0.86	–				3	0.77
CAU6		0.74	0.85	–				3	0.77
CAU7		0.67	0.86	–				3	0.77

[a]For general standing of each variable, see Table 1 in Sect. 2.3; for full details of 100 variables, please refer to the Appendix C

[b]Extraction Method: Principal Component Analysis; Rotation Method: Varimax with Kaiser normalisation; Eigenvalues greater than 1; Suppress absolute values less than 0.3

Cronbach's Alpha and EFA results at group A4. The factor loadings and Cronbach's alpha are deemed adequate.

3.3 Re-modelling and Correlation Structure

Figure 1 finalises the correlation structure between key variables. This model is a new theory generated by the authors of this paper, developed from current empirical data but without reference to any others' model. Using AI and EPS, the diagram depicts a network of nodes and links. Each node represents a variable, and each link delineates dependency between two nodes: the target and the determinant. Targets and determinants were formulated from the Cronbach' Alpha and Exploratory factor analyses, following the component they belong to. This paper is unique in that it notices that the psycho-cultural dimension has no impact on the community's decision about transport modes. This finding is discussed further in the conclusion section.

4 Limitations

The first limitation of this paper stemmed from time constraint. While the original preferred method aimed to split the survey into two phases to increase the validity, limited time boundaries made the twin survey impossible. The second limitation fell onto difficult target segments during both qualitative and quantitative data collection phases. Interviewing high-rank opinion leaders and soliciting government officials' responses were both challenging. These difficulties have led to arid interviews and unequal proportions between clusters.

Another issue comes from the difference in concept between this research and another paper. Hundreds of tests into more than 600 valid responses to this research de-emphasised the psycho-cultural dimension as having no impact on the community's decision about transport modes under context. Private transport vehicle ownership is "empowered" as a symbol of social status and culture-bound decision.

4.1 Implications Applicable to Researchers

Given the conceptual difference under limitations, further empirical studies into the psycho-cultural effect on transport mode selection, if any, may become the first potential for researchers to develop.

The second implication to researchers is theory-wise, coming from the following arguments: As congestion would become worse if the decrease of motorcycles is accompanied by a growth of private cars (Nguyen et al., 2008, p. 09), [and] "if the

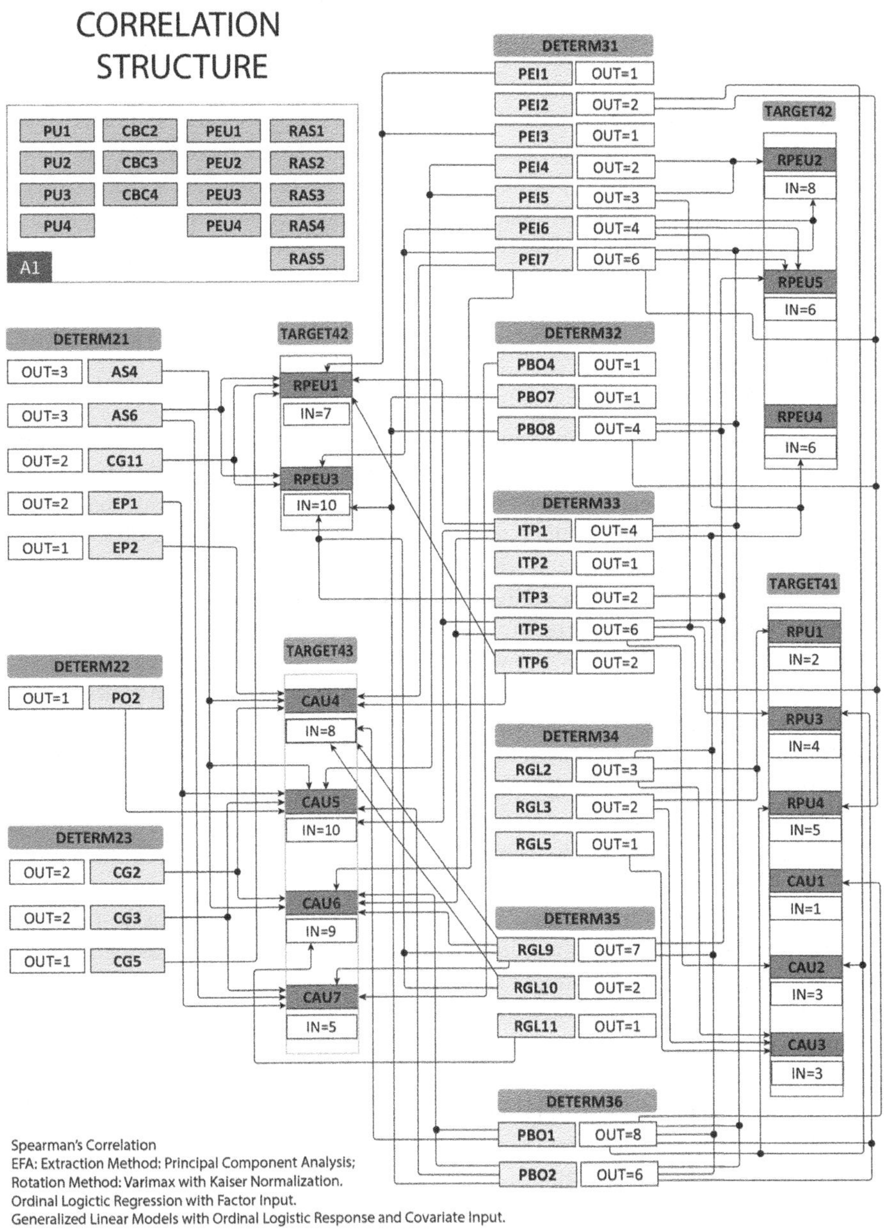

Fig. 1 Re-modelling and Correlation structure: authors' self-produced theory (source: AI and EPS)
Note: For general standing of each variable, see Table 1 in Sect. 2.3; for full details of 100 variables, refer to Appendix C
TARGET 4j set of variables in group 4 and assembled in component j (by EFA)
DETERM ij set of variables in group i and assembled in component j (i = 1,2,3; j = 1–6)

number of buses increases, the traffic problems like congestion will also increase" (Nguyen & Yoshitaka, 2018, p. 7); how to minimise congestion? What situational approach would help? This case study is waiting for subsequent answers.

Finally, this paper has explored the midstream and proposed solutions to the debate between two-wheel figurehead and public transport modes, but the downstream is still intact. What specific programs would suit the 'A' series of urgent tasks? How can policymakers induce follow-up and accountability? These typical questions are also waiting for researches.

5 Conclusions

To fill the research gap and reconcile public transport with two-wheel vehicle, the paper applied the Sequential exploratory mixed methodology to achieve its objectives. This original research was validated longitudinal and multidimensional by four sources of data: (a) documentary review; (b) current experts' interviews; (c) the authors' own accountability; and (d) more than 600 valid responses from different sectors in a recent survey. The study combined four statistical methods to filter and skim the ordinal-scale results before concluding. Going through rigorous screening processes, the ultimate results show 87 correlations between "targets" and "determinants." Targets measure the community readiness to transform from motorcycle to public transport in response to selected improvements in the legal, social and environmental sectors; expressed by: (α) motorcyclists' perceived usefulness of sustainable public transport; (β) perceived ease of use; or (γ) community' self-realisation and actual decision. Determinants stipulate the conditions that must be met in order to reach the targets. Table 4 in Appendix A provides full descriptions of those 87 relations.

In term of priority, the paper recommends an 'A' series of urgent tasks. Table 5 in Appendix B describes six utmost important actions for commensurate adaptations between two-wheel figurehead and sustainable public transport. Emerging urgency would include: setting more bus lines and routes; propaganda and legal sanctions against motorcyclists' lack of traffic awareness and safety; educating bus drivers and operators to behave friendly with motorcyclists and communities, and setting feedback channels and participative problem solving with communities.

Implications to policymakers cover a range of commensurate adaptations such as: (1) Due to the current shortage of traffic regulations, additional laws and safety regulations should be amended to motorcyclists and also to public transport modes, with specific sanction levels against traffic violations; (2) Laws and regulations should not stand alone, but paired with propaganda and constructive training on traffic law; (3) Specific control on routes and traffic time to motorcycles should be considered; (4) "Silo" regulations should be minimised, urban planning and land-use orientation must be synchronised, and traffic areas in metropolitan cities should increase relatively; (5) MRT and Metro Line 1 must be coupled with other modes of sub-networks, and the coming Metro line 2 should also receive the same;

(6) Intermodal travel patterns should be added, e.g. park-and-ride, bike-and-ride, etc.; (7) Feedback channels and participative problem solving with commuters must be set up; (8) Additional policy must be given to assist disabilities; (9) and for longer-term, public transport should receive better infrastructure.

This research also proposes recommendations to managers and entrepreneurs working in the transport industry. The first emphasis is to open more bus lines and routes. Secondly, bus drivers and operators must be educated to drive safely and behave friendly with motorcyclists and communities. Positive and negative reinforcement must apply in parallel. Thirdly, although social mobility and private cooperative business are two different disciplines, they must be reconciled. Sustainable public transport is currently "flagged" by the government, but the implementation phase relies on private cooperatives that prefer shortcut and resource-saving. The fourth recommendation is that infrastructure system intelligence should not be neglected. Smart traffic light systems, flexible lane dividers to smart roads, route allocation during peak hours, etc., are among the examples that entrepreneurs can invest in. The fifth recommendation stays at the intersection between leaders working in the transport industry and business managers. This "soft" measure calls for flextime operation strategy and flexible work hours applied to companies and schools.

Appendices

Appendix A

Table 4 87 correlations between the readiness of communities for sustainable public transport and its determinants

No.	VAR in group A4	VAR in group A3 and A2	Generalised linear model B	Exp (B)	Conclusions
1	CAU1	PBO1	0.399	1.490	The community prefers to use other transport modes (bus, metro) instead of motorbikes if there are more bus lines and routes.
2	CAU2	ITP5	0.437	1.549	The community will recommend and encourage their relatives and friends to use other transport modes if they are provided with intermodal travel patterns (park-and-ride, bike-and-ride, etc.).
3		PBO1	0.250	1.284	The community will recommend and encourage their relatives and friends to use other transport modes if there open more bus lines and routes.

(continued)

Table 4 (continued)

No.	VAR in group A4	VAR in group A3 and A2	Generalised linear model B	Exp (B)	Conclusions
4		PEI2	0.301	1.351	The community will recommend and encourage their relatives and friends to use other transport modes if sanction levels against traffic violations are well propagated.
5	RPU4	PBO1	0.445	1.560	The community would adjust their individual/family behavior to adapt to public transport if there are more bus lines and routes.
6		PBO8	0.360	1.433	The community would adjust their individual/family behavior to adapt to public transport if the buses are equipped with additional equipment to assist disabilities.
7		PEI2	0.441	1.555	The community would adjust their individual/family behavior to adapt to public transport if sanction levels against traffic violations are well propagated.
8		ITP5	0.266	1.305	The community would adjust their individual/family behavior to adapt to public transport if intermodal travel patterns are added (park-and-ride, bike-and-ride, etc.).
9		PEI7	0.341	1.407	The community would adjust their individual/family behavior to adapt to public transport if bus drivers and assistants are trained to become friendly, especially with motorcyclists.
10	RPEU4	ITP1	0.534	1.706	Synchronising between urban planning and land-use orientation would help the community adapt immediately to the change.
11		PBO2	0.335	1.398	The community would adapt immediately to the changes if more bus lines are provided to reduce waiting times.
12		PEI6	0.214	1.239	The community would adapt immediately to changes if traffic demand is well propagandised: e.g., not riding motorbikes as an unnecessary habit.
13		RGL2	−0.267	0.766	The community would adapt immediately to changes if there exist regulations on traffic time constraints.
14		RGL9	0.357	1.429	The community would adapt immediately to changes if MRT has additional transport sub-networks.
15		PBO1	0.274	1.316	The community would adapt immediately to changes if more bus lines and routes are added.

(continued)

Table 4 (continued)

No.	VAR in group A4	VAR in group A3 and A2	Generalised linear model		Conclusions
			B	Exp (B)	
16	RPEU5	ITP5	0.312	1.366	Adding intermodal travel patterns (park-and-ride, bike-and-ride, etc.) will make public transport modes much easier to be selected.
17		PBO8	0.391	1.479	Additional equipment in buses that assist disabilities will make public transport modes much easier to be selected.
18		PEI6	0.267	1.306	If the traffic demand by motorcyclists is reduced with unnecessary motorbike trips, public transport modes become much easier to be selected.
19		PEI7	0.449	1.567	If bus drivers and operators are trained to become friendly with communities, public transport modes become much easier to be selected.
20		ITP3	0.339	1.403	Adding flexible lane dividers to smart roads will make other transport modes much easier to be selected.
21		RGL9	0.298	1.347	Adding sub-networks along MRT will make public transport much easier to be selected.
22	RPEU1	CG5	0.252	1.286	Improving infrastructure by increasing traffic areas to reduce traffic jams will make it easier to use public transport.
23		AS6	0.495	1.641	It will be easier to select public transport if infrastructure is improved to reduce accidents and to stop motorcyclists taking the wrong lanes.
24		CG11	0.325	1.384	It will be easier to select public transport if sub-networks and connections are added to the infrastructure.
25		ITP1	0.680	1.975	It will be easier to select public transport if urban planning and land-use orientation are synchronised with infrastructure.
26		ITP6	0.402	1.495	It will be easier to select public transport if smart traffic light systems are added to infrastructure.
27		PEI1	0.506	1.659	There exists a correlation between self-awareness of riding motorbike, infrastructure improvement, and the intended use of public transport.
28		PEI3	−0.518	0.595	There exists a correlation between propagating the adverse effects of using alcohol in traffic, infrastructure improvement, and the intended use of public transport.

(continued)

Table 4 (continued)

No.	VAR in group A4	VAR in group A3 and A2	Generalised linear model B	Exp (B)	Conclusions
29	RPU3	PBO1	0.409	1.506	Change in the bus operating system with more lines and routes will motivate the community to use public bus.
30		PBO2	0.277	1.319	Change in the bus operating system with more lines to shorten waiting times will motivate the community to use public bus.
31		ITP5	0.416	1.516	Change in the bus operating system with additional intermodal travel (park-and-ride, bike-and-ride) will motivate the community to use public bus.
32		PEI5	0.424	1.528	Changes in the bus operating system by setting up feedback channels and participative problem solving with commuters will motivate the community to use public bus.
33	RPEU2	ITP2	0.525	1.690	There exists a correlation between lane and route allocation during peak hours, quality and quantity of buses, and the ease of selecting traffic modes to reach destinations.
34		PBO1	0.323	1.382	Improving the quality of bus and adding new bus routes will increase the ease to select traffic modes to reach destinations.
35		PBO2	0.587	1.799	Improving the quality of bus and adding more buses to shorten waiting times will increase the ease to select traffic modes to reach destinations.
36		PEI5	0.644	1.903	Feedback channels and participative problem solving with commuters together with bus improvement will increase the ease to select traffic modes to reach destinations.
37		PEI6	0.304	1.356	Traffic demand reduction by motorcyclists with unnecessary motorbike trips together with bus improvement will increase the ease to select traffic modes to reach destinations.
38		PBO8	0.341	1.407	Additional equipment to assist disabilities together with bus improvement will increase the ease to select traffic modes to reach destinations
39		PEI4	−0.651	0.521	Law propaganda and training together with bus improvement will increase the ease to select traffic modes to reach destinations
40		PEI7	0.448	1.564	Educating bus drivers and operators together with bus improvement will increase the ease to select traffic modes to reach destinations.

(continued)

Table 4 (continued)

No.	VAR in group A4	VAR in group A3 and A2	Generalised linear model B	Exp (B)	Conclusions
41	CAU4	CG2	0.489	1.631	The community supports improvements to public bus because traffic jams ruin the health and life of communities.
42		AS4	0.395	1.485	The community supports changes to public bus because a number of motorcyclists lack traffic awareness and adversely impact safety.
43		EP2	0.453	1.573	The community supports changes to public bus because of traffic noise pollution in megacities.
44		PBO1	0.555	1.742	The community supports changes to public bus and expects more bus lines and routes.
45		RGL10	0.320	1.377	The community supports changes to public bus in conjunction with flextime strategy applied to businesses and school.
46		RGL9	0.313	1.367	The community supports changes to public bus in conjunction with additional transportation networks along the main route of MRT.
47		ITP6	0.362	1.436	The community supports changes to public bus in conjunction with smart traffic light systems.
48		PEI7	0.456	1.578	The community supports changes to public bus in conjunction with educating bus drivers and operators.
49	CAU5	CG3	0.325	1.384	The community supports infrastructure improvements as traffic jam induces losses to financial resources and infrastructure facilities.
50		PO2	0.562	1.754	The community supports infrastructure improvements considering the shortage of traffic regulations.
51		AS4	0.585	1.795	The community supports infrastructure improvements, given that a number of motorcyclists lack traffic awareness and endanger traffic safety.
52		EP1	0.484	1.623	The community supports infrastructure improvements, taking into account the increasing number motorcycles and endangered environment.
53		ITP5	0.445	1.561	The community supports infrastructure improvements in connection to intermodal travel patterns.
54		PBO2	0.279	1.322	The community supports infrastructure improvements which lead to reducing elapsed waiting times.

(continued)

Table 4 (continued)

No.	VAR in group A4	VAR in group A3 and A2	Generalised linear model		Conclusions
			B	Exp (B)	
55		PEI5	0.716	2.046	The community supports infrastructure improvements in conjunction with feedback channels and participative problem solving with commuters.
56		RGL9	0.341	1.406	The community supports infrastructure improvements together with additional sub-networks along the main route of MRT.
57		ITP1	0.393	1.482	The community supports infrastructure improvements considering urban planning and land-use orientation.
58		PEI4	−0.692	0.500	The community supports infrastructure improvements in conjunction with propaganda and training on traffic law.
59	CAU6	AS4	0.381	1.464	The community supports the government in promoting the benefits of public transport, given that a number of motorcyclists lack traffic awareness.
60		CG2	0.339	1.403	The community supports the government in promoting the benefits of public transport, because traffic jams ruin the health and life of communities.
61		ITP5	0.338	1.402	The community supports the government in promoting the benefits of public transport in connection to intermodal travel patterns.
62		PBO1	0.283	1.327	The community supports the government in promoting the benefits of public transport in favor of additional bus lines and routes.
63		PBO2	0.241	1.273	The community supports the government in promoting the benefits of public transport in conjunction with shortening bus waiting times.
64		RGL9	0.370	1.448	The community supports the government in promoting the benefits of public transport with additional sub- networks along MRT.
65		ITP1	0.534	1.705	The community supports the government in promoting the benefits of public transport in line with urban planning and land-use orientation.
66		PEI7	0.332	1.393	The community supports the government in promoting the benefits of public transport provided that bus drivers and assistants are educated to become friendly.

(continued)

Table 4 (continued)

No.	VAR in group A4	VAR in group A3 and A2	Generalised linear model		Conclusions
			B	Exp (B)	
67		RGL11	0.198	1.219	The community supports the government in promoting the benefits of public transport in condition that the number of cars is controlled, not only pointing out motorcycles.
68	CAU7	CG3	0.329	1.389	The community supports the government in endorsing traffic laws and safety regulations, given that traffic jam is getting worse.
69		EP1	0.555	1.742	The community supports the government in endorsing traffic laws and safety regulations to decrease the rising number of vehicles.
70		AS6	0.498	1.645	The community supports the government in endorsing traffic laws and safety regulations to stop motorcyclists taking the wrong lanes.
71		PBO4	0.459	1.583	The community supports the government in endorsing traffic laws and safety regulations to ensure the punctuality of public bus.
72		RGL9	0.292	1.339	The community supports the government in endorsing traffic laws and safety regulations considering the additional sub- networks along MRT.
73	RPEU3	AS6	0.712	2.039	Tentative improvement will support disabilities to use public bus because two-wheel vehicles may take the wrong lanes.
74		CG11	0.352	1.423	Tentative improvement will support disabilities to use public bus provided that networks and connections are also added.
75		PBO2	0.349	1.418	Tentative improvement will support disabilities to use public bus especially when more bus lines and routes are added.
76		PBO8	0.995	2.705	Tentative improvement will support disabilities to use public bus especially if equipment assistance is added.
77		PEI7	0.458	1.581	Tentative improvement will support disabilities to use public bus especially if bus drivers are trained to be friendly.
78		RGL10	0.273	1.314	Tentative improvement will support disabilities to use public bus, in addition to flexible work hours.
79		ITP3	0.405	1.499	Tentative improvement will support disabilities to use public bus in conjunction with flexible lane dividers.
80		PBO7	−0.346	0.708	Tentative improvement will support disabilities to use public bus with emphasis on bus drivers' behavior.

(continued)

Table 4 (continued)

No.	VAR in group A4	VAR in group A3 and A2	Generalised linear model B	Exp (B)	Conclusions
81		PEI6	0.280	1.323	Tentative improvement will support disabilities to use public bus, taking control of unnecessary motorcycle trips.
82		RGL9	0.292	1.339	Tentative improvement will support disabilities to use public bus in combination with additional sub-networks along MRT.
83	RPU1	RGL2	0.198	1.219	Public transport would save time compared to using a motorbike, provided that traffic time for motorcycle is regulated.
84		RGL3	0.238	1.269	Public transport would save time compared to using a motorbike in condition that routes for motorcycles is controlled.
85	CAU3	RGL2	0.268	1.307	The community agrees with time restriction against motorcycles.
86		RGL3	0.230	1.258	The community agrees with route restriction against motorcycles.
87		RGL5	0.491	1.634	The community agrees with the usage restriction of motorcycles by increasing motorbike ownership tax.

B parameters in Generalised linear models with Ordinal responses and covariates
Exp(B) values of odds; Exp(B) >1 implies a positive relationship between the dependent variable and its predictor

Appendix B

Table 5 High-priority recommendations to policymakers and the transport industry

VAR	Category	IN/ OUT	Description	Priority[a]
PEI5	A3	3	Setting feedback channels and participative problem solving with communities.	A
PEI6		4	Propaganda on traffic demand reduction against unnecessary motorbike trips.	B
PEI7		6	Propagating/educating bus drivers and operators to behave friendly with motorcyclists and communities.	A
AS4	A2	3	Propaganda and legal sanctions against motorcyclists' lack of traffic awareness and safety.	A
AS6		3	Propaganda and legal sanctions against motorcyclists taking the wrong lanes.	A
PBO1	A3	8	Setting more bus lines and routes.	A
PBO2		6	Setting more buses to shorten waiting times.	A

(continued)

Table 5 (continued)

VAR	Category	IN/ OUT	Description	Priority[a]
PBO8		4	Setting additional equipment to assist disabilities using public transport.	B
ITP1		4	Synchronising between urban planning and land-use orientation.	B
ITP5		6	Adding intermodal travel patterns; e.g., park-and-ride, bike-and-ride.	B
RGL2		3	Limiting the traffic time against motorcycles.	B
RGL9		7	Installing additional sub-networks along the main route of MRT.	B

[a]Priorities are based on the quantities of IN/OUT in Fig. 1. All selections were rigorously screened by Ordinal logistic regression, Generalised linear models, and Spearman's correlations

Appendix C

List of 100 variables with full descriptions

Variables	Code	Questions
A1: COMMUNITY PSYCHOLOGY AND CULTURE The following questions involve the psychological and cultural behavior of the Vietnamese community towards specific vehicles below:		
Perceived usefulness(PU)	PU. How do you agree/disagree with the following statements about the usefulness of using a motorcycle:	
	PU1	Using motorcycles helps me save my time.
	PU2	Using motorcycles helps me save my money.
	PU3	Motorcycles bring a lot of benefits to my life.
	PU4	The motorcycle is the transportation I mostly use.
	PU5	Motorcycles can help me make with some earnings (e.g., Grab, Gojek, etc.)
Culture-bound Comfort (CBC)	CBC. How do you agree/disagree with the following statements about Vietnamese behavior:	
	CBC1	I usually walk to the destination just within a few hundred meters away.
	CBC2	I do not get used to using other transport modes except motorcycles.
	CBC3	I find it is difficult to use other transport modes.
	CBC4	I prioritise riding a motorbike over walking.
	CBC5	Motorcycles also express personal property ownership.
Perceive Ease of Use (PEU)	PEU. How do you agree/disagree with the following statements related to ease of use of motorcycles:	
	PEU1	It is easy to learn how to ride a motorcycle.
	PEU2	It is easy to have a motorcycle maintained.

(continued)

Variables	Code	Questions
	PEU3	It is easy to own a motorcycle rather than other vehicles.
	PEU4	It is easy to use my motorcycle for riding to alleys or crowded places.
Reasons Against Substitution (by Community) (RAS)	RAS. How do you agree/disagree with the following reasons for not choosing other transport modes?	
	RAS1	Using a motorbike is more useful than other transport modes.
	RAS2	Motorbikes are easier to use than other vehicles.
	RAS3	I always encourage family and friends to use motorbikes.
	RAS4	I cannot give up my motorbike riding habit.
	RAS5	Other transport modes cannot meet my needs.
A2: GOVERNMENT/INSTITUTIONAL CONCERN		
Congestion (CG)	CG. How do you agree about the current traffic jam?	
	CG1	The transport infrastructure cannot meet all the needs of using motorbikes.
	CG2	Traffic jams harm the health as well as the daily life of the residents.
	CG3	Traffic jam causes physical damage and transport infrastructure.
	CG4	The increasing number and volume of motorcycles is the primary cause of traffic jams.
	CG5	Insufficient traffic area (roads, bridges, tunnels, etc.) is the cause of traffic jams.
	CG6	Traffic jams do harm to socio-economic development.
	CG7	The traffic jam is getting to an uncontrollable level.
	CG8	Traffic laws play a decisive role in decreasing traffic congestion.
	CG9	The self-awareness of traffic participants will significantly reduce traffic jams.
	CG10	Macro investment solutions (metro line, subway, MRT, etc.) will completely reduce traffic jams.
	CG11	The above macro investment solutions can partly reduce traffic congestion, if there are no networks and connectivity solutions.
Environmental Pollution (EP)	EP. How do you think about the current environmental pollution?	
	EP1	The number and volume of motorcycles are increasing, which lead to do harm to the living environment (air pollution).
	EP2	High traffic density in big cities causes noise pollution.
	EP3	The current legal framework's sanctions are not strong enough to solve the environmental pollution caused by traffic.

(continued)

Variables	Code	Questions
	EP4	Traffic participants' self-awareness is not good enough, which affects environmental pollution.
Accident and Safety (AS)	AS. How do you feel about the following statements related to traffic accidents and traffic safety?	
	AS1	The increase in motorbike leads to a higher rate of traffic accidents.
	AS2	Many motorcycles pass the traffic light, break the speed limit, occupy the roadside… affecting traffic safety.
	AS3	Using mobile phones while riding a motorcycle is the direct cause of traffic accident.
	AS4	A number of participants lack traffic awareness while riding a motorbike, affect other traffic and adversely impact traffic safety.
	AS5	Drinking alcohol and being drunk while riding a motorbike is directly related to traffic safety.
	AS6	Two-wheel motorised vehicles (and other vehicles) encroach or go in the opposite direction related to traffic safety.
Other Transport Modes (OTM)	OTM. How do you agree/disagree with the following statements regarding other transport modes?	
	OTM1	Public transport is not supported by the residents.
	OTM2	Public transport does not completely meet the needs of the people.
	OTM3	The residents have not been widely propagated about the benefits of other means of transport (bus, metro...)
Policies (PO)	PO. How do you agree/disagree with the following statements regarding the policies?	
	PO1	Responsibility assignment to authorities is not clear.
	PO2	The policies ensuring traffic safety are still lacking.
	PO3	The policies ensuring traffic safety are not appropriate.
	PO4	The legality of road traffic safety policies is low.
A3: TENTATIVE SOLUTIONS Here are a number of tentative solutions, how do you agree/disagree with the followings:		
Public Bus Operation improvement (PBO)	PBO. How do you agree/disagree with the solutions to improve the current public bus system?	
	PBO1	I would like to have more bus lines to serve more routes.
	PBO2	I want to have more buses to shorten bus waiting times.
	PBO3	I want the bus to improve the quality of the seats and its smell.
	PBO4	I would like the bus to operate on time.
	PBO5	I want the bus to be equipped with WiFi, a clock, surveillance cameras for higher security.

(continued)

Variables	Code	Questions
	PBO6	I would like to have more automated information about bus stops and bus positioning.
	PBO7	I want the bus drivers to become friendlier to the bus passengers and with the motorbike community.
	PBO8	The bus should be equipped with additional equipment to assist the disabilities.
	PBO9	It is necessary to expand and improve the quality of bus stops (add roofs, seats, maps...)
	PBO10	It is necessary to improve the appearance of the bus.
	PBO11	Buses should avoid abuse running into the roadway for two-wheel vehicles and pinching them.
	PBO12	Buses should limit honking and reduce the emission into the environment.
	PBO13	Smaller buses should be mobilised to avoid unused seats on the bus.
Infrastructure/Travel Patterns Improvement (ITP)	ITP. How do you agree with the solutions to improve the current transport infrastructure?	
	ITP1	Synchronise with urban planning and land-use orientation.
	ITP2	It is crucial to allocate lanes and routes properly during peak hours in the city. Avoid overcrowding in one lane and empty flow in the other lane.
	ITP3	Adding many automatic movable smart road dividers on some main city routes.
	ITP4	Limiting some unsuitable means of transport during peak hours.
	ITP5	Adding intermodal travel patterns for the traffic participants (park-and-ride, bike-and-ride)
	ITP6	Researching and installing smart traffic light systems (can increase/decrease the traffic signal timing depending on the presence of vehicles at that time).
Regulation change (RGL)	RGL. How do you agree with the policy change below?	
	RGL1	It is necessary to have policies for restricting new motorcycle registration.
	RGL2	Limiting the traffic time for motorcycles.
	RGL3	Restricting some routes against motorcycles.
	RGL4	Seriously punish motorcyclists who do not have licenses.
	RGL5	Increasing motorbike ownership tax.
	RGL6	Changing the motorbike price.
	RGL7	Reducing urbanisation. Distancing between urban zones.
	RGL8	Eliminating the old, low-quality motorbikes and tricycles.
	RGL9	Installing additional transportation networks along the main route of MRT.

(continued)

Variables	Code	Questions
	RGL10	Encourage businesses and schools to apply flexible work hours.
	RGL11	Controlling the increase in the number of cars (some studies indicate that if you reduce motorbikes but increase cars, traffic jams will get even worse).
Propaganda/Education Implementation (PEI)	PEI. How do you agree with the implementation of communication/education sessions for traffic participants?	
	PEI1	Improve the self-awareness of riding a motorbike.
	PEI2	Propagating some sanction levels for traffic violations.
	PEI3	Propagating about the adverse effects of using alcohol in traffic.
	PEI4	It is necessary to educate about the traffic law as long as is suitable for each individual (the traditions, culture, religion, and customs).
	PEI5	Setting up feedback systems from residents; listen and seriously deal with each traffic problem.
	PEI6	Traffic demand management: Propaganda to avoid riding motorbikes as an unnecessary habit, providing motivation for the young generation to live at home.
	PEI7	Propagating/educating bus drivers (and bus assistants) to make them more friendly with residents, especially motorcycle communities.
A4: COMMUNITY ADAPTED BEHAVIOR If those changes are applied (or a majority of them will be applied), how will you have new perspectives on the use of public transport instead of motorcycles?		
Reconciliation Perceived Ease of Use (RPEU)	RPEU. How do you think about the ease of use of other transport modes after making the changes above?	
	RPEU1	Improving infrastructure (especially roads) will make it easier for me to use public transport.
	RPEU2	Changing the quality and adding more buses will make it easier for me to find out the means to get to my destination.
	RPEU3	The change of the bus system will make it easier for the disabilities to use.
	RPEU4	I am able to adapt immediately to these changes.
	RPEU5	In general, after the change, the use/selection of other means will become much easier than before.
Reconciliation Perceived Usefulness (RPU)	RPU. How do you think about the usefulness of other transport modes after making the changes above?	
	RPU1	Using other transportation (especially public transport) will save time compared to using a motorbike.
	RPU2	Using other transportation (especially public transport) will save more money than using a motorbike.
	RPU3	These changes in the bus operating system give me more motivation to use this type of service.
	RPU4	With the benefits of the above changes, we are able to adjust individual/family behavior in order to adapt to public transport.

(continued)

Variables	Code	Questions
Community Actual Usage (CAU)	CAU. Do you intend to use other transport modes instead of motorcycles after the changes as above?	
	CAU1	I will prefer to use other transport modes (bus, metro...) instead of motorbikes.
	CAU2	I will recommend and encourage my relatives and friends to use other transport modes.
	CAU3	I agree with the usage restriction of motorcycles on the road.
	CAU4	I agree with the aforementioned changes to the bus system.
	CAU5	I agree with the above-mentioned changes relating to transport infrastructure.
	CAU6	I encourage the government to promote the benefits of using other transport modes.
	CAU7	I encourage positive changes in traffic laws, ensuring traffic safety as mentioned above.

References

Bakker, S., Contreras, K. D., Kappiantari, M., Nguyen, T. A., Guillen, M. D., Gunthawong, G., et al. (2017). Low-carbon transport policy in four ASEAN countries: Developments in Indonesia, the Philippines, Thailand and Vietnam. *Sustainability*.

Boltze, M., & Vu, A. T. (2016). *Approaches to achieve sustainability in traffic management*. In *Sustainable development of civil, urban and transportation engineering conference* (pp. 205–212). Elsevier.

Chu, X. N., & Thi, H. D. (2017). Actual situation and solutions for reducing the traffic jams and congestion in Vietnam. In *Advances in natural and applied sciences*. AENSI Publication.

Cohen, J., Cohen, P., West, S. G., & Aiken, L. S. (2003). *Applied multiple regression/correlation analysis for the behavioral sciences* (3rd ed.). Lawrence Erlbaum Associates.

Cooper, D. R., & Schindler, P. S. (2014). *Business research methods* (12th ed.). McGraw-Hill.

Dapice, D., Gomez-Ibanez, J. A., & Thanh, N. X. (2010). Ho Chi Minh City: The challenges of growth. Prepared under *UNDP – Harvard Policy Dialogue Papers*.

Dobson, A. J., & Barnett, A. G. (2018). *An introduction to generalised linear models* (4th ed.). Taylor & Francis/CRC Press.

Dung, N. T., & Yoshitaka, K. (2018). Study on traffic situation after operating bus rapid transit system in Hanoi. In *International symposium of transport simulation (ISTS'18) and the international workshop on traffic data collection and its standardization (IWTDCS'18)*. Elsevier Ltd.

Dunteman, G. H., & Ho, M.-H. R. (2006). *An introduction to generalised linear models*. Sage.

Fujii, S., & Van Hong, T. (2009). Psychological determinants of the intention to use the bus in Ho Chi Minh City. *Journal of Public Transportation, 12*(1).

Hair, J. F., Celsi, M., Ortinau, D. J., & Bush, R. P. (2017). *Essentials of marketing research* (4th ed.). McGraw-Hill Education.

Ho, C. Q., & Yamamoto, T. (2011). The role of atitudes and public transport service on vehicle ownership in Ho Chi Minh, Vietnam. In *The 34th Australasian Transport Research Forum (ATRF) proceedings* (pp. 1–15). World Transit Research.

Hoang, Q., & Okamura, T. (2018). Analysing behavioral intentions in new residential developments of motorcycle dependent cities: The case of Ho Chi Minh City, Vietnam. In *2018 World conference on transport research society – Case studies on transport policy* (pp. 163–172). Elsevier.

Jonker, J., & Pennink, B. (2010). *The essence of research methodology*. Springer.

Kleinbaum, D. G., & Klein, M. (2002). *Logistic regression – A self-learning text* (2nd ed.). Springer.

Nguyen, N. T., Miwa, T., & Morikawa, T. (2018). Switching to public transport modes for commuting trips: Considering latent motivations in Ho Chi Minh City. *Asian Transport Studies, 5*(1), 117–136.

Nguyen, M. Q., Pham, T. T., & Phan, T. T. (2019). Traffic congestion – A prominent problem in Vietnam: Current situation and solutions. *EJERS, European Journal of Engineering Research and Science, 4*(9).

Nguyen, H., Montgomery, F., & Timms, P. (2008). *Should motorcycle be blamed for traffic congestion in Vietnamese cities?* Codatu XIII.

Phan, Y. T., Yano, T., Phan , A. T., Nishimura, T., Sato, T., Hashimoto, Y., et al. (2008). Social surveys on community response to road traffic noise in Hanoi and Ho Chi Minh City. In *9th International Congress on noise as a public health problem.* ICBEN.

Saunders, M., Lewis, P., & Thornhill, A. (2016). *Research methods for business students* (7th ed.). Pearson Education.

Shibata, T. (2007). Social costs of traffic congestion in developing metropolises. *Urban Justice & Sustainability*.

Tabachnick, B. G., & Fidell, L. S. (2013). *Using multivariate statistics* (6th ed.). Pearson.

Tien-Pen, Sadullah, A. F. M., & Dao, N. X. (2003). A comparison study on motorcycle traffic development in some Asian countries – Case of Taiwan. In *Malaysia and Vietnam*. Transportation Studies (EASTS).

Tracy, S. J. (2013). *Qualitative research methods: Collecting evidence, crafting*. Communicating. Blackwell Publishing – John Wiley & Sons.

Tran, M. T. (2019). Sustainabilization of Hanoi mobiity approached from new residential areas. *Journal of Science and Technology in Civil Engineering*, 89–99.

Decentralised Urban Waste Management: A Case Study of Solid Waste Management in Two Indian Cities - Thiruvananthapuram and Bengaluru

Namitha Madhukumar

Abstract India generates 62 million tons of waste every year, of which 60% gets collected and only 15% processed. With the huge spike in urban population and shrinking spaces, it is imperative for an efficient waste management system. Unscientific waste disposal augments the emission of Greenhouse Gases like methane (6% in India). Waste to Energy plant is not viable in India due to the high concentration of organic content and inadequate segregation. Under such a situation, a Centralised treatment facility will not only culminate in irrevocable environmental and health hazards but further aggravate prevailing socio-political injustice in the country. The best possible alternative to this systemic hurdle is Decentralised Waste Management. This paper looks at two urban cities, Thiruvananthapuram and Bengaluru, where the former follows a decentralised waste management system and the latter centralised. The Waste Management system in Thiruvananthapuram city champions concepts of circular economy adopted by developed countries, which contest the unsustainable linear model. The city's strategies adopted under Decentralised Waste Management are a catalyst towards achieving '*no burn city*', an initiative against incineration and greenhouse gas emissions. The case studies of Bengaluru and Thiruvananthapuram city highlight the impact of systemic changes through progressive interventions towards the eradication of structural disparities. It analyses different aspects, the labour, the public, the governance and the environment in the context of waste management. The paper delves further into the question of welfare and beneficiary from state's point of view. Through the system of Decentralised Waste Management, the paper advocates the importance of devolution of power and dissolution of responsibilities for a sustainable environment and an empowered and equitable society.

Keywords Waste management · Governance · Decentralisation · Circular economy · Labour · Sustainable development · Welfare

---

N. Madhukumar (✉)
Programme Coordinator (Research), Thanal, Thiruvananthapuram, Kerala, India

© The Author(s), under exclusive license to Springer Nature Singapore Pte Ltd. 2022

T. Chaiechi, J. Wood (eds.), *Community Empowerment, Sustainable Cities, and Transformative Economies*, https://doi.org/10.1007/978-981-16-5260-8_14

1 Introduction

India is the second-largest populous country (1.3 billion) in the world and is predicted to outgrow China before 2050 (US Census Bureau, 2021; Ghosh, 2020). In a report on population projection by the Indian Ministry of Health and Family welfare, 70% of the estimated population growth will be in urban areas (Agarwal, 2020; National Commission on Population, 2019). Urbanisation in India is often accounted to be unsustainable and disordered due to large socio-economic disparity and ecological degradation (Shaban, Kourtit, & Nijkamp, India's Urban System: Sustainability and Imbalanced Growth of Cities, 2020) One of the major concerns related to urbanisation and population growth is the mounts of unmanaged waste and India, is the best example (D'Souza & Nagendra, 2011; Baviskar & Gidwani, 2019). The country generates about 62 million tonnes of waste every year, of which 60% gets collected and only 15% processed (Swaminathan, 2018). Between 2001 and 2011, the quantity of waste generated in India grew by 50%, and under similar conditions, it might reach 230 million tons by 2041 (Annepu, 2012). Dorron and Jeffrey (2018 see p.43 in [2]) in their book writes,

> Never in history have so many people had so much to throw away and so little space to throw it as the people of India in the second decade of the twenty-first century.

With the huge spike in urban population and shrinking spaces, it is imperative to devise an efficient waste management system. To tackle the problem of limited space to dump waste, the most common strategy adopted in India is burning, which carries high environmental risk (Bhalerao, 2019; Bhat, 2019). These unscientific waste disposal and processing augment the emission of Greenhouse Gases like methane (6% in India). The management of waste is not confined to mitigating climate crises but also to tackle the deep-rooted social, cultural and economic disparity that has crippled the quality of life of many in India (Gupta, 2012). The study aims to understand the effect of solid waste management strategies adopted by Urban Local Bodies on governance, public, and environment aspects. Here, the study looks at two urban cities in India, Thiruvananthapuram, and Bengaluru, where the former follows a decentralised system of waste management and the latter, centralised.

2 Literature Review

Over the past decades, reports by international agencies and national governments extensively emphasised the importance of managing the accumulating amount of waste across the globe (Hoornweg & Tata, 2012); Environment Protection Agency,

2020; Wilson et al., 2015). The waste management in developed countries such as the United States, Germany, and Sweden are remarkable compared to developing and under-developed countries (Hui et al., 2006). One of the major reasons is the utilisation of advanced technologies in incineration, biological treatment, sanitary landfilling, and recovery technology for managing waste (Vujic et al., 2015). But it often carries the possibility of creating high environmental degradation due to emissions from these practices. Though technological interventions play a pivotal role (Singh, 2015; Pujara et al., 2019), to manage waste properly and sustainably, an efficient governance structure is imperative especially in developing countries due to deficiency in finances, and evident social and ecological vulnerabilities (Bhuiyan, 2010). Most of the developing countries face difficulties related to collection, transfer, and transportation which hamper the processing and treatment of waste (Owolabi et al., 2016). Since 70–80% of waste generated in Asia is organic with low net caloric value, following a centralised model similar to developed countries such as waste to energy incineration is redundant (Narayana, 2009; Zhang et al., 2010). The model of decentralisation has been explored in scholarships as an alternative method of waste management in developing and under-developed counties (Massoud et al., 2019; Nzeadibe, 2009; Zurbrugg et al., 2005; Korner et al., 2008). But, inadequacies in decentralised model can create negative socio-economic, health, and environmental implications if people are inactive actors (Ahlheim et al., 2019). When (Grindle, 2010) defined the concept of 'good governance' one of the prominent aspects across government character, normative concerns, politics of left and right was the public role and its impact. One of the major hindrances towards efficient waste management is the lack of segregation, the first step of the cycle, which predominantly requires people's participation (Narayana, 2009; Zhang et al., 2010). For an efficient working of decentralised model, it is imperative to include the public into the system (Das et al., 2019; Metin et al., 2003).

The previous and current lapses in the decentralised model of waste management in India revolve around the lacunae in the systemic integration of people. The Municipal Solid Waste (Management and Handling) Rule, 2000, flag-shipped on 'Recycle before Dispose' but the limited segregation resulted in mounts of waste across the nation (Zurbrugg et al., 2004). The amended rule of 2016 provides guidelines for segregation and terminate exploitation of landfills but, it still gives a window for repeating the past errors. The article by (Bjerkli, 2013) highlights conflicts in Addis Ababa due to the existence of older power dynamics in new structures of decentralisation. Therefore, with the help of the empirical examples from India, the study advocates entailing the true essence of the decentralised model of waste management. The examples from Bengaluru locate the negative socio-economic and political dynamics in waste management. And the case of Thiruvananthapuram shows the effect of incentivising people participation to eradicate lacunae stated by (Nilsson et al., 2009) between national policies goals and local level implementation.

3 Methodology

The study uses a comparative design for analysing the governance structure of waste management (centralised and decentralised) and its impact in two cities of India. Here, the area under Thiruvananthapuram Municipal Corporation (TMC) and Bruhat Bengaluru Mahanagara Pallike (BBMP) are considered to understand the waste management strategies adopted by Urban Local Bodies (ULBs). The population considered for the study are people engaged in waste management such as private service providers, contract waste workers, government department officials, experts from non-governmental organisations, scrap dealers, and residents. The study has utilised convenience sampling to locate and contact the selected stakeholders for data collection. The data collection was planned in two phases, first during October and November 2019 in Thiruvananthapuram and second between March and April 2020 in Bengaluru. The study has used a qualitative method for data collection and analysis. The key informants were enlisted based on literature review and selected after close consultation with field experts from NGOs (Thanal) and universities (National Law School of India University). An interview guide was prepared, with semi-structured questions. Most of the interviews were recorded with the consent of the participant and later transcribed, coded, and categorised to capture the main points required for the study. During data collection, five field visits were undertaken to Material Recovery Facilities in Thiruvananthapuram. The basis for selecting these five was on two criteria, the type of material processed (biodegradable or non-biodegradable) and the location (residential, public, commercial). The primary objective of the study is to critically engage with the impact of governance structure in the waste management system. The study leans towards a constructive epistemology as the data acquired from the key informants is scrutinised for capturing the intersectionalities. The paper also uses narrative structure to critically engage with literature and field data. Though the first phase of data collection was completed, the second was hampered by the Covid-19 outbreak. But the lapses in fieldwork were compensated through telephonic interviews and secondary data such as government and NGO reports- published and unpublished (sent by the organisation), academic research papers, and legal documents.

3.1 Limitations and Ethical Consideration

The interpretation might cause redundancies as secondary data (predominantly quantitative values) can be dated and vary from the status quo. Since the study was conducted based on convenience sampling, the population is limited to the selected area and not exhaustive of the population. The purpose of the study was explained to interviewees, and conversations recorded after seeking permission. The participants were free to refrain from answering questions they wanted to evade. The paper has only mentioned names of participants who agreed on citing them in quotes. The rest of the participants' names are not disclosed instead, a general description of their profile is specified.

4 Status of Waste Management

4.1 Thiruvananthapuram

Located in the southernmost part of Kerala, Thiruvananthapuram (Fig. 1) is the capital hub of the state and is home to 9.7 lakh people. The city is divided into 100 wards for effective governance, comprising both rural and urban segments, and Thiruvananthapuram Municipal Corporation (TMC) as the administrative body. Spread over an area of 214.86 km^2, the city produces 350 tonnes of waste every day, and households contribute about 49% to the total (TMC, 2019).

The relation of waste with the city and its people has evolved through the years. Currently, the administrative body adheres to the 2016 SWM rule and follows a Decentralised Solid Waste Management System, but till 2011, it had a Centralised Model. The major factor that enabled the city's shift in solid waste management is not only the legislative amendment but vociferous 'people's movements. In 2000, TMC along with a private firm, established a Centralised facility in *Vilappilsala*, a village 16 km away from the Capital city. Since the waste generated was not

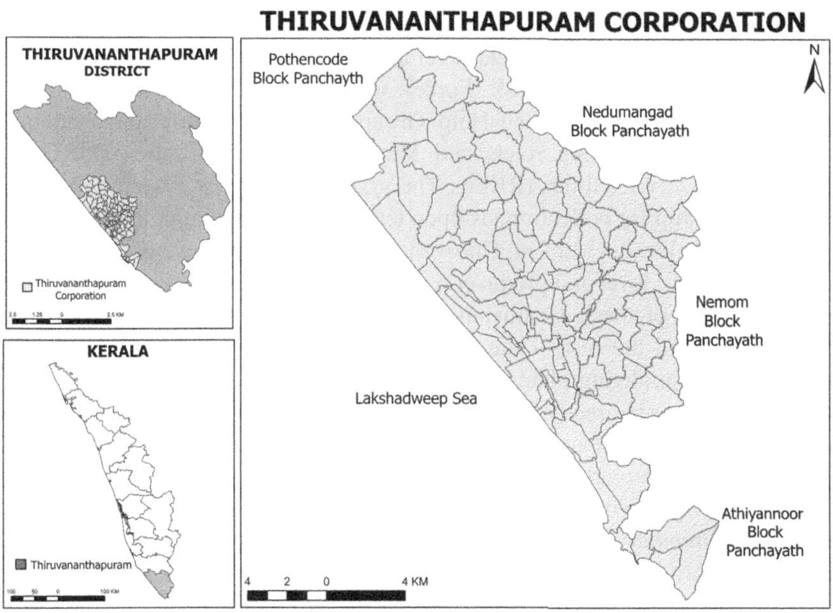

Fig. 1 Thiruvananthapuram Map. (Thanal, 2021)

segregated and beyond the plant capacity, processing was dogged by technical hitches, resulting in the accumulation of waste in the plant.

> They kept dumping waste for almost 12 years, we watched the pile grow above our heads in seconds, resembling like mountains above 30 feet high
> –A 66-year-old resident from *Vilappilsala*

The inefficacy of the system created health, environmental and economic hazards in the rural area. In 2010, the villagers in the *Vilappil* panchayat united and formed a movement of protest for the closure of the Waste Processing Plant and against the leachate contaminating Killiyar River, a major source of drinking water in the district. This struggle for clean land and water brought like-minded people into the protest. The mass movement was spread across 2 years and became chaotic due to partisan politics but ultimately, the plant was shut down. But this opened window for illegal dumping and burning of waste across the city. The unfortunate situation prompted the adoption of decentralised management in 2013 but the model became efficient after the 2017 campaign on 'Freedom from Waste' (Ramachandran et al., 2018). The Decentralised model adopted by TMC advocates the concept of 'My waste, My Responsibility' against 'Not in my Backyard' (Arya, 2017; Narain & Sambyal, 2016). Therefore, the local body adopted strategies to abide by the notion through a circular model.

In the Decentralised waste management followed by TMC, the local body is, directly and indirectly, engaged in managing (collection, processing, and reusing) waste in the city. The new system introduced devolution of responsibility to the lowest unit, the household, which is the highest contributor of waste in the city. A government entity under TMC called Suchitwa Paripalana Samithi (SPS) is responsible for monitoring and assisting in the waste management within the city. Further, the local body has established field level assistance in the form of *Haritha Karma Sena* (translates to Green Task Force) *who* are predominantly members of *Kudumbashree*, a women's Self-Help Group (SHG) in Kerala, engaged in dry waste collection, sweeping roads and Material Recovery Centres (MRCs) and Resource Recovery Facilities (RRFs). The system also opens a window to public-private partnership for collection, as open tenders are floated to collect dry waste.

The Decentralised system in Thiruvananthapuram mandates segregation of the waste at the source level and producer responsibility to Commercial Establishments. Since only 10% of these establishments have fulfilled source-level management, TMC has directed the rest of the 90% of organic waste to authorised piggeries, plantations, and rendering plants (Table 1).

TMC directly or indirectly manages about 58% of the solid waste generated in the city through source level and community level facilities. Around 42% of wards have authorised service providers for collecting dry waste and assisting with kitchen and bio compost bins. To avoid creating black spots around the city, TMC has established *Thumboormozhi*, an aerobic composting facility, across the city to manage wet waste at a community level. Currently, there are 44 *Thumboormozhis* and Material Recovery Facilities (MRF) each across the wards. The organic compost procured from these facilities are supplied in subsidies or free of cost to farmers as

Table 1 Waste facilities under TMC and their capacity. (TMC, 2019)

Facilities	No of units	Total capacity (TPD)	Facility utilisation (%)
Kitchen bins	19,000	19.00	80
Bio bins	109	2.72	60
Biogas plants	3982	3.98	60
Pipe compost	87,000	87.00	50
Organic waste converters	2	0.50	100
Aerobic bins	383	11.49	100
Mobile composting units	154	4.62	100
Community biogas plants	23	23.00	80
Dry waste collection bins	2	0.20	100
Dry leaves collection bins	3	0.30	100
Material recovery facilities (MRF)	44	44.00	100
Resource recovery Centre (RRC)	2	10.00	100
Facilities in private sector (rendering plants, farms, piggeries)	19	150.00	60
Total		356.81	67.89

manures. The city is a major hub for scrap dealers therefore efficient segregation and collection can assist in enhancing their market. Additionally, the district collector has issued guidelines to prohibit the use of single use plastics in Thiruvananthapuram.

Along with SPS, the city's entire routine of collection and processing activities is monitored by the Health Inspectors (HIs). It is facilitated through a digital platform called the 'Trivandrum Smart App' where the HIs can track the activities related to waste management by service providers and households. The adverse impact from the shut-down of the waste processing plant in 2012 was the reckless dumping of waste across the city by people who were left with no other waste management option. To prevent this illegal dumping, TMC launched an Anti-Littering Enforcement Team called 'ALERT' comprising officials from the health wing of the corporation in 2019. Though orders for segregation and source management of organic waste were issued, the awareness drives through multiple initiatives are the impetus for the success of the current waste management system. The accomplishment of policy objectives depends highly on its acceptance and support from the target population. Thus, to involve people in the initiative of decentralised waste management, TMC along with other non-governmental organisations (NGOs) came up with the idea of Green Army. It consists of volunteers from different spectrums such as students from schools and universities, environmental enthusiasts, NGOs, government and private agencies. The members of the Green Army are involved in spreading awareness and enhancing the monitoring of waste management. With the help of the smart app, anyone can notice the authorities if they happen to witness any violation of directives. The facilities available in the Thiruvananthapuram city are concrete proofs of the success achieved through the combined efforts of a local self-government and the residents. TMC has many projects in its pipeline to upgrade its existing facilities to convert the city into a 'zero waste' zone and achieve the ultimate objective of 'no burn' (Praveen, 2020).

4.2 Bengaluru

Here, the study considers the waste management system in the greater Bengaluru metropolitan area which is spread across 741 km^2 (Fig. 2). For administrative ease, the urban city is divided into 198 wards across eight zones and is headed by the Municipal Corporation, Bruhat Bengaluru Mahanagara Palike (BBMP), which was established in 1976. This capital region of Karnataka is the third largest populous city in India, with 84 lakh people residing in the urban agglomeration (Sharma, 2018). In the past four decades, Bengaluru faced a dramatic surge in population with a growth rate of 46.68% (Ramachandra et al., 2018).

The major reasons for growth are the expansion of city boundaries and concentrated activities for economic development (Ramachandra & Bachmanda, 2007; Ramachandra & Aithal, 2016). The United Nations report on World Urbanisation Prospects (2014) predicted the population of Bengaluru to reach ten crores by 2030. The condition of waste management in the fast-growing city is a matter of concern.

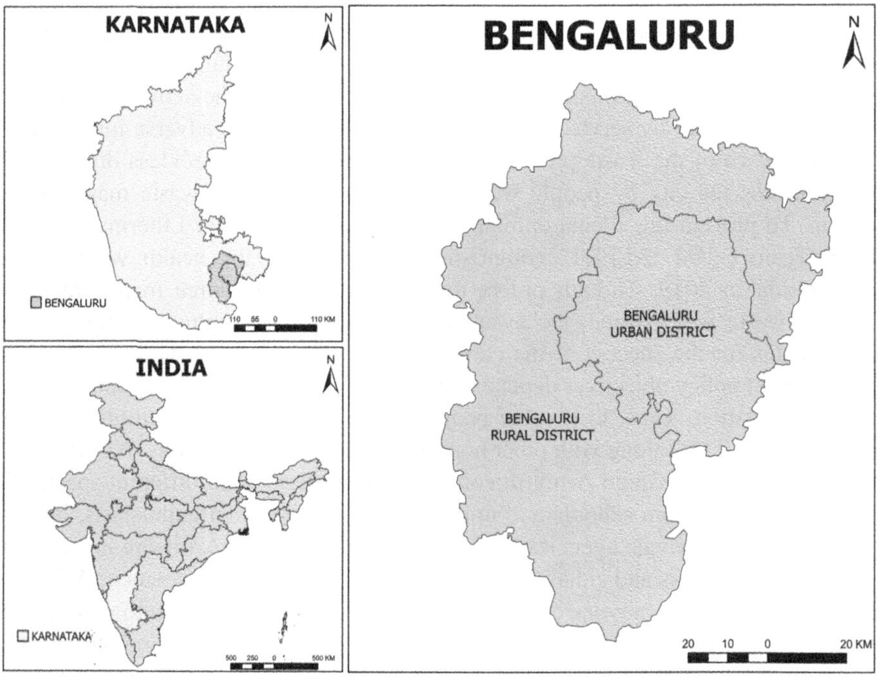

Fig. 2 Bengaluru map. (Bengaluru Development Authority, 2017)

Table 2 Waste management facilities under BBMP and its capacity (BBMP, 2020)

Facilities	No of units	Capacity
Wet waste processing plants	7	1570
Bio Methanation plants	13	65
Sanitary landfill	1	3000
Dry Waste Collection Centre (DWCC)	164	Varies across ward
Total	185	4635[a]

[a]Excluding DWCC

Bengaluru produces 5000 tonnes of waste per day and BBMP follows a centralised system based on the 2000 Solid Waste (Management and Handling) act (Naveen & Sivapullaiah, 2020).

The BBMP has contracted workers and private entities to collect, transport, and process waste generated in the city. The contract for door-to-door services is assigned after the fulfilment of the public tender requirements. HIs and Junior HIs under the BBMP are assigned to monitor waste management and conditions of workers in the city. The local body has workers known as Pourakarmikas engaged in sweeping roads and clearing common bins in the city. About 18,500 Pourakarmikas are working directly under the local body payment (BBMP, 2020). Until 2019, these workers were contracted via private agencies, which led to protest by workers unions such as BBMP Guttige Pourakarmika Sangha and Pourakarmika union affiliated with the All-India Central Council Trade Unions (AICCTU). The reasons for the protest can be traced to the non-regularisation of work, default payments by private entities, and poor work conditions of the Pourakarmikas. Though BBMP has agreed to accommodate the workers' demands, the conditions are yet to improve as these workers are subjected to social and political disparities[1] (Ramani, 2018).

In addition to the contracted service providers, various non-governmental organisations (NGOs) have started engaging in waste management. These organisations assist in launching awareness campaigns among the stakeholders. Some of the active organisations in the city are Saahas Zero Waste, Hasirudala and SWMRT. They work with Residents Associations, Corporates, and institutions to manage waste, deploying sustainable methods such as segregation, establishing source-level processing and sometimes imparting training and awareness programmes to a wider audience (Table 2).

As per the BBMP data, Bengaluru has seven wet waste processing plants, 13 Bio methanation units, one sanitary landfill and 164 dry waste collection centres. The waste management system was installed in the backdrop of the 2013 movement towards a Kasa Mukta (Garbage-free) city and Swachh Bharat Abhyan (Clean India Initiative) by the State and Central Government in 2015. The devised technological strategies were targeted to resolve the health and environmental hazards from landfills and illegal waste dumps in the city. Albeit it paved the way for the

[1]About 90% of *Pourakarmikas* are women and belong to Scheduled Caste.

installation of multiple waste management facilities in the city, the waste situation in Bengaluru has not improved. Around 1.04 lakh tonnes of mixed waste were generated in a month across the eight zones in Bengaluru, of which, only 18.65% was sent to the plants for processing (BBMP, 2020). The poor efficacy of the processing units is linked to the non-segregation of waste and inadequate facilities to store waste within the plants. (Ramachandra et al., 2018; Environment and Support Group, 2018; Tiwari, 2021). The inadequate waste management in the city has resulted in both private and government entities using landfills (such as Bellahalli) beyond its thresholds and creating illegal black spots in the city.[2] The inefficiency and failure of BBMP to implement the 2016 SWM rule in the city has resulted in litigations against the local body in the National Green Tribunal. The city continues to depend on landfills and inefficient processing units to manage waste even after noticing the environmental degradation. Rather than resolving the segregation problem in the city, in December 2020 the State has announced its plan to install Waste to Energy Plants by 2022 for resolving the issue of waste in the city (The Hindu, 2020).

5 Discussion

The Waste Management system in Thiruvananthapuram champions concepts of circular economy that contest the unsustainable linear model of centralised management (Frosch & Gallopoulos, 1989; Korhonen et al., 2018). The impact of the different models by TMC and BBMP can be analysed from three aspects – segregation, collection and processing – correlated with each other. The first step towards waste management is segregation, which both Thiruvananthapuram and Bengaluru follow (Figs. 3 and 4).

Through the decentralised system followed by TMC, about 80% of the household waste in the city gets segregated at the source. But the Centralised model of BBMP can segregate only 40% which often gets mixed at collection points (Sambyal, 2016; The Hindu, 2020). The factor conditioning this aspect of segregation is closely linked to the accountability of waste generators. The reluctance towards managing waste can be traced to its association with ideas on impurity and obsolesce created by humans (Eriksen & Schober, 2017). The success of TMC lies in its progressive interpretation of the 2016 Solid Waste Management Act, which enabled creating positive value to waste through its innovative strategies.

> We can create mineral-rich manure at home than buying harmful synthetic fertilisers. Through proper segregation, discarded waste becomes valuable
> – Official from Upcycle

The knowledge about the efficacy of waste through segregation was spread across the city through multiple awareness programmes with the help of the Green Army.

---

[2]Kavitha Shankar vs BBMP and ors (ESG, 1995).

Fig. 3 Transfer of waste in Bengaluru (Author)

Fig. 4 Processed waste in Thiruvananthapuram

The participatory model adopted by TMC ensures public support and cooperation to facilitate interventions. The directive by the local body to service providers to collect only dry waste, other than the 3.4%, further ensures segregation of waste. BBMP provides guidelines for segregation based on the composition of waste but the limited efforts for implementation hinder the process.

> People throw garbage in random parts of the street and road. This makes waste segregation extremely difficult. The only difference is the punctuality of rickshaws that comes to collect the garbage. Other than that, wages are still low and people treat us with disgust
> –Bengaluru's Paurakarmika

India has a long history of oppression towards people from the marginalised section. Predominantly, people from the lower sections of the society are engaged in menial hazardous jobs that further aggravates their socio-economic, political and health vulnerabilities (Darokar, 2018). The above anecdote is by a Pourakarmika contracted by BBMP who recalled the poor conditions at work. Bengaluru's centralised waste management system fails to eradicate the social and economic disparities faced by waste workers in the city. The approach by TMC protects the conditions of waste workers in the city by reducing their interface with an unpleasant and unhealthy environment. Their work is recognised and respected by designating them as Green Technicians, who are assisting the Generators in managing their waste. It breaks the traditional division of labour engaged in waste management and involves all sections of the society for managing waste. Such a system manoeuvres removal of disparity connected to waste management in a traditionally hierarchical society.

The collection is well defined in Thiruvananthapuram due to constant monitoring by multiple stakeholders in a system. The regularity of door-to-door waste collection fluctuates across Bengaluru, resulting in illegal dumping and accumulation of mixed waste (Ramachandra et al., 2018; Fathima, 2020). Interview with an organisation[3] engaged in waste management advocacy in Bengaluru indicated the strong lobbying by private contractors and submission of wrong details such as overestimating resources (workers, pushcarts and autos) for receiving legal tenders. The improper segregation and collection contribute to the inefficiency of processing units in Bengaluru. Five out of seven wet-waste processing units in Bengaluru are currently causing a risk of leachate contamination into soil and water sources (Environment and Support Group, 2018; National Green Tribunal, 2021). The inadequate segregation, collection and processing of waste in Bengaluru have subscribed towards irrevocable environmental degradation. The city has depended on natural and manmade lakes for drinking and irrigation needs, but the water sources remain unsafe due to the illegal dumping into lakes. (D'Souza & Nagendra, 2011; Ramachandra et al., 2018). The mismanagement of, and the malpractices embedded in the existing system, affect the water and ecological sustainability in Bengaluru.

The adoption of a decentralised model of waste management has reduced the financial burden of TMC. This is evident from the cost reduction from 33 lakhs to 7 lakhs per month, with the largest share of the reduction in transportation (Sambhyal, 2016). Though there are strict mandates to segregate waste, source-

[3]The name of the organization and individuals are not revealed to maintain the anonymity clause ensured during interviews.

level management by households is the only promoted and not forced by TMC. The subsidisation of facilities and the tireless awareness programmes are the key factors that acted as an impetus in more than 50% source level management of the biodegradable waste (TMC, 2019). The proper segregation in TMC facilitates Reuse and Recycling of waste. The organic produce from waste is not only utilised as manure but also as an inoculant for composting thus, the recycled product gets 'Revalued'.

Fluctuations are inevitable in a diverse society but, the governing body through the power vested in it by the Constitution, must facilitate and ensure the welfare of all its citizens. The analysis of waste management in Thiruvananthapuram and Bengaluru emphasise the notion of governance and welfare. Compared to Karnataka, the state of Kerala has been following a decentralised model of development which adheres to the devolution of power to the lowest unit in a system (Isaac & Tharakan, 1995; Isaac & Harilal, 1997). Therefore, the high level of public participation, which is the crux of a democratic system, became a catalyst towards successful Decentralised waste management by TMC. The governance structure in Bengaluru reciprocates the idea of the 74th Constitutional amendment through the establishment of BBMP. But, in the context of waste management, the power hierarchy within the system restricts public participation and eventually affects their welfare. Public cohesion is a necessary tool in implementing and successfully carrying any policy intervention. TMC acknowledges the significance of public support from the fallout during the *Vilappilsala* protest. Therefore, their strategies devised for efficient management of waste revolve around the increased role of people in every step of waste management. In both Thiruvananthapuram and Bengaluru, households are the largest generators, predominantly with an organic composition in waste. The mechanism adopted by TMC ensures accountability by households and other generators towards their solid waste. BBMP, though it has guidelines, fails to devise strategies that promote accountability among producers of waste. Under such a circumstance, the responsibility to manage waste gets divided among fewer units, and the burden is concentrated to specific sections, predominantly the marginalised. Due to the linear model followed in Bengaluru, the burden of poor waste management is faced by the frontline workers and inhabitants in the periphery. This condition resembles the situation in Thiruvananthapuram before the decentralised system of waste management.

The previous section elucidated that, unlike TMC, BBMP is callous about the waste management situation in Bengaluru even after instances of acute pollution and multiple protests especially by waste workers. This is evident from the lack of initiative to promote segregation and management at the source level. Most of the landfill and processing sites exist in 28% of the city which predominantly lies on the outskirts of Bengaluru (Ramachandra et al., 2018). The centralised waste management adopted by BBMP reflects on the notion of selective welfare in governance (Badlock et al., 2012). This further intensifies the power dichotomy between city and periphery and different sections in the society. Bengaluru is an example of a capitalist system that ignores equity of power and resources. The selective welfare in the context of waste management by BBMP indicates how the quality of life is compromised. The city is developing through infrastructural expansions[4] but at the cost of its sustainability.

The impact of waste management strategies by TMC and BBMP reflects on the idea of waste as 'midwife of all creation or most formidable obstacle' (Bauman, 2013). Due to the linear model of BBMP, waste creates negative externality like environmental degradation, social exclusion and ultimately the concentration of power among few. TMC has opted for ward-level and household-level waste processing, as it reduces the burden on land, water, and air, unlike the centralised landfill. The decentralised system in Thiruvananthapuram collaborates a cross-section of people irrespective of their socio-economic status, integrating the labour of the marginalised into the mainstream fold. The involvement of self-help groups and scrap dealers contribute to a wider dimension of economics, as it inducts unorganised labour into a formal framework.

6 Conclusion

The study provides empirical evidence on the multiple implications – social, economic, political and environmental – of waste and its management. Both Thiruvananthapuram and Bengaluru have experienced the adverse impact of improper waste management. The decision by TMC to shift from a centralised model to a people-centred decentralised approach highlights the effect of progressive institutional intervention in mitigating negative impact. But the approach adopted by BBMP reflects negligence towards rectifying proven mistakes. Though the 2016 SWM rule directs termination of landfill utilisation, the private and government entities in Bengaluru continue to depend on landfills, beyond the threshold (refer to Sect. 4.2). BBMP fails to understand that the waste situation in Bengaluru cannot be eradicated through new technological interventions such as WTEIs. It must devise strategies to mobilise people and establish norms or incentives to segregate. The literature section and example from TMC elucidated the importance of the first step in waste management to reduce, reuse and recycle waste generated.

The examples from both the cities highlight the adverse effect of concentration of power and limited participation by people. Bengaluru echoes the rural-urban power dichotomy with the concentrated establishment of waste management facilities in the former area. The ideal option to avoid environmental and social stress will be to decentralise waste management practices to smaller units. Although, it is imperative to strategise decentralised models that will be suitable for the designated area. Elinore Ostrom (2008), in her study about common property resources, reflect on adopting strategies to best fit the existing structure and the influence of surrounding conditions in the result chain. The management strategy followed by TMC is based

[4]The 2020 order for case WP 24739/2021 indicated building permission to 9188 application between 1st January 2019 to 31st January 2020.

on the Solid Waste Management rules of 2016. The current rate of success is a consequence of progressive interpretation of SWM rule by the ULB for adapting to the conditions in the city. To tackle the waste situation across the nation, the most sustainable practice is through decentralisation catered through people participation but, it is imperative to understand the ground realities for efficiency.

References

Ahlheim, M., Becker, M., Trastl, H., & Losada, Y. A. (2019). Wasted! Resource recovery and waste management in Cuba. *International Journal of Cuban Studies*, 147–173.

Annepu, R. K. (2012). *Sustainable solid waste management in India*. http://www.seas.columbia.edu/earth/wtert/sofos/Sustainable%20Solid

Arya, U. R. (2017, August 12). *The Times of India*. https://timesofindia.indiatimes.com/city/kochi/your-garbage-your-responsibility-saysthiruvananthapuram/articleshow/60023376.cms.Narain. Accessed 31 March 2021.

Badlock, J., Mitton, L., Manning, N., & Vickerstaff, S. (2012). *Social Policy*. Oxford University Press.

Bauman, Z. (2013). *Wasted lives: Modernity and its outcasts*. John Wiley & Sons.

Baviskar, A., & Gidwani, V. (2019). The lives of waste and pollution. *Economic and Political Weekly*, 33–35.

BBMP. (2020). *Bruhat Bengaluru Mahanagar Palike.*. https://bbmp.gov.in/departmentwebsites/swm/index.html. Accessed 31 March 2021.

Bhalerao, S. (2019, March 26). *Fire breaks out at Mumbai's Deonar dumping ground, as temperature soars*. Hindusthan Times. https://www.hindustantimes.com/mumbai-news/firebreaks-out-in-mumbai-s-deonar-dumping-ground-as-temperatures-soar/story-eca6OWCIbpm9VUYoK82c4I.html. Accessed 30 August 2019.

Bhat, P. (2019). *What garbage burning does to Bengaluru: Asthma and heart attacks on the rise*. https://www.thenewsminute.com/article/what-garbage-burning-does-bengaluru-asthma-and-heart-attacks-rise-88739. Posted on 21 September 2018. Accessed on 14 September 2019.

Bhuiyan, S. H. (2010). A crisis in governance: Urban soild waste management in Bangladesh. *Habitat International*, 125–133.

Bjerkli, C. L. (2013). Government on the ground: A study of solid waste management in Addis Ababa, Ethiopia. *International Journal of Urban and Regional Research*, 1273–1287.

D'Souza, R., & Nagendra, H. (2011). Changes in public commons as a consequence of urbanisation: The Agara Lake in Bangalore, India. *Environment Management*, 840–850.

Darokar, S. (2018). *Manual scavengers: A blind spot in urban development discourse*.

Das, S., Lee, S. H., Kumar, P., Kim, K. H., Lee, S. S., & Bhattacharya, S. S. (2019). Solid waste management: Scope and challenges of sustainability. *Journal of Cleaner Production*, 658–678.

Doron, A., & Jeffery, R. (2018). Waste of a nation: Garbage and growth in India. In I. A. Doron & R. Jeffery (Eds.), *Growth and garbage* (p. 43). Harvard University Press.

Environment Protection Agency. (2020, October). Retrieved from https://www.epa.gov/sites/production/files/2020-10/documents/master_swmg_10-20-20_0.pdf

Environment and Support Group. (2018). *Bangalore's toxic legacy Intensifie*. Environment and Support Group.

Environment Support Group India (Bengaluru). (1995). https://esgindia.org/new/pils/swm-pils/esgsinitiatives-onsocially-just-and-ecologically-progressive-management-ofmunicipal-solid-waste-including-pils/. Accessed 30 April 2020.

Eriksen, T. H., & Schober, E. (2017). Waste and the superfluous: An introduction. *Social Anthropology, 25*(3), 282–287.

Fathima, I. (2020, February 22). *New Indian Express*. https://www.newindianexpress.com/cities/bengaluru/2020/feb/22/irregular-waste-collection-leaves-residents-in-a-fix-2106860.html. Accessed 27 April 2020.

Frosch, R. A., & Gallopoulos, N. E. (1989). Strategies for manufacturing. *Scientific American, 261* (3), 144–153. http://www.jstor.org/stable/24987406. Accessed 18 January 2021

Ghosh, A. (2020, August 13). *The Print*. https://theprint.in/india/indiaspopulation-to-cross-152-crore-in-next-16-years-more-people-will-be-of-working-age/481018/. Accessed 31 March 2021.

Grindle, M. S. (2010). *Good governance: The inflation of an idea* (HKS faculty research working paper series, RWP10–023, John F). Harvard University.

Gupta, S. K. (2012). Integrating the informal sector for improved waste management. *Private Sector and Development, 15*, 12–17.

Hoornweg, D., & Tata , P. B. (2012, March). *What a waste: A global review of solid waste management*. Retrieved from World Bank Group: https://openknowledge.worldbank.org/handle/10986/17388

Hui, Y., Li'ao, W., Fenwei, S., & Gang, H. (2006). Urban solid waste management in Chongquing: Challenges and opportunities. *Waste Management*, 1052–1062.

Isaac, T., & Harilal, K. N. (1997). Planning for empowerment: People's campaign for decentralised planning in Kerala. *Economic and Political Weekly*, 53–58.

Isaac, T., & Tharakan, M. (1995). *Kerala: Towards a New Agenda. Economic and Political Weekly 1993–2004*.

Korhonen, J., Nuur, C., Feldmann, A., & Birkie, S. E. (2018). Circular economy as an essentially contested concept. *Journal of Cleaner Production, 175*, 544–552.

Korner, I., Sanchez, S. I., & Corrales, A. Y. (2008). Proposal for the integration of decentralised composting of the organic fraction of municipal soild waste into the waste management system of Cuba. *Waste Management*, 64–72.

Massoud, M. A., Mokbel, M., Alawieh, S., & Yassin, N. (2019). Towards improved governance for sustainable solid waste managemnt in Lebanon: Centralised vs decentralised approaches. *Waste Management & Research*, 686–697.

Metin, E., Erozturk, A., & Neyim, C. (2003). Solid waste management practices and review of recovery and recycling operations in Turkey. *Waste Management*, 425–432.

Narayana, T. (2009). Municipal solid waste management in India: From waste disposal to recovery of resources? *Waste Management*, 1163–1166.

Nilsson, M., Eklund, M., & Tyskeng, S. (2009). Environmental integration and policy implementation: Competing governance modes in waste management decision making. *Environment and Planning*, 1–18.

National Commission on Population. (2019, November). *Reports*. Retrieved from Ministry of Health and Wefare. https://nhm.gov.in/New_Updates_2018/Report_Population_Projection_2019.pdf

National Green Tribunal. (2021, February 2). *Karnataka State Pollution Control Board*. https://kspcb.karnataka.gov.in/sites/default/files/inlinefiles/2.2.21%20BBMP%20limit%20NGT%20SLC%20meeting%20proceedings.pdf. Accessed 25 March 2021.

Naveen, B. P., & Sivapullaiah, P. V. (2020). Solid waste management: Current scenario and challenges in Bengaluru. In *Sustainable sewage sludge management and resource efficiency*. IntechOpen.

Nzeadibe, T. C. (2009). Solid waste reforms and informal recycling in Enugu urban area, Nigeria. *Habitat International*, 93–99.

Ostrom, E. (2008). Institutions and the environment. *Economic Affairs, 28*(3), 24–31.

Owolabi, S. A., Mmereki, D., Baldwin, A., & Li, B. (2016). A comparative analysis of solid waste management in developed, developing and lesser developed countries. *Environmental Technology Reviews*, 120–141.

Praveen, R. S. (2020, February 17). *Waste to energy plants not necessary* (p. 2). The Hindu.

Pujara, Y., Pathak, P., Sharma, A., & Govani, J. (2019). Review on Indian municipal solid waste management practices for reduction of environmental impacts to acheieve suitable development goals. *Journal of Environmental Management*, 1–12.

Ramachandra, T. V., & Aithal, B. H. (2016). Bengaluru's reality: Towards unlivable status with unplanned urban trajectory. *Current Science, 110*(12), 2207–2208.

Ramachandra, T. V., & Bachamada, S. (2007). Environmental audit of municipal solid waste management. *International Journal for Environmental Technology and Management*, 369–391.

Ramachandra, T. V., Bharath, H. A., Kulkarni, G., & Han, S. S. (2018). Municipal solid waste: Generation, composition and GHG emission in Bengalore, India. *Renewable and Sustainable Energy Reviews*, 1122–1136.

Ramani, C. V. (2018). *Pourakarmikas still wait for service regularisation*. The Hindu.

Sambhyal, S. S. (2016). *Solid waste management in Indian cities*. Centre for science and environment.

Sambyal, S. S. (2016). *Swachh Bharat Mission—Performance in figures*. https://www.downtoearth.org.in/feature/two-years-of-swachhbharat- mission-55883. Posted on 1 October 2016. Accessed on 29 April 2020.

Sambyal, Swati singh. (LinkedIn). https://www.LinkenIn.com/posts/swatisambhyal_thiruvananthapuramzerowaste-zerowaste-activity-6635471247696322560-EJLL. Accessed on 12 April 2020.

Shaban, A., Kourtit, K., & Nijkamp, P. (2020). India's urban system: Sustainability and imbalanced growth of cities. *Sustainability*, 1–20.

Sharma, M. (2018, May 12). *Bangalore Mirror*. Retrieved January 5, 2021, from https://bangaloremirror.indiatimes.com/bangalore/cover-story/ec-data-reveals-citys-exponential-growth-there-are-now-over-1-25-crore-of-us-bengalureans/articleshow/64129198.cms

Singh, S. (2015). Cities- the 21st century India. In S. Singh (Ed.), *Decentralised solid waste Management in India: A perspective on technological options* (pp. 289–302). Bookwell Publishers.

Swaminathan, M. (2018). *How can India's waste problem see a systemic change. Economic and Political Weekly Engage*. https://www.epw.in/engage/article/institutional-framework-implementingsolid-waste-management-india-macro-analysis. Accessed 28 August 2019.

The Hindu. (2020, December 3). https://www.thehindu.com/news/cities/bangalore/state-to-get-waste-to-energy-plant-in-2022/article33234145.ece#:~:text=State%20to%20get%20waste%2Dto%2Denergy%20plant%20in%202022,-Staff%20Reporter&text=Yediyurappa%20on%20Wednesday%20laid%20the,WtE%20plant%2. Accessed 20 March 2021.

Tiwari, D. (2021, January 2). *Deccan Herald*. https://www.deccanherald.com/specials/point-blank/fixing-bengalurus-waste-management-issues-beyond-activism-934212.html. Accessed 20 March 2021.

TMC (Thiruvananthapuram Municipal Corporation). (2019). *Status of solid and liquid waste management*. Thiruvananthapuram Municipal Corporation.

US Census Bureau. (2021, January 18). *United States Census Bureau*. https://www.census.gov/popclock/print.php?component=counter. Accessed 31 March 2021.

Vujic, G., Roof, A. G., Stanisavljevic, N., & Ragossnig, A. (2015). Municipal solid waste developement phases: Evidence from EU27. *Waste Management & Research*, 1112–1120.

Wilson, D. C., Rogero, A. C., Modak, P., Velis, C., Rodic, L., Soos, R., . . . Iyer, M. (2015). *Global Waste Management Outlook*. Retrieved from United Nations Environment Programme: https://www.unep.org/resources/report/global-waste-management-outlook

Zhang, D. Q., Tan, S. K., & Gersberg, R. M. (2010). Municipal soild waste management in China: Status,problems and challenges. Journal of Environmental Management, 1623–1633.

Zurbrugg, C., Drescher, S., Patel, A., & Sharatchandra, H. C. (2004). Decentralised composting of urban waste- An overview of community and private initiatives in India. *Waste Management*, 655–662.

Zurbrugg, C., Drescher, S., Rytz, I., Sinha, A. M., & Enayetullah, I. (2005). Decentralised composting in Bangladesh, a win-win situation for all stakeholders. *Resources, Conservation and Recycling*, 281–292.

The Major Underlying Factors Behind the Rise of Cairns as a First World Tropical City

W S (Bill) Cummings

Abstract The development of technology suited to the tropics has been one of four major underlying factors behind the rapid growth of Cairns as a major regional city in Australia. Much of the technological developments of importance have related to industry sectors like agriculture, mining, fisheries and tourism. However, arguably, those relating to development of technology related to everyday living in the tropics have been of equal importance. This Paper seeks to identify these major developments in technology related to everyday living that have been of importance to Cairns' progress, including some in which the city has played a key role of global significance. The Paper records the views of the 1930s, set out in the American Geographical Society Study "White Settlers in the Tropics", about the challenges and progress in tropical Queensland. The Paper looks at data on life expectancies compared to other parts of Australia. The Paper discusses the role of cooling devices from water cooled safes, iceboxes, ceiling fans, refrigeration and air-conditioning. It will discuss the impact of satellite technology on cyclone warnings and work on cyclone proofing structures with consequent avoidance of loss of life. The Paper will also record how these developments, combined with "success breeds success" factors, the development of improved medical, education, sporting, cultural, arts and entertainment facilities, have seen Cairns and the tropical north progress over the years from being a "hardship posting" to being a "desired place to live".

Keywords Global Markets · Technology · Tropical City · Cairns · Economic Growth

W. S. (Bill) Cummings (✉)
Cummings Economics, Cairns, Australia
e-mail: cummings@cummings.net.au

© The Author(s), under exclusive license to Springer Nature Singapore Pte Ltd. 2022

T. Chaiechi, J. Wood (eds.), *Community Empowerment, Sustainable Cities, and Transformative Economies*, https://doi.org/10.1007/978-981-16-5260-8_15

1 Introduction

The Census held in 1947 after the end of the Pacific War recorded Cairns City Council population at 16,400 (Queensland Year Book, 1957). This compares with a population of over 160,000 today (Australian Bureau of Statistics cat. no. 3218.0, n. d.). This Paper outlines the basic underlying factors behind the city's growth to pass seven other Australian regional cities in size since 1976 to become the hub (capital) city of northern Australia's most populous region and one of the largest in regional Australia.

The first thing to understand is that Cairns' primary economic role is that of being a hub city servicing a region 1½ times the size of Victoria, as large in area as the British Isles and almost as large as California. In biological resources, this is one of Australia's richest regions. The region accounts for 26% of Australia's water run-off. Its tropical rainforests account for the continent's most intense plant growth. The northern half of the biologically rich waters of the Great Barrier Reef stretch along the region's eastern coastline.

The second major thing to understand is that the area lies deep into the tropics from 9^0 to 19^0 south. The area posed an immense challenge to a young nation with most of its technology and population derived from cold climate north-western Europe. Sydney was almost 100 years old before Cairns commenced being established as a port in 1876. Early progress was slow, with plenty of setbacks.

The major industries that underpinned the development of southern Australia, wheat and sheep, did not prosper in the northern regions. A fledgling pastoral industry based on cattle received a major setback in the 1890s when susceptible British breeds died in their thousands as tick-borne Redwater fever from Asia swept through the herds.

Although Federation brought protection of the sugar industry, the White Australia Policy required the industry to change from a plantation system to small farmers supplying to central mills. World War 1 came along in 1914 and by the 1920s, an early mining boom that had underpinned much early development faded leaving a hinterland dotted with ghost towns. Over exploitation of fisheries saw an early pearling boom fade. The depression and World War II followed with its brief influx of thousands of defence personnel, mainly on their way to the New Guinea battlefields.

In the early post war period, the economy of the region was almost entirely based on a protected sugar industry that had grown steadily over the years. While Queensland as a whole was being referred to as the "Cinderella State" (Hughes and McFarlane, 1964) that had failed to share in the development of Australia's manufacturing industries, the Cairns region was calling itself the forgotten Far North at the end of the line, 1000 miles north from the state capital.

However, the region's potentially rich natural resource base was still there in plant growth potential, in marine resources, in minerals, and of increasing importance, in natural tourism resources. A strong local pioneering spirit of self-help and a willingness to follow its own path based on a realistic appraisal of its position saw the region leap forward from the 1960s on. This leap forward was aided by four underlying global economic factors that were to underpin a massive growth in the region's earnings from the rest of Australia and the world that, in turn, underpinned a major growth in population and the city of Cairns.

2 Growing Global Markets

The first of these was the growth in world markets reaching out for previously marginal resources of minerals, primary produce and for the region's tourism resources. Of great importance to the region was the fact that it was relatively close to the largest global growth area of the period in eastern Asia. Strong growth also occurred in the Australian economy under the influence of a change in economic policy from protection aimed at building up manufacturing, to one of pursuing freer international trade.

3 Advances in Transport and Communications Technology

Apart from being remote from national markets, the region was located in a continent remote from international markets. Major developments in transport and communication were to break down the high-cost penalties of remoteness in a big way.

Australia's and this region's early mining boom was based on high value metals. The post-war development of bulk ore carriers was to open out the development of a major new mining boom based on sedimentary type deposits with coal and iron ore leading the way but importantly for this region, the opening up of bauxite and silica sand deposits in the Cape.

The advent of superior semi-trailers and subsequent road trains along with the sealing of roads, especially of the Bruce Highway, proved Bruce Davidson's gloomy view of prospects for development of agriculture in the north in his 1960s book, "The Northern Myth" (Davidson, 1965) were wrong.

Falling transport costs relative to other costs saw the region's advantages in production of tropical crops and offseason produce come to the fore. The Cairns region is now Australia's third largest fruit producing region (Australian Bureau of Statistics cat. no. 7503.0, n.d.).

The whole history of tourism in the region can be written in terms of transport development. The underlying attractions of the "Tropical Wonderland" of the reefs and rainforest have been there from the beginning. Before the 1920s, tourists came north on winter cruises on the Manunda and Manoora. The 1920s saw the railway linked to Brisbane and the age of the Sunshine Express began. The post war period saw a surge based on the family car and coach. Wide bodied jets and the major upgrading of Cains airport in 1984 to take jets direct from overseas brought a further surge. In turn, the international air routes would open the doors for air export of high value fishery and horticulture products.

Communication developments have shrunk the world. Backpackers from Europe can call home on their mobiles and use their home credit card to pay for goods anywhere, any time.

However, the picture would not be complete without recording the dark side of transport development. The region has lost a great deal of local manufacturing – notably in fields like the brewery, brickworks, softdrink manufacturing.

4 Development of Technology Suited to the Tropics

When British settlers first arrived in Australia, they brought with them the world's most advanced technology in many fields. But much of it relating to the environment of north-western Europe. This included a suite of highly productive plants and animals, housing, clothing, disease and climate control.

However, for a young nation with most of its people and technology derived from north-western Europe, the tropics represented a massive challenge. Sydney was almost 100 years old before Cairns was established as a port in 1876.

A great deal of the progress made in the region has been due to the development of technology related to the tropics. Standing behind the sugar industry coming through in the 1980s to throw off the need for protection was the locally developed mechanisation of sugar cane harvesting and bulk handling of sugar. Tropical Australia now has more beef cattle per square kilometre than southern Australia with the introduction of tropical type Brahman breeds into the herds being a major factor. The explosion of horticultural crops in the region has followed, in part, local Rare Fruits Society members scouring the world in the 1970s for new tropical types.

In reef tourism, the region has led the world starting with the underwater observatory at Green Island in the 1950s. The introduction of fast passenger catamaran technology enabled visitors to be carried to the outer reefs swiftly and with major reduction in sea sickness. Cableway technology has been introduced to rainforest viewing. Four-wheeled drives have opened up wilderness touring.

But of very great importance, technology has been introduced that has revolutionised everyday living in the tropics.

Cairns was established in 1876 in the late Victorian age of immense optimism and technological advances. From experiences elsewhere in the tropics, the new settlers in the Cairns region brought with them adaptation of house design, widespread use of cotton clothing, mosquito nets and subsequently, an ability to manufacture ice blocks to assist with food storage. They also brought with them tropical ornamental trees from around the tropical world for their gardens.

However, there were substantial problems with tropical diseases and in dealing with hot wet summers. By the 1930s, as the American Geographical Society book "*White Settlers in the Tropics*" (Grenfell Price, 1939) indicates, serious doubts were still being expressed about the ability of people living in the tropics (especially those of European origin), to live healthy and productive lives.

"*All things considered, this chapter on the white settlers of north-eastern Queensland must end with a question mark. Up to the present, with an adequate living standard supported (and justly so) by the whole Australian nation* (Queensland Year Book, 1957), *the progress of this tropical penetration has been excellent. But past successes are no certain proof of further advances, and the people of Australia who are making substantial contributions toward* one of the most important experiments in world history, *should see that while the national government treats north-eastern Queensland with sympathy and kindness, it at the same time subjects the area to continuous and vigorous scientific research.*" (Our underlining.) (Note: Queensland Year Book, 1957, reference to protection of the sugar industry.)

Historically, there has been a widespread belief in the population in southern Australia that the tropics were uncomfortable to live in and unhealthy. Advances in more recent decades have seen many of the negatives of living in the tropics overcome.

4.1 Health

Children growing up in Cairns up to the 1930s were exposed to widespread incidence of Malaria, Dengue Fever and Hookworm. Elimination of Hookworm was a matter of public sanitation.

Cairns based Dr. Koch had played a role in the earlier identification of mosquitos as a vector for Malaria and Dengue Fever. There was a plaque at the old Cairns North school now Community Health Centre setting out the role the wartime hospital (established at the school), played in combatting Malaria during the Pacific War.

American engineers and Council efforts in the early post-war period to drain swamps and introduce fogging saw Malaria effectively eliminated not just in Cairns but throughout Queensland, as recorded in Cilento and Lacks 1959 Queensland Centenary History "*Triumph in the Tropics*" (Cilento Sir Raphael and Lack C Snr, 1959).

Cairns' more recent role and that of James Cook University in bringing Dengue Fever under control is well known. Our firm's market research arm, Compass Research, was pleased to provide the community research and feedback to assist in the implementation of the Eliminate Dengue Program. This program has now morphed into the Dengue World Mosquito Program. Problems with rat-borne "Wells Disease" among canecutters was brought under control by burning the cane before harvesting in the 1930s, and with mechanical harvesting these days is now a thing of the past.

An analysis our firm carried out of comparative life expectancies (Cummings, 2014) in the early 2000s, which separated out the still unacceptably low life expectancies in the Aboriginal and Islander population throughout Australia, indicated there was no foundation for any belief these days that life expectancies in the region's population were any lower than other parts of regional Australia.

4.2 Temperature Control

There is a view in literature on the subject (Markham, 1942) that the rise of north-western Europe in a global context can be traced back to the invention of the hearth and chimney in about the 12th and 13th centuries. Certainly, immigrants from north-western Europe brought with them superior ability to combat winter cold through housing design and heating and in suitable clothing.

The challenge in the tropics has been the reverse – the need to cool. The punkah from India, old Queenslander house design, cotton clothing, hessian ceilings that could be wet, air-cooled water bags, ice block safes were all early advances in this direction. By the 1940s, electric ceiling fans were being installed in public buildings but they were extremely heavy and expensive.

Three more recent advances have had a major impact as follows.

1. Widespread introduction of household refrigerators.
2. Installation of light cheap ceiling fans. (Apart from cooling, mosquitos are unable to fly in the breeze created. Mosquito nets are a thing of the past.)
3. The widespread introduction of air-conditioning in homes and work places.

Against this background, household electricity bills have soared to Canberra winter oil-heating bill levels. But intolerable hot muggy summer nights with mosquitos buzzing are gone.

4.3 Clothing

Early settlers in the area quickly transitioned to lighter cotton clothing for work and leisure if not for formal occasions. However, cotton fabrics required starching and ironing to look good, and hot and humid conditions required frequent change of clothing and heavy washing-day burdens. Introduction of washing machines and new fabric types have been of disproportionate value in a tropical household.

4.4 Gardening and Household Maintenance

For an area that experiences very strong plant growth, the replacement of hand push mowers by motor mowers and whipper snippers have cut down time spent and difficulties in garden maintenance. Jet sprays, superior detergents and paints have been particularly important in an area that traditionally experiences wet season mould growth. Apart from benefitting individual households, these advances have had a major impact on public gardens and spaces.

4.5 Hazard Reduction

The introduction of satellite tracking and superior building codes have greatly reduced the impact of tropical cyclones. Antivenenes have been developed that reduce snake and insect bite and marine stinger hazards. Insect control has been of special importance, especially in this area to combat ticks on family pets.

5 Success Breeds Success

As population, industry and infrastructure has built up, new activities have become feasible that replace imports or replace a need to travel elsewhere to access.

With the growth of marine activity in the area – the fishing fleet, the reef fleet, trading vessels, work vessels, government vessels, the Navy, Cairns has become a major skills-based marine servicing centre in national terms as well as leading the north. Similarly, in aircraft activity, Cairns has become a skills-based aircraft servicing centre of national significance.

Based on population growth, higher education facilities have been established, specialist medical services expanded, improved facilities for arts and entertainment activities and sporting facilities. Effectively, these developments have lowered the real costs of living in the area and made the region a more attractive place to live and work.

6 Looking Forward

In the past ten years, growth of the city and region has slowed but remained above the rest of the north. A number of recent shocks, not least the recent Covid experience, has led to concern about where the city and region go next to get back to strong growth again.

Just as the city came to realise in the 1960s that it could not just lazily rely on sugar expansion to continue underpinning its progress – today, there needs to be a realisation to embrace all the opportunities that the city and region presents.

The four underlying factors remain. Although checked by Covid, the world economy can be expected to continue growing although the situation with China is a worry. The speed of transport development appears to have slowed but we are seeing road links expanding into the Peninsula and direct routes to Melbourne and Darwin developing. However, communication technology, especially through the internet, is exploding. The big improvement in technology related to the tropics appears to have slowed but the rest of the world, especially southern Australia, can probably be made more aware that some of the old negatives in terms of comfort and health are things of the past and the area has become a desirable place to live.

We are yet to capitalise on some of the possibilities for development coming out of our new position as the most populous region in northern Australia. But with Cairns now featuring on global TV network weather maps, the world is becoming more aware of it – a far cry from the past.

Although strong progress has been achieved, in the scale of Australia and the world, population in the region (1½ times the size of Victoria and as large as the British Isles), is just passing 300,000. With 26% of Australia's water runoff, we are still only producing about 3% of Australia's primary industry output.

In looking forward, there are three major opportunities.

The first is to continue to seize the opportunities to build our earnings from the rest of the world based on our resources – to get tourism back on track, to exploit opportunities to expand agriculture, mining and marine industries.

The second is to continue to expand on outside earnings into skills-based sectors like the marine sector, aviation servicing, international education and other services we are good at. While the situation with China is a negative for substantial amounts of trade, there are some offsetting positives for the city in defence.

Our population size now gives us an opportunity to catch up with other cities of our size in fields like higher education, health services and sporting and cultural facilities in which we have been lagging.

Finally, the position of the region as the largest in population in the north opens up new opportunities for Cairns in relation to its position in the wider North Australia, Tropical Southwest Pacific region that need to be pursued.

References

Queensland Year Book. (1957)

Australian Bureau of Statistics cat. no. 3218.0. (n.d.)

Hughes, G., & McFarlane, P. (1964). *Queensland industrial enigma*. Melbourne University Press.

Davidson, B. R. (1965). *The northern myth. A study of the physical & economic limits to agricultural & pastoral development in northern Australia*. Melbourne University Press.

Australian Bureau of Statistics cat. no. 7503.0. (n.d.)

Grenfell Price, A. (1939). White settlers in the tropics. American geographical society, special publication no 23, New York.

Cilento Sir Raphael and Lack C Snr. (1959). *Triumph in the tropics. An historical sketch of Queensland. Completed & edited by for the Historical Committee of the Centenary Celebrations Council of Queensland*. Brisbane: Smith & Patterson Pty Ltd.

Cummings, W.S. (2014). Australia's Tropical North. Initial challenges, historical development, current progress and future prospects. Exhibit 76 Pivot North Inquiry into the Development of Northern Australia, Final Report.

Markham, S.F. (1942). Climate and the energy of nations.

Sustainable Cities and Modern Built Heritage: The Value of Art Deco in Brisbane

Andrea Schurmann, Josephine Pryce, and Taha Chaiechi

Abstract It is incumbent for city planners seeking to achieve sustainable cities that they utilise their modern built heritage resources. The built environment contributes significantly to the carbon footprint of a city. Buildings account for 50% of raw materials used and produce waste from demolition and new construction. It is often more sustainable to re-use and repurpose existing buildings than to build anew. Protected heritage buildings are often re-used and repurposed; however, the future of heritage buildings that are not valued is dubious, precarious and, it can be said, even perilous. Modern built heritage (MBH) is defined by UNESCO as a built heritage from the 'modern' era 1920–1970. MBH is currently in focus in the heritage preservation literature as it is considered at risk of demolition due to rapid urbanisation, weak legal protection, and low awareness of its value among the public. MBH is available in many cities as the heritage of tomorrow. However, to assume this standing requires identification and an understanding of its value. This paper explores the value of Art Deco as a form of modern built heritage through in-depth interviews with stakeholders in Brisbane. An argument is made for the further conservation of MBH by linking value with sustainable city goals.

Keywords Sustainable cities · Modern built heritage · Art Deco · Value · Brisbane · Preservation · Heritage conservation

A. Schurmann (✉) · J. Pryce
Business, Law, and Governance, Division of Tropical Environment & Societies, James Cook University, Cairns, Australia
e-mail: andrea.schurmann@my.jcu.edu.au; Josephine.pryce@jcu.edu.au

T. Chaiechi
College of Business, Law and Governance, James Cook University, Townsville, QLD, Australia
e-mail: Taha.chaiechi@jcu.edu.au

© The Author(s), under exclusive license to Springer Nature Singapore Pte Ltd. 2022

T. Chaiechi, J. Wood (eds.), *Community Empowerment, Sustainable Cities, and Transformative Economies*, https://doi.org/10.1007/978-981-16-5260-8_16

1 Introduction- Why a Sustainable City?

The world is urbanising at an unprecedented rate. Predictions indicate that by 2050 9.8 billion people will live in urban areas (UNDESA, 2018). This equates to 70% of the world's population. Many cities are struggling with environmental degradation, traffic congestion, inadequate urban infrastructure, and a lack of basic services, such as water supply, sanitation, and waste management (UNEP, 2021). The environmental footprints of cities are alarming. Cities account for more than 76% of CO_2 emissions (UN-Habitat, 2021). The focus on developing sustainable cities has gained momentum due to increased pressures in the face of finite resources. As a result, strategies are becoming increasingly focused on appropriate city planning as being essential to sustainable development (UN, World Bank, multilateral banks, GEF). This reality places cities at the forefront of the climate change and sustainability agenda (Jabareen, 2006).

The 2030 Agenda for sustainable development sets out a global framework with 17 Sustainable development goals and 169 targets. Goal 11 focuses on sustainable cities and communities. Sustainable cities are defined as those dedicated to achieving green sustainability, social sustainability and economic sustainability (UNDESA, 2018). The literature discusses features of a sustainable city (Bibri & Krogstie, 2017; Kenworthy, 2006; Moore, 2007, Yanarella & Levine, 2020). This includes minimising city inputs such as energy from non-renewable sources (Nijkamp & Pepping, 1998), water consumption, and the consumption of finite resources. Cities also need to reduce outputs by drastically reducing waste, water pollution, heat, greenhouse gases and air pollution (Jenks & Jones, 2009). References are frequently made to sustainable transport modalities, biodiversity, and green spaces (Kenworthy, 2006; Ashraf & Garvey, 2020). Carbon neutrality, self-sufficiency, climate change, and the circular economy have been incorporated into environmental policies and planning. Increasingly, concepts such as resilience, liveability, quality of life, and wellbeing have been used as goals for city planners to work toward.

The built environment contributes significantly to the carbon footprint of a city. Buildings account for 50% of raw materials used and produce waste from demolition and new construction (UN-Habitat, 2021). Sustainable cities incorporate 'green buildings' through green assessment schemes on new construction. However, it is often more sustainable to re-use and repurpose existing buildings than to build anew (Bullen & Love, 2010). Less embodied energy is involved in refurbishing or adapting a heritage building rather than building anew (Martinez-Molina et al., 2016; Yung & Chan, 2012). Many heritage buildings are constructed of materials and techniques that require half the maintenance of more recent buildings (Carroon, 2010). However, the value of MBH is yet to be fully determined in this discussion. It is timely to consider the value of MBH in the sustainable city context.

2 Review of the Literature: The Value of Modern Built Heritage

Modern built heritage (MBH) is defined by UNESCO (2013) as a built heritage from the 'modern' era 1920–1970. MBH is currently in focus in the heritage preservation literature (Lenticchia et al., 2016; Mualam & Sybblis, 2016). This is because it is at risk of demolition due to rapid urbanisation, weak legal protection, and low awareness of its value among the public (World Monuments Fund, 2021). These buildings are currently undervalued as they are neither contemporary architecture nor heritage buildings but exist in the space in between, potentially being the built heritage of tomorrow. Many cities around the world do not have a great track record of caring for their built heritage. Societies often realise the value of the world as it existed in past generations only after destroying it. This is further evident in the neglect of buildings from the modern era. Scholarly interest in MBH is growing, yet significant works of this era are underrepresented on heritage registers. Much of the world's heritage from this period remain at risk and in need of identification, conservation, and protection. For MBH to survive, it needs to be considered worthy of preservation and transmission to future generations (Willson & McIntosh, 2007). If MBH is not protected now, then it will be lost forever. MBH is available in many cities as the heritage of tomorrow. However, for it to assume this standing requires identification and an understanding of its value.

The Australian International Council on Monuments and Sites (ICOMOS) Charter for Places of Cultural Significance (Burra Charter, 2013) is considered the best practice standard for managing cultural heritage places in Australia. It recognises the following value of built heritage: enriches people's lives; provides a deep and inspirational sense of connection to community and landscape; provides a deep connection to the past and lived experiences; reflects the diversity of our communities; considered irreplaceable and precious and therefore should be conserved for future generations. The numerous benefits for communities associated with the conservation of built heritage are detailed extensively in scholarly articles. Table 1 outlines key dimensions from the literature, which highlight the value of built heritage for communities.

Built heritage preservation results in the preservation of memories and connections to the past as well as the contribution to sense of place and character and identity (Allsopp, 1974). Similarly, Francesco and Oers (2012) assert that preservation includes the preservation of memory, the conservation of artistic and architectural achievements, the valuing of places of significance and collective meaning. Built heritage is considered an important dimension of civic identity and memory and a cultural resource for social and economic development. Nasser (2003) also recognises the link between built heritage and the past, along with its influence on the sense of place as an important dimension of sustainable places, strengthening local identity, contributing to investment, and retaining communities. While discussions in the literature are predominantly focused on built heritage in general, there is an opportunity to focus on the value of MBH for communities.

Table 1 The value of built heritage for communities

Authenticity	Greffe (2004), ICOMOS (1994)
Sense of place	Allsopp (1974), Cresswell (2004), Florida (2005), Nasser (2003)
Place identity	Florida (2005)
Identity	Allsopp (1974), Ashworth (2013), Elkadi (2007), Nasser (2003)
Civic pride	Francesco and Oers (2012)
Character	Allsopp (1974), Smith (2006)
Uniqueness	Licciardi and Amirtahmasebi (2012)
Aesthetic appeal	Allon (2008), Cresswell (2004), Seresinhe et al. (2015), Smith (2006)
Artistic and architectural achievement	Francesco and Oers (2012)
Collective meaning for communities	Aplin (2002), Aplin (2009), Francesco and Oers (2012), Steinberg (1996)
Emotional attachment	Bertella and Droli (2018), Madgin (2019), Mason (2002)
Enriches people's lives	Burra Charter (2013)
Connection to the past	Allsopp (1974), Burra Charter (2013)
Connection to community	Burra Charter (2013), Fund and Heritage (2006)
Connection to place/landscape	Burra Charter (2013), Cresswell (2004)
Diversity of community	Burra Charter (2013), Billore (2021), de Boer (2006), Elkadi (2007)
Memory	Allsopp (1974), Francesco and Oers (2012)
Continuity/stability	Khan (2015), Pillai (2019)
More sustainable to adapt buildings than to build anew	Armitage and Irons (2013), Hu (2017), Minner (2016)
Social development	Aplin (2002), Francesco and Oers (2012), Steinberg (1996), Yung and Chan (2012)
Contributing to investment	Allen (2012), Nasser (2003)
Increased property values	Elliott et al. (2015), Rypkema (2012), Shipley (2000)
Economic development	Allen (2012), Florida (2005), Francesco and Oers (2012), Mason (2005)

3 Why Should Sustainable Cities Utilise their Modern Built Heritage?

Built heritage has long been absent from the mainstream sustainable development debate. The 2030 Agenda for sustainable development now integrates culture and heritage into its goals as an enabler of sustainable development. Target 11.4 in particular; aims to "protect and safeguard the world's cultural and natural heritage" in order to "make cities and human settlements inclusive, safe, resilient and sustainable".[1] In this context, built heritage is a key ingredient in sustainable city planning. However, it has yet to be allocated a clear role.

On an international level, UNESCO has taken the initiative to integrate a sustainable development perspective into its World Heritage Convention. This move aligns cultural heritage with the 2030 agenda for sustainable development (UNESCO, 2021). As a result, World Heritage Site managers are now applying innovative approaches to sustainability (Larsen & Logan, 2018). This raises the question of whether national, state, and locally protected sites are also being integrated with the sustainability agenda. While this association is being established in terms of built heritage, it does not include built heritage from the modern era. MBH has limited representation on both the World Heritage list as well as local heritage lists as its values are in the process of being determined.

Built heritage is underfunded (Misiura, 2006; Van Oers & Pereira Roders, 2012). In the future, an additional allocation of resources for built heritage maintenance and preservation will need to be balanced against resources required for other community needs.[2] With the increased pressures of population growth and sustainability, governments are going to have less money available to meet community needs. Heritage preservation should not compete for diminishing resources as an extra cost burden. Rather than the usual built heritage preservation versus development tension, there needs to be more consideration of how these goals align. Preservation in the future must become increasingly resourceful. The arguments for preservation need to be reframed to link with the sustainable city agenda. This creates a positive solution-based focus, providing access to current funding sources while solving many of the complex problems currently facing the city.

Energy efficiency, green building materials, and sustainable technologies are becoming increasingly used in new construction. However, sustainable retrofits of historic buildings, particularly MBH, lag behind. Costs of repair versus replacement are often used as an argument against preservation. Applying sustainability audits as a way of comparing the environmental impact of new construction to the adaptation of existing structures may result in new ways of valuing MBH. Economists, preservationists, and others grapple with developing methodologies for valuing built cultural resources. The range of costs and benefits of preservation need to be fully examined to consider value. This study concentrates on the value of Art Deco MBH in Brisbane as a sustainable city.

---

[1] Refer to https://sdgs.un.org/2030agenda

[2] Refer to https://www.getty.edu/conservation/publications_resources/pdf_publications/pdf/assessing.pdf

4 Scope of the Study: Brisbane as a Sustainable City

Brisbane's commitment to sustainability has twice earned it the accolade of Australia's most sustainable city. Recent Council strategic plans such as the Brisbane 2022 New World City Action Plan, Creative Brisbane Creative Economy, and City Centre Master Plan all include ambitious sustainability goals. The Brisbane Clean, Green, Sustainable 2017–2031 Plan takes Brisbane City Council's commitment to sustainability further. It includes practical actions for achieving the Brisbane Vision 2031 long-term plan for the city. There are nine themes in the plan; clean air, biodiversity, low carbon, sustainable CityShape, parks, green transport, waste and resource recovery, WaterSmart city, and urban forest which are outlined in Table 2. With the increased focus on cities being essential to sustainable development, this paper considers the value of Art Deco MBH in the context of Brisbane as a sustainable city. As an introduction to that exploration, Table 2 aligns references to Art Deco with each theme of The Brisbane Clean, Green, Sustainable 2017–2031 Plan.

When considering how the value of Art Deco MBH could be linked to the sustainable city agenda through Brisbane's Clean, Green, Sustainable 2017–2031 Plan's themes, as noted in Table 2, it is evident that some themes appear to have more relevance than others. Heritage buildings were only mentioned in two of the nine themes; low carbon and Sustainable CityShape. More importantly, there was no mention of MBH, in particular Art Deco, in relation to the nine themes. This highlights the need to explore these relationships. The value of Art Deco MBH to Brisbane is extended further in the next section.

5 Art Deco Preservation in Brisbane

According to ICOMOS, there are many forms of MBH; these include the Modern Movement, Industrial heritage, Art Nouveau/Jugendstil, Expressionism, Rationalism, Constructivism, Eclecticism/Beaux-Arts, and Art Deco. ICOMOS suggests further research on Art Deco is required (UNESCO, 2013). Based on this recommendation, Art Deco has been selected as an understudied form of MBH for the context of this study. Brisbane, Australia, was selected due to the fact it had a local conservation society, "Art Deco Brisbane" that is a member of the International Coalition of Art Deco Societies (ICADS), which provides evidence of Art Deco MBH.[3] Brisbane City Council is the largest local government area (LGA) in Australia in terms of population and budget.[4] In terms of protection, specific buildings and places of heritage significance are protected at the international level

[3]Refer to http://www.icads.info/members/

[4]Refer to https://www.brisbane.qld.gov.au/about-council/governance-and-strategy/business-in-brisbane/business-opportunities/brisbane-community-profiles

Table 2 Brisbane: clean, green, sustainable 2017–2031 plan

Theme	Where we want to be	Identification of Art Deco in The Plan
Clean air	Brisbane will consistently have clean, healthy air.	**No mention of relationship between heritage buildings & clean air** **No mention of relationship between Art Deco MBH & clean air**
Biodiversity	Brisbane will grow and connect its natural areas to protect its rich biodiversity.	**No mention of relationship between heritage buildings & biodiversity** **No mention of relationship between Art Deco MBH & biodiversity**
Low carbon	Council is recognised as a leader in reducing carbon.	**Mentions relationship between heritage buildings & low carbon** *Brisbane city council is largest carbon neutral organisation in Australia. It builds and leases green buildings to reduce the carbon intensity of the built environment. Some of these are heritage-listed.* **No mention of relationship between Art Deco MBH & low carbon**
Sustainable CityShape	Brisbane embraces development that enhances our city's subtropical lifestyle	**Mentions relationship between heritage buildings & sustainable CityShape** *Brisbane City hall achieved Australia's first green star rating for a heritage-listed public building. New development is being concentrated in areas where it makes sense to grow, such as the inner city and around bus and train stations to preserve our green spaces, quiet suburbs and the city's important historic 'timber and tin' homes.* **No mention of relationship between Art Deco MBH & sustainable CityShape**
Parks	Brisbane parks are diverse and accessible.	**No mention of relationship between heritage buildings & parks** **No mention of relationship between Art Deco MBH & parks**
Green transport	More trips will be made by public and active transport, helping to reduce congestion, fossil fuel consumption and emissions.	**No mention of relationship between heritage buildings & green transport** **No mention of relationship between Art Deco MBH & green transport**

(continued)

Table 2 (continued)

Theme	Where we want to be	Identification of Art Deco in The Plan
Waste and resource recovery	Brisbane will reduce, re-use and recycle waste.	**No mention of relationship between heritage buildings & waste & resource recovery** *Focused on domestic household waste,* *No focus on construction waste from new or heritage buildings* **No mention of relationship between Art Deco MBH & waste & resource recovery**
WaterSmart City	Brisbane is a resilient, water-smart city that uses water sustainably and protects its waterways.	**No mention of relationship between heritage buildings & watersmart city** **No mention of relationship between Art Deco MBH & watersmart city**
Urban forest	Brisbane will value, nurture and protect its urban forest.	**No mention of relationship between heritage buildings & urban forest** **No mention of relationship of Art Deco MBH & urban forest**

Source: Brisbane City Council, 2017 (https://www.brisbane.qld.gov.au/clean-and-green/2017-31)

Table 3 Examples of protected Art Deco MBH in Brisbane City Council LGA

List/Register/Scheme	Example
World Heritage List	N/A
Commonwealth Heritage List	N/A
National Heritage List	N/A
Queensland Heritage Register	McWhirters Marketplace
	Morningside State School
	Yeronga State School
Local Heritage Register	55 listings of Art Deco = 2.4% of local heritage register
Local planning scheme	All houses and commercial buildings before 1946 protected

as a world heritage site; the national level on the National Heritage List; the state level on the Queensland Heritage Register; and the local level on the Local Heritage Register under the Queensland Heritage Act 1992. Local-level protection is also afforded by inclusion in the planning scheme or overlay. Table 3 provides examples of the limited number of Art Deco MBH that are protected in Brisbane City Council Local Government Area (LGA). Searching the Queensland Heritage Register uncovered three Art Deco buildings deemed of State significance in Brisbane City Council LGA: McWhirter's Marketplace, Morningside State School, and Yeronga State School (see Table 3 and Figs. 1, 2, and 3 below). Coronet Flats (Fig. 4) is an example of Art Deco on the local heritage register.

Art Deco MBH is currently protected at the local level in Brisbane. Houses and commercial character buildings built during or before 1946 are to be retained, and

Fig. 1 McWhirters Marketplace; from west (2009), Queensland Heritage Register https://apps.des.qld.gov.au/heritage-register/detail/?id=600214 (CC BY 4.0)

Fig. 2 Morningside State School; Depression-era Brick Infants School Building (Block A), from North (2018), Queensland Heritage Register https://apps.des.qld.gov.au/heritage-register/detail/?id=650057# (CC BY 4.0)

Fig. 3 Yeronga State School; Brick Infants' School Building, Block L; view from south (2016), Queensland Heritage Register https://apps.des.qld.gov.au/heritage-register/detail/?id=650025

Fig. 4 Coronet Flats, Brunswick St (2010), Local Heritage Places https://heritage.brisbane.qld.gov.au/heritage-places/1134 (CC BY 4.0)

any extensions or alterations should complement the Art Deco building style.[5] However, other forms of MBH from 1946 onwards are not afforded the same protection.

6 Methodology

This paper reports on the findings for the question "What is the value of Art Deco modern built heritage?" This question formed part of a PhD thesis where the overarching aim was to understand whether modern built heritage tourism contributes to community wellbeing, and if so, how? Brisbane was selected due to the fact it has a local conservation society, "Art Deco Brisbane" that is a member of the International Coalition of Art Deco Societies (ICADS), which provides evidence of concentrations of MBH.[6] There is also a recently published book on Brisbane Art Deco (Wilson, 2015).

The Brisbane case study was designed as an exploratory case study. It served to provide an opportunity for testing the research design and research instruments, but more broadly, it was intended to provide an overview of the role of Art Deco as a modern built heritage in tourism and its effect on community wellbeing. The researcher conducted 12 in-depth interviews with key stakeholders having knowledge of Art Deco MBH and/or tourism. This included tourism professionals, built heritage professionals, and residents from Brisbane. A list of potential interviewees was made from a preliminary internet search and from documentary evidence. A snowball sampling or (chain-referral sampling) approach was then used to ensure that further possible interviewees were uncovered. This involved locating primary data sources, which led to further data sources to be used in the research (Atkinson & Flint, 2004). The research was deemed low negligible risk, and ethics approval granted.

The aim of an in-depth interview is to explore the insider perspective to capture rich, descriptive data about people's behaviours, attitudes, perceptions, and unfolding complex processes (Seidman, 1991). Questions were designed and informed from the literature review. Interviewees were also asked questions to elucidate the background contextual information as required. Qualitative data was analysed following the coding procedures and identification of themes detailed by Miles and Huberman (1994). The coding exercise used was thematic analysis, an inductive approach to identify patterns within a data set (Attride-Stirling, 2001). Being an inductive process, NVivo 12 was used to derive nodes directly from the data (Strauss, 1987). A separate researcher verified the nodes and coding themes initially devised by the primary researcher to ensure reliability of the findings (Patton, 2002). This iterative process allowed for levels of interpretation of the data from nodes to themes (refer to Table 4).

[5]Refer to https://www.brisbane.qld.gov.au/planning-and-building/planning-guidelines-and-tools/brisbane-city-plan-2014/supporting-information/heritage-and-character-buildings

[6]Refer to http://www.icads.info/members/

Table 4 Themes for Research Question "What is the value of Art Deco MBH?"

Researcher 1	Researcher 2
Buildings	Buildings
Art Deco	People
People	Place
Place	Heritage
Time	History
Heritage	Connection
History	Stories
Connection	
Stories	

Fig. 5 The value of Art Deco modern built heritage in Brisbane: Word cloud 50 words

Table 4 shows that the main themes emerging from the thematic analysis were: buildings, people, place, heritage, history, connection, and stories.

Further to thematic analysis, data from the interview research question "what is the value of Art Deco modern built heritage?" was used to produce the word cloud (Fig. 5). A word cloud is a word frequency query used to generate a visualisation for commonly used words and phrases (Jackson & Bazeley, 2019). The bigger and bolder the word appears, and the more often it is mentioned within the text, the more important it is. At the core of the word cloud are buildings, people, and heritage. These paralleled themes that had emerged from the thematic analysis of the interview data (refer to Table 4). The themes that emerged from the word cloud were: buildings, people, place (including heritage and history); connections, and stories. As the data from the interviews were explored more deeply, key aspects of these themes emerged. This paper focuses on the theme of 'buildings' and the associated subthemes.

7 Results and Discussion

7.1 The Value of Art Deco Modern Built Heritage in Brisbane

For buildings, subthemes included: authenticity, aesthetic appeal, artistic and aesthetic achievement, and character, as discussed below.

7.1.1 Authenticity

Authenticity explains the notion that an item is original and genuine (Boorstin, 1961). The Art Deco architectural style is not currently considered authentic to Brisbane. Most interviewees considered it an international style that could be found anywhere in the world, as indicated by the following comment,

> It is an international style. The examples in Australia are borrowing from international trends . . . buildings would present to the world they were ahead of the curve, that they were bringing ideas in that were international.

The Art Deco style originated in 1925 at the Paris L'Exposition Internationale des Arts Decoratifs et Industriels Modernes which was shortened to Art Deco. This exhibition heralded the recognition of a new international decorative style formed without reliance on Greco-Roman traditions. As a result, respondents did not consider Art Deco to be authentic to Brisbane or Australia. However, a strong connection to the international Art Deco era was passionately described by many, for example,

> Art Deco was a really exciting period of time. It tells us a lot about how we lived. It was the spirit of progress. It was exciting.
>
> it really was that cusp of modernity. All of those things are amazing legacies that we benefit from today.

The Art Deco era was associated with modernity, a focus on feminism, independence, and new technologies. Many referred to the fact that women had started working for the first time and were beginning to live independent lives. New modes of transport became accessible such as airplanes, trains, ships, and cars. This allowed for more freedom of movement and travel. These are ideas that resonate strongly today. "The Roaring twenties and the Jazz age" were often used to describe the Art Deco era. The Roaring twenties was associated with freedom, celebration, optimism and living life to the full. This lifestyle was to be experienced through music, dancing, speakeasies, and fashion, with Art Deco buildings as the setting. Frequent references were made to the glamour of Hollywood movies and Art Deco theatres.

Interviewees felt an authentic connection to the international Art Deco era and lifestyle. The study uncovered a group of people in Brisbane who call themselves "Art Decophiles" or "Art Deco enthusiasts", who are fans of all things Art Deco. This included members of the Brisbane Art Deco Society, vintage car clubs, creatives, artists, designers, fashion designers, musicians, and collectors. The Great

Gatsby movie, directed by Baz Luhrmann, and Miss Fisher's murder mysteries were often cited as having reignited the appeal of the Art Deco era. A connection was also made between the twenty-twenties and the nineteen-twenties, as evidenced in the following comment by one of the interviewees,

> We are coming into the 100th anniversary of Art Deco. So, everything that is 1920s is now going to be antique. It will be legitimised as antique rather than vintage. The consensus on the definition of antique is 100 years old around the world. In 2020, we will see that gaining momentum as it is one hundred years.

Art Deco MBH was considered representative of Australia's waves of immigration and an increased international outlook during the interwar period. The origins of Art Deco in Australia were linked to returning soldiers and the wave of European immigration following World War 1. Australians felt more strongly connected to Europe, the UK and USA. In these countries, the Art Deco era was considered to have commenced around the early to mid-nineteen twenties. The Art Deco style arrived later in Brisbane, with most buildings being built in the thirties. At the time, Brisbane had a conservative government, resulting in a more inwardly focused population than other Australian and international cities. Queensland had been adversely affected by drought, the Great Depression, and high unemployment. As a result, the Great Depression Building Scheme was initiated to reduce high unemployment, with many civic and infrastructure projects being constructed. There was also a Queensland government initiative to build more schools. Therefore, civic buildings, bridges, roads, scenic lookouts, and schools were often built in the Art Deco style. Art Deco MBH allows insight into this era of Brisbane history.

The interviews in Brisbane uncovered evidence of regional variation of the Art Deco international style. According to Harris (2011), Art Deco is considered an international style with regional variations. The Art Deco style signified modernity and a particular sense of cosmopolitanism on the one hand, and yet resonated with or extended pre-existing cultural traditions in a distinctly local manner on the other, as indicated by one interviewee in the following,

> . . . there is an Australian very restrained version of Art Deco. Brisbane takes that to another level. It is particularly restrained. Very simple

The extensive decoration is typical of Art Deco style, although its purpose is strictly ornamental and not integral to building design (Lampugnani, 1988). In the case of Brisbane, the decoration was more restrained. As a predominantly working-class city, there was a limited budget for architects and consequently, few glamour homes compared to Sydney, Melbourne, and international cities like Paris. Art Deco decorative motifs are usually geometric in form and often theme-oriented, such as chevrons, arcs, sunbursts, maidens, fountains and liberated women. In Brisbane, these motifs were evident but more restrained, with a novel appearance of Australian fauna and flora motifs.

A majority of Brisbane Art Deco MBH was built from brick, which is typical of the Art Deco architectural style. However, there were examples built with Brisbane tuff stone that were uncovered during the interviews. Brisbane tuff is a form of welded ignimbrite rock, formed as a result of a volcanic eruption. Brisbane tuff comes in a variety of colours: pink, green, blue, and purple that is only found in Brisbane. Convicts originally quarried tuff stone to build many of the buildings in Brisbane. Local materials give a building authenticity. Other regional variations of Art Deco MBH included the incorporation of balconies and verandahs to help accommodate airflow. These climatic responses to Art Deco MBH were characteristic of many buildings Queensland wide, rather than particular to Brisbane. Many Respondents commented that there was value in buildings from every period being represented. For example,

> I think I value all built heritage. It tells us something about a particular time. In cities we need those layers. We need to be able to read where we have come from. Art Deco was a really exciting period of time. It tells us a lot about how we lived. The layout of the buildings, the materials we used, the reasons we made architectural decisions. So, I think that I see it the way I see all twentieth century built heritage or even older. That we need all those layers. That is an important chapter in the twentieth century.

Areas with larger concentrations of Art Deco MBH, such as West End, New Farm, and Sandgate, were considered to have a greater heritage value and more authenticity as a result.

7.1.2 Aesthetic Appeal

Art Deco architecture in Brisbane was considered to have aesthetic appeal. Beauty was a strong theme used to describe architectural features such as cornice work, ceiling work, colour, curves, curved corners, and beautiful finishes. As one interviewee said,

> "Appreciating visually, appreciating the beauty" expertise and the craftmanship that went into the construction of those buildings.

The Art Deco style was considered interesting due to its streamlined, modern, futuristic aesthetic. Glamourous, elegant, simple, and timeless were other defining attributes. Respondents valued Art Deco architectural style over other styles based on aesthetics. For example,

> As far as Art Deco buildings go, they are elegant. Some older buildings, the Victorian buildings are very fussy. If you look at a Victorian living room it is crowded, there are thousands of little things in it. You look at an Art Deco living room and its clean lines, geometric and peaceful. Simplicity. I don't find it harsh. I can see an Art Deco building and it appeals to me.

Some forms of Art Deco MBH were valued more than others, such as houses, main streets, churches, and the city hall. Buildings considered ugly were less likely to inspire people to protect them. This finding has relevance when determining the value of other forms of MBH.

7.2 Artistic and Architectural Achievement

Art Deco MBH was associated with architectural achievement, where architectural design is considered high quality. Most examples of Art Deco MBH in Brisbane were designed by architects, as noted in the following comment,

> Art Deco was sold as a high-class style like in the suburbs of Ascot and Hamilton. Metal finishes in stairways, a lot more chrome, beautiful ceiling work, beautiful finishes in the house. A lot more classy.

The architectural legacy of Walter Taylor in Brisbane was revealed by a couple of respondents. Walter Taylor bridge is well known for being the longest span suspension bridge in Australia. The bridge was built in the Art Deco style using cables that were surplus to requirements during the construction of the Sydney Harbour Bridge. It is also the only inhabitable bridge in the Southern hemisphere, with many of the toll keepers and their families having lived inside the bridge pylons. Walter Taylor was a pioneer with reinforced concrete construction techniques. This represented a distinct departure from preceding construction material modes. There are other examples of his technical innovation around Brisbane that are less well known and interviewees valued the aesthetic value of these buildings, for example,

> "Appreciating visually, appreciating the beauty" expertise and the craftmanship that went into the construction of those buildings.

Daphne Mayo, Vida Lahey, and William Bustard were presented as examples of artists working on Art Deco MBH in Brisbane. Daphne Mayo was a significant twentieth-century Australian artist, most prominently known for her work in sculpture. The tympanum of Brisbane City Hall, the Women's War Memorial in ANZAC Square, and Art Deco friezes in the Tattersalls building being the more well-known examples of her work during the interwar period. Vida Lahey's work is represented in major Australian art galleries, including the National Gallery of Australia. She founded the Foundation of the Queensland Art Fund in 1929 with Daphne Mayo. Her paintings were often of buildings being constructed during the interwar period, such as the Brisbane City Hall. William Bustard was an artist who immigrated to Queensland in 1921. His stained-glass work features in many heritage-listed buildings from 1921 onwards.

7.2.1 Character

Art Deco MBH was seen to have character. Respondents valued character. Although heritage buildings in general have character, some respondents value particular architectural styles over others. Most interviewees believed new buildings lacked character, stating that new buildings left them cold.

Art Deco MBH was seen as different and unique because in Brisbane they were rare. Not many Art Deco buildings were built in Brisbane in the first instance, and many have been demolished.

What is the value of Art Deco modern built heritage? To summarise, value included aesthetic appeal, artistic and aesthetic achievement, and character. Aesthetic appeal referred to the beauty of the architectural style, particularly as a crossover between highly decorative heritage buildings and minimalist new buildings. Artistic and architectural achievement was due to most buildings of this style being designed by architects, and utilisation of expensive local building materials of higher quality. The architectural legacy of Walter Taylor and his reinforced concrete technological innovations, and the work of artisans such as Daphne Mayo, Vida Lahey, and William Bustard were cited as examples of value. Art Deco MBH was not considered an authentic Brisbane architectural style, but rather an international style. However, the interviews uncovered the potential to further increase value through association with the authenticity of the philosophy and lifestyle of the international Art Deco era through "Art Decophiles" or "Art Deco enthusiasts", who are fans of all things Art Deco. Authenticity could also be achieved by communicating Brisbane's built history during the interwar period. This includes The Queensland Government's Great Depression Building Scheme which resulted in many civic and infrastructure projects being built in the Art Deco style. Finally, the interviews uncovered evidence of Art Deco MBH being built with local Brisbane tuff stone and being appropriated for the Brisbane climate which increase authenticity and value.

8 Art Deco MBH and Brisbane Sustainable City

The results from the interviews were mapped against the Brisbane Clean, Green, Sustainable 2017–2031 plan in Table 5. These results increased the connections between Art Deco MBH and the sustainable city themes. The potential links between low carbon, sustainable CityShape, and waste and resource recovery were identified. Low carbon objectives can be achieved when embodied energy is saved by re-using Art Deco MBH compared to its demolition for new construction. Brisbane City Council is the largest carbon-neutral organisation in Australia. Therefore there is further opportunity to explore how heritage buildings, particularly Art Deco MBH, can reduce the carbon intensity of the built environment. Brisbane City Hall is an example of how heritage buildings can achieve Green Star ratings. More sustainable heritage buildings, and particularly MBH, should be incorporated as part of the Brisbane City Council portfolio. Sustainable CityShape can be achieved by preserving Art Deco MBH of 3–4 storey height to maintain the connection with the street which helps create a sense of community. Streetscapes and precincts of higher concentrations of Art Deco MBH have higher heritage value and authenticity for communities. These ideas could be incorporated into Brisbane's Sustainable CityShape. In terms of waste and resource recovery, the longer the Art Deco MBH are used, the better for the environment. As compared to using new materials in new construction and the disposal of the old into landfill.

Table 5 Art Deco MBH and Brisbane as a Sustainable City: Results from interviews

Theme	Where we want to be	Interviews
Clean air	Brisbane will consistently have clean, healthy air.	**N/A**
Biodiversity	Brisbane will grow and connect its natural areas to protect its rich biodiversity.	**N/A**
Low carbon	Council is recognised as a leader in reducing carbon.	**Embodied energy is saved by re-using Art Deco MBH**
Sustainable CityShape	Brisbane embraces development that enhances our city's subtropical lifestyle	**Art Deco MBH Streetscapes and precincts have higher heritage value and authenticity for communities Art Deco MBH is usually less than 3 storeys and has a closer connection to the street which helps to create a human scale and sense of community**
Parks	Brisbane parks are diverse and accessible.	**N/A**
Green transport	More trips will be made by public and active transport, helping to reduce congestion, fossil fuel consumption and emissions.	**N/A**
Waste and resource recovery	Brisbane will reduce, re-use and recycle waste.	**The longer the materials are used, the better it is for the environment because you are not using new materials or disposing of the old**
WaterSmart City	Brisbane is a resilient, water smart city that uses water sustainably and protects its waterways.	**N/A**
Urban forest	Brisbane will value, nurture and protect its urban forest.	**N/A**

The Brisbane "Greeters" program, which is part of the Brisbane Sustainable city initiative, was mentioned once during the interviews. The Greeters is a community-based ambassador program that enabled residents to connect with visitors worldwide. The Greeters communicated stories about new buildings with sustainable design principles to visitors. This is a great initiative, however, it demonstrated how MBH is not currently considered part of the Brisbane sustainable city story.

Philosophically, the concepts of heritage conservation and sustainable development both focus on preserving items of value for future generations. Interview respondents expressed the value of Art Deco MBH for individuals and communities now, with limited mentions of its importance for future generations. The interviews elucidated that the connection between Art Deco MBH and sustainability were not well understood. It was not the purpose of this paper to assess the relationship between heritage buildings and sustainability, but rather to demonstrate how the value of heritage buildings, MBH in particular, is often not linked to sustainability.

9 Conclusion

In conclusion, there is an increased focus on sustainable cities being essential to sustainable development. MBH is available in many cities as the heritage of tomorrow. However, to assume this standing, requires identification and an understanding of its value. This paper considered the value of Art Deco, as a form of MBH, in the context of Brisbane as a sustainable city. Key findings indicated Art Deco MBH was valued for aesthetic appeal, artistic and aesthetic achievement, and character. Value could be increased through authenticity. Authenticity was linked to the philosophy and lifestyle of the international Art Deco era, Brisbane's built history during the interwar period, and showcasing examples of Art Deco MBH built with Brisbane tuff stone and/or design features appropriated for the local climate. More importantly, this paper demonstrated how MBH is not currently integrated with the sustainable city plan in Brisbane. Potential links with sustainable city goals of low carbon, sustainable CityShape, and waste and resource recovery were identified. Australia is home to a substantial range of significant twentieth-century built heritage and there is growing interest and attention in its conservation (Art Deco and Modernism Society of Australia, 2015). Built heritage is a key ingredient in sustainable city planning; however it has yet to be allocated a clear role. It is suggested that further research is needed to explore links between MBH and sustainable city initiatives. Community wellbeing (CW) has recently been explored in the sustainability literature as an approach to sustainable development. It is suggested that a 'community wellbeing' framework could be a useful approach for assessing the value of MBH from a sustainability dimension.

References

Allen, A. D. (2012). Economics of historic preservation: Dollars and sense. *Transylvanian Review of Administrative Sciences, 8*, 11–18.

Allon, F. (2008). *Renovation nation: Our obsession with home*. UNSW Press.

Allsopp, B. (1974). *Towards a humane architecture*. Frederick Muller.

Aplin, G. (2009). Australian attitudes to heritage. *AQ-Australian Quarterly, 81*(3), 19.

Aplin, G. (2002). *Heritage: Identification, conservation, and management*. Oxford University Press.

Armitage, L., & Irons, J. (2013). The values of built heritage. *Property Management, 31*(3), 246–259.

Art Deco and Modernism Society of Australia. (2015). https://www.artdeco.org.au/brisbane-chapter/

Ashraf, A., & Garvey, T. (2020, July). *A conceptual model for designing sustainable city development*. In International conference on applied human factors and ergonomics (pp. 360–369). Cham: Springer.

Ashworth, G. J. (2013). From history to heritage–from heritage to identity. In *Building a new heritage: Tourism, culture and identity in the new Europe* (pp. 13–30).

Atkinson, R., & Flint, J. (2004). Snowball sampling. In: Lewis-Beck, M.S., Bryman, A. and Liao, T.F. (eds.) *The Encyclopaedia of social science research methods*. Sage. ISBN 978076192363.

Attride-Stirling, J. (2001). Thematic networks: An analytic tool for qualitative research. *Qualitative Research, 1*(3), 385–405.

Australia ICOMOS Incorporated. (2013). *The Burra Charter: The Australia ICOMOS charter for places of cultural significance.* Retrieved from: https://australia.icomos.org/wp-content/uploads/The-Burra-Charter-2013-Adopted-31.10.2013.pdf

Bertella, G., & Droli, M. (2018). Creative practices of local entrepreneurs reinventing built heritage. In *Creating heritage for tourism* (pp. 179–191). Routledge.

Bibri, S. E., & Krogstie, J. (2017). Smart sustainable cities of the future: An extensive interdisciplinary literature review. *Sustainable Cities and Society, 31*, 183–212.

Billore, S. (2021). Cultural consumption and citizen engagement – Strategies for built heritage conservation and sustainable development. A case study of Indore City, India. *Sustainability, 13* (5), 2878.

Boorstin, D. J. (1961). *The image*. Harper and Row.

Brisbane City Council. (2021). *Community profiles.* Retrieved from https://www.brisbane.qld.gov.au/about-council/governance-and-strategy/business-in-brisbane/business-opportunities/brisbane-community-profiles

Brisbane City Council. (2019). *Creative Brisbane, creative economy.* Retrieved from https://www.brisbane.qld.gov.au/sites/default/files/20191213%20-%20Creative%20Brisbane%20Creative%20Economy%20Strategy.pdf

Brisbane City Council. (2017). *Brisbane clean, Green, Sustainable 2017–2031*. Retrieved from https://www.brisbane.qld.gov.au/clean-and-green/2017-31

Brisbane City Council. (2014). *Brisbane city centre master plan 2014 a vision for our open city.* Retrieved from https://www.brisbane.qld.gov.au/sites/default/files/20140417-City%20Centre%20Master%20Plan-full%20document.pdf

Brisbane Marketing. (2015). *Brisbane 2022 New World City Action Plan (Brisbane 2022).* Retrieved from https://www.choosebrisbane.com.au/~/media/choose/pdf/brisbane2022planpdf.ashx

Bullen, P. A., & Love, P. E. (2010). The rhetoric of adaptive re-use or reality of demolition: Views from the field. *Cities, 27*(4), 215–224.

Carroon, J. (2010). *Sustainable preservation: Greening existing buildings*. Wiley.

Cresswell, T. (2004). *Place: A short introduction*. Blackwell Publishing.

de Boer, S. (2006). Diffusion or diversity in cultural heritage preservation? Comparing policy arrangements in Norway, Arizona and The Netherlands. In *Institutional dynamics in environmental governance* (pp. 161–181). Springer.

Elkadi, H. A. (2007). Whose identity? Valuing the culture built heritage in diverse and tensioned societies. *A| Z ITU Journal of the Faculty of Architecture, 4*(1), 45–55.

Elliott, P., Warren, C., & Staines, J. (2015). *The effects of demolition control precincts on property values* (no. eres2015_273). European Real Estate Society (ERES).

Florida, R. (2005). *The flight of the creative class: The new global competition for talent.* Harper.

Francesco, B., & Oers, R. (2012). *The historic urban landscape: Managing heritage in an urban century.* Wiley.

Fund, H. L., & Heritage, E. (2006). *Capturing the public value of heritage: The proceedings of the London conference, 25-26 January 2006.*

Greffe, X. (2004). Is heritage an asset or a liability? *Journal of Cultural Heritage, 5*(3), 301–309.

Harris, C. M. (2011). *Dictionary of architecture & construction* (4th ed.). McGraw-Hill.

Hu, M. (2017). Balance between energy conservation and environmental impact: Life-cycle energy analysis and life-cycle environmental impact analysis. *Energy and Buildings, 140*, 131–139.

ICOMOS. (1994). *The Nara document on authenticity.* ICOMOS. Retrieved from https://www.icomos.org/charters/nara-e.pdf

International Coalition of Art Deco Societies. (2021). http://www.icads.info/members/

Jabareen, Y. R. (2006). Sustainable urban forms: Their typologies, models, and concepts. *Journal of Planning Education and Research, 26*(1), 38–52.

Jackson, K., & Bazeley, P. (2019). *Qualitative data analysis with NVivo.* Sage.

Jenks, M., & Jones, C. (Eds.). (2009). *Dimensions of the sustainable city*.

Khan, H. U. (2015). Architectural conservation as a tool for cultural continuity: A focus on the built environment of islam. *ArchNet-IJAR: International Journal of Architectural Research, 9*(1), 1.

Kenworthy, J. R. (2006). The eco-city: Ten key transport and planning dimensions for sustainable city development. *Environment and Urbanisation, 18*(1), 67–85.

Lampugnani, V. M. (1988). Thames and Hudson encyclopaedia of 20th-century architecture. In *New York*. Thames & Hudson.

Larsen, P. B., & Logan, W. (Eds.). (2018). *World heritage and sustainable development: New directions in world heritage management*. Routledge.

Lenticchia, E., Ceravolo, R., & Chiorino, C. (2016). Optimal sensor placement for modern heritage spatial structures. In *Structural analysis of historical constructions: Anamnesis, diagnosis, therapy, controls* (pp. 716–723). CRC Press.

Licciardi, G., & Amirtahmasebi, R., (Eds.). (2012). *The economics of uniqueness: Investing in Historic City cores and cultural heritage assets for sustainable development*. Urban development series. Washington, DC: World Bank. http://hdl.handle.net/10986/12286

Madgin, R. (2019). A place for urban conservation? The changing values of Glasgow's built heritage. In *Transforming Glasgow: Beyond the post-industrial city* (p. 221).

Martínez-Molina, A., Tort-Ausina, I., Cho, S., & Vivancos, J. L. (2016). Energy efficiency and thermal comfort in historic buildings: A review. *Renewable and Sustainable Energy Reviews, 61*, 70–85.

Mason, R. (2005). *Economics and historic preservation: A guide and review of the literature*. Brookings Institution.

Mason, R. (2002). Assessing values in conservation planning: Methodological issues and choices. In *Assessing the values of cultural heritage*, Report (pp. 5–30). Getty Conservation Institute.

Miles, M. B., & Huberman, A. M. (1994). *Qualitative data analysis: An expanded sourcebook* (2nd ed.). Sage.

Minner, J. (2016). Revealing synergies, tensions, and silences between preservation and planning. *Journal of the American Planning Association, 82*(2), 72–87.

Misiura, S. (2006). *Heritage marketing*. Routledge.

Moore, S. A. (2007). *Alternative routes to the sustainable city: Austin, Curitiba, and Frankfurt*. Lexington Books.

Mualam, N., & Sybblis, M. (2016). The functional threshold of modern heritage: Form versus function and the struggle over Tel aviv's concert hall. *International Journal of Heritage Studies, 22*(2), 145. https://doi.org/10.1080/13527258.2015.1103299

Nasser, N. (2003). Planning for urban heritage places: Reconciling conservation, tourism, and sustainable development. *Journal of Planning Literature, 17*(4), 467–479.

Nijkamp, P., & Pepping, G. (1998). A meta-analytical evaluation of sustainable city initiatives. *Urban Studies, 35*(9), 1481–1500.

Patton, M. Q. (2002). *Qualitative research and evaluation methods* (3rd ed.). Sage.

Pillai, J. (2019). Cultural mapping: A guide to understanding place, community and continuity (2013). *Historic Cities: Issues in Urban Conservation, 8*, 267.

Rypkema, D. D. (2012). Economics and historic preservation. *Forum Journal, 27*(1), 46–54. National Trust for Historic Preservation.

Seidman, I. (1991). *Interviewing as qualitative research: A guide for researchers in education and the social sciences*. Teachers College Press.

Seresinhe, I., Preis, T., & Moat, H. (2015). Quantifying the impact of scenic environments on health. *Nature, 5*, 16899.

Shipley, R. (2000). Heritage designation and property values: Is there an effect? *International Journal of Heritage Studies, 6*(1), 83–100.

Smith, L. (2006). *Uses of heritage*. Routledge.

Strauss, A. L. (1987). *Qualitative analysis for social scientists*. Cambridge University Press.

Steinberg, F. (1996). Conservation and rehabilitation of urban heritage in developing countries. *Habitat International, 20*(3), 463–475.

UNESCO. (2021). *Culture for sustainable development*. Accessed 20 Mar 2021. https://en.unesco.org/themes/culture-sustainable-development

UNESCO. (2013). *Identification and documentation of modern heritage*. World heritage papers. World Heritage Centre. Retrieved from http://whc.unesco.org/en/modernheritage

United Nations Department of Economic and Social Affairs. (2018). *Transforming our world: The 2030 Agenda for sustainable development*. Retrieved from: https://sdgs.un.org/2030agenda

United Nations Environment Programme. (2021). *Sustainable cities*. Retrieved from https://www.unep.org/regions/asia-and-pacific/regional-initiatives/supporting-resource-efficiency/sustainable-cities

UN-Habitat. (2021). *Climate action for cities*. Retrieved from https://unhabitat.org/topic/climate-change

van Oers, R., & Pereira Roders, A. (2012). Historic cities as model of sustainability. *Journal of Cultural Heritage Management and Sustainable Development, 2*(1), 4–14.

Willson, G. B., & McIntosh, A. J. (2007). Heritage buildings and tourism: An experiential view. *Journal of Heritage Tourism, 2*(2), 75–93. https://doi.org/10.2167/jht024.0

Wilson, K. (2015). *Brisbane Art Deco: Stories of our built heritage*. Jubilee Studio.

World Monuments Fund. (2021). *Modernism at risk*. Retrieved from https://www.wmf.org/project/modernism-risk

Yanarella, E. J., & Levine, R. S. (2020). *From eco-cities to sustainable city-regions: China's uncertain quest for an ecological civilisation*. Edward Elgar Publishing.

Yung, E. H., & Chan, E. H. (2012). Implementation challenges to the adaptive re-use of heritage buildings: Towards the goals of sustainable, low carbon cities. *Habitat International, 36*(3), 352–361.

The Application of Netnography as a Tool for Understanding Visitors' Resilience: The Case of Villages in Central Java

Dwi Sugiharti, Taha Chaiechi, and Josephine Pryce

Abstract Since the tourism industry plays a critical role in economic development, tourism resilience from both the supplier and demand sides needs to be considered. The tourism industry's resilience is partly dependent on the adaptability and absorbability of visitors, without which the perpetuity of the industry would be threatened. This paper examines socio-economic resilience by exploring visitors' reviews of the UNESCO World Heritage-listed Borobudur Temple in Central Java, Indonesia. The paper adopts a netnography approach to identify factors that could be used to build a visitors' resilience index. Netnography is a naturalistic and predominantly unobtrusive technique developed for exploring online contributions. Using NVivo 12 Plus software, thematic analysis is conducted on a sample of 255 visitor reviews shared on TripAdvisor.com between March 2018 and March 2020. An interpretive coding approach was conducted by examining the reviews, selecting theoretically significant features from the reviews, coding the selected features systematically across the entire set of 255 reviews, and collating the reviews relevant to each code. The paper concludes that a visitors' resilience index can be constructed using a range of multidimensional variables, including spiritual and cultural awareness, emotional aspect, educational aspect, care for the natural environment, physical challenges, recreational and tourist aspect, and economic and social aspect. Findings show that visitors' resilience is reflected in online reviews by conveying their perceptions, experiences, personal feelings, and challenges during the visit. The results are significant as they demonstrate the critical role visitors' resilience plays in building a resilient tourism industry. This paper complements the existing literature on developing resilience in the tourism industry as it improves our understanding of visitor's characteristic and adaptive resilience.

D. Sugiharti (✉) · J. Pryce
James Cook University, Cairns, Australia
e-mail: dwi.sugiharti@my.jcu.edu.au; josephine.pryce@jcu.edu.au

T. Chaiechi
College of Business, Law and Governance, James Cook University, Townsville, QLD, Australia
e-mail: taha.chaiechi@jcu.edu.au

© The Author(s), under exclusive license to Springer Nature Singapore Pte Ltd. 2022

T. Chaiechi, J. Wood (eds.), *Community Empowerment, Sustainable Cities, and Transformative Economies*, https://doi.org/10.1007/978-981-16-5260-8_17

Keywords Netnography · Thematic analysis · Borobudur Temple · Visitors' resilience · Experience · Perception

1 Introduction

In social settings, resilience is often defined as a system's ability to absorb shocks and disturbances and maintain the same connections between the people and their surroundings and regenerate after the shocks (Espiner et al., 2017; Felicetti, 2016). At the individual level, resilience can refer to a host of biological, psychological, social and cultural factors that interact with one another to determine how individuals respond to stressful experiences (Southwick et al., 2014).

Economic resilience was first defined as innate and adaptive responses to disasters that enabled individuals and communities to avoid potential losses (Rose & Liao, 2005). It is used in the literature to examine the ability and speed of adjustment an economic system to recover from an external shock such as a disaster (Östh et al., 2015; Rose & Krausmann, 2013). Economic resilience may take place at the following three levels: micro (including individual business, household or government), meso (including individual industry or market), and macro (including a combination of all economic entities) (Rose & Krausmann, 2013; Rose & Liao, 2005). In general, regions with a more substantial economic profile tend to experience less economic losses and require a shorter time to recover from a disaster shock than regions with weaker economic systems (Kim & Marcouiller, 2015; Schmude et al., 2018).

Apart from individual and economic resilience, the literature also talks about the concept of community resilience which is often referred to as the physical infrastructure, economic resources, and community capacities and capabilities necessary to respond to adversity (Berkes & Ross, 2013; Lew, 2014; Magis, 2010). The exposure or sensitivity to change in a community and its adaptive capacity in responding to disruptions determines the degree of the community's vulnerability and resilience (Gallopín, 2006; Smit & Wandel, 2006).

The tourism sector is consistently subject to battering from changes and disturbances occurring externally as well as from within and at various levels (B. King & Berno, 2002). Shifts in the social and economic domains of communities can impact the tourism sector (Tovar & Lockwood, 2008). Therefore, the resilience of the tourism industry at various levels depends on inherent and adaptive capacities (Sugiharti et al., 2021).

2 Resilience in the Tourism Industry

The tourism industry is a complex network sector that comprises several complementary goods and services contributing to tourism products (Cellini & Cuccia, 2015). This sector is also characterised by dynamic changes and developments that respond to supply (a range of tourism products and services) and demand (diverse needs of tourists) (Decelle, 2004; Garin-Munoz & Montero-Martín, 2007; Novelli et al., 2006).

As a dynamic and competitive industry because of its interrelatedness among visitors and tourism suppliers (Dwyer et al., 2009; Mihalič, 2000), the tourism industry requires the capacity to adjust when external shocks are imposed (Becken, 2013). Therefore, planning for resilience by incorporating flexibility and adaptive capacities into the complex social and economic systems is crucial for all tourism stakeholders and their increasingly complex interrelations (Brown et al., 2018; Luthe & Wyss, 2014).

In this evolving context, both suppliers and travellers can face stressful, challenging or overwhelming situations that put their resilience to the test. However, most of the existing literature on tourism resilience have mainly focused on the adaptive capacity and the resilience of operators on the supply side of the equation, and the visitor's resilience on the demand side has been largely ignored (Sugiharti et al., 2021).

There are four important elements in tourism resilience: identifying capacities, controlling capacities, social capital, and stakeholders relatedness (Cheer & Lew, 2017; Cochrane, 2010). The first element is the capacity to identify problems as well as tourism potentials in a region. This element is crucial because it opens up opportunities for actions, adjustments, changes and transformations (Leach, 2008). This first element must be supported by the capacity to control socio-economic and environmental impacts. The third element is social capital which is the ability and willingness of community members to participate in actions directed to community objectives when changes and disruptions occur (Sherrieb et al., 2010). This social capital is an essential ingredient in fostering local resilience in communities as community members have the collective capacity to respond to changes, sustain, and renew the community if needed (Magis, 2010). The last element is the interrelatedness among all stakeholders, including private, public, and third sectors whose roles and contributions to tourism development are different. All these stakeholders must work and synergise themselves, showing their resilience to have sustainable tourism development (Cheer & Lew, 2017; Cheer et al., 2019). This is important because, without all stakeholders' successful engagement with the tourism market and its dynamics, the system will fail (Cochrane, 2010).

The above mentioned four elements call for strong and committed leadership, either from individuals or institutions with a clear vision and accountable management (Ruiz-Ballesteros, 2011). Effective leadership and preparedness is needed to lead all elements to capture the nature of the disruptions and then set up strategies for quick adaptation and consistent adaptability (Pike et al., 2010).

3 Theoretical Framework

The subjection of the tourism sector to a range of disruptions such as economic recession, fast-paced technological changes, natural disasters, and unpredictable public health emergencies presents it as a good example of a Complex Adaptive System (CAS) (Farrell & Twining-Ward, 2004; Schianetz & Kavanagh, 2008). In

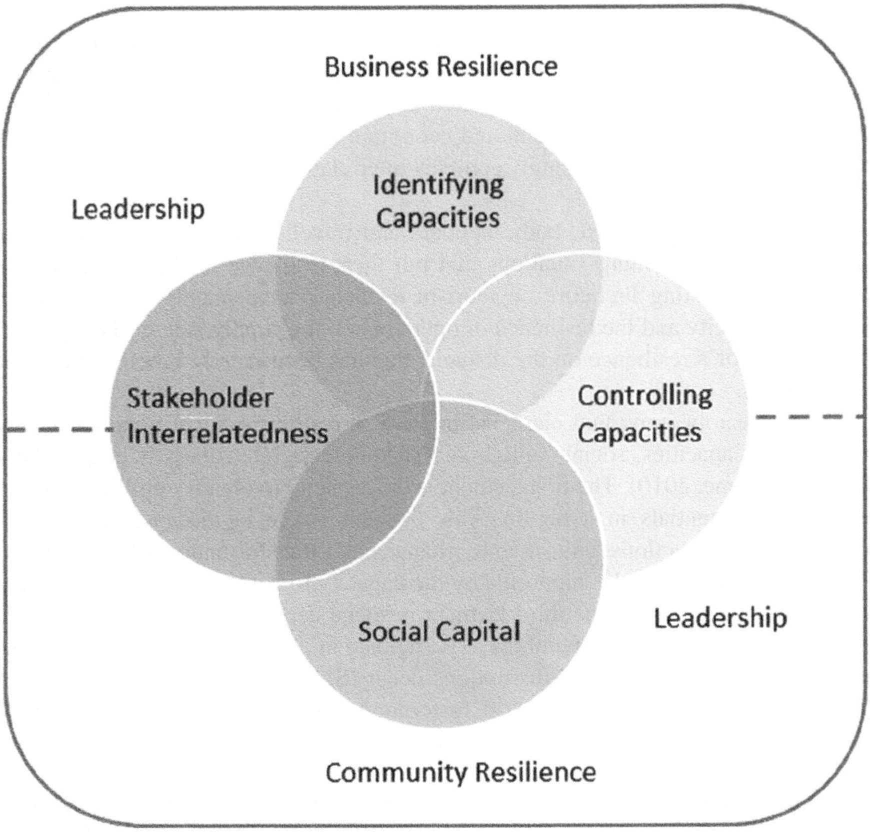

Fig. 1 The elements of resilience in tourism. (Source: Author's elaboration adopted from (Calgaro et al., 2014; Cheer & Lew, 2017; Cochrane, 2010)

the long run, the system's consistent adaptive capacity to the continuous changing competitive environment, technological and market pressures determines the success, resilience, and sustainability of tourism development (Boschma, 2004). This paper proposes a theoretical model for Resilience in Tourism that captures both the social (community) and economic (business) aspects (Fig. 1).

The proposed model in Fig. 1 illustrates that tourism resilience as a whole system comprises two kinds of resilience: business resilience and community resilience (Cheer & Lew, 2017). Business Resilience defines the ability of enterprises to absorb, adapt, and innovate when faced with the changing business environment by utilising their resources and capacities (Orchiston et al., 2016). Business resilience also covers how business stakeholders can self-organise and recalibrate business operating conditions to external disturbances and possible conflicts from within (Dahles & Susilowati, 2015). In the meantime, community resilience defines the empowerment of community members and the engagement of community resources to learn and survive in an uncertain environment with constant changes and disruptions (Magis, 2010).

The social capital and stakeholder cohesiveness in the model are closely related to the 'visitors' resilience (Sugiharti et al., 2021). For example, the willingness of locals who are part of tourism stakeholders to get involved in the tourism development influences the 'visitors' experiences during their visits. Moreover, local communities play an important role in developing sustainable tourism, as they are the agents of cultures and local wisdom in which tourism is delivered (Gonzales et al., 2018). This interconnectedness exemplifies the importance of social and economic resilience and lends support for the use of the Resilience in Tourism framework proposed in Fig. 1. That framework is used to guide the research.

4 Knowledge Gap

The importance of visitor's behaviour and resilience as one of the key stakeholders in the tourism industry has been neglected in previous studies on tourism resilience, even though the industry is largely dependent on travellers' adaptability, without which the industry's perpetuation would likely be risky. Hence, the combined individual, social and economic contexts of resilience assisting in building tourism systems' resilience is suggested (Sugiharti et al., 2021).

The related information provided on the Internet has recently gained popularity and become one of the prominent sources of information for travellers (Heinonen & Medberg, 2018; Libai et al., 2010). Travellers share their experiences, either positive or negative, contribute knowledge, experience to other travellers, and save other potential travellers' time, especially travellers who want to visit certain places for the first time (Bae et al., 2017; Lehto et al., 2004; Nash & Smith, 1989).

Tourist information shared via online travel community platforms such as TripAdvisor, Yahoo! Travel, and Lonely Planet have been utilised in many studies (H. Y. Kim & Yoon, 2013; Lee et al., 2011; Miguéns et al., 2008). The analysis of the utilisation of tourist information by reviewers show how the information has its effects on the decision-making of other tourists (Lee et al., 2011; Papathanassis & Knolle, 2011), and research indicates that travellers trust online reviews shared by other tourists more than the online information advertised by the tourist industry (Kladou & Mavragani, 2015; Xiang & Gretzel, 2010). Furthermore, the analysis of the qualitative data posted by tourists on the Internet can play an important role in understanding tourist experiences, destination branding, destination image formation, and structural and cultural changes in tourism markets (Bosangit et al., 2015; Hsu et al., 2009).

Previous research on assessing online visitor reviews shows that visitor reviews shared on the online platforms are utilised to improve marketing strategy (Weaver et al., 1994) as the success and failure of a destination can be influenced by 'tourists' evaluation of the destination (Meng et al., 2008); and to understand the competitiveness of a destination (Enright & Newton, 2004) as the reviews used to access the destination attributes that make the destination attractive and competitive is critical for the destination to achieve economic sustainability (Rodríguez-Díaz et al., 2018). While this paper analyses what the online reviews reveal about tourist destination that relates to the resilience of the visitors as one of the main stakeholders in the tourism industry that has not been highlighted in the previous studies on tourism resilience.

5 Scope of the Study

The scope of this study is the Borobudur Temple in Central Java, Indonesia. As the world's biggest Buddhist Temple, Borobudur is well-known as one of the most favourite heritage tourism destinations (Canny & Hidayat, 2012). Built in the eighth and ninth centuries during the reign of the Syailendra Dynasty (UNESCO, 2020), Borobudur Temple was constructed gradually over a long period of time. Around the year 780 AD, the early stages of the construction began. The process continued until about the year 792 AD. Another phase began in the year 824 AD, and finished in 833 AD (Dumarçay, 1991).

The Temple is located in central Java. Its pyramidal structure with three tiers and a monumental stupa at the top draws domestic and international visitors. (Table 1)

The table above illustrates the numbers of visitors to Borobudur temple in the past few years. Even though the number of visitors has been continuously increasing since 2017, the incremental number of visitors fluctuates. In 2020 as the travel restrictions were imposed in April, there have been no international visitors visiting the Temple. In contrast, domestic visitors have declined sharply following the restrictions for public gatherings, events and ceremonies, travel, and *visitors* to tourist sites.

As an exemplar of tourist destinations in Central Java and as a magnet for tourists, Borobudur Temple has been in the spotlight of national and regional tourism development programs. To increase the benefits of the development and preservation of Borobudur, the local government has launched the partnership concept to allow locals to start or expand their tourism supporting businesses. These programs include improving partnerships between local producers and the government in terms of management, training, product marketing, financial assistance, and tourism promotion to support the tourism sector's sustainability in the Borobudur Temple area (Taman Wisata Candi Borobudur, 2017).

Table 1 The number of tourists visiting Borobudur temple from 2017–2020

Year	Number of visitors	Incremental visitors (%)
2017	3,900,677	
2018	4,008,667	2.77%
2019	4,039,153	0.76%
2020	997,250	−3.05%

Source: (Disporapar, 2020)

6 Methodology

In this paper, a qualitative research approach is adopted. Netnography, as the study of online communities with its origins in ethnography, is selected for an in-depth description and explanation of the multi-faceted phenomenon of tourist resilience. Compared to traditional ethnography, netnography is faster, simpler, and less expensive (Kozinets, 2006; Maulana & Eckhardt, 2007). Netnography is also more descriptive than traditional ethnography as it provides information from customers using the Internet to share their experiences, expressing their subjective reality and emotional truth, which can be used as recommendations as well as warnings for other customers (Heinonen & Medberg, 2018; Narayan et al., 2010) Moreover, this method minimises the respondents' possible shyness and social anxiety as opposed to traditional ethnography approaches (Rageh et al., 2013; Wu & Pearce, 2014). And since travellers usually write their reviews after their visit, this method is considered an adequate approach to observing customer experience (Kozinets, 2002).

7 Data and Data Sources

TripAdvisor, the largest online travel community platform, was chosen as the source of data. The platform offers approximately 867 million reviews and feedback on tourist destinations, accommodation, restaurants, airline tickets, and cruises (TripAdvisor, 2019).

Online reviews for "Borobudur Tour" posted on TripAdvisor from March 2018–2020 were selected to describe tourists' types of tourist experiences when visiting Borobudur temple and classify them into aspects related to resilience.

7.1 Data Collection and Preparation

The first step of data collection involves identifying the most relevant online travel communities to cover the tourist experience. Data collection was conducted by selecting reviews based on a set of inclusion criteria (as per Table 2).

The selection process of reviews is shown in Fig. 2. From a total of 270 reviews, 15 reviews were discarded as they were either written in the Indonesian language or irrelevant to the topic. For improved reliability, 27 posts with unknown place of origin were removed. The reviews then were screened for brevity, and three further reviews consisting of fewer than ten words were removed. The final sample included 225 reviews.

Table 2 Inclusion Criteria for Reviewers posted on TripAdvisor from March 2018–2020

Inclusion criteria	
Name of the place	Borobudur Temple and surrounding
Language	English
Visitor's place of origin	City and country
Time frame	March 2018 to March 2020
Traveller rating	All ratings (terrible, poor, average, very good, excellent)
Travel companions	All
Brevity	Comments with ten words or more

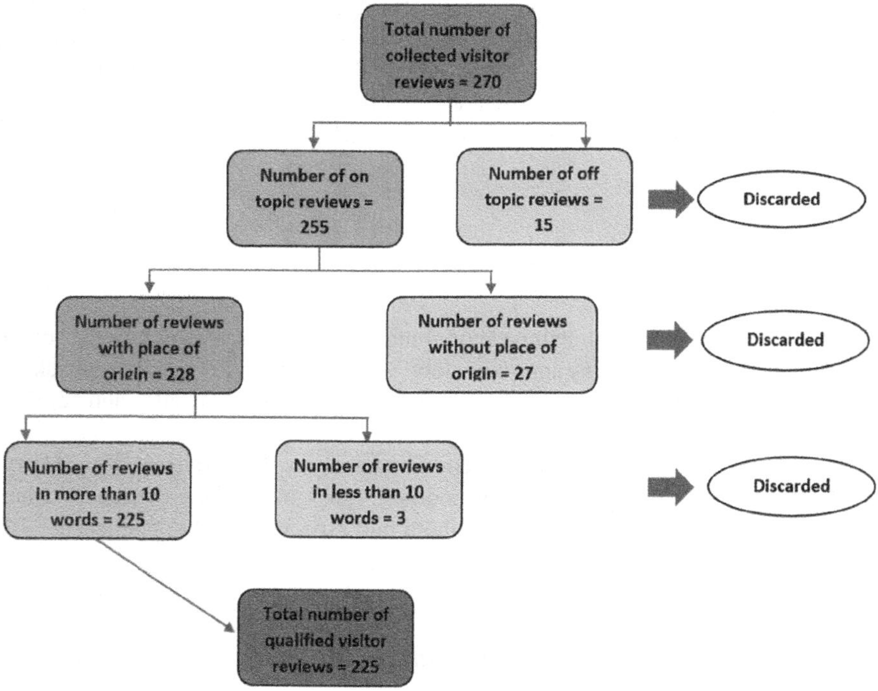

Fig. 2 Visitor Reviews Selection Process

This study used NVivo 12 Plus, a computer-aided qualitative data analysis software that enables researchers to reveal evidence-based insight from qualitative data. The software also allows researchers to search, count for index specific words, themes, and clusters across multiple text documents (Leech & Onwuegbuzie, 2011; Sotiriadou et al., 2014). The analytical tools of NVivo assisted the research team in the process of themes identification.

8 Charting of the Data

Providing insight into data through visual representations is important to query the data from multiple angles and reveal patterns/trends. The visualisation provides the ability to comprehend the data set and clarify the data categories (Bazeley & Jackson, 2013). The following figure presents the countries from where the visitor originated based on the visitor place of origin. (Fig. 3)

The pie chart shows the origins of the visitors who came to Borobudur Temple from March 2018 to March 2020. We have only included the countries of origin in the above chart if they have at least appeared twice in the reviews. From 255 visitors who wrote their reviews on TripAdvisor, the top three portions measured in terms of the number of visitors were the USA, Indonesia, and Australia.

As shown in Table 1, the number of visitors to Borobudur Temple increased annually in the years leading to 2020 and the start of the COVID-19 pandemic. However, the number of international visitors only formed a tiny portion of total visitors, as depicted in Fig. 4.

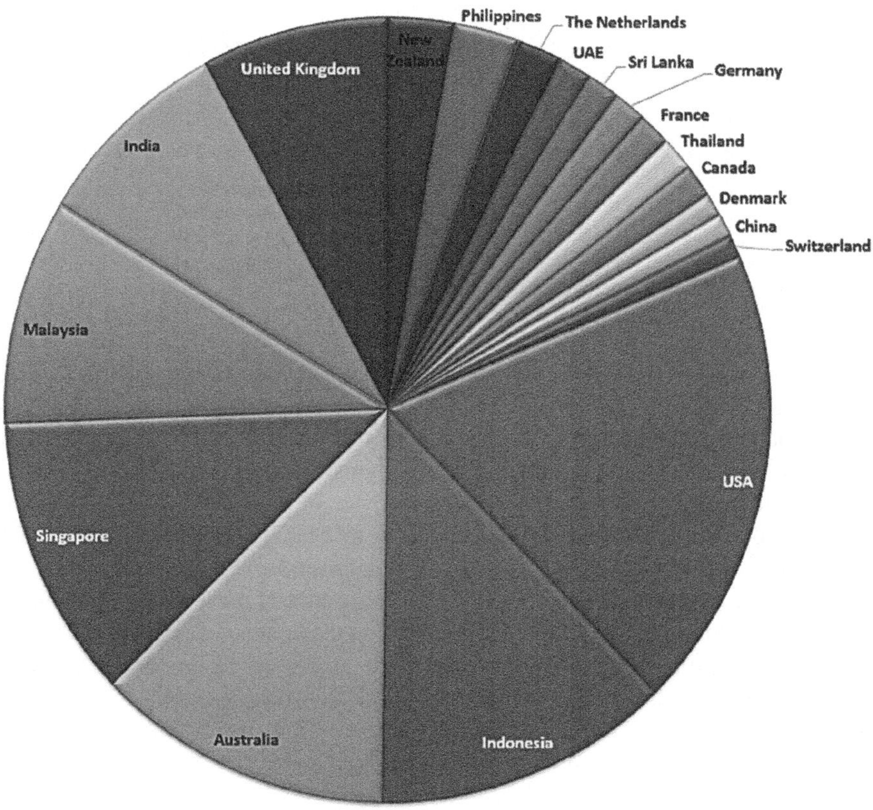

Fig. 3 Number of scoped reviews concerning the "place of Origin (Country)"

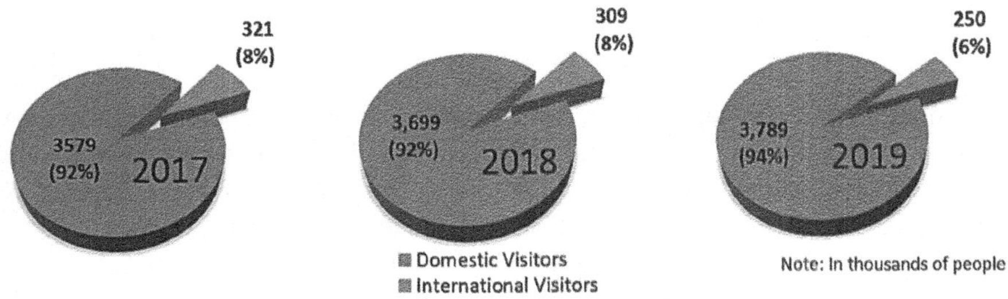

Fig. 4 The proportion of international and domestic visitors to Borobudur Temple in 2017, 2018 and 2019

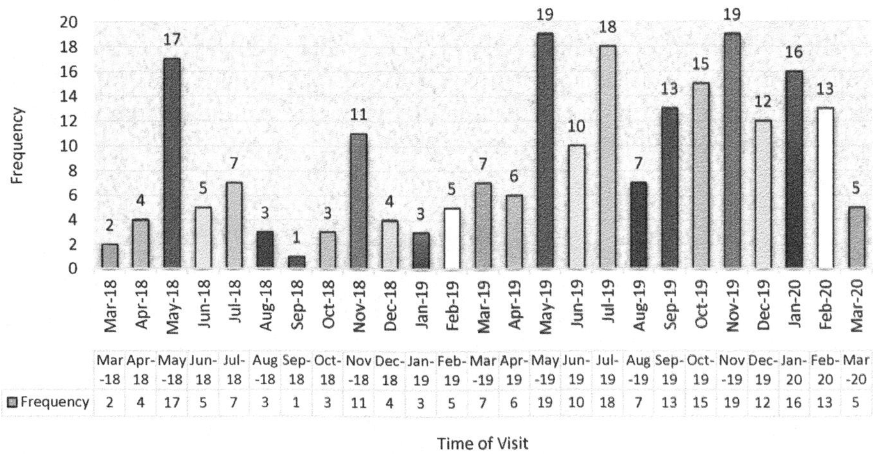

Fig. 5 The occurrence of the reviews from March 2018–March 2020

It is also noteworthy that the online reviews only represent a small fraction of the total visitors coming to Borobudur Temple. And, unfortunately, neither the destination management companies nor government tourism agencies has classified the international visitors based on their country origins.

The following bar chart displays the occurrence of reviews shared by travellers visiting Borobudur temple from March 2018 to March 2020. Even though the number of reviews only depicts a fraction of total visitors. (Fig. 5)

The above bar chart shows the fluctuating occurrence of the reviews based on the time of visits. In May of 2018 and 2019, a spike in the number of reviews is detected because a Buddhist event named *Vesak Day* annually occurs in May. The event attracts many Buddhist and non-Buddhist travellers worldwide who wish to celebrate the event at the Temple. Another sharp increase in the number of online reviews is observed in November 2018 and 2019 when the annual international sports event named *Borobudur Marathon* is held. July is the month of the local school holiday; expectedly, more reviews were shared in that month.

The following map of countries shows the distances of the travellers' place of origin from Borobudur Temple. Visitors from many parts of the world come to the Temple despite the long journey they have to take. This indicates the perceived resilience of visitors on Borobudur Temple to the distance. (Fig. 6)

9 Thematic Analysis

We have adopted a thematic analysis to investigate the data further. Thematic Analysis is a qualitative method commonly used to identify, report, and analyse qualitative data for the meanings produced and by people, situations, and events (Braun & Clarke, 2006; Nowell et al., 2017).

The thematic analysis began with creating 'free nodes' extracted from the data which the 225 visitors reviews. The research team developed themes within raw data by identifying important elements. The team then proceeded to the encoding stage, which is the primary process prior to the interpretation stage (Boyatzis, 1998; Ozkan, 2004). The main aim of creating free nodes was to find the basic relative content (King et al., 2018). Creating free nodes started by removing some insignificant words from the 225 verbatim comments made by reviewers, which yielded a total of 101 free nodes. The result of the pre-coding Word Frequency Query is presented in Fig. 7.

The following table presents The List of Top Quartile words of Word Frequency Query. The Word Frequency List in Table 3 and the word Cloud in Fig. 7 show the most frequently occurring words that appeared in the online reviews. The authors used the feature of word frequency in NVivo to identify the most frequently occurring words. The most frequently used words were viewed as a proxy representing respondents' perception (Jackson & Trochim, 2002; Westergren, Edin, & Christianson, 2021). The more frequently the words used in online reviews, the more important and significant they are (Carley, 1993). Moreover, analysing word frequency improves logical consistency and can help researchers to avoid subjectivity (Leech & Onwuegbuzie, 2011; Onwuegbuzie & Leech, 2007).

The authors selected these words based on the narratives opined in Trip Advisor by visitors to the Borobudur Temple Tour. Some words with similar meanings were highlighted in the same colours. For example, sunrise, morning, and sunset are coded with the same colour.

Each of the reviews was examined manually and coded systematically across the entire set of reviews. This step of the process is referred to as interpretive coding. Reviews relevant to each code were organised using the colour coding from Table 3 to build interpretative codes.

The data in interpretive codes used phrases rather than single words. This interpretive coding was to capture the deeper nuances from the reviews. These interpretative codes were further categorised into primary themes (as presented in Table 4). A primary theme summarises the essence of several related codes and covers different reviews to reveal subthemes' core concepts. Two members of the

Fig. 6 Map of countries from where the reviewers are originated. (Source: Authors)

Fig. 7 Word frequency from 225 TripAdvisor reviews on Borobudur Tour

research team were involved in this process to ensure no important elements from free codes are neglected. They also conducted cross-coding to increase the validity and reliability of the results.

10 Interpretations and Discussion

There were 101 free codes from a total of 225 reviews in the first step. The 101 free codes were then reduced to 29 interpretive codes in the second step. And finally, these 29 interpretive codes were reduced to seven primary themes (Table 4), namely: spiritual aspects, emotional aspects, educational aspects, natural environmental aspects, physical aspects, recreational and tourist aspects, and economic and social aspects. These primary themes are discussed further in the following sections.

10.1 Spiritual Aspects and Cultural Awareness

The reviews relating to spiritual aspects and cultural awareness were the most discussed in the text data set. The interpretive codes identified therein were Stone

Table 3 List of top quartile words based on weighted percentage

Word	Count	Weighted percentage (%)	Word	Count	Weighted percentage (%)
Sunrise	96	2.09	Best	18	0.39
Visit	88	1.92	Entrance	18	0.39
World	83	1.81	Hours	18	0.39
Amazing	67	1.46	Tourists	18	0.39
Buddhist	66	1.44	Breakfast	17	0.37
Stone	62	1.35	Bucket	17	0.37
Carvings	60	1.31	Recommend	17	0.37
Buddha	55	1.20	Stones	17	0.37
Tour	50	1.09	Sunset	17	0.37
History	48	1.05	Ancient	16	0.35
Guide	46	1.00	Stories	16	0.35
Beautiful	43	0.94	Views	16	0.35
Heritage	40	0.87	Story	15	0.33
Unesco	36	0.79	Biggest	14	0.31
Structure	32	0.70	Buddhism	14	0.31
People	31	0.68	Visiting	14	0.31
Great	26	0.57	Culture	13	0.28
Morning	26	0.57	Details	13	0.28
View	26	0.57	Spectacular	13	0.28
Complex	24	0.52	Wonder	13	0.28
Statues	24	0.52	Wonderful	13	0.28
Huge	23	0.50	Crowds	12	0.26
Carving	22	0.48	Incredible	12	0.26
Magnificent	22	0.48	Sight	12	0.26
Experience	21	0.46	Stunning	12	0.26
Architecture	20	0.44	Ticket	12	0.26
Largest	19	0.41	Walking	12	0.26
Local	19	0.41	Walls	12	0.26

Wall Carvings, Stories of historical events, Life of Buddha, Beautiful Arts, Religious site, Mystical and Magical, and Inspirational.

As the world's biggest Buddhist Temple, Borobudur is undoubtedly rich in history and spiritual significance. It is the central place for all Buddhists worldwide to gather on Vesak Day to commemorate the birth, enlightenment, and death of Gautama Buddha – the founder of Buddhism. Such significance given to visiting Borobudur indicates the value of the visits in helping visitors absorb and adapting to "life's shocks and changes, indicating the contribution of the visits to 'individuals' resilience (Pyke et al., 2018). Equally, the restorative power of the visits is evident in comments such as the following:

Table 4 Primary themes and subthemes

Primary themes	Subthemes/interpretive codes	Free codes
Spiritual aspect	Stone wall carvings Stories of historical events Life of Buddha Beautiful arts Religious site Mystical & magical Inspirational	Sunrise, morning, sunset, Buddhist, stone, carvings, Buddha, statues, carving, Buddhism, stones, details, story, wonder, experience, stories, bucket [list], walls
Emotional aspect	Worth the visit Peaceful and serene Wonder of the world	Amazing, beautiful, great, magnificent, spectacular, incredible, stunning, best, wonderful, recommend
Educational aspect	Historical site Heritage site Amazing architecture Real-world heritage	World, history, heritage, UNESCO, structure, complex, huge, architecture, ancient, biggest, story, culture, largest
Natural environmental aspect	Breathtaking nature Surrounding gardens Fog, clouds Mountainous surrounding area	View, views, sight
Physical aspect	Tropical heat Fitness Climbing Walking Water	Walking
Recreational & tourist aspects	Tours & Guides Photo opportunities Tourists, crowds, people	Visit, tour, guide, crowds, people, tourists, visiting, ticket, entrance, breakfast, hours
Economic and social aspect	Preservation and maintenance Local friendliness Local vendors Food providers Souvenir sellers Museum	Local

We went here for the sunrise and was not disappointed. It was a place that if you let it could be a spiritual experience. The bells are just amazing in their constuction with Buda statues hidden inside every bell. If you take the time to take in the atmosphere it truly is amazing.

Yet another reviewer spoke of the cultural significance of Borobudur Temple:

Temple has the largest and most complete ensemble of Buddhist reliefs in the world. It is one of the greatest Buddhist monuments in the world. Once a year, Buddhists in Indonesia celebrate Vesak Day at the monument. Borobudur is Indonesia's single most visited tourist attraction. You've not visited Indonesia if you've not been to Borobudur Temple.

For Buddhists, Borobudur Temple is a sacred and spiritual place to visit. The Temple has many symbols reflecting Buddhist teachings, while non-Buddhist visitors will learn wisdom and peace by visiting this place. Even though the local community is mostly Muslim, Vesak Day is officially established as a national holiday to respect

Buddhists. Local communities, together with religious leaders, prepare the event in the Temple as well as the accommodation for Buddhist pilgrims coming from all over the world, as shown by the following review:

> *Borobudur Temple is quite an impressive temple. Even though the Temple was originally Buddhist, the tourists, according to our guide, is 80% locals, and mostly Muslims since the local population shifted over the centuries. Our tour guide was also quite excellent, explaining a lot of historic events depicted by the carvings.*

The spiritual aspect theme shows how religious and spiritual motivations successfully drive people from many parts of the world to travel to visit Borobudur Temple. This motivation indicates that for the visitors to Borobudur Temple, travelling the distance to get there is worthwhile because the rewards are enriching and restorative. This indicates that the perceived gains from visits to Borobudur Temple are spiritually nourishing and culturally inspiring for the visitors, all factors which are recognised as contributing to individuals' resilience (Han & Cheer, 2018).

10.2 Emotional Factors

Emotional aspects described the admiration shown by visitors when visiting Borobudur Temple. The "'peaceful' atmosphere when visiting the Temple was described as providing unexpected experiences to visitors that captured the transformative power of the site and so, contributed to building 'visitors' resilience. Many respondents mentioned feelings full of admiration upon seeing Borobudur and this is captured in the following review:

> *... The Temple is magnificent from the outside and has beautiful 8th-9th century stone carvings... There are 3 levels to climb. The temple complex and its surroundings is very peaceful and quiet. All in all I had a wonderful experience walking to and around in one of the most breathtaking wonders of the world.*

Emotions were also expressed by the tourist impressions when comparing Borobudur to other Buddhist temples, and the memories created when visiting the Temple:

> *Everyone must be proud of this world heritage. I have visited many temples around SEA but I can say Borobudur was the most memorable experience due to the stunning location between the mountains - paradise! But I was impressed by the architecture with its history carved on the stones that build the whole Temple - amazing. It doesn't consist of Temple complexes like Angkor, it is more like a giant temple. And the view at the top... OMG.. the view is indescribably awesome! It felt like I had reached the (real) Nirvana.*

Such reviews captured how visits to such places as Borobudur Temple promoted holistic wellbeing, allowing for people to connect with oneself, others, nature and the beauty of the world. The reviews showed how wonders such as those presented by Borobudur Temple and its surrounds can contribute to positive emotions. This is in line with the literature which shows that enjoyment can create positive emotions and build resilient thinking (Arewasikporn et al., 2019).

10.3 Educational Aspects

Several reviewers described Borobudur as a place where visitors can gain knowledge about historical events, for example:

> *Borobudur Temple is an amazing UNESCO Heritage... a must when in Indonesia and go to the museum to read about the history and its existence. I did not do the sunrise tour... too lazy to get up at 3 am get ready and take a 1 hour trip just to see the sunrise!! Nevertheless, the visit was just as great.*

The educational elements of the temple setting were also evident in reviewers comments that highlighted that the structures contained many symbols, as in the following review:

> *Borobudur Temple is stunning and has such a rich history behind it. Visually it is stunning to experience the architecture, as the Temple has several tiers. Walk around each tier before you ascend to the next and admire the stone relief walls and carvings you being to get a sense of the amount of thought and work that has been executed.*

The educational aspects relates to Borobudur's status as a World Heritage Area renowned for its historical and cultural significance. Visits to Borobudur then offer time to focus on deep-rooted connections with traditions and history and encourage care of oneself, as highlighted by the previous two themes, and building understanding of natural wonders and sites of spiritual and cultural significance. Recognition of historical buildings and the times the represent, creates an appreciation of the need to balance good and bad times and in that acknowledgement build resilience (Holtorf, 2018).

10.4 Physical Challenges

Physical activity can push people beyond their capabilities, and this was evident from some of the comments of visitors to the Temple who questioned their fitness in climbing up the narrow stairs to the top. Such physical challenges can create stress and be overwhelming for individuals. For example, the following review showcased that the tropical heat and climb required capabilities and endurance:

> *The side of the Borobudur is very spacious. Surrounded by a nice park with plenty of trees providing the necessary shade. The way up to the Temple is easy accessible, once there you can climb the monument, but this not suitable for everyone. Very steep stairs makes is sometimes a challenge (especially on the way down). Visit early in the day to beat the heat and the crowds. Definitely a bucket list item to check off!!!!*

Equally, the physical accomplishment of reaching the top of the Temple can be rewarding and this was noticeable in some of the reviews, such as the following one:

> *The highlight of the tour was definitely seeing the Borobudur Buddhist Temple - one of the seven wonders of the world & the world's biggest Buddhist Temple. A very popular tourist destination so be prepared for the crowds!! There's quite a few steps so carry water and a hat with you, but it's worth the climb - the view is spectacular. – Jessica from London.*

Physical aspects relate to individual engagement in beneficial physical activity. Such activity can be rewarding and build resilience. Studies have shown that physical activity can increase resilience to stress (Hegberg & Tone, 2015) Such studies highlight the parallel of physical exertion in climbing the steps at temples such as Borobudur to enhancing resilience.

10.5 Care for the Natural Environmental

Some people were fortunate to view the perfect sunrise. They reported that it was fascinating to see the Temple with its breathtaking surrounding, as is evident in the following review:

> *Must visit, it's a must!!! if you have a chance to arrive early in the morning for the sunrise tour, be better be.…!!! the greatest Temple in Indonesia, no wonder as one of the world heritage sites by UNESCO, you should spare at least 3 hours to get details about the site, also have a guide to explain its much better!!*

Others observed the magical view of a mountainous background. Overall, the surrounding nature added up Borobudur's attractiveness:

> *Borobodur is really stunning - plus incredible views, so much history and amazing art work of the carvings in the stones (Buddha's history) - beautiful views, the amazing stupas and Mount Merapi in the back ground. I would go back again.*

Natural environmental aspects reflected in the online reviews are based on the appeal of Borobudur Temple as a tourism attraction which is located in a beautiful mountainous area. The literature presents evidence that connection with nature can positively affect an "individual's psychological resilience (Ingulli & Lindbloom, 2013). It is argued that immersing oneself in natural settings can help in coping during challenging and difficult times and so, enhance 'individuals' resilience (Ryan et al., 2010).

10.6 Recreational Aspect

Services provided by drivers and tour guides were mentioned as value-adding to tourists' experiences. For example, one reviewer said:

> *We got a guide, who was over 70 and his insight and passion for the Temple was amazing, he was so friendly it really added an extra dimension to the trip to see this amazing wonder.*

Similarly, another reviewer commented:

> *The driver and our guide still did a really good job telling us the history of the volcano and showing us some sights*

Some reviewers depicted Borobudur temple as "clean and pleasant to walk around" and as being "large and well maintained and picturesque", picking up on the value of Borobudur as a recreational area being enhanced by the commitment to the maintenance of the Temple. As one reviewer elaborated:

> *In the early morning hours in soft sunlight, both the Temple and the surrounding areas down the Temple was simply unforgettable. The whole Temple is huge and while going down from the top we could get a feel the vastness of this stunning Temple. The Temple is very well maintained. Definitely this is one of the most spectacular Temple we have ever seen*

Recreational aspects in the reviews related to the maintenance of the infrastructure and services showed how these issues influenced visitors' satisfaction. Such services impact 'visitors' experiences and inadvertently affect 'individuals' resilience. The literature shows that positive experiences enhance resilience and contribute to the positive functioning of individuals (Arewasikporn et al., 2019).

10.7 Economic Aspect

Local services and amenities were two interpretive codes that were prominent in the findings. There were comments about services provided for the visitors, such as:

> *We went here for the sunrise and was not disappointed. It was a place that if you let it could be a spiritual experience. If you take the time to take in the atmosphere it truly is amazing. When we booked our hotel packed us breakfast as we were not going to be at the hotel for breakfast but they did not need to as the entrance fee included breakfast at their restaurant which was just as good as what you get at most hotels, this was on our bucket list which was worth the trip.*

Also, satisfactory tour packages and excellent service were two prominent features highlighted by some reviewers, for example:

> *It was fabulous. The Temple is surreal. You really need to see it to believe it. With the tour came a nice luncheon with entertainment at the restaurant of the local hotel. Ten flights of rather steep steps to reach the top but you can take your time.*

Economic factors related to the visitors' excellent local services and amenities highlight that visitation to Borobudur can enhance the resilience of businesses and communities through economic ways (Buultjens et al., 2015).

11 Conclusion

This paper used netnograhy and thematic analysis as a qualitative research approach to explore tourists' resilience. The total sample of 225 TripAdvisor reviews resulted in the identification of seven themes relating to tourism experiences at Borobudur Temple: spiritual and cultural awareness, emotional aspect, educational aspect, care for the natural environment, physical challenges, recreational and tourist aspect, and economic and social aspect. Overall, the tourists had positive attitudes towards their visits, with spiritual and cultural awareness discussed the most by reviewers (i.e. visitors). The online reviews suggest that places such as Borobudur Temple could be used as part of a comprehensive strategy to enhance socio-economic resilience through the range of tourism activities that bring rewards to visitors and locals. The results also indicate that a visitors' resilience index can be constructed using a range of multidimensional variables that are based on the seven themes that emerged from this research.

Findings show that visitors' resilience is reflected in online reviews by conveying their perceptions, experiences, personal feelings, and challenges during the visit. The results are significant as they demonstrate the critical role visitors' resilience plays in building a resilient tourism industry. Across all seven themes, visitors comments aligned with the literature relating to individuals' resilience, indicating that the themes are robust and worthy of including in a visitors' resilience index. To advance the index, future research should include a scoping review that captures other variables that could be included in the visitors' resilience index. In addition, extending the research to surveys and interviews to capture more participants and a deeper understanding of resilience. Equally, it would be worthwhile to conduct research relating to other heritage sites in other places and countries.

Visitor's reviews affect destination choices, the visitors spending, and their decision to return. Accordingly, this study posits that it is essential to give voice to visitors and communities and incorporate their views in strategies to build a resilient tourism sector. In achieving that goal, this paper recommends governments take a more active role in developing and implementing initiatives that strengthen multilevel stakeholder relationships. It is also suggested that further work in building the visitors' resilience index can contribute to advancing the sustainability of tourism into the future.

References

Arewasikporn, A., Sturgeon, J. A., & Zautra, A. J. (2019). Sharing positive experiences boosts resilient thinking: Everyday benefits of social connection and positive emotion in a community sample. *American Journal of Community Psychology, 63*(1–2), 110–121.

Bae, S. J., Lee, H., Suh, E.-K., & Suh, K.-S. (2017). Shared experience in pretrip and experience sharing in posttrip: A survey of Airbnb users. *Information & Management, 54*(6), 714–727.

Bazeley, P., & Jackson, K. (2013). *Qualitative data analysis with NVivo*. SAGE Publications Limited.

Becken, S. (2013). Developing a framework for assessing resilience of tourism sub-systems to climatic factors. *Annals of Tourism Research, 43*, 506–528.

Berkes, F., & Ross, H. (2013). Community resilience: Toward an integrated approach. *Society & Natural Resources, 26*(1), 5–20.

Bosangit, C., Hibbert, S., & McCabe, S. (2015). "If I was going to die I should at least be having fun": Travel blogs, meaning and tourist experience. *Annals of Tourism Research, 55*, 1–14.

Boschma, R. (2004). Competitiveness of regions from an evolutionary perspective. *Regional Studies, 38*(9), 1001–1014.

Boyatzis, R. E. (1998). *Transforming qualitative information: Thematic analysis and code development*. Sage.
Braun, V., & Clarke, V. (2006). Using thematic analysis in psychology. *Qualitative Research in Psychology, 3*(2), 77–101.
Brown, N. A., Orchiston, C., Rovins, J. E., Feldmann-Jensen, S., & Johnston, D. (2018). An integrative framework for investigating disaster resilience within the hotel sector. *Journal of Hospitality and Tourism Management, 36*, 67–75.
Buultjens, J., Ratnayake, I., & Gnanapala, A. (2015). From tsunami to recovery: The resilience of the Sri Lankan tourism industry. *B. Ritchie, B. & K. Campiranon (Eds.). Tourism crisis and disaster management in the Asia-Pacific*, 132–148.
Calgaro, E., Lloyd, K., & Dominey-Howes, D. (2014). From vulnerability to transformation: A framework for assessing the vulnerability and resilience of tourism destinations. *Journal of Sustainable Tourism, 22*(3), 341–360.
Canny, I., & Hidayat, N. (2012). The influence of service quality and tourist satisfaction on future behavioral intentions: The case study of Borobudur Temple as a UNESCO world culture heritage destination. *International Proceedings of Economics Development & Research, 50* (19), 89–97.
Carley, K. (1993). Coding choices for textual analysis: A comparison of content analysis and map analysis. *Sociological Methodology*, 75–126.
Cellini, R., & Cuccia, T. (2015). The economic resilience of tourism industry in Italy: What the 'great recession' data show. *Tourism Management Perspectives, 16*, 346–356.
Cheer, J. M., & Lew, A. A. (2017). *Tourism, resilience and sustainability: Adapting to social, political and economic change*. Routledge.
Cheer, J. M., Milano, C., & Novelli, M. (2019). Tourism and community resilience in the Anthropocene: Accentuating temporal overtourism. *Journal of Sustainable Tourism, 27*(4), 554–572.
Cochrane, J. (2010). The sphere of tourism resilience. *Tourism Recreation Research, 35*(2), 173–185.
Dahles, H., & Susilowati, T. P. (2015). Business resilience in times of growth and crisis. *Annals of Tourism Research, 51*, 34–50.
Decelle, X. (2004). A conceptual and dynamic approach to innovation in tourism.
Disporapar, J. T. (2020). Buku Saku 2020. Retrieved from http://disporapar.jatengprov.go.id/portal/page/ppid/395/disporapar-jateng-buku-saku
Dumarçay, J. (1991). Borobudur.
Dwyer, L., Edwards, D., Mistilis, N., Roman, C., & Scott, N. (2009). Destination and enterprise management for a tourism future. *Tourism Management, 30*(1), 63–74.
Enright, M. J., & Newton, J. (2004). Tourism destination competitiveness: a quantitative approach. *Tourism Management, 25*(6), 777–788.
Espiner, S., Orchiston, C., & Higham, J. (2017). Resilience and sustainability: A complementary relationship? Towards a practical conceptual model for the sustainability–resilience nexus in tourism. *Journal of Sustainable Tourism, 25*(10), 1385–1400.
Farrell, B. H., & Twining-Ward, L. (2004). Reconceptualizing tourism. *Annals of Tourism Research, 31*(2), 274–295.
Felicetti, G. (2016). The concept of resilience applied by local communities in protected area as Social-Economic-Ecological Systems (SEES). *Quality-Access to Success, 17*(153).
Gallopín, G. C. (2006). Linkages between vulnerability, resilience, and adaptive capacity. *Global Environmental Change, 16*(3), 293–303.
Garin-Munoz, T., & Montero-Martín, L. F. (2007). Tourism in the Balearic Islands: A dynamic model for international demand using panel data. *Tourism Management, 28*(5), 1224–1235.
Gonzalez, V. M., Coromina, L., & Gali, N. (2018). Overtourism: residents' perceptions of tourism impact as an indicator of resident social carrying capacity-case study of a Spanish heritage town. *Tourism Review*.

Han, X., & Cheer, J. M. (2018). Chinese tourist mobilities and destination resilience: Regional tourism perspectives. *Asian Journal of Tourism Research, 3*(1), 159–187.
Hegberg, N. J., & Tone, E. B. (2015). Physical activity and stress resilience: Considering those at-risk for developing mental health problems. *Mental Health and Physical Activity, 8*, 1–7.
Heinonen, K., & Medberg, G. (2018). Netnography as a tool for understanding customers: Implications for service research and practice. *Journal of Services Marketing*.
Holtorf, C. (2018). Embracing change: How cultural resilience is increased through cultural heritage. *World Archaeology, 50*(4), 639–650.
Hsu, S.-Y., Dehuang, N., & Woodside, A. G. (2009). Storytelling research of consumers' self-reports of urban tourism experiences in China. *Journal of Business Research, 62*(12), 1223–1254.
Ingulli, K., & Lindbloom, G. (2013). Connection to nature and psychological resilience. *Ecopsychology, 5*(1), 52–55.
Jackson, K. M., & Trochim, W. M. (2002). Concept mapping as an alternative approach for the analysis of open-ended survey responses. *Organizational Research Methods, 5*(4), 307–336.
Kim, H., & Marcouiller, D. W. (2015). Considering disaster vulnerability and resiliency: The case of hurricane effects on tourism-based economies. *The Annals of Regional Science, 54*(3), 945–971.
Kim, H. Y., & Yoon, J. H. (2013). Examining national tourism brand image: Content analysis of lonely planet Korea. *Tourism Review*.
King, B., & Berno, T. (2002). Tourism and civil disturbances: An evaluation of recovery strategies in Fiji 1987–2000. *Journal of Hospitality and Tourism Management, 9*(1), 46–61.
King, N., Horrocks, C., & Brooks, J. (2018). *Interviews in qualitative research*. SAGE Publications Limited.
Kladou, S., & Mavragani, E. (2015). Assessing destination image: An online marketing approach and the case of Trip Advisor. *Journal of Destination Marketing & Management, 4*(3), 187–193.
Kozinets, R. V. (2002). The field behind the screen: Using netnography for marketing research in online communities. *Journal of Marketing Research, 39*(1), 61–72.
Kozinets, R. V. (2006). Click to connect: Netnography and tribal advertising. *Journal of Advertising Research, 46*(3), 279–288.
Leach, M. (2008). Re-framing resilience: Trans-disciplinarity, reflexivity and progressive sustainability – A symposium report.
Lee, H. A., Law, R., & Murphy, J. (2011). Helpful reviewers in TripAdvisor, an online travel community. *Journal of Travel & Tourism Marketing, 28*(7), 675–688.
Leech, N. L., & Onwuegbuzie, A. J. (2011). Beyond constant comparison qualitative data analysis: Using NVivo. *School Psychology Quarterly, 26*(1), 70.
Lehto, X. Y., O'Leary, J. T., & Morrison, A. M. (2004). The effect of prior experience on vacation behavior. *Annals of Tourism Research, 31*(4), 801–818.
Lew, A. A. (2014). Scale, change and resilience in community tourism planning. *Tourism Geographies, 16*(1), 14–22.
Libai, B., Bolton, R., Bügel, M. S., De Ruyter, K., Götz, O., Risselada, H., & Stephen, A. T. (2010). Customer-to-customer interactions: Broadening the scope of word of mouth research. *Journal of Service Research, 13*(3), 267–282.
Luthe, T., & Wyss, R. (2014). Assessing and planning resilience in tourism. *Tourism Management, 44*, 161–163.
Magis, K. (2010). Community resilience: An indicator of social sustainability. *Society and Natural Resources, 23*(5), 401–416.
Maulana, A. E., & Eckhardt, G. M. (2007). Just friends, good acquaintances or soul mates? An exploration of web site connectedness. *Qualitative Market Research: An International Journal*.
Meng, F., Tepanon, Y., & Uysal, M. (2008). Measuring tourist satisfaction by attribute and motivation: The case of a nature-based resort. *Journal of Vacation Marketing, 14*(1), 41–56.
Miguéns, J., Baggio, R., & Costa, C. (2008). Social media and tourism destinations: TripAdvisor case study. *Advances in Tourism Research, 26*(28), 1–6.

Mihalič, T. (2000). Environmental management of a tourist destination: A factor of tourism competitiveness. *Tourism Management, 21*(1), 65–78.
Narayan, P. K., Narayan, S., Prasad, A., & Prasad, B. C. (2010). Tourism and economic growth: A panel data analysis for Pacific Island countries. *Tourism Economics, 16*(1), 169–183.
Nash, D., & Smith, V. L. (1989). *Hosts and guests: The anthropology of tourism*. University of Pennsylvania Press Philadelphia.
Novelli, M., Schmitz, B., & Spencer, T. (2006). Networks, clusters and innovation in tourism: A UK experience. *Tourism Management, 27*(6), 1141–1152.
Nowell, L. S., Norris, J. M., White, D. E., & Moules, N. J. (2017). Thematic analysis: Striving to meet the trustworthiness criteria. *International Journal of Qualitative Methods, 16*(1), 1609406917733847.
Onwuegbuzie, A. J., & Leech, N. L. (2007). Validity and qualitative research: An oxymoron? *Quality & Quantity, 41*(2), 233–249.
Orchiston, C., Prayag, G., & Brown, C. (2016). Organizational resilience in the tourism sector. *Annals of Tourism Research, 56*, 145–148.
Östh, J., Reggiani, A., & Galiazzo, G. (2015). Spatial economic resilience and accessibility: A joint perspective. *Computers, Environment and Urban Systems, 49*, 148–159.
Ozkan, B. C. (2004). Using NVivo to analyze qualitative classroom data on constructivist learning environments. *The Qualitative Report, 9*(4), 589–603.
Papathanassis, A., & Knolle, F. (2011). Exploring the adoption and processing of online holiday reviews: A grounded theory approach. *Tourism Management, 32*(2), 215–224.
Pike, A., Dawley, S., & Tomaney, J. (2010). Resilience, adaptation and adaptability. *Cambridge Journal of Regions, Economy and Society, 3*(1), 59–70.
Pyke, J., Law, A., Jiang, M., & de Lacy, T. (2018). Learning from the locals: The role of stakeholder engagement in building tourism and community resilience. *Journal of Ecotourism, 17*(3), 206–219.
Rageh, A., Melewar, T., & Woodside, A. (2013). Using netnography research method to reveal the underlying dimensions of the customer/tourist experience. *Qualitative Market Research: An International Journal.*
Rodríguez-Díaz, M., Rodríguez-Díaz, R., Rodríguez-Voltes, A. C., & Rodríguez-Voltes, C. I. (2018). A model of market positioning of destinations based on online customer reviews of lodgings. *Sustainability, 10*(1), 78.
Rose, A., & Krausmann, E. (2013). An economic framework for the development of a resilience index for business recovery. *International Journal of Disaster Risk Reduction, 5*, 73–83.
Rose, A., & Liao, S. Y. (2005). Modeling regional economic resilience to disasters: A computable general equilibrium analysis of water service disruptions. *Journal of Regional Science, 45*(1), 75–112.
Ruiz-Ballesteros, E. (2011). Social-ecological resilience and community-based tourism: An approach from Agua Blanca, Ecuador. *Tourism Management, 32*(3), 655–666.
Ryan, R. M., Weinstein, N., Bernstein, J., Brown, K. W., Mistretta, L., & Gagne, M. (2010). Vitalizing effects of being outdoors and in nature. *Journal of Environmental Psychology, 30*(2), 159–168.
Schianetz, K., & Kavanagh, L. (2008). Sustainability indicators for tourism destinations: A complex adaptive systems approach using systemic indicator systems. *Journal of Sustainable Tourism, 16*(6), 601–628.
Schmude, J., Zavareh, S., Schwaiger, K. M., & Karl, M. (2018). Micro-level assessment of regional and local disaster impacts in tourist destinations. *Tourism Geographies, 20*(2), 290–308.
Sherrieb, K., Norris, F. H., & Galea, S. (2010). Measuring capacities for community resilience. *Social Indicators Research, 99*(2), 227–247.
Smit, B., & Wandel, J. (2006). Adaptation, adaptive capacity and vulnerability. *Global Environmental Change, 16*(3), 282–292.
Sotiriadou, P., Brouwers, J., & Le, T.-A. (2014). Choosing a qualitative data analysis tool: A comparison of NVivo and Leximancer. *Annals of Leisure Research, 17*(2), 218–234.

Southwick, S. M., Bonanno, G. A., Masten, A. S., Panter-Brick, C., & Yehuda, R. (2014). Resilience definitions, theory, and challenges: interdisciplinary perspectives. *European Journal of Psychotraumatology, 5*(1), 25338.
Sugiharti, D., Chaiechi, T., & Josephine, P. (2021). *The role of visitor's resilience in understanding tourism resilience: A conceptual framework.* Paper presented at the transformations in uncertain time: Future perfect in tourism, hospitality and events.
Taman Wisata Candi Borobudur, P. d. R. B. (2017). Balkondes Borobudur. Retrieved from http://balkondesborobudur.com/desa-wisata/
Tovar, C., & Lockwood, M. (2008). Social impacts of tourism: An Australian regional case study. *International Journal of Tourism Research, 10*(4), 365–378.
TripAdvisor. (2019). TripAdvisor Fact Sheet. Retrieved from https://tripadvisor.mediaroom.com/au
UNESCO. (2020). Borobudur Temple Compounds. Retrieved from https://whc.unesco.org/en/list/592
Weaver, P. A., McCleary, K. W., Lapisto, L., & Damonte, L. T. (1994). The relationship of destination selection attributes to psychological, behavioral and demographic variables. *Journal of Hospitality & Leisure Marketing, 2*(2), 93–109.
Westergren, A., Edin, K., & Christianson, M. (2021). Reproducing normative femininity: Women's evaluations of their birth experiences analysed by means of word frequency and thematic analysis. *BMC Pregnancy and Childbirth, 21*(1), 1–13.
Wu, M.-Y., & Pearce, P. L. (2014). Appraising netnography: Towards insights about new markets in the digital tourist era. *Current Issues in Tourism, 17*(5), 463–474.
Xiang, Z., & Gretzel, U. (2010). Role of social media in online travel information search. *Tourism Management, 31*(2), 179–188.

Learning from the COVID-19 Pandemic: Media Representations of Responsible Coffee Tourism Practices in Indonesia

Heri Setiyorini, Tingzhen Chen, and Josephine Pryce

Abstract This paper reviews the media representations of responsible coffee tourism practices during the pandemic of COVID-19 in Indonesia. The key aim is to identify the leading actor and the themes of responsible coffee tourism practices by critically analysing the stakeholders' roles in coping with the disruption. The archival information from internet media in 2020 was collected via the Google search engine. The data were classified in three different time frames: the initial (January–April), the second midpoint (May–August), and the third midpoint (September–December). Subsequently, Leximancer was employed to assist the analysis of the collected 128 articles. The results indicated that the government institutions were the leading actors in encouraging responsible coffee tourism practices during the pandemic. Different themes of responsible coffee tourism practices emerged from the three-time periods investigated: operating business as usual, raising awareness of potential risks, and edification. The contribution of media representation to the business' learning curve is discussed. The pandemic is not over yet. Nevertheless, the first-year discourses analysis could provide some guidelines for stakeholders' future directions of managing crisis in tourism responsibly.

Keywords Responsible tourism · Coffee tourism · Pandemic · COVID-19

H. Setiyorini (✉)
James Cook University, Townsville, Australia

Universitas Pendidikan Indonesia, Bandung, Indonesia
e-mail: heri.setiyorini@upi.edu

T. Chen · J. Pryce
James Cook University, Townsville, Australia
e-mail: tingzhen.chen@jcu.edu.au; josephine.pryce@jcu.edu.au

© The Author(s), under exclusive license to Springer Nature Singapore Pte Ltd. 2022

T. Chaiechi, J. Wood (eds.), *Community Empowerment, Sustainable Cities, and Transformative Economies*, https://doi.org/10.1007/978-981-16-5260-8_18

1 Introduction

The pandemic of COVID-19 is a novel problem faced globally. In the first year of the crisis, countries relied on the Non-Pharmaceutical Interventions (NPI) program, such as social distancing, limiting people mobility, and modifying behaviour by practising health protocols (Gössling et al., 2020). The program had a significant economic impact on the tourism industry, such as on accommodation (Cai et al., 2021), restaurants (Madeira et al., 2021), MICE (Aburumman, 2020), cruise ships (Benjamin et al., 2020; Ocheni et al., 2020; Stankov et al., 2020), sports events (Borovcanin et al., 2020), and outbound tour activities (Hasenzahl & Cantoni, 2021). The tourism growth dropped to 60–80%, and the international tourists' arrival, particularly in Asia and the Pacific, plummeted to −35% (UNWTO, 2021).

The substantial impacts of the pandemic on tourism have affected many countries' economy and social condition. Hence, public policy was set up to tackle pandemic problems and the multiple impacts on the societal environment. On the other hand, the pandemic also forced the public to learn fast on mitigating the pandemic and surviving the economic crisis. This situation also created a moral dilemma for setting up the public policy agenda. Ethical values are being contested. Implementing NPI and maintaining tourism activities for economic reason were the two opposite concepts: limiting and encouraging people mobility. The pros and cons of this dilemma were also discussed by tourism scholars in the debates of boosterism and tourism reform (Higgins-Desbiolles, 2020). Boosterism is the idea of developing tourism for increasing social and economic benefits. In contrast, tourism reform focuses on pausing development, degrowth, and anti-consumerism, which is aligned with limiting people's mobility.

Coffee tourism is the context for this study. Ethical and moral practices of coffee emphasise the environmental concerns of its production and consumption. Coffee tourism is also developed with the aim to improve the local community livelihood (Lyon, 2015; Vellema et al., 2015; Woyesa & Kumar, 2020). The coffee industry has a long supply chain. Many stakeholders are involved in the coffee production from seed to cups, including the farmers, plantation owners, coffee processing services, coffee roasting facilities, retailers, cafés and the end consumers. For some small farmers, the income is insufficient for living. Hence, tourism is expected to give added value to the coffee farmers livelihood.

Further, the current pandemic is categorised as a wicked problem, which is defined by Yankelovich (2014) as those problems that are: 1) novel and unique, 2) complex and multifaceted, 3) less likely solved by the conventional method (legislation, regulation, money, power, technology), 4) requiring ample time for the learning and remedy, and 5) depending on how the problem is framed for the solution. As a public communication channel, media plays a vital role in framing the problems (Afzal, 2016). The crisis often requires public attention. Framing focuses on how a problem is expressed in news media, which may affect the way individuals perceive the problem (Scheufele & Tewksbury, 2006). Subsequently, the media and its framing can help shape the public's perception of the crisis (De Vreese, 2003 as cited in Afzal 2016; Yankelovich, 2014).

Entman (1993) specified four elements in framing: the actors involved in the issues, the causal interpretation, the moral values, and the potential solution's recommendation. The actors and the interpretation of the framing were two elements that would be discussed in this study. Hence, two research questions were developed: 1) who are the key actors in Indonesia coffee tourism during the pandemic as represented in the media discourses? 2) what are the main practices for Indonesian coffee tourism during the pandemic as a discourse in the media? Analysing the actors and the themes helps to understand the future direction in coping with the pandemic crisis.

2 Literature Review

2.1 *Defining the Responsible Coffee Tourism*

This article will take coffee tourism as an example to explore responsible practices in tourism. Coffee symbolises ethical consumption and production practices. For instance, the Fairtrade of Coffee Certification illustrates that the social construct of market-based coffee consumption can enforce the implementation of responsible practices on coffee production, such as ensuring fair prices for farmers and employees (Thompson, 2014). Subsequently, the upstream stakeholders in the coffee supply chain, such as coffee plantations and processing owners, are motivated to take responsible practices in coffee production. The spirit of stakeholders' alignment is a key for implementing responsible practices in coffee commodities.

The same spirit also exists in coffee tourism development. Yun (2014, p.35) defined coffee tourism as:

> *".. a form of commodity tourism that provides opportunities for tourists to engage in coffee experiences of all aspects in places that contain unique nature, and/or culture associated with coffee. It is not simply a combination of coffee and tourism. Coffee tourism works as a development vehicle for people or countries involved in the coffee industry. It can be conducted in both rural and urban areas while providing benefits to coffee growers and coffee workers. Coffee tourism is situated between commercial and ethical dimensions."* (Yun, 2014)

Moreover, developing coffee tourism aims to improve the local community well-being and conserve the natural environment (Lyon, 2007, 2015; Woyesa & Kumar, 2020). Accordingly, responsible tourism practices seek to improve the local community's social well-being (economically and culturally) and support environmental conservation (Carasuk et al., 2016). Responsible tourism also pays attention to the coordination of stakeholders to ensure the negative impacts of tourism development could be managed to achieve sustainability (Goodwin & Boekhold, 2010; Weeden, 2005; UNWTO, 2013).

Therefore, responsible coffee tourism describes the behaviour of stakeholders engaged in coffee experiences with the awareness and action of social and environmental concern. Coffee tourism takes place in urban and rural settings. Urban coffee tourism emphasises the coffee culture, leisure, and luxurious coffee lifestyle (Harris, 2007; Kim & Jang, 2017; Laniyonu, 2018; Montgomery, 1997; Shaker & Rath, 2018). On the other hand, rural coffee tourism links agricultural, natural, and social contexts with tourist activities (Lyon, 2015; Renard, 2011; Ricketts et al., 2004; Wang et al., 2019). Both coffee tourism settings are also subjected to practice coffee tourism development responsibly. The examples of the responsible coffee tourism research are as follows: the green practices in the city's cafés (Filimonau et al., 2019; Hicks, 2018; Jang et al., 2015), and supporting wildlife and nature conservation in rural coffee tourism (Anbalagan & Lovelock, 2014; Lyon, 2009, 2015). The pandemic brings in further scope for sustainable tourism development (Bhuiyan et al., 2020). Coffee tourism businesses responded with resilience by enticing customers to transact online and with long-term recovery and solution in mind (Opoku et al., 2021).

Coffee tourism also has the potential to connect urban and rural development. Urban-rural linkages have received more policy attention because they are seen as a way to achieve economic diversification in rural areas while still ensuring that urban areas have access to essential resources (Mayer et al., 2016). The elements of capital, goods, technology and information (Mayer et al., 2016) flow from urban to rural, and vice versa through coffee tourism. Hence, coffee tourism could contribute to the fluidity of urban and rural development (Gillen, 2016). Further, the urban-rural connection in coffee tourism can help understand the discourses' locality, such as the social, economic, political, legal, and cultural backgrounds.

2.2 *Pandemic in Indonesia & Crisis Management*

The COVID-19 virus was firstly detected in Indonesia in early March 2020. The outbreak grew exponentially afterwards. The data retrieved on 5 April 2021 stated that the curve had not flattened yet. Up until this paper is written, there were still 3712 new cases in a day found in Indonesia (Satuan Tugas Penanganan Covid 19, 2021).

The pandemic hits the Indonesian economics significantly. Indonesian statistics (BPS, 2021) reported that the economic growth plummeted to 2.07%, and the GDP per capita decreased to US$ 3911.7. Tourism, as Indonesia primary sector, is also negatively affected. Tourism development contributed as the fourth exporting income source after palm oil, coal, and oil. However, during the pandemic, tourism income dropped sharply in 2020 (CNBC Indonesia, 2020). The closing of the international flight and managing the pandemic through people mobility limitation have affected hotels, restaurants, tour operators, and destination's activities. During this crisis, the seamless coordination between the government and the citizens is proved to be the key contributor to prompt and efficient reaction (La et al., 2020). In

Indonesia, the Indonesian Ministry of Tourism and Creative Economic coordinated the public policy on tourism. The policy included monetary support and COVID-safe protocols implementation in the tourism industry. Grants were provided for tourism businesses mainly to support the operational cost, such as building and site maintenance and salary for the employees. The COVID-safe protocols and certification, known as CHSE (*Cleanliness, Health, Safety, and Environmental Sustainability*), were also established.

2.3 *Media Effects on the Public Learning Curve*

There are two important approaches to analyse media discourses: framing and representations. Media framing is to analyse how the media selects topics, issues, and information to be disseminated. Accordingly, media representation evaluates the meaning of the news or articles' topic, issues, information, and social practices. However, the outcomes of both effects are relatively similar; for example, they both function well in building destination image (Kapuściński & Richards, 2016; Santos, 2004), evaluating tourism impacts (Robertson & Rogers, 2009), and understanding tourist behaviour (Hansen, 2020; Hasenzahl & Cantoni, 2021; Li et al., 2018; Pearce et al., 2015). This paper integrates media framing and representations, mainly for understanding the actors (framing) and themes discoursed (representation).

Media shapes public opinion and learning (Yankelovich, 2014; Hansen, 2020). The public learning curve is the process of understanding complex problems and deciding the best course of action to resolve them (Yankelovich, 2011 as cited in Raisio & Vartiainen, 2015). Hence, learning contains opinion and actions. The public learning curve consists of three stages: consciousness-raising, impediments for learning or working-through process, and resolutions (Yankelovich & Elman, 2009), as shown in Fig. 1.

The stage of raising consciousness is simpler and can be done quickly, and the media is an excellent instrument at this stage (Yankelovich & Elman, 2009). In particular, the proliferation of misinformation on social media spreads faster than the coronavirus (Barua et al., 2020); however, the media also plays a significant role in stopping the spread of misinformation and educating and promoting the public to protect themselves and the community (La et al., 2020). Therefore, the two following stages are more significant but challenging as they require repetitive activities and more extended time to gain public resolution. However, through discourses in the media, the public could understand the critical impediments in their learning process. Hence, the key stakeholders might use this information to anticipate the problems and ensure the people keep climbing the learning curve.

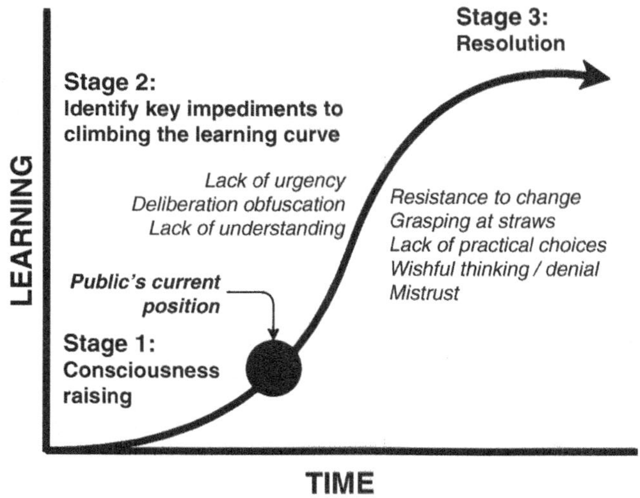

Fig. 1 Stages in public learning curve. (Source: Yankelovich & Elman, 2009)

3 Method

This was a qualitative study using a content analysis approach assisted by Leximancer. The archival information was collected from the Google search engine. The search engine is used because it can capture public opinion, intention, and social representation (de Lange & Dodds, 2017; Kornfield et al., 2015; Li et al., 2018; Moscardo, 2011; Oktadiana et al., 2020). Keywords were employed to collect archives published on the various platforms, including the cyber-news media, government and organisational websites, and blogs. The combinations of keywords in *Bahasa Indonesia* that represented the coffee tourism (*pariwisata, wisata, kopi, destinasi*), pandemic (*pandemic, corona, COVID, COVID 19*) and responsible practices (*protokol kesehatan, masyarakat, alam, lingkungan*) were applied. The time set for the query was from January to December 2020. The archives were collected between 4 February and 15 March 2021.

Subsequently, the inclusion and exclusion criteria for the archives were set. The archive information from social media, non-coffee tourism activities, letters, regulations, and coffee tourism outside Indonesia, was excluded. Moreover, the news and features from news media, such as national and local e-newspapers and e-magazines, from the government and/or organisational websites, and blogs were included. (Fig. 2)

The Leximancer was employed to assist with data analysis. Leximancer is an unsupervised software for qualitative data analysis. It is useful for exploring the textual data, particularly for finding some essential factors (Sotiriadou et al., 2014). The unit analysis was the text of the news and features in the cyber-media. The data were classified into three different periods: the initial (T1: January–April), the

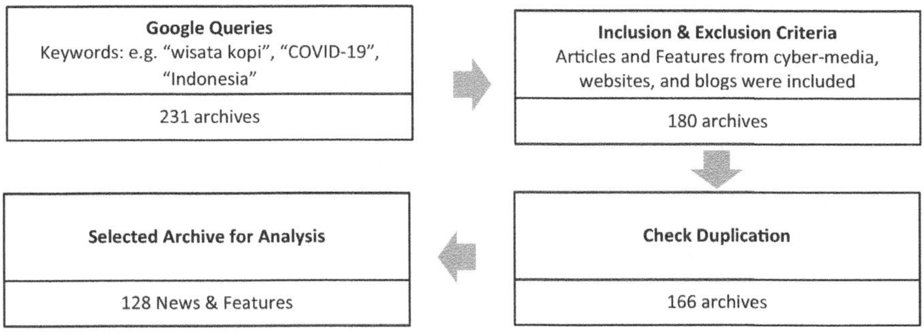

Fig. 2 Archive selection illustration

second midpoint (T2: May–August), and the third midpoint (T3: September–December). Subsequently, Leximancer examined the data within the three time periods, respectively.

The initial concept generation automatically identified some *word-like* concepts. Due to the language nature of Bahasa Indonesia, there is a need to apply a manual selection of the concepts. First of all, unmeaningful *word-like* concepts, such as conjunctions (*dan* (and), *di* (in), *ke* (to), *dari* (from), and *yang* (which, that), etc.) were removed from the automatic concept list. Secondly, the words with the same meaning were merged (e.g. *wisatawan* and *pengunjung* (tourist and visitor); *pengembangan* and *pembangunan* (growing and developing); *kementrian, kabupaten, kecamatan and pemerintah* (the ministry, municipality, and district were merged as the government (*pemerintah*)). In addition, the *user-defined concept* was also employed to add more *word-like* concepts to help capture ideas of the responsible practices, such as the economy (*ekonomi*) and nature (*alam*). The above procedures allow creating a thematic summary of Indonesian responsible coffee tourism practices in COVID-19 pandemic.

4 Result

4.1 The archive's Profile

The classification of the types of the collected archives shows they can be grouped into news (64%), features (27%), and press release (9%). News is an article that covers current events, such as everyday activities, incidents, and regulations. In comparison, features expose special issues or topics that do not have a time concern and contain deeper analysis than the news. The press release is the news disseminated by the organisation for disseminating information of new programs or initiatives.

The number of archival articles that discussed coffee tourism in the initial period (T1) was low (7%). During that period, the media focused on the new crisis. Coffee

Table 1 The archives profile

The type of article	*No. of articles*	*Percentage*	*The type of media*	*No. of articles*	*Percentage*
News	82	64%	***Cyber media***		
Features	34	27%	*e-newspaper*	92	72%
Press release	12	9%	*News portal*	10	8%
Total	**128**	**100%**	*e-magazine*	4	3%
Period	***No. of articles***	***Percentage***	**Institutional websites**		
Initial (T1)	9	7%	*Government*	8	6%
2nd MP (T2)	41	32%	*Organisation*	9	7%
3rd MP (T3)	78	61%	*Personal blog*	5	4%
Total	**128**	**100%**	**Total**	**128**	**100%**

tourism might not be affected as much as other sectors, such as the aviation and the hotel industry, where the press intensively exposed. The coffee tourism archival information gradually increased during the second (32%) and third midpoint (61%) periods.

Most of the archival articles were found in the cyber media (83%): e-newspaper, news portal, and e-magazine. The news portal is the convergent platform that also has internet TV and e-newspaper. There were also small portions of institutional websites (17%), such as government and organisation, as well as personal blogs archives. (Table 1)

4.2 The Actors of the Discourses

Manual coding was applied to understand the actors discoursed on the archival information. The actors were categorised as academics, government, coffee association, tourism businesses, local community, and public opinion. An article could contain one to six actors. In summary, the government was mentioned in 76 out of 128 (59%) articles, followed by tourism businesses (43%), coffee association (24%) and local community (24%), public opinion/journalists (20%), and academics (8%). The result is displayed in Fig. 3.

The government was derived from such terms: The Ministry of Tourism and Creative Economy, The Ministry of Foreign Affairs, The Regional Offices (*Dinas, Pemerintah Daerah*) at the Provincial Level, Municipality (*Kabupaten*) and District (*Kecamatan*) Level. Those terms represented several institutions from national to regional levels. The government played a role in disseminating information about programs and developing coffee tourism during the pandemic. For instance, the Ministry of Tourism and Creative Economic launched the "Cleanliness, Health, and Sustainable Environment (CHSE) Standardisation and Certification" campaign. Some articles also use coffee tourism development as the materials for their political

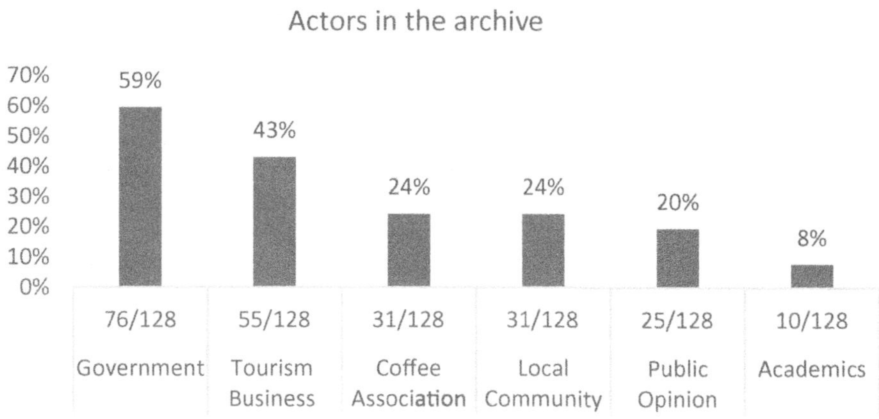

Fig. 3 Actors discoursed in the archive

campaign and public relations. For example, one of the regional leader candidates had a plan to develop coffee tourism to improve the local community's well-being.

4.3 *Thematic Summary from Leximancer*

Leximancer provides a heat map to display the themes and related concepts for the textual analysis. The cluster of the *word-like* concepts was derived from the algorithms and words co-occurrence from the archive. The analysis employed 100% visibility of the concepts and 50% theme size. The visibility and size helped to display the dominant themes. The concepts that often appear together in the text are close to each other on the map. The concepts are grouped as a theme according to their context. The themes have different colours on the map. The hot colours (red and orange) represent the most important themes.

In comparison, the cool colours (blue and green) describe the least important themes. The interpretation process involved understanding the social and cultural context of Indonesia. The analysis of the thematic summary maps from the three periods is as followed:

4.3.1 The Initial Time Themes (T1)

The themes that appeared in the early time of the pandemic (January – April 2020) encompassed coffee (*kopi*), East Nusa Tenggara (*NTT*), farmer (*petani*), community (*masyarakat*), Pontianak, and corona. Coffee was the most important theme shown in that bubble.

Further, based on the social-cultural interpretation, the textual themes indicated three meaning: the responsible coffee tourism practices, the region, and the pandemic discourse. First, the responsible coffee tourism practices were described by the path drawn from the red colour bubble. The path showed the connection between concepts and theme. The line was drawn to link the concepts of coffee (*kopi*), tour (*wisata*), village (*desa*), and community (*masyarakat),* and nature (*alam*). The connection indicates that coffee tourism has strong linkages to village, community, and nature. It also explained the responsible coffee tourism practice on the social aspects ("community" and "village") and natural environment ("nature") (Carasuk et al., 2016).

Second, the region was described by the name of two areas: East Nusa Tenggara (NTT) and Pontianak. NTT is a small island group in the southern part of Indonesia. In contrast, Pontianak is a city in Kalimantan, the largest island in the northern part of Indonesia. NTT has a famous specialty coffee and more coffee plantations than Pontianak. The articles described how coffee production could leverage the local community well-being in NTT. This notion also contributed to the economic aspects of responsible coffee tourism practices (Carasuk et al., 2016). In addition, the articles that contained Pontianak discussed the coffee culture and lifestyle in that area.

The two different regional characteristics indicated the growing number of regions of coffee tourism destination and new potential resources for coffee tourism: the physical and cultural coffee resources. This finding may contribute to the notion of associating coffee as a food consumption with the cultural capital (Mkono et al., 2013).

Third, the term related to the pandemic, "corona", was found in the purple bubble. The track of the concepts showed its connection with tour (*wisata*). Purple represents the cool colour or less important topic. It showed that the notion of the pandemic had already been exposed in the discourses. Hence, people might have cancelled their tour (*wisata*) to the coffee destinations due to mobility restrictions.

The thematic summary of the initial period is described in Fig. 4 (English explanation is provided in Table 2).

4.3.2 The Second Midpoint Themes (T2)

The themes emerged in the second midpoint include: pandemic (*pandemik*), coffee (*kopi*), tour (*wisata*), health (*kesehatan*), community (*masyarakat*), tourists (*wisatawan*), and together (*bersama*). The most important theme in the second midpoint (T2) was the pandemic (*pandemic*). The link between coffee tourism and pandemic was prevalent in this period. The path connected coffee (*kopi*), Indonesia, tourism (*pariwisata*), pandemic to COVID and health (*kesehatan*), as well as to community (*masyarakat*). The conncection of coffee, tourism, pandemic and "community" represented the social aspects of responsible coffee tourism practices. Moreover, the "health" concept is also found in another path. This concept extended the notion of responsible coffee practices during the pandemic. "Community" and

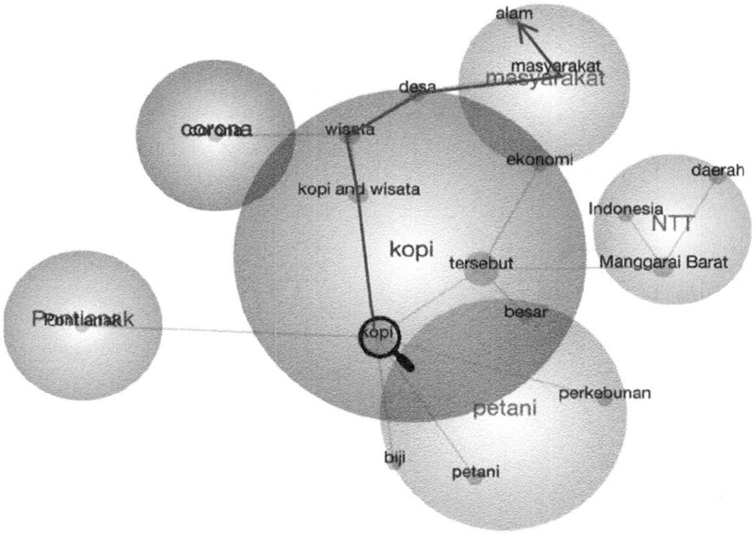

Fig. 4 Thematic summary of initial period (T1)

Table 2 The English explanation of the themes and concepts in Fig. 4

No	Color	Theme	Concept
1	●	*Kopi* (coffee)	*Desa* (rural area or village), *wisata* (tour), *kopi dan wisata* (coffee and tour), *tersebut* (aforemention)
2	●	*NTT* = Nusa Tenggara Timur (East Nusa Tenggara)	*Manggarai Barat* (West Manggarai, a district in East Nusa Tenggara), Indonesia, *daerah* (region)
3	●	*Petani* (farmer)	*Perkebunan* (plantations), *besar* (big, significant), *biji* (bean)
4	●	*Masyarakat* (community)	*Alam* (nature)
5	●	*Pontianak*	*Pontianak* (name of capital city for West Kalimantan)
6	●	*Corona*	Corona

"health" become the highlight of implementing responsible tourism during the pandemic.

Another interesting finding was observed in the connection of the pandemic, tourism, Indonesia, coffee, coffee association (*komunitas*), and together (*bersama*). This linkage indicated that the possibility of collaboration ("together") between tourism stakeholders with the coffee association was stronger during the pandemic.

The thematic summary of the second midpoint (T2) is described in Fig. 5. (Table 3)

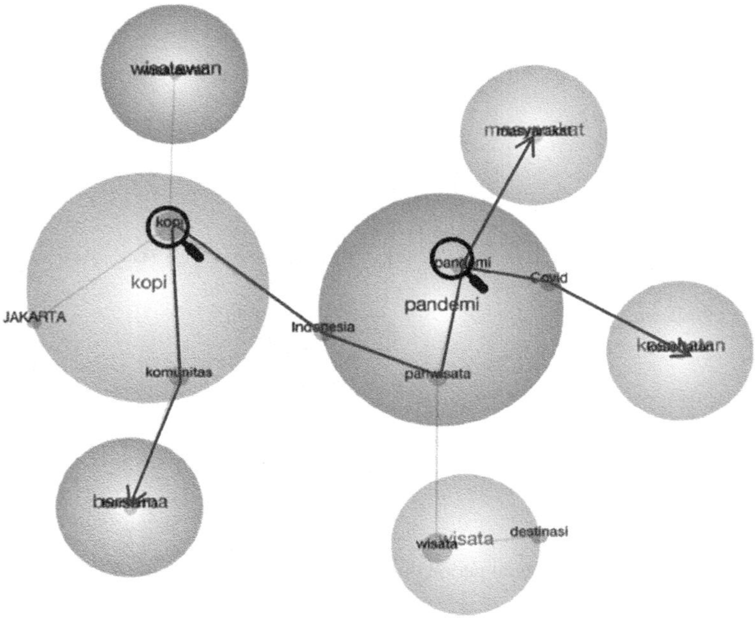

Fig. 5 Thematic summary of the second midpoint (T2)

Table 3 The English explanation of the themes and concepts in Fig. 5

No	Color	Theme	Concept
1	●	*Pandemi* (pandemic)	*Pariwisata* (tourism)*, COVID, pandemic, Indonesia*
2	●	*Kopi* (coffee)	*Kopi, komunitas* (society club)*, Jakarta* (capital city of Indonesia)
3	●	*Wisata* (tour)	*Wisata* (tour)*, destinasi* (destination)
4	●	*Kesehatan* (health)	*Kesehatan* (health)
5	●	*Bersama* (together)	*Bersama* (together)
6	●	*Wisatawan* (tourist)	*Wisatawan* (tourist)

4.3.3 The Third Midpoint Themes (T3)

There are five themes emerged during the third midpoint time period: tour (*wisata*), coffee (*kopi*), Indonesia, tidak (*no*), and pandemic; and these five themes are surrounded with a richer set of concepts, compared to that in T1 and T2. The most important theme in the third mid point (T3) is tourism (*wisata*). The map showed three interesting paths: 1) coffee (*kopi*), community (*masyarakat*), many (*banyak*), and new (*baru*); 2) coffee, community, many, no (*tidak*), visitor (*pengunjung*); 3) coffee, community, many, no, us (*kita*), COVID, pandemic, and economy. The first path indicated that there were new coffee tourism destinations in the community. Some articles showed the topic of launching a new coffee tourism destination.

The second path extended the first path to include the negative expression (no) and visitor. This path indicated that the responsible action was connected with the community and limited the number of visitors at the destination. The third path shows the relationship between responsible coffee tourism practices and the pandemic, which is represented by the link between the terms of community and economy. The thematic summary of the third midpoint (T3) is described in Fig. 6. (Table 4)

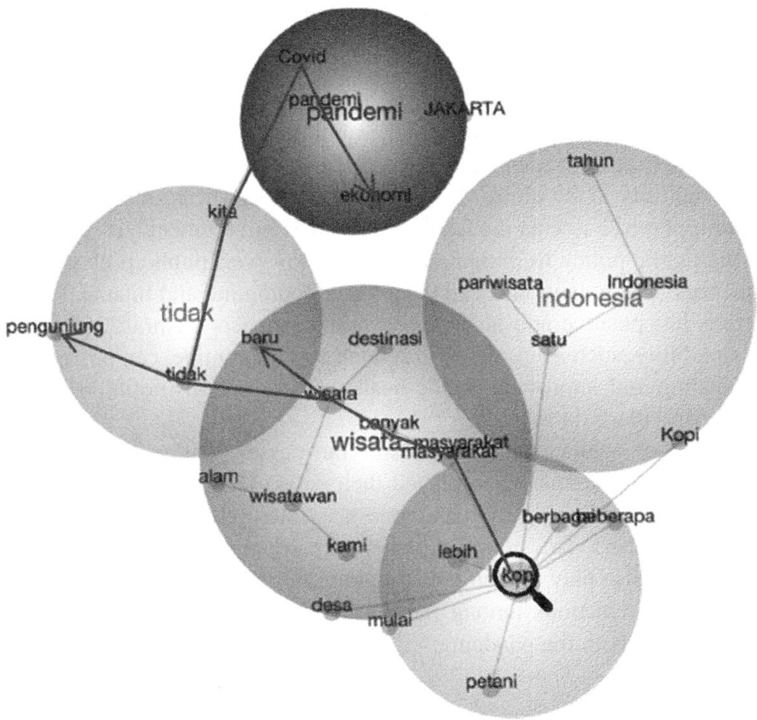

Fig. 6 Thematic summary of the third mid point (T3)

Table 4 The English explanation of the themes and concepts in Fig. 6

No	Color	Theme	Concept
1	●	*Wisata* (tour)	*Wisata* (tour), *destinasi* (destinasi), *banyak* (banyak), *masyarakat* (masyarakat), *desa* (rural, village), *kami* (us), *wisatawan* (tourist), *alam* (nature).
2	●	*Kopi* (coffee)	*Kopi* (coffee), *berbagai* (various), *beberapa* (several), *petani* (farmer), *mulai* (start)
4	●	Indonesia	Satu (one), pariwisata (tourism), tahun (year), kopi (coffee)
5	●	*Tidak* (no)	Tidak (no), pengunjung (visitor), kita (us)
6	●	*Pandemi* (pandemic)	Pandemic, COVID, *ekonomi* (economy), Jakarta

5 Discussion

5.1 Key Actor of Responsible Coffee Tourism Discourse During the Pandemic

The pandemic is categorised as a wicked problem that requires some time to solve. It is challenging to accelerate public learning to tackle the problems (Raisio & Vartiainen, 2015). However, the community, businesses, government, and tourists are forced to learn fast to anticipate these problems. Media is the sources that can help to facilitate information and public learning. As the way media presents the news, media framing is used to analyse the media effectiveness in delivering this information. Hence, knowing the actors who speak on the news contributes to understanding how the media framed the information. The credentials of actors in the discourses are important, particularly in building trust and attract public participation. The source of credentials can come from expertise (Thon & Jucks, 2017), power or authority, and culture (Denner et al., 2019). The results showed that the government played a role as the leading actor. The government has the authority to set out the public policy to mitigate the crisis. However, public policy comes with consequences. The policy on social distancing, quarantine and financial support for the citizens has positive and negative economic impacts (Ashraf, 2020). Limiting people's mobility, such as in social distancing and quarantine, can prevent the virus from spreading and improving public health. However, this notion will affect the economy, particularly in tourism.

Further, other actors, such as tourism businesses, coffee associations, local community, and academics, also played their roles. The findings showed how the public policy for mitigating the pandemic was interpreted and reproduced by the social group members. This notion explains the particular relevance of discourse that the social actors also play in their constructions and reproduction (Van Dijk, 1998). Therefore, the interactions among the social groups could enhance the learning process in coping with the pandemic.

5.2 The Themes of Responsible Coffee Tourism Practices During the Pandemic

The Leximancer result identified different themes in three defined period: coffee, pandemic, and tour. This finding also indicated the learning curve of implementing the responsible coffee tourism practice as illustrated in Fig. 7.

The discourse showed how the coffee tourism stakeholders learnt to practice responsible tourism. During the first period (T1), coffee tourism was treated as a usual business. The awareness of the crisis during the first period was low. However, the sense of crisis increased significantly in the second period (T2), indicating awareness of the problem. Tourism public policy was developed to mitigate the

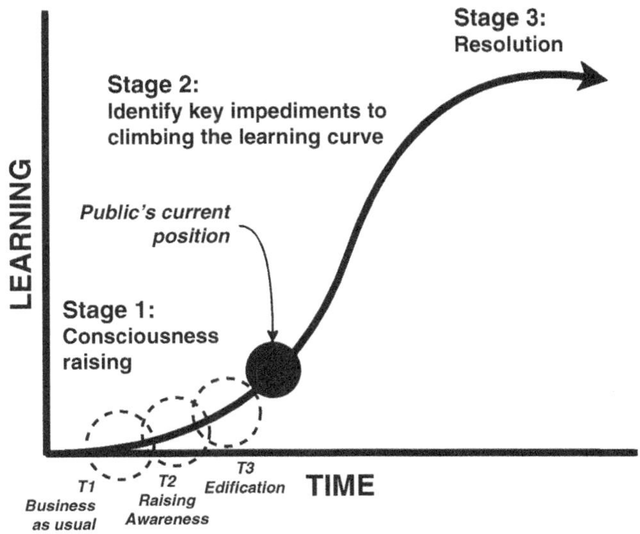

Fig. 7 The learning curve of responsible coffee tourism practices. (Source: Adapted from Yankelovich & Elman, 2009)

pandemic crisis. The pandemic also remained in discourse in the third period (T3), but tourism has become the main topic of discussion.

(a) *Coffee Theme: Business as Usual and Boosterism*

Coffee was the main theme in the first period (T1). The media discoursed the benefits of developing coffee tourism for local communities, farmers, rural development, and the natural environment. The coffee-producing (NTT) and non-producing region (Pontianak) showed opportunities to develop coffee tourism. The discourses showed exploration of coffee tourism that was developed based on the current agricultural and cultural resources. Therefore, in this period, coffee tourism was discussed akin to business as usual. The public has not considered COVID 19 as a pandemic yet. It was shown by the word "Corona" that had been frequently used in the discourse rather than the pandemic.

Coffee tourism is not like other tourism sectors directly affected by COVID-19, such as the airlines industry (Albers & Rundshagen, 2020; Tisdall & Zhang, 2020) and accommodation businesses (Bonfanti et al., 2021; Wong et al., 2021; Yang et al., 2020). The focus on coping with the pandemic was still limited during the initial period, as explained above. Hence, the result from the first period emphasised the practice of responsible coffee tourism development for improving the community livelihood and environmental conservation (Carasuk et al., 2016).

(b) *Pandemic and Raising Awareness: Adjusting Boosterism*

The pandemic was an essential theme in the second period (T2). The coffee and tourism industry has been affected significantly. The media also discoursed the connection between pandemic, tourism, coffee, and togetherness. It indicated collaboration among stakeholders in mitigating the crisis. Moreover, health appeared as a theme. It signified the importance of health concern in conducting tourism responsibly.

The pandemic disrupted coffee consumption and production. Cafés and coffee houses are associated with the people' third-place, where most people find more joy to drink coffee outside their first and second places, the home and workspace (Bookman, 2014; Hickman, 2013; Manzo, 2015). Pandemic prevented the occasions at the cafes and coffee houses; hence it affected coffee consumption. The price of coffee bean has plummeted because of the closing of cafés and the disruption of exporting goods.

Further, the media discoursed that the government introduced a virtual coffee tour in Jakarta during the second period. The virtual tour connects some coffee places and coffee culture in Jakarta, the capital city of Indonesia – a vibrant and metropolitan city. Later, the virtual coffee story could also encourage visits to a coffee plantation in a rural area. This notion strengthens the fluidity of the urban-rural context (Gillen, 2016).

City people are the potential market for rural coffee tourism. On the other hand, farmers are also the market for coffee festivals held in the city. The capital flows from the city to rural areas and vice versa; for instance, investment for coffee plantation comes from the city. Conversely, farmers open distribution channels in the city to suffice the needs of cafes and expand the markets. Some cafés provide coffee plantation ornaments and send their baristas to rural areas to get the coffee story to tell the visitors. Hence, the cafes do not only bring the countryside atmosphere for their coffee scape, but also the narratives. Moreover, the strong connection of urban and rural development in coffee tourism also encourages the boosterism approach.

(c) *Tour and Edification: Enhanced Responsible Practices*

Tour was the main theme in the third period (T3). The media discussed coffee and tourism more frequently. The boosterism approach for coffee tourism was also strong in this period. New coffee tourism destinations have been launched. The interesting part was that the theme of limiting visitor ("no" and "visitor" concepts) also emerged. It implies that responsible practice has enhanced to not only considering the number of tourist's arrival at the destination, but also the health concern for the community.

In the 2020–2024 Strategic Plan, the Indonesian Ministry of Tourism and Creative Economy started to focus on the quality of tourism (Kemenparekraf, 2020). The focus refers to improving the quality of tourist experience and quality of life of the local people. Subsequently, the measurement for tourism performance of the destination does not only depend on the number of tourist's arrival. Hence, limiting the number of tourists might also become a part of responsible practices for measuring the destination performance.

The learning curve has been escalated from awareness to edification, where more considerate practices implemented to adjust the boosterism approach. However, this approach may contradict the previous policy of limiting people mobility to prevent the virus spread. Implementing boosterism during the pandemic was contested as the irresponsible capitalism practice (Higgins-Desbiolles, 2020; Spinks in Hudson, 2020 p. 53).

The government endeavoured to find a win-win solution by implementing ethical concerns, such as emphasising health and community consideration. The government introduced the Cleanliness, Health, Safety, and Environment Sustainability (CHSE) standardisation certification programs for tourism stakeholders.

The CHSE program enables tourism businesses to run the operation if they meet the standard requirements, such as providing a clean environment, managing the visitor capacity, and the concern for the local community. The certification serves as both business practice recognition and a message to tourist. Hence, putting ethical concern in the business process can be seen as a part of *enlightened capitalism* (Yankelovich 2014).

One of the regional Government also launched a mobile application that compiles data of CHSE certified tourism businesses. Later, the tourists can access this information for their consideration before visiting places. This certification also represented the responsible marketing practices to tourists because it provides information about the risk and how to anticipate it.

This result also showed how the government's intervention to help tourism businesses survive during the pandemic. However, the intervention needs collective participation from stakeholders to run the tourism development responsibly. The notion of responsibility needs more than just being "aware". It requires collaborative action to participate in responsible tourism (Goodwin & Francis, 2003).

The recovery of the impact on the pandemic is still in process. The public has not come to the resolution stage yet. However, the discourses show that the public has learned to adjust to the disruption.

6 Conclusion

This study explored the discourse of responsible coffee tourism practices in Indonesia in the COVID 19 pandemic. The research was based on 128 articles on Indonesia internet archive information, particularly on the news, features, press release, and blogs. The first objective of this research is to analyse the actors in the discourse. The government played as the leading actor in the discourse. It represents the importance of authority and power to set priority in tackling wicked problems. Tourism is also their priority to secure the economic wheel is running. The responsible practices, such as implementing COVID-safe standardisation and certification protocols, were implemented. The second objective is to investigate the themes of the discourses. The different theme in each period showed the climbing of the public learning curve. The dimension of responsible coffee tourism practices was extended by including the "health" concern, after the natural environment, social, and economic dimensions.

Understanding how the media used the actors to frame the priority information and how the media represented the responsible coffee tourism themes during the pandemic also taught *enlightened capitalism.* This kind of capitalism articulated the ethical practices to balance the economic objectives (Yankelovich, 2014). The key limitation of this research lies in its single analytical context, namely a specific tourism form – coffee tourism. The future research may explore more discourses in a broad tourism context and evaluate how to measure the tourism policy effectiveness and the responsible practices in tourism during this pandemic.

References

Aburumman, A. A. (2020). COVID-19 impact and survival strategy in business tourism market: The example of the UAE MICE industry. *Humanities and Social Sciences Communications, 7*(1), 141. https://doi.org/10.1057/s41599-020-00630-8.

Afzal, N. (2016). Elements of pathos and media framing as scientific discourse: A newspaper perspective on Rohingya crisis. *International Journal of Advanced and Applied Sciences, 3*(10), 89–99. https://doi.org/10.21833/ijaas.2016.10.014.

Albers, S., & Rundshagen, V. (2020). European airlines' strategic responses to the COVID-19 pandemic (January-May, 2020). *Journal of Air Transport Management, 87*(June), 101863. https://doi.org/10.1016/j.jairtraman.2020.101863

Anbalagan, K., & Lovelock, B. (2014). The potential for coffee tourism development in Rwanda – Neither black nor white. *Tourism and Hospitality Research, 14*(2), 81–96. https://doi.org/10.1177/1467358414529579.

Ashraf, B. N. (2020). Economic impact of government interventions during the COVID-19 pandemic: International evidence from financial markets. *Journal of Behavioral and Experimental Finance, 27*, 100371. https://doi.org/10.1016/j.jbef.2020.100371.

Barua, Z., Barua, S., Aktar, S., Kabir, N., & Li, M. (2020). Effects of misinformation on COVID-19 individual responses and recommendations for resilience of disastrous consequences of misinformation. *Progress in Disaster Science, 8*. https://doi.org/10.1016/j.pdisas.2020.100119.

Benjamin, S., Dillette, A., & Alderman, D. H. (2020). "We can't return to normal": Committing to tourism equity in the post-pandemic age. *Tourism Geographies, 22*(3), 476–483. https://doi.org/10.1080/14616688.2020.1759130.

Bhuiyan, M. A. H., Hassan, S., Darda, A., & Habib, M. W. (2020). *Aspects of sustainable tourism development and COVID-19 pandemic*. August: Preprints. www.preprints.org.

Bonfanti, A., Vigolo, V., & Yfantidou, G. (2021). The impact of the Covid-19 pandemic on customer experience design: The hotel managers' perspective. *International Journal of Hospitality Management, 94*, 102871–. https://doi.org/10.1016/j.ijhm.2021.102871

Bookman, S. (2014). Brands and urban life: Specialty coffee, consumers, and the co-creation of urban café sociality. *Space and Culture, 17*(1), 85–99. https://doi.org/10.1177/1206331213493853.

Borovcanin, D., Cuk, I., Lesjak, M., & Juvan, E. (2020). The importance of sport event on hotel performance for restarting tourism after COVID-19. *Societies, 10*(4), 90. https://doi.org/10.3390/soc10040090.

Badan Pusat Statistik (BPS). (2021, February 5). *Pertumbuhan Ekonomi Indonesia Triwulan IV 2020* [Berita Resmi Statistik] (Indonesia Economic Growth 4th Quarter 2020, [Press Release]). https://www.bps.go.id/pressrelease/2021/02/05/1811/ekonomi-indonesia-2020-turun-sebesar-2-07-persen--c-to-c-.html

Cai, G., Hong, Y., Xu, L., Gao, W., Wang, K., & Chi, X. (2021). An evaluation of green ryokans through a tourism accommodation survey and customer-satisfaction-related casbee–ipa after COVID-19 pandemic. *Sustainability (Switzerland), 13*(1), 1–24. https://doi.org/10.3390/su13010145.

Carasuk, R., Becken, S., & Hughey, K. F. D. (2016). Exploring values, drivers, and barriers as antecedents of implementing responsible tourism. *Journal of Hospitality and Tourism Research, 40*(1), 19–36. https://doi.org/10.1177/1096348013491607.

CNBC Indonesia. (2020). Kemenparekraf Sebut Devisa Wisata 2020 Hanya Mencapai USD 3 M., *CNBC Indonesia*, 01.11.2020, Broadcast Network.

de Lange, D., & Dodds, R. (2017). Increasing sustainable tourism through social entrepreneurship. *International Journal of Contemporary Hospitality Management, 29*(7), 1977–2002. https://doi.org/10.1108/IJCHM-02-2016-0096.

Denner, J., Bean, S., Campe, S., Martinez, J., & Torres, D. (2019). Negotiating trust, power, and culture in a research–practice partnership. *AERA Open, 5*(2), 233285841985863. https://doi.org/10.1177/2332858419858635

Entman, R. M. (1993). Framing: Toward clarification of a fractured paradigm. *Journal of Communication, 43*(4), 51–58. https://doi.org/10.1111/j.1460-2466.1993.tb01304.x

Filimonau, V., Krivcova, M., & Pettit, F. (2019). An exploratory study of managerial approaches to food waste mitigation in coffee shops. *International Journal of Hospitality Management, 76*, 48–57. https://doi.org/10.1016/j.ijhm.2018.04.010.

Gillen, J. (2016). Bringing the countryside to the city: Practices and imaginations of the rural in Ho Chi Minh City, Vietnam. *Urban Studies, 53*(2), 324–337. https://doi.org/10.1177/0042098014563031.

Goodwin, H., & Boekhold, H. (2010). Beyond fair trade: Enhancing the livelihoods of coffee farmers in Tanzania. In L. Jolliffe (Ed.), *Coffee culture, destination, and tourism* (pp. 181–196). Channel View Publications.

Goodwin, H., & Francis, J. (2003). Ethical and responsible tourism: Consumer trends in the UK. *Journal of Vacation Marketing, 9*(3), 271–284. https://doi.org/10.1177/135676670300900306.

Gössling, S., Scott, D., & Hall, C. M. (2020). Pandemics, tourism and global change: A rapid assessment of COVID-19. *Journal of Sustainable Tourism, 29*(1), 1–20. https://doi.org/10.1080/09669582.2020.1758708.

Hansen, T. (2020). Media framing of Copenhagen tourism: A new approach to public opinion about tourists. *Annals of Tourism Research, 84*, 102975. https://doi.org/10.1016/j.annals.2020.102975.

Harris, C. (2007). Libraries with lattes: The new third place. *Australasian Public Libraries and Information Services, 20*(4), 145.

Hasenzahl, L., & Cantoni, L. (2021). "Old" and "new" media discourses on Chinese outbound tourism to Switzerland before and during the COVID-19 outbreak. An exploratory study lea. *Information and Communication Technologies in Tourism, 2021*, 530–542. https://doi.org/10.1007/978-3-030-65785-7.

Hickman, P. (2013). "Third places" and social interaction in deprived neighbourhoods in Great Britain. *Journal of Housing and the Built Environment, 28*(2), 221–236. https://doi.org/10.1007/s10901-012-9306-5.

Hicks, A. L. (2018). Environmental implications of consumer convenience: Coffee as a case study. *Journal of Industrial Ecology, 22*(1), 79–91. https://doi.org/10.1111/jiec.12487.

Higgins-Desbiolles, F. (2020). The "war over tourism": Challenges to sustainable tourism in the tourism academy after COVID-19. *Journal of Sustainable Tourism, 29*(4), 551–569. https://doi.org/10.1080/09669582.2020.1803334.

Hudson, S. (2020). COVID-19 and travel: Impacts, responses and outcomes. ProQuest Ebook Central https://ebookcentral.proquest.com

Jang, Y. J., Kim, W. G., & Lee, H. Y. (2015). Coffee shop consumers' emotional attachment and loyalty to green stores: The moderating role of green consciousness. *International Journal of Hospitality Management, 44*, 146–156. https://doi.org/10.1016/j.ijhm.2014.10.001.

Kapuściński, G., & Richards, B. (2016). News framing effects on destination risk perception. *Tourism Management, 57*, 234–244. https://doi.org/10.1016/j.tourman.2016.06.017.

Kemenparekraf. (2020). Rencana Strategis Kemenparekraf/Baparekraf 2020–2024 (*The Strategic Plan of The Ministry/The Council of Tourism and Creative Economy 2020–2024).* Kemenparekraf, 1–136. https://www.kemenparekraf.go.id/asset_admin/assets/uploads/media/pdf/media_1598887965_Rencana_strategis_2020-2024.pdf

Kim, D., & Jang, S. (Shawn). (2017). Symbolic consumption in upscale cafés: Examining Korean gen Y consumers' materialism, conformity, conspicuous tendencies, and functional qualities. *Journal of Hospitality and Tourism Research, 41*(2), 154–179. https://doi.org/10.1177/1096348014525633.

Kornfield, R., Smith, K. C., Szczypka, G., Vera, L., & Emery, S. (2015). Earned media and public engagement with CDC's "tips from former smokers" campaign: An analysis of online news and blog coverage. *Journal of Medical Internet Research, 17*(1), e12. https://doi.org/10.2196/jmir.3645.

La, V. P., Pham, T. H., Ho, M. T., Nguyen, M. H., Nguyen, K. L. P., Vuong, T. T., Nguyen, H. K. T., Tran, T., Khuc, Q., Ho, M. T., & Vuong, Q. H. (2020). Policy response, social media and science journalism for the sustainability of the public health system amid the COVID-19 outbreak: The Vietnam lessons. *Sustainability (Switzerland), 12*(7). https://doi.org/10.3390/su12072931.

Laniyonu, A. (2018). Coffee shops and street stops: Policing practices in gentrifying Neighborhoods. *Urban Affairs Review, 54*(5), 898–930. https://doi.org/10.1177/1078087416689728.

Li, J., Pearce, P. L., & Low, D. (2018). Media representation of digital-free tourism: A critical discourse analysis. *Tourism Management, 69*(June), 317–329. https://doi.org/10.1016/j.tourman.2018.06.027.

Lyon, S. (2007). Fair trade coffee and human rights in Guatemala. *Journal of Consumer Policy, 30*(3), 241–261. https://doi.org/10.1007/s10603-007-9040-7.

Lyon, S. (2009). "What good will two more trees do?" the political economy of sustainable coffee certification, local livelihoods and identities. *Landscape Research, 34*(2), 223–240. https://doi.org/10.1080/01426390802390673.

Lyon, S. (2015). Coffee tourism and community development in Guatemala. *Human Organization, 72*(3), 188–198. https://doi.org/10.17730/humo.72.3.0011g4xj1m83x68j.

Madeira, A., Palrão, T., & Mendes, A. S. (2021). The impact of pandemic crisis on the restaurant business. *Sustainability (Switzerland), 13*(1), 1–13. https://doi.org/10.3390/su13010040.

Manzo, J. (2015). "Third-wave" coffeehouses as venues for sociality: On encounters between employees and customers. *The Qualitative Report, 20*(6). https://doi.org/10.1007/978-1-4615-2373-4.

Mayer, H., Habersetzer, A., & Meili, R. (2016). Rural-urban linkages and sustainable regional development: The role of entrepreneurs in linking peripheries and centers. *Sustainability (Switzerland), 8*(8). https://doi.org/10.3390/su8080745.

Mkono, M., Markwell, K., & Wilson, E. (2013). Applying Quan and Wang's structural model of the tourist experience: A Zimbabwean netnography of food tourism. *Tourism Management Perspectives, 5*, 68–74. https://doi.org/10.1016/j.tmp.2012.10.007.

Montgomery, J. (1997). Cafe culture and the city: The role of pavement cafes in urban public social life. *Journal of Urban Design, 2*(1), 83–102. https://doi.org/10.1080/13574809708724397.

Moscardo, G. (2011). Exploring social representations of tourism planning: Issues for governance. *Journal of Sustainable Tourism, 19*(4–5), 423–436. https://doi.org/10.1080/09669582.2011.558625.

Ocheni, S. I., Agba, A. M. O., Agba, M. S., & Eteng, F. O. (2020). COVID-19 and the tourism industry: Critical overview, lessons and policy options. *Academic Journal of Interdisciplinary Studies, 9*(6), 114. https://doi.org/10.36941/ajis-2020-0116.

Oktadiana, H., Pearce, P. L., & Li, J. (2020). Let's travel: Voices from the millennial female Muslim travellers. *International Journal of Tourism Research*. https://doi.org/10.1002/jtr.2355.

Opoku, E. K., Wang, S. M.-J., & Muñoz, K. E. (2021). A better brew: COVID-19 and sustainable outcomes for coffee tourism in Ali mountain, Taiwan. *Journal of Responsible Tourism Management, 1*(1), 71–87. https://doi.org/10.47263/jrtm.01-01-06.

Pearce, P. L., Wu, M. Y., & Chen, T. (2015). The spectacular and the mundane: Chinese tourists' online representations of an iconic landscape journey. *Journal of Destination Marketing and Management, 4*(1), 24–35. https://doi.org/10.1016/j.jdmm.2014.11.001.

Raisio, H., & Vartiainen, P. (2015). Accelerating the public's learning curve on wicked policy issues: Results from deliberative forums on euthanasia. *Policy Sciences, 48*(3 (September 2015)), 339–361. https://doi.org/10.1007/s11077-015-9221-1.

Renard, M. C. (2011). Chapter 5: Free trade of coffee, exodus of coffee workers: The case of the Southern Mexican border region of the state of Chiapas. *Research in Rural Sociology and Development, 17*, 147–165. https://doi.org/10.1108/S1057-1922(2011)0000017008.

Ricketts, T. H., Daily, G. C., Ehrlich, P. R., & Michener, C. D. (2004). Economic value of tropical forest to coffee production Can economic forces be harnessed for biodiversity conservation? *PNAS, 101*(34), 12579–12582. www.pnas.org/cgi/doi/10.1073/pnas.0405147101.

Robertson, M., & Rogers, P. (2009). Festivals, cooperative stakeholders and the role of the media: A case analysis of newspaper media. *Scandinavian Journal of Hospitality and Tourism, 9*(2–3), 206–224. https://doi.org/10.1080/15022250903217019.

Santos, C. A. (2004). Framing Portugal representational dynamics. *Annals of Tourism Research, 31*(1), 122–138. https://doi.org/10.1016/j.annals.2003.08.005.

Satuan Tugas Penanganan COVID-19. (2021, April). *Peta Sebaran COVID-19*. https://covid19.go.id/peta-sebarancovid19

Scheufele, D. A., & Tewksbury, D. (2006). Framing, agenda setting, and priming: The evolution of three media effects models. *Journal of Communication, 56*(4), 864–866. https://doi.org/10.1111/j.1460-2466.2006.00326.x.

Shaker, R., & Rath, J. (2018). *The coffee scene in Glasgow's West End: On the class practices of the new urban middle classes*. doi:https://doi.org/10.1016/j.ccs.2018.08.001.

Sotiriadou, P., Brouwers, J., & Le, T. A. (2014). Choosing a qualitative data analysis tool: A comparison of NVivo and Leximancer. *Annals of Leisure Research, 17*(2), 218–234. https://doi.org/10.1080/11745398.2014.902292.

Stankov, U., Filimonau, V., & Vujičić, M. D. (2020). A mindful shift: An opportunity for mindfulness-driven tourism in a post-pandemic world. *Tourism Geographies, 22*(3), 1–10. https://doi.org/10.1080/14616688.2020.1768432.

Thompson, C. (2014). Ethical consumerism as a human rights enforcement mechanism: The coffee cultivation model. *Transnational Law & Contemporary Problems, 24*, 161–192. http://www.ilo.org/dyn/normlex/en/f?p=NORMLEXPUB:11001:0::NO.

Thon, F. M., & Jucks, R. (2017). Believing in expertise: How authors' credentials and language use influence the credibility of online health information. *Health Communication, 32*(7), 828–836. https://doi.org/10.1080/10410236.2016.1172296

Tisdall, L., & Zhang, Y. (2020). Preparing for 'COVID-27': Lessons in management focus – An Australian general aviation perspective. *Journal of Air Transport Management, 89*(May), 101922. https://doi.org/10.1016/j.jairtraman.2020.101922

UNWTO. (2013). *Sustainable Tourism for Development Guidebook - Enhancing capacities for Sustainable Tourism for development in developing countries*. World Tourism Organization (UNWTO). https://doi.org/10.18111/9789284415496

UNWTO. (2021). International tourism highlights, 2020 edition. In *International tourism highlights, 2020 edition*. World Tourism Organization (UNWTO). https://doi.org/10.18111/9789284422456.

Van Dijk, T. A. (1998). *Ideology: A multidisciplinary approach*. ProQuest Ebook Central https://ebookcentral.proquest.com

Vellema, W., Buritica Casanova, A., Gonzalez, C., & D'Haese, M. (2015). The effect of specialty coffee certification on household livelihood strategies and specialisation. *Food Policy, 57*, 13–25. https://doi.org/10.1016/j.foodpol.2015.07.003.

Wang, M., Chen, L. H., Su, P., & Morrison, A. M. (2019). The right brew? An analysis of the tourism experiences in rural Taiwan's coffee estates. *Tourism Management Perspectives, 30*(February), 147–158. https://doi.org/10.1016/j.tmp.2019.02.009.

Weeden, C. (2005). A qualitative approach to the ethical consumer: The use of focus groups for cognitive consumer research in tourism. *Tourism Research Methods: Integrating Theory with Practice, 2005*, 179–190. https://doi.org/10.1079/9780851999968.0179.

Wong, A. K. F., Kim, S. (Sam), Kim, J., & Han, H. (2021). How the COVID-19 pandemic affected hotel employee stress: Employee perceptions of occupational stressors and their consequences. *International Journal of Hospitality Management, 93*(December 2020), 102798. https://doi.org/10.1016/j.ijhm.2020.102798

Woyesa, T., & Kumar, S. (2020). Potential of coffee tourism for rural development in Ethiopia: A sustainable livelihood approach. *Environment, Development and Sustainability, 23*(1), 815–832. https://doi.org/10.1007/s10668-020-00610-7.

Yankelovich, D. (2011). How to achieve sounder public judgment. In D. Yankelovich & W. Friedman (Eds.), *Toward wiser public judgment* (pp. 11–32). Nashville, TN: Vanderbilt University.

Yankelovich, D. (2014). *Wicked problems, workable solutions: Lessons from a public life*. ProQuest Ebook Central. https://ebookcentral.proquest.com

Yankelovich, D., & Elman, J. (2009). Academy meetings the new pragmatism: Coping with America's problems. *Bulletin of the American Academy of Arts and Sciences*, 62(3), 25–30.

Yang, Y., Liu, H., & Chen, X. (2020). COVID-19 and restaurant demand: Early effects of the pandemic and stay-at-home orders. *International Journal of Contemporary Hospitality Management, 13*(12), 3809–3834. https://doi.org/10.1108/IJCHM-06-2020-0504

Yun, O. (2014). *Coffee tourism in Ethiopia: Opportunities, challenges, and initiatives*. University of Exeter.

Community Resilience: Do Differences in COVID-Induced Regional Economic Impacts Draw Different Community Initiatives in Response? A Thematic Analysis

Someek Basu, Josephine Pryce, and Riccardo Welters

Abstract COVID-19 affected every part of Australia - disrupting businesses and livelihoods, creating uncertainty for communities. This paper examined how COVID-19 impacted Cairns and Townsville with the specific aim to explore the proposition that, for similar levels of base-line resilience within a community, the number and type of community-based initiatives generated for the two tropical cities were directly related to the impact of this disruptive pandemic. This research employed a thematic analysis to examine community-based initiatives mentioned in articles published in: *The Cairns Post* and *The Townsville Bulletin*, for the year 2020. It also implemented a deductive approach in aligning these initiatives to community resilience capacities (viz. absorption, adaptive, and restorative capacities), leading to an interpretive and comparative understanding of the responses of the Cairns and Townville communities to COVID-19.

Results indicated Cairns and Townsville were impacted differently by COVID-19 and responses varied accordingly. Firstly, more initiatives were generated in Cairns, likely due to its strong reliance on tourism and related sectors, which were severely affected by COVID-19, upsetting Cairns' economy more than Townsville. Secondly, different types of initiatives were observed in the two cities, which focused on different capacities of community resilience. Initiatives in Cairns reinforced the community's restorative capacity while Townsville, had no restorative initiatives and focused on strengthening absorption and adaptive capacities due to less severe impact of COVID-19. This supports the initial proposition that the number and type of community-based initiatives varies with the severity of the disruption and can therefore be used as an indicator of the severity of the disruption. Cairns and Townsville both developed various social and community initiatives to cushion the effects of COVID-19 which demonstrate their ingenuity and resilience. The

S. Basu (✉) · J. Pryce · R. Welters
College of Business, Law and Governance, DTES, James Cook University, Townsville, Australia
e-mail: someek.basu@my.jcu.edu.au; josephine.pryce@jcu.edu.au; riccardo.welters@jcu.edu.au

© The Author(s), under exclusive license to Springer Nature Singapore Pte Ltd. 2022
T. Chaiechi, J. Wood (eds.), *Community Empowerment, Sustainable Cities, and Transformative Economies*, https://doi.org/10.1007/978-981-16-5260-8_19

initiatives provide a silver lining to the pandemic and should help in long-term sustainable recovery of Cairns and Townsville as regional cities servicing Tropical North Queensland.

Keywords COVID-19 · Community initiatives · Tourism · Thematic analysis · Community resilience · Tropical North Queensland

1 Introduction

The COVID-19 pandemic has had extensive negative impacts. It has transformed the way people live, how they communicate and interact with neighbors and other members of the community and hold community events (Shigemoto, 2021). Consequently, countries are trying to establish 'rapid response methods' to prevent, detect, and treat coronavirus by promoting medical and health research (Peeters et al., 2020). Though lives and health are considered as top priorities, it is crucial to also monitor the economy (Shen & Taska, 2020).

COVID-19's adverse socio-economic impacts have presented many challenges in the year 2020. Australia has managed to limit community spread and deaths by comparison to other countries but has had its own challenges, as COVID-19 touched every part of community. The negative consequences and health problems linked to COVID-19 are disproportionately distributed across the population (Shigemoto, 2021). For businesses, it created uncertainty as some floundered and others surrendered to ongoing lockdowns and downturn in business activities. Yet, this crisis also galvanised community.

The response to COVID-19 and its impact on activities (such as social-distancing rules applicable to businesses and domestic border closures) varied across states and territories due to their own mandates and procedures in line with the Australian government policy (Foster, 2020). Moreover, the impact of COVID-19 has been heterogeneous within states because the impact of the restrictions is economic sector-dependent, e.g., tourism industry, education, agriculture, and bricks and mortar retail. That is, if a regional economy draws more heavily on those industries, the impact on those communities is more severe. Consequently, the intensity and the impact of the pandemic varied from place to place within the community.

In order to gain a better understanding of the heterogeneity of the impacts of the pandemic, this paper examines, applying insights from the community resilience literature, how COVID-19 affected two major regional cities in Tropical North Queensland: Cairns and Townsville. These two cities afforded a valuable comparative study because of their regional proximity and similar restrictions to COVID-19 but significantly different industry compositions, implying different socio-economic COVID-19 impacts. The basic assumption underpinning this paper is that the inherent community resilience prior to the insurgence of the pandemic was comparable in both cities, because of their geographical proximity, similar size and demographics. Based on this assumption the paper then proposes that the number of community-based initiatives would be higher and its composition different (focused more on restorative initiatives) in the city that—given its economic structure—has been impacted more by COVID-19 and so, requires a greater effort to bring its community back to normal.

To examine this proposition, this research employs thematic analysis to examine relevant newspaper articles published in the two main local newspapers: *The Cairns Post* and *The Townsville Bulletin*, for the year 2020. We argue that newspapers are still one of the most commonplace modes of mass communication. Hence it is likely that most community-based initiatives would be communicated to the community through this medium to encourage active participation. If some initiatives remain unreported, there is no reason to assume that the share of reported initiatives or the type of reported initiatives varies among the two newspapers because the same research criteria were applied to both newspapers.

This paper begins by examining the concept of community resilience, exploring various definitions of the concept to find common elements and a working definition. The paper continues by investigating the connection between the development of community resilience and community initiatives. It then presents the socio-economic profiles of Cairns and Townsville to understand the impact of the pandemic on the respective economies. This comparative analysis reveals why the Cairns economy was more severely affected than Townsville's. With this knowledge, the paper then presents the approach to data collection, specifically locating community initiatives initiated in the region using predefined search parameters as outlined in the search strategy section. The results are captured in the next section, with the first part presenting the various initiatives in the two cities and the second documenting the comparative analysis of the community resilience aspects of Townsville and Cairns as determined from the initiatives. This is followed by concluding comments.

2 Community Resilience and Community-Based Initiatives

The novel coronavirus (causing COVID-19) has increased uncertainty and stress in the lives of people (Shigemoto, 2021) and the pandemic has affected communities and peoples, across all demographics regardless of age, race, social status, and gender. The permeability of COVID-19 has tested the resilience of communities. Epidemics of the past, such as the Ebola virus disease (EVD) of 2014–2016, have contributed to the increased recognition of "community resilience" as a key instrument in recovering from similar health shocks, but the concept and its constituting factors are still not fully understood (Alonge et al., 2019). Resilience can be attributed to systems, individuals as well as communities. It is an active process of coping, adaptation, and growth in response to a threat (South et al., 2019). Concepts of resilience within the context of a community can have opposing definitions and philosophies (Berkes & Ross, 2013). It has been approached from various academic disciplines, such as social and behavioral sciences and ecology (Vaneeckhaute et al., 2017). Equally, understanding of community resilience has been drawn from mental health perspectives and social–ecological systems (Berkes & Ross, 2013). Consequently, various researchers have defined community resilience in their own way, based on their perspectives and findings.

In the context of this paper to articulate the relation between community resilience and community-based initiatives, we find the following definitions as closely aligned. The first is that community resilience can be defined as the "existence, development and engagement of community resources by community members to thrive in an environment characterised by change, uncertainty, unpredictability and surprise" Magis (2010, p. 401). Hence resilience largely depends on the obtainability of various local resources and the ability of a community to mobilise those (Revell & Henderson, 2019). In other words, the resilience of a community is often understood through its social system's capability to get together to work towards achieving a common objective (Berkes & Ross, 2013). Hence, properly-developed communal resources and agency are important for building community resilience (Vaneeckhaute et al., 2017).

Secondly, Norris et al. (2008, p. 127) defined resilience as "a process linking a network of adaptive capacities (resources with dynamic attributes) to adaptation after a disturbance or adversity." They added, community resilience developing from four primary sets of adaptive capacities viz. Social Capital, Economic Development, Information and Communication, and Community Competence, require engagement of local people and linkages with organizations to collectively create a strategy for disaster readiness.

Thirdly, Bond et al. (2017, p. 2) define resilience as "the capacity of a system—a household, a community, an organization, or a coupled natural-human system—to prepare for disruptions from outside the system, to recover from shocks and stresses, and to adapt to and grow from a disruptive experience." The key element of this definition of resilience is that it extends the concept to the notion of growth; not just the capability to endure and recover from a disruptive influence. They further spread the idea to include "co-benefits" associated with the resilience project—as a key difference between a resilience and an intervention project where "co-benefits" are benefits not directly related to the shock or stressor.

Bond et al. (2017) found three main commonalities among all the diverse definitions of community resilience, which are:

1. Absorption capacity, which aims to comprehend the capacity of a community to withstand shock but still function as in a pre-event scenario.
2. Adaptive capacity, which focuses on understanding the capability of a community to adapt to shocks while continuing to function.
3. Restorative capacity, which investigates the capacity of a community to return to its 'normal' operation or pre-event scenario after a shock.

Based on the above definitions and commonalities, we argue that community-based initiatives are intrinsically linked to community resilience development. A resilient community would generate initiatives to restore its societal balance to pre-disruption times in the face of an unsettling stimulus to its absorption, adaptive and restorative capacities. We also argue that the number of initiatives required for the restoration of the community is directly correlated to the level of impact it endured because of the disruptive stimulus. It is acknowledged that initiatives that align with restorative capacity may not be fully exposed until 'normal' or 'pre-event' status is attained. The situation with COVID-19 has presented extraordinary circumstances with much talk of 'the new normal". Nonetheless, the literature shows that some restorative capacity can be assessed and measured early (quick recovery), rather than later (slow recovery) (Proag, 2014; Tariq et al., 2021).

The importance of community initiatives in building community resilience is illustrated in the Victorian Compendium of Community-Based Resilience Building Case Studies. It was developed to encourage the sharing of achievable, practical resilience building activities, to inspire community members to build expertise, reduce program duplication, and save valuable resources to reinforce disaster resilience (Spencer et al., 2019). The online Compendium offers free access for all communities to explore activities before, during, and after disasters. It includes 30 "Expression of Interests" presented at the MUDRI Advancing Community Resilience Forums over six years between 2012 and 2018. A thematic analysis of these case studies identified four critical success factors including community-based initiatives along with others viz. (1) strong governance, board support, leadership, and trust; (2) partnerships and (3) commitment, adaptability, and stamina. Several community-based initiatives are emerging even in small geographic communities of place to build resilience needed to cope with various interconnected random challenges due to an increase in the instability and stresses of our socio-ecological systems at local and global levels (Revell & Henderson, 2019).

3 Socio-Economic Profile of Townsville and Cairns

In this paper our focus is on the two Far North Queensland cities of Cairns and Townsville. They are comparable due to the proximity of their geographical locations, size, and other similar demographics. Hence, our basic assumption is that their inherent community resilience prior to the insurgence of the pandemic was comparable. We however argue that the economic impact of COVID-19 pandemic was more intense in Cairns than in Townsville. The rationale behind this argument can be attributed to the heavy reliance of Cairns on international tourism as an economic sector. With the international travel bans due to the pandemic, the Cairns economy was hit harder than Townsville's as the industry subsectors depending on international tourism struggled with the dwindling international tourist numbers. Furthermore, Australian consumer demand changed due to behavioral amendments and associated government policy in response to COVID-19 (e.g. restrictions on economic activity including lockdowns, and stimulus programs such as JobKeeper) affecting both labor supply and demand (Foster, 2020). Hence, domestic tourist numbers would have seen some likely reduction as well which would have further exacerbated the economic impact on Cairns.

Tourism activity does not easily fit within the boundaries of the standard Australian and New Zealand Standard Industrial Classification (ANZSIC) that the Australian Bureau of Statistics (ABS) uses. Instead, it has many crossovers between sectors. The Productivity Commission (2005) have attempted to identify the main sectors to which tourism activity contributes. They differentiate between tourism characteristic industries and tourism connected industries. The main tourism characteristic industries in the ANZSIC are 'Travel Agency and Tour Arrangement Services', 'Water Passenger Transport', 'Air and Space transport', 'Accommodation', and 'Cafes, Restaurants and Takeaway Food Services'. The main tourism connected industries are 'Pubs Taverns and Bars', 'Fuel Retailing', 'Other Store-Based Retailing', 'Gambling Activities', 'Amusement and Other Recreation Activities', and 'Museum Operations'.

Summarising and aggregating tourism characteristics and connected industries to the ANZSIC main industry classification, tourism activity elevates economic activity in three sectors: 'Retail Trade', 'Accommodation and Food Services' and 'Arts and Recreation Services'. To visualise the importance of tourism to the Cairns economy relative to the Townsville economy we compare industry employment shares for Cairns and Townsville in Fig. 1, which demonstrates the relative importance of tourism in Cairns. 'Retail Trade', 'Accommodation and Food Services' and 'Arts and Recreation Services' are more important industries in Cairns than they are in Townsville.

Consequently, while it was largely 'business as usual' in Townsville, Cairns was brought to a halt given its reliance on tourism which according to Cairns Regional Council (2020) is one of its five strategic industry sectors. Data from the Regional Tourism Satellite Accounts (RTSA) shows that in, "2018-19, the tourism industry contributed an estimated $2.9 billion to the Tropical North Queensland (TNQ) regional economy (16.9% of TNQ's gross regional product) and supported about 25,600 jobs (18.6% of employment in TNQ)" (TEQ, 2021). This information highlights the value of the tourism industry to CAIRNS.

3.1 Methods

In order to explore the proposition that the number and type of community-based initiatives generated for the two tropical cities of Cairns and Townsville was directly related to the impact of COVID-19, this research employed a qualitative design utilizing thematic analysis to examine relevant newspaper articles published in the two main local newspapers: *The Cairns Post* and *The Townsville Bulletin*, for the year 2020. In line with approach outlined by Crabtree and Miller (1999), an *a priori* approach was adopted where the categories of community resilience (absorptive, adaptive, and restorative) were used as the themes to align the initiatives as detailed below, leading to an interpretive and comparative understanding of the responses of the communities of Cairns and Townville, to COVID-19. Hierarchical coding utilising an inductive thematic analysis as described by Braun and Clarke (2006)

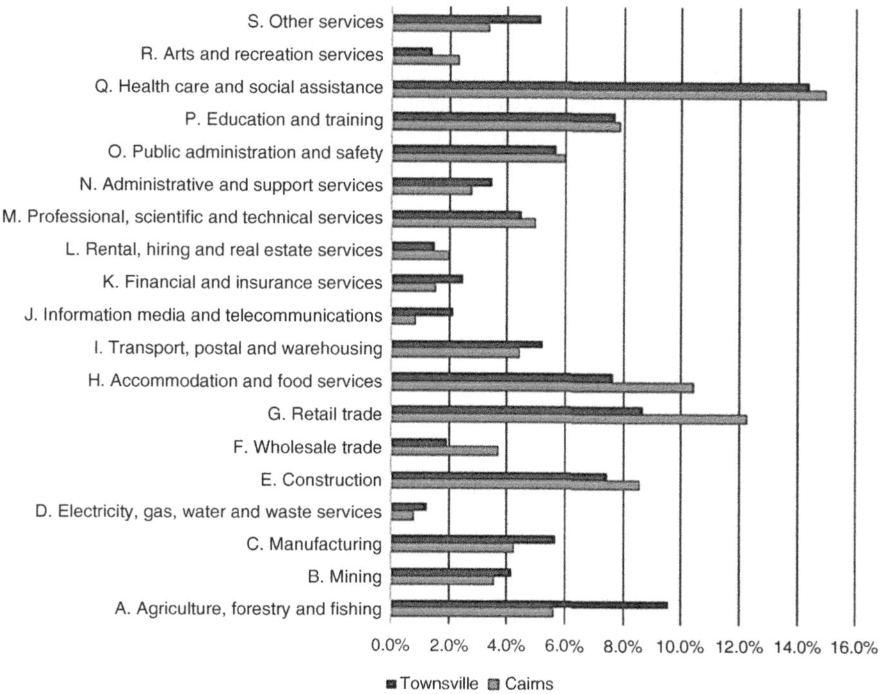

Fig. 1 Industry structure comparison Cairns and Townsville November 2020, ABS. (Source: ABS (2020) [Tourism contributes significantly to the 'Air and Space transport' industry, particularly international tourists. However, that contribution (at least the air traffic component) typically does not benefit the city, which the tourist visits, but rather the city in which the airline company resides (which is not Townsville or Cairns). Hence, this industry is not very important to our analysis])

allowed for subthemes to be identified and encompassed in the analysis. This process involved five main phases: detailed reading of the newspaper articles to ensure familiarization with the data, identification of themes/subthemes that were relevant to the research question, re-reading of the data to refine themes/sub-themes, categorisation of themes/subthemes based on relevant concepts, and drawing of extracts from the raw data to illustrate the themes/subthemes. To maintain rigour and accuracy, NVivo 12 Plus, a qualitative data analysis software program, was utilised. As a further measure and to ensure validity and fitness of each theme, two of the authors discussed and negotiated the results till consensus was reached.

The search focused on newspaper articles sourced from *The Cairns Post* and *The Townsville Bulletin* that presented stories on community-based initiatives. Search words and phrases included: COVID-19/Coronavirus; Initiatives; Well-being/wellbeing; Job/work; and combinations of these search criteria.

The results were further filtered for articles reporting on initiatives developed specifically in Cairns and Townsville, excluding reported initiatives in the adjoining towns of Port Douglas and Charters Towers (which are in the reporting realm of the newspapers). We only looked at social and community initiatives which were initiated due to impact of the pandemic and excluded government initiatives. We investigated constructs like work, wellbeing, and resilience to better understand the contrast between Cairns and Townsville in their reaction to the pandemic.

Overall, 24 newspaper articles were gathered with 4 articles from *The Townsville Bulletin* and 20 from *The Cairns Post*. Utilising an *a priori* approach, the resulting initiatives were then collated in accordance with the commonalities of the various definitions of community resilience as per Bond et al. (2017): Absorption capacity; Adaptive capacity; and Restorative capacity. Each article aligned with one or more of the capacities of community resilience, as detailed in Table 1 in the next page.

3.2 Results and Discussion

Analysis of the community initiatives data shows differences in both the number of initiatives and the types of initiatives in Townsville and Cairns.

4 Townsville

A word frequency analysis was undertaken using NVivo software and the top ten words that emerged from the four articles as most frequent were: student(s), support, pandemic, community, expansion, business, university, local, people and workers (Fig. 2). This is indicative of the situation in Townsville where one of the main focuses was to support the students during the time of the pandemic. James Cook University's Townsville campus attracts many international students who form a vital part of the local economy by not only bringing in overseas funds but also contributing to the local casual workforce. JCU Townsville, with more than 13,000 students, including 1500 international students, contributes about 5.6% of the region's employment (James Cook University, 2018). Many of these international students lost their often hospitality-related employment and combined with their ineligibility to access the government's JobKeeper support program, they lost an important source of their income due to COVID-19. Hence, their wellbeing and support requirements were highly topical in both the university as well as the broader community, as evidenced by the prevalence of related stories in *The Townsville Bulletin*. In response to the community concern and as part of its corporate social responsibility, James Cook University initiated incentives such as the food pantry and the Student Success Support Package (SSSP). The SSSP included financial support, along with an academic safety net to protect students from being academically disadvantaged in addition to various health and wellbeing support initiatives.

As a way to identify and understand how the initiatives aligned with community resilience, a selection of the top ten words for Townsville initiatives was applied to the three capacities of community resilience: absorption, adaptive, and restorative (Bond et al., 2017). Table 2 below shows the top ten words that emerged as part of

Table 1 Selected newspaper articles from 2020 that show initiatives for Cairns and Townsville and alignment with respective community resilience capacity

CAIRNS: Articles obtained from *The Cairns Post* (2020)				
Date	**Initiative**	**AB**	**AD**	**RS**
March 20	COVID-19 Cairns: Yorkeys Knob butcher delivering to elderly, posting record sales	■	■	
March 25	Cairns coronavirus: Donations grow as city prepares for COVID-19 hit	■	■	
March 28	Malanda property Rose Gums Wilderness Retreat offers 'a place of comfort' during crisis	■	■	■
April 2	Coronavirus: Cairns Private Hospital to get on with the job of fighting COVID-19 in Far North	■		
April 3	Coronavirus: Croc Piss manufacturer FNQ Spirits making hand sanitizer to fight pandemic	■	■	
April 5	Cairns coronavirus: Businesses open in city	■	■	■
April 8	Northern Pride eager to be part of Cairns sports working group	■		
May 2	Cairns funerals: Burkin Svendsens Funerals helping grieving families during COVID-19 restrictions	■	■	
May 29	Far North pubs and clubs get helping hand to stay afloat	■		■
June 1	JCU provides nearly half a million dollars in financial support to help students	■		
June 16	Cairns retail jobs: VPG hosts virtual recruitment drive for hundreds of young workers		■	
June 17	Cairns Hockey: More girls can Aspire to be Deadly as program set to expand	■	■	
June 19	Cairns' Grant Westthorp gives boost to Men's Health Week during coronavirus	■	■	
July 1	Cairns Wellness Centre set for reopening after coronavirus shutdown	■	■	
July 7	Signage released to protect visitors ahead of tourism influx		■	
August 11	Kuranda traders prepare for ways to attract visitors back post-COVID	■	■	■
August 12	Coronavirus: Aged care homes in Cairns receive kind gestures from school kids	■	■	
August 13	Cairns' Holy Cross School lifts coronavirus-hit FNQ businesses' spirits with Christmas initiative	■		■
August 18	Cairns cinemas at Earlville and Smithfield to reopen after lengthy COVID closure	■		■
December 3	Real-time health tracker could change the game on air travel	■	■	■
TOWNSVILLE: Articles obtained from *The Townsville Bulletin (2020)*				
Date	**Initiative**	**AB**	**AD**	**RS**
March 25	Townsville Brewery to deliver beers to homes during COVID-19 pandemic	■	■	
April 25	Townsville's Chinese community fundraises for healthcare workers to combat racism	■	■	
May 25	Sun Metals speeds contractor payments at refinery expansion	■	■	
May 29	JCU students in line for COVID-19 assistance package	■		

Abbreviations: *AB* absorptive capacity, *AD* adaptive capacity, *RS* restorative capacity

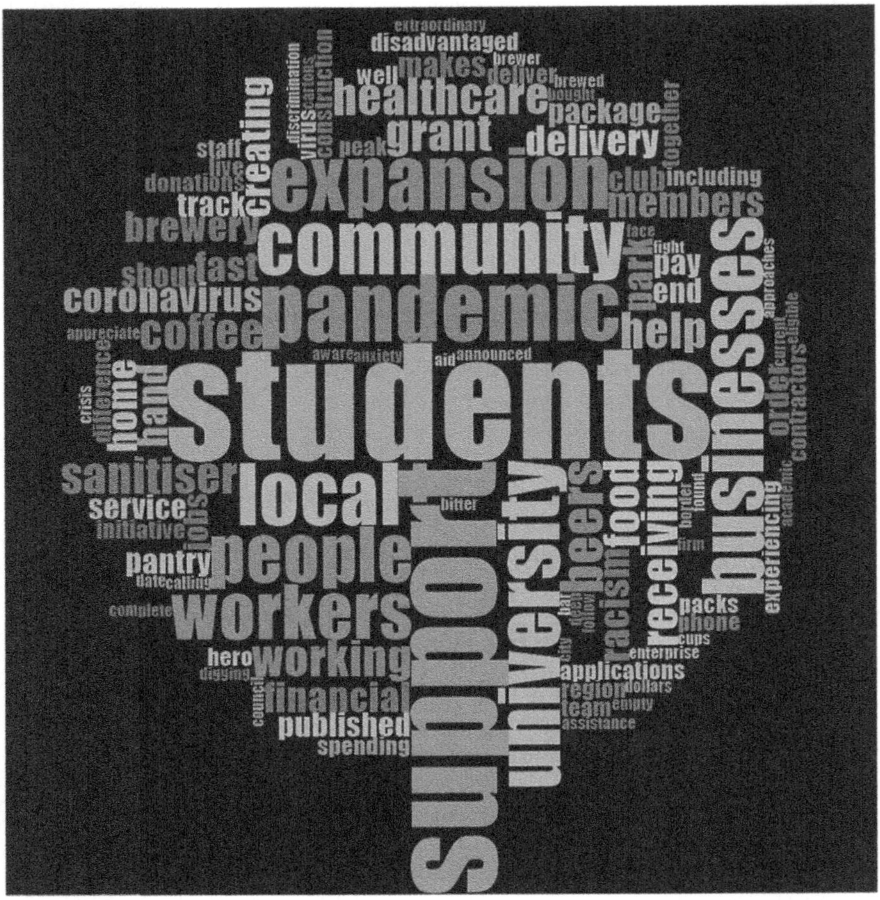

Fig. 2 NVivo Word cloud frequency for Townsville initiatives

the NVivo analysis of the initiatives data and highlights that there were no restorative initiatives. The absence of restorative initiatives lends support to the notion that Townsville's economy was not severely impacted and had the ability to absorb and adapt to the disruptive influences of COVID-19.

Looking closely at the words for the absorption and adaptive capacities, the top ten words are mostly similar to the main words as per the word cloud (Fig. 2). These indicate that the initiatives for Townsville focused on providing 'support' to the 'university' 'students' and other 'disadvantaged' 'people' within the 'community' while helping 'local' 'businesses' to absorb the 'financial' impacts of the 'pandemic'.

Furthermore, the graphic below shows the hierarchical relationship between the various capacities and their elements, which emerged from the initiatives undertaken in Townsville (Bond et al., 2017). From the articles analysed some initiatives were focused towards strengthening one particular capacity of community resilience while

Table 2 Townsville initiatives in terms of the community resilience capacities

Top ten words comparison for the different initiative capacities				
Townsville				
S/L No.:	Initiatives	Absorption	Adaptive	Restorative
1	Students	Pandemic	Support	X
2	Support	Support	Financial	X
3	Pandemic	Financial	Pandemic	X
4	Community	Students	Students	X
5	Expansion	Academic	Academic	X
6	Local	Disadvantaged	Disadvantaged	X
7	University	Aid	Aid	X
8	Businesses	Approaches	Beer	X
9	People	Beer	Business	X
10	Workers	Business	Coffee	X

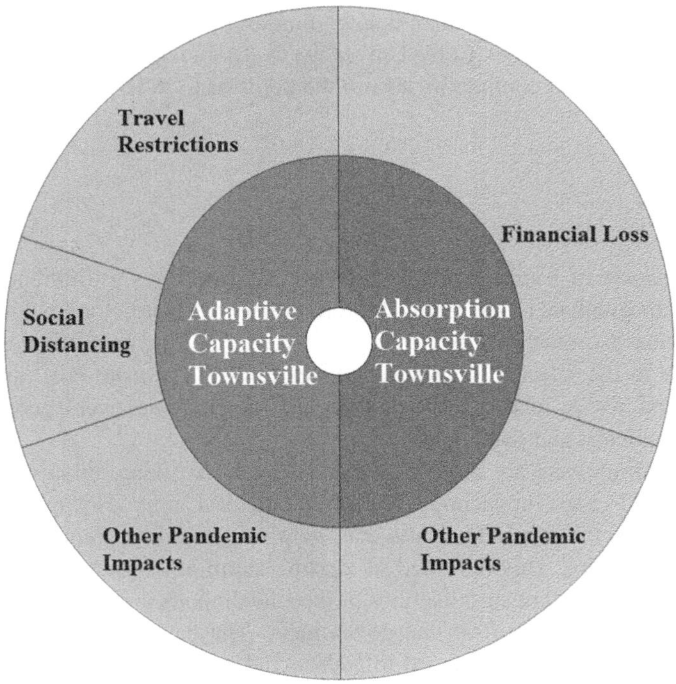

Fig. 3 NVivo Hierarchical chart for Townsville initiatives and associated capacities

others were effective across more than one. Therefore, some initiatives were included in more than one capacity. For example, Sun Metals, a major employer in the region, had a big impact on strengthening community resilience. Its effort in producing hand sanitisers (listed under other pandemic impacts in Fig. 3 above) to adapt to the acute shortage in the local market, helped in bolstering the adaptive capacity of Townsville. Also, Sun Metals' partnership with Townsville City Council to have the sanitisers distributed to a seniors' health facility helped the community absorb the impact of the shortage of hand sanitisers. Moreover, Sun Metals' initiative of fast-tracking contractor payments helped the local community absorb some of the financial losses generated due to the pandemic. Figure 3 highlights the prominence of the subthemes of adaptive and absorption capacities, such as 'financial loss' and 'other pandemic impacts'.

Similarly, the initiative of Townsville Brewery to deliver cartons and six-packs of its locally brewed beers to homes across Townsville not only helped keep the brewers and core staff working by generating much needed revenue, but also helped local consumers to adapt to the laws of social distancing and travel restrictions. Another initiative was launched by the members of Townsville's Chinese community, to offer coffee to healthcare workers, not only to absorb the ill effects of racism which was an unfortunate impact of the COVID-19 pandemic, but also to adapt to change in community outlook towards Asians in general. Therefore, this initiative was shown as other pandemic impact under both the absorption and adaptive capacities in the hierarchy chart below. Furthermore, half a million dollars in financial support by James Cook University to its students impacted by COVID-19 helped the student community absorb the perils of COVID-19.

5 Cairns

Similar analysis of Cairns data on the other hand portrays a different picture as shown in the graphics below (Fig. 4). From the NVivo word cloud below it can be observed that 'Coronavirus' and 'business' were two of the most frequently occurring words in the selected newspaper articles from *The Cairns Post*. Some of the other topical words related to community-associated issues were people, health, hospital, residents, and pandemic.

These findings were not surprising considering the evolving situation of COVID-19 as a health issue impacting the community of Cairns. However, what was noticeable from the word cloud was that 'help' was the most frequently occurring word in the articles. This indicated of a rising alarm amongst residents and businesses around the future sustainability of their livelihoods and the repeated request for assistance, especially from the government. The data also reflect the parallel emergence of initiatives that aimed to address the cries for help. For example, one article highlighted Carlton & United Breweries' (CUB) "For The Love of Your Local campaign", which is an initiative to help pubs and clubs survive the coronavirus crisis. Bluewater Bar and Grill at Trinity Park is one of several Far North venues to have been given a helping hand. As part of this campaign, people can nominate their participating local pub online and then purchase a pint of CUB beer. The funds will go to the venue directly and CUB will then match that support, pint for pint in donated stock, which means patrons will get 2 for 1 pint when their local pub re-opens. This is one of several initiatives that was developed to 'help' keep the

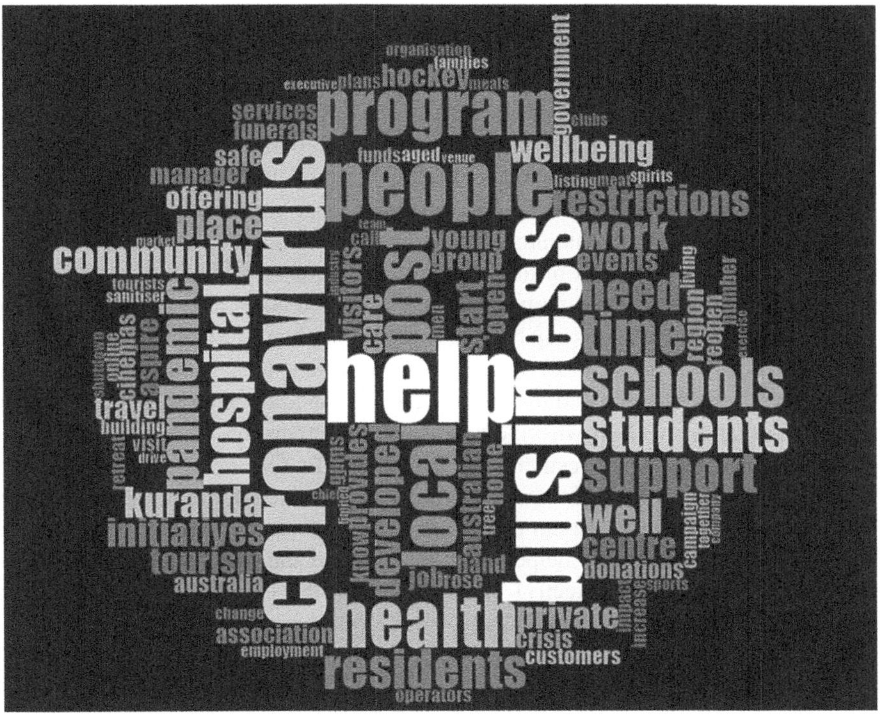

Fig. 4 NVivo Word cloud frequency for Cairns initiatives

Table 3 Cairns initiatives in terms of the community resilience capacities

Top ten words comparison for the different initiative capacities				
Cairns				
S/L No.:	Initiatives	Absorption	Adaptive	Restorative
1	Help	Coronavirus	Residents	Tourists
2	Business	Time	Centre	Business
3	Coronavirus	Local	Group	Donations
4	People	Centre	Tourists	Pint
5	Local	Help	Business	Workers
6	Health	Residents	Coronavirus	Association
7	Post	Call	Donated	Away
8	Program	Crisis	Drive	Banding
9	Schools	Developed	Employed	Boat
10	Hospital	Donated	Friends	Breakfast

'businesses' from collapsing following the debilitating effects of the pandemic like lock downs and customer number capping at venues.

Table 3 below shows the top ten words that emerged as part of the NVivo analysis of the initiatives data for Cairns. It shows that help was the most prevalent word, followed by business, coronavirus, and people. These words are similar to the main words in the word cloud shown earlier (Fig. 4) and indicate that the main focus of the community initiatives in Cairns was to provide help and support to the businesses and people of the city. Also looking at the top words for the different capacities of community resilience, it can be interpreted that the initiatives were mainly aimed at adapting the residents of Cairns to absorb the impact of the coronavirus by reviving the economy of the city by restoring tourism and other businesses.

Looking further into the hierarchical chart obtained from NVivo (Fig. 5), it can be observed that more than half of the initiatives in Cairns were directed to bolster the absorption capacity of community resilience. With reference to the three capacities of community resilience, this can be interpreted as –Cairns was significantly affected by COVID-19 and hence more initiatives were started to help the community to absorb the effects as compared to those related to adaptation and restoration. Similar to our observations with Townsville data, some initiatives in Cairns also influenced more than one capacity of resilience. For example, BCC Cinemas in Earlville and Event Cinemas in Smithfield offered half-price adult tickets for a limited time when they reopened after a five-month closure due to the pandemic. This initiative as per our interpretation, not only helped in the revival of the local cinemas and other associated businesses (indirectly) but also helped the community to absorb the negative sentiment due to the pandemic by offering an option for patrons to enjoy

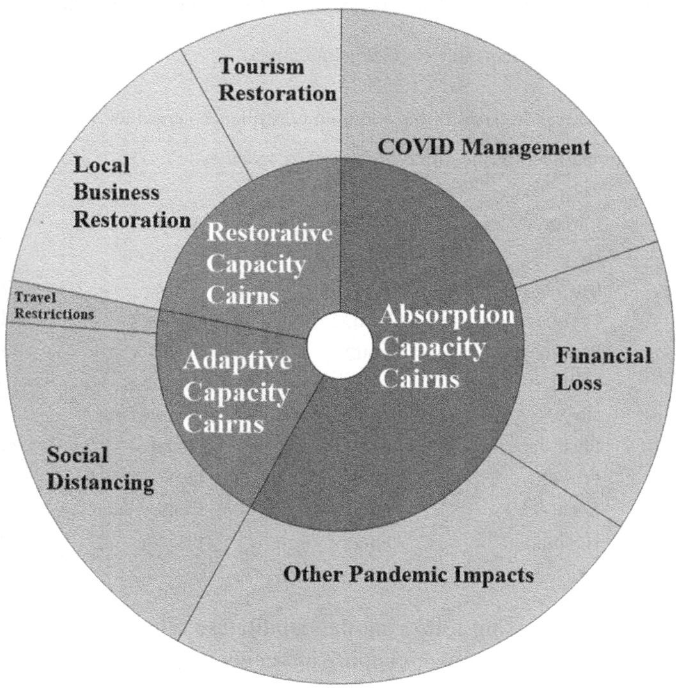

Fig. 5 NVivo Hierarchical chart for Cairns initiatives and associated capacities

some normalcy in their life by going to the movies. Similarly, the deal between Cairns Private Hospital and the Federal government to allow for hospital capacity to be offered on a cost recovery basis is beneficial for both the hospital and the local community. The initiative would help the local business absorb some financial loss due to COVID-19 while at the same time help the community with the management of COVID-19 through the provision of their hospital services.

The community initiative articles analysed as a part of this paper are in Table 1. It shows which capacity of community resilience was affected by the initiatives. It can be observed from the table that not all initiatives impacted community resilience in the same way. While some improved the absorption capacity of the community to build resilience against the coronavirus, so some others helped revive local businesses and the economy from the disruptive effects of the virus. Also, certain initiatives have a bigger impact than others where their effects flowed on to more than one capacity of community resilience as mentioned earlier. One such example that arguably enhanced all the three capacities of community resilience, is the initiative by the owners of "Rose Gums Wilderness Retreat" to turn the place into a sanctuary for Australians aged over 60 to provide them with security, comfort, and wellbeing during the COVID-19 crisis (Nally, 2020). It not only helped a vulnerable section of the community to absorb and adapt to the challenges of the pandemic but in turn also helped restore a lot of 'businesses' in the area devastated due to lack of 'tourists' and kept 'workers' from losing their jobs. This observation is also demonstrated through our explanation of the hierarchy charts earlier.

6 Conclusions

The aim of this paper was to explore the proposition that, for similar level of baseline resilience across two tropical communities, the number and type (absorptive, adaptive, or restorative) of community-based initiatives generated is directly related to the impact of a disruptive influence such as COVID-19. An *a priori* approach was adopted where the categories of community resilience (absorptive, adaptive, and restorative) were used as the themes to align community-based initiatives identified from newspaper articles in *The Cairns Post* and *The Townsville Bulletin* in the respective cities of Cairns and Townsville. Subsequent thematic analysis showed that these two tropical cities, which had similar base-line community resilience levels, endured different COVID-19 impacts (Cairns worse than Townsville) as a result of different economic structures.

Firstly, it was found that more initiatives were generated in Cairns than in Townsville. It is thought this is likely due to the more severe impact of COVID-19 on the economy of Cairns as compared to Townsville, due to the region's strong reliance on tourism and other related sectors for revenues, sectors which were hit hard by COVID-19. This is in line with the work of (Fransen et al., 2021) who found that community resilience initiatives generally address vulnerable areas or people.

Secondly, it was observed that there were some differences in the types of initiatives in the two cities with regards to which capacity of community resilience they focused on. The Cairns economy was more heavily impacted, hence required initiatives that bolstered the restorative capacity of community resilience to encourage a revival of the local community. In contrast, in Townsville where the impact of COVID-19 was less severe, the initiatives were mainly focused on strengthening the absorption and adaptive capacities of community resilience, and there were no initiatives developed specially to restore any element of the local community. The literature is largely mute on the relationship between initiatives and resilience capacities. Hence, this is a contribution of this paper, but further research is required to confirm this relationship and to know if restorative capacities lead to long-term and sustainable recovery and benefits, as is suggested by researchers such as (Murray & Zautra, 2011).

Consequently, we find support for the notion that the number and type of community-based initiatives varies with the severity of the disruption and can therefore be used as an indicator of the severity of the disruption. Despite differences between the two cities, both developed various social and community initiatives, which helped cushion the effects of the pandemic. These initiatives demonstrate the ingenuity and resilience of the respective local communities where businesses and their clientele, both adapted to the changing needs to recover and survive through this crisis. The initiatives provide a silver lining to the pandemic and should help in the long-term sustainable recovery of Cairns and Townsville as regional cities servicing Tropical North Queensland.

7 Limitations

There are largely three main limitations to this study. First, the classification of initiatives was based on individual interpretation by the researchers and can lead to bias. Second, assuming *The Cairns Post* and *The Townsville Bulletin* have not covered all community-based initiatives, our analysis is necessarily confined to only a subset of the full spectrum of initiatives in both cities, which may also bias the result. Third, four articles from Townsville Bulletin were included in the paper compared to twenty articles from Cairns Post. This creates certain limitations in terms of breadth and depth of insights into the various resilience capacities covered within Townsville.

References

Alonge, O., Sonkarlay, S., Gwaikolo, W., Fahim, C., Cooper, J. L., & Peters, D. H. (2019). Understanding the role of community resilience in addressing the Ebola virus disease epidemic in Liberia: A qualitative study (community resilience in Liberia). *Global Health Action, 12*(1). https://doi.org/10.1080/16549716.2019.1662682.

Berkes, F., & Ross, H. (2013). Community resilience: Toward an integrated approach. *Society & Natural Resources, 26*(1), 5–20. https://doi.org/10.1080/08941920.2012.736605.

Bond, C. A., Strong, A., Burger, N., Weilant, S., Saya, U., & Chandra, A. (2017). Resilience dividend valuation model: Framework development and initial case studies. RAND Corporation. https://doi.org/10.7249/RR2129.

Braun, V., & Clarke, V. (2006). Using thematic analysis in psychology. *Qualitative Research in Psychology, 3*, 77–101.

Cairns Regional Council. (2020). Strategic industry sectors. Retrieved 4 April from https://www.cairns.qld.gov.au/building-planning-business/business-and-economic-development/data/strategic-industry-sectors

Crabtree, B., & Miller, W. (1999). A template approach to text analysis: Developing and using codebooks. In B. Crabtree & W. Miller (Eds.), *Doing qualitative research* (pp. 163–177). Newbury Park, CA: Sage.

Foster, G. (2020). Early estimates of the impact of COVID-19 disruptions on jobs, wages, and lifetime earnings of schoolchildren in Australia. *Australian Journal of Labour Economics, 23*(2), 129–151. https://search-proquest-com.elibrary.jcu.edu.au/docview/2470411907/93436EC8E90248D1PQ/2?accountid=16285.

Fransen, J., Peralta, D. O., Vanelli, F., Edelenbos, J., & Olvera, B. C. (2021). The emergence of urban community resilience initiatives during the COVID-19 pandemic: An international exploratory study. *The European Journal of Development Research*. https://doi.org/10.1057/s41287-020-00348-y.

James Cook University. (2018). JCU Impact Report. Retrieved March, 31 from https://www.jcu.edu.au/__data/assets/pdf_file/0012/649299/JCU-Impact-Report-2018-Web.pdf

Magis, K. (2010). Community resilience: An indicator of social sustainability. *Society & Natural Resources, 23*(5), 401–416. https://doi.org/10.1080/08941920903305674.

Murray, K., & Zautra, A. (2011). Community resilience: Fostering recovery, sustainability, and growth. In *The social ecology of resilience: Culture, context, resources, and meaning* (pp. 337–346). Springer New York. https://doi.org/10.1007/978-1-4614-0586-3_26.

Nally, A. (2020, March 28). Malanda property rose gums wilderness retreat offers 'a place of comfort' during crisis. *The Cairns Post*. https://www.cairnspost.com.au/news/cairns/malanda-property-rose-gums-wilderness-retreat-offers-a-place-of-comfort-during-crisis/news-story/abb95bfe0843201fe1c4e66f4430494c

Norris, F. H., Stevens, S. P., Pfefferbaum, B., Wyche, K. F., & Pfefferbaum, R. L. (2008). Community resilience as a metaphor, theory, set of capacities, and strategy for disaster readiness. *American Journal of Community Psychology, 41*(1), 127–150. https://doi.org/10.1007/s10464-007-9156-6.

Peeters, A., Mullins, G., Becker, D., Orellana, L., & Livingston, P. (2020). COVID-19's impact on Australia's health research workforce. *The Lancet, 396*(10249), 461. https://doi.org/10.1016/S0140-6736(20)31533-6.

Proag, V. (2014). The concept of vulnerability and resilience. *Procedia Economics and Finance, 18*, 369–376. https://doi.org/10.1016/S2212-5671(14)00952-6.

Revell, P., & Henderson, C. (2019). Operationalising a framework for understanding community resilience in Europe. *Regional Environmental Change, 19*(4), 967–979. https://doi.org/10.1007/s10113-018-1390-y.

Shen, K., & Taska, B. (2020). Measuring the impacts of COVID-19 on job postings in Australia using a reweighting-estimation-transformation approach. *Australian Journal of Labour Economics, 23*(2), 153–171. https://search-proquest-com.elibrary.jcu.edu.au/docview/2470412011/93436EC8E90248D1PQ/3?accountid=16285.

Shigemoto, Y. (2021). Exploring state-level variabilities between perceived community resilience and posttraumatic stress symptoms during the COVID-19 pandemic: Multilevel modeling approach. *Traumatology: An International Journal*. https://doi.org/10.1037/trm0000303.

South, J., Jones, R., Stansfield, J., & Bagnall, A. M. (2019). OP107 how can we measure community resilience for population health? An evidence synthesis for WHO Europe heath equity network. *Journal of Epidemiology and Community Health, 73*(Suppl 1). https://doi.org/10.1136/jech-2019-SSMabstracts.110.

Spencer, C. D., Cross, S. M., McArdle, D. M., & Archer, F. P. (2019). Victorian compendium of community-based resilience building case studies – Critical success factors help communities strengthen resilience to disasters. *Prehospital and Disaster Medicine, 34*(s1), s12. https://doi.org/10.1017/S1049023X1900044X.

Tariq, H., Pathirage, C., & Fernando, T. (2021). Measuring community disaster resilience using Q-methods: A physical resilience perspective. Built environment project and asset management, ahead-of-print (ahead-of-print). https://doi.org/10.1108/BEPAM-03-2020-0053.

TEQ. (2021). Regional Tourism Satellite Accounts. Retrieved April, 4 from https://cdn1-teq.queensland.com/~/media/28462eb87510468eb0d661c409dc2e1b.ashx?vs=1&d=20200917T150438

Vaneeckhaute, L. E., Vanwing, T., Jacquet, W., Abelshausen, B., & Meurs, P. (2017). Community resilience 2.0: Toward a comprehensive conception of community-level resilience. *Community Development, 48*(5), 735–751. https://doi.org/10.1080/15575330.2017.1369443.

Towards Developing a Multisensory Scale to Capture Attributes of Heritage Boutique Hotels

Zahra Pourabedin, Tracey Mahony, and Josephine Pryce

Abstract Heritage tourism is one of the fastest-growing global segments of the Tourism and Hospitality industry, with associated products and experiences generating substantial benefits for tourism operators, promoting economic growth and making social contributions to the local communities. Heritage tourism should rely on recognition and valuation of attributes including aesthetics, uniqueness, cultural elements, and historical significance by tourism operators, visitors, and communities to be successful and sustainable. As an emerging field of study, knowledge and promotional use of specific heritage attributes to target visitors' needs are still being developed. This study seeks to fill that important gap by focusing on 'heritage boutique hotels' (HBHs), where heritage buildings are being repurposed or refurbished to accommodate visitors. The purpose of this study is to identify if, and how, customers are recognising and communicating satisfaction on attributes unique to HBHs. This study forms the first phase of a larger research project examining (HBHs) practices in Singapore and Malaysia with a view to later expanding the study to more widely cover the Asia-Pacific region following JCU's focus on the tropics. Using a qualitative and inductive approach, thematic analysis was utilised for online customer reviews that were collected from a promotional website for six HBHs located across Singapore and Malaysia. Leximancer analysis assisted the contextual and relational analysis affording an opportunity to identify the important attributes and explore relationships between respective attributes. The analysis showed that experiences were multisensory, drawing on visitors' affective, cognitive, and social complexities to gain satisfaction from their experiences of visiting HBHs. These findings provide preliminary insights into the key drivers for the economic, social and cultural sustainability of HBHs and inform operators and communities on strategic planning for future use.

Z. Pourabedin (✉)
James Cook University, Singapore, Singapore
e-mail: zahra.pourabedin@jcu.edu.au

T. Mahony · J. Pryce
James Cook University, Townsville, Australia
e-mail: tracey.mahony@jcu.edu.au; josephine.pryce@jcu.edu.au

© The Author(s), under exclusive license to Springer Nature Singapore Pte Ltd. 2022

T. Chaiechi, J. Wood (eds.), *Community Empowerment, Sustainable Cities, and Transformative Economies*, https://doi.org/10.1007/978-981-16-5260-8_20

Keywords Heritage tourism · Boutique hotels · Visitor experiences · Multisensory · Hotel attributes

1 Introduction

Heritage tourism is one of the growing segments of the travel and tourism industry. Alongside cultural tourism, heritage tourism plays an important role in sustainability, sometimes being the only measure to preserve and keep heritage from degradation, for as long as possible in the most authentic form (Wells et al., 2015; Yu Park, 2010). The word 'heritage' is generally associated with the word 'inheritance' and is understood to mean something that is transferred from one generation to another (Little, 2020). When associated with 'tourism', 'heritage tourism' is defined as "an economic activity that makes use of socio-cultural assets to attract visitors" (Garrod & Fyall, 2000, p. 213). It is in this space that 'heritage marketing' plays a key role. Heritage marketing helps make heritage accessible and meaningful to more than just the specialist cultural visitors (Fullerton et al., 2010). Hence, being able to identify and understand the attributes of heritage products is important.

In the context of hospitality and heritage, the relationship between these two is marked by a shortage of literature, especially regarding heritage attributes and their impact on visitors' needs. The area of heritage lodgings has not been well studied, although it is unique because it provides heritage experiences and accommodation simultaneously (Lee & Chhabra, 2015). More specifically, 'heritage boutique hotels' (HBHs), being boutique hotels housed in heritage properties, have attracted growing interest (Aksoy, 2017). The increasing number of HBHs in South-East Asia (Henderson, 2011) highlights the need to study visitors' experience in such accommodations. For instance, the number of HBHs in George Town (Malaysia) has increased sharply since 2008, with 18 boutique hotels to be found a decade later (Rahman, 2018). Similarly, other researchers have identified boutique hotels in different countries. For example, Henderson (2011) explored HBHs in Singapore with a view to understanding the blend of modern design with heritage elements of old buildings as they were repurposed for visitors. Lim and Endean (2009) examined the aesthetic and operational attributes of boutique hotels in the UK. They found that HBHs are not necessarily privately owned and that they have "distinct individual character' because each property tries to preserve the unique heritage of the building (p. 48). Equally, Lim and Endean (2009, p. 48) found that the properties contained "contemporary luxuries' and that the service was traditional, personal and friendly. The presence of a restaurant was also an important feature of HBHs. These factors can be used as specific indicators of HBH which them form other types of hotels.

Culture and heritage play an important role in developing competitive tourism products (Almeida et al., 2020; Timothy, 2020) and creating income for destinations (Astuti et al., 2017). Transforming heritage resources into heritage tourism-based products leads to the generation of economic, cultural, and educational value for societies within the local area and beyond (Astuti et al., 2017). The increasing

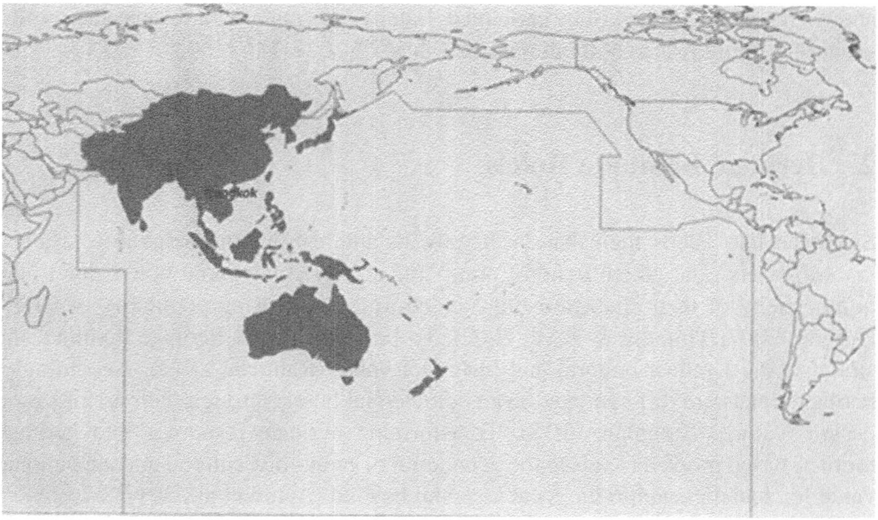

Fig. 1 Map of Asia Pacific (APAC) region with member states indicated in blue shading. (ICAO, 2021)

popularity of HBHs in Southeast Asia has increased investment in HBHs in Singapore (Henderson, 2011) and World Heritage listed cities of Malaysia (George Town and Melaka) (Rahman, 2018). Culture and heritage play important roles in developing competitive tourism products (Almeida et al., 2020; Timothy, 2020), creating and increasing income for participating destinations (Astuti et al., 2017). In order to understand the key characteristics of HBHs that contribute to quality visitors' experiences, online hotel reviews are recognised as major information sources for hoteliers and visitors (Fong et al., 2018).

Although online hotel reviews have been addressed in the general hotel marketing literature, it has largely been ignored in the context of HBHs (Yoo & Lee, 2015). This study seeks to fill this gap by investigating online reviews available in the public domain on HBHs from the TripAdvisor website to ascertain the attributes perceived by visitors that enhanced their experiences. This research is important for strengthening understanding of the heritage and boutique features and provides insights for owners/managers of HBHs seeking to create quality heritage experiences that appeal to visitors, promote satisfaction, and create competitive advantage.

This preliminary study focuses on HBHs in Malaysia and Singapore and will contribute to advancing a wider project covering the Asia-Pacific (APAC) region with a view to explore usefulness of a multisensory scale development for HBHs. The APAC region covers East Asia, South Asia, Southeast Asia and Oceania, as indicated in Fig. 1.

Commencing the study with hotels selected in Singapore and Malaysia reflects the practicalities of conducting research during COVID travel restrictions and the strategic emphasis of the authors' university. The following section describes the concept of HBHs and previous research in the area of HBHs. Next, the methodology and results of the study will be explained. Finally, this paper will discuss the results, providing future research directions.

2 Heritage Boutique Hotels

Since the late 1980s there has been growing interest among hospitality scholars toward HBHs. The global trend of non-popularity of commercial hotels due to the homogeneity of their characteristics has led to the increasing popularity of HBHs (Aggett, 2007; Timothy & Teye, 2009). To be considered a heritage building, the structure must reflect cultural and historical value (Rahman, 2013). Accordingly, heritage hotels are differentiated from commercial hotels through their architectural design features (Rahman, 2018). Transforming heritage resources into heritage tourism-based products leads to the generation of economic, cultural and educational value for societies within the local area and beyond (Astuti et al., 2017).

HBHs are defined as "*the concept of the hotels being unique and small, primeval architecture, culturistic interior decorations, with less than 100 room occupancy, as well as, history and cultural identity offered to the customers*" (Henderson, 2011, p. 218). More recently, researchers acknowledge that HBHs are not necessarily defined by the number of rooms but rather the ambience of the hotel and service provided (Zhovkva, 2020). Ghaderi et al. (2020) note that the number of rooms for HBHs is often constrained by the original capacity of the building and its style and design. This evolving definition of HBHs confirms that there is a lack of standard criteria specific to HBHs (Ghaderi et al., 2020). A growing interest in art, culture and history, which started in the 1980s, and increasing dissent standards large hotel chain properties, were the underlying factors that contributed to the appearance and acceptance of HBHs (Băltescu & Boşcor, 2016; Freund & Munsters, 2004; Henderson, 2011; Lim & Endean, 2009). Boutique style hotels have become an attractive market even for chain hotels to adopt (Chan, 2012) a larger market, commercial hotels have enhanced their heritage aspects to gain competitive advantage and HBHs can no longer be distinguished through their capacity by smaller room numbers only (Ghaderi et al., 2020). Raffles Hotel and Fullerton Hotel in Singapore are two examples of large, luxury, and modern boutique hotels that leverage their long histories and are now recognised as HBHs (Henderson, 2011).

One of the emerging characteristics of HBHs has been attention to aspects of authenticity. Rahman (2018) noted that "Culture and heritage are common attractions for cultural tourists, who seek authenticity and an experience of the past" (p., 105). He also pointed out that although the commodification of heritage buildings enhances the sustainability of the buildings, the commercialisation process can decrease the authenticity of these buildings by converting these buildings to hotels and seeking to accommodate the needs of the visitor market. Terzano (2014) argues that commodification of ethnic enclaves, such as 'Little Italy' communities in the USA, have raised questions about the sustainability of their authenticity as they have become commodified spaces. Rahman (2018) draws on Terzano (2014) work to suggest that such loss of authenticity can be observed with HBHs. So, he emphasises that the commodification of heritage and historical buildings needs to preserve their intrinsic value as heritage resources and not be driven by a sole focus on profits. Rahman (2018) raises this warning for the commodification of built heritage in George Town (Malaysia) and advances caution in ensuring that authenticity is preserved (Terzano, 2014).

However, Henderson (2013) also stress that retaining authenticity in HBHs should not be at all costs. There is a need to balance economic, sociocultural, and environmental goals in the sustainable development of heritage buildings. Ghaderi et al. (2020) suggest guidance can be gained for the sustainable development of HBHs to reflect the characteristics of local lifestyles creating a sense of place. Rahman (2018) by focusing on the commodification process of a heritage building in Penang, Malaysia, identified factors of size, location, architecture and design, theme, interior design, specialised service, unique ambience, unforgettable experience, and price as the key attributes of HBHs.

Beyond Rahman's (2018) findings, beautiful architecture and unique interiors have been identified as the main motivations for staying at HBHs (Aliukeviciute, 2011; Khosravi et al., 2014). Unique designs of HBHs as well as their cultural service create a unique cultural experience for hotel visitors (Henderson, 2013; Lee & Chhabra, 2015). However, Hussein and Hapsari (2020) expanded knowledge on HBHs' beyond that of traditional definitions that focused on visual aesthetics of the buildings and their architecture and interior design. Instead, they investigated the dimensions of heritage experiential quality of Indonesian heritage hotels, including physical, experiential quality, heritage aspects and interactional experiential quality. The results of Hussein and Hapsari's (2020) work revealed the influence of heritage experience on marketing constructs such as heritage hotel image, heritage experiential satisfaction, experiential heritage value and behavioural intentions.

However, as visitors are human beings there is the capacity to engage multiple senses to engage visitors outside of visual aesthetics such as architecture and interior design fixtures and fittings and enhance visitors' experiences of HBHs (Manthiou et al., 2016; Xu & Chan, 2010). Previous research revealed the importance of creating sensory experience in hotels via smell, touch, sound, and sight to create competitive advantage (Manthiou et al., 2016). Exploration of sensory perceptions in terms of visitors' experiences and the ability of sensory perceptions to provide a unique leverage for HBHs' needs further research identifies how visitors are engaging multiple sense in HBHs. The next section explores visitors' multisensory experiences further.

2.1 *Importance of Multisensory Experiences*

Hospitality and tourism products have an experiential nature and so, there is growing interest in research that examines the multisensory nature of hospitality and tourism experiences (Brochado et al., 2021). It is recognised that 'stimulating the senses' engages visitors at both emotional and cognitive levels thereby increasing more memorable experiences (Qu et al., 2011), leading to brand knowledge and loyalty (Manthiou et al., 2016). This is why researchers such as Brochado et al. (2021) and Qu et al. (2011) recommend hospitality and tourism products, particularly those targeting niche markets such as HBHs, provide multisensory experiences for visitors. Brochado et al.'s (2021) research focused on multisensory experiences in wine tourism and argued that by creating visitor experiences that stimulate the five senses in a holistic way results in memorable experiences that promote aesthetic and functional elements of the product. Multisensory experiences present a holistic approach to visitors' experiences (Agapito & Chan, 2019) and here it is argued that investigating HBHs through a multisensory lens can add to the understanding of the attributes of HBHs that enhance visitors' experiences and contribute to the sustainability of the heritage buildings and spaces that shape such experiences.

Various researchers have highlighted the importance of heritage in the attractiveness of HBHs in Singapore (Chang, 2017; Henderson, 2011; Panchal et al., 2018). Rahman (2018) presented a framework that incorporated internal and external factors that define HBHs. In their study, they interviewed boutique hotel hoteliers to identify main heritage attributes. The framework presented by Rahman (2018) highlights external factors such as location, branding and image are an important aspect. Internal factors were identified as tangible and intangible values. The tangible aspects included the buildings' heritage or colonial architectural features and unique interior design; intangible aspects included history, culture, price, and rare experience. Rahman (2018) identified characteristics of HBHs that further clarified the tangible and intangible values into attributes. The result was eight (8) attributes with four (4) each for tangible values (size of the hotel, location, architecture and design, and interior design/furniture) and intangible values (specialised service, unique ambience, unforgettable experience, and price).

HBHs are rich in terms of tangible (e.g. visual aesthetic) and intangible attributes (e.g., nostalgia) (Fuentes-Moraleda et al., 2020) which can be used to develop sensory strategies, providing unique hotel experience (Kim et al., 2017). Sensory experiences can be developed via touch, smell, sound, touch, and sight (Manthiou et al., 2016). Multisensory elements have been found to enhance hotel visitors' experiences; however, the body of knowledge concerning how visitors' senses are being reached by hotels and perceived by visitors is not fully developed and requires future research. This study seeks to address this dearth in the research and bring understanding to how HBHs can develop holistic multisensory experiences.

3 Methodology

This study used secondary data obtained from a publicly available visitor online travel website, TripAdvisor (https://www.tripadvisor.com.au/). The TripAdvisor website provides a service that advertises hotels, makes visitor comparisons possible and makes online customer reviews available for viewing. The dataset contains all online customer reviews from each of the selected hotels from 1 January 2020 to 31 March 2021. A total of 397 reviews were collected to form the database. Data was transferred from the TripAdvisor website onto an excel document. The data was screened prior to processing, including correcting spelling, removing blank lines, punctuation errors, and in-text numbering of dot points within the visitor review text. Emoji's were also removed from within the text responses. The dataset was peer reviewed to ensure accuracy.

The study methodology consisted of two phases of analysis of this database; the first phase was a thematic analysis of the review text and the second phase was a natural language processing (NLP) coding of the multisensory elements identified within the review text. As there was scant literature on HBHs' characteristics and their importance in market offerings, this study adopted a largely inductive approach to the first phase of the analysis. By taking this approach no existing structures were presumed from the literature. Rather, the heritage characteristics were allowed to emerge directly from the online customer reviews on aspects that were pertinent to their customer experience. Inductive reasoning is applicable in circumstances such as the proposed scale development in this study where HBHs' observations are needed to form broad generalisations to develop new theory (Hinkin, 1995; Pijls et al., 2017).

A content analysis was used to do the data analysis, which is a widely accepted approach in analysing visitors' review by previous researchers in the field of tourism marketing (e.g. Boo & Busser, 2018; Dinçer & Alrawadieh, 2017; Lei & Law, 2015). Content analysis is useful to get insights regarding the reviewers' comments. Leximancer software that is used for content analysis can produce a conceptual structure of the text buy extracting key themes (Leximancer, 2018). It is a useful finding in our research as there is no prior set of factors (Sotiriadou et al., 2014). The data was uploaded to Leximancer 4.5 (Leximancer), a software that assists with mining the dataset for efficient analysis. Leximancer is commonly applied in visitor engagement and communication in online environments (Vincent et al., 2016), social media studies (Kilgour et al., 2015), and hotel studies (Boo & Busser, 2018). Given these previous studies, it was deemed that Leximancer would be suitable for the analysis of the data for this project. Leximancer uses an automated coding process reported to reduce bias by providing increased objectivity (Sotiriadou et al., 2014). (Frey, 2018). An interactive map was generated using the Topical mapping functions to show direct relationships in the data as it is considered more stable than the alternate Gaussian mapping function (Leximancer, 2018). The test-retest process was applied to this dataset. The data was shown to be reliable, with three (3) central hubs being, (1) hotel (2) staff and (3) room and consistent concepts and linking between concepts in 8 of 10 iterations. The remaining themes link directly or indirectly into one of these hubs and rotate around the hub depending upon each test-retest iteration with minor variations only. The concept links were found to be consistently formed in each iteration of 'the concept map' showing the data was suitable for analysis using Leximancer.

A thematic content analysis systematically reduces text into themes for interpretation and is a suitable methodology for this study's inductive approach (Frey, 2018).

Concepts and themes were generated from the dataset rather than applying a presupposed structure on the data through the researchers' modifications (Weber, 1990) other than for minor matters such as joining plural forms of words, e.g., hotel and hotels (Frey, 2018). The content analysis contained two parts: a conceptual analysis to identify the existence of themes within the text, and a relational analysis to consider the proximity and strength of links between the identified themes (Price et al., 2015).

The second phase of the analysis was deductive in approach to locate multisensory aspects contained within the customer online review text. As the multisensory categories were known from the literature and human experience (sight, smell, hear, taste, touch, feel), a deductive natural language coding process was used to identify their existence within the text. A codebook was created and applied to the review text. As 'heritage' had been identified in the thematic analysis as a distinct concept separate to visitor, it was added to the codebook. A secondary coder verified this with minimal adjustment (<5%) required for an agreed finalisation of data categorisation and confirm intercoder reliability(O'Connor & Joffe, 2020). The results of the multisensory coding were then tabled in the form of descriptive statistics and analysed in context of the current literature. The below section outlines the results of both the thematic analysis of the review text using Leximancer and the NPS coding for multisensory elements.

4 Sample Overview

The hotels selected for collection of online customer reviews are from high end HBHs advertising on their websites as providing a 5-star experience. Three (3) hotels were selected from each country. The data collection was limited to online customer reviews mentioning the term 'heritage' in the text for manageability. From Singapore, 162 online customer reviews were collected, comprising of Raffles Hotel (40), The Fullerton (47), and the Duxton Reserve (75). From Malaysia, 239 online customer reviews were collected being from The Seven Terraces (113), The Majestic Melaka (79) and the Cheong Fatt Tze (47) (Table 1).

As this study is a desktop review, the website images and text for each hotel was reviewed to ensure comparable heritage features were present in each of the selected hotels external building facade as identified in the literature review (Hussein & Hapsari, 2020). For example, the period features present in the Raffles Hotels Singapore.[1]

[1] https://www.raffles.com/singapore/

Table 1 Sample Heritage Boutique Hotels

Location	Hotel	Nu of Rooms	Approx. Price Range 2 person, single night stay (AUD)	Overall Star Rating (Trip Advisor)	Nu of online customer reviews retained
Singapore	Raffles	115	AUD 1026 – AUD 1300	4.5	40
Singapore	Fullerton	400	AUD 360 – AUD 450	4.5	47
Singapore	Duxton Reserve	306	AUD 319-AUD 350	4.5	75
Malaysia (Penang)	Cheong Fatt Tze	38	AUD 150-AUD 250	4.5	47
Malaysia (Penang)	Seven Terraces	45	AUD 120-AUD 150	5	113
Malaysia (Melaka)	The Majestic Melaka	54	AUD 180-AUD 650	4.5	79

Note: TripAdvisor provides reviewers an option to provide an overall rating for their customer experience on a scale from 1 (worst) through to 5 (excellent) represented on the website by star icons. The Overall rating was only used in this project to ensure hotels were chosen with similar overall ratings

The website review for each hotel also encompassed viewing the hotel interior fixtures and finishes, for example, the ornately carved bed in a room at the Seven Terraces Hotel, George Town Penang in Malaysia.[2]

5 Results – *Phase 1 Thematic Analysis*

The use of Leximancer to assist with the content analysis of the dataset allowed for both conceptual and relational analysis. The conceptual analysis enabled the establishment of the existence of themes within the text of the customer reviews in the dataset (Weber, 1990). Figure 1 shows the main themes: hotel, room, staff, breakfast, tour, bathroom, and Chinese. The themes (Fig. 2) identified by the content analysis through Leximancer are indicated by size order and heat mapped as 'hotel' (red), 'staff' (orange), 'room' (lime green), 'breakfast' (mint green), 'tour' (aqua), 'bathroom' (blue) and 'Chinese' (purple). This diagram forms the basis of the initial analysis discussions. The Leximancer visualisation was set at 100% visibility of themes and the recommended 50% visibility of theme sizing (Leximancer, 2018).

The relational analysis considered the proximity between the themes (Frey, 2018). Leximancer plots the position of the themes on 'the concept map' according to their proximity of use with each other in the customer review text. For example, the theme of 'hotel' is indicated by a larger dot, indicating it is an important theme

[2] See the images here https://www.traveller.com.au/seven-terraces-hotel-review-penang-malaysia-an-elegant-tribute-to-a-bygone-era-h0ut0c

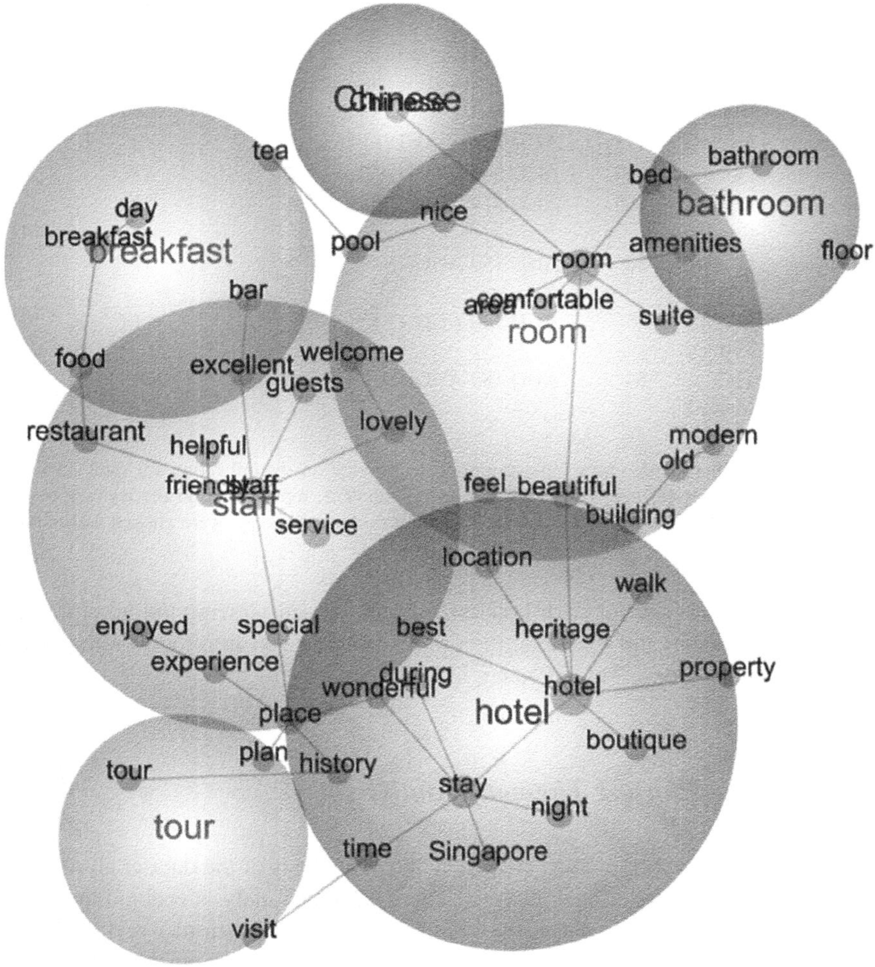

Fig. 2 Key themes in online reviews using Leximancer

identified in the text than 'walk'. The theme of 'hotel' is closer positioned with the theme of 'location' than the theme of 'breakfast' (refer to Fig. 2).

To enable further analysis to determine the story emerging from the data, the word 'hotel' was examined in more detail. The Leximancer output provides evidence of the existence of the identified theme, through a direct count of the number of mentions in the text and a percentage of relevance of the theme proximity to the leading theme in the dataset. For example, the theme of 'hotel' is the most frequently occurring theme with 574 direct mentions in the online visitor review texts and given a relative percentage of 100%. The theme of 'room', which was the next main theme in Fig. 1, has a direct count of 414 and a relevance of 72% to the theme of 'hotel'. Similarly, the theme of 'staff', which was the third main theme in Fig. 1, has a direct

Table 2 Full concept listing for words related to 'hotel'

Word-Like Concept	Direct Count	Likelihood	Word-Like Concept	Direct Count	Likelihood
Hotel	574	100%	Excellent	79	14%
Room	414	72%	History	77	13%
Stay	339	59%	Feel	73	13%
Staff	271	47%	Tea	72	13%
Beautiful	156	27%	Old	70	12%
Breakfast	154	27%	Enjoyed	69	12%
Service	148	26%	Wonderful	68	12%
Night	128	22%	Bed	62	11%
Restaurant	115	20%	Building	61	11%
Experience	113	20%	Special	61	11%
Pool	108	19%	Day	60	10%
Friendly	103	18%	Best	58	10%
Time	96	17%	Visit	58	10%
Location	93	16%	Boutique	57	10%
Food	91	16%	Bathroom	55	10%
Place	88	15%	Walk	53	9%
Helpful	87	15%	Property	49	9%
Bar	87	15%	Modern	45	8%
Heritage	86	15%	Welcome	44	8%
Area	86	15%	Suite	42	7%
Comfortable	85	15%	During	41	7%
Tour	84	15%	s	40	7%
Lovely	82	14%	Amenities	40	7%
Nice	81	14%	Floor	28	5%

Note: Leximancer separates themes into categories of 'Name-Like concepts' (nouns) and 'Word-like concepts' (non-nouns) in all outputs

count of 339, with a relevance of 59% to the theme of 'hotel'. Therefore, from this 'concept listing', in customer reviews where 'hotel' is mentioned, the 'room' theme is more likely to be mentioned in the same review rather than 'staff' but there is a good chance that both 'room' and 'staff' will be mentioned collectively with 'hotel'. A full concept listing is listed in Table 2.

Further to the focus on 'hotel', attention was given to the project aim, which was to identify customer reviews of HBHs. Hence, it was considered necessary to explore the words 'heritage', 'boutique', and 'hotel'. From the analysis, the reviews have identified distinct themes for each of these words. Table 2 shows that the theme of 'heritage' has a direct count of 86, with a relevance of 15% to the theme of 'hotel'; and that of 'boutique' has a direct count of 57, with a relevance of 10% to 'hotel'.

Still staying with the key themes that emerged from the data, a look at the relationship between 'room' and 'hotel' shows that 'room' has a direct count of 414, with a relevance of 72% to 'hotel', suggesting that the features of the room are important to visitors visiting HBHs. A closer look at the subthemes associated with

Table 3 Comparison of top 10 co-occurring themes with sentiment X

	Heritage	Boutique	Hotel
Word-like concept	Building	Hotel	Boutique
	Property	Heritage	Heritage
	Boutique	Property	Location
	History	Beautiful	Walk
	Lovely	Wonderful	Best
	Old	Night	Modern
	Location	Location	Beautiful
	Tour	Experience	Feel
	Hotel	Best	Wonderful
	Modern	Excellent	During

the room, highlights that 'amenities', 'comfort', 'suite' and 'bed' were features that the visitors prioritised. The emergence of 'bathroom' as a key theme linked to 'room' is also worth noting. In relation to 'hotel', 'bathroom', has a direct count of 55, with a relevance of 10% to 'hotel'. By contrast, 'staff' has a direct count of 271 to 'hotel', with a relevance of 47% to 'hotel', indicating that the staff can play a key role in visitors' experiences. An equally important attribute is 'beautiful', which has a direct count of 156, with a relevance of 27% to 'hotel', suggesting that aesthetic aspects are important to visitors.

Another main theme was 'breakfast', which has a direct count of 154, with a relevance of 27% to 'hotel', suggesting that eating is an important part of the visitor experience. This finding is not surprising given that the provision of hospitality entails extending to visitors' opportunities for a rest (e.g., 'bed'), eating (e.g., 'restaurant', 'food', 'bar', 'tea') and entertainment or activities (e.g., 'pool', 'walk', 'tour'). Combined with the importance of 'beautiful' and other subthemes from Table 2, such as 'experience', 'friendly', 'place', 'helpful', 'feel', the data shows that the experience for the visitor is 'a multisensory one', that is elaborated on in the next section.

In this dataset there were two (2) 'name-like concepts', being 'Singapore' and 'Chinese'. It is reasonable to suggest that the 'name-like concept' is more likely to be mentioned in relation to a hotel in customer reviews where it is of relevance to individuals in terms of recall for the particular hotel and also as a search term on the Web. It can also be considered in terms of the importance of 'location' and the meaning of 'place' to the visitors. In addition, it may be representative of the cultural element associated with the stay, as distinct from its historical aspect. Upon reviewing the concepts associated text there was insufficient consistent common context to assign meaning as other than the name-like mention. Further primary research would be required to determine the significance of the 'name-like concepts'.

Further exploration of the relationship between these three (3) themes was conducted through a comparison of the top 'Word-Like concepts' for each of these words/themes is known as a 'sentiment analysis' in Leximancer; Table 3 presents the top 10 concepts that comprise each theme listed highest (1) to lowest ranking (10).

Table 3 shows that the 'heritage' 'word-like concepts' referred to physical features of the exterior and interior of the premises itself. Of note for the 'boutique' is the focus on 'experience', 'best', and 'excellence', all terms indicating levels of luxury, stylishness and exceptionality consistent with the 5-star experience advertised by each hotels and the customer ratings received for the hotels selected. Common words of the 'hotel' theme bring 'heritage', 'boutique', and 'hotel' concepts together, including 'walk', 'modern' and 'feel', although the positioning of the concepts is prioritised differently in each.

The top two (2) concepts listed within Heritage, Boutique and Hotel show the focus on the building structure's visual aesthetics; this finding is consistent with the existing literature (Henderson, 2011).

The ability to take historical tours in and around the HBHs was mentioned throughout the reviews of all hotels.

> 'I found myself daydreaming in splendour whisked away to a golden era as soon as we stepped into the bright and opulent lobby. Our experience kicked off with a historical tour about the hotel's rich history, architecture, and past guests', (Reviewer 10, Raffles Hotel, Singapore).

However, within the 'Tour' theme it was observed a deeper connection (beyond the aesthetic appreciation of the HBHs experience), was present where the Tour was served to provide a connection between the HBHs-History-Visitor experience. This connection was particularly prominent in the Malaysian HBHs. For example,

> 'The Blue Mansion tour is exceptional. Terry is a knowledgeable and engaging storyteller', (Reviewer 66, Cheong Fatt Tze, Malaysia).
>
> 'Sally has been able to bring us back to the olden days by her way of telling the story. Strongly recommend for those who enjoys history and architecture', (Reviewer 57, Cheong Fatt Tze, Malaysia).
>
> 'We enjoyed trying the unique Kristang food prepared by the two Chefs in the hotel. Our spa treatment was lovely and relaxing, and the historical tour by the hotel's historian was very interesting', (Reviewer 356, Majestic Melaka, Malaysia).

Observed within the related concept listing were concepts that did not relate to physical visual aspects of HBH such as the building itself. There were also concepts that related to multisensory elements other than sight such as lovely, beautiful and feel, as underlined in Table 3. The sensory concepts were explored in terms of their quotations. An example quote for 'lovely' within the Heritage listing being,

> 'I'm overall very positive about Six Senses Duxton, but a few minor quibbles: one, it's a <u>lovely</u> calm environment in the rooms, so you really notice it when doors of the other guest rooms slam, and boy do they slam. Like prison cells', (Reviewer 157 Duxton Reserve, Singapore).

The use of the word lovely relates to what was commonly also referred to in the text excerpts as ambience or atmosphere of the HBHs producing the sense of 'feel' within the multisensory literature (Joy & Sherry Jr., 2003). The example quote also demonstrates that noise from slamming doors was a negative sentiment for the sense of hearing within the multisensory literature. To explore the existence of what other senses could be imbedded in the review text, Phase 2 of the analysis was undertaken.

6 Results – *Phase 2 Multisensory Elements*

The online reviews were then examined for evidence of multisensory perception included in the text. The online review was corded in accordance with the multisensory importance recommended in the literature review by identifying words related to all/any of the human senses of smell, hearing, taste, sight, touch, and feel. The main themes and illustrative quotes presented in Table 4 from the online reviews to showcase how the themes can be mapped to the dimensions of such a multisensory framework. Further examples were located included the mention of SMELL ('bathroom luxuriously perfumed', 'mouldy smell', 'musty smell'); HEARING ('piped music', 'classical music', 'quiet', 'Christmas carols' 'noisy'); TASTE ('Food was delicious', 'taste great', 'yummy'); SIGHT ('Raffles. Love at first sight'); TOUCH ('comfortable'). Often the sense of taste could be depicted from gastronomic experiences that of sight determined from the aesthetic appreciation of the physical features, and touch from the ambience and emotions stirred. An example of coded illustrative quotes for each of the themes identified in the Leximancer analysis is provided in Table 4.

The multisensory coding of the review text was then tabled as percentages to account for the different numbers of reviews from each hotel grouped by country location (refer Table 5). It was noted that this grouping also produced a grouping by size of the hotel with Singapore Hotels meeting the more flexible definition of HBHs and the Malaysian hotels closer to the original 100 room size classification of HBHs.

Observed from the Table 5 summary is that the most commonly mentioned sense located in the reviews was 'sight'. There were differences noted between the senses reported when the hotel reviews were grouped by country, with Malaysian Hotels customer reviews reporting higher numbers of multisensory elements in their reviews for Taste, Sight, Touch and Feel. Where multiple senses were included in the online review, the most common combination of senses was Sight with Feel. The existence of the main themes and observations of the multisensory perceptions evidenced in the online reviews are now discussed in terms of the extant literature where the greatest opportunities have been observed for HBHs improvement.

7 Discussion

The experience of staying at HBHs for customers is captured in the main themes (hotel, staff, room, breakfast, bathroom, tour, and Chinese), refer Fig. 2. The themes located in the analysis are consistent with the existing wider literature on hotel reviews (Holjevac et al., 2010). It is feasible that HBHs as a subset of Hotel literature online reviews would sit within the wider hotel review expectations. The 'hotel' theme is at the core of the accommodation and all the other elements work to shape the visitors' experiences. The following review quotes are provided as examples to

Table 4 Sample of illustrative quotes from the online reviews

Theme	Illustrative quotes from the reviews	Mapped to multisensory element
HOTEL	Excellent. Well-appointed quiet room. Fine dining at La dame du pic and writers Bar. Very attentive staff. Beautiful hotel. Great location. Thank you very much raffles hotel and staff for a great experience. Very enjoyable and relaxing. (SINGAPORE)	*Sight* *Taste* *Feel* *Hearing*
STAFF	If you're looking for a unique experience in Georgetown, I recommend staying here. It's a great location - walking distance to coffee shops, food stalls, live music, restaurants, and street art. The hotel is beautiful and has a fascinating history. If you're free, I recommend taking the free tour of the facility. (MALAYSIA)	*Sight* *Feel* *Heritage*
ROOM	Thoroughly enjoyed my stay. I had an enormous room, with everything present I could want and more importantly the ambience is wonderful. You sense the history in the walls and if you miss that, there are free house tours and a small museum as well. Breakfast was delicious every day and the staff friendly and helpful. Would have been happy to stay longer. Highly recommended. (MALAYSIA)	*Sight* *Taste* *Feel* *Heritage*
BREAKFAST	This five star heritage hotel lives up to its fame for all details. Room is specious and very clean. Bathroom is in decent size and I love the automatic toilet with auto open when you enter. Breakfast is superb with lots of choice. Lobby is really majestic in heritage building. Recommend. (SINGAPORE)	*Sight* *Taste* *Feel* *Heritage*
BATHROOM	Luxurious, food exceptional, staff exceptional, service exceptional. Had a suite in the palm court the oldest part of the hotel, enter the parlour, then into large bedroom come with four (4) poster bed, tv, then into a very luxurious bathroom. Lights, temperature, tv controls on tablet, very simple to use. And a butler to assist. What's not to like. (SINGAPORE)	*Sight* *Taste* *Feel*
TOUR	I had a great guided tour of the mansion today with an excellent guide ... She was engaging and very knowledgeable. The mansion is a beauty with a rich and interesting history. Wish I'd visited sooner. (MALAYSIA)	*Sight* *Feel* *Heritage*
PLACE	Unique, beautiful and charming. Good sized rooms as standard, all with air con, in this unique old Chinese mansion. Staff are lovely, location is excellent. Breakfast is good, with really friendly staff. Not a cheap hotel for Georgetown, but is special; worth a stay. (MALAYSIA)	*Sight* *Taste* *Feel*

provide an understanding of the themes and the relationship between concepts in terms of customer expectation and satisfaction.

The literature review identified authenticity in the heritage renovations was important for HBHs, although not to be achieved at all costs. This study supported

Table 5 Summary of review multisensory perceptions by Hotel, Country & Sample as percentages

	Smell	Hearing	Taste	Sight	Touch	Feel	Heritage
	%	%	%	%	%	%	%
Raffles (SNG)	0	33	43	65	5	60	60
Fullerton (SNG)	0	9	43	66	4	79	60
Duxton reserve (SNG)	1	19	53	87	12	65	96
Cheong Fatt Tze (MY)	2	32	38	72	2	87	81
Seven terraces (MY)	1	4	57	57	11	65	99
The majestic Melaka (MY)	0	10	70	81	29	78	95
SNG hotels (n = 162)	1	19	48	75	8	15	77
MY hotels (n = 239)	1	12	57	83	15	74	95
Total sample (N = 397)	0	15	54	81	12	72	89

authenticity and consistency in renovations in the interior design as appreciated by customers, for example,

> 'This extends to the rooms which, despite a smattering of old furniture, are mostly fitted out in a gaudy faux-antique pastiche. The bathroom is very utilitarian, with no bathtub', (Review 352, Majestic Melaka Hotel, Malaysia).

However, from Fig. 1, bathroom facilities (heat mapped blue) are distant from the concepts of heritage and boutique within the theme of hotel (heat mapped red). Even while appreciating the historic nature of a building as the HBH, customers sought modernity in bathroom facilities themselves, for example,

> 'We can enjoy staying in a historic house in traditional Peranakan style. One weak point of this hotel is its bathroom', (Review 269, Seven Terraces Hotel, Malaysia).

And positively noted the use of today's technology applied in that space,

> 'We were given thorough explanations as to the modernity of the beautiful, huge room and bathroom. Using the iPod, you can control everything that is electric', (Review 3, Raffles Hotel, Singapore).

While evidence was located of customer's perceptions of multisensory aspects of their HBHs stays impacting their experiences, there were clear opportunities to build stronger unique experiences through the development of many of the senses. The three senses with the least evidence located in the review text were Smell, Hearing and Touch. The identification of smell occurred in only 1% of the Sample (N = 397). Where smell was mentioned, by enlarging it was with negative sentiment, for example, where it related to a maintenance issue for the hotel,

> 'It rained during our stay and immediately an unbearable moldy smell was overpowering, to the extent we were planning to change hotels. Opening all windows, keeping fan and A/C running together with air freshener made us acceptable, but we did not enjoy', (Reviewer 75, Cheong Fatt Tze, Malaysia).

Only on a single occasion was smell mentioned positively,

> 'The room is all about quietness, aromatherapy and no stress, colors and ambient just make you mind float into a peaceful sleep', (Reviewer 153, Duxton Reserve, Singapore).

This was a surprising defining for HBHs, as the Tourism industry, through commercial hotels, airlines and high-end events, have been using specifically designed fragrances evoking customer sense of smell and memory association through signature scents ability to create a positive emotional impact (Boswell, 2008; Errajaa et al., 2020; Girard et al., 2019; Spence et al., 2014). Signature scenes are fragrances created purely to reflect the Hotel branding and create ambience in hotels, thereby inducing customer recall. The practice of using signature scents has been reported in studies for over a decade. The study identified an opportunity for HBHs to increase uptake and/or make this known to visitors.

Touch was the next lowest mentioned sense forming only 12% of the total reviews (N = 397). Touch was most frequently mentioned in areas akin to expectations across standard commercial 5-star hotels with luxurious soft furnishings and bathroom attire or massage facilities, for example,

> 'The room is huge and I absolutely love the interior decoration and their attention to details. The bed is super comfy and most importantly, the linen is fresh and crisp', (Reviewer 212, Seven Terraces, Malaysia).

There were no reviews located that mentioned Touch in relation to features specific to the features of HBHs and this provides further opportunity for strengthening unique competitive advantages, for example.

The final sense that was left at the bottom of the list was Hearing, forming only 15% of the total mentions of senses I the review text (N = 397). There were few positive mentions evidenced for Hearing with the majority relating to noise of the location,

> 'The only issue was with the open air restaurant/food market right beside the hotel: there are loud singers there who go on for hours in the evening...on our final night we went over and had a couple of quarts of beer (can't beat 'em, join 'em); at least the singers had fun...and it was culturally interesting; too bad for the hotel to be located beside it'. (Reviewer 76, Cheong Fatt Tze, Malaysia)

Where the use of background mood setting music had been poorly implement by the hotel,

> 'The piped music was so repetitive I asked the manager to change it, which she did. The next morning at breakfast we had Christmas carols. In April!', (Reviewer 310, Seven Terraces, Malaysia).

Or related to maintenance issues of the hotel,

> 'Can be improved/bad Delayed check in timing - overbooked themselves Creeky floor Connecting hdmi to tv. No view', (Reviewer 15, Raffles Hotel Singapore).

Where it was of positive sentiment, the most frequent identification of 'Hearing' was on the quietness of the room,

> 'The room is all about quietness, aromatherapy and no stress, colors and ambient just make you mind float into a peaceful sleep. Location is juts spot on next to one of the hot locations for night out and good drink', (Reviewer 153, Duxton Reserve, Singapore).

The storytelling ability of staff providing inhouse historical tours to hotel guest,

> 'Clement was really knowledgeable and clear in his explanation of the history behind the mansion and Kapitan Cheong. We really enjoyed the informative tour and are thankful for this experience to appreciate the beauty and rich heritage of the Blue Mansion and Penang', (Reviewer 84 Cheong Fatt Tze, Malaysia).

And in relation to service personalisation even where not full coverage was made by the hotel,

> 'All staffs are very friendly. Serving staffs even went around singing birthday songs to each individual birthday person together with a piece of cake. But they did not come to my table', (Reviewer 102, The Fullerton Hotel, Singapore).

In reviewing the websites of the selected hotels there was clear communication on each site as to the aesthetic beauty of the architecture, visualisation through stylised photographs. However, there was little communication on any of the websites to communicate the availability to connect with other customer senses. To leverage multisensory opportunities hospitality and tourism establishments should address product design and marketing strategies that communicate engagement with multiple human senses, being touch, sight, hearing, smell and taste (Brochado et al., 2021) and their ability to report on their experience through review functionality on websites and associated feedback tools to capture same. The results highlighted 6 main themes: staff, room, breakfast, bathroom, tour, and place The finding of this research reveals that sensory features of HBHs contributes to visitors 'experience. Visitors mention multisensory aspects when evaluation HBHs.. The result highlights the importance of the sight dimension of sensory experience, writing about visual aesthetic of HBH (e.g. ancient furniture, unique architecture). The results further show a focus on taste.

8 Conclusion

This study contributes to the hospitality literature, especially hospitality marketing studies by building the knowledge surrounding the unique aspects of HBHs as perceived by customers in their online reviews. A gap in the literature was located in terms of HBHs attributes of importance to visitors and the inclusion of multisensory experiences reflected in reviews. The literature gap was consistent with the opportunities presented by the themes and underdeveloped sensory experiences reported by the online reviews. The results include seven (7) main themes identified as of priority to visitors satisfaction being 'hotel', 'staff', 'room', 'breakfast', 'bathroom', 'tour' and 'culture/place'. Hotel visitors are distinguishing between Hotel, Boutique and Heritage as separate concepts demonstrating an opportunity for HBHs to develop their offerings in these respects to influence visitor satisfaction. The analysis of the reviews for multisensory elements confirmed the literature position that this area of research is still developing. The sense of 'sight' leading the senses reported confirmed the existing literature and industry practice to ensure a high level of visual aesthetics to hotel visitors. Opportunities were identified for

HBHs to develop 'smell', 'hearing' and 'touch' to further leverage that visitor satisfaction for future recall and positive word of mouth recommendation. These findings of this preliminary study support the call for further research to explore the development a novel multisensory framework that holistically captures the attributes important to both HBHs and their visitors. It is the intent of the authors to advance the current research and work toward developing such a framework. Beyond this value of the research, by gaining a better understanding of HBHs attributes, this research assists hotel operators in differentiating their properties for the sustainable enjoyment of current and future generations. Hence, future research should explore the development of a framework that includes a multisensory experience measurement tool for use across HBHs so that operators can draw and engage visitors, differentiate their properties and sustain interest in HBHs.

References

Agapito, D., & Chan, C. S. (2019, July). The contribution of a multisensory approach to responsible management in community-based tourism: The case of Yim Tin Tsai village in Hong Kong. In *9th Advances in Hospitality and Tourism Marketing and Management Conference Proceedings* (pp. 314–322).

Aggett, M. (2007). What has influenced growth in the UK's boutique hotel sector? *International Journal of Contemporary Hospitality Management, 19*(2), 169–177.

Aksoy, E. (2017). Refunctioning of alaçati houses with cultural heritage as boutique hotels. *Proceedings book*, 55.

Aliukeviciute, M. (2011). *Boutique hotels evolution.*

Almeida, A., Machado, L. P., & Silva, T. P. (2020). Heritage as a source of competitive advantage: Lessons from Madeira. In *Multilevel approach to competitiveness in the global tourism industry* (pp. 177–197). IGI Global.

Astuti, W., Permana, A. S., Qomarun, Q., & Andisetyana, R. (2017). Integrated planning model of creative industry-based kampung tourism in Jayengan Surakarta, Indonesia. *Planning Malaysia, 15*(3).

Băltescu, C. A., & Boşcor, D. (2016). The development of boutique hotels in Braşov city. *Ovidius University Annals: Economic Sciences Series, 16*(1), 274–278.

Boo, S., & Busser, J. A. (2018). Meeting planners' online reviews of destination hotels: A twofold content analysis approach. *Tourism Management, 66*, 287–301.

Boswell, R. (2008). Scents of identity: Fragrance as heritage in Zanzibar. *Journal of Contemporary African Studies, 26*(3), 295–311.

Brochado, A., Stoleriu, O., & Lupu, C. (2021). Wine tourism: A multisensory experience. *Current Issues in Tourism, 24*(5), 597–615.

Chan, C. (2012). Lodging subsector report: Boutique hotels.

Chang, T. (2017). Heritage boutique hotels as 'Experienscapes': Three views from Singapore. *Asian Journal of Tourism Research, 2*(1), 50–76.

Dinçer, M. Z., & Alrawadieh, Z. (2017). Negative word of mouse in the hotel industry: A content analysis of online reviews on luxury hotels in Jordan. *Journal of Hospitality Marketing & Management, 26*(8), 785–804.

Errajaa, K., Legohérel, P., Daucé, B., & Bilgihan, A. (2020). Scent marketing: linking the scent congruence with brand image. *International Journal of Contemporary Hospitality Management.*

Fong, S. W. L., Kian, T. P., Fern, Y. S., & Quan, S. L. (2018). The impact of online consumer review to online hotel booking intention in Malaysia. *International Journal of Supply Chain Management, 7*(2), 140–145.

Freund, D., & Munsters, W. (2004). *Developments in the hotel industry: Design meets historis properties*.

Frey, B. B. (2018). *The SAGE encyclopedia of educational research, measurement, and evaluation* (Vol. 1–4). Sage.

Fuentes-Moraleda, L., Villacé-Molinero, T., Lafuente-Ibáñez, C., & Muñoz-Mazón, A. (2020). Do the managers of boutique hotels value their tangible and intangible attributes in the same way as their guests? *International Journal of Management Practice, 13*(5), 521–546.

Fullerton, L., McGettigan, K., & Stephens, S. (2010). Integrating management and marketing strategies at heritage sites. *International Journal of Culture, Tourism and Hospitality Research.*

Garrod, B., & Fyall, A. (2000). Managing heritage tourism. *Annals of Tourism Research, 27*(3), 682–708.

Ghaderi, Z., Dehghan Pour Farashah, M. H., Aslani, E., & Hemati, B. (2020). Managers' perceptions of the adaptive reuse of heritage buildings as boutique hotels: Insights from Iran. *Journal of Heritage Tourism, 15*(6), 696–708.

Girard, A., Lichters, M., Sarstedt, M., & Biswas, D. (2019). Short-and long-term effects of nonconsciously processed ambient scents in a servicescape: Findings from two field experiments. *Journal of Service Research, 22*(4), 440–455.

Henderson, J. C. (2011). Hip heritage: The boutique hotel business in Singapore. *Tourism and Hospitality Research, 11*(3), 217–223.

Henderson, J. C. (2013). Selling the past: Heritage hotels. *Tourism: An International Interdisciplinary Journal, 61*(4), 451–454.

Hinkin, T. R. (1995). A review of scale development practices in the study of organisations. *Journal of Management, 21*(5), 967–988.

Holjevac, I. A., Marković, S., & Raspor, S. (2010). *Customer satisfaction measurement in hotel industry: content analysis study.* Paper presented at the 4th International Scientific Conference Planning for the future learning from the past: Contemporary Developments in Tourism, Travel & Hospitality.

http://www.raffles.com/singapore

http://www.georgetownheritage.com

Hussein, A. S., & Hapsari, R. (2020). Heritage experiential quality and behavioural intention: Lessons from Indonesian heritage hotel consumers. *Journal of Heritage Tourism*, 1–20.

ICAO. (2021). Retrived from https://icao.int

Joy, A., & Sherry, J. F., Jr. (2003). Speaking of art as embodied imagination: A multisensory approach to understanding aesthetic experience. *Journal of Consumer Research, 30*(2), 259–282.

Khosravi, S., Malek, A., & Ekiz, E. H. (2014). *Why tourists are attracted to boutique hotels: Case of Penang Island, Malaysia*.

Kilgour, M., Sasser, S. L., & Larke, R. (2015). The social media transformation process: curating content into strategy. *Corporate Communications: An International Journal, 20*(3), 326–343. https://doi.org/10.1108/CCIJ-07-2014-0046

Kim, B., Wang, S., & Heo, C. Y. (2017). Sensory marketing in hotels. *Routledge Handbook of Hospitality Marketing, 245*.

Lee, W., & Chhabra, D. (2015). *Heritage hotels and historic lodging: Perspectives on experiential marketing and sustainable culture*. Taylor & Francis.

Lei, S., & Law, R. (2015). Content analysis of TripAdvisor reviews on restaurants: A case study of Macau. *Journal of Tourism, 16*(1).

Leximancer. (2018). *Introduction to Leximancer and content analysis*. Retrieved from https://info.leximancer.com/

Lim, W. M., & Endean, M. (2009). Elucidating the aesthetic and operational characteristics of UK boutique hotels. *International Journal of Contemporary Hospitality Management.*

Little, S. (2020). Whose heritage? What inheritance?: Conceptualising family language identities. *International Journal of Bilingual Education and Bilingualism, 23*(2), 198–212.

Manthiou, A., Kang, J., Sumarjan, N., & Tang, L. (2016). The incorporation of consumer experience into the branding process: An investigation of name-brand hotels. *International Journal of Tourism Research, 18*(2), 105–115.

O'Connor, C., & Joffe, H. (2020). Intercoder reliability in qualitative research: Debates and practical guidelines. *International Journal of Qualitative Methods, 19*, 1609406919899220.

Panchal, J. H., Tang, C. M., & Bradshaw, A. (2018). Guest impressions of boutique hotels in Singapore. *Journal of Economic & Management Perspectives, 12*, 742–746.

Pijls, R., Groen, B. H., Galetzka, M., & Pruyn, A. T. (2017). Measuring the experience of hospitality: Scale development and validation. *International Journal of Hospitality Management, 67*, 125–133.

Price, P., Chiang, I. C. A., Jhangiani, R., Project, B. C. O. T., Open Textbook, L., & Bccampus. (2015). *Research methods in psychology* (2nd Canadian ed.). BC campus, BC Open Textbook Project.

Qu, H., Kim, L. H., & Im, H. H. (2011). A model of destination branding: Integrating the concepts of the branding and destination image. *Tourism Management, 32*(3), 465–476.

Rahman, S. (2013). Heritage management challenges in historic town of Ludlow, England. *World Applied Sciences Journal, 24*(12), 1589–1596.

Rahman, S. (2018). Emerging built heritage commodification of boutique hotels in world heritage site: Evidence from George Town, Penang, Malaysia. *Planning Malaysia, 16*(8).

Sotiriadou, P., Brouwers, J., & Le, T.-A. (2014). Choosing a qualitative data analysis tool: A comparison of NVivo and Leximancer. *Annals of Leisure Research, 17*(2), 218–234.

Spence, C., Puccinelli, N. M., Grewal, D., & Roggeveen, A. L. (2014). Store atmospherics: A multisensory perspective. *Psychology & Marketing, 31*(7), 472–488.

Terzano, K. (2014). Commodification of transitioning ethnic enclaves. *Behavioral Sciences, 4*(4), 341–351.

Timothy, D. J. (2020). 5 looking for something real: Heritage, tourism and elusive authenticity. In *Cultural heritage and tourism* (pp. 111–133). Channel View Publications.

Timothy, D., & Teye, V. (2009). *Tourism and the lodging sector*. Routledge

Vincent, D., Eva, L. G., & Versailles, D. W. (2016). CSR communications strategies through social media and influence on e-reputation: An exploratory study. *Management Decision, 54*(2), 363–389. https://doi.org/10.1108/MD-01-2015-0015

Weber, R. P. (1990). *Basic content analysis* (2nd ed.). Sage.

Wells, V. K., Manika, D., Gregory-Smith, D., Taheri, B., & McCowlen, C. (2015). Heritage tourism, CSR and the role of employee environmental behaviour. *Tourism Management, 48*, 399–413.

Xu, J. B., & Chan, A. (2010). A conceptual framework of hotel experience and customer-based brand equity. *International Journal of Contemporary Hospitality Management.*

Yoo, K.-H., & Lee, W. (2015). Use of Facebook in the US heritage accommodations sector: An exploratory study. *Journal of Heritage Tourism, 10*(2), 191–201.

Yu Park, H. (2010). Heritage tourism: Emotional journeys into nationhood. *Annals of Tourism Research, 37*(1), 116–135.

Zhovkva, O. I. (2020). *Designing modern boutique hotels*. Paper presented at the International conference on Research in Engineering, Science and Technology.

Exploring the Role of Reef-Friendly, Edible Packaging in Reducing Plastic Pollution: Proposition of a Conceptual Model Explaining Purchase Intentions

Breda McCarthy and Pengji Wang

Abstract The aim of this paper is to highlight the ways in which the sustainable packaging industry, in conjunction with consumers, can help to reduce environmental damage to fragile ecosystems. We discuss several theoretical models that have been widely used to explain behavourial change. The literature review suggests that lifestyle segmentation, and concepts from the extended theory of planned behaviour and adoption of innovation literature provide rich explanations for why individuals are likely to purchase and adopt novel forms of sustainable packaging. We propose a model identifying several factors that influence purchase intentions and further research is recommended with a focus on market segments defined by sustainable lifestyles.

Keywords Sustainable packaging · Pro-environmental behaviour · Lifestyle segmentation · Spill-over effects

1 Introduction

Plastic is pervasive in our environment, it is embedded in everyday practices and their use can only be understood in terms of the services they provide, and the "wider networks and relations of which they are part." (Evans et al., 2020). Although it has a significant role to play in food packaging – keeping food fresh and safe to eat, making products easy to transport and consume - plastic packaging is both easy to dispose of and a pollutant. According to recent estimates, only 9% of all plastics ever produced have been recycled, meaning most ends up in landfills or elsewhere in the

---

B. McCarthy (✉)
College of Business, Law & Governance, James Cook University, Townsville, QLD, Australia
e-mail: breda.mccarthy@jcu.edu.au

P. Wang
Business, James Cook University, Singapore, Singapore
e-mail: pengji.wang@jcu.edu.au

© The Author(s), under exclusive license to Springer Nature Singapore Pte Ltd. 2022
T. Chaiechi, J. Wood (eds.), *Community Empowerment, Sustainable Cities, and Transformative Economies*, https://doi.org/10.1007/978-981-16-5260-8_21

environment (Geyer et al., 2017). Plastic waste is now so alarming that it is seen as a geological marker of the Anthropocene era (Vince & Hardesty, 2017). The cumulative amount produced, as of 2015, was around 5 billion tons of plastic, which is enough to wrap the Earth in a layer of cling-film (Zalasiewicz et al., 2016).

When plastic was first invented, it was hailed as a miracle, "the material of a thousand uses", but today it is seen as an environmental disaster (UNEP, 2018). An estimated 6 to 12 million tonnes of plastic enters the ocean each year, resulting in a global pollution problem (Vince & Hardesty, 2017). There is a rapidly expanding literature on plastics, documenting its effects on the land, lakes, rivers and the sea, and on animals and marine mammals (Baird & Hooker, 2000). Plastic kills marine fauna such as turtles through ingestion (Gregory, 2009), and it is noted that all but one species of marine turtles are classified as threatened (Nelms et al., 2015). Surveys show that most micro-plastics (which are fragments of plastic invisible to the naked eye, typically <5 mm), collected from rivers (Rowley et al., 2020) and the offshore marine environment, are polyethylene (PE) and polypropylene (PP), two resins commonly used in single-use plastic food packaging (Zettler et al., 2013). Single use packaging is prevalent in plastic bottles, food wrappers and bags.

Communicating environmental sustainability through packaging can convey positive customer experiences and influence purchase intentions (Signori et al., 2019). There is a vast literature on pro-environmental behaviour (PEB), which refers to any practice (such as purchasing, use, post-use, management and activism) that consciously seeks to limit the impact of human activities on the environment. However, the number of studies assessing the effect of sustainable packaging on consumer decisions are relatively scarce (Boz et al., 2020). Since consumer perceptions of environmentally friendly packaging are not well understood, this research responds to the call by Ketelsen, Janssen, & Hamm (2020, p.15) to focus on consumer response to specific packaging solutions. It is critical to understand the response of consumers to novel forms of packaging, such as edible packaging, since consumers have market power and ultimately it is consumers who decide whether to buy, or not buy, products that are sustainably packaged. According to Steenis et al. (2017), p. 286), "one of the key challenges for packaging managers, marketers and designers is to develop sustainable packaging designs that are acceptable to consumers."

The research question of this study is as follows:

1. What are the factors affecting a consumer's decision to purchase edible packaging?

The research objective is to develop a research model and formulate research propositions related to the consumer's purchase of edible packaging, drawing on the theory of planned behaviour.

The outline of this paper is as follows. We provide a context by outlining the plastic pollution crisis and policy responses to plastic waste. This is followed by a discussion of theoretical models to explain consumer response to sustainable food packaging. Lastly, recommendations for future consumer-oriented research are laid down accordingly.

2 Context: The Plastic Packaging Crisis

2.1 Food Packaging and Plastic Pollution

Plastic is used in many industry sectors due to its flexibility, durability, water resistance and affordability and demand for plastic has grown exponentially (Sharma et al., 2020). In the food and beverage industry, packaging plays an essential role such as protecting products throughout the supply chain and ensuring their safe delivery (Politis et al., 2019). Food packaging serves numerous functions, such as maintaining freshness, extending shelf life and avoiding food waste (Wikström et al., 2014). It also plays a critical role in differentiating brands and serves as a means of marketing communications (Davison & Redhill, 1998). The recent Covid-19 pandemic has further increased reliance on plastics for food safety and hygienic purposes, and there is growing concern that the pandemic could fuel a rise in the throw away culture (Sharma et al., 2020).

Despite the utility of plastic in food packaging, a major side effect is its contribution to plastic pollution. Such that plastic pollution not only threatens the biodiversity, but also our economy. Plastic rubbish in marine environments is a major environmental issue, with many studies documenting the magnitude of the negative impact on wildlife (Eagle et al., 2016; Pettipas et al., 2016; Wilcox et al., 2016). Such a hazard for wildlife remains for a considerable period of time given that plastics degrade very slowly (Jakovcevic et al., 2014). In addition, pollution of beaches via plastic and other debris may impact adversely on visitor numbers, with potential negative impacts on tourism-based economies (Pettipas et al., 2016). Another consideration is that the majority of plastic packages are produced from fossil fuels, resulting in a large carbon footprint (Spierling et al., 2018). According to the World Economic Forum (2016), an estimated cost of externalities related to the use of plastics is US$40 billion annually. Such externalities may be attributed to greenhouse gas emissions resulting from the production phase (which consumes fossil feed-stocks) and after-use incineration, damage to natural systems such as the ocean and other urban infrastructure for example clogging sewers, and health and environmental impacts from synthetic substances and additives. Calls are made for the adoption of a radically different model of consumption – one that does not involve single-use packaging – to help solve the plastic waste challenge (World Economic Forum, 2016).

2.2 Public Policy Response to the Plastic Waste Challenge

In Australia and elsewhere, bans on single-use plastic bags for grocery shopping have been enacted to reduce environmental harm (Australian Government Department of Agriculture, Water and the Environment, 2020) on account of their volume, the resource intensiveness (i.e. energy use) of their manufacture and the fact that

90% are used only once before being consigned to rubbish (Muralidharan & Sheehan, 2016). However, plastic bags are part of a much wider marine pollution problem in which other forms of plastics play a significant role (Duhec et al., 2015). For instance, it is reported that a third of all forms of plastic food packaging that are too small or too complex to be recycled often find their way into the ocean, for example, coffee cup lids, food wrappers, take-away boxes, drink pouches and sachets (MacArthur, 2017).

In the European Union (EU), the circular economy approach is increasingly embraced by both industry and policy spheres, as evident in the EU waste legislation and directives to reduce plastic pollution (Foschi & Bonoli, 2019). There is growing commitment internationally to solving plastic waste, and policy measures are being taken by the Group of Twenty (G20) countries to discourage single-use plastics, encourage bio-based and biodegradable plastic substitutes, and improve plastic waste collection and recycling (Fadeeva & Van Berkel, 2021). The voluntary Australian Packaging Covenant (Covenant, 2010) have assisted the packaging supply chain to rethink the design of packaging materials and formats to reduce their environmental impacts.

In Australia, it is reported that only 11.5% of plastics are recovered for recycling or energy. Furthermore, "*... away-from-home plastic packaging collection systems are underdeveloped... and most of these products continue to be disposed to landfill at end of life*" (Australian Government Department of Agriculture, Water and the Environment, 2020, p. 9). To ensure the development of more sustainable materials for packaging, and the correct disposal thereof there is a need for collaboration between industry and government. Interest in the plastic problem had markedly increased in social science in the last few years (Heidbreder et al., 2019). While the problem is complex and no one single solution is likely to have an immediate impact, a diverse range of stakeholders working collaboratively have the potential to make an impact (Heidbreder et al., 2019; Veiga et al., 2016; Vince & Hardesty, 2017).

2.3 Industry Response: Bioplastics and Edible Packaging

Sustainable packaging initiatives are aligned with the goal of sustainable development, i.e., development that meets the needs of the present, without compromising the needs of future generations (World Commission on Environment and Development, 1987). Sustainable packaging goals are linked to the United Nations Sustainable Development Goals, notably goal 12 (responsible consumption and production) and goal 14 (life below water) (United Nations, n.d.). Sustainable packaging is defined as "packaging that has a comparatively low environmental impact as measured by life cycle models" (Steenis et al., 2017, p. 278). One of the sustainable alternatives are packages that are bio-based (derived from biomass), and at least partially made from plant-based materials such as crops, wood or grasses, and are either recyclable or compostable (Taufik et al., 2020). However, terms such as bio-plastics and biodegradable are not unambiguously defined and labels confuse consumers (Van den Oever et al., 2017). Despite the dynamic research and development on bio-sourced and/or biodegradable materials, market demand is hampered by green washing suspicion, confusion on the part of consumers and controversies about its environment benefit, such as resource utilization, greenhouse gas emissions (GHG) and pollution (Guillard et al., 2018). In addition, considering potential impacts on end users' health and safety is critical to securing public acceptance (Falcone & Imbert, 2018). Therefore, studies on consumers' responses to edible packaging are needed.

Edible packaging goes a step further than bio-based packaging, since it has plant-based coatings and films that are edible. Edible films are derived from proteins, lipids and polysaccharide molecules, found in plant-based materials such as cassava, potato starch and seaweed (Umaraw et al., 2020). The films or coatings may be transparent or translucent, flavourless and colourless, but they may also have a particular taste. The main purpose of edible coatings is to increase the natural barrier of perishable fruits and vegetables, but applications are expected to grow, such as in the use of ready-to-eat products (Aguirre-Joya et al., 2018). Edible packaging has gained wide interest among food scientists and industry (Parente Ribeiro Cerqueira, 2019) and falls within the mandates of the circular economy. It may help mitigate the problem of single-use packaging, linked to convenient consumption, which is a feature of the modern economy (MacArthur, 2017).

While edible packaging is a better option than using plastic, it is still in the development phase, with all the technical challenges, associated uncertainties around consumer acceptance and commercial viability (Jeya-Jeevahan et al., 2020). Furthermore, the production of some types of edible packaging may have externalities, including land use and biodiversity (Patel, 2019), and if the costs and benefits of sustainable packaging are not clear to consumers, this could reduce consumer acceptance. Practical applications are limited due to the high cost of the raw materials and limited production (Galgano, 2015). While there are niche opportunities for plant-derived packaging, such as edible water pouches for participants in marathons and for some single-use items (i.e., seasoning sachets, wraps for fast food and fresh goods, packets used in meal kits and straws), the higher price could limit its marketability (Patel, 2019). Furthermore, the edible package needs to be disposed of properly, if consumers do not wish to eat it. Studies have shown that consumers are not familiar with compostable bio-based plastic packaging, and this negatively affects disposal behaviour (Taufik et al., 2020). Despite these limitations, edible packaging has the potential to contribute to a cleaner environment, as the use of bio-based materials in general has lower greenhouse gas emissions than fossil-based materials (Bos et al., 2016).

3 Literature Review: Theoretical Models

In this paper, we advance the literature by developing a conceptual model (see Fig. 1) to explain the determinants of consumer purchase of edible packaging. We draw primarily on research into pro-environmental behaviour as well as sustainable

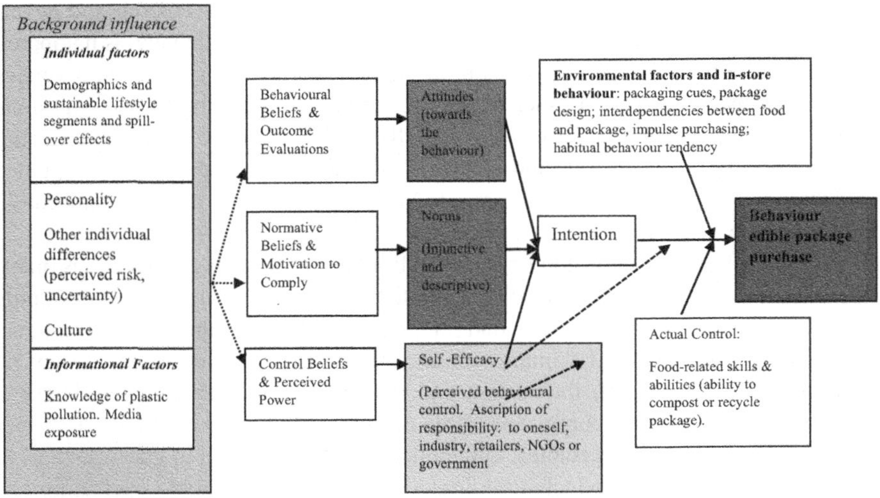

Fig. 1 An integrative Model of the Determinants of Sustainable Packaging Purchase. (Source: Adapted from Fishbein & Cappella, 2006)

lifestyles. The conceptual model draws on the well-known theory of planned behaviour originally developed by Fishbein and Ajzen in 1975, which has been extensively cited, extended and used to predict behaviour in various consumption domains (Bosnjak et al., 2020). The adapted model, outlined in Fig. 1, can be used to guide future research into edible packaging.

4 Pro-Environmental Behaviour

There is a vast literature on pro-environmental behaviour (PEB), which refers to any practice (such as purchasing, use, post-use, management, activism behaviors) that consciously seeks to limit the impact of human activities on the environment (Boz et al., 2020). Pro environmental behaviour is understood to be a mixture of self-interest and pro-social motives such as concern for other people, the next generation, other species and eco-systems (Bamberg & Möser, 2007). Research into the field of consumers and their response to sustainable packaging dates back more than 20 years (Herbes et al., 2018). For example, an early study focused on German consumers and their response to environmentally-friendly packaging (Thøgersen, 1996). Rational models of buyer behaviour, such the theory of planned behaviour (Van Birgelen et al., 2009) and the theory of reasoned action (TRA) (Prakash & Pathak, 2017), are frequently used in studies of sustainable packaging.

The model that informs this paper (see Fig. 1) shows that the critical variables that underpin intentions are attitudes towards a specific behaviour, norms and self-efficacy. These concepts are influenced by beliefs and background influences further back in the causal chain. If perceived behavioural control or self-efficacy is weak (i.e. an individual's belief about their ability to positively influence outcomes such as solving an environmental problem), then a given behaviour may not be performed. Researchers have adopted and adapted these 'behavioural' frameworks and have sought to explore a broader set of influences on environmental behaviour, such as values (Schwartz, 1994) and moral norms (Schwartz, 1977), as well as environmental concern and socio-demographics (Barr et al., 2011). For instance, studies have emphasised particular socio-demographic variables, such as gender, education and income, as antecedents of individual ecological concern (Magnier & Schoormans, 2015).

Attitudes are a key variable in the theory of reasoned action (TRA) and they have received considerable attention in the packaging context. For example, scholars have found that consumers who have positive attitudes towards the environment are more likely to purchase eco-friendly products and dispose of packaging in a sustainable manner (Van Birgelen et al., 2009). Studies have also revealed positive attitudes towards 'environmentally friendly' packaging, in particular towards end-of-life attributes, such as recyclability, reusability and biodegradability (Herbes et al., 2018). However, confusion and greenwashing concerns exist (Lynch et al., 2017). Among various packages, it is found that compostable bio-based packages have the most environmental appeal for consumers, although a lack of familiarity of the disposal process hampers proper disposal (Taufik et al., 2020).

It is widely acknowledged in the consumer behaviour literature that attitudes have cognitive and affective components (Thøgersen, 1999). For instance, consumers with a higher level of bio-based product familiarity generally have more positive attitudes towards bio-based products (Reinders et al., 2017). Therefore, some awareness or knowledge is needed to guide behaviour. Earlier research has shown that a low salience is given to environmentally friendly packaging since cues were not obvious and consumers lacked awareness and knowledge of packaging waste (Thøgersen, 1996). In line with such a finding, recent literature shows that consumers do not have a clear idea of what sustainable packaging is (Boz et al., 2020), such as the materials used in bio-based containers and disposal methods available after use (Koutsimanis et al., 2012). On another note, eco-labels as a tool to communicate the information about the environmental outcomes, are seen as an enabler of consumer adoption in the literature on green purchase behaviour (Nath et al., 2013). It is further found that eco-label knowledge is positively associated with attitudes towards the environment, and trust in eco-labels affects 'green' purchasing behaviour (Taufique et al., 2017). While there is an the assumption that increased knowledge will lead to pro-environmental behaviour is the subject of much debate in the literature (Ardoin et al., 2015), scholars have concluded that building consumer knowledge and trust in eco-labels is imperative (Taufique et al., 2017).

Limitations of behavioural models have been widely debated. Research has found a weak correlation between general environmental attitudes and specific behaviour

(Alwitt & Pitts, 1996) and the attitudes-behaviour gap is well recognised in the literature (Ketelsen et al., 2020). One study on Romanian consumers found that the main barriers to adoption of green packaging are the price and lack of information (Orzan et al., 2018). Likewise, a review of reusable packaging systems found that inconvenience, lack of availability, cost and pricing issues are barriers to adoption (Coelho et al., 2020).

The theory of reasoned action (TRA) has been applied to sustainable packaging. A study of young Indian consumers confirmed that purchase intention is significantly influenced by personal norms, attitudes, environmental concern and willingness to pay (Prakash & Pathak, 2017). Another study, based on structural equation modelling, revealed that environment- and health-related concerns associated with plastics are key drivers of plastic avoidance (Cavaliere et al., 2020). Environmental concern is frequently measured in the literature on the response of consumers to 'green' packaging (Ketelsen et al., 2020). In the context of green purchase behaviour, studies have found that peer influence is a top predictor of green purchase behaviour (Taufik et al., 2020).

4.1 Habitual Behaviour and Consumer Response to Packaging Design

The theoretical frameworks discussed above largely imply that individuals make reasoned choices and tend to over-rationalise behaviour (Burgess et al., 1998). However, in many cases, behaviour is habitual and guided by automated cognitive processes, rather than being preceded by elaborate reasoning (Jakovcevic et al., 2014). Therefore, the application of these behavioural models to habitual practices, such as grocery shopping, may require further explanations.

Packaging plays an important role in influencing in-store purchasing decisions, especially for food products where purchase decisions are characterized by low involvement, habits or impulsive processes (Liao et al., 2015). In food purchasing literature, a distinction is often made between intrinsic and extrinsic cues. The former refers to cues, which if changed, would produce a change in the physical or chemical aspects of the product (such as colour, flavor, aroma, alcohol content), while the latter refers to non-physical characteristics (such as package design) (Szybillo & Jacoby, 1974). Design plays an important role in purchasing decisions and cues such as the packaging material, aesthetic elements such as the colour and graphics, and text elements, have been found to influence expectations and attitudes in relation to sustainable packaging (Rebollar et al., 2017). The literature on package design shows that consumers make use of simple visual elements with limited cognitive effort to make fast decisions in grocery stores (Clement et al., 2013). Therefore, quick, emotional responses and not just cognitive deliberations to packaging must be taken into account.

5 Market Segmentation and Sustainable Lifestyles

Segmentation studies are common in the literature, where attempts are made to assign individuals to particular groups or segments, based on a complex array of behaviours and attitudes (Barr et al., 2011). For instance, studies have identified three sustainability-related segments: 'greens', 'potential greens', and 'non-greens' (Verain et al., 2012). Scholars have argued that lifestyle segmentation is a sophisticated means of interpreting groups, rather than focusing exclusively on socio-demographic variables (Lubowiecki-Vikuk et al., 2021). Sociologists, however, adopt a different perspective and question the notion of individualistic lifestyle choices, and frame consumption as a set of day-to-day practices and habits that are interdependent and socially embedded (Shove & Warde, 2002).

5.1 *Sustainable Lifestyles and Spill-Over Effects*

The notion of sustainable lifestyles has been critiqued within the context of the ongoing debate concerning 'spillover' effects. The concept of spill-over effects asserts that one pro-environmental behaviour increases the likelihood of performing additional pro-environmental behaviours (Truelove et al., 2014). On the one hand, positive spillovers have been observed, where recycling positively correlates with the avoidance of excess packaging (Thøgersen, 1999). On the other hand, scholars have found that behaviours performed in one consumption setting, such as in the home, do not automatically lead to change in another setting, such as a reduction in air travel within leisure and tourism settings (Barr et al., 2011). The absence of spillovers may be explained by different factors such as decision making mode, motives and the characteristics of the behaviour, whether it is difficult or new (Truelove et al., 2014). Counter-arguing is put forward as another explanation, particularly when individuals are asked to take responsibility for solving problems they did not cause, and therefore the balance between personal cost and benefits needs to be adjusted (Thøgersen, 1999). Inconsistent findings in the literature suggest the need for further research.

5.2 *Personal Factors: Perceived Risk and Uncertainty*

Perceived risk and uncertainty are key influences on consumer purchasing decisions (Koenig-Lewis et al., 2014). Perceived risk is related to the functional or physical properties of the new sustainable materials, as well as to health-related risks (Chen & Chang, 2013). In the case of products made of recycled ocean plastic, it is proposed that consumers might be are afraid of contamination risk and this risk is high for food and drink products (Magnier et al., 2019). A recent study on bio-based products found that highly ambivalent consumers are more sensitive to risks than less ambivalent consumers, and such a sensitivity is negatively associated with purchase intentions (Onwezen et al., 2017).

5.3 Interdependencies Between the Food Product and Packaging Attributes

The adoption of new forms of packaging depends not only on the package, but also the product within it, so the interdependencies between packaging and products (i.e., foods) need to be analysed (Boz et al., 2020). One study reported that framing an edible package as one with environmental benefits can negatively judge the product attributes, such as health and taste (Aldred Cheek & Wansink, 2017). Several studies have found that environmentally-friendly packaging is less important to consumers than other product attributes, such as price, product quality (Martinho et al., 2015) and healthiness. Inconsistent findings in the literature suggest the need for further research.

6 Propositions

Based on the literature review and contradictory findings in the literature, we propose a research model, illustrated in Fig. 2.

This model deals with sustainable packaging from the consumer's point of view. A list of measurement scales obtained from prior literature can be found in Appendix 1. Consumers who are committed to being environmentally responsible are likely to buy edible packaging, due to positive spill-over effects. An adoption of sustainable patterns of living should reflect positive attitudes towards pro-environmental behaviour. Thus, we propose:

Proposition 1

The adoption of a sustainable lifestyle has a direct and positive influence on purchase intentions of edible packaging.

The literature review shows that attitudes have a cognitive component (Thøgersen, 1999) and therefore some familiarity with edible packaging is needed to guide purchase. We propose:

Proposition 2

Familiarity with edible packaging has a direct and positive influence on purchase intentions of edible packaging.

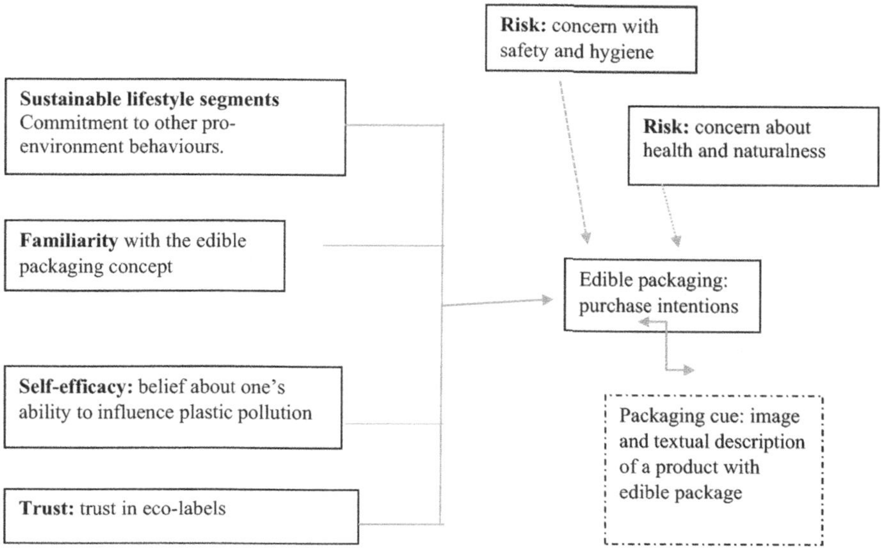

Fig. 2 The research model

The adoption of sustainable packaging is found to be influenced by the interdependencies between food attributes and the package. Consumers may find it difficult to accept edible packaging due to reservations about safety and hygiene.

Proposition 3

Concern about safety will weaken purchase intention of edible packaging.

Pro environmental behaviour is understood to be a mixture of self-interest and pro-social motives. Concern about personal costs and risks are emphasized in the literature. Therefore, the following propositions are formulated:

Proposition 4

Concern about healthiness and naturalness will weaken purchase intentions of edible packaging.

The literature emphasizes the concept of self-efficacy and this factor reflects the belief that one's action can, or cannot, contribute to solving environmental problems. The proposition is as follows:

Proposition 5

Belief in one's ability to influence environmental outcomes, such as plastic pollution, has a direct and positive influence on purchase intentions.

The literature highlights that trust is an enabler of consumer acceptance of sustainable packaging and the final proposition is as follows:

Proposition 6

Trust in eco labels has a direct and positive influence on purchase intentions.

7 Summary

In the face of growing societal concerns about plastic pollution, the packaging industry is bringing new forms of packaging to the marketplace. The success of next-generation sustainable packaging forms is strongly linked to consumer acceptance, so it is important to understand the factors underlying pro-environmental behaviour. Innovation models remain in the background. This paper contributes to the literature by reviewing theories relevant to the adoption of innovation and the theory of reasoned action, lifestyle segmentation, and the concept of spill-over effects. A model is proposed to explain purchase intentions in the context of edible packaging.

Appendix 1

Table 1 Summary of Measures of Sustainable Consumption

Scale name	Authors	Description	Items
Purchase intention	Prakash and Pathak (2017)	I would prefer to buy products with packaging materials that are environmentally-friendly.	2 items; 5 point Likert scale, from strongly agree to strongly disagree.
		I would buy products with packaging materials that are environmentally friendly, even if they belong to a less well-known company.	
Sustainable consumption behaviour	Geiger et al. (2018)	Four key dimensions of sustainable consumption behaviour (SCB) and impact. Covering phases from acquisition, to usage and disposal of products and services; covering consumption domains such as food, housing, mobility and clothing.	16 item; 5 point frequency scale, never to always.
Behaviours related to use of	Schnurr et al. (2018),	I use single use plastic bags	2 items; 5 point frequency scale, never to always.
		I use plastic water bottles	

(continued)

Table 1 (continued)

Scale name	Authors	Description	Items
single-use plastics.	Bartolotta and Hardy (2018)		
Behaviours related to recycling and mindful consumption	Schnurr et al. (2018), Bartolotta and Hardy (2018)	I recycle as much as I can	3 items; 5 point frequency scale, never to always
		I try to reduce my amount of rubbish.	
		I try to reduce my consumption.	
Familiarity with edible packaging	Herbes et al. (2018)	Hygiene and safety: The product with edible packaging may not be as safe as standard products.	1 item; 5 point familiarity scale, not at all to very familiar.
Concern about healthiness	Aldred Cheek and Wansink (2017)	Healthiness: The ingredients may not be as nutritious as other foods	1 item; 5 point concern scale, from not at all concerned to very concerned
Concern about naturalness	Author-derived	Naturalness: The ingredients of the edible package may not be as natural or as pure as other products	1 items; 5 point concern scale, from not at all concerned to very concerned
Self-efficacy (ascription of responsibility)	Adapted from Herbes et al. (2018)	Protecting the environment from plastic pollution is the responsibility of the consumer.	5 items, 5 point scale, most responsible to least responsible.
		Protecting the environment from plastic pollution is the responsibility of our government.	
		Protecting the environment from plastic pollution is the responsibility of environmental organisations (like WWF or Greenpeace).	
		Protecting the environment from plastic pollution is the responsibility of business / corporations.	
Trust in eco-labels	Taufique et al. (2017)	The labels are genuinely committed to environmental protection.	3 items, 5 point Likert scale, ranging from strongly agree to strongly disagree.
		Most of what labels say about its products is true.	
		If the label makes a claim or promise about its product, it's probably true.	

References

Ardoin, N. M., Wheaton, M., Bowers, A. W., Hunt, C. A., & Durham, W. H. (2015). Nature-based tourism's impact on environmental knowledge, attitudes, and behavior: A review and analysis of the literature and potential future research. *Journal of Sustainable Tourism, 23*(6), 838–858.

Aguirre-Joya, J. A., De Leon-Zapata, M. A., Alvarez-Perez, O. B., Torres-León, C., Nieto-Oropeza, D. E., Ventura-Sobrevilla, J. M., … Ramos-Aguiñaga, M. E. (2018). Basic and applied concepts of edible packaging for foods. In A. M. Grumezescu & A. M. Holban (Eds.), *Food packaging and preservation* (pp. 1–61). Academic.

Aldred Cheek, K., & Wansink, B. (2017). Making it part of the package: Edible packaging is more acceptable to young consumers when it is integrated with food. *Journal of Food Products Marketing, 23*(6), 723–732.

Alwitt, L. F., & Pitts, R. E. (1996). Predicting purchase intentions for an environmentally sensitive product. *Journal of Consumer Psychology, 5*(1), 49–64.

Baird, R. W., & Hooker, S. K. (2000). Ingestion of plastic and unusual prey by a juvenile harbour porpoise. *Canadian Journal of Fisheries and Aquatic Sciences, 51*, 172–178.

Bamberg, S., & Möser, G. (2007). Twenty years after Hines, Hungerford, and Tomera: A new meta-analysis of psycho-social determinants of pro-environmental behaviour. *Journal of Environmental Psychology, 27*(1), 14–25.

Barr, S., Shaw, G., & Coles, T. (2011). Times for (Un)sustainability? Challenges and opportunities for developing behaviour change policy. A case-study of consumers at home and away. *Global Environmental Change, 21*(4), 1234–1244. https://doi.org/10.1016/j.gloenvcha.2011.07.011

Bartolotta, J. F., & Hardy, S. D. (2018). Barriers and benefits to desired behaviors for single use plastic items in Northeast Ohio's Lake Erie basin. *Marine Pollution Bulletin, 127*, 576–585.

Bos, H. L., Meesters, K. P., Conijn, S. G., Corré, W. J., & Patel, M. K. (2016). Comparing biobased products from oil crops versus sugar crops with regard to non-renewable energy use, GHG emissions and land use. *Industrial Crops and Products, 84*, 366–374.

Bosnjak, M., Ajzen, I., & Schmidt, P. (2020). The theory of planned behavior: Selected recent advances and applications. *Europe's Journal of Psychology, 16*(3), 352–356.

Boz, Z., Korhonen, V., & Koelsch Sand, C. (2020). Consumer considerations for the implementation of sustainable packaging: A review. *Sustainability, 12*(6), 2192.

Burgess, J., Harrison, C. M., & Filius, P. (1998). Environmental communication and the cultural politics of environmental citizenship. *Environment and Planning A, 30*(8), 1445–1460.

Cavaliere, A., Pigliafreddo, S., De Marchi, E., & Banterle, A. (2020). Do consumers really want to reduce plastic usage? Exploring the determinants of plastic avoidance in food-related consumption decisions. *Sustainability, 12*(22), 9627. https://doi.org/10.3390/su12229627

Chen, Y. S., & Chang, C. H. (2013). Greenwash and green trust: The mediation effects of green consumer confusion and green perceived risk. *Journal of Business Ethics, 114*(3), 489–500.

Clement, J., Kristensen, T., & Grønhaug, K. (2013). Understanding consumers' in-store visual perception: The influence of package design features on visual attention. *Journal of Retailing and Consumer Services, 20*(2), 234–239.

Coelho, P. M., Corona, B., ten Klooster, R., & Worrell, E. (2020). Sustainability of reusable packaging-current situation and trends. *Resources, Conservation & Recycling: X, 100037*.

Covenant, A. P. (2010). *A commitment by governments and industry to the sustainable design, use and recovery of packaging* (Vol. 8). APC Secretariat.

Davison, L., & Redhill, D. (1998). Structural packaging design: Building and protecting brand value. *Journal of Brand Management, 6*(1), 13–26. https://doi.org/10.1057/bm.1998.41

Duhec, A. V., Jeanne, R. F., Maximenko, N., & Hafner, J. (2015). Composition and potential origin of marine debris stranded in the Western Indian Ocean on remote Alphonse Island, Seychelles. *Marine Pollution Bulletin, 96*(1), 76–86.

Eagle, L., Hamann, M., & Low, D. R. (2016). The role of social marketing, marine turtles and sustainable tourism in reducing plastic pollution. *Marine Pollution Bulletin, 107*(1), 324–332.

Evans, D. M., Parsons, R., Jackson, P., Greenwood, S., & Ryan, A. (2020). Understanding plastic packaging: The co-evolution of materials and society. *Global Environmental Change, 65*, 102166.

Fadeeva, Z., & Van Berkel, R. (2021). Unlocking circular economy for prevention of marine plastic pollution: An exploration of G20 policy and initiatives. *Journal of Environmental Management, 277*, 111457.

Falcone, P. M., & Imbert, E. (2018). Social life cycle approach as a tool for promoting the market uptake of bio-based products from a consumer perspective. *Sustainability, 10*(4), 1031.

Fishbein, M., & Cappella, J. N. (2006). The role of theory in developing effective health communications. *Journal of Communication, 56*(Suppl_1), S1–S17.

Foschi, E., & Bonoli, A. (2019). The commitment of packaging industry in the framework of the European strategy for plastics in a circular economy. *Administrative Sciences, 9*(1), 18.

Galgano, F. (2015). Biodegradable packaging and edible coating for fresh-cut fruits and vegetables. *Italian Journal of Food Science, 27*(1), 1–20.

Geiger, S. M., Fischer, D., & Schrader, U. (2018). Measuring what matters in sustainable consumption: An integrative framework for the selection of relevant behaviors. *Sustainable Development, 26*(1), 18–33.

Geyer, R., Jambeck, J. R., & Law, K. L. (2017). Production, use, and fate of all plastics ever made. *Science Advances, 3*(7), e1700782.

Gregory, M. R. (2009). Environmental implications of plastic debris in marine settings—Entanglement, ingestion, smothering, hangers-on, hitch-hiking and alien invasions. *Philosophical Transactions of the Royal Society of London B: Biological Sciences, 364*(1526), 2013–2025.

Guillard, V., Gaucel, S., Fornaciari, C., Angellier-Coussy, H., Buche, P., & Gontard, N. (2018). The next generation of sustainable food packaging to preserve our environment in a circular economy context. *Frontiers in Nutrition, 5*, 121.

Heidbreder, L. M., Bablok, I., Drews, S., & Menzel, C. (2019). Tackling the plastic problem: A review on perceptions, behaviors, and interventions. *Science of the Total Environment, 668*, 1077–1093.

Herbes, C., Beuthner, C., & Ramme, I. (2018). Consumer attitudes towards biobased packaging–A cross-cultural comparative study. *Journal of Cleaner Production, 194*, 203–218.

Jakovcevic, A., Steg, L., Mazzeo, N., Caballero, R., Franco, P., Putrino, N., & Favara, J. (2014). Charges for plastic bags: Motivational and behavioral effects. *Journal of Environmental Psychology, 40*, 372–380.

Jeya-Jeevahan, J., Chandrasekaran, M., Venkatesan, S. P., Sriram, V., Britto Joseph, G., Mageshwaran, G., & Durairaj, R. B. (2020). Scaling up difficulties and commercial aspects of edible films for food packaging: A review. *Trends in Food Science & Technology, 100*, 210–222. https://doi.org/10.1016/j.tifs.2020.04.014

Ketelsen, M., Janssen, M., & Hamm, U. (2020). Consumers' response to environmentally-friendly food packaging – A systematic review. *Journal of Cleaner Production, 254*, 120123. https://doi.org/10.1016/j.jclepro.2020.120123

Koenig-Lewis, N., Palmer, A., Dermody, J., & Urbye, A. (2014). Consumers' evaluations of ecological packaging–rational and emotional approaches. *Journal of Environmental Psychology, 37*, 94–105.

Koutsimanis, G., Getter, K., Behe, B., Harte, J., & Almenar, E. (2012). Influences of packaging attributes on consumer purchase decisions for fresh produce. *Appetite, 59*(2), 270–280.

Liao, L. X., Corsi, A. M., Chrysochou, P., & Lockshin, L. (2015). Emotional responses towards food packaging: A joint application of self-report and physiological measures of emotion. *Food Quality and Preference, 42*, 48–55. https://doi.org/10.1016/j.foodqual.2015.01.009

Lubowiecki-Vikuk, A., Dąbrowska, A., & Machnik, A. (2021). Responsible consumer and lifestyle: Sustainability insights. *Sustainable Production and Consumption, 25*, 91–101.

Lynch, D. H., Klaassen, P., & Broerse, J. E. (2017). Unraveling Dutch citizens' perceptions on the bio-based economy: The case of bioplastics, bio-jetfuels and small-scale bio-refineries. *Industrial Crops and Products, 106*, 130–137.

MacArthur, E. (2017). Beyond plastic waste. *Science, 358*(6365), 843.
Magnier, L., & Schoormans, J. (2015). Consumer reactions to sustainable packaging: The interplay of visual appearance, verbal claim and environmental concern. *Journal of Environmental Psychology, 44*, 53–62.
Magnier, L., Mugge, R., & Schoormans, J. (2019). Turning Ocean garbage into products–consumers' evaluations of products made of recycled ocean plastic. *Journal of Cleaner Production, 215*, 84–98.
Martinho, G., Pires, A., Portela, G., & Fonseca, M. (2015). Factors affecting consumers' choices concerning sustainable packaging during product purchase and recycling. *Resources, Conservation and Recycling, 103*, 58–68.
Muralidharan, S., & Sheehan, K. (2016). "Tax"and "fee"message frames as inhibitors of plastic bag usage among shoppers: A social marketing application of the theory of planned behavior. *Social Marketing Quarterly, 1*, 18.
Nath, V., Kumar, R., Agrawal, R., Gautam, A., & Sharma, V. (2013). Consumer adoption of green products: Modeling the enablers. *Global Business Review, 14*(3), 453–470.
Nelms, S. E., Duncan, E. M., Broderick, A. C., Galloway, T. S., Godfrey, M. H., Hamann, M., ... Godley, B. J. (2015). Plastic and marine turtles: A review and call for research. *ICES Journal of Marine Science: Journal du Conseil*, fsv165.
Onwezen, M. C., Reinders, M. J., & Sijtsema, S. J. (2017). Understanding intentions to purchase bio-based products: The role of subjective ambivalence. *Journal of Environmental Psychology, 52*, 26–36. https://doi.org/10.1016/j.jenvp.2017.05.001
Orzan, G., Cruceru, A. F., Bălăceanu, C. T., & Chivu, R.-G. (2018). Consumers' behavior concerning sustainable packaging: An exploratory study on Romanian consumers. *Sustainability, 10*(6), 1787.
Parente Ribeiro Cerqueira, M. Â. (2019). Edible packaging. In L. Melton, F. Shahidi, & P. Varelis (Eds.), *Encyclopedia of food chemistry* (pp. 173–176). Academic.
Patel, P. (2019). Edible Packaging. *ACS Central Science, 5*(12), 1907–1910.
Pettipas, S., Bernier, M., & Walker, T. R. (2016). A Canadian policy framework to mitigate plastic marine pollution. *Marine Policy, 68*, 117–122.
Politis, A. E., Sarigiannidis, C., & Voutsinas, V. (2019). The environmental aspects of packaging: Implications for marketing strategies. In *Strategic innovative marketing and tourism* (pp. 965–972). Springer.
Prakash, G., & Pathak, P. (2017). Intention to buy eco-friendly packaged products among young consumers of India: A study on developing nation. *Journal of Cleaner Production, 141*, 385–393.
Rebollar, R., Gil, I., Lidón, I., Martín, J., Fernández, M. J., & Rivera, S. (2017). How material, visual and verbal cues on packaging influence consumer expectations and willingness to buy: The case of crisps (potato chips) in Spain. *Food Research International, 99*, 239–246.
Reinders, M. J., Onwezen, M. C., & Meeusen, M. J. (2017). Can bio-based attributes upgrade a brand? How partial and full use of bio-based materials affects the purchase intention of brands. *Journal of Cleaner Production, 162*, 1169–1179.
Rowley, K. H., Cucknell, A.-C., Smith, B. D., Clark, P. F., & Morritt, D. (2020). London's river of plastic: High levels of microplastics in the Thames water column. *Science of the Total Environment, 740*, 140018. https://doi.org/10.1016/j.scitotenv.2020.140018
Schnurr, R. E., Alboiu, V., Chaudhary, M., Corbett, R. A., Quanz, M. E., Sankar, K., ... Walker, T. R. (2018). Reducing marine pollution from single-use plastics (SUPs): A review. *Marine Pollution Bulletin, 137*, 157–171.
Schwartz, S. H. (1977). Normative influences on altruism. *Advances in Experimental Social Psychology, 10*(1), 221–279.
Schwartz, S. H. (1994). Are there universal aspects in the structure and contents of human values? *Journal of Social Issues, 50*(4), 19–45.
Sharma, H. B., Vanapalli, K. R., Cheela, V. S., Ranjan, V. P., Jaglan, A. K., Dubey, B., ... Bhattacharya, J. (2020). Challenges, opportunities, and innovations for effective solid waste

management during and post COVID-19 pandemic. *Resources, Conservation and Recycling, 162*, 105052.

Shove, E., & Warde, A. (2002). Inconspicuous consumption: The sociology of consumption, lifestyles and the environment. *Sociological Theory and the Environment: Classical Foundations, Contemporary Insights, 230*(51).

Signori, P., Gozzo, I., Flint, D. J., Milfeld, T., & Nichols, B. S. (2019). Sustainable customer experience: Bridging theory and practice. In *The synergy of business theory and practice* (pp. 131–174). Palgrave Macmillan.

Spierling, S., Knüpffer, E., Behnsen, H., Mudersbach, M., Krieg, H., Springer, S., ... Endres, H.-J. (2018). Bio-based plastics-a review of environmental, social and economic impact assessments. *Journal of Cleaner Production, 185*, 476–491.

Steenis, N. D., van Herpen, E., van der Lans, I. A., Ligthart, T. N., & van Trijp, H. C. (2017). Consumer response to packaging design: The role of packaging materials and graphics in sustainability perceptions and product evaluations. *Journal of Cleaner Production, 162*, 286–298.

Szybillo, G. J., & Jacoby, J. (1974). Intrinsic versus extrinsic cues as determinants of perceived product quality. *Journal of Applied Psychology, 59*(1), 74.

Taufik, D., Reinders, M. J., Molenveld, K., & Onwezen, M. C. (2020). The paradox between the environmental appeal of bio-based plastic packaging for consumers and their disposal behaviour. *Science of the Total Environment, 705*, 135820. https://doi.org/10.1016/j.scitotenv.2019.135820

Taufique, K. M. R., Vocino, A., & Polonsky, M. J. (2017). The influence of eco-label knowledge and trust on pro-environmental consumer behaviour in an emerging market. *Journal of Strategic Marketing, 25*(7), 511–529.

Thøgersen, J. (1996). *The demand for environmentally friendly packaging in Germany*. Handelshøjskolen i Århus, Center for markedsovervågning,-vurdering og-bearbejdning til fødevaresektoren.

Thøgersen, J. (1999). Spillover processes in the development of a sustainable consumption pattern. *Journal of Economic Psychology, 20*(1), 53–81.

Truelove, H. B., Carrico, A. R., Weber, E. U., Raimi, K. T., & Vandenbergh, M. P. (2014). Positive and negative spillover of pro-environmental behavior: An integrative review and theoretical framework. *Global Environmental Change, 29*, 127–138.

Umaraw, P., Munekata, P. E. S., Verma, A. K., Barba, F. J., Singh, V. P., Kumar, P., & Lorenzo, J. M. (2020). Edible films/coating with tailored properties for active packaging of meat, fish and derived products. *Trends in Food Science & Technology, 98*, 10–24. https://doi.org/10.1016/j.tifs.2020.01.032

United Nations. (n.d.). *Sustainable development goals*. Retrieved 12 May, 2021 https://www.un.org/sustainabledevelopment

UNEP-WCMC, I. U. C. N. (2018). NGS (2018). Protected planet report, 70.

Van Birgelen, M., Semeijn, J., & Keicher, M. (2009). Packaging and proenvironmental consumption behavior: Investigating purchase and disposal decisions for beverages. *Environment and Behavior, 41*(1), 125–146.

Van den Oever, M., Molenveld, K., van der Zee, M., & Bos, H. (2017). *Bio-based and biodegradable plastics: Facts and figures: Focus on food packaging in the Netherlands*. Wageningen.

Veiga, J. M., Vlachogianni, T., Pahl, S., Thompson, R. C., Kopke, K., Doyle, T. K., ... Loizidou, X. I. (2016). Enhancing public awareness and promoting co-responsibility for marine litter in Europe: The challenge of MARLISCO. *Marine Pollution Bulletin, 102*(2), 309–315.

Verain, M. C., Bartels, J., Dagevos, H., Sijtsema, S. J., Onwezen, M. C., & Antonides, G. (2012). Segments of sustainable food consumers: A literature review. *International Journal of Consumer Studies, 36*(2), 123–132.

Vince, J., & Hardesty, B. D. (2017). Plastic pollution challenges in marine and coastal environments: From local to global governance. *Restoration Ecology, 25*(1), 123–128.

Wikström, F., Williams, H., Verghese, K., & Clune, S. (2014). The influence of packaging attributes on consumer behaviour in food-packaging life cycle assessment studies – A neglected topic. *Journal of Cleaner Production, 73*, 100–108. https://doi.org/10.1016/j.jclepro.2013.10.042

Wilcox, C., Mallos, N. J., Leonard, G. H., Rodriguez, A., & Hardesty, B. D. (2016). Using expert elicitation to estimate the impacts of plastic pollution on marine wildlife. *Marine Policy, 65*, 107–114.

World Economic Forum. (2016). *The new plastics economy rethinking the future of plastics*. World Economic Forum.

Zalasiewicz, J., Waters, C. N., do Sul, J. A. I., Corcoran, P. L., Barnosky, A. D., Cearreta, A., . . . Leinfelder, R. (2016). The geological cycle of plastics and their use as a stratigraphic indicator of the Anthropocene. *Anthropocene, 13*, 4–17.

Zettler, E. R., Mincer, T. J., & Amaral-Zettler, L. A. (2013). Life in the "plastisphere": Microbial communities on plastic marine debris. *Environmental Science & Technology, 47*(13), 7137–7146.

The Kaleidoscope of Changing Values: Are We Heading Towards Responsible Consumption and Sustainable Society? Lessons from Pune, India

Mansi Kapoor, Taha Chaiechi, Shilpa Deo, Pooja Darda, Anjali Sane, and Ravikumar Chitnis

Abstract Values are inherently personal constructs that influence individuals' choices and help navigate many personal and professional dilemmas. Using the Basic Human Values by Schwartz as the theoretical framework, the aim of this paper is to examine the substitutability of self-enhancement values by self-transcendence values in promoting responsible consumption behaviours in society. The paper further examines whether Self Transcendence values are instrumental in driving responsible consumption among individuals.

The paper relies on Focus Group studies to explore the topic. To ensure the accuracy of our analysis, representative samples of 88 Generation Z (48 – Under Graduates; 40 – Post Graduates) college students, 25 Generation Y employees, and 25 Generation X home-makers were selected for focus group discussions. The interaction in each group was for 60 minutes. All interviews were recorded with permission and transcribed. Data thus obtained was manually coded and analysed using the thematic analysis technique. The findings of the paper provide meaningful insights about the changing human values and their influence on consumption behaviour.

In addition to the contribution to the existing literature in intercultural and consumer behaviour research, this study also contributes to the current

M. Kapoor (✉) · S. Deo · P. Darda
Faculty of Management, MIT-World Peace University, Pune, Maharashtra, India
e-mail: mansi.kapoor@mitwpu.edu.in; shilpa.deo@mitwpu.edu.in; pooja.darda@mitwpu.edu.in

T. Chaiechi
College of Business, Law and Governance, James Cook University, Townsville, QLD, Australia
e-mail: taha.chaiechi@jcu.edu.au

A. Sane
Faculty of Commerce, MIT-World Peace University, Pune, Maharashtra, India
e-mail: anjali.sane@mitwpu.edu.in

R. Chitnis
MIT-World Peace University, Pune, Maharashtra, India
e-mail: ravikumar.chitnis@mitwpu.edu.in

© The Author(s), under exclusive license to Springer Nature Singapore Pte Ltd. 2022

T. Chaiechi, J. Wood (eds.), *Community Empowerment, Sustainable Cities, and Transformative Economies*, https://doi.org/10.1007/978-981-16-5260-8_22

understanding of how changing values are encouraging individuals for responsible consumption. The findings of the study will be useful to both researchers and practitioners in the field of consumer behaviour.

Keywords Responsible consumption · Individual values · Generation-X · Millennials · Post-millennials · Sustainability · Qualitative research

1 Introduction

The staggering level of consumption is depleting the earth's resources rapidly and has grave consequences for land, air and water. Consumption expenditure represents 60% of the global GDP.[1] In 1990, approximately 8.1 tonnes of natural resources were used to satisfy individuals consumption demands (aka per-capita material footprint); this figure showed a global increase of almost 50% and rose to 12.2 tonnes per person in 2017 (Fig. 1). If no intervention is made, by 2030, annual consumption is expected to reach $8.2 trillion in China and $ 6 trillion in India (Gonzalez, 2019).

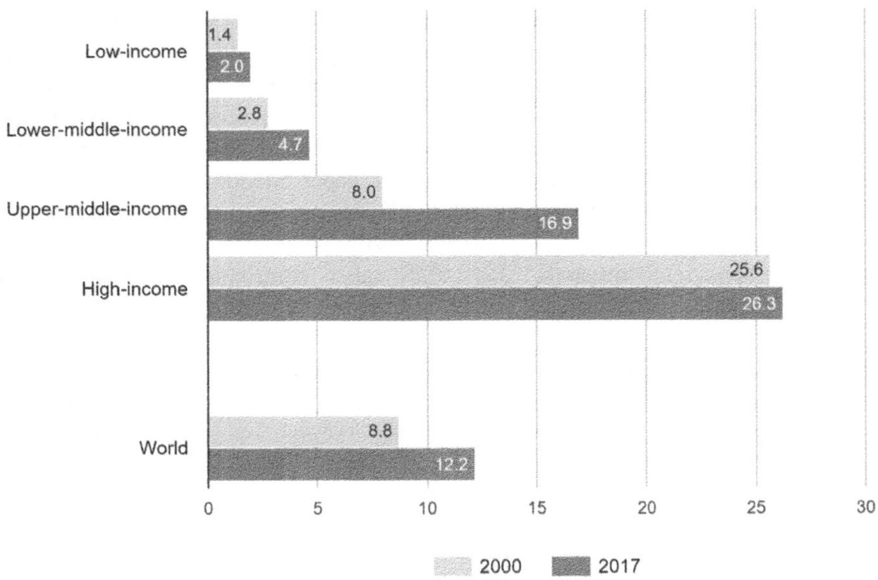

Fig. 1 Material footprint per capita, 2000 and 2017 (metric tons per person Source: United Nations, Department of Economic and Social Affairs, Statistics Division, 2019 Report on Sustainable Development Goal 12. (https://unstats.un.org/sdgs/report/2019/goal-12/)

[1] https://www.weforum.org/platforms/shaping-the-future-of-consumption

India is home to 18% of the world's population but has only 4%of global water resources. Only 19.9% of India's urban waste is processed; India is the third-highest emitter of carbon dioxide. It is responsible for 6.9% of global emissions.

According to the 2019 revision of the World Population Prospects, India is the second-most populous nation, with nearly 1.367 billion people. In 2017, India became the sixth-largest economy globally.[2] In terms of purchasing power parity (PPP), India ranks third behind the US and China.[3] As reported by the UN, the country only processes 19.9% of its urban wastes, and at the same time, it is responsible for almost 7% of global emissions.[4] India's rapidly growing middle class (aka consuming class) and swiftly expanding cities are the main drivers behind domestic demand for a broad range of consumer goods from cosmetics to cars and household items. Domestic consumption constitutes nearly 60% of India's GDP, which expectedly puts enormous pressure on its natural resources. For example, while the country is home to 18% of the world's population, it only poses 4% of global water resource.

While the increase in national consumption levels was once a political goal back in the 1980s and 1990s (Kennedy, 2014), the government has started to shift its focus away from an increase in consumption to resource efficiency in recent years; an economic policy move that started by establishing India Resource Panel in 2015 (Becker et al., 2019). Moreover, some emerging reports seem to suggest that the COVID-19 pandemic is changing consumption patterns in India. For example, weekly surveys between April 2020 and June 2020 by Bain & Co. and People Research on India's Consumer Economy (PRICE) reveal that 50% of surveyed households have reported a reduction in their overall consumption.[5] Consumer research by Accenture (2020) reported a rise in consumer's concern during the COVID-19 pandemic, leading to changes in consumers' priorities. Part of this change is a noticeable delay in purchasing non-essential items and a desire to shop locally to support local businesses. But is consumer behaviour shifting towards more sustainable consumption in India? This question is a matter of paramount importance.

Subsequently, this study is interested in uncovering motivational factors that influence individuals to adjust their consumption habits to increase sustainable consumption. This study's initial proposition is that some of the potential motivational factors behind behavioural change could range between peer influence, environmental regulation, and reactions to grassroots activism within the society. The paper aims at exploring these motivational factors using the Theory of Basic

---

[2] https://indianexpress.com/article/business/economy/india-becomes-sixth-largest-economy-in-the-world-overtakes-france-5256279/

[3] https://www.businesstoday.in/current/economy-politics/india-remains-3rd-largest-economy-in-purchasing-power-parity-still-way-behind-china-us/story/407776.html

[4] https://in.one.un.org/page/sustainable-development-goals/sdg-12/

[5] https://www.livemint.com/companies/news/india-gears-up-for-the-new-normal-as-consumer-behaviour-shifts-11591293072080.html

Human Values. This theoretical framework was developed by Schwartz (1992a, b and 2012a, b) based on ten fundamental human motivational values that are grouped into four dimensions of openness to change, conservation, self-enhancement, and self-transcendence. The framework brought about a resurgence of research on motivationally distinct values and their interactions. This paper utilises the Schwartz theoretical framework because of its adaptability to intercultural research. The paper then adopts the thematic analysis of focus group interviews as a research method.

The paper is structured as follows. The study begins with a literature review on responsible consumption and linkages to human values as drivers of change. The paper then introduces Schwartz's Theory of Human Values and explains it as the study's theoretical framework. The paper is structured thereafter using Braun and Clarke's (2006) six-steps thematic analysis of focus group interviews. A detailed and systematic discussion of all the six steps has been given, which is followed by a definitive and action-oriented conclusion.

2 Literature Review

Understanding individuals and society's motivational construct started with the simplistic yet profound theory of Maslow's hierarchy of needs (1943), which equipped researchers to understand the motivational goals. Much research has subsequently been done to understand the complexity, and there have been multiple theories since then, specifically in the field of psychology. Examples include Feather and Peay (1975), Hofstede (1980), Braithwaite and Law (1985), Crosby et al. (1990), Cawley et al. (2000), Park et al. (2004), Schwartz (1994, 2012a, b).

Changing consumer behaviour could be a long-term process. It has a strong location and time dependencies (Howard & Sheth, 1969). Consumer choices are being influenced by a complex integration of social, psychological, political, and marketing factors (Wood & Hayes, 2012; Vikuk et al., 2021). Realising this, White et al. (2019) developed a new and comprehensive framework through which they have conceptualised and encouraged sustainable consumer behaviour. To achieve this, the authors have suggested that the marketing messages should leverage Social influence, Habit formation, Individual self, Feelings and cognition, and Tangibility.

Kopnina (2011) showed how the household income level plays a substantial role in determining environmental awareness and promoting responsible consumption behaviour. The study found that children attending economically advantaged schools had greater awareness and concern about their consumption behaviour than pupils belonging to less economically advantaged and ethnically mixed schools. In addition to this, other studies found that certain other socio-economic variables can also help us influence sustainable behaviour. For example, Asmuni et al. (2012) found that university students' conservation behaviour had a significant relationship with rural background & parents' highest education level.

As the UN deadline of 2030 to meet the Sustainable Development Goals (SDGs) is nearing, experts believe that COVID-19 has provided the world with an opportunity to build recovery plans focusing on changing consumption and production patterns.[6] Another challenge is the fast-growing urban areas globally that are putting immense pressure on resources, increasing demand for consumption, and threatens food security in some regions (Islam & Karim, 2019; Giudice et al., 2020). Other researchers point out the importance of circular economy in directing both production and consumption towards protecting the environment (Korhonen et al., 2018; D'Adamo, 2018).

The choice architecture that any individual builds for the self could be based on myriad factors, some mindful and some conditioned by prevailing cultural norms. However, personal values exert a powerful influence on an individual's choice matrix and collectively create a paradigm shift in society. Values are what we consider useful, desirable and excellent. They form a fundamental part of how an individual, a culture or society defines itself. Within the myriad folds of complex societies, they articulate a vision, aspiration for self and society (Dahl, 2001). Personal values are broad and varying in importance, affecting a person's attitude and behaviour (Schwartz, 1992a, b).

Schwartz's Basic Human Values Framework is a powerful and widely used conceptual framework for furthering research based on value systems. Within this framework, the study focuses specifically on the movement from self-enhancement towards self-transcendence. According to the Values theory, values serve as guiding principles in our lives. Moving from self-enhancement to self-transcendence involves deviating from power and achievement and going closer to universalism and benevolence values (Schwartz, 2006).

Furthermore, research confirms that value systems play a crucial role in explaining the social and individual reactions to change (Weber, 1958; Durkheim, 1954). Accordingly, this research aims to probe into what links the individual to the larger whole. More specifically, the study aims to explore the kaleidoscope of changing values and understand how these changes impact responsible consumption.

The demographic variables are linked to a person's basic characteristics such as age, gender, income, and other factors influencing consumer purchasing behaviour. Age, gender, household income, education, social status, and other demographic variables all impact customers' perceptions of green goods. The age of the consumers had a huge impact on the purchase of organic foods (Davies et al., 1995). Similar findings were published in other papers (e.g., Lea & Worsley, 2005), which identified the influence of age on customers' confidence in organic goods. People in their forties and fifties have a deep belief in the benefits of organic foods, which they see as an alternative to traditional foods (Lea & Worsley, 2005). According to many studies, household income positively impacts organic food and cosmetics use and purchase (Davies et al., 1995; Lea & Worsley, 2005; Chinnici et al., 2002). It was

[6] https://www.un.org/sustainabledevelopment/sustainable-consumption-production/

also discovered that the composition of a family indicates that households with children, especially women members of those households, tend to purchase more green products than households without children (Davies et al., 1995). Hence, homemakers were considered as sample unit for the focus group interview. The buying behaviour for organic goods is often influenced by a higher formal educational degree (Lockie et al., 2002; Ahmad and Juhdi, 2010). This is because increased education raises consumer awareness of the environment, which influences their buying decisions. Therefore, generation Y and Z were considered as sample unit for the focus group interview.

Organisations can use more successful advertising efforts to raise awareness of the benefits of green goods. Promotional campaigns should be targeted at all geographies, from urban to rural. When consumers have mixed feelings about purchasing green goods, companies should make a concerted effort to alleviate their concerns. As a result, before pursuing green advertising, businesses should determine their target consumers' ambiguity toward purchasing green goods (Polonsky et al., 1998). They can also attempt to chart the demographics-ambivalence attitude relationship. Effective demographic or psychographic segmentation should be introduced so that various green product segments can be targeted based on the consumer segment chosen. Overall, these measures will assist the company in further promoting green goods, resulting in a rise in the number of green customers and a reduction in environmental degradation (Ottman, 1998).

This will aid in the sustainability of both the environment and humanity. The categorisation of the factors into the primary, middle, and peripheral factors and their inclusion within a hierarchically organised process explains the frequently observed attitude-behaviour gap in academia. It shows that even personally concerned customers, who will consciously announce their positive attitudes regarding purchasing sustainably, may consider various other factors that will ultimately prevent them from acting in an attitude-consistent manner (Majumdar, 2015).

Knowledge of customer justifications for conscious consumption will help businesses and government policymakers mitigate unfounded assumptions and raise awareness of the consequences of consumers' decisions (Arcury, 1990). This research offers valuable product positioning guidelines for businesses. The findings have significant managerial consequences, as they specifically indicate that businesses should incorporate sustainability aspects in low involvement categories, select other-centred benefits within hedonic product categories, and segment customers based on their education and income levels, as these subject-specific covariates have the greatest effect on preference structures (Puohiniemi, 2002).

3 The Theoretical Framework

This study is modelled on ten basic human values, four higher-order values and two underlying motivational sources (Schwartz, 2015) of the original Schwartz's Theory of Basic Human Values. The theory defines values as individual concepts with

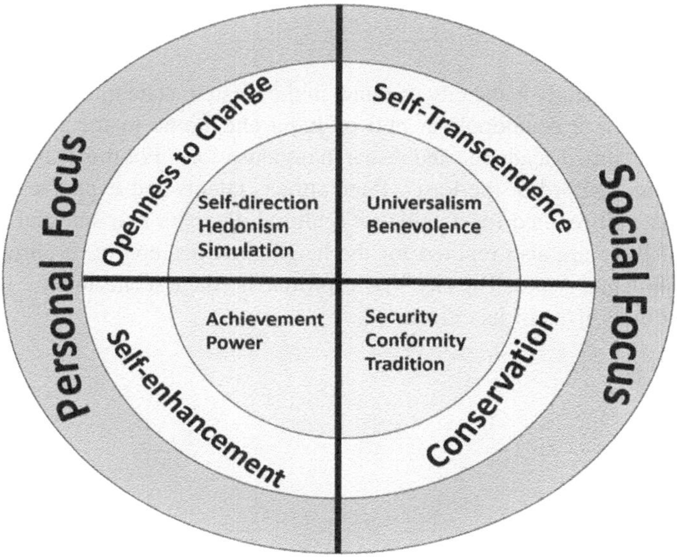

Fig. 2 The circular model of ten basic human values, four higher-order values and two underlying motivational sources. (Source: adapted from Schwartz, 2015)

"trans-situational" goals that guide the selection or evaluation of individuals' actions (Schwartz et al., 2012a, b). The structure of the Schwartz assumes a circular form, and it is portrayed in Fig. 2. The values listed in the circular model are considered to be broad goals with varying importance (Schwartz 1992a, b and a more elaborated version in 2012a, b). In proposing this circular structure, Schwartz also assumes a polarity between the values with personal focuses and values with social focuses. Furthermore, the adjoining domains are interrelated, and those that are non-adjoining represent opposing domains.

Under the self-transcendence domain, Schwartz et al. (2012a, b) defined three types of universalism: concern, nature and tolerance. The study also assumed two types of benevolence under the same domain: caring and dependability. Under the openness to change domain, the study proposed two types of self-direction: thought and action; under the conservation domain, Schwartz et al. (2012a, b) defined two types of conformity: rules and interpersonal, and two types of security: personal and societal. Finally, under the self-enhancement domain, the study defined two types of power: dominance and resources. In our approach to basic human values, we follow Giménez and Tamajón (2019) assuming that values listed in the circular model (Fig. 2) form a continuum meaning that values do not have exact limits might have a shared load amongst them.

4 Scope of the Study

The scope of this study is the city of Pune, in the western state of Maharashtra, India (Fig. 3). Pune is a cosmopolitan hub of India and home to the IT industry and numerous acclaimed academic and research organisations. For this reason, the city is known as the "Oxford of the East". Pune attracts talents and expertise from across India and is well-reputed for its citizens' cultural diversity and spiritual awareness. Citizens of Pune are also reputed for the heightened perception of climate change and environmental issues. The city's rich spiritual heritage seems to have interwoven into the ordinary lives of its citizens.

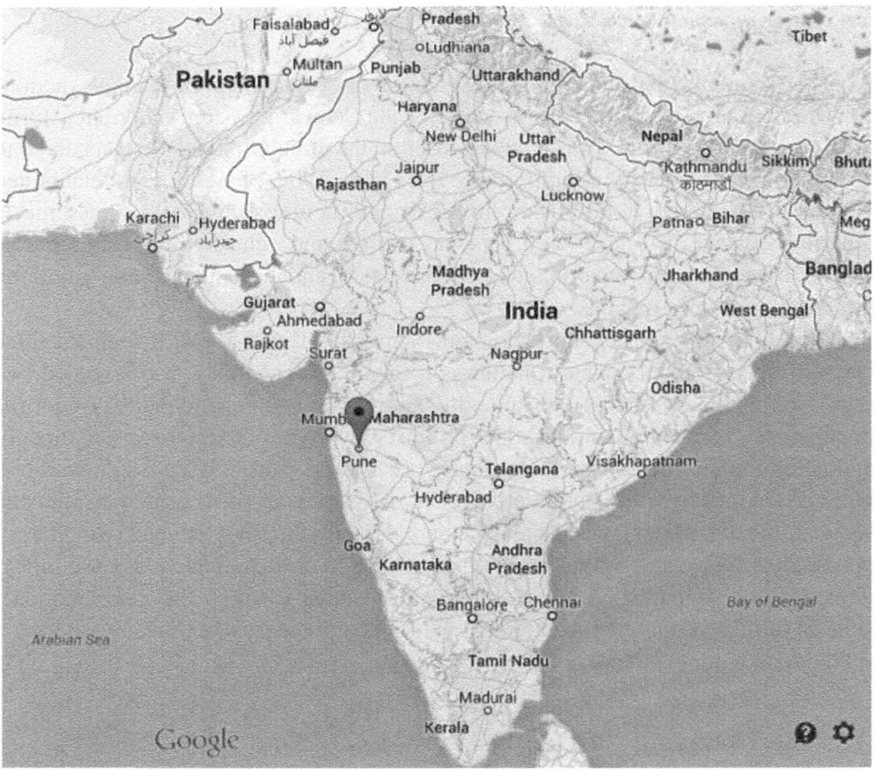

Fig. 3 Location of City of Pune in Inida. (Source: Google maps)

5 Methods and Sources of Data

This paper adopts a qualitative approach to the research question. Thematic analysis of focus group interview data has been selected as the research method as it provides a theoretically flexible approach to collecting and analysing qualitative data. Focus groups interviews were an advantageous method of data collection for this study. The group dynamic and social interaction element provided an opportunity to collect deeper and richer data than those collected in one-on-one interviews. Literature confirms that another advantage of focus group interviews is allowing the research team to structure the discussion around themes rather than direct questions, enabling participants to take control of the discussion and share their valuable insights more freely (Fielden et al., 2011).

Following Braun and Clarke (2006), this paper utilises a thematic analysis of focus group interviews in six steps. Step 1 is to become familiar with the focus group interview data. Step 2 is to generate initial codes. Step 3 involves searching for emerging themes. Step 4 focuses on reviewing themes. Step 5 defines finalised themes, and step 6 is the write-up of the findings in a replicable and systematic manner.

Ethics approval was sought from the Dean, Research and Innovation at MIT -World Peace University to organise focus group interviews. Understanding the consumers' perception of consumption choices requires detailed probing and various rounds of Q & A to gain insights into the individuals' minds. Accordingly, rounds of questions were designed based on the Schwartz Theory of Basic Human Values as focus group interview questions, aiming to unravel the complex and nuanced consumers' motivational values the way individuals perceive responsible consumption.

To identify the various themes and the relationship among them, data has been manually labelled and categorised. Labels were assigned to words and phrases that represented important themes (Braun & Clarke, 2006).

The qualitative data was broken into smaller samples. Using the data sample, we have read the data carefully and tried to interpret the lines. Based on this, codes have been created for the sample. After this step we read another sample of data and applied the codes we already set up for the first one we read (Braun & Clarke, 2006). The researchers have repeated this step until the entire data has been coded.

Flat code framework is easier and faster in use. In this research flat coding framework was assigned where each code in the database is given the same degree of specificity and significance, regardless of context. In this research code frames were versatile enough to make the most of the findings and be applicable in various situations. When developing codes, the researchers made sure that they cover a variety of responses, contrast one another, and strike a balance between too much and too little data.

6 The Sampling Process and the Participants

The research team adopted a purposive sampling technique for the focus group discussions. Purposive sampling has been widely recommended in the literature as it relies on participants' aptitude and capability to provide the relevant information (Morgan, 1988). This type of sampling technique involves the targeted recruitment of potential participants on the basis of their ability to elucidate a specific theme, concept, or phenomenon (Cresswell & Plano Clark, 2011; Robinson, 2014). Subsequently, the research team created a common pool of participants from college students and middle to high-income earners and grouped them further to conduct focus group discussions. Given the above composition, the study's conclusions would be more applicable to the working class (aka consuming class) and higher education students in India. All the participants belong to the city of the cosmopolitan city of Pune, India and represented cultural diversity. Although the sampling for the focus group was purposeful and not random, it inherently captures diversity. Overall, 40 undergraduate students, 48 postgraduate students, 25 working professionals, and 25 home-makers consented to participate in the study. For Post Millennials, the percentage of female respondents was 50%, for millennials, the percentage of the female respondents was 65%, and for home-makers, the group comprised 100% women. Since Pune is considered the education hub of India, with over 1247 colleges,[7] the representation of higher-education students in our sample is substantial.

Following the selection procedure, the researchers categorised participants into three cohorts of Millennials, Post-millennials and Generation X, to explore each generation's characteristics, including their world views and values systems. The Post Millennial group comprised of college students, both undergraduates and postgraduates, in separate groups. The Millennials group comprised working professionals in the early or mid-career journey, and the third group comprised home-makers from Generation X. The classification was based on the generation cohort and not career types or occupations. This is because the literature confirms generational cohorts are formed on shared values and experiences that shape collective aspirations. Hence, the classification was more suited for this study's purpose (Yogamalar & Samuel, 2018).

7 The Process of Data Collection

This study used dual moderator focus-group interviews as a qualitative approach to understanding responsible consumption patterns and the consumer's preferences. Two researchers were assigned to each group as group moderators to facilitate discussions. Due to social distancing and pandemic-related restricted mobility in

[7] https://www.shiksha.com/colleges/pune

the city of Pune, discussion groups took place online using the Zoom platform. A total of 14 focus groups were conducted; four sessions for undergrad(UG) students, four sessions for postgrad(PG) students, three sessions for working professionals and three sessions for the home-makers(Gen X). The number of participants in each group varied between 8 and 10. Sessions lasted between 60 min, except for UG focus groups, where the sessions got extended to nearly 90 min each due to high levels of engagement and enthusiasm from participants.

A schedule, including a list of 10 questions, was prepared by the researchers beforehand to be used as guidance for each group discussion session. The schedule also included tips for moderators, including welcome message, consent process, introduction to the study, logistics and ground rules. Two moderators were present for all the discussions. The moderators' role was to nurture discussions amongst the participants by ensuring maximum participation in the time allotted. Each session started with a "warm-up time". The moderators spent a few minutes introducing themselves, introducing the topic and providing ground rules and guidelines to create a friendly and relaxed environment. The moderators exercised mild yet unobtrusive control throughout the sessions.

7.1 Focus Group Questions

Using focus group interview data, this study examines whether consumers exhibit patterns of an attitudinal shift from focusing on self-enhancement values such as power and achievement to self-transcendence values such as universalism and benevolence, eventually leading to more sustainable and responsible consumption behaviour.

Three different types of questions were developed to gather as much information from participants as possible. These types included:

1. Engagement questions: questions used to establish the topic of the study
2. Exploration questions: questions used to probe into the subject of the study
3. Exit questions: questions asked to ensure nothing gets left out.

Engagement questions were written to spark discussion about the topics at hand. These questions focused on factors affecting personal purchase decisions and the importance of social approval in making personal or household purchases. For the exploration questions, this study followed Krueger and Casey (2000) as a useful guide on the progressiveness of the questioning and how they ought to be used throughout the interview. An experience question was included in this section related to three R's of Reduce, Reuse, and Recycle to understand lifestyle changes and choices. A transition question was asked to determine if there was a shift towards responsible consumption by probing into factors like animal cruelty, pollution, climate change and sustainability. A key question was asked about values that drive purchase decisions and contribute to community and people and a sense of achievement and purpose. Sessions ended with an exit question, asking the respondents if they wished to add anything else pertaining to the discussion that was not included in the interview questions.

8 Thematic Analysis

Step 1: to become familiar with the focus group interview data

All focus groups sessions were recorded using the recording feature on Zoom. Field notes were also taken by one of the two moderators in each session. After each session, the moderators immediately checked the recording to ensure the technical quality and compared the field notes and the recording to confirm all essential points had been taken down, and nothing important was left out.

Once all the responses were manually transcribed, detailed coding was done by identifying repeated patterns within the data. The research team followed (Braun & Clarke, 2006) to immerse themselves in the interview data by repeated readings of the field notes, transcribing the data by listening to the Zoom recordings as many times as required.

Step 2: generate initial codes, and Step 3: searching for themes

The moderators systematically read and re-read it to understand the frequent responses across the cohorts. The line by line and open coding methods were used for generating initial codes. The moderators developed codes independently and then discussed and modified them. The UG students (95%) believed that they could work as climate change activists and actually change society. It was realised from the conversations with PG students (70%) that residence and infrastructural availability play an influential role in determining the purchase of eco-friendly products. These themes are captured in Fig. 4. The students and home-makers believed in contributing to society through volunteering. It was observed that the undergraduate students (80%) are aware of their requirements and so "*Convenience is important than ambience*" for them. Furthermore, they seem to be adapting to the changes in society (90%) as they expressed that "*Ours is a status-driven society, which increases the usage of brands*".

For around 95% of the working professionals, comfort, priority, affordability, proximity seem to be important parameters in making decisions. They were found to be providing financial assistance (90%) as a way of contributing to society. As also captured in Fig. 5, these young professionals focussing on finding the right work-life balance. They are looking at products, services and experiences which enhance their sense of well being (80%) and are also looking for products that improve health, like bicycles, yoga classes etc. They appreciate corporations that follow environmentally friendly practices. As compared to older generations, they prefer sharing services (70%). They prefer to save money rather than spend heavily on luxury goods.

Home-makers (96%) strongly believe in the ideology of "*Being the change yourself*" and make optimum use of resources by using and reusing them as much

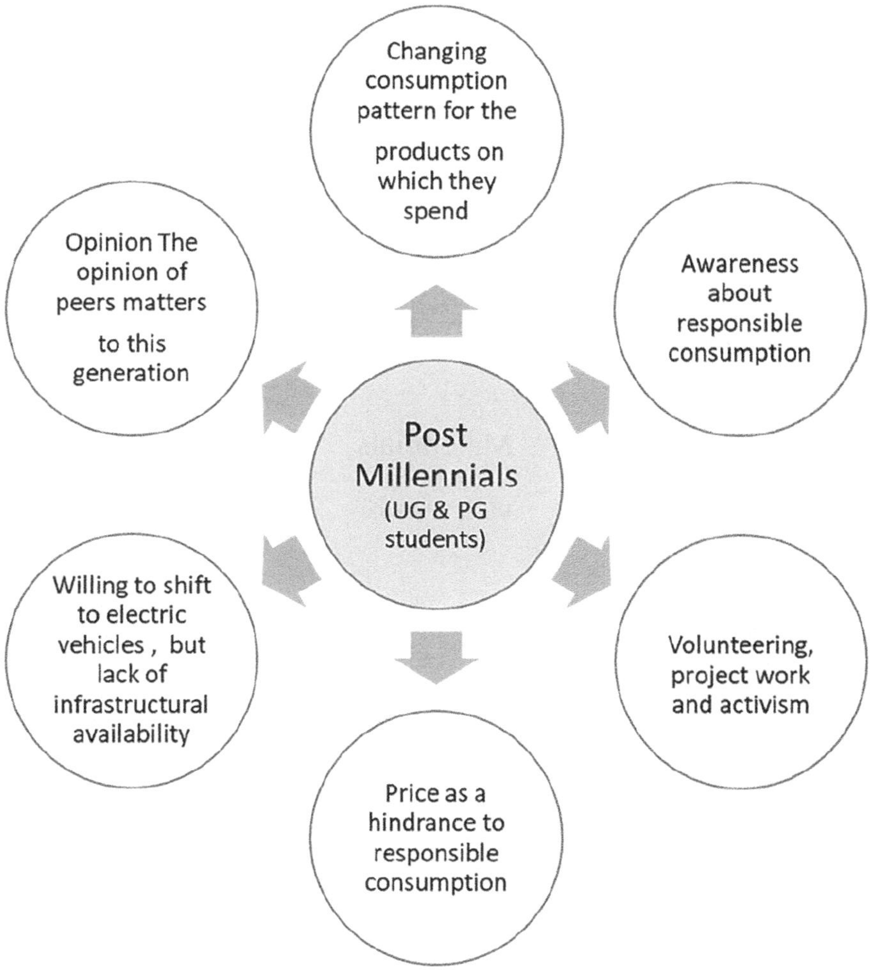

Fig. 4 Emerging themes from post-millennial focus group interviews data

as possible. As illustrated in Fig. 6, the concept of reuse, recycling, and reduction has been handed down from generations. Also, Indian home-makers are highly benevolent (90%). They not only care for the health and well being of their children but have a deep sense of connection with the community at large (92%).

Step 4 and 5: Reviewing and finalising themes

A. The Allure of Activism and Awareness for Post Millennials

The focused group discussions gave rich insights into the complex value system and aspirations of the group. The shift towards Self-Transcendence, particularly universalism, is significant. Most respondents have displayed Nature, Concern and Tolerance values by demonstrating the following volunteering for NGOs, working

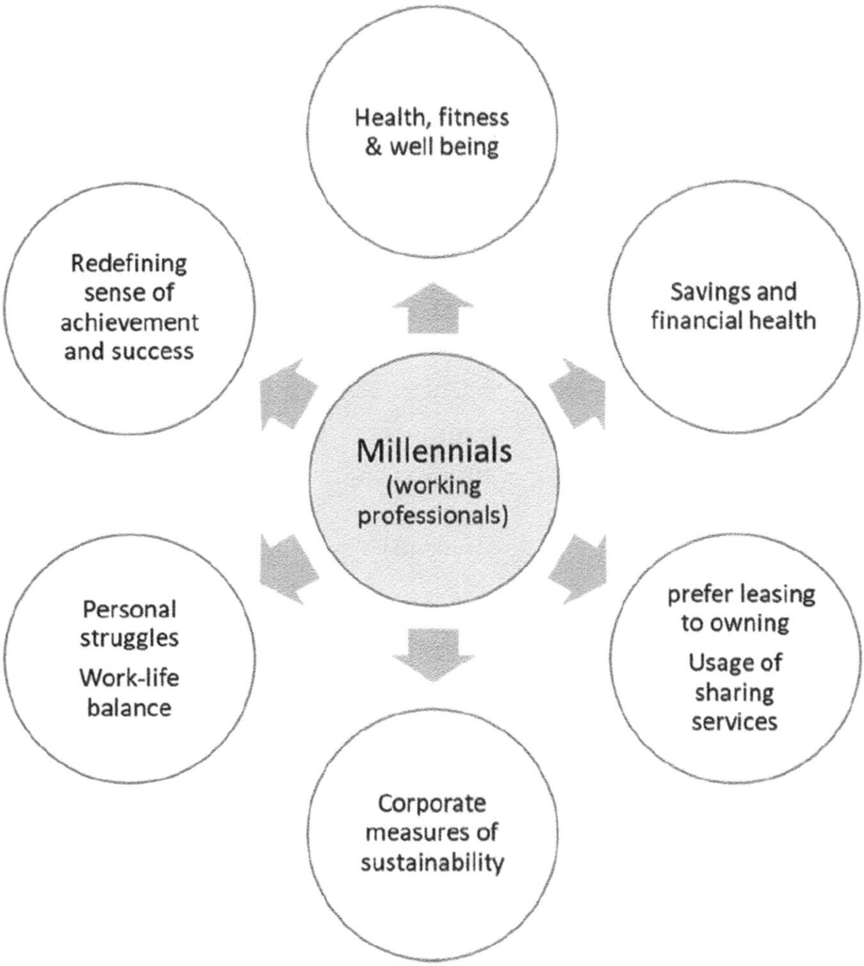

Fig. 5 Emerging themes from millennial focus group interviews data

on climate change and sustainability projects, participating in awareness programs on college campuses, etc. Human values are influenced by social, educational, and economic conditions. These principles, in turn, have an effect on how different students view Corporate Social Responsibility (CSR). It is recommended that the universities should raise awareness of the importance of incorporating human values and CSR into the curricula of potential business and social leaders (Gonzalez-Rodriguez et al., 2016).

Regarding responsible consumption, since all the respondents are graduate or postgraduate students who are currently not earning and depend on their parents or part-time jobs, their expenditure could give details about consumption on goods like clothes, cosmetics, grocery items, mobile phones and bikes.

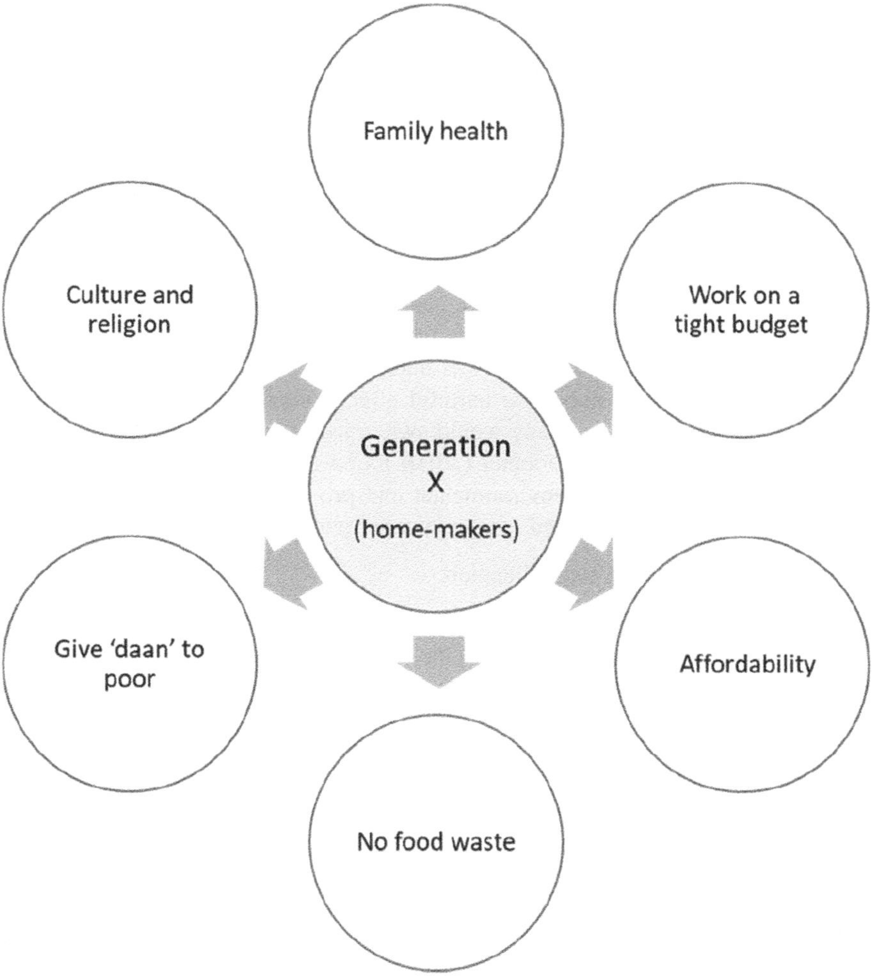

Fig. 6 Emerging themes from generation X focus group interviews data

The highest level of responsible consumption was witnessed in clothes and cosmetics by the group. Many said that they do not buy cosmetics that have been tested on animals; many prefer cosmetics with minimum harmful chemicals and are environmentally friendly in production processes. Simple things like using bamboo toothbrushes instead of the regular ones available and using jute bags instead of plastic ones have been heavily adopted. The awareness regarding the detrimental effects of fast fashion is constantly increasing, and those who were aware of the same prefer to buy clothes (specifically jeans and clothes using denim) from corporates who follow environmentally-friendly policies; the example of Lewis was given by some students who have gone through the latest initiatives. Also, the idea of renting and reusing old clothes is now not being looked upon with disdain by many young respondents who thought that this was a pragmatic way to save personal expense and reduce carbon footprint too. The reason why this was a significant revelation is that wearing old or worn clothes is considered to be a big taboo. This indicates a subtle yet profound shift from Hedonism (Self Enhancement) to Nature and Concern (Self Transcendence).

The respondents acknowledged the benefits of organic food and staples; however, they are reluctant to switch because of high prices and lack of credibility in packaging and labelling norms. Most respondents currently use fossil fuels; they said they wish to switch to electronic bikes. However, they are reluctant in doing so because of a lack of infrastructure like charging stations etc. Gadgets like mobile phones are usually passed off to others who need them or resold and not merely thrown away. While the discussion was underway, many respondents said that if there is more awareness about the harmful effects of producing certain products, given the same price range, many would switch to environmentally friendly products. Moreover, Uitto and Saloranta (2010) found that the human-centric values, biocentric nature value, pro-environmental and pro-social attitudes, interests, and motivations were interconnected for the younger generation.

B. Balance is the Mantra for Millennials

The millennials comprise the young working professionals in the age group of 25 to 35 years. The respondents were in the early and mid-stages of their careers and the early stages of parenting. This group, too, like the post-millennials, comprised both men and women.

The discussion was intriguing because most participants were in an age when self-enhancement is the key focus. However, and most interestingly, there is a palpable shift in how this generation is viewing achievement. Most respondents are striving to balance: balance in work/life, balancing family expectations and personal choices in finding the right partner and, where applicable, balancing traditional education with modern methods for their children and finally balancing savings with expenditure. A consumption pattern has emerged in the balancing act, covering health equipment, holidays, cars and homes, etc.

The millennial generation has faced the maximum disruption caused by the pandemic and is still facing an uncertain future. The impact was most visible in the group discussions conducted with this cohort. The emergent theme is a conscious and pragmatic consumption pattern which optimises health and well-being but affordable and convenient at the same time. Conspicuous consumption like spending on luxury goods, fancy gadgets is not considered necessary. Furthermore, Rickaby et al. (2020) have articulated the relationship between working professionals' personal values and sustainability performance. 'Feeling of oneness', 'moral obligation', 'creativity', 'challenge', 'change', and 'compliance' are the major theoretical concepts developed by them.

This group has given importance to buying fitness equipment like bicycles, yoga mats, sports gear, comfortable and multi-use furniture. Big purchases such as buying cars or taking out a mortgage are being postponed as of now. Many respondents emphasised the importance of sharing services and preferred leasing instead of owning. This is a big shift in what defines a sense of achievement. Many participants stated that working for an organisation that follows green practices and actively engages in sustainable policies adds meaning to their lives. While many would not be actively working in climate change or sustainability, they choose to work with such organisations. While earlier, many in the group would spend heavily on gratification and impulse purchases, are now giving more importance to saving and thrift.

C. Cultural Conditioning of Indian Home-makers

The strongest theme emerging from the discussion with home-makers belonging to generation X is Benevolence. The priority for most respondents is the health and well-being of family members and also of the community. This was the group that only comprised of women, given the patriarchal structure of Indian society.

Reduce, Reuse and Recycle is a way of being for Indian home-makers and culturally conditioned since previous generations. Almost all respondents regularly reuse and recycle products that are used in the houses. For example, as narrated by some respondents, old sarees are reused to make quilt covers or remodelled to make dresses. Worn out clothes will be shaped into kitchen mops and dusters. Used tea leaves and eggshells will find their way into the rose pot to become an organic fertiliser. Not even a mortal of food is wasted in Indian homes because food is considered a form of God and is respected. Left-over food is again refashioned to a new snack or given away to domestic help or fed to birds and stray animals.

Rather, the home-makers play a crucial role in influencing the household's consumption habits since they are mostly in charge of family shopping. In this regard, they constitute the world's largest consumer group (Financial Tribune, 2021). Hence, tapping home-makers as a target group while implementing certain policies to ensure sustainable consumption can be a long way to achieve that goal.

Similarly, many Indian festivals are cantered around nature and community, and hence, many medicinal herbs and plants are cultivated and offered in worship and prayer as part of many rituals. Giving back to the community happens automatically because such acts are programmed in the ritual associated with many festivals which follow lunar cycles and hence come periodically. Consequently, the cultural orientation of Indian home-makers makes them the biggest contributors to sustainability practice. It's just that the work that they do is undocumented and unappreciated.

9 Limitations

Although the findings from this study offer valuable insights into Generation Y and Z's sustainable consumption, the research can be improved further. Sample size in future studies could be increased to improve the interpretation of the results. The geographical distribution of the study area could be expanded to include various cities and studies in India. Finally, in addition to consumers, the producers should also be included in future studies to allow for an inclusive contribution of both sides of the dialogue.

10 Step 6- Conclusion

This paper explored the motivational factors influencing individuals to adjust their consumption habits and move towards more sustainable consumption. The paper used Schwartz Theory of Basic Human Values as a theoretical framework to design focus group interview questions and then used thematic analysis to examine the qualitative interview data. With a focus on the city of Pune, India, a total of 14 focus groups were conducted for four groups of undergraduate students, postgraduate students, working professionals and home-makers, with a total sample size of 138. This study's significance is to take the UN's Sustainable Development goal 12 of Responsible Consumption and Production right into people's hearts and minds and understand how sustainability is now becoming a part of a person's choice matrix at a very personal level.

The study finds that Post-millennials are influenced by climate activists and draw inspiration from social media platforms such as Instagram, where influencers actively post content and stories of environmentally friendly practices. This generation feels responsible for the future and takes up initiatives. This cohort values "universalism" and is keen to be actively engaged in sustainable practices. The idea of personal activism has a very high appeal for this generation, and working for a social cause makes them feel fulfilled and connected. The paper also finds that Millennials groups value work-life balance; this generation strives for meaningful work and social connections. The study finds evidence of "openness to change" amongst this group and their willingness to change the workplace's narrative by promoting sustainable practices.

Finally, the study finds that home-makers value "benevolence". The study finds this group exhibit solid and positive character traits such as caring for others and dependability. This generation had made an inherently sustainable lifestyle choice. Tapping into best practices of Indian home-makers and encouraging them to share their stories on social media platforms by engaging post-millennials with them as part of research projects or corporate social responsibility by Universities can prove to be a game-changer in encouraging responsible consumption. This strategy can also help bridge the gap between the two generations and enliven community-building programs.

The study has captured a subtle but powerful shift in how the change in personal values changes the paradigm of consumption as a whole. This shift is primarily caused by the underlying continues 'search for meaning life' in the consumerist society that we have largely become. A society where we have been conditioned to want more and to chase a moving target constantly is collectively staring at the unintended consequences of capitalism, technological progress and globalisation. None of these three forces can be reversed, despite the political rhetoric. However, the pandemic has taught us that the natural world has no boundaries. Global problems could best be solved by localisation and by involving the community and finally individuals themselves. This study uncovered how individuals are on the move from self-enhancement values towards transcendence. People are ready to embrace a lifestyle that is driven by more conscious choices that bring long term value, well being and nourishment for the mind, body and soul and a sense of connectedness with nature.

Several important implications and contributions for both academia and business practice can be learned from this research. This study gives academics and managers a greater understanding of consumers' decision-making processes and the factors that must be met to consider social or environmental factors in final product selection. The findings of the study will aid organisations in identifying the main factors that lead to greater acceptance of green cosmetic and food products in the Indian market, especially in Pune and the surrounding Maharashtra districts. It will also assist all concerned parties in identifying the factors that serve as roadblocks to the popularity of green goods and taking corrective steps to resolve these roadblocks. Customers will be educated about the benefits of green cosmetics and foods, and as a result, they can consider them for everyday use.

References

Accenture. (2020). *Covid-19: Fast-changing consumer behaviour*. Retrieved March 23, 2021, from https://www.accenture.com/us-en/insights/consumer-goods-services/coronavirus-consumer-behavior-research

Ahmad, S., & Juhdi, N. (2010). Organic food: A study on demographic characteristics and factors influencing purchase intentions among consumers in Klang Valley. *Malaysia International Journal of Business and Management., 5*(2), 105–118.

Arcury, T. (1990). Environmental attitude and environmental knowledge. *Human Organization, 49*(4), 300–304.

Asmuni, S., Khalili, J., & Zain, Z. (2012). Sustainable consumption practices of students in an urban setting: A case in Selangor. *Procedia – Social and Behavioral Sciences, 36*, 716–722. https://doi.org/10.1016/j.sbspro.2012.03.078

Becker, U., Fernandes, T., Arora, R., Banerjee, A., & Saluja, M. S. (2019). The Indian resource panel: A mechanism to promote resource efficiency policy throughout the Indian economy. In S. Ghosh (Ed.), *Waste management and resource efficiency*. Springer. https://doi.org/10.1007/978-981-10-7290-1_24

Braithwaite, V. A., & Law, H. G. (1985). Goal values inventory, mode values inventory, and the social values inventory. *Psyctests Dataset*. https://doi.org/10.1037/t02235-000.

Braun, V., & Clarke, V. (2006). Using thematic analysis in psychology. *Qualitative Research in Psychology, 3*(2), 77–101. https://doi.org/10.1191/1478088706qp063oa

Cawley, M. J., Martin, J. E., & Johnson, J. A. (2000). A virtues approach to personality. *Personality and Individual Differences, 28*(5), 997–1013. https://doi.org/10.1016/s0191-8869(99)00207-x

Chinnici, G., D'Amico, M., & Pecorino, B. (2002). A multivariate statistical analysis on the consumers of organic products. *British Food Journal, 104*(3/4/5), 187–199.

Cresswell, J. W., & Plano Clark, V. L. (2011). *Designing and conducting mixed-method research* (2nd ed.). Sage.

Crosby, L. A., Bitner, M. J., & Gill, J. D. (1990). Organisational structure of values. *Journal of Business Research, 20*(2), 123–134. https://doi.org/10.1016/0148-2963(90)90056-j
D'Adamo, I. (2018). The profitability of residential photovoltaic systems. A new scheme of subsidies based on the Price of CO_2 in a developed PV market. *Social Sciences, 7*, 148.
Dahl, R. (2001). Democracy. *International Encyclopedia of the Social & Behavioral Sciences*, 3405–3408. https://doi.org/10.1016/b0-08-043076-7/01131-1
Davies, A., Titterington, A., & Cochrane, C. (1995). Who buys organic food? A profile of the purchasers of organic food in Northern Ireland. *British Food Journal, 97*(10), 17–23. https://doi.org/10.5772/intechopen.85919
Durkheim, E. (1954). *The elementary forms of religious life*. Free Press.
Feather, N. T., & Peay, E. R. (1975). The structure of terminal and instrumental values: Dimensions and clusters. *Australian Journal of Psychology, 27*(2), 151–164. https://doi.org/10.1080/00049537508255247
Fielden, A., Sillence, E., & Little, L. (2011). Children's understandings' of obesity, a thematic analysis. *International Journal of Qualitative Studies on Health and Well-Being, 6*(3). https://doi.org/10.3402/qhw.v6i3.7170
Financial Tribune. (2021). *Home-makers key to sustainable consumption patterns*. Retrieved from https://financialtribune.com/articles/people/23345/homemakers-key-to-sustainable-consumption-patterns
Giménez, A. C., & Tamajón, L. G. (2019). Analysis of the third-order structuring of Shalom Schwartz's theory of basic human values. *Heliyon, 5*(6). https://doi.org/10.1016/j.heliyon.2019.e01797
Giudice, F., Caferra, R., & Morone, P. (2020). Covid-19, the food system and the circular economy: Challenges and opportunities. *Sustainability, 2020*(12), 7939. https://doi.org/10.3390/su12197939
Gonzalez, F. (2019). *Why responsible consumption is everyone's business*. Retrieved from https://www.weforum.org/agenda/2019/09/why-responsible-consumption-is-everyone-s-business/
Gonzalez-Rodriguez, M., Diaz-Fernandez, M., Spers, V., & Leite, M. (2016). Relation between background variables, values and corporate social responsibility. *Revista de Administração de Empresas, 56*(1), 8–19.
Hofstede, G. (1980). Culture andorganizations. *International Studies of Management & Organization, 10*(4), 15–41. https://doi.org/10.1080/00208825.1980.11656300
Howard, J. A., & Sheth, J. N. (1969). *The theory of buyer behavior*. Wiley.
Islam, S. M. F., & Karim, Z. (2019). *World's Demand for food and water: The consequences of climate change*. Retrieved from https://www.intechopen.com/books/desalination-challenges-and-opportunities/world-s-demand-for-food-and-water-the-consequences-of-climate-change
Kennedy, L. (2014). *The politics of restructuring in India_ economic governance and state spatial rescaling*. Routledge.
Kopnina, H. (2011). What is (responsible) consumption? Discussing environment and consumption with children from different socio-economic backgrounds in the Netherlands. *Environmentalist, 31*, 216. (2011). https://doi.org/10.1007/s10669-011-9324-y
Korhonen, J., Honkasalo, A., & Seppälä, J. (2018). Circular economy: The concept and its limitations. *Ecological Economics, 143*, 37–46.
Krueger, R. A., & Casey, M. A. (2000). *Focus groups: A practical guide for applied research* (3rd ed.). Sage Publications.
Lea, E., & Worsley, T. (2005). Australians' organic food beliefs, demographics and values. *British Food Journal, 107*(11), 855–869.
Lockie, S., Lyons, K., Lawrence, G., & Mummery, K. (2002). Eating 'green': Motivations behind organic food consumption in Australia. *European Society for Rural Sociology, 42*(1), 23–40.
Majumdar, S. (2015). *Analysis of factors influencing consumer preferences for green cosmetic and food products: A study in and around Kolkata*. ICFAI University.
Maslow, A. H. (1943). A theory of human motivation. *Psychological Review, 50*(4), 370–396. https://doi.org/10.1037/h0054346

Morgan, D. L. (1988). *Focus group as qualitative research*. Sage Publications Inc. *Online Readings in Psychology and Culture, 2*(1). https://doi.org/10.9707/2307-0919.1116.

Ottman, J. (1998). *Green marketing: Opportunity for innovation*. NTC: McGraw-Hill.

Park, N., Peterson, C., & Seligman, M. E. (2004). Strengths of character and well-being. *Journal of Social and Clinical Psychology, 23*(5), 603–619. https://doi.org/10.1521/jscp.23.5.603.50748

Polonsky, J., Bailey, J., Baker, H., Basche, C., Jepson, C., & Neath, L. (1998). Communicating environmental information: Are marketing claims on packaging misleading? *Journal of Business Ethics, 17*(3), 281–294.

Puohiniemi, M. (2002). *Arvot, asenteet ja ajankuva [Values, attitudes, and zeitgeist]*. Limor. In Finnish.

Rickaby, M., Glass, J., & Fernie, S. (2020). Conceptualising the relationship between personal values and sustainability – A TMO case study. *Administrative sciences, 10*(15), 1–22.

Robinson, R. S. (2014). Purposive sampling. In A. C. Michalos (Ed.), *Encyclopedia of quality of life and Well-being research*. Springer. https://doi.org/10.1007/978-94-007-0753-5_2337

Schwartz, S. (2012a). An ethics of the unconscious. *British Journal of Psychotherapy, 28*(2), 221–234. https://doi.org/10.1111/j.1752-0118.2012.01282.x

Schwartz, S. H. (1992a). Universals in the content and structure of values: Theoretical advances and empirical tests in 20 countries. *Advances in Experimental Social Psychology*, 25.1–25.2565.

Schwartz, S. H. (1992b). Universals in the content and structure of values: Theoretical advances and empirical tests in 20 countries. *Advances in Experimental Social Psychology, 25*, 1–65.

Schwartz, S. H. (1994). Schwartz values scale. *Psyctests Dataset*. https://doi.org/10.1037/t55949-000.

Schwartz, S. H. (2006). Basic human values: Theory, measurement, and applications. *Revue française de sociologie, 42*, 249–288.

Schwartz, S. H. (2012b). An overview of the Schwartz theory of basic values. *Online Readings in Psychology and Culture, 2*(1). https://doi.org/10.9707/2307-0919.1116

Schwartz, S. H. (2015). Basic individual values: Sources and conse-quences. In D. Sander & T. Brosch (Eds.), *Handbook of value*. Oxford University Press.

Uitto, A., & Saloranta, S. (2010). The relationship between secondary school students' environmental and human values, attitudes, interests and motivations. Procedia social and Behavioral. *Sciences, 9*, 1866–1872.

Vikuk, A., Dabrowska, A., & Machnik, A. (2021). Responsible consumer and lifestyle: Sustainability insights. *Sustainable Production and Consumption, 25*, 91–101. https://doi.org/10.1016/j.spc.2020.08.007

Weber, M. (1958). *The Protestant ethic and the spirit of capitalism*. Scribner's.

White, K., Habib, R., & Hardisty, D. J. (2019). How to SHIFT consumer Behaviors to be more sustainable: A literature review and guiding framework. *Journal of Marketing, 83*(3), 22–49. https://doi.org/10.1177/0022242919825649

Wood, W., & Hayes, T. (2012). Social Influence on consumer decisions: Motives, modes, and consequences. *Research Dialogue, 22*(3), 324–328. https://doi.org/10.1016/j.jcps.2012.05.003

Yogamalar, I., & Samuel, A. A. (2018). Classification of shared values for educational research. *International Journal of Human Resource Studies, 8*(2), 47. https://doi.org/10.5296/ijhrs.v8i2.12818

Exploring Sustainable Meat Consumption Intentions in a Pakistani Collectivist Culture: Utilising the Theory of Planned Behaviour

Sadaf Zahra, Breda McCarthy, and Taha Chaiechi

Abstract Increased globalisation, urbanisation, and a growing middle class in developing countries significantly impact food sustainability, especially within the livestock industry. The way meat is produced, processed, transported and consumed has an immense effect on environmental sustainability. From an environmental perspective, it is vital to understand better how consumers can be motivated to restrict meat consumption, particularly in non-Western countries where this area is less explored. The current study proposes a model for an emerging economy, Pakistan, where meat consumption has increased rapidly. The empirical study employed the Theory of Planned Behaviour, integrating pro-environmental attitude, perceived behaviour control and collectivist culture, to investigate sustainable meat consumption intentions (SMCI) grounded in a specific context. Data were collected from 300 meat consumers and analysed through a two-step structural equation modelling (SEM) approach, i.e. measurement and structural models. Results reported that perceived behaviour control and collectivistic culture positively influence SMCI, and the model is partially mediated through pro-environmental attitude. The study findings can help managers and policymakers to understand consumer intentions and develop actionable strategies.

Keywords Sustainable meat consumption intentions (SMCI) · Collectivist culture · Theory of planned behaviour (TPB) · Emerging economy · Environmental sustainability · Structural equation modelling (SEM)

S. Zahra (✉)
College of Business, Law and Governance, James Cook University, Townsville, QLD, Australia

Department of Management Sciences, National University of Modern Languages, Islamabad, Pakistan
e-mail: sadaf.zahra@my.jcu.edu.au

B. McCarthy · T. Chaiechi
College of Business, Law and Governance, James Cook University, Townsville, QLD, Australia
e-mail: breda.mccarthy@jcu.edu.au; taha.chaiechi@jcu.edu.au

© The Author(s), under exclusive license to Springer Nature Singapore Pte Ltd. 2022
T. Chaiechi, J. Wood (eds.), *Community Empowerment, Sustainable Cities, and Transformative Economies*, https://doi.org/10.1007/978-981-16-5260-8_23

1 Introduction

Meat production and consumption patterns are significant contributors to greenhouse gas emissions (GHG) and environmental deterioration worldwide (Apostolidis & McLeay, 2019; de Boer & Aiking, 2019). The livestock industry pollutes freshwater with antibiotics, hormones, and chemical substances, depletes freshwater availability, contributes to biodiversity loss, and is a significant source of anthropogenic greenhouse gas emissions (Sanchez-Sabate & Sabaté, 2019; Zur & Klöckner, 2014). Addressing threats from global meat production requires an in-depth knowledge of consumer intentions to reduce meat consumption and purchase more quality eco-friendly organic meat. Animals raised free from antibiotics, growth hormones, and enough space for grazing produce organic meat and contribute less GHGs emissions (Burnier et al., 2021; Hoang Viet et al., 2021; Yu et al., 2020). Consumers' sustainable meat choices can contribute to controlling environmental degradation.

Sustainable meat consumption allowed consumers to eat meat within planetary boundaries. As defined by FAO (2010), "Sustainable diets are protective and respectful of biodiversity and ecosystems, culturally acceptable, accessible, economically fair and affordable; nutritionally adequate, safe and healthy; while optimising natural and human resources". Motivating consumers' towards a more sustainable meat consumption is a great challenge. People consider meat a rich source of protein and associate meat with their traditional food culture (Apostolidis & McLeay, 2016; Paloviita, 2021) and are reluctant to change their meat consumption intentions. Therefore, globally, marketers and policymakers have been exploring effective ways to persuade consumers towards sustainable meat consumption by creating awareness about the social, environmental and economic consequences of unsustainable meat consumption. Studies have shown that increasing consumer awareness about the meat production process, improving society's knowledge about sustainable consumption, eco-labelling, group conformity pressures, and organic meat availability have all improved sustainable meat choices (Burnier et al., 2020; Peschel et al., 2016; Xie et al., 2015).

Numerous dietary studies are based on developed countries consumer markets in literature, although their attitudes, perceptions, and consumption patterns differ from developing nations. In addition, the culture, religion and country greatly influence consumers mindsets (Anam et al., 2018; de Boer et al., 2017; Minton et al., 2018; Mullee et al., 2017). These perspectives provide an interesting lens to view sustainable meat consumption intentions (SMCI) in an emerging economy context. The present empirical study suggests a new domain to capture the impacts of a collectivist culture on SMCI. The conceptual framework in the current study is based on the well-known Theory of Planned Behaviour (TPB). The authors propose that environmentally sensitive cultural values would better predict consumers' sustainable intentions in the context of an emerging economy, Pakistan. The cultural influence on meat consumption less explored in the literature, especially in the current behavioural change theories. The authors believe that the present avenue would eventually cultivate and apply more effective livestock industries' sustainable strategies in the Pakistani context. Further to providing a conceptual framework, the paper also empirically examines the relationship between perceived behaviour control, pro-environmental attitude and collectivist culture on sustainable meat consumption intentions (SMCI).

Accordingly, the structure of this paper is as follows. Section 2 provides an overview of the literature about sustainable meat consumption and utilises the constructs perceived behaviour control, a pro-environmental attitude of the Theory of Planned Behaviour with an additional construct collectivist culture to develop the hypotheses. Section 3 illustrates the scope of the study. Section 4 describes the methodology considering the sample description, sampling technique and measurement scales. Section 5 reports analysis and results. Section 6 presents the discussion on findings and implications of the study, followed by Sect. 7 elucidates limitations and future research directions.

2 Literature Review

In recent years a stream of literature has attempted to analyse drivers that underlie consumer sustainable meat consumption behavioural intentions, including the curtailment of meat from the diet, the consumption of organic meat or plant-based protein, are pro-environmental attitude, perceived behaviour control, personal norms, environmental concern and animal welfare (Austgulen et al., 2018; Azzurra et al., 2019; Taufik, 2018; Vandenbroele et al., 2018). Culture is usually ignored when predicting behavioural intentions (Mancha & Yoder, 2015; Nair & Little, 2016). Several theories are reported in the food literature to explain sustainable behavioural intentions. The current study utilised TPB to understand the effect of collectivist culture on sustainable meat consumption intentions in the Pakistani context.

2.1 Sustainable Meat Consumption

Increasing environmental deterioration due to escalating meat consumption attracts global attention (Liobikienė & Bernatonienė, 2017; Taufik, 2018). Therefore, a deep understanding of consumers about sustainable meat consumption intentions has become crucial for policymakers and marketers. The literature defines sustainable meat consumption as the curtailment of meat consumption at an individual level (Austgulen, 2014). The food literature explains three interlinked strategies to achieve the target of sustainable meat consumption. These strategies are named efficiency, sufficiency and consistency (Allievi et al., 2015). Firstly, optimising the use of resources (land, water, crops) for meat production is called efficiency. Secondly, sufficiency is delineated as the consumer's responsibility to reduce the amount of meat consumed, which is also linked to improved health and avoidance of obesity (Alexander et al., 2015; Tosun & Yanar Gürce, 2018). Thirdly, consistency is associated with farm-based animal welfare (AWE) (Allievi et al., 2015; Pohjolainen et al., 2016). AWE is related to the attributes related to the natural, green, organic and eco-friendly production of meat (Burnier et al., 2021). Consumers consider these factors when making purchase decisions through AWE labels on the packaging. It demands to replace animal-based protein with plant-based protein or eat eco-friendly meat such as organic (Lazzarini et al., 2018; Nijdam et al., 2012; Śmiglak-Krajewska & Wojciechowska-Solis, 2021).

2.2 *The Theory of Planned Behaviour (TPB)*

Consumer buying behaviour exacerbates most environmental problems, and therefore, the literature highlights that consumers have become aware of the need to buy environmentally friendly products (Medeiros & Ribeiro, 2017; Panda et al., 2020). The Theory of Planned Behaviour (TPB) (Ajzen, 1991) has become one of the most widely used rational choice models to explore the decision-making framework related to sustainable or ethical behaviour (Chang & Chuang, 2005; Hoeksma et al., 2017) across a wide range of eco-friendly contexts, such as organic food purchase intention (e.g. Pacho, 2020), sustainable seafood consumption (e.g. Honkanen & Young, 2015) and green consumption (e.g. Taufique & Vaithianathan, 2018). The TPB captures significant factors that explain the behaviour towards a particular issue (Ajzen, 1991). It permits various related variables like environmental concern, environmental knowledge, cultural values, religion and uniqueness seeking a lifestyle that may significantly affect specific behaviour (Marija Ham & Ana Pap, 2018; Minton et al., 2018; Nguyen et al., 2017; Pham et al., 2019). TPB models' flexibility allows researchers to incorporate additional variables and/or replace constructs of the underlying theory with other variables of interest to clarify consumer behavioural intentions (Kumar et al., 2017).

2.2.1 Perceived Behavioural Control

The Perceived Behavioural Control (PBC) states an individual's degree of self-control and willingness to execute specific behaviour is mainly determined by attitude and subjective norms (Ajzen, 1991). PBC can be divided into external and internal PBC. A person with high internal PBC has more control over personal resources, like confidence, planning and ability to perform a particular behaviour (Armitage & Conner, 1999). External PBC explains the control of external parameters, such as time, money and social pressure. Research in the Western context reports that PBC positively affects the organic food purchase decision (Hoeksma et al., 2017; Sultan et al., 2020). However, a study conducted in the United Kingdom showed that PBC has no impact on sustainable seafood consumption intentions

(Honkanen & Young, 2015). A study conducted in Asian context, supported that PBC enhance the purchase intention for green products (Maichum et al., 2016).

2.2.2 Collectivist Culture

The culture in which consumption activities occur embraces a dynamic array of entities, processes, events, and rituals that drive SMCI. Hofstede (1980, p.25) defines culture as "a collective programming of the mind which distinguishes one group from another". According to this definition, culture is likely rooted in each individual, forming a different school of thoughts and practices. Traditional culture may help to shape personal and collective identities (Milfont et al., 2010). Cultural traditions may improve consumers knowledge to choose more quality, eco-friendly organic meat dishes or move towards plant-based protein. Previous studies showed that food is a form of cultural heritage. People preferred those foods related to their specific traditions and festivals as they are familiar and culturally attached to and grown-up eating (Kapelari et al., 2020; Mancha & Yoder, 2015).

Cultural values can be separated at the collective and individual level. Followers of collectivist cultures tend to make decisions according to the group members' opinion (Xu-Priour et al., 2014). The literature shows that Western consumers tend to be more individualistic than Asian cultures, which are more collectivist (Cho et al., 2013; Nair & Little, 2016; Qi & Ploeger, 2019). In a collectivist culture, people's decisions closely bind with group conformity and place importance on the greater good for their extended family (Halder et al., 2020). To further explore the effect of collectivist culture on SMCI in more depth, the current study substituted subjective norms by incorporating collectivist culture.

2.2.3 Pro-Environmental Attitude

Regarding the TPB, people's intention to perform a specific behaviour is determined by their attitude, subjective norms, and perceived behavioural control (Ajzen, 1991). Attitude towards a behaviour is interpreted as the extent of an individual's favourable or unfavourable assessment of a particular behaviour (Ajzen, 1991). Several studies have verified that pro-environmental attitude is one of the most robust predictor influencing environmental behaviour (Hoang Viet et al., 2021; Taufique & Vaithianathan, 2018; Wang et al., 2018). Consumers' pro-environmental attitude can drive organic food consumption (Shin et al., 2017). Environmentally sensitive consumers are ready to pay premium prices for organic food, especially meat products, to protect the environment for society (Campbell-Arvai et al., 2014; Xie et al., 2015) and food safety concern (Yang, 2020). Pro-environment attitude varies between humans living in different geographic areas. An individual's pro-environmental attitude can be influenced by cultural values (Kim & Choi, 2005). The culture was a key predictor shaping pro-environmental attitude; people who belong to collectivistic culture more engaged in pro-environmental attitude because of their intentions

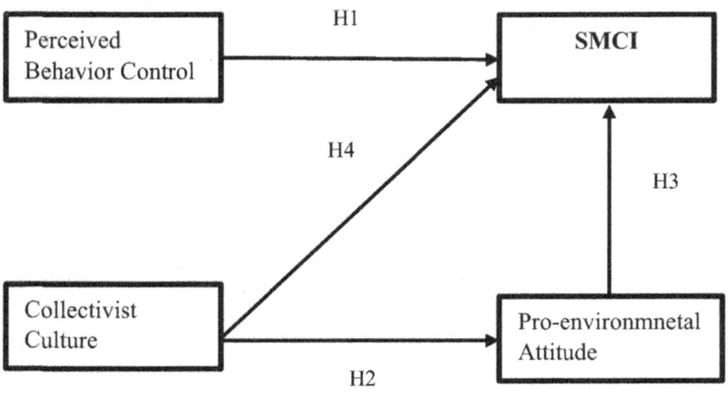

Fig. 1 Conceptual framework of sustainable meat consumption intentions (SMCI) model illustrating collectivist culture based on the amended structure of TPB

towards others, whereas individualists preferred personal goals (Mancha & Yoder, 2015; Milfont et al., 2010).

Based on the literature, the present study modifies the existing framework of TPB to examine the impact of collectivist culture instead of subjective norms on sustainable meat consumption intentions (SMCI) and proposes the following framework (Fig. 1).

2.3 Research Hypotheses

Based on the above discussion, this study proposes the following hypotheses:

H1: Perceived behaviour control affects SMCI
H2: Collectivist culture supports the pro-environmental attitude
H3: Pro-environmental attitude has an impact on SMCI
H4: Collectivist culture affects SMCI
H5: Pro-environmental attitude mediates the relationship between collectivist culture and SMCI

3 Scope of the Study

Pakistan is ranked as the fifth most populated country globally with a population of 233 million, as of July 2020, increasing 2 per cent yearly (CIA, 2020). Pakistan is one of the Muslim states with rich cultural, ethnic, religious and traditional festivals. Food, especially meat dishes, are dominant in Pakistani festivals and with consumers preferring Halal meat due to religious teachings (Sohaib & Jamil, 2017). Annual meat consumption is expected to reach up to 20 kg per capita by 2022, compared to 16 kg, 19 kg reported in 2016 and 2018, respectively **(OECD,** 2019**).** Rising meat consumption in Pakistan is accelerating environmental hazards (Rehman et al., 2017; Ullah et al., 2018). Therefore, the current study adds to the literature on sustainable meat consumption by focusing on an emerging nation and proposing a model to capture cultural values' effect on consumer's purchase decision.

4 Methods

The current empirical study utilises an online survey technique to recruit respondents through purposive sampling. The online survey technique is appropriate and cost-effective to recruit a geographically diverse population (Pearson et al., 2016; Ritter & Sue, 2007). SPSS 26.0 was utilised for demographics description and data cleaning. PLS-SEM is the most robust technique in explaining complex consumer behaviour in marketing research (Hair et al., 2014; Hair et al., 2012). The present research employed SmartPLS v.3.3.2 for path analysis.

4.1 Survey Instrument

The current research survey was divided into two main sections: the first section contained questions related to respondents demographic profile such as age, income, education, marital status, gender, employment status and location. The second section was comprised of items related to the theoretical model of the current study. The pro-environmental attitude was measured through a four-item scale adapted from Biswas and Roy (2015). In this study, PBC refers to consumers' perceived control over reducing meat from diet or eating more quality organic meat. The current study utilised a six-item scale adapted from Fishbein and Ajzen (2010) to measure PBC. The collectivist culture was measured through a six-item scale adapted from Yoo et al. (2011). SMCI was measured on a three-dimensional scale developed in the Pakistani context by the study authors having ten- items. This scale explicitly measured the consumers' meat attachment, meat curtailment intentions and organic meat purchase intentions in Appendix 1. All the responses were measured on a seven-point Likert-type scale (1 = strongly agree to 7 = strongly disagree).

4.2 Data Collection Procedure and Analysis Technique

A survey link was created through 'Qualtrics' software for online data collection purpose. A half-page statement related to the importance of the sustainable meat consumption project followed by a survey link was published on three grocery store websites having branches nationwide. The purposive (non-probability) sampling technique was used to recruit consumers responsible for grocery shopping for their household. Results may be biased due to the purposive sampling method. Even though literature support that purposive sampling results reliable and robust (Jupp, 2006; Zhao, 2018; Zikmund, 2003). The purposive sampling technique was employed in the absence of an adequate sampling frame and appropriate for theoretical generalizability (Akbar et al., 2019; Bukhari et al., 2018; Cooper & Schindler, 2008; Creswell & Plano Clark, 2018). An incentive was used to increase the response rate whereby the respondents could register separately in a draw and win a 32GB tablet.

Statistical analyses of the data were conducted through SPSS v. 26.0 and SmartPls v 3.2.2. Initially, Exploratory Factor Analysis (EFA) was performed for sampling adequacy (Hair et al., 2014) and followed by the partial least squares-structural equation modelling (PLS-SEM) for hypotheses testing. The two-step approach was applied for model analysis (Hair et al., 2014). Firstly, the embedded two-stage was utilised to confirm the validity and reliability of the measurement model. Secondly, the disjoint two-stage method was applied for hypotheses testing (Sarstedt et al., 2019).

5 Analysis and Results

Literature supports that a sample size of 200 is sufficient for structural equation model (SEM) analysis (Henseler & Sarstedt, 2013; Hoelter, 1983). SEM analysis demands at least five or, ideally, 10 cases per parameter (Bentler & Chou, 1987). As per the current study, the survey consisted of 26 items; therefore, the study required 260 (10*26) respondents. The online survey for the current research was conducted from 15th October 2020 to 15th December 2020. Overall, 525 respondents started to fill the survey, and only 300 completed it (57% response rate). A low response rate is prevalent in the online survey (see e.g. Sultan et al., 2018; Tandon et al., 2020). Larger sample size is always desired to reduce the sampling error (Randall & Gibson, 1990). Hence, the completed responses were sufficient for SEM analysis.

5.1 Demographics of Respondents

Firstly, the demographic characteristics of the respondents were examined and presented in Table 1. The total of 300 respondents consisted of 54% of males and 46% of females. Of the total respondents, 56.3% were married, 25.7% were students, and 20% owned a business. In terms of educational attainment, 40.3% of respondents have Inter-Bachelors degrees (14 years of education). Half of the respondents (51.3%) lived in cities, 35.7% lived in the suburbs and 13% in rural areas.

Table 1 Demographics characteristics of the sample

Variables	Category	Percentage
Gender	Male	54.0
	Female	46.0
Age	20–29	43.7
	30–39	27.0
	40–49	16.3
	50 or above	10.6
	Prefer not to say	2.30
Marital status	Married	56.3
	Widowed	2.50
	Divorced	1.30
	Single	39.9
Income[a]	Less than 25,000	8.0
	25,000–49,999	12.0
	50,000-74,999	13.0
	75,000-99,999	18.0
	100,000-124,999	8.3
	125,000-149,999	10.7
	150,000-174,999	8.7
	175,000 and more	21.3
Employment status	Landlord	13.0
	Own business	20.0
	Unemployed	16.7
	Employed, part-time	6.0
	Employed, full-time	18.7
	Student	25.7
Education	Primary (year 5)	6.0
	Middle- Matric (Year 10)	13.7
	Inter- Bachelors	40.3
	Master- PhD	30.3
	Professional education	9.7
Location	City	51.3
	Suburb	35.7
	Countryside	13.0

[a]Income: given in Pak Rupees (Rs)

5.2 *Measurement Model*

Initially, EFA was conducted using the Principle Component Analysis (PCA) with varimax rotation. Kaiser-Meyer-Olkin (KMO) measure (KMO = 0.875) and Bartlett's test ($X^2 = 2582.234$, $p < 0.001$) confirmed the appropriateness of data for EFA analysis (Sultan et al., 2020). The items (ColCul3, ColCul4 and PBC1) having communalities less than 0.50 were deleted iteratively (Kaiser, 1974). Results of EFA are reported in Table 2. According to Ringle et al. (2015), before accessing

Table 2 Measurement Model assessment (First-order)

Constructs	Comm.	Outer Loading	AVE's	α	CR
A. Collectivist Culture			0.574	0.753	0.843
ColCul1	0.572	0.773			
ColCul2	0.620	0.755			
ColCul5	0.587	0.746			
ColCul6	0.687	0.756			
B. Meat Attachment Intention			0.649	0.729	0.847
MAI1	0.564	0.773			
MAI2	0.706	0.824			
MAI3	0.664	0.818			
C. Meat Curtailment Intention			0.628	0.705	0.835
MCurlI1	0.642	0.771			
MCurlI2	0.603	0.792			
MCurlI3	0.623	0.814			
D. Organic Meat Purchase Intention			0.609	0.785	0.861
OMPI1	0.600	0.755			
OMPI2	0.608	0.785			
OMPI3	0.789	0.845			
OMPI4	0.533	0.732			
E. Perceived Behaviour Control			0.548	0.725	0.829
PBC2	0.562	0.714			
PBC4	0.547	0.763			
PBC5	0.556	0.714			
PBC6	0.553	0.768			
F. Pro-Environmental Attitude			0.699	0.857	0.903
ATT1	0.660	0.748			
ATT2	0.734	0.855			
ATT3	0.765	0.891			
ATT4	0.687	0.844			

Note: AVE: Average variance extracted, CR: Composite reliability, α: Cronbach alpha

the proposed hypotheses (the inner model), the outer model's reliability and validity should be maintained. Accordingly, the outer model in the current study was evaluated by assessing convergent and discriminant validity.

5.3 *Convergent Validity*

Three measures may be used collectively to identify the levels of convergent validity. Factor loading is the first measure that should be statistically robust, significant and greater than 0.7. The average variance extracted (AVE) of every construct should be greater than 0.5, which is the second measure (Fornell &

Larcker, 1981). The SMCI, the dependent variable, was revealed as a second-order construct with three dimensions; therefore, the AVE of SMCI was measured based on its first-order constructs (Souki et al., 2019). The third measure is the composite reliability (CR) which should be greater than 0.7. All the required criteria, as reported in Tables 2 having acceptable values.

5.4 Discriminant Validity

Discriminant validity is established through the Fornell and Larcker (1981) estimates. Each AVE's square root in the diagonal with the correlation coefficients (off-diagonal) of each construct in the relevant rows and columns are compared. The AVE square roots must be larger than the correlations among the constructs. The results (Table 3) indicated that the AVE square roots for all analysed constructs were superior to Pearson correlations; hence, the measurement model presents discriminant validity (Hair et al., 2010).

5.5 Structural Modeling and Hypotheses Testing

This study assessed the structural model to meet the criteria of the three most robust methods: (1) the path coefficients with t-statistics values; (2) the coefficient of determination (R^2); and (3) the stone-Geisser criterion (Q^2) (Geisser, 1975). Bootstrapping sample of 5000 with a bias-corrected confidence interval method (0.05) was utilised to test all hypotheses.

Table 4 presented the path coefficients (β), t-statistics and P-values for all hypotheses. Results showed that all the hypotheses show significant values ($\beta > 0.1$, $t > 1.96$, $P < 0.05$) and accepted. The result also analysed the indirect effect of collectivist culture on SMCI with a mediating effect of Pro-environmental attitude and accepted the hypothesis. The results showed a partially mediated model.

The R^2 values for both pro-environmental attitude (0.198) and SMCI (0.379) indicated that the proposed model has good predictive accuracy (Hair et al., 2014).

Table 3 Fornell-Lacker estimates for Discriminant validity

Constructs	A	B	C	D	E	F
A. Collectivistic culture	**0.758**					
B. Meat attachment intention	0.453	**0.806**				
C. Meat curtailment intention	0.423	0.442	**0.792**			
D. Organic meat purchase intention	0.472	0.492	0.437	**0.78**		
E. Perceived behaviour control	0.438	0.34	0.278	0.366	**0.74**	
F. Pro-environmental attitude	0.445	0.334	0.213	0.476	0.446	**0.836**

Note: Diagonal values show the square root of AVE for each construct

Table 4 Hypotheses results

Hypotheses	β	t-statistics	P-values	Decision
H1: Perceived Behaviour_ control - > SMCI	0.148	2.590	0.011	Supported
H2: Collectivist _Culture- > Pro_Environmental_Attitude	0.445	8.216	0.000	Supported
H3: Pro_Environmental_Attitude - > SMCI	0.191	2.991	0.003	Supported
H4: Collectivist _Culture - > SMCI	0.414	6.625	0.000	Supported
H5: Collectivist _Culture - > Pro_Environmental_Attitude- > SMCI	0.143	2.794	0.005	Supported

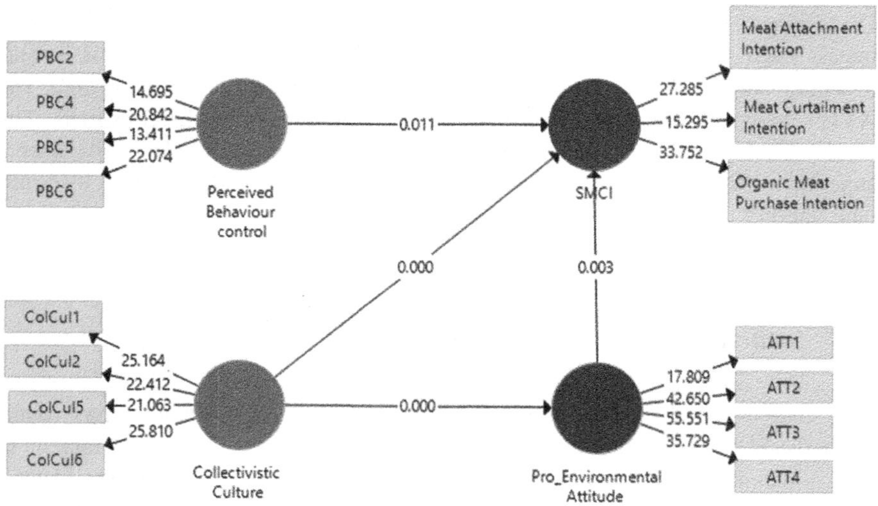

Fig. 2 The structural model with T-values (outer-model) and P-values (inner-model)

The current study also analysed Q^2 values greater than zero by using a blindfolding procedure to cross-validate the predictive relevance of the constructs pro-environmental attitude (0.131) and SMCI (0.223) (Ringle et al., 2015) (Fig. 2).

6 Discussion and Implications

The present empirical study was designed entirely around the TPB model (Ajzen, 1991) to understand different antecedents' effects on Pakistani consumers' SMCI. Food choice is a complex behaviour highly intertwined with culture (Wang & Basso, 2019). Therefore, adding collectivist culture in the TPB model increased the explanatory capability of the model significantly in the Pakistani context, where the people lived in an extended family system and are bounded in their decisions (Ahmad et al., 2020).

The findings of the study have some policy implications. First, the results revealed that consumers' pro-environmental attitudes are strongly related to sustainable meat consumption intentions. The result is consistent with the recent study conducted in the context of young Indian consumers' pro-environmental behaviour (Taufique & Vaithianathan, 2018). Similarly, the current study results recommend that livestock marketers and environmentalists communicate environmental and sustainability-related information on the meat packages to create favourable attitudes towards eco-friendly organic meat in a developing country such as Pakistan.

Second, the statistical findings verified that PBC influences SMCI. Therefore, the concept of PBC and its application to products were considered effective in promoting favourable attitudes and SMCI. A sustainable meat consumption intention may occur when an individual has the ability and motivation to perform a specific behaviour. The findings are consistent with previous studies conducted in green hotels (Han & Kim, 2010), organic food (Maichum et al., 2016; Zhu et al., 2013) and sustainable consumption (Wong & Aini, 2017) areas. The study findings are suggesting that the Government, organic meat producers, NGO's should develop strategies that motivate consumers for sustainable meat consumption to reduce environmental degradation in Pakistani culture.

Third, the results proved that collectivist culture is the most strong predictor of SMCI. This phenomenon is most likely a consequence of the Pakistani culture, where consumers rely on others' opinions and past experiences instead of rationally analysing the product's features during the food purchase stage. The study finding is consistent with another recent research conducted in another emerging country, china, that showed that group conformity enhances sustainable food consumption intentions (Qi & Ploeger, 2019). The results guide the policymakers and livestock producers who want to recognise sustainable marketers to create and develop more efficient advertising campaigns; by introducing self-enhancing promotional messages, such as "step forward for the societal good" in traditional societies. In other words, promoting general sustainable attitudes requires an understanding of the consumers' specific sustainable behaviours (Minton et al., 2018; Thøgersen, 2010). Policymakers, social marketers and sustainable activists need to help consumers build positive impressions of sustainable consumption before expecting consumers to engage in sustainable meat consumption. The current study helps to fill a gap in the literature by investigating how consumers who belong to an emerging nation react to sustainable meat consumption using the lens of collectivist culture.

7 Limitations and Future Research Direction

The present study provides interesting information but still has some limitations. First, the study is limited only to measuring intentions and not actual consumer behaviour, although there is evidence that intentions are related to behaviour (Sudbury-Riley & Kohlbacher, 2016). A longitudinal study is required to measure actual behaviour. Second, the study is conducted in Pakistani culture, and the results are not generalisable to consumers living in other emerging nations. This study contributed to the literature by examining the predictors' antecedents of SMCI in an emerging country, where sustainable consumption research is at a nascent stage.

Appendix 1: Research Survey

Response Scale

1	2	3	4	5	6	7
Strongly Agree	Agree	Somewhat Agree	Neutral	Somewhat Disagree	Disagree	Strongly Disagree

Theoretical Constructs

Perceived behaviour control								
1	I am confident that if I want, I can buy organic meat.	1	2	3	4	5	6	7
2	To buy or not to buy organic meat is entirely up to me.	1	2	3	4	5	6	7
3	It's inconvenient to purchase organic meat, although I have the purchase intention	1	2	3	4	5	6	7
4	I understand the environmental phrases and symbols on the product package.	1	2	3	4	5	6	7
5	I am very knowledgeable about environmental and social issues.	1	2	3	4	5	6	7
6	I know how to select products and packages that reduce the amount of waste ending up in landfills	1	2	3	4	5	6	7
Attitude								
7	Buying organic meat is a good idea.	1	2	3	4	5	6	7
8	Buying organic meat is a wise choice.	1	2	3	4	5	6	7
9	I like the idea of buying organic meat.	1	2	3	4	5	6	7
10	Buying organic meat would be pleasant.	1	2	3	4	5	6	7
Collectivist culture								
11	Individuals should sacrifice self-interest for the group	1	2	3	4	5	6	7
12	Individuals should stick with the group even through difficulties	1	2	3	4	5	6	7
13	Group welfare is more important than individual reward	1	2	3	4	5	6	7
14	Group success is more important than individual success	1	2	3	4	5	6	7
15	Individuals should only pursue their goals after considering the welfare of the group	1	2	3	4	5	6	7
16	Group loyalty should be encouraged even if individual goals suffer	1	2	3	4	5	6	7
Sustainable meat consumption intentions								
Meat attachment intention								
17	My meal is incomplete without meat	1	2	3	4	5	6	7

(continued)

Perceived behaviour control								
18	I am attracted to more meat dishes.	1	2	3	4	5	6	7
19	I can't reduce meat from my diet.	1	2	3	4	5	6	7
Meat curtailment intention								
20	By eating meat, I engage with industry responsible for significant environmental damage	1	2	3	4	5	6	7
21	I know my meat consumption habit harms the environment.	1	2	3	4	5	6	7
22	I feel motivated when I see that other people also reduce meat from their diet.	1	2	3	4	5	6	7
Organic meat purchase intention								
23	I prefer to buy organic meat due to my health concerns.	1	2	3	4	5	6	7
24	I know if I buy organic meat, it is a step towards sustainability.	1	2	3	4	5	6	7
25	I would like to pay more for organic meat for a quality of life.	1	2	3	4	5	6	7
26	If I have a choice, I prefer to buy organic meat.	1	2	3	4	5	6	7

References

Ahmad, M. S., Jamil, A., Latif, K. F., Ramayah, T., Ai Leen, J. Y., Memon, M., & Ullah, R. (2020). Using food choice motives to model Pakistani ethnic food purchase intention among tourists. *British food journal (1966), 122*(6), 1731–1753. https://doi.org/10.1108/BFJ-01-2019-0024.

Ajzen, I. (1991). The theory of planned behavior. *Organisational Behavior and Human Decision Processes, 50*(2), 179–211. https://doi.org/10.1016/0749-5978(91)90020-T.

Akbar, A., Ali, S., Ahmad, M. A., Akbar, M., & Danish, M. (2019). Understanding the antecedents of organic food consumption in Pakistan: Moderating role of food Neophobia. *International Journal of Environmental Research and Public Health, 16*(20), 4043. https://doi.org/10.3390/ijerph16204043.

Alexander, P., Rounsevell, M. D. A., Dislich, C., Dodson, J. R., Engström, K., & Moran, D. (2015). Drivers for global agricultural land use change: The nexus of diet, population, yield and bioenergy. *Global Environmental Change, 35*, 138–147. https://doi.org/10.1016/j.gloenvcha.2015.08.011.

Allievi, F., Vinnari, M., & Luukkanen, J. (2015). Meat consumption and production – Analysis of efficiency, sufficiency and consistency of global trends. *Journal of Cleaner Production, 92*, 142–151. https://doi.org/10.1016/j.jclepro.2014.12.075.

Anam, J., Sany Sanuri, B. M. M., & Ismail, B. L. O. (2018). Conceptualising the relation between halal logo, perceived product quality and the role of consumer knowledge. *Journal of Islamic Marketing, 9*(4), 727–746. https://doi.org/10.1108/JIMA-02-2017-0019.

Apostolidis, C., & McLeay, F. (2016). Should we stop meating like this? Reducing meat consumption through substitution. *Food Policy, 65*, 74–89. https://doi.org/10.1016/j.foodpol.2016.11.002.

Apostolidis, C., & McLeay, F. (2019). *To meat or not to meat?* Comparing empowered meat consumers' and anti-consumers' preferences for sustainability labels. Food Quality and Preference. https://doi.org/10.1016/j.foodqual.2019.04.008

Armitage, C. J., & Conner, M. (1999). Distinguishing perceptions of control from self-efficacy: Predicting consumption of a low-fat diet using the theory of planned Behavior1. *Journal of Applied Social Psychology, 29*(1), 72–90. https://doi.org/10.1111/j.1559-1816.1999.tb01375.x.

Austgulen, M. H. (2014). Environmentally sustainable meat consumption: An analysis of the Norwegian public debate. *Journal of Consumer Policy, 37*(1), 45–66. https://doi.org/10.1007/s10603-013-9246-9.

Austgulen, M. H., Skuland, S. E., Schjøll, A., & Alfnes, F. (2018). Consumer readiness to reduce meat consumption for the purpose of environmental sustainability: Insights from Norway. *Sustainability (Switzerland), 10*(9), 3058. https://doi.org/10.3390/su10093058.

Azzurra, A., Massimiliano, A., & Angela, M. (2019). Measuring sustainable food consumption: A case study on organic food. *Sustainable Production and Consumption, 17*, 95–107. https://doi.org/10.1016/j.spc.2018.09.007.

Bentler, P. M., & Chou, C.-P. (1987). Practical issues in structural modeling. *Sociological Methods & Research, 16*(1), 78–117. https://doi.org/10.1177/0049124187016001004.

Biswas, A., & Roy, M. (2015). Leveraging factors for sustained green consumption behavior based on consumption value perceptions: Testing the structural model. *Journal of Cleaner Production, 95*, 332–340. https://doi.org/10.1016/j.jclepro.2015.02.042.

Bukhari, S. F. H., Woodside, F. M., Hassan, R., Shaikh, A. L., Hussain, S., & Mazhar, W. (2018). Is religiosity an important consideration in Muslim consumer behavior: Exploratory study in the context of western imported food in Pakistan. *Journal of Islamic Marketing, 0*(0), null. https://doi.org/10.1108/JIMA-01-2018-0006

Burnier, P. C., Spers, E. E., & Barcellos, M. D. d. (2021). Role of sustainability attributes and occasion matters in determining consumers' beef choice. *Food Quality and Preference, 88*, 104075. https://doi.org/10.1016/j.foodqual.2020.104075.

Burnier, P. C., Spers, E. E., & Guerra, D. (2020). Effect of production process and attitudes on the intent to buy sustainable beef. *Journal of International Food & Agribusiness Marketing, 32*(2), 168–197. https://doi.org/10.1080/08974438.2019.1599755.

Campbell-Arvai, V., Arvai, J., & Kalof, L. (2014). Motivating sustainable food choices: The role of nudges, value orientation, and information provision. *Environment and Behavior, 46*(4), 453–475. https://doi.org/10.1177/0013916512469099

Chang, & Chuang. (2005). The study of subculture and consumer behavior: An example of Taiwanese university students' consumption culture. *Journal of American Academy of Business, 7*(2), 258–264.

Cho, Y.-N., Thyroff, A., Rapert, M. I., Park, S.-Y., & Lee, H. J. (2013). To be or not to be green: Exploring individualism and collectivism as antecedents of environmental behavior. *Journal of Business Research, 66*(8), 1052–1059. https://doi.org/10.1016/j.jbusres.2012.08.020.

CIA. (2020, July). *Central Intelligence Agency*. https://www.cia.gov/library/publications/the-world-factbook/geos/pk.html

Cooper, D. R., & Schindler, P. S. (2008). *Business research methods* (10th ed.). McGraw-Hill Irwin. http://jcu.summon.serialssolutions.com/2.0.0/link/0/eLvHCXMwdV3JCsIwEB1cQAQPrlg3-gOKbZPGnkURvIh412yiHkRQ_99J0rp7SiYMIQkhkxlm3gOIwtF4-PEmGBAXqqUSO5HgFxldMiFDNJ1xKAVLbAXAS8Hcgx1ofziPjvL2D1Dwg9b6LV4dG9yXBNs85MnEkDosV2vnlkURIfiNTgV0MBhlTmBo0HB1KTBPphk9ZascPGSnb-zSMWM6snZpXoWCqVWoQU6f61DKktgb4GVdPwXz2fuOKvrSBG8-20wXQ5xqm8Zutm4XYQsq3CS8n662ME61wVeEJlxRxSlXRMeSU6ml4DqYCM4CHXtQ-56o82uwC2WXBGHiCj0o7vDe677d0sCe2h3Gtna7

Creswell, J. W., & Plano Clark, V. L. (2018). *Designing and conducting mixed methods research* (3rd ed.). SAGE.

de Boer, J., & Aiking, H. (2019). Strategies towards healthy and sustainable protein consumption: A transition framework at the levels of diets, dishes, and dish ingredients. *Food Quality and Preference, 73*, 171–181. https://doi.org/10.1016/j.foodqual.2018.11.012.

de Boer, J., Schösler, H., & Aiking, H. (2017). Towards a reduced meat diet: Mindset and motivation of young vegetarians, low, medium and high meat-eaters. *Appetite, 113*, 387–397. https://doi.org/10.1016/j.appet.2017.03.007.

FAO. (2010). *Biodiversity and sustainable diets united against hunger*. Rome: International Scientific Symposium.

Fishbein, M., & Ajzen, I. (2010). *Predicting and changing behavior: The reasoned action approach*. New York: Routledge. https://doi.org/10.4324/9780203838020.

Fornell, C., & Larcker, D. F. (1981). Evaluating structural equation models with unobservable variables and measurement error. *Journal of Marketing Research, 18*(1), 39–50. https://doi.org/10.2307/3151312.

Geisser, S. (1975). The predictive sample reuse method with applications. *Journal of the American Statistical Association, 70*(350), 320–328. https://doi.org/10.1080/01621459.1975.10479865.

Hair, Black, W., Babin, B., & Anderson, R. (2010). *Multivariate data analysis*. London: Prentice Hall.

Hair, Sarstedt, M., Hopkins, L., & Kuppelwieser, V. (2014). Partial least squares structural equation modeling (PLS-SEM): An emerging tool in business research. *European Business Review, 26*(2), 106–121. https://doi.org/10.1108/EBR-10-2013-0128.

Hair, Sarstedt, M., Ringle, C. M., & Mena, J. A. (2012). An assessment of the use of partial least squares structural equation modeling in marketing research. *Journal of the Academy of Marketing Science, 40*(3), 414–433. https://doi.org/10.1007/s11747-011-0261-6.

Halder, P., Hansen, E. N., Kangas, J., & Laukkanen, T. (2020). How national culture and ethics matter in consumers' green consumption values. *Journal of Cleaner Production, 265*, 121754. https://doi.org/10.1016/j.jclepro.2020.121754.

Han, H., & Kim, Y. (2010). An investigation of green hotel customers' decision formation: Developing an extended model of the theory of planned behavior. *International Journal of Hospitality Management, 29*(4), 659–668. https://doi.org/10.1016/j.ijhm.2010.01.001.

Henseler, J., & Sarstedt, M. (2013). Goodness-of-fit indices for partial least squares path modeling. *Computational Statistics, 28*(2), 565–580. https://doi.org/10.1007/s00180-012-0317-1.

Hoang Viet, N., Ninh, N., Bach Khoa, N., & Steven, G. (2021). Sustainable food consumption: Investigating organic meat purchase intention by Vietnamese consumers. *Sustainability (Basel, Switzerland), 13*(2), 953. https://doi.org/10.3390/su13020953.

Hoeksma, D. L., Gerritzen, M. A., Lokhorst, A. M., & Poortvliet, P. M. (2017). An extended theory of planned behavior to predict consumers' willingness to buy mobile slaughter unit meat. *Meat Science, 128*, 15–23. https://doi.org/10.1016/j.meatsci.2017.01.011.

Hoelter, J. W. (1983). The analysis of covariance structures: Goodness-of-fit indices. *Sociological Methods & Research, 11*(3), 325–344. https://doi.org/10.1177/0049124183011003003.

Hofstede, G. H. (1980). *Culture's consequences: International differences in work-related values*. Sage Publications.

Honkanen, P., & Young, J. A. (2015). What determines British consumers' motivation to buy sustainable seafood? *British Food Journal, 117*(4), 1289–1302. https://doi.org/10.1108/BFJ-06-2014-0199.

Jupp, V. (2006). *The SAGE dictionary of social research methods*. London: SAGE. https://doi.org/10.4135/9780857020116.

Kaiser, H. F. (1974). An index of factorial simplicity. *Psychometrika, 39*(1), 31–36. https://doi.org/10.1007/BF02291575.

Kapelari, S., Alexopoulos, G., Moussouri, T., Sagmeister, K. J., & Stampfer, F. (2020). Food heritage makes a difference: The importance of cultural knowledge for improving education for sustainable food choices. *Sustainability (Basel, Switzerland), 12*(4), 1509. https://doi.org/10.3390/su12041509.

Kim, Y., & Choi, S. M. (2005). Antecedents of green purchase behavior: An examination of collectivism, environmental concern, and PCE. *Advances in Consumer Research, 32*(1), 592–599.

Kumar, B., Manrai, A. K., & Manrai, L. A. (2017). Purchasing behaviour for environmentally sustainable products: A conceptual framework and empirical study. *Journal of Retailing and Consumer Services, 34*, 1–9. https://doi.org/10.1016/j.jretconser.2016.09.004.

Lazzarini, G. A., Visschers, V. H. M., & Siegrist, M. (2018). How to improve consumers'environmental sustainability judgements of foods. *Journal of Cleaner Production, 198*, 564–574. https://doi.org/10.1016/j.jclepro.2018.07.033.

Liobikienė, G., & Bernatonienė, J. (2017). Why determinants of green purchase cannot be treated equally? The case of green cosmetics: Literature review. *Journal of Cleaner Production, 162*, 109–120. https://doi.org/10.1016/j.jclepro.2017.05.204.

Maichum, K., Parichatnon, S., & Peng, K.-C. (2016). Application of the extended theory of planned behavior model to investigate purchase intention of green products among Thai consumers. *Sustainability (Switzerland), 8*(10), 1077. https://doi.org/10.3390/su8101077.

Mancha, R., & Yoder, C. (2015). Cultural antecedents of green behavioral intent: An environmental theory of planned behavior. *Journal of Environmental Psychology, 43*. https://doi.org/10.1016/j.jenvp.2015.06.005.

Ham, M., & Ana Pap, M. S. (2018). What drives organic food purchasing? – Evidence from Croatia. *British Food Journal, 120*(4). https://doi.org/10.1108/BFJ-02-2017-0090.

Medeiros, J. F., & Ribeiro, J. L. D. (2017). Environmentally sustainable innovation: Expected attributes in the purchase of green products. *Journal of Cleaner Production, 142*, 240–248. https://doi.org/10.1016/j.jclepro.2016.07.191.

Milfont, T. L., Duckitt, J., & Wagner, C. (2010). A cross-cultural test of the value–attitude–behavior hierarchy. *Journal of Applied Social Psychology, 40*(11), 2791–2813. https://doi.org/10.1111/j.1559-1816.2010.00681.x.

Minton, Jeffrey Xie, H., Gurel-Atay, E., & Kahle, L. R. (2018). Greening up because of god: The relations among religion, sustainable consumption and subjective well-being. *International Journal of Consumer Studies, 42*(6), 655–663. https://doi.org/10.1111/ijcs.12449.

Mullee, A., Vermeire, L., Vanaelst, B., Mullie, P., Deriemaeker, P., Leenaert, T., De Henauw, S., Dunne, A., Gunter, M. J., Clarys, P., & Huybrechts, I. (2017). Vegetarianism and meat consumption: A comparison of attitudes and beliefs between vegetarian, semi-vegetarian, and omnivorous subjects in Belgium. *Appetite, 114*, 299–305. https://doi.org/10.1016/j.appet.2017.03.052.

Nair, S. R., & Little, V. J. (2016). Context, culture and green consumption: A new framework. *Journal of International Consumer Marketing, 28*(3), 169–184. https://doi.org/10.1080/08961530.2016.1165025.

Nguyen, T. N., Lobo, A., & Greenland, S. (2017). The influence of cultural values on green purchase behaviour. *Marketing Intelligence & Planning, 35*(3), 377–396. https://doi.org/10.1108/MIP-08-2016-0131.

Nijdam, D., Rood, T., & Westhoek, H. (2012). The price of protein: Review of land use and carbon footprints from life cycle assessments of animal food products and their substitutes. *Food Policy, 37*(6), 760–770. https://doi.org/10.1016/j.foodpol.2012.08.002.

OECD. (2019). *Meat consumption*. https://www.oecd-ilibrary.org/agriculture-and-food/meat-consumption/indicator/english_fa290fd0-en

Pacho, F. (2020). What influences consumers to purchase organic food in developing countries? *British food journal (1966), 122*(12), 3695–3709. https://doi.org/10.1108/BFJ-01-2020-0075.

Paloviita, A. (2021). Developing a matrix framework for protein transition towards more sustainable diets. *British food journal (1966), 123*(13), 73–87. https://doi.org/10.1108/BFJ-09-2020-0816.

Panda, T. K., Kumar, A., Jakhar, S., Luthra, S., Garza-Reyes, J. A., Kazancoglu, I., & Nayak, S. S. (2020). Social and environmental sustainability model on consumers' altruism, green purchase intention, green brand loyalty and evangelism. *Journal of Cleaner Production, 243*, 118575. https://doi.org/10.1016/j.jclepro.2019.118575.

Pearson, D., Mirosa, M., Andrews, L., & Kerr, G. (2016). *Reframing communications that encourage individuals to reduce food waste* (Vol. 3). https://doi.org/10.1080/22041451.2016.1209274.

Peschel, A. O., Grebitus, C., Steiner, B., & Veeman, M. (2016). How does consumer knowledge affect environmentally sustainable choices? Evidence from a cross-country latent class analysis of food labels. *Appetite, 106*, 78–91. https://doi.org/10.1016/j.appet.2016.02.162.

Pham, T. H., Nguyen, T. N., Phan, T. T. H., & Nguyen, N. T. (2019). Evaluating the purchase behaviour of organic food by young consumers in an emerging market economy. *Journal of Strategic Marketing, 27*(6), 540–556. https://doi.org/10.1080/0965254X.2018.1447984.

Pohjolainen, P., Tapio, P., Vinnari, M., Jokinen, P., & Räsänen, P. (2016). Consumer consciousness on meat and the environment — Exploring differences. *Appetite, 101*, 37–45. https://doi.org/10.1016/j.appet.2016.02.012.

Qi, X., & Ploeger, A. (2019). Explaining consumers' intentions towards purchasing green food in Qingdao, China: The amendment and extension of the theory of planned behavior. *Appetite, 133*, 414–422. https://doi.org/10.1016/j.appet.2018.12.004.

Randall, D. M., & Gibson, A. M. (1990). Methodology in business ethics research: A review and critical assessment. *Journal of Business Ethics, 9*(6), 457–471. https://doi.org/10.1007/BF00382838.

Rehman, A., Jingdong, L., Chandio, A. A., & Hussain, I. (2017). Livestock production and population census in Pakistan: Determining their relationship with agricultural GDP using econometric analysis. *Information Processing in Agriculture, 4*(2), 168–177. https://doi.org/10.1016/j.inpa.2017.03.002.

Ringle, C., Wende, W. S., & Becker, J.-M. (2015). *"SmartPLS 3." Boenningstedt: SmartPLS GmbH"*. Retrieved 15 June from https://www.smartpls.com

Ritter, L. A., & Sue, V. M. (2007). Systematic planning for using an online survey. *New Directions for Evaluation, 2007*(115), 15–22. https://doi.org/10.1002/ev.231.

Sanchez-Sabate, R., & Sabaté, J. (2019). Consumer attitudes towards environmental concerns of meat consumption: A systematic review. *International Journal of Environmental Research and Public Health, 16*(7), 1220. https://doi.org/10.3390/ijerph16071220.

Sarstedt, M., Hair, J. F., Cheah, J.-H., Becker, J.-M., & Ringle, C. M. (2019). How to specify, estimate, and validate higher-order constructs in PLS-SEM. *Australasian Marketing Journal, 27*(3), 197–211. https://doi.org/10.1016/j.ausmj.2019.05.003.

Shin, Y. H., Moon, H., Jung, S. E., & Severt, K. (2017). The effect of environmental values and attitudes on consumer willingness to pay more for organic menus: A value-attitude-behavior approach. *Journal of Hospitality and Tourism Management, 33*, 113–121. https://doi.org/10.1016/j.jhtm.2017.10.010.

Śmiglak-Krajewska, M., & Wojciechowska-Solis, J. (2021). Consumption preferences of pulses in the diet of polish people: Motives and barriers to replace animal protein with vegetable protein. *Nutrients, 13*(2), 454. https://doi.org/10.3390/nu13020454.

Sohaib, M., & Jamil, F. (2017). An insight of meat industry in Pakistan with special reference to halal meat: A comprehensive review. *Korean Journal for Food Science of Animal Resources, 37*(3), 329–341. https://doi.org/10.5851/kosfa.2017.37.3.329

Souki, G. Q., Antonialli, L. M., Barbosa, Á. A. D. S., & Oliveira, A. S. (2019). Impacts of the perceived quality by consumers' of à la carte restaurants on their attitudes and behavioural intentions. *Asia Pacific Journal of Marketing and Logistics, 32*(2), 301–321. https://doi.org/10.1108/APJML-11-2018-0491.

Sudbury-Riley, L., & Kohlbacher, F. (2016). Ethically minded consumer behavior: Scale review, development, and validation. *Journal of Business Research, 69*(8), 2697–2710. https://doi.org/10.1016/j.jbusres.2015.11.005.

Sultan, P., Tarafder, T., Pearson, D., & Henryks, J. (2020). Intention-behaviour gap and perceived behavioural control-behaviour gap in theory of planned behaviour: Moderating roles of communication, satisfaction and trust in organic food consumption. *Food Quality and Preference, 81*, 103838. https://doi.org/10.1016/j.foodqual.2019.103838.

Sultan, P., Wong, H. Y., & Sigala, M. (2018). Segmenting the Australian organic food consumer market. *Asia Pacific Journal of Marketing and Logistics, 30*(1), 163–181. https://doi.org/10.1108/APJML-10-2016-0211.

Tandon, A., Dhir, A., Kaur, P., Kushwah, S., & Salo, J. (2020). Why do people buy organic food? The moderating role of environmental concerns and trust. *Journal of Retailing and Consumer Services, 57*, 102247. https://doi.org/10.1016/j.jretconser.2020.102247.

Taufik, D. (2018). Prospective "warm-glow" of reducing meat consumption in China: Emotional associations with intentions for meat consumption curtailment and consumption of meat substitutes. *Journal of Environmental Psychology, 60*, 48–54. https://doi.org/10.1016/j.jenvp.2018.10.004.

Taufique, K. M. R., & Vaithianathan, S. (2018). A fresh look at understanding green consumer behavior among young urban Indian consumers through the lens of theory of planned behavior. *Journal of Cleaner Production, 183*, 46–55. https://doi.org/10.1016/j.jclepro.2018.02.097.

Thøgersen, J. (2010). Country differences in sustainable consumption: The case of organic food. *Journal of Macromarketing, 30*(2), 171–185. https://doi.org/10.1177/0276146710361926.

Tosun, P., & Yanar Gürce, M. (2018). Consumer comments about meat anti-consumption. *British Food Journal, 120*(10), 2439–2453. https://doi.org/10.1108/BFJ-12-2017-0685.

Ullah, A., Khan, D., Khan, I., & Zheng, S. (2018). Does agricultural ecosystem cause environmental pollution in Pakistan? Promise and menace. *Environmental Science and Pollution Research, 25*(14), 13938–13955. https://doi.org/10.1007/s11356-018-1530-4.

Vandenbroele, J., Slabbinck, H., Van Kerckhove, A., & Vermeir, I. (2018). Curbing portion size effects by adding smaller portions at the point of purchase. *Food Quality and Preference, 64*, 82–87. https://doi.org/10.1016/j.foodqual.2017.10.015.

Wang, F., & Basso, F. (2019). "Animals are friends, not food": Anthropomorphism leads to less favorable attitudes toward meat consumption by inducing feelings of anticipatory guilt. *Appetite, 138*, 153–173. https://doi.org/10.1016/j.appet.2019.03.019.

Wang, J., Wang, S., Wang, Y., Li, J., & Zhao, D. (2018). Extending the theory of planned behavior to understand consumers' intentions to visit green hotels in the Chinese context. *International Journal of Contemporary Hospitality Management, 30*(8), 2810–2825. https://doi.org/10.1108/IJCHM-04-2017-0223.

Wong, S. S., & Aini, M. S. (2017). Factors influencing purchase intention of organic meat among consumers in Klang Valley, Malaysia. *International Food Research Journal, 24*(2), 767–778.

Xie, B., Wang, L., Yang, H., Wang, Y., & Zhang, M. (2015). Consumer perceptions and attitudes of organic food products in eastern China. *British food journal (1966), 117*(3), 1105–1121. https://doi.org/10.1108/BFJ-09-2013-0255.

Xu-Priour, D.-L., Truong, Y., & Klink, R. R. (2014). The effects of collectivism and polychronic time orientation on online social interaction and shopping behavior: A comparative study between China and France. *Technological Forecasting and Social Change, 88*, 265–275. https://doi.org/10.1016/j.techfore.2014.07.010.

Yang, X. (2020). Potential consequences of COVID-19 for sustainable meat consumption: The role of food safety concerns and responsibility attributions. *British food journal (1966), 123*(2), 455–474. https://doi.org/10.1108/BFJ-04-2020-0332.

Yoo, B., Donthu, N., & Lenartowicz, T. (2011). Measuring Hofstede's five dimensions of cultural values at the individual level: Development and validation of CVSCALE. *Journal of International Consumer Marketing, 23*(3–4), 193–210. https://doi.org/10.1080/08961530.2011.578059.

Yu, W., Han, X., Ding, L., & He, M. (2020). Organic food corporate image and customer co-developing behavior: The mediating role of consumer trust and purchase intention. *Journal of Retailing and Consumer Services*. https://doi.org/10.1016/j.jretconser.2020.102377.

Zhao, L. (2018). Social media and Chinese consumers' environmentally sustainable apparel purchase intentions. *Asia Pacific Journal of Marketing and Logistics, 31*(4), 855–874. https://doi.org/10.1108/APJML-08-2017-0183.

Zhu, Q., Li, Y., Geng, Y., & Qi, Y. (2013). Green food consumption intention, behaviors and influencing factors among Chinese consumers. *Food Quality and Preference, 28*(1), 279–286. https://doi.org/10.1016/j.foodqual.2012.10.005.

Zikmund, W. G. (2003). *Exploring marketing research* (8th ed.). Thomson/South-Western.

Zur, I., & Klöckner, C. (2014). Individual motivations for limiting meat consumption. *British Food Journal, 116*(4), 629–642. https://doi.org/10.1108/BFJ-08-2012-0193.

Financialisation and Environmental Goals of 2030 Agenda

Mateusz Racławski

Abstract One of the phenomena impacting economies around the world is the process called financialisation. Changes in regulations and behaviour of both financial and nonfinancial firms shifted the balance of power away from the real economy and towards the financial sector. Some economists argue that financialisation has had negative effects on society, e.g., it has increased inequalities and made economies more prone to crises. This paper aims to identify and analyse three categories of risk arising from financialisation that may pose a threat to the environmental goals of the 2030 Agenda. According to some predictions, the first category pertains to class division; the negative effects of climate change will not be shared equally. Since financial markets are deemed to be partially responsible for the increasing class inequalities, there is indeed a risk that working- and middle-class people will bear the burden of climate change. This leads to the second category of risk: the risk of insufficient regulation concerning unsustainable financial activity. While some steps have been taken in recent years to regulate financial markets, there may not be enough incentive to switch towards environmentally sustainable financial activities. The third category of risk concerns the change in rhetoric imposed by financialisation. Financial markets are seen more and more as the economy and not as an extension of it. There is a risk that adhering to the 2030 Agenda's goals may be seen primarily as a hindrance for financial markets instead of perceiving these goals as necessary steps required to mitigate the negative consequences of climate change.

Keywords 2030 Agenda · Climate change · Financialisation · Financial markets · Financial regulation · Inequalities

---

M. Racławski (✉)
Faculty of Management and Social Communication of the Jagiellonian University, Kraków, Poland
e-mail: mateusz.raclawski@doctoral.uj.edu.pl

© The Author(s), under exclusive license to Springer Nature Singapore Pte Ltd. 2022

T. Chaiechi, J. Wood (eds.), *Community Empowerment, Sustainable Cities, and Transformative Economies*, https://doi.org/10.1007/978-981-16-5260-8_24

1 Introduction

In 2015, the United Nations set 17 Sustainable Development Goals (SDGs) in the resolution called the 2030 Agenda. These goals are meant to achieve sustainable development by mitigating climate change, reducing inequalities, and solving various humanitarian issues like poverty or hunger. This paper aims to identify trends and opportunities in the field of financialisation connected with SDGs. Financialisation is an ambiguous term, as there are many different approaches to defining it. The most general approach is to define financialisation as a process during which the role of financial markets increases in the economy. A more specific way is to define it as the increase of value added by financial firms to Gross Domestic Product (GDP) (Naples & Van Arnum, 2013: 1169). Another approach sees financialisation mainly as the increasing involvement of nonfinancial firms in financial markets (Krippner 2005: 181–182). Yet another way is to define financialisation as a growing influence of financial markets on previously nonfinancial sectors. No matter how financialisation is defined, the growing importance of the financial markets has been observed in the member countries of the Organisation for Economic Cooperation and Development (OECD) economies since around 1980 (Lin & Tomaskovic-Devey, 2011).

The paper is based on the theoretical framework the Radical Political Economics school of economic thought put forth. Radical economics is aimed at examining economic structures, the structures of power, and how these structures affect people (Kim, 2018). The school treats economics normatively and goes to the root of structures in order to identify issues present in the economy and society. With that in mind, financialisation may be seen as a part of economic structure that influences the well-being of people – identifying trends connected with financialisation, and climate change may help understand harmful structures of power present in the economy. With the looming threat of climate change, this paper is intended to contribute to bridging the gap in knowledge regarding how financialisation may impede the enforcement of SDGs. Since SDGs were set just 6 years ago, it is still too early to judge the effectiveness of the 2030 Agenda decisively. Therefore, the paper is limited simply by the lack of knowledge and data, which economists and statisticians will gather in the coming decade. However, knowing how financialisation affected the economy in the past, it is possible to predict how financialisation may affect the implementation of SDGs. Therefore, this discussion paper aims to identify and discuss the risks stemming from financialisation in achieving the environmental goals of the 2030 Agenda connected with climate change. Doing so is important, since global society cannot possibly afford the risk of financialisation obstructing climate change mitigation.

The paper is divided into three sections, each of which describes risks posing a threat to the sustainable path to the 2030 Agenda. The first section discusses the risks stemming from the effect financialisation has on economic inequality, particularly income and wealth inequality. While inequalities are not directly connected with the environment, high inequalities were linked to the increase in the risks stemming from climate change. These risks can be divided into two general categories: physical risks involve economic damages arising from climate-related events and transition risks from society transitioning towards a low-carbon economy (Dafermos et al., 2018: 219). The second section identifies the risks coming from financial regulation. Financial entities were observed to either tend to evade regulations or use regulatory policies for financial gain. Contemporary financial rhetoric is discussed in Sect. 3. There is a risk that financial rhetoric may influence climate change action.

1.1 Inequality

The first category of risk regards the effect financialisation has on class division and inequalities. A significant amount of evidence from the early 2010s supports the claim that financialisation has led to more income and wealth inequalities (e.g., Zalewski & Whalen, 2010; Assa, 2012; Kus, 2012; Lin & Tomaskovic-Devey, 2013; Naples & Van Arnum, 2013). Two general conclusions can be gathered from these studies. First, financialisation had a negative impact on inequality. Second, financialisation caused downward pressure on wages (Lin & Tomaskovic-Devey, 2013: 1313) and increased capital income (Zalewski & Whalen, 2010: 766), thus widening the income gap. More recent studies focused on further explanations as to how financialisation leads to inequalities. Hyde et al. (2018: 207–208) argued that credit expansion, financial crises, and employment increase in the finance, insurance, and real estate sectors led to more inequalities. Godechot (2020) points to the financial labour market (particularly the increase of income for the top earners) as the main channel of financialisation-induced inequality. Huber et al. (2020) argued that the shareholder value model of corporate governance and demand for financial professionals exacerbated inequalities by increasing the income earned by the top 1%. Daud et al. (2020: 3) found that the improvement of digital technology in the financial sector has an added effect on widening inequality.

Although there is no unanimous agreement on how financialisation causes inequality, the cause-and-effect relationship between financialisation and inequality seems certain. By increasing income and wealth inequalities, financialisation strengthens the underlying class division in market societies. While the modern class division is definitely less overt than in the nineteenth century, it still stands at the core of society. Bryan et al. (2009: 468) argued that financialisation had changed class relations, but it has not removed class contradictions. However, with the growing threat of climate change, inequalities and class division may become increasingly explicit. High inequalities are linked to increased physical and transition risks for those at the bottom of the socioeconomic hierarchy. Specifically, it means that disadvantaged people are more likely to suffer from the negative effects of climate change itself than rich people (unequal physical risk) and that they are more susceptible to unjust climate change mitigation policies (unequal transition risk). The disparity in physical risk is a rather well-known issue regarding inequalities across countries. Populations of low-income countries were found to be more endangered by direct climate change damages (Roberts, 2010; King & Harrington, 2018). The scientific effort is coupled with the increasing media attention concerning the physical risks of climate change, e.g., the well-known case of Kiribati Island (Pala, 2019) or a tragic yet symbolic death over a water dispute during a heatwave in India (Giordano, 2019). However, the literature regarding financialisation focuses more often on inequalities within countries, and therefore, this type of inequality is more relevant to the paper. Islam and Winkel (2017) found that low-income people and other disadvantaged groups (such as women, children, or the elderly) are more endangered by the physical risks of climate change. Consequently, low-income people may suffer disproportionately from climate change, which they will face on top of the usual hardships.

Regarding the transition risks, the issue is comparable. Some climate change mitigation policies may increase income and wealth inequalities and decrease the quality of life in areas such as transportation or health (Markkanen & Anger-Kraavi, 2019: 832–835). Therefore, transition risks are twofold: first, there is a risk that pre-existing inequalities will cause the disadvantaged groups to be negatively affected by climate change mitigation policies and second, there is a risk that these policies will effectively increase inequalities. The concern for these risks generated discussion both among social scientists and policymakers. As Baer et al. noted (2009: 1124) "the poor must, at a minimum, be spared the burdens of the climate transition". The framework of Just Transition emerged to merge the climate change mitigation effort with the improvement in quality of life for working-class people (Velicu & Barca, 2020: 264). According to the Just Transition Centre (2017), in the 1990s, the framework was primarily connected with job losses caused by environmental policies, but now it "offers the opportunity to solve three key challenges at once: climate change, growing inequality and social inclusion" (JTC, 2017: 2). A vision of the International Labour Organization's similarly linked environmental transition reduces inequalities (ILO, 2015: 4).

The United Nations adopted this multidimensional approach in the 2030 Agenda, and aside from SDGs focused on climate change, the 10th goal of the resolution aims to reduce inequalities within and among countries. Target 10.5 is particularly relevant in regard to the role of financialisation in causing inequalities: "improve the regulation and monitoring of global financial markets and institutions and strengthen the implementation of such regulations" (UN, 2015: 21). The report published in 2020 by the Economic and Social Council states that some progress has been made regarding reducing income inequalities, but the COVID-19 pandemic may exacerbate inequalities, particularly in the poorest countries (UN, 2020: 12). To summarise the preceding argument: financialisation has been proved to increase income and wealth inequalities; inequalities strengthen class division; high inequalities are connected with increased physical and transition risks stemming from climate change; the concept of just transition emerged, and it has been expressed in the form of SDGs; some progress in reducing inequalities has been observed in the past few years.

Therefore, the risk in question is twofold: financialisation may further cause inequalities and, by extension, cause disadvantaged groups to suffer more severely

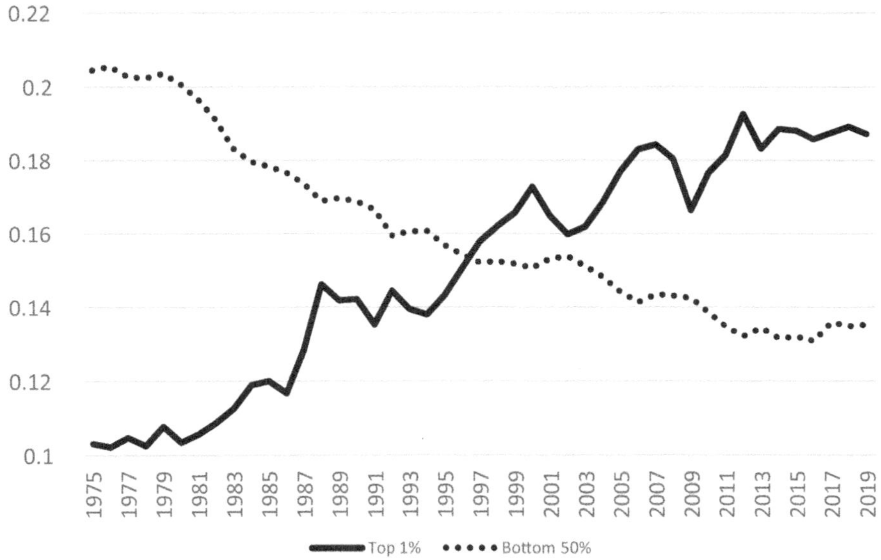

Fig. 1 Top 1% and bottom 50% income shares in the United States 1975–2019. (Source: World Income Inequality Database (2021))

from transition and physical risks arising from climate change. One could ask the problem since the risk has been identified by social scientists and incorporated by international organisations in their goals and guidelines. The issue is that the progress which has been made so far was minuscule. Figure 1 shows the top 1% and bottom 50% income shares in the United States from 1975 to 2019. Income inequalities have been increasing at an alarming rate since 1980, and beginning from 1997, the top 1% share has exceeded the share of the bottom 50%. Between 2015 and 2019, the bottom 50% share increased by 0.3 percentage points, which is far too slow to achieve any substantial progress. The bottom 50% income share would need to increase, on average, by 0.14 pp yearly between 2019 and 2030 to offset the exacerbating inequalities in the 15 years preceding the publishing of the 2030 Agenda. Achieving such a rate is rather improbable under existing conditions.

The case of income inequality is the most explicit in the United States, but a similar process has been observed in other OECD countries. Table 1 shows the bottom 40% income share[1] in all OECD countries and several world regions. The bottom 40% share has increased in 27 countries in the four years since SDGs were set in 2015, and it has decreased in the remaining 10 countries. While progress has been made in most countries, the share in 28 countries is still lower than in 1980. Additionally, the share is higher than 16% only in 10 countries, the same could be said about 20 countries for 1980. The situation is much worse in regions outside of

[1] Increasing the bottom 40% income share has been set as a target in SDG 10.

Table 1 Bottom 40% income share (%), OECD member states and selected regions

Country	1980[a]	2015	2019	Country	1980[a]	2015	2019
Australia	15.64	13.12	13.13	Luxembourg	15.95	13.76	13.57
Austria	15.19	16.53	17.26	Mexico	4.82	4.68	5.27
Belgium	14.85	14.29	14.34	Netherlands	19.33	15.91	15.56
Canada	14.54	13.99	13.16	New Zealand	13.06	15.8	15.88
Chile	5.79	5.89	6.36	Norway	19.01	18.68	18.07
Colombia	5.13	6.84	6.97	Poland	21.77	12.97	13.18
Czech Republic	25.58	19.07	20.13	Portugal	16.01	12.36	12.9
Denmark	18.72	15.99	16.02	Slovakia	21.39	18.04	17.47
Estonia	17.54	12.39	13.37	Slovenia	20.31	15.44	16.55
Finland	17.74	15.92	16.32	Spain	13.75	14.59	14.94
France	16.29	14.37	14.56	Sweden	20.13	17.18	17.63
Germany	16.75	12.25	12.67	Switzerland	17.29	16.51	16.31
Greece	11.45	11.39	12.26	Turkey	10.52	12.57	12.57
Hungary	28.34	15.64	15.28	USA	13.21	8.24	8.42
Iceland	16.44	18.24	18.52	United Kingdom	15.71	13.69	14.81
Ireland	17.2	13.96	15.33	World	4.35	5.65	5.85
Israel	12.85	11.58	11.72	Africa	4.58	5.01	5.26
Italy	18.95	13.62	13.7	Asia (excl. Middle East)	9.51	7.71	7.85
Japan	14.04	12.81	12.83	Eastern Europe	18.15	11.52	11.87
Korea	15.77	12.67	12.6	Western Europe	15.89	13.44	13.86
Latvia	17.52	12.86	12.77	Latin America	5.66	6.15	6.05
Lithuania	19.63	12.13	12.1	Middle East	7.17	8.22	8.38

[a]1990 for Japan, Korea, Africa, Middle East

OECD countries. The bottom 40% share has increased in Africa, Latin America, and the Middle East; it still is below acceptable levels.

While it is too early to evaluate the effectiveness of the 2030 Agenda, the progress made so far is negligible. The aforementioned report by the Economic and Social Council acknowledged this issue, underlining that "inequality still persists in all forms" (UN, 2020: 12). Despite some noticeable improvements in reducing inequalities and emissions, income inequalities remain at unacceptable levels, and the emission gap[2] is still increasing (UN, 2020). Since financialisation is one of the main sources of increasing inequality, new financial regulation must be enforced swiftly to mitigate physical and transition risks stemming from climate change. However, any effort connected with financial regulation poses another risk, which will be discussed in the following point.

[2]Emission gap is "the difference between the greenhouse gas emission levels consistent with a specific probability of limiting the mean global temperature rise to below 2 °C or 1.5 °C in 2100 above pre-industrial levels and the GHG emission levels consistent with the global effect of the NDCs, assuming full implementation from 2020." (UN, 2020: X)

2 Financial Regulation

Achieving SDGs can be linked to two kinds of financial regulation. The first type concerns the restoration of regulatory policies abolished in the last 40 years, which allowed financialisation to flourish in a neoliberal landscape. While financial deregulation was particularly excessive in the United States, similar processes have been happening in many other OECD countries, e.g., in the United Kingdom, Sweden, Japan, or Australia (see: Bayoumi, 1993; Turner, 1997; Honda, 2003; Nevile, 1997). The substantial role of financial deregulation in increasing inequalities was acknowledged by the Department of Economic and Social Affairs of the United Nations Secretariat (UN, 2020: 13). The idea of regulating the financial markets to decrease inequalities was also expressed in the aforementioned 10.5 targets of the 2030 Agenda. The second type of financial regulation concerns changing the financial system with environmental goals in mind. The Network for Greening the Financial System (NGFS) was established in 2017 by central banks and international organisations to "mobilise mainstream finance to support the transition toward a sustainable economy" (NGFS, 2018: 3). The European Green Deal aims to reduce greenhouse gas emissions within the European Union (EU) in part by directing private capital to green investment, promoting long-term and sustainable development strategies, and obligating financial institutions to disclose the impact they have on the environment (European Commission, 2019: 16–17). Admittedly, there is an institutional effort to impose financial regulation to decrease inequalities and mitigate physical and transition risks stemming from climate change.

However, reviewing particular regulatory policies is beyond the scope of this paper. The excess of financialisation in the last four decades will be discussed instead. Economies in the OECD countries are vastly different when compared to their state in 1980, and there is a risk that it is too late to achieve any substantial progress within the contemporary financial paradigm. In other words, the question that needs to be addressed is whether regulatory evolution, instead of revolution, is enough to prepare society for the dangers associated with climate change? Regulatory evolution is to be understood as implementing new green regulations without changing the contemporary financial paradigm. Financialisation-induced inequalities and unsustainable financial systems are the products of a systematic transformation of financial markets undertaken in the span of several decades. Therefore, achieving SDGs within contemporary financial systems may prove futile. Financial markets need to benefit the real economy and income distribution instead of aggravating external costs stemming from financial activity (Aiginger, 2016: 102).

Targets set by the 2030 Agenda do not sufficiently acknowledge the systematic risks connected with financial markets, neither do they acknowledge the possibility that an outright transformation of financial markets may be needed to achieve SDGs in time. Some authors argue for a more revolutionary approach to the role of the financial markets in mitigating climate change. Davis argues (2019) that climate change mitigation policies cannot be based around market mechanisms or for-profit financial systems. Pettifor (2019). goes so far as to say that the contemporary financial system has to be dismantled for the public sphere to regain control over ecosystems. The more evolutionary approach may be the reason why unsatisfactory progress has been reported by the Economic and Social Council not only in the case of inequalities but also regarding the 13th goal of the agenda - private investments in renewable energy were deemed "relatively small concerning the scale of annual investment needed for a low-carbon, climate-resilient transition" (UN, 2020: 15). In the European Green Deal case, Pianta argued (2020: 3) that businesses have no incentive to invest in sustainable production. Relying on private investment may prove to be an inadequate measure to combat climate change if financial and nonfinancial firms decide that investing in other sectors is more profitable in the short term.

The shortcomings of the contemporary financial paradigm are best exemplified by financial actors having a history of circumventing regulations. Even if suitable regulations were in place, there is a risk that they would be either exploited to achieve financial gains or avoided altogether. While financialisation was undeniably caused by deregulation (Lin & Tomaskovic-Devey, 2011), a change in banks and other business behaviour occurred in the United States prior to the first financial deregulation in 1978. In the 1960s and 1970s, the financial system in the United States was still heavily regulated by Glass-Steagall Act and other regulations. However, the reduced profits observed in this period incentivised businesses to take advantage of financial markets (Krippner, 2005; Marazzi, 2010: 31–32). While nonfinancial businesses simply began to invest more capital into financial markets, banks bypassed regulations forbidding them from nonbanking activities to increase profits (Naples & Van Arnum, 2013: 1159–60). Lapavitsas argued (2013: 794) that the rise of finance in that era was partly caused by banks focusing more on financial trading than their primary functions - lending and borrowing. Essentially, banks were able to change their method of capital accumulation despite widespread regulations prohibiting them from doing so. More recent examples include "financial innovations" – techniques praised for positively affecting growth and prosperity, which in reality are used by financial firms to circumvent regulations (Nesvetailova & Palan, 2013). Offshoring, securitisation, and shadow banking – these innovations make it possible to avoid tax or disguise risky underlying assets as reliable financial instruments. This phenomenon has already extended its reach to climate change mitigation. Vlachou and Pantelias showed (2020) that the European Union's Emission Trading System, an emissions trading market mechanism, has led to the creation of profit-oriented financial innovations and had a mildly effective impact on the environment. See Mol (2012); Schneider and La Hoz Theuer (2019) for other reviews of flawed financial and market mechanisms in combating climate change.

There are at least four general views on financial regulation and climate change. The first approach treats climate change as a danger to the stability of financial markets. Advocates of this view stress the importance of securing financial markets since climate change may damage both the financial markets and the economy (see Campiglio et al., 2018; Chenet et al., 2021). The second view focuses on market-based policies as a solution to climate change. Creating carbon markets and incentivising private green investment falls into this approach. The third view involves improving the regulation and monitoring of financial markets within the contemporary financial paradigm. Finally, the fourth approach perceives a complete transformation of the financial system as a necessary step to combat climate change. Currently, employed policies are a mixture of the first three views. However, there is no reason to think that climate change regulations will be free of issues stemming from the financial system. Just as regulations were being evaded in the past, they may be evaded today.

3 Financial Rhetoric

The whole of production and exchange constitutes the real economy, which serves as the main institution used to satisfy needs and wants. In accordance with the basic approach to the economy, the financial sphere serves as a supplementary institution used to improve production by raising finance or reducing transaction costs. The third and final category of risk concerns the rise of the financial narrative, which puts financial markets in the spotlight instead of manufacturing and service production.

The financialisation of the economy went in pair with a financial narrative, which legitimised the growing importance of financial markets. Share-holder-value conception of the firm is at the core of this narrative (Kus, 2012: 484). It is a corporate governance model, which evaluates a firm's performance based on the price of its shares. In this approach, long-term growth is a secondary goal in comparison with achieving short-term profits. Short-termism dominated the governance of nonfinancial corporations since around 1980 (Crotty, 2003: 272), which is the reason some firms started to focus less and less on achieving real profits. Sawyer proposed (2013: 16) that one way to understand financialisation is to understand it as the rise of a new form of capitalism, where financial markets have a dominant position. Since advanced financial markets make it possible to accumulate wealth in separation from economic reality, there may be no incentive to care for long-term sustainability. Additionally, financialisation is not limited to markets and firms – financialisation was found to influence households (Bryan et al. 2009; De Vita and Luo 2020), healthcare (Hunter & Murray, 2019) or education (Eaton et al., 2016). Financialisation has not only changed the economy but also how people think about the economy. Hansen argued (2014: 622) that since the 1970s top managers started to be seen as "heroes", while politicians became "servants" obliged to design an institutional framework for business and finance. Hansen applies the servant/master metaphor to the whole of economy and finance (ibid. 2014: 610): "historically, the dominant narrative has constructed and legitimised finance as either master or servant of the economy and society (. . .)".

Essentially, financialisation has changed the traditional paradigm. Wealth accumulation by financial means does not inherently require any real production, which, aside from benefiting investors, does not lead to creating any substantial ends in society. Financial rhetoric influenced nonfinancial firms and parts of society previously associated with the public sector. How does it relate to climate change?

Mitigating the effects of climate change is one of such ends, which has to be accomplished using scarce resources. How these resources are used depends on the currently employed rhetoric in the economy and society. There is a risk that adhering to the 2030 Agenda's goals may be heavily influenced by financial rhetoric. While inequalities and insufficient regulation act as direct risks, financial rhetoric acts as indirect risk as it may impede the implementation of necessary policies. The omission of the top 1% income share from the 2030 Agenda's targets may serve as an example. SDGs do not explicitly acknowledge that the low-income share of the bottom 40% was partly caused by financialisation inflating the share of the top 1% (Huber et al., 2020).

In regard to regulation, market mechanisms mentioned in the previous point are an example of financial rhetoric influencing climate change mitigation. These mechanisms apply financial rhetoric to solving a nonfinancial problem, which may have some benefits - e.g., a reduction in greenhouse gas emissions is attributed to the European Emissions Trading System (European Commission, 2020). However, the question persists if it is enough. Altvater and Mahnkopf argue that mitigating climate change with market-based policies and within contemporary capitalism is "at best dishonest", since the emissions gap continues to increase. Schor argues (2015: 532–533) that climate change mitigation must be reframed as an inherently positive activity. As one of the possible solutions, Schor proposed using economic growth to reduce work hours (and by that carbon emissions) instead of expanding output. However, the point here is not to argue that mitigating climate change within the contemporary financial paradigm is impossible. Rather, the point is to stress that financial rhetoric cannot impede progress if staying below 1,5C, or 2C requires reducing the strength of financial markets. While enforcing new financial regulations is itself a problem, overcoming financial rhetoric acts as an additional hurdle. Louche et al. see (2019: 10–11) dominant logics in finance as incompatible with climate change mitigation; they propose a change toward long-termism or "reconnecting society to capital markets" as a chance to successfully transition to low-carbon economies.

4 Conclusion

The paper aimed to identify risks stemming from financialisation, which may impede climate change mitigation policies. Risks have been found in each of the researched aspects. In the field of inequality, financialisation poses two risks. First, it may further increase economic inequality, and second, financialisation may increase both transition and physical risks arising from climate change. When it comes to financial regulation, financialisation has been showing to be historically linked with circumventing regulations for financial gain. The same may happen again in the process of enforcing climate change mitigation policies. Another risk arises from the contemporary financial rhetoric. Financial markets are primarily oriented at shareholder value, and the activity stemming from financial markets may be incompatible with mitigating climate change.

Risks identified in the paper have severe implications both for future research and in the policy domain. In the 2020s, once data becomes available, social scientists should consider researching whether financial markets impede climate change mitigation expressed within SDGs. Mitigating climate change means focusing on long-term goals and society's well-being, which stands in contradiction to the financial narrative promoting short-term profit-seeking nature. Since global warming may reach 1.5C as early as 2030 (IPCC, 2018: 4), financial markets cannot be left without scientific oversight. Regarding climate change mitigation policies, any effort to revert the negative impact of the financial market on climate change needs to be both extensively and promptly enforced since global society is running out of time. To ensure the success of these policies in the field of financialisation, a three-step strategy is proposed:

1. Aforementioned scientific oversight over financial markets and the effectiveness of currently employed financial regulations.
2. If contemporary financial regulations prove to be insufficient in connecting financial markets with SDGs, government and international organisations should consider further regulatory measures within the current financial system.
3. If these additional regulations also prove to be ineffective in mitigating climate change, a complete overhaul of the contemporary financial system has to be considered by policymakers.

This strategy concerns the idea that immensely dangerous physical and transition risks stemming from climate change should not be seen as a hindrance to financial markets. Rather, if contemporary financial paradigm proves to be a hindrance to climate change mitigation efforts, transforming the core of financial systems should be, at least, seriously considered. The overhaul of financial system could start by strenghtening financial regulation and oversight over financial markets to levels comparable with the era prior to the rise of financialisation in 1980s. While ineffective market mechanisms mentioned in the paper serve as an example of harmful effect of financial markets, the highest priority should be given to regulating financial markets in order to decrease income and wealth inequalities. One of the reasons why *SDG 10: reduced inequalities* had to be established in the first place was the process of financialisation. OECD member countries have already experienced relatively low economic inequality in 1960s and 1970s – physical and transition risks stemming from climate change would be much less of a threat had inequality remained at those levels. Overall, objectives set within SDGs are dependent on financial markets. Since financialisation leads to increasing economic inequality and circumventing regulations, it is one factor impeding the enforcement of Just Transition and mitigating the physical risk of climate change. The traditional financial paradigm, which sees financial markets as a supplementary institution enhancing the real economy, would be more in line with achieving SDGs.

References

Aiginger, K. (2016). *New dynamics for Europe: Reaping the benefits of socio-ecological transition. Part I: Synthesis*.

Assa, J. (2012). Financialisation and its consequences: The OECD experience. *Finance Research, 1*(1), 35–39.

Baer, P., Kartha, S., Athanasiou, T., & Kemp-Benedict, E. (2009). The greenhouse development rights framework: Drawing attention to inequality within nations in the global climate policy debate. *Development and Change, 40*(6), 1121–1138. https://doi.org/10.1111/j.1467-7660.2009.01614.x

Bayoumi, T. (1993). Financial deregulation and consumption in the United Kingdom. *The Review of Economics and Statistics, 75*(3), 536–539. https://doi.org/10.2307/2109471

Bryan, D., Martin, R., & Rafferty, M. (2009). Financialisation and Marx: Giving labor and capital a financial makeover. *Review of Radical Political Economics, 41*(4), 458–472. https://doi.org/10.1177/0486613409341368

Campiglio, E., Dafermos, Y., Monnin, P., Ryan-Collins, J., Schotten, G., & Tanaka, M. (2018). Climate change challenges for central banks and financial regulators. *Nature Climate Change, 8*, 462–468. https://doi.org/10.1038/s41558-018-0175-0

Chenet, H., Ryan-Collins, J., & van Lerven, F. (2021). Finance, climate-change and radical uncertainty: Towards a precautionary approach to financial policy. *Ecological Economics, 183*. https://doi.org/10.1016/j.ecolecon.2021.106957

Crotty, J. (2003). The neoliberal paradox: The impact of destructive product market competition and impatient finance on nonfinancial corporations in the neoliberal era. *Review of Radical Political Economics, 35*(3), 271–279. https://doi.org/10.1177/0486613403255533

Dafermos, Y., Nikolaidi, M., & Galanis, G. (2018). Climate change, financial stability and monetary policy. *Ecological Economics, 152*, 219–234. https://doi.org/10.1016/j.ecolecon.2018.05.011

Davis, A. E. (2019). Salvation or commodification? The role of money and markets in global ecological preservation. *Review of Radical Political Economics, 51*(4), 536–543. https://doi.org/10.1177/0486613419859688

De Vita, G., & Luo, Y. (2020). Financialisation, household debt and income inequality: Empirical evidence. *International Journal of Finance and Economics*, 1–21. https://doi.org/10.1002/ijfe.1886

Eaton, C., Habinek, J., Goldstein, A., Dioun, C., Godoy, D. G. S., & Osley-Thomas, R. (2016). The financialisation of US higher education. *Socio-Economic Review, 14*(3), 507–535. https://doi.org/10.1093/ser/mwv030

European Commission. (2019). *Communication from the commission to the european parliament, the european council, the council, the european economic and social committee and the committee of the regions*. https://eur-lex.europa.eu/resource.html?uri=cellar:b828d165-1c22-11ea-8c1f-01aa75ed71a1.0002.02/DOC_1&format=PDF. Accessed 19 Feb 2021.

European Commission. (2020). *Report from the commission to the european parliament and the council*. https://ec.europa.eu/clima/sites/default/files/news/docs/com_2020_740_en.pdf

Giordano, C. (2019). *Man killed in fight over water as India grapples with heatwave*. Independent. https://www.independent.co.uk/news/world/asia/india-heatwave-fight-death-water-shortage-dead-a8949281.html

Godechot, O. (2020). Financialisation and the increase in inequality. In P. Mader, D. Mertens, & N. van Der Zwan (Eds.), *The Routledge international handbook of financialization* (pp. 413–424). Routledge. https://doi.org/10.4324/9781315142876

Hansen, P. H. (2014). From finance capitalism to financialization: A cultural and narrative perspective on 150 years of financial history. *Enterprise and Society, 15*(4), 605–642. https://doi.org/10.1093/es/khu047

Honda, E. (2003). Financial deregulation in Japan. *Japan and the World Economy, 15*(1), 135–140. https://doi.org/10.1016/S0922-1425(02)00015-4

Huber, E., Petrova, B., & Stephens, J. D. (2020). Financialisation, labor market institutions and inequality. *Review of International Political Economy*, 1–28. https://doi.org/10.1080/09692290.2020.1808046

Hunter, B. M., & Murray, S. F. (2019). Deconstructing the financialisation of healthcare. *Development and Change, 50*(5), 1263–1287. https://doi.org/10.1111/dech.12517

Hyde, A., Vachon, T., & Wallace, M. (2018). Financialisation, income inequality, and redistribution in 18 affluent democracies, 1981–2011. *Social Currents, 5*(2), 193–211. https://doi.org/10.1177/2329496517704874

International Labour Organization. (2015). *Guidelines for a just transition towards environmentally sustainable economies and societies for all.* https://www.ilo.org/wcmsp5/groups/public/%2D%2D-ed_emp/%2D%2D-emp_ent/documents/publication/wcms_432859.pdf

IPCC. (2018). Summary for Policymakers. In *Global Warming of 1.5°C. An IPCC Special Report on the impacts of global warming of 1.5°C above pre-industrial levels and related global greenhouse gas emission pathways, in the context of strengthening the global response to the threat of climate change.* https://doi.org/10.1016/j.oneear.2019.10.025.

Just Transition Centre. (2017). *Just transition.* https://www.oecd.org/environment/cc/g20-climate/collapsecontents/Just-Transition-Centre-report-just-transition.pdf

Kim, M. (2018). What is radical political economics? *Review of Radical Political Economics, 50*(3).

King, A. D., & Harrington, L. J. (2018). The inequality of climate change from 1.5 to 2°C of global warming. *Geophysical Research Letters, 45*, 1–4. https://doi.org/10.1029/2018GL078430

Krippner, G. (2005). The financialization of the American economy. *Socio-Economic Review, 3*, 173–208. https://doi.org/10.1093/SER/mwi008

Kus, B. (2012). Financialisation and income inequality in OECD nations: 1995–2007. *The Economic and Social Review, 43*(4), 477–495.

Lapavitsas, C. (2013). The financialisation of capitalism: "Profiting without producing". *City, 17*(6), 792–805. https://doi.org/10.1080/13604813.2013.853865

Lin, K. H., & Tomaskovic-Devey, D. (2011). Income dynamics, economic rents, and the financialisation of the U.S. economy. *American Sociological Review, 76*(4), 538–559. https://doi.org/10.1177/0003122411414827

Lin, K. H., & Tomaskovic-Devey, D. (2013). Financialisation and U.S. income inequality, 1970–2008. *American Journal of Sociology, 118*(5), 1284–1329. https://doi.org/10.1086/669499

Louche, C., Busch, T., Crifo, P., & Marcus, A. (2019). Financial markets and the transition to a low-carbon economy: Challenging the dominant logics. *Organisation and Environment, 32*(1), 3–17. https://doi.org/10.1177/1086026619831516

Marazzi, C. (2010). *The violence of financial capitalism.* Semiotext(e).

Markkanen, S., & Anger-Kraavi, A. (2019). Social impacts of climate change mitigation policies and their implications for inequality. *Climate Policy, 19*(7), 827–844. https://doi.org/10.1080/14693062.2019.1596873

Mohd Daud, S. N., Ahmad, A. H., & Ngah, W. A. S. W. (2020). Financialisation, digital technology and income inequality. *Applied Economics Letters*, 1–5. https://doi.org/10.1080/13504851.2020.1808165

Mol, A. P. J. (2012). Carbon flows, financial markets and climate change mitigation. *Environmental Development, 1*, 10–24. https://doi.org/10.1016/j.envdev.2011.12.003

Naples, M. I., & Van Arnum, B. M. (2013). Financialisation and Income Inequality in the United States, 1967–2010. *American Journal of Economics and Sociology, 72*(5), 1158–1182. https://doi.org/10.1111/ajes.12036

Nesvetailova, A., & Palan, R. (2013). Minsky in the shadows: Securitisation, Ponzi Finance, and the crisis of Northern Rock. *Review of Radical Political Economics, 45*(3), 349–368. https://doi.org/10.1177/0486613412470090

Network for Greening the Financial System. (2018). *First progress report.*

Nevile, A. (1997). Financial deregulation in Australia in the 1980s. *The Economic and Labour Relations Review, 8*(2), 273–292. https://doi.org/10.1177/103530469700800206

Pala, C. (2019). *Kiribati's president's plans to raise islands in fight against sea-level rise This article is more than 6 mon.* The Guardian. https://www.theguardian.com/world/2020/aug/10/kiribatis-presidents-plans-to-raise-islands-in-fight-against-sea-level-rise
Pettifor, A. (2019). *The case for the green new deal.* Verso.
Pianta, M., Lucchese, M., Nascia, L. (2020). The policy space for a novel industrial policy in Europe. *Industrial and Corporate Change, 29*(3), 779–795. https://doi.org/10.1093/icc/dtz075
Roberts, J. T. (2010). Global inequality and climate change. *Society and Natural Resources, 14*(6), 501–509. https://doi.org/10.1080/08941920118490
Sawyer, M. (2013). What Is Financialization? *International Journal of Political Economy, 42*(4), 5–18. https://doi.org/10.2753/IJP0891-1916420401
Schneider, L., & La Hoz Theuer, S. (2019). Environmental integrity of international carbon market mechanisms under the Paris Agreement. *Climate Policy, 19*(3), 386–400. https://doi.org/10.1080/14693062.2018.1521332
Schor, J. (2015). Climate inequality and the need for reframing climate policy. *Review of Radical Political Economics, 47*(4). https://doi.org/10.1177/0486613415576114
Turner, B. (1997). Housing cooperatives in Sweden: The effects of financial deregulation. *Journal of Real Estate Finance and Economics, 15*(2), 193–217.
UN General Assembly. (2015). *Transforming our world: The 2030 agenda for sustainable development.* https://www.un.org/ga/search/view_doc.asp?symbol=A/RES/70/1&Lang=E
UN Economic and Social Council. (2020) Progress towards the Sustainable Development Goals. In *International organization.* https://digitallibrary.un.org/record/1627573
UN Department of Economic and Social Affairs. (2020). Inequality in a rapidly changing world. *World Social Report 2020.* https://www.un.org/development/desa/dspd/wp-content/uploads/sites/22/2020/02/World-Social-Report2020-FullReport.pdf
UN Environment Programme. (2020). *Emissions gap emissions gap report 2020.* https://www.unep.org/emissions-gap-report-2020
Velicu, I., & Barca, S. (2020). The just transition and its work of inequality. *Sustainability: Science, Practice, and Policy, 16*(1), 263–273. https://doi.org/10.1080/15487733.2020.1814585
Vlachou, A., & Pantelias, G. (2020). The EU emissions trading system in crisis-ridden Greece: Climate under neoliberalism. *Review of Radical Political Economics, 53*(1). https://doi.org/10.1177/0486613420910546
Winkel, J. (2017). Climate change and social inequality. *UN Department of Economic and Social Affairs Working Papers, 152.* https://doi.org/10.18356/2c62335d-en
World Income Inequality Database. (2021). https://www.wider.unu.edu/project/world-income-inequality-database-wiid#:~:text=The%20latest%20version%20of%20the,year%20observations%20in%20the%20database
Zalewski, D. A., & Whalen, C. J. (2010). Financialisation and income inequality: A Post Keynesian Institutionalist analysis. *Journal of Economic Issues, 44*(3), 757–777. https://doi.org/10.2753/JEI0021-3624440309

Geography, Climate and Life Satisfaction

Phil Lignier, Diane Jarvis, Daniel Grainger, and Taha Chaiechi

Abstract Individual life satisfaction (LS), used as a proxy measure of human wellbeing, has been a growing topic of research in the discipline of economics over the last 30 years. The underpinning rationale is the need to determine the extent to which various contextual factors contribute to LS, thereby informing policymaking decisions designed to enhance LS in the population. Empirical studies have predominantly focused on economic factors like income and employment and socio-demographic variables, e.g., age, gender, education and health. This paper presents a review of the LS research literature, focusing on the less widely researched influences of geography, environmental factors, and climate. The review identifies knowledge gaps in these specific areas and develops a research agenda to address these gaps. The review finds evidence of significant variations in individual LS, and in influencing factors, between different locations within the same country. While these variations' nature and significance appear largely dependent on the scale of geographic aggregation used in the data, clear patterns for these spatial variations are yet to be identified and understood. Building on recent studies undertaken in Australia, further research using techniques such as geographically weighted regression at different scales of observation could provide insights into both where and why spatial clusters occur.

The paper also examines the evidence regarding the contribution of environmental and climatic factors to individual LS. Variables associated with environmental amenities (such as urban greenspace or the presence of a world heritage area) generally have statistically significant positive coefficients in LS regression models; conversely, variables representing environmental dis-amenities like air or noise pollution have been found to be negative contributors. The evidence on the impact of climatic variables is more patchy, and their association with individual LS appears

P. Lignier (✉) · D. Jarvis · D. Grainger
James Cook University, Townsville, Australia
e-mail: phil.lignier@my.jcu.edu.au; diane.jarvis1@jcu.edu.au; daniel.grainger@jcu.edu.au

T. Chaiechi
College of Business, Law and Governance, James Cook University, Townsville, QLD, Australia
e-mail: taha.chaiechi@jcu.edu.au

© The Author(s), under exclusive license to Springer Nature Singapore Pte Ltd. 2022

T. Chaiechi, J. Wood (eds.), *Community Empowerment, Sustainable Cities, and Transformative Economies*, https://doi.org/10.1007/978-981-16-5260-8_25

to be more ambiguous. This may be linked to context-specific conditions creating a high level of correlation between the different climate factors and other environmental factors: e.g., a positive correlation between precipitation levels and LS may be driven by the fact that high rainfall is generally associated with lush landscapes and scenic beauty. The paper argues that the investigation of the contribution of the climate and environment on individual LS requires the building of complex regression models integrating multiple variables. The research agenda proposed in the final section of this paper articulates two research objectives based on the above research gaps. It formulates research questions and lays out a research strategy to answer these questions.

Keywords Life satisfaction · Climate · Environment · Spatial amenities · Geography · Geographically weighted regression

1 Background and Introduction

Good policymaking is fundamentally important to improving human wellbeing. To achieve this goal, the current orthodoxy of economics attempts to maximise utility. However, the link between maximal utility and determinants of wellbeing arguably requires deeper consideration. If the objective of policymakers is to design a policy that improves human wellbeing, a requirement for designing effective and appropriate policy is to have a good understanding of what factors most significantly impact on wellbeing, and to get this understanding; they need to be able to define and measure wellbeing, and then define and measure the relationship between the many economic, social, cultural and environmental factors that may influence wellbeing. This paper reviews the literature to ascertain the depth of research with regard to the relationship between utility and determinants of utility. In the following, non-trivial research gaps are identified and an agenda of research to elicit a deeper understanding is proposed. In short, this literature review begs the following questions:

- Do individual and contextual factors influence variations in individual LS differently depending on the geographical location?
- Do individual and contextual factors influence variations in individual LS differently depending on the scale of aggregation?

Happiness and human wellbeing have long been topics of interest in the fields of philosophy and psychology. Philosophers, as far back as Aristotle, have attempted to *define* the concept of wellbeing (Gasper, 2004), while studies in psychology have mainly focussed on the *measurement* of wellbeing based on self-reported subjective wellbeing (Kahneman, Diener, & Schwarz, 1999). The widely shared position is that wellbeing extends beyond hedonism and instead involves self-actualisation and the realisation of one's true potential (Newton, 2007).

The current orthodoxy of economists arguably uses the "utility" concept rather than "wellbeing" concept. Utility, being considered the calculus of pleasure and pain (Fishburn, 1968), is arguably a subset of the broader notion of wellbeing (Larson et al., 2019). Unlike psychologists, economists have, for a long time, rejected the cardinal measurement and interpersonal comparisons of utility based on self-reported wellbeing on the grounds that it was an arbitrary and subjective measure (Gasper, 2004; Kristoffersen, 2010). Thus, for a long time, the utility was deemed measurable only in the ordinal sense. The resulting difficulty and paradoxes of measuring ordinal utility led economists to rely on variables such as income and wealth as a proxy for utility (Kristoffersen, 2010). But, as discussed further below, money is not an appropriate proxy for utility (Stiglitz, Sen, & Fitoussi, 2009).

The newly found interest in measuring wellbeing in the field of economics stems from the growing realisation that reliance on income measures such as Gross Domestic Product (GDP), the paramount indicator of economic progress, has its limitations. Many authors have pointed out the conceptual shortcomings of GDP in measuring economic welfare (Daly & Cobb, 1989; Stiglitz et al., 2009), but there are also growing claims that there is much more to human wellbeing than just economic welfare (Costanza, Hart, Posner, & CJ, 2009; Kubiszewski et al., 2013; Nordhaus & Tobin, 1973; Stiglitz et al., 2009).

Empirical evidence tends to support the argument that GDP may not be a good indicator of individual wellbeing: while GDP per capita increased dramatically over the past five decades, other measures of wellbeing show either a flat trend or even a decrease over the same period (Easterlin, 1995; Easterlin et al., 2010; Kubiszewski et al., 2013). In response to these criticisms of GDP, alternative indicators measuring human progress have been proposed in the literature and by global institutions. Examples of such indicators include adjusted economic indicators such as the Index of Sustainable Economic Welfare (ISEW) (Daly & Cobb, 1989) or composite indices like the United Nations Human Development Index (HDI) that capture various relevant aspects of welfare and wellbeing (Bleys, 2012).

Table 1 presents an overview of the best-known economic indicators and composite indices. As shown in the "critique" column in Table 1, neither adjusted economic indicators nor composite indices completely remedy the shortcomings of GDP. Furthermore, whereas the method for calculating GDP has been standardised, there are issues around the availability, reliability, comparability and timeliness of the data used in the calculation of many alternative indicators (Costanza et al., 2009). A fresh approach to finding an ideal indicator was put forward by various authors (Kahneman et al., 2004; van den Bergh, 2009); it starts from the findings of the psychology research on happiness and subjective wellbeing.

The ultimate objective of this paper is not to present a comprehensive review of wellbeing research in economics but to identify non-trivial research gaps in the empirical literature and make recommendations for future research. We particularly focus on two specific topics canvassed by LS research: the geographic variations in LS and factors influencing LS; and the impact of the natural environment and climate on individual LS. To this end, the remainder of this paper is logically structured as follows. Section "Wellbeing Research in Economics" presents a brief overview of the wellbeing/LS research in economics. In section "Life satisfaction in context: The relevance of geography, the contribution of the natural environment and climate," we discuss the current research relating to the two topics of special interest and identify knowledge gaps. Section "Proposed research agenda" proposes a research

Table 1 Overview of economic indicators and composite indices

Name	Type	Authors	Description	Critique
Index of sustainable economic welfare (ISEW)	Adjusted economic indicator	Daly & Cobb (1989)	Adjusts GDP for non-market activities, capital depletion and environmental degradation.	Lack of theoretical foundations. Some methodological flaws (Atkinson 1995, Neumayer 1999, 2000).
Genuine Progress index (GPI)	Adjusted economic indicator	Talberth, Cobb & Slattery (2007)	Same as ISEW. In addition. Takes into account income distribution, changes in environmental conditions and social capital.	Same as ISEW
Genuine savings (GS)	Adjusted economic indicator	Hamilton & Clements (1999) World bank	Focuses on maintaining or increasing wealth defined as the sum of economic, human and natural capital.	Weak sustainability: neglects capital depreciation, only partially recognises informal activities (van den Bergh, 2009).
Human development index (HDI)	Composite index	United Nations	Composite of gross National Income pc, education index and life expectancy index.	Unit-less indices, components equally weighted (Diener & Suh 1997). Data reliability and comparability issues (Costanza et al. 2009).
Happy planet index (HPI)	Composite index	New economic foundation	Composite of subjective wellbeing, life expectancy, income distribution and ecological footprint.	
Better life index (BLI)	Composite index	OECD	Composite of 11 indicators that represent conditions essential to the quality of life.	

agenda aiming to address the research gaps identified in the previous section. A brief conclusion follows in section "Conclusion".

2 Wellbeing Research in Economics

2.1 *The Literature Review Strategy*

This paper aims to critically review the wellbeing research literature in economics. In order to do so, the research team pursued the following strategy. First, the relevant literature was collated using the searching terms "subjective wellbeing", "happiness" and "life satisfaction". As there has been an abundance of research on these topics (particularly "happiness") in the field of psychology, only papers that had relevance to economics were selected. Once the relevant literature was identified, papers were classified into two broad categories: papers that focused on conceptual issues, including concept definitions and measurement, and empirical papers. In some cases, papers could be classified into both categories as some empirical literature also deals with conceptual issues; examples of these include Frey and Stutzer (2000) and Welsch and Ferreira (2014).

Although our literature review was broad and covered both types of papers, the main focus of the review presented in this paper is on the empirical literature, in particular the investigation of contextual factors that influence wellbeing. It became apparent that some topics were under-researched and that other researched topics called for further investigation. The two research areas that drew our particular attention were the relevance of geography and the influence of natural capital factors on wellbeing.

2.2 Subjective Wellbeing and Utility

The concept of subjective wellbeing has similarities with the economic concept of utility (Krueger & Schkade, 2008). Jeremy Bentham described the latter term as referring to pleasure and pain, happy and unhappy states (Kristoffersen, 2010). Under the utilitarian approach, people use preference ordering when making choices to allocate scarce resources (Kahneman, Wakker, & Sarin, 1997). This process can then be represented by a utility function where people's choices and the ensuing utility is inferred from observable individual behaviour (Diener & Suh, 1997). Wellbeing, on the other hand, closely aligns with traditional welfare economic *ex-ante* decision utility (Kristoffersen, 2010). Notable is that experienced utility (i.e. *ex-post* satisfaction related to the outcome of the decision), once believed to be non-measurable, is now considered measurable (Ferrer-i-Carbonell, 2013; Welsch & Ferreira, 2014). In short, there is now a broad acceptance (particularly in the economics of life-satisfaction and happiness literature) that self-reported wellbeing is a valid and reliable proxy for individual utility measurement (Ferrer-i-Carbonell, 2013; Kristoffersen, 2010).

2.3 Subjective Wellbeing, Happiness and Life Satisfaction

The terms life satisfaction,[1] happiness and subjective wellbeing tend to be used interchangeably in the literature (Easterlin, 2003); however they are conceptually distinct (OECD, 2013). The psychology literature traditionally distinguishes between the hedonic component (affect) of wellbeing and the eudaimonic[2]

[1]The terminology "Quality of Life" is sometimes used in the literature.

[2]Eudaimonia is a Greek term meaning "psychological flourishing"(OECD, 2013, p. 34).

component (cognitive evaluation of achievements in one's life) (Deci & Ryan, 2008, p. 2). While happiness is generally associated with hedonic wellbeing (short-lived emotions), life satisfaction (LS) is more closely related to cognitive judgements and intrinsic goals (in the Aristotelian tradition) (Engelbrecht, 2009). Many authors have argued that the use of LS is preferable in wellbeing studies as it correlates better with national predictors (Helliwell, 2003; Vemuri & Costanza, 2006). There is some evidence of a reasonably strong relationship between the different concepts: correlation between psychological wellbeing and LS was found to be 0.62 while the correlation between psychological wellbeing and affect balance was 0.56 (Diener et al., 2009). In the field of economics, LS is generally accepted as the preferred measure, although the terms "happiness" and "subjective wellbeing" are also used, and comparisons across the different measures are common in the literature (Engelbrecht, 2009).

2.4 The Life Satisfaction Method and Its Domains

Life satisfaction (LS) research endeavours to investigate which factors influence overall individual wellbeing. Typically, the methodology adopted in the research is to build a model similar to a utility function of the form $Y = f(x1, x2, \ldots xi, \ldots xn)$ where Y is self-reported overall individual LS and $(x1, x2, \ldots xi, \ldots xn)$ represents a string of explanatory variables relating to various domains of life (Stiglitz et al., 2009). The underlying assumption is that interpersonal comparability of LS levels is allowed (Kristoffersen, 2010; Van Praag et al., 2003). The fundamental rationale behind LS research is that if the appropriate indicators of LS are ascertained, then policymakers can identify the levers that can be used to improve LS in the population.

The nature of the explanatory variables included in the regression model will depend on the factors expected to contribute positively or negatively to overall LS. Factors that can potentially influence variations in overall individual LS can be grouped into two broad categories: genetic factors (Tellegen et al., 1988) and contextual factors (Emmons & Diener, 1986; Larsen & Ketelaar, 1991).

LS domains are subjective collections of correlated factors and ideally weighted by relative importance (McAllistair, 2005). In wellbeing research conducted in tropical North Queensland, (Larson, 2009, 2010) and among indigenous communities (Larson et al., 2020) the methodology was guided by the idea that local communities should determine their own set of wellbeing factors. Twenty-seven wellbeing factors were thus identified in the 2010 study and grouped into three domains: family and community; economy and services; natural environment (Larson, 2010).

Costanza et al. (2013) propose an integrative approach to identify important LS domains, which takes into account opportunities (measured by objective indicators) and human needs (measured by subjective indicators). The authors identify

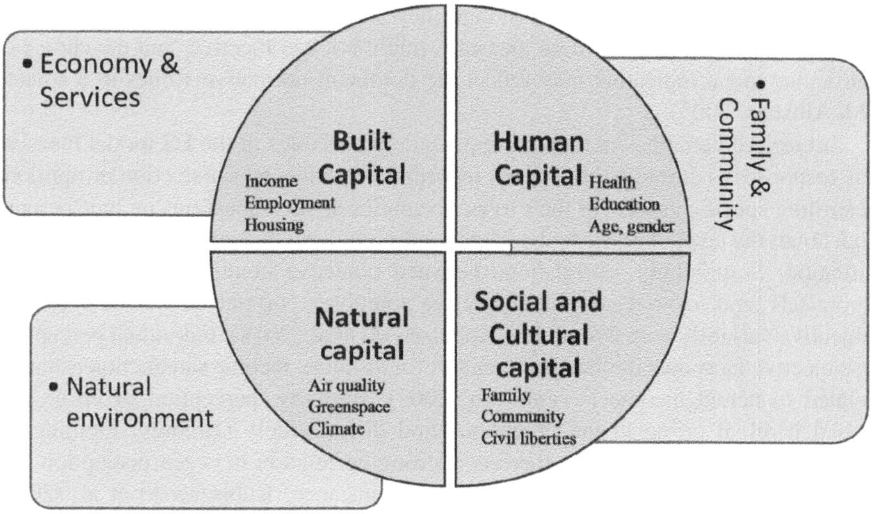

Fig. 1 Opportunities "capital" and Life satisfaction domains: comparison between Costanza et al. (2013) (pie) and Larson (2010) (rectangles) frameworks

opportunities by grouping them into four basic types of assets or "capital"[3] "that are necessary to support wellbeing: built (physical) capital, human capital, social and cultural capital, and natural capital"(Costanza et al., 2013, p. 9). Although the approach differs from Larson's, the LS domains identified by each author largely overlaps as shown in Fig. 1.

2.5 *Objective and Subjective Variables*

Explanatory factors in the LS model can be either objective or subjective variables. Objective variables include demographic variables such as age, gender, or education level and social indicators that reflect people's circumstances in a particular cultural and geographical setting, based on quantitative statistics (e.g., unemployment level). Social indicators are assumed to measure "objective" aspects of life that can help identify the appropriate policy lever to be used for corrective action (Diener & Suh, 1997). However, social indicators are not infallible: they can be contaminated by measurement errors or be biased. It is also contended that they do little to inform policymakers about public preferences (Veenhoven, 2002). Social indicators also

[3]The term "Capital" or "Assets" here have a much broader meaning than when associated with capitalism. They are used in the sense of "a stock or accumulation or heritage, a patrimony received from the past and contributing to the welfare of the present and future. These assets overlap and interact in complex ways to produce all benefits that will contribute to quality of life" (Costanza et al., 2013, p. 10).

have a selectivity problem: even though they are derived from objective measures, the process of selection of these measures might not be objective, and the choice of particular social indicators may reflect the dominant normative values in a society (McAllistair, 2005).

Subjective variables included as explanatory variables in the LS model measure the responses to attitudinal questions reporting respondents' satisfaction or opinions regarding specific aspects of their lives. Examples of such questions include perception about the level of crime in the neighbourhood or satisfaction with one's financial situation. Surprisingly, correlations between objective conditions and subjective appraisals tend to be weak, but subjective appraisals correlate more strongly than objective variables with overall LS (Kubiszewski et al., 2018). Individual perception of objective facts may deviate from reality: for instance, income satisfaction is hardly related to actual income (Veenhoven, 2002); similarly, perception of crime and actual level of crime in the neighbourhood differ widely (Ambrey, Fleming, & Manning, 2014). Even where there is a strong correlation between perception and reality, the relationship can be complex. For instance, Kubiszewski et al. (2018) found that satisfaction with the financial situation was positively correlated with household income, but it was also correlated with demographic factors such as age and gender.

2.6 Factors Found to Influence Variations in LS

The empirical evidence about factors that were found to significantly influence variations in individual LS is presented in Table 3. Most factors had either a positive or negative influence; however, in some cases, the relationship was found to be ambiguous or nonlinear.

An example of a nonlinear relationship is the correlation between income and LS. While there seems to be a positive correlation between income and LS at the country level, rising income over time is not associated with increased LS at a certain point in time. Easterlin (1974) explains this paradox by the fact that material norms increase at the same rate as the actual income of society. At a micro level, there is an indication that in developed countries, "relative" income is more important to individual wellbeing than "absolute" income (Ambrey & Fleming, 2014; Bonini, 2008; Shields, Price, & Wooden, 2009). The relative income hypothesis is confirmed in both space and time: social comparison, which means that relative income is at least twice as important to LS as actual income; income adaptation which means that the majority of individual effect of an increase in income on LS "evaporates" within two years (Clark, Frijters, & Shields, 2008; Daly, 1987; Diener, Suh, Lucas, & Smith, 1999; Stutzer & Frey, 2010). Overall, the importance of income in explaining variations in individual LS should not be overstated. Blanchflower and Oswald (2004) note that while the evidence indicates that richer people in Britain were generally more satisfied with their lives and that people got happier the closer their

Table 3 Factors frequently found to influence variations in LS

Factor	Positive influence	Negative influence	Ambiguous/ nonlinear relationship
Higher income	Higher income generally associated with higher levels of LS both at country level and micro-level.		Strong evidence that relative income is more important to individual LS than absolute income (Ambrey & Fleming, 2014; Bonini, 2008; Shields, Price, & Wooden, 2009).
Employed rather than unemployed	Blanchflower & Oswald, 2004; Bonini, 2008; Brereton, Clinch, & Ferreira, 2008; Clark & Oswald, 1994; Helliwell, 2003)		Retired persons, full time students and part-time employees report higher LS than full-time employees (Ambrey & Fleming, 2014; Shields et al., 2009).
Age			U shape relationship between age and LS with a minimum at late 30s or early 40s (Blanchflower & Oswald, 2004; Ferrer-i-Carbonell & Gowdy, 2007; Helliwell, 2003; Ambrey & Fleming 2014).
Gender			Ambiguous: some report that females have higher levels of LS (Blanchflower & Oswald, 2004; Brereton et al., 2008; Ferrer-i-Carbonell & Gowdy, 2007) others that gender is an insignificant factor (Stutzer & Frey, 2010).
Being married or in a de-facto relationship	(Ambrey & Fleming, 2014; Blanchflower & Oswald, 2004; Brereton, Clinch, & Ferreira, 2008; Frey & Stutzer, 2000; Helliwell, 2003)		
Being healthy	(Brereton et al., 2008; Diener et al., 1999; Helliwell, 2003; Kubiszewski et al., 2018)		
Quality of social capital	At a macro- level, good governance, democracy and political freedom associated with higher levels of LS (Abdalah, Thompson, & Marks, 2008; Frey & Stutzer, 2000; Helliwell,		

(continued)

Table 3 (continued)

Factor	Positive influence	Negative influence	Ambiguous/ nonlinear relationship
	2003; Inglehardt, 1990; Inglehardt et al., 2008)		
Crime levels		Actual crime levels, perception of high crime level (Ambrey et al., 2014)	
Family relations and friendships	Deemed important by 68% of respondents (Larson 2010) Neighbourly social interaction (Shields et al. 2009) (Myers & Diener 1995)		

income came to that of rich people around them, the non-economic variables in happiness equations enter with large coefficients, relative to that of income.

Other variables found to positively influence individual LS were "being employed", "being healthy", "being in a relationship" and family relations and friendships. Conversely, high crime levels were associated with lower levels of LS. The influence that age and gender may have on overall individual LS is both ambiguous and controversial (Ambrey & Fleming, 2014; Frijters & Beatton, 2012; Stutzer & Frey, 2010).

3 Life Satisfaction in Context: The Relevance of Geography, the Contribution of the Natural Environment and Climate

3.1 The Relevance of Geography: Regional Variations and Scale of Observation

Geography matters when it comes to the satisfaction of individual preferences: as people are generally free to move where they wish within the same country, people will move to areas where their individual preferences are better satisfied, leading to a general state of equilibrium (Tiebout, 1956). Although this hypothesis was partly confirmed by studies of regional variations in LS in the United States (Oswald & Wu, 2011), regional comparisons of LS have sometimes delivered puzzling results, including the following research outcomes:

- Ambrey and Fleming (2014) identified significant variations in the level of LS between metropolitan areas (lower LS) and remote communities (higher LS) in Australia.

- Kubiszewski, Jarvis, and Zakariyya (2019a, b) noted that average LS scores in Australia varied across statistical areas (SA2) from 3 to almost 10 (on a scale of 0 to 10) but could not identify any discernible pattern.
- In China, one study concluded that urban residents were happier than residents of rural areas (Asadullah et al., 2018).
- Also, in China, another study found no significant variations in the average level of individual LS between different regions (Zhou & Xie, 2016).

These diverging results may be partly explained by the varying scales of aggregation of the data among studies. The data in both Chinese studies were aggregated at a large scale (countrywide and large region), while the statistical unit (SA2 Statistical area) considered by LS research undertaken in Australia was a relatively small area with an average population of 10,000. Researchers that examined the impact of scale on LS models noted that some of the explanatory power of the LS regression model and information about which specific variables contribute to wellbeing was lost through aggregation (Ballas & Tranmer, 2012; Kubiszewski et al., 2019a, b).

It is also possible that at different locations, factors influence overall LS differently. Two studies that used Geographically Weighted Regressions (GWR) analysis (Jarvis et al., 2017; Kubiszewski et al., 2019a, b) show that the relative importance of the variables with the most significant impact on LS (positively and negatively) vary considerably across different areas. For instance, in some areas of Australia (Queensland, Tasmania, Melbourne area), increased age was found to have the greatest positive impact on LS, whereas in the southern parts of Western Australia, household income was the variable with the highest positive coefficient (Kubiszewski et al., 2019a, b).

From this evidence regarding the impact of scale and regional variations, a number of questions arise. The first question is "what is the ideal scale of observation to examine LS contributors?". Aggregated observations are useful to evaluate population wellbeing, but small scale observation allows to identify communities that are most at risk (Kubiszewski et al., 2019a, b). Secondly, while recent has identified regional variations in LS and LS contributors, we still do not know why clusterings happen. A further question related to that observation is "Do people move to live near others with shared values or does moving into a community change an individual's values?" (Kubiszewski et al., 2019a, b). It is believed that further investigation of geographic variations building on the recent studies by Kubiszewski et al. will help find answers to these questions. The investigation will use techniques such as GWR to help identify how different factors contribute to overall LS in different locations. It will also examine geographic variations at different scales of aggregation.

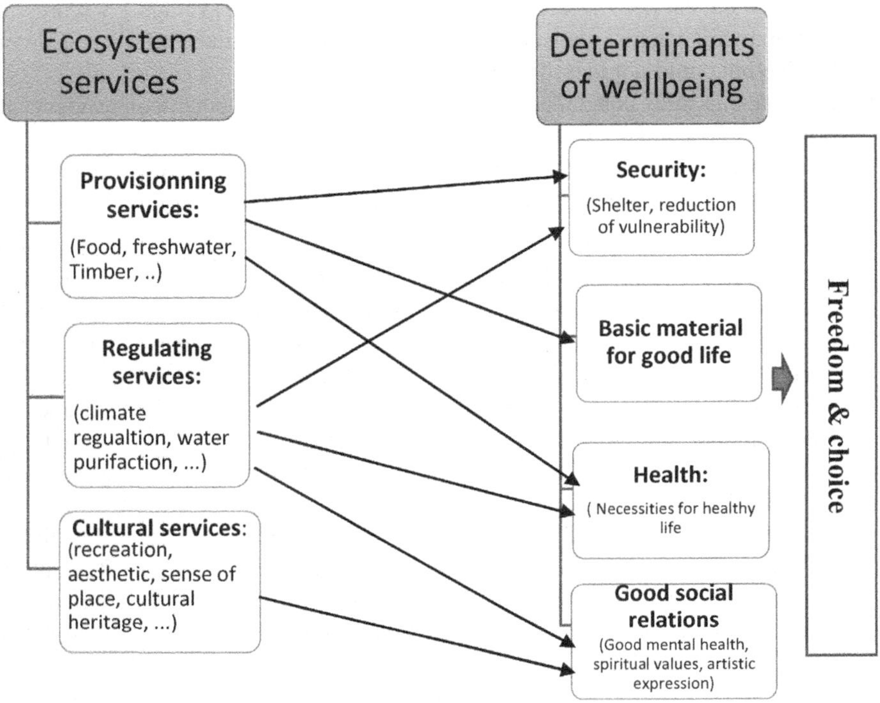

Fig. 2 The MEA framework: ecosystem services and their links to human wellbeing. (Source: MEA (2003) p 5 (adapted))

3.2 Contribution of the Natural Environment and Climate to LS

Much has been written about the contribution of nature to human wellbeing. Existing research from various fields of inquiry provides evidence that nature fundamentally impacts human wellbeing both physically and mentally (Newton, 2007).[4] The Millennium Ecosystem Assessment (MEA) is a useful framework to analyse the links between nature and human wellbeing (Fig. 2). Under this framework, ecosystem services contribute to human wellbeing by providing the basic necessities of life, security and health (Millenium Ecosystem Assessment, 2003). They also support good social relations by enhancing mental and spiritual wellbeing; they contribute to social cohesion by promoting a sense of place (Newton, 2007).

The links identified within the MEA theoretical framework are illustrated by evidence from the empirical literature. Nature seems to have both quantity and quality effects on LS: quantity effects as in how much we can actually use and

[4]For a comprehensive review of the evidence on the impact of the natural environment on wellbeing, see Newton (2007).

Table 4 Natural capital factors frequently found to influence variations in LS

Factor	Positive influence	Negative influence
Proxy variables: Ecosystem product value per sq. km, Natural capital per capita Normalised Difference Vegetation Index (NDVI)	Macro proxy values found to be significant factors. (Abdalah, Thompson, & Marks, 2008; Engelbrecht, 2009; Vemuri & Costanza, 2006) NDVI highly significant at **lower** scales of aggregation (regional local level). (Kubiszewski, Zakariyya, et al., 2019a, b)	
Environmental dis-amenities: Air pollution, water pollution, noise pollution		Significant negative influence at both macro and micro levels: air pollution (Ferreira & Moro, 2013; Levinson, 2009; Luechinger, 2009; MacKerron & Mourato, 2009; Welsch, 2002, 2006); water pollution (Ferreira & Moro, 2013)proximity to land fill (Ferreira & Moro, 2013); airport noise (Van Praag & Baarsma, 2005).
Environmental amenities: Greenspace, proximity to the coast, cultural value of ecosystems	Urban greenspace (Ambrey & Fleming, 2013); proximity to the coast (Ferreira & Moro, 2013); engagement with nature (Biedenweg et al., 2017) cultural value of Great Barrier Reef (Jarvis et al., 2017).	

enjoy nature, for instance, proximity and accessibility to parks, beaches etc.,... (Ambrey & Fleming, 2013; Takano et al., 2002); quality effects as in an environment that is not polluted or degraded (Speldewinde et al., 2011). However, research has also shown that we don't necessarily have to live close to nature to benefit from it: the feeling of being connected to nature (regardless of whether we actually interact with and live in nature), has been linked to LS and wellbeing (Howell et al., 2011).

The findings of empirical LS research that investigated the influence of natural capital factors on LS are summarised in Table 4. Proxy variables such as Normalised Difference Vegetation Index (NDVI)[5] adopted by Kubiszewski, Zakariyya, et al. (2019a) and Kubiszewski, Jarvis, et al. (2019b) in their Australian study were found to be a significant positive predictor of individual LS when measured at a small spatial scale (local level). Empirical evidence provides support that proximity to

[5]"NDVI is an index measuring the difference between visible light absorbed and infrared radiation reflected by vegetation. This measure changes due to vegetation density and greenness. The index value lies between-1 and + 1. Higher values are associated with greater density and greenness, decreasing as vegetation comes under water stress, becomes diseased, or dies" (Kubiszewski, Jarvis, et al., 2019a,b).

green space (Ambrey & Fleming, 2013) and interaction with nature (Biedenweg et al., 2017) contributes positively to LS, and that the quality of the environment also matters (Ferreira & Moro, 2013). The positive correlation between LS and cultural ecosystem services from the Great Barrier Reef (Jarvis et al., 2017) indicates that nature can also contribute positively to LS regardless of use and proximity.

Despite this significant gathering of evidence, two major issues have hampered empirical research on the influence of environmental factors on LS. Firstly, data is not always available at the right level of aggregation and often spatially incomplete: for instance, data on air quality is generally reported as a single value for whole countries or cities rather than at a local level (Welsch, 2006). Secondly, the framework of analysis developed by the MEA (Fig. 2) shows that links between environmental factors and human wellbeing are likely to be complex and intertwined. Thus, a key gap in knowledge about the influence of environmental factors could be addressed by a holistic approach where the influence of these factors is considered simultaneously. Moreover, as suggested in the Brereton et al. (2008) study, it is likely that natural environment variables interact with climate variables when influencing individual life satisfaction.

Climate and weather[6] affect physiological, psychological, social and economic conditions and as such are expected to have an impact on human wellbeing (Parker, 1995). The weather was found to have a transient effect on responses to LS survey: cloudiness prior to the day of interview negatively influenced reported LS in two Canadian surveys, but other weather variables such as temperature and precipitation on the day of the interview did not have any significant impact (Barrington-Leigh, 2008). Most of the evidence regarding the influence of climate comes from country-level studies (Maddison & Rehdanz, 2011; Rehdanz & Maddison, 2005; Van de Vliert, Huang, & Parker, 2004). There is some evidence that variations in temperatures and precipitation levels across countries were significant in explaining variations in LS. This concurs with conclusions from earlier research by Frijters and Van Praag (1998) that harsh climatic conditions in Russia (cold winters and high humidity in Summer) negatively affected both financial welfare and wellbeing.

Since people actually experience the climate in their immediate surroundings, it is important to disaggregate climate data at the lowest possible level, i.e., at the regional or even local level (Brereton et al., 2008). It is also important to understand the combined effect of all climatic factors on LS. Barrington-Leigh (2008) noted that any attempt to estimate the influence of regional variations in climate on LS will need to resolve the challenge presented by the confounding effect of variations in multiple climate variables and in other geographic amenities. Such an attempt was undertaken by Brereton et al. (2008) in Ireland. Although many climate variables (sunshine, windiness and precipitation) had significant coefficients, it was unclear whether their influence was the result of a direct impact or correlation with other

[6]"Climate is what you expect, weather is what you get...". Weather refers to short-term changes in the atmosphere; climate depicts what the weather is like in a specific area over a long period of time (National Centers for Environmental Information, 2018).

hidden factors. For instance, high precipitation levels were associated with higher LS. Still, the authors speculated that this might have been linked to the fact that areas with high rainfall offered more lush and beautiful scenery. Thus, a key gap in the literature needs to be addressed. This requires examination of the combined influence of climate and natural environment factors at a low level of aggregation. We also need to undertake this research in different climate zones. It is highly possible that a higher level of precipitation will positively affect LS where rainfall is generally scarce; conversely, frequent and heavy rainfall may have a negative influence on LS for people living in the wettest regions.

Existing research has also investigated the *incidence* of single extreme climate events on LS in particular locations. These include:

- drought in rural Australia (Caroll et al., 2009),
- floods in the Philippines (Fernandez et al., 2019)
- hurricanes in Louisiana (Calvo et al., 2015).

The impending *risk* associated with extreme weather needs also to be considered as it may have a variety of impacts on LS: financial (higher insurance costs, higher building costs) and psychological (anxiety). Extreme weather risk may also affect people's decision to move to a particular area. This knowledge is particularly relevant to Australia, but it also has wider significance since it is widely predicted that climate change will increase the frequency of such events (CSIRO, 2011).

In this section, we have highlighted a number of knowledge gaps and made suggestions for further investigation. Two broad topics warranting further research are identified:

- the first topic relates to geographical variations in LS and LS factors and scale of observation;
- the second topic relates to the combined impact of climate factors and natural environment factors on LS.

These two topics are articulated into two separate research objectives that form part of an overall research agenda aiming to contribute to LS empirical research in the field of economics. Australian data and the Australian context will be used for this research; however, it is anticipated that the findings will be generalisable to other contexts. This all informs research objectives that are stated in the next section.

4 Proposed Research Agenda

4.1 *Research Objective 1: Investigate Geographic Variations in LS and LS Contributing Factors and Explain Possible Patterns*

Research objective 1 will address the need for further investigation of the impact of geography on LS. Building on the recent studies by Kubiszewski, Jarvis, et al. (2019a) and Kubiszewski, Zakariyya, et al. (2019b), this project will use GWR to further examine how contextual and individual factors influence overall individual variations LS at different geographic locations. It will also explore how the relationship might vary depending on the scale of aggregation. Following this analysis, patterns in geographic variations may emerge. Different patterns may emerge for different locations at different scale of observation. If so, the research will explore the possible reasons for these patterns. Research questions linked to this research objective are formulated as follows:

RQ1: Do individual and contextual factors influence variations in individual LS differently depending on the geographical location?
RQ2: Do individual and contextual factors influence variations in individual LS differently depending on the scale of aggregation?

To answer these questions, the research team will use data collected through the Household, Income and Labour Dynamics in Australia (HILDA)[7] surveys. The HILDA surveys have been carried out annually across all Australian states and territories since 2001 (The Melbourne Institute, 2019). The latest data currently available is for 2019 (Wave 19). The data is from a representative sample of around 13,000 people from more than 7500 households interviewed every year; however, not all individuals in the dataset have responded to every year surveys (The Melbourne Institute, 2019, p. 166). The same data source (up to Wave 16) was used in the Kubiszewski et al. studies in 2019. Even though different approaches of the investigation will be used in this project, a comparison of results is likely to be meaningful.

The process that will be followed to answer the research questions linked to this objective is represented by the diagram in Fig. 3.

[7] HILDA Survey website: https://melbourneinstitute.unimelb.edu.au/hilda

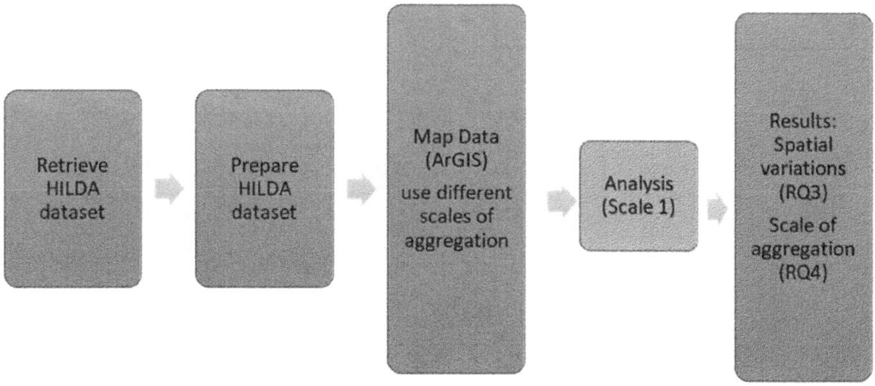

Fig. 3 Method, data and analysis: Investigate geographic variations in LS and LS contributing factors at different scales of aggregation. Investigate possible patterns

4.2 Research Objective 2: Explore and Investigate the Combined Effect of Climate and Environmental Variables on LS at a Local Level

As part of Research objective 2, researchers will explore and investigate the combined influence of climatic variables and environmental variables on individual LS variations at a low scale of aggregation (SA2 Statistical area). Due to its geographic size and its wide variety of climates, Australia presents the ideal context for this investigation. The research will be extended by an estimation of the anticipated cost of climate change based on climate projections. This estimation will adopt hedonic pricing based on the LS method, a technique used in previous LS research on climate (Caroll et al., 2009; Maddison & Rehdanz, 2011). Specific research questions linked to this second objective are formulated as follows:

RQ3: To what extent and how significantly do variables associated with local climatic and environmental conditions influence variations in individual LS?

RQ4: What will be the individual welfare impact of changing local climatic conditions due to the projected effects of climate change?

To answer these research questions, two parallel processes of data collection and analysis will be implemented. The first process will use the HILDA data sources as well as climate data available from the Bureau of Meteorology. The second process will use data collected from a separate survey. The use of additional data collection for this research is justified on several methodological and theoretical grounds. Firstly, the HILDA survey data is skewed towards metropolitan areas. The additional survey will be targeted towards respondents in regional and rural areas; this will allow comparing the influence of climate variables between metropolitan areas and regional areas. Secondly, the additional survey will target respondents in different climate zones and investigate whether different variables influence LS in the same

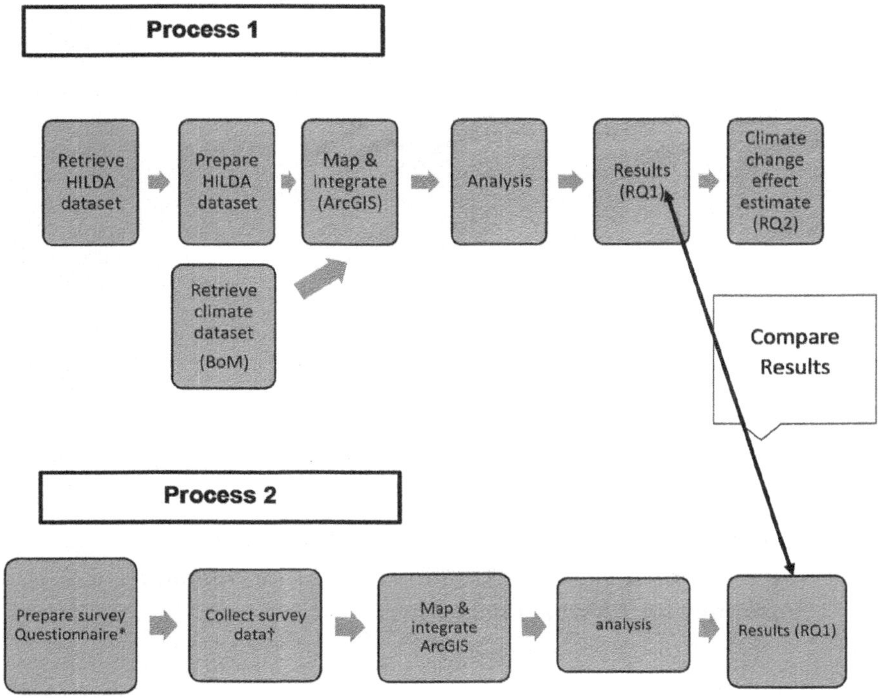

Fig. 4 Method, data & analysis: Explore and investigate the combined effect of climate and environmental variables on LS at a local level

way across different climate zones. Thirdly, the additional survey will include attitudinal questions asking respondents about the climate in their area. This will allow the testing of the relationship between perception and actual climate data and climate perception and LS.

The dual-process that will be followed to answer the research questions linked to objective 2 can be represented by the diagram in Fig. 4.

5 Conclusion

LS research is a vibrant, well-developed field of enquiry in the discipline of economics. The literature review of LS undertaken in this paper has identified a number of non-trivial research gaps. It proposes that in order to use LS to inform policy, various determinants of LS across space and time that affect individual wellbeing needs to be properly considered. This finding suggests a research agenda as follows.

1. The proposed research agenda aims to contribute to the growing knowledge in this field of research by addressing knowledge gaps in two specific areas. Firstly,

it will explore further how geographic variations affect the relationship between contributing factors and LS at multiple scales of observation and attempt to identify distinctive spatial patterns. This investigation should provide further insight into the interaction between local contextual factors and individual LS.
2. Secondly, it will investigate how climate factors and variables representing local environmental attributes and conditions combine to influence individual LS in a local context.

The proposed approach is novel insofar as, to the best of our knowledge, the only prior study that investigated the influence of environmental and climate factors on LS at a local level was undertaken in a small country (Ireland) that doesn't have the variation in climate zones that Australia can offer. Australia is a perfect study area as it offers different climate and environmental zones within the same country, and so controls for governance systems, social norms etc., that you wouldn't get if trying to compare two different small countries that had different climates. Our approach is also innovative as it proposes to evaluate the relationship between subjective perception and objective variables relating to the climate and the environment and their respective correlation with overall LS. In combining this novelty and innovation, one can readily see that informed regional policy can result. Moreover, this knowledge about the geographic and climate overlap and its impact on wellbeing is particularly critical at a time of widely predicted climate change and the likely resultant terraformation.

References

Abdalah, S., Thompson, S., & Marks, N. (2008). Estimating worldwide life satisfaction. *Ecological Economics, 65*(1), 35–47.

Ambrey, C., & Fleming, C. (2013). Public greenspace and life satisfaction in urban Australia. *Urban Studies, 51*(6), 1290–1321.

Ambrey, C., & Fleming, C. (2014). Life satisfaction in Australia: Evidence from ten years of the HILDA survey. *Social Indicators Research, 115*, 691–714.

Ambrey, C., Fleming, C., & Manning, M. (2014). Perception or reality: What matters more when it comes to crime in your neighbourhood. *Social Indicators Research, 119*(2), 877–896.

Asadullah, N., Xiao, S., & Teoh, E. (2018). Subjective wellbeing in China: The role of relative income, gender and location. *China Economic Review, 48*, 83–101.

Atkinson, G. (1995). Measuring sustainable economic welfare a critique of the UK ISEW.. Retrieved from Norwich (UK).

Ballas, D., & Tranmer, M. (2012). Happy people or happy places? A multilevel modeling approach to the analysis of happiness and well-being. *International Regional Science Review, 75*(1), 70–102. https://doi.org/10.1177/0160017611403737.

Barrington-Leigh, C. (2008). *Weather as a transient influence on survey-reported satisfaction with life*. Department of Economics, University of British Columbia.

Biedenweg, K., Scott, R., & Scott, T. (2017). How does engaging with nature relate to life satisfaction? Demonstrating the link between environment specific social experiences and life satisfaction. *Journal of Environmental Psychology, 50*, 112–124.

Blanchflower, D., & Oswald, A. (2004). Well-being over time in Britain and the USA. *Journal of Public Economics, 88*, 1359–1386.

Bleys, B. (2012). Beyond GDP: Classifying alternative measures for Progress. *Social Indicators Research, 109*, 355–376.

Bonini, A. (2008). Cross-national variations in indiviudual life satisfaction: Effects of national wealth, human development and environmental conditions. *Social Indicators Research, 87*, 223–236. https://doi.org/10.1007/s11205-007-9167-6.

Brereton, F., Clinch, J.-P., & Ferreira, S. (2008). Happiness, geography and the environment. *Ecological Economics, 65*, 386–396.

Calvo, R., Arcaya, M., Baum, C., Lowe, S., & Waters, M. (2015). Happily ever after? Pre-and-post disaster determinants of happiness among survivors of Hurricane Katrina. *Journal of Happiness Studies, 16*, 427–442. https://doi.org/10.1007/s10902-014-9516-5.

Caroll, N., Frijters, P., & Shields, M. (2009). Quantifying the costs of drought: New evidence from the life satisfaction data. *Journal of Population Economics, 22*, 445–461.

Clark, A., & Oswald, A. (1994). Unhappiness and unemployment. *The Economic Journal, 104* (424), 648–659.

Clark, A., Frijters, P., & Shields, M. (2008). Relative income, happiness and utility: An explanation of the Easterlin paradox and other puzzles. *Journal of Economic Theory, 46*(1), 95–144.

Costanza, R., Alperowitz, G., Daly, H., Farley, J., Franco, C., Jackson, T., . . . Victor, P. (2013). *Building a sustainable and desirable economy-in-society-in -nature*. Canberra: ANU Press.

Costanza, R., Hart, M., Posner, S., & CJ, T. (2009). *Beyond GDP: The need for new measures of Progress*. The Pardee Papers, (4). Boston.

CSIRO (Ed.). (2011). *Climate change: Science and solutions for Australia*. Canberra: CSIRO Publishing.

Daly, H. (1987). The economic growth debate: what some economists have learned but many have not. *Journal of Environmental Economics and Management*, 14.

Daly, H., & Cobb, J. (1989). *For the common good*. Boston: Beacon Press.

Deci, E., & Ryan, R. (2008). Hedonia, eudaimonia, and wellbeing: An introduction. *Journal of Happiness Studies, 9*, 1–11. https://doi.org/10.1007/s10902-006-9018-1.

Diener, E., Kahneman, D., Arora, R., Harter, J., & Tov, W. (2009). Income differential influence on judgements of life versus affective well-being. In E. Diener (Ed.), *Assessing well-being: The collected works of Ed Diener, social indicators research Series* (Vol. 39, pp. 247–266). Dordrecht: Springer.

Diener, E., & Suh, E. (1997). Measuring quality of life: Economic, social and subjective indicators. *Social Indicators Research, 40*, 189–216.

Diener, E., Suh, E., Lucas, R. E., & Smith, H. L. (1999). Subjective well-being: Three decades of progress. *Psychological Bulletin, 125*(2), 1276–1302.

Easterlin, R. (1974). Does economic growth improve the human lot? In P. David & M. Reder (Eds.), *Nations and households in economic growth: Essays in honour of Moses Abramovitz*. New York: Academic.

Easterlin, R. (1995). Will rasing the incomes of all increase the happiness of all? *Journal of Economic Behavior and Organization, 27*, 35–47.

Easterlin, R. (2003). Explaining happiness. *Proceedings of the National Academy of Sciences, 100* (19), 11176–11183.

Easterlin, R., McVey, L., Switek, M., Sawangfa, O., & Smith Zweig, J. (2010). The happiness-income paradox revisted. *Proceedings of the National Academy of Sciences of the United States of America, 107*(52), 22463–22468.

Emmons, R., & Diener, E. (1986). An interactional approach to the study of personality and emotion. *Journal of Personality, 54*, 375–384.

Engelbrecht, H.-J. (2009). Natural capital, subjective wellbeing and the new welfare economics of sustainability: Some evidence from cross-country regressions. *Ecological Economics, 69*, 380–388.

Fernandez, C., Stoeckl, N., & Welters, R. (2019). The cost of doing nothing in the face of climate change: A case study, using the life satisfaction approach to value the tangible and intangible costs of flooding in the Philippines. *Climate and Development, 11*(9), 825–838. https://doi.org/10.1080/17565529.2019.1579697.

Ferreira, S., & Moro, M. (2013). Income and preferences for the environment: Evidence from the subjective wellbeing data. *Environment and Planning, 45*, 650–667. https://doi.org/10.1068/a4540.

Ferrer-i-Carbonell, A. (2013). Happiness economics. *SERIEs, 4*, 35–60. https://doi.org/10.1007/s13209-012-0086-7.

Ferrer-i-Carbonell, A., & Gowdy, J. (2007). Environmental degradation and happiness. *Ecological Economics, 60*, 509–516.

Fishburn, P. (1968). Utility theory. *Management Science, 14*(5), 335–378.

Frey, B., & Stutzer, A. (2000). Happiness, economy and institutions. *The Economic Journal, 110*, 918–938.

Frijters, P., & Beatton, T. (2012). The mystery of the U-shaped relationship between happiness and age. *Journal of Economic Behavior and Organization, 82*, 525–542.

Frijters, P., & Van Praag, B. (1998). The effcets of climate on welfare and Well-being in Russia. *Climatic Change, 39*, 61–81.

Gasper, D. (2004). *Human wellbeing: Concepts and conceptualisation*. Discussion Paper No 2004/6. Helsinki.

Hamilton, K., & Clemens, M. (1999). Genuine savings rates in developing countries. *The World Bank Economic Review, 13*(2), 333–356.

Helliwell, J. (2003). How's life? Combining individual and national variables to explain subjective wellbeing. *Economic Modelling, 20*, 331–360.

Howell, A., Dopko, R., Passmore, H.-A., & Buro, K. (2011). Nature connectedness: Association with wellbeing and mindfulness. *Personality and Individual Differences, 51*(166–71).

Inglehardt, R. (1990). *Culture shift in advanced industrial society*. Princeton University Press.

Inglehardt, R., Foa, R., Peterson, C., & Welzel, C. (2008). Development, Freedon, and rising happiness. A global perspective (1981-2007). *Perspectives on Psychological Science, 3*(4).

Jarvis, D., Stoeckl, N., & Liu, H. (2017). New methods for valuing, and for identifying spatial variations, in cultural services: A case study of the Great Barrier Reef. *Ecosystem Services, 24*, 58–67.

Kahneman, D., Diener, E., & Schwarz, N. (1999). Wellbeing: Foundations of hedonic psychology.

Kahneman, D., Krueger, A., Schkade, D., Schwarz, N., & Stone, A. (2004). Toward national well-being accounts. *American Economic Review, 94*(2), 429–434.

Kahneman, D., Wakker, P., & Sarin, R. (1997). Back to Bentham? Exploration of experienced utility. *Quarterly Journal of Economics, 112*(2), 375–406. https://doi.org/10.1162/003355397555235.

Kristoffersen, I. (2010). The metrics of subjective wellbeing: Cardinality, neutrality and additivity. *The Economic Record, 86*(272), 98–123. https://doi.org/10.1111/j.1475-4932.2009.00598.x.

Krueger, A., & Schkade, D. (2008). The reliability of subjective well-being measures. *Journal of Public Economics, 92*, 1833–1845.

Kubiszewski, I., Costanza, R., Franco, C., Lawn, P., Talberth, J., Jackson, T., & Aylmer, C. (2013). Beyond GDP: Measuring and achieving global genuine progress. *Ecological Economics, 93*, 57–68.

Kubiszewski, I., Jarvis, D., & Zakariyya, N. (2019a). Spatial variations in contributors to life satisfaction: An Australian case study. *Ecological Economics, 164*, 1–10.

Kubiszewski, I., Zakariyya, N., & Costanza, R. (2018). Objective and subjective indicators of life satisfaction in Australia: How well do people perceive what supports a good life? *Ecological Economics, 154*, 361–372.

Kubiszewski, I., Zakariyya, N., & Jarvis, D. (2019b). Subjective wellbeing at different spatial scales for individual satisfied and dissatisfied with life. *Peer J, 7*, 1–25.

Larsen, R., & Ketelaar, T. (1991). Personality and suceptibility to positive and negative emotional states. *Journal of Personality and Social Psychology, 61*, 132–140.

Larson, S. (2009). Communicating stakeholders priorities in the great barrier reef region. *Society and Natural Resources, 22*, 650–664.

Larson, S. (2010). Regional wellbeing in tropical Queensland, Australia: Developping a dissatisfaction index to inform government policy. *Environment and Planning, 42*, 2972–2989.

Larson, S., Stoeckl, N., Jarvis, D., Addison, J., Grainger, D., Watkin Liu, F., & Walalakoo Aboriginal Corporation, B. D. A. C. R., Ewamian Aboriginal Corporation RNTBC, Yununijarra Aboriginal Corporation RNTBC. (2020). Indigenous Land and Sea Management Programs (ILSMPs) Enhance the Wellbeing of Indigenous Australians. . *International Journal of Environmental Research and Public Health, 17*.

Larson, S., Stoeckl, N., Jarvis, D., Addison, J., Prior, S., & Esparon, M. (2019). Using measures of wellbeing for impact evaluation: Proof of concept developed with an indigenous community undertaking land management programs in northern Australia. *Ambio, 48*, 89–98. https://doi.org/10.1007/s13280-018-1058-3.

Levinson, A. (2009). Valuing public goods using happiness data: The case of air quality. In *WP 15156*. Cambridge: MA.

Luechinger, S. (2009). Valuing air quality using the life satisfaction approach. *The Economic Journal, 119*, 482–515.

MacKerron, G., & Mourato, S. (2009). Life satisfaction and air quality in London. *Ecological Economics, 68*, 1441–1453. https://doi.org/10.1016/j.ecolecon.2008.10.004.

Maddison, D., & Rehdanz, K. (2011). The impact of climate on life satisfaction. *Ecological Economics, 70*, 2437–2445.

McAllistair, F. (2005). Wellbeing: Concepts and challenges. Discussion Paper. Retrieved from http://www.sd-research.org.uk/wellbeing/documents/SDRNwellbeingpaper-Final_000.pdf

Millenium Ecosystem Assessment. (2003). Ecosystems and human wellbeing: A framework for assessment. Retrieved from New York:

Myers, D., & Diener, E. (1995). Who is happy? *Psychological Science, 6*(1), 10–19.

National Centers for Environmental Information. (2018, 07/08/2020). What's the Difference between Weather and Climate? Retrieved from https://www.ncei.noaa.gov/news/weather-vs-climate

Neumayer, E. (1999). The ISEW: Not an index of sustainable economic welfare. *Social Indicators Research, 48*(1), 77–101.

Neumayer, E. (2000). On the methodology of ISEW, GPI and related measures: Some constructive suggestions an some doubts on the 'threshold' hypothesis. *Ecological Economics, 30*, 347–361.

Newton, J. (2007). *Wellbeing and the natural environment: a brief review of the evidence.* Retrieved from

Nordhaus, W., & Tobin, J. (1973). Is growth obsolete? In M. Moss (Ed.), *The measurement of economic and social performance* (pp. 509–564). New York: National Bureau of Economic Research.

OECD. (2013). OECD guidelines on measuring subjective wellbeing. Retrieved from.

Oswald, A., & Wu, S. (2011). Well-being across America. *The Review of Economics and Statistics, 93*(4), 1118–1134.

Parker, P. M. (1995). *Climate effects on individual, social and economic behavior: A physioeconomic review of research across disciplines*. Westport, CT: Greenwood Press.

Rehdanz, K., & Maddison, D. (2005). Climate and happiness. *Ecological Economics, 52*, 111–125.

Shields, M., Price, S., & Wooden, M. (2009). Life satisfaction and the economic and social characteristics of neighbourhoods. *Journal of Population Economics, 22*, 421–443.

Speldewinde, P., Cook, A., Davies, P., & Weinstein, P. (2011). The hidden health burden of environmental degradation: Disease comorbidity and dryland salinity. *EcoHealth, 8*(1), 82–92.

Stiglitz, J., Sen, J., & Fitoussi, J.-P. (2009). Report of the commission on the measurement of economic performance and social Progress. Retrieved from: https://ec.europa.eu/eurostat/documents/8131721/8131772/Stiglitz-Sen-Fitoussi-Commission-report.pdf

Stutzer, A., & Frey, B. (2010). Recent advances in the economics of individual subjective well-being. *Social Research: An International Quaterly, 77*(2), 679–714.

Takano, T., Nakamura, K., & Watanabe, M. (2002). Urban residential environments and senior citizens, longevity in megacity areas: The importance of walkable green spaces. *Journal of Epidemiology and Community Health, 56*(12), 913–918.
Talberth, C., Cobb, C., & Slattery, N. (2007). *The genuine Progress indicator 2006, a tool for sustainable development*. Redefining Progress.
Tellegen, A., Lykken, D., Bouchard, T., Wilcox, K., Segal, N., & Rich, S. (1988). Personality similarity in twins reared apart and together. *Journal of Personality and Social Psychology, 54*, 1031–1039.
The Melbourne Institute. (2019). *The household, income and labour dynamics in Australia survey: Selected findings from waves 1 to 17*. Retrieved from Melbourne:
Tiebout, C. (1956). A pure economy of local expenditures. *Journal of Political Economy, 64*(5), 416–424.
Van de Vliert, E., Huang, X., & Parker, P. (2004). Do colder and hotter climate make richer societies more, but poorer societies less happy and altruistic? *Journal of Environmental Psychology, 24*, 17–30.
van den Bergh, J. (2009). The GDP paradox. *Journal of Economic Psychology, 30*, 117–135.
Van Praag, B., & Baarsma, B. (2005). Using happiness surveys to value intangibles: The case of airport noise. *The Economic Journal, 115*, 224–246.
Van Praag, B., Frijters, P., & Ferrer-i-Carbonell, A. (2003). The anatomy of subjective wellbeing. *Journal of Economic Behavior and Organization, 51*(1), 29–49.
Veenhoven, R. (2002). Why social policy needs subjective indicators. *Social Indicators Research, 58*, 33–45.
Vemuri, A., & Costanza, R. (2006). The role of social, human, built and natural capital in explaining life satisfaction at the country level: Toward a Nation Wellbeing Index (NWI). *Ecological Economics, 58*, 119–133.
Welsch, H. (2002). Preferences over prosperity and pollution: Environmental valuation based on happiness surveys. *Kyklos, 55*(4), 473–494.
Welsch, H. (2006). Environment and happiness: Valuation of air pollution using life satisfaction data. *Ecological Economics, 56*, 801–813.
Welsch, H., & Ferreira, S. (2014). *Environment. Well-being and experienced preference*. Oldenburg Discussion Papers in Economics, (V347-14). Oldenburg Germany.
Zhou, J., & Xie, Y. (2016). Does economic development affect life satisfaction? A spatial-temporal-contextual analysis in China. *Journal of Happiness Studies, 17*, 643–658.

Sustainable and Resilient Community in the Times of Crisis: The Greater Sydney Case

Khandakar Farid Uddin and Awais Piracha

Abstract With more than 86% of people residing in large metropolitans, Australia is one of the world's most urbanised countries. Sydney, the state capital of New South Wales (NSW), is Australia's economic heart, and its vibrance is essential to drive both the NSW and Australian economies. Due to rapid economic and population growth, Greater Sydney has been expanding, and its demographics have been transforming. However, Greater Sydney is divided into advantaged and disadvantaged areas considering various indicators. A slanted imaginary line running from north-west to the south-east divides the advantaged north and east from the disadvantaged (Greater Western Sydney) south-west and west. This study reveals that Greater Western Sydney lacks sustainable and resilient communities due to the uneven distribution of opportunities and lack of community capacity. This study also argues that the disadvantaged communities experience higher vulnerability to risks in emergencies, such as the COVID-19 pandemic, which resulted in an even more disadvantaged condition. Creating resilient communities is imperative to progress individuals or communities' ability to adapt and overcome any crisis and transform their collective ability to face challenges. The disadvantaged Western Sydney communities require sustainable urban growth with evidence-based, long-term, and inclusive strategic responses to build community resilience to reduce vulnerability. This paper points toward the need for shaping resilient communities and emphasises the need for community empowerment, provision of urban amenities, and provision of socio-economically and infrastructurally balanced sustainable growth for the underprivileged communities in Sydney.

Keywords Community resilience · Sustainability · Crisis · Disadvantaged · Western Sydney

---

K. Farid Uddin (✉) · A. Piracha
School of Social Sciences, Western Sydney University, Penrith, Australia
e-mail: K.FaridUddin@westernsydney.edu.au; A.Piracha@westernsydney.edu.au

© The Author(s), under exclusive license to Springer Nature Singapore Pte Ltd. 2022

T. Chaiechi, J. Wood (eds.), *Community Empowerment, Sustainable Cities, and Transformative Economies*, https://doi.org/10.1007/978-981-16-5260-8_26

1 Introduction

Communities are lively and dynamic social domains that have chased community life and wellbeing throughout history (Zautra et al., 2008). Communities are bounded by numerous complex and influential built, natural, social, and economic settings central to generating progressive growth (Norris et al., 2008). In this process of growth, resilience, that is, the adaptive capacities of individuals, is vital for maintaining communities vibrant livelihoods (Norris et al., 2008). Besides, the community is the primary component of sustainable development and sustainability capacity (Xia et al., 2015). Sustainable communities are essential to utilise all available social infrastructure and facilities for community wellbeing and to maintain a quality life in a safe environment (Teriman et al., 2011). Community resilience and sustainability is encompassed by the stability of livelihoods, socio-economic opportunities, equitable distribution of resources, and balanced growth (Houston, 2018). Our world system has become increasingly connected and complex, and communities worldwide are increasingly confronting various challenges (Norris et al., 2008); some are familiar but unpredictable, such as bushfires or floods, and some are new as Coronavirus 2019 (COVID-19).

People cannot foretell much earlier where or when or how the disaster will occur. Also, individuals are not acquainted with some novel crises until they occur. However, a sustainable and resilient community would face any challenges and pull through from any uncertain situation. The ability to adjust to individuals, communities, and cities' changing settings is considered resilience (Norris et al., 2008). A sustainable and resilient community depends on its socio-economic structures and character. However, it is undeniable that communities' ability in a city differs significantly considering their capacity, skills, distribution of opportunities and inadequate prospects (Pickett & Wilkinson, 2015). Thus, this paper intends to explore Sydney's community capacity to understand their sustainability and resiliency aptitude.

Sydney is ranked one of the world's most liveable cities. It is a modern and vibrant city and is home to a substantial global business and economy concentration. Greater Sydney metropolitans cover 12,300 square kilometres and have a population of 5,312,163 (2019),[1] almost two-thirds of the NSW state's total population. Greater Sydney comprises 33 Local Government Areas (LGAs) and more than 900 suburbs.

Greater Western Sydney is a large metropolitan region of Greater Sydney that generally embraces the north-west, south-west, central-west, and far western sub-regions within Sydney's metropolitan areas.[2] It comprises 13 local government areas of Blacktown City, Blue Mountains City, Camden Council, Campbelltown City, the City of Canterbury-Bankstown, Cumberland Council, Fairfield City, Hawkesbury City, Liverpool City, the City of Parramatta, Penrith City, The Hills

[1] .idcommunity, https://profile.id.com.au/australia/about?WebID=250

[2] Western Sydney University, https://www.westernsydney.edu.au/rcegws/rcegws/About/about_greater_western_sydney

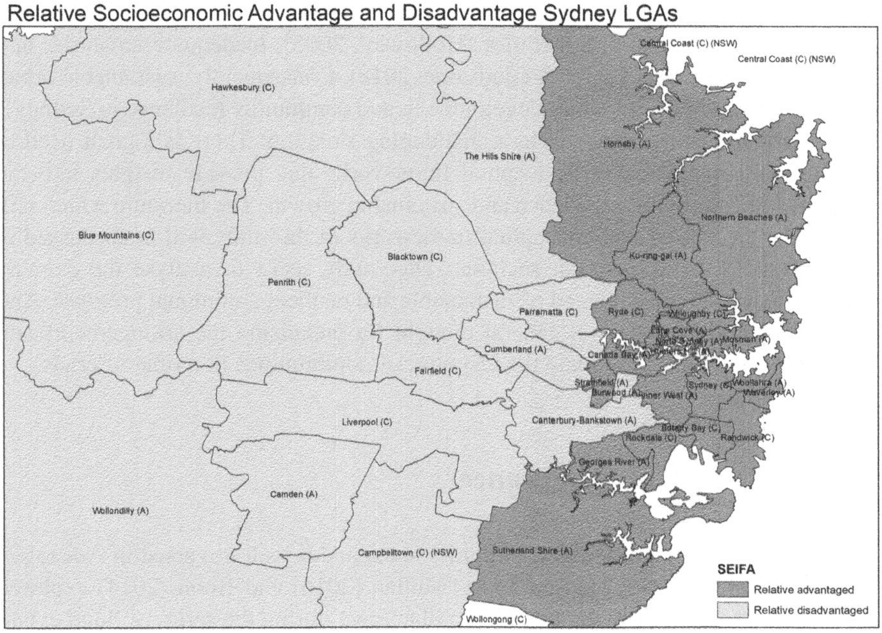

Fig. 1 The socio-economic advantage areas in Sydney
Source: Drawn by authors using Australian Bureau of Statistics (ABS) Socio-Economic Indexes for Areas (SEIFA – 2016, The Index of Relative Socio-economic Advantage and Disadvantage (IRSAD)) at Statistical Area Level 2. Local government boundaries are superimposed

Shire and Wollondilly Shire.[3] Western Sydney contains about 9% of Australia's population and 44% of Sydney's population. Western Sydney's population is expected to reach 3 million by 2036 and absorb two-thirds of the Greater Sydney population growth, making the Western Sydney region one of Australia's largest growing urban populations.[4]

Though substantial urban growth and development are taking place in Sydney, some regions lag in providing residents with the necessary opportunities. The socio-economically underprivileged residents are geographically concentrated in Greater Sydney's western and south-western suburbs; conversely, socio-economically privileged regions are situated in the other parts of the city (Roggema, 2019; Scheurer et al., 2017). Figure 1 shows that the below-average advantage areas are in the Greater Western Sydney areas, and the above-average advantage areas are situated in Eastern and Northern Sydney.

The rapid urban growth of Sydney is mostly being accommodated in below-average advantage areas which have fewer and low-grade jobs (Lee et al., 2018),

[3] .idcommunity, https://profile.id.com.au/cws/about

[4] Western Sydney University, https://www.westernsydney.edu.au/rcegws/rcegws/About/about_greater_western_sydney

more deficient earnings (Stilwell & Hardwick, 1973), reduced services (Holloway, 2002), not as much of ICT facilities (Holloway, 2005), inadequate amenities and much higher densities (Taylor & Gladstone, 2018). Consequently, sustainable urban growth, sustainable community development, and community resilience in Sydney's most accommodating areas are in a challenging situation. There is a great need to develop and operationalise conceptual frameworks that provide insights into the dynamics of community resilience and sustainable growth. The literature which will lead to the theoretical and conceptual frameworks of the study will be discussed in more detail in the subsequent sections. This study seeks to analyse the existing community capabilities in need of sustainable and resilient communal progress. And finally, the study proposes a general thought for enhancing the arrangements and capacities which may stimulate the response of communities in a time of crisis.

2 Objectives and Significance

Research on sustainability and community resilience is well-traversed in Australian academia. For example, Madsen and O'Mullan (2016) and Boon (2014) explored community resiliencies in the rural Australian town during the series of flood event; and West et al. (2020) discussed community resilience and Australian bushfires. Besides, Burnside-Lawry and Carvalho (2016) studied the approach to building community resilience, and Morley et al. (2018) examined the status of community resilience in two remote towns of Australia. Likewise, Farmer et al. (2012) examined rural health services contribute to community sustainability; Xia et al. (2015) compared various sustainable community rating tools in Australia, and Teriman et al. (2011) explored social infrastructure and sustainable development essentials for a sustainable community. However, research on the combination of community resilience and community sustainability, specifically, study on communities' ability and available opportunities related to sustainable growth and resilient communities, have not been conducted. In addition, this research feels a lack of work on the implications of urban discrepancies, community resilience and sustainability in terms of resilient and sustainable community strategies and locational deprivation.

Across the globe, community resilience and sustainability increasingly gain researchers' and policymakers' attention as communities face the effects of numerous disasters (Madsen & O'Mullan, 2016). Specifically, Australia has experienced three particular large-scale economic shocks during 2006–2011 and is particularly at risk to the effects of climate change, heatwaves, bushfires, droughts, floods and the recent COVID-19 catastrophe is a new addition (Dinh et al., 2017; Kippen et al., 2020; Shakespeare-Finch et al., 2020; Singh-Peterson & Lawrence, 2015).

In addition, there are place-based disparities of the consequences of the crisis, and it is evident that some communities are better able to cope and recover while others are less capable; consequently, less capable communities face a threat of declining resources and quality of life (Madsen & O'Mullan, 2016; Steiner et al., 2018). Thus, this research is a noteworthy contribution in understanding the global and modern city Sydney's community disparities concerning sustainability and resiliency at the time of crisis.

In addition, there is a lack of empirical evidence about community resilience levels across geographic and time precincts amongst Australian communities, which is a substantial inadequacy for the advance of hands-on policy actions to support communities (Dinh et al., 2017).

This paper concentrates on the assessment and analysis of the capacities theorised to produce community resilience and sustainability. Finally, the study reflects how the current crisis COVID-19 is challenging the residents of Greater Western Sydney. This research argues that socio-economic disparities and the crisis generate significant challenges to Greater Western Sydney's regions communities. It emphasises the need to search for an appropriate strategy and highlights the need for rational distribution of opportunities to the disadvantaged Western Sydney communities.

3 Methodology

This study explores community resilience and sustainability across different local government areas (LGAs) in the Sydney Metropolitan area. Sociodemographic characteristics of the study areas are provided at the start. Based on the literature review, the study established four key indicators and two variables for each indicator. The selection of indicators was made to cover the main aspects of sustainability, i.e. social, economic, ecological and built environment. This study investigated whether differences exist in community resilience and sustainability among different communities in Sydney Metro. The community was classified into two groups: the rest of Sydney LGAs and Western Sydney LGAs.

A set of Australian Bureau of Statistics (ABS) census 2016 sociodemographic publicly available data is used to measure and analyse community capacities. The ABS data is most valid, authentic, and publicly available to use from its official website. The research limited the focus to eight types of data of 34 local government areas (2016 boundaries) of entire metropolitan Sydney. During the census period in 2016, there were 34 LGAs in metropolitan Sydney; however, later, Rockdale and Botany Bay council were merged into the Bayside Council, resulting in 33 LGAs. The study combined the data of these two LGAs to fit with the existing administrative boundaries.

The study has explored quantitative data from the ABS web portal and analysed human, social, physical, and economic capitals related statistics. The numerical analysis has produced statistical evidence to define the sustainability and resiliency difference between the Greater Sydney communities. This study also explored newspapers articles, journal articles, reports, websites, and other materials. Besides, the ArcGIS mapping software is applied to create maps illustrating the demographical difference.

4 Conceptual Framework

The concept of community is very challenging to unpack. However, in general, a community is a group of people in a comparatively small confined area that can take collective action (Akamani, 2012). A community is a cluster in a specific geographical precinct and has common natural, social, economic backgrounds and targets (Norris et al., 2008). Over time, the term 'Community Stability', was shaped in Germany in the eighteenth century to improve the segregated communities; however, over the eighteenth century, some blunders exposed with the approaches, consequently, finally, in the 1990s, the criticisms lead to the new paradigms of 'community resilience' and 'community capacity' (Akamani, 2012). On the other hand, the term resilience can be defined in various ways. Norris et al. (2008) define resilience as the ability to recover from stress, the improvement of resources, and the capacity of applied approach in challenging situations. Scherzer et al. (2019) explicate community resilience as the constructive ability to increase the community's potentials to upkeep any crisis. Also, community capacity is the public's shared capability to generate and utilise opportunities, cope with anxieties, and fulfil residents' fundamental necessities (Akamani, 2012). Thus, community resilience and community capacity are strongly connected to understanding its residents' ability.

The community's essential features, obtainability of capitals and organised systems are acute in swaying communities' skill to react to various challenges and to accomplish practical results (Akamani, 2012). Community resilience signifies a community's aptitude and is necessary to reinstall its situation after a short-term adverse disruption, such as a disaster or crisis (Houston, 2015, 2018). Communities resilience supports the community to get ready and plan to face ups and downs more magnificently and adapt to the actual or potential adverse actions in a timely and efficient manner (Scherzer et al., 2019).

The notion of 'sustainable development' was first widely pronounced in 1987s Brundtland Report of World Commission on Environment and Development (WCED) from the United Nations, and it defines sustainable development as "development that meets the needs of the present without compromising the ability of future generations to meet their own needs" (WCED, 1987). Besides, Johnston et al. (2007) argue that sustainability is an assumed action or accomplishment that is adept at being persistent and unlocks ways of living and working that enable people to lead healthy and secured life by fulfilling their needs without destroying the future welfare of people and the planet. A community that is building capability is one that strategies for positive advancement (Zautra et al., 2008) and a sustainable community are about continuing and increasing the superiority of community's life, welfares, desires and ethos by resolving the economic, environmental and social health concerns (Teriman et al., 2011).

The provisions of urban sustainability, sustainable city and sustainable community refer to the suitable socio-economic condition and equal concern to social and economic sustainability (Shen et al., 2011). Sustainable development, or sustainability of communities, maintains a dominant role as the preferred development paradigm and plays a critical role in successfully achieving urban sustainability (Lew et al., 2016; Shen et al., 2011). A sustainable community ensures its members' wellbeing by equal access to opportunities and resources, with the capacity to compete with various challenges in the time of crisis (Rogers & Ryan, 2001). Thus, the literature discussed above defines and highlights the importance of community. The issue of sustainability and resilience is an important term to explore the disparities among communities in Sydney.

5 Analytical Framework

Community capacity and sustainability are connected to numerous resources, and many different authors have explored the different capitals and their roles in underpinning economic growth, human wellbeing and sustainability, focusing on various capitals' economic, social, biophysical, and ecological economic viewpoints (Akamani, 2012; Magis, 2010; Norris et al., 2008; Roberts & Townsend, 2016; Rogers & Ryan, 2001; Valentin & Spangenberg, 2000). Different authors have used different terms for these community capitals and resources. For example, Roberts and Townsend (2016) refer to social, economic, natural, and cultural capital, while Akamani (2012) identifies five types of capital to ensure community resilience: social, economic, physical, human, and human natural capital. Besides, Norris et al. (2008) reviewed various literature, identified economic development, social capital, information and communication, and community competence as four principal means of community development and Magis (2010) calls for natural, built, human, cultural, social, political, and financial resources.

Regarding the sustainability indicators, Valentin and Spangenberg (2000) define sustainability based on four social, economic, environmental, and institutional elements. Also, Rogers and Ryan (2001) identify social, environmental and economic wellbeing performance and Shen et al. (2011) recognise environmental, economic and social signs as an approach to sustainable community development.

Population flow, growing inequity, increasing migration, and mounting development in incompatible and hazard-prone zones situate individuals and belongings in more risks and add people and assets in danger from catastrophe each year (Aldrich & Meyer, 2015). Thus, various community capitals such as social capital, human capital, economic capital, physical capital, and environmental or natural capital embody the numerous scopes of community welfare and the capacity to face any crisis (Akamani, 2012). Besides, sustainable community development aims to synchronise and incorporate the economic, environmental, social, and human capitals to ensure a participatory, universal, wide-ranging and sustainable community development practice (Xia et al., 2015).

Table 1 defines five capitals and explains their applications and associated indicators applied in this study to evaluate the community capacity and

Table 1 Definition, applications and associated indicators of five capitals applied in this study

Capital	Definition and applications	Indicators
Social	Communities ability, support for social participation, mutual social contact and network of relationships that collectively regulate social trajectories (Aldrich & Meyer, 2015; Norris et al., 2008; Sherrieb et al., 2010)	Education, families, skill base, leisure, social support, social participation, organisational cooperation, leadership roles and community understanding (Norris et al., 2008; Payne et al., 2021; Rogers & Ryan, 2001; Sherrieb et al., 2010).
Human	The skills, knowledge and other elements enable communities to engage in creative activities and enhance their wellbeing (Akamani, 2012).	Skills, jobs, qualifications, education and health (Dinh et al., 2017)
Physical/Built	Physical capital comprises all forms of infrastructure that support the wellbeing of people directly through its role as a production input and indirectly by reducing costs (Akamani, 2012; Dinh et al., 2017).	Effective transportation systems, infrastructure, roads, rails, equipment, and housing (Akamani, 2012; Dinh et al., 2017)
Financial	Economic capital refers to opportunities for income and employment and other sources of livelihoods that contribute to the wellbeing of communities and the local economy performance (Akamani, 2012; Rogers & Ryan, 2001).	Financial assets, employment, infrastructure, technology, innovation, economic development, diverse economic resources, equal distribution of resources (Akamani, 2012; Norris et al., 2008; Payne et al., 2021).
Natural/environmental	Nature's capacity to continue peoples activities and opportunities to promote community growth (Dinh et al., 2017; Rogers & Ryan, 2001).	Climate change, land, water, landscape, biodiversity, plants, rain (Dinh et al., 2017; Payne et al., 2021; Valentin & Spangenberg, 2000).

Source: Generated by authors by analysing various literature

sustainability. The chosen five community capitals are regarded as combined resources endowed into productive actions and outcomes, which constitute an essential source of resilience and sustainability (Dinh et al., 2017; Valentin & Spangenberg, 2000).

Thus, there is a need to develop analytical frameworks that provide insights into the dynamics of community resilience and sustainability and provide the theoretical foundation for the exploration. After analysing various variables and indicators guided by various literature (Akamani, 2012; Norris et al., 2008; Rogers & Ryan, 2001; Shen et al., 2011; Valentin & Spangenberg, 2000), this study has considered social, human, physical, financial and natural capital and related indicators to analyse the Greater Sydney community's capacity (Fig. 2). The selection of indicators has been made following the rich understanding of various related literature cited above, suitability with the study, appropriateness with analyses and availability of statistics.

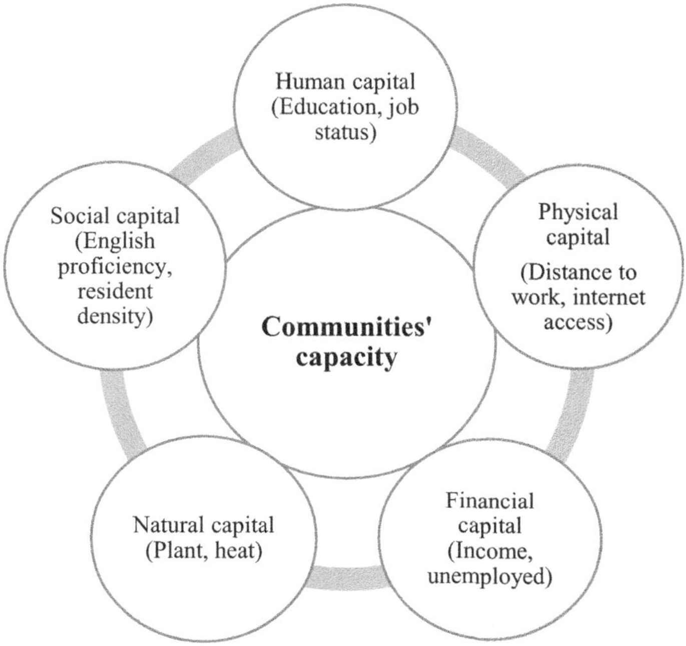

Fig. 2 Communities' capacity indicators applied in this study
Source: Generated by authors by collecting ideas from various literature

6 Findings and Analysis

After analysing the data guided by the indicators outlined in the conceptual framework, this study claims that Western Sydney is in poor condition in the human, social, physical, and financial indicators. Table 1 shows that dwellings with excessive residents are primarily located in Western Sydney.

Data (Table 2) shows that the residents of Western Sydney work in other regions and must travel far for work. 76.78% of the Greater Sydney residents travelling between 30 and 50 km for work reside in Western Sydney. The residents of Western Sydney's have lower education levels. The Bachelor degree level qualified residents to have a significant presence in the rest of Sydney compared to Western Sydney. The people of Western Sydney are mainly involved with manual jobs. Nearly 65% of the Sydney residents who do manufacturing jobs live in Western Sydney. The ethnic migrants' communities have an intense concentration in Western Sydney and are mainly from non-English speaking countries. Greater Sydney's people who have poor proficiency in native English are primarily concentrated in the Western Sydney region. Due to the higher involvement in low-paid work, Western Sydney has a high concentration of less earning individuals. Data shows that the individuals who have $3000 or more income are concentrated in the rest of the Sydney LGA areas.

Table 2 Community's capacities

	Western Sydney			Rest of Sydney		
Indicators	%	Mean	Std. Dev	%	Mean	Std. Dev
Number of dwelling with eight residents or more	77.32%	641.31	509.31	22.68%	116.57	88.92
Distance to work (30 km to less than 50 km)	76.78%	11024.08	7782.69	23.22%	2064.43	3143.58
Job status (manufacturing)	64.31%	6040.77	3058.10	35.69%	2075.05	1598.42
Spoken English proficiency not at all	64.51%	3673.54	3646.95	35.49%	1250.57	1014.35
Unemployed (looking for full-time work)	60.05%	3295.00	2079.34	39.95%	1356.05	857.83
Internet not accessed from dwellings	55.50%	7370.15	4711.93	44.50%	3659.24	2555.40
Education (bachelor's degree level)	36.41%	20316.69	13247.35	63.59%	21963.62	13581.39
Weekly personal income ($3000 or more)	18.86%	2487.46	1875.43	81.14%	6621.43	4565.61

Source: Generated by authors using Australian Bureau of Statistics (ABS) 2016 Census data

Besides, the labour force which is out of work is concentrated in Western Sydney. A significant number of dwellings in Sydney that do not have access to the internet from home are high in Western Sydney.

The table above shows that the mean for the number of dwellings with eight residents or more in Western Sydney is six times than the rest of Sydney, and the mean for the Distance to work (30 km to less than 50 km) in Western Sydney is five times higher than the rest of Sydney. Besides, the mean for the Job status (Manufacturing) and Spoken English proficiency not at all in Western Sydney is three times higher compared to the rest of Sydney. Besides, the standard deviation is also significantly different between Western Sydney and the rest of Sydney.

Sydney is also environmentally or naturally divided, and Western Sydney is also climatically underprivileged. The area is often 5–10 °C hotter in summer and has half the annual rainfall of other parts of Sydney (Allchin, 2019). Table 3 shows that the average hot days are significantly higher in Western Sydney areas; conversely, annual rainfall and the tree canopy cover is the lowest compared to the other parts. In January 2020, when bushfires and heatwaves pounded Sydney, parts of Western Sydney recorded a temperature of up to 52.0 °C, making it one of the hottest places on the earth (Pfautsch et al., 2020; Purtill, 2021).

Considering the social, human, economic, physical, and environmental or natural capital, the situation of the Western Sydney region is below standard. Given the above analysis, this research contends that Western Sydney communities are experiencing poor resilience and lower sustainability (Fig. 3).

Table 3 Environmental characteristics of various parts of Sydney

Sydney Regions (GSC, 2018)	Average annual rainfall	Average annual days over 35 degrees Celsius	Existing urban area tree canopy
Western Parkland City (mostly Penrith, parts of Blacktown, Liverpool, Campbelltown, Fairfield LGAs under Greater Western Sydney region)	683 mm (Badgerys Creek)	21 days (Penrith)	16%
Central River City (mostly greater Parramatta, parts of Blacktown Cumberland, Canterbury-Bankstown, the hills LGAs under Greater Western Sydney region)	973 mm (Parramatta)	11 days (Parramatta)	17%
Eastern Harbour City (rest of Sydney LGAs – To the east of the River City)	1215 mm (Observatory Hill)	3 days (Observatory Hill)	32%

Source: A Metropolis of Three Cities – the Greater Sydney Region Plan (2018), Greater Sydney Commission (https://www.greater.sydney/metropolis-of-three-cities)

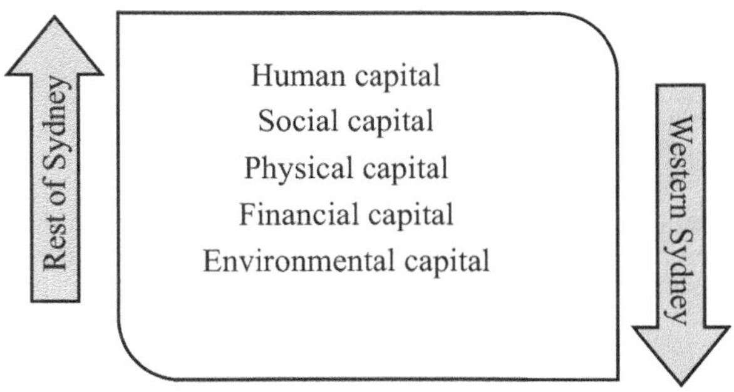

Fig. 3 Community's resilience and sustainability situation
Source: Generated by authors analysing various literature and evidence cited above

7 Discussion

The sociodemographic features of cities worldwide have been changing for a long time, consequently generating diverse and complex waves on the various regions of metropolises' (Foote & Walter, 2017). Sydney's ongoing urban growth is nothing different; Sydney has been undergoing socio-economic transformations for a long time (Stilwell & Hardwick, 1973). Consequently, Sydney's urban growth and development provisions intensify human, social, physical, and financial capital disparities among its residents (Vogel et al., 2020).

Communities are inspired to become accustomed to socio-economic transformation and possess the ability to develop into more vigorous, more dynamic and pre-emptive approaches (Steiner et al., 2018). However, community resilience and sustainability is contingent on the community's resources, the community's ability to advance, and the community's capacity to face challenges. Cities need to establish a baseline for their residents to strengthen a community's resilience and sustainability, and an initial measure that allows strengthening its communities' capacities is needed. However, the Sydney Metropolitan areas' situation is that the residents of

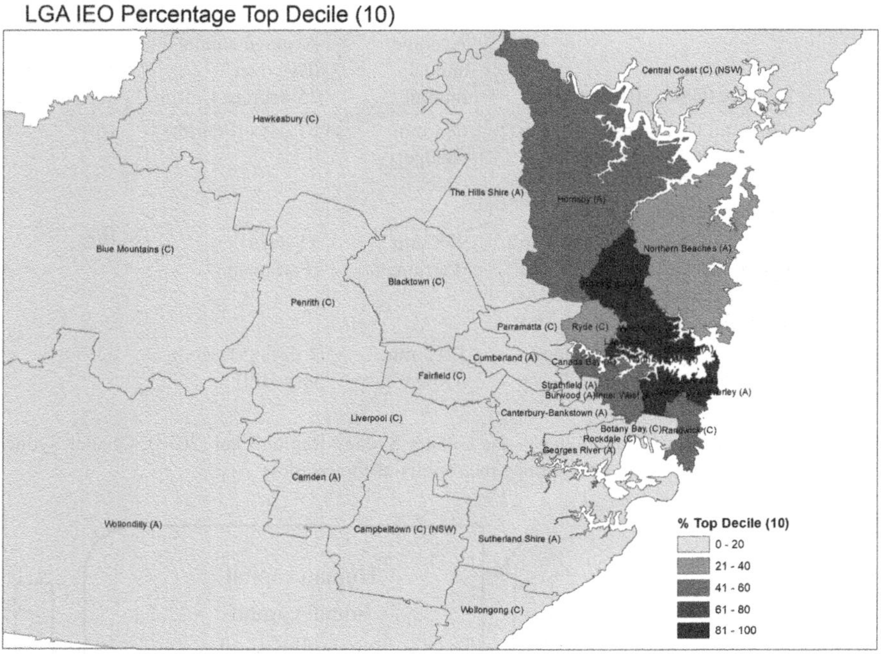

Fig. 4 Sydney LGAs Index of Education and Occupation (IEO) percentage of decile 10
Source: Drawn by authors using Australian Bureau of Statistics (ABS) 2016 Census data

specific areas face significant resilient and sustainability challenges due to lack of facilities. Figure 4 shows Sydney LGAs Index of Education and Occupation (IEO) percentage of decile ten areas, revealing communities' educational and occupational levels. The map shows the percentage of the population in each LGA that belongs to the top decile where 100% population of Hunters Hill, Ku-ring-gai, Lane Cove, Mosman, North Sydney, Sydney City, Waverley, Willoughby and Woollahra LGAs population belongs to IEO top decile. On the other hand, 0% of Blacktown, Blue Mountains, Camden, Campbelltown, Canterbury-Bankstown, Cumberland, Fairfield, Hawkesbury, Liverpool, Penrith and Wollondilly LGAs belongs to the top decile. 11 of 13 Western Sydney LGAs educational and occupational level to communities is at the bottom line.

The existing human, social, economic, physical and environmental resources are essential to adapt to a crisis and eventually overcome adversity, get back to a normal situation, and even sometimes perform well in the restored situation (Rapaport et al., 2018). While 78%of residents of the Eastern City District live and work within their district, this compares with 57% in Western City District and 52% in Central City District; also, the proportion of jobs in the knowledge and professional services sector is highest in the Eastern City District and lowest in the other districts (GSC, 2019). The socio-economic impacts of the coronavirus pandemic were geographically segregated in Sydney due to unequal socio-economic and environmental situations. It was estimated that the COVID-19 crisis most impacted areas regarding job losses were hospitality with 689,800, real estate with 130,000, sports and physical recreation with 114,000, hotel and other accommodation with 97,800 (Molloy, 2020). Western Sydney has a high reliance on jobs in these sectors; about 70–80% of people in Western Sydney are involved in non-professional and non-managerial jobs that were the most affected by the COVID-19 pandemic crisis (Farid Uddin & Piracha, 2020). While JobKeeper allowance from the Commonwealth government maintained some of these jobs, others were affected more severely. It was estimated that the Coronavirus disaster would surge Australia's unemployment rate from 5.1% to closer to 15% (Worthington, 2020). Unemployment is higher in Western Sydney, and the COVID-19 crisis have devastating effects on the Western Sydney areas' unemployment rates. Also, Western Sydney residents have a lower ICT skill level, and the internet is not accessible from 10 to 20% of its dwellings (Farid Uddin & Piracha, 2020). Many western residents are thus struggling to work and study from home – also, Western Sydney residents employed in sectors that do not fit to work from home situation.

The outcomes of community resilience are significant from the sustainability perspective (Akamani, 2012). Sustainable urban growth is a dynamic process that denotes the well-balanced relationship between urban development and the existing human, social, financial, physical and environmental resources in society to undertake sustainable life (Shen et al., 2011). The latest five financial years ABS data on building approvals in Greater Sydney shows Western Sydney has been the centre of urban expansion. In the financial year 2016–2017, among the total 55,995 buildings approval in Greater Sydney, 55.44% of the approvals were in the Western Sydney region. The amount was also higher in the subsequent years, 61.30% in 2017–2018, above 70% in 2018–2019, nearly 70% in 2019–2020 and around 88% dwellings were approved in the current 2020–2021 financial year (July to September) in Western Sydney LGAs (Fig. 5).

Hot days and heatwaves represent a significant hazard in the Western Sydney region, and the urban heat island effect across Sydney shows it is highest in the Western City District and lowest in the North District, and the percentage of residents with exposure to high urban heat is highest in Western City District with 46% and lowest in North City District with only 2% (GSC, 2019). There are substantial adverse environmental impacts on Western Sydney resident lifestyles. For example, walking trips are highest in Eastern City District and lowest in Western City District and have the most considerable difference between access to open space (GSC, 2019). Increasing tree canopy in the urban area is a means to recover urban heat and make a sustainable city; however, tree canopy cover is also lower in Western Sydney. With the higher amount of housing approvals, many highly disadvantaged Western Sydney residents live in poor quality houses. New dwellings in Western Sydney are constructed on small lands, leaving little space between neighbours and minimal front or rear gardens (Roggema, 2019) that permits fewer options for added trees.

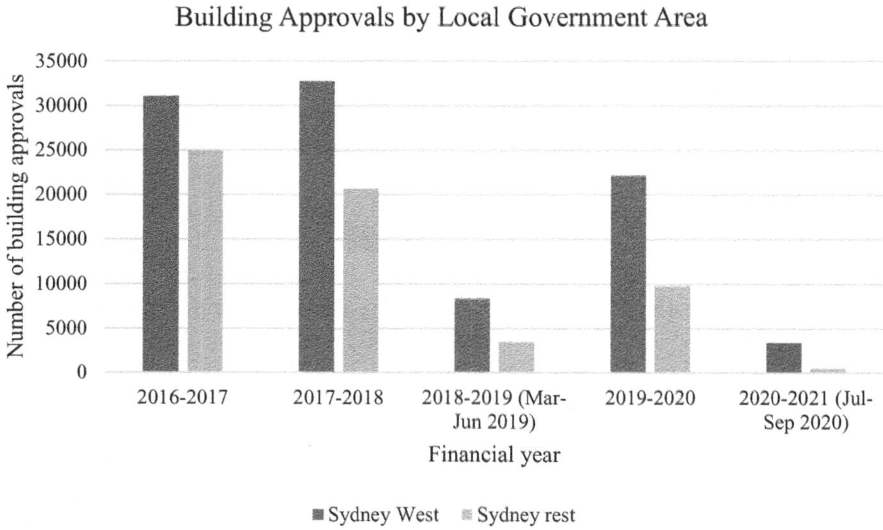

Fig. 5 Building approvals in Greater Sydney
Source: Generated by authors by using ABS data. (http://stat.data.abs.gov.au/Index.aspx?DataSetCode=ABS_BLDG_APPROVALS_LGA201)

Unsustainable development and unequal distribution of opportunities have undesirable impacts on residents' everyday lives (Burton, 2001). A wide range of community resources and their effects are connected with disadvantages in the social order, and community problems are prevalent in unequal societies (Pickett & Wilkinson, 2015). There has been widespread concern about inequality, and inequality has huge adverse socio-economic impacts; besides, many of the undesirable features of the effects of inequality may indicate further fundamental societal problems (Whiteford, 2015). Besides, inequality has significant psychosocial and behavioural special effects on communities, and many social problems are acute in the uneven peoples (Pickett & Wilkinson, 2010; Wilkinson, 2004). People who live in more impoverished socio-economic situations tend to face worse consequences (Whiteford, 2015).

On the other hand, the community has improved opportunities and a better life in inequitable societies (Wilkinson, 2009). Besides, physical health and wellbeing are better, and confidence levels are higher in equal societies (Pickett & Wilkinson, 2010). The existing urban development trends have complex effects on Sydney residents. Urban expansion in the areas where they are more and more detached from opportunities and less capacity to develop leads to unsustainable Western Sydney communities. The far distanced location from job, fewer employment opportunities, poor socio-economic condition, and urban development harshness has placed western Sydney residents in an unfavourable and imbalanced situation. Consequently, instead of minimising urban inequality, the situation deteriorates progressively (Vogel et al., 2020).

8 The Way Forward: Rethinking Urban Living

Cities' success depends on the community's ability to adapt to changes and challenges. Cities ensure their residents' opportunity by their innovations to further equitable, sustainable and resilient futures (Frantzeskaki et al., 2021). The best effective methods of constructing a community's ability and making community resilient are to produce positive urban growth, foster community ties, and ensure essential amenities and key community capital vigorous (Miles & Chang, 2011; Zautra et al., 2008). Global city Sydney got caution from the recent bushfire, flood, and COVID-19 crisis that communities need to be more equipped for any challenges. Sydney needs to rethink urban planning and community development strategies. Thus this research realises the needs to introduce a critical combined approach to tackle crisis and build community capacity for sustainable and resilient cities and communities (Fig. 6).

In this regard, building a smart city and community through technical knowledge, modern technology, innovation, and technical infrastructure should be the foundation of city and community building strategies. Sustainable urban growth must be ensured with a creative economy, creative people, adequate transport, active mobility, better health, sustainable cities, sustainable energy, and smart living. Knowledgebase communities are essential to face any challenges (Florida, 2003; Satterthwaite, 1997). Similarly, Satterthwaite (1997) emphasises the commitment to other sustainable development and emphasises integrating the discussions about sustainable cities and confirming that urban concerns are thoroughly deliberated in the environmental plans and national strategies. Modern universities, comprehensive

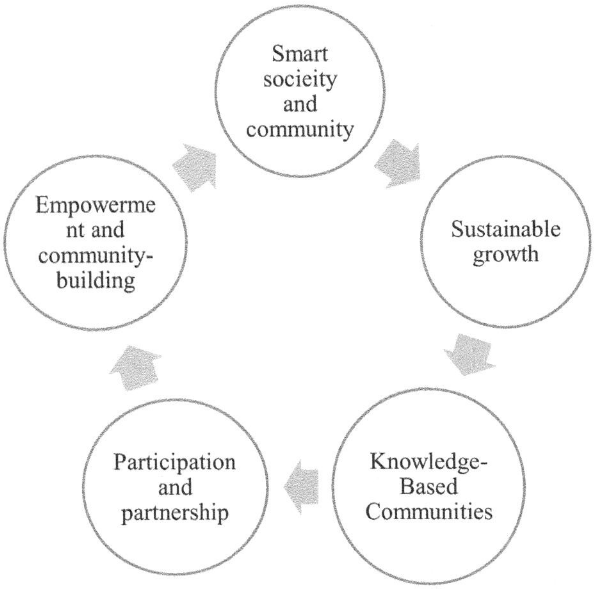

Fig. 6 Critical and combined approach developed by authors concerning a sustainable and resilient community Source: Generated by authors analysing various literature mentioned above

education, smart classrooms, intelligent learning environments, and active learning are essential in forming a knowledge base and empowerment, community-building, community participation, and partnership should be at the centre of policymaking to form a resilient and inclusive city (Florida, 2003; Godschalk, 2003). Unequal resilience in communities jeopardise the economic, social and political resources, and it is crucial to expand the prospects for the disadvantaged groups for the radical city (Vale, 2014). Cities must reconsider the socio-economic opportunities and public services delivery and prioritise budgets and investments in the less advantaged regions.

9 Conclusions

The concept of a sustainable and resilient community is highly relevant for cities. This study's comprehensive critical analyses suggest that Sydney is lagging in promoting equality regarding the communities' opportunities and capacities. This study argues that a comprehensive measure is needed for ensuring sustainable and resilient urban growth. The study's importance lies in its academic debate and, ultimately, its implications for existing urban strategic transformation. This study is limited to some variables and indicators which fulfil its objectives—also inadequate to preliminary statistical analysis. However, this research can serve as an outline to understand the socio-economic split in Sydney. Future research can explore community resiliency and sustainability more broadly by including broader indicators and applying robust statistical packages.

Acknowledgments The authors are thankful to the Centre for International Trade and Business in Asia (CITBA) team at the College of Business, Law, and Governance (CBLG) of the James Cook University, Australia, for their sincere efforts and is also grateful to two anonymous reviewers for their insightful observations in the earlier version of the paper.

References

Akamani, K. (2012). A community resilience model for understanding and assessing the sustainability of forest-dependent communities. *Human Ecology Review*, 99–109.

Aldrich, D. P., & Meyer, M. A. (2015). Social capital and community resilience. *American Behavioral Scientist, 59*(2), 254–269.

Allchin, C. (2019). The future of urban planning in Australia: A big deal. In *Contemporary urban design thinking* (pp. 11–38). Springer.

Boon, H. J. (2014). Disaster resilience in a flood-impacted rural Australian town. *Natural Hazards, 71*(1), 683–701.

Burnside-Lawry, J., & Carvalho, L. (2016). A stakeholder approach to building community resilience: Awareness to implementation. *International Journal of Disaster Resilience in the Built Environment.*

Burton, E. (2001). *The compact city and social justice.* Paper presented at the housing, Environment and Sustainability, housing studies association spring conference.
Dinh, H., Freyens, B., Daly, A., & Vidyattama, Y. (2017). Measuring community economic resilience in Australia: Estimates of recent levels and trends. *Social Indicators Research, 132* (3), 1217–1236.
Farid Uddin, K., & Piracha, A. (2020). *A tale of two cities*. May 14. Retrieved from https://www.openforum.com.au/a-tale-of-two-cities/
Farmer, J., Prior, M., & Taylor, J. (2012). A theory of how rural health services contribute to community sustainability. *Social Science & Medicine, 75*(10), 1903–1911.
Florida, R. (2003). Cities and the creative class. *City & Community, 2*(1), 3–19.
Foote, N., & Walter, R. (2017). Neighborhood and socio-economic change in emerging megapolitan nodes: Tracking shifting social geographies in three rapidly growing United States metropolitan areas, 1980–2010. *Urban Geography, 38*(8), 1203–1230.
Frantzeskaki, N., McPhearson, T., & Kabisch, N. (2021). Urban sustainability science: Prospects for innovations through a system's perspective, relational and transformations' approaches. *Ambio*, 1–9.
Godschalk, D. R. (2003). Urban hazard mitigation: Creating resilient cities. *Natural Hazards Review, 4*(3), 136–143.
GSC. (2018). *Greater Sydney region plan a metropolis of three cities*. Sydney: Greater Sydney Commission. Retrieved from https://gsc-public-1.s3.amazonaws.com/s3fs-public/greater-sydney-region-plan-0318.pdf
GSC. (2019). *The pulse of greater Sydney 2018–2019*. Greater Sydney Commission. Retrieved from https://gsc-public-1.s3.amazonaws.com/s3fs-public/gsc_pulse_of_greater_sydney-july_2019_updated_0.pdf
Holloway, D. (2002). Disparities in Internet access: A case study of the digital divide in Western Sydney. *Australian Journal of Social Issues, 37*(1), 51–69.
Holloway, D. (2005). The digital divide in Sydney: A sociospatial analysis. *Information, Community & Society, 8*(2), 168–193.
Houston, J. B. (2015). *Bouncing forward: Assessing advances in community resilience assessment, intervention, and theory to guide future work.* Sage.
Houston, J. B. (2018). Community resilience and communication: Dynamic interconnections between and among individuals, families, and organizations. *Journal of Applied Communication Research, 46*(1), 19–22.
Johnston, P., Everard, M., Santillo, D., & Robèrt, K.-H. (2007). Reclaiming the definition of sustainability. *Environmental Science and Pollution Research International, 14*(1), 60–66.
Kippen, R., O'Sullivan, B., Hickson, H., Leach, M., & Wallace, G. (2020). A national survey of COVID-19 challenges, responses and effects in Australian general practice. *Australian Journal of General Practice, 49*(11), 745.
Lee, C. L., Piracha, A., & Fan, Y. (2018). *Another tale of two cities: access to jobs divides Sydney along the 'latte line'.* Retrieved from https://theconversation.com/another-tale-of-two-cities-access-to-jobs-divides-sydney-along-the-latte-line-96907
Lew, A. A., Ng, P. T., & Ni, C.-c., & Wu, T.-c. (2016). Community sustainability and resilience: Similarities, differences and indicators. *Tourism Geographies, 18*(1), 18–27.
Madsen, W., & O'Mullan, C. (2016). Perceptions of community resilience after natural disaster in a rural Australian town. *Journal of Community Psychology, 44*(3), 277–292.
Magis, K. (2010). Community resilience: An indicator of social sustainability. *Society and Natural Resources, 23*(5), 401–416.
Miles, S. B., & Chang, S. E. (2011). ResilUS: A community based disaster resilience model. *Cartography and Geographic Information Science, 38*(1), 36–51.
Molloy, S. (2020, March 27). Coronavirus in Australia: Industries most at risk of job losses in COVID-19 crisis. *news.com.au*. Retrieved from https://www.news.com.au/finance/work/careers/coronavirus-in-australia-industries-most-at-risk-of-job-losses-in-covid19-crisis/news-story/e4bd4f5b9cc3e1bc794131bb04742784

Morley, P., Russell-Smith, J., Sangha, K. K., Sutton, S., & Sithole, B. (2018). Evaluating resilience in two remote Australian communities. *Procedia Engineering, 212*, 1257–1264.

Norris, F. H., Stevens, S. P., Pfefferbaum, B., Wyche, K. F., & Pfefferbaum, R. L. (2008). Community resilience as a metaphor, theory, set of capacities, and strategy for disaster readiness. *American Journal of Community Psychology, 41*(1), 127–150.

Payne, P., Kaye-Blake, W., Kelsey, A., Brown, M., & Niles, M. (2021). Measuring rural community resilience: Case studies in New Zealand and Vermont, USA. *Ecology and Society, 26*(1).

Pfautsch, S., Wujeska-Klause, A., & Rouillard, S. (2020). *Benchmarking summer heat across Penrith, New South Wales*. Retrieved from Sydney: https://researchdirect.westernsydney.edu.au/islandora/object/uws:57237

Pickett, K. E., & Wilkinson, R. G. (2010). Inequality: An underacknowledged source of mental illness and distress. *The British Journal of Psychiatry, 197*(6), 426–428.

Pickett, K. E., & Wilkinson, R. G. (2015). Income inequality and health: A causal review. *Social Science & Medicine, 128*, 316–326.

Purtill, J. (2021, January 24). Heatwaves may mean Sydney is too hot for people to live in 'within decades'. *ABC News*. Retrieved from https://www.abc.net.au/news/science/2021-01-24/heatwaves-sydney-uninhabitable-climate-change-urban-planning/12993580

Rapaport, C., Hornik-Lurie, T., Cohen, O., Lahad, M., Leykin, D., & Aharonson-Daniel, L. (2018). The relationship between community type and community resilience. *International Journal of Disaster Risk Reduction, 31*, 470–477.

Roberts, E., & Townsend, L. (2016). The contribution of the creative economy to the resilience of rural communities: Exploring cultural and digital capital. *Sociologia Ruralis, 56*(2), 197–219.

Rogers, M., & Ryan, R. (2001). The triple bottom line for sustainable community development. *Local Environment, 6*(3), 279–289.

Roggema, R. (2019). Australian urbanism; state of the art. In R. Roggema (Ed.), *Contemporary urban design thinking. The Australian approach* (pp. 1–10). Springer.

Satterthwaite, D. (1997). Sustainable cities or cities that contribute to sustainable development? *Urban Studies, 34*(10), 1667–1691.

Scherzer, S., Lujala, P., & Rød, J. K. (2019). A community resilience index for Norway: An adaptation of the baseline resilience indicators for communities (BRIC). *International Journal of Disaster Risk Reduction, 36*, 101107.

Scheurer, J., Curtis, C., & McLeod, S. (2017). Spatial accessibility of public transport in Australian cities: Does it relieve or entrench social and economic inequality? *The Journal of Transport and Land Use, 10*(1), 911–930. https://doi.org/10.5198/jtlu.2017.1097

Shakespeare-Finch, J., Bowen-Salter, H., Cashin, M., Badawi, A., Wells, R., Rosenbaum, S., et al. (2020). COVID-19: An Australian perspective. *Journal of Loss and Trauma, 25*(8), 662–672.

Shen, L.-Y., Ochoa, J. J., Shah, M. N., & Zhang, X. (2011). The application of urban sustainability indicators–A comparison between various practices. *Habitat International, 35*(1), 17–29.

Sherrieb, K., Norris, F. H., & Galea, S. (2010). Measuring capacities for community resilience. *Social Indicators Research, 99*(2), 227–247.

Singh-Peterson, L., & Lawrence, G. (2015). Insights into community vulnerability and resilience following natural disasters: Perspectives with food retailers in northern NSW, Australia. *Local Environment, 20*(7), 782–795.

Steiner, A., Woolvin, M., & Skerratt, S. (2018). Measuring community resilience: Developing and applying a 'hybrid evaluation'approach. *Community Development Journal, 53*(1), 99–118.

Stilwell, F., & Hardwick, J. (1973). Social inequality in Australian cities. *The Australian Quarterly, 45*(4), 18–36.

Taylor, A., & Gladstone, N. (2018, May 18). The parts of Sydney with the most development – And those with the least. *The Sydney Morning Herald*. Retrieved from https://www.smh.com.au/national/nsw/the-parts-of-sydney-with-the-most-development-and-those-with-the-least-20180518-p4zg1y.html

Teriman, S., Yigitcanlar, T., & Mayere, S. (2011). *Social infrastructure planning and sustainable community: Example from south East Queensland, Australia.* Paper presented at the proceedings of the business and social science research conference 2011.

Vale, L. J. (2014). The politics of resilient cities: Whose resilience and whose city? *Building Research & Information, 42*(2), 191–201.

Valentin, A., & Spangenberg, J. H. (2000). A guide to community sustainability indicators. *Environmental Impact Assessment Review, 20*(3), 381–392.

Vogel, R. K., Ryan, R., Lawrie, A., Grant, B., Meng, X., Walsh, P., et al. (2020). Global city Sydney. *Progress in Planning, 136*. https://doi.org/10.1016/j.progress.2018.09.002

WCED. (1987). *Our common future: Report of the World commission on environment and development*. Retrieved from Oxford: Oxford University Press.

West, S., Visentin, D. C., Neil, A., Kornhaber, R., Ingham, V., & Cleary, M. (2020). Forging, protecting, and repairing community resilience informed by the 2019–2020 Australian bushfires. Wiley Online Library.

Whiteford, P. (2015). Inequality and its socio-economic impacts. *Australian Economic Review, 48* (1), 83–92.

Wilkinson, R. (2004). Why is violence more common where inequality is greater? *Annals of the New York Academy of Sciences, 1036*(1), 1–12.

Wilkinson, R. (2009). What difference does inequality make. *MR Magazine, 16*.

Worthington, B. (2020, March 25). People urged to go home as lines form around Centrelink offices due to coronavirus, Stuart Robert admits not anticipating MyGov demand. *ABC News*. Retrieved from https://www.abc.net.au/news/2020-03-24/centrelink-minister-stuart-robert-not-anticipate-coronavirus/12080612

Xia, B., Chen, Q., Skitmore, M., Zuo, J., & Li, M. (2015). Comparison of sustainable community rating tools in Australia. *Journal of Cleaner Production, 109*, 84–91.

Zautra, A., Hall, J., & Murray, K. (2008). Community development and community resilience: An integrative approach. *Community Development, 39*(3), 130–147.

Mining the Future: A Meta-ethnographical Synthesis of the Broken Hill Mining Community

Graeme Cotter, Taha Chaiechi, and Narayan Gopalkrishnan

Abstract The mining industry is today the largest contributor to Australia's commodity-based export economy. With an international market orientation from colonial times to the present, and by virtue of its corporate structure, the metalliferous mining industry may be considered a suitably representative proxy to reflect on the broader sphere of Australian economic and industrial activity. Equally, as the nature of work changes with advances in technology, the future sustainability of work communities has become of increasing concern.

A feature of mining communities in Australia, in both historical and contemporary times has been the recurring conflict between capital and labour. This has at times severely impacted mine profitability, which in some cases has led to premature closure of mining operations. It has also caused widespread immiseration of working class families during the extended strikes and lockouts which have ensued.

In *The Great Transformation*, Karl Polanyi (1944) outlined his thesis of a *double-movement* which occurs as a protective counter-movement whenever human society has been threatened by market liberalism. The trade-union movement has been arguably the most effective of such *double-movements*, from its inception during the Industrial Revolution, until a resounding defeat at the hands of market liberalism in the mining industry at Broken Hill in 1986. The union movement has yet to show any convincing signs of recovery from this defeat.

This paper employs a meta-ethnographical synthesis of the literature relating to the historic mining community of Broken Hill in New South Wales to explore the capital-labour conflict in industry. The meta-ethnography was conducted following the approach outlined by Noblit and Hare (1985). Key themes from a selection of five books and fourteen journal articles on the industrial history of Broken Hill were encoded in NVivo to facilitate the synthesis. Tracing the cyclical fortunes of the

G. Cotter (✉) · T. Chaiechi
College of Business, Law, and Governance, James Cook University, Townsville, QLD, Australia
e-mail: graeme.cotter@my.jcu.edu.au; taha.chaiechi@jcu.edu.au

N. Gopalkrishnan
College of Arts, Society, and Education, James Cook University, Townsville, QLD, Australia
e-mail: narayan.gopalkrishnan@jcu.edu.au

© The Author(s), under exclusive license to Springer Nature Singapore Pte Ltd. 2022
T. Chaiechi, J. Wood (eds.), *Community Empowerment, Sustainable Cities, and Transformative Economies*, https://doi.org/10.1007/978-981-16-5260-8_27

capital-labour conflict through the lens of the mining industry in this district, the study, aided by a proposed culture interpretive theory (CIT), outlines implications for industry development, employment, and community sustainability in a future Australia, finding evidence that capitalism may be finally ridding itself of the need for the working-class.

Keywords Community · Mining · Capital · Working-class · Unions · Market liberalism · Polanyi · Conflict · Sustainability

1 Introduction

1.1 Polanyi's 'Double-Movement'

In 1944, anthropological economist Karl Polanyi, in his book *The Great Transformation,* described the transformation of European civilisation from a pre-industrial world to the era of industrialisation. In this most powerful critique of market liberalism, he developed his thesis of the *double-movement.* Polanyi proposed that market societies were constituted by two opposing forces. On the one hand, the laissez-faire attempts to expand the scope of the free market; and on the other hand, a resultant protective counter-force which emerges as elements in society move to prevent the attempt to establish such a market. Together, it is these two that constitute the *double-movement* (Polanyi, 2001). Examples of social protection that Polanyi elaborates include the Elizabethan Poor Laws, the Statute of Artificers, the Speenhamland Law, the Corn Laws, the Chartists, and the emergence of the working-class as a coherent entity.

Polanyi (2001) contended that the emergence of working-class unions during the Industrial Revolution in England was the most significant example of the *double-movement.* The immediate self-interest of the working-class, Polanyi believed, destined them to become the protectors of society against the intrinsic dangers of a free market. Particularly destructive to society, in Polanyi's view, were attempts by liberal capitalists to establish free markets in what he termed the *fictitious* commodities of *land, money, and labour* (Polanyi, 2001). It is the attempts to establish the latter, a free and unrestrained market in labour that has absorbed the attention of working-class unions ever since, and to which they have opposed themselves at every suggestion of its emergence.

1.2 Social Class Theory, or Culture Theory?

In Karl Marx's system of social class categorisation he focussed his attention on the capitalist-class and the working-class as being the primary divisions of the production process. Although acknowledging the existence of other classes, Marx believed that the capitalist market tended to eliminate other non-capitalist classes, rendering them of lesser importance to his analysis (Barbalet, 1986). Changes in the division of labour since the beginning of the twentieth century have seen the emergence of an increasingly divergent middle class. Professional and semi-professional positions that are not directly related to the production process such as managerial, technical, scientific, administrative, sales and accounts, have been designated as 'new' middle class, to distinguish them from the 'old' middle class of independent trade workers and merchants (Barbalet, 1986). From a Marxian perspective, given that this 'new' middle class remains economically constrained to seek employment through the labour market, it is still plausible for social class theory to consider contemporary capitalist society as divided simply into employers and employees (Barbalet, 1986), although a considerable diversity will be obscured in the process. An attempt to capture aspects of this obscured diversity by divisions into 'upper middle class' and 'lower middle class', 'unionised working class' and 'unorganised working class', or even Weber's 'status' divisions of class would seem to provide little clarification, leading some proponents of class theory to call for a renewal "which would entail a wider and deeper concept of class" (Bottero, 2004, p. 986).

Building on this discussion, this research proposes a *culture interpretive theory* (CIT) which is based on the analysis of the observed behaviour, actions and processes such as manifestos or artefacts, of sub-cultural divisions identifiable in a complex society. Such observation may be either direct, as in a participant-observer ethnography, or indirect, based on a meta-ethnographical synthesis of existing qualitative case studies and ethnographies. The application of such a theory would allow for a greatly expanded identification of relationships, including conflictual interactions and underlying motivations, within Marx's bipartite capitalist society division into employers and employees. The adaptation by the author of a *culture interpretive* perspective allowed the exploration of counter-cultural and sub-cultural influences, which often had a profound influence on the outcome of disputes (Fig. 1).

The theoretical conceptualisation captured in Fig. 1 allowed for the bringing together of Tajfel's *Minimal Group Paradigm*, Stewards *Cultural Ecology*, and Anthropological and *Organisational Culture* theories, to build what is being proposed as *Culture Interpretive Theory* (CIT).

1.3 Research Question

The research question guiding the study is: *What implications might the recurrent and cyclical nature of the tensions between capital and labour hold for the future of industry development and employment in Australia in the twenty-first century and beyond?* A capital/labour antipathy in mining communities in Australia has formed a prominent example of Polanyi's *double-movement* at work. This paper contends that the metalliferous mining industry, as a most significant contributor to Australia's commodity-based export economy, and by virtue of its corporate structure, can be considered a suitable proxy to reflect on the broader sphere of Australian economic

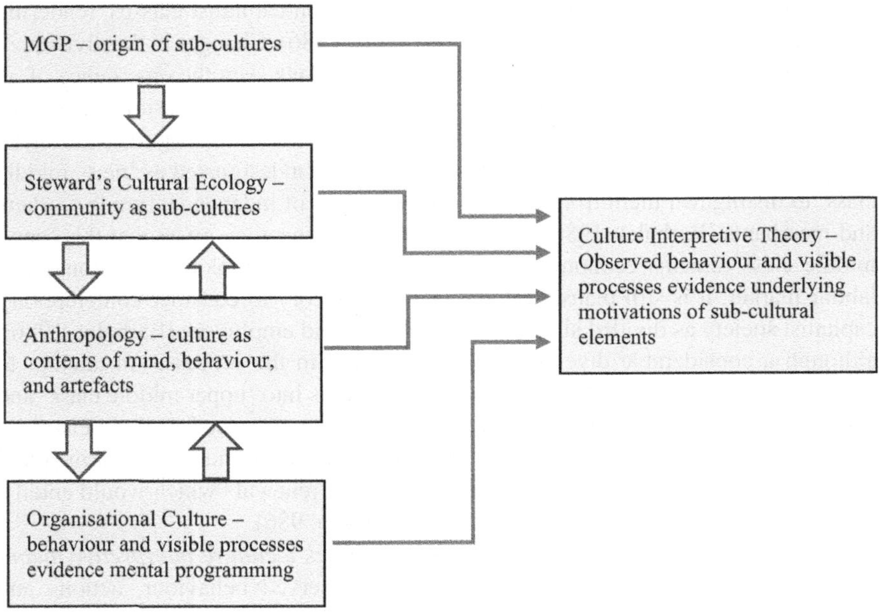

Fig. 1 Culture Interpretive Theory. Adaptation by author showing input development from Minimal Group Paradigm (MGP) (Tajfel, 1970), Cultural Ecology (Steward, 1972), Anthropology (Taylor, 1948), and Organisational Culture (Schein, 1992)

and industrial activity. It is anticipated that this meta-ethnographic synthesis of the literature relating to the historic mining community of Broken Hill will provide insight into the reasons behind the capital-labour conflict. This in turn will inform understanding of the potential future course and sustainability of industry development and employment in Australia in the twenty-first century.

2 Methodology

In exploring the literature relating to Broken Hill, the prevalence of qualitative case studies became apparent, suggesting that an interpretive approach be adopted.

As methodologies within the interpretive paradigm were considered, there emerged a realisation that a meta-ethnography might be the methodological option best suited to addressing this research focus, as explained below.

First described by Noblit and Hare (1988) as a seven phase methodology, meta-ethnography may be used to synthesise existing qualitative case studies. They further explain

> [a] meta-ethnography seeks to go beyond single accounts to reveal the analogies between the accounts. It reduces the accounts while preserving the sense of the account through the selection of key metaphors and organizers. The 'senses' of different accounts are then

> translated into one another. The analogies revealed in these translations are the form of the meta-ethnographic synthesis (p. 15).

In this context Strike and Posner (cited in Noblit & Hare, 1988, p. 18) offered the following definition of synthesis.

> Synthesis is usually held to be activity or the product of activity where some set of parts is combined or integrated into a whole ... [Synthesis] involves some degree of conceptual innovation or employments of concepts not found in the characterization of the parts as means of creating the whole.

Accordingly, to achieve such conceptual innovation as was being sought to understand the capital-labour conflict, it was decided to conduct a meta-ethnographical synthesis of existing qualitative case studies, as well as academic papers and grey literature sources, of the historic mining community of Broken Hill in New South Wales. The interpretation of these sources and the encoding of NVivo nodes was aided by culture interpretive theory (CIT), which sought to discern the hidden motivations and "basic underlying assumptions" (Schein, 1992, p. 17) of the main protagonists under consideration. Through the interpretive and systematic comparison of the available monographs and literature sources referring to this community, such a meta-ethnographic synthesis stood to uncover novel insights into the nature and causes of the relentless class warfare that appears to have been an inescapable feature of both mining and industrial enterprises in Australia since earliest times.

3 Methods

Noblit and Hare (1988, p. 27) identified a seven phase procedure in the development of a meta-ethnography, adding that "[i]n practice, the[se] phases overlap and may be parallel". How these seven phases proposed by Noblit and Hare were applied to the meta-ethnography of the selected mining communities is outlined below.

Phase 1: Getting started – The identification of an intellectual interest that qualitative research might inform.

It is scarcely arguable that in human society there has always arisen a minority who have been able to achieve dominance over the majority, who then become subjected under that power imbalance. Nowhere is this more plainly evident than with the emergence of a minority ruling-class capitalism during the Industrial Revolution in England. Such a situation prevailed, scarcely relieved by occasional government intervention, until the working-class was finally able to organise itself into a mass unionism to counter the power of the capitalists. This mass organisation of the working-class was referred to by Polanyi (2001) as a *double-movement*, which he proposed would always emerge in some form whenever the structure of human society was threatened by an unrestrained market.

The meta-ethnography of the Broken Hill mining community explores the continuation of this power struggle as it has played out over the last 135 years in Australia. In this contest, power ascendency has shifted between unions and management several times. At Broken Hill in 1986, judging by subsequent events in Australia, the forces of capitalism delivered a mortal blow from which the ranks of working-class unionism have to date shown no convincing signs of recovery.

Phase 2: Deciding what is relevant to the initial interest – will the research be exhaustive, or will It be targeted by a substantive interest?

The substantive interest of this research is the outworking of the antipathy between capital and labour. Given the implications of this antipathy for the future of industry development and employment in Australia in the twenty-first century and beyond, only monographs and journals which directly address this theme, or aspects of it, were selected to maintain the focus of the research. Ultimately, five books and fourteen journal articles featured predominantly in the final Broken Hill synthesis.

Phase 3: Reading the studies – requires extensive attention to details in the monographs and How They inform Your substantive interests.

Beginning with the earliest publication, each of the books was read closely, recording themes relating to industrial action in the community. The themes were initially arranged in chronological order in Table 1 to give an overall appreciation of the main sequence of events and to ensure that the chronology was preserved in the narrative. Relevant journal articles were added to the table to extend the period of coverage to the present-day, concluding the meta-synthesis. Following this, a more comprehensive analysis of both books and journal articles was undertaken in NVivo, by adopting an inductive approach in the selection of NVivo nodes, which served the purpose of delineating the relevant themes and interpretive metaphors found in the texts. An adherence to the research question during this process ensured that appropriate focus was maintained.

Phase 4: Determining How the studies are related – create a list of the key metaphors, and themes used in Each account and juxtapose Them.

Concurrent with Phase 3 above, the NVivo coding was guided by the research question, here restated for clarity: *What implications might the recurrent and cyclical nature of the tensions between capital and labour hold for the future of industry development and employment in Australia in the twenty-first century and beyond?* Adherence to the research question facilitated the identification of key themes and interpretive metaphors centred around industrial relations in the individual studies which, when combined with data from the chronological tables, allowed the comparison and synthesis of the key themes across the studies (Fig. 1).

There are not a few authors, including Noblit and Hare (1988), in their seminal book, who have appeared to use 'themes', 'concepts', 'key ideas', and 'metaphors' almost interchangeably, and certainly without adequate definition. This paper has regarded 'themes', 'concepts', and 'key ideas' as essentially synonymous, and are defined herein as themes. The relevance and selection of themes were determined by

Table 1 Chronological order of main themes (First page only, 1 of 10; shown for illustration)

	Dale, 1918	Blainey, 1968	Kennedy, 1978	Koenig, 1983	Journal Articles & etc.
1884			Barrier Ranges Miners' Association formed at Silverton "to promote the mining interests of the silver fields by the close union and cooperation amongst the classes ... the absurd antagonism which sometimes appears to exist between labour and capital was positively to be avoided by all"	The BH union movement born at Silverton Sept 20th, 1884 ... public meeting at Adelaide Club hotel resolved "miner's assoc. to be called the Barrier Ranges Miner's Association" ... July 5th, headquarters moved to BH.	(Journal articles take up from 1903)
1885		BHP floated into a public company June 1885. Difficult overland routes from Sydney of 900 miles ... or by steamer to Adelaide 1200 miles then overland 2 days & nights.	Silverton more egalitarian ... the struggle for existence linked men together ... the hub of Barrier unionism moved to BH ... Robert Griffin militant secretary. Survey of April 1, 1886, showed BH had 23 houses, 15 huts, 30 tents, 3 hotels, a store, 2 smithies, and various sheds & stables.	First BHP smelter blown in, May 6th, 1886. Carbonate of lead was the most plentiful ore at BH in the early days ... lead-rich dust carpeted the town ... SA extended the narrow gauge rail to the border ... Silverton Tramway Co extended the line to BH in 1886.	

(continued)

Table 1 (continued)

	Dale, 1918	Blainey, 1968	Kennedy, 1978	Koenig, 1983	Journal Articles & etc.
1887		W H Patton recruited from Nevada . . . most expensive manager . . . repaid his salary many times over in 1st year.	By Oct 1887 BH population of 4–5 K had outstripped Silverton, pop. declined to 1695. Rumoured in late April that BHP was contemplating introducing contract . . . American managers sought . . . hostility to Sydney . . . typhoid 1/3 of deaths	Patton (BHP) introduced the square-set timber method in 1888. Maze of timber became a fire hazard.	
		Silverton Tramway opened in early 1888. Forty-seven hotels in BH . . . dominance of single men			
1889 Union membership	Union membership drive . . . "the usual skull-dragging" . . . many refused . . . Strike on Nov. 7th lasted until 15th Nov . . . booming market – directors recognise compulsory unionism . . . "infringement on the sacred rights of the master class" – would not be tolerated long	"Knowledge of how to minimise lead poisoning, and even how to diagnose it, was still imperfect. How many people died from an overdose of the lead is unknown". Symptoms include lassitude; loss of appetite; weakness of hands, spreading to shoulders and legs . . . effect on nervous system.	Richard Sleath elected president of AMA . . . proposed establishment of 'closed shop' . . . 2500 of 3000 men were unionists . . . hardcore unionists were the underground miners . . . united community behind union . . . in the first 6 months of 1889 more than ¾ of union's expenditure was accident & funeral benefits . . . November strike.	Miners' union claimed 2200 members of 3000 employed at BH . . . First strike for union recognition . . . management agreed to collect dues . . . several non-unionists tarred & feathered.	

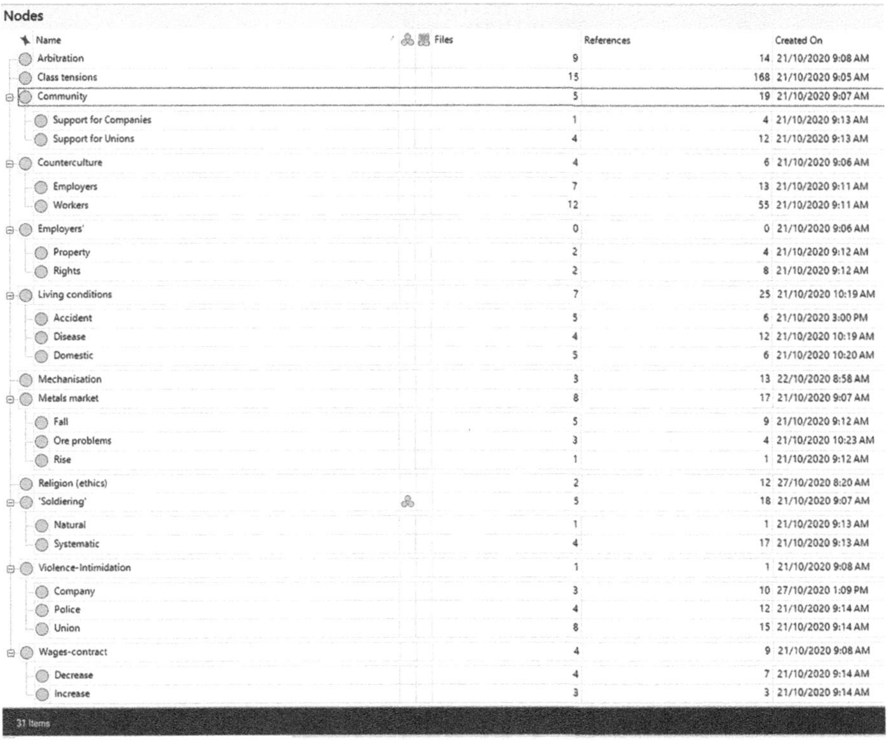

Nodes

Name	Files	References	Created On
Arbitration	9	14	21/10/2020 9:08 AM
Class tensions	15	168	21/10/2020 9:05 AM
Community	5	19	21/10/2020 9:07 AM
Support for Companies	1	4	21/10/2020 9:13 AM
Support for Unions	4	12	21/10/2020 9:13 AM
Counterculture	4	6	21/10/2020 9:06 AM
Employers	7	13	21/10/2020 9:11 AM
Workers	12	55	21/10/2020 9:11 AM
Employers'	0	0	21/10/2020 9:06 AM
Property	2	4	21/10/2020 9:12 AM
Rights	2	8	21/10/2020 9:12 AM
Living conditions	7	25	21/10/2020 10:19 AM
Accident	5	6	21/10/2020 3:00 PM
Disease	4	12	21/10/2020 10:19 AM
Domestic	5	6	21/10/2020 10:20 AM
Mechanisation	3	13	22/10/2020 8:58 AM
Metals market	8	17	21/10/2020 9:07 AM
Fall	5	9	21/10/2020 9:12 AM
Ore problems	3	4	21/10/2020 10:23 AM
Rise	1	1	21/10/2020 9:12 AM
Religion (ethics)	2	12	27/10/2020 8:20 AM
'Soldiering'	5	18	21/10/2020 9:07 AM
Natural	1	1	21/10/2020 9:13 AM
Systematic	4	17	21/10/2020 9:13 AM
Violence-Intimidation	1	1	21/10/2020 9:08 AM
Company	3	10	27/10/2020 1:09 PM
Police	4	12	21/10/2020 9:14 AM
Union	8	15	21/10/2020 9:14 AM
Wages-contract	4	9	21/10/2020 9:08 AM
Decrease	4	7	21/10/2020 9:14 AM
Increase	3	3	21/10/2020 9:14 AM

31 Items

Fig. 2 NVivo screenshot showing nodes used to encode themes and interpretive metaphors identified in the Broken Hill monographs

reference to the research question when reading the texts. Some examples of themes from Fig. 2 are 'Arbitration'; 'Living Conditions'; 'Mechanisation'; 'Metals Market'; 'Violence-Intimidation'; and 'Wages-Contract'.

Interpretive metaphors are less easy to define. Some sources may not contain what might strictly be termed 'metaphors', but for practical purposes this paper has defined metaphors as less constraining than themes, in that nodes, again from Fig. 2, such as 'Class Tensions'; 'Counterculture'; 'Employers Rights'; and 'Soldiering', may each stand for a number of themes that can be aggregated under that metaphorical head. The synthesis occurs as the narrative is constructed by combining the sense and interpretation of the themes and metaphors across the chosen texts, to arrive at the meta-ethnography.

Phase 5: Translating the studies into one Another ... compares Both the metaphors or themes and Their interactions in one account with the metaphors or themes and Their interactions in the other accounts.

Fig. 3 NVivo word clouds enabled visualisation of weighting of metaphors and themes

Concurrent with Phases 3 and 4 above, Phase 5 was substantially enabled by the flexibility of NVivo to handle the data, facilitating the comparison of metaphors and themes across the different authors, as well as providing a range of visual applications of the data (Fig. 3).

Phase 6: Synthesizing translations – making something more Than the parts alone imply.

Phase 7: Expressing the synthesis – choose a form suited to the intended audience, e.g., narrative form for an academic audience?

Phases 6 and 7 evolved during the crafting of the narrative, with reference to the themes and interpretive metaphors that emerged during Phases 4 and 5. Occasional recourse was also taken to period newspaper articles and other relevant grey literature, to enlarge upon themes either barely alluded to, or omitted from the encoded monographs. As the meta-ethnography had a significant temporal extension, continual reference to Table 1 was also required to direct the evolution of the narrative. This permitted the observation of the cycles of industrial unrest, and the circumstances that promoted those cycles. For example, the 1892 timeline of Table 1 (not illustrated in full due to space limitations) indicates in that year the metal market was falling, and that the companies had begun to strike the intractable sulphide ore, placing them in a difficult financial position. Cross-referencing to NVivo reveals George Dales' (1976) observations of the industrial unrest of 1892 under the NVivo 'Wages-Contract' node. Dale also recorded circumstances contributing to the 1892 industrial action which were captured under the 'Class Tensions' node, as did Dickey (1966); Kennedy (1978), and Solomon (1988). Observations by various authors pertaining to the 1892 strike are also to be found under NVivo nodes 'Community-Support for Unions', 'Counterculture', 'Employers-Rights', 'Living Conditions', 'Metals Market', 'Soldiering', 'Violence-Company', and 'Violence-Union', all of which contributed to the crafting of the meta-ethnography. A continual cross-referencing between the Table 1 chronology of events and the NVivo nodes allowed the meta-ethnography to be synthesised in a temporal narrative form spanning 100 years.

4 Broken Hill: The 'Mecca of Unionism'

Broken Hill (Fig. 4) has entered into the folklore of industrial relations in this country as the 'Mecca of Unionism' (Kennedy, 1978). At first take, it may be difficult to understand the reason for the town achieving this sobriquet. Between 1889 and 1920 Broken Hill had just seven significant strike actions, which, outside of the Barrier District itself, inconvenienced the nation very little. By contrast, over

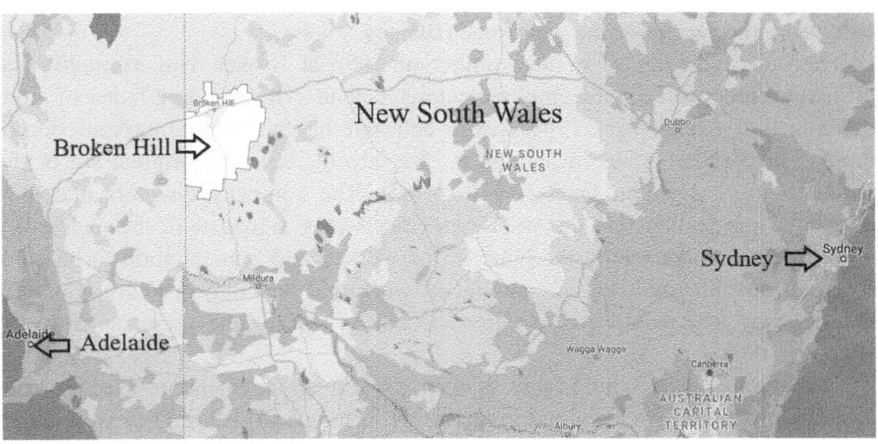

Fig. 4 Broken Hill location. (Map data © 2021 Google)

the same period the coal mining industry, centred at the time in New South Wales, regularly held the entire eastern seaboard of the country to ransom by strike actions that threatened the critical energy supplies of the day (Gibson, 1984). Energy needed for the generation of electricity, heating, and the powering of locomotives and shipping. So disruptive were these strikes that they provided the impetus for Queensland and Victoria to establish independent coal industries (Gibson, 1984).

This paper contends that the seeds of the folklore legend of the 'Mecca of Unionism' were planted in the very significant industrial action which occurred in the town in 1892. This action came in the wake of successful union strikes in 1889, which saw the companies agree to employ only union labour, and in 1890, in which the companies conceded a reduction in hours and agreed to refer any future dispute to arbitration. These successful actions which wrested the balance of power from the companies must have buoyed union spirits substantially. George Dale, in his *Industrial History of Broken Hill* crowed 'thus the Barrier [union] had had its first strike, had badly beaten the boss in eight days, and had won conditions never previously obtaining in this country ...' (1976, p. 11).

5 1892: 'The Great Depression'

By 1892 the companies faced entirely changed circumstances (Blainey, 1968), of which, to judge by their actions, the unions appear to have had little appreciation. The 1890s depression, which was to last most of the decade, had settled on the land. Some scholars have recently considered that this was more severe than the Great Depression of the 1930s (Merrett, 2013). In addition, the companies were beginning to encounter the underlying sulphide ore, which the technology of the time was unable to process (Blainey, 1968). In a bid to reduce costs, the companies, led by BHP, decided to introduce mining by contract. They believed that more men were employed than the work required, but were unwilling to antagonise the workers by reducing either wages or the workforce (Blainey, 1968).

The underlying issues of the conflict of 1892 at Broken Hill exemplify the difficulties inherent in many employment agreements. The founding father of modern industrial management, F. W. Taylor believed that the "conscious restriction of output" or 'soldiering' as he termed it, "has always been the original sin of the working-class" (cited in Davis, 1975, p. 83). The company directors had long harboured the feeling that the wage agreements they signed with the men every 2 years while guaranteeing the hours to be worked and remuneration to be paid, specified no obligation for the amount of work that was due in return. Contract mining, they felt, would give a fairer accounting of the time spent underground (Blainey, 1968).

The unions, quite comfortable in their present arrangement, refused even to consider mining by contract, and immediately went out on strike. They were rather arrogantly confident that they could dictate to the companies the terms under which they would agree to work, as there was no other skilled mining workforce available

("The Great Strike at Broken Hill, 1892"). Their actions belied an understanding of the true situation of unemployment outside of Broken Hill during the depression. In the great cities of the land, suffering as they were under the weight of the depression, there were too many unemployed men glad to find work at much lower wages than the miners of Broken Hill had been paid.

BHP manager John Howell responded to the strike by sacking the entire unionised workforce. He replaced them with labour contracted from the Melbourne firm of Baxter & Sadler which he turned to open-cut mining at the top of the lode ("The Labour War at the Barrier, 1892"). BHP director John Darling vowed to devote his life to the beating out of unionism (Dale, 1976). Three thousand unionists were blacklisted by the companies with no option but to leave the town to look for work elsewhere. Just how comfortable the miners had been with their previous arrangement is indicated by John Howell's boast a few months later that "we have extracted 22,000 tons more of ore, with just under 40% less men" (Kennedy, 1978, p. 71).

In this action, the balance of power returned to the companies and would largely remain with them until the Big Strike of 1919–20. This was the source of the bitterness that the unions felt towards BHP, which eventually spread to include all of the companies. Radicals and militants from all over Australia flocked to the Mecca of Unionism, attracted by the opportunity to bring down the upstart BHP.

These events at Broken Hill were just a microcosm of what was occurring around Australia during the 1890s depression as employers attacked the hard-won conditions of workers around the country. The Queensland shearers dispute looked like descending into a country-wide civil war as the squatters armed themselves. They would rather shoot unionists than pay them a living wage (Spence, 2013). Back in Broken Hill, violence was barely avoided when the managers armed themselves and their supervisors while having the police confiscate firearms from the local rifle club premises (Dale, 1976).

At Federation, the national government was so alarmed at this narrow escape from anarchy that it moved to institute protectionism in the form of compulsory arbitration to ensure workers would receive a living wage. Manufacturer's profits were to be guaranteed by a system of import tariffs and duties (Kelly, 1994). Just when it seemed that Polanyi's *double-movement* protection in the form of working-class unionism had failed, other forces in society had moved to avoid social destruction.

6 Collins House

Although there were a further three strikes by the Broken Hill unions in the intervening period, it was not until the Big Strike of 1919–20 that the balance of power could be said to have returned decisively to the unions. In the interim, BHP, with its ore supply almost exhausted and able to work only when markets were favourable, had surrendered leadership on the field to the Collins House group of mines which were finally becoming profitable (Blainey, 1968). BHP would never again rise to the prominence in Broken Hill that it had once enjoyed. Its future lay in steelmaking, and it would retire from the field disillusioned by the militant unionism that it had done so much to promote.

The Collins House group favoured a more conciliatory approach to managing their workforce over the confrontational approach adopted by BHP. This had already produced favourable results at their Port Pirie smelters, and they hoped the same would be well received at Broken Hill. Unfortunately, by this time the Broken Hill miners were so far alienated that they viewed the conciliatory policies as, in the words of Kennedy (1978, p. 161) "delusions, palliatives, sops, and doles; for them nothing less than the complete overthrow of capitalism could emancipate the class-conscious worker".

7 The Big Strike

The Big Strike, which was to last for 18 months, began after the collapse of negotiations for the 1919 employment agreement. Cyril Emery, the current Mining Manager's Association president chairing the meeting, was a throwback to the confrontational BHP style of management. Arguing the merits of a good long strike, he stated that "once Broken Hill men owned the earth they would clamour for the moon" (Kennedy, 1978, p. 148). His attitude only hardened the miner's resolve, and the union leaders readied for a protracted and bitter strike.

As negotiations to end the strike reached an impasse the Collins House directors took the lead, inviting union leaders to a Melbourne conference. It was here that they learned, to their complete surprise, of the health issues that were foremost in the miner's claims for a 35 hour week. A subsequent inquiry, examining the health of almost four thousand miners revealed the prevalence of disease and disability induced by the working and living conditions at Broken Hill (Kennedy, 1978).

The settlement of the Big Strike in 1921 was a high point in the union's long struggle for recognition of the difficulties of living and working in remote Broken Hill. Disease affected miners were retired with a lump sum compensation of £2000. A 35 hour week was awarded for all underground men, and the night shift was abolished. The miners had won some of the best working conditions in Australia, but this would come at a significant cost to the companies (Blainey, 1968).

8 The Big Easy: The Lead Bonus

In 1925, in a bid to forestall a further campaign for higher wages and shorter hours from a resurgent union in a booming metal market, the Collins House directors agreed to introduce a lead bonus payment. This was to be indexed to the prevailing market price of lead. After the failure of their welfare initiatives, the directors hoped that this might re-acculturate workers to a more harmonious commitment to company objectives (Shields, 1997). In this, they were doomed to be disappointed.

As the Great Depression of the 1930s began to ease, the miners' union instituted restrictive job-control measures. Prominent among these was a ban on the employment of anyone who had not been born in Broken Hill or had lived within a 100-mile mile radius for at least 8 years. Extra-union, communist-inspired 'job committees' also used go-slow tactics to force increases in contract rates. Restrictive staffing levels were enforced, such as the rule of 'two men, one machine' (Shields, 1997). Such job-control measures were doubtless, union attempts at maintaining employment levels in the face of the increasing mechanisation beginning to be introduced throughout the 1930s. Once again, as in 1892, the union was presuming to dictate to the companies how they might manage their business.

Leading up to the Second World War, Broken Hill had been transitioning from manual mining techniques to more mechanised ore retrieval. The hand drills had long been replaced by compressed air drills. Picks and shovels were now being replaced by mechanical loaders and underground diesel and electric locomotives, allowing for much greater tonnages of ore to be handled. Despite these innovations, however, productivity per man continued to decrease post-war, and bargaining power remained firmly with the unions (Shields, 1997).

While the mining industry has often cited worker safety as one of the principal reasons for introducing mechanisation (Stewart, 2015), it is logical that capitalist owners will only introduce mechanised methods if doing so is profitable (Mahnkopf, 2019). Not so readily admitted behind the drive for mechanisation in mining is the desire to reduce a troublesome labour force as far as possible (Stewart, 2015). Frustrating this motivation of the Collins House directors at Broken Hill were the job-control and restrictive work practices of the miners, who also began to moderate their work effort in response to a steep rise in the lead bonus. By the late 1940s, the price of lead had boomed so that the lead bonus constituted as much as half of a miner's take-home pay (Shields, 1997).

Contract mining had been introduced at Broken Hill in 1892 precisely in a bid to counter the 'systematic soldiering' that the managers believed had been occurring under conditions of waged mining. At the time it resulted in a greatly increased output per man, but with the affluent pay conditions resulting from a runaway lead bonus in the 1950s, the problem of systematic soldiering had obviously re-emerged. Despite this evident disadvantage of the lead bonus, in a booming market the companies were able to absorb the increased labour costs and were reluctant to provoke a confrontation that might lead to strike action and a consequent reduction in profits.

9 CRA: A Final Reckoning

After 1952, the Collins House companies were superseded by new mining conglomerates such as Conzinc Riotinto Australia (CRA), who favoured a partial reversion to a more confrontational and 'Taylorist' style of management. In the mid-1970s, ongoing technological development underpinned the first sustained increase in productivity since the 1950s. This, despite a steady decline in workforce numbers, achieved predominantly by voluntary redundancy. The further decline in workforce numbers that accompanied the adoption of mechanised long-hole stoping in the CRA mines also contributed to a weakening of union influence (Shields, 1997). Such technology-labour substitution was to set the stage for a later offensive by CRA against restrictive union work practices.

In the decade after the first OPEC oil price shock of 1973, Australian mining industries faced heavy price competition for exports in a world that was becoming increasingly connected in the process of globalisation. The CRA company, with mining operations in Western Australia and Queensland as well as Broken Hill, had been undergoing a decade of management restructuring under the guidance of CEO Roderick Carnegie, to enable the company to meet the challenges of globalisation. Chief among Carnegie's concerns was the inefficiency of the workforce and the high level of industrial conflict at some of the company's operations (McKinnon, 2007). By the end of 1985, the company was preparing to test the mettle of Australian mining unions at that 'Mecca of Unionism', Broken Hill.

In February 1986, CRA made the shock announcement that their Broken Hill mining and processing operations were no longer profitable under present conditions and would close the following week. The city's fourth major mine, North Broken Hill Limited announced shortly afterwards that it also would be retrenching part of its workforce. The total workforce across the four mines was 3010 workers. The registered association of Broken Hill mine managers, the MMA, subsequently served a log of claims on the unions, citing 63 restrictive work practices as contributing to low productivity, making the companies uncompetitive on world markets (Flynn, 1988).

The unions, unaware that the companies intended to replace previous contract agreements with an award, presented at the conciliation conference convened by Justice Fisher prepared only to discuss the dispute. They had no legal representation, and no prepared evidence to counter the companies' well supported legal submissions to substantiate their claims. Part of the evidence presented by the companies compared production at Broken Hill at 1100 tons per employee per annum, with production at Cobar at 3200 tons per employee per annum. The unions were unable to counter this submission. Justice Fisher's recommendation that the unions accept the companies' log of claims was rejected by the unions, leading the companies to apply for arbitration and the granting of an award (Flynn, 1988).

At the subsequent arbitration hearing, again convened by Justice Fisher, the unions were represented by the general secretary of the Miners Federation, a part-time law student. The companies were represented by a Queen's Counsel, a barrister, and a solicitor. Counsel for the unions, unable to counter the companies' statement as to their financial position, was criticised by Justice Fisher for the lack of evidence to support the unions' position when he subsequently handed down the Metalliferous Mining (Broken Hill) Interim Award in May 1986 (Flynn, 1988).

Of all the industrial actions in the long history of Broken Hill, two stand out as a signal lesson in industrial relations for both unions and companies. In 1892, amid a global recession, a haughty and disdainful union thought to dictate to the companies the terms under which they would agree to carry out their work. Again in 1986, a union grown fat on the lead bonus thought by restrictive practices to circumscribe a company's prerogative in managing its business. In doing so, on each occasion, the union made the mistake to its ultimate cost, of not appreciating the changed international circumstances and conditions of profitability in which the companies were operating.

10 Mining the Future

Six months after the Broken Hill dispute began, in July of 1986, in what cannot be considered mere coincidence, mining company Peko Wallsend, soon to be known as 'North Broken Hill Peko Ltd.', also served a log of claims on its troublesome unionised workforce at the Robe River iron ore operations in the Pilbara District of Western Australia. The protracted legal dispute which followed became the basis for the de-unionisation of the Pilbara iron ore industry, and the beginning of a new era of industrial relations in Australia (Ellem, 2015). At the time of writing in 2021, there has been no indication of a resurgence of Polanyi's *double-movement* in favour of the dispossessed working-class. Capital, for its part, continues to move relentlessly closer to full automation of its mining operations in Australia.

11 Conclusion

This paper has employed a meta-ethnographical synthesis of the literature relating to the historic mining community of Broken Hill in New South Wales to explore the capital labour conflict which appears to be inherent in industry in the Western world. Tracing the cyclical fortunes of the capital-labour conflict through the lens of the mining industry in this district, the study, aided by Culture Interpretive Theory (CIT), outlines implications for industry development, employment, and community sustainability in a future Australia, finding evidence that capitalism may be finally ridding itself of the need for the working-class.

Polanyi's *double-movement* thesis in *The Great Transformation* has experienced something of a resurgence of interest among contemporary scholars (Lacher, 1999). As present-day dilemmas facing a globalising society begin to echo the events leading up to the First World War, the Great Depression, and the rise of Fascism, it is as though Polanyi is speaking directly to present-day issues. Although in penning *The Great Transformation* in 1944, Polanyi may not have envisaged the disruptive power capable of being wielded by a militant and powerful union, he does seem to have anticipated that the *double-movement* could be a two-edged sword. He stated that even capitalists had been involved at times in efforts to increase the stability of society (Polanyi, 2001), a fact that contemporary scholars may not have fully appreciated.

This study illustrates unequivocally that the *double-movement* as conceived by Polanyi is not intrinsically a movement of social forces against the excesses of capitalism. It may rather take the form of a social movement against the excessive use of coercive power in society, from whichever direction it might arise. As capitalism closes in on its goal of fully automated mining operations in the Pilbara, such a realisation, although too late for the mining communities and unions of the Pilbara District, portends ominously for working communities and the future of industry employment across Australia.

References

Barbalet, J. M. (1986). Limitations of class theory and the disappearance of status: The problem of the new middle class. *Sociology, 20*(4), 557–575.

Blainey, G. (1968). *The rise of Broken Hill*. Macmillan.

Bottero, W. (2004). Class identities and the identity of class. *Sociology, 38*(5), 985–1003.

Dale, G. (1976). *The industrial history of Broken Hill*. Adelaide.

Davis, M. (1975). The stop watch and the wooden shoe: Scientific management and the industrial workers of the world. *Radical America, 9*(1), 69–95.

Dickey, B. (1966). The Broken Hill Strike, 1892. *Labour History, 11*, 40–53.

Ellem, B. (2015). Robe River revisited: Geohistory and industrial relations. *Labour History: A Journal of Labour and Social History, 109*(1), 111–131.

Flynn, B. (1988). Trade unions and the law: The Broken Hill dispute. *Journal of Industrial Relations, 30*(1), 32–53.

Gibson, K. D. (1984). Industrial reorganisation and coal production in Australia, 1860–1982: An historical materialist analysis. *Australian Geographical Studies, 22*(2), 221–242.

Kelly, P. (1994). *The end of certainty: Power, politics and business in Australia*. Allen and Unwin.

Kennedy, B. (1978). *Silver, sin, and sixpenny ale: A social history of Broken Hill*. Melbourne University Press.

Koenig, K. (1983). *Broken Hill: 100 years of mining*. NSW Department of Mineral Resources.

Lacher, H. (1999). The politics of the market: Re-reading Karl Polanyi. *Global Society, 13*(3), 313–326.

Mahnkopf, B. (2019). *The '4th wave of industrial revolution' - A promise blind to social consequences, power and ecological impact in the era of 'digital capitalism'* (No. 01). EuroMemo Group. Discussion Paper.

McKinnon, B. H. (2007). *Behind workchoices: How one company changed Australia's industrial relations*. Heidelberg Press.

Merrett, D. T. (2013). The Australian bank crashes of the 1890s revisited. *Business History Review, 87*(3), 407–429.

Noblit, G., & Hare, R. (1988). *Meta-ethnography: Synthesizing qualitative studies*. Sage.

Polanyi, K. (2001). *The great transformation*. Beacon Press.

Schein, E. H. (1992). *Organizational culture and leadership*. Jossey-Bass.

Shields, J. (1997). 'Lead bonus happy': Profit–sharing, productivity and industrial relations in the Broken Hill mining industry, 1925–83. *Australian Economic History Review, 37*(3), 222–255.

Solomon, R. J. (1988). *The richest lode: Broken Hill 1883–1988*. Hale & Ironmonger Pty. Limited.

Spence, W. G. (2013). *History of the AWU*. Melbourne University Press.

Steward, J. (1972). *Theory of culture change: The methodology of multilinear evolution*. Chicago University Press.

Stewart, P. (2015). Accelerated mechanisation and the demise of a mass-based labour force? Platinum mines in South Africa. *Review of African Political Economy, 42*(146), 633–642.
Tajfel, H. (1970). Experiments in intergroup discrimination. *Scientific American, 223*(5), 96–103.
Taylor, W. W. (1948). A study of archaeology. *American Anthropologist, 50*(3), 5–202.
The Great Strike at Broken Hill. (1892, July 21). *Bendigo Independent*, p. 4.
The Labour War at the Barrier. (1892, September 12). *Melbourne Herald*, p. 1.

Integrated Risk Management, a Conduit to Building Resilient and Sustainable Local Government Communities: A Scoping Review

Christina Rutendo Mushaya, Taha Chaiechi, and Josephine Pryce

Abstract The management of risk and its integration with business strategy (corporate plan) and performance is important to building resilient and sustainable local communities. Local Governments fulfil a series of vital roles worldwide. There has been increasing recognition of the need to implement holistic and integrated Enterprise Risk Management (ERM) approaches, given that risk is an unavoidable occurrence. At the same time, there has been a drive towards evidence-based practice, which has led to scoping reviews, a relatively new approach to the literature review. Of interest was Arksey & O'Malley's (Int J Soc Res Methodol 8(1):19–32, 2005) framework that provided a distinctive process to follow given that ERM is a broad and multidisciplinary topic, where different organisations are applying many different risk standards.

The authors used One Search and Google Scholar electronic databases and Google search engine to search for relevant studies using search terms, which resulted in 1690 studies. Some inclusion and exclusion criteria were applied to narrow the search results. 210 studies were found to be eligible to be included in the scoping review. The authors complemented the scoping review with thematic analysis of those selected studies using NVivo 12 Plus, and results were synthesised using Excel.

The paper finds that only 2% of studies were published concerning risk management at Local Government levels. The paper also finds that while there has been an increase in the number of publications in ERM between 2010 and 2020, research appears to be more interested in the integration of ERM than the traditional silo approaches to managing risk.

It appears risk management is a "tick in a box exercise" where risk management processes are not significantly integrated into the delivery of strategic goals that, in

C. R. Mushaya (✉) · T. Chaiechi · J. Pryce
College of Business, Law and Governance, James Cook University, Townsville, QLD, Australia
e-mail: christina.mushaya@my.jcu.edu.au; taha.chaiechi@jcu.edu.au; josephine.pryce@jcu.edu.au

© The Author(s), under exclusive license to Springer Nature Singapore Pte Ltd. 2022
T. Chaiechi, J. Wood (eds.), *Community Empowerment, Sustainable Cities, and Transformative Economies*, https://doi.org/10.1007/978-981-16-5260-8_28

turn, benefits communities. Research gaps indicate the need to establish a methodology to integrate ERM with strategy and performance as three concepts in a Local Government setting.

Keywords Scoping review · Enterprise Risk Management (ERM) · Local government · NVivo · Thematic analysis

1 Background

Enterprise Risk Management (ERM) is a significant factor that affects organisational strategies such as sustainability initiatives and performance, which are important to building resilient and sustainable local communities (Chen et al., 2020; Cokins, 2009; Hoyt & Liebenberg, 2011; Shad et al., 2019). Local Governments fulfil a series of vital roles worldwide to their citizens, from remote towns to capital cities (Brunet-Jailly & Martin, 2017). They are representative of communities and deliver the Governments' priorities, locally and regionally (Dollery et al., 2006). The role of Local Government can be classified into four goals of economic sustainability, social sustainability, environmental sustainability, and responsible governance referred to as the Quadruple Bottom Line by Alibasic (2018). "Sustainability risk management requires holistic and systematic integration of ecological, socioeconomic, and corporate risk factors" (Yilmaz & Flouris, 2010, p. 162; Hanggraeni et al., 2019; Mauelshagen et al., 2014). However, ineffective ways of managing risk create problems in both the administration and performance of organisations, inclusive of the Local Government (Abuzarqa, 2019; Oulasvirta & Anttiroiko, 2017; Sharma & Gadenne, 2011; QAO, 2019).

There is increasing recognition of the need to manage risk, given that risk is inherent to all functions of a business and is unavoidable (Acharyya, 2008; Meyer et al., 2017; Tekathen & Dechow, 2013; Saguil et al., 2008). Risk management practices have been evolving over the years (Crockford, 1982). Tools to build resilience to external shocks and disasters are becoming important in most Local Governments. Resilient communities are seen to be those that quickly bounce back to their pre-crisis state (Platts-Fowler et al., 2016). However, the complex environment and tremendous advances in technology and processes have contributed to a more dynamic and challenging environment, as organisations continue to be exposed to unanticipated risks that affect performance (Bhaumik et al., 2017; Pelling et al., 2004). Such challenges have encouraged organisations to continuously adjust their scope of risk (Choi et al., 2016; Soltanizadeh et al., 2016). The need to improve ways of managing risk has led to the introduction of Enterprise Risk Management (ERM), a holistic and integrated approach to managing positive (opportunities) and negative (threats) risk (Arena et al., 2010; Bharathy & McShane 2014; Chen et al., 2019; Choi et al., 2016; Khan, 2016; Lam, 2014). Simultaneously, there is also a drive towards evidence-based practice, which has led scholars to adopt different literature review approaches for their studies (Snyder, 2019).

With that introduction in mind, this paper aims at understanding and synthesising knowledge by mapping key concepts and evidence about integrated ERM. Gaps in how ERM is integrated with strategy and performance are identified. Generating outcomes and impact beyond the walls of academia is what the researchers are aiming for. Senior management and staff in Local Government, policymakers, independent assurance, and statutory bodies may leverage findings to institute change in how risk is managed in Local Government.

Of interest in this study is the scoping review. Scoping studies have been used across a range of disciplines for a wide variety of purposes (Anderson et al., 2008; Moher et al., 2009; Peters et.al., 2015; Tricco et al., 2016). While approaches to the literature review are named differently, generally, they have common characteristics: collecting, evaluating, and presenting the available research evidence (Arksey & O'Malley, 2005; Levac et al., 2010). Accordingly, the layout of this paper is as follows. The second section introduces the methodology where the importance of qualifying criteria used for the study and the scoping review protocol with six stages are discussed. The third section presents and discusses the study results. The conclusions of this study are given in section four.

2 Method

Arksey and O'Malley (2005) are the first scholars to propose a protocol for a scoping review of the literature. This scoping review will follow the methodological six stages, given that Arksey and O'Malley's (2005) work has been cited over 7000 times.

While scoping reviews are a relatively new approach to literature review (Munn et al., 2018), a scoping review is the most appropriate approach to use for this study given that Enterprise Risk Management (ERM) is a broad and multidisciplinary topic, where many different risk standards are being applied by different organisations of any type, size, or industry (Haimes, 2009; ISO, 2018).

2.1 *Importance of Qualifying Criteria*

According to Patino and Ferreira (2018), establishing inclusion and exclusion criteria is a standard practice that is important when designing high-quality research in academia. Following Chaiechi (2020), who details apriori protocol, including specific inclusion and exclusion criteria, this study established a set of qualifying criteria to assist with search results and screening. These qualifying criteria are listed in Table 1 below.

Table 1 Inclusions and exclusions table

Criteria	Inclusions	Exclusions
Language	English	Non-English sources
Publication dates	Between 1980 and 2020	Before 1980
Country of publication	Any studies with depth relevant to titles and abstracts regardless of country of publication	Studies that seem not to be authentic
Relevance	Relevance in titles and abstracts and/full articles: Enterprise risk management, organisational performance, corporate strategy, and Local Government	If the title and abstract are outside this range
Access	Accessible studies	Broken links
		Removed content
Publications	Reputable publishers and websites: experienced in the field with an objective view of the study area	Lack of reputation or experience in the field, specifically on google
Document type	Citable studies such as Academic Journal articles, conference papers, books, Local Government, and leading organisations reports (grey literature)	Drafts or work in progress
	Full-text documents	Local Government policies and frameworks, blogs, commercial type
		Abstract-only papers
Additions:		
Models through subscription	ISO 31000 (2018) and COSO (2017)	Risk standards not relevant to Local Government
Websites	Local Government Websites, e.g., The Department of Local Government, Racing and Multicultural Affairs.	All other Government websites
	Local Government Association of Australia	

Source: Authors generated

2.2 *The Protocol*

Arksey and O'Malley (2005) develop a six-stage methodological framework that is iterative rather than linear. Researchers are encouraged to engage with each stage intuitively and, where necessary, repeat steps such that the literature is covered comprehensively.

Stage 1: Identifying the Guiding Question

Identifying the guiding question is the first stage of the framework. A pilot search is an important process to identify clearly defined but not too focused guiding search questions or phrases. A pilot search using different phrases and search questions is conducted. This review is guided by the following guiding questions:

- How can key concepts and evidence on Enterprise Risk Management be integrated with strategy and performance to be a conduit for resilience and sustainability in Local Government?
- Can senior management and staff in Local Government, policymakers, independent assurance, and statutory bodies leverage on research findings to institute change on how risk is integrated into Local Government, such that impact beyond the walls of academia is generated?

The search query consist of terms considered by the authors to describe the scoping review.

"Enterprise Risk Management, strategy, and performance in Local Government" search terms are used to yield focused results given that ERM is a broad and multidisciplinary topic. This understanding is consistent with the literature by Colquhoun et al. (2014) that the search question or terms must be clearly defined as they play an important role to shape the study and in all subsequent stages, including search strategy. While limits are applied to conduct a search aligned to "Local Government" in the search phrase, the other common forms of Local Government terms, such as Local Authorities and Cities, are also co-opted in an Advanced Search. While Stage 1 helps to identify the search terms for this research, it is also aimed at including ways to draw as many relevant studies as possible into the search results.

Stage 2: Identifying Relevant Studies
This stage allows for search limits to be applied using the inclusion and exclusion criteria. Reflecting time and countries of publication were important criteria included, where a broad and generous approach versus a narrow and restrictive approach is undertaken. Publications with relevance to the study, regardless of country, published between 1980 and 2020 are considered. This is because there seems not to be many Local Government studies in the academic realm. This approach is seen to complement Arksey and O'Malley's (2005) recommendation of tapping into as many relevant studies as possible for the under-researched area. Only material published in English was included.

One Search and Google Scholar electronic databases and Google search engine are identified as sources that are most likely to produce the type of studies the research is seeking. One Search yields 500 search results, and Google Scholar yields 980 results, giving a total of 1440 studies. Google search engine is used to access grey literature and yielded 210 documents, including government reports. A total of 1690 are identified as potentially relevant studies made available for a detailed study selection.

Stage 3: Study Selection
The first level of screening is conducted using relevant titles and abstracts and 965 results are excluded from the study. The remaining 725 citations are imported into the Endnote library, a Citation Management System. A query in Endnote is conducted to exclude 92 duplicate studies and the remaining 633 studies were exported into an Excel workbook file. The second level of comprehensive screening

is then conducted. Any abstracts with broken links to full text, work in progress documents, commercial material, and Local Government policies are excluded from the study. This detailed process excludes a total of 397 studies, retaining 236 studies for a subsequent review based on the full-text reading. While reading the full text, a further 33 studies are excluded based on the overall quality of study and outcomes not relevant to the study, leaving 203 studies. To align the process in this study to Arksey and O'Malley (2005), where processes are not linear, citations for the 33 excluded studies are deleted in Endnote and Excel workbook as they were now irrelevant to the study. A post hoc inclusion and exclusion criteria can be applied to add more studies based on familiarity with the subject matter through reading the studies (Colquhoun et al., 2014). Risk Management Standards are subscribed to and government departments are added to access relevant Local Government reports. Based on this additional inclusion criteria, seven studies are included, giving a total of 210 studies to be charted before informing the literature review process.

Stage 4: Charting the Data

At this stage, decisions about the type of information that needs to be extracted and recorded from the primary studies are made. This is the stage where the variables to be used to extract information that answers the guiding question are determined (Arksey & O'Malley, 2005; Colquhoun et al., 2014; Levac et al., 2010). The spreadsheet holds information such as author, year of publication, title, abstract, discipline area, and key takings from the full text. On the other hand, NVivo has features useful to support the qualitative data analysis using organised categories of references, referred to as "nodes". Nodes allow for information to be organised into themes (discussed under Thematic Presentations).

Stage 5: Collating, Summarising, and Reporting the Results

This stage involves collating, summarising, and reporting the results of the scoping review. Results should be seen to be answering the guiding question (Daudt et al., 2013). A range of data and information contributed to satisfy a varied range of areas of interest, making it easier to envisage the desired trends to the study, as the similarities and differences started to show. This is the stage that allows for analytics and thematic processes to provide an overview of the breadth of the literature. In this study, both numerical analyses using tables and charts, and qualitative analysis were presented using information that was collated and analysed. A thematic analysis was presented using information that was collected mostly in NVivo and the data from the spreadsheet was quantified to produced graphs and charts.

Stage 6: Consultation (Optional)

The consultation stage is an optional stage that provides stakeholder involvement opportunities to suggest additional references and provide insights beyond those in the literature (Arksey & O'Malley, 2005). While this is optional and has not been used in this study due to time constraints, it is recommended to inform future studies. It is put forward that findings from stage 5 are used for consultation with independent assurance and statutory bodies and government entities such as the Audit Office.

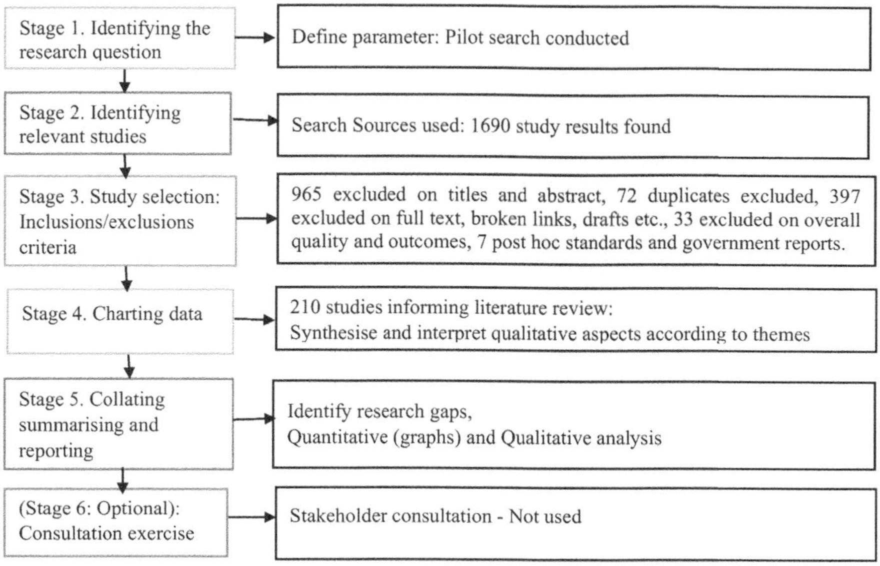

Fig. 1 Flow of information through the different stages of a scoping review. (Source: Adapted Arksey & O'Malley's 2005)

Figure 1 below summarises an explicit yet rigorous approach that is applied in the various stages to increase the reliability of the scoping review process. It also highlights the multi-step approach taken to compile the appropriate search terms, inclusion, and exclusion criteria to meet the research protocol.

3 Results and Discussion

3.1 Mapping the Research Landscape

Studies have been mapped according to the discipline in which the studies were carried out. As observed in Fig. 2 below, of the sample of 210 studies, the two major disciplines of the literature were Banking, Finance, and Insurance (21%) and the supply chain (18%). 16% of the studies were just discussed in general, an undesirable state that should encourage more research in the academic realm targeted at specific industries. Only 2% of the studies were published relating to Local Government.

While it was encouraging to find some studies published relating to Local Government, this is the discipline with the lowest empirical studies out of the sample followed by the public sector in general. Evidence shows that there is a dire need for case studies in Local Government regarding how risk management can be integrated

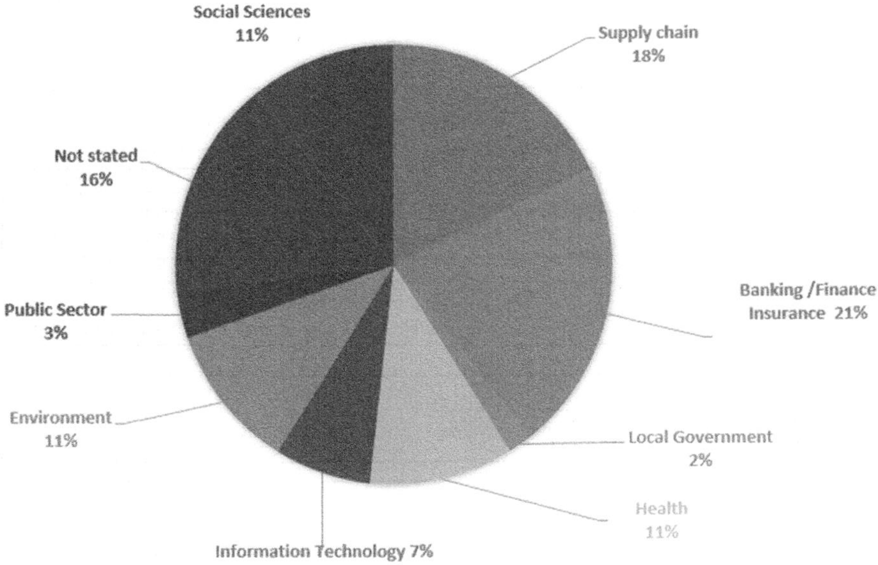

Fig. 2 Disciplines of publications in integrated enterprise risk management

with strategy and performance to achieve corporate objectives that have a flow-on effect to sustain local communities.

These findings are in line with reported significant deficiencies of the Local Government, which requires the need to improve how risk is being managed such as, The Local Government Risk Report for Australian Local Government by Aon (2018), revealed how more than 50% of all Australian local councils are failing to execute practices to "rein in" some of their greatest risks (Aon, 2018). According to Climate Council (2017), while local councils and their communities are considered leading State and Federal Governments in tackling climate change, they are at risk of worsening climate impacts such as rising sea levels, floods, pollution, and bushfires. Studies specific to local councils will help establish effective ways to mitigate these risks.

The review considers the trend in published content on the transition of risk from a silo approach to a more holistic and integrated approach to managing risk. A notable finding in Fig. 3 is that researchers are now more interested in integrating ERM with governance processes including strategy and performance, from around 2000, which saw a drastic decline in risk discussed as a silo approach. Although the concept of ERM has existed for a number of years, it is still in its progressive mode (Kerstin et al., 2014; Lin et al., 2012; Lundqvist, 2014, 2015; Meulbroek, 2002; Razali & Tahir, 2011; Sarker et al., 2016). The evidence clearly shows the need for more empirical studies in the academic realm regarding an integrated ERM.

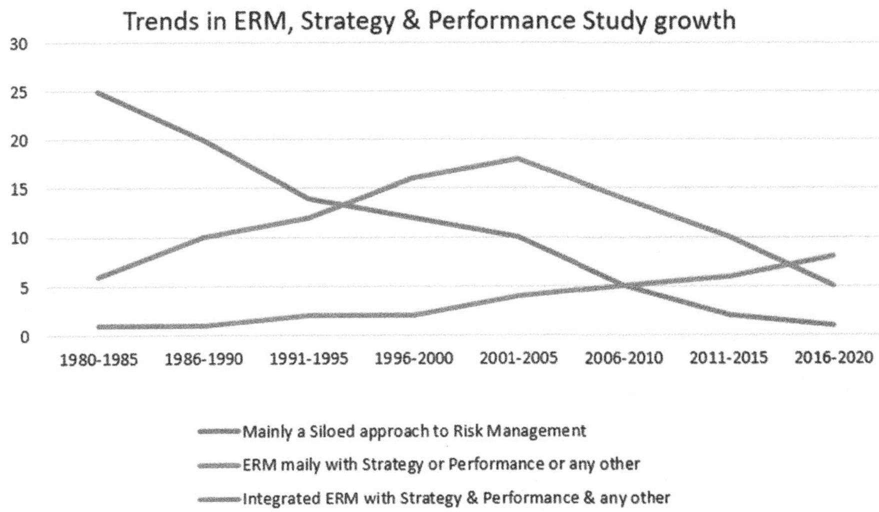

Fig. 3 Articles showing the progressive nature from a siloed to an integrated ERM approach

3.2 Gaps Identification

The scoping review identified four important study gaps: unclear integration of risk management processes, an unclear process that can be used to cascading long term strategy, no overarching legislative mandate to implement Risk Appetite Statements (RAS) and risk frameworks, and lack of methodology to integrate the three concepts of risk management, strategy, and performance. NVivo Nodes (discussed later under Thematic Presentations) have let the researchers gather related material in one place to allow for the identification of emerging patterns and ideas. The analysis of NVivo nodes assisted in identifying the gap in the literature regarding the integrated relationship in all three concepts of risk management, strategy, and performance. These study gaps are of concern given that Local Governments fulfil a series of vital roles worldwide to their citizens (Brunet-Jailly & Martin, 2017). How will then, resilient and sustainable Local Government communities be established on an unstable foundation? The study gaps are depicted in Fig. 4 and elaborated in the following sections.

3.3 Study Gap 1: Integration of Risk Management with Strategy and Performance

While there are important aspects of Enterprise Risk Management (ERM) and its integration, there are some gaps in the existing body of risk management research. Leading scholars (Bromiley et al., 2015; Cooper et al., 2019; Hardy, 2014;

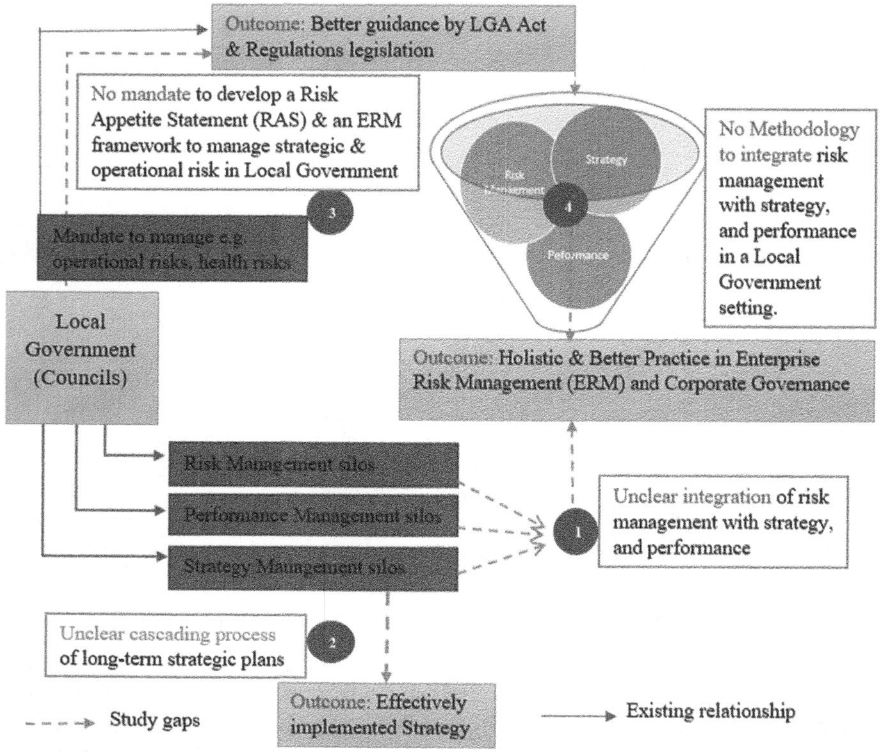

Fig. 4 Overview of study gaps. (Source: Authors generated)

Soltanizadeh et al., 2016) discuss the importance of ERM and its maturity over the years but there seems to be no written application integrating all the three concepts of risk management, strategy, and performance in a Local Government setting. There is clear evidence of the three concepts discussed separately or with one other concept, such as Ben-Amar et al. (2014) discusses the link between the firm's corporate strategic choices and its risk management approach while Lam (2014) concentrates on the effective enterprise risk management practices and Cooper et al. (2019) explores risk management critical success factors to municipalities.

Some articles did discuss the interrelatedness of risk management such as Rehman & Anwar, (2019) and Soltanizadeh et al. (2016) that focuses on the influence of business strategy on ERM adoption and organisational performance in the public sector while Oulasvirta and Anttiroiko, (2017) discusses comprehensive ERM in Local Government. Abolfazli (2019) discusses the relationship between main dimensions in the strategy-making process, environmental complexity, and performance. There has been a little reference in specifying how the concepts of risk, strategy, and performance can be integrated, yet it is such an important concept to holistically manage interrelated risk processes because no matter the size or maturity of the local council, communities still expect effective governance processes that create sustainability and resilience around them (Hastings et al., 2016). The scoping review revealed the fact that holistic approaches to managing risk create and protect value, which makes it important to effectively manage risk (Abrams et al., 2007; Beasley et al., 2007; Choi et al., 2016; Shad et al., 2019; Viscelli et al., 2016)

3.4 Study Gap 2: Process to Cascade/Deploy a Long-Term Strategic Plan

Strategic planning is one of the critical means for organisations to achieve their set vision, mission and strategic goals (Achampong, 2010; Bowman et al., 2001; Berry, 1994; Epstein & Manzoni, 1998; Feldman, 2020). All local councils in Australia have a long-term strategic planning document to meet the legislative requirement. However, the scoping review uncovers that there is no documented process guiding organisations and Local Governments on how to effectively align or cascade long-term strategic plans to short-term operational plans and effectively report quarterly and annually to the community. Some articles discuss performance indicators such as Brusca et al. (2016) and Ryan et al. (2002), reveal that performance reporting has been introduced as a mechanism to control local government activities to enhance performance. Anchor et al. (2015); Kaplan & Norton (1996) and Kloot & Martin (2000) support the scoping review results that there should be a strong linkage between strategic plans and performance measures, both financial and non financial. However, studies on performance reporting seem not to reflect a spread-out achievement of commitments in a fashion that reflects the link and achievement of the long-term strategy.

3.5 Study Gap 3: Legislated Mandate to ERM Implementation

Some studies from the scoping review concentrated on reporting requirements such as Montesinos et al. (2013) discussed the mandatory requirements from the central government for organisations to adopt performance indicators that they report on. There is no explicit mandate for the Local Government to develop an ERM framework, a Risk Appetite Statement (RAS) representing risk taken to assume consistently with its strategy and its related risk tolerances as processes that anchor implementation of ERM (Cremonino, 2011; Davison, 2011; Fehring, 2018; Qadan & Idilbi-Bayaa, 2020; Segal, 2006). The legislation only gives a mandate for the annual operational plan to state how the Local Government manages operational risk. The legislation does not define or differentiate strategic from operational risk, nor does it consider emerging risks. Current legislation does not enforce the existence and implementation of a conceptual guiding framework and RAS and yet their absence supports the argument by Oulasvirta and Anttiroiko, (2017) that, if ERM is not obligatory, it is not widely used in Local Government.

3.6 Study Gap 4: Methodology

Liu et al. (2020) discusses the emergency planning using a risk-based integration methodology for river chemical spills while COSO's (2017) framework "Enterprise Risk Management- Integrating with Strategy and Performance", emphasises a collection of case studies about how the ERM Framework is put to use. Each case study by COSO (2017) describes how a specifically chosen organisation adapts to the framework principles. However, further analysis of the literature reveals that there seems not to be any methodology in use to integrate risk management with strategy and performance in a Local Government Setting or a specific industry. There is no step-by-step guidance in Local Government to achieve ERM integration. However, risk management is not a very old concept after the Second World War II, which signifies a lot of room for improvement (G Dionne, 2013).

The ERM standards are commonly and widely used, as they are very generic, a one size fits all that applies to any organisation irrespective of the industry or sector such as Dali and Lajtha (2012) discusses how the framework has been widely adopted around the world by most of the G20 countries and concentrates on things to watch for, while Muzaimi et al. (2017) discusses the implementation of the

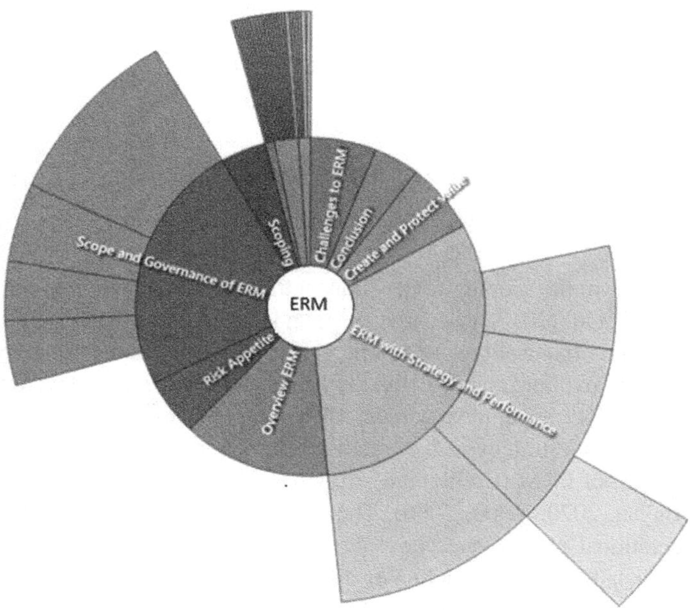

Fig. 5 NVivo Sunburst showing segments and related hierarchy levels of data distribution

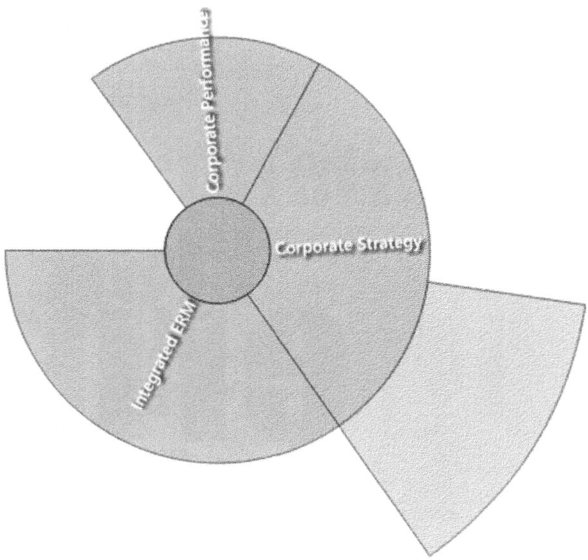

Fig. 6 NVivo main theme showing further segmentation into more segments

different integrated management system and how they share common goals for better quality management. A gap exists on how to implement and adapt them following a guide in specific industries. The question remains how well the risk models established in Local Government are being implemented effectively integrate with corporate strategy and performance.

3.7 Thematic Presentations

Figure 5 below is a sunburst showing the hierarchy levels of data being presented in nodes. Sunburst charts are used to visualise hierarchical data. The innermost node ERM is the top level of the hierarchy with the main themes, such as the Overview of ERM, Risk Appetite, Scope and Governance of ERM, Scoping, Challenges to ERM, Create and Protect Value, ERM with Strategy and Performance and the Conclusion.

A segment is further divided into more segments, representing a parent child relationship in the hierarchy. For example, Fig. 6 shows how the parent theme, ERM with Strategy and Performance in Fig. 5 (parent) is further divided into sub segments of Corporate Performance, Integrated ERM and Corporate Strategy (children). Corporate strategy is further segmented into another segment as seen in Fig. 6. The more the parent or child node is drilled down on, the more the segments themes are displayed.

To find out the main concepts associated with the research, a query was run for word frequency using NVivo. Figure 7 below shows the frequently used words generated using Word Cloud. Results show that the top five keywords are clearly in line with the purpose of this research, namely, risk, ERM, management, strategy, and

Fig. 7 Word Cloud showing frequently used research word

performance. While these are the main terms guiding the research, their relationship cannot be explained using the word cloud. Of interest is the term "Local Government" which has not appeared as one of the most used words, a sign pointing towards a lack of empirical studies in Local Government and highlighting the importance of the proposed research.

4 Conclusion

There is a desire to investigate the nature and the extent to which the three concepts of risk management, strategy, and performance are concurrently implemented as the integrated process that acts as a conduit to building resilient and sustainable communities. It appears that the integration of ERM in Local Government has not been reviewed comprehensively as discussed outside of the academic realm. It was necessary to give a descriptive account of how the relevant information collected for the literature review was arrived at. There has been a drive towards evidence-based practice and of interest is the Arksey and O'Malley (2005) framework that provides a clear and distinctive process to carry out a scoping review. This framework provides procedural and methodological rigor with six stages that were applied to this research.

Search results gave a total of 1690 potentially relevant studies. The inclusion and exclusion criteria were applied, and 210 studies were eligible for a scoping review. Documents with titles and abstracts not relevant to the study, duplicate documents, documents with broken links, commercial type of material, Local Government entity policies and frameworks, were excluded from the study. The scoping review identified four research gaps relating to the integration of risk management processes, the cascading process of corporate strategy, the overarching legislative mandate to the implementation of RAS and risk frameworks, and methodology to integrate risk management with strategy and performance. This review suggests that the integration of the three concepts, especially in the Australian Local Government is an under-researched area of study.

The findings of this study benefit Local Governments to avoid managing risk as a "tick in a box exercise" (Beeri & Navot, 2014). The development of an ERM integration methodology offers a conceptual versus a theoretical approach to risk management. Policymakers can call for policy reforms and enact effective regulation that makes mandatory, the implementation of RAS and ERM frameworks. Results can be used by independent assurance bodies to inform audits and training programs aimed at improving ERM processes and risk management self-assessment tools.

Lessons learnt in the course of conducting the scoping review are insights on the need to effectively set inclusion and exclusion criteria to identify and scope in-depth content that relates to a broad and multidisciplinary topic. This approach made it possible to yield meaningful results as different risk standards are being applied by different organisations of any type, size, or industry. ERM concept can be difficult to define and expound when being referred to by many disciplines. However, following Arksey and O'Malley's (2005) framework provided a broad and inclusive process that enabled the researchers to draw in relevant studies for scoping. Results of a scoping review are a necessary means to establish a roadmap to integrated ERM processes that act as a conduit to building resilient and sustainable Local Government communities.

References

Abolfazli, S. A., Mohammadzadeh, M., Peiravian, F., Zonoozi, J., Sharifnia, H., & Vasheghani, A. (2019). Strategy-making process and firm performance in Iranian pharmaceutical industry. *Iranian Journal of Pharmaceutical Research: IJPR, 18*(1), 531.

Abrams, C., Von Kanel, J., Muller, S., Pfitzmann, B., & Ruschka-Taylor, S. (2007). Optimised enterprise risk management. *IBM Systems Journal, 46*(2), 219–234.

Abuzarqa, R. (2019). The relationship between organisational culture, risk management and organisational performance. *Cross-Cultural Management Journal, 21*(1), 13–20.

Achampong, F. K. (2010). Integrating risk management and strategic planning: Integrated risk management and strategic planning leverages the benefits of both processes and makes them mutually reinforcing. *Planning for Higher Education, 38*(2), 22–28.

Acharyya, M. (2008). In measuring the benefits of enterprise risk management in insurance: An integration of economic value added and balanced score card approaches. *ERM Monograph*, 1–25.

Alibašić, H. (2018). *Sustainability and resilience planning for local governments: The Quadruple Bottom Line Strategy* (pp. 15–103). Springer.

Anchor, J. R., Amhalhal, A., & Dastgir, S. (2015). The use of multiple performance measures and organisational performance in an emerging market. *In Liberec Economic Forum, 233*.

Anderson, S., Allen, P., Peckham, S., & Goodwin, N. (2008). Asking the right questions: Scoping studies in the commissioning of research on the organisation and delivery of health services. *Health Research Policy and Systems, 6*(1), 1–12.

Aon. (2018). *2018 risk report: A focus on Australian Local Government*, 5–6.

Arena, M., Arnaboldi, M., & Azzone, G. (2010). The organisational dynamics of enterprise risk management. *Accounting, Organisations and Society, 35*(7), 659–675.

Arksey, H., & O'Malley, L. (2005). Scoping studies: Towards a methodological framework. *International Journal of Social Research Methodology, 8*(1), 19–32.

Beasley, M. S., Frigo, M. L., & Litman, J. (2007). Strategic risk management: Creating and protecting value. *Strategic Finance, 88*(11), 24.

Beeri, I., & Navot, D. (2014). Turnaround management strategies in local authorities: Managerial, political and national obstacles to recovery. *Journal of Management and Organization, 20*(1), 121–138.

Ben-Amar, W., Boujenoui, A., & Zéghal, D. (2014). The relationship between corporate strategy and enterprise risk management: Evidence from Canada. *Journal of Management and Strategy, 5*(1), 1.

Berry, F. S. (1994). Innovation in public management: The adoption of strategic planning. *Public Administration Review*, 322–330.

Bharathy, G. K., & McShane, M. K. (2014). Applying a systems model to enterprise risk management. *Engineering Management Journal, 26*(4), 38–46.

Bhaumik, S. K., Estrin, S., & Mickiewicz, T. (2017). Ownership identity, strategy and performance: Business group affiliates versus independent firms in India. *Asia Pacific Journal of Management, 34*(2), 281–311.

Bowman, E. H., & Helfat, C. E. (2001). Does corporate strategy matter? *Strategic Management Journal, 22*(1), 1–23.

Bromiley, P., McShane, M., Nair, A., & Rustambekov, E. (2015). Enterprise risk management: Review, critique, and research directions. *Long Range Planning, 48*(4), 265–276.

Brunet-Jailly, E., & Martin, J. F. (2017). Local government in a global world: Australia and Canada in comparative perspective. In *Local government in a global world* (pp. 1–34).

Brusca, I., & Montesinos, V. (2016). Implementing performance reporting in local government: A cross-countries comparison. *Public Performance & Management Review, 39*(3), 506–534.

Chaiechi, T. (2020). Sustainable tropical cities: A scoping review of multidisciplinary methods for urban planning. *eTropic: Electronic Journal of Studies in the Tropics, 19*(2), 25–51.

Chen, J., Jiao, L., & Harrison, G. (2019). Organisational culture and enterprise risk management: The Australian not-for-profit context. *Australian Journal of Public Administration, 78*(3), 432–448.

Chen, Y. L., Chuang, Y. W., Huang, H. G., & Shih, J. Y. (2020). The value of implementing enterprise risk management: Evidence from Taiwan's financial industry. *The North American Journal of Economics and Finance, 54*, 100926.

Choi, Y., Ye, X., Zhao, L., & Luo, A. C. (2016). Optimising enterprise risk management: A literature review and critical analysis of the work of Wu and Olson. *Annals of Operations Research, 237*(1), 281–300.

Cokins, G. (2009). Performance management: Integrating strategy execution, methodologies, risk, and analytics v (21).

Colquhoun, H. L., Levac, D., O'Brien, K. K., Straus, S., Tricco, A. C., Perrier, L., & Moher, D. (2014). Scoping reviews: Time for clarity in definition, methods, and reporting. *Journal of Clinical Epidemiology, 67*(12), 1291–1294.

Cooper, T., Downer, P., & Faseruk, A. (2019). Assessing risk management in small rural municipalities in Canada. *Journal of Accounting & Finance, 19*(5), 2158–3625.

COSO. (2017). *Enterprise risk management integrating with strategy and Committee of Sponsoring Organisations of the Treadway Commission*, 1–16.

Cremonino, A. (2011, March). Risk appetite as a core element of ERM: Definition and process. In *Enterprise Risk Management Symposium, Society of Actuaries*, 1–29.

Crockford, G. N. (1982). The bibliography and history of risk management: Some preliminary observations. *Geneva Papers on Risk and Insurance*, 169–179.

Dali, A., & Lajtha, C. (2012). ISO 31000 risk management- "The gold standard". *EDPACS, 45*(5), 1–8.

Daudt, H. M. L., van Mossel, C., & Scott, S. J. (2013). Enhancing the scoping study methodology: A large, inter-professional team's experience with Arksey and O'Malley's framework. *BMC Medical Research Methodology, 13*(1), 48.

Davison, A. (2011). Enterprise risk management: Risk appetite and risk tolerance: How robust are yours. *Water: Journal of the Australian Water Association, 38*(5), 65–68.

Dionne, G. (2013). Risk management: History, definition, and critique. *Risk Management and Insurance Review, 16*(2), 147–166.

Dollery, B., Crase, L., & Johnson, A. (2006). *Australian local government economics* (pp. 49–137). UNSW Press.

Epstein, M., & Manzoni, J. F. (1998). Implementing corporate strategy: From tableaux de Bord to balanced scorecards. *European Management Journal, 16*(2), 190–203.

Fehring, A. (2018). Risk management: Putting the appetite into risk management: Is it time to delete your risk matrix? *Governance Directions, 70*(7), 390–402.

Feldman, E. R. (2020). Corporate strategy: Past, present, and future. *Strategic Management Review, 1*(1), 179–206.

Haimes, Y. Y. (2009). On the complex definition of risk: A systems-based approach. *Risk analysis: An International Journal, 29*(12), 1647–1654.

Hanggraeni, D., Ślusarczyk, B., Sulung, L. A. K., & Subroto, A. (2019). The impact of internal, external and enterprise risk management on the performance of micro, small and medium enterprises. *Sustainability, 11*(7), 2172.

Hardy, K. (2014). *Enterprise risk management: A guide for government professionals* (pp. 7–36). Wiley.

Hastings, C., Wortley, L., Ryan, R., & Grant, B. (2016). Community expectations for the role of local government in regional Australia: Meeting the challenges of 'slow burn'. *Australasian Journal of Regional Studies, 22*(1), 158.

Hoyt, R. E., & Liebenberg, A. P. (2011). The value of enterprise risk management. *Journal of Risk and Insurance, 78*(4), 795–822.

International Standards Organization (ISO). (2018). *Risk management: guidelines: International Organization for Standardization*, 1–16.

Kaplan, R. S., & Norton, D. P. (1996). Linking the balanced scorecard to strategy. *California Management Review, 39*(1), 53–79.

Kerstin, D., Simone, O., & Nicole, Z. (2014). Challenges in implementing enterprise risk management. *ACRN Journal of Finance and Risk Perspectives, 3*(3), 1–14.

Khan, M. J. (2016). Why do firms adopt enterprise risk management (ERM) Empirical evidence from France? *Management Decision, 54*(8), 1886–1907.

Kloot, L., & Martin, J. (2000). Strategic performance management: A balanced approach to performance management issues in local government. *Management Accounting Research, 11* (2), 231–251.

Lam, J. (2014). *Enterprise risk management: From incentives to controls* (pp. 5–67). Wiley.

Levac, D., Colquhoun, H., & O'Brien, K. K. (2010). Scoping studies: Advancing the methodology. *Implementation Science, 5*(1), 1–9.

Lin, Y., Wen, M. M., & Yu, J. (2012). Enterprise risk management: Strategic antecedents, risk integration, and performance. *North American Actuarial Journal, 16*(1), 1–28.

Liu, J., Jiang, D., Guo, L., Nan, J., Cao, W., & Wang, P. (2020). Emergency material location-allocation planning using a risk-based integration methodology for river chemical spills. *Environmental Science and Pollution Research International, 27*(15), 17949–17962.

Lundqvist, S. A. (2014). An exploratory study of enterprise risk management: Pillars of ERM. *Journal of Accounting, Auditing & Finance, 29*(3), 393–429.

Lundqvist, S. A. (2015). Why firms implement risk governance–stepping beyond traditional risk management to enterprise risk management. *Journal of Accounting and Public Policy, 34*(5), 441–466.

Mauelshagen, C., Smith, M., Schiller, F., Denyer, D., Rocks, S., & Pollard, S. (2014). Effective risk governance for environmental policy making: A knowledge management perspective. *Environmental Science & Policy, 41*, 23–32.

Meulbroek, L. (2002). A senior manager's guide to integrated risk management. *Journal of Applied Corporate Finance, 14*, 56–70.

Meyer, N., Meyer, D., & Kot, S. (2017). The development of a process tool for improved risk management in local government. *Quality - Access to Success, 18*(S1), 425–429.

Moher, D., Liberati, A., Tetzlaff, J., Altman, D. G., & PRISMA Group. (2009). Preferred reporting items for systematic reviews and meta-analyses: The PRISMA statement. *BMJ, 339*(jul21 1), b2535–b2535.

Montesinos, V., Brusca, I., Rossi, F. M., & Aversano, N. (2013). The usefulness of performance reporting in local government: Comparing Italy and Spain. *Public Money & Management, 33* (3), 171–176.

Munn, Z., Peters, M. D., Stern, C., Tufanaru, C., McArthur, A., & Aromataris, E. (2018). Systematic review or scoping review? Guidance for authors when choosing between a systematic or scoping review approach. *BMC Medical Research Methodology, 18*(1), 1–7.

Muzaimi, H., Chew, B. C., & Hamid, S. R. (2017, March). Integrated management system: The integration of ISO 9001, ISO 14001, OHSAS 18001 and ISO 31000. *AIP Conference Proceedings, 1818*(1), 020034.

Oulasvirta, L., & Anttiroiko, A. V. (2017). Adoption of comprehensive risk management in local government. *Local Government Studies, 43*(3), 451–474.

Patino, C. M., & Ferreira, J. C. (2018). Inclusion and exclusion criteria in research studies: Definitions and why they matter. *Jornal Brasileiro de Pneumologia, 44*(2), 84–84.

Pelling, M., Maskrey, A., Ruiz, P., Hall, P., Peduzzi, P., Dao, Q.-H., & Kluser, S. (2004). *Reducing disaster risk: A challenge for development*, 26–136.

Peters, M. D. J., Godfrey, C. M., Khalil, H., McInerney, P., Parker, D., & Soares, C. B. (2015). Guidance for conducting systematic scoping reviews. *International Journal of Evidence-Based Healthcare, 13*(3), 141–146.

Platts-Fowler, D., & Robinson, D. (2016). Community resilience: A policy tool for local government? *Local Government Studies, 42*(5), 762–784.

Qadan, M., & Idilbi-Bayaa, Y. (2020). Risk appetite and oil prices. *Energy Economics, 85*, 104595.

QAO. (2019). *Fraud risk management Report* 6, 2017–18.

Razali, A. R., & Tahir, I. M. (2011). Review of the literature on enterprise risk management. *Business Management Dynamics, 1*(5), 8.

Rehman, A. U., & Anwar, M. (2019). Mediating role of enterprise risk management practices between business strategy and SME performance. *Small Enterprise Research, 26*(2), 207–227.

Ryan, C., Stanley, T., & Nelson, M. (2002). Accountability disclosures by Queensland local government councils: 1997–1999. *Financial Accountability & Management, 18*(3), 261–289.

Saguil, A., & Farnel, E. (2008). Risks unavoidable and worth taking. *Canadian Medical Association Journal (CMAJ), 178*(12), 1533–1533.

Sarker, S., Engwall, M., Trucco, P., & Feldmann, A. (2016). Internal visibility of external supplier risks and the dynamics of risk management silos. *IEEE Transactions on Engineering Management, 63*(4), 451–461.

Segal, S. (2006, July). Defining risk appetite. In *ERM Symposium* Presentation, March 29, 2007.

Shad, M. K., Lai, F.-W., Fatt, C. L., Klemes, J. J., & Bokhari, A. (2019). Integrating sustainability reporting into enterprise risk management and its relationship with business performance: A conceptual framework. *Journal of Cleaner Production, 208*, 415–425.

Sharma, B., & Gadenne, D. (2011). Balanced scorecard implementation in a local government authority: Issues and challenges: Balanced scorecard implementation in an LGA. *Australian Journal of Public Administration, 70*(2), 167–184.

Snyder, H. (2019). Literature review as a research methodology: An overview and guidelines. *Journal of Business Research, 104*, 333–339.

Soltanizadeh, S., Abdul Rasid, S. Z., Mottaghi Golshan, N., & Wan Ismail, W. K. (2016). Business strategy, enterprise risk management and organisational performance. *Management Research Review, 39*(9), 1016–1033.

Tekathen, M., & Dechow, N. (2013). Enterprise risk management and continuous re-alignment in the pursuit of accountability: A German case. *Management Accounting Research, 24*(2), 100–121.

Tricco, A. C., Lillie, E., Zarin, W., O'Brien, K., Colquhoun, H., Kastner, M., & Straus, S. E. (2016). A scoping review of the conduct and reporting of scoping reviews. *BMC Medical Research Methodology, 16*(1), 15–10.

Viscelli, T. R., Beasley, M. S., & Hermanson, D. R. (2016). Research insights about risk governance. *Implications from a Review of ERM Research*, 6(4).

Yilmaz, A. K., & Flouris, T. (2010). Managing corporate sustainability: Risk management process based perspective. *African Journal of Business Management, 4*(2), 162–171.

Does Covid-19 Spark the End of Globalisation?

Benedict Atkinson, Jacob Wood, and Haejin Jang

Abstract Scholars have argued that the spread of the Covid-19 virus is undermining globalisation and may ultimately prove a catalyst for de-globalisation. We debate this issue. Covid-19 is speeding the changing of the process of globalisation, which continues. In this sense, it can be viewed as a black swan event which, by arresting the free movement of people globally and constricting supply chains, is inhibiting trade. At the same time, Covid-19 has accelerated the uptake of digital communication via platforms such as zoom and skype. In support of our thesis that Covid-19 is accelerating a change in the nature of globalisation, we argue that globalisation had not ceased since the time when European powers first began venturing across the globe in pursuit of trade between the fifteenth and nineteenth centuries. The study is intended to briefly survey the modern history of globalisation to create a platform for analysing the effect of Covid-19. The social and economic effect of pandemics in history is also discussed, in particular the Plague of Justinian, the Black Death and the Spanish flu. While the Economic Cycles theory does not provide an explanation for the effect of the pandemic on societies and economies, the theory of Hegemonic Cycles is more explanatory, enabling us to view the pandemic as an event that will probably affect global power relations. The purpose of this paper is to identify how the Covid-19 virus has brought into stark relief the apparent hegemonic rivalry of the United States and China. One country is, to date, the worst affected by the virus, the other is its place of origin. Our study shows that both countries are proponents of globalisation but expound different narratives concerning how the world can trade and prosper in the future.

Keywords COVID-19 · Globalisation · International trade · Nationalism

JEL Codes F6, P16

B. Atkinson (✉) · J. Wood · H. Jang
James Cook University Singapore Business School, Singapore, Singapore
e-mail: benedict.atkinson@jcu.edu.au; jacob.wood@jcu.edu.au; haejin.jang@jcu.edu.au

© The Author(s), under exclusive license to Springer Nature Singapore Pte Ltd. 2022
T. Chaiechi, J. Wood (eds.), *Community Empowerment, Sustainable Cities, and Transformative Economies*, https://doi.org/10.1007/978-981-16-5260-8_29

1 Introduction

The COVID-19 pandemic has turned the global economy on its head. Initially seen as a disease confined to China and later South-East Asia, many experts believed the disease could be contained and controlled within the region. However, unlike SARS which was relatively well controlled, claiming only 774 lives between 2002–2004 (WHO, 2020a), COVID-19 has created the kind of global health emergency not seen since the Spanish Flu Pandemic of 1918/19. Since the disease first emerged at the end of 2019, the World Health Organization has now registered 153,954,491 confirmed cases of COVID-19, including 3,221,052 deaths (WHO, 2020b).[1]

As the health and human toll grows, the economic damage is already evident and represents the largest economic shock the world has experienced since the end of World War II, with World Bank forecasts predicting that the global economy will shrink by 5.2% in 2020 (World Bank, 2020). Moreover, economic activity among advanced economies is expected to fall by as much as 7% in 2020, with significant declines in domestic demand and supply, trade, and finance being the primary reasons. Emerging market and developing economies are expected to contract by 2.5% in 2020, their first contraction as a group in more than 60 years (World Bank, 2020).

Given these health and economic impacts, many scholars have begun to assess how the disease influences the broader global landscape and in particular, the issue of globalisation, which has been at the forefront of policy agendas since the end of WW2 in 1945. In order to assess this impact, we identify how global response to the Covid-19 virus has made stark the contrasting ideologies of the United States and China as those ideologies influence response to globalisation. The pandemic appears to have accelerated a fissure in the political relationship between these two powers which will itself have implications for the future of globalisation. We also debate whether or not the pandemic is a so-called black swan event. In this debate, consideration of business cyclic theory and hegemonic theory is fundamentally important. We first explore whether Covid-19 fits into the analysis of the occurrence and effect of economic cycles. We then discuss how hegemonic cycles and rivalries are affected by, and affect, a global pandemic.

2 Is Covid-19 a Threat to Globalisation?

Covid-19 is the latest of many lethal outbreaks of mass contagion in history. The Plague of Justinian (541–549) named after the Byzantine emperor who contracted the plague (and survived) wreaked havoc on the population of Constantinople. The Black Death (1346–1353), a bubonic plague like the Justinian plague, killed between one third and one half of Europe's population (De Witte, 2014), while the Spanish

[1]Case numbers and deaths correct as at May 5, 2021.

Flu (1918–1920) killed at least 50 million people worldwide (Centers for Disease Control and Prevention, 2019). The Justinian Plague, the Black Death and the Spanish Flu all radically destabilised society.

In the case of the Black Death, the plague precipitated the steady breakdown of European feudalism. The death toll from the Spanish Flu was so alarming that it may have contributed towards creating a politics and culture of nihilism and violence in the years between WW1 and WW2. (Time, 2020) It is noteworthy that both the Black Death and Spanish Flu preceded long periods of expansion as countries attempted to find prosperity through trade.

So far as Covid-19 is concerned, countries today have responded to the spread of the virus by quarantine and border closure, resulting in a drop in a 65% number of people travelling (UNTWO). Some supply chains are halted, some upended and others constricted. Enormous increases in public debt are accompanied by the shrinking of national income. Since extinguishment of the virus is unlikely in the short term it can be guessed that in most countries, output will continue to be relatively low and travel between jurisdictions low.

The character of globalisation has changed to the extent that communication within and between countries has become a simulacrum, meaning that digital video link permits video communication to function as a surrogate for physical meetings. Video conferencing has dematerialised the economy, demonstrating that business can be viable without the various business actors meeting in person. Could Covid-19, therefore, contribute to *deglobalisation* or is the more relevant question whether, in the long run, the social and economic effects of the virus will change the *character* of globalisation?

3 Is Covid-19 a Black Swan Event?

An argument can be made that the Covid-19 pandemic is a 'black swan' event. A black swan signifies the occurrence of a unique, unpredictable and potentially cataclysmic event the impact of which may be unprecedented (Taleb, 2007). A black swan event contrasts with everyday white swan events. Until the sighting of black swans in 1697 by a Dutch maritime exploration expedition traversing the coast of Western Australia (Museum WA) Europeans thought that only white swans existed. The discovery of black swans overturned the previous unchallenged belief swans are always white in colour. Viewed from this perspective, Covid-19 is an exogenous shock to most of world society, and while it is not the first plague to have descended on the world, it seems to be aptly described as a black swan event (Taleb, 2007).

An important question is whether this putative black swan portends still-worse effects for societies across the globe.[2] Governments have responded to the virus by, among other things, instituting 'lockdowns', bans on non-essential travel and quarantining of travellers. At the time of writing, numerous parts of the globe were acutely experiencing the mal-effects of the disease in the second wave of infections. Two parts of governmental response stand out: the first is a mandating of mass migration of the employed from conventional workplace to home workplace; the second is the extraordinary subsidy provided in developed countries to ensure that workers, both active and redundant, could remain solvent.

The ultimate effect on the globalisation of the pandemic is difficult to predict. It seems highly probable that the effect will be great and long-lasting. This proposition is supported by history. Numerous plagues or pandemics have erupted throughout history, but, as noted above, three, in particular, stand out for severity and long-lasting effect. The first was the Plague of Justinian (541–549), which killed approximately one fifth (and possibly much more) of the population in Constantinople alone (North, 2011). The plague weakened the armies of the Byzantine Empire, which could not resist localised invasions by the Lombards and Arabs. The second event is the Black Death (1347–51), the bubonic plague carried by rats on ships sailing from China to Europe. The Black Death killed one third to one half of Europe's population (Firth, 2012). The third is the Spanish Flu (1918–1920) which killed, in the United States, Europe and elsewhere, approximately 50 million people (Centers for Disease Control and Prevention, 2019) and contributed to the psychological trauma afflicting populations after WW1. The toll of Covid-19, material and psychological, can be expected to be, in some ways at least, similar to those of the earlier pandemics.

In practical terms, the Plague of Justinian prevented the Byzantine Empire from the reconquest of Italy and reunification of the eastern and western Roman empires. The Black Death hugely reduced the servile population of Europe, advantaging labour in economic bargaining. Labourers could travel to find better working conditions and consequently the Black Death can be seen to have precipitated the breakdown of feudalism. To some extent, continuing grief over WW1, and a desire to forget the horror of that war, subsumed reactions to the Spanish Flu. It can be speculated, however, that apart from the mortality rate causing labour shortage, the toll of the Spanish flu encouraged in the European interwar populations a sense of futility. A likely consequence was over-engagement in politics (thus widespread

[2]Nassim Nicholas Taleb the author of *The Black Swan: The Impact of the Highly Improbable* Random 2007 has asserted that Covid-19 threatens globalisation (see Bernard Avishai 'The Pandemic Isn't a Black Swan but a Portent of a More Fragile Global System' *New Yorker* 21 April 2020). In his book Taleb advanced the idea of black swan occurrences as unique, rare and significant in effect. Taleb has argued that Covid-19 is not a black swan because its occurrence was predictable. While the rapid spread of a deadly virus is neither unpredictable nor unprecedented, the particular character of the virus and its social effect (mass 'lockdowns' for instance) are novel.

support for extremist parties) or under-engagement (apathy leading to the election of extremist parties).

4 Economic Cycles

One theoretical economic explanation for Covid-19 is that it represents the working of the economic cycle. The theory of economic cycles, discussed briefly below, is multifarious but all cyclical theories have in common the idea of economic expansion and regression (Morgan, 1990). Caution is necessary: if Covid-19 is a Black Swan it must be understood on its own terms, and not artificially fitted into a cyclical model. If it is sui generis, its impact is hard to accurately predict precisely because it cannot be explained by a model or comparison to analogous events. Even if the virus continues to kill a large number of people (noting that both the Black Death and Spanish flu ceased to be epidemiological threats within a few years of their irruption) its social effects in the long run could be positive as well as negative in ways that are not strictly predictable.

The primary hypotheses about economic cycles are Kondratievian, Keynesian, Austrian and Monetarist. Each hypothesis is discussed below to help to identify traits or factors that may be relevant to analysis of Covid-19's effect on globalisation.

4.1 Kondratiev's Waves

Nikolai Kondratiev theorised that significant innovation occurring at intervals of 40–60 years creates cycles or waves of prosperity or abundance (Kondratiev, 1985). Kondratiev's first postulated wave related to the invention of the steam engine and lasted from 1780 to 1830. The second wave (1830–80) followed the use of steel and the growth of rail transport. The invention of electricity and growth in the chemical industry led to a third wave that lasted from 1880–1930. The fourth wave (not hypothesised by Kondratiev himself) involved the ascendancy of the motor and petrochemical industries and lasted from 1930 to 1970. Information technology precipitated a fifth wave, starting in 1970 and extending to the present. It can be argued that the developed world has entered the sixth wave of digital communication and biotechnology.

Kondratiev's theory is not accepted in mainstream economics because it makes teleological assumptions about the connection between innovation and growth. Why, for example, are air transport or medical advances not identified as innovations critically affecting economic growth and social welfare? However, wave theory is useful in demonstrating recurrence in economic life. It has considerable utility in showing the effect of innovation on human development by reference to history, but it is a poor predictor of future effect. For this reason, the theory cannot, in the present, provide a reason for black swan events or explain the future of globalisation.

4.2 Keynesian Cycles

John Maynard Keynes argued that that asymmetry in investment and consumption creates cycles of increased or decreased output (Keynes, 1936). According to Keynes, in a period of output expansion, the marginal efficiency of capital (profit) rises and the business environment is characterised by optimism, high demand, high investment and high income. In time, the marginal efficiency of capital drops as costs rise and profits reduce. Then demand/investment become asymmetrical and must be stimulated by government intervention. Keynes's remedy for a black swan event would be to increase government spending since only the government *will* and *can* spend effectively in a time of output and demand shortfall. However, extraordinary spending over time raises the possibility of moral hazard if that spending involves ad nauseum printing of money and purchase of debt.

4.3 Austrian School

The Austrians, notably represented by Ludwig von Mises (von Mises, 1954) and Friedrich Hayek (Hayek, 1944) argued against Keynes that monetary manipulation by central banks distorted the economic process. According to the Austrians, government monetary intervention benefits non-productive sectors such as real estate while demand for constructive investment in innovation dwindles. Ultimately the consequence of misdirected investment is insolvency and bankruptcy is followed by recession.

4.4 Monetarism

Monetarist theory, propounded by Milton Friedman (Friedman, 1962) and other economists, proposes that control of the money supply determines economic contraction or expansion. According to monetarists, by raising or reducing interest rates a central bank can stimulate or depress economic activity. Higher rates make access to money more expensive, which contracts the money supply and suppresses activity. By contrast lower rates induce greater borrowing and expenditure. Monetary controls are exerted to increase or reduce supply as circumstance dictate. The monetarist model accommodates the possibility of exogenous shock, the effect of which is supposedly mitigated by the application of monetary policy.

4.5 *Is Covid-19 Part of an Economic Cycle?*

There seems little doubt that Covid-19, if it can be related to economic cycles, is an exogenous occurrence and so does not fit into the pattern of recurrence applicable to endogenous events occurring in a boom-bust cycle. If we posit that an economy rises and falls in keeping with, for instance, Kondratiev cycles, we can say that an exogenous event like Covid-19 is exactly the kind of unpredictable event that could precipitate the ending of a cycle and the beginning of a new one. It can be seen that Covid-19's effects could presage a new cycle of economic relationship, and indeed innovation, based on new conceptions of production, work, migration and consumption.

If, by contrast, we analyse Covid-19 by reference to the Austrian or monetarist views of economic cycles we can say that Covid-19 has presented spending choices to governments, and government has made choices the merit of which is difficult to judge in the short term. Keynesians would probably argue that government actually has one choice and that is to spend. So far as globalisation is concerned, the government response to the virus has been to retard the free movement of people, while both government and business response has been to retard the movement of capital.

Assuming that the virus in the next few years either becomes extinct, or is contained by vaccination, it is likely that the complexion of globalisation will change considerably. Free movement and mass travel may continue to be curtailed and localism may govern economic and social choices. If this is the case, inequality within and between nations might become the predominant concern of policymakers since more restricted globalisation might be accompanied by asset consolidation, risk mitigation and focus on regional and national concerns as opposed to international ones (Rapoza, 2020; Economist, 2019).

5 Hegemonic Cycles

Much has been written about economic cycles but less about hegemonic cycles. The literature on hegemonic cycles is, nonetheless, extensive. An event like Covid-19 is probably explained by that literature as a destructive occurrence in the sense that it potentially ends one cycle and begins another. The idea of hegemonic power is tied to the reality that throughout history dominant states have arisen and achieved economic and often military ascendancy over rival states. The effect of Covid-19 may be to help effect a realignment of international power that could have positive or negative effects for globalisation (Harkavy, 2020).

The theory of hegemonic cycles is diverse. Realist theory, systemic theory, hegemonic stability theory, power transition theory, long cycle theory, world systems theory, liberal theory, constructivist theory, Marxist theory, all provide perspectives on the growth and exercise of hegemonic power and its consequences for other states. In essence, hegemonic cycle theory proposes that in different periods of history a hegemon with the wherewithal to dominate other states exerts coercive power (sometimes passively, that is, cooperatively) to achieve hegemonic objects (imperial control, institutional dominance etc.). Globalisation in different forms (mercantilist or free trade blocs, associative blocs – e.g., the World Trade Organization- and imperial blocs) is intrinsic to the exercise of hegemonic power.

Most theory about hegemonic cycles is focused on modern European (and later American) capitalism but hegemons are identifiable from near the beginning of recorded history. A hegemon's outward extension of power to subjugate or conciliate other states and rivals is a powerful expression of internationalism over localism. One common principle articulated in hegemonic cycle theory is that hegemons stabilise the international state system either oppressively or cooperatively – or both. This proposition is the cornerstone of hegemonic stability theory (Boswell & Sweat, 1991). According to the theory, in the absence of a hegemon, international state relations become unpredictable, and because a leader does not coordinate a response, black swan occurrences are maladroitly handled by different actors. At the time of the Great Depression, for example, the absence of hegemonic leadership contributed to disparate and sometimes catastrophic government responses to a global stock market contagion. At this time, the United States already possessed the capacity of a superpower but it declined to assert world leadership, adopting instead an inward response to the economic crisis.

Long cycle theory proposes that hegemonic activity can be observed over a historical period and the decline and failure of a hegemon causes international instability. Long cycle theory purports to accurately measure the length of hegemonic cycles, which may range in length from about 70 years to about 120 years. The originator of this theory, George Modelski (Modelski, 1987), adopted Kondratiev's wave theory as a model. He identified a first hegemonic wave in Portugal's expansion during the sixteenth century, followed in the seventeenth century by the Netherlands (or its proxy the Dutch East India Company). The next wave of hegemonic power emerged as Great Britain founded two empires in the eighteenth and nineteenth centuries. Then after WW2, having previously spurned the role of hegemon, the United States adopted it wholeheartedly, establishing the architecture of international relations that continues to the present (Modelski, 1987).

5.1 Hegemons

Another way of looking at hegemonic cycles is to analyse hegemonic behavior in the ancient as well as modern world. We can see that from 3000 BC Egypt succeeds Mesopotamia as the predominant civilisation. The Persian Empire becomes the next hegemon to and is succeeded by the Greek states and Macedonia. From about 197 BC, when Rome conquered Macedonia, the Roman republic – later the Roman Empire – was world hegemon, its dominance lasting until the fifth century AD. In the East, the Indus Valley civilisation exerted a local hegemony from

2500 BC–1500 BC and from 2000 BC Chinese dynasties asserted China's hegemonic status.

Following the dissolution of the Western Roman Empire in the fifth century, the Byzantine Empire became the new Mediterranean/European hegemon. Then came new imperial hegemonies. The Spanish Empire between the sixteenth and nineteenth centuries spanned Latin America, a large part of North America and the Philippines. In the same period, the Portuguese empire comprised Brazil and certain territories in Africa and Asia. Then France, the Netherlands and England/Great Britain established empires between the sixteenth and nineteenth centuries, the British Empire being established in two time periods. In Europe, Sweden established a Baltic Empire in the sixteenth and seventeenth centuries. Until the nineteenth century, the governments of the largest empires, Spain, France and Britain pursued mercantilism, a practice of obtaining and protecting, through force if necessary, favourable terms of trade to accumulate wealth for the mercantilist country (Friedman & Chase-Dunn, 2005).

In the later nineteenth century, when it established its second empire, Great Britain began to institute free trade policies *within* the empire. As the United States grew in power in the nineteenth century it pursued mostly protectionist policies intended to encourage the growth of industries protected by tariffs. These various hegemonies competed with each other for territory and influence and, before the nineteenth century, prosecuted various wars with one another (Kennedy, 1987). At the same time, hegemonic crowding also opened to imperial countries hitherto little known parts of the world and created new and extensive trade routes. It also caused disequilibrium because the trade policy of contesting for territory resulted in wars, notably between England/Great Britain and the Netherlands and France, and these countries against Spain (Webb & Krasner, 1989).

Imperial contest ensured that in the period of the fifteenth–nineteenth centuries no overwhelming hegemon arose in Europe. The result of competition was frequent war or fractured peace which nonetheless established a rudimentary process of globalisation. Empires might not trade especially with each other but their existence depended on the annexation and control of territory which meant perforce that the hitherto little known parts of the globe became integrated in the trading systems of the imperialist powers (Kennedy, 1987).

Eventually mercantilism, an insular and imperialist system collapsed (Braudel, 1979) and free trade arguments came to dominate legislatures in the United Kingdom and United States (from the 1930s onwards). But for most of the fifteenth–nineteenth centuries mercantilist ideas dominated the trade thinking of various powers. Crowded sovereignties meant that while empires might not compete very much with one another no empire established hegemonic status. In the later nineteenth century a free trading Britain, and a protectionist United States, became dominant though not hegemonic powers. Then from the 1930s onwards, the United States adopted free trade policies which informed its establishment, from the time of the Bretton Woods Agreement (1944), of the beginnings of a global free trade system (Bordo, 2017).

5.2 *Globalisation and Hegemony*

In the modern era (after 1800) hegemon cycles can be observed in world politics. Each cycle ends with the containment or defeat of a hegemon. Thus the Congress of Vienna (1815) conciliated the defeated French hegemon and ushered in 100 years of largely peaceful relations in Europe. That peaceful settlement vanished in 1914 on outbreak of WW1. The next hegemonic cycle ended in WW2 and the defeat of Nazi Germany (and Japan). Postwar, the United States and the USSR contended for hegemonic supremacy and after the dissolution of the USSR in 1991, the United States emerged victorious as the sole world hegemon (Kennedy, 1987). In our present era, the hegemon at odds with the United States (and other countries) is China and the consequences of that contest remain uncertain (Mendes, 2018).

If we adopt the hegemonic thesis, we can argue that Covid-19 is indeed an exogenous event but one which, rather than being strictly destructive, may (or may not) be leading to the containment of one hegemon, China. Whether or not this speculation is correct, it seems undoubted that one effect of Covid-19 will be a reassessment of the purpose and meaning of globalisation. The way in which globalisation occurs is likely to change radically. To some extent this proposition is demonstrated by the widespread adoption of the phrase, the 'new normal'. A 'new normal' implies a fundamental contradistinction between an old normalcy and a new normalcy and acceptance of new norms.

The old normalcy and new normalcy can be broken into periods in the modern era: (1) Non-hegemonic peace (for the most part) between the Congress of Vienna in 1815 and the outbreak of WW1 in 1914; (2) Hegemonic contest between 1914 and 1945 (Germany as aspirant hegemon); (3) Hegemonic superpower rivalry in the period between the Bretton Woods Agreement (1944) and establishment of the United Nations (1945) and the dissolution of the USSR (1991); and (4) The current period of monetary expansion and China's assumption of hegemon status.

Each period is defined by the activity of, or response to, hegemons. The Congress of Vienna in 1815 promulgated treaties intended to contain the recently vanquished French hegemon. It succeeded in its purpose by securing for a century a general European peace.[3] That peace ended in 1914, when a world war broke out. The period from 1914 until 1945 is then shaped by the actions of a hegemonic – or would-be hegemonic – Germany, which eventually provoked a second world war.

6 Current Politics

During the postwar period until the dissolution of the USSR in 1991, two hegemons, the United States and USSR, contended for dominance in a bifurcated world. In the succeeding period (1991 until the present), the United States, the dominant

[3] Interrupted by the Prussian-Danish (1864) and Franco-Prussian (1870–71) wars.

hegemon, confronted the challenge of China, a would-be hegemon. During this period, the United States has espoused the ideology of globalisation, which proposes that free trade between nations, involving the free movement of people and the capital, benefits all trading nations (Litan, 2000).

As the term is understood, globalisation theory can be traced to the Bretton Woods Agreement (1944), which sought to secure peace by establishing a mechanism for developing free markets throughout the globe. The Bretton Woods Agreement established the International Monetary Fund, the World Bank and the International Bank for Reconstruction and Development, the latter created to assist in reconstructing postwar Europe. As well as functioning as a country lender of last resort, the IMF encourages, among other things, international monetary co-operation, international trade and high employment. The World Bank lends money to less developed countries to fund development projects. The intellectual roots of the World Trade Organization also lie in the Bretton Woods meeting. It is the successor organisation to the General Agreement on Tariffs and Trade, which was established in 1947 and became effective in 1948 (Benn Steil, 2013).

As to the effect of Covid-19 on globalisation, it can be seen from the previous discussion that Covid-19 is best understood as an external shock to a prevailing system that may have far-reaching consequences (Ampudia et al., 2020). Covid-19 may not threaten globalisation or cause it to lose dynamism because communications technology has been integrated in economies and societies. Populations are unlikely to tolerate much diminution of the conveniences and choices afforded by globalisation. But globalisation, as a process, could change shape and trajectory (Altman, 2020).

7 The New Normal

So what is the new normal? And how will it shape our future? Covid-19 has caused globalising nations – assuming globalisation to be an object pursued under the auspices of the WTO – to adopt, for health and safety reasons, a policy of insularity. Thus borders are closed and measures such as isolation, quarantining, and non-socialising have been adopted. However, the insular tendency is to some extent counteracted by the use of internet communication platforms such as Zoom to enable people both to work and escape social isolation. In the Covid-19 era, work continues in a changed way (Guardian, 2020).

What then is the new normal? One manifestation of the new normal appears to be risk aversion (Angrisani et al., 2020). If people fear deadly infection they may develop a risk-averse attitude to life matters generally. In other words, if preservation of health – or, more bluntly, life – is a paramount consideration in everyday activity, then most likely the preservation priority is likely to govern most aspects of a person's behaviour. If this is the case, an individual is likely to spend less time thinking creatively and more time in risk-mitigation activity (Financial Times, 2020). And what applies to the individual can apply to the collective.

Accordingly, it can be predicted that in the Covid-19 era investment will drop meaning further economic contraction and quiescence in labour relations, since labour is focused on jobs retention (International Labour Organization, 2020). Falling investment does not automatically mean falling stock prices. A curious feature of economic contraction during the Covid-19 period is that while GDP has declined, equities have boomed. The dissonance between economies threatened by insolvency and booming markets is, however, easily explained: government is committed to underwriting asset inflation in the hope that this action will ensure market stability and conjure growth.

The financialisation of government (Trampusch, 2019), means that governments accept as a tenet of globalisation that asset values must be preserved, a presumption that leads to policies that result in credit and debt growth, and rising prices in stocks and property – even as GDP falls. Governments have become financialised in outlook because maintaining asset values is critical to maintaining economic well-being. The financial sector, which underwrites debt, is heavily invested in property assets.

The new normal is currently a new normal introduced during the 2008 financial crisis, which is for the government to create money or buy debt to ensure money market liquidity. Whether the new normal will become a newer normal is open to question. In this respect, the onset of Covid-19 suggests that a newer normal is actually coming into being. Workplaces have become disembodied in the real sense that a majority, or significant minority, of working populations, have departed the workplace to work from home. This fact probably facilitates globalisation because it means that online communications platforms, such as Zoom, become widely used to facilitate work communications. Such platforms can be readily used for international communication.

A second possibility is that governments may begin to pay attention to social deficits previously neglected, such as the effects of unemployment, work alienation and casualisation (Bailey & Shibata, 2019). Governments may reconsider arguments for austerity given that if many work from home, increasingly they will demand social spending to ensure the provision of infrastructure and amenity to support work-from-home populations.

7.1 The Future

As noted above, globalisation in the short and even long run may be shaped by competition between two hegemons, the United States and China. As we have seen, hegemonic conflict is not new. 200 years ago France-as-hegemon established military ascendancy in Europe but was ultimately defeated in war. The peace negotiated that confirmed that defeat created a peace that lasted with some interruptions for a century.

Then from 1914–45, two world wars were fought to defeat the would-be German hegemon and ultimately the victory/peace settlement imposed in Europe was one determined by the United States. After Germany's defeat in 1945, the USSR emerged as a new hegemon competing with the United States. The USSR's economic implosion in the late 1980s initially conferred on the United States the status of super-hegemon. Now China appears to be seeking to challenge US hegemony. Covid-19 and globalisation need to be evaluated in light of that challenge.

In this respect, the epidemiological consequences of Covid-19 are critically important. The virus emerged in China and quickly leapt borders but while China appeared to limit the incidence of the virus by draconian quarantining methods, the United States reported the highest incidence of deaths from the virus of any country in the world. Thus to external eyes, the virus appears to have caused chaos in the United States but in China appears to have been effectively contained, allowing life in that country to resume its old pattern. It could be argued that a permanent shift in power relations is occurring and the newer-normal may be a normal enjoined by China.

Against this thesis is the fact of the extraordinary resilience and creative capacity of the United States which has created a Covid-19 vaccine and may lead to a resumption of its upward hegemonic trajectory. This is all the more likely since hegemonic power can exist even though the hegemon's society appears to be failing. In the United States, the most critical social issue is that of inequality but it is worth noting that the Roman Empire endured for 500 years without solving a chronic problem of inequality.

8 Summary and Conclusion

As a black swan event, Covid-19 has thrown the world, if not into chaos, into disequilibrium. As an exogenous event the onset and spread of the virus do not seem to fit within a narrative of economic cycles. While a number of country-crossing lethal viruses have occurred in the world in the last 20 years, the outbreak of so pervasive and life-threatening a virus was probably not predictable. In any case, if we call the Covid virus a black swan event, we can say its occurrence is not accounted for by connecting it to the operation of trade cycles. This is not to say that Covid-19 has not exerted a very powerful depressing effect on global trade (Pak et al., 2020). But that effect was not strictly predictable – the outbreak of a deadly virus that spreads across the globe might be predicted but the particular virulence and contagiousness of Covid-19 probably was not. Thus cyclical theory does not seem to explain the virus nor its social and economic effect. We can probably say with reasonable cause that the virus's undoubtedly arresting effect on globalisation – in the sense of retarding the movement of capital and people – is not predictable by reference to any model (Inoue et al., 2014).

On the other hand, although the epidemiological consequences of the virus are still not fully understood, and societies around the world continue to grapple with the crisis, we can say that hegemonic theory gives some context to discussion of present and future effect of the virus on globalisation. If we say that two hegemons, one the originator of the virus, and other the worst affected by the virus, are competing to dominate a post-virus future, we can suggest that Covid-19 has radically altered the nature of globalisation – now the competition between these two powers is stark (Edel & Rapp-Hooper, 2020).

Now two trade camps are clearly identifiable and each proposes itself as the more ontologically correct proponent and explicator of a new globalisation. The United States propounds positive legal norms while China proposes commercial bargains. Globalisation to date has been an exercise in legal positivism and the United States the champion of that positivism. China by contrast is shy of ethical-legal positivism and propounds a deontological trade position which is transactional: join our enterprise for material benefit. But for Covid-19, it is unlikely that hegemonic rivalry would have resulted in so stark a choice for a particular vision of globalisation.

References

Altman, S. (2020, May 20). *Will Covid-19 have a lasting impact on globalisation?* Harvard Business Review. https://hbr.org/2020/05/will-covid-19-have-a-lasting-impact-on-globalization

Ampudia, M., Baumann, U., & Fornari, F. (2020). Coronavirus (COVID-19): Market fear as implied by options prices. *ECB Economic Bulletin*. https://www.ecb.europa.eu/pub/economic-bulletin/focus/2020/html/ecb.ebbox202004_02~26672a3808.en.html

Angrisani, M., Cipriani, M., Guarino, A., Kendall, R., & Ortiz de Zarate, J. (2020, May). *Risk references at the time of COVID-19: An experiment with professional traders and students staff report No. 927*. Federal Reserve Bank of New York. https://www.newyorkfed.org/medialibrary/media/research/staff_reports/sr927.pdf

Bailey, D., & Shibata, S. (2019). Austerity and anti-austerity: The political economy of refusal in 'Low-Resistance' models of capitalism. *British Journal of Political Science, 49*(2), 683–709. https://doi.org/10.1017/S0007123416000624

Bordo, M. (2017, April 23). The operation and demise of the Bretton woods system: 1958 to 1971. *Vox EU CEPR*. https://voxeu.org/article/operation-and-demise-bretton-woods-system

Boswell, T., & Sweat, M. (1991). Hegemony, long waves, and major wars: A time series analysis of systemic dynamics, 1496–1967. *International Studies Quarterly, 35*(2), 123–149. https://doi.org/10.2307/2600467

Braudel, F. (1979). *Civilisation and capitalism, 15th–18th century: The wheels of commerce*. William Collins Sons & Co Ltd. https://epdf.pub/civilization-and-capitalism-15th-18th-century-volume-ii-the-wheels-of-commerce.html

Centers for Disease Control and Prevention. (2019). *The 1918 Pandemic (H1 N1 Virus)*. Retrieved from https://www.cdc.gov/flu/pandemic-resources/1918-pandemic-h1n1.html

De Witte, S. N. (2014). Mortality risk and survival in the aftermath of the medieval black death. *PLoS ONE, 9*(5), e96513. https://doi.org/10.1371/journal.pone.0096513

Economist. (2019, January 8). Globalisation is dead and we need to invent a new world order. *Economist*. https://www.economist.com/open-future/2019/06/28/globalisation-is-dead-and-we-need-to-invent-a-new-world-order

Edel, C., & Rapp-Hooper, M. (2020, May 18). The 5 ways U.S.-China competition is hardening. *Foreign Policy*. https://foreignpolicy.com/2020/05/18/united-states-competition-coronavirus-pandemic-tensions/

Firth, J. (2012, April). The history of plague – Part 1. The three great pandemics. *Journal of Military and Veterans' Health, 20*(2), 11–16. http://jmvh.org/wp-content/uploads/2012/12/JMVH_History-of-Plague.pdf
Friedman, J., & Chase-Dunn, C. (2005). *Hegemonic declines: Past and present*. Paradigm Publishers.
Friedman, M. (1962). *Capitalism and freedom*. University of Chicago Press.
Harkavy, R. (2020). COVID-19 and the world of work. International Labor Organization. https://www.ilo.org/global/topics/coronavirus/lang%2D%2Den/index.htm
Hayek, F. (1944). *The road to serfdom*. Routledge.
Inoue, A., Kuo, C.-H., & Rossi, B. (2014, November 24). When economic models are unable to fit the data, what can researchers do? *Vox*. https://voxeu.org/article/when-economic-models-are-unable-fit-data
Kennedy, P. (1987). *The rise and fall of the great powers: Economic change and military conflict from 1500 to 2000*. Vintage Books.
Keynes, J. M. (1936). *The general theory of employment, interest and money*. Palgrave Macmillan.
Kondratiev, N. (1985). *The major economic cycles*. E. P. Dutton Publishing.
Litan, R. (2000, March 1). The 'Globalisation' challenge: The U.S. role in shaping world trade and investment. *Brookings*. https://www.brookings.edu/articles/the-globalization-challenge-the-u-s-role-in-shaping-world-trade-and-investment/
Mendes, M. V. I. (2018). Is it the end of North-American hegemony? A structuralist perspective on Arrighi's systemic cycles of accumulation and the theory of hegemonic stability. *Brazilian Journal of Political Economics, 38*(3), 434–449. https://doi.org/10.1590/0101-35172018-2799
Mises, L. V. (1954). *Theory and history: An interpretation of social and economic evolution*. Arlington House.
Modelski, G. (1987). *Long cycles in world politics*. Palgrave Macmillan.
Morgan, M. (1990). The history of econometric ideas. *Journal of the History of Economic Thought, 13*(2), 273–275. https://doi.org/10.1017/S1053837200003631
North, J. (2011). *The death toll of Justinian's plague and its effects on the Byzantine Empire*. https://www.medievalists.net/2013/04/the-death-toll-of-justinians-plague-and-its-effects-on-the-byzantine-empire/
Pak, A., Oyelola, A., Adegboye, A., Adekunle, I., Rahman, K., McBryde, M., & Eisen, D. (2020, May 29). Economic consequences of the COVID-19 outbreak: The need for epidemic preparedness. *Frontiers in Public Health, 8*(241), 1–4. https://doi.org/10.3389/fpubh.2020.00241
Rapoza, T. (2020, April 3). The post-Coronavirus world may be the end of globalisation. *Forbes*. https://www.forbes.com/sites/kenrapoza/2020/04/03/the-post-coronavirus-world-may-be-the-end-of-globalisation/?sh=399163657e66
Steil, B. (2013). *The Battle of Bretton Woods: John Maynard Keynes, Harry Dexter White, and the making of a New World Order*. Princeton University Press.
Taleb, N. N. (2007). *The black swan: The impact of the highly improbable*. Random House.
Trampusch, C. (2019). The financialisation of the state: Government debt management reforms in New Zealand and Ireland. *Competition and Change, 23*(1), 3–22. https://doi.org/10.1177/1024529418800778
Webb, M., & Krasner, S. (1989). Hegemonic stability theory: An empirical assessment. *Review of International Studies, 15*, 183–198. https://doi.org/10.1017/S0260210500112999
World Bank. (2020, June 8). *COVID-19 to Plunge Global Economy into Worst Recession since World War II*. https://www.worldbank.org/en/news/press-release/2020/06/08/covid-19-to-plunge-global-economy-into-worst-recession-since-world-war-ii
World Health Organization. (2020a). *Summary of probable SARS cases*. https://www.who.int/csr/sars/country/table2004_04_21/en/
World Health Organization. (2020b). *WHO coronavirus disease (COVID-19) dashboard*. Retrieved May 7, 2021 from https://covid19.who.int/

The Role of Political Leadership in Shaping Integrated Urban Policy Frameworks in the City of Semarang, Indonesia

Faruq Ibnul Haqi and Stefanie Dühr

Abstract Since the introduction of regional autonomy legislation in 1999, Indonesia has been pursuing a major process of democratic decentralisation. The resulting administrative and political processes of restructuring have had considerable impacts on the urban planning system in Indonesian cities (Firman, 2014). There seem to be considerable differences in how Indonesia's rapidly growing cities are dealing with urban challenges (Dethier, 2017). Urban policymaking processes in Indonesian cities are characterised by complexity and can be hampered by unclear responsibilities of central and local government as a result of the decentralisation process. The political leadership of cities appears to play a major role in shaping urban policies that are inclusive, equitable, and consider environmental sustainability.

This paper discusses the role of urban political leadership in defining urban policies aimed at providing a strong framework for coordinating plans and projects that meet the requirements of current and future generations. The study focuses on analysing the role of political leadership in the urban policy initiatives in Semarang, the capital city of Central Java Province. The analysis leads to the identification of key features and elements affecting urban policy on urban infrastructure provisions. The empirical analysis in this paper results from in-depth interviews with key policymakers and stakeholders in the City of Semarang. The findings presented in this paper allow critical reflection on the role of urban political leadership in shaping integrated urban policies aimed at urban development.

Keywords Political leadership · Urban policy · Urban development · Indonesia · Semarang

F. I. Haqi (✉) · S. Dühr
University of South Australia, Adelaide, Australia
e-mail: faruq.haqi@mymail.unisa.edu.au; Stefanie.Duehr@unisa.edu.au

© The Author(s), under exclusive license to Springer Nature Singapore Pte Ltd. 2022

T. Chaiechi, J. Wood (eds.), *Community Empowerment, Sustainable Cities, and Transformative Economies*, https://doi.org/10.1007/978-981-16-5260-8_30

1 Introduction

The Central Bureau of Statistics of Indonesia (BPS (2015) stated that Indonesia currently has a population of 269 million people or 3.49 per cent of the total world population. Indonesia is ranked as the fourth most populous country in the world after China (1.42 billion people), India (1.37 billion people), and the United States (328 million people). As cited by the Indonesian Ministry of Home Affairs (Kemendagri, 2018), Indonesia has 514 cities and districts spreading across 34 provinces. According to recent statistics, 56 per cent of Indonesia's population or 150 million inhabitants live in urban areas (BPS, 2014). Data on global trends in urbanisation and city growth are critical for evidence-based policymaking and planning. For example, urban sprawl is a significant challenge for Indonesia as capital cities are experiencing rapid urbanisation. This phenomenon could be serious challenges for mayors and policymakers to ensure sustainable urban development (Haqi & Pandangwati, 2021; Haqi & Pieters, 2019). Urban policies formulated by the city government to provide urban infrastructure, which is part of urban development, should be able to maintain a balance between the city and its environment. That is why cities undergoing rapid urbanisation processes require strong political leadership. This condition has consequences and poses crucial challenges for mayors in managing their region, especially related to what urban policies will be taken in the process of city development.

Besides the reason for urbanisation, which impacts urban issues such as uncontrolled urban sprawl in Indonesia, another influence is decentralisation (Firman, 2010). Firman stated that the concept of decentralisation for Indonesia may not be a new idea because Indonesia has implemented a system of regional autonomy in several cities and districts over the past decades. The central government has increasingly emphasised the role of local governments in the provision of urban services and infrastructures. One of the effects is that the local governments achieve more influential authority to control development objectives in their regions (Fahmi et al., 2015). This will be advantageous when the urban development process is carried out based on needs and supported by accurate data. Hence, data on general trends in urbanisation and city growth are essential for evidence-based urban policy making and planning (Bunce, 2017). In conjunction with this, Fahmi et al. (2015) argued that local leaders have a strategic position to handle the decision-making process, as they know how to meet the local demands by surpassing professional boundaries, integrating different development dimensions within a coordinated action, and developing networks between stakeholders (Cullen et al., 2010).

The rapid pace of urban growth results in extensive demands for the capacity of the government to provide appropriate urban services, including transportation, education, health, housing, sanitation, and employment. Decentralisation which has been introduced in Indonesia over the last few decades, has had an impact on the policy-making process. This process has become the authority of local governments to deal with and address increasingly complex urban problems (Firman, 2014). Decentralisation has given the local governments immense authority to formulate urban development agendas and programmes, but the capacity of local governments to answer the decentralisation has varied noticeably depending on the level of local-government abilities. As stated by Anwar and Theresa (2004), decentralisation is a step and a decision to reduce local governments' dependence on the central government. Anwar and Theresa mentioned that the power and authority for managing the budget for public expenditure have moved from the central government to the local governments. Aside from that, with the conditions and advantages of regional autonomy, the local governments are expected to take initiatives to promote sustainable urban development and manage their investment projects (Alm & Indrawati, 2004).

The progress of decentralisation, which is being implemented for more than two decades since the fall of the New Order in 1999, has not yielded uniform outcomes. Some cities and districts may have been able to develop impressively, but several other areas in Indonesia are experiencing worsening urban conditions. One of the main reasons is that the regions still depend on the quality of leadership of local elites, especially regents and mayors. In fact, many heads of municipalities and districts have been able to bring economic development and better public service provisions to their regions. As von Luebke (2009) argues:

> *[Under Indonesia's decentralisation reform] the quality of government leadership ... emerges as a salient force driving the quality of policy outcomes ... [The] district heads with strong managerial skills and long-term career aspirations have successfully used their official powers to initiate broad-based reform and supervise bureaucratic performance. (p. 202)*

Hence, this study aims to investigate the role of urban political leadership in the making of urban policies in Semarang city. This study examines the approach and concept of leadership of the city leaders of Semarang in the policy-making process. It provides a brief overview of the urban development policies planned in Semarang as one of the results of government activities.

Considering the aims of the study, the research question is how political leadership influences the making of urban policy in the context of urban infrastructure provisions be a part of urban development, which can maintain the relationship between the city and its natural environment to remain balanced? That is why cities undergoing rapid urbanisation processes require strong political leadership. This condition has consequences and poses crucial challenges for mayors in managing their region, especially related to what urban policies will be taken in the process of city development.

This paper discusses the role of urban political leadership in defining urban policies aimed at providing a strong framework for coordinating plans and projects that meet the requirements of current and future generations. The study focuses on analysing the role of political leadership in the urban pol-icy initiatives in Semarang, the capital city of Central Java Province. The analysis leads to the identification of key features and elements affecting urban policy on urban infrastructure provisions. The empirical analysis in this paper results from in-depth interviews with key policymakers and stakeholders. The findings presented in this paper allow a critical reflection on the role of urban political leadership in shaping integrated urban policies aimed at urban development.

This paper is divided into four sections. The first section outlines the background of the research, identifying the research gap and study area. The second section explores the research methods which discussesd about data collection process and data analysis. The third section discusses the findings of the research on decentralisation, urban development, and urban political leadership. The last section of this paper proposes conclusion the study.

1.1 Research Significance and Knowledge Gap

This study is significant because it improves the function of political leadership, which plays an essential role in the initiation of urban policies in Semarang, the capital city of Central Java Province. Scholarly attention to the role of political leadership in urban policies in Indonesia has been limited to date. The urgency of the urban policy issues to be responded may have forced academics and experts to investigate the issues deeply in terms of prescriptive and normative aspects rather than the empirical aspects. This research also fills a significant gap in knowledge of urban studies that substantially impacts urban policies to promote the eminence of leadership aspect in urban management.

Particularly in Indonesia, this study helps fulfil common goals of municipal institutions by identifying factors that influence the innovativeness of urban policies in the municipal government. Additionally, this work will enrich the body of literature by showing the importance of policymakers' underlying factors and learning experience and augments the prior research from developing countries by discussing the rich 'external environment' background of the study.

Lastly, the research contributes to discussions on political leadership practices, expanding the understanding of the role of urban leadership and key players in planning and development. It considers the extent to which elements of leadership character influence the success of the planning system and how they could be used to support the effectiveness of spatial planning programs in developing countries, especially in Indonesia.

1.2 Literature Review and Theoretical Framework

Different definitions of leadership have been proposed. Predominantly in the context of local development, it is not a straightforward concept. There have been numerous published studies that have methodically analysed the nature of leadership. Nevertheless, it is essential to describe what leadership is in the context of urban development. A leader is commonly defined as a 'great person' (Hoffman et al., 2011; Isaac Mostovicz, Kakabadse, & Kakabadse, 2009; Spector, 2016). Leadership models have changed from the great man theory and trait theory to transformational leadership theory (MaloŞ, 2012). He also states that the previous concepts put emphasis on traits and individual figure of leaders. On the word of these hypotheses, Bolden, Gosling, Marturano, and Dennison (2003) expressed that leaders are extraordinary people who have specific characteristics and exceptional qualities, and certainly those born to be leaders. Therefore, the situational leadership theory reveals that there is no method that is appropriate for everything, but it should be adapted to the situation. Bolden et al. (2003) injunction method could be apposite for highly repetitive, monotonous, and systematic settings, while for active, alive, and vibrant environments, a participatory approach will possibly a better fit.

Because these theories, as described previously, are considered too narrow and not representing the reality, recent leadership theories tend to disregard such person-centred approaches (Morse et al., 2010). The current understanding is no longer looking at the leadership figure as the starring role or single person, but rather as a collective action where numerous stakeholders are able to participate, collaborate and work together in making decisions for common purposes (Rondinelli & Heffron, 2009; Stimson et al., 2009). Planners and policymakers work together for various purposes in the policy process and for different type of territories.

Furthermore, previous research has shown that the main challenge in the city development is the initiation urban policies which are largely determined by leadership and governance factors (Barber & Eastaway, 2010; Bochel & Bochel, 2010; Bossink, 2007; Collinge & Gibney, 2010; Hambleton & Sweeting, 2014; John & Cole, 1999; Reiter, 2012; Stimson et al., 2009). Therefore, it needs to be well prepared in the process of making policies so that the city development objectives are on target and successful. Considering the urgency of leadership in the planning system in the era of regional autonomy, it is necessary to study the importance of urban political leadership in commencing urban policies.

1.3 Study Area

The decision-making process for determining urban policies is not easy, and it is done in different levels of the management structure of Indonesian cities. The mayor is in the highest position of decision-making, and senior officers of the municipalities are in the second level. Meanwhile, the bottom layer consists of lower-level administrators and officers responsible for the technical implementation of urban policies. It requires a strong leader who is able to manage complex bureaucratic systems at each level of the management structure. The mayoral leadership plays an essential role in the decision-making process. (Table 1)

The City of Semarang is struggling to deal with city problems and trying to improve in the last few decades. They improve urban development by employing several urban policies (Joewono et al., 2016; OECD, 2014). As an example, their local task is to formulate an effective urban design program to improve the image of their city. The formulated program impacts various areas of urban policies such as

Table 1 City of Semarang profile

Size Area (km2)	Total population	Population density	Total districts	Mayoral election
373,780	1.602.717	4.289/ km2	16 districts & 177 sub-districts	Directly elected

Source: BPS (2014)

infrastructure, including roads, sidewalks, transport, and housing. The program and strategy formulated should be able to highlight the significance of urban policies for sustainable development, especially related to harmony with nature and surroundings (Homsy et al., 2016).

Remarkably, in line with several pieces of literatures for instance Getimis and Grigoriadou (2005); Getimis and Hlepas (2006) found that different city leaders have very different styles and approaches to dealing with urban challenges. The differences in approach are also influenced by both internal and external factors (Getimis & Hlepas, 2006). Conversely, because of the decentralisation, the urban governance system and the bureaucracy structures employed in the city of Semarang has the autonomy to manage their respective regions. Considering challenges and factors that can influence the process of initiating urban policies, this study highlights the need for collaboration between multiple levels of government and all stakeholders, including non-governmental stakeholders such as developers, planners, and communities, to ensure the success of urban policies. Therefore, this research will focus on understanding the role of political leadership in the City of Semarang, Indonesia in initiating urban policies.

2 Methods

A simple 3-step methodology is followed here. In the beginning, this study attempted to identify the key concepts of political leadership by analysing existing urban political leadership frameworks and their themes and components. Afterwards, these components were classified after passing them through a specified sorting condition to get the final composition of the framework consisting of components and features. As a final step, concluded the key findings based on the qualitative descriptive approach. (Fig. 1)

2.1 Data Collection

In the case study design, it is essential to develop and design how the study will be addressed to answer the research question. Therefore, it is important to make sure that the data collection is appropriate. The study used a case study design based on

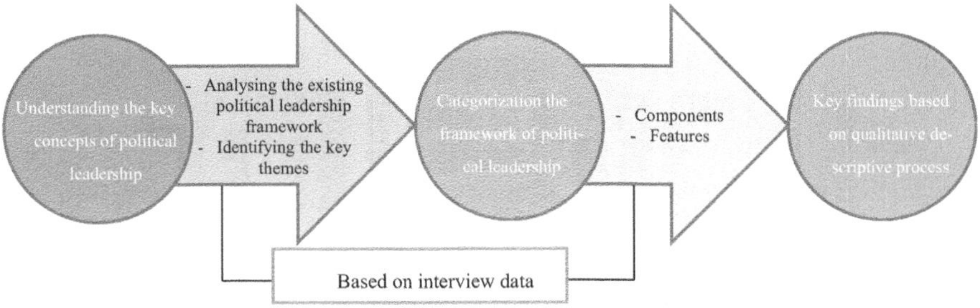

Fig. 1 The methodology followed to establish the political leadership framework

political leadership model introduced by Sweeting (2002) to investigate the policymaking processes. The design for this study employed semi-structured interviews with the key policymakers as the primary data collection technique. Interviews were analysed using thematic qualitative analysis.

Data collection for the purposes of this study was carried out between August and October 2021 in the city of Semarang using one-on-one, semi-structured and audio-recorded interview. Before the interview commenced, the researcher sent participant information sheets a few weeks before the interview to the potential participants. This has been done by the researcher so that the participants have the opportunity to read all the information related to this research. In addition, to allow them to ask any questions they may have had before agreeing to participate and signing the consent form. Field notes were taken in parallel with the interview to support the dependability aspect of this study. Each interview lasted approximately 60–75 minutes and was conducted in Bahasa Indonesia, the native language of the participants.

Approvals to conduct the study were obtained from accredited human research ethic committees (HREC) in the University of South Australia. Written informed consent was obtained from each participant prior to the interview.

2.2 *Data Analysis*

The data generated were subject to qualitative thematic analysis and coding using the QSR NVivo 12 qualitative research software. As noted previously, this study uses qualitative components. All the interview data has been transcribed and categorised, then organised for code analysis using QSR NVivo 12 software. This software provides several tools for qualitative data analysis. (Fig. 2)

Overall, this research was analysed through successive phases. All data and conversations audio recordings have been transcribed in the initial stage, and the transcripts have been gathered and categorised. The data were then thematically analysed following the framework using NVivo 12 (QSR International). Then commenced to separate and disassembled data by coding them into several themes. After that, the codes reassembled to generate a comprehensive portrait. At the final

Fig. 2 The word clouds of interview analysis (*in Bahasa Indonesia*)

stage, the data in the previous phase interpreted and concluded based on the theoretical concepts in this study.

3 Discussions and Findings

3.1 Decentralisation and Development Planning Process

Numerous academics and urban experts have examined and discussed general urban issues and challenges at metropolitan or regional scales. Urban problems are very complex and will always arise. The government should address these challenges. Generally, municipalities will explore what urban policies are needed to appropriately address urban problems. According to Hudalah, Firman, and Woltjer (2014), the decentralisation strategy has been connected as a tracking down of political reform and '*modality of democratisation'* which corresponds to Indonesia as developing country. This strategy has changed the existing planning system in Indonesia which was previously concentrated at the central government (Firman 2010). This devolution process has been carried out in Indonesia using a bottom-up approach model which has replaced the previously centralised and top-down system as explained earlier. One of the effects is that the local governments obtain more influential authority to control the development objectives in their regions (Fahmi et al. 2015).

Numerous respondents of this study have commented about urban development process and their issues. One of senior officers in the Semarang City stated that:

> *"'During my time as a policy maker in Semarang City, I have experienced 3 different mayors. Each of these leaders has different priorities for what policies will be done to deal with the problems of the city. .... It can be said that this is the positive seed of the decentralisation policy because we (the city of Semarang) can decide what policies to take ....."*

Another view is from a senior key policymaker who in relation to thequestion of what the city is required to be able to solve their problems stated that:

> *"In the past, all policies were from the central government, now we are obliged to be able to manage urban policies to deal with problems in the city."*

Another perspective is come from senior officer in urban planning who further commented:

> *"The biggest problem in the city of Semarang is flooding. This is because the position of our city is slightly above sea level. Slowly but surely, the Semarang City Government has been able to handle this problem even though it is not finished."*

This is in line with what has been stated by Firman (2010), decentralisation has enabled urban governance institutions to overcome inter-local government development problems. This would be a challenge for local governments and active participation from all elements is needed. Active participation from all levels of government, policymakers and the public are needed to find a solution. Therefore, good city governance is required to activate all these lines (Bunnell, Miller, Phelps, & Taylor, 2013). Governance is much more multifaceted than the government. One of the objectives of governance is to promote vibrant and environmentally sustainable communities. To be more wide-ranging, the UNDP (2004) defines governance broadly as:

> *Governance is the system of values, policies and institutions by which a society manages its economic, political and social affairs through interactions within and among the state, civil society and private sector. It is the way a society organises itself to make and implement decisions—achieving mutual understanding, agreement and action. It comprises the mechanisms and processes for citizens and groups to articulate their interests, mediate their differences and exercise their legal rights and obligations. It is the rules, institutions and practices that set limits and provide incentives for individuals, organisations and firms. Governance, including its social, political and economic dimensions, operates at every level of human enterprise, be it the household, village, municipality, nation, region or globe.*

There are two boundless challenges in urban and regional governance, namely competitiveness and quality of life (Freire et al., 2001). Reform of urban and regional governance institutions is absolutely critical to sustainable urban development.

Consistent with Healey (2006b) what is needed for institutional improvement of extended metropolitan areas is the resolution of metropolitan policy issues at the macro and micro levels which traditional local governments cannot provide alone and the development of new forms of coordination. In the case study presented in this paper, one respondent who is also a senior policy maker also stated that:

> *"…..Semarang City Government really needs collaboration between all stakeholders to provide urban infrastructure in order to support the success of city development ..."*

The basis of Indonesia's decentralisation policy reforms is the shift of some of the functions, tasks and responsibilities of the central government to local governments. Local government that consists of Provincial and Municipalities (cities and regencies) will have a greater role and function in several crucial tasks. As stated by the Ministry of Home Affairs (MOHA) or Kemendagri (2018), the decentralisation has altered the structure of responsibilities from the national level to the regions which consist of 514 autonomous municipal level (cities and regencies); with 34 provinces doing coordinating functions. This is recognising Indonesia's diversity and widespread geography that is too wide to cover centrally. This is realistic because it is difficult for the central government to cover all regions in Indonesia. The difficulty of the central government in overcoming urban problems was also acknowledged by the senior policy maker in the city of Semarang who said that:

> *"several regulations in Indonesia were still overlapping, and this made us "dizzy" in the local government as the lowest executor. Carefulness is needed to anticipate it, so that innovative policies will come out but do not violate existing rules ..."*

It is necessary to recognise how complex the current Indonesian administrative system is. Indonesia is a Unitary State, in the form of a Republic under Article 1 of the 1945 Indonesian Constitution. Recently, Indonesia is divided into 34 provinces and 514 cities and regencies. Its management system has six levels of government operations or administrative levels, namely: provincial *(propinsi)*, municipal/ regency *(kotamadya/kabupaten)*, district *(kecamatan)*, village *(kelurahan)*, community *(Rukun Warga or RW)*, and neighbourhood (*Rukun Tetangga or RT*). (Table 2)

The official name of government level and the title of heads of the regions clearly reflect the unitary system of government in Indonesia. The design of the hierarchy is structured to help reach the authority of the central government to the lowest level of government. Interestingly, the lowest level in the hierarchy is the community, consisting of RWs and RTs as informal structures. Even though they are non-formal, their role is important to the local government. From this level, the local government filters and gets input from the community for the types of policies that will be formulated in urban policies. This process is called *Musrenbang* or development planning discussions, which is carried out in a face-to-face format in which policy makers and the public directly discuss the issues faced by the communities and decide priorities for short-term improvements. Local communities (*RWs* and *RTs*) and governments now have a greater responsibility and obligation to shape the future of their neighbourhoods. From this process, municipalities have more freedom to explore innovative policies and practices in integrated solutions.

Table 2 Organization of the governmental system in Indonesia

Government Level	Head	Structure	Structure
Provincial	Governor	Indonesia = 34 provinces 1 province = 5–10 municipalities/regencies	Formal
Municipal *(Kota)* or Regency *(Kabupaten)*	Mayor *(walikota)* or Regent *(Bupati)*	1 municipal/regency = 5–10 districts *(kecamatan)* depends on size of area	Formal
District *(Kecamatan)*	District head *(Camat)*	1 *kecamatan* = 10–20 *kelurahans*	Formal
Sub-district / village *(Kelurahan)*	Village head *(Lurah)*	1 *kelurahan* = 10–20 *RWs*	Formal
Community association *(RW)*	RW chairperson	1 *RW* = 5–15 *RTs*	Informal
Neighbourhood association *(RT)*	RT chairperson	1 RT = 15–100 households	Informal

Source: Own compilation based on Kemendagri (2019)

The development planning meeting is a discussion for deliberation among all stakeholders and the communities to draft and develop national and regional development plans. The *Musrenbang* is regulated in Indonesian Law No. 25 of 2004 concerning the National Development Planning System. *BAPPENAS* (National Development Planning Agency) is a government agency who has responsibilities for the national planning level, whereas *BAPPEDA* (Regional Development Planning Agency) has responsibilities at the regional or city level. The *Musrenbang* is a participatory or top-down approach that involves all levels of the governmental organisation from the suburb (neighbourhood and community association) to the sub-district or village, district, and city levels. This series of forums become part of developing a plan and budgeting system as a means of shaping policies for realising the development activities each year (Bappenas, 2019). Through the discussion forum, the community has the chance to propose and deliver their aspirations as well as participate in producing development plan documents based on their needs.

The respondent who is also senior policymaker in Semarang, also commented on the *Musrenbang*. The senior policymaker at Bappeda stated that

> *".... In fact, this forum has a very noble goal, namely, to accommodate the aspirations of the community. Therefore, the government really needs input from the public on what policies are urgent to solve the problem ... "*

However, what is surprising was the criticism from city planners who were also community leaders who said that

> *"Musrenbang has a good aim to get input from the community. But unfortunately, this forum still has the impression that it is only a formality. This has been done for several years, and the process is still the same".*

Remarkably, one of the difficulties and challenges in the *Musrenbang* forum, as acknowledged by Padawangi (2019), is dominance by more established and influential groups or individuals who understand the development process and can influence it. This is also recognised by Taylor (2019) in his investigation found that they often pursue based on the desires of individuals or their groups, without prioritising the common interests. Basically, the *Musrenbang* has great goals. One of which is the emergence of non-government stakeholders and community participation in the development process to reach consensus on developing and arranging development planning policies (Buchori & Sugiri, 2016). But unexpectedly, numerous previous studies (Hidayat, 2017; Sopanah, 2012; Taylor, 2019) have detected that the deliberation process on the *Musrenbang* forum does not authentically involve citizens to their full potential. Instead, the findings discovered that it is more a bureaucratic forum and ceremonial with a centralistic, top-down approach.

The *Musrenbang* is a 'way of approaching' by bringing together various stakeholders in a forum at the same time, which is typically led by public agencies to take consensus decisions. The principle emphasised in the forum is that the approach taken leads to results, and achievements that can satisfy all parties involved in the process. This model is similar to collaborative governance in the Western concept which has been developed since early 2000 (Westerink et al., 2016). The analysis of Innes and Booher (2004) showed that there are common attributes such as consensus rule-making, community visioning, policy consensus, and collaborative network structures in collaborative governance. They also argue that collaborative governance models must be involved in "authentic dialogue" with various stakeholders legitimately representing their interests, but with 'special note' that they must have an 'open minded' commitment and willingness in order to 'seek mutual solutions'.

This is advocated by numerous academics and experts (Booher & Innes, 2002; Healey, 1998; Purbani, 2017; Westerink et al., 2016) who have agreed on the new paradigm of planning as collaborative planning. It can also be said that people can build up relational networks and resolve complex conflicts through collaborative planning based on interpretive approaches (Healey, 2006a). In particular, she also noted that collaborative planning systems play an essential role in dealing with the complexity and diversity of the city governance fields. In other words as mentioned by Johnston, Hicks, Nan, and Auer (2011), appropriate and efficient management by involving all elements of stakeholders in the collaborative governance process would be able to produce power to create a strengthening cycle of trust, understanding, commitment and communication.

3.2 The Local Political Leadership

There has been growing awareness from scholars and professionals in discussions on the importance of leadership in the urban planning literature (Balducci & Calvaresi, 2004; Borraz & John, 2004; Svara, 1990). Several published pieces of literature state that leadership aspect indicates how to cultivate an effective collaboration on the urban renewal process (Horita et al., 2009; Westerink et al., 2016). A practical leadership concept, which is designed for specific a governance setting, can foster dialogues, help mobilise resources, overcome conflicts and encourage participation between stakeholders (Crosby & Bryson, 2005; Cullen et al., 2010; Innes & Booher, 2018).

The role of local political leadership is a critical component of the transformation schema in Indonesian regional governance. This is also acknowledged by the companion of the Mayor of Semarang who stated that:

> *"... The mayor leadership genuinely determines the direction of the city, where it is going and what it looks like. With the tagline "Great Semarang", it should also be balanced with strong leadership to bring about changes for the better city."*

It can be said that leadership is the single most momentous driver of change and enhancement in local authorities. Leadership is essential for arranging and supporting comprehensible basic rules, assisting dialogue, fostering trust, and discovering mutual gains. Bolden et al. (2003) argue that leadership has a vital role in embracing and empowering stakeholders to engage in certain objectives, and then mobilise them to advance collaboration. Scholars and experts stress that collaborative governance involves specific sorts of leadership. Purbani (2017) described collaborative leaders as individuals who were able to serve, transform or facilitate the public interest, rather than individual leaders who took decisive actions.

Related to the leadership style of the mayor of Semarang, several respondents gave their views. The senior policymaker in the planning field stated that:

> *"The mayor of Semarang has a background as a politician, so he can communicate his politics very well. So that the policy proposals submitted at the DPRD do not experience too much friction ..."*

Another view was also shared by members of the local council, he stated that:

> *"... The program proposed by the mayor is currently more collaborative with the community. Programs like this are sure to get more support. By involving public participation, of course, it will be easy to overcome complex urban problems and the needs that exist at the grassroots, for example repairing damaged roads, sanitation and street lighting."*

The idea of redesigning or reforming local governance structure to improve local leadership is common in Western countries. In addition to the UK in 1999 and 2000, which agreed regulation announcing mayoral models of governance, the following European countries, Slovakia in 1990, Italy in 1993, Hungary in 1994 (only some cities then since 1998 all municipalities), and Poland in 2002, have introduced directly elected mayors to their systems of local government (Hambleton & Sweeting, 2014). The notion of strengthening local leadership by announcing directly elected mayors in the UK has moved on and off several times from the policy agenda (Fenwick & Elcock, 2014; Hambleton & Sweeting, 2014). Furthermore, during the 1990s until the early 2000s, several countries outside Europe such as Costa Rica, New Zealand and Australia also adopted direct elections for mayors. Lately, directly elected mayors are on the rise internationally, including Asian countries like Indonesia, which commenced when the reform era after the new-order era collapsed in 1998. From the discussion above, it seems plausible to assert that despite the differences between Western nations and Indonesia in the context of the commencement, Indonesia's direct elections are the beginning of a change in the local government bureaucratic system, which was previously chosen through a parliamentary system representative. Changes to the mayor election system are the single most momentous driver of change and enhancement in local authorities.

According to John and Cole (1999), there are four themes identified in international public discourse related to urban leadership. The first theme is the institutional design of local government: to which extent the design of local government organisations has significance. This is supported, for example on the Western local government leadership literature which analysed the work of political leaders and senior officers, the work of Brown and Mouritzen (2003) that concluded 'Institutions matter, and the choice of political-administrative structure makes a difference'. The second theme is the drive for outward-facing leadership focused on the shifting environment within which civic leadership is exercised. It can be said that the forces of globalisation need a distinctive sort of locality leadership than the one that has functioned local government well in the past. The third theme is that the relationship between politicians and officers has changed. This is described as the interconnection between 'politician as elected' and 'professional being appointed officials' functions in executive leadership. The last is the changing relationship between city leaders and followers, including officers in a work environment. As stated by Hambleton and Sweeting (2004), there are unavoidable anticipation and frictions in this relationship. This crack arises when followers may be less trusting and create fewer creative forms of officialdom and politics. In contrast, particular local political cultures have high social capital and cultivate co-operative forms of urban governance.

Leadership studies have proposed a variety of typologies. There are two characteristics in organisational institutions. The first one is the range between directive and responsive leaders. The other is the difference between leaders who are selfish in the narrow sense and those who produce capacity. This is portraying the notion that leadership can improve the ability of the community to govern. The range is captured by Stone and Pierre (1991) distinction. (Fig. 3)

As Fig. 3 indicates, there are four types of leader functions in the crisscross. The caretakers are the frail political leaders who have the capability to deal with the elaborate alliances that have been revealed in local governance. Such leaders, both as city leaders and party chief, feel difficult to overcome the rapidity of the policy change and the complexity of policymaking process. The consensual facilitator is the other type of responsive leaders. These leaders can adapt quickly and have gained knowledge about the urgency of networks and partnerships. These leaders may be popular and are able to generate capacity, but over the time, they have difficulties in developing policies that are driven by the demands of other local actors.

In contrast, strong leaders are on the other side of the axis. The city bosses can be said to have similarities to caretakers, and they have a character that does not adapt well to the new urban governance environment. These leaders have no desire to find alternatives and solutions when they no longer work to manage management strategies. The city boss does not provide innovative policymaking, complex manoeuvring, and understanding of networking which are required (John & Cole,

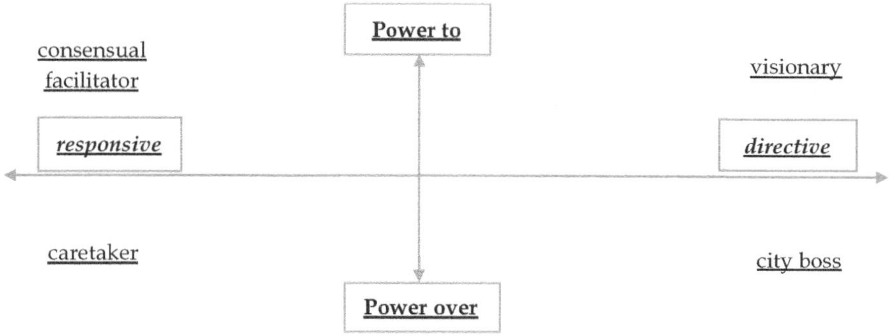

Fig. 3 Leadership typology in urban governance. (Source: Adapted from John and Cole, 1999)

1999). Finally, the visionary combines essentials of capacity generation and strong leadership. The visionary is the who can establish more innovative urban policies and effective coordination amongst officers, who is able to work together with whoever for several purposes, who can knock down some of the recalcitrance, dissension, and disaffection in urban politics (John & Cole, 1999). These leaders have the ability to communicate well with their extensive personal contacts within the public and private sectors. Leadership plays a crucial function in the new urban governance. The politics of bureaucratic reform, decentralisation, rapid policy change, networks, central intervention, partnerships, and participation require powerful but innovative and creative figures who offer a direction to urban policy making (John & Cole, 1999).

This research offers a new standpoint to investigate the role of leadership by employing *Political Leadership Theory (PLT)* for examining the types and factors that influence urban leadership to shape urban policies in Semarang city. The PLT developed by Sweeting (2002) has four components which are formal and informal characteristics (*institutional arrangements*). Then, *external environment* refers to the wide-ranging context or background within which leadership is exercised. Moreover, *local environment* comprises features that are particular to the city including the specific concerns on the local agenda. Lastly, *personal characteristics* of leaders include personal background, skills and psychological traits that contribute to their leadership style. The Table 3 below presents an operationalisation of the key concepts and elements of political leadership in this study.

Conclusion Urban problems are very complex and rarely is there are a simple solution. The government should address these challenges. Generally, municipalities will explore what sort of urban policy will be carried out to overcome urban problems. The decentralisation strategy in Indonesia has been connected as a tracking down of political reform and *'modality of democratisation'*, which reflects the status of Indonesia as a developing country. This strategy has changed the existing planning system in Indonesia, which was previously concentrated at the central government. This devolution process has been carried out in Indonesia using

Table 3 Operationalisation of key concepts

	Description	Examples of what to look for
Institutional arrangement	Formal and informal structures. Formal authority, identity, power and context from which exercise leadership	Empirical pieces of evidence for newly established organisations (or changes in municipal organisational structure), platforms, applications or letter of intents to collaborate on urban development
External environment	National and international which leadership is exercised	References to urban, regional, national or international policy frameworks, agendas and formalised collaboration frameworks
Local environment	The specific characteristics that are particular to the city, and the issues on the local agenda.	References to prioritizations of what city leaders should be in action within local agenda to address local issues, and through which means and through whose involvement they should be developed.
Personal characteristics	Personal background, skills and psychological traits that contribute to their leadership style	Data of the city leaders' profile (such as educational background, experience organisational, training and skills that they have) in the case study cities

Source: Own compilation based on Sweeting (2002)

a bottom-up approach model, replacing the previously centralised and top-down system. One of the effects is that the local governments obtain more influential authority to control the development objectives in their region. Decentralisation has given the local governments immense authority to formulate urban development agendas and programs. Still, the capacity of the local governments to answer the decentralisation has varied noticeably depending on the level of local-government abilities.

The leadership aspect indicates how to cultivate an effective collaboration on the urban renewal process. Based on the evidence of this study in Semarang, leadership is a substantial aspect in shaping what policies will formulate. Evidence shows that leadership plays critical roles in urban governance in facilitating and advising urban policy, primarily related to urban development, such as urban infrastructure provisions through *musrenbang*. The development planning meeting is actually a discussion for deliberation among all stakeholders and the communities to draft and develop national and regional development plans. In fact, the forum does not authentically involve citizens to their full potential. Instead, the findings discovered that it is more a bureaucratic forum and ceremonial with a centralistic, top-down approach.

Drawing on the key findings from the interviews and based on a qualitative approach, this study found a close relationship between mayoral leadership and the urban development process. Based on the case in this study, the quality of the mayor's leadership who can communicate the program well to stakeholders, local councils, and the community will quickly get support in passing the program.

Acknowledgements The authors thank the anonymous reviewers and the editors for their constructive comments on this paper.

References

Alm, J., & Indrawati, S. M. (2004). Decentralization and local government borrowing in Indonesia. In J. Alm, J. Martinez-Vazquez, & S. M. Indrawati (Eds.), *Reforming intergovernmental fiscal relations and the rebuilding: The 'big bang' program and its economic consequences* (pp. 234–260). Edward Elgar Publishing.

Anwar, S., & Theresa, T. (2004). Implementing decentralized local government: A treacherous road with potholes, detours and road closures. In J. Alm, J. Martinez-Vazquez, & S. M. Indrawati (Eds.), *Reforming intergovernmental fiscal relations and the rebuilding: The 'big bang' program and its economic consequences* (pp. 301–337). Edward Elgar Publishing.

Balducci, A., & Calvaresi, C. (2004). Participation and leadership in planning theory and practices. In M. Haus, H. Heinelt, & M. Stewart (Eds.), *Urban governance and democracy: Leadership and community involvement* (1st ed., pp. 234–252). Routledge Taylor & Francis Group.

Bappenas. (2019). *Pedoman musrenbangnas 2019 (guidelines on national development plans deliberation 2019)*. Jakarta: Bappenas Retrieved from https://musrenbangnas.bappenas.go.id/files/musrenbang/petunjuk/2019-05-02%20PEDOMAN%20MUSRENBANG%202019_rev.pdf

Barber, A., & Eastaway, M. P. (2010). Leadership challenges in the inner city: Planning for sustainable regeneration in Birmingham and Barcelona. *Policy Studies, 31*(4), 393–411. https://doi.org/10.1080/01442871003723309

Bochel, H., & Bochel, C. (2010). Local political leadership and the modernisation of local government. *Local Government Studies, 36*(6), 723–737. https://doi.org/10.1080/03003930.2010.523199

Bolden, R., Gosling, J., Marturano, A., & Dennison, P. (2003). *A review of leadership theory and competency frameworks*. Retrieved from United Kingdom: https://ore.exeter.ac.uk/repository/bitstream/handle/10036/17494/mgmt_standards.pdf?sequence=1

Booher, D. E., & Innes, J. E. (2002). Network power in collaborative planning. *Journal of Planning Education and Research, 21*(3), 221–236. https://doi.org/10.1177/0739456X0202100301

Borraz, O., & John, P. (2004). The transformation of urban political leadership in Western Europe. *International Journal of Urban and Regional Research, 28*(1), 107–120. https://doi.org/10.1111/j.0309-1317.2004.00505.x

Bossink, B. A. G. (2007). Leadership for sustainable innovation. *International Journal of Technology Management and Sustainable Development, 6*(2), 135–149.

BPS. (2014). *Persentase penduduk daerah perkotaan menurut provinsi (Percentage of urban population by province), 2010–2035*. BPS. Retrieved from https://www.bps.go.id/statictable/2014/02/18/1276/persentase-penduduk-daerah-perkotaan-menurut-provinsi-2010-2035.html

BPS. (2015). *Proyeksi penduduk Indonesia 2015–2045 berdasarkan hasil SUPAS 2015 (The projected population of Indonesia in 2015–2045 based on the 2015 SUPAS' results)*. BPS.

Brown, A., & Mouritzen, P. (2003). Leadership at the Apex: Politicians and administrators in Western local governments. *Australian Journal of Political Science, 38*(3), 576–576.

Buchori, I., & Sugiri, A. (2016). An empirical examination of sustainable metropolitan development in Semarang City, Indonesia. *Australian Planner, 53*(3), 163–177. https://doi.org/10.1080/07293682.2016.1151905

Bunce, S. (2017). *Sustainability policy, planning and gentrification in cities* (Vol. 1). Taylor and Francis.

Bunnell, T., Miller, M. A., Phelps, N. A., & Taylor, J. (2013). Urban development in a decentralized Indonesia: Two success stories? *Pacific Affairs, 86*(4), 857–876. https://doi.org/10.5509/2013864857

Collinge, C., & Gibney, J. (2010). Connecting place, policy and leadership. *Policy Studies, 31*(4), 379–391. https://doi.org/10.1080/01442871003723259

Crosby, B. C., & Bryson, J. M. (2005). *Leadership for the common good: Tackling public problems in a shared-power world* (2nd ed.). John Wiley & Sons.

Cullen, D., McGee, G. J. A., Gunton, T. I., & Day, J. C. (2010). Collaborative planning in complex stakeholder environments: An evaluation of a two-tiered collaborative planning model. *Society & Natural Resources, 23*(4), 332–350. https://doi.org/10.1080/08941920903002552

Dethier, J. J. (2017). Trash, cities, and politics: urban environmental problems in Indonesia. *Indonesia (Ithaca), 103*, 73–90.

Fahmi, F. Z., Prawira, M. I., Hudalah, D., & Firman, T. (2015). Leadership and collaborative planning: The case of Surakarta, Indonesia. *Planning Theory, 15*(3), 294–315. https://doi.org/10.1177/1473095215584655

Fenwick, J., & Elcock, H. (2014). Elected mayors: Leading locally? *Local Government Studies, 40* (4), 581–599. https://doi.org/10.1080/03003930.2013.836492

Firman, T. (2010). Multi local-government under Indonesia's decentralization reform: The case of Kartamantul (the greater Yogyakarta). *Habitat International, 34*(4), 400–405. https://doi.org/10.1016/j.habitatint.2009.11.005

Firman, T. (2014). Inter-local-government partnership for urban management in decentralizing Indonesia: From below or above? Kartamantul (Greater Yogyakarta) and Jabodetabek (Greater Jakarta) compared. *Space and Polity, 18*(3), 215–232. https://doi.org/10.1080/13562576.2014.959252

Freire, M. E., Stren, R. E., & Stren, R. (2001). *Challenge of urban government: Policies and practices*. Washington: World Bank Publications.

Getimis, P., & Grigoriadou, D. (2005). Changes in urban political leadership: Leadership types and styles in the era of urban governance. In M. Haus, H. Heinelt, & M. Stewart (Eds.), *Urban governance and democracy: Leadership and community involvement* (pp. 168–199). Routledge.

Getimis, P., & Hlepas, N.-K. (2006). Aspects of leadership styles: An interaction of context and personalities. In H. Bäck, H. Heinelt, & A. Magnier (Eds.), *The European mayor: Political leaders in the changing context of local democracy* (pp. 177–199). VS Verlag für Sozialwissenschaften.

Hambleton, R., & Sweeting, D. (2004). U.S.-style leadership for English local government? *Public Administration Review, 64*(4), 474–488. https://doi.org/10.1111/j.1540-6210.2004.00393.x

Hambleton, R., & Sweeting, D. (2014). Innovation in urban political leadership. Reflections on the introduction of a directly-elected mayor in Bristol, UK. *Public Money & Management, 34*(5), 315–322. https://doi.org/10.1080/09540962.2014.945793

Haqi, F. I., & Pandangwati, S. T. (2021). Mayoral leadership in shaping urban beautification in Surabaya and aspects influencing its capacity. *EMARA: Indonesian Journal of Architecture, 6* (2), 91–104. https://doi.org/10.29080/eija.v6i2.1035

Haqi, F. I., & Pieters, J. (2019). The role of leadership influencing the health equality through urban design in the city of Surabaya, Indonesia. *International Journal of Engineering & Technology, 8* (1.9), 434–438. https://doi.org/10.14419/ijet.v8i1.9.26703

Healey, P. (1998). Collaborative planning in a stakeholder society. *Town Planning Review, 69*(1), 1–21. https://doi.org/10.3828/tpr.69.1.h651u2327m86326p

Healey, P. (2006a). *Collaborative planning: Shaping places in fragmented societies* (2nd ed.). Palgrave Macmillan.

Healey, P. (2006b). Transforming governance: Challenges of institutional adaptation and a new politics of space. *European Planning Studies, 14*(3), 299–320. https://doi.org/10.1080/09654310500420792

Hidayat, R. (2017). Political devolution: Lessons from a decentralized mode of government in Indonesia. *SAGE Open, 7*(1). https://doi.org/10.1177/2158244016686812

Hoffman, B. J., Woehr, D. J., Maldagen-Youngjohn, R., & Lyons, B. D. (2011). Great man or great myth? A quantitative review of the relationship between individual differences and leader effectiveness. *Journal of Occupational and Organizational Psychology, 84*(2), 347–381.

Homsy, G. C., Warner, M. E., & Liao, L. (2016). Sustainability and local governments: Planning helps balance environmental, economic, and social equity priorities. *Public Management, 98* (11).

Horita, M., Koizumi, H., Okata, J., & Koizumi, H. (2009). *Innovations in collaborative urban regeneration* (Vol. 6). Springer Japan.

Hudalah, D., Firman, T., & Woltjer, J. (2014). Cultural cooperation, institution building and metropolitan governance in decentralizing Indonesia. *International Journal of Urban and Regional Research, 38*(6), 2217–2234. https://doi.org/10.1111/1468-2427.12096

Innes, J. E., & Booher, D. E. (2004). Reframing public participation: Strategies for the 21st century. *Planning Theory & Practice, 5*(4), 419–436. https://doi.org/10.1080/1464935042000293170

Innes, J. E., & Booher, D. E. (2018). *Planning with complexity: An introduction to collaborative rationality for public policy* (2nd ed.). Routledge.

Isaac Mostovicz, E., Kakabadse, N. K., & Kakabadse, A. P. (2009). A dynamic theory of leadership development. *Leadership and Organization Development Journal, 30*(6), 563–576.

Joewono, T. B., Tarigan, A. K. M., & Susilo, Y. O. (2016). Road-based public transportation in urban areas of Indonesia: What policies do users expect to improve the service quality? *Transport Policy, 49*, 114–124. https://doi.org/10.1016/j.tranpol.2016.04.009

John, P., & Cole, A. (1999). Political leadership in the new urban governance: Britain and France compared. *Local Government Studies, 25*(4), 98–115. https://doi.org/10.1080/03003939908433969

Johnston, E. W., Hicks, D., Nan, N., & Auer, J. C. (2011). Managing the inclusion process in collaborative governance. *Journal of Public Administration Research and Theory, 21*(4), 699–721. https://doi.org/10.1093/jopart/muq045

Kemendagri. (2018). *Pembentukan daerah-daerah di Indonesia sampai dengan tahun 2014 (Formation of regions in Indonesia until 2014)*. Kementerian Dalam Negeri.

Kemendagri. (2019). *Kode dan data wilayah administrasi pemerintahan (code and data on government administrative areas)*. Kementerian Dalam Negeri. Retrieved from https://www.kemendagri.go.id/page/read/48/peraturan-menteri-dalam-negeri-no72-tahun-2019

MaloŞ, R. (2012). The most important leadership theories. *Annals of Eftimie Murgu University Resita, Fascicle II, Economic Studies*, 413–420. Retrieved from https://web.b.ebscohost.com/ehost/pdfviewer/pdfviewer?vid=2&sid=383121df-4ea2-4f07-8b3c-d8a19245cd1d%40pdc-v-sessmgr06

Morse, R. S., Buss, T. F., & Kinghorn, C. M. (2010). *Transforming public leadership for the 21st entury*. M.E. Sharpe.

OECD. (2014). National policy options for managing the impact of urbanisation on green growth. In OECD (Ed.), Towards green growth in Southeast Asia (pp. 147–184). : OECD Publishing.

Padawangi, R. (2019). In R. Padawangi (Ed.), *Routledge handbook of urbanization in Southeast Asia* (1st ed.). Routledge.

Purbani, K. (2017). Collaborative planning for city development. A perspective from a city planner. *Scientific Review Engineering and Environmental Sciences, 26*(1), 136–147. https://doi.org/10.22630/PNIKS.2017.26.1.12

Reiter, A. (2012). Liveable city – Sustainable quality of life as success driver for urban branding. In R. Conrady & M. Buck (Eds.), *Trends and issues in global tourism 2012* (1st ed., pp. 69–76). Springer.

Rondinelli, D. A., & Heffron, J. M. (2009). *Leadership for development: What globalization demands of leaders fighting for change*. Kumarian Press.

Sopanah, A. (2012). Ceremonial budgeting: Public participation in development planning at an Indonesian local government authority. *Journal of Applied Management Accounting Research,*

10(2), 73–84. Retrieved from https://search-proquest-com.access.library.unisa.edu.au/scholarly-journals/ceremonial-budgeting-public-participation/docview/1366365783/se-2?accountid=14649

Spector, B. A. (2016). Carlyle, freud, and the great man theory more fully considered. *Leadership, 12*(2), 250–260.

Stimson, R., Stough, R. R., & Salazar, M. (2009). *Leadership and institutions in regional endogenous development*. Edward Elgar Publishing Limited.

Stone, C., & Pierre, J. (1991). Regime politics – Governing Atlanta, 1946–1988. *Scandinavian Political Studies, 14*(1), 93.

Svara, J. H. (1990). *Official leadership in the city: Patterns of conflict and cooperation*. Oxford University Press.

Sweeting, D. (2002). Leadership in urban governance: The mayor of London. *Local Government Studies, 28*(1), 3–3. https://doi.org/10.1080/714004134

Taylor, J. (2019). Citywide participatory community mapping. In R. Padawangi (Ed.), *Routledge handbook of urbanization in Southeast Asia* (1st ed., pp. 469–477). Routledge.

UNDP. (2004). *Governance indicators: A users' guide*. UNDP. Retrieved from https://www.un.org/ruleoflaw/files/Governance%20Indicators_A%20Users%20Guide.pdf

von Luebke, C. (2009). The political economy of local governance: Findings from an Indonesian field study. *Bulletin of Indonesian Economic Studies, 45*(2), 201–230. https://doi.org/10.1080/00074910903040310

Westerink, J., Kempenaar, A., van Lierop, M., Groot, S., van der Valk, A., & van den Brink, A. (2016). The participating government: Shifting boundaries in collaborative spatial planning of urban regions. *Environment and Planning C: Politics and Space, 35*(1), 147–168. https://doi.org/10.1177/0263774x16646770

Funding Social Protection from Data After COVID-19: Potential Contribution of the Right to Benefit from Scientific Progress

Jayson S. Lamchek

Abstract The paper engages the challenge of expanding social protection after Covid-19 by examining new ideas about funding universal social protection from data. It argues that thinking about the right to benefit from scientific progress (RBSP) in the digital age can have important implications for articulating and understanding the economic fairness issue in the wealth accumulation of Big Tech through Big Data. The paper introduces the need for rebuilding social protection by discussing how the socio-economic crisis brought by COVID-19 put a spotlight on social protection. It then surveys and examines policy-relevant literature that proposes feasible measures for radically expanding social protection post-pandemic, highlighting specifically novel measures that call for taxation of data to fund expanded social protection. The paper then discusses how a human rights approach based on RBSP extends the human rights argument for social protection floors and tax reform. It concludes that RBSP can help articulate novel measures for funding social protection from data.

Keywords Social protection · Right to benefit from scientific progress · Big Data · Human rights · Pandemic

1 Introduction

The social impact of the pandemic, primarily in terms of job loss, ought to be addressed with new insights and creativity commensurate with the unprecedented nature of the pandemic.

This paper engages this challenge by examining new ideas about social protection funded from the taxation of data. Social protection is a human right,[1] yet before

[1] Art. 22, Universal Declaration of Human Rights.

J. S. Lamchek (✉)
ANU College of Law, Acton, ACT, Australia
e-mail: jayson.lamchek@anu.edu.au

© The Author(s), under exclusive license to Springer Nature Singapore Pte Ltd. 2022
T. Chaiechi, J. Wood (eds.), *Community Empowerment, Sustainable Cities, and Transformative Economies*, https://doi.org/10.1007/978-981-16-5260-8_31

COVID-19 struck, most of humanity had no access to any form of social protection program and were vulnerable to disruption to their jobs and livelihoods. The pandemic revealed the extreme inadequacy of existing social protection coverage as millions lost incomes and were pushed into poverty.

In the economic rebuilding that will transpire if and when COVID-19 is managed, policies that allow nations to leapfrog their way into more resilient economies should be favoured over policies that reflected "more of the same" thinking. The painful lessons of the pandemic should goad countries to include in their economic rebuilding the establishment of systems of social protection that will safeguard people against the ruining effects of the next pandemic. A strategy to "recover better" (United Nations Department of Global Communications, 2021) from the pandemic that engaged with proposals to radically strengthen social protection systems is plausible if states put new funding mechanisms on the table.

In recent years, human rights scholars have seriously engaged the problem of extreme poverty and income inequality and have debated the redistributive potential of international human rights law (Alston, 2017, 2019a; Aguilar & Saiz, 2015). As a UN special rapporteur on extreme poverty, Philip Alston championed a human rights argument for social protection floors in the form of a Universal Basic Income (Alston, 2019b). His argument comes in the context of a turn to structural reforms, particularly the reform of tax and fiscal policies, as core human rights issues and concerns (Alston, 2019a). However, this argument does not directly address or engage with novel proposals for the taxation of data.

An extension of the human rights argument for social protection floors takes into consideration the less-commented right to benefit from scientific progress (RBSP), which is a human right provided under article 27.1 of the Universal Declaration of Human Rights (UDHR). This paper explores the implication of implementing RBSP to Big Data progress in terms of instituting a concrete benefit-sharing scheme (Lamchek, 2020). It argues that the novel proposal for data-funded social protection is helpfully thought of as an interpretation of RBSP. It also notes that RBSP allows human rights advocates to grasp the issues of Big Tech's accumulation of wealth through Big Data and data science, especially during the pandemic, and the need to tax or share that wealth as human rights issues.

Article 27.1 UDHR provides that "Everyone has the right . . . to share in scientific advancement and its benefits". Article 15.1(b) of the International Convention of Economic, Social and Cultural Rights (ICESCR) reiterates the right to "enjoy the benefits of scientific progress and its applications". Originally, the framers of the Universal Declaration of Human Rights had intended article 27.1 to play a role in the redistribution of material resources, both domestically and internationally. The French delegate Rene Cassin explained that the right was precisely "intended to give those who had played no part in making scientific progress an indisputable right of access to the benefits of that progress".[2] Moreover, the framers made the recognition

[2]UNGA Third Committee (3rd Session), Hundred and Fiftieth Meeting (20 November 1948), UN Doc A/C.3/SR.150, 619.

of that public interest at par with the already well-recognised and domestically legally protected private intellectual property interests of scientists and investors in scientific production. As Smith observes, the recognition of people's right to benefit from scientific advancement under article 27.1 UDHR and article 15.1(b) ICESCR was precisely intended as a means "to overcome ... obstinate intellectual property hurdles and the construction of monopolies which could ultimately prevent individuals from sharing in the benefits of science" (Smith, 2020).

While much less discussed than other human rights, RBSP has been implemented in medicine, and some scholars have also considered the meaning of RBSP in light of advances in agriculture (De Schutter, 2011). Commentators have traditionally understood "benefits" to refer to scientific information or technological know-how, and that benefit-sharing means sharing information, promoting scientific cooperation, and transferring technology (Schabas, 2007; Morgera, 2015). However, according to Marks and Benedict, in medicine, the "benefits" that article 27.1 UDHR and article 15.1(b) ICESCR mandate everyone "to share" refer to concrete rather than intangible benefits, namely, vaccines and essential medicines and critical medical technologies. Thus, benefit-sharing in the context of medicine means vaccines, essential medicines, and critical medical technologies should be free or easily accessible to even the poorest of the poor who may not afford the market price of such technologies (Marks & Benedict, 2013). Thanks to advocacy around the HIV pandemic and the leadership of the World Health Organization (WHO), states generally recognise that access to essential medicines and vaccines are universal human rights that are superior to private intellectual property interests (Meier et al., 2012; Meier & Yamin, 2011; Heywood, 2009). Access to vaccines and critical medicines are widely understood today as a right deriving not only from the right to health (art. 25 UDHR; art. 12 ICESCR) but also RBSP.[3] In the context of the COVID-19 pandemic, the World Health Organization implements the right to access vaccines through the WHO co-led COVAX program that aims to make COVID-19 free or accessible to developing countries (World Health Organization, 2021). RBSP should also be seen as partly responsible for enabling debate around the legality of preventing developing countries from having access to COVID-19 vaccines through intellectual property hurdles (BBC News, 2021).

The present paper discusses RBSP in relation to progress in Big Data and the digital economy. It contributes to the discussion of social protection post-pandemic and new funding sources by relating RBSP thereto. First, it introduces the problem by discussing how the socio-economic crisis brought by COVID-19 put a spotlight

[3]UN Commission on Human Rights (57th session, 2001) Resolution 2001/33, Access to medication in the context of pandemics such as HIV/AIDS, UN Doc. E/CN.4/RES/2001/33; UN Human Rights Council (2009) Resolution 12/24, October 2009; UN CESCR (2006) General Comment No. 17, paras. 2 and 35; UN General Assembly, 2008, Human Rights Guidelines for Pharmaceutical Companies in Relation to Access to Medicines, Report of the Special Rapporteur on the right of everyone to the highest attainable standard of physical and mental health, Paul Hunt, UN Doc. A/63/338; World Health Assembly (61st Session, 2008, paras. 7 and 10) Resolution 61.21 – Global strategy and plan of action on public health, innovation and intellectual property, WHA61/21.

on social protection. Second, it surveys and examines policy-relevant literature that proposes feasible measures for radically expanding social protection post-pandemic, highlighting specifically novel measures that call for taxation of data to fund expanded social protection. Thirdly, it discusses how a human rights approach based on RBSP extends the human rights argument for social protection floors and tax reform. Finally, it concludes that RBSP can help articulate novel measures for funding social protection from data.

2 Social Protection During COVID-19

The COVID-19 pandemic has generated a global socio-economic crisis. The imposition of restrictions on movement to contain the pandemic has resulted in immense losses in trade and tourism (Farge, 2020; World Trade Organization, 2020), the dwindling of remittances (World Bank, 2020b, 2021), and a standstill in economic activities in general. In June 2020, the World Bank projected a global economic contraction of 5.2% for 2020, the deepest recession in decades. It predicted a contraction of per capita GDP in 2020 for more than 90% of countries, the highest share since 1871 (World Bank, 2020a). The effect on employment and livelihoods proved to be devastating. The International Labor Organization (ILO) estimated in April 2020 that lockdown measures would destroy the livelihoods of 1.6 billion informal workers globally or half of the world's workforce. The percentage is higher in low-income (68%) and lower-middle-income countries (80%), where the workforce consists overwhelmingly of informal workers (International Labor Organization, 2020a). The World Economic Forum announced that unemployment figures in the developed countries alone showed tens of millions reported losing work, more than 12% of the workforce in both the United States and Canada by the second quarter of 2020 (World Economic Forum, 2020).

Social protection is the provision of cash or in-kind income assistance to the population, whether unconditional or made on the basis of an income test (Barrientos, 2010, 1). Social protection generally encompasses social assistance, social insurance, and labour market protection, aiming to reduce poverty and economic and social vulnerability of the poor and marginalised (Food and Agriculture Organization, 2015, xii). Social protection measures are obviously important during the pandemic. They provide the lifeline for people who would otherwise have very little to nothing to pay for food, rent and other necessities. Social protection affects states' health response to COVID-19, as ensuring that populations comply with movement restrictions largely depends on whether people could afford to stay at home. They ensure the health crisis does not turn into a crisis of malnutrition and starvation as well. Moreover, they stimulate aggregate economic demand, which keeps businesses going (United Nations Development Program, 2020; United Nations Department of Social and Economic Affairs, 2020; International Labor Organization, 2021).

During the pandemic, developed countries instituted temporary measures to provide emergency supplemental income to citizens who were unemployed or whose employments have been impacted negatively. For example, in the United States, both the Trump and Biden administrations passed relief packages that included direct cash transfers to citizens. In Australia, this was paralleled by the temporary increase in social security payments through the JobKeeper and JobSeeker programs, which according to one study, saved 2.2 million Australians from falling under the poverty line (Philipps et al., 2020). The study further showed that JobKeeper and JobSeeker, in fact, reduced the number of people in poverty by 32% compared to before COVID-19, though the poverty rate has increased again with subsequent reductions in JobKeeper and JobSeeker payments (Philipps et al., 2020).

In developing countries, the provision of social protection during the pandemic has been severely limited by a lack of resources and/or political will. A study published by the United Nations Development Program (UNDP) in June 2020 noted that low and middle-income countries had only spent a negligible $7 per capita on average in social assistance during the pandemic compared to $121–123 in high-income countries. For this reason, senior officials of the United Nations (UN) urged developing countries to institute emergency schemes for unconditional cash transfers to the most vulnerable during a nine- to twelve-month period (UN News, 2020; United Nations Development Program, 2020). In the accompanying UNDP report, it was argued that rolling out a "Temporary Basic Income" that provided "poor and near-poor households" in 132 developing countries with cash transfers to supplement their income to just above the poverty rate would cost from 0.27% to 0.63% of GDP.

The UNDP report argued that a "Temporary Basic Income" was financially plausible given that the amount represents just 12% of the projected total financial response to COVID-19 in 2020. However, given that this amount was already equivalent to one-third of the amount developing countries owed in external debt payments in that year, it was likely to exacerbate developing country's indebtedness if funded through borrowing. Alternatively, it could be funded if payments for debt servicing were redirected to the provision of social protection (Molina & Ortiz-Juarez, 2020). This was precisely why the UN Secretary-General has called on the International Monetary Fund, the World Bank and the G20 countries to suspend debt collection from all developing nations during the pandemic (United Nations, 2020).

Unfortunately, however, the cooperation of the creditors to this call has been limited to debt relief to the least developed states (Jones & Shalal, 2020). More disturbing, some debtor countries have prioritised external debt servicing and obtaining more debts for their COVID response and recovery but still provided little social protection to their citizens. For example, in the Philippines, the government rejected a proposed debt moratorium fearing this could lead to reduced creditor's trust in the country and inability to borrow further for its economic recovery (Philippines Department of Finance, 2020).

The inadequacy of pre-existing systems of social security is clearly part of the problem. According to the International Labor Organization (ILO), less than 22% of the world's workers are covered by unemployment protection. The majority of 55% of the world population is not covered by any form of social security scheme, such as child benefit, maternity benefit, disability or old age pension and the like (International Labor Organization, 2017). Thus, even had pre-existing programs operated fully during the pandemic, a huge number of people would still have been left out. Moreover, countries with no or underdeveloped social protection systems in place would have struggled to improvise delivery of social protection during the pandemic.

Importantly, strengthening social protection forms part of the UN's Global Development Goals before the pandemic. The ILO in its Social Protection Floors Recommendation, had called on nations to define a social protection floor that should ensure a basic level of social security to all regardless of contribution, and progressively wider scope and higher levels of benefits (International Labor Organization, 2012). States have committed to the adoption of social protection floors as reflected in the 2030 Agenda for Sustainable Development, most explicitly in SDG 1.3 (implement nationally appropriate social protection systems for all, including floors). During the pandemic, the ILO reiterated its call and drew attention to the role of strong social protection systems in cushioning the impact of future pandemics (International Labor Organisation, 2020b, 2021). Clearly, social protection needs to be part of the preparation for the next pandemic.

3 Social Protection and Rebuilding Better

As the United Nations Secretary-General António Guterres has underscored, the economic rebuilding after the pandemic should be turned into "a real opportunity to do things right for the future" (United Nations Department of Global Communications, 2021). The socio-economic impact of COVID-19 has set back progress in the achievement of the Sustainable Development Goals (United Nations Department of Social and Economic Affairs, 2020). But recovery efforts could allow developing countries to leapfrog their way into more resilient economies with innovative policies that result in the faster achievement of SDGs.

Addressing low and middle-income countries specifically, Barbier and Burgess (2020) argued that several criteria defined what innovative policies meant in the context of sustainable post-pandemic recovery. These are policies that: (1) "remove existing policy distortions and correct perverse incentives that inhibit sustainable development"; (2) "create synergies across several SDGs simultaneously", for example, achieving poverty reduction, job creation and economic goals at the same time as improving environmental and health outcomes; (3) "are cost-effective, raise or save revenue, and be quickly and effectively implemented" (Barbier & Burgess, 2020, 2). In other words, innovative policy solutions continued progress towards the 17 SDGs, including the five environmental SDGs 11–15, while delivering immediate socio-economic returns cost-effectively. As they suggested:

> This calls for prioritising policies that yield immediate progress towards several SDGs together without sacrificing other SDGs, require little external financing, generate the necessary funding for any additional investments and have a proven track record.

These criteria, they argued, was satisfied by "subsidy swaps" (Barbier & Burgess, 2020, 1). For example, removing fossil fuel subsidies and investing these subsidies instead in clean energy reduced not only greenhouse gas emissions but also energy poverty across developing countries (Barbier & Burgess, 2020, 2).

Similarly, Guterres emphasised that the transition to green economies was the "better" way to rebuild economies post-COVID. The UN Secretary-General counselled tying new public expenditure for business recovery to the creation of green jobs and sustainable growth. He also pushed to remove fossil fuel subsidies and make "polluters pay for their pollution" to raise funding for these new public expenditures (United Nations Department of Global Communications, 2021).

From the viewpoint of preventing the next pandemic, societies need to rethink how industries are organised (Chebly et al., 2020). For example, to begin with, large-scale agricultural enterprises, intensive poultry and industrial meat production in the grey economy have made the spread of zootonic viruses more likely and more global (Specht, 2020). Thus, economic rebuilding which takes a pandemic prevention approach, will likely involve localising our supply chains and "greening" our food production systems. Societies will also need to rethink mass transportation systems in cities post-COVID so that work commutes are short and safe. This may involve not only rearranging work schedules across industries to eliminate the "rush hour", but anything from installing better ventilation mechanisms into trains and buses to reducing urban density with open spaces and parks (Chebly et al., 2020). Moreover, regardless of whether countries transition to green economies, the uncertainty that businesses faced as governments balanced avoidance of a resurgence or outbreak of cases and the need to reopen businesses will push business towards greater automation (Chernoff & Warman, 2020). Already, many businesses are considering permanently moving part of their workforce online and investing more in technology (Chavez-Dreyfuss, 2020).

As mentioned, grossly inadequate social protection worldwide not only hindered the achievement of SDGs by states but actually caused their setting back in most developing countries during the pandemic, so that the removal or remedying of this policy distortion should be an imperative of post-pandemic rebuilding. Moreover, expanding social protection was an SDG in itself and created synergies across other SDGs, importantly, poverty eradication and health; hence, investing in social protection was a smart way to rebuild especially in developing countries. However, to satisfy the criteria for policy innovation defined by Barbier and Burgess (2020), post-pandemic social protection policy must find a funding mechanism that did not adversely affect the achievement of other SDGs.

In a paper that ILO published, several measures had been identified to fund social protection floors in developing countries. These measures are: reallocating public expenditures; increasing tax revenues; expanding contributory revenues from expanded social security programs; lobbying for international aid; eliminating illicit financial flows; using fiscal and Central Bank foreign exchange reserves; managing debt; and adopting a more accommodating macroeconomic framework (Ortiz et al., 2017). Some of these measures, such as reallocating public expenditures and expanding contributory revenues, may have limited traction in view of the overall contraction of national and individual wealth for most of the population because of Covid-19. However, increasing tax revenues, particularly from new sources such as large technology companies, digital services and billionaires, is apposite (Duran-Valverde et al., 2020, 41; United Nations Department of Social and Economic Affairs, 2012).

Of these potential solutions, new taxation on Big Tech, digital services and billionaires in both developed and developing countries is the most directly intended to have a redistributive effect. It is the most attractive solution in view of the exacerbation of extreme inequality between the poorest and the wealthiest during the pandemic. While Covid-19 negatively impacted most people's livelihoods, the pandemic was a boon to some of the largest companies and wealthiest individuals. According to Oxfam, 17 United States companies alone, including Microsoft, Johnson & Johnson, Facebook, Pfizer, and Visa, made $85 billion more profits in 2020 than they made in the previous 4 years on average. Compared to huge losses across the economy, the top 25 companies in the US made an average of 11% more net profit in 2020 than in previous years. Almost all of these profits were expected to be distributed to shareholders in 2020, increasing the net worth of the wealthiest individuals, unless new taxes are instituted such as a "pandemic profit tax" that Oxfam advocates (Oxfam America, 2020). Fifty new Americans became billionaires during the pandemic, and the total wealth of all US billionaires grew by $1.3 trillion in just the first 11 months of the pandemic with Jeff Besoz and Elon Musk leading the list (Americans for Tax Fairness and The Institute for Policy Studies – Inequality Program, 2020). Globally, there were 30% more billionaires in 2020 than the previous year; it was estimated that all together the world's billionaires were $5 trillion richer in 2020 than the year before (Dolan et al., 2021). Thus, the billionaire's tax is probably the most intuitive solution to the question of funding post-pandemic recovery.

Other proposed novel tax measures on big tech companies, the Google tax, and a tax on diverted corporate profit draw attention to the underlying inadequacy of laws governing corporate taxes that allow the wealthiest companies to avoid being taxed. The Organization for Economic Cooperation and Development (OECD) is coordinating the discussion of a global strategy for "digital taxation". The discussion involves 134 countries and is anchored on the proposition that large corporations whose assets are digital platforms rather than factories should pay taxes, not where they are headquartered or where they register their intellectual properties but where they actually generate profit or where their users are. The OECD and G20 estimated that countries lose about US$100 to 240 billion annually from corporations' "base erosion and profit-shifting" (BEPS) practices, which was equivalent to 4% to 10% of global corporate income tax revenue. In comparison, taxes on international billionaires could generate about US$ 40–50 billion per year (United Nations Department of Social and Economic Affairs, 2012; Christie, 2021). Some economists argue that simplified rules setting a global corporate tax rate would achieve the same purpose as the OECD's proposal but generate higher revenues and distribute revenues more equitably across developed and developing countries (Picciotto et al., 2021).

4 Funding Social Protection from Data: Human Rights Arguments

The aforementioned proposed new taxes on billionaires and digital platforms may expand the fiscal space for post-pandemic recovery measures in general. In the rest of the paper, I examine human rights arguments supporting the elaboration of these new tax measures.

In recent years, human rights scholars have seriously engaged the problem of extreme poverty and income inequality and have debated the redistributive potential of international human rights law (Alston, 2017, 2019a; Aguilar & Saiz, 2015; Dehm et al., 2020; Brinks et al., 2020). Prominently, Philip Alston championed a human rights argument for a universal basic income (UBI) in the form of social protection floors (Alston, 2019b). As UN special rapporteur on extreme poverty, Alston called on the international community to accord prominence to the rights to work, social security, and an adequate standard of living in the human rights agenda, traditionally dominated by civil and political rights. Alston supported UBI to alleviate extreme poverty and income inequality based on the broadly worded human right to an adequate standard of living (Art. 25.1 UDHR). The boldness and simplicity of the idea of UBI, Alston argued, were precisely the qualities that traditional state solutions to material inequality – namely, contributor-supported social insurance or welfare systems – lack.

Linked to this UBI advocacy is the need to acknowledge the role of states in ensuring fair taxation and fiscal policies, and redistributive justice. For the human rights movement, taxation and fiscal policies are key to the move away from the narrow focus on civil and political rights and simple calls to ratify treaties and end violent state practices, which are mere starting points, towards advocacy for structural changes that deal directly with inequality and extreme poverty. As Alston explained, a nation's tax policy, and the larger transnational issues of corporate corruption, tax evasion, illicit financial transfers, and the like, have a crucial effect on the human rights situation, particularly on inequality and extreme poverty in and between countries (Alston, 2015; Alston & Reisch, 2019). Most importantly, refusing to tax or failure to collect, a very common practice in many countries, results in the lack of resources to fund human rights measures such as social security (Alston, 2015). Tax policy also clearly reveals to whom privileges and burdens in terms of tax incentives and obligations are assigned in society and whether resources are redistributed progressively to the poor or regressively to the rich (Alston, 2015). Tax havens, such as Ireland, also affect how resources are distributed or flow across developed and developing countries and inequality between countries (Alston, 2015).

Therefore, human rights advocates will need to take on tax policy as a human rights issue. This imperative will be even more salient in the post-Covid reconstruction. As we have seen, the elaboration of new tax policies will be crucially important to have resources to undertake recovery measures, including new social protection systems.

In the United States, universalising social protection through a UBI scheme has attracted public attention and has been linked to a concern about the lack of fairness in the way Big Tech creates wealth for its shareholders but not for users of their digital platforms. During the US Democratic Party presidential debates leading to the 2020 elections, candidate Andrew Yang ran for President on the singular issue of instituting a UBI scheme for the US in light of increasing automation of work, hence, joblessness due to advances in Artificial Intelligence. At the same time, he argued that digital platforms such as Google and Facebook should be footing the bill. Following the characterisation of Big Data to oil and mineral resources, Yang opined that digital platform users should share in the profits obtained by companies from mining and monetising their data on an ongoing or regular basis (Clifford, 2019). Relatedly, the governor of California is leading a campaign to legislate users' right to be paid by companies a "data dividend", or a share in profits derived by companies from users' data (Cowan, 2019). These policy proposals reflect thinking about work displacement due to automation, UBI, and Big Tech's social license that a range of corporate and intellectual figures have already been considering (e.g., Hughes, 2018; Sadowski, 2016; Schneider, 2015).

In this context, I have argued that Yang's proposal to fund UBI through some mechanism by which the economic value derived by Big Tech from Big Data is shared with users may be seen as a way of implementing RBSP in the context of Big Data progress (Lamchek, 2020). Thinking about RBSP in the digital age can breathe new life to RBSP, a largely neglected human right with an originally huge redistributive ambition. It can also be seen as supporting the human rights turn to structural reforms and redistributive measures, including taxation. Already, the establishment of a UBI scheme is a significant structural and redistributive reform that directly addressed inequality and extreme poverty within countries that will institute them. But there are at least two added claims that the argument based on RBSP in Big Data makes that are relevant to new taxation proposals.

The first claim is that RBSP should be applied to data science or Artificial Intelligence and not just to medicine and agriculture. This is because progress in data science and Artificial Intelligence underpin the wealth of the wealthiest companies in the world. Intellectuals and human rights advocates have been justifiably concerned with the implications of data science and Artificial Intelligence for privacy rights, subversion of democracy and other harms to individuals and society. Perhaps an emblematic example of these concerns, Zuboff has emphasised that Big Tech's Big Data-driven business model has led to the development of highly intrusive means of users' surveillance to sell behaviour prediction and modification products targeting them (Zuboff, 2019a). As have been revealed in an explosive way in the Cambridge Analytica scandal, these products have not only been sold to advertisers but have also been used by political campaign operations to undermine democratic elections, for example (Davies & Rushe, 2019). As Yang's presidential campaign shows, quite apart from these privacy and political concerns, there is also a growing public awareness of economic fairness issues involved in the amassing of wealth through the mining and monetising of data from users of digital platforms.

Owners of intellectual properties in these technologies have so far shut out ordinary people from the benefit, narrowly understood as corporate profits. Indeed, businesses based on monetising data have amassed data from their users in exchange for nothing else but the free use of their digital platforms. Google, Facebook and Amazon, the most successful of these tech giants, have treated users' data as a free resource to be taken and mined. Zuboff has argued that the legality of this business model should be an issue for public debate (Zuboff, 2019b). Without going so far as to foreclose data mining and monetisation altogether, however, one can use RBSP as a legal language that also underscores the basic fairness problem with Big Tech's exploitative business model. RBSP articulates that progress in Big Data and data science applications that only enlarged Big Tech's coffers and didn't share benefits to the people was contrary to the human rights vision for science and scientific progress.

This leads to the second claim: there is a duty to establish a benefit-sharing scheme in Big Data that dispenses concrete and substantial benefit to everyone. As advocates and scholars in medicine and agriculture understand, for art. 27.1 UDHR and art. 15.1(b) ICESCR to have a substantial redistributive impact, "benefit" has to be given a clear, material, and substantial meaning. The interpretation and revitalisation of RBSP in the digital age has hardly really begun. Thus, the forms of benefit-sharing and the meaning of "benefit" are not really foreclosed. Nevertheless, as I have argued, the current discussion on data-funded UBI and data dividends can be regarded as an attempt to provide that clear, material and substantial meaning of "benefit" and benefit-sharing in Big Data (Lamchek, 2020).

Operationalising a data-funded UBI will have to involve some computation both of the economic value of data derived by Big Tech and the portion to be distributed back to users. Presumably, there are similar operational issues being considered by states as they figure out whether and how to levy and collect digital taxes. In this sense, the proposal for a data-funded UBI is in synergy with new taxation proposals.

5 Conclusion

The COVID-19 pandemic has demonstrated the imperative for countries to radically expand their social protection systems in accordance with the Sustainable Development Goals. In the economic rebuilding after the COVID-19 pandemic, it will be wise for states, especially developing countries, to invest in social protection. Fiscal space for the economic rebuilding in general will be provided by new taxes, including digital taxation, which recognised that businesses made profits from users' data. The same recognition and the proposition that users should directly share in the economic value generated by large companies from their data underpin demands for data-funded universal basic income or data dividends. This paper introduced RBSP as providing a legal language within international human rights law for these specific claims. It reinforces and extends the human rights argument for social protection floors. An RBSP-based argument for radically expanding social protection after COVID-19 may help define the terms of an acceptable and meaningful benefit-sharing scheme in the field of data science and Artificial Intelligence.

References

Aguilar, G. O., & Saiz, I. (2015). Introducing the debate on economic inequality: can human rights make a difference? *OpenDemocracy*, October 27. https://www.opendemocracy.net/en/openglobalrights-openpage/introducing-debate-on-economic-inequality-can-human-ri/

Alston, P. (2015). *Tax policy is human rights policy: The Irish debate.*

Alston, P. (2017). *Report of the special rapporteur on extreme poverty and human rights*. A/HRC/35/26.

Alston, P. (2019a). Taxation, human rights, and a universal basic income. In P. Alston & N. Reisch (Eds.), *Tax, inequality, and human rights* (pp. 553–564). Oxford University Press.

Alston, P. (2019b). Universal basic income as a social rights–based antidote to growing economic insecurity. In K. Young (Ed.), *The future of economic and social rights*. Cambridge University Press.

Alston, P., & Reisch, N. (Eds.). (2019). *Tax, inequality, and human rights*. Oxford University Press.

Americans for Tax Fairness and The Institute for Policy Studies – Inequality Program. (2020). Growth in total wealth of U.S. billionaires during the pandemic. *Billionaires by the Numbers*. https://americansfortaxfairness.org/billionaires/

Barbier, E. B., & Burgess, J. C. (2020). Sustainability and development after COVID-19. *World Development, 135*.

Barrientos, A. (2010). *Social protection and poverty* (42. Social Policy and Development Paper). United Nations Research Institute for Social Development.

BBC News. (2021). Covid: US backs waiver on vaccine patents to boost supply. *BBC.Com*, May 6. https://www.bbc.com/news/world-us-canada-57004302

Brinks, D., Dehm, J., & Engle, K. (2020). Introduction: Human rights and economic inequality. *Humanity: An International Journal of Human Rights, Humanitarianism, and Development, 10*(3).

Chavez-Dreyfuss, G. (2020). Permanently remote workers seen doubling in 2021 due to pandemic productivity: Survey. *Reuters.Com*, October 23. https://www.reuters.com/article/us-health-coronavirus-technology-idUSKBN2772P0

Chebly, J., Schiano, A., & Mehra, D. (2020). The value of work: Rethinking labor productivity in times of COVID-19 and automation. *American Journal of Economics and Sociology, 79*(4), 1345–1365.

Chernoff, A. W., & Warman, C. (2020). *Covid-19 and implications for automation* (Working Paper 27249). National Bureau of Economic Research. https://www.nber.org/system/files/working_papers/w27249/w27249.pdf

Christie, R. (2021). Digital services taxes take shape in the shadow of the pandemic. *International Monetary Fund*. Spring. https://www.imf.org/external/pubs/ft/fandd/2021/03/taxing-big-tech-and-the-future-of-digital-services-tax-christie.htm?fbclid=IwAR3YUfJ8kwti2q2E_H7tqlxl_-kd3n2FPQcz0Y8GyTx0BrX4Owlt8ZIrgl4

Clifford, C. (2019). Andrew Yang: You should get a check in the Mail from Facebook, Amazon, Google for Your Data. *CNBC.Com*, October 17. https://www.cnbc.com/2019/10/17/andrew-yang-facebook-amazon-google-should-pay-for-users-data.html
Cowan, J. (2019). How much is your data worth? *New York Times*, March 25. https://www.nytimes.com/2019/03/25/us/newsom-hertzberg-data-dividend.html
Davies, R., & Rushe, D. (2019). Facebook to pay $5bn fine as regulator settles Cambridge Analytica complaint. *The Guardian*, July 24. https://www.theguardian.com/technology/2019/jul/24/facebook-to-pay-5bn-fine-as-regulator-files-cambridge-analytica-complaint
De Schutter, O. (2011). The right of everyone to enjoy the benefits of scientific progress and the right to food: From conflict to complementarity. *Human Rights Quarterly, 33*(2), 304–350.
Dehm, J., Golder, B., & Whyte, J. (2020). Introduction: 'Redistributive human rights?' Symposium. *London Review of International Law, 8*(2), 225–232.
Dolan, K. A., Wang, J., & Peterson-Withorn, C. (2021). The richest in 2021. *Forbes*, April 7. https://www.forbes.com/billionaires/
Duran-Valverde, F., Pacheco-Jimenez, J. F., Muzaffar, T., & Elizondo-Barbosa, H. (2020). *Financing gaps in social protection: Global estimates and strategies for developing countries in light of the COVID-19 crisis and beyond* (ILO Working Papers). International Labor Organization.
Farge, E. (2020). Global tourism stands to lose up to $3.3 trillion from COVID-19: U.N. study. *Reuters.Com*, July 1. https://www.reuters.com/article/us-health-coronavirus-tourism-idUSKBN2425YI
Food and Agriculture Organization. (2015). *The state of food and agriculture: Social protection and agriculture: Breaking the cycle of rural poverty*. Food and Agriculture Organization.
Heywood, M. (2009). South Africa's treatment action campaign: Combining law and social mobilization to realise the right to health. *Journal of Human Rights Practice, 1*(1), 14–36.
Hughes, C. (2018). The wealth of our collective data should belong to all of us. *The Guardian*, April 27. https://www.theguardian.com/commentisfree/2018/apr/27/chris-hughes-facebook-google-data-tax-regulation
International Labor Organization. (2012). *R202 – Social protection floors recommendation, 2012* (No. 202). ILO 101st ILC Session.
International Labor Organization. 2017. "World social protection report 2017–19: Universal social protection to achieve the sustainable development goals." .
International Labor Organization. (2020a). ILO: As job losses escalate, nearly half of global workforce at risk of losing livelihoods. *International Labor Organization*, April 29. https://www.ilo.org/global/about-the-ilo/newsroom/news/WCMS_743036/lang%2D%2Den/index.htm
International Labor Organization. (2020b). *Financing gaps in social protection: Global estimates and strategies for developing countries in light of the COVID-19 crisis and beyond* (ILO Brief: Social Protection Spotlight). International Labor Organization.
International Labor Organization. (2021). *Towards solid social protection floors? The role of non-contributory provision during the COVID-19 crisis and beyond* (ILO Brief: Social Protection Spotlight). International Labor Organization.
Jones, M., & Shalal, A. (2020). Debt relief plans for world's poor countries inch forward. *Reuters*, May 29. https://www.reuters.com/article/us-health-coronavirus-debt-private-idUSKBN2342PS
Lamchek, J. (2020). The right to benefit from big data progress: Another argument for universal basic income. *Voelkerrechtsblog*, August 6. https://voelkerrechtsblog.org/the-right-to-benefit-from-big-data-progress/
Marks, S. P., & Benedict, A. L. (2013). Access to medical products, vaccines, and medical technologies. In J. M. Zuniga (Ed.), *Advancing the human right to health* (pp. 305–324). Oxford University Press.
Meier, B. M., Brugh, K. N., & Halima, Y. (2012). Conceptualising a human right to prevention in global HIV/AIDS policy. *Public Health Ethics, 5*(3), 263–282.
Meier, B. M., & Yamin, A. E. (2011). Right to health litigation and HIV/AIDS policy. *Journal of Law, Medicine and Ethics, 39*, 81–84.

Molina, G. G., & Ortiz-Juarez, E. (2020). *Temporary basic income: Protecting poor and vulnerable people in developing countries* (Transitions Series Working Papers). United Nations Development Program.

Morgera, E. (2015). Fair and equitable benefit-sharing at the cross-roads of the human right to science and international biodiversity law. *Laws, 4*, 803–831.

Ortiz, I., Cummins, M., & Kurananethy, K. (2017). *Fiscal space for social protection options to expand social investments in 187 countries* (Extension of Social Security Working Paper ESS 048). International Labor Organization.

Oxfam America. (2020). *Pandemic profits exposed*. https://webassets.oxfamamerica.org/media/documents/Pandemic_Profiteers_Exposed.pdf

Philippines Department of Finance. (2020). Dominguez says 'unequivocal' no to debt moratorium, PHL to honor its obligations through coronavirus crisis. *Department of Finance, Republic of the Philippines*. April 14. https://www.dof.gov.ph/dominguez-says-unequivocal-no-to-debt-moratorium-phl-to-honor-its-obligations-through-coronavirus-crisis/

Philipps, B., Gray, M., & Bidlle, N. (2020). *COVID-19 JobKeeper and JobSeeker impacts on poverty and housing stress under current and alternative economic and policy scenarios*. Australian National University Centre for Social Research and Methods.

Picciotto, S., Faccio, T., Kadet, J. M., Jansky, P., Cobham, A., & Garcia-Bernardo, J. (2021). *For a better GLOBE. METR: A minimum effective tax rate for multinationals*. https://papers.ssrn.com/sol3/papers.cfm?abstract_id=3796030

Sadowski, J. (2016). Why Silicon Valley is embracing universal basic income. *The Guardian*, June 22. https://www.theguardian.com/technology/2016/jun/22/silicon-valley-universal-basic-income-y-combinator

Schabas, W. (2007). Study of the right to enjoy the benefits of scientific and technological progress and its applications. In Y. Donders & V. Volodin (Eds.), *Human rights in education, science and culture: Legal developments and challenges* (pp. 273–308). UNESCO Publishing; Ashgate.

Schneider, N. (2015). Why the tech elite is getting behind universal basic income. *Vice*, January 7. https://www.vice.com/en/article/mv5d3y/something-for-everyone-0000546-v22n1

Smith, T. (2020). Understanding the nature and scope of the right to science through the Travaux Préparatoires of the universal declaration of human rights and the international covenant on economic, social and cultural rights. *The International Journal of Human Rights*.

Specht, L. (2020). Modernising meat production will help us avoid pandemics. *Wired*, March 13. https://www.wired.com/story/opinion-modernizing-meat-production-will-help-us-avoid-pandemics/

UN News. (2020). Senior UN official calls for universal basic income to tackle growing inequality. *UN News*, May 6. https://news.un.org/en/story/2020/05/1063312

United Nations. (2020). *Debt and COVID-19: A global response in solidarity*. United Nations.

United Nations Department of Global Communications. (2021). Climate change and COVID-19: UN urges nations to 'Recover better.' *United Nations COVID-19 Response*. https://www.un.org/en/un-coronavirus-communications-team/un-urges-countries-%E2%80%98build-back-better%E2%80%99. Accessed Mar 24.

United Nations Department of Social and Economic Affairs. (2012). *World economic and social survey 2012: In search of new development finance* (E/2012/50/Rev.1ST/ESA/341). United Nations.

United Nations Department of Social and Economic Affairs. (2020). UN report finds COVID-19 is reversing decades of progress on poverty, healthcare and education. *United Nations Department of Social and Economic Affairs*. July 7. https://www.un.org/development/desa/en/news/sustainable/sustainable-development-goals-report-2020.html

United Nations Development Program. (2020). Temporary basic income to protect the world's poorest people could slow the surge in COVID-19 cases, says UNDP. *UNDP*, July 23. https://www.undp.org/content/undp/en/home/news-centre/news/2020/Temporary_Basic_Income_to_protect_the_worlds_poorest_people_slow_COVID19.html?fbclid=IwAR2SNyFHJr3pkrLZ_PjYxF7JnAHygAlc8MzESI6yrQCCAUARBDLx14_sG9k

World Bank. (2020a). The global economic outlook during the COVID-19 pandemic: A changed world. *The World Bank*, June 8. https://www.worldbank.org/en/news/feature/2020/06/08/the-global-economic-outlook-during-the-covid-19-pandemic-a-changed-world
World Bank. (2020b). COVID-19: Remittance flows to shrink 14% by 2021. *WorldBank.Org*, October 29. https://www.worldbank.org/en/news/press-release/2020/10/29/covid-19-remittance-flows-to-shrink-14-by-2021
World Bank. (2021). Defying predictions, remittance flows remain strong during COVID-19 crisis. *WorldBank.Org*, May 12. https://www.worldbank.org/en/news/press-release/2021/05/12/defying-predictions-remittance-flows-remain-strong-during-covid-19-crisis
World Economic Forum. (2020). How coronavirus has hit employment in G7 economies. *World Economic Forum*, May 13. https://www.weforum.org/agenda/2020/05/coronavirus-unemployment-jobs-work-impact-g7-pandemic/
World Health Organization. (2021). COVAX: Working for global equitable access to COVID-19 vaccines. *World Health Organization*. https://www.who.int/initiatives/act-accelerator/covax. Accessed Apr 16.
World Trade Organization. (2020). Trade set to plunge as COVID-19 pandemic upends global economy. *WTO.Org*, April 8. https://www.wto.org/english/news_e/pres20_e/pr855_e.htm
Zuboff, S. (2019a). *Surveillance capitalism: The fight for a human future at the new frontier of power*. Public Affairs Hachett Book Group.
Zuboff, S. (2019b). It's not that we've failed to rein in Facebook and Google. We've not even tried. *The Guardian*, July 2. https://www.theguardian.com/commentisfree/2019/jul/02/facebook-google-data-change-our-behaviour-democracy

Fiscal Implications – Inclusive Growth and Climate Change Resilience: A Scoping Study of Existing Policy in Selected ASEAN Countries

Max Weber and Taha Chaiechi

Abstract Inclusive growth and climate change resilience have been enthusiastically debated issues at the global and local levels even before the COVID-19 pandemic. It has been argued that they have increasingly threatened to destabilise the economy while interfering with the fiscal goals of stability, full employment, sustainable growth and development for shared prosperity and welfare.

Governments, institutions and the private sector now acknowledge the importance and urgency for coordinated action toward inclusive and sustainable outcomes and government actions. However, tweaking existing policies by adding discretionary programs within the "one size fits it all" paradigm could not address these issues effectively. It has been argued that pro-equity policies can reduce inequality and pro-green policies can strengthen climate change resilience and thus achieve sustainable outcomes under an integrated fiscal policy.

This study reviews the existing literature in this field by employing a structured qualitative methodology to scope, contextualise and map the literature in this field. The paper focuses on inclusive and sustainable fiscal policy, which, through coordination and integration, achieves economic stability, inclusive growth, and sustainable development outcomes concurrently, i.e. the challenge of internalising economic activity's social costs to render a net social surplus and neutralise environmental impact.

This study evaluates the extent of the existing programs and policies by adopting a mixed-method qualitative analysis methodology that incorporates a scoping review and document analysis. It performs a structured analysis to uncover the effective policy variables, drivers and impediments. The document analysis method complements the scoping review to extract the thematic meaning, article design and metadata of the analysed documents in the context of the declared sustainability

M. Weber (✉)
Winterthur, Switzerland
e-mail: max.weber1@my.jcu.edu.au

T. Chaiechi
College of Business, Law and Governance, James Cook University, Townsville, QLD, Australia
e-mail: taha.chaiechi@jcu.edu.au

© The Author(s), under exclusive license to Springer Nature Singapore Pte Ltd. 2022

T. Chaiechi, J. Wood (eds.), *Community Empowerment, Sustainable Cities, and Transformative Economies*, https://doi.org/10.1007/978-981-16-5260-8_32

goals. Data repositories include pertinent literature and topical reports from private and public economic, policy and industry research and advisory institutions and firms.

Keywords Fiscal policy · Inclusive growth · Climate change · Scoping review · Document analysis

1 Introduction

Inclusive growth and climate change have been long debated topics at the global, regional and local levels (Jacobs & Mazzucato, 2016), not only in academia but also by independent institutions (Gaspar et al., 2019; and Tang et al., 2021) like the Organisation of Economic Development (OECD), United Nations Development Program (UNDP), World Bank (WB), International Monetary Fund (IMF), World Economic Forum (WEF), Asian Development Bank (ADB) and others. Through global fora like the G20 and the World Economic Forum (Samans et al., 2015), governments acknowledge the importance of the inequality and climate change challenges and the urgency of addressing these issues effectively at the multilateral and policy level to maintain social, ecological and economic stability (Esty, 2017). Even the private sector has recently recognised the severity of the situation and included an account of sustainability action and achievements in their corporate responsibility reporting (CSR) (Belal & Momin, 2009; Rahman & Momin, 2009).

Many governments have committed to remedial, mitigating and/or affirmative policy action by recognising the mounting risks and ramifications emanating from these unresolved externalities of economic activity (Meade, 1973). Governments now realise that the global trends of inequality and climate change are not favourable and will not recede but cumulate to threaten and destabilise the short-term economic goals, erode comparative advantage and disrupt the inter-generational sustainable development plans of the nation (Tavoni et al., 2011). Moreover, many developing nations' rapid growth will tend to "hide" the social costs imposed by externalities. At the same time, intermediate and longer-term effects of inequality and climate change have a mostly negative impact on developing and the developed economies. Research has confirmed this phenomenon worldwide, particularly in the ASEAN (Klenow & Rodriguez-Clare, 2005).

With the Kyoto Protocol (1997), which was originally organised by the United Nations Framework Convention (UNFC/IPPC) and superseded by the Paris Agreement in 2015, 196 member states committed to coordinated climate action for greenhouse-gas (GHS) reduction on a multilateral level. However, the implementation of national policy has been fragmented due to the lack of coordination and integration (Hogl et al., 2016). Contrary, since the new millennium, governments have tabled inequality (and climate change) as a top priority at global fora (G20, WEF, etc.), but despite widespread support for the sustainable development goals, have failed to agree on a multilateral approach to address the issue through policy coordination at the global level (Hickel, 2017). Nevertheless, some governments like Indonesia have committed to the Voluntary National Reviews reporting scheme under the United Nation Development Program framework of the 2030 Sustainable Development Goals. Despite strong academic, institutional, and governmental interest in both multidisciplinary issues, a preliminary literature scan suggests that the research landscape in this field is thematically and methodologically fragmented, with substantial diversification in the design, perspective and findings of individual studies and articles. However, the research community struggles with these global trends' inter-relationships and how to address the rampant challenges effectively at the macroeconomic (fiscal) policy level. Evidence points out a knowledge gap in the literature for research toward a robust approach to internalise the socio-economic and ecological costs of the inequality and climate change externalities from economic activity into an integrated fiscal policy framework, as conceptualised in Fig. 1.

Answering the research question of *the extent of existing inclusive and sustainable fiscal policy, instruments, drivers and impediments*, this paper asserts that systematic research in the field of inclusive and sustainable fiscal policy in combination with multilateral policy coordination can assist policymakers in developing and maintaining robust pro-green and pro-equity policies by design, rather than by discretionary add-on programs. This study aims to review the existing literature in this field by employing a structured qualitative analysis methodology. By combining the scoping review and document analysis methods, this study seeks to reveal the pertinent constructs, contexts, concepts, and paradigms towards the research question while identifying the knowledge gaps for future research.

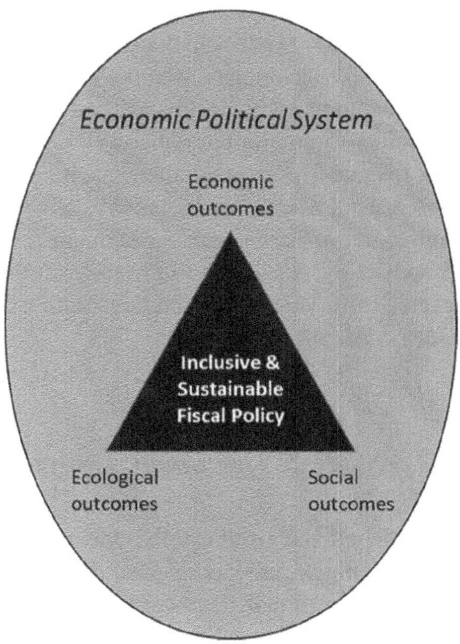

Fig. 1 Research paradigm of inclusive and sustainable fiscal policy. (Source: authors)

2 Methodology & Methods

This study uses a qualitative analysis approach to investigate the extent of existing literature on inclusive and sustainable fiscal policy and the drivers and impediments – and to assess this literature's relevance for pro-equity and pro-green fiscal policy development two-stages which combines a scoping review and document analysis. Scoping review is adopted to map the relevant documents in this field, and document analysis is adopted to expose and contextualise the thematic constructs relative to the research objective. Each stage involves an iterative process that is continued until exhausted, when a saturation point is reached when no further improvements in the search results can be achieved.

2.1 Stage 1: Scoping Review – Method

The first stage follows the scoping review method by Arksey and O'Malley (2005) in exploratory mode to identify and map the relevant literature in this field based on the guiding question and search criteria (a priori protocol). This step involves a focused, positive search process to identify a representative subset of all relevant literature in scope from pre-selected online libraries, databases and repositories, article reference lists, reverse citations and proximity searches. According to Arksey and O'Malley the method for identifying literature in a scoping study needs to achieve in-depth and broad results across different source domains, regardless of the individual article design. The suggested scoping framework in Fig. 2 enlists five guiding principles and a voluntary sixth step that describe a systematic and transparent analysis process and suitable techniques, which are repeatable.

In exploratory mode, this method should not be restrained by restrictive inclusion or exclusion criteria but rather follow an interactive inductive or deductive process that tolerates different article types and designs within the given thematic boundaries and general search parameters as defined in the a priori protocol (i.e. time, space, source, etc.). To conduct the scoping review, we follow the five-stage framework proposed by Arksey and O'Malley (2005). The optional sixth step, "consultation exercise" to validate the findings with external stakeholder groups, is outside this study's scope.

2.2 Stage 2: Document Analysis – Method

The second stage follows the document analyse the method by Bowen (2009) to examine the documents selected during the scoping review in Stage 1 while further reducing the initial document set by concentrating and interpreting the contents under investigation. The aim is to expose, conceptualise and map the relevant

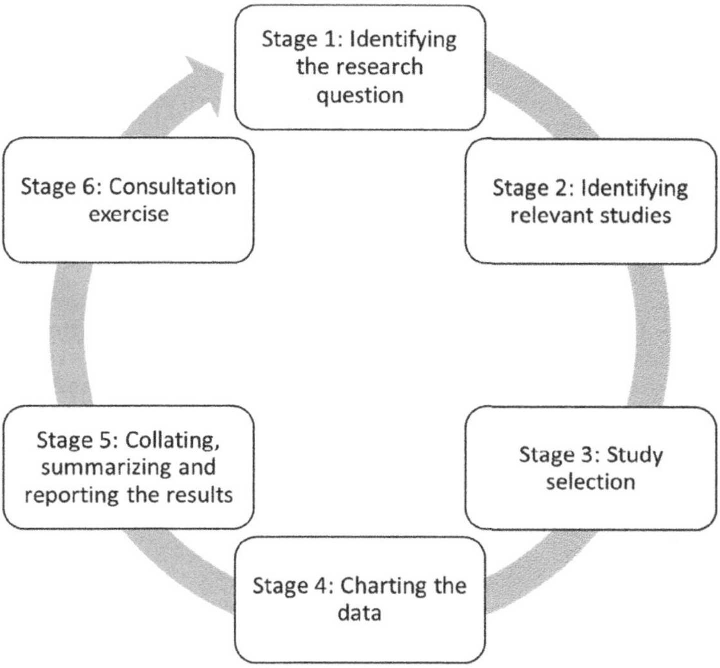

Fig. 2 Scoping review method with 5-steps. (Adapted from Arksey and O'Malley 2005)

thematic constructs as identified in this second stage of the process, and visualise the relationships, concepts, paradigms and article design in accordance with the research objective and the protocol, as depicted in Fig. 3.

To mine and analyse the document content requires a systematic process with multiple passes through the text, the bibliographic and meta-data. The full-text search uses word frequency and proximity techniques to identify relevant thematic references and contexts. A further iteration seeks to expose the relationship between the identified thematic constructs, including synonyms, patterns and irregularities, i.e. unexplainable instances of passages in the text. A further pass searches the text specifically for relevant features of document design, methodology and methods, etc. A validation pass may search the document for evidence of authenticity, diversity or congruence of citations, other styles, form and quality attributes, and abnormalities or irregularities, etc., as relevant to the research objective.

3 Execution of Methods

This section discusses the results from the scoping review in Stage 1 and the document analysis in Stage 2, and then integrates and summarises the findings.

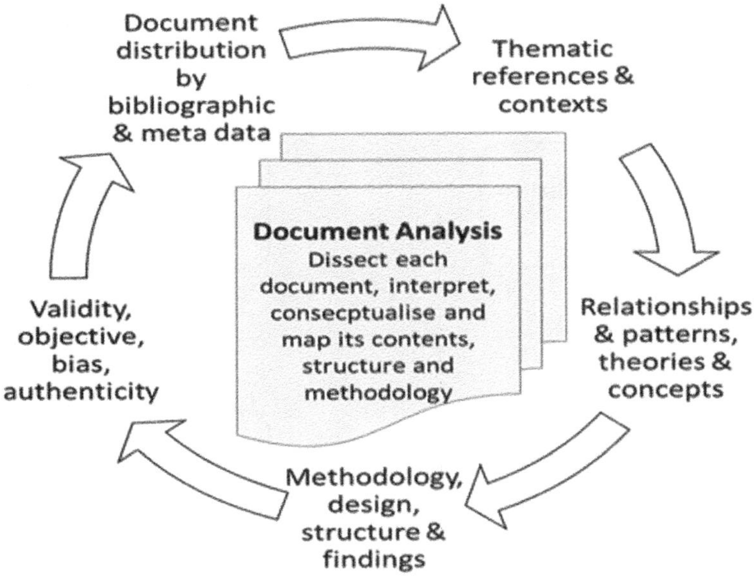

Fig. 3 Document analysis method. (Adapted from Bowen 2009)

3.1 Scoping Review

The scoping review procedure included the initial search performed within the pre-selected search domains to which we applied structured and customised online queries. The search domains included the leading search engines that cover peer-reviewed and grey literature, i.e., Google Scholar and Goole Search, Microsoft Academic, Semantic Scholar, JCU e-Library, and the global government summits (G7, G20, WEF), as well as repositories and databases of independent institutions, i.e., the Government Revenue Dataset (*GRD,* UNU-WIDER), the SDG-2030 database (UNDP), work papers, reports and policy advisory of OECD, WB, IMF, and the local ministries for their policies and development plans. In an iterative process, the initial search terms were adjusted to optimise the search results. Following Chaiechi (2020), an a priori protocol has been developed to guide this process, which defines the following guiding question for this study: the inclusion and exclusion criteria, secondary screening criteria, and the reporting and presentation techniques, as listed in Table 1.

The guiding question was derived from the broad research question below; the search terms were optimised for recall and specificity of the result, i.e., reducing the chances of missing relevant articles while keeping the number of retrieved documents manageable:

Guiding question: What is the extent of existing literature about "inclusive and sustainable fiscal policy, programs, instruments, drivers and impediments in the ASEAN"?

Table 1 Eligibility criteria

Criterion	Inclusion	Exclusion
Publication year	2001–2020	Studies outside this period
Search language	English	Non-English literature
Type of literature	Peer-reviewed original research, conference proceedings, working papers, governmental reports	Non-scholarly, non-official or non-reputable sources
	Grey literature including reputable advisory reports and pertinent published articles and books	
Concepts	Documents that discuss dimensions of Inclusive Sustainable Fiscal Policy (ISFP), including fiscal policy in the context of pro-equity and pro-green and sustainable development outcomes	Documents without thematic relevance
Coverage	The document must cover Inequality, Climate Change issues in Sustainable Fiscal Policy context	Documents with only partial coverage
Relevance	Title and abstract relevant to the guiding question	Irrelevant titles and abstracts

Adapted from Chaiechi (2020)

The initial selection criteria were further optimised in subsequent iterations based on the relevance of the retrieved titles and abstracts in peer-reviewed articles or executive summaries in grey literature. Where warranted, a full-text search was performed to uncover more details or context (Chaiechi, 2020). The criterion for the time-span was set to 2001–2020 as this period reflects the recent increase in public interest in the inequality and climate change challenges in the context of externalities of economic activity, as well as the associated topics of fiscal remedial, mitigation and affirmative policy action in the new millennium (Pawson, 2002). This era is characterised by regional and global economic crises (i.e., Asian Financial Crisis 1998, Global Financial Crisis 2001 and 2008) followed by moderating world growth in the wake of the booming World-War-II rebuilding phase that accelerated globalisation, mass production and consumerism. The threat to economic stability emanating from these socio-economic and ecological risks have brought about new multilateral mechanisms to foster inter-government communication, policy coordination and collaboration, including the G20 Summit, the annual World Economic Forum, the United Nations Conference on Environment and Development (UNCED) World Summit on Sustainable Development, and the United Nations Framework Convention on Climate Change (NFCCC). Particularly, the Kyoto Protocol in 1997, which the Paris Treaty superseded in 2015, where 196 signatory countries agreed to coordinated policy action to curb global warming – the topic of "inclusive and sustainable fiscal policy" was defining this year's moments. Therefore, these cut-off points were deemed appropriate to capture the literature in this field.

The identified documents were screened for eligibility, and duplicates were removed. The articles were classified according to the bibliographic and meta-data and prepared for document analysis in this second stage of the methodology, based

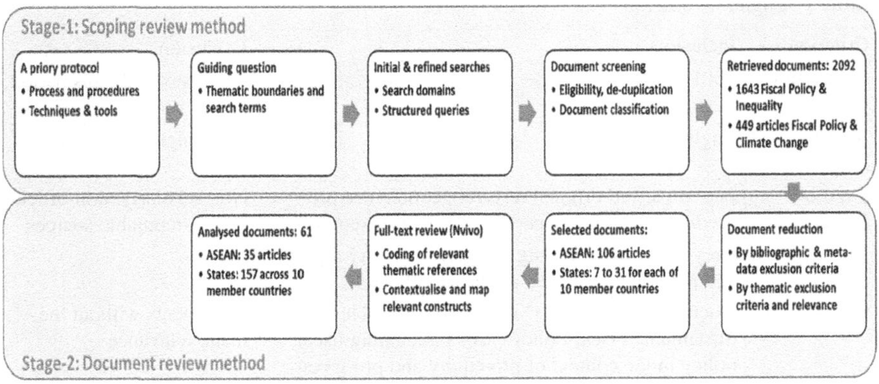

Fig. 4 A priori protocol for 2-stage qualitative analysis methodology. (Adapted from Chaiechi 2020)

on the diagram in Fig. 4. The process yielded 2091 matches, thereof 1643 documents within the thematic space of socioeconomically inclusive fiscal policy (inclusive growth) and 449 documents within the thematic space of ecologically sustainable fiscal policy (climate change) across the three policy goals of remedial policy action, mitigation policy action and affirmative policy action.

3.2 Document Analysis

Using the Nvivo 12 Plus software with its built-in techniques for structured content analysis, the selected documents from the scoping review in stage 1 were prepared for the document analysis, which entailed a systematic and iterative process with four steps, each using appropriate techniques and tools. The first pass involved a full-text search with a word-frequency distribution to construct a thematic vocabulary of the document. The second pass involved a grammatical proximity search with the selected vocabulary terms to expose the related expressions, sentences, paragraphs and sections of the document. The third pass consisted of the "coding" procedures to extracts pertinent text passages and linked them to other thematic references from this and other documents in the batch. The fourth pass exposed conceptualised constructs, paradigms and relationships, and the fifth pass mapped these in thematic space for subsequent interpretation (Fig. 6).

3.3 Themes Identification

The conceptual model was defined by deductive logic to include the three topical dimensions of the research objective i.e., inclusive and sustainable fiscal policy.

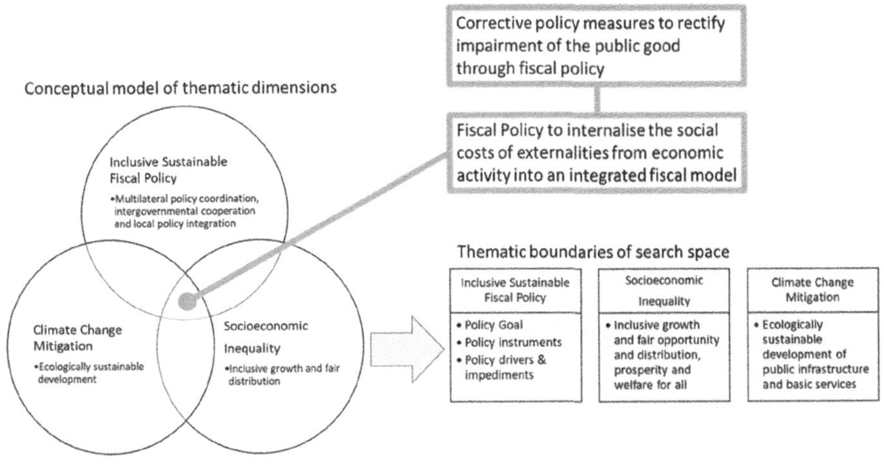

Fig. 5 Thematic boundaries for systematic and structured document search. (Source: authors)

Within this model, an iterative inductive process helped to further focus the search terms and techniques on defining the search space's thematic boundaries. This exploratory approach culminated in identifying three themes to guide the content analysis of the pre-selected documents in the batch.

As shown in Fig. 5, the three-dimensional search model was developed to structure the queries by the identified themes, the policy goal, and the political sovereignty of the ASEAN region and the ten member states:

- Research dimensionality: inequality, climate change, and sustainable fiscal policy
- Thematic boundaries: Fiscal policy goals, instruments, drivers and impediments, i.e., remedial policy action, mitigating policy action, and affirmative policy action
- Research scope: Political sovereignty, i.e., ASEAN (region) and 10 member states

Each query was then augmented with the identified search terms within the defined thematic boundaries and the relevance criteria (filters) for the time span, authenticity, article design, etc. We conducted an iterative search process through a list of pre-qualified repositories and databases, including online search engines covering peer-reviewed and grey literature (i.e., JCU e-Library, Google Scholar and Goole Search, Microsoft Academic, Semantic Scholar and government repositories). To further optimise the search terms for best-fit results, we employed the confusion matrix concept with the simple F-measure (F-score) optimisation technique as described in Mengarelli (2020). Each thematic space was systematically searched with a structured query that including specific search terms to retrieve documents by fiscal policy type, objective, instruments, drivers and impediments. Retrieved documents were classified according to the attributes implied by the search criteria, including the country, organisation, and publishing time. To expose the relevant constructs, the search task was segregated into multiple search

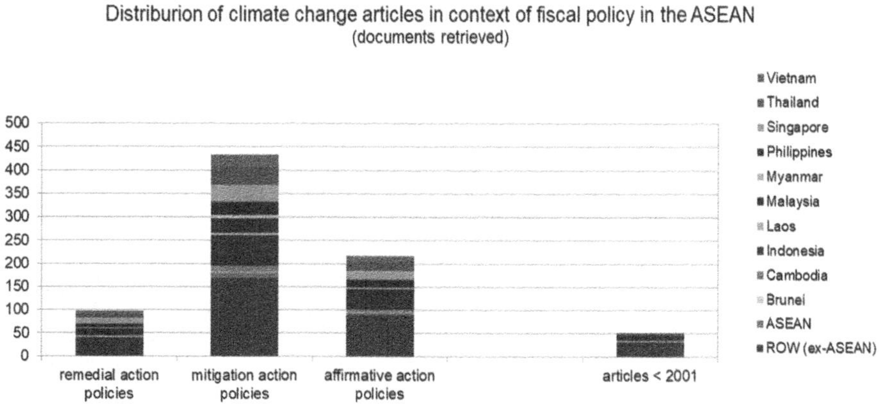

Fig. 6 Distribution of fiscal policy documents in the context of climate change. (Source: authors)

procedures and the partial results were interpreted, contextualised and conceptually integrated to reveal the relevant thematic constructs, patterns, and paradigms.

Firstly, we focused on the cluster of relevant documents in the thematic intersection of ecologically sustainable fiscal policy and climate change, as depicted in Fig. 6. Worldwide, the search retrieved 747 documents, thereof 434 in the classes of "mitigation policy action", 216 in "affirmative policy action" and 97 in "remedial policy action". The ASEAN publishing instance indicates the relatively stronger policy focus on mitigation than on affirmative and remedial fiscal policy action to address the discussed challenges. Across these three classes of policy goals/focus, the search identified, worldwide, 316 relevant documents, thereof 18 that were published under the ASEAN regional banner and 298 by Rest of World countries (i.e. ROW-ex ASEAN). The number of published articles retrieved from individual ASEAN member states varied considerably, led by Indonesia (110), then Singapore (70), and at the other end of the spectrum, Myanmar (11) and Laos (7).

Secondly, we focused on the cluster of relevant documents in the thematic space of inclusive fiscal policy and the inequality challenge, as depicted in Fig. 7. Worldwide, the search retrieved 2437 documents, thereof 1471 in the class of "affirmative policy action", 716 in "mitigation policy action" and 250 in "remedial policy action". This shows that there is significantly stronger published interest in forward-thinking policies within the ASEAN than in mitigation or corrective policy action. Across the three classes of policy goals and outcomes, the search identified worldwide 882 relevant documents, thereof 88 that were published under the ASEAN regional banner and 794 by Rest of World countries (where ROW is ex-ASEAN). The number of published articles retrieved from individual ASEAN member states varied considerably, led by Indonesia (321), then Singapore (253), and at the other end of the spectrum, Laos (37) and Brunei (27).

Globally, about 2/3rd of all received articles as relevant for the research objective and the guiding question was from within the ASEAN region or about it. Only a relatively small percentage of relevant articles were published by or under the

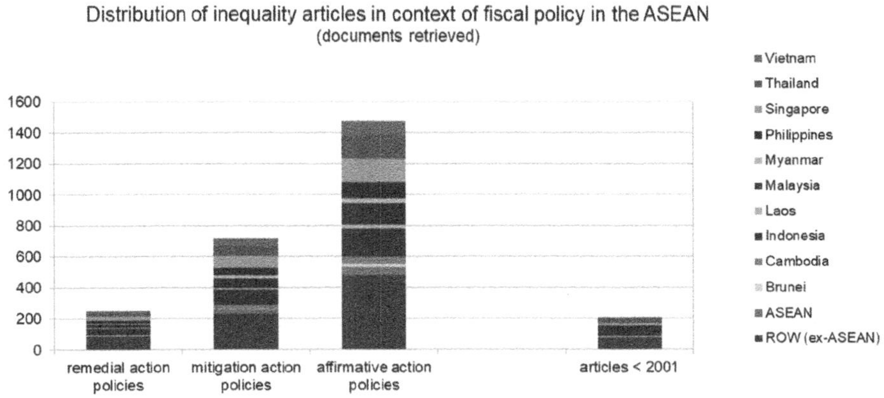

Fig. 7 Distribution of fiscal policy documents in the context of inequality. (Source: authors)

ASEAN regional banner, indicating that research interest at the regional level was relatively small compared to that of its member states. Particularly, Indonesia and Singapore stood out through strong publishing activity, followed by Thailand, Malaysia and Vietnam. This tendency could be observed across both thematic spaces within inclusive and sustainable fiscal policy within and among the ASEAN. It has been noted above that from a thematic perspective, the inequality challenge produced most publications in affirmative policy action, while with the climate change challenge, the fiscal policy focus was clearly on mitigation action both at the regional and the national level. Furthermore, it is interesting to note that individual nations' number of published documents does not correlate with the macroeconomic variables, particularly the population size, per-capita income, fiscal stance, public-debt, and neither the GINI-coefficient nor the per-capita-emission footprint.

To expose and contextualise the thematic constructs within the selected articles, we focused on the relationships between the publication activity of a particular country and its form of governance, i.e., the economic system ideology and the political orientation, and on other external variables that could exert political pressure, including foreign direct investment and tourism, etc. To focus the analysis on the most informative articles, the selected documents from Stage 1 were further reduced to a manageable number by applying filter criteria for thematic quality (i.e., relevance, focus, coverage, redundancy, authenticity, etc.). The iterative process yielded 118 articles for full-text analysis, using Nvivo 12 Plus Software and its specific procedures and techniques for construct identification and extraction, "coding" of relevant text sequences within and across the selected final batch documents, conceptual modelling and visualisation techniques. Following the qualitative framework analysis methodology for applied policy research (Srivastava & Thomson, 2009) combined with the contextual narratives techniques (Pawson, 2002) the authors developed the following conceptual model to keep the document analysis process focused and relevant within the research objective and the guiding question.

3.4 Thematic Analysis of the Documents

The model in Fig. 8 guided the content analysis task to identify the relevant constructs within and across the mined documents and to collate a vocabulary of contextualised expressions, sentences and text passages in a structured and balanced manner. Using the text analysis features, coding and linking techniques of Nvivo in an iterative process, the relevant constructs were identified and analysed for the relationships and patterns with other constructs and then linked to ideas, concepts and paradigms, as guided by the research question. This analysis led to a structured thematic map with four thematic policy spaces within the study's economic, social and ecological dimensions of the inclusive and sustainable fiscal policy paradigm.

The analysis revealed that literature associates the economic and social, and ecological dimension with the concept of an "inclusive and sustainable fiscal policy". The sub-themes within each dimension identified further important qualities of an integrated fiscal policy model to effectively address the ASEAN countries' inequality and climate change challenges. With the thematic map (Fig. 9) in place, the document analysis focused on particular aspects of the model, looking for further evidence in the literature about the drivers and impediments for an integrated fiscal policy model. Literature evidence pointed at several determinants that advocate the inclusive and sustainable fiscal policy model and the impediments that would have to be considered in policy development.

Further analysis of the policy drivers based on the thematic map in Fig. 10 uncovered additional aspects of increasing public concern about non-sustainable policy action and lack of policy effectiveness and the potential ramifications of this neglect for future generations. We found evidence of the growing global consent of a

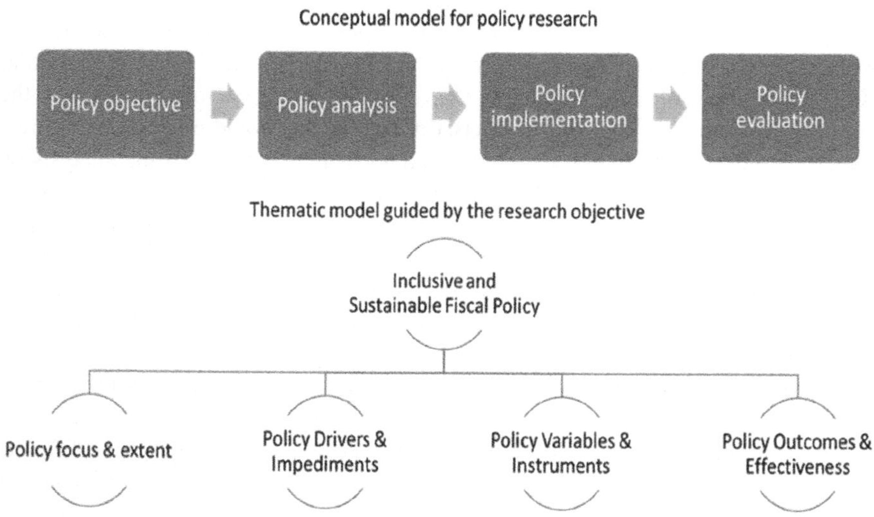

Fig. 8 The conceptualised thematic model used for the document analysis. (Source: authors)

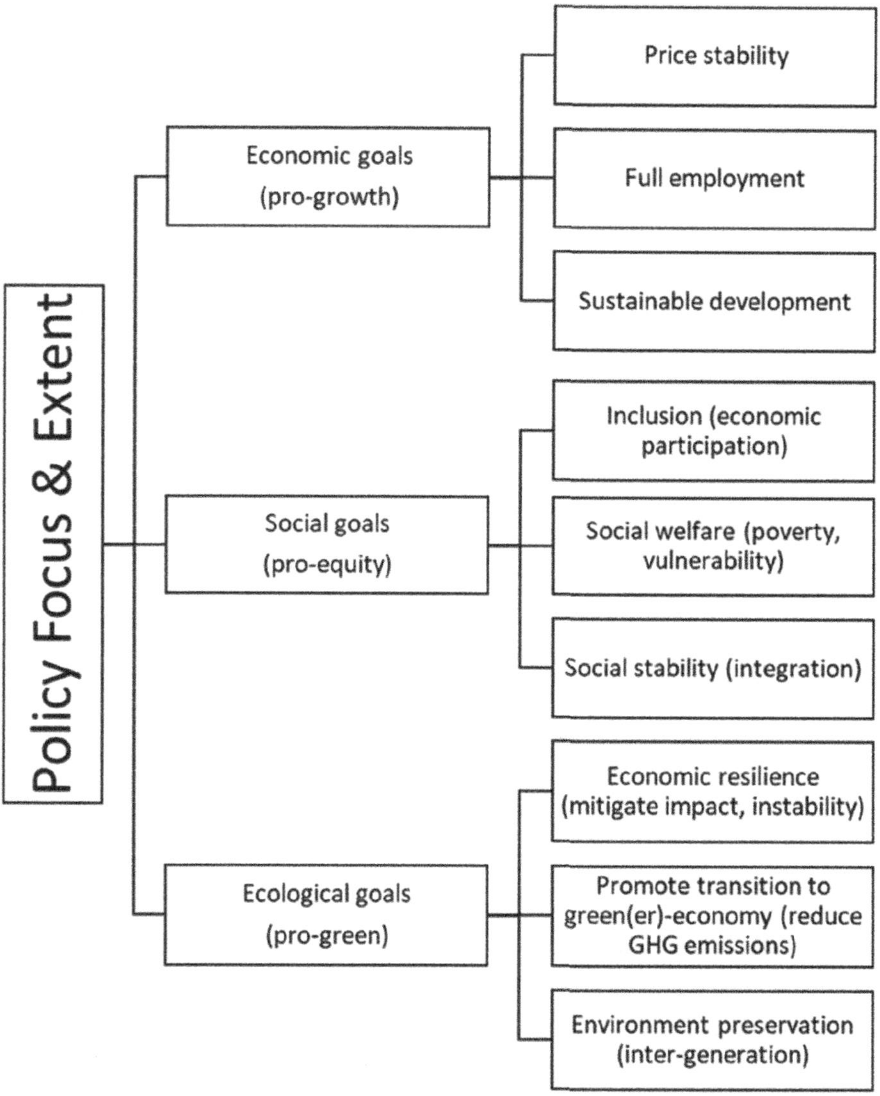

Fig. 9 Conceptualised thematic map of the "policy focus and extent" theme within the three sustainability dimensions. (Source: authors)

causal relationship between the unresolved inequality and climate change trends and the socio-economic stability, sustainable growth and development, and the negative direct and indirect effects on our quality of life and very existence (Human Development Index, United Nations Development Program; and World Happiness Index, Sustainable Development Solutions Network). Moreover, there is increasing global pressure for government conformance with multilateral standards and institutional and policy advisory recommendations with an urgent call to action. For policy

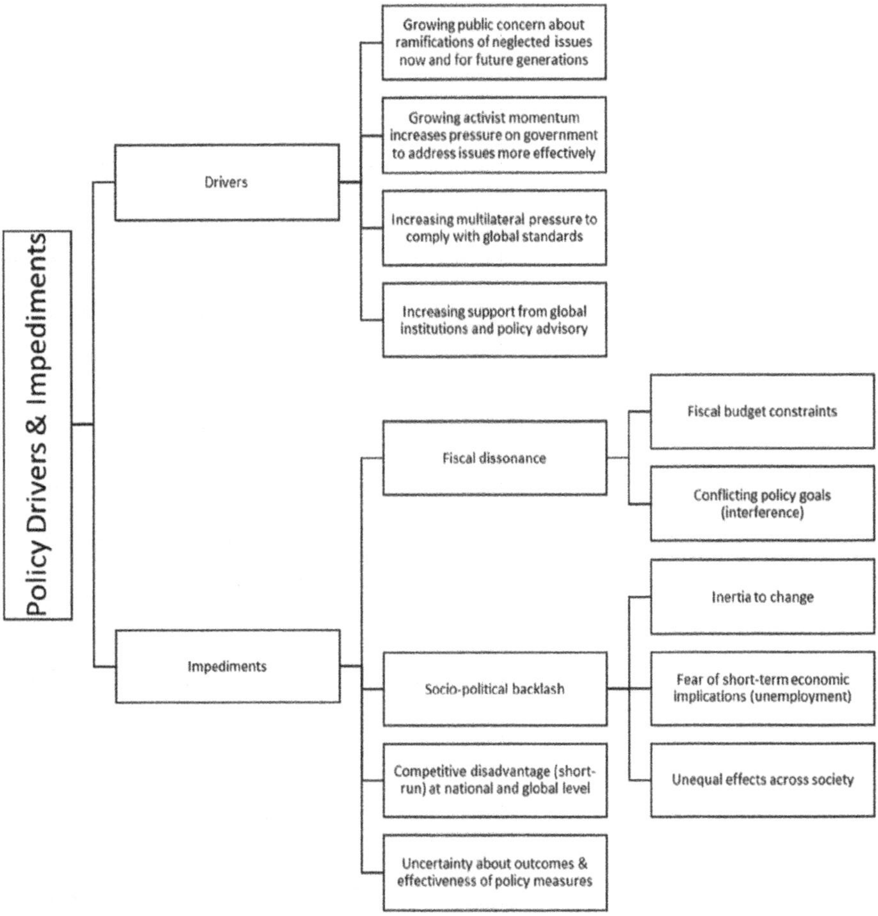

Fig. 10 Conceptualised thematic map of the policy drivers and impediments. (Source: authors)

impediments, the analysis revealed socio-political backlash (i.e., the inertia or resistance to change), a competitive disadvantage in the short-run (i.e., first-mover disadvantage) and uncertainty about the policy effectiveness. For both dimensions, the policy drivers and the impediments, the analysis revealed additional explanatory details.

Guided by the overall conceptual model, we examined literature evidence about the policy variables and instruments for an inclusive and sustainable fiscal policy. This process exposed five dimensions of policy variables (Fig. 11), including taxation (i.e., direct and indirect tax schemes), expenditure (i.e. spending for public services and infrastructure and social transfers), fiscal budget and stance (i.e., expansionary, contractionary) and public debt, as well as specific levers for policy targeting, progressivity schemes, inequality and climate change incidences (i.e., dynamic feedback loops).

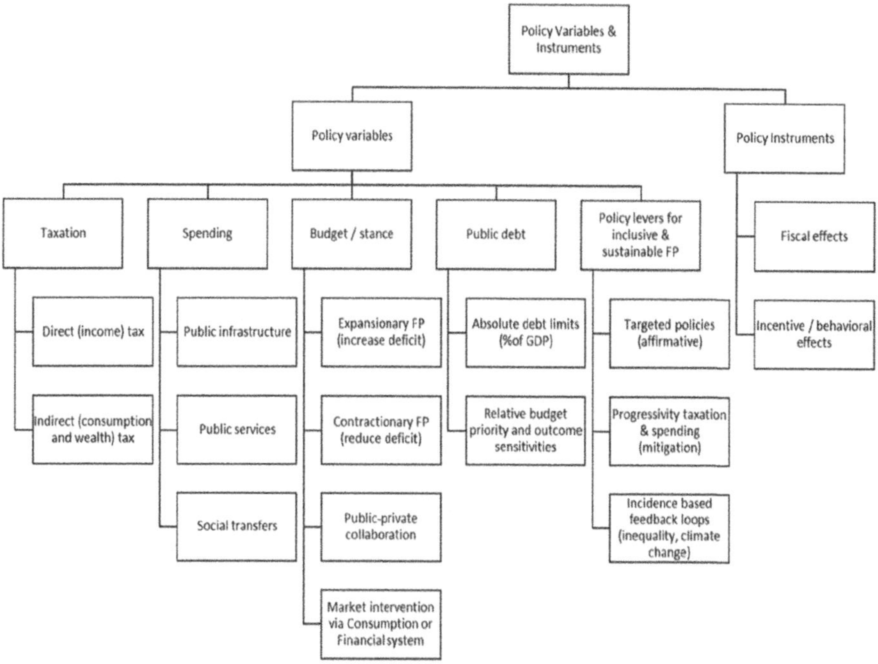

Fig. 11 Conceptualised thematic map of the policy variables and instruments. (Source: authors)

In this analysis step, the literature revealed many instruments that worked on one or several policy variables. These were classified into two categories, those with a primary fiscal effect and those aiming to incentivise behaviour change through positive or negative reinforcement (i.e., tax/fee/fine or subsidy/transfers, etc.). The final analysis step identified specific literature evidence of the policy focus, outcomes and effectiveness. Literature on policy action was classified into three clusters: remedial policy action aiming to rectify damage, mitigation policy action that seeks to build resilience, and affirmative action to prevent unfavourable future trends. The classification in Fig. 12 allows clustering policy by intent, which facilitates the analysis of the literature by policy outcomes and effectiveness regarding inequality and climate change challenges.

3.5 *Identified Gaps*

This study found robust evidence of broad knowledge about policy frameworks, programs, instruments, and variables in the ASEAN. We also uncovered significant evidence in existing academic and grey literature about the inequality and climate change challenges, their causes and effects, drivers and impediments. However, our analysis suggests that existing literature lacks a multilateral approach to an inclusive

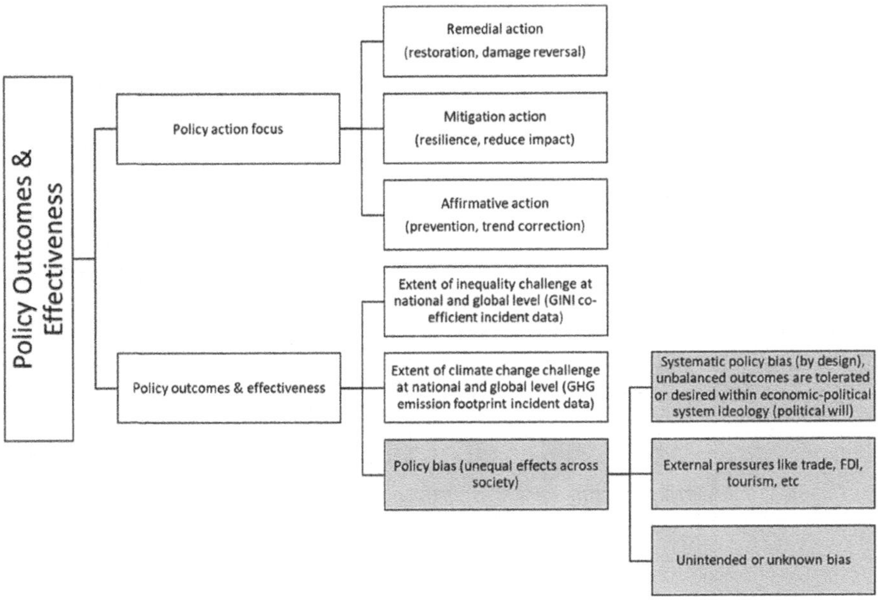

Fig. 12 Conceptualised thematic map of policy outcome and effectiveness. The shaded branches denote a literature gap. (Source: authors)

and sustainable fiscal policy in an integrated macroeconomic model to effectively address the inequality and climate change issues in ASEAN and worldwide. Particularly, policy bias and its consequences are not well understood and call for further research.

4 Conclusion

This study's objective was to search for evidence of inclusive and sustainable fiscal policy practices that aim to internalise the social costs of inequality and climate change into an integrated fiscal model. The paper adopted a qualitative approach to search for existing evidence of structured knowledge, using two methods. The scoping review to map the literature in this field and the document analysis method to dissect and contextualise the content. The scoping review method identified pertinent academic and grey literature sources in an iterative process, applying content-sensitive inclusion and exclusion criteria, de-duplication and other eligibility criteria. The second step involved applying the document analysis method to investigate the content of the selected documents, expose the thematic constructs, relationships and patterns, interpret and visualise the extracted ideas, concepts and paradigms of these documents.

The study produced evidence of substantial research coverage of the inequality and climate change challenges at the global and national levels and growing interest in the new policy discipline of inclusive, sustainable fiscal policy to mitigate the effects. Global government fora, independent institutions and private sector policy advisors have further contributed to the international momentum and public awareness of this topic while pressing for policy action. The analysis revealed that in the ASEAN the inequality issue attracted significantly more (publication) interest than climate change. Only with the recent event of the Paris Agreement (2015), as a multilateral approach to GHG reduction, has the ASEAN's climate change issue gained serious traction. However, existing literature did not reconcile the structural commonalities between the inequality and climate change issues, in that both of these multi-dimensional phenomena have natural and manmade causes. These occur inevitably in the economic conduct of the private and the public sectors and they are linked to the country's endowments, its economic ideology and political orientation. Furthermore, we found solid evidence of growing interest and support in the concept of an inclusive and sustainable fiscal policy with targeted and dynamic instruments (through progressivity and incidences) to internalise the socio-economic and ecological costs from externalities of economic activity into an integrated fiscal model. In the paradigm of an inclusive and sustainable fiscal policy, the goal is to render a net social surplus and neutralise the environmental impact from economic activity across generations. Our research confirmed the complex and multi-dimensional nature of both issues and the need for a multilateral approach through policy coordination at the global level and policy integration at the national and sub-national levels. Finally, this analysis surfaced the question of the extent of policy bias in design, implementation and evaluation, and the importance of government's political will to effectively address these issues within the paradigm of the economic system ideology and political orientation i.e., capitalism versus interventionism.

References

Arksey, H., & O'Malley, L. (2005). Scoping studies: Towards a methodological framework. *International Journal of Social Research Methodology, 8*(1), 19–32.

Belal, A. R., & Momin, M. (2009). *Corporate social reporting (CSR) in emerging economies: A review and future direction*. Accounting in Emerging Economies.

Bowen, G. A. (2009). *Document analysis as a qualitative research method*. Qualitative Research Journal.

Chaiechi, T. (2020). Sustainable tropical cities: A scoping review of multidisciplinary methods for urban planning. *ETropic: Electronic Journal of Studies in the Tropics, 19*(2), 25–51.

Esty, D. C. (2017). Toward a sustainable global economy: An initiative for G20 leadership. *Journal of Self-Governance and Management Economics, 5*(2), 46–60.

Gaspar, V., Amaglobeli, M. D., Garcia-Escribano, M. M., Prady, D., & Soto, M. (2019). *Fiscal policy and development: Human, social, and physical investments for the SDGs*. International Monetary Fund.

Hickel, J. (2017). *The divide: A brief guide to global inequality and its solutions*. Random House.

Hogl, K., Kleinschmit, D., & Rayner, J. (2016). Achieving policy integration across fragmented policy domains: Forests, agriculture, climate and energy. *Environment and Planning C: Government and Policy, 34*(3), 399–414.

Jacobs, M., & Mazzucato, M. (Eds.). (2016). *Rethinking capitalism: Economics and policy for sustainable and inclusive growth*. Wiley.

Klenow, P. J., & Rodriguez-Clare, A. (2005). Externalities and growth. *Handbook of Economic Growth, 1*, 817–861.

Meade, J. E. (1973). *The theory of economic externalities: The control of environmental pollution and similar social costs* (Vol. 2). Brill Archive.

Pawson, R. (2002). Evidence-based policy: In search of a method. *Evaluation, 8*(2), 157–181.

Rahman, B. A., & Momin, M. (2009). Corporate social reporting (CSR) in emerging economies: A review and future direction. In M. Tsamenyi & S. Uddin (Eds.), *Accounting in emerging economies* (Vol. 9, pp. 119–143). Emerald Group Publishing Limited.

Samans, R., Blanke, J., Corrigan, G., & Drzeniek, M. (2015, September). *The inclusive growth and development report 2015* (Vol. 13). World Economic Forum.

Srivastava, A., & Thomson, S. B. (2009). Framework analysis: A qualitative methodology for applied policy research, *4*(2), 8.

Tavoni, A., Dannenberg, A., Kallis, G., & Löschel, A. (2011). Inequality, communication, and the avoidance of disastrous climate change in a public goods game. *Proceedings of the National Academy of Sciences, 108*(29), 11825–11829.

Community Empowerment as a Tool to Reduce Unemployment: Contrasting Cases of Iceland and Ireland

Pawel Gralewicz

Abstract Iceland and Ireland conduct radically different anti-crisis policies to reduce unemployment. Their strategies differ in the approach to the concept of community empowerment. After the Crisis of 2008, Iceland introduced measures to expand social partnership and vocational training, whereas the Irish government broke dialogue with trade unions and deprived them of their influence. This paper compares not only the two contrasting strategies but also their economic outcomes in the labour market. Thus, it aims to verify whether community empowerment enables a faster and more effective way out of the unemployment crisis. For this purpose, a statistical analysis of selected labour market indicators was performed. Results show that both countries have managed to reduce the unemployment and youth unemployment rate. However, this reduction should be interpreted, bearing in mind the fact that the Labour Force Participation Rate (LFPR) in Ireland is only 62%. The efficiency of the Irish approach has been undermined by detailed unemployment indicators. Until 2016, the long-term unemployed in Ireland accounted for over 50% of the unemployed. Long-term unemployment and underemployment have never returned to their pre-crisis levels. On the contrary, in Iceland, long-term unemployment is almost non-existent. Over 80% of the working-age population has been professionally active. Visible underemployment has remained below 10%. The differences between Irish performance and Icelandic performance in this research seem to be located in the governmental responses to the previous crisis. By following the rules of community empowerment, Iceland appears to have different unemployment conditions. Investment in human capital and efficient communication with citizens have resulted in higher economic resilience. Community empowerment may help reduce unemployment and develop a stable and inclusive labour market.

Keywords Community empowerment · Labour market · Unemployment · Iceland · Ireland

---

P. Gralewicz (✉)
Institute of Economics and Management, Jagiellonian University, Kraków, Poland
e-mail: pawel.gralewicz@doctoral.uj.edu.pl

© The Author(s), under exclusive license to Springer Nature Singapore Pte Ltd. 2022

T. Chaiechi, J. Wood (eds.), *Community Empowerment, Sustainable Cities, and Transformative Economies*, https://doi.org/10.1007/978-981-16-5260-8_33

1 Introduction

Despite its importance for the reduction of inequality, poverty eradication, and community development, the concept of community empowerment is rarely associated with employment (Angeles, 2004; Travers, 1997). Certainly, community empowerment mentions education as an empowering tool that can provide people with knowledge and skills (Cervero et al., 2001; Freire, 2000). It clearly affects employment. However, in terms of human capital, this concept is more elaborate and implementing its rules could be an instrument to combat unemployment.

It is a relatively new concept. Insomuch as the value of sustainable and inclusive growth becomes more visible, community empowerment develops. The world economy today differs vastly from the 1930s, nevertheless, unemployment still preoccupies and perplexes economists and politicians. It is a notable constant. Thus, using new concepts to find ideas for restructuring the labour market is necessary and may prove productive. Involvement of citizens from different regions of the country, giving them decision-making power through participation in designing the labour market, continuous improvement of vocational training, offering education to long-term jobseekers, all of this helps reduce unemployment (Garrouste et al., 2010; Mondschean & Oppenheimer, 2011). Moreover, such government initiatives could help build a transformative economy that is resilient to external shocks.

The research in this paper explores the relationship between community empowerment and the reduction of unemployment. A comparative analysis presents the labour market policies introduced in two European states, Iceland and Ireland. Both countries were severely hit by the Financial Crisis of 2008. Both entailed a collapse of the banking system, in both cases a deep recession was triggered, and both needed to resort to outside financial assistance. Nevertheless, there was a significant difference between them. In the years following the crisis, Iceland and Ireland conducted radically different anti-crisis policies regarding unemployment. Icelandic government started a transformation of the economy with new demand-driven vocational training for the unemployed. The idea of community empowerment has been brought into a sharp focus. Oppositely, Ireland has paid particular attention to paying off the country's debt obligations. The system of activating and training the unemployed, which required reform, has changed but not much. Social partnership disappeared for several years.

The comparative analysis presents the differences between the Irish and Icelandic responses to the unemployment crisis. To verify their effectiveness in the labour market, the unemployment indicators are compared over time. Labour market measures introduced in Iceland and Ireland, provide information on the compliance with community empowerment rules in both labour markets. The comparative analysis of the indicators, such as youth unemployment rate and long-term unemployment rate, depicts how these contrasting approaches influenced unemployment. The main objective of the analysis is to verify whether the use of community empowerment can offer a faster and more effective way out of the unemployment crisis.

2 Literature Review

In recent years, community empowerment has been seen as a tool for making people powerful, aware of options, able and active to participate in the economy and its growth. This concept has a diverse nature and translates into both collective power over the economy and power to create something individually or collectively for oneself or for others (Brophy et al., 2017). There are various ways in which community empowerment has been defined. The literature reiterates that it is crucial for people to participate in the development process (Hjorth, 2003). Empowerment and participation are closely interrelated (Laverack, 2001). Empowering people means promoting and giving opportunities for their active participation, whereas participation requires the empowerment of people to entitle them to exercise this right (Sidorenko, 2006). This means an increase in their access to and control over the resources (Speer et al., 2001). Community empowerment equips local citizens with more political power or social influence (Corbett & Keller, 2004) by developing confidence in their own capacities (Wallerstein, 2006). These changes may result in such important development outcomes as a reduction in poverty, inequality and social exclusion, protection of resources, and improvements in quality of life (Itzhaky & York, 2000; Gutberlet, 2009; Sreberny, 2006). Bennet (2002) defines community empowerment as an enhancement of the capabilities and assets of communities to engage, influence, and hold accountable the institutions that affect them. It is rather used to characterize approaches that rely on social mobilization. It is not a static, single experience but a continuous process (Brophy et al., 2017). The concept can translate into the functioning of the entire economy through education.

Education plays a significant role in community empowerment at both the individual and collective level. It equips people and local communities with knowledge and skills of trade which make them more competitive in the specific productive field (Freire, 2000). It is amplifying people's possibilities to hold or create a job or a business to have a career that would make them more confident and increase their living standards (Cervero et al., 2001). On a macroeconomic scale, enhanced skills of local workers mean a higher quality of human capital which can attract foreign investors and firms (Blanton & Blanton, 2007). Economic growth achieved by investment in human capital can also lead to inclusive growth. By inclusive growth, one can understand growing the economy in such ways that positively affect the distribution, in which more and more people participate in an increased wealth (Saad-Filho, 2010).

Economic development professionals begin to consider not only innovation systems, technology, and governance, but also the deployment and development of strong human capital as the key levers of the new market dynamics – "growing from the inside out". A more inclusive economic development approach is currently emerging, one which can generate "transformative economies". National and regional competitiveness may be driven predominantly not by consumption, but by increasing productivity and production (Brophy et al., 2017). By definition, transformative economies rely on identifying their potential and using the synergies of the concentration of business, technology assets and their human capital (Brophy et al., 2017). All this translates into engaging the whole spectrum of people and places within a country or region to drive inclusive prosperity. The movements of the transformative economy are forward-looking and aware of the need to sustain continuous development. (Suriñach-Padilla, 2017). The engaged countries or regions are receptive to socio-economic reorganization and attempt to transform the current model or to mitigate its negative effects (Suriñach-Padilla, 2017). Human capital is an important part of transformative economies where the labour market and the workforce education systems are being constantly retooled. Such adjustments are implemented to make workforce training and courses more employer- and demand-driven, more specialized, and tailored (Brophy et al., 2017). New technologies help better project labour demand and enable workers to better find suitable jobs (Utting, 2018). Consequently, it is necessary for economic development planners to figure out how to deploy and train the workforce – including some of the traditionally disadvantaged into emerging occupations. Transformative economies create an environment for continuous skill development and are ready for propelling inclusive growth by offering the right workers the right jobs (Brophy et al., 2017).

This strategy and transformation of power between the government and communities may be a tool in fighting unemployment. There is still not much research about the relationship between community empowerment and the reduction of unemployment. Several authors claim that community empowerment may be enabled through the removal of structural obstacles such as unequal access to employment (Laverack & Pratley, 2018; Popay, 2010). On the other hand, in the research conducted in the Mahenye community in Zimbabwe, the cause-and-effect sequence was reversed. Gohori and Van der Merwe (2021) presented evidence that adherence to the concept of community empowerment created employment opportunities. This discrepancy in the literature may serve as an interesting background for the conducted research.

3 Methodology

The analysis compares two European states, Iceland and Ireland, both severely hit by the Financial Crisis of 2008. There are numerous similarities between the Irish and Icelandic crises. Both countries entailed a collapse of the banking system, in both cases, a deep recession was triggered, and both needed to resort to outside financial assistance. Furthermore, during the crisis and over the last 12 years, Iceland and Ireland had almost identical dynamics of economic growth (OECD, 2021). Therefore, different outcomes in the labour market in Iceland and Ireland can be attributed precisely to different policy measures taken in these countries.

In the case of Ireland, particular attention was paid to studies by Seamus McGuinness and Philip O'Connell. Their research activity majored in the evaluation of the labour market and government initiatives to tackle unemployment. Furthermore, to obtain more information on unemployment activation programmes, the training system for the unemployed, and social partnership in Ireland, the following documents were used:

- "Public Employment Services – Mapping Activation. Spending Review" written by Orlagh Lavelle and Niamh Callaghan under the auspices of IGEES,[1]
- "Pathways to Work 2016 to 2020 Report" submitted by the Department of Employment Affairs and Social Protection,
- "The Impact of anti-crisis measures, and the social and employment situation: Ireland" compiled by the European Economic and Social Committee.

The information regarding initiatives taken by the Icelandic government was gained from government reports:

- "Conclusions of the 2020 – Moving Iceland Forward Initiative" compiled by the Initiative's Steering Committee for the Icelandic Prime Minister's Office,
- "Iceland's fourth Periodic Report under Articles 16 and 17 of the International Covenant on Economic, Social and Cultural Rights" submitted by the Icelandic Government,
- "Welfare Watch. Report to the Althing" written by the Icelandic Ministry of Social Affairs and Social Security.

Studies by Katrin Ólafsdóttir, Geir Gunnlaugsson, and Jónína Einarsdóttir were also used to learn more about vocational training for the unemployed, social partnership and programmes implemented in Iceland during the Crisis of 2008.

The comparative analysis of unemployment indicators in Iceland and Ireland is a second part of the study. The analysis is based on data from OECD Employment and Labour Market Statistics. This section aims to assess how the anti-crisis measures introduced in both countries have translated into their labour market outcomes. The community empowerment concept intends to provide people with skills and knowledge that empower them to be financially independent and professionally fulfilled. Therefore, the following unemployment indicators are particularly important in this analysis: the unemployment rate, long-term unemployment rate, labour force participation rate, youth unemployment rate, and visible underemployment rate. The unemployment rate appears only to illustrate how both Iceland and Ireland managed to reduce it, despite conducting such contrasting anti-crisis policies. Further indicators are to examine the situation in both labour markets more closely. Long-term unemployment prevents an individual from empowerment, as it deprives them of independently earned income and makes them heavily dependent on the

[1] Irish Government Economic and Evaluation Service (IGEES) is a cross-government service. Through economic evaluation and analysis, it supports better policy formulation and implementation in the civil service.

government. Statistics on youth unemployment rates are important in the context of the development of human capital. These indicators may be a certain prediction of the future in the labour market. LFPR measures the number of individuals who are either working or actively looking for a job as a share of the working-age population. This indicator gives a more in-depth picture of the labour market than the unemployment rate. While the national unemployment rate takes into account only the people in the workforce, the LFPR presents the entire working-age population. Underemployment occurs when employees are involuntarily working part-time. They would take full-time positions if that were available. Visible underemployment rate reveals the real situation in the labour market. It may remain unnoticed by researchers who base their assessment only on the unemployment rate.

4 Labour Market Policies – Comparative Analysis

The labour market measures aim to reduce unemployment, help job seekers remain active in the labour market, and create ways for them to enhance their prospects. The first part of the study is a comparative analysis of the labour market measures introduced in Iceland and Ireland, such as: (1) activation of the unemployed, (2) wages, (3) social partnership in the labour market, (4) training programmes and education.

Activation of the Unemployed Public Employment Services (PES) has been established in both Iceland and Ireland to perform as a key intermediary between job seekers and employers. Although structured diversely in each country, PES embrace a series of externally contracted and internally managed services that are responsible for paying benefits to the unemployed, and for matching in the labour market.

Giving consideration to fiscal constraints, the initiatives of tackling unemployment in Ireland should have been cost-neutral. By definition, in such a scenario, a wide range of labour market activation measures should be taken into sharp focus. According to the previous research of Grubb et al. (2009), the matching function of PES in Ireland was detached from the benefit function. Later on, it transpired that failures in communication between PES and benefits organisations brought about great numbers of qualifying claimants falling out of the activation net (McGuinness et al. 2011a, b). Regardless of that, people were activated right after 3 months of presence on the Irish register, however, the claimants who, under the previous unemployment period, had already been interviewed, were automatically excluded from activation during the ensuing claims. For claimants qualifying for assistance and benefits, attending the first interview was the only quasi-obligatory contact with employment assistance (Lavelle & Callaghan, 2018).

In Iceland, since the first year of the crisis, the Directorate of Labour has been responsible not only for accepting applications and handling benefits but also for running Public Employment Services. Therefore, the matching and benefits function in the Icelandic labour market has been consolidated. To meet the criteria of the Unemployment Insurance Act, for unemployment benefit, an individual must partake in all scheduled interviews and meetings. When a benefit recipient did not appear at the interview or meeting, of which they had been given notice, and could not provide a documented and valid explanation, a penalty was imposed. (Government of Iceland, 2010) Throughout the crisis, individuals registered as unemployed were contacted within the first 3 months after submitting the application. According to "Iceland's fourth Periodic Report under Articles 16 and 17 of the International Covenant on Economic, Social, and Cultural Rights" (2010), registered unemployed received a schedule covering their search for employment and engagement in labour market measures based on the assessment.

Wages In the face of the crisis, the reaction of politicians often comes down to lower wages in the public sector. Governments, however, can take initiatives to maintain effective demand. An example of this type of activity are subsidies for companies guaranteeing employee retention or an increase in the tax-free rate.

In 2009, Irish public sector unions proposed a shorter work time in the public sector as an alternative to planned wage cuts. The proposal has been rejected, and tiered wage cuts in the public sector were applied as follows:

- a 5% cut in annual income until €30,000;
- a 7.5% cut in annual income until €40,000;
- a 10% cut in annual income above €55,000.

In 2011, the government cut the minimum wage by 12.5% from €8.65 per hour to €7.65 per hour (Rigney and Irish Congress of Trade Unions 2012). In the years of the Great Recession, there were no employer benefits offered in Ireland. In this regard, the government did not take any action to keep people employed.

In 2009 and 2010, in Iceland, there was an average wage cut of 9.3% in wages in both public and private sectors (Ólafsdóttir, 2020a). In 2010, due to collective bargaining, the wage increases had more than offset the nominal wage cuts during the recession (Ólafsdóttir, 2020b). At the advent of the crisis, the Icelandic Directorate of Labour introduced part-time benefits from the unemployment benefits fund. The list of jobs with wage subsidies was widely expanded (Andersen et al., 2011). Therefore, firms could afford to hold more people on their payrolls. Self-employed individuals could apply for the benefit as well. The part-time benefit was offered as a temporary measure. Due to the weakened currency, and therefore inflation, in 2010, the minimum wage in Iceland was increased by 30%. The government intervention was intended to maintain the purchasing power of the Icelandic people.

Social Partnership in the Labour Market In 2009, after wage cuts in the public sector, the social partnership in Ireland collapsed. In fact, the social partnership has been atrophying from the onset of the crisis (Rigney and Irish Congress of Trade Unions Rigney, 2012). The role of the public sector union was minimized and the meetings with the government ceased. The unions were left with neither access nor influence. Due to protests, the government and public unions re-engaged in 2010 (Tassinari & Donaghey, 2020). The National Economic and Social Council was productively stood down by the government. This independent institution had previously served as the central forum for social dialogue. Its tenure expired, and the council did not meet for most of the crisis.

In Iceland, already in 2008, the union density was high, with nearly 85% of employees covered (Andersen et al., 2011). Collective bargaining agreements had a status equal to law.

During the Great Recession, the new government aimed to shelter the low-income groups from the impact of the crisis. The emphasis was on reducing the nominal wages of the higher paid, while remaining the status of the lowest paid (Ólafsdóttir, 2020b). In 2009, as part of "2020 - Moving Iceland Forward Initiative", a work team was set up to analyse Iceland's competitiveness and advise on what measures must be taken to rebuild the economy.

Over 1200 participants came together representing all regions of the country to develop a common vision for the future (Forsætisráðuneyti, 2010). The most important new policy, shaping Icelandic wages was the Stability Pact signed by the government, unions, and employers. This outcome of the dialogue provided stability in the labour market. It addressed some of the pressing needs, such as a reduction in interest rates, job creation, and expanded efforts in rehabilitation. The Stability Pact also addressed the main goals for government finances. The emphasis on collective bargaining agreements has translated into the share of the working poor being the lowest among the OECD countries (Ólafsdóttir, 2020b).

One of other initiatives was the Welfare Watch, established in February 2009 (Welfare Watch, 2010; Velferðarráðuneytið, 2013). This multidisciplinary platform consisted of various sectors of society, including representatives from the labour market, non-governmental organisations, municipalities, government ministries, and institutions. The Welfare Watch aimed to monitor the economic and social impact of the crisis on the population, offer ideas to policy makers, and evaluate the actions taken by the government (Gunnlaugsson & Einarsdóttir, 2016).

Training Programmes and Education In Ireland, Specific Skills Training (SST) received about 60% of expenditures on training programmes. SST included courses that provided learners with formal vocational qualifications. McGuinness et al. (2011a) claims that specific skills programmes in Ireland were unsuccessful and increased the probability of getting hired only by 9%. Job search training (17.9%) and special high skill training (22.4%) were estimated to be the most productive (McGuinness et al., 2011b). Job search training courses informed the unemployed how and where to look for job offers. Special high skills training allowed the unemployed to find a career path that would match their interests and skills. Unfortunately, most training programmes in Ireland have been designed to provide less effective, general and low-level skills, which proved to have a minimum impact on reducing unemployment (Barrett & McGuiness, 2012). To restructure the composition of training options, the Irish Government launched the "Pathways to Work" initiative in 2012 (Department of Employment Affairs and Social Protection, 2016). Nevertheless, training programmes in Ireland have not been reoriented away from ineffective general and low skills initiatives (Barrett & McGuiness, 2012).

In Iceland, education was an important part of the adjustment to the unemployment crisis. The basic support programmes have been focused on strengthening and empowering an individual. In 2010, 60% of the registered unemployed participated in these measures (Andersen et al., 2011). Vocational training offered various specific courses, like computing, programming, office-work training, business, and bookkeeping. In 2009, the government targeted distinct groups of the workforce. The needs of unemployed young individuals were addressed in the programme *Ungt fólk til athafna* (Eng. Young People to Action). As an effect of the crisis and the incapacity of many companies to offer training for students and fresh graduates, Iceland offered incentives for firms to train students in the workplace. Over 50 firms were provided with IKR 54.4 million (EUR 470,000). In the period between 2012 and 2014, an additional IKR 450 million (around EUR 2.8 million) was sent to the workplace training fund. Individuals with more experience and long-term unemployed were covered by another program – *ÞOR –Þekking og reynsla* (Eng. DARE – Knowledge and Experience) (Vilhjálmsdóttir, 2016). To expand the general training programmes, the government signed new contracts with the private sector. A variety of courses, ranging from language studies to specific vocational training in different industries, have been offered. ÞOR aimed at keeping the unemployed active, and the programme involved collaboration with various schools and even sports clubs in a spirit that inactivity was not considered as an option. Next, in 2011, the government encouraged the unemployed to attend school within the programme *Nám er vinnandi vegur* (Eng. Education is a working Road). The overall aim was to improve their qualifications in the labour market. While in school, individuals kept unemployment benefits for the first semester, along with support to acquire study loans to enable them to pursue their studies. In 2013, the final initiative – *Liðsstyrkur* (Eng. Support) – was introduced as a support for the long-term unemployed. (Gunnlaugsson & Einarsdóttir, 2016).

5 Unemployment Indicators – Comparative Analysis

The second part of the analysis aims to assess how the anti-crisis policies introduced in Iceland and Ireland have translated into labour market outcomes. Figure 1 displays the unemployment rate in the years closely preceding and following the Crisis of 2008. By the end of 2007, right before the crisis, the unemployment rates in Iceland and Ireland were rather similar. With the outbreak of the crisis, the unemployment rate in both countries increased rapidly. Importantly, however, in Iceland as early as 2009, the increase in unemployment began to slow down sharply, to decline from 2010 (7.6%) until 2018 (2.7%). The steep rise in unemployment in Ireland continued, reaching 15.5% in 2012. Afterwards, it began to decline at an impressive pace until 2019 when, at 5%, it approached the Icelandic level (3.5%). Despite the longer period of struggle against rising unemployment, Ireland's final outcome in reducing the unemployment rate is astonishing. Thus, it is worth taking a closer look at the

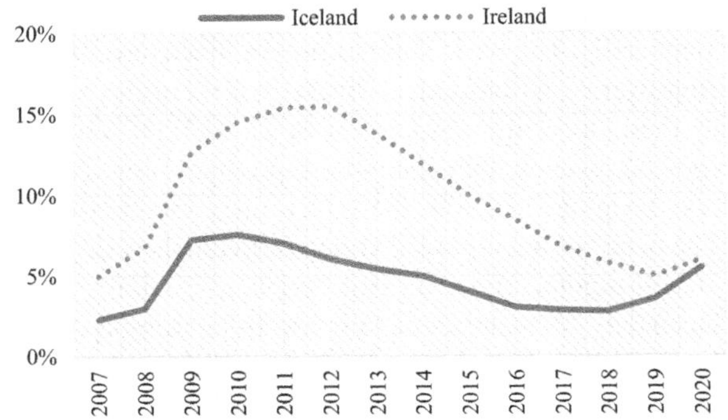

Fig. 1 The unemployment rate (%) (OECD Employment and Labour Market Database)

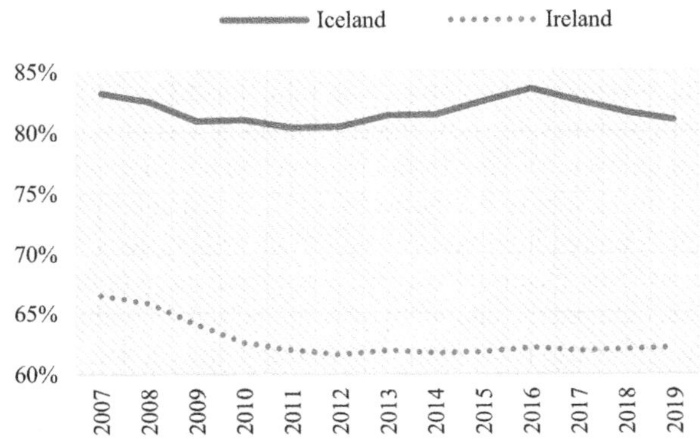

Fig. 2 Labour force participation rate (%) (OECD Employment and Labour Market Database)

other unemployment statistics to study whether the Irish labour market is indeed an example of exceptional recovery.

The participation rate is the percentage of the whole population of working age that is either employed or actively looking for employment. As shown in Fig. 2, in Iceland, economically active people consistently account for over 80% of the working-age population.

In Ireland, LFPR only in 2007 and 2008 exceeded 65%. During the post-crisis period, it was around 62% and has not been able to return to its pre-crisis level. Thus, the low unemployment rate in Ireland has been obtained in the context of low economic activity within the society.

In the period from 2008 to 2011, the long-term unemployment rate in Iceland closely resembled the pattern observed in Ireland (see Fig. 3). During the first years of the crisis in both countries, the rate increased sharply. However, only in Iceland did it begin to decline rapidly, in 2014 getting closer to the pre-crisis level. After 2016, the long-term unemployment rate in Iceland has been below 10%, matching pre-crisis levels. The situation was different in Ireland. Until 2015, the long-term unemployment rate was close to 60%. It is worth mentioning here that before the crisis, this rate was 30%. From 2016, the index began to decline at a faster pace, but only in 2019 it was approaching the pre-crisis level. Thus, it took Ireland 11 years to

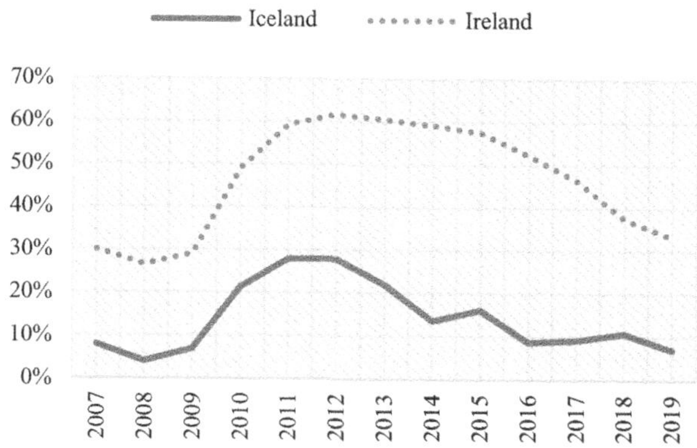

Fig. 3 Long-term unemployment rate (%) (OECD Employment and Labour Market Database)

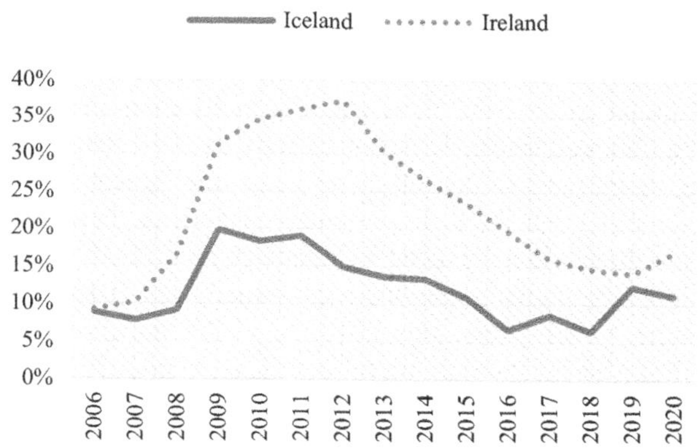

Fig. 4 Youth unemployment rate (%) (OECD Employment and Labour Market Database)

return to pre-crisis values, and despite the boom in Europe after 2012, the country continued to struggle with the fight against long-term unemployment.

Figure 4 displays the youth unemployment rate. In 2006, in Ireland and Iceland, the youth unemployment rates were almost identical – around 9%. The rapid growth of the youth unemployment rate in Iceland was halted a year after the crisis - in 2009 at the level of 20%. Afterwards, the indicator began to fall steadily, except in 2010. From 2015, youth unemployment in Iceland was on average 10%. In 2016, its level was lower than before the crisis, which can be considered a great achievement for Iceland. Youth unemployment in Ireland continued to increase longer, until 2013, and what is essential, its level was as high as 35%. After 2013, along with the good economic situation in Europe, Ireland experienced a sharp drop in the youth unemployment rate. In 2019, Ireland and Iceland again had a similar rate of roughly 14%, but only for a year. In 2020, Ireland experienced a rise in youth unemployment, whereas, in Iceland, the indicator decreased.

Visible underemployment rate presents how well the labour force is being utilized in terms of availability to work. Involuntary part-time workers are part-timers because they were not able to find a full-time job. They usually work less than 30 h per week. Underemployment differs from unemployment in that an individual

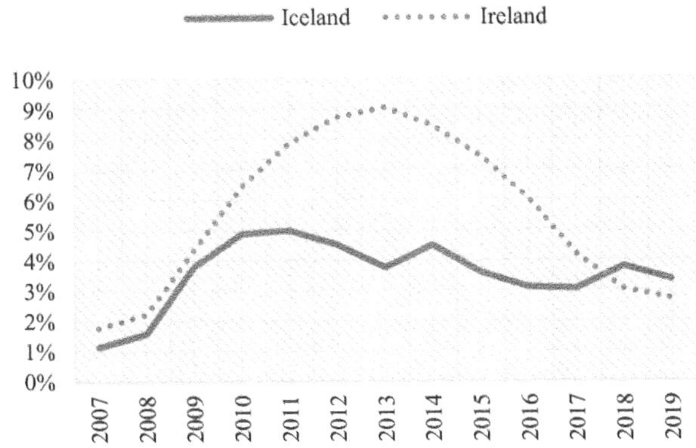

Fig. 5 Visible underemployment rate (%) (OECD Employment and Labour Market Database)

is working, albeit not at their full capability. As depicted in Fig. 5, one year before the crisis, the visible underemployment rates in Iceland and Ireland were very similar. After 2008, there was an equally sharp increase in visible underemployment in both countries. However, as early as 2010, underemployment in Iceland stopped growing, and in the following years, the indicator began to decline rapidly, except for 2010 and 2018. Importantly, in both of these years, the increase in underemployment did not exceed 1 percentage point. In the case of Ireland, the sharp increase in visible underemployment continued until 2013, amounting to almost 10% at the time. Nevertheless, after 2013, the visible underemployment rate in Ireland began to drop sharply, amounting to less than 3% in 2019.

6 Discussion and Concluding Remarks

In the research conducted by Jennie Popay (2010), Laverack and Pratley (2018), community empowerment has been linked with the reduction of unemployment. According to these authors, facilitating access to employment contributed to community empowerment. Apparently, this relation of influence may also take place in the opposite direction. The experiences highlighted in this research are in line with the conclusions of Gohori and Van der Merwe (2021). In their experience in Zimbabwe, adherence to community empowerment principles may lead to a reduction in unemployment. This is what happened in Iceland.

Icelandic approach has brought positive results in terms of faster exit from the unemployment crisis. Although the Irish approach is not that fast, it results in a similar reduction of unemployment, youth unemployment, and visible underemployment. Nevertheless, in Ireland, it took 4 years for youth unemployment to recede, while in Iceland, it took only a year. A similar pattern can be observed in the case of underemployment. In Iceland, it only took 2 years to stem the surge in underemployment. In Ireland, the unrestrained increase of underemployment lasted over 5 years and led to almost 10% of Irish employees working part-time involuntarily. Furthermore, the efficiency of the Irish approach has been undermined by detailed unemployment indicators. The country has been struggling with long-term unemployment and continuously decreasing LFPR that never returned to the pre-crisis level. Icelandic labour market seems more stable. Long-term unemployment is almost non-existent in Iceland. Despite the perturbation in the economy, the visible underemployment is still low, whereas the LFPR has remained over 80%. Therefore, adjustment to the rules of community empowerment seems able to reduce unemployment not only faster but also more effectively. There are also surplus effects. The economy may become more resilient to negative external shocks. Meanwhile, the efficient flow of information from the citizen to the government level, from the periphery right to the centre, may build more conscious and inclusive development. Providing inclusive development and helping more people gain valuable labour market skills is another step towards building a transformative economy. In such conditions, the concept of growing from the inside out expands.

References

Andersen, T., Frøhlich Hougaard, K., & Ólafsson, S. (Eds.). (2011). *Assessment of the labour market in Iceland – Final report*. Aarhus: Danish Technological Institute.

Angeles, L. C. (2004). Grassroots democracy and community empowerment: The quest for sustainable poverty reduction in Asia. In F. Quadir & J. Lele (Eds.), *Democracy and civil society in Asia* (pp. 182–212). New York: Palgrave Macmillan.

Barrett, A., & McGuiness, S. (Eds.). (2012). The Irish labour market and the great recession. *CESifo DICE Rep, 10*, 27–33.

Bennet, L. (Ed.). (2002). *Using empowerment and social inclusion for pro-poor growth: A theory of social change* (Working Draft of Background Paper for the Social Development Strategy Paper). Washington, DC: World Bank.

Blanton, S. L., & Blanton, R. G. (2007). What attracts foreign investors? An examination of human rights and foreign direct investment. *Journal of Politics, 69*(1), 143–155.

Brophy, P., Weissbourd, R., & Beideman, A. (2017). *Transformative economies: Emerging practices for aligning growth and inclusion*. Philadelphia: Federal Reserve Bank of Philadelphia.

Cervero, R., Wilson, A., & Associates. (2001). *Power in practice: Adult education and the struggle for knowledge and power in society*. San Francisco: Jossey Bass.

Corbett, J., & Keller, P. (2004). Empowerment and participatory geographic information and multimedia systems: Observations from two communities in Indonesia. *Information Technologies and International Development, 2*(2), 25–44.

Department of Employment Affairs and Social Protection. (2016). *Pathways to work 2016 to 2020 report*. Department of Employment Affairs and Social Protection.

Forsætisráðuneyti. (2010). *Conclusions of the 2020 – Moving Iceland forward initiative*. The Steering Committee. http://www.forsaetisraduneyti.is/media/2020/2020Moving-Iceland-Forward-Initiative.pdf. Accessed 7 Jan 2021.

Freire, P. (2000). *Pedagogy of indignation*. Sao Paulo: UNESP.

Garrouste, C., Kozovska, K., & Perez, E. A. (2010). *Education and long-term unemployment. JRC scientific and technical reports*. Luxembourg: European Commission. https://mpra.ub.uni-muenchen.de/25073/1/MPRA_paper_25073.pdf. Accessed 13 Jan 2021.

Gohori, O., & Van der Merwe, P. (2021). Tourism and community empowerment: The perspectives of local people in Manicaland Province. *Zimbabwe, Tourism Planning & Development*. https://doi.org/10.1080/21568316.2021.1873838.

Government of Iceland. (2010). *Iceland's fourth periodic report under articles 16 and 17 of the international covenant on economic social and cultural rights*. Government of Iceland.

Grubb, D., Singh, S., & Tergeist, P. (2009). *Activation policies in Ireland. Employment and migration* (Working papers 75). OECD Social.

Gunnlaugsson, G., & Einarsdóttir, J. (2016). All's well in Iceland? Austerity measures, labour market initiatives, and health and well-being of children. *Nordisk Välfärdsforskning*, 30–42.

Gutberlet, J. (2009). Solidarity economy and recycling co-ops: Micro-credit to alleviate poverty. *Development in Practice, 19*(6), 737–751.

Hjorth, P. (2003). Knowledge development and management for urban poverty alleviation. *Habitat International, 27*, 381–392.

Itzhaky, H., & York, A. S. (2000). Empowerment and community participation: Does gender make a difference. *Social Work Research, 24*(4), 225–234.

Lavelle, O., & Callaghan, N. (2018). *Public employment services – Mapping activation* (Spending review). IGEES – Irish Government Economic & Evaluation Service.

Laverack, G. (2001). An identification and interpretation of the organizational aspects of community empowerment. *Community Development Journal, 36*(2), 134–145.

Laverack, G., & Pratley, P. (2018). *What quantitative and qualitative methods have been developed to measure community empowerment at a national level*. Health Evidence Network (HEN) synthesis report 59, WHO Regional Office for Europe, Copenhagen.

McGuinness, S., O'Connell, P. J., Kelly, E., & Walsh, J. (2011a). *Activation in Ireland: An evaluation of the National Employment Action Plan*. ESRI Research Series 20.

McGuinness, S., O'Connell, P. J., & Kelly, E. (2011b). *One dummy won't get it: The impact of training program type and duration on the employment chances of the unemployed in Ireland*. ESRI working paper 410.

Mondschean, T., & Oppenheimer, M. (2011). Regional long-term and short-term unemployment and education in transition: The case of Poland. *The Journal of Economic Asymmetries, 8*(2), 23–48.

OECD Annual National Accounts Statistics. (2021). https://stats.oecd.org/. Accessed 21 Feb 2021.

OECD Employment and Labour Market Statistics. (2021). https://stats.oecd.org/. Accessed 12 Feb 2021.

Ólafsdóttir, K. (2020a). A deep recession came with deep wage cuts. *Economics Letters, 189*.

Ólafsdóttir, K. (2020b). The labour market in Iceland 2000-2018. *IZA World of Labour, 474*.

Popay, J. (2010). Community empowerment and health improvement: The English experience. In A. Morgan, M. Davies, & E. Ziglio (Eds.), *Health assets in a global context*. New York: Springer.

Rigney, P. (2012). *The impact of anti-crisis measures, and the social and employment situation: Ireland*. European Economic and Social Committee.

Saad-Filho, A. (2010). *Growth, poverty and inequality: From Washington consensus to inclusive growth* (UN/DESA working paper 100). New York: United Nations Department of Economic and Social Affairs.

Sidorenko, A. (2006). *Empowerment & participation in policy action on ageing*. Rovaniemi: UN Program on Ageing, International Design for All Conference 2006.

Speer, P. W., Jackson, C. B., & Peterson, N. A. (2001). The relationship between social cohesion and empowerment: Support and new implications for theory. *Health Education and Behavior, 28*(6), 716–732.

Sreberny, A. (2006). Gender, empowerment, and communication: Looking backwards and forwards. *International Social Science Journal, 57*(184), 197–201.

Suriñach-Padilla, R. (2017). *Economias transformadoras de Barcelona*. Barcelona: Marge Books.

Tassinari, A., & Donaghey, J. (2020). Social Partnership in Europe in the Aftermath of the Great Recession. In D. Pohler (Ed.), *Reimagining the governance of work and employment* (pp. 113–142). Chicago: Labour Employment Relations Association.

Travers, K. D. (1997). Reducing inequalities through participatory research and community empowerment. *Health Education & Behaviour, 24*(3), 344–356.

Utting, P. (2018). *Achieving the sustainable development goals through social and solidarity economy: Incremental versus transformative change* (UNRISD knowledge hub working paper) (pp. 28–31).

Velferðarráðuneytið. (2013). Skýrsla velferðarvaktarinnar, p. 36. http://bit.ly/1xjg6Zy. Accessed 15 Jan 2021.

Vilhjálmsdóttir, G. (2016). *Viðbrögð við hruninu og þáttur náms- og starfsráðgjafar. Hrunið – hvað gerðist svo? Sýn félags- og mannvísinda. Málþing Félags- og mannvísindadeildar.* Reykjavík: University of Iceland.

Wallerstein, N. (2006). *What is the evidence on effectiveness of empowerment to improve health.* Copenhagen: Health Evidence Network report, WHO Regional Office for Europe. http://www.euro.who.int/Document/E88086.pdf. Accessed 10 Jan 2021.

Welfare Watch. (2010). *Report to the Althingi* (p. 17). Reykjavik: Ministry of Social Affairs and Social Security.

Impact of Covid-19: How to Achieve Resilience in the Indonesian Agricultural Sector?

Renie Oelviani, Sodiq Jauhari, Wahyudi Hariyanto, Seno Basuki, Joko Triastono, and Aryana Citra Kusumasari

Abstract As the impact of Covid-19 arises, world economic development is severely being distressed, the agricultural sector in Indonesia, as previously proven in facing economic disturbances, is expected to be resilient. The objective of this study was to analyse comprehensively the impact of covid-19 to the agricultural sector in Indonesia. This review analysed and interpreted literature, government reports, and other secondary data to understand how the negative impact of covid-19 affected the agricultural sector and what solution should be taken into account. The result showed that covid-19 caused increased risk and uncertainty, disturbed the food supply chain, and decreased farmer households' income. Meanwhile, the political will of the government to support agricultural development is essentially important, such as setting production priority across regions, distribution of agricultural products, and relief package for farmers exposed to covid-19. This finding is expected to push agriculture to be more resistant in dealing with any emergencies this country might face in the future. Furthermore, this study identifies that factors affecting farmers signifies their importance and must be considered by the government in the pre and post cases. It is; therefore, suggested that resolving and mitigating mechanism might be adopted to keep agricultural growth moving forward.

Keywords Covid-19 · Agriculture · Farmer · Agricultural sector · Agriculture institution

1 Introduction

Unlike previous pandemics, such as Spanish influenza in 1918, Hong Kong Flu in 1968, N1H1 in 2009, Severe Acute Respiratory Syndrome (SARS) in 2002, Middle East Respiratory Syndrome (MERS) in 2012, and Ebola in 2013–14 (Wren-Lewis,

R. Oelviani (✉) · S. Jauhari · W. Hariyanto · S. Basuki · J. Triastono · A. C. Kusumasari
AIAT Central Java, Ministry of Agriculture, Ungaran, Central Java, Indonesia
e-mail: renieoelviani@pertanian.go.id

© The Author(s), under exclusive license to Springer Nature Singapore Pte Ltd. 2022

T. Chaiechi, J. Wood (eds.), *Community Empowerment, Sustainable Cities, and Transformative Economies*, https://doi.org/10.1007/978-981-16-5260-8_34

2020), the Covid-19 pandemic has caused a serious global crisis (Wren-Lewis, 2020; Aktar et al., 2021). WHO reported 102 million positive cases, and more than two million died from covid-19 (https://covid19.who.int/table, February 3 2021). Economists predict this unpredictable contagious pandemic to impact many aspects of human life, particularly related to health and the economy (Wren-Lewis, 2020; Adu-Gyamfi et al., 2021). One of the frightening impacts is related to its implication on food security (Workie et al., 2020; Mandal et al., 2021). according to the (Food and Agriculture Organization, 2020) report, the Covid-19 pandemic affects food supply, people's purchasing power, food production, and distribution. Further, all of these are predicted to have a strong and negative impact on the poor (Rasul, 2021; Rivera-Ferre et al., 2021).

The pandemic and its social and economic reverberations trigger particularly salient challenges in many aspects of life (Food and Agriculture Organization, 2020; Organisation for Economic Co-operation and Development, 2020). In the agricultural sector, FAO identified possible impacts of covid-19 (FAO, 2020; Goswami et al., 2021a). Many articles expressed concern that farmers would stop producing because of the pandemic (as they get sick), and less food will be available, if at all, at higher prices (Coopmans et al., 2021). As to demand-related impacts, probably the most important impact described by the articles was panic shopping and stockpiling. In fear of being locked down for a longer period, people have started to buy up huge stocks of durable food in a relatively short time period, thereby causing difficulties for supermarkets [https: //www.dailydemocrat.com/2020/03/11/will-fears-of-corona virus-change-demand-for-farm-goods/ (accessed on April 2 2020)].

Many scholars concerned about the implication of covid-19 develop anticipated models to deal with the worse scenario (Wren-Lewis, 2020). And, they propose a model that converts the epidemiological assumptions into economic shocks to save the existence of human beings globally, as the world has never been experienced such a bizarre state of emergency (Chakraborty & Maity, 2020). (Wren-Lewis, 2020) provide an example of countries severely hit; US, China, Japan, Germany, Britain, France, and Italy, are all in the top-ten most affected by the disease that affects 60% of world supply and demand (GDP), 65% of world manufacturing, and 41% of world manufacturing exports, as the supply and demand sides weakened (Wren-Lewis, 2020).

Among the shocks affecting human being to survive, the agricultural sector should be taken into account as the globally essential issue (Goswami et al., 2021b), as every person needs food to live (Lin & Zhang, 2020), yet every nation should be setting a plan in exploring, promoting, and developing its competitive advantages based agricultural products. Many agricultural-based countries, including Indonesia, are being suffered from the impact of border controlling policy applied to control the spread of the virus. For Indonesia, exports and import have been slowdown (Yofa & Suryani, 2020), the stability of food price and food supply are being disturbed (Perdana et al., 2020; Pertanian, 2020; Priyadarshini & Abhilash, 2021; Varshney et al., 2021) a slowdown in poverty alleviation, an increase in unemployment from 8% (2019) to 12% (Yusuf et al., 2020), and an increase in rural poverty to 68%, half of whom are farmers (Krisnamurthi, 2021).

This paper is structured as follows; Part two briefly describes the methods and data, section three provides results and discussion, section four outlines some of the policy implications, and section five outlines conclusions and future research.

2 Method and Data

Our data collection process took place from February 1 to April 30 2021. The search process consisted of three steps (Table 1).

2.1 *Data*

This study combined qualitative and quantitative information to describe and analyse the impact of disturbances and how agriculture should survive amid the covid-19 lockdown that began in March 2020. Sources of information used for this descriptive analysis include data from the Republic of Indonesia's Central Bureau of Statistics (BPS). Indonesia, publications, FAO, WHO, and the World Economic Forum, Bappenas, Ministry of Agriculture, government-released reports and other official information, media articles, and research results to determine the impact of agriculture from the pandemic and how agriculture survives.

Table 1 The search process

Step1		Step 2	Step 3
Keywords of Search	Results (Number)	Relevant Articles on the Topic (Number)	Analysed Articles without Overlaps (Number)
Pandemic + agriculture	13	7	4
Farmers + pandemic	15	6	3
Resilience + agriculture + pandemic	7	4	3
NTP of Indonesian farmers + pandemic	3	3	3
Food availability + pandemic	4	3	3
Needs + distribution + pandemic	3	3	2
Trade + agricultural commodities + pandemic	9	6	4
Transformation + agricultural + pandemic	5	4	3
Logistics system + pandemic	6	4	3
Supply chain + pandemic	9	5	4

Step 1: We use science direct, google search, and government websites with several pairs of keywords tailored to the materials needed. A "keyword" search returned 74 articles

Step 2: We select relevant articles on the topic from the search results. A "keyword" search returned 45 articles

Step 3: In the last step, we filtered the overlap. After this process we generated a total of 119 articles and data that were to be analysed

2.2 The Impact of the Covid-19 Pandemic on Agriculture

The impact of the Covid-19 pandemic on agriculture has been the subject of research by several researchers. For example, (Stephens et al., 2020) stated that a pandemic could lead to food scarcity. According to (Lioutas & Charatsari, 2021), disruption to the agricultural sector threatens the socio-economic strength of a country. The Indonesian government, through the Ministry of Agriculture, strives to create food security for the community, for example, refocusing activities & reallocation of activities focused on activities to increase food production immediately, increasing the volume of agricultural production facilities & infrastructure in order to fulfill food for the community, and economic stimulus in the context of economic recovery farmers (Ministry of Agriculture, 2020b). The anticipatory strategy is as follows.

3 Agriculture and Farmers

The agricultural sector in Indonesia has managed to get through the crisis period in the first year of the pandemic even though the results have not optimal. In 2020, the contribution of agriculture to GDP was 15.46%. In the first quarter of 2020, the expansive growth of food plants was 57.37% leading to grow business fields by 9.46% (Central Bureau of Statistics, 2020) (Central Bureau of Statistics, 2020b). However, at the same time, there was an economic contraction of as much as 2.41% (Statistics, 2020c). In the second quarter, the agricultural sector was able to grow positively by 2.19%, while other sectors experienced a contraction, but the growth was not able to withstand the economic contraction of 5.32% (Statistics, 2020c) due to low people's purchasing power (Zhan & Chen, 2021). In the third quarter of 2020, when economic conditions began to improve with a contraction of 2.03% (q to q), agriculture, forestry, and fisheries sectors grew positively by 1.52% due to a major harvest of both rice crops and increased demand for fruit and vegetables (Bappenas, 2020). In quarter IV/2020, the agricultural sector grew 2.59% (q to q) due to an increase in harvested area and production of food crop commodities as well as demand for fruit and vegetables (Statistics, 2020b) (Central Bureau of Statistics, 2020a). Meanwhile, in the fourth quarter of 2020, economic conditions grew by 0.42%; seen from the production side, the deepest growth contraction occurred in Agriculture, Forestry and Fishery Business Fields by 20.15%.

From the farmer's point of view, Covid-19 also hurts workers, subsidised fertilisers, seed prices, access to information, sales of agricultural products, and prices for harvested commodities (PRISMA, 2020b; Lioutas & Charatsari, 2021). Social restrictions result in limited and expensive planting labourers, and the planting time is delayed (Yusuf et al., 2020; Ilesanmi et al., 2021; Rasul, 2021). The scarcity of subsidised fertilisers, due to quantity and distribution constraints, has an impact on cultivation techniques because fertilisers contribute 9% to the cost of planting (Asmanto et al., 2020; OECD, 2020). Farmers in Java confirm the increase in fertiliser and seed prices, NTT and NTB by 10–30% (PRISMA, 2020a).

Another negative impact is the difficulty in selling crops because the number of middlemen from the outside village is limited, and some markets do not operate (PRISMA, 2020b). As a result, the price of horticultural commodities has fallen, except for shallots due to reduced production of shallots in production centres (Pertanian, 2020; PRISMA, 2020c; Saliem et al., 2020). In general, people's purchasing power has decreased due to layoffs in various business sectors and reduced social activities that require large amounts of food ((Ashari et al., 2020; Ilesanmi et al., 2021).

As food crop farmers are under heavier pressure, these rice producers with a micro-scale business dominate (47.5%) the group of agricultural business households (Ministry of Agriculture, 2020a), among whom 58.7% have less than 0.5 hectares of land (Asmanto et al., 2020). The average age of most farmers is in the pre-elderly and elderly range, 45–60 years, so they are vulnerable to exposure to covid-19 (Ministry of Agriculture, 2020a; Yusuf et al., 2020). In addition, their understanding of the importance of health protocols is very limited (Yusuf et al., 2020), which is thought to be due to the low level of education of farmers; 25% - 40% only graduated from elementary school, and 36% did not attend school/did not complete primary school (Ministry of Agriculture, 2020a).

In a broader context, fluctuating farmer exchange rates, below the value of 100, occurred in most parts of Indonesia and reached the lowest value in May and June 2020 (99.47) (Statistics, 2019, 2020a), even the NTP of Lampung (91.5) was lower than that of national NTP (Ministry of Agriculture, 2020b). According to (Mahendra Dev & Sengupta, 2020), this phenomenon is a result of the harvest that is not maximally absorbed during the main harvest (May) due to a decrease in purchases as a result of large-scale social restrictions imposed by the government. On the other hand, production costs are higher due to the increase in input prices followed by erratic production and crop marketing.

Gradually, the exchange rate of farmers increased in August, except for the livestock sub-sector, which was still at 98.72 in December (Fig. 1). This occurred due to a decrease in the price index received by farmers in the commodity groups of broilers and beef cattle (Statistics, 2019; Central Bureau of Statistics, 2020) and reduced demand as a result of social restrictions imposed by the government (Rachmat et al., 2016). In his survey, it was stated that this pandemic caused a sharp decrease in farmers' income by 16%, 56% of farmers' income decreased, and only 19% of farmers' income did not experience changes in income (Krisnamurthi, 2021; Lioutas & Charatsari, 2021).

3.1 Food Availability, Needs, and Distribution

During the pandemic, economic sectors hit the hardest: transportation and warehousing services, contracted by −30.84% in the second quarter of 2020 (y to

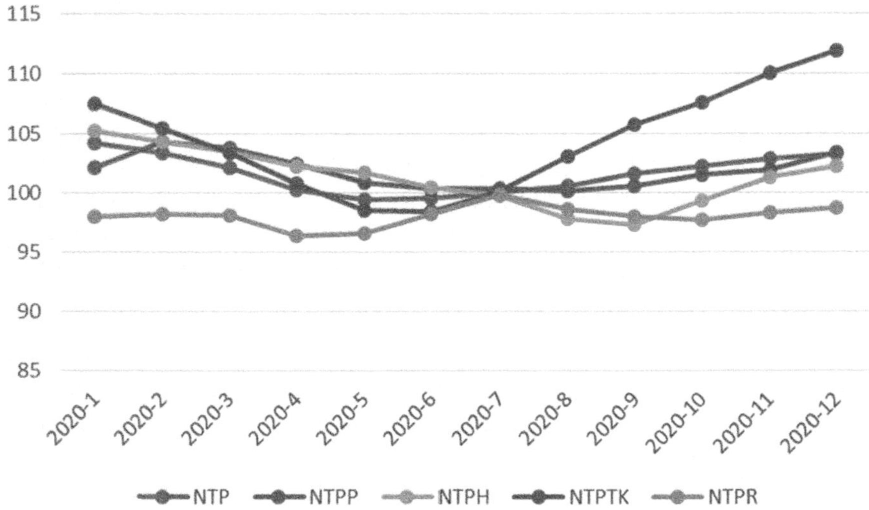

Fig. 1 Farmer Exchange Rate of Indonesian Farmers, 2020. (Source: Bappenas, 2020)

y) (Central Bureau of Statistics, 2020; Statistics, 2020b). This disruption to the national logistics system significantly affects food availability, needs, and distribution (Perdana et al., 2020). At the same time, there is a decrease in food production by 5% (Food and Agriculture Organization, 2020) due to limitations and an increase in the price of production facilities and distribution (Dermoredjo et al., 2020; Pertanian, 2020). This condition will be exacerbated by the presence of panic buying from the community, which results in an increase in food needs by 5% (Ministry of Agriculture, 2020a; Pertanian, 2020), which needs to be addressed so that it does not have a sustainable impact (Hobbs, 2020). On the one hand, an increase in food needs must be balanced with an adequate and well-distributed supply (Marusak et al., 2021), while large-scale social restrictions imposed by the government have an effect on food availability especially staple food commodities (Adewopo et al., 2021).

In fact, the data show that (1) supply is available but is constrained in delivery resulting in the buildup, which causes commodity prices to fall or commodity destruction (Lioutas & Charatsari, 2021); (2) supply decreases due to a lack of manpower, hampered distribution of production facilities, and limited imports; and (3) distribution of products to consumers is uneven or hampered because consumer demand is very volatile and difficult to predict (Dermoredjo et al., 2020; Coluccia et al., 2021) (Fig. 2).

According to the Food Security Agency report, the national staple food needs are in a surplus condition, both at the beginning of the pandemic (April–June 2020) and at the end of 2020 (September–December) (Fig. 3). However, commodity production from one island is a surplus, while commodity production from other islands is a deficit. Most of the commodities produced by Java and South Sulawesi islands, except eggs, mostly come from North Sumatra.

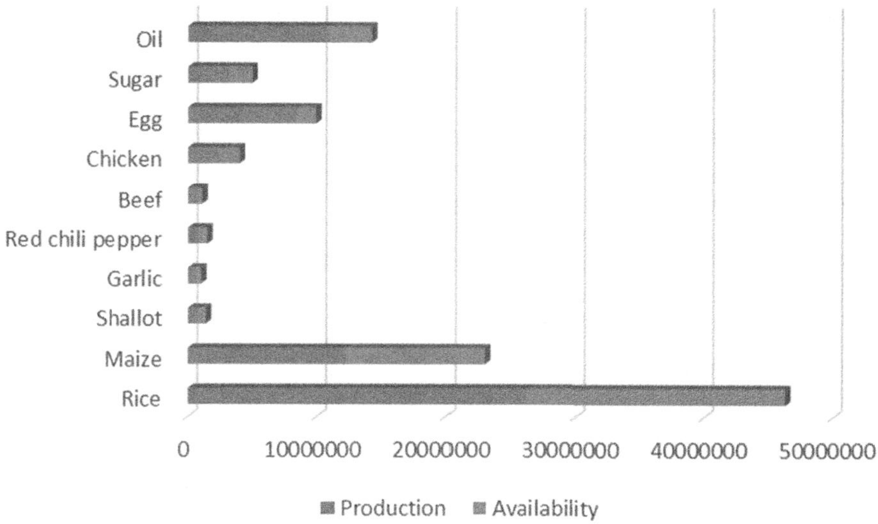

Fig. 2 Availability and Basic Food Needs in 2021. (Sources: Ministry of Agriculture, 2020)

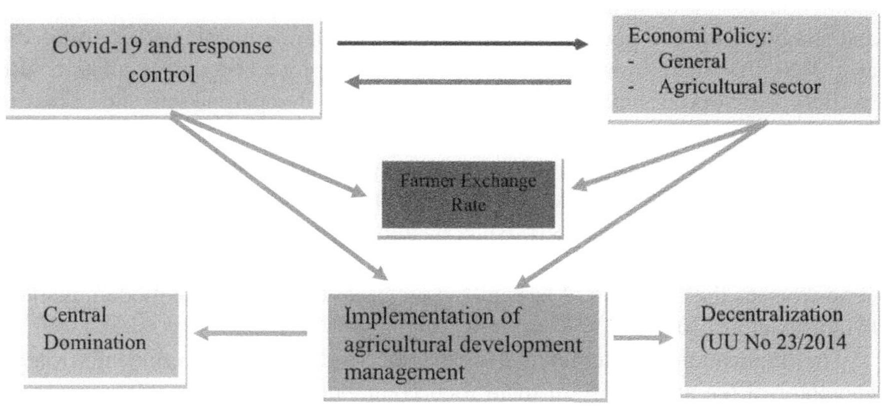

Fig. 3 Framework implementation of development management. (Source: Sumedi et al. (2020) and modification)

Therefore, the government intervene by distributing several commodities from Java to several commodity deficit areas. Red chillies from Central Java are supplied to Kalimantan, Riau Islands, and NTT; shallots from Central Java are distributed to DKI Jakarta, Sumatra Island and Kalimantan. Chicken eggs from East Java to Kalimantan and South Sulawesi (BPPP, 2020).

The impact of the pandemic, which has resulted in instability in food commodity prices, both due to scarcity and the impact of commodity distribution, is also influenced by the size of Indonesia's territory; 1.9 million km^2 consisting of more than 16 thousand islands (Statistics, 2020a, 2020c) and weaknesses in food logistics management (Dermoredjo et al., 2020). Prices tend to be high at the consumer level due to supply constraints, whereas prices tend to be low at the farm level due to a large decline in demand from hotels, restaurants, and others (Saliem et al., 2020; Adewopo et al., 2021; Coluccia et al., 2021).

A significant price disparity occurs in food commodities, while red chillies have the highest disparity of 65.57% (Dermoredjo et al., 2020). In South Sulawesi Province, the price of red chilli at the producer level is Rp. 13,091 per kg, while the retail price of red chilli in the province of deficit in Papua is Rp. 78,977 per kg or 600% higher. The price of shallots at the producer level in South Sulawesi is IDR 17,800 per kg, while the retail price of shallots in Maluku Province is IDR 49,714 per kg or 282% higher (BKP, 2020).

3.2 Trade-in Main Agricultural Commodities

The covid-19 pandemic has also changed the trading system for agricultural commodity trading. The Ministry of Trade issued Decree No. 317 / M-DAG / SD / 04/2020 dated April 3, 2020, to the Governor of DKI Jakarta and Regents/Mayors throughout Indonesia so that during the large-scale social restrictions, the availability and smooth supply of goods for community needs can be maintained (Dermoredjo et al., 2020). Apart from being related to health protocols, this regulation also controls the working hours of traditional markets and supermarkets and access to the distribution of staple goods. This regulation implies that most farmers lose their market due to limited operating time for traditional markets. Still, on the other hand, supermarkets or modern markets experience an increase in sales turnover of 50% compared to normal conditions (Bayu & Kamim, 2020). There is a change in buying patterns. Consumers prefer to shop at the nearest mini-market online. This phenomenon worsens the condition of farmers but increases the turnover of modern markets (Marusak et al., 2021).

The implications of the Covid-19 pandemic underlie the government's role as guarantor of the availability of main food commodities so that people's needs are met, and inflation can be suppressed such as the main food commodities including rice, corn, soybeans, chillies, beef, onions and garlic (Ministry of Agriculture, 2020b). The very high rice trade was triggered by a very high level of public consumption, which was 97.1 kg in 2018 (Rachmat et al., 2016; Badan Ketahanan Pangan, 2019). However, the government makes an effort not to import rice because the stock is deemed sufficient, which was 6.1 million tons by December 2020 (Arif et al., 2020) (Asian Development Bank, Bappenas and International Food Policy Research Institute, 2019), although from 2013 to 2019, the government always imported grain as many as 0.9 million tons in average per year (Arif et al., 2020).

Entering the beginning of the pandemic, the price of rice rose from March to July 2020 with a monthly price coefficient of diversity (KK) of 0.62% at a high price level of IDR 10,650 per kilogram (BPPP, 2020). This increase was due to rising un-hulled rice prices and government policies to close several access to production centres

(BPPP, 2020). Measured from international standards, approximately IDR 10,000 per kilogram, the price of rice in Indonesia is relatively high, especially when compared to the standard international rice price of IDR 6000 per kilogram (Asian Development Bank, Bappenas and International Food Policy Research Institute, 2019; BPPP, 2020).

Meanwhile, (BPPP, 2020) reported that nationally the average price of shelled corn in 2020 decreased by 1.11% compared to the 2019 average price, which was in the range of IDR 7700 per kilogram. This condition was due to a decline in chicken prices which caused chicken farmers to reduce the number of chickens raised. In 2020, the soybean trade was still dominated by imported ones with an average price of 10,300 per kilogram, with the highest price in October 2020. This condition was motivated by the lack of imported soybeans due to a decrease in soybean supply from the United States to meet China's soybean needs. As a result, local soybean production slumped at 2.1 million tons, unable to compete with imported soybean, which was still high. Indonesia's dependence on soybean imports increased from 69.7% of domestic consumption in 2013 to 88.1% in 2019.

Red chillies and shallots are the most sought-after horticultural commodities in the domestic trade, even though their prices fluctuate constantly. Red Chili is one of the source commodities of inflation in 2020 because the price has increased by 74.05% compared to the price in December 2019 (BPPP, 2020). The significant increase in chilli prices is due to weather factors that disrupted supply from production centres (PRISMA, 2020a). Stock shortages are due to limited farmer capital during the Covid-19 pandemic, and farmers' interest in planting is reduced due to decreased demand during the harvest season (PRISMA, 2020c). The price of shallots that increased significantly (in the range of Rp. 52,000 per kilogram) at the beginning of the pandemic, April to June, was due to community panic buying, poor production, and damaged crop stocks in several shallot production centre areas. However, prices gradually fell in July and August due to improved supply and distribution of shallots. Still, prices rose again in December by IDR 35,000 per kilogram due to the harvest accompanied by high demand due to Christmas and year-end celebrations.

4 Mitigation Mechanisms for the Impact of Covid-19 and Efforts to Achieve Agricultural Resilience

4.1 Implementation of Agricultural Development Management in Times of Crisis and Beyond

The Covid-19 pandemic is the momentum for the government to reassess the implementation of centralised agricultural development management to be decentralised. Law No. 23/2014 on the provisions of the division of central and regional authority in the context of regional autonomy sets the agricultural sector to be a concurrent and optional affair in which duties and responsibilities are shared between the central and regional governments. However, in its implementation, the central government dominates the execution of this policy in terms of program determination, budgeting, and implementation beyond the roles and initiatives of the local governments (Sumedi et al., 2020). As pandemic has forced every region to be adaptable to a specific need, considering areas specified by their constraints and potentials are essential, as the regions are the executors of the activities (Dutta & Fischer, 2021).

Amongst programs being developed by the central and local governments is sustainable agricultural development. China has developed a similar model through the transformation of small-scale agricultural development with the participation of private sectors and entrepreneurs at all levels (Lele & Goswami, 2020). Through the agricultural sector, Romania reforms its domestic economic policies (Vasile et al., 2017), while Nepal strengthens its local governments with agricultural infrastructure development strategies, innovative policies, legal instruments, and institutional arrangements (Thapa Magar et al., 2021).

The policy model that favours farmers, as producers of food providers for the benefit of mankind, is a logical choice under the responsibility of both central and local government, especially during the Covid-19 pandemic. The United States has spent $ 19 billion (Coronavirus Food Assistance Program) to ensure that farmers and supply chain actors will continue producing and distributing food amid the pandemic (U.S. Department of Agriculture, 2020). Canada has allocated its budget to increase lending capacity and ease loan repayments to farmers (Rivera-Ferre et al., 2021), and India provides financial assistance to farmers (Priyadarshini & Abhilash, 2021). The Nepalese government provides cash assistance for farmers to cultivate promising fallow land (Adhikari et al., 2021).

The Indonesian government has promoted short-term a KUR program of IDR 50 trillion (an increase of more than 100% from 2019), but its implementation has not been maximised due to limited farmers accessing it (Ashari et al., 2020). For the long term, the government establishes a program to increase the production of agricultural commodities. Yet, its implementation has been likely to ignore farmer's welfare even put the burdensome upon them (Nuhung, 2014; Sumedi et al., 2020; Haqiqi & Bahalou Horeh, 2021). These policies include MA Decree No.70 of 2014, which dropped Presidential Decree No. 31/2007 on the imposition of 10% VAT for all fresh agricultural products produced by farmers, both fresh agricultural products, plantations, horticulture, and forest products (RI, 2014).

The facts show that an increase does not follow the achievement of government policies in farmers' welfare to compensate for an increase in the price of non-agricultural products (Nuhung, 2014; George, 2020). The farmer exchange rate (FER) has been at 100–105 since 2010, even decreases during the pandemic (Arif et al., 2020), far below the RPJMN lower limit target, which is 115–120 (RI, 2014) (Asian Development Bank, Bappenas and International Food Policy Research Institute, 2019). In addition, it is difficult for farmers to access agricultural infrastructure in several areas because of limited facilities and increased price (PRISMA, 2020b) during the government assistance program (Ministry of Agriculture, 2020b).

This suggests that there are problems related to distribution and policy in this context. In general, the framework of this concept is presented in Fig. 3.

4.2 Accurate and Fair Logistics System

Two aspects that need to be built are improving the existing logistics system and the development of the information system. The current logistic system that cannot record accurately, authentically, and transparently leads to leaking and exploitation (food adulteration) opportunities along the chain (IPB, 2020). For this reason, an intelligent and accurate information system is needed to manage data and information related to the availability and needs of food from various regions (Nimmagadda et al., 2019). One alternative is the use of AI and blockchain to ensure accuracy, precision, real-time, authenticity, and transparency (Neethirajan & Kemp, 2021). In its agricultural policy, China applies this approach to increase transparency and support the end-to-end visibility of the logistics system (Choi, 2021).

Another improvement is the existence of a food reserve institution that functions to stabilise supplies and prices within the community (Nehring et al., 2016; Rachman & Purwantini, 2020). In 2017, Brazil pursued institutional implementation as one of its agricultural development strategies that targeted price stability, income generation, and food security (Nehring et al., 2016). Furthermore, North Uganda implements Produce Lane that connects agricultural and financial sectors oriented towards sustainable agri-food as a form of food supply (Alpha & Fouilleux, 2018). In times of crisis such as today, this institution can be formed to accommodate farmers' harvest and distribute it to workers or the poor in need. This institution might function as a container for excess yields in a surplus area at a set price and distribute it to deficit areas in an advanced stage. This institution is also expected to be able to help small farmers in need in the production process.

The government once formed the Food Reserve Institution Program in collaboration with big companies within industrial systems based on science and technology, capital, and modern organisation and management (Nasution & Bangun, 2020). Yet, the negative implication occurred due to land acquisition by big companies, marginalisation of farmers, and environmental degradation (Santosa, 2014). In response, the government introduced a food security program with a target of growing village-based food estate institutions as a means of strengthening food reserves and logistics systems (Ministry of Agriculture, 2020b) with a budget of 104.2 trillion (Nasution & Bangun, 2020) in Central Kalimantan, South Sumatra, and Papua (Merauke).

4.3 Supply Chain Management During the Pandemic

The development of information technology (IT) is an alternative in solving supply chain problems during a pandemic, considering that one of the impacts of IT is a change in spending behaviour from cash to non-cash (Sumedi et al., 2020; Coluccia et al., 2021). The Chinese Ministry of Agriculture allocates a large budget to build an online public service platform. It uses public-private partnerships to collaborate with e-commerce companies to sell agricultural products ((Zhan & Chen, 2021). Limitations in the agricultural food supply chain and the food industry can be overcome with innovation and technological tools to improve the quality and efficiency of the production chain (Rejeb et al., 2021).

In this context, the government of Indonesia may act as an agent of facilitator in preparing regulations and supporting facilitation. Public-private collaboration to build supply chains is needed to regulate market availability and needs (Marusak et al., 2021). Complex and long supply chains make farmers lose price power (Huang et al., 2021). There are more than 42 agri-tech platforms in Indonesia, including TaniHub, Aruna, eFishery, Hara, Keday Sayur, Eden Farm, Crowde, MSMB, Sayurbox, and Jala (Jurnal agro.com, 2020). Apart from focusing on downstream products, Agri-tech also pays attention to education for farmers from cultivation to post-harvest (Beheraa et al., 2015). Therefore, the government of Indonesia's support for agri-tech is urgently needed to change the direction of marketing of harvested commodities so that they are absorbed, farmers get a decent price, and impact the welfare of farmers and Indonesian agriculture.

5 Conclusion

The lessons learned from the COVID-19 pandemic are that the impact of the major crisis or disaster on agriculture that have been discussed promotes an opportunity for Indonesian agriculture to deal with unexpected problems. Shared responsibility between central and regional government concerning agricultural development policies must be clearly defined in terms of policy, implementation, and responsibility.

In a time of crisis, the government should control all aspects related to agricultural commodities, such as price stability, distribution, and logistic system. In addition, the establishment of agricultural information technology might help the food estate program to be effective.

Agricultural start-up is an alternative solution for absorption of production constrained during the pandemic and afterwards. Start-up, which is already present in almost all major cities in Indonesia, might become an alternative to refreshing Indonesian agriculture. From them, we get new energy in the form of technology, Social Impact, and game changers to build agriculture through the pandemic period and afterwards towards better agriculture. It needs more serious support and initiatives from the government to make this even bigger.

These three mechanisms can be combined to increase agricultural capacity amid crises or disasters. The existence of the crisis and international trade restrictions provide room for experimentation on how we should survive and become better.

References

Adewopo, J. B., et al. (2021). Using crowd-sourced data for real-time monitoring of food prices during the COVID-19 pandemic : Insights from a pilot project in northern Nigeria. *Global Food Security, 29*, 100523. https://doi.org/10.1016/j.gfs.2021.100523.

Adhikari, J., et al. (2021). COVID-19 impacts on agriculture and food systems in Nepal: Implications for SDGs. *Agricultural Systems, 186*(June 2020), 102990. https://doi.org/10.1016/j.agsy.2020.102990.

Adu-Gyamfi, S., et al. (2021). A COVID in the wheels of the world: A contemporary history of a pandemic in africa. *Research in Globalization, 3*(April), 100043. https://doi.org/10.1016/j.resglo.2021.100043.

Aktar, M. A., Alam, M. M., & Al-Amin, A. Q. (2021). Global economic crisis, energy use, CO2 emissions, and policy roadmap amid COVID-19. *Sustainable Production and Consumption, 26*, 770–781. https://doi.org/10.1016/j.spc.2020.12.029.

Alpha, A., & Fouilleux, E. (2018). How to diagnose institutional conditions conducive to inter-sectoral food security policies ? The example of Burkina Faso. *NJAS – Wageningen Journal of Life Sciences, 84*(July 2017), 114–122. https://doi.org/10.1016/j.njas.2017.07.005.

Arif, S., et al. (2020). *Tinjauan Strategis Ketahanan Pangan dan Gizi di Indonesia*. Jakarta.

Ashari, Syukur, M., & Pasaribu, S. M. (2020). Pembiayaan Usaha Pertanian Merespons Dampak Pandemi Covid1–19. In *Dampak Pandemi Covid-19: Perspektif Adaptasi dan Resilensi Ekonomi Pertanian* (pp. 6–8). Bogor: IAARD Press. Available at: https://www.acehtrend.com/.

Asian Development Bank, Bappenas and International Food Policy Research Institute. (2019). *Policies to support investment requirements of Indonesia's food and agriculture development during 2020–2045*. Manila: Asian Development Bank.

Asmanto, P. et al. (2020) Menjaga Ketahanan Pangan di Tengah Pandemi Covid-19, Bhirawa Online. jakarta. Available at: http://tnp2k.go.id/download/92111PB8. Ketahanan PanganFA-Jul2020.pdf.

Badan Ketahanan Pangan. (2019). *Direktori Perkembangan Konsumsi Pangan, Badan Ketahan Pangan*. Jakarta: Badan Ketahanan Pangan.

Bappenas. (2020). Laporan Perkembangan Ekonomi Indonesia dan Dunia Triwulan III Tahun 2020, Www.Bappenas.Go.Id. Jakarta. Available at: https://www.bappenas.go.id/id/berita-dan-siaran-pers/laporan-perkembangan-ekonomi-indonesia-dan-dunia-triwulan-i-tahun-2020/.

Bayu, A., & Kamim, M. (2020). Wabah Virus Korona Dan Momentum Evaluasi Rezim Ketahanan Pangan Di Indonesia (Covid-19 Pandemic and Momentum of Food Security Evaluation in Indonesia). *jurnal kependudukan Indonesia, 2902*, 87–92. Available at: https://ejurnal.kependudukan.lipi.go.id/index.php/jki/article/view/569/pdf_1.

Beheraa, B. S., et al. (2015). Information communication technology promoting retail marketing in agriculture sector in India as a study. *Procedia Computer Science, 48*(C), 652–659. https://doi.org/10.1016/j.procs.2015.04.148.

BKP. (2020). *Kebijakan Strategis Ketahanan Pangan dan Gizi 2020–2024*. Jakarta: BKP.

BPPP. (2020). Analisis Perkembangan Harga Bahan Pangan Pokok di Pasar Domestik dan Internasional Desember 2020, Kementerian Perdagangan RI. Jakarta: Kementerian Perdaganangan RI. https://doi.org/10.22487/j24775398.2016.v2.i2.6719.

Central Bureau of Statistics. (2020). *PDB Indonesia Triwulanan 2016-2020, Central Bureau of Statistics*. Jakarta: BPS RI. Available at: https://www.bps.go.id/publication/download

Chakraborty, I., & Maity, P. (2020). COVID-19 outbreak: Migration, effects on society, global environment and prevention. *Science of the Total Environment, 728*, 138882. https://doi.org/10.1016/j.scitotenv.2020.138882.

Choi, T. M. (2021). Risk analysis in logistics systems: A research agenda during and after the COVID-19 pandemic. *Transportation Research Part E: Logistics and Transportation Review, 145*(December 2020). https://doi.org/10.1016/j.tre.2020.102190.

Coluccia, B., et al. (2021). Effects of COVID-19 on the Italian Agri-food supply and value chains. *Food Control, 123*(December 2020), 107839. https://doi.org/10.1016/j.foodcont.2020.107839.

Coopmans, I., et al. (2021). COVID-19 impacts on Flemish food supply chains and lessons for Agri-food system resilience. *Agricultural Systems, 190*(April), 103136. https://doi.org/10.1016/j.agsy.2021.103136.

Dermoredjo, S. K., Saputra, Y. H., & Azahari, D. H. (2020). Dampak pandemi covid-19 terhadap perdagangan dalam negeri komoditas pertanian. In *Dampak Pandemi Covid-19: Perspektif Adaptasi dan Resilensi Ekonomi Pertanian* (pp. 127–148). Jakarta: IAARD Press.

Dutta, A., & Fischer, H. W. (2021). The local governance of COVID-19: Disease prevention and social security in rural India. *World Development, 138*, 105234. https://doi.org/10.1016/j.worlddev.2020.105234.

FAO. (2020). *FAO Regional Conference For Asia and The Pacific The impact of COVID-19 on food and agriculture in Asia and the Pacific and FAO's response*. Available at: http://www.fao.org/partnerships/resource-partners/covid-19/en/. Accessed 5 May 2021.

Food and Agriculture Organization. (2020). *Addressing the impacts of COVID-19 in food crises*. Food and Agriculture Organization of the United Nations.. https://doi.org/10.4060/ca9123en.

George, T. (2020). A new look at agricultural development and the non-agriculture economy in low-income countries. *Global Food Security, 26*(October), 100449. https://doi.org/10.1016/j.gfs.2020.100449.

Goswami, R., et al. (2021a). Multi-faceted impact and outcome of COVID-19 on smallholder agricultural systems: Integrating qualitative research and fuzzy cognitive mapping to explore resilient strategies. *Agricultural Systems, 189*(December 2020), 103051. https://doi.org/10.1016/j.agsy.2021.103051.

Goswami, R., et al. (2021b). Multi-faceted impact and outcome of COVID-19 on smallholder agricultural systems: Integrating qualitative research and fuzzy cognitive mapping to explore resilient strategies. *Agricultural Systems, 189*(January), 103051. https://doi.org/10.1016/j.agsy.2021.103051.

Haqiqi, I., & Bahalou Horeh, M. (2021). Assessment of COVID-19 impacts on U.S. counties using the immediate impact model of local agricultural production (IMLAP). *Agricultural Systems, 190*(September 2020), 103132. https://doi.org/10.1016/j.agsy.2021.103132.

Hobbs, J. E. (2020). Food supply chains during the COVID-19 pandemic. *Canadian Journal of Agricultural Economics, 68*(2), 171–176. https://doi.org/10.1111/cjag.12237.

Huang, S. M., Che-Hao (Valagas Gadeljeman), H., & Chang, Y. H. (2021). The paradox of cultivating community resiliency: Re-agrarianisation and De-peasantisation of indigenous farmers in Taiwan. *Journal of Rural Studies, 83*(February), 96–105. https://doi.org/10.1016/j.jrurstud.2021.02.017.

Ilesanmi, F. F., Ilesanmi, O. S., & Afolabi, A. A. (2021). The effects of the COVID-19 pandemic on food losses in the agricultural value chains in Africa: The Nigerian case study. *Public Health in Practice, 2*(January), 100087. https://doi.org/10.1016/j.puhip.2021.100087.

IPB. (2020). *Mengamankan Logistik Pangan di Masa Pandemi COVID-19, IPB*. Available at: https://dpis.ipb.ac.id/mengamankan-logistik-pangan-di-masa-pandemi-covid-19/.

jurnal. agro.com. (2020). *Startup Pertanian, Solusi Regenerasi Petani dengan Pendekatan Teknologi, jurnal agro.com.* Available at: https://jurnalagro.com/startup-pertanian-solusi-regenerasi-petani-dengan-pendekatan-teknologi/. Accessed 4 May 2021.

Krisnamurthi, B. (2021). *Economic growth rate : Indonesia and Indonesia Agriculture*. Makassar.

Lele, U., & Goswami, S. (2020). Agricultural policy reforms: Roles of markets and states in China and India. *Global Food Security, 26*(October 2018), 100371. https://doi.org/10.1016/j.gfs.2020.100371.

Lin, B. X., & Zhang, Y. Y. (2020). Impact of the COVID-19 pandemic on agricultural exports. *Journal of Integrative Agriculture, 19*(12), 2937–2945. https://doi.org/10.1016/S2095-3119(20)63430-X.

Lioutas, E. D., & Charatsari, C. (2021). Enhancing the ability of agriculture to cope with major crises or disasters: What the experience of COVID-19 teaches us. *Agricultural Systems, 187* (August 2020), 103023. https://doi.org/10.1016/j.agsy.2020.103023.

Mahendra Dev, S., & Sengupta, R. (2020). Covid-19: Impact on the Indian Economy. *Working paper 2020-013*, (April), 41.

Mandal, S. C., et al. (2021). The impact of the COVID-19 pandemic on fish consumption and household food security in Dhaka city, Bangladesh. *Global Food Security, 29*(August 2020), 100526. https://doi.org/10.1016/j.gfs.2021.100526.

Marusak, A., et al. (2021). Resilient regional food supply chains and rethinking the way forward: Key takeaways from the COVID-19 pandemic. *Agricultural Systems, 190*(February), 103101. https://doi.org/10.1016/j.agsy.2021.103101.

Ministry of Agriculture (2020a). *Analisis Kesejahteraan Petani Tahun 2019* (Hakim, M. L., & Wahyuningsih, S.). Jakarta: Pusat Data dan Sistem Informasi Pertanian. Available at: http://epublikasi.setjen.pertanian.go.id/publikasi/perstatistikan

Ministry of Agriculture. (2020b). Kebijakan dan Program Kementerian Pertanian dalam Menjamin Ketahanan Pangan di Era New Normal Pandemi Covid-19, Disampaikan pada Webinar "Strategi Ketahanan Pangan di Era New Normal Pandemi Covid 19" yang diselenggarakan oleh Badan Keahlian DPR RI Bekerjasama dengan Sekolah Bisnis Institut Pertanian Bogor, tanggal 9 Juni 2020. Jakarta.

Nasution, M., & Bangun, O. V. (2020). Tantangan Program Food Estate dalam Menjaga. *Buletin APBN*, 2–15.

Neethirajan, S., & Kemp, B. (2021). 'Sensing and bio-sensing research digital livestock farming. *Sensing and Bio-Sensing Research, 32*(February), 100408. Available at: https://doi.org/10.1016/j.sbsr.2021.100408.

Nehring, R., Miranda, A., & Howe, A. (September 2016). (2017) 'Making the case for institutional demand : Supporting smallholders through procurement and food assistance programmes'. *Global Food Security, 12*, 96–102. https://doi.org/10.1016/j.gfs.2016.09.003.

Nimmagadda, S. L., et al. (2019). Design science information system framework for managing the articulations of digital agroecosystems. *Procedia Computer Science, 159*, 1198–1207. https://doi.org/10.1016/j.procs.2019.09.289.

Nuhung, I. A. (2014). Revitalisasi Pertanian Terbelenggu. In Haryono (Ed.), *Reformasi Kebijakan Menuju Transformasi Pembangunan Pertanian* (pp. 283–301). Jakarta: IAARD Press.

OECD. (2020). 'COVID-19 and the Food and Agriculture Sector: Issues and policy Responses. Oecd, (April), pp. 1–12. Available at: https://read.oecd-ilibrary.org/view/?ref=130_130816-9uut45lj4q&title=Covid-19-and-the-food-and-agriculture-sector-Issues-and-policy-responses

Organisation for Economic Co-operation and Development. (2020). Coronavirus: The world economy at risk. *OECD Interim Economic Assessment*, (March), pp. 1–15. Available at: http://www.oecd.org/berlin/publikationen/Interim-Economic-Assessment-2-March-2020.pdf

Perdana, T., et al. (2020). Scenarios for handling the impact of COVID-19 based on food supply network through regional food hubs under uncertainty. *Heliyon, 6*(10), e05128. https://doi.org/10.1016/j.heliyon.2020.e05128.

Pertanian, B. P. K. (2020). Buletin Perencanaan Pembangunan Pertanian. *Bulletin Perencanaan Pembangunan Pertanian*, April, pp. 1–74. Available at: http://perencanaan.setjen.pertanian.go.id/public/upload/file/20200415123744BULETIN-EDISI-KHUSUS.pdf

PRISMA. (2020a). *Applying an inclusive Lens while addressing Covid-19 crisis*. Jakarta.

PRISMA. (2020b). *Dampak COVID-19 di Pertanian – Perspektif Petani*. Jakarta.

PRISMA. (2020c). *Impact of COVID-19 to Farmers Design & Respondent*. Jakarta.

Priyadarshini, P., & Abhilash, P. C. (2021). Agri-food systems in India : Concerns and policy recommendations for building resilience in post COVID-19 pandemic times. *Global Food Security, 29*(April), 100537. https://doi.org/10.1016/j.gfs.2021.100537.

Rachman, B., & Purwantini, T. B. (2020). Penguatan Lumbung Pangan Masyarakat Berbasis Desa pada Era Covid-19. In *Dampak Pandemi Covid-19: Perspektif Adaptasi dan Resilensi Ekonomi Pertanian* (pp. 885–900). Jakarta: IAARD Press.

Rachmat, M., et al. (2016). Lumbung Pangan Masyarakat: Keberadaan dan Perannya dalam Penanggulangan Kerawanan Pangan. *Forum penelitian Agro Ekonomi, 29, 43*(1). https://doi.org/10.21082/fae.v29n1.2011.43-53.

Rasul, G. (2021). Twin challenges of COVID-19 pandemic and climate change for agriculture and food security in South Asia. *Environmental Challenges, 2*(December 2020), 100027. https://doi.org/10.1016/j.envc.2021.100027.

Rejeb, A., et al. (2021). Integrating the internet of things in the halal food supply chain: A systematic literature review and research agenda. *Internet of Things, 13*, 100361. https://doi.org/10.1016/j.iot.2021.100361.

RI, S. D. (2014). Permasalahan dan Upaya Peningkatan Produktivitas Pertanian. *Bulletin APBN*. Available at: https://www.dpr.go.id/doksetjen/dokumen/apbn_PERMASALAHAN_DAN_UPAYA_PENINGKATAN_PRODUKTIVITAS_PERTANIAN20140821143024.pdf. Accessed 2 May 2021.

Rivera-Ferre, M. G., et al. (2021). The two-way relationship between food systems and the COVID19 pandemic: Causes and consequences. *Agricultural Systems, 191*(October 2020), 103134. https://doi.org/10.1016/j.agsy.2021.103134.

Saliem, H. P., Agustian, A., & Perdana, R. P. (2020). Dinamika Harga, Permintaan, dan Upaya Pemenuhan Pangan Pokok pada Era Pandemi Covid-19. In *Dampak Pandemi Covid-19: Perspektif Adaptasi dan Resiliensi Sosia Ekonomi Pertanian* (pp. 361–379). Jakarta: IAARD Press.

Santosa, E. (2014). Percepatan Pengembangan Food Estate Untuk Pangan Nasional. *Rislah Kebikakan Pertanian dan Lingkungan, 1*(2), 80–85.

Statistics, C. B. of. (2019). *Statistik nilai tukar petani di indonesia*. Jakarta: Central Bureau of Statistics.

Statistics, C. B. of. (2020a). *Berita resmi statistik, Central Bureau of Statistics*. Available at: https://www.bps.go.id/pressrelease/2020/08/05/1737/-ekonomi-indonesia-triwulan-ii-2020-turun-5-32-persen.html

Statistics, C. B. of. (2020b). Pendapatan Nasional (National Income of Indonesia), National Income of Indonesia 2015–2019. Jakarta: Central Bureau of Statistics. Available at: https://www.bps.go.id/publication/2020/06/12/7fe8d749c43bad46b1601662/pendapatan-nasional-indonesia-2015-2019.html

Statistics, C. B. of. (2020c). *Statistik Pertumbuhan Ekonomi Indonesia Triwulan IV-2020, central bureau of statistics*. Jakarta: Central Bureau of Statistics. Available at: https://www.bps.go.id/pressrelease/2020/02/05/1755/ekonomi-indonesia-2019-tumbuh-5-02-persen.html

Stephens, E. C., et al. (2020). Editorial: Impacts of COVID-19 on agricultural and food systems worldwide and on progress to the sustainable development goals. *Agricultural Systems, 183* (May), 102873. https://doi.org/10.1016/j.agsy.2020.102873.

Sumedi, Yofa, R. D., & Savitri, S. (2020). Transformasi Manajemen Pembangunan Pertanian Masa dan Pasca Pandemi Covid-19. In *Dampak Pandemi Covid-19: Perspektif Adaptasi dan Resilensi Ekonomi Pertanian* (pp. 657–678). Jakarta: IAARD Press.

Thapa Magar, D. B., et al. (2021). Pathways for building resilience to COVID-19 pandemic and revitalising the Nepalese agriculture sector. *Agricultural Systems, 187*(December 2020), 103022. https://doi.org/10.1016/j.agsy.2020.103022.

U.S. Department of Agriculture. (2020). *USDA Announces Coronavirus Food Assistance Program | USDA, Press release*. Available at: https://www.usda.gov/media/press-releases/2020/04/17/usda-announces-coronavirus-food-assistance-program

Varshney, D., et al. (2021). India's COVID-19 social assistance package and its impact on the agriculture sector. *Agricultural Systems, 189*(December 2020), 103049. https://doi.org/10.1016/j.agsy.2021.103049.

Vasile, A. J., Mihai, M., & Mirela, P. (2017). Transformations of the Romanian agricultural paradigm under domestic economic policy reforms: An analysis during 1960–2011. *Land Use Policy, 67*(April), 288–297. https://doi.org/10.1016/j.landusepol.2017.06.008.

Workie, E., et al. (2020). Deciphering the impact of COVID-19 pandemic on food security, agriculture, and livelihoods: A review of the evidence from developing countries. *Current Research in Environmental Sustainability, 2*, 100014. https://doi.org/10.1016/j.crsust.2020.100014.

Wren-Lewis, S. (2020). *The economic effects of a pandemic, economics in the time of COVID-19* (Baldwin, R., & Mauro, B. W., eds.). London: CEPR Press. Available at: https://voxeu.org/content/economics-time-covid-19

Yofa, R. D., & Suryani, E. (2020). Dampak Pandemi Covid-19 Terhadap Ekspor dan Impor Komoditas Pertanian. In *Dampak Pandemi Covid-19: Perspektif Adaptasi dan Resiliensi Sosial Ekonomi Pertanian*. Jakarta: IAARD Press.

Yusuf, A. A., et al. (2020). Strategi Ekonomi Sektor Pertanian di Tengah Pandemi Covid-19. In *Perspektif 2030: SDGs center policy brief*. Bandung: Center for Sustainable Developmet Goals Studies.

Zhan, Y., & Chen, K. Z. (2021). Building resilient food system amidst COVID-19: Responses and lessons from China. *Agricultural Systems, 190*(February), 103102. https://doi.org/10.1016/j.agsy.2021.103102.

Strategies to Enhance the Development of Organic Coffee to Support Local Economic Resource Growth. The Case of Wonokerso Village, Temanggung Regency, Central Java, Indonesia

Alfina Handayani

Abstract The development of organic coffee in Indonesia has been progressing insignificantly, although the country is one of the leading coffee producers. One of the reasons slowing down the development of Organic coffee is because the farmers encounter several obstacles at the farm. This study aims to create strategies for the development of organic coffee in Wonokerso Village because there have been previous researches and the location for some superior coffee clones since 2004 from the Indonesian Coffee and Cocoa Research and organic coffee demonstration plot in farmer's land. This study was conducted in Wonokerso Village in 2019. Through in-depth interviews and analysis by Strengths Weaknesses Opportunities and Threats (SWOT) and strategy formulated by Treats Opportunities Weaknesses Strengths (TOWS) matrix, data collection was conducted. The respondents consisted of coffee farmers, extension workers, and village officials in Wonokerso. The results show that developing organic coffee is in quadrant III (turn around), which means weaknesses are higher than strengths. Potential opportunities are much more than threats. Strategies include increasing the standardization of organic coffee quality, price guarantee, and improving productivity. The action plan that should be implemented, firstly, facilitating the organic coffee certification. Secondly, establishing Village-Owned Enterprises that accommodate, process and market organic coffee directly to consumers, and lastly, improving technology adoption by training and technology incentive.

Keywords Strategy · Organic coffee · SWOT analysis

A. Handayani (✉)
Regional Planning Research and Development Agency of Central Java, Semarang, Indonesia

© The Author(s), under exclusive license to Springer Nature Singapore Pte Ltd. 2022
T. Chaiechi, J. Wood (eds.), *Community Empowerment, Sustainable Cities, and Transformative Economies*, https://doi.org/10.1007/978-981-16-5260-8_35

1 Introduction

While economic development in Indonesia over the past decade has had a huge impact on poverty reduction (Farwati, 2013; Suryahadi et al., 2006, 2020), unfortunately, the outcomes have not been evenly distributed at all levels of society (Wicaksono et al., 2017). Data from Statistical Bureau says that there were 24.79 million poor people in Indonesia in 2019, which is 9.2% of the total population, and most of them live in rural areas with 12 million (Badan Pusat Statistik, 2020).

According to Myrdal (1968), although there has been an increase in economic growth, development has so far relied more on urban areas while leaving rural areas, which has led to the backwash effect, namely the depletion of resources in rural areas (Hasan & Azis, 1999; Stimson, 2006). Therefore, economic development based on local resources is one of the influential efforts to provide improvements for community welfare, poverty alleviation and also reduce inequality between rural and urban areas (Anríquez, 2007; Azunu & Mensah, 2019; Pavel & Moldovan, 2019; Rogerson, 2015; Susanti, 2013).

Coffee is Indonesia's leading plantation commodity, in 2019, 70% of which is an export commodity with a value of US $ 815.9 million, where 96% of the coffee production in Indonesia comes from smallholder plantations. Export destination countries include the US, Malaysia, Japan, Egypt, and Italy. (BPS-Statistics Indonesia, 2018; Directorate General of Estate Crops, 2020).

One of the coffee producers is located in Temanggung, Central Java, Indonesia, more precisely, in a small village called Wonokerso, which is the locus of this study. Like most coffee farmers in Temanggung, coffee cultivation is an embedded life in Wonokerso Village. Even though coffee is not the solely main commodity for the community, coffee still contributes significantly to farmers' household income. However, many farmers live in pre-prosperous conditions (Handayani, 2018, unpublish). Coffee has been cultivated traditionally from generation to generation, making the quality of the coffee produced low because the level of knowledge of farmers in post-harvest handling is also low (Handayani, 2013, 2015), for example, instead of using chemical fertilizers and pesticides, many farmers still use manure or even without chemical fertilization. Therefore, it is crucial to improve the potential of its resources.

The development of organic coffee in Wonokerso has several drawbacks, but there are opportunities to encourage its growth. The prospects for developing organic coffee over the last two decades have shown an increasing trend both at domestic and globally. According to Van Der Vossen, the demand for organic coffee in Western Europe, North America, and Japan exceed the present supply, which is still small (<1% of annual world production). More than 85% of organic coffees come from Latin America, and practically all is (washed) arabica coffee (Van Der Vossen, 2005). Meanwhile, organic coffee producers remain small, based on the Indonesian Organic Association (AOI), only 8% of the total coffee cultivation in Indonesia (AOI, 2019; Fadillah et al., 2019) means that there are opportunities for the organic coffee market. There are still many local potentials that have not been explored to meet market demands.

Hence, this study aims to create strategies for developing organic coffee in Wonokerso Village and an effort to improve the local economy by developing its local potential. It is expected to provide inputs to policymakers in developing local resources, especially in Temanggung Regency and other areas with similar characteristics.

2 Literature Review

2.1 Strategy to Support Local Economic Resource Growth

The term of strategy, derived from the Greek word 'strategos', meaning general, has been used in different ways (Weihrich, 1982). Weihrich collects several sources and defines (Strategy are) programs or actions in utilizing resources to achieve comprehensive long-term goals or the detailed action plans for reaching a goal or shortly. Strategy means a detailed action plan for reaching a goal. In the context of planning, a strategic means actions that will be carried out in the future which are arranged based on various selected alternatives (Steiner, 1979).

Local economic resource growth, mostly known as local economic development (LED), is a process by which the public sector, business, and civil society work collectively to create better economic growth and employment generation (Rogerson, 2015). Its purpose is to build up the economic capacity of a local area to improve its economic future and the quality of life for all (Villanueva, 2014). Moreover, according to Villanueva, a LED Strategic Plan is a detailed action plan that explains the procedure for strengthening local resources in economic development, becomes a general reference for actions, including how to prioritize, select appropriate resources to achieve goals. In addition, it is also a direction in developing local economic, physical, social, and environmental strengths in overcoming various challenges.

Internal and external factors affecting a local resources potency are identified to form strategies. Hence, it is necessary to have the right strategies to boost local resources; the strategies made by organizations are strongly influenced by the internal and external environment so that proper planning will facilitate management and minimize the impact of several internal and external factors (Alam et al., 2018).

2.2 Organic Coffee Development

Organic agriculture is one of the efforts to achieve sustainable economic development because it uses lower external inputs and is safe for the environment to provide higher profits (Aher et al., 2012; Torres et al., 2016). However, the development of organic farming in Indonesia has remained insignificant, even though the government has launched various policies (Mayrowani, 2016). According to IFOAM (2012), organic agriculture has four main pillars: health, ecology, fairness, and care. First, health means agriculture should preserve and boost the robustness of soil, plant, animal, and human as single and inseparable. Second, ecology means organic agriculture should be established on living ecological schemes and chain, work together, copy them and maintain them. Third, fairness means should build on an accord that protects equity respecting the natural surrounding and life opportunities. Lastly, care defines organic agriculture should be managed in a discrete and liable mode to protect the health and welfare of recent and forthcoming generations and the environment (Freyer & Bingen, 2015).

In developing local economic resources, the development of organic coffee is aimed at human health and the environment and pays attention to farmers' welfare (Bacon, 2005). However, the impact of organic production on farmer welfare is an important issue since organic coffee production has been suggested to lower yields and farmer income compared with what can be achieved using conventional methods (Van Der Vossen, 2005). Organic yields are typically lower than conventional yields because of low external input, even though these yield differences are highly circumstantial depending on system and site characteristics (Seufert et al., 2012). Several studies on various commodities in Indonesia show that organic agriculture increases income for farmers and is economically viable (Emiria & Purwandari, 2015; Jamil et al., 2019; Leksono et al., 2018; Setiawati et al., 2015). In contrast, other studies show the opposite condition (S. Putri, 2018; Saroja RAZ & T. Karyani, 2021; Tinubaya et al., 2011). Nonetheless, organic farming has a long-term effect on the environment and improves soil quality (Velmourougane, 2016).

According to Borella, during the last decade, the coffee industry is experiencing commoditization, tendering an opportunity for farmers to distinguish their coffee in terms of sustainability and quality and market it more directly. However, smallholders coffee growers face productivity and transactional restrain prohibiting them from penetrating these higher-value market segments. Intermediaries are needed to connect them with this recent market (Borrella et al., 2015). Furthermore, previous research has shown that some factors must be considered in the development of organic coffee, namely demand for intensive and skill-based management of organic coffee plantations, high cost of certification, and market penetration (Ayalew, 2014). Sarirayu and Aprianingsih suggest to improving smallholders coffee farmers productivity in Indonesia include fair trade certification, technology adoption, and intensive farmer training (K. Sarirahayu & A. Aprianingsih, 2018).

Therefore, the development of organic coffee is one of the efforts to maintain environmental sustainability and, at the same time, make a positive contribution to the economy of the local community. Reviewing the literature leads back to the question: What is the right strategy to develop organic coffee to support the growth of local economic resources?

3 Methodology

The study uses a mixed-method using both qualitative and quantitative data. Quantitative data were analyzed using SWOT and qualitative data using the TOWS matrix.

3.1 Methods

The data collection was conducted from March to June 2019 in Wonokerso Village, Temanggung Regency, Central Java, Indonesia. The sampling location was selected purposively by considering: Wonokerso is one of the largest robusta coffee-producing villages in Temanggung Regency, the availability of preliminary data and key informants. The type of data was primary data that was collected by in-depth interviews. The key informants were eight, consisting of coffee farmers, extension workers, and village officials.

In-depth interviews with informants were complemented by filling out questionnaires to determine the weight and rating of internal and external factors that affect the development of organic coffee in Wonokerso. Identification of internal factors consists of strengths and weaknesses. Strength is a comparative advantage, either human or natural resources, which are the main drivers of the growth of organic coffee. Meanwhile, weakness is a problem and obstacle that hinders the development of organic coffee. In terms of external factors, there are opportunities and challenges. Opportunity is a favourable environmental factor for organic development. Threats are external environmental factors that hamper the development of organic coffee. In this analysis, both internal and external factors are only three main priorities assessed. Questionnaire statement of internal and factors in Tables 1 and 2, respectively.

4 Scope of Study

Wonokerso is located in the Pringsurat sub-district between –7°16.7637 – 110°18′4.23″ in the upper northernmost Temanggung regency of Central Java, Indonesia. Being in a high altitude area, 840 above sea level, Wonokerso has limited rice fields, only 4.5% of its total area (505 ha), and most of its are non-rice fields. The majority of the region consists of state plantations, community plantations, and private forests, covering about 316 ha or 62% of the total area. (BPS Kabupaten Temanggung, 2020). (Fig. 1).

Because rice fields are limited, the people in Wonokerso depend on forest and plantation products for their livelihoods. Wonokerso has numerous potentials, including staple food, vegetables, fruits, and livestock. Coffee is one of the main

Table 1 Questionnaire statement of internal factors

No	Strengths	No	Weaknesses
S1	Suitability of local natural resources	W1	Organic product certification
S2	Low use of chemical fertilizers and pesticides	W2	Prices for organic and conventional coffee beans are the same
S3	Local government support	W3	Low productivity

Table 2 Questionnaire statement of external factors

No	Opportunities	No	Treats
O1	The low number of organic coffee producers	T1	Competition with other organic coffee products
O2	The demand for organic coffee is increasing	T2	Pests and plant diseases attack
O3	Digital technology development	T3	Climate change, increasing temperature

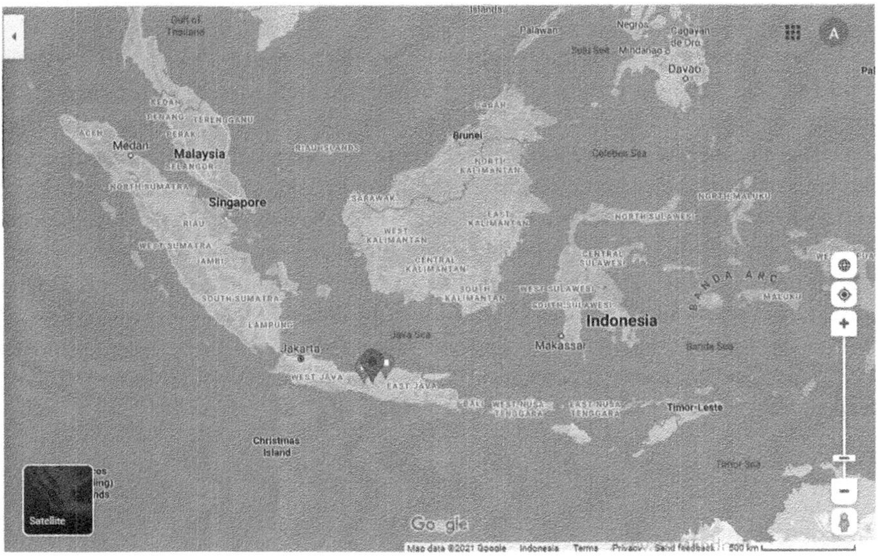

Fig. 1 Maps of Wonokerso Village, Temanggung Regency, Central Java, Indonesia. Source: Google maps 2021

sources of income for the local community, which has been cultivated traditionally for generations with other annual commodities such as timber, vanilla, cubeb, etc.

Administratively, Wonokerso has three sub-villages, there are Pakistan, Ngadirojo, and Krajan. In 2019, the population is 2662 people, consisting of 1372 men and 1290 women. Most of them are in productive age, accounted for 68%. The main profession is a farmer, approximately 60%. The number of land ownership is quite high, namely 733 families or 89.6 per cent are landowners. The majority of the people (81%) have low education. This is also due to the limited educational facilities.

5 Data Analysis

The stages of SWOT analysis are based on Chang and Huang (2005) with modification in the weight of key factors using the Likert scale. The steps for a SWOT analysis are as follows:

(a) Identification of internal and external factor
(b) Measuring the internal factors by weighing and rating both strengths and weaknesses while weighing and rating opportunities and threats. Weights then were allocated to each internal and external variable based on the level of importance using a Likert scale. After that, the rating was carried out for each factor on a scale of 1 to 5, based on the influence of these factors on the development of organic coffee. The result is shown in the IFAS and EFAS table.
(c) Calculating and comparing the coordinate values of internal and external assessment then show them on the 4- quadrant coordinate, with the following quadrant categories:

If the total score created from internal and external assessment plotted in the first quadrant, then the development of organic need to use an aggressive strategy;
If it plotted in the second quadrant, then the development of organic need to use a conservative strategy;
If it plotted in the third quadrant, then the development of organic need to use turnaround strategy and;
If it is plotted in the fourth quadrant, the development of organic needs to use a defensive strategy

(d) Furthermore, this study used the Treats Opportunities Weaknesses Strengths (TOWS) matrix to facilitate strategy formulation. The TOWS matrix is a complementary tool to the SWOT for implementing strategy and is widely used when creating strategies (Dandage et al., 2019). SWOT and TOWS are more useful when used together than when individually in strategy formulation. The TOWS matrix helps to identify systematic relationships between threats, opportunities, weaknesses, and strengths and offers a structure for generating strategies based on these relationships (Weihrich, 1982). A previous study by Aslan used the SWOT and TOWS matrix in creating strategies for sustainable development of the Kipaş Group (Aslan et al., 2012). Based on this analysis, an organic coffee development was formulated. The analysis examines threats and opportunities first, followed by weaknesses and strengths. According to (Weihrich, 1982), TOWS involves four possible types of strategy:

1. WT Strategy (mini-mini) aims to minimize both weaknesses and threats.
2. WO Strategy (mini-maxi) attempts to minimize weaknesses and maximize opportunities
3. ST strategy (maxi-mini) intends to maximizing strengths and minimizing threats
4. SO strategy (maxi-maxi) uses to maximizing both strengths and opportunities

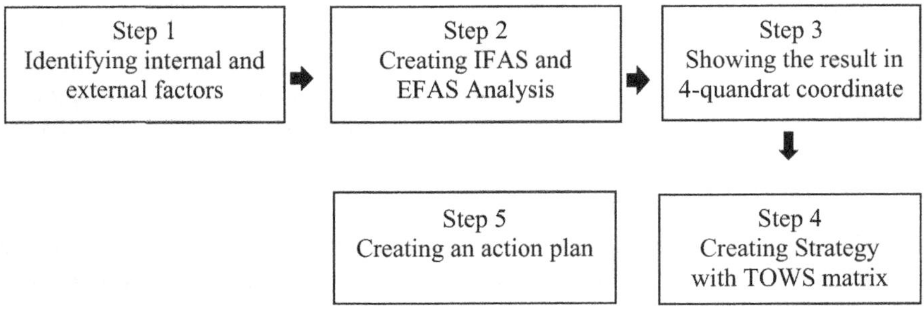

Fig. 2 The Steps for constructing organic coffee development strategies in Wonokerso Village

(e) Creating action plan

Action plans are prepared to describe strategies in the form of either programs or activities accompanied by actors and funding.

Finally, the steps for developing an organic coffee development strategy are shown in Fig. 2, while the action plan is in Attachment 1.

6 Result and Discussion

6.1 Internal Factor Analysis Summary (IFAS)

The results of the analysis of internal factors are shown in Table 3. The IFAS indicates that the greater impact to a factor is, the higher weighting be. The rating was given based on stakeholder's preferences. The higher this factor position, the higher the total value be. Low productivity is the lowest metric of this development of organic coffee in Wonokerso Village compared to the other factors. The difference between strength and weakness is 2.27–2.40 = − 0.133; this shows that the weaknesses factor is higher than the strengths factor.

6.2 External Factor Analysis Summary (EFAS)

The steps to analyze the external factors are the same as in IFAS. The result of EFAS can be seen in Table 3. As shown in Table 4, we can see that competition with other organic coffee products is the lower position of this organic coffee development than the other factors. The difference between opportunities and threats is 2.13–1.74 = 0.397; this shows that the opportunities factor is higher than the threats factor.

Table 3 Internal factor analysis summary (IFAS)

No	Factors	Weight	Value	Weight x Value
	Strengths			
1	Suitability of local resources	0.20	5	1.00
2	Low use of chemical fertilizers and pesticides	0.20	5	1.00
3	Local government support	0.07	4	0.27
		0.47		2.27
	Weaknesses			
4	Organic certification	0.13	4	0.53
5	Prices for organic and conventional coffee beans are the same	0.33	5	1.67
6	Low productivity	0.07	3	0.20
		0.53		2.40
	Total IFAS	1.00		4.67

Table 4 External Factor Analysis Summary (EFAS)

No	Factors	Weight	Value	Weight x Value
	Opportunities			
1	The low number of organic coffee producers	0.13	4	0.53
2	The demand for organic coffee is increasing	0.13	4	0.53
3	Digital technology development	0.27	4	1.07
		0.53		2.13
	Threats			
4	Competition with other organic coffee products	0.27	4	1.07
5	Pests and plant diseases attack	0.13	3	0.40
6	Climate change, increasing temperature	0.07	4	0.27
		0.47		1.74
	Total EFAS	1	4	3.87

6.3 Cartesian Diagram of Organic Coffee Development in Wonokerso Village

Moreover, based on analyzed data from IFAS, Strength is 2.27, whether Weaknesses is 2.40 and the difference between them is – 0.133. In the EFAS, Opportunity is 2.134, whether Threat is 1.74, and the difference between them is 0.399. These data are then displayed to the Cartesian diagram in Fig. 3.

As can be seen from the Cartesian diagram, the development of organic coffee in Wonokerso lies on quadrant III Turn Around, which means that the strategy applied is based on exploiting existing opportunities by minimizing weaknesses, namely the W-O strategy (mini-maxi). Regarding the position in this quadrant, the development of organic coffee in Wonokerso Village needs to minimize its weaknesses to take advantage of the best possible opportunities.

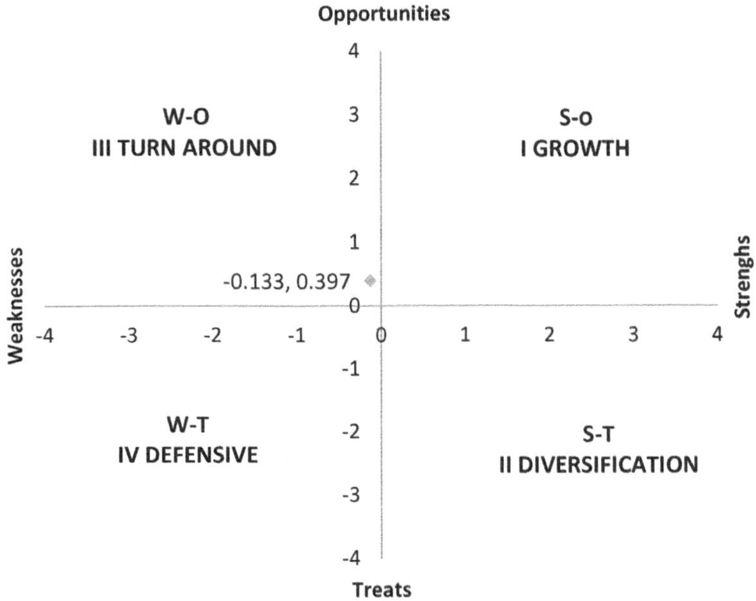

Fig. 3 Cartesian Diagram of Organic Coffee Development in Wonokerso Village

6.4 *Strategy Using TOWS matrix*

The formulation of an organic coffee development strategy using the TOWS matrix refers to Weihrich (Weihrich, 1982). This matrix is used to make it easier to juxtapose internal and external factors in strategy formulation. (Table 5).

a. SO Strategy (Maxi-Maxi)

The development of organic coffee is supported by its comparative advantages, namely suitability with local resources, the minimal use of chemical compounds and pesticides, especially coffee grown in community forest areas, and local government support in developing specialty coffee. Meanwhile, the opportunity is quite large because there are still a few organic coffee producers and the increasing demand for coffee both inside and outside the country and the development of digital technology that allows farmers to access the market directly. Therefore, in general, a strategy is directed to improve all aspects from on-farm to off-farm (production, harvest and post-harvest, processing technology, and marketing).

b. ST Strategy (Maxi-Mini)

Paying attention to the strengths possessed in the form of conformity with resource conditions and support from local governments and also paying attention to threat factors so far have not affected the stability of coffee production, especially related to pest attacks and climate change, but also need to pay attention to

Table 5 The TWOS matrix of organic coffee development in Wonokerso

Internal / External	Strengths (S) 1. Suitability of local resources 2. Low use of chemical fertilizers and pesticides 3. Local government support	Weaknesses (W) 1. Organic product certification 2. Prices for organic and conventional coffee beans are the same 3. Low productivity
Opportunities (O) 1. The low number of organic coffee producers 2. The demand for organic coffee is increasing 3. Digital technology development	Strategies SO Improving all aspects (production, harvest and post-harvest, processing technology, and marketing)	Strategies WO 1. Providing organic certification (W1,O1,O2) 2. Improving organic coffee price (W2, O1,O2,O3) 3. Improving productivity (W3, O1,O2) 4. Increasing the ability of farmers to market coffee with digital technology (W2, O3) 5. Improved communication network access (W3,O3)
Treats (T) 1. Pests and plant diseases attack 2. Climate change, increasing temperature 3. Competition with other organic coffee products	Strategies ST Improving all aspects (production, harvest and post-harvest, processing technology, and marketing)	Strategies WT Improving all aspects (production, harvest and post-harvest, processing technology, and marketing)

competition with other organic coffee products. Therefore, a strategy is directed to improve all aspects from on-farm to off-farm (production, harvest and post-harvest, processing technology, and marketing).

c. WO Strategy (Mini-Maxi)

There are three main obstacles in developing organic coffee in Wonokerso, namely low coffee productivity, no guaranteed price, and organic certification, which is burdensome for farmers even though there is still a low chance for organic coffee producers, high demand in international markets, and easy market access through online marketing. The strategy that needs to be done is (1) Providing organic certification, (2) Improving organic coffee price, (3) Improving productivity, (4) Increasing the ability of farmers to market coffee with digital technology, (5) Improved communication network access.

d. WT Strategy (Mini-Mini)

Regarding WT strategy, the factors of both weaknesses and threats are considered. Weaknesses include low productivity, no guarantee of price, and a certification process that is burdensome for farmers. While threats related to environmental factors, such as pests and diseases, and climate change have not considerably affected coffee production, if organic coffee is developed and significantly increases farmers' income, paramount importance to make improvements in all aspects.

Based on the results of the TOWS matrix, the action plan is then prepared as a frame of guidance in carrying out the strategy. The action plan includes programs and activities needed to develop organic coffee, including actors and funding. Overall, the description of the action plan is attached (Attachment 1).

In the short term, strategies are needed to develop organic coffee through a WO strategy, namely:

(i) First, facilitation of organic certification. Organic certification is strongly important to get a premium price and increase farmers' income, but the certification procedure is quite complicated and expensive. Hence the role of local governments through their technical services to facilitate organic farmers is significantly needed. Facilitation is given mainly to farmer groups who have been carrying out organic cultivation. Previous research has shown that some factors must be considered in the development of organic coffee, including the high cost of certification (Ayalew, 2014; K. Sarirahayu and A. Aprianingsih, 2018).

(ii) Second, the improvement of organic coffee prices. Second, the improvement of organic coffee prices. Price is the main obstacle for farmers in developing organic coffee. The price of both organic and conventional coffee generally still the same, as well as good quality coffee. According to farmers, coffee prices have been determined by the middleman because there is no specific marketing channel, the distribution channels were still long; this is in line with a study conducted by Neilson that the distribution chain is still long (Neilson, 2013). Although coffee outlets demand coffee that sell specialty coffee that directly orders coffee beans from farmers, the demand is still small and not yet continuous (Neilson, 2013). If organic coffee is developed, efforts need to cut these long distribution channels. Therefore, an institution is needed that can cut the distribution chain. The institution plays a role in buying farmers' organic coffee, processing it, and marketing it directly to consumers. The institution can be in the form of a village-owned enterprise (BUMDES). Borella's research shows that the need for intermediary institutions that can connect farmers to global markets (Borrella et al., 2015).).

Price is the main obstacle for farmers in developing organic coffee. The price of both organic and conventional coffee remained the same, as well as good quality coffee. According to farmers, a middleman has determined coffee prices because there is no specific marketing channel; the distribution channels were still long; this is in line with a study conducted by Neilson that the distribution chain is still long (Neilson, 2013). Although there is a demand from coffee outlets that sell specialty coffee that directly order coffee beans from farmers, the demand is still small and not continuous (Neilson, 2013). If organic coffee will be developed, efforts need to cut the long distribution channel. Therefore, an institution is needed that can cut the distribution chain. The institution plays a role in buying farmers' organic coffee, processing it, and marketing it directly to consumers. The institution can be in the form of a village-owned enterprise (BUMDES). The results of research conducted by Borella show that the need for intermediary institutions that can connect farmers to global markets

(iii) The third is to increase the productivity of organic coffee. Coffee productivity in Wonokerso has typically remained small because most of the coffee plants are cultivated in forest areas along with other annual crop commodities, irregular spacing, old trees, and minimal production inputs. The research that took place in Margamulya Village, West Java, Indonesia showed similar conditions, the production of organic coffee farmers lower than conventional, because farmers have just implemented this system, they had not received a premium price for their products (Saroja RAZ & T. Karyani, 2021). This result also supports Saufert's study using a comprehensive meta-analysis to examine the relative yield performance of organic and conventional farming systems globally, which shows that overall organic yields are in most cases lower than conventional yields (Seufert et al., 2012). Hence, it is necessary to improve plants' cultivation according to organic procedures through training and to provide technology packages and plant rejuvenation.

(iv) Fourth, improve the ability of farmers to market their products online. Most farmers in Wonokerso still do not take advantage of online coffee marketing due to limited ability to access digital technology and poor communication network infrastructure, especially the internet network. In general, in other strategies, ST, SO, and WO or in the long term, improvements are needed throughout the coffee production chain, starting from cultivation, harvesting, post-harvest, processing, and marketing so that organic coffee production in Wonokerso can be sustainable and increase farmers' income.

7 Conclusion

In this study, strategy creates the relationship between local economy resource and the shifting environment. Developing organic coffee in Wonokerso requires a comprehensive approach both on-farm and off-farm. The result of the SWOT analysis shows that the existing conditions are in quadrant III or turnaround, which means the strategy applied is based on exploiting existing opportunities by minimizing weaknesses. Hence, in the short term, if the development of organic coffee will be successful, it will refer to the WO strategy. The WO's strategies include providing organic certification, improving coffee price, improving productivity, increasing farmers' ability to the coffee market with digital technology, improving communication network access. Meanwhile, in the long term, the strategy is directed at improving all aspects of production, harvest and post-harvest, processing, and marketing, including the WT, ST, and SO strategies.

The important action plans that need to be carried out are: 1) The local government facilitates organic coffee certification to improve the standardization quality of organic coffee, 2) the improvement of selling price of organic coffee by forming a Village-Owned Enterprise (BUMDES) to accommodate farmers' organic coffee beans in processing and marketing directly to consumers, 3) Increasing the production and the quality of organic coffee by providing training and technology packages to increase farmers' knowledge and skills related to SOPs for cultivation, post-harvest, and processing of organic coffee and 4) Increasing skills of farmers in utilizing digital technology to market organic coffee products. Attached is the action plan for the development of organic coffee in Wonokers. These action plans have accommodated all aspects.

Attachment 1 The Action Plan of Organic Coffee Development in Wonokerso

Strategy	Programs and Activities	Time	Success Indicator	Actor	Budget Source
PRODUCTION	Provision of production fasilities (qualified coffee seed and clones, regenerating old plants, organic fertilizer, organic pesticide, wire, poles)		Availability of production fasilities	Agricultural development, farmer, university, R&D institution	Local government, CSR
	Increasing farmer skill in cultivation organic coffee, including the ability to produce organic fertilizer and pesticide.		Improving skill of farmers in organic coffee production	Agricultural development, farmer, university, R&D institution	Local government, CSR
HARVEST AND POST HARVEST	Provision of harvest and post harvest facilities		Availability of post harvest fasilities	Agricultural development, farmer, university, R&D institution	Local government, CSR
	Increasing farmer skill in harvest and post harvest.		Improving skill of farmers in harvest and post harvest	Agricultural development, farmer, university, R&D institution	Local government, CSR
PROCESSING TECHNOLOGY	Provision of processing technology facilities		The availability of processing technology facilities	Food security department, farmer, university, R&D institution	Local government, CSR

(continued)

Strategy	Programs and Activities	Time	Success Indicator	Actor	Budget Source
	To increase farmer skill in processing technology		Improving skill of farmers in processing technology	Food security department, farmer, university, R&D institution	Local government, CSR
MARKET	Providing organic certification	Sort term	Certified organic coffee	Food security department, farmer, university, R&D institution	Local government, CSR
	To establish processing agricultural products units in village or a village-owned Enterprise	Sort term	Establising processing agricultural products units in village or a village-owned Enterprise	Food security department, farmer, university, R&D institution	Local government, CSR
	Provision of market facilities		Availibilty market facilities	Department of Industry and Commerce farmer, university, R&D institution	Local government, CSR
	Improving farmer skill to sell their product with digital platform and		Increasing farmer skill to sell their product	Department of Industry and Commerce farmer, university, R&D institution	Local government, CSR
	Open network and patnership with domestic and international company		Availibility of network and parnership	Department of Industry and Commerce farmer, university, R&D institution	Local government, CSR

References

Aher, S. B., Swami, B., & Sengupta, B. (2012). Organic agriculture: Way towards sustainable development. *International Journal of Environmental Sciences, 3*(1), 209–216. https://doi.org/10.6088/ijes.2012030131021

Alam, K., Erdiaw-Kwasie, M. O., Shahiduzzaman, M., & Ryan, B. (2018). Assessing regional digital competence: Digital futures and strategic planning implications. *Journal of Rural Studies, 60*(March), 60–69. https://doi.org/10.1016/j.jrurstud.2018.02.009

Anríquez, G., & Kostas, S. (2007). Rural development and poverty reduction: Is agriculture still the key? Electronic. *Journal of Agricultural and Development Economics, 4*(1), 5–46.

AOI. (2019). Statistik Pertanian Organik Indonesia 2019. In *Aliansi Organis Indonesia*.

Aslan, I., Çinar, O., & Kumpikaitė-Valiūnienė, V. (2012). Creating strategies from tows matrix for strategic sustainable development of Kipaş Group. *Journal of Business Economics and Management, 13*(1), 95–110. https://doi.org/10.3846/16111699.2011.620134

Ayalew, T. (2014). Organic coffee Carter. *Asian Journal of Agricultural Research, 8*(4), 170–180.

Azunu, R., & Mensah, J. K. (2019). Local economic development and poverty reduction in developing societies: The experience of the ILO decent work project in Ghana. *Local Economy, 34*(5), 405–420. https://doi.org/10.1177/0269094219859234

Bacon, C. (2005). Confronting the coffee crisis: Can fair trade, organic, and specialty coffees reduce small-scale farmer vulnerability in Northern Nicaragua? *World Development, 33*(3), 497–511. https://doi.org/10.1016/j.worlddev.2004.10.002

Badan Pusat Statistik. (2020). Catalog : 1101001. *Statistik Indonesia, 2020*(1101001), 790. https://www.bps.go.id/publication/2020/04/29/e9011b3155d45d70823c141f/statistik-indonesia-2020.html

Borrella, I., Mataix, C., & Carrasco-Gallego, R. (2015). Smallholder farmers in the speciality coffee industry: Opportunities, constraints and the businesses that are making it possible. *IDS Bulletin, 46*(3), 29–44. https://doi.org/10.1111/1759-5436.12142

BPS Kabupaten Temanggung. (2020). Kecamatan Pringsurat dalam Angka. BPS Kabupaten Temanggung.

BPS-Statistics Indonesia. (2018). *Indonesian Coffee Statistic*, 2018.

Chang, H., & Huang, W. C. (2005). Application of a quantification SWOT analytical method. *Mathematical and Computer Modelling, 43*(1–2), 158–169. ISSN 0895-7177, https://doi.org/10.1016/j.mcm.2005.08.016.

Dandage, R. V., Mantha, S. S., & Rane, S. B. (2019). Strategy development using TOWS matrix for international project risk management based on prioritization of risk categories. *International Journal of Managing Projects in Business, 12*(4), 1003–1029. https://doi.org/10.1108/IJMPB-07-2018-0128

Directorate General of Estate Crops. (2020). Tree Crop Estate Statistics of Indonesia. *Tree Crop Estate Statistics of Indonesia* 2018-2020, 1–82. https://drive.google.com/file/d/1FVxpBNihnuB3ayAALBi-FtsBShIUxMTD/view

Emiria, F., & Purwandari, H. (2015). Pengembangan Pertanian Organik di Kelompok Tani Madya, Desa Kebonagung, Kabupaten Bantul, Daerah Istimewa Yogyakarta. *Jurnal Penyuluhan, 10*(2). https://doi.org/10.25015/penyuluhan.v10i2.9919

Fadillah, A., Indrawan, D., & Achsani, N. A. (2019). Indonesian coffee in the global value chain: The comparison of global partnership sustainability standards implementation. *Jurnal Manajemen Dan Agribisnis, 16*(2), 191–198. https://doi.org/10.17358/jma.16.2.191

Farwati, R. (2013). Pro-poor growth: Does it work in Indonesia ? *Perencanaan Pembangunan, BAPPENAS, XIX*(01).

Freyer, B., & Bingen, J. (2015). Re-thinking organic food and farming in a changing world. In *International library of environmental, agricultural and food ethics* (Vol. 22). Springer. https://doi.org/10.1007/978-94-017-9190-8_12

Handayani, A. (2013). Penerapan Sistem Nilai Cacat pada Komoditas Kopi Robusta (Studi Kasus di Wonokerso, Pringsurat, Temanggung). *Jurnal Litbang Provinsi Jawa Tengah, 11*(2), 201–209.

Handayani, A. (2015). Evaluasi Tingkat Penanganan Pasca Panen Kopi Robusta Sesuai GMP (Good Manufacturer Practices). 2015(190), 109–116. http://prosiding.upgris.ac.id/index.php/pangan/pangan/paper/viewFile/688/642

Handayani, A. (2018). Development of organic coffee in Wonokerso Village, Temanggung regency, *Central Java Indonesia Lesson learned from Japan*.

Hasan, M., & Azis, M. (1999). Pembangunan Ekonomi & Pemberdayaan Masyarakat.

IFOAM. (2012). *The IFOAM norms for organic production and processing*. Retrieved from http://www.ifoam.org/en/ifoam-norms.

Jamil, A. S., Saleh, I., Sungkawa, I., & Mardhatilla, F. (2019). Analisis Perbandingan Kelayakan Usahatani Padi Organik Dan Konvensional (Studi Kasus: Kecamatan Cigugur Kabupaten Kuningan Jawa Barat). *Seminar Nasional Pembangunan Pertanian Berkelanjutan Berbasis Sumber Daya Lokal*, 530–539. https://conference.unja.ac.id/SemnasSDL/article/view/59

Leksono, T. B., Supriyadi, S., & Zulkarnain, Z. (2018). Analisis Perbandingan Pendapatan Usahatani Padi Organik Dan Anorganik Kecamatan Seputih Banyak Kabupaten Lampung Tengah. *Jurnal Wacana Pertanian*, *14*(2), 69. https://doi.org/10.37694/jwp.v14i2.45.

Mayrowani, H. (2016). Pengembangan Pertanian Organik di Indonesia. *Forum Penelitian Agro Ekonomi, 30*(2), 91. https://doi.org/10.21082/fae.v30n2.2012.91-108

Myrdal, G. (1968). *Asian drama: An inquiry into the poverty of nations*. Pantheon.

Neilson, J. (2013). The value chain for Indonesian coffee in a green economy. *Buletin RISTRI*, *4*(3), 183–198. https://doi.org/10.21082/jtidp.v4n3.

Pavel, A., & Moldovan, O. (2019). Determining local economic development in the rural areas of Romania. *Exploring the role of exogenous factors. Sustainability (Switzerland)*, *11*(2). https://doi.org/10.3390/su11010282

Putri, S., S. I. S. dan W. D. P (2018). *Analisis Komparasi Pendapatan Petani Cabai Merah Keriting Organik dan Non Organik di Desa Batur, Kecamatan Getasan, Kabupaten Semarang. December*, 1–14.

Rogerson, C. M. (2015). Local economic development. In *International Encyclopedia of the Social & Behavioral Sciences: Second Edition* (Second Edi, Vol. 14). Elsevier. https://doi.org/10.1016/B978-0-08-097086-8.72111-8.

Sarirahayu, K., & Aprianingsih, A. (2018). Strategy to improving smallholder coffee farmers Productivty. *The Asian Journal of Technology Management*, *11*(1), 1–9.

Saroja, R. A. Z., & Karyani, T. (2021). Comparison of income organic and conventional coffee farmers (case in Margamulya Village, Pangalengan regency, Bandung regency, West Java). *Jurnal Pemikiran Masyarakat Ilmiah Berwawasan Agribisnis.*, *7*(1), 25–37.

Setiawati, S., & I., & Djelantik, A. (2015). Analisis Pendapatan Usahatani Padi Bersertifikat Organik (Kasus Kelompok Tani Gana Sari Kabupaten Badung). *E-Journal Agribisnis Dan Agrowisata (Journal of Agribusiness and Agritourism)*, *4*(5), 355–364.

Seufert, V., Ramankutty, N., & Foley, J. A. (2012). Comparing the yields of organic and conventional agriculture. *Nature, 485*(7397), 229–232. https://doi.org/10.1038/nature11069

Steiner, G. A. (1979). *Strategic planning what every manager must know* (pp. 1–393).

Stimson, R. J. et al. (2006). Regional economic development. In M. M. Fischer & G. J. D. H. P. N. F. S. (Coordinating Editor) (Eds.), *(Advances in spatial science*. Springer. https://doi.org/10.1007/978-3-662-04911-2.

Suryahadi, A., Suryadarma, D., & Sumarto, S. (2006). Economic growth and poverty reduction in Indonesia: The effects of location and sectoral components of growth. In *SMERU Research Institute* (Issue August).

Suryahadi, A., Al Izzati, R., & Suryadarma, D. (2020). Estimating the impact of Covid-19 on poverty in Indonesia*. Bulletin of Indonesian Economic Studies, *0*(0), 175–192. doi:https://doi.org/10.1080/00074918.2020.1779390.

Susanti, E. (2013). Pengembangan Ekonomi Lokal Dalam Sektor Pertanian (Studi Pada Kecamatan Pagelaran Kabupaten Malang). *Jurnal Administrasi Publik Mahasiswa Universitas Brawijaya*, *1*(4), 31–40.

Tinubaya, E., Priyono, B. S., Rasyid, W., Sosial, J., & Pertanian, E. (2011). Analisis Komparasi Usahatani Padi Sawah Sistem Tanam SRI dan Konvensional di Desa Bukit Peninjauan I Kecamatan Sukaraja Kabupaten Seluma. *AGRISEP*, *10*(2), 188–206.

Torres, J., Valera, D. L., Belmonte, L. J., & Herrero-Sánchez, C. (2016). Economic and social sustainability through organic agriculture: Study of the restructuring of the citrus sector in the "Bajo Andarax" district (Spain). *Sustainability (Switzerland)*, *8*(9), 1–14. https://doi.org/10.3390/su8090918

Van Der Vossen, H. A. M. (2005). A critical analysis of the agronomic and economic sustainability of organic coffee production. *Experimental Agriculture, 41*(4), 449–473. https://doi.org/10.1017/S0014479705002863

Velmourougane, K. (2016). Impact of organic and conventional systems of coffee farming on soil properties and culturable microbial diversity. *Scientifica, 2016*. https://doi.org/10.1155/2016/3604026

Villanueva, M. (2014). Creating a strategic plan for local economic development: A guide. *The Federation of Canadian Municipalities – Caribbean local economic development project (FCM-CARILED), Trinidad a*, 54.

Weihrich, H. (1982). The TOWS matrix – A tool for situational analysis. *Long Range Planning, 15*(2), 54–66. https://doi.org/10.1136/bcr-2017-222123

Wicaksono, E., Amir, H., & Nugroho, A. (2017). The source of income inequality in Indonesia: A regression-based inequality decomposition. *ADBI Working Paper, 667*, 1–16. https://www.adb.org/publications/sources-income-inequality-indonesia

The Impact of the COVID-19 Pandemic on the Socio-Economic Conditions of Rural Communities in Central Java

Tri Risandewi and Arif Sofianto

Abstract Based on data from the Indonesian Ministry of Finance, the COVID-19 pandemic is expected to cause a decline in Indonesia's economic growth to depreciate to a level of 2.5% and to 0%, so it is feared that the poverty rate will increase by more than 5%. Currently, the number of poor people in Central Java Province in 2020 has reached 3.98 million people or 11.41%, where the majority were in rural areas (2.18 million people). Rural areas (villages) are considered less attractive due to limited employment opportunities, despite having considerable potential as an alternative to post-COVID-19 recovery. This study aims to determine the impact of the COVID-19 pandemic on the socio-economic sector and the problems faced by rural communities in Central Java. This research is a qualitative descriptive study using mixed methods. The research was conducted in 29 regencies in Central Java. The results showed that the sectors most affected were the tourism, trade, and small industry sectors i.e. Micro, Small, and Medium Enterprises (MSMEs). The problems faced were an increase in the poverty rate, the number of unemployed and the crime rate, and a decrease in people's purchasing power. The recommendations are: (1) in the short term, increase purchasing power by reducing miscellaneous expenses and increasing income, food availability, and disaster mitigation budget, and (2) in the medium term create growth centres in the periphery and remote areas.

Keyword COVID-19 impact · Rural communities · Socio-economic · Central java

1 Introduction

The COVID -19 pandemic has spread widely to most parts of Indonesia. Based on data from the COVID-19 Task Force of the Indonesian Ministry of Health on July (revise) 6, 2020, the number of positive cases reached 64,958 people with 3241

T. Risandewi (✉) · A. Sofianto
Regional Planning, Research and Development Board of Central Java Province, Semarang, Central Java, Indonesia

© The Author(s), under exclusive license to Springer Nature Singapore Pte Ltd. 2022
T. Chaiechi, J. Wood (eds.), *Community Empowerment, Sustainable Cities, and Transformative Economies*, https://doi.org/10.1007/978-981-16-5260-8_36

deaths (Anwar, 2020). The spread of COVID-19 resulted in various negative impacts for all sectors, namely the economic, social, cultural, health, and education (Fahrika & Roy, 2020). The spread of COVID-19 has had a large impact on job losses due to large-scale public restriction policies on various activities that cause the economy to run slowly and stagnant (Rahmansyah et al., 2020). The Ministry of Finance of the Republic of Indonesia predicted that there would be a decline in Indonesia's economic growth to a level of 2.5–0% in 2020 (Yamali & Putri, 2020). Consequently, the poverty rate will increase by more than 5% (Yamali & Putri, 2020).

In the meantime, the Ministry of Manpower of the Republic of Indonesia reported that as many as 1.94 million workers have been laid off or affected by layoffs due to the pandemic (Yamali & Putri, 2020). At the same time, the Indonesian Employers' Association (Apindo) noted that the number of workers affected by layoffs due to the COVID-19 pandemic has so far reached seven million (CNBC Indonesia, 8 May 2020).

In Central Java, the number of poor people in 2020 reached 3.98 million people or 11.41%, and most of them are in villages (2.18 million people or 12.80%) (BPS Jawa Tengah, 2020b). In addition, there was also an increase in unemployment by 0.03% from 4.22% in February 2019 to 4.25% in February 2020 (equaling approximately 300 thousand) (BPS Jawa Tengah, 2020c).

Research by Livana et al. (2020) shows that many rural communities affected by the pandemic have caused businesses to close causing layoffs due to restrictions on activities by the government. In addition, the COVID -19 pandemic has also caused panic, confusion, and depression for those directly affected (Livana et al., 2020; Yanuarita & Haryati, 2021). Therefore, a study is needed to identify the social and economic impacts and problems in rural areas due to the COVID -19 pandemic in Central Java.

2 Methodology

Mixed method research will consider a combination of qualitative and quantitative techniques to formulate a research problem. In social science research, two types of instruments are often used, namely questionnaires and interview guides. The questionnaire used consists of questions that are formulated systematically, directed, and carefully and makes it easy to collect data from large numbers of respondents in a relatively short time (Suyanto et al., 2005).

This study aims to analyze the impact of the COVID-19 pandemic on rural communities and what problems are faced directly by the community in rural areas in Central Java. This research was conducted by the Regional Development Planning, Research and Development Agency of Central Java Province in collaboration with related agencies. Using online survey (google form) and in-depth interviews with relevant stakeholders in 13 districts in Central Java Province (Grobogan, Wonogiri, Wonosobo, Batang, Tegal, Klaten, Pati, Kebumen, Purworejo,

Temanggung, Semarang, Demak, and Magelang district, the sample was taken from four groups, namely the affected community, village government, sub-district, and business actors. The question in google form was based on the results of the Central Java Statistics Agency (Badan Pusat Statistik Jawa Tengah /BPS Jawa Tengah) survey, and was accepted by the ethics committee (BPS Jawa Tengah, 2020a).

3 Results and Discussion: The Impact of the COVID-19 Pandemic in Rural Central Java

3.1 *Result*

In general, based on the results of in-depth interviews with rural communities in 13 research locations, the sectors most affected by the COVID-19 pandemic are tourism, small and micro industries (craftsmen, ironworkers, metal casting, food processing, etc.), art workers (puppets, singers, traditional artists, etc.), catering and party equipment rental, fishermen, farmers, labourers. Only a few types of work are not significantly affected, including “gula semut” farmer (Kebumen), farmers of food crops such as rice, goat breeders (Klaten), managers of natural tourism (Magelang).

Based on the in-depth interview data, several things can be seen as a result of mapping the impacts of the COVID-19 pandemic. First, Tourism sector was the most negatively impacted sector, especially if tourism is the main core business, there will be a strong decline in economic income. The follow-on impact is on the traders who usually sell at tourist attractions. Second, the agricultural sector has the lowest impact even though the price of agricultural food products has decreased due to the lack of market demand (Ferdi, 2020). However, rural food security can still be relied upon. Although the price of food plants has fallen due to low consumer demand, there are several types of herbal plants (ginger, turmeric) whose prices tend to rise because consumer demand increases due to claims that these spice plants can protect the body from the attack of the coronavirus (Perdani & Hasibuan, 2021).

Third, the trade sector in the village, especially retail, experienced a quite heavy impact given the decline in market demand. Mobile vegetable traders still exist, but traders of cooked food and products for tourist attractions have stopped because tourist attractions have closed in the villages. Cooked food traders are also affected by schools conducting learning at home, resulting in limited mobility within the community. Fourth, the industrial sector has also been quite strongly affected, especially in villages with house tile and materials, for example, because the demand for those products has dropped dramatically.

In addition to the in-depth interview results, this study also uses an online survey method using google forms, which were filled in by the four categories of respondents as described above. The respondents include 155 sub-districts, 337 villages, 3062 rural business actors, and 1828 communities affected by the pandemic (Fig. 1).

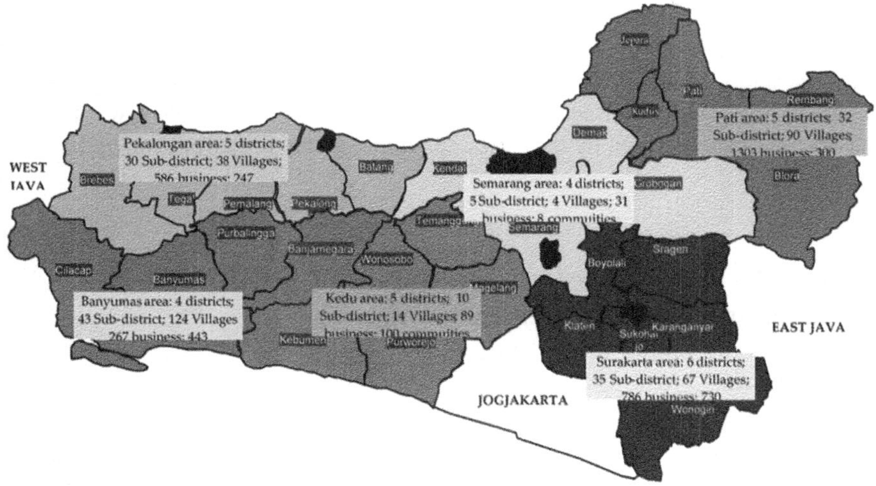

Fig. 1 Distribution of research respondents by region

This survey uses several indicators as listed in the google form, namely: (1) Main Occupation of Respondents Before and During the COVID-19 Pandemic, (2) The Influence of the COVID-19 Pandemic on the Life of Village Communities, (3) The Influence of the COVID-19 pandemic on the poverty rate and the number of unemployment in the village, (4) Changes in Rural Community Income During the Pandemic.

Based on primary data from the results of the questionnaire, Table 1 below summarizes the main occupations of respondents before and after being affected by the COVID-19 pandemic in Central Java. While Milzam et al. (2020) research on Pekalongan City shows that MSMEs income decreased by 53.5% due to the COVID-19 pandemic and the most affected was the fashion business, our data shows that the most affected were industrial workers/MSMEs with a total of 188 people who lost their jobs. In the carpentry service, construction, and transportation services as many as 46 people lost their jobs, and in the financial services, 16 people lost their jobs. The loss of jobs in Central Java was directly related to the reduced number of construction projects and the enactment of the large-scale social restrictions/Pembatasan Sosial Berskala Besar (PSBB) due to the pandemic.

However, several jobs in agriculture (farmers, breeders, forestry, plantations), accommodation providers such as hotels, inns, restaurants, and cafes), educational services, and odd jobs have absorbed more labour force. This shows that the COVID-19 pandemic has a negative impact on economic growth and has a positive impact on economic growth in certain sectors. When being asked about how COVID-19 has affected their lives, the online survey data analysis results identified that just over 43% of people in the village community were greatly affected. According to perceptions of the village community, 47% were quite affected and

Table 1 Main occupation of respondents before and during the COVID-19 pandemic in Central Java

No.	Main Job	Before COVID-19	During COVID-19
1.	Farming/livestock/plantation/forestry	140	191
2.	Fishermen/Fisheries	5	7
3.	Trade	419	407
4.	Carpentry/Construction service	121	75
5.	Transportation service	95	49
6.	Electronic/automotive services	38	28
7.	Information technology, mass media, and broadcasting	11	4
8.	Art/creative industry workers/	44	34
9.	Farmworkers/fishermen	21	30
10.	Industrial works/SMEs	285	97
11.	Mining/quarrying	4	1
12.	Travel and entertainment	21	21
13.	Accommodation (hotel, inns, restaurant, caffe, etc)	48	54
14.	Education service	54	55
15.	Health service	12	7
16.	Financial service	19	3
17.	Odds job	158	289
18.	Taking care of household	51	89
19.	Unemployment/not working	25	331
20.	Several types of work	227	35
21.	Other work	31	22
	Total	**1.829**	**1.829**

Fig. 2 The Influence of the COVID-19 Pandemic on the Life of Village Communities in Central Java

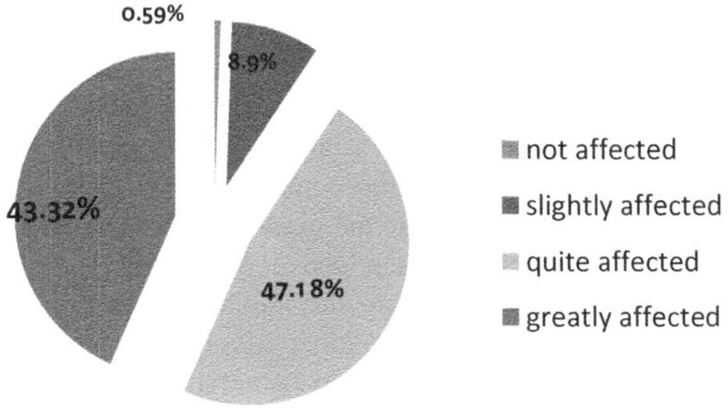

nearly 9% were slightly affected; less than 1% were not affected at all, as seen in Fig. 2.

Livana et al. (2020) study regarding the impact of the COVID-19 pandemic in rural areas found that all informants said that COVID-19 had a profound impact on their lives. They also said that the COVID-19 pandemic caused stress, confusion,

Table 2 The influence of the COVID-19 pandemic on the poverty rate and the number of unemployment in the village

No.	Information	Poverty		Unemployment	
		Number of villages	%	Number of villages	%
1.	Constant	34	10.09	13	3.86
2.	Increase <= 2.5%	143	42.43	143	42.43
3.	Increase 2.6–5%	75	22.26	87	25.82
4.	Increases above 5%	85	25.22	94	27.89
	Amount	337	100	337	100

Table 3 Poverty rate in Central Java

	Urban	Rural	Urban+Rural
March 2019	9.20	12.48	10.80
September 2019	8.99	12.26	10.58
March 2020	10.09	12.80	11.41
September 2020	10.57	13.20	11.84

Source: BPS Jawa Tengah (2021)

and panic, although some felt that COVID-19 had a positive impact, which supports the results of this study. Where people were anxious, their anxiety occurs because of difficulties in fulfilling their daily needs because some of them no longer work or trade. The groups in Livana et al. (2020) study that felt the most economic hardship or decreased income were those who worked in the informal sector (e.g. street vendors, transportation workers, small traders) who had a low income on average since before the COVID 19 pandemic. This study is in line with another study's findings, where the parties that experienced the most decline in income were those with the lowest income levels (BPS Jawa Tengah, 2020c). The policy of limiting activities (PSBB) caused many people to lose their jobs or decrease their income, which resulted in increased poverty and unemployment.

The effect of the COVID-19 pandemic on the lives of rural communities can be seen in the increased number of poverty and unemployment in 337 sample villages, as shown in Table 2. According to the village community (42.43%), there was an increase in poverty and the number of unemployed up to 2.5% in 143 villages in 2020. In fact, there is also the perception of the village community that poverty and unemployment have risen above 5%. Only 10.09% of the village community thought it did not increase the number of poor people and 3.86% thought there was no increase in the number of unemployed. The impact of the COVID-19 pandemic in Central Java also occurred in various aspects, social and economic. Since March 2020, the poverty rate in Central Java has increased.

According to BPS (2020a, 2020b, 2020c), the number of poor people in Central Java was 3.98 million (11.41%) in September 2020, an increase compared to September 2019 of 3.68 million (10.58%), see Table 3. The poverty rate increased in urban areas from 8.99% (2019) to 10.09% (2020); in rural areas, it increased from 12.26% (2019) to 12.80% (2020). Inequality based on the Gini Ratio increased from 0.358 in 2019 to 0.362 in 2020. The need for foodstuffs contributed 74.14% to

Table 4 Percentage of decrease in income due to COVID based on income level

No	Income level (rupiah)	Decrease income (%)
1	<= 1.8 million	42.8
2	1.8–3 million	24.2
3	3–4.8 million	11.6
4	4.8–7.2 million	10.7
5	> = 7.2 million	10.7

Source: BPS Jawa Tengah (2021)

poverty; the rest were non-food needs such as housing, gasoline, electricity, and education (BPS Jawa Tengah, 2021).

Based on the results of a Central Java BPS survey (2020a) involving 10,570 respondents, it was found that 27.1% of respondents were unemployed, as many as 2.5% of respondents were laid off as a result of the COVID-19 pandemic, while 14.9% had the status of being laid off. While, as many as 41.6% of respondents experienced a decrease in income due to COVID-19. Some of the people affected by the pandemic are still working and some are being laid off or are already laid off. As many as 64.6% of workers who were temporarily laid off experienced a decrease in income, while those who were still working, 35.3% of them, experienced a decrease in income.

The survey results show that for most people with an income below IDR 1.8 million (42.8%) and an income of between IDR1.8 million to 3 million, their income has decreased due to the COVID-19 pandemic. It is different for people who earn above IDR 3 million experienced only a slight decrease in income, as shown in Table 4. The COVID-19 pandemic disrupted rural economic activities and experienced a shrinkage or decrease in income (Ferdi, 2020).

The survey also found that as many as 42.8% of low-income people (IDR1.8 million and below) experienced a decrease in income due to the COVID-19 pandemic. While the above income group was lower, namely income IDR 1.8–three million by 24.2%, income IDR 3–4.8 million by 11.6%, income IDR 4.8–7.2 million by 10.7%, and income of IDR 7.2 million and above 10.7%. Therefore, the poor who work in the informal sector is the most vulnerable group due to the COVID 19 pandemic.

About 95% of respondents admitted that they have experienced a decline in income in this pandemic era. On the other hand, more than 55% of respondents admitted that their spending has increased in this pandemic era. These results are in accordance with the Central Java BPS survey (2020a), where the poor who work in the informal sector are the group most affected by this pandemic. In this survey, 42.8% of people with the lowest income experienced a decrease in income. From the expenditure side, 56.1 respondents admitted that their expenditure had increased in the era of the COVID 19 pandemic. The foodstuffs contributed the biggest increases in expenditure (48.3%), followed by health (20.1%), and internet access (18.4%). These changes in spending are the impact of government policies so that people stay at home (BPS Jawa Tengah, 2020b) (Table 5).

Table 5 Changes in rural community income during the pandemic

Change	Income (%)	Spending (%)
Increase > = 20%	0.55	35.16
Increase <20%	0.16	20.28
Constant	4.10	31.38
Decrease <20%	24.44	6.56
Decrease > = 20%	70.75	6.62

Table 6 A source of income for the village community

No.	Source of income	Percentage
1	Working	35.65
2	Help family or relatives	12.41
3	Assistance from other parties/neighbors	1.69
4	Government assistance	5.69
5	Debt	7.22
6	Work, help, debt, savings	26.19
7	Debt, family assistance, government, other parties	9.95
8	No income/not working	0.66
9	Savings/severance pay	0.55
	Amount	100

Table 7 An increase in crime due to the COVID -19 pandemic on Central Java

No.	Increased crime	Amount	Percentage
1.	Constant	214	63.50
2.	Slightly increased	96	28.49
3.	Quite increased	23	6.82
4.	Greatly increased	4	1.19
	Amount	337	100

Some people rely on help from other parties to meet their daily needs. As many as 35.65% admitted to making work their main source of income, while 26.19% said that in addition to working, they also rely on fulfilling their needs from help from others, go into debt, or use savings. As many as 12.41% really depend on their families, 7.22% rely on debt, and the rest is assistance from other parties (Table 6).

This situation can lead to increased crime due to economic difficulties. According to (Dermawanti et al., 2015) crime is strongly influenced by factors of poverty and increasing unemployment. However, in this study, according to the perception of most rural communities (63.50%), there was no increase in crime due to the COVID pandemic, only a small proportion (1.19%) thought that crime had increased significantly as can be seen in Table 7.

The table data above shows that there has been an increase in criminal cases in some rural areas. A decrease in income or job loss has an impact on increasing crime rates because people need quick solutions in addressing shortages during this pandemic. Economic difficulties are one of the factors that influence the occurrence of crime during the COVID-19 pandemic (Millah, 2020). According to Susanto

Table 8 The Influence of the Pandemic on People's Purchasing Power

No.	People's purchasing power	Amount	Percentage
1.	Fixed	25	7.42
2.	Slightly decreased	98	29.08
3.	Quite decreased	185	54.90
4.	Greatly decreased	29	8.61
	Amount	337	100

(2011), the factors influencing the occurrence of crime include economic factors, social environment, opportunities, and imitating other regional crimes. Especially during the COVID -19 pandemic, there is an increase in social inequality and decreasing public welfare, which encourages an increase in crime. Therefore policies are needed both from the government through the Police and the Community to further maintain security and safety.

In addition to causing an increase in poverty, unemployment, and crime, according to 92.6% of the respondents, the COVID-19 pandemic also caused a decrease in purchasing power. Only 7.42% thought there was no decrease in people's purchasing power as seen in Table 8.

3.2 *Discussion*

Most people are affected by the pandemic through a decrease in turnover, loss of a job, and decreased income (BPS Jawa Tengah, 2020b). The purchasing power in rural communities tends to be stable because their basic necessity can be fulfilled from agricultural land, gardens, and yards. However, other needs such as electricity, water, and others (transportation, telecommunications, etc.) still heavily burden the household finances in rural communities. During the pandemic, peoples prioritize purchasing food and health necessities over other things (Milzam et al., 2020). The government issued direct cash assistance (Bantuan Langsung Tunai/BLT), subsidized electricity and fuel, and free medical examinations (Mufida et al., 2020).

The government issued a policy to provide social assistance in the form of foodstuffs, money, health facilities, and production facilities assistance for capital entrepreneurs (Suryahadi et al., 2020). The Ministry of Villages, Development of Disadvantaged Areas, and Transmigration also mandated that the Village Fund allocation during this pandemic focused on providing social assistance (cash, foodstuffs, health needs) to the community as implementing cash-intensive projects to provide job opportunities for unemployed people. While this social assistance has many benefits, contrastingly, it negatively impacts rural communities, making the people increasingly dependent on assistance and becoming reluctant to rise in difficult situations (Sarip et al., 2020).

In accordance with the survey participant's responses, they did not only expect material assistance but also hoped for the opportunity to work again. It is hoped that the government will reopen job opportunities, open new job opportunities, facilitate capital for them to start businesses, or increase their capacity.

In addition to the impact on individuals, the pandemic also affects micro, small and medium enterprises (MSMEs) in rural areas. Types of businesses in rural areas are dominated by processed food catering, cakes and bread, batik, textiles, garments, food stalls, agriculture, handicrafts, souvenirs, accessories, creative industries, tourism, and entertainment. The tourism (tourism village) and entertainment sectors have been closed since the pandemic occurred. According to other survey findings from BPS Central Java, tourism, transportation, accommodation, and food and beverage are the sectors most affected (BPS Jawa Tengah, 2020c).

Other sectors are struggling; some are still surviving. Some of the difficulties experienced by the business sector in rural areas are capital, raw materials, production equipment, and marketing. As many as 907 respondents (29.62%) stated that they did not have capital, while 1.924 other people (62.83%) experienced a lack of capital. As many as 292 people (9.54%) admitted that raw materials were no longer available, while 1.544 other people (50.42%) admitted that they had difficulty obtaining raw materials. Difficulties in production consisted of difficulty in obtaining spare parts (6.01%), high costs (43.21%), delayed distribution (13.10%), and lack of maintenance (5.85%). In terms of productivity and marketing, most of them experienced a decline. More than 65% of business operators in rural areas admit that they have experienced a decline in production and marketing of over 20%. Meanwhile, only about 2.5% experienced an increase.

4 Conclusion

There are several important conclusions obtained from the results of this study, regarding the results of mapping the impact of the COVID-19 pandemic in rural Central Java. Firstly, the sectors most affected by COVID-19 in rural areas are the tourism sector, MSMEs, art actors, craft, and materials. Secondly, the pandemic's professions are industrial workers, MSME workers, construction, and transportation services. Thirdly, the pandemic has quite affected the lives of rural people, both in terms of an increase in the poverty rate and the number of unemployed (=<2.5%) as well as a decrease in people's purchasing power.

From the social aspect, there is a situation of vulnerability due to increased unemployment, reduced income, and the potential for conflict due to the unequal distribution of social assistance. It is feared that this situation will lead to other social problems such as an increase in criminal cases or a situation of disharmony.

5 Recommendation

Economic recovery can be started from some aspects of productivity, market and labour by implementing some strategies aiming to provide a foothold for strategic sectors in rural areas as well as for the workforce to survive in the COVID-19 pandemic crisis. Both central and regional governments with their authorities should provide subsidies such as capital / easy access, grants for production tools, seeds, fertilizers, materials. More subsidies for electricity, fuel, water are needed as well as tax incentives and rescheduling of credit instalments.

References

Anwar, F. (2020). Update Corona RI 6 Juli: 64.958 Positif, 29.919 Sembuh, 3.241 Meninggal. https://Health.Detik.Com/. https://health.detik.com/berita-detikhealth/d-5082078/update-corona-ri-6-juli-64958-positif29919-sembuh3241-meninggal

BPS Jawa Tengah. (2020a). *Hasil survei Sosial Demografi Dampa COVID 19 Jawa Tengah 2020*. https://jateng.bps.go.id/news/2020/06/03/379/hasil-survei-sosial-demografi-dampak-COVID-19.html

BPS Jawa Tengah. (2020b). Kemiskinan Provinsi Jawa Tengah Maret 2020. In *15 Juli* (Issue 06). https://jateng.bps.go.id/pressrelease/2020/07/15/1225/persentase-penduduk%2D%2Dmiskin-maret-2020-naik-menjadi-11-41-persen%2D%2Ddibanding-september-2019%2D%2Dyang-sebesar-10-58-persen.html

BPS Jawa Tengah. (2020c). Tingkat Ketimpangan Pengeluaran Penduduk Maret 2020. In *15 Juli* (Issue 57). https://jateng.bps.go.id/pressrelease/2020/07/15/1226/gini-ratio-maret-2020-tercatat-sebesar-0-362%2D%2Dnaik-dibanding-september-2019-yang-sebesar-0-358.html

BPS Jawa Tengah. (2021). Provinsi Jawa Tengah Dalam Angka 2021. https://jateng.bps.go.id/publication/2021/02/26/c5709cd0419788a55827d58f/provinsi-jawa-tengah-dalam-angka-2021.html

Dermawanti, Hoyyi, A., & Rusgiyono, A. (2015). Faktor-Faktor Yang Mempengaruhi Kriminalitas Di Kabupaten Batang Tahun 2013 Dengan Analisis Jalur. *Jurnal Gaussian, 4*(2), 247–256.

Fahrika, A. I., & Roy, J. (2020). Dampak Pandemi COVID-19 terhadap Perkembangan Makro Ekonomi di Indonesia dan Respon Kebijakan yang Ditempuh the impact of the COVID-19 pandemic on macroeconomic developments in Indonesia and the policy response taken. *Inovasi, 16*(2), 206–213.

Ferdi. (2020). Dampak Pandemi COVID-19 Terhadap Aktivitas Ekonomi Masyarakat di Desa Salumpaga, Kecamatan Tolitoli Utara. *Geography Science Education Journal, 1*(2), 3–43. https://doi.org/10.29303/resiprokal.v2i2.46

Livana, P. H., Suwoso, R. H., Febrianto, T., Kushindarto, D., & Aziz, F. (2020). Dampak Pandemi COVID-19 Bagi Perekonomian Masyarakat Desa. *Indonesian Journal of Nursing and Health Sciences, 1*(1), 37–48.

Millah, I. A. (2020). Penanggulangan Kejahatan Di Masa Pandemi COVID-19 (Dalam Perspektif Kriminologi Dan Viktimologi). *Jurnal Komunikasi Hukum (JKH), 6*(2), 2356–4164. https://mediaindonesia.com/read

Milzam, M., Mahardika, A., & Amalia, R. (2020). Corona virus pandemic impact on sales revenue of micro small and medium enterprises (MSMEs) in Pekalongan City. *Journal of Vocational Studies on Applied Research, 2*(1), 7–10. https://doi.org/10.14710/jvsar.2.1.2020.7-10

Mufida, S., Timur, F. G. C., & Waluyo, S. D. (2020). Strategi Pemerintah Indonesia Dalam Menangani Wabah COVID-19 Dari Perspektif Ekonomi. *Independen, 1*(2), 121–130. https://doi.org/10.24853/independen.1.2.121-130

Perdani, M. S., & Hasibuan, A. K. (2021). Analisis Informasi Tanaman Herbal melalui Media Sosial ditengah Masyarakat pada Pandemi COVID-19 : Sebuah Tinjauan Literatur. *Bencoolen Journal of Pharmacy, 1*(1), 11–25. https://ejournal.unib.ac.id/index.php/bjp/article/download/15589/7585

Rahmansyah, W., Qadri, R. A., Sakti, R. R. A., & Ikhsan, S. (2020). Pemetaan Permasalahan Penyaluran Bantuan Sosial Untuk Penanganan COVID-19 Di Indonesia. *Jurnal Pajak Dan Keuangan Negara, 2*, 90–102.

Sarip, Syarifudin, A., & Muaz, A. (2020). Dampak COVID-19 Terhadap Perekonomian Masyarakat dan Pembangunan Desa. *Al-Mustashfa: Jurnal Penelitian Hukum Ekonomi Islam, 5*(1), 10–20. https://www.syekhnurjati.ac.id/jurnal/index.php/al-mustashfa

Suryahadi, A., Al Izzati, R., & Suryadarma, D. (2020). *The impact of COVID-19 outbreak on poverty: An estimation for Indonesia* (draft). SMERU working paper, April, 1–20. http://smeru.or.id/en/content/impact-COVID-19-outbreak-poverty-estimation-indonesia

Susanto, I. (2011). *Kriminologi*. Genda Publishing.

Suyanto, B., Sutinah, Oetomo, D., Singgih, D. S., Susanti, E., Subiakto, H., Siahaan, H. M, Wirawan, I., Glinka, J., Karnaji, P.L. D., & Isfironi, M. (2005). Metode Penelitian Sosial Berbagai Alternatif Pendekatan (B. Suyanto & Sutinah (eds.), 3rd ed.). Kencana Prenamedia Group.

Yamali, F. R., & Putri, R. N. (2020). Dampak COVID-19 Terhadap Ekonomi Indonesia. *Ekonomis: Journal of Economics and Business, 4*(2), 384. https://doi.org/10.33087/ekonomis.v4i2.179

Yanuarita, H. A., & Haryati, S. (2021). Pengaruh COVID-19 Terhadap Kondisi Sosial Budaya Di Kota Malang Dan Konsep Strategis Dalam Penanganannya. *Jurnal Ilmiah Widya Sosiopolitika, 2*(2), 58. https://doi.org/10.24843/jiwsp.2020.v02.i02.p01

The Impact of the COVID-19 Pandemic on the Prices Volatility of the Main Foodstuffs in Indonesia

Agus Hermawan, Komalawati Komalawati, Cahyati Setiani, Joko Triastono, Miranti Dian Pertiwi, Forita Dyah Arianti, and Indrie Ambarsari

Abstract The coronavirus, originally an endemic in Wuhan Province, China, quickly spread throughout the world and turned into a pandemic. In Indonesia, COVID-19 was officially announced on March 2, 2020. Several policies were taken to prevent the spread of the coronavirus, particularly in social distancing, self-isolation, and travel restrictions. This policy has reduced employment in all sectors of the economy and the loss of many jobs. The study was conducted to determine the impact of COVID-19 on the volatility of the leading food commodities that strongly trigger inflation (rice, fresh chicken meat, beef, eggs, onions, garlic, curly red chillies, red chillies, cooking oil, and sugar). The analysis was carried out by dividing the daily food price data into two periods: before (July 31, 2017 – March 1, 2020) and during (March 2, 2020 – October 14, 2020) COVID-19. Price volatility was analysed using the ARCH/GARCH Model. Analysis was also carried out by correlating food price movements with the progress of COVID-19 cases. The results show that most food prices tend to be stable after COVID-19 cases except for chicken, meat and eggs. A significant correlation was also found between the price movements with the COVID-19 cases. The results indicated that the impact of COVID-19 on food price volatility related to the intrinsic character or the nature of foods, the benefits of the foods to health, and government protection policies for these food staples. In general, the government must guarantee those food staples' movement, and thus, their distribution would not be disrupted. Social security policies are still essential to maintain purchasing power, access the poor to food, and prevent a decline in the performance of the agricultural sector.

Keywords COVID-19 · ARCH/GARCH · Volatility · Food prices · Indonesia

---

A. Hermawan (✉) · K. Komalawati · C. Setiani · J. Triastono · M. D. Pertiwi · F. D. Arianti · I. Ambarsari
Assessment Institute for Agricultural Technology Central Java, Semarang Regency, Central Java, Indonesia

© The Author(s), under exclusive license to Springer Nature Singapore Pte Ltd. 2022

T. Chaiechi, J. Wood (eds.), *Community Empowerment, Sustainable Cities, and Transformative Economies*, https://doi.org/10.1007/978-981-16-5260-8_37

1 Introduction

In December 2019, the world was shocked by pneumonia cases that started in Wuhan City, China. China identified the case as a new type of Coronavirus on January 7, 2020. A virus that attacks humans and animals' respiratory tract with early flu symptoms to cause severe acute respiratory syndrome (SARS) has quickly evolved from a provincial health scare to a global meltdown (Ali et al., 2020). On January 30, 2020, WHO declared the Coronavirus a Public Health Emergency of International Concern. On February 11, 2020, the WHO named the illness associated with the 2019 novel coronavirus disease / 2019-nCoV or COVID-19 (Dong et al., 2020). World Health Organization (WHO) declare COVID-19 firstly as a global emergency on February 20, 2020, and then a pandemic on March 11, 2020 (Ali et al., 2020).

COVID-19 then spread throughout the world. In Indonesia, COVID-19 was officially announced on March 2, 2020. As in other countries, several policies were taken to prevent the spread of the corona virus. Common steps taken are applying social distancing, avoiding unnecessary travel, and prohibiting gatherings (Nicola et al., 2020). The policy in controlling virus spread that exponentially increases has reduced employment in all sectors, and job losses make a shock source to the global economy. There are two reasons why the health crisis has turned into a financial crisis, namely (i) a contagious virus that has resulted in a lockdown in the business world and the economy and (ii) a rapidly growing virus that has created uncertainty about the initiation of investment among traders unsafe. The COVID-19 pandemic has even sparked fears of an economic crisis and recession (Nicola et al., 2020).

The impact of COVID-19 on both the stock market and commodity markets has been widely analysed. Several researchers reported the impact of COVID-19 on falling stocks and their high volatility (Ali et al., 2020; Sharif et al., 2020; Baek et al., 2020). COVID-19 also impacts the volatility of the money/foreign exchange market and even the crypto index (Umar & Gubareva, 2020). The analysis results by Baker et al. (2020) showed that the highest peak value of financial volatility was recorded in March 2020. A spike in financial uncertainty is usually associated with decreased activity in the real sector (Caggiano et al., 2020). COVID-19 has triggered volatility in commodity market prices, including oil (Sharif et al., 2020; Shruthi & Ramani, 2020), perishable meat and vegetables (Nicola et al., 2020), agricultural commodity (maise, sugar, and wheat), and oil market volatility (Shruthi & Ramani, 2020). Demand in the food sector had increased, triggered by public panic to buy and stockpile food products (Nicola et al., 2020). The main factors driving price volatility are weather changes, domestic production, storage levels, imports, delivery constraints, and market information. The three last factors seem strongly related to the COVID-19 issue.

It is interesting to know the extent of the impact of COVID-19 on the volatility of agricultural commodity prices in Indonesia, especially agricultural commodities, which have a significant impact on inflation. The calculation of inflation in Indonesia is based on fluctuations in the price of 744 commodities (goods and services), and several food commodities play a vital role in the formation of national inflation (volatile foods), which is 27.2% (Prastowo et al., 2008). These commodities are rice, cooking oil, chicken meat, sugar, beef, eggs, chicken, red chillies, bananas, tuna, and shallots (Prastowo et al., 2008). In addition to bananas and cobs, Darma et al. (2018) have analysed the effect of these food commodities' price, with the addition of garlic, on inflation. The analysis results showed that three of them are significant (rice, red chillies, and shallots) (Darma et al., 2018). Apart from these two researchers, several researchers have analysed the effect of commodity prices on inflation; among others were Surya (2015) (rice, shallots, red chilies); Rahmanta and Maryunianta (2020) (rice, onions, garlic, curly red chillies, red chillies), Rahmanta et al. (2020) (rice, fresh chicken meat, eggs, red chillies, and cooking oil), Apriyadi and Hutajulu (2020) (fresh chicken meat, beef, eggs); Rizaldy (2017) (onions and red chillies), and Kurnianti and Sugiarti (2018) (curly red chillies). According to the previous research (Prastowo et al., 2008), there was an influence of distribution factors on commodity prices that affecting inflation, especially for perishable commodities, do not have stock management, a company does not control their distribution channels. Most of the food commodities contributing to inflation meet these criteria.

This paper describes the research results to determine the impact of COVID-19 on the volatility of the main food commodities that are considered strongly triggered inflation. This inflation is due to one of the policies implemented to control COVID-19, namely travel restrictions and market closures, which impact distribution delays that trigger an increase in the price of goods and services, including food commodities contributing to inflation.

2 Research Methods

The time series daily data analysed came from two sources. Daily data of the other COVID-19 incidences come from Indonesian government releases (https://COVID19.go.id/). In contrast, daily price data of Jakarta-Indonesia food commodity prices (rice, fresh chicken meat, cattle meat, eggs, onion, garlic, curly red chilly, cayenne pepper, cooking oil, and sugar) comes from the National Strategic Food Price Information Center of Indonesia (https://hargapangan.id/). The range of data analysed was from March 2, 2020, to October 14, 2020, for COVID-19 data, while for food commodity prices was from July 31, 2017, to October 14, 2020. The analysis was carried out by dividing the daily food price data into two periods, namely before COVID-19 (July 31, 2017 - March 1, 2020) and during COVID-19 (March 2, 2020 - October 14, 2020). March 2, 2020, was the date of the official announcement of the COVID-19 incident in Indonesia, so it was chosen as the cut period.

Data dividing to determine the impact of a shock on price volatility has been widely used. Gozgor and Memis (2015), who analysed the price volatility spillovers among the crude oil, soybeans, corn, wheat, and sugar futures markets as the impact of the financial crisis of 2008–2009, dividing data throughout January 1, 2006, to November 29, 2013, into three periods of the pre-crisis, the crisis, and the post-crisis. Regarding the impact of COVID-19, several researchers also divided the data and compared the time before and during COVID-19, including the impact on volatility transmission over the financial crisis of agricultural commodity and oil markets (Shruthi & Ramani, 2020); on the cross-correlations of multifractal characteristics between the Brent Crude Oil and future agricultural markets (London Sugar, London Wheat, USA Cotton, USA Orange Juice) (Wang et al., 2020); on US stock market volatility (Baek et al., 2020); and the electricity sector (Ruan et al., 2020).

The data will be analysed with correlation analysis to determine the relationship between the development of COVID-19 and the development of commodity prices. Correlation analysis is widely used to determine whether there is a relationship between two variables. Regarding the relationship between several commodity prices, correlation analysis has been used to determine the relationship between the prices of biodiesel, ethanol, and related fuels and agricultural commodities before and during the food crisis, which is then continued with a use of minimal spanning trees and hierarchical trees (Kristoufek et al., 2012). Correlation analysis is also used to determine the relationship between the volatility of rice commodity prices and the level of climate change vulnerability for each province in Indonesia (Rum & Sihaloho, 2017), correlations between supply shocks and volatility of prices (von Braun & Tadesse, 2012), conditional correlation among each commodity market and the crude oil market and evaluate the time-differing qualities of correlations (Shruthi & Ramani, 2020), and cross-correlation of multi-fractality between Brent Crude Oil and selected agricultural future markets (Wang et al., 2020). In this study, the relationship between the development of COVID-19 and the price of food commodities contributing to inflation is measured by the bivariate Pearson correlation coefficient.

Referring to von Braun and Tadesse (2012), who divided Commodity price changes into three types, namely trends (in the long term), volatility, and spikes (in short to medium terms), this paper analyses price volatility. Price volatility describes the price fluctuations of a commodity. Because the price is a function of supply and demand, high volatility levels reflect the extraordinary supply and/or demand characteristics and show price uncertainty in markets.

Price volatility is a condition where prices fluctuate with excessive variations over time. Volatility can also be connoted with unstable conditions, which tend to vary and are difficult to predict (Dewi, 2016). Prices become volatile when high price fluctuations are followed by low price fluctuations and then return to high (Juanda and Junaidi 2012). Volatility can be definite or predictable and unpredictable (Gilbert & Morgan, 2010; Christanty & Wahyudi, 2012). It is natural for agricultural commodity prices to fluctuate rapidly all the time because prices are always adjusting to various changes. If the excessive variation in price can be predicted following a certain pattern, then the price variation is not a problem. Problems arise when these price variations become very large, cannot be anticipated, and create uncertainty about the future. This uncertain price variability is a problem because it can increase the risk of decision-making for economic actors (producers, consumers and the government), and can even affect the macroeconomic conditions of a country through inflation or increases in the price of other goods. If all the prices of goods increase, with a fixed income, people's purchasing power will decrease, and in the end, it can affect food security and even people's welfare.

A simple volatility analysis could be conducted by calculating Coefficient Variation. Recently, many researchers are using autoregressive conditional heteroscedasticity (ARCH) and generalised autoregressive conditional heteroscedasticity (GARCH) model to measure volatility. There are several procedures in analysing volatility using ARCH/GARCH models:

1. Test the stationarity of time series data, which is a condition where the data fluctuations are around a constant average value, independent of time, and the variance of these fluctuations remains constant for each time. Testing the mean stationarity (unit root in the model) was carried out using the Dicky Fuller test. The stationarity test is a necessity to prevent the spurious regression that could cause biased results either in the sign or the magnitude. Testing of stationarity of the data (unit root in the model) was carried out using the Dicky Fuller test with the formula as follows:

$$\Delta X_t = \alpha + \beta X_{t-1} + \delta_t + u_{tu}$$

ΔX_t is differences of time series data between t-1 period and t period; $u_t =$ *disturbance term*, and t = *trend*. The hypotheses used to test the stationarity data are: H0: $\beta = 0$, the data has a unit root or the data does not have stationarity; and H1: $\beta \neq 0$, the data does not have a unit root or stationarity. If the null hypothesis of $\beta = 0$ is rejected, the time series data is stationary, and when the null hypothesis of $\beta = 0$ is not rejected, the time series data is not stationary. Data that is not stationary will be differentiated until it becomes stationary and does not contain biased data. The differencing process is the process of looking for differences between data from one period to another sequentially. In Time Series data modelling, a model will be selected with the assumption of data stationarity, model residual normality, and no correlation between residuals in the model and homogeneous residual variants.

2. The identification and determination of Mean Equation. The average equation in the ARCH/GARCH model could consist of only the intercept, the price of the previous period (ARIMA model), dummy variables, and other explanatory variables. This study uses the ARIMA model (p, d, q). The best ARIMA model is determined based on the smallest Akaike Information Criterion (AIC) and Schwartz Criterion (SC) values and the largest log-likelihood value. The ARIMA model should follow the criteria such as (a) the model has a random residual and a parsimonious model; (b) the estimated parameters of a model should be significantly different from zero; (c) the stationarity conditions are met as indicated by the number of AR and MA coefficients each of which is less than one; (d) the iteration process must be convergent; and (e) the model has a small MSE value.

3. The determination of the ARCH / GARCH model can be done if the residuals obtained from the average equation contain Autoregressive Conditional Heteroscedastic (ARCH) effects or contain heteroscedasticity. The ARCH effect was tested using the Lagrange Multiplier test (ARCH-LM test). Based on the null hypothesis (H0) there was no ARCH error. If the test results do not reject the null hypothesis, the ARCH effects do not exist, and the ARCH-GARCH model could not be used.
4. The residual variant modelling is carried out if the residual variant is not homogeneous, namely the Autoregressive Conditional Heteroscedastic (ARCH) and Generalised Autoregressive Conditional Heteroscedastic (GARCH) models. The general form of the GARCH model (p, q) is:

$$\sigma_t^2 = \alpha_0 + \alpha_1 \varepsilon_{t-1}^2 + \ldots + \alpha_p \varepsilon_{t-p}^2 + \beta_1 \sigma_{t-1}^2 + \ldots + \beta_q \sigma_{t-q}^2$$

In the GARCH model, the residual variant depends not only on the previous residual but also on the previous residual variant. Based on this equation, if the order of p = 0, then it becomes the ARCH (q) model. In the ARCH model, the residual variants are now influenced by the previous residuals. The criteria of the ARCH / GARCH model are: (b) the model must have significant coefficients; (b) the number of coefficients less than 1 ($\alpha + \beta < 1$); and (c) the coefficient must have a positive value ($\alpha 0 > 0$, $\alpha > 0$, $\beta > 0$). The level of price volatility can be seen from the α value or the ARCH effect. The value of $\alpha + \beta$ close to unity shows the tendency of persistence of volatility in the long run. $\alpha + \beta > 1$ indicates the time series data jumped higher than the average value.

Many researchers have used ARIMA and ARCH / GARCH to analyse food price volatility, contributing to inflation in Indonesia (Table 1). The contribution of this paper is to find out the significance of COVID-19 on the volatility of food prices.

3 Results and Discussions

3.1 The Price Movement of 10 Main Food Commodities in Indonesia

Figure 1 illustrates the price movement of 10 main food commodities in Indonesia before and during COVID-19. The period before COVID-19 from August 2017 to the beginning of March 2020 shows that the prices of 10 main commodities fluctuated except for cattle meat, rice, cooking oil and sugar. The prices of cattle meat were relatively stable in the higher prices compared to the other prices, while rice, cooking oil and sugar were relatively stable in the lower prices. During COVID-19, the prices of 10 main food commodities in Indonesia had a slower fluctuation than the previous period except for cattle meat, rice, cooking oil, and sugar. Similar to the previous period, the prices of cattle meat, rice, cooking oil, and sugar remain

Table 1 Previous research on the volatility of inflation-supporting food prices in Indonesia

Commodity	Data	Site research	Models results	Source
1. Rice	Weekly price of 2010–2013	Indonesia	ARIMA (1,1,1); GARCH (2,1)	Larasati et al. (2016)
	The monthly price of Januari 1984–June 2009	Indonesia	AR (1); ARCH (1)	Sumaryanto (2009)
2. Fresh chicken meat	Daily price of February 2003–February 2013	Indonesia	MA (1); ARCH (1)	Burhani et al. (2013)
	Weekly price of 2010–2013	Indonesia	ARIMA (0,1,2); GARCH (1,1)	Larasati et al. (2016)
3. Cattle meat	Daily price of February 2003–February 2013	Indonesia	ARIMA (1,0,1); GARCH (1,1)	Burhani et al. (2013)
	The monthly price of Januari 2007–Desember 2016	Provinsi Kepulauan Bangka Belitung.	AR(12) AR (28) MA (12) MA (28); GARCH (1,1)	Pipit and Evahelda (2019)
4. Eggs	Weekly price of 2010–2013	Indonesia	ARIMA (1,1,1) GARCH (2,1)	Larasati et al. (2016)
	The monthly price of Januari 1984–June 2009	Indonesia	AR(1); ARCH – not significant	Sumaryanto (2009)
5. Onion	Daily price of 2006–2009	Indonesia	Arima (0,1,1) dan (1,1,2); ARCH (1)	Sumantri et al. (2016)
	Weekly price of 2010–2013	Indonesia	ARIMA (1,1,1) GARCH (1,1)	Larasati et al. (2016)
	Monthy price of Januari 1984–Juni 2009	Indonesia	AR (1), MA (1) ARCH (1)	Sumaryanto (2009)
6. Garlic	Monthy price of 1992–2012	East Java Province, Indonesia	AR (1); ARCH (1)	Wijaya et al. (2014)
	Monthy price of January 2015–March 2019	Menado, North Sulawesi, Indonesia	ARIMA (0,1,1); GARCH (1,1)	Kalengkongan et al. (2020)
7. Curly red chilly	Daily price of 2006–2009	Indonesia	ARIMA (0,1,1), (1,1,2); ARCH (1)	Sumantri et al. (2016)
	The daily price of January 2011–December 2015	Indonesia	ARIMA (1,1,2), (1,1,1); ARCH (1)	Nugrahapsari and Arsanti (2018)
	Weekly price of 2010–2013	Indonesia	ARIMA (0,1,2) GARCH (1,1)	Larasati et al. (2016)
	Monthy price of Januari 1984–Juni 2009	Indonesia	AR (2), MA (1) ARCH (1)	Sumaryanto (2009)

(continued)

Table 1 (continued)

Commodity	Data	Site research	Models results	Source
8. Cayenne pepper	Monthy price of 2014–2017	Bangkalan regency, East Java, Indonesia	MA (1); GARCH (2,2)	Kurnianti and Sugiarti (2018)
9. Cooking oil	Weekly price of 2010–2013	Indonesia	ARIMA (0,1,2); GARCH (1,1)	Larasati et al. (2016)
	The monthly price of 2000–2012	Indonesia	AR (1); GARCH (1,1)	Bakari et al. (2013)
	Monthy price of Januari 1984–Juni 2009	Indonesia	AR (1) MA (1) ARCH-not significant	Sumaryanto (2009)
10. Sugar	Weekly price of 2010–2013	Indonesia	ARIMA (0,1,2) GARCH (2,1)	Larasati et al. (2016)
	Monthy price of Januari 2002–April 2013	Indonesia	AR(1) MA(1); GARCH (1,1)	Laili et al. (2014)
	Monthy price of Januari 1984–Juni 2009	Indonesia	AR(2); GARCH (1,1)	Sumaryanto (2009)

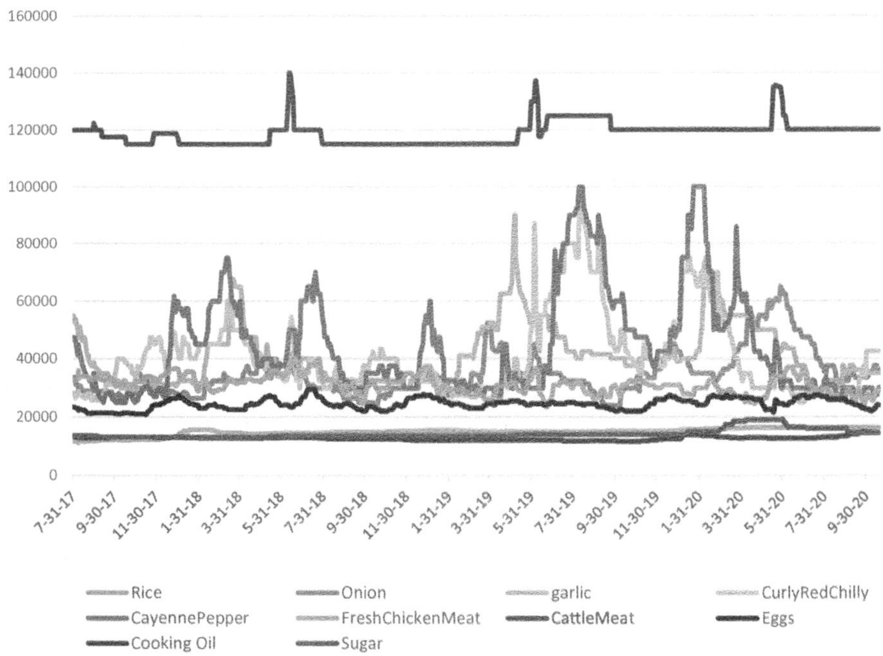

Fig. 1 The price trend of 10 main food commodities in Indonesia before and during COVID-19

stable. The relative stability of prices for cattle meat, rice, cooking oil and sugar were related to the government intervention either in the form of floor prices policy or import policy for those commodities.

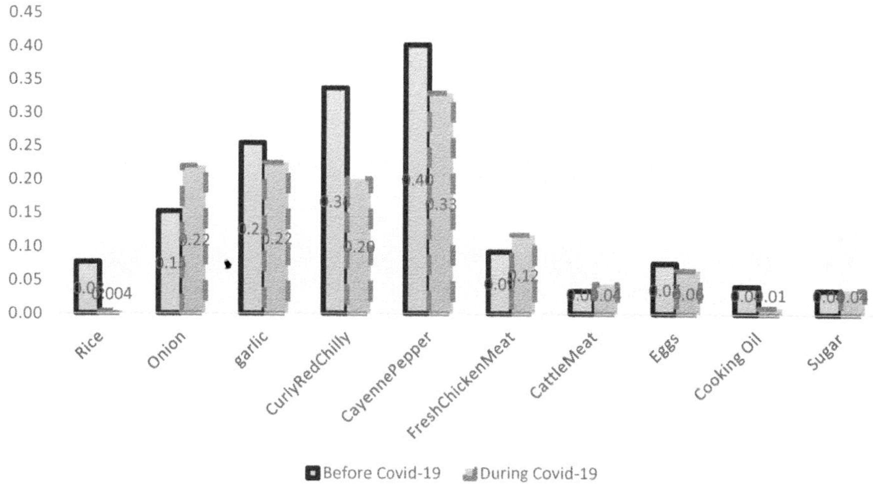

Fig. 2 The coefficient variation of 10 main food commodities before and during COVID-19

The simple way of calculating price fluctuation is by using coefficient variation (CV). According to Fig. 2, the price fluctuation is higher on five main commodities: rice, onion, garlic, curly red chilly, and cayenne pepper before and during COVID-19 cases. Eggs, cooking oil and sugar were relatively stable before and during COVID-19 cases. There was a decreasing fluctuation of main food commodities after the COVID-19 outbreaks except for fresh chicken meat and cattle meat. The decreasing fluctuation of main food commodities was related to decreasing people's purchasing power to food. At the same time, the increasing fluctuation for chicken meat and cattle meat was probably caused by the increasing assumption of the middle and higher-income classes about the importance of protein to increase their immunity to the virus. However, the calculation of CV only gives an overall picture of the price fluctuation. Still, it could not give the fluctuation in detail, whether the fluctuation would be persistent or the causes of the fluctuation or whether the fluctuation would lead to uncertainty. Therefore, this paper would analyse further the price fluctuation using ARCH/GARCH models.

3.2 COVID-19 Cases

As previously mentioned, COVID-19 cases were formally announced by the Indonesian President by March 2, 2020. Cases continue to increase from time to time. COVID-19, which was initially identified in Depok, West Java, continues to spread throughout Indonesia. The number of COVID-19 cases continues to increase. Up to the third week of March 2020, the average number of cases was less than 100 people per day; in the first week of April, the cases increased by an average of more than 275 people. In the first week of June 2020, the COVID cases even exceeded 1000

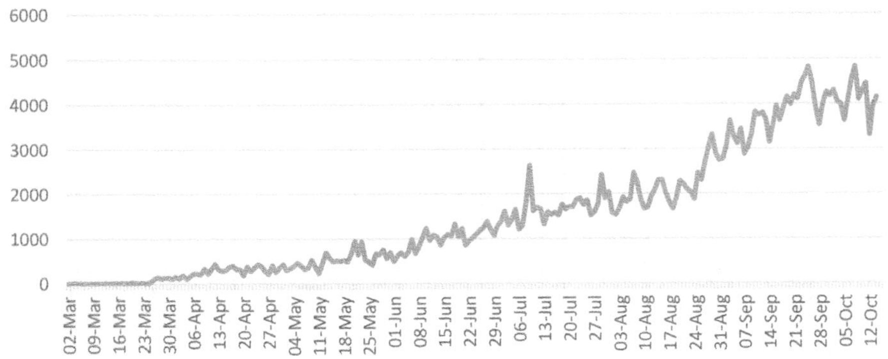

Fig. 3 Confirmed cases of COVID-19 in Indonesia

people. The number of confirmed cases of COVID-19 continues to increase, so that starting of the first week of October, around 4000 people are reported contiguous by COVID-19 every day.

As of October 14, 2020, it was reported that the number of confirmed COVID-19 cases in Indonesia was 344,079 people, with 12,112 deaths. Figure 3 shows the increase in daily COVID-19 cases in Indonesia.

3.2.1 Correlation Analysis

Correlation analysis is used to determine whether there is a relationship between commodity prices and the development of the COVID-19 case. A significant correlation was found between the price movements with the COVID-19 cases. The analysis results show that seven out of 10 daily prices of food commodities that support inflation in Indonesia were significantly correlated at 10% level with the increase in the number of COVID-19. Furthermore, of the seven commodities, two commodities (rice and cooking oil) have a positive correlation, while the other six negatively correlate. Only the prices of shallots, fresh chicken meat, and cattle meat were not significantly correlated.

The significance of the correlation coefficient and the direction of the relationship between food commodity prices and the daily development of the COVID-19 case is closely related to food life storage. Commodities resistant to storage, such as rice and cooking oil, have a very significant positive correlation or prices increase in line with the increase in the number of COVID-19 cases. It might be related to the tendency of people to hoard goods.

Meanwhile, other commodities have a very significant negative correlation. It means that prices tend to fall with the increasing confirmation of the COVID-19 case. Policies to restrict social activities (parties, weddings, restaurants, and entertainment) encourage a decrease in demand. Meat commodities that could not be stored or only lasted less than one day at room temperature were not significantly correlated. For two cases, this food price may be explained by Indonesia's relatively

Table 2 Life storage and correlation coefficient between confirmed cases of COVID-19 and food commodity prices

	Commodity	Correlation coefficient	Life storage under room temperature
1	LnRice	0.874**	6 months (Jumali et al., 2011; Subarna et al., 2005)
2	LnFreshChickenMeat	0.038	9 hours (Edi and Rahmah, 2018).
3	LnCattleMeat	0.003	18 hours (Aritonang, 2007)
4	LnEggs	−0.368**	<10 days (Fibrianti et al., 2012)
5	LnOnion	−0.104	1,5–2 months (Mutia et al., 2014)
6	LnGarlic	−0.754**	6 months (Titisari et al., 2019)
7	LnCurlyRedChilly	−0.688**	12–16 days (Astutik et al., 2017)
8	LnCayennePepper	−0.799**	<12 days (Edowai et al., 2016; Rachmawati et al., 2009)
9	LnCookingOil	0.373**	2–3 months (Permata, 2018)
10	LnSugar	−0.504**	No expired date (Lestari, 2017)

Note: ***, **, * significant at 5%, 10%, 15%

low level of meat consumption. Meat is mainly consumed by middle to upper-income people who are relatively well-off financially, so the demand for these two types of food is not influenced by the development of the COVID-19 case (Table 2).

3.2.2 Price Volatility Analysis

Table 3 provides the results of unit root tests which were analysed using ADF test. According to Table 3, most variables were stationary at the first difference except for the prices of beef, eggs, and chicken meat before COVID-19 outbreaks and rice prices during COVID-19 outbreaks. The next step after determining the stationarity of prices was to determine the mean equation explained in the next section.

Price Volatility Before COVID-19 Pandemic

The prices data were transformed into real data with the basic year of 2012 and a natural logarithm to clear the data from inflation, trend, and seasonal effect. Therefore, the measurement of volatility only used the unpredicted part of the prices. The next step of volatility measurement was to determine the mean model. The best mean equation was different for every food commodities before and during COVID-19 pandemic. Before the pandemic, the best model of the mean equation for majority food commodities (cayenne pepper, eggs, cooking oil, and sugar were ARIMA(1,1). Meanwhile, the best model of the mean equation for onion, cattle meat and garlic were MA(1). Other commodities (rice, curly red chilly and chicken meat) were ARIMA(2,2), ARIMA(2,1) and AR(1) models. Those mean equations were substantially tested using ARCH-LM test.

Table 3 Results of unit root tests using Augmented Dickey-Fuller (ADF) test

	Before COVID-19			During COVID-19		
	Level	*First diff.*	Critical value 1%	Level	*First diff.*	Critical value 1%
ADF test						
Real Price of rice	−2.44	−7.42	−3.44	−4.92	–	−3.47
	0.13	0.00		0.00	–	
Real price of onion	−2.82	−19.20	−3.44	−0.94	−11.57	−3.47
	0,06	0.00		0.77	0.00	
Real price of garlic	−2.15	−23.14	−3.44	−1.63	−12.08	−3.47
	0.22	0.00		0.46	0.00	
Real price of curly red chilly	−2.69	−19.16	−3.44	−2.66	−14.20	−3.47
	0.08	0.00		0.08	0.00	
Real price of Cayenne pepper	−2.48	−23.20	−3.44	−1.69	−9.42	−3.47
	0.12	0.00		0.43	0.00	
Real price of beef	−6.02	–	−3.44	−2.24	−11.49	−3.47
	0.00			0.19	0.00	
Real price of eggs	−3.84	–	−3.44	−2.07	−9.14	−3.47
	0.003			0.26	0.00	
Real price of chicken meat	−4.15	–	−3.44	−2.06	−9.59	−3.47
	0.00			0.26	0.00	
Real price of cooking oil	−1.73	−21.47	−3.44	0.35	−10.45	−3.47
	0.42	0.00		0.98	0.00	
Real price of sugar	0.50	−24.74	−3.44	−0.22	−6.59	−3.47
	0.99	0.00		(0.93)	(0.00)	

Table 4 Results of heteroscedasticity test of mean equation of 10 main food commodities prices before COVID-19 (End of July 2017–Beginning of March 2020)

	Rice	**Onion**	**Garlic**	**Curly Red Chilly**	**Cayenne Pepper**
F-statistic	145.65*	3.66**	0.08	4.60**	1.10
	(0.00)	(0.06)	(0.77)	(0.03)	(0.29)
Obs *R-squared	120.06*	3.65**	0.08	4.59**	1.10
	(0.00)	(0.06)	(0.77)	(0.03)	(0.29)
	Meat	**Eggs**	**Chicken meat**	**Cooking oil**	**Sugar**
F-statistic	20.59***	1.17	23.13***	93.57***	4.10**
	(0.00)	(0.28)	(0.00)	(0.00)	(0.04)
Obs *R-squared	20.15***	1.17	22.56***	82.41***	4.09**
	(0.00)	(0.28)	(0.00)	(0.00)	(0.04)

Note: the number in the brackets is the probability value; ***, **, * = significant at 1%, 10%, and 15%

Table 4 shows the results of ARCH-LM test of the mean equation models of 10 main food commodities before COVID-19. The results of ARCH-LM test show that the majority of models have a significant probability value ($p < 0.01$) except for garlic and cayenne pepper. It implied the existence of ARCH effect in the mean equation models of majority food commodities and the models could be estimated using ARCH/GARCH models. Meanwhile, the unavailability of ARCH effect in the mean equation models of garlic and cayenne pepper indicate the tendency of those commodities to be stable relative to other commodities.

Table 5 presents the estimated parameters of price volatility models (GARCH (p, q)) of 7 main food commodities before COVID-19 from end of July 2017 to the beginning of March 2020. According to Table 5, GARCH models chosen are between GARCH(1,1) and GARCH(1,0). GARCH models chosen have already had the highest value of log-likelihood and the smaller value of AIC and SIC. Furthermore, those models had the significant value of parameter coefficients of the mean equations and GARCH models. ARCH-LM test in all GARCH (p,q) models chosen showed no ARCH in the GARCH models and the models had already been well specified.

The estimation result of GARCH (p,q) models showed that most food commodities have lower price volatility, except for sugar. The relatively low price volatility of food commodities could be seen from the coefficient value of ARCH or residual squares (α) that were between 0.08 and 0.17. Meanwhile, sugar was the most volatile commodity since the value of α was 0.83. The value of the parameter coefficient of GARCH (β) could indicate the persistence of shock that was occurred in the variance. A smaller α value than the value of β illustrated the movement of beef prices which was more influenced by its variance than the external turmoil or dynamic markets. The sum of α and β values are close to one, which indicates the volatility of beef price tended to persist for a long time. According to the value of β and the sum of α and β values, cattle meat volatility was more persistent compared to onions, curly red chilly and chicken meat. This means once the price of beef becomes volatile, it would persist for a long time. The low volatility and persistence of beef price were supported by the study of Burhani et al. (2013), Komalawati et al. (2019).

Price Volatility During COVID-19 Pandemic

The prices data during COVID-19 pandemic consisted of data from the beginning of March 2020 to October 2020. These prices data were also transformed into real data and a natural logarithm as previously mentioned to test the stationarity and determine the mean equation. Before COVID-19, the best mean equation of 10 main food commodities was also different for every food commodity during COVID-19 pandemic. The best model of the mean equation was determined based on the highest value of log-likelihood and the smallest value of AIC and SC. According to the determination of the mean equation, the mean equation of majority food commodities was ARIMA(1,1) and MA(1), except for chicken meat (AR(1)) and garlic. Those mean equations determined were substantially tested using ARCH-LM test.

Table 6 shows the results of the ARCH-LM test of the mean equation models of 10 main food commodities during COVID-19. The results of the ARCH-LM test

Table 5 Estimation results of price volatility models of main food commodities in Jakarta Province before COVID-19 (the End of July 2017–Beginning of March 2020)

Coefficient	Rice ARIMA(2,2)-GARCH (1,0)	Onion MA(1)-GARCH (1,1)	Curly Red Chilly ARIMA(2,1)-GARCH(1,1)	Beef MA(1)-GARCH(1,0)
Mean equation				
AR(1)	0.33***		0.67***	
AR(2)	0.69***		−0.54***	
MA(1)	−0.14***	0.16***	−0.20***	0.25***
MA(2)	−0.62***		–	
Residual equation				
ω (konstanta)	0.00***	0.00***	0.00**	0.00***
α (ARCH)	0.17***	0.15***	0.15**	0.08***
β (GARCH)	–	0.48***	0.60***	0.78***
α + β	0.17	0.63	0.75	0.86
ARCH-LM test				
Prob. F-statistic	0.13	0.48	0.57	0.95
Prob. Chi-Square	0.13	0.48	0.57	0.95
Coefficient	Chicken meat AR(1)-GARCH (1,1)	Cooking oil ARIMA(1,1)-GARCH(1,0)	Sugar ARIMA(1,1)-GARCH (1,0)	
Persamaan rata-rata				
AR(1)	0.33***	0.99***	−0.89***	
AR(2)				
MA(1)		0.24***	0.94***	
MA(2)				
Persamaan Ragam				
ω (konstanta)	0.00***	0.00***	0.00***	
α (ARCH)	0.14***	0.16***	0.83***	
β (GARCH)	0.60***			
α + β	0.74	0.16	0.83	
Uji ARCH-LM				
Prob. F-statistic	0.27	0.62	0.91	
Prob. Chi-Square	0.27	0.62	0.91	

Note: ***, **, * = significant at 1%, 10%, 15%

show that the majority of models do not have a significant probability value ($p < 0.01$) except for rice, beef, chicken meat, and eggs. There were ARCH effects in the mean equation models of majority food commodities, and the models could be estimated using ARCH/GARCH models. Meanwhile, the unavailable of the ARCH

Table 6 Results of heteroscedasticity test of mean equation of 10 main food commodities prices during COVID-19 (the beginning of March 2020–October 2021)

	Rice	Onion	Garlic	Curly Red Chilly	Cayenne Pepper
F-statistic	85788.32***	0.70		0.00	1.54
	(0.00)	(0.40)	–	(0.95)	(0.22)
Obs *R-squared	161.70***	0.70		0.00	1.55
	(0.00)	(0.40)		(0.95)	(0.21)
	Beef	**Eggs**	**Chicken meat**	**Cooking oil**	**Sugar**
F-statistic	9.05***	14.44***	4.20**	0.00	0.04
	-(0.00)	(0.00)	(0.04)	(0.96)	(0.85)
Obs *R-squared	8.67***	13.40***	4.14**	0.00	0.04
	(0.00)	(0.00)	(0.04)	(0.96)	(0.85)

Note: number in the bracket is the probability value; ***, **, * = significant at 1%, 10%, 15

Table 7 Estimation results of price volatility models of main food commodities in Jakarta Province during COVID-19 (the beginning of March 2020–October 2020)

Coefficient	Rice MA(1)-GARCH (1,0)	Eggs ARIMA(1,1)-GARCH(1,1)	Chicken Meat AR(1)-GARCH (1,0)	Beef MA(1)-GARCH (1,0)
Persamaan rata-rata				
AR(1)		−0.53***	0.37***	
AR(2)				
MA(1)	0.25***	0.88***		0.65***
MA(2)				
Persamaan Ragam				
ω (konstanta)	61.13	0.00***	0.00***	0.00***
α (ARCH)	0.17	0.17**	0.17***	0.17**
β (GARCH)	–			
α + β	0.17	0.17	0.17	0.17
Uji ARCH-LM				
Prob. F-statistic	0.13	0.84	0.58	0.10
Prob. Chi-Square	0.13	0.84	0.57	0.10

Note: ***, **, * significant at 1%, 10%, 15%

effect in the mean equation models of other commodities could imply the tendency of those commodities to be stable during the pandemic.

The estimation result of GARCH (p,q) models showed that all volatile food commodities have lower price volatility (Table 7). The relatively low price volatility of food commodities could be seen from the coefficient value of ARCH or residual squares (α) that were around 0.17. The value of the parameter coefficient of GARCH (β) could indicate the persistence of shock that was occurred in the variance. According to Table 7, there were no GARCH models with β value, which concludes that the price volatililty of food commodities during COVID-19 was not persistent.

If the price volatility of the food commodities were compared between before and during COVID-19, there was decreasing price volatility during the pandemic, specifically beef and chicken meat. However, the price volatility of rice was still similar since the α value was 0.17 before and during the COVID-19 pandemic. The similar price volatility of rice was related to the Government policy.

Meanwhile, the commodities such as onion, curly red chilly, cooking oil, and sugar were not volatile anymore. During the COVID-19 pandemic, those commodities (onion, curly red chilly, cooking oil and sugar) were tend to be stable. Among those food commodities, only eggs had increasing price volatility. Before COVID-19, eggs were not volatile, while during the pandemic, eggs were volatile, although with lower price volatility. The relative volatile of beef, chicken meat and egg prices during the COVID-19 pandemic were probably related to the awareness of Indonesian people to the importance of protein to increase their immunity or the benefits of the foods to health.

4 Conclusion

This study shows the impact of COVID-19 on to price volatility of 10 main food commodities in Jakarta. Most commodities were relatively stable during COVID-19 compared to before COVID-19, specifically onion, curly red chilly, cooking oil, and sugar. At the same time, food commodities that are a source of protein, such as beef, chicken meat and eggs, tend to be volatile even after the pandemic happened, although with lower price volatility. There was a tendency for people to increase the consumption of protein, while the supply of the commodities was disrupted because of COVID-19. Therefore, this research indicated the impact of COVID-19 on food price volatility related to the intrinsic character or the nature of foods, the benefits of the foods to health, and government protection policies for these food staples. In general, the government must guarantee the price movement of those food staples, and thus, their distribution would not be disrupted. Social security policies are still essential to maintain purchasing power, access the poor to food, and prevent a decline in the agricultural sector's performance.

References

Ali, M., Alam, N., & Rizvi, S. A. R. (2020). Coronavirus (COVID-19)—An epidemic or pandemic for financial markets. *Journal of Behavioral and Experimental Finance, 27*, 100341. https://doi.org/10.1016/j.jbef.2020.100341

Apriyadi, R., & Hutajulu, D. M. (2020). Pengaruh Harga Komoditas Pangan Hewani Asal Ternak terhadap Inflasi di Provinsi D.I. Yogyakarta. *Jurnal ECOBISMA, 7*(2).

Aritonang, S. N. (2007). Pengaruh Lama Perendaman dalam Larutan Natrium Laktat terhadap Daya Awet Daging Sapi pada Penyimpanan Suhu Ruang. *Journal of the Indonesian Tropical Animal Agriculture, 32*(1), 41–43.

Astutik, W., Rahmawati, D., & Sjamsijah, N. (2017). Uji Daya Hasil Galur MG1012 Dengan Tiga Varietas Pembanding Tanaman Cabai Keriting (Capsicum annum L.). *Agriprima, Journal of Applied Agricultural Sciences, 1*(2), 164–173. https://doi.org/10.25047/agriprima.v1i2.30

Baek, S., Mohanty, S. K., & Glambosky, M. (2020). COVID-19 and stock market volatility: An industry level analysis. *Finance Research Letters, 37*(July), 101748. https://doi.org/10.1016/j.frl.2020.101748

Bakari, Y., Anindita, R., & Syafrial. (2013). Analisis Volatilitas Harga, Transmisi Harga, dan Volatiility Spillover pada Pasar Dunia Crude Palm Oil (CPO) dengan Pasar Minyak Goreng di Indonesia. *AGRISE, XIII*(3), 253–264.

Baker, S. R., Bloom, N., Davis, S. J., Kost, K. J., Sammon, M. C., & Viratyosin, T. (2020). *The unprecedented stock market reaction to COVID-19* (No. 26945).

Burhani, F. J., Fariyanti, A., & Jahroh, S. (2013). Analisis volatilitas harga daging sapi potong dan daging ayam broiler di Indonesia. *Forum Agribisnis, 3*, 19–39.

Caggiano, G., Castelnuovo, E., & Kima, R. (2020). The global effects of COVID-19-induced uncertainty. *Economics Letters, 194*(July 1992), 109392. https://doi.org/10.1016/j.econlet.2020.109392

Christanty, R., & Wahyudi, S. T. (2012). Pengaruh Volatilitas Harga terhadap Inflasi di Kota Malang: Pendekatan Model ARCH/GARCH. *Jurnal Ilmiah Mahasiswa FEB, 1*(2).

Darma, D. C., Pusriadi, T., & Hakim, Y. P. (2018). Dampak Kenaikan Harga Komoditas Sembako Terhadap Tingkat Inflasi di Indonesia. In *Prosiding Seminar Nasional dan Call for Paper: Manajemen, Akuntansi dan Perbankkan* (pp. 1048–1074). UIN Maulana Malik Ibrahim.

Dewi, I. (2016). *Price volatility analysis in Indonesian beef market [Tesis]*. Program Pascasarjana IPB.

Edi, S., & Rahmah, R. S. N. (2018). Pengaruh Lama Penyimpanan Daging Ayam pada Suhu Ruang dan Refrigerator Terhadap Angka Lempeng Total Bakteri dan Adanya Bakteri Salmonella Sp. *Jurnal Biosains, 4*(1), 23–31.

Edowai, D. N., Kairupan, S., & Rawung, H. (2016). Mutu Cabai Rawit (Capsicum frutescens L) pada Tingkat Kematangan dan Suhu yang Berbeda Selama Penyimpanan. *Agrointek, 10*(1), 12–20.

Fibrianti, S. M., Ketut Suada, I., & Rudyanto, M. D. (2012). Kualitas Telur Ayam Konsumsi yang Dibersihkan dan Tanpa Dibersihkan Selama Penyimpanan Suhu Kamar. *Indonesia Medicus Veterinus, 1*(3), 408–416.

Gilbert, C. L., & Morgan, C. W. (2010). Food price volatility. *Philosophical Transactions of the Royal Society B, 365*, 3023–3034. https://doi.org/10.1098/rstb.2010.0139

Gozgor, G., & Memis, C. (2015). Price volatility spillovers among agricultural commodity and crude oil markets: Evidence from the range-based estimator. *Agricultural Economics (Czech Republic), 61*(5), 214–221. https://doi.org/10.17221/162/2014-AGRICECON

Juanda, B., & Junaidi. (2012). *Ekonometrika Deret Waktu: Teori & Aplikasi*. IPB Press.

Jumali, J., Indrasari, S. D., & Kusbiantoro, B. (2011). Pengaruh Bahan Pengemas terhadap Mutu Beras Padi Aromatik selama Penyimpanan. *Penelitian Pertanian Tanaman Pangan, 30*(3), 154–163.

Kalengkongan, C. S., Langi, Y. A. R., & Nainggolan, N. (2020). Analisis Volatilitas Harga Bawang Putih di Kota Menado Menggunakan Model GARCH. *Jurnal Matematika dan Aplikasi, 9*(1), 43–49.

Komalawati, R. W., Asmarantaka, R. N., & Hakim, D. B. (2019). Modeling price volatility and supply response of beef in Indonesia. *Tropical Animal Science Journal, 42*(2), 159–166. https://doi.org/10.5398/tasj.2019.42.2.159

Kristoufek, L., Janda, K., & Zilberman, D. (2012). Correlations between biofuels and related commodities before and during the food crisis: A taxonomy perspective. *Energy Economics, 34*(5), 1380–1391. https://doi.org/10.1016/j.eneco.2012.06.016

Kurnianti, R., & Sugiarti, T. (2018). Volatilitas Harga Komoditas Cabai Rawit (Capsium Frutescent L.) Antara Pasar Ki Lemah Duwur Dan Pasar Baru Bancaran Di Kabupaten Bangkalan. In *Prosiding Seminar Nasional "Peran Sektor Pertanian dalam Pembangunan Ekonomi Nasional di Era Revolusi Industri 4.0"*. diedit oleh Markus Patiung, Dwi Haryanta, Elika Joeniarti, Basuki, Moch Thohiron, dan Endang Siswati, 4:64–75. BSA UIN.

Laili, F., Anindita, R., & Setiawan, B. (2014). Volatilitas Harga Gula Dunia dan Harga Gula Domestik. *AGRISE, XIV*(3), 191–204.

Larasati, E. N., Hendikawati, P., & Zaenuri. (2016). Analisis Volatility Forecasting Sembilan Bahan Pokok Menggunakan Metode GARCH dengan Program R. *UNNES Journal of Mathematics, 5*(1), 90–99.

Lestari, R. (2017). *6 Makanan yang Tak Memiliki Batas Kadaluarsa – Medcom*. medcom.id. 2017. https://www.medcom.id/rona/kesehatan/0Kv3g0lN-6-makanan-yang-tak-memiliki-batas-kadaluarsa

Mutia, A. K., Aris Purwanto, Y., & Pujantoro, L. (2014). Penyimpanan Pada Tingkat Kadar Air dan Suhu yang Berbeda. *Jurnal Pascapanen, 11*(2), 108–115.

Nicola, M., Alsafi, Z., Sohrabi, C., Kerwan, A., Al-jabir, A., Iosifidis, C., Agha, M., & Agha, R. (2020). The socio-economic implications of the coronavirus pandemic (COVID-19): A review. *International Journal of Surgery, 78*(April), 185–193. https://doi.org/10.1016/j.ijsu.2020.04.018

Nugrahapsari, R. A., & Arsanti, I. W. (2018). Analisis Volatilitas Harga Cabai Keriting di Indonesia dengan Pendekatan ARCH GARCH. *Jurnal Agro Ekonomi, 36*(1), 25–37.

Permata, S. (2018). Setelah Dibuka dari Kemasan Minyak Goreng Harus Segera Dihabiskan, Ini Sebabnya. *detikFood*, 2018. https://food.detik.com/info-kuliner/d-3799024/setelah-dibuka-dari-kemasan-minyak-goreng-harus-segera-dihabiskan-ini-sebabnya

Pipit, P., & Evahelda, Y. S. (2019). Analisis Volatilitas Harga Daging Sapi di Provinsi Kepulauan Bangka Belitung. *Jurnal Ekonomi Pertanian dan Agribisnis, 3*(3), 619–630.

Prastowo, N. J., Yanuarti, T., & Depari, Y. (2008). *Pengaruh distribusi dalam pembentukan harga komoditas dan implikasinya terhadap inflasi*. WP/07/2008.

Rachmawati, R., Defiani, M. R., & Suriani, N. L. (2009). Pengaruh Suhu dan Lama Penyimpanan terhadap Kandungan Vitamin C pada Cabai Rawit Putih (Capsicum Frustescens). *Jurnal Biologi, XIII*(2), 36–40.

Rahmanta, & Maryunianta, Y. (2020). Pengaruh Harga Komoditi Pangan Terhadap Inflasi di Kota Medan. *Agrica, 13*(1), 35–44.

Rahmanta, S. F., Ayu, E. F. F., & Sitorus, R. S. (2020). Pengaruh Fluktuasi Harga Komoditas Pangan Terhadap Inflasi di Provinsi Sumatera Utara. *Agrica, 13*(2), 81–92.

Rizaldy, D. Z. (2017). Pengaruh Harga Komoditas Pangan terhadap Inflasi di Kota Malang Tahun 2011-2016. *Jurnal Ekonomi Pembangunan, 15*(2), 171–183.

Ruan, G., Wu, D., Ruan, G., Wu, D., Zheng, X., Zhong, H., & Kang, C. (2020). Report a cross-domain approach to analysing the short-run impact of COVID-19 on the US electricity sector a cross-domain approach to analysing the short-run impact of COVID-19 on the US electricity sector. *Joule*, 1–16. https://doi.org/10.1016/j.joule.2020.08.017

Rum, I. A., & Sihaloho, E. D. (2017). Menjawab Anomali Harga Komoditas Beras berdasarkan Tingkat Kerentanan Perubahan Iklim di Indonesia. *ISEI Economic Review, I*(2), 42–45.

Sharif, A., Aloui, C., & Yarovaya, L. (2020). COVID-19 pandemic, oil prices, stock market, geopolitical risk and policy uncertainty nexus in the US economy: Fresh evidence from the wavelet-based approach. *International Review of Financial Analysis, 70*(April), 101496. https://doi.org/10.1016/j.irfa.2020.101496

Shruthi, M. S., & Ramani, D. (2020). Materials today: Proceedings statistical analysis of impact of COVID 19 on India commodity markets. *Materials Today: Proceedings, xxxx*. https://doi.org/10.1016/j.matpr.2020.07.729

Subarna, S., Budijanto, S., & Sutrisno. (2005). Perubanan Kualitas Beras Selama Penyimpanan. In J. Munarso, S. Prabawati, S. Abubakar, F. K. Risfaheri, & F. Suaib (Eds.), *Prosiding Seminar*

Nosional Teknologi lnovotif Pascopanen untuk Pengembangan lndustri Berbosis Pertanion (pp. 387–398). Bolol Besor Penelltion don Pengembongon Pascoponen Pertonion.

Sumantri, A. T., Junaidi, E., & Sari, R. M. (2016). Volatilitas Harga Cabai Merah Keriting dan Bawang Merah. *Jurnal Agribisnis Terpadu, 9*(2), 1–11.

Sumaryanto. (2009). Analisis Volatilitas Harga Eceran Beberapa Komoditas Pangan Utama dengan Model ARCH/GARCH. *Jurnal Agro Ekonomi, 27*(2), 135–163.

Surya, T. A. (2015). Pengendalian Inflasi Komoditas Pangan Menjelang Bulan Ramadhan. *Info Singkat Ekonomi dan Kebijakan Publik, VII*(11), 13–16.

Titisari, A., Setyorini, E., Sutriswanto, S., & Suryantin, H. (2019). *Kiat Sukses Budi Daya Bawang Putih* (E. Setyorini & N. Rachmawati, Eds.). Pusat Perpustakaan dan Penyebaran Teknologi Pertanian.

Umar, Z., & Gubareva, M. (2020). A time – Frequency analysis of the impact of the COVID-19 induced panic on the volatility of currency and cryptocurrency markets. *Journal of Behavioral and Experimental Finance, 28*, 100404. https://doi.org/10.1016/j.jbef.2020.100404

von Braun, J., & Tadesse, G. (2012). *Global food price volatility and spikes: An overview of costs, causes, and solutions* (ZEF-Discussion Papers on Development Policy, No. 161). University of Bonn, Center for Development Research (ZEF). https://doi.org/10.22004/ag.econ.120021

Wang, J., Shao, W., & Kim, J. (2020). Analysis of the impact of COVID-19 on the correlations between crude oil and agricultural futures. *Chaos, Solitons and Fractals: Nonlinear Science, and Nonequilibrium and Complex Phenomena, 136*, 109896. https://doi.org/10.1016/j.chaos.2020.109896

Wijaya, M. A., Anindita, R., & Setiawan, B. (2014). Analisis Volatilitas Harga, Volatilitas Spillover, dan Trend Harga Pada Komoditas Bawang Putih (Allium sativum, L.) di Jawa Timur. *AGRISE, XIV*(2), 127–143.

Impact of Covid-19 on Empowering Garlic Farmers in Indonesia

Wahyudi Hariyanto, Aryana Citra Kusumasari, Renie Oelviani, Seno Basuki, Sodiq Jauhari, Intan Gilang Cempaka, and Francisċus Rudi Prasetyo Hantoro

Abstract One of the impacts of the lockdown policy due to COVID-19 has caused decreased growth of the agricultural sector in Indonesia. The availability of garlic, 95% imported from China, India, United States of America, Malaysia, Switzerland, Germany, dan Australia, while 5% is produced in Indonesia, declines persistently. The objective of this study was to analyze factors affecting the availability of garlic during the COVID-19 pandemic. Mix-method was used to illustrate the phenomena through analyzing secondary data and semi-structured interviews with key informants in the regencies of Karanganyar, Tegal, and Temanggung, Central Java Province. The snowball sampling method was used to identify informants chosen based on cultivation experiences and post-harvest handling. The results showed that local varieties of garlic had been preferred by other countries for medication ingredient due to its strong aroma and spicy taste, although its price is relatively competitive. On the other hand, most households in Indonesia preferred imported garlic for cooking because of its large size. Consequently, improved quality for local garlic should be continually improved to increase both quantity and quality. To keep efforts sustainable, farmers should always be assisted in empowering their potential.

Keywords COVID-19 · Garlic farmers · Community empowerment

1 Introduction

As the COVID-19 pandemic forced many countries to close their borders to control the spread of the virus, it has also caused dramatic loss of human life worldwide and creating unprecedented problems for public health, food systems, businesses (Chriscaden Kimberly, 2020), global economy, human activities, and policy (Kumar et al., 2021; Workie et al., 2020; Sperling et al., 2020). For Indonesia,

W. Hariyanto (✉) · A. C. Kusumasari · R. Oelviani · S. Basuki · S. Jauhari · I. G. Cempaka · F. R. P. Hantoro
Assessment Institute for Agricultural Technology (AIAT) Central Java, Semarang Regencey, Central Java, Indonesia

© The Author(s), under exclusive license to Springer Nature Singapore Pte Ltd. 2022
T. Chaiechi, J. Wood (eds.), *Community Empowerment, Sustainable Cities, and Transformative Economies*, https://doi.org/10.1007/978-981-16-5260-8_38

exports have slowed down, although at the same time, it has accelerated domestic production (D. A. D. Nasution et al., 2020). Negative disturbances occurred in the stability of food price and food supply (Hermanto, 2020), such as garlic, one of the important vegetables for spicy food and household medicine: high cholesterol, high blood pressure, skin problems, and fungal infections. The *allicin* in garlic has an anti-oxidant effect ((Pawar et al., 2011). In addition to its consumption use as a food flavouring, garlic is also used as traditional medicines and in nurseries.

In 2017, before the pandemic, the consumption of garlic was 482.19 thousand tons in Indonesia, yet the available production was only 20.45 thousand tons; 461.74 thousand tons deficit (Ministry of Agriculture, 2017) (Fig. 1). This imbalance led to importing of garlic continues to increase (I'anatus Shofiyah, 2020). Besides being pressured by the impact of COVID-19 in the form of reduced imports, garlic production is also facing unfavourable weather, pests, and diseases.

Indonesia imports garlic from other countries to meet domestic needs, the largest importer is China (99.53%), and the volume continues to increase from year to year (Hadianto et al., 2020). In 2018, the total volume of imported garlic was 583 thousand tons, increased by 4.16% from the previous year, in 2019 was 465,344 tons (USD 529.9 million); meanwhile, the realization of import from January to July 2020 was 335,229 ton (Fig. 2) (Kementan, 2018). The dependence on imports causes the price of garlic vulnerable to shock (Hermawan et al., 2017) and increased price is also triggered by panic buying behaviour (Hermanto, 2020).

The gap in availability compared to domestic needs of garlic requires an approachable solution through the provision of superior quality seeds at the farmer level, optimal land use, expansion of the planting area, and timeliness planting, all of

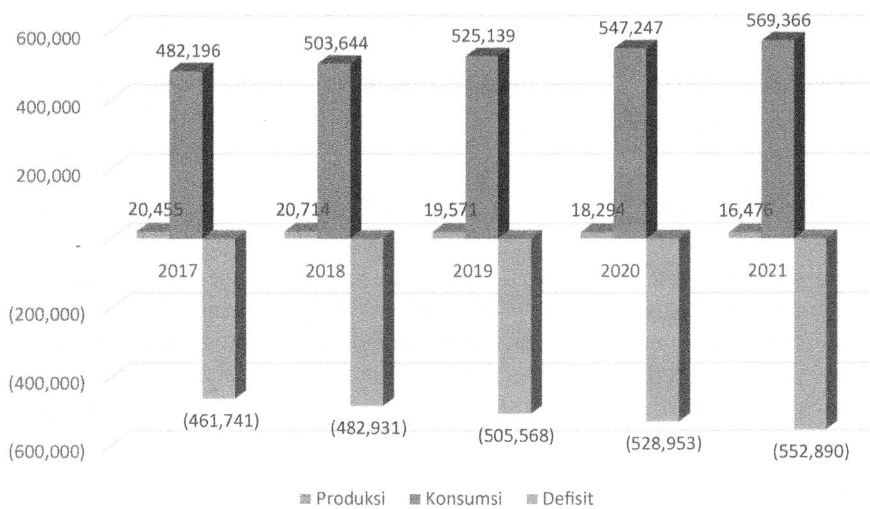

Fig. 1 National projection of garlic production, consumption, and deficit (2017–2021). (Source: Ministry of Agriculture-Director General of Horticulture, 2018)

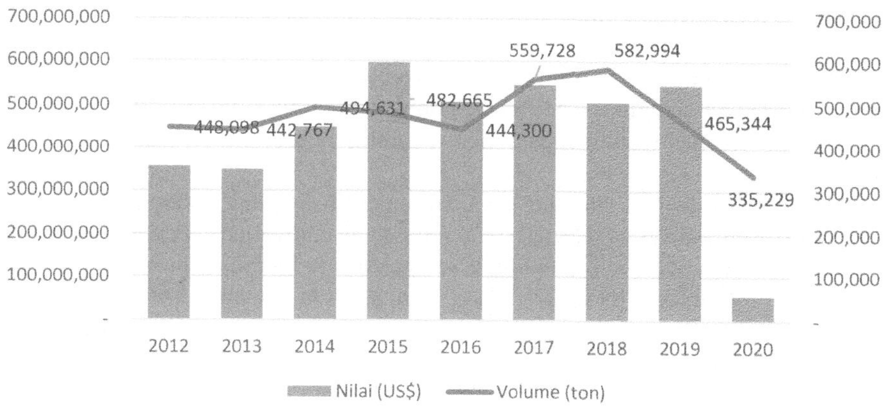

Fig. 2 Volume and value of imported garlic to Indonesia. (Source: Ministry of Agriculture-Directorate General of Horticulture)

which is preceded by improving the performance of farmers' resources towards garlic technology innovation.

The liberalization policy implemented by the Indonesian government due to the economic crisis in 1997/1998 has reduced farmers' enthusiasm to cultivate garlic (Hermawan et al., 2017). The reasons are a land mismatch, higher costs, difficult maintenance, relatively equal advantages as other vegetables, and inability to compete with imported garlic products (Suryarandika, 2018; Fauzi, 2017; Deny, 2017). For this reason, the government introduced the 2030–2045 garlic self-sufficiency program through the development of centres garlic program and import arrangements in 2016–2019, regional development in 2020–2024, and stabilization of the area in 2024–2029 (Ministry of Agriculture, 2017).

In Indonesia, Central Java province is one of the garlic production that are centered in Karanganyar, Tegal, Magelang, and Temanggung Regencies (Kurniawan et al., 2020). These four districts contributed 30.57% of national garlic production, based on the average production in 2012–2016 (Rahmawati & Jamhari, 2019). However, the problems being faced are limited planting area, high production costs, limited seed breeders at the farmer level, and a very low price of imported garlic. This condition causes the price of garlic to fluctuate (Harinta & Basuki, 2018; Setiawan, 2020). Based on this description, the objective of this study was to analyze factors affecting the availability of garlic in Indonesia during the COVID-19 pandemic.

2 Methods and Data

The mixed-method was used to illustrate phenomena through focused surveys using semi-structured interviews with key informants and explore current problem; meanwhile, the follow-up exploration was carried out using quantitative data; both of which are combined and integrated so that the understanding of the problem being observed can be obtained (Molina-Azorin, 2016). Interviews were conducted with researchers and key informants (extension agents and farmer cooperators) involved in garlic seeding activities. Their descriptions were used to identify, describe, and analyze various factors influencing the availability of garlic during the COVID-19 pandemic.

The Linear Snowball sampling (or Chain-referral-sampling) method was used to identify key informants as selected sources based on cultivation experience and post-harvest handling. Snowball sampling is an approach to identify key informants who have a lot of information. Primary sources will assist in obtaining another necessary resource (referral) person through recommendations based on directions in the research study (Nurdiani, 2014, Naderifar et al., 2017). The referrals are recruited into the sample group one by one as each referral intum recruits another subject, and the sample group expands. This pattern is continued until the sample group is fully formed (Bali & Club, 2021). Interview techniques and field surveys also supported this technique.

All data obtained from interviews and relevant literature reviews, and grey literature such as national and international news website columns published in online mass media during the COVID-19 outbreak in Indonesia, were treated as supporting references.

Sources of information used for descriptive analysis included data from BPS Indonesia, scientific publications, reports of the results of assessment activities, articles in the mass media, and empirical data obtained from telephone interviews (video calls), including official information issued by institutions/organizations, government, as well as personal communications collected representing a variety of views and expertise.

Data were analyzed to determine the impact of COVID-19 on the empowerment of garlic farmers in Indonesia. The variables observed included technical aspects, namely the provision of high-quality, superior seeds at the farmer level, the right cultivation technology, optimal land use, expansion of the planting area, and choosing the right planting time, while the non-technical aspects, namely assistance in empowering farmers to innovate garlic, and pro-farmer policies.

3 Result and Discussion

In Indonesia, the impact and the solution of COVID-19 on health and the economy have become a public debate. Health impact causing death can be caused by lack of preparation, such as personal protective equipment (PPE) for health workers, hospital equipment, sanitation equipment, toilet paper, and insufficient water (Kaye et al., 2020). The impact on the economy is in the form of job losses of millions of people (Chriscaden Kimberly, 2020), causing misery in almost every field of human business (transportation industry, sports, entertainment) because people are obliged to stay at home (Ozili & Arun, 2020).

The threats to health opposite to one of the economies; therefore, the anticipatory efforts must be in balance. The government then issues Presidential Regulation (Perpres) Number 7 of 2020 concerning the Task Force for the Acceleration of Handling of Corona Virus Diseases 2019 and Presidential Regulation Number 9 of 2020 by authorizing Governors to direct and evaluate the handling of COVID-19 in their respective regions (Wicaksono, 2020). From an economic point of view, the government has issued policies to increase people's purchasing power, reduce the risk of layoffs, maintain economic productivity and people productivity throughout Indonesia (Ihsanuddin, 2020).

In the food sector, the impact of export-import restrictions between countries has resulted in increasing complexity. For example, the price of garlic in Indonesia has risen sharply, more than 26%, in February 2020 compared to January 2020 (WFP, 2020). The increased price always occur every year, so that the government must pay attention to supply and demand, and it is estimated that the price of garlic will continue to rise until March 2021 (Berita SATU, 2021, Jawa Pos, 2021). The widening gap between the availability and demand for garlic makes this commodity vulnerable to be speculated.

Figure 3 explains that garlic consumption tended to increase until its peak in 2018; it was inversely proportional to production figures, which declined until 2017. Then in 2018, garlic production began to show an increase and has been predicted to continue increasing until 2023. This increase is believed to result from the program development of the garlic area that the government has initiated since 2016 throughout the archipelago (Table 1) (Ministry of Agriculture, 2017).

The total area of garlic covering 5453 ha across 16 provinces in Indonesia (Table 1) aims to increase production by expanding planted areas. In addition, the Ministry of Agriculture also applies compulsory planting regulations for business actors who obtain import recommendations for horticultural products (RIPH). These recommendations require importers to cultivate at least 5% of the total volume of imported garlic in the form of compulsory planting and production. Usually, importers partner with one another or lease land (Ministry of Agriculture, 2021b) to meet these requirements. The stock of garlic that must be available indicates that culturally this commodity is very important for the Indonesian people so that their needs must always be fulfilled even through imports.

Table 1 also shows that Central Java is a government supported area to develop the largest garlic area (29%) compared to other provinces. Central Java's garlic production contributed 83.64% to national production from 2014–2018, supported by Karanganyar Regency of 77.77% and Temanggung Regency as much as 71.24%.

The government's development program to cover the scarcity of garlic in Indonesia will open opportunities for farmers to cultivate it independently. Technically, Indonesian agroecology is suitable for the development of garlic. This agroecological approach emphasizes ecological and social bases to conserve and empower small farmers, focusing on input-saving technologies and reducing costs for intensifying production (Amekawa et al., 2010). Socially, community empowerment has the opportunity to strengthen factors of production, distribution and marketing, and gain access to knowledge and skills (Mar'Atusholikha et al., 2019). Economically,

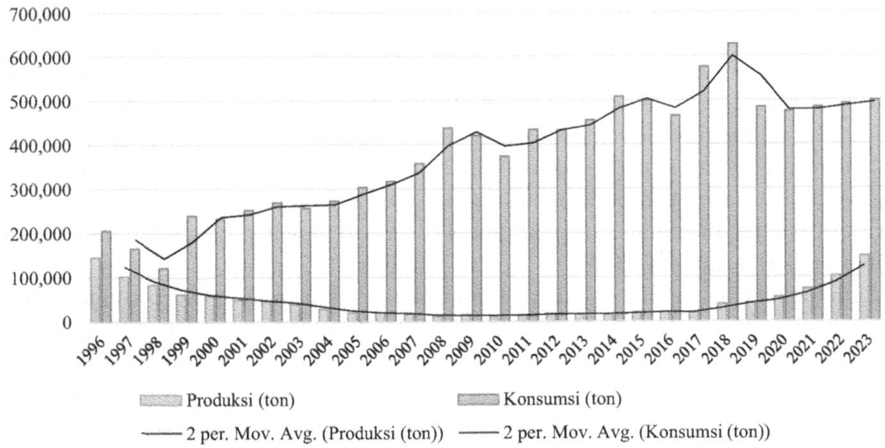

Fig. 3 Development of garlic production and consumption in Indonesia, 1996–2023. (Source: Ministry of Agriculture (2019) processed)

Table 1 Development of garlic areas in Indonesia

No.	Province	Luas Areal (ha)	Percentage
1.	Aceh	100	2%
2.	Sumatera Utara	505	9%
3.	Sumatera Barat	150	3%
4.	Bengkulu	225	4%
5.	Jambi	75	1%
6.	Sumatera Selatan	50	1%
7.	Lampung	160	3%
8.	Jawa Barat	185	3%
9.	**Jawa Tengah**	**1.581**	**29%**
10.	Jawa Timur	636	12%
11.	Bali	195	4%
12.	Nusa Tenggara Barat (NTB)	811	15%
13.	Nusa Tenggara Timur (NTT)	50	1%
14.	Sulawesi Utara	170	3%
15.	Sulawesi Tengah	200	4%
16.	Sulawesi Selatan	360	7%
	Total:	**5.453**	

Source: Antara (2020), processed

the demand for garlic in Indonesia is very high compared to its production. In addition, through the regional development program, the government will focus on increasing seed production, not consumption (Antara, 2020). The seeds for farmers will always be available, and opportunities for farmers to cultivate garlic will be properly facilitated. Opportunities in developing and increasing garlic production can be approached through technical and non-technical aspects.

3.1 Technical Aspects

3.1.1 Availability of Superior Quality Seeds at Farmer Level

Among factors affecting the quality of garlic seeds are temperature and storage. High temperatures may cause tubers to shrink, and high humidity will cause fungi and moulds that stimulate shoot growth (Nurmalia et al., 2019). In addition, farmers generally use uncertified seeds, as seed sources are not continuously available, the number of breeders is insufficient, and breeders lack experience (Nuswardhani, 2019). This important variable is an obstacle for farmers not to use certified seeds so that genetic purity and seed quality cannot be accounted for.

In general, most farmers mix up various varieties of garlic seeds. The Ministry of Agriculture has identified local garlic seeds indicated to be mixed up (broken and unbroken dormant) in one area, causing the purity of the variety is not in accordance with the morphological character of the description, physical quality, physiological quality, and health status (Kepmentan RI, 2018), later this practice can harm farmers and government programs (Kementan, 2021a). In addition, the availability of local garlic seeds is very limited as a result of the continuous import of garlic (Ammurabi, 2019), while imported seeds are not suitable for the Indonesian climate (Setjen Kementan, 2019).

According to (FAO, 2010), the three basic parameters that characterize quality seeds, the main factors of plant growth, are physiological, genetic, and seed health qualities. Further, to produce good quality seeds, plants must be planted in optimal soil conditions. For this reason, choosing a location and planting area, suitable soil texture, pH, and fertility status are essential in producing good quality seeds (Rao, 2016). Based on these considerations, the production of garlic seeds in several development centres in Central Java needs to be well maintained.

Most of the garlic production centers are located in highlands (>700 m above sea level) such as in Tawangmangu (Karanganyar), Parakan and Kledung (Temanggung), Kaliangkrik (Magelang), Pulosari (Pemalang), Paguyangan (Brebes), and Bojong (Tegal).[1] The varieties cultivated in the area are Tawangmangu Baru, Lumbu Hijau, Lumbu Putih, Lumbu Kuning, and Sembalun (Table 2). Lumbu Putih, Lumbu Kuning, Lumbu Hijau, and Tawangmangu Baru (TMB) are local varieties that are suitable to be advanced as they are still being cultivated by farmers (Ministry of Agriculture, 2019).

The provision of quality seeds must incorporate both the level of seed purity and the types of varieties having large tuber size genes. Exploration, characterization, and evaluation conducted by on several varieties of garlic showed that the variety of Tawangmangu Baru has larger tuber size genes than other varieties. In addition, tuber diameter, tuber weight/plant, the weight of garlic cloves, and productivity are greater than other varieties. A variety that also has the potential to have large tuber genes and high productivity is Lumbu Hijau. Therefore, Tawangmangu Baru and

[1] http://inaagrimap.litbang.pertanian.go.id/

Table 2 Characteristics of several local varieties of Indonesian garlic

Characteristic	Lumbu Putih	Lumbu Kuning	Lumbu Hijau	Tawangmangu Baru	Sembalun
Harvesting Age (DAP)	100–110	105–116	112–120	120–140	105–110
Plant Height (cm)	52–65	57–58	63–75	60–80	80–85
Leaf Color	Slightly grayish	Light green, slightly yellowish	Light green, slightly reddish purple	Bluish green	Light green
Bulb Color	White with purple stripes uneven at the edges	White slightly purplish	Purplish white	Purplish white	Purplish white
Growing Environment (masl)	6–200	600–900	900–1100	>1000 m	Uplands
Productivity (tons/ha dry tuber)	4–8	6–8	8–10	8–12	8.75

Source: Sandrakirana (2018)

Lumbu Hijau can be developed as a large bulb of garlic, which can increase garlic agribusiness while reducing imports.

Farmers can also increase garlic production using double chromosome garlic seeds. Double chromosome technology (Moebi, 2021) is a technology developed by Prof. Sobir, Professor of the Department of Agronomy and Horticulture, Faculty of Agriculture, IPB.[2] Although not yet providing consistent results, this technology could be considered an alternative to enlarging tubers. This technology is being improved to gain technological stability so that it can be adopted easily. According to farmers cultivating this double chromosome garlic to be G3 seeds, this seed still provides large tuber yields (Personal Communication, 2021). The potential yield of double chromosome garlic in an area of 0.5 ha reaches 20 tons/ha if the weather conditions are favourable (Firdaus, 2020). Shortly, double chromosome garlic is expected to compete with imported garlic, especially the one from China.

In addition to developing garlic which has the characteristics of large tubers released (Tawangmangu Baru and Lumbu Hijau), study the diversity of local Indonesian garlic germplasm, potentially having high productivity and large tubers and cloves, is still being carried out. The research and Development Agency of the Indonesian Ministry of Agriculture is releasing local garlic bulbs, Jangkiriah Adro from Sakoduo Village, Kayuaro Barat District, Jambi Province,[3] and Geol from Petarangan Village, Kledung District, Temanggung Regency, Central Java Province.

[2] https://repository.ipb.ac.id/handle/123456789/93076

[3] http://pvtpp.setjen.pertanian.go.id

3.1.2 Cultivation Technology

Garlic cultivation technology that is currently being developed in Indonesia is Double Production Technology (Proliga). According to (Basuki and Efendi, 2019), Proliga technology increases productivity (>20 tons/ha), tuber size (>4 cm), and clove size (>2 cm). The technological components include prerequisites for planting time, availability of water and suitable location, use of quality seeds and suitable varieties, use of organic fertilizer of mature layer chicken manure (15 tons/ha), balanced fertilization, dense spacing (10 × 10 cm), one seed per planting hole, and the use of straw mulch (Rofik Sinung Basuki, 2019). Implementing Proliga technology, Vegetables Research Center conducted a study in 2018 in Karanganyar Regency. The results showed that the Tawangmangu Baru variety produced 26.9 tons/ha, 90% of which categorized as AB class tubers, Lumbu Hijau variety produced 23.3 tons/ha of which 87% were AB class tubers. Meanwhile, in 2019, the Tawangmangu Baru variety produced 37.5 tons/ha and the Lumbu Hijau variety produced 29.6 tons/ha (R.S. Basuki, 2020).

3.1.3 Optimal Land Use

The most suitable growing prerequisites for garlic cultivation are an average temperature of 16–8 °C, altitude of 1100–1500 m above sea level, rainfall during the growing period of 350–600 mm, soft to medium textured soil with a soil depth >50 cm, soil pH of 6–7.8, and flat slope of <3% (Muslim & Mulyani, 2019).

Garlic grows well in the highlands with a temperature of 15–25 °C (Ministry of Agriculture, 2019) for tuber formation and enlargement. Until now, the utilization of the highlands for garlic plants has not been optimal (Djodhi Indra Septiyan, 2019, Titisari, 2019). In 2016, the existing area of garlic was 2027 ha, while the available potential was approximately 26,999 ha (Dirjen Hortikultura, 2017). According to the Center for Agricultural Land Resources of IAARD that, extensification and diversification can increase the availability of garlic in Indonesia. Extensification can be carried out in currently abandoned land (scrub, open land, scrub forest), while diversification can be implemented in dry land /upland usually used for cultivating less profitable vegetables (Ministry of Agriculture, 2019). In 2017, 279,506 ha land in Indonesia was identified to be potentially diversified (115,371 ha) and intensified (279,506 ha).

3.1.4 Expansion of Planting Area

The expansion area for garlic (extensification) while optimizing cultivated land management in Indonesia, especially in Central Java, is an option for increasing garlic production (Table 3). This program can be done in collaboration with garlic

Table 3 Projection of harvested area, productivity, and production of Indonesian garlic

Year	Producer price (Rp/Kg)	Harvested area (Ha)	Productivity (Ton/Ha)	Production (Ton)
2018	25.980	5.013	7,84	39.300
2019	31.661	4.530	9,19	41.603
2020	35.861	5.703	9,56	54.503
2021	40.680	7.385	9,97	73.580
2022	46.215	9.837	10,41	102.375
2023	52.585	13.478	10,90	146.822
Average	**38.830**	**7.658**	**9,65**	**76.364**

Source: Setjen Kementan (2019)

importers who are obliged to plant 5% from the volume of garlic import applications (Hadianto et al., 2019).

The intensity of land management greatly determines the yield of garlic tubers, especially in terms of soil cultivation, irrigation, fertilization and mulching (organic and inorganic), and pest control (Septiyan, 2019). Setjen Kementan (2019) reported that garlic production during 1981–2018 tends to increase in line with the expansion of the harvested area (Fig. 4. West Nusa Tenggara is the largest contributor (45.71%) of the national garlic production, followed by Central Java (37.94%), West Java (5.86%), and East Java (5.24%). Nationally, there are still many opportunities to expand garlic planting areas outside Java.

Figures 4 and 5 show that in aggregate, the harvested area and production of garlic continue to increase from 1981 to 1997 and after that decrease constantly until 2017. The implementation of the import liberalization policy influenced the decline in harvested area and garlic production in all garlic production centres. Yet, Temanggung Regency, one of the centres for garlic production in Central Java, is still consistently producing garlic. In 2017 the Ministry of Agriculture appointed Temanggung Regency to plant garlic (Hermawan et al., 2017).

Viewed from the planted area, during 1981–2018, the harvested garlic area in Java was higher than that outside Java; 60.49% and 39.51%, respectively. The average annual growth of the harvested area in Java was 6.51%, and outside Java was 2.25%. Meanwhile, the harvested area for garlic in the next 5 years (2019–2023) is projected to be 31.40% per year, the growth of productivity and production is projected to be 4.37% and 37.14% per year, respectively. In 2021, the consumption of garlic per year is projected to be 483.53 thousand tons, an increase to 491.63 thousand tons in 2022 and 498.85 thousand tons in 2023 (Setjen Kementan, 2019).

Based on the cropping area, in 1981–2018, the harvested area of garlic in Java was higher than that outside Java; 60.49% and 39.51%, respectively, with annual growth of 6.51% (Java) and 2, 25% (Outside Java) (Fig. 3). Meanwhile, the harvested area for garlic during 1981–2018 in Java had an average annual growth of 6.51%, while outside Java, it tended to increase by 2.25%.

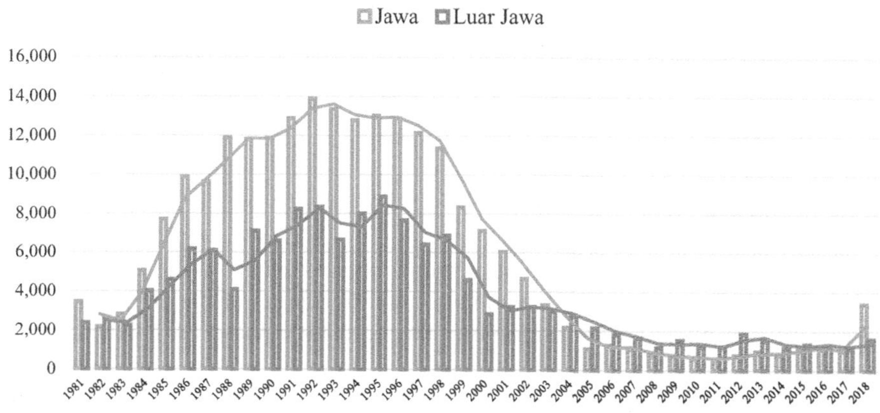

Fig. 4 Garlic harvest area in Java and Outside Java, 1981–2018

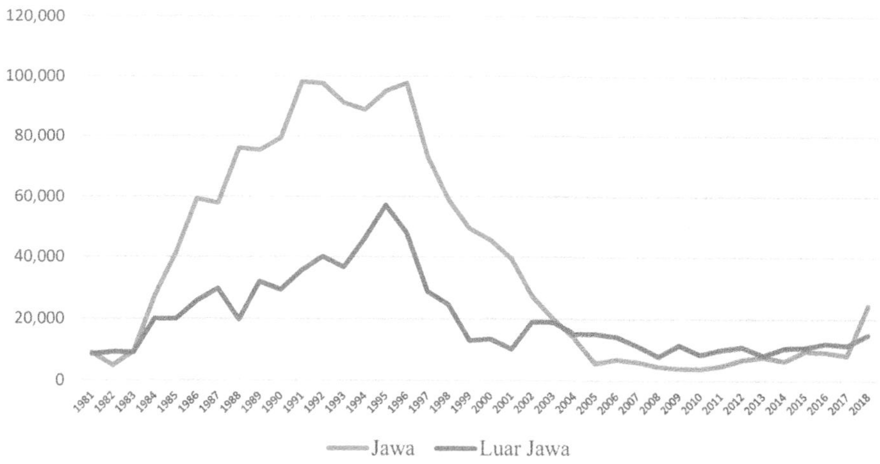

Fig. 5 Development of garlic production in Java, and Outside Java, 1981–2018. (Source: Ministry of Agriculture (2019) processed)

The projected area of harvested garlic for the next 5 years (2019–2023) increases by an average of 31.40% per year. The average productivity and production are projected to grow by 4.37% and 37.14% per year (Table 3) garlic consumption is projected to increase by 0.80% per year. In 2021, the consumption of garlic is projected to be 483.53 thousand tons, then increase to 491.63 thousand tons in 2022, and again increase to 498.85 thousand tons in 2023 (Secretariat General of the Ministry of Agriculture, 2019).

The projection of harvested area, productivity, and production tends to increase in line with the government's plan to proclaim garlic self-sufficiency in 2033. The plan was set in 2016, as shown in Table 3. The goal is to meet domestic consumption needs, reduce imports, and be an independent garlic country. The Ministry of Agriculture is optimistic that the volume of imported garlic throughout 2021 will decrease. The decline is claimed to be due to domestic garlic production, which continues to grow and is starting to be consumed by the public.

3.1.5 Planting Time

The timeliness of planting determines the quantity and quality of the yield (Titisari, 2019). The best time is at the beginning of the dry season or the end of the rainy season so that water is still available at the vegetative phase. In contrast, at the generative phase, dry conditions, full sun, and low temperature will support the formation and enlargement of garlic tubers (Dirjenhorti, 2009). In addition, farmers also need to pay attention to information related to weather forecasts obtained from BMKG. Weather forecast information can determine the correct planting time to anticipate unwanted things in bad weather.

Planting garlic in the dry season results in healthier garlic production both in the crop and after harvesting. The intensity of the pest attack is lower, the maintenance will be more efficient, the production is higher, and the yield is also greater than the garlic grown in the rainy season.

The planting time of garlic in the highlands of Central Java is (1) April–May (Banjarnegara, Batang and Brebes Districts); (2) Early dry season (May/June) (Karanganyar and Tegal Districts); (3) Early rainy season (November/December) (Temanggung, Magelang, Wonosobo, and Batang Districts). The highland areas where garlic is planted in the dry season have a vegetable planting pattern (leek/carrot) – garlic. In contrast, those in the rainy season have a garlic-tobacco cropping pattern (Jateng, 2021). Even though the production is not optimal in the rainy season, farmers still keep doing it because tobacco should be planted in the dry season, and water is available only in the rainy season.

3.2 Non-technical Aspect

3.2.1 Empowering Farmers on Garlic Technology Innovations

Top-down and bottom-up approaches are modelled to develop and disseminate technological innovations based on farmer demands/needs. Technological innovation assistance in the framework of producing scattered seeds in Karangnyar Regency is carried out in cooperation with related stakeholders; among which are BPSB as a seed certification assistance, AIAT as the source of technology introducing biological agents as a means of environmentally friendly garlic cultivation, IPB as an institution introducing planting based double chromosome treatment, LPPM as a cultivator of garlic from bulbils or air tubers which is an alternative of planting material in garlic propagation, PHP Laboratory as biological agents assistance, and

Bank Indonesia as an institution providing capital and independent selection of sustainable seeds. Each of these stakeholders has a complementary role in terms of technology, institutions, and capital. Even though amid the COVID-19 pandemic, farmers are still planting, yet after harvesting, the price of consumption garlic has decreased sharply.

One of the garlic assistance activities carried out by Bank Indonesia (BI) is in Tuwel Village, Bojong District, Tegal Regency, Central Java (Firdaus, 2020). Meanwhile, AIAT Central Java has also assisted in seed technology innovation in Jeruk Village, Jatiyoso District, Karanganyar Regency by producing garlic seeds in collaboration with cooperative farmers. Several approaches were taken while assisting cooperator farmers, including improving management in quality-oriented production and approaches that were oriented towards agro-ecosystem and agro-climatic approaches in accordance with the requirements of garlic seed production.

3.2.2 Pro Farmers Policy

Indonesia is the world's largest importer of garlic (24.46%), most of which are imported from China (Table 4) because only China has met the requirements for the international standard Good Agricultural Practices (GAP) certification from the Ministry of Agriculture (Bisnis.com, 2021). GAP is one of the requirements to obtain a Garlic Horticultural Product Import Recommendation (RIPH) to ensure imported products are safe to be consumed by people (Antara, 2021; I'anatus Shofiyah, 2020).

To meet domestic garlic needs, coordination involving all stakeholders is supported by policies including simplifying access to finance, insurance policies, land access policies, assigning BUMNs as stock buffers, fair-trade policies, utilization of warehouse receipts and so on (Rahmawati & Jamhari, 2019, I).

The excerpt from interviews with garlic farmers in Tegal Regency shows that:

1. Covid-19 pandemic has not affected garlic cultivation activities from planting, maintaining, or harvesting, but farmers depend on government policies.
2. Imports recommendations of horticultural products (RIPH) article 36 Permentan RI No 38/Permentan/HR. 060/11/2017 (Kementan RI, 2017) requires importers to produce garlic as much as 5% of the volume of the RIPH application, only after which the importer can obtain RIPH. However, the current government policy is reversed, that importer is allowed to import first, and after that, they are required to plant with a one-year grace period. The time period for carrying out the obligation follows one year after the RIPH is issued. Meanwhile, importers who have obtained RIPH, but have not succeeded in obtaining an Import Approval Letter (SPI) from the Ministry of Trade, will not be subject to compulsory planting (D. D. Nasution, 2021).
3. One of the impacts caused by government policy on garlic farmers is the low absorption of the harvest. Initially, the garlic harvest is used as seeds, then farmers

Table 4 Garlic importers and exporters in the world, 2013–2017

Importer	Average volume of imports (Ton)	Contribution (%)	Exporter	Average volume of imports (ton)	Contribution (%)
Indonesia	**481.005**	**24,46%**	**China**	**1.674.871**	**81%**
Brazil	167.613	9%	Spain	140.383	7%
Vietnam	132.446	7%	Argentina	74.740	4%
Malaysia	120.361	6%	Netherlands	29.505	1%
USA	83.682	4%	India	21.741	1%
Bangladesh	55.176	3%	Malaysia	16.664	1%
United Arab Emirate	54.182	3%	Mexico	13.087	1%
Russia	52.301	3%	French	11.303	1%
Thailand	51.297	3%	Italia	10.576	1%
Pakistan	45.112	2%	Chili	10.206	0%
Arab Saudi	43.209	2%	Others	69.419	3%
Others	680.381	35%			
World	1.966.765			2.072.495	

Source: Secretariat General of the Ministry of Agriculture, 2019, processed

distributed them to several areas, but many were not absorbed, leading to the damaged ones.

4. Farmers expect the government to issue a new policy for importers to be obliged to plant and buy crops from partner farmers. If there is no new policy, local garlic will not be able to compete with the imported one.

The results of the evaluation of Indonesia's garlic import policy recommends expanding garlic farming land, providing urea subsidies, providing protection to domestic garlic farmers through renegotiating garlic import tariffs for a long term basis, and maintaining exchange rate stability in the short term in order to create conducive conditions for garlic farmers (Putra A.H. et al., 2015). Price incentive is needed so that farmers get a decent reward for their efforts, especially when the weather is bad and overproduction (Thornton, 2017).

4 Conclusion

This paper aimed at analyzing the factors affecting the availability of garlic during the COVID-19 pandemic in Indonesia. Mix-method was used to illustrate the phenomena through analyzing secondary data and semi-structured interviews with key informants in the regencies of Karanganyar, Tegal, and Temanggung, Central Java Province. The snowball sampling method was used to identify informants chosen based on cultivation experiences and post-harvest handling. During the pandemic, farming activities are not significantly disrupted, as farmers continue to carry out cultivation activities as they usually do. The most influential factors to keep garlic cultivation sustainable are the availability of seeds at the farmer level and the reduction in technology innovation assistance at the field level due to refocusing of the government budget (APBN) in the agricultural sector. However, farmer empowerment activities can still be done online, yet it is not optimal.

The government issues a Horticultural Product Import Recommendation (RIPH) policy that requires importers to produce garlic as much as 5% of the RIPH application volume to fulfil the supply of garlic. In the future, the strategic food commodities needed by the majority of Indonesians as household consumption can be fulfilled in Indonesia independently.

The paper finds that a pro-farmer policy is needed, especially in providing quality garlic seeds in quantity and quality on time; besides, the harvest price should be maintained at a reasonable level. It is necessary to expand research about garlic production technology that can increase productivity and enlarge the size of garlic tubers and cloves so that national garlic products can compete with the imported ones.

Acknowledgments The authors would like to appreciate the resource persons for cooperative farmers in Temanggung, Tegal, and Karanganyar regencies, Central Java Province, to provide valuable information and input for this research. Our appreciation also goes to Kuscahyo BP for providing constructive input and correction of this manuscript.

References

Amekawa, Y., Sseguya, H., Onzere, S., & Carranza, I. (2010). Delineating the multifunctional role of agroecological practices: Toward sustainable livelihoods for smallholder farmers in developing countries. *Journal of Sustainable Agriculture, 34*(2), 202–228. https://doi.org/10.1080/10440040903433079

Ammurabi, S. D. (2019). Diserbu Impor, Varietas Bawa Putih Lokal Terus Tergerus. *Gatra.Com*, 1–3. https://www.gatra.com/detail/news/439847/ekonomi/diserbu-impor-varietas-bawa-putih-lokal-terus-tergerus-

Antara. (2020). Kementan Alokasikan Rp 220 Miliar Kembangkan Kawasan Bawang Putih. *Tempo.Co*.

Antara. (2021). Rekomendasi Impor Diterbitkan Lagi Jadi 450 Ribu Ton Bawang Putih 1x Datang, Mobil. *Tempo.Co*, 54–57.

Bali, N., & Club, G. (2021). Snowball sampling application of snowball sampling: An example gain credits from peer reviews disadvantages of snowball sampling. 1–3.

Basuki, R. S. (2020). *Proliga Bawang Putih*. Balai Penelitian Tanaman Sayuran.

Basuki, R. S. (2019). Teknologi Inovatif Budidaya Bawang Putih. In *Balai Penelitian Tanaman Sayuran*. Balai Penelitian Tanaman Sayuran.

BeritaSATU. (2021). Klaim Stok Aman, Harga Bawang Putih Justru Naik. *Berita Satu*, 2–5.

Bisnis.com. (2021). *Ini Sebabnya Impor Bawang Putih hanya dari China* (pp. 1–11).

Chriscaden Kimberly. (2020). *Impact of COVID-19 on people's livelihoods, their health and our food systems*. World Health Organization, 1. https://www.who.int/news/item/13-10-2020-impact-of-covid-19-on-people's-livelihoods-their-health-and-our-food-systems

Deny, S. (2017). *Sebab Petani Enggan Menanam Bawang Putih*. 5–6.

Dirjenhorti. (2009). *Standar Operasional Prosedur (SOP) Budidaya Bawang*. Direktorat Budidaya Tanaman Sayuran dan Biofarmaka.

Djodhi Indra Septiyan, S. (2019). Karakteristik Lahan Untuk Tanaman Bawang Putih (Allium sativum L.) pada Inceptisol dan alfisol di Kecamatan Pujon, Malang. *Jurnal Tanah Dan Sumberdaya Lahan, 6*(2), 1391–1403. https://doi.org/10.21776/ub.jtsl.2019.006.2.20

FAO. (2010). Seeds in emergencies: A technical handbook. In *Plant production*. FAO.

Fauzi, F. (2017). Petani Ogah Tanam Bawang Putih, Kenapa? *DetikFinance*, 2–3.

Firdaus, G. (2020, September 2). Tekan Impor, BI Terus Kembangkan Bawang Putih Tegal. *Gatra. Com*, 2–3. https://www.gatra.com/detail/news/489190/ekonomi/tekan-impor-bi-terus-kembangkan-bawang-putih-tegal

Hadianto, A., Amanda, D., & Asogiyan, P. K. (2019). An Analysis of Garlic Self-Sufficiency in Indonesia. *Sosial Dan Ekonomi Pertanian, 13*(1), 25–24. https://jurnalfp.uisu.ac.id/index.php/sep/article/view/34

Hadianto, A., Amanda, D., Asogiyan, P. K., Divisi, D., Pertanian, E., Ekonomi, D., Ekonomi, F., & Bogor, I. P. (2020). An analysis of garlic self-sufficiency in Indonesia an analysis of garlic self-sufficiency in Indonesia Analisis Pencapaian Swasembada Bawang Putih Indonesia Email: prisiliakristin@gmail.com Allium sativum L. merupakan komoditas yang sangat dibutuhkan m. September.

Harinta, Y. W., & Basuki, J. S. (2018). Potensi pengembangan bawang putih sebagai komoditas unggulan di kabupaten Karanganyar. *Agrisaintifika-Jurnal Ilmu-Ilmu Pertanian, 2*(2), 123–130.

Hermanto. (2020). Dampak Ekonomi Penyebaran COVID-19 Terhadap Kinerja Sektor Pertanian. *Buletin Perencanaan Pembangunan Pertanian, 6*.

Hermawan, A., Haryanto, W., Ambarsari, I., Pengkajian, B., Pertanian, T., Jawa, B., Soekarno, J., Km, H., Lor, B., & Asia, N. (2017). DAN IMPOR DI JAWA TENGAH DAN IMPLIKASINYA ANALYSIS OF PRICE IN TEGRATION AND IT' S I MPLICATIONS OF LOCAL AND IMPORTED GARLIC IN CENTRAL JAVA terpuruk karena gairah petani untuk. *Semnas BAPPEDA Provinsi Jawa Tengah*, 492–498.

Hortikultura, D. (2017). Pengembangan Bawang Putih Nasional.

I'anatus Shofiyah, T. S. (2020). Tren Dan Faktor-Faktor Yang Mempengaruhi Volume Impor Bawang Putih Di Indonesia, *1*(2017), 1–16.

Ihsanuddin. (2020). *9 Kebijakan Ekonomi Jokowi di Tengah Pandemi Covid-19*. Kompas.Com.

Jateng, P. (2021). *Kebijakan dan spek benih bawang merah -bawang putih di Jawa Tengah*. Dinas Pertanian dan Perkebunan Provinsi Jawa Tengah.

JawaPos. (2021). Harga Bawang Putih Naik, Stok Diperkirakan Sampai Maret 2021. *Jawa Pos*, 1–9.

Kaye, A. D., Okeagu, C. N., Pham, A. D., Silva, R. A., Hurley, J. J., Arron, B. L., Sarfraz, N., Lee, H. N., Ghali, G. E., Gamble, J. W., Liu, H., Urman, R. D., & Cornett, E. M. (2020, January). Economic impact of COVID-19 pandemic on healthcare facilities and systems: International perspectives. *Best Practice and Research: Clinical Anaesthesiology*. https://doi.org/10.1016/j.bpa.2020.11.009

Kementan. (2017). *Pengembangan Bawang Putih Nasional*.

Kementan. (2018). *Berapa Volume dan Nilai Impor Bawang Putih ke Indonesia? Vol. d*.

Kementan. (2019). *Varietas Tawangmangu Baru Didorong Untuk Swasembada Bawang Putih*. Kementan. https://www.pertanian.go.id/home/?show=news&act=view&id=3365

Kementan. (2021a). *Kementan Ingatkan Semua Pihak untuk Mewaspadai Benih Bawang Putih Oplosan*. Kementerian Pertanian RI. https://www.pertanian.go.id/home/?show=news&act=view&id=4025

Kementan. (2021b). *Uniknya Strategi Menuju Swasembada Bawang Putih*. Kementerian Pertanian RI.

Kepmentan RI. (2018). http://hortikultura.pertanian.go.id/wp-content/uploads/2015/06/pemurnian-varietas-hortikultura-cetak.pdf

Kumar, P., Singh, S. S., Pandey, A. K., Singh, R. K., Srivastava, P. K., Kumar, M., Dubey, S. K., Sah, U., Nandan, R., Singh, S. K., Agrawal, P., Kushwaha, A., Rani, M., Biswas, J. K., &

Drews, M. (2021). Multi-level impacts of the COVID-19 lockdown on agricultural systems in India: The case of Uttar Pradesh. *Agricultural Systems, 187*(December 2020), 103027. https://doi.org/10.1016/j.agsy.2020.103027

Kurniawan, A., Yulivan, I., Nasional, P., & Jakarta, V. (2020). Pengaruh Learning Organization dan Innovation Strategy terhadap Daya Saing Budidaya Bawang Putihdi Kabupaten Temanggung Mahasiswa Program Studi Magister Manajemen Fakultas Ekonomi dan Bisnis, Universitas Fakultas Ekonomi dan Bisnis, Universitas Pembangu. *Sosial Humaniora Dan Pendidikan, 4*(2), 93–112.

Mar'Atusholikha, V., & Widiatmaka, & Firmansyah, I. (2019). Sustainability of garlic cultivation at Tegal Regency, Central Java Province, Indonesia. *IOP Conference Series: Earth and Environmental Science, 399*(1). https://doi.org/10.1088/1755-1315/399/1/012027

Moebi, N. (2021). *Petani Bawang Putih Tegal Bingung Jual Hasil Panen.* Suara Baru. https://suarabaru.id/2020/09/03/petani-bawang-putih-tegal-bingung-jual-hasil-panen/

Molina-Azorin, J. F. (2016). Mixed methods research: An opportunity to improve our studies and our research skills. *European Journal of Management and Business Economics, 25*(2), 37–38. https://doi.org/10.1016/j.redeen.2016.05.001

Muslim, R. Q., & Mulyani, A. (2019). Land characteristics and suitability for development of garlic in East Lombok Regency, West Nusa Tenggara Province. *IOP Conference Series: Earth and Environmental Science, 393*(1). https://doi.org/10.1088/1755-1315/393/1/012079

Naderifar, M., Goli, H., & Ghaljaie, F. (2017). Snowball sampling: A purposeful method of sampling in qualitative research. *Strides in Development of Medical Education, 14*(3). https://doi.org/10.5812/sdme.67670

Nasution, D. A. D., Erlina, E., & Muda, I. (2020). Dampak Pandemi COVID-19 terhadap Perekonomian Indonesia. *Jurnal Benefita, 5*(2), 212. https://doi.org/10.22216/jbe.v5i2.5313

Nasution, D. D. (2021). Kementan Optimistis Impor Bawang Putih 2021 Turun 5, 3 Persen. *Republika Online*, 5–6.

Nurdiani, N. (2014). Teknik Sampling Snowball dalam Penelitian Lapangan. *ComTech: Computer, Mathematics and Engineering Applications, 5*(2), 1110. https://doi.org/10.21512/comtech.v5i2.2427

Nurmalia, N., Purwanto, Y. A., Sobir, S., Sulassih, S., & Naibaho, N. (2019). Effect of low temperature and period of storage on the quality of Garlic Seeds (Allium sativum L). *IOP Conference Series: Materials Science and Engineering, 557*(1). https://doi.org/10.1088/1757-899X/557/1/012088

Nuswardhani, S. K. (2019). Kajian Serapan Benih Padi Bersertifikat Di Indonesia Periode 2012–2017. *Agrika, 13*(2), 162. https://doi.org/10.31328/ja.v13i2.1207

Ozili, P. K., & Arun, T. (2020, April). Spillover of COVID-19: Impact on the global economy. *SSRN Electronic Journal.* https://doi.org/10.2139/ssrn.3562570

Pawar, S. S., Pharm, I. J., Sci, B., Bharude, N. V., Sonone, S. S., Deshmukh, R. S., Raut, A. K., & Umarkar, A. R. (2011, June). Chillies as food, spice and medicine: A perspective. *International Journal of Pharmacy and Biological Sciences*, 2230–7605. www.ijpbs.com

Putra, A. H., Ratya, A., & Suhartini, S. (2015). The Evaluation of Indonesia Import Policies of Garlic. *Greener Journal of Business and Management Studies, 5*(1), 016–030. https://doi.org/10.15580/gjbms.2015.1.081414329

Rahmawati, F., & Jamhari, N. (2019). Efisiensi Teknis Usaha Tani Bawang Putih Pola Tumpang Sari Di Kabupaten Karanganyar, Provinsi Jawa Tengah. *Jurnal Agro Ekonomi, 36*(2), 135. https://doi.org/10.21082/jae.v36n2.2018.135-147

Rao, N. K. (2016). A review of factors that influence the production of quality seed for long-term conservation in genebanks. *Genetic Resources and Crop Evolution, 64*(June), 1061–1074. https://doi.org/10.1007/s10722-016-0425-9

Sandrakirana, R. (2018). *Panduan Budidaya Bawang Putih Kementerian. Balai Pengkajian Teknologi Pertanian Jawa Timur.*

Setiawan, S. R. D. (2020, September). Menurut Pengamat, Ini Penyebab Produksi Bawang Putih RI Rentan Fluktuasi. *Kompas.Com*, 2020.

Sperling, L., Louwaars, N., de Ponti, O., Smale, M., Baributsa, D., & van Etten, J. (2020). Viewpoint: COVID-19 and seed security response now and beyond. *Food Policy, 97*-(September), 102000. https://doi.org/10.1016/j.foodpol.2020.102000

Suryarandika, R. (2018, May). Mengapa Petani Garut tak Mau Menanam Bawang Putih? *Rupublika Online*, 2–3.

Thornton, G. (2017). Value chain analysis.

Titisari, A. (2019). *Budi Daya Bawang Putih*. Kementerian Pertanian.

WFP. (2020, March). *Indonesia Food price update – March 2020. Focus: Effect of COVID-19 outbreak on food prices. March.* https://reliefweb.int/sites/reliefweb.int/files/resources/WFP-0000113732.pdf

Wicaksono, R. M. T. A. D. (2020). *Examining the policies and priorities of the Indonesian Government*. Gajah Mada University.

Workie, E., Mackolil, J., Nyika, J., & Ramadas, S. (2020). Deciphering the impact of COVID-19 pandemic on food security, agriculture, and livelihoods: A review of the evidence from developing countries. *Current Research in Environmental Sustainability, 2*, 100014. https://doi.org/10.1016/j.crsust.2020.100014

Correction to: Vietnam and Motorcycles: Dialectics and Commensurate Adaptations

Quang Chinh Nguyen, Sanjay Mishra, Dyen Thanh My Nguyen, and Duyen Hong Thuc Nguyen

Correction to: Chapter 13 in: T. Chaiechi, J. Wood (eds.), *Community Empowerment, Sustainable Cities, and Transformative*, Economies, https://doi.org/10.1007/978-981-16-5260-8_13

The chapter was inadvertently published with incorrect author's name "Tasya Aspiranti" instead of "Dyen Thanh My Nguyen".

This error has now been corrected by updating the correct author's name as "Dyen Thanh My Nguyen".

The correct author group for chapter 13 entitled "**Vietnam and Motorcycles: Dialectics and Commensurate Adaptations**" is as follows:

Quang Chinh Nguyen, Sanjay Mishra, Dyen Thanh My Nguyen, and Duyen Hong Thuc Nguyen

---

The updated online version of the chapter can be found at
https://doi.org/10.1007/978-981-16-5260-8_13

© The Author(s), under exclusive license to Springer Nature Singapore Pte Ltd. 2022
T. Chaiechi, J. Wood (eds.), *Community Empowerment, Sustainable Cities, and Transformative Economies*, https://doi.org/10.1007/978-981-16-5260-8_39

The manufacturer's authorised representative in the EU is Springer Nature Customer Service Centre GmbH, Europaplatz 3, 69115 Heidelberg, Germany. If you have any concerns regarding our products, please contact ProductSafety@springernature.com

Printed and bound by CPI Group (UK) Ltd, Croydon, CR0 4YY
30/09/2026
02225290-0020